For Uncle Peter

May 2016

CW00719899

OXFORD STUDIES IN
MEDIEVAL EUROPEAN HISTORY

General Editors
JOHN H. ARNOLD   PATRICK J. GEARY
and
JOHN WATTS

The Shape of the State in Medieval Scotland, 1124–1290

ALICE TAYLOR

OXFORD
UNIVERSITY PRESS

OXFORD

UNIVERSITY PRESS

Great Clarendon Street, Oxford, OX2 6DP,
United Kingdom

Oxford University Press is a department of the University of Oxford.
It furthers the University's objective of excellence in research, scholarship,
and education by publishing worldwide. Oxford is a registered trade mark of
Oxford University Press in the UK and in certain other countries

© Alice Taylor 2016

The moral rights of the author have been asserted

First Edition published in 2016

Impression: 1

Published in the United States of America by Oxford University Press
198 Madison Avenue, New York, NY 10016, United States of America

British Library Cataloguing in Publication Data
Data available

Library of Congress Control Number: 2015944459

ISBN 978–0–19–874920–2

Printed in Great Britain by
Clays Ltd, St Ives plc

Acknowledgements

This book has taken a long time to write and so has accumulated many debts. It grew out of my doctoral thesis at the University of Oxford (2005–09), which was funded by the Arts and Humanities Research Council. My DPhil thesis was supervised primarily by John Maddicott and I am profoundly grateful for his patience and exacting criticism. Hector MacQueen and James Campbell examined the thesis in 2009 and it is partly thanks to their constructive feedback that this book has taken the vast shape it has. I would like to give particular thanks to John Watts, George Garnett, and Jenny Wormald for supporting this book in its initial and rather shaky post-thesis life and to Henrietta Leyser, Mark Whittow, and Lawrence Goldman, as well as Annabel Smith and Margaret Davies, for their endurance during earlier times at St Peter's College, Oxford, and NLCS respectively.

The commissioning editors at OUP, Stephanie Ireland and Terka Acton, did not baulk at the sheer size of this manuscript, and I am very grateful to them both, as well as to Robert Faber. Cathryn Steele expertly saw this manuscript through to publication. I am extremely grateful to the three anonymous peer reviewers, who came back with such helpful suggestions, and to the series editors of the Oxford Studies in Medieval European History for including this book in their series. Scottish medieval history has, on occasion, wrongly been seen as a rather parochial sub-section of British history (let alone European history writ large) and I am very pleased that this book is being included in an explicitly European framework. Ed Merritt drew all the maps (online at <http://www.merrittcartographic.co.uk/>), and the Centre for Scottish and Celtic Studies at the University of Glasgow and Boydell and Brewer Press gave permission to republish extracts from articles originally published with them.

Much of the research for this book was on manuscripts held at the National Records of Scotland (NRS) and the National Library of Scotland (NLS) in Edinburgh. All the staff there have been very helpful but Alan Borthwick of the NRS took time to supervise my consultation of the Melrose archive at Thomas Thomson House in Edinburgh Park back in 2007. King's College, Cambridge, awarded me a Research Fellowship between 2008 and 2011 and with it the most wonderful environment in which to build on my doctoral work. I am grateful to all friends and colleagues there, especially Anastasia Piliavsky.

There have been many readers of parts and drafts of this book, some of whom did not always see them in the most pristine of conditions: Amanda Beam-Frazier, Michael Clanchy, John Reuben Davies, Alexander Grant, Tom Lambert, Hector MacQueen, George Molyneaux, and Keith Stringer. I am also very grateful for the wider support of David Bates, Robert Bartlett, Julia Crick, John Gillingham, Elisabeth van Houts, Bruce O'Brien, David Sellar, Richard Sharpe, Simon Taylor, Nicholas Vincent, Tessa Webber, Jenny Wormald, and Alex Woolf. Keith Stringer has been very generous in sharing his thoughts and research on Alexander II's *acta* for *Regesta Regum Scottorum*, Volume 3, and I have greatly appreciated this. Matthew Hammond has not only been an encouraging friend and reader but also the source of much stimulating and useful discussion. The support and advice of Chris Wickham has been exacting and invaluable.

Since 2011, I have been lucky enough to work at King's College London and have accumulated many debts there, particularly to its community of medievalists; these debts are too many to list here. The friendship and intellectual warmth of David Carpenter and Alice Rio have, however, made being an academic historian far better than I could ever have hoped. Alice even read the entire book; I could not have written it without her friendship. My greatest debt is to Dauvit Broun. Since meeting him in April 2005, he has been a constant source of support, encouragement and inspiration. It is rare to meet that level of academic generosity so early in a career.

My final thanks are to my family and stepfamilies, particularly to my father, David Taylor, and my sister, Myfanwy Taylor. I would also like to acknowledge gratefully the help and thoughtfulness of my late stepfather, Peter Scott. My partner, Emily Fedouloff, has had to endure much as a result of this book's long gestation period; its publication not only sees my release but also hers. This book, however, is dedicated to my mother, Toni Griffiths, who has always been there, every step of the way.

Alice Taylor
King's College London
May 2015

Contents

PART II: THE EMERGENCE OF A BUREAUCRATIC STATE, *c.*1170–1290?

List of Maps

List of Tables

List of Abbreviations

ABB	*Collections for a History of the Shires of Aberdeen and Banff*, ed. J. Robertson, and *Illustrations of the Topography and Antiquities of the Shires of Aberdeen and Banff*, ed. J. Robertson, 5 volumes in total (Aberdeen, 1843–69).
Aberdeen Burgh Chrs	*Charters and Other Writs Illustrating the History of the Royal Burgh of Aberdeen MCLXXI–MDCCCIV*, ed. P. J. Anderson (Aberdeen, 1890).
Aberdeen Reg.	*Registrum Episcopatus Aberdonensis: Ecclesie Cathedralis Aberdonensis Regesta que extant in unum collecta*, ed. C. N. Innes, 2 vols (Edinburgh, 1845).
Anderson, *Diplomata*	*Diplomata Scotiae: Selectus Diplomatum et Numismatum Scotiae Thesaurus*, ed. J. Anderson (Edinburgh, 1739).
Anderson, *Oliphants*	J. Anderson, *The Oliphants in Scotland* (Edinburgh, 1879).
ANS	*Anglo-Norman Studies: Proceedings of the Battle Conference*, 1978–present (various editors) (Woodbridge, 1979–present).
APS	*The Acts of the Parliaments of Scotland*, vol.1: *1124–1423*, ed. T. Thomson and C. N. Innes (Edinburgh, 1844). All references are to the red foliation.
Arbroath Liber	*Liber S. Thome de Aberbrothoc*, 2 vols, ed. C. N. Innes and P. Chalmers (Edinburgh, 1848–56).
ARD	*Assise Regis David*, in *APS*, i, pp. 315–25.
ARW	*Assise Regis Willelmi*, in *APS*, i, pp. 369–84.
ASC	*The Anglo-Saxon Chronicle: A Collaborative Edition*, vol. 3: *MS A*, ed. Janet M. Bately (Cambridge, 1986); vol. 5: *MS C*, ed. Kathleen O'Brien O'Keeffe (Cambridge, 2001); vol. 7: *MS E*, ed. Susan Irvine (Cambridge, 2004).
AU	*The Annals of Ulster AD 431–1202*, electronic edition compiled by Pádraig Bambury and Stephen Beechinor, CELT: The Corpus of Electronic Texts, online at <http://www.ucc.ie/celt/published/T100001A/index.html>. All references cited from here.
AT	*The Annals of Tigernach*, ed. and trans. Gearóid Mac Niocaill; electronic edition compiled by Emer Purcell and Donnchadh Ó Corráin, online at <http://www.ucc.ie/celt/published/T100002A/index.html>. All references cited from here.
Ayr Burgh Charters	*Charters of the Royal Burgh of Ayr*, ed. W. S. Cooper, Ayrshire and Wigtownshire Archaeological Association (Edinburgh, 1883).
Balmerino Liber	*Liber S. Marie de Balmorinach*ed. W. B. D. D. Turnball (Edinburgh, 1840).
Bamff Chrs	*Bamff Charters, AD 1232–1703*, ed. J. H. Ramsay (Oxford, 1915).
BL	British Library, London.

Bower, *Scotichronicon*	*Scotichronicon by Walter Bower*, 9 vols, gen. ed. Watt (Aberdeen and Edinburgh, 1989–98).
Brechin *Reg.*	*Registrum Episcopatus Brechinensis cui accedunt Cartae quamplurimae originales*, ed. P. Chalmers, J. I. Chalmers and C. N. Innes, 2 vols (Edinburgh, 1856).
Cambuskenneth Reg.	*Registrum Monasterii S. Marie de Cambuskenneth A.D. 1147–1535*, ed. W. Fraser (Edinburgh, 1872).
CD	*Capitula Assisarum et Statutorum Domini David Regis Scocie.*
CDI	*The Charters of David I: the Written Acts of David I, King of Scots, 1124–53, and of His Son, Henry, Earl of Northumberland, 1139–52*, ed. G. W. S. Barrow (Woodbridge, 1999).
CDS	*Calendar of Documents Relating to Scotland, Preserved in Her Majesty's Public Record Office*, ed. J. Bain, 5 vols (Edinburgh, 1881–88).
Chron. *Melrose*	*The Chronicle of Melrose: A Stratigraphic Edition*, vol. 1: *Introduction and Facsimile*, ed. D. Broun and J. Harrison, Scottish History Society (Woodbridge, 2007). All citations are from the facsimile included in this edition, available on CD-rom.
Cold Corr.	*The Correspondance, Inventories, Account Rolls and Law Proceedings of the Priory of Coldingham*, ed. J. Raine, Surtees Society (London, 1841).
Coupar Angus Chrs	*Charters of the Abbey of Coupar Angus*, ed. D. E. Easson, 2 vols, Scottish History Society, 3rd ser., vol. 40 (Edinburgh, 1847).
Coupar Angus Rental	*Rental Book of the Cistercian Abbey of Cupar-Angus with the Breviary of the Register*, ed. C. Rogers, 2 vols (London, 1879–80).
Douglas, 'Culross'	W. Douglas, 'Culross Abbey and Its Charters, with Notes on a Fifteenth-Century Transumpt', *Proceedings of the Society of Antiquaries of Scotland*, vol. 60 (1925–26), pp. 67–94.
Dryburgh Liber	*Liber S. Marie de Dryburgh: Registrum Cartarum Abbacie Premonstratensis de Dryburgh*, ed. J. Spottiswoode (Edinburgh, 1847).
Dunf. *Reg.*	*Registrum de Dunfermelyn*, ed. C. N. Innes (Edinburgh, 1842).
EHR	*English Historical Review*
ER	*Rotuli Scaccarii Regum Scotorum: The Exchequer Rolls of Scotland,*vol. 1: *AD 1264–1359*, ed. J. Stuart and G. Burnett (Edinburgh, 1878).
Foedera	*Foedera, Conventiones, Literae, et cuiuscunque generis acta publica intere reges Angliae et alios quosvis imperatores, reges, pontifices, principes vel communitates*, ed. T. Rymer (London, 1704–45).
Fraser, *Carlaverock*	William Fraser, *The Book of Carlaverock: Memoirs of the Maxwells, Earls of Nithsdale, Lords Maxwell and Herries*, 2 vols (Edinburgh, 1873).
Fraser, *Douglas*	William Fraser, *The Douglas Book*, 4 vols (Edinburgh, 1885).
Fraser, *Grant*	William Fraser, *The Chiefs of Grant*, 3 vols (Edinburgh, 1883).
Fraser, *Keir*	William Fraser, *The Stirlings of Keir and Their Family Papers* (Edinburgh, 1858).

Fraser, *Lennox*	William Fraser, *The Lennox*, 2 vols (Edinburgh, 1874).
Fraser, *Menteith*	William Fraser, *The Red Book of Menteith*, 2 vols (Edinburgh, 1880).
Fraser, *Southesk*	William Fraser, *History of the Carnegies, Earls of Southesk*, 2 vols (Edinburgh, 1867).
Fraser, *Sutherland*	William Fraser, *The Sutherland Book*, 3 vols (Edinburgh, 1892).
Glanvill	*The Treatise on the Laws and Customs of the Realm of England, Commonly Called Glanvill*, ed. and trans G. D. G. Hall, with comments by M. T. Clanchy, Oxford Medieval Texts (Oxford, 1993).
Glasgow Reg.	*Registrum Episcopatus Glasguensis: Munimenta Ecclesie Metropolitane Glasguensis a sede restaurata seculo ineunte XII ad reformatam religionem*, 2 vols, ed. C. N. Innes (Edinburgh, 1843).
HMC	Historical Manuscripts Commission (Royal Commission on Historical Manuscripts).
Holyrood Liber	*Liber Cartarum Sancte Crucis: Munimenta Ecclesie Sancte Crucis de Edwinesburg*, ed. C. N. Innes (Edinburgh, 1840).
Howden, *Chronica*	*Chronica Magistri Rogeri de Houedene*, ed. W. Stubbs, Rolls Series, 4 vols (London, 1868–71).
Howden, *Gesta*	*Gesta Regis Henrici Secundi Benedicti Abbatis: The Chronicle of the Reigns of Henry II and Richard I AD 1169–1192*, ed. W. Stubbs, 2 vols (London, 1867).
Inchaffray Chrs	*Charters, Bulls and Other Documents Relating to the Abbey of Inchaffray*, ed. W. A. Lindsay, J. Dowden, and J. Maitland Thomson, Scottish History Society, 2nd ser., vol. 56 (Edinburgh, 1908).
Inchcolm Chrs	*Charters of the Abbey of Inchcolm*, ed. D. E. Easson and A. Macdonald, Scottish History Society, 3rd ser., vol. 32 (Edinburgh, 1938).
Kelso Liber	*Liber S. Marie de Calchou: Registrum Cartarum Abbacie Tironensis de Kelso 1113–1567*, ed. C. N. Innes, 2 vols (Edinburgh, 1846).
Kinloss Recs.	*Records of the Monastery of Kinloss*, ed. J. Stuart, (Edinburgh, 1868).
Lawrie, *ESC*	*Early Scottish Charters Prior to A.D. 1153*, ed. A. C. Lawrie (Glasgow, 1905).
LBS	*Leges inter Brettos et Scotos*
Lennox Cart.	*Cartularium Comitatus de Levenax ab initio seculi decimi tertii usque ad annum M.CCC.XCVIII*, ed. J. Dennistoun (Edinburgh, 1833).
Lindores Cart.	*Chartulary of the Abbey of Lindores 1195–1479*, ed. J. Dowden, Scottish History Society, 2nd ser., vol. 42 (Edinburgh, 1903).
LS	*Leges Scocie*, edited and translated in Alice Taylor, 'Leges Scocie and the Lawcodes of David I, William the Lion and Alexander II', *Scottish Historical Review*, vol. 88 (2009), pp. 207–88.
LW	*Leges Willelmi Regis*

May Recs.   Records of the Priory of the Isle of May, ed. J. Stuart,
             (Edinburgh, 1868).
Melrose Liber   Liber S. Marie de Melros: Munimenta Vetustiora Monasterii
             Cisterciensis de Melros, ed. C. N. Innes, 2 vols (Edinburgh,
             1837).
Moray Reg.   Registrum Episcopatus Moraviensis e pluribus codicibus
             consarcinatum circa AD MCCCC, ed. C. N. Innes (Edinburgh,
             1837).
National MSS Scot.   Facsimiles of the National Manuscripts of Scotland, ed. W. G.
             Craig, 3 vols (Edinburgh, 1867–71).
Newbattle Reg.   Registrum S. Marie de Neubotle: Abbacie Cisterciensis Beate
             Virginis de Neubotle Chartarium Vetus, 1140–1528, ed. C. N.
             Innes (Edinbugh, 1849).
NLS   National Library of Scotland, Edinburgh.
NRS   National Records of Scotland, Edinburgh.
Paisley Reg.   Registrum Monasterii de Passelet: Cartas, Privilegia,
             Conventiones, ed. C. N. Innes (Edinburgh, 1832).
Panmure Reg.   Registrum de Panmure: Records of the Families of Maule, de
             Valoniis, Brechin and Brechin-Barclay, united in the line of the
             Barons and Earls of Panmure, compiled H. Maule, ed. J. Stuart
             (Edinburgh, 1874).
PNF   The Place-Names of Fife, ed. Simon Taylor with Gilbert
             Márkus, 5 vols (Donnington, 2006–12).
PSAS   Proceedings of the Society of Antiquaries of Scotland
Raine, North Durham   James Raine, The History and Antiquities of North Durham, as
             Subdivided into the Shires of Norham, Island and Bedlington
             (London, 1852).
RM   Regiam Majestatem, edited by Thomas Thomson in APS, i,
             pp. 597–641.
RMS   Registrum Magni Sigilli Regum Scotorum: The Register of the
             Great Seal of Scotland, ed. J. M. Thomson, J. B. Paul, J. H.
             Stevenson, W. K. Dickson., 11 vols (Edinburgh, 1882–1914).
RPS   The Records of the Parliaments of Scotland to 1707, ed. K. M.
             Brown, G. H. MacIntosh, A. J. Mann, P. E. Ritchie, R. J.
             Tanner (St Andrews, 2007–9), online at <http://www.rps.
             ac.uk>.
Rot. Scot.   Rotuli Scotiae in Turri Londonensi et in Domo Capitulari
             Westmonasteriensi Asservati, vol. 1: the Reigns of Edward I,
             Edward II and Edward III (1291–1377), ed. D. MacPherson
             (London, 1814).
RRS, i   Regesta Regum Scottorum, vol. 1: The Acts of Malcolm IV,
             1153–65, ed. G. W. S. Barrow (Edinburgh, 1960).
RRS, ii   Regesta Regum Scottorum, vol. 2: The Acts of William I,
             1165–1214, ed. G. W. S. Barrow with the collaboration of
             W. W. Scott (Edinburgh, 1971).
RRS, iv, 1.   Regesta Regum Scottorum, vol. 4, part 1: The Acts of Alexander
             III, king of Scots, 1249–86, ed. C. J. Neville and G. G.
             Simpson (Edinburgh, 2013).

RRS, v	*Regesta Regum Scotorum*, vol. 5: *The Acts of Robert I 1306–29*, ed. A. A. M. Duncan (Edinburgh, 1988).
S	P. H. Sawyer, *Anglo-Saxon Charters: An Annotated List and Bibliography* (London, 1968), revised by Susan E. Kelly in *The Electronic Sawyer*, online at <http://esawyer.org.uk/about/index.html>.
SA	*Statuta Regis Alexandri* (MS version).
Scone Liber	*Liber ecclesie de Scon: Munimenta Vetustiora monasterii Sancte Trinitatis et Sancti Michaelis de Scon*, ed. W. Smythe (Edinburgh, 1843).
SHR	*Scottish Historical Review*
Skene, *Fordun*	*Johannis de Fordun Chronica Gentis Scotorum*, 2 vols, ed. W. F. Skene, trans. Felix Skene (Edinburgh, 1871–2).
Spalding Misc.	*Miscellany of the Spalding Club*, vol. 2, ed. J. Stuart (Aberdeen, 1842); vol. 5, ed. J. Stuart (Aberdeen, 1852).
SRA	*Statuta Regis Alexandri* in *APS*, i, pp. 395–404.
St Andrews Liber	*Liber Cartarum Prioratus Sancti Andree in Scotia e Registro ipso in Archivis Baronum de Panmure hodie asservato*, ed. T. Thomson and O. Tyndall Bruce (Edinburgh, 1841).
Stevenson, *Documents*	*Documents Illustrative of the History of Scotland from the death of Alexander the Third to the accession of Robert Bruce MCCLXXXVI–MCCCVI*, ed. J. Stevenson, 2 vols (Edinburgh, 1870).
Stirling Charters	*Charters and Other Documents Relating to the Royal Burgh of Stirling, A.D. 1124–1705*, ed. R. Renwick (Glasgow, 1884).
Stubbs, *Select Charters*	*Select Charters and Other Illustrations of English Constitutional History from the Earliest Times to the Reign of Edward I*, ed. W. Stubbs, 9th edn, revised by H. W. C. Davis (Oxford, 1921).
Thanes of Cawdor	*The Book of the Thanes of Cawdor: A Series of Papers Selected from the Charter Room at Cawdor 1236–1742*, ed. C. N. Innes (Edinburgh, 1859).
Theiner, *Monumenta*	*Vetera Monumenta Hibernorum et Scotorum historiam illustrantia 1216–1547*, ed. A. Theiner (Rome, 1864).
TNA	The National Archives, London.
TRHS	*Transactions of the Royal Historical Society*
Wilson, 'Cupar charters'	James Wilson, 'Original Charters of the Abbey of Cupar, 1219–1448', *SHR*, vol. 10, no. 39 (1913), pp. 272–86.

Preliminary Notes

The representation in modern scholarship of personal names in the kingdom of the Scots during the central Middle Ages requires some explanation. Until recently, most Gaelic personal names were anglicized: Donnchad was rendered Duncan; Mael Coluim, Malcolm; and Gille Brigte, Gilbert. This is no longer the case: recent scholarship, in general, presents personal names in Gaelic. I have thus taken the decision in this book to render all personal names in their Gaelic form as far as possible. I have also chosen to use Scots legal terminology. Thus, *feudum* is translated as 'feu', not 'fief'; I use 'infeftment' rather than 'enfeoffment'; 'teind' instead of 'tithe'; 'dissasine' instead of 'disseisin' (and all the variants); 'mortancestry' or 'mortancestor' instead of '*mort d'ancestor*'; 'essonzie' instead of 'essoin', and so on.

One major corpus of evidence used in this book is the statutes and assizes issued by kings of Scots over the twelfth and thirteenth centuries. The current edition of these texts—that produced by Thomas Thomson for volume 1 of the *Acts of the Parliaments of Scotland* (1844)—is, however, seriously problematic, for reasons which this book will set out. I am preparing an edition of these texts, provisionally entitled *The Auld Lawes of Scotland*, which will not appear before the publication of this book. I have only used the manuscript texts of these laws. Their position in *APS*, volume 1, is set out in Table A.1 in the Appendix to this book. By consulting this table, the reader will know where in *APS* they can find at least a version of the particular text. My new edition of *Leges Scocie* is already in print (A. Taylor, '*Leges Scocie* and the Lawcodes of David I, William the Lion and Alexander II', *SHR*, vol. 88, no. 226 (2009), pp. 207–88, at pp. 246–88), and is referenced throughout this book. I have not, however, always followed the translation provided in my *SHR* article because my understanding of these texts has naturally altered over the five years since preparing the translation and finishing this book. Readers should therefore not assume that the translations given in this book always match those provided back in 2009. References to the edition of *Leges Scocie* in this book refer only to the Latin text.

A major narrative source of the period covered by this book is *Gesta Annalia*, long attributed to the fourteenth-century chronicler John of Fordun. In 1999, however, Dauvit Broun showed that *Gesta Annalia* was not the work of Fordun but in fact consisted of two separate works, dubbed *Gesta Annalia* I and *Gesta Annalia* II (Dauvit Broun, 'A New Look at *Gesta Annalia* attributed to John of Fordun', in B. E. Crawford ed., *Church, Chronicle and Learning in Medieval and Early Renaissance Scotland* (Edinburgh, 1999), pp. 9–30; and now Dauvit Broun, *Scottish Independence and the Idea of Britain from the Picts to Alexander III* (Edinburgh, 2007)). *Gesta Annalia* I was in existence by early 1285; Broun (2007) has since shown that it belonged to an even longer work, which drew on a now lost history of the Scottish people, probably written by Richard Vairement. The standard edition of the whole text of *Gesta Annalia* is still, however, W. F. Skene's edition and

Felix Skene's translation of the *Chronica* of John of Fordun, published in 1871 and 1872 respectively. In order to distinguish between Fordun's *Chronica* and *Gesta Annalia* I, citations from *Gesta Annalia* I will be given as '*Gesta Annalia* I in Skene, *Fordun*, vol. no., p. 0' while those from John of Fordun's *Chronica* will be given as 'Skene, *Fordun*, vol. no., p. 0'.

While I was in the process of writing this book, the database *The People of Medieval Scotland* (PoMS) was launched (<http://db.poms.ac.uk>). It is, essentially, a prosopographical database (but also so much more than this), based on the evidence of all surviving charters from medieval Scotland, 1094–1314. This is a remarkable resource, born out of two AHRC-funded projects, *The Paradox of Medieval Scotland* (2007–10) and *The Breaking of Britain* (2010–13). These were run by a combination of the Universities of Glasgow, Lancaster, and Edinburgh, and King's College London. The project was the brainchild of Dr Matthew Hammond and was headed by Professor Dauvit Broun, along with Dr Hammond, Dr Amanda Beam, Professor John Bradley, Professor David Carpenter, Dr John Reuben Davies, Dr Beth Hartland, Professor Roibeard Ó Maolalaigh, Dr Michele Pasin, and Professor Keith Stringer, among others (for a full list, see <http://www.poms.ac.uk/about/project-team/>). I have obviously made use of this database in this book, and have checked most of my citations against it. Where I have been led through the database to a document which I would not otherwise have found, I have cited the PoMS reference number after the document in question. Where I have taken material directly from the PoMS database, the database is my sole reference point. For information about how to cite the PoMS database, see <http://www.poms. ac.uk/information/how-to-cite/>. It cannot be stressed enough how extraordinary and helpful this database is.

The acts of Alexander II are soon to be available as the third volume in the series *Regesta Regum Scottorum* (*RRS*), published by Edinburgh University Press. Professor Keith Stringer has been editing these *acta*, and the volume will also include Dr John Reuben Davies's analysis of the diplomatic of Alexander II's *acta*. As this edition will be the standard edition of Alexander II's *acta*, this presents a problem of referencing for this book. I have referenced the already published texts of Alexander II's charters (many in nineteenth-century editions) but have also added the references to *RRS*, volume 3, in square brackets following the reference in question. In this way, it will be clear to which text I am referring when Professor Stringer's edition is published. All the references to *RRS*, iii, have been checked against the list provided on the PoMS website (which also uses the *RRS*, iii, references), online at <http://www.poms.ac.uk/information/reference-information/rrs-iii-references/>. All citations to online sources were accessed on 22 May 2015. All internal cross-references in this book refer to the relevant chapter and then the page number. If the cross-reference is to a section in the same chapter, then the reference reads: 'see above/below, pp. 00–00'.

Finally, the decision to expand my doctoral research into a book was taken sometime after the completion of my doctorate (2009). This book therefore completely supersedes the thesis. As a result, some elements of the book have already been published or are, at the time of writing, forthcoming. As stated earlier, I am grateful to the publishers (Boydell and Brewer and the Centre for Scottish and Celtic Studies) for granting permission for the reuse of this material.

Chapter 2 is a shortened form of:

A. Taylor, 'Common Burdens in the *Regnum Scottorum*: the evidence of charter diplomatic', in Dauvit Broun ed., *The Reality behind Charter Diplomatic: Studies by Dauvit Broun, John Reuben Davies, Richard Sharpe and Alice Taylor* (Glasgow, 2011), pp. 166–234.

Chapter 3 contains extracts from:

A. Taylor, 'Crime without Punishment: Medieval Scottish Law in Comparative Perspective', *Anglo-Norman Studies*, 35, ed. David Bates (Woodbridge, 2013), pp. 287–304.

Chapters 6 and 7 contain extracts from:

A. Taylor, 'Auditing and Enrolment in Thirteenth-Century Scotland', in *The Growth of Royal Government under Henry III*, ed. David Crook and Louise Wilkinson (Woodbridge, 2015), pp. 85–103.

Map 1. Frequently mentioned places and regions in north Britain

Introduction

This book is not about politics nor is it concerned with the deeds of kings. Rather, it is concerned with the changing form of royal government in the kingdom of the Scots during the twelfth and thirteenth centuries—or, in other words, the shape of the state in medieval Scotland. The chronological limits chosen for this book, 1124–1290, encompass the time when the way kings of Scots ruled, and what records their rule produced, changed dramatically: permanent institutions of government were introduced, the geographical reach of their kingdom extended to cover almost all of what is now Scotland, and royal authority was felt much more intensively in the localities than previously. In short, this period was when kings in Scotland started governing as a matter of administrative routine, through institutions and officials, and produced records of their government. How this happened and what form this state took is the subject of this book; its focus is on changing political structures, rather than actors.

The shape of the state in Scotland in the central Middle Ages has never been examined fully in a single study; this book fills this gap. It is an important subject. The introduction and development of governmental institutions are key to our understanding of the European central Middle Ages as a whole. Throughout Western Europe, the central Middle Ages are understood to be the period when kings started to govern in ways that look familiar to us now; not for nothing did Joseph Strayer concentrate on the central Middle Ages in his influential book *On the Medieval Origins of the Modern State*.[1] But Scotland is rarely integrated into this narrative, either by historians of Scotland or by historians of European government. The most recent book on the subject by Thomas N. Bisson did not mention Scotland but concentrated mainly on the 'core' kingdoms of Europe: France, the German Empire, England, as well as taking in parts of Spain and Italy.[2] One aim of this book is thus to integrate Scotland into wider European narratives. This is not to say that this book adopts a comparative approach but, at the end, it does analyse the example of government in Scotland as part of a wider, rather than

---

[1] Joseph R. Strayer, *On the Medieval Origins of the Modern State*, with forewords by Charles Tilly and William Chester Jordan (Princeton, 2005), pp. 3–56; but see Charles Tilly, 'Reflections on the History of European State-Making', in *The Formation of National States in Western Europe*, ed. Charles Tilly (Princeton, 1975), pp. 3–83; see also Fredric L. Cheyette, 'The Invention of the State', in *The Walter Prescott Memorial Lectures: Essays on Medieval Civilisation*, ed. R. E. Sullivan, B. K. Lachner and K. R. Philp (Austin and London, 1978), pp. 143–78.

[2] Thomas N. Bisson, *The Crisis of the Twelfth Century: Power, Lordship and the Origins of European Government* (Princeton, 2009).

nationally particularistic, phenomenon that is of key importance to the European central Middle Ages as a whole.[3]

As a result, this book contributes to our conceptualizations of medieval states. State is a controversial word among medieval historians and some question whether it should be used as an analytical or comparative concept. It is, after all, not contemporary to the period and it is often thought that medieval power was too 'privatized', held too much by a non-royal elite, to really develop a sense of the abstract public, a concept so key to modern understandings of state power.[4] But the term is adopted here in order to understand better how power and political form worked in one particular kingdom in order to work towards a more nuanced understanding of medieval statehood. The key contribution this book will make to the study of medieval statehood is its understanding that the heavy presence of non-royal elite power was not inimical to the emergence of relatively intensive public institutions of power; indeed, in medieval Scotland, elite power was formally part of state structures. This should allow for more fruitful synchronic and diachronic comparisons to be made with other places and periods.

Existing concepts of state in the central Middle Ages are normally drawn from modern ones and invariably start with or are influenced by the work of the sociologist Max Weber. Weber's core concept of the bureaucratic state stresses the importance of a public order, separate from private interests, which are themselves supposed to be protected by governmental authority and institutional structures. The central authority exercises a monopoly over legitimate violence: it defines what violence is legitimate, what illegitimate, and exercises this authority within a geographically and administratively defined political unit, such as a nation or country (whence the term, nation-state).[5] Moreover, bureaucratic states have a structure of officialdom whereby people with a private existence serve and work for state institutions (such as the judicial system, the civil service, the police force, or fire service, to take some examples from today). These people serve the state in a public, abstract capacity in order to provide for the needs of the people who, in theory, submit to the authority of the state. Many of these elements have been used as the benchmarks of determining the existence (or otherwise) of medieval states.

---

[3] For the methodology of comparative history, see Chris Wickham, 'Problems in Doing Comparative History', reprinted in *Challenging the Boundaries of Medieval History*, ed. Patricia Skinner (Turnhout, 2009), pp. 5–28; for the ambiguities and tensions in national historiographies, see Chris Wickham, 'The Early Middle Ages and National Identity', in *Die Deutung der mittelalterlichen Gesellschaft in der Moderne (19.–21. Jahrhundert)*, ed. Natalie Fryde, Pierre Monnet, Otto Gerhard Oexle, and Leszek Zygner. (Göttingen, 2006), pp. 107–22.

[4] For work on medieval states, see, among many, the collection of essays in Walter Pohl and Veronika Wieser ed., *Der frühmittelalterliche Staat—europäishe Perspektiven*, Forschungen zur Geschichte des Mittelalters 16 (Vienna, 2009); see further, Susan Reynolds, 'The Historiography of the Medieval State', in *Companion to Historiography*, ed. Michael Bentley (London, 1997), pp. 117–38; R. R. Davies, 'The Medieval State: the Tyranny of a Concept?', *Journal of Historical Sociology*, vol. 16 (2003), pp. 280–300; Susan Reynolds, 'There were States in Medieval Europe: A Response to Rees Davies', *Journal of Historical Sociology*, vol. 16 (2003), pp. 550–5.

[5] Max Weber, *Economy and Society: An Outline of Interpretative Sociology*, ed. Guenther Roth and Claus Wittich, 2 vols (Berkeley and Los Angeles, 1987), ii, pp. 901–1005, particularly pp. 956–1005.

However, if one adopts only modern criteria of statehood as barometers for medieval states, then we run the risk of misunderstanding their form: elements in a society that correspond with the above criteria, such as royal judicial institutions, may be identified as facets of a 'state', while those which are seen as private interests and privileges, such as aristocratic jurisdictions, can be relegated to other areas of historical study, such as lordship.[6]

As its broadest possible aim, therefore, this book seeks to challenge as a fallacy the notion that royal and aristocratic power serve fundamentally different interests (the 'public' and the 'private' respectively) and thus are structurally opposed forces of political power. What may look like autonomous elite power (and thus a potentially weak or non-existent state) was, in fact, the constitution of medieval states that kings relied on to greater or lesser degrees. Scotland is a good case study for such a position: the developing intensity of royal government and the introduction of royal courts did not develop at the expense of the 'private' power of aristocrats; instead, such developments formally relied upon that power. Major aristocrats served as the king's central and local officials and their courts were a necessary part of royal justice. Elite power was, in fact, the basis of Scotland's statehood. The dynamic between kings, aristocrats and administrative institutions is thus put forward in the conclusion to set the framework for further comparative work on medieval states. How far aristocratic power was incorporated into the government of a particular kingdom, and how that affected, and was affected by the dynamic between local and central power structures, allows us to understand better the governmental varieties that existed in Europe during the central Middle Ages.

Given the importance and complexity of the subject of the state to the history of Europe in the central Middle Ages, it is surprising that no previous monograph has tackled this subject directly in relation to Scotland, even more so since states and royal governments were the first real interests of academic historians across Western Europe when the discipline first began to be taught as an autonomous subject in universities during the second half of the nineteenth century.[7] This does not mean that historians of medieval Scotland have never examined its government. On the contrary, some consensus has developed concerning the chronology and form of administrative, judicial and institutional change, a consensus which this book will challenge.[8] But it remains that there is no monograph on the subject and current historians have to rely on scattered articles written at different points

---

[6] Thomas N. Bisson, 'Medieval Lordship', *Speculum*, vol. 70, no. 4 (1995), pp. 743–59.
[7] For this development in England (mainly in Oxford and Cambridge), see Reba N. Soffer, *Discipline and Power: The University, History and the Making of an English Elite, 1870–1930* (Stanford, 1994). It is possible that the reason why the twelfth and thirteenth centuries were not ripe for a more nationalist-inspired 'origins of Scottish statehood' was not only the ambiguous position of Scotland within the Union but also the concentration of Scottish national identity on the Gaelic past, to which the changes of the twelfth and thirteenth centuries stand in an ambivalent position; see, for the early modern position, Colin Kidd, *British Identities before Nationalism: Ethnicity and Nationhood in the Atlantic World 1600–1800* (Cambridge, 1999), pp. 123–45; and, for its effect on the historiography, see Matthew H. Hammond, 'Ethnicity and the Writing of Medieval Scottish History', *SHR* vol. 85, no. 219 (2006), pp. 1–27.
[8] Fuller bibliographies are given at the start of each chapter, so only a few will be cited here: for administration, see *RRS*, i, pp. 27–56; *RRS*, ii, pp. 28–67; G. W. S. Barrow, 'The Justiciar', in

over the last 100 years or so. In part, the absence of a monograph must be the result of the loss of the majority of the written outputs of royal government during the twelfth and thirteenth centuries. In this, Scotland stands almost in complete opposition to its southern neighbour, England, in that its records have not survived and cannot be used. How can academic interest in government be sustained and, moreover, develop, when faced with such a scarcity of surviving material?[9] Those historians who have worked on government in twelfth- and thirteenth-century Scotland have predominantly used royal and non-royal charters, which predominantly have come down to us in beneficiary archives, on the assumption that other types of source material either do not survive or survive in a form too late and suspect to be used with any authority.[10] But this book shows that some other types of written sources—in particular, the legal evidence—can be used with confidence and it is this corpus of relatively untapped material which has enabled a new narrative on the subject to be written.

THE EXPANSION OF ROYAL POWER OVER NORTH BRITAIN

The period covered by this book is unified in two ways. First, it is given coherence through the patterns of survival of the evidence: 1124 is the earliest possible date for the earliest surviving record of dispute settlement in Scotland north of the Forth; 1290 is the latest year covered in our earliest set of royal account rolls (which survive only in seventeenth-century transcripts). But it is also given unity through political history: 1124 is the year of the accession of David I, an important king in traditional histories of royal government, while 1290 is the date of the death of his great-great-great-great-granddaughter, Margaret, in September 1290, a cataclysmic event in the history of the kingdom of the Scots, which prompted a competition for the kingship, invasion by Edward I, and temporary conquest.[11] But, before this occurred, between 1124 and 1290, the kingdom of the Scots in the twelfth and thirteenth centuries was ruled by a single royal line which, until the death of Alexander III in 1286, all inherited directly in the male line.

This dynasty descended from Mael Coluim III (1058–93), son of Donnchad (d.1040), and Mael Coluim's second wife, Margaret (later a canonized saint), who

G. W. S. Barrow, *The Kingdom of the Scots. Government, Church and Society from the eleventh to the fourteenth century*, 2nd edn (Edinburgh, 2003), pp. 68–111; for developments in law, see Hector L. MacQueen, *Common Law and Feudal Society in Medieval Scotland* (Edinburgh, 1993).

[9] John Maitland Thomson, *The Public Records of Scotland* (Glasgow, 1922); for an introduction to the sources, see Bruce Webster, *Scotland from the Eleventh Century to 1603* (London, 1975).

[10] Most obviously, *RRS*, i, pp. 27–56; *RRS*, ii, pp. 28–67; A. A. M. Duncan, *Scotland: the Making of the Kingdom* (Edinburgh, 1975), who did use the legal material more than Geoffrey Barrow.

[11] For two recent analyses of the post-1286, pre-war period, see Michael Brown, 'Aristocratic Politics and the Crisis of Scottish Kingship, 1286–1296', *SHR*, vol. 90, no. 229 (2011), pp. 1–26; A. A. M. Duncan, *The Kingship of the Scots, 842–1292: Succession and Independence* (Edinburgh, 2002), pp. 175–254. For the war and the career of Robert I (1306–29), see G. W. S. Barrow, *Robert Bruce and the Community of the Realm of Scotland*, 4th edn (Edinburgh, 2005), and now Michael Penman, *Robert the Bruce: King of the Scots* (New Haven, 2014), which focuses on Bruce's kingship and government.

was the daughter of Edward the Exile and great-granddaughter of Æthelred II, king of England (978–1016).[12] The direct line descending from Mael Coluim and Margaret produced kings until Alexander III, Mael Coluim's great-great-great-grandson, died in March 1286 after accidentally falling from his horse. The first king of this line to succeed after Mael Coluim III was one of his elder sons, Edgar. Back in 1097, Edgar obtained the kingship of the Scots after a bloody period of struggle for the kingship after Mael Coluim III's death in 1093.[13] Edgar's brothers, Alexander I (1107–1124) and David I (1124–53), ruled after him and, following the latter's death in 1153, David's grandsons, Mael Coluim IV (1153–65) and William the Lion (1165–1214), ruled until 1214.[14] William's son, Alexander II (1214–49), succeeded him, while Alexander II was followed by his son, Alexander III (1249–86).[15] In 1290, Alexander III's granddaughter, Margaret, known as the 'Maid of Norway', died en route to Scotland. Mael Coluim III and his direct descendants thus ruled the kingdom of the Scots for 228 years; their direct line was finally extinguished after 232 years on the Maid of Norway's death.

[12] Mael Coluim III (now more commonly Mael Coluim mac Donnchada) was the son of Donnchad (Duncan), son of Crínán. Crínán was not a member of Clann Chinaeda, the royal kindred of *Alba*; instead, he may well have married the daughter of Mael Coluim mac Cinaeda (1005–34), Bethóc. For discussion, see Alex Woolf, *From Pictland to Alba 789–1070*, The New Edinburgh History of Scotland 2 (Edinburgh, 2007), pp. 249–55, 256; Duncan, *Kingship of the Scots*, pp. 34–49. For Mael Coluim III's assumption of the kingship, see Woolf, *Pictland to Alba*, pp. 263–71; Duncan, *Kingship of the Scots*, pp. 41–3. For Queen Margaret, see Catherine Keene, *Saint Margaret, Queen of the Scots: A Life in Perspective* (Basingstoke, 2013), particularly pp. 1–80; Joanna Huntington, 'St Margaret of Scotland: Conspicuous Consumption, Genealogical Inheritance and Post-Conquest Authority', *Journal of Scottish Historical Studies*, vol. 33, no. 2 (2013), pp. 149–64; Valerie Wall, 'Queen Margaret of Scotland (1070–93): Burying the Past, Enshrining the Future', in *Queens and Queenship in Medieval Europe*, ed. Anne Duggan (Woodbridge, 1997), pp. 27–38; for the later use of Margaret's Anglo-Saxon ancestry, see Alice Taylor, 'Historical Writing in Twelfth- and Thirteenth-Century Scotland: the Dunfermline Compilation', *Historical Research*, vol. 83, no. 220 (2010), pp. 228–52; and, for all potential family connections, Keene, *Saint Margaret*, pp. 95–117.
[13] This massively simplifies the period 1093–7: see the most recent account in Richard Oram, *Domination and Lordship: Scotland 1070–1230*, The New Edinburgh History of Scotland 3 (Edinburgh, 2011), pp. 38–46; for later retellings of this period, in order to delegitimize later twelfth-century claims to the kingship from the descendants of Donnchad II, Mael Coluim III's son from his previous marriage, see Dauvit Broun, 'Contemporary Perspectives on Alexander II's Succession: the Evidence of King-lists', in *The Reign of Alexander II, 1214–49*, ed. Richard Oram (Leiden, 2005), pp. 79–98.
[14] There is a large body of scholarship on David I, some of which is noted below, note 62. There is far less on Alexander I, although see Duncan, *Kingship of the Scots*, pp. 59–60, 84–9; and Kenneth Veitch, ' "Replanting Paradise": Alexander I and the reform of religious life in Scotland', *Innes Review*, vol. 52, no. 2 (2001), pp. 136–66. There has been more attention paid to Mael Coluim IV recently but this work more focuses on his internal problems: see, in part, Alasdair Ross, 'The Identity of the Prisoner at Roxburgh: Malcolm son of Alexander or Malcolm MacHeth?', in *Fil súil nglais: A Grey Eye Looks Back. A Festschrift in Honour of Colm Ó Baoill*, ed. Sharon Arbuthnot and Kaarina Hollo (Brig O' Turk, 2007), pp. 269–82; Alex Woolf, 'The Song of the Death of Somerled and the Destruction of Glasgow in 1153', *Journal of the Sydney Society for Scottish History*, vol. 14 (2013), pp. 1–11, at pp. 4–8. William the Lion has been slightly better served, see G. W. S. Barrow, 'The Reign of William the Lion', in G. W. S. Barrow, *Scotland and its Neighbours in the Middle Ages* (London, 1992), pp. 67–89; for the most recent treatment of the reigns of Mael Coluim IV and William the Lion, see Oram, *Domination and Lordship*, pp. 109–14, 115–51, 152–75.
[15] For his minority, see D. E. R. Watt, 'The minority of Alexander III of Scotland', *TRHS*, 5th ser. 21 (1971), pp. 1–23.

Despite its longevity, this line of kings experienced serious challenges to their hold on their kingdom, particularly in the twelfth and early thirteenth centuries. The main threats came from two branches of their very own family which had support not only from within the kingdom but also, at various points, from the Western Isles, Ulster, Orkney, and Norway.[16] The first and earlier challenges came from one Mael Coluim, an illegitimate son of Alexander I, and then Mael Coluim's own descendants, who violently challenged David I, Mael Coluim IV and, just possibly, William the Lion.[17] The second branch, known as the 'MacWilliams', descended from Donnchad II (Duncan), a son from Mael Coluim III's first marriage to Ingibjorg. Donnchad had become king of Scots briefly in 1094 before being killed.[18] Donnchad's son, known as William fitz Duncan, appears to have supported the kingship of his half-uncle, David I, but William's son, Domnall (and then Domnall's sons) had other ideas and sections of the 'MacWilliam' family made serious bids for the kingship of the Scots in the late 1170s–80s, 1211–15, and the late 1220s.[19] The last recorded action against the 'MacWilliams' (the brutal execution of an infant) was in 1230: Alexander II and Alexander III saw no further significant internal challenges to their family's hold on the kingship. These challenges were thus intermittent in the twelfth and early thirteenth centuries but their significance and potential consequences have not been underestimated, particularly in more recent scholarship.[20]

During the central Middle Ages, the area over which kings of Scots ruled expanded significantly; by 1290, it covered almost all of modern Scotland. Where the kingdom of the Scots actually was at the start of the period examined in this book is, however, rather more difficult to establish. In the tenth and eleventh centuries, kings of 'Scots' were, in Gaelic, called *rí Alban*—'kings of *Alba*' ('Britain').[21]

---

[16] R. Andrew McDonald, *Outlaws of Medieval Scotland: Challenges to the Canmore Kings, 1058–1266* (East Linton, 2003), but see the important correctives by Alasdair Ross, cited in notes 14 and 17, and in Alex Woolf, 'The Origins and Ancestry of Somerled: Gofraid mac Fergusa and "The Annals of the Four Masters"', *Medieval Scandinavia*, vol.15 (2005), pp. 199–213.

[17] The identity and importance of Mael Coluim, son of Alexander I, was finally established in Ross, 'Identity', and reiterated in Alasdair Ross, *The Kings of Alba c.1000–c.1130* (Edinburgh, 2011), pp. 195–205. The sons of Mael Coluim, son of Alexander I, challenged Mael Coluim IV in 1154 and it is possible that a grandson of Mael Coluim, son of Alexander, challenged William.

[18] For the argument that Mael Coluim III might had Orkney's support when he obtained the kingship in 1057–8, see Duncan, *Kingship of the Scots*, pp. 42–3, and Woolf, *Pictland to Alba*, pp. 265–70. The only reference to Mael Coluim's marriage to Ingibjorg is in *Orkneyinga Saga*, in *Icelandic Sagas and Other Historical Documents Relating to the Settlement and Descent of the Northmen of the British Isles*, ed. Gudbrand Vigfusson, 4 vols, Rolls Series 88 (London, 1887–94), i, pp. 1–221, at p. 60. For Donnchad, see Broun, 'Contemporary Perspectives', pp. 87–96.

[19] Alasdair Ross, 'Moray, Ulster and the MacWilliams', in *The World of the Galloglass: Kings, Warlords and Warriors in Ireland and Scotland 1200–1600*, ed. Seán Duffy (Dublin, 2007), pp. 24–44.

[20] Ross, 'Identity'; Ross, 'Moray'; Broun, 'Contemporary Perspectives'.

[21] The first appearance of the term *Alba* is in 900. For *Alba*, see, among many, Dauvit Broun, '*Alba*: Pictish homeland or Irish offshoot?', in *Exile and Homecoming: Papers from the 5th Australian Conference of Celtic Studies*, ed. Pamela O'Neill (Sydney, 2005), pp. 234–75, and now Dauvit Broun, *Scottish Independence and the Idea of Britain from the Picts to Alexander III* (Edinburgh, 2007), pp. 71–97; and Dauvit Broun, 'Britain and the beginnings of Scotland', Sir John Rhŷs Memorial Lecture, *Journal of the British Academy*, vol. 3 (2015), pp. 107–37. For an earlier view, which saw the coinage of *Alba* as representing a new 'politically defined grouping', see Máire Herbert, '*Rí Éirenn, Rí*

Alba could be Latinized as *Albania* but it could also be denoted by the word *Scotia*—Scotland—although *Scotia* first appears as a name for *Alba* as late as *c*.980.[22] This area of 'Scotland' denoted a rather smaller area than it does today.[23] *Scotia* meant the region bounded by the River Forth in the South, the River Spey in the north, and the mountain range known as Druim Alban (often now referred to as 'Drumalban', meaning the 'ridge' or 'spine' of *Alba* or 'Britain').[24] *Scotia*— or Scotland—was not only distinguishable from Moray in the north (Gaelic: *Muréb*), which lay west of the River Spey, but also greater Lothian in the south, which encompassed the area between the Tweed and Forth.[25] The 'E' text of the Anglo-Saxon Chronicle reported that, in 1091, Mael Coluim III went 'out of *Scotlande* into Lothian in *Englaland*', revealing that he saw Lothian as in England, not in Scotland, which lay north of the Forth.[26] *Scotia*—meaning 'modern Scotland north of the Forth, south and east of the Spey and east of Druim Alban'—should really be translated as 'Scotland', as the Anglo-Saxon Chronicler did in 1091.[27] However, I will refer to it as 'Scotia' in this book, in order to keep the country conceptually separate from our territorial understanding of modern Scotland.

The kings of *Alba* were not, however, confined to Scotia at the end of the eleventh century; Moray and Lothian were, in different ways and at different points, integral to their authority. Until 1034, all the kings of *Alba* descended from the later ninth-century kings Caustantín and Áed, both sons of Cinaed mac Ailpín

Alban: kingship and identity in the ninth and tenth centuries', in *Kings, Clerics and Chronicles in Scotland 500–1297: Essays in Honour of Marjorie Ogilvie Anderson*, ed. Simon Taylor (Dublin, 2000), pp. 62–72.

[22] Woolf, *Pictland to Alba*, p. 248, note 35.

[23] 'Scotland' (Latin: *Scotia*; Old Norse: Skotland) was also used of the kingdom of Dál Riata; for which see Alex Woolf, 'Reporting Scotland in the Anglo-Saxon Chronicle', in *Reading the Anglo-Saxon Chronicle: Language, Literature, History*, ed. Alice Jorgensen (Turnhout, 2010), pp. 221–39, at pp. 233–4. That Dál Riata could also be called *Albania* (or *Alba*) by later writers is demonstrated by the text 'de situ Albanie' ['On the location of *Alba*'], compiled 1165×84, which states that 'Fergus, son of Erc himself was first of the seed of Conaire who received the realm of *Alba* (*regnum Álban*), that is from the mountain Druimm-nAlbain or Druimm-nErenn as far as the sea of Ireland and as far as Inchgal [i.e. the Hebrides]'; translation taken from David Howlett, *Caledonian Craftsmanship: The Scottish Latin Tradition* (Dublin, 2000), pp. 29–39, at p. 31 (Latin), p. 34 (English).

[24] For an in-depth study of the 'spine of Britain', see Philip M. Dunshea, '*Druim Alban, Dorsum Britanniae*—"the Spine of Britain"', *SHR*, vol. 92, no. 235 (2013), pp. 275–89. For the relocation of the earlier Pictish kingdom of Fortriu (previously thought to have been in later Scotia), see Alex Woolf, 'Dún Nectáin, Fortriu and the Geography of the Picts', *SHR*, vol. 85, no. 220 (2006), pp. 182–201.

[25] The first mention of *Muréb* is in the 'Chronicle of the Kings of Alba', which states that Mael Coluim mac Domnaill, king of Alba in the mid-tenth century, 'marched into Moray (*in Moreb*) and killed Cellach'; see Benjamin T. Hudson, 'The "Scottish Chronicle"', *SHR* vol. 77, no. 204 (1998), pp. 129–61, at p. 150. In the late 1130s, Geoffrey of Monmouth recorded that Auguselus's kingdom was called *Albania* 'which is now called *Scotia*'. *Alba/Scotia* was distinguished from *Murefensium*, and *Lodonesiae*, given by Arthur to Uranius and Loth respectively; *Geoffrey of Monmouth: The History of the Kings of Britain*, ed. Michael Reeve, trans. Neil Wright (Woodbridge, 2007), 156.328. I owe this reference to Alex Woolf, 'Geoffrey of Monmouth and the Picts', in *Bile ós Chrannaibh: A Festschrift for William Gillies*, ed. W. McLeod, A. Burnyeat, D. U. Stiùbhart, T.O. Clancy and R. Ó Maolalaigh (Brig O' Turk, 2010), pp. 269–80, at pp. 270–1, 278, note 11.

[26] *ASC* E *s.a.* 1091.

[27] As was done in, for example, Broun, 'Britain and the beginnings of Scotland', pp. 109–10.

(d.858), once seen as the Scottish 'conqueror' of Pictland (the reality is, of course, much more complex).[28] This large royal kin-group is known as Clann Chinaeda meic Ailpín in recent modern scholarship—'the kin (or clann) of Cinaed mac Ailpín'. Both Alex Woolf and Dauvit Broun have suggested that at least one branch of Clann Chinaeda (descending from Áed) had its landed base around the Moray Firth, while the other (descending from Caustantín) had its base in southern Scotia. Thus, when the 'Áed' branch of Clann Chinaeda held the kingship of *Alba* in the tenth and early eleventh centuries, it did so from a powerbase in Moray (*Muréb*).[29] Over the eleventh century, however, this changed. During Mael Coluim III's reign as king of *Alba* (1058–93), Irish annalists record in 1085 the existence of the first *king* of Moray.[30] At the end of the eleventh century, therefore, the relationship between kings of *Alba* and the region of Moray had changed. In a record of his death in 1093, Mael Coluim III was described as the *ardrí* ('high-king') of *Alba*, perhaps to reflect a looser relationship with Moray by the end of the eleventh century than could ever have been predicted at its beginning.[31] The last *rí Muréb* on record is one Óengus, who died fighting against the forces of David I in 1130.[32]

Lothian was once part of the old kingdom of Northumbria, and was seen as an English-speaking region. In the early 730s, Bede wrote in his *Ecclesiastical History* that Abercorn (near Edinburgh) was located in a 'region of the English (*regione Anglorum*) but near the barrier [the Forth] which divides the lands of the English (*Anglorum terras*) and the Picts'.[33] Over the tenth century and early eleventh century, kings of *Alba* gradually gained control over Lothian.[34] *The Chronicle of the Kings of Alba* records that in the reign of Ildub, king of *Alba* (954–62), Edinburgh (*opidum Eden*) was abandoned (by whom we are not told) and left 'to the Scots' (*Scottis*).[35] Later sources state that different English kings gave or ceded Lothian to the kings of Scots at some point in the late tenth or eleventh century; we do not

---

[28] Woolf, *Pictland to Alba*, pp. 93–102, 106–17, 122–9, 223–4; Dauvit Broun, 'Dunkeld and the origin of Scottish identity', *Innes Review*, vol. 48, no. 2 (1997), pp. 112–24.

[29] Alex Woolf, 'The "Moray Question" and the Kingship of Alba in the Tenth and Eleventh centuries', *SHR*, vol. 79, no. 208 (2000), pp. 145–64, at pp. 154–6; Dauvit Broun, 'The Origins of the *mormaer*', in *The Earl in Medieval Britain*, ed. David Crouch and Hugh F. Doherty (forthcoming).

[30] *AU* 1085.1. The tangled politics of the eleventh century (of which the above represents a considerable simplification) are explored in Woolf, *Pictland to Alba*, pp. 240–2, 244–8, 252–71, and Woolf, 'Moray Question', *passim*.

[31] *AU* 1093.5. This may reflect only the period *after* Mael Coluim III became king. Lulach and Macbethad were both called *ardrí* in their obituaries in the Annals of Ulster; *AU*, 1058.2; *AU*, 1058.6. Macbethad was the son of Findláech, who was called *mormaer* of Moray and *rí Alban* in the Annals of Tigernach and the Annals of Ulster respectively; for discussion, see Woolf, *Pictland to Alba*, pp. 227–30; Broun, 'Origins of the *mormaer*'.

[32] *AU*, 1130.4.

[33] Bede, *Ecclesiastical History of the English People*, ed. and trans. B. Colgrave and R. A. B. Mynors (Oxford, 1969), pp. 428–9; commented on in George Molyneaux, *The Formation of the English Kingdom in the Tenth Century* (Oxford, 2015), pp. 5–7.

[34] For the extension of Scottish control over Lothian, see Marjorie O. Anderson, 'Lothian and the Early Scottish Kings', *SHR*, vol. 39, no. 128 (1960), pp. 98–112; Bernard Meehan, 'The Siege of Durham, the Battle of Carham and the Cession of Lothian', *SHR*, vol. 55, no. 159 (1976), pp. 1–19; A. A. M. Duncan, 'The Battle of Carham, 1018', *SHR*, vol. 55, no. 159 (1976), pp. 20–8; Woolf, *Pictland to Alba*, pp. 232–40.

[35] Hudson, 'Scottish Chronicle', p. 151.

need to accept the chronological difficulties in the accounts of such gifts to acknowledge that some sort of formal recognition of Scottish possession of Lothian was made on more than one occasion between the late tenth and the late eleventh century.[36] That Lothian had become an area under the king of *Alba*'s authority did not mean that it was seen as being *in Alba*. As we have already seen, in 1091, the Anglo-Saxon Chronicle text referred to Lothian as 'in England' but, as Molyneaux has shown, 'England' did not mean part of the English kingdom but, instead, an area inhabited by English-speaking people.[37] That Lothian was the 'land of the English' was again stressed in the later twelfth century. In *c*.1180, Adam of Dryburgh, writing at the Premonstratensian house of Dryburgh in the modern Scottish borders, described himself as living 'in the land of the English and the kingdom of the Scots'.[38] In the 'Life of Margaret', written (probably) between 1100 and 1107, Turgot, prior of Durham, described how Queen Margaret, caused 'little dwellings' to be built on 'each bank of the sea dividing Lothian (*Lodoneia*) and Scotland (*Scotia*)' so that poor men and pilgrims could rest after visiting St Andrews in Fife.[39] There is no sense in Turgot's testimony that Lothian was not part of Mael Coluim and Margaret's kingdom; only that, therein, there existed a sea which divided two areas—Lothian and Scotland, divided by the Firth of Forth.[40]

Until the mid-eleventh century, there was an expectation that there would be kings in Cumbria, the area of Britain once known as Strathclyde which, at its greatest extent, stretched up into Clydesdale (as far east as Peebles), with its pre-mier church perhaps at Govan, and down into the Solway region.[41] The last king

---

[36] The 'gift' of Lothian to kings of Scots is mentioned (in very different ways) in *De obsessione Dunelmi* and *De primo Saxonum adventu*, both printed in *Symeonis Monachi Opera Omnia*, ed. T. Arnold, Rolls Series 75, 2 vols (London, 1882–5), i, pp. 215–20, ii, pp. 365–84, at p. 218 and p. 382 respectively; Orderic Vitalis, *The Ecclesiastical History of Orderic Vitalis*, ed. and trans. M. Chibnall, 6 vols (Oxford, 1968–80), iv, pp. 268–71.

[37] Molyneaux, *Formation*, p. 6.

[38] Adam of Dryburgh, *De tripartito tabernaculo*, in *Patrologia Latina Cursus Completus*, ed. J. P. Migne, 221 vols (Paris, 1844–64), vol. 198, cols 609–796, at col. 723. That the borders did gradually start to see themsleves as 'Scottish' in the thirteenth century is discussed with reference to the Melrose Chronicle in Dauvit Broun, 'Becoming Scottish in the Thirteenth Century: The Evidence of the Chronicle of Melrose', in *West over Sea: Studies in Scandinavian Sea-Borne Expansion and Settlement before 1300. A Festschrift in Honour of Dr Barbara E. Crawford*, ed. Beverley Ballin Smith, Simon Taylor and Gareth Williams (Leiden, 2007), pp. 19–32.

[39] Turgot, *Vita Sancte Margarete*, in *Symeonis Dunelmensis Opera et Collectanea*, ed. I. H. Hinde, Surtees Society 51 (Durham, 1868), pp. 234–54, at p. 247.

[40] A charter of Mael Coluim's son, Edgar, issued in 1095 when he was claiming the kingship of the Scots (but now only surviving in rather complicated forms), refers to his possession of 'the whole land of Lothian (*Lodoneio*) and the kingdom of Scotland (*regnum Scotie*)', which he claimed by 'paternal inheritance' and the gift of William Rufus; Lawrie, *ESC*, no. 15. This charter has been deemed spurious but is defended in A.A.M. Duncan, 'Yes, the earliest Scottish Charters', *SHR*, vol. 78, no. 205 (1999), pp. 1–38.

[41] For the name Cumbria, see P. A. Wilson, 'On the use of the terms "Strathclyde" and "Cumbria"', *Transactions of the Cumberland and Westmorland Antiquarian and Archaeological Society*, vol. 66 (1966), pp. 57–92; Dauvit Broun, 'The Welsh Identity of the Kingdom of Strathclyde *c*.900–*c*.1200', *Innes Review*, vol. 55, no. 2 (2004), pp. 111–80, at pp. 111–13, 127–9; Woolf, *Pictland to Alba*, pp. 152–4; for Govan, see Stephen T. Driscoll, 'Church Archaeology in Glasgow and the kingdom of Strathclyde', *Innes Review*, vol. 49, no. 2 (1998), pp. 95–114; for the argument that 'Cumbria' was adopted as the

of the region on record was Owain (once denoted as 'king of the Clydesmen'), who allied with Mael Coluim mac Cinaeda of *Alba* in, perhaps, 1018, against Uhtred, earl of Northumbria.[42] There may well have been an attempt in the mid-eleventh century to restore another Mael Coluim, a 'son of the king of the Cumbrians' (perhaps the son of Owain), to the kingship of Cumbria but this attempt seems to have been short-lived.[43] Under Mael Coluim III, there is no reference to a king of the Cumbrians; indeed Symeon of Durham's *Historia Regum* records in 1070 that Mael Coluim III invaded *Cumbreland* which became 'possessed not through right but subjugated through force'.[44] In 1092, William Rufus captured Carlisle but even after his reign the area could still be seen by some as under the control of the kings of *Alba*.[45] The future David I was described as *princeps* ('prince' or 'ruler') of the 'Cumbrian region' in the reign of his elder brother, Alexander I (1107–24).[46]

At the end of the eleventh century, therefore, kings of Scots controlled *Alba*, Lothian and probably Cumbria (Strathclyde). Their relationship with Moray appears to have changed: although the region was once key to the royal kin-group (and indeed provided kings of *Alba* well into the mid-eleventh century), it seems to have become more detached by the century's end, sporting its own kings. By 1290, however, the areas over which kings of Scots exercised their authority had increased significantly. Galloway lies in the extreme south-west of modern Scotland: the last king of Galloway so titled died in 1161; his sons, grandson, and great-grandson were all lords in Galloway thereafter under the authority of the kings of Scots.[47] In 1234, the male line failed and the lordship of Galloway was divided among three co-heiresses after a short but violent struggle against the king in 1235 (which was nonetheless remembered as a 'war' (*guerra*) within ten years of the event).[48] In the west, Alexander II took campaigns into Argyll from the 1220s onwards and, in 1266, Magnus, king of Norway, sold Man and the Western Isles to the kingdom of the Scots for 4000 marks.[49] In the very far north, Sutherland was detached from the earldom of Caithness before 1222.[50] From the late eleventh century, the earldom

---

new name of the expanding kingdom of Strathclyde south of the Clyde valley in the early tenth century, see Fiona Edmonds, 'The Emergence and Transformation of Medieval Cumbria', *SHR*, vol. 93, no. 237 (2014), pp. 195–216.

[42] Woolf, *Pictland to Alba*, pp. 236–40; for the suggestion that 'king of the Clydesmen' denoted a Northumbrian, expansionist, perspective, see Edmonds, 'Medieval Cumbria', p. 209.

[43] Woolf, *Pictland to Alba*, pp. 261–3; Edmonds, 'Medieval Cumbria', pp. 209–10.

[44] Symeon of Durham, *Historia Regum*, ed. Arnold, ii, p. 191; Woolf, *Pictland to Alba*, pp. 270–1; Edmonds, 'Medieval Cumbria', pp. 210–11.

[45] *ASC* E, *s.a.* 1092.   [46] *CDI*, no. 15.

[47] For Galloway, see Richard Oram, *The Lordship of Galloway* (Edinburgh, 2000).

[48] *Glasgow Reg.*, i, no. 187 [AII/301]; Duncan, *Making of the Kingdom*, pp. 530–2.

[49] Richard Oram, *Alexander II, king of Scots, 1214–1249* (Edinburgh, 2012), pp. 79–81, 85–94, 99–103, 179–91; Noel Murray, 'Swerving from the Path of Justice: Alexander II's Relations with Argyll and the Western Isles, 1214–49', in *Reign of Alexander II*, ed. Oram, pp. 285–305; Edward J. Cowan, 'Norwegian Sunset – Scottish Dawn: Hakon IV and Alexander III', in *Scotland in the Reign of Alexander III, 1249–1286*, ed. N. H. Reid (Edinburgh, 1990), pp. 103–31; for an in-depth study of the treaty, see Richard I. Lustig, 'The Treaty of Perth: A Re-Examination', *SHR*, vol. 58, no. 165 (1979), pp. 35–57.

[50] Barbara E. Crawford, *The Northern Earldoms: Orkney and Caithness from AD 870 to 1470* (Edinburgh, 2013), pp. 264–7; Barbara E. Crawford, 'The Earldom of Caithness and the Kingdom of

of Caithness itself was held from the kings of Scots but, uniquely, was held jointly with the earldom of Orkney, which was itself under the control of the kings of Norway. The title of earl of Orkney, however, took precedence over that of Caithness. The *jarl* of Orkney submitted to the Norwegian king before assuming the title and only after that could he obtain the title of earl of Caithness from the king of Scots.[51] During the 1230s, however, this process was reversed when the earls of Angus claimed the joint earldom: on this occasion, the new earls of Caithness first submitted to Scottish kings and only afterwards to Norway. In short, by 1290, kings of Scots had formal authority over all of what is now mainland Scotland in a way that would have been unimaginable two centuries earlier.

This brief narrative of the politics of the twelfth and thirteenth centuries is necessarily simplified and thus, in many ways, is misleading, tending towards teleology. Indeed, some territorial gains made during these two centuries did not last: the most obvious example is David I's gain of Northumberland in the late 1130s.[52] In 1139, Northumberland was formally ceded to David I's son, Henry, by King Stephen of England to be held of the English king; in 1157, however, David's grandson, Mael Coluim IV, probably had no alternative but to give it back to Stephen's successor, Henry II, along with Cumberland (in north-west England, inclusive of the southern part of the old kingdom of Cumbria). Attempts to regain Northumberland in particular were made by Mael Coluim's brother, William, and continued by William's son, Alexander II.[53] Most ended in complete failure, particularly in 1173–4, which resulted in William's temporary imprisonment and the imposition of English overlordship over Scotland. The northern counties were only formally ceded in 1237.[54] The emergence of the larger kingdom of the Scots by 1290 was thus in no way inevitable; it could have been a much smaller entity, under the domination of the English king, or, conversely, if northern England had been retained and incorporated into the Scottish kingdom, the geopolitics of north Britain would have been completely different.[55] The kingdom of the Scots could have been a coherent region from, perhaps, the Tyne to the Forth,

Scotland, 1150–1266', in *Essays on the Nobility of Medieval Scotland*, ed. Keith J. Stringer (Edinburgh, 1985), pp. 25–43, at pp. 32–8.

[51] Crawford, *Northern Earldoms*, pp. 276–7.

[52] For comment, see Keith J. Stringer, 'State-building in Twelfth-century Britain: David I, king of Scots, and Northern England', in *Government, Religion and Society in Northern England, 1000–1700*, ed. John C. Appleby and Paul Dalton (Stroud, 1997), pp. 40–62.

[53] For context, see Judith Green, 'Anglo-Scottish Relations, 1066–1174', in *England and her Neighbours, 1066–1453: Essays in Honour of Pierre Chaplais*, ed. Michael Jones and Malcolm Vale (London, 1989), pp. 53–72; Duncan, *Kingship of the Scots*, pp. 99–105; R. R. Davies, *Domination and Conquest: The Experience of Ireland, Scotland and Wales 1100–1300* (Cambridge, 1990), pp. 66–87; Geoffrey [G. W. S.] Barrow, 'Scotland, Wales and Ireland in the Twelfth Century', in *The New Cambridge Medieval History*, vol. 4: *c.1024–1198*, ed. David Luscombe and Jonathan Riley-Smith (Cambridge, 2004), pp. 581–610, at pp. 587–8.

[54] D. W. Hunter Marshall, 'Two Early English Occupations of Southern Scotland', *SHR*, vol. 25, no. 97 (1927), pp. 20–40, at pp. 20–3, 37; Duncan, *Making of the Kingdom*, pp. 228–33; Duncan, *Kingship of the Scots*, pp. 99–102.

[55] For the Scottish-held liberty of Tynedale in the thirteenth century, see M. L. Holford and K. J. Stringer, *Border Liberties and Loyalties: North-East England, c.1200–c.1400* (Edinburgh, 2010), pp. 231–358.

which looked south towards a smaller England, with 'Scotland' (*Scotia*) as its northern outlier. If this had happened, kings of Scots, perhaps losing their control over Moray anyway, might have been more content to leave the far north and west primarily to the politics of the Norwegian-Irish sea-world.[56]

Moreover, it is important to acknowledge that the political expansion of the kingdom did not mean that regional specificity disappeared. The first chapter of the legal compilation known as *Leges Scocie*, probably issued some time in the later twelfth century, delineated the area of Scotia as between the Forth, Spey, and Druim Alban, and contrasted that with the land *ultra Forth* ('beyond' or 'over' the Firth of Forth, denoting 'Galloway or other places', presumably Lothian).[57] This is interesting because it shows that Scotia was the spatial focus for the assize itself, with the southern part of the kingdom merely being described as 'beyond' Scotia's southern limit. A statute issued by Alexander II in 1244 pertained only to Lothian: it mentioned Galloway but only to note that the region had its own 'special laws'.[58] In 1264, the royal chamberlain accounted for all the king's revenue and stated that he was returning the income from sheriffdoms 'on each side of the sea of Scotland', meaning north and south of the Firth of Forth.[59] A chronicle known as *Gesta Annalia* I, written before 1285, referred to King William journeying from Moray through Scotia and down into Lothian.[60] Thus, even though the authority of kings of Scots expanded over north Britain during the twelfth and thirteenth century, a significant level of regional specificity remained.

THE AIMS OF THIS BOOK

Over the two centuries covered by this book, the power of kings of Scots increased over north Britain. This process must have involved the increase of the population of their kingdom, in a period when, across Western Europe, population levels were in general on a sharp rise. This book will not show the practical mechanisms of the extension of royal power through, for example, diplomacy and military activity; these subjects have been dealt with in detail by others.[61] It is instead devoted to

---

[56] Although many lords anyway operated in England, Scotland and Ireland: see, for example, Keith J. Stringer, 'Nobility and Identity in Medieval Britain and Ireland: The de Vescy Family, *c.*1120–1314', in *Britain and Ireland, 900–1300: Insular Responses to Medieval European Change*, ed. Brendan Smith (Cambridge, 1999), pp. 199–239.

[57] *LS*, *c.*1; the later version in *SA* provides the reading 'Lothian or Galloway or elsewhere'; see Alice Taylor, '*Leges Scocie* and the Lawcodes of David I, William the Lion and Alexander II', *SHR*, vol. 88, no. 226 (2009), pp. 207–88, at p. 254, notes 278–9.

[58] *SA*, *c.*2, see also Alice Taylor, 'The Assizes of David I, king of Scots, 1124–53', *SHR*, vol. 91, no. 232 (2012), pp. 197–238, at pp. 230–1.

[59] *ER*, i, p. 10.

[60] *Gesta Annalia* I, in Skene, *Fordun*, i, p. 279 (see also another reference of the king 'advancing' into Moray, in *Gesta Annalia*, in Skene, *Fordun*, i, p. 268); for further examples of this definition of 'Scotland' (*Scotia*), see Dauvit Broun, 'Defining Scotland and the Scots before the Wars of Independence', in *Image and Identity: The Making and Re-Making of Scotland through the Ages*, ed. Dauvit Broun, R. J. Finlay, and Michael Lynch (Edinburgh, 1998), pp. 4–17, particularly pp. 4–9.

[61] Most recently, Oram, *Domination and Lordship*; Michael Brown, *The Wars of Scotland 1214–1371*, New Edinburgh History of Scotland 4 (Edinburgh, 2004).

changes in how royal power was exercised during this period. One of its essential arguments is that permanent, formal, and uniform institutions of government developed later than historians have often thought. As a result of this later chronological development, the book explores how kings of Scots, for much of the twelfth century, could rule without such uniform institutions. In addition, it investigates how the emergence and development of governmental institutions affected the dynamics of power relations, particularly between the king and his lay aristocracy.

In so doing, this book seeks to overturn or refine four prevailing trends in the historiography of medieval Scotland which relate to royal government: the role of David I as the 'founder' of Scottish royal government; the causal force of 'Anglo-Normans' in Scotland in shaping this government; the adoption of English law and governmental practices; and the relationship between aristocratic and royal power. Some of these views are over forty or fifty years old and many current historians would not accept the positions outlined in what follows without at least a degree of qualification. However, because there is a lack of recent work on the structures of government (which many historians have pointed out), it is necessary to sketch these four positions here because, insofar as they relate to royal government, they reflect a consensus which has not yet been overturned in writing. As such, what follows is not a full survey of the scholarship on Scotland during the central Middle Ages but, instead, a description of the present state of published scholarship (some of which is now quite old) on royal government in the twelfth and thirteenth centuries.

First, this book will reject the notion that the introduction of administrative institutions of royal government was a process fundamentally accomplished during the reign of David I, king of Scots (1124–53), and continued—but was not substantially changed—by his grandsons Mael Coluim IV (1153–65) and William the Lion (1165–1214). The development of institutional government in Scotland has primarily been seen, with one key exception, as a twelfth-century phenomenon, with particular importance attached to the reign of David I. From the nineteenth-century work of E. W. Robertson and W. F. Skene, it has become axiomatic to associate with David I the introduction of not only a network of local governmental units—sheriffdoms—but also a royal judicial official (the 'justiciar'), who held his own court.[62] As a result of these innovations, royal government is thought to have become institutionally distinct from other forms of power, allowing the king to govern his kingdom intensely and routinely for the first time, through formal institutions as well as personal networks.

The importance attached to the twelfth century as a whole is partly the result of the research and work of the late G. W. S. Barrow, who died in 2014. Barrow was

---

[62] E. W. Robertson, *Scotland under Her Early Kings*, 2 vols (Edinburgh, 1862), i, pp. 235–320, at pp. 317–20; W. F. Skene, *Celtic Scotland: A History of Ancient Alban*, 3 vols (Edinburgh, 1876–80), i, pp. 457–9; G. W. S. Barrow, 'David I: the Balance of New and Old', and G. W. S. Barrow, 'The Reign of William the Lion', both in Barrow, *Scotland and its Neighbours*, pp. 45–65, 67–89; Richard Oram, *David I: the King who Made Scotland* (Stroud, 2004); Steve Boardman and Alasdair Ross ed., *The Exercise of Power in Medieval Scotland c.1200–1500* (Dublin, 2003), pp. 15–17.

one of the premier charter scholars of the twentieth century and produced, among much else, editions of the charters of the twelfth-century kings of Scots, David I, Mael Coluim IV, William the Lion, as well as those of David's son, Henry, earl of Northumberland (d.1152).[63] It was from the basis of his unparalleled knowledge of the charter material that Barrow established and developed a narrative of twelfth-century governmental development, although he never built up his views into a full study and instead published them as discrete articles, or within the introductions to his editions of charters.[64] In this narrative, Scottish kings started to introduce local administrative units of government—the sheriffdom, modelled on the English shire or county—in the reign of David I (1124–53). David's grandsons and successors (Mael Coluim IV and William) carried on this policy and, by William's death in 1214, the kingdom from Berwick in the south to Inverness in the north and Dumfries in the west was governed through these units.[65] In addition, royal judicial officers ('justiciars') were introduced, again in the reign of David I. By William's death, there were three justiciars, in charge of Scotia, Lothian, and Galloway respectively.[66] Barrow also posited that probative accounting sessions were introduced during William's reign (the development of an 'Exchequer').[67] In this way, government has been seen as a twelfth-century phenomenon, the structures of which were essentially set and formed by the accession of Alexander II in 1214. Any further developments (such as the introduction of common law procedures) were introduced within this structure, rather than substantially changing it.[68]

By contrast, the thirteenth century has, with one exception, been analysed less in terms of government writ large and more in terms of political expansion (into Argyll and the Western Isles) and the kingdom's internal aristocratic politics.[69] As a whole, scholarship interested in power relations and rulership has focused on the question of noble families and noble faction: the rise of certain powerful families (the Comyns, Durwards, Stewarts, Bruces, Balliols) and how their factional politics affected and contributed to royal power, both negatively and positively.[70] Part

---

[63] *RRS*, i (1960); *RRS*, ii (1971); *CDI* (1999).

[64] *RRS*, i, pp. 27–56; *RRS*, ii, pp. 28–67; see also the relevant collected essays in Barrow, *Scotland and its Neighbours* and Barrow, *Kingdom of the Scots*, 1st edn 1973; 2nd edn, 2003. All references in what follows are to the second edition. In a review of the second edition, Alex Woolf noted that *The Kingdom of the Scots* 'has not been superseded after thirty years'; Alex Woolf, Review of G. W. S. Barrow, *The Kingdom of the Scots*, *SHR*, vol. 86, no. 221 (2007), pp. 126–7, at p. 127.

[65] *RRS*, i, pp. 36–49; *RRS*, ii, pp. 39–42.   [66] Barrow, 'Justiciar'.

[67] *RRS*, ii, pp. 58–9; see also Duncan, *Making of the Kingdom*, pp. 596–600, 606–7.

[68] Barrow, 'Justiciar'.

[69] A recent biography of Alexander II actively eschews discussing governmental development in the absence of Keith Stringer's forthcoming edition of the charters of Alexander II; Oram, *Alexander II*, p. 3. There are single volumes on the reigns of Alexander II and Alexander III, published in 2005 and 1990 respectively; Oram, ed., *Reign of Alexander II*; Reid, ed., *Scotland in the Reign of Alexander III*. Although political expansion and internal politics are a feature of both volumes, there is no treatment fully devoted to governmental developments, apart from the single chapters on the law.

[70] See, among many, Alan Young, *Robert the Bruce's Rivals: The Comyns, 1212–1314* (East Linton, 1997), particularly pp. 34–65, 90–120; for a relatively positive assessment, see Alan Young, 'Noble Families and Political Factions in the Reign of Alexander III', in *Scotland in the Reign of Alexander III*,

of the reason for this concentration must lie in the major divisions in the aristocracy which sprang up on the death of Alexander III in 1286 and then his only direct heir, Margaret, in 1290. In this later period, the nobility was again divided into familial factions, focused on key figures (Comyn, Bruce, Balliol), which not only resulted in some fairly high-profile murders (such as the murder of Donnchad, earl of Fife, in 1289 and, indeed, John Comyn by Robert Bruce himself in 1306) but also the 'competition' for the kingship, which saw candidates from the three most powerful families in Scotland (again, Comyn, Bruce, and Balliol) vie with each other for the kingship itself.[71] The upshot of this is that thirteenth-century aristocratic factions and feudings (which resulted in some fairly gruesome behaviour, such as the murder of Patrick, heir to the earldom of Atholl, in 1242) cannot but be seen as somehow foreshadowing the factional politics of the late thirteenth and early fourteenth centuries, the very period when the famous language of the 'community of the realm' is now seen as acting as a fig-leaf to hide such masked internal discord.[72]

The main exception to this narrative lies in legal history and particularly in the work of David Sellar and Hector MacQueen.[73] Here, the twelfth century stands only as a backdrop against which to view the much more important thirteenth. It was during the reign of Alexander II that kings of Scots introduced standard written procedures by which civil disputes could be settled in their own courts.[74] Particularly through the introduction of three 'pleadable brieves' (written commands which initiated pleading in royal courts), the royal judicial system grew stronger, and accordingly so too did the structures of royal power. The thirteenth

---

ed. Reid, pp. 1–30; Alan Young, 'The Political Role of Walter Comyn, Earl of Menteith, during the Minority of Alexander III of Scotland', in *Essays on the Nobility*, ed. Stringer, pp. 131–49; Amanda Beam, *The Balliol Dynasty 1210–1364* (Edinburgh, 2008), pp. 58–70; The subject of the 'political community' has, however, been given recent attention in Keith J. Stringer, 'The Scottish 'Political Community' in the reign of Alexander II (1214–49)', in *New Perspectives on Medieval Scotland, 1093–1286*, ed. Matthew Hammond (Woodbridge, 2013), pp. 53–84.

[71] For the most recent account, see Brown, 'Aristocratic Politics'.

[72] This is a point made in Young, 'Noble Family and Political Factions', pp. 1–3; For the long-standing position of Alexander III's adult reign as a 'golden age', a time of peace, see Norman H. Reid, 'Alexander III: The Historiography of a Myth', in *Scotland in the Reign of Alexander III*, ed. Reid, pp. 181–213; for the rhetoric of community see Roland J. Tanner, 'Cowing the Community? Coercion and Falsification in Robert Bruce's Parliaments, 1309–1318', in *The History of the Scottish Parliament: Parliament and Politics in Scotland, 1235–1560*, ed. Keith Brown and Roland J. Tanner (Edinburgh, 2004), pp. 50–73. The point above is a general observation: for an exception, see John Gillingham, 'Killing and Mutilating Political Enemies in the British Isles from the late Twelfth to the Early Fourteenth Century: A Comparative Study', in *Britain and Ireland, 900–1300*, ed. Smith pp. 114–34, at pp. 123–5, which stresses that the killing of Patrick of Atholl should be seen as an extremely unusual event of the high politics of the thirteenth-century kingdom.

[73] As stated above, the volumes on the reigns of Alexander II and Alexander III each contained an important article on thirteenth-century legal history; see Hector L. MacQueen, 'Canon Law, Custom and Legislation in the Reign of Alexander II', in *Reign of Alexander II*, ed. Oram, pp. 221–51; Hector L. MacQueen, 'Scots Law under Alexander III', in *Scotland in the Reign of Alexander III*, ed. Reid, pp. 74–102. The major study of medieval common law is MacQueen, *Common Law*, and, in addition, the important observations in W. D. H. Sellar 'The Common Law of Scotland and the Common Law of England', in *The British Isles 1100–1500: Comparisons, Contrasts and Connections*, ed. R. R. Davies (Edinburgh, 1988), pp. 82–99.

[74] MacQueen, 'Canon Law, Custom and Legislation'.

century saw the emergence of a Scottish common law, a system of pleading and courts that not only remained firm throughout the politically tortuous fourteenth and fifteenth centuries (once seen as a 'Dark Age' for Scottish legal history) but also developed.[75] Over the thirteenth century, therefore, there did develop a regularized system of royal law, applied in royal courts, which was based on that in England, although it was not so extensive.[76] But even this important exception ignores one major corpus of evidence, commonly known as the Auld Lawes. This is a body of legal material with a very complex manuscript tradition which was subject to the best and worst of nineteenth-century editorial practices. As a result, legal historians have generally neglected this material. But unpacking the manuscript tradition has revealed live and useable legal texts which make a significant impact on how we view the twelfth- and thirteenth-century Scottish kingdom. The textual nature of this material is set out in places throughout this book, but is given particular attention in the Appendix.[77]

In sum, therefore, the twelfth and thirteenth centuries are often examined separately, with the twelfth century taking credit for basic governmental development, and the thirteenth being seen as an age of political expansion, internal politicking, and common law. This book seeks to bring the twelfth and thirteenth centuries together, using (in particular), the neglected body of legal evidence, and aims to challenge the notion that David I somehow introduced a governmental structure, which was then dutifully followed through by his successors. Indeed, the question of how far David's reign did in fact see the establishment of these institutions of government in his kingdom is rarely addressed in more recent scholarship. The most recent synthesis of Scottish governmental transformation in the twelfth and thirteenth centuries concluded that '[by the 1230s] the Scottish kingdom had been transformed from a largely notional entity... into a sophisticated state with a bureaucratic royal administration, effective local representatives of crown authority, and a regional magnate group responsive to the needs and demands of the king'.[78] But the chronology of these changes is not made explicit; there has been little attention paid to *how* and *when* this transformation actually happened nor has it really been acknowledged that institutions, once introduced, have the capacity to change and develop.[79] One of the major arguments of this book is that it was not until the last two decades of the twelfth century that there was a relatively uniform network of institutions of Scottish government in the kingdom and even these were concentrated in a large core region: in Scotia, Moray, and Lothian. But

---

[75] T. M. Cooper [Lord Cooper of Culross], 'The Dark Age of Scottish Legal History, 1350–1650', in T. M. Cooper, *Selected Papers 1922–1954* (Edinburgh, 1957), pp. 219–36.

[76] MacQueen, *Common Law*, chapters 4–7.

[77] See the Appendix, 'A Note on Legal Sources', pp. 457–60, and Table A.1.

[78] Oram, *Domination and Lordship*, p. 363.

[79] The need for a study of the sheriffdom, for example, was stressed in Alexander Grant, 'Lordship and Society in Twelfth-Century Clydesdale', in *Power and Identity in the Middle Ages: Essays in Memory of Rees Davies*, ed. Huw Pryce and John Watts (Oxford, 2007), pp. 98–124. For important comments, see Duncan, *Making of the Kingdom*, pp. 151–63, 170–2, 200–15, 538–41, 595–611. Duncan, however, never worked up these comments into a single study so they have not had as much impact as one might have hoped.

this did not mean that a static system had emerged: governmental development is as live and dynamic as, for example, political diplomacy. We should thus discard the notion that David I was somehow fully responsible for these governmental changes and instead see them as part of living and much longer-term processes, which only become recognizable as permanent institutions of government during the last few decades of the long reign of David's grandson, William the Lion (1165–1214), and then changed significantly over the reigns of Alexander II (1214–49) and Alexander III (1214–86). In short, governmental developments must be seen over a longer *durée*.

The second narrative this book seeks to overturn is the explanatory power held by the so-called Anglo-Norman Era on our understandings of the changing form of royal government in Scotland. The term itself was the title of G. W. S. Barrow's 1977 Ford lectures in the University of Oxford and is so neat and so useful a phrase that it has retained purchase in modern historiography.[80] Put broadly, the Anglo-Norman era refers to the twelfth and thirteenth centuries, during which Scotland was affected by the political and social culture of Anglo-Norman England, itself profoundly affected by Norman French culture as a result of the Norman Conquest. This period of cultural transformation in Scotland was caused not by conquest but primarily by royally-sponsored aristocratic migration, involving those aristocrats who settled in Scotland either directly from northern continental Europe or via England, with the express encouragement of the then kings of Scots, particularly (but not exclusively) David I.[81] Together with the Scottish kings, these aristocrats are thought to have introduced a whole set of political, social and cultural norms to the kingdom of the Scots: knighthood, fiefs, and even Latin charters, which also transformed the political and social culture of the native elite. It thus used to be unproblematic to say that David and his successors 'feudalized' Scotland.[82] In the same way, the Anglo-Norman era also saw the adoption by Scottish kings of governmental forms from Anglo-Norman England. This process of 'Normanization' or 'Anglo-Normanization' made Scotland in the period prior to the twelfth century look extremely different from the Anglo-Norman era—different in political culture and different in governmental structure.

There have already been many challenges to this narrative.[83] Continuity, rather than change, in the political culture of Gaelic-speaking Scottish aristocrats has

---

[80] G. W. S. Barrow, *The Anglo-Norman Era in Scottish History* (Oxford, 1980); see also G. W. S. Barrow, 'Scotland's 'Norman' Families', in Barrow, *Kingdom of the Scots*, pp. 279–95, responding to R. L. Graeme Ritchie, *The Normans in Scotland* (Edinburgh, 1954).

[81] Barrow, *Anglo-Norman Era*, chapters 1–4.

[82] G. W. S. Barrow, 'The Beginnings of Military Feudalism', in Barrow, *Kingdom of the Scots*, pp. 250–78; see, however, the suggestions in Susan Reynolds, 'Fiefs and Vassals in Scotland: A View from the Outside', *SHR*, vol. 82, no. 214 (2003), pp. 176–93; and the response in Hector L. MacQueen, 'Tears of a Legal Historian: Scottish Feudalism and the *Ius Commune*', *Juridical Review*, new ser. (2003), pp. 1–28.

[83] See the survey of the field by Richard Oram, 'Gold into Lead? The State of Early Medieval Scottish History', in *Freedom and Authority: Scotland c.1050–c.1650—Historical and Historiographical Essays Presented to Grant G. Simpson*, ed. Terry Brotherstone and David Ditchburn (East Linton, 2000), pp. 32–43. More recently, important work has been done by Keith Stringer, showing how 'Anglo-Norman' lords in Scotland did in fact keep and maintain important links with their 'home'

been stressed. In addition, the live element of Irish ancestry in the identity of the kings of Scots in the twelfth and early thirteenth century has been identified and stands as an important corrective.[84] The effect of this second group of work on Scottish identity, spearheaded by Dauvit Broun, has been to transform our understanding of historical writing in Scotland.[85] We now know that there were several coherent written legends about the origins of the Scottish people circulating in thirteenth century, which appear to have been skilfully knitted together in a now lost history of the Scottish people written in the 1260s, which was eventually used first in the 1280s, and then by John of Fordun in the 1380s.[86] Nor is it just the dominance of the 'Anglo-Norman Era' which has been problematized; its technologies have also been the subject of critical attention. Most importantly, the notion that kings of Scots in the first half of the twelfth century granted out land to lay aristocrats in return for knight service, and routinely recorded that gift in a formulaic Latin charter has been questioned.[87] In addition, feudalism itself is no longer seen as a portable social system that rulers could introduce by *fiat* into their own kingdom; the narrative which sees David as 'feudalizing' Scotland is thus automatically problematic and there has been no further explanation put forward for structural governmental change other than aristocratic settlement (which *did* change the personnel of the political elite, at least partly). Moreover, if government took longer to develop than previously thought—one of the arguments presented here—what was going on during the twelfth century (the main period of Anglo-Norman settlement)?[88] This book will argue that there was indeed a significant change

region; see Keith J. Stringer, 'Aspects of the Norman Diaspora in Northern England and Southern Scotland', in *Norman Expansion: Connections, Continuities and Contrasts*, ed. Keith J. Stringer and Andrew Jotischky (Farnham, 2013), pp. 9–48. For a survey of the evidence of material culture, see Stuart D. Campbell, 'The Language of Objects: Material Culture in Medieval Scotland', in *New Perspectives*, ed. Hammond, pp. 183–201.

[84] The essays in *The Exercise of Power* stress 'the varied experience of 'native' lords', in the central and later Middle Ages; *Exercise of Power*, ed. Boardman and Ross, pp. 17–19. For work that stresses the more 'conservative' position of 'Gaelic' lords, see Cynthia Neville, *Native Lordship in Medieval Scotland: The Earldoms of Strathearn and Lennox, c.1140–1365* (Dublin, 2005); and Cynthia Neville, 'A Celtic Enclave in Norman Scotland: Earl Gilbert and the Earldom of Strathearn', in *Freedom and Authority*, ed. Brotherstone and Ditchburn, pp. 75–92. For the live and continuing Irish element in Scottish identity, see, among many works by the same historian, Dauvit Broun, 'Anglo-French Acculturation and the Irish Element in Scottish Identity', in *Britain and Ireland*, ed. Smith, pp. 135–53; Dauvit Broun, *The Irish Identity of the Kingdom of the Scots in the Twelfth and Thirteenth Centuries* (Woodbridge, 1999).

[85] Broun, *Scottish Independence*; Dauvit Broun, 'The Birth of Scottish History', *SHR*, vol. 76, no. 201 (1997), pp. 4–22.

[86] Broun, *Scottish Independence*, pp. 215–68.

[87] Matthew Hammond, 'The Adoption and Routinization of Scottish Royal Charter Production for Lay Beneficiaries, 1124–1195', *ANS*, vol. 36 (2014), pp. 91–115. Hammond here was developing and expanding the work of Dauvit Broun, mostly cited in Chapter 1, p. 25, note 1, but see, as an example, Dauvit Broun, 'The Changing Face of Charter Scholarship: A Review Article', *Innes Review*, vol. 52, no. 2 (2001), pp. 205–11. Both Broun and Hammond were reacting to the position set out by Barrow in, for example, G. W. S. Barrow, 'The Pattern of Non-Literary Manuscript Production and Survival in Scotland, 1200–1300', in *Pragmatic Literacy, East and West, 1200–1330*, ed. Richard Britnell (Woodbridge, 1997), pp. 131–45.

[88] As shown in Dauvit Broun, 'The Property Records in the Book of Deer as a Source for Early Scottish Society', in *Studies on the Book of Deer*, ed. Katherine Forsyth (Dublin, 2008), pp. 313–60, in part re-evaluating the strength of David I's power in the north-eastern part of his kingdom.

in the way in which elite power in general was conceptualized; it became territorialized, a process which affected 'newcomer' and 'native' alike. Moreover, the territorialization of elite power was a key part of the institutional growth of royal power.

The third aim of this book is to understand the form of Scottish government as
a phenomenon separate from that in England. The kingdom of the Scots was not
an England in miniature: Scottish kings and their counsellors took inspiration
from English governmental practices but adapted them significantly.[89] This adaptation has not been dealt with fully and instead has been the subject of discrete
studies of different aspects of this English/Norman influence.[90] Certainly, the
existing work which stresses difference has not been enough to permeate fully the
non-Scottish historiographical world. In 2000, Sir Rees Davies characterized
Scotland as undergoing a process of 'Anglicization' in the twelfth and thirteenth
centuries, of which a major part was the adoption of methods of governing taken
directly from England: the sheriff and sheriffdom, the justiciar, the common law
and even a comparable system of royal judicial courts.[91] While certain procedural
and institutional borrowings have already been studied, such as common law
brieves, and the justiciar, this book will take a wider view and show that, although
Scottish kings did draw on English example, they adapted and changed their
model, revealing significant differences in the relative power, complexity, and
intensity of the royal governments of England and Scotland during the central
Middle Ages.[92] Again, the excavation of the so-called *Auld Lawes* of Scotland has
made this re-examination possible.[93]

Finally, how we understand royal government needs to be refined. In Scottish
historiography on the central Middle Ages, the subject of government is often
treated in an isolated context, giving the impression that it was a process that
either developed independently or at the expense of any other type of power.[94]

---

[89] James Campbell, 'The United Kingdom of England: The Anglo-Saxon Achievement', in *Uniting the Kingdom? The Making of British History*, ed. Alexander Grant and Keith J. Stringer (London, 1995), pp. 31–47, at p. 47.

[90] Barrow, *Anglo-Norman Era*, pp. 118–44 [stressing feudalism as a system of government]; for those that stress the 'Norman' influence on government, coming into Scotland as a result of the Norman Conquest, see Ritchie, *Normans in Scotland*, pp. 305–41; for law, see T. M. Cooper, 'From David I to Bruce, 1124–1329: The Scoto-Norman Law', in *Introduction to Scottish Legal History*, Stair Society 20 (Edinburgh, 1958), pp. 3–17.

[91] R. R. Davies, *The First English Empire: Power and Identities in the British Isles 1093–1343* (Oxford, 2000), pp. 142–71, at pp. 156–9, 160–1. Matthew Hammond has recently problematized Davies's concept of Anglicization in relation to Scotland; see Matthew Hammond, 'Domination and Conquest? The Scottish Experience in the Twelfth and Thirteenth Centuries', in *The English Isles: Cultural Transmission and Political Conflict in Britain and Ireland, 1100–1500*, ed. Seán Duffy and Susan Foran (Dublin, 2013), pp. 80–95. Robin Frame, *The Political Development of the British Isles 1100–1400* (Oxford, rev edn, 1995), is an important exception.

[92] See for a recent study, David Carpenter, 'Scottish Royal Government in the Thirteenth Century from an English Perspective', in *New Perspectives*, ed. Hammond, pp. 117–59; also G. W. S. Barrow, 'Kingship in Medieval England and Scotland', in Barrow, *Scotland and its Neighbours*, pp. 23–44.

[93] For a description of the scholarly history of this legal material, see the Appendix, pp. 457–9.

[94] The exception is Alexander Grant, 'Franchises North of the Border: Baronies and Regalities in Medieval Scotland', in *Liberties and Identities in the Medieval British Isles*, ed. Michael Prestwich (Woodbridge, 2008), pp. 155–99. The Baronial Research Group has, understandably, concentrated on the aristocracy in its own right; *Essays on the Nobility*, ed. Stringer; *Exercise of Power*, ed. Boardman

Thus, studies on the exercise of power in Scotland have either emphasized kings and government but not aristocrats, or aristocrats at the expense of kings and their government.[95] This is not the case for fifteenth- and sixteenth-century Scotland, where the co-dependent power of kings and the nobility has received a lot of attention and generated a great deal of debate.[96] This book shows how dependent royal power was on elite power during the very period in which formal institutions of government first appear. When administrative institutions of power developed, as they began to do in a regular way only in the last quarter of the twelfth century, they redefined elite power and worked alongside it.[97] As a result, the royal bureaucracy that had emerged midway through the reign of Alexander III (1249–86) was more limited and less intensive than has perhaps been assumed; royal institutional power did not need to become more complex because aristocrats, bishops, and the king were all fundamentally part of the same system. The small size of the core of the Scottish kingdom meant that 'local officials' were not only major aristocrats but also firmly integrated with royal business at regnal level.

A better understanding of the form of royal government will thus show how aristocratic power was, in the Scottish case, constitutive of state power, rather than structurally separate from it. This feeds into larger narratives concerned with the emergence of bureaucratic government during the central Middle Ages.[98] There remains a tendency to think of royal power and aristocratic power as engaged in some sort of zero-sum game. The emergence of bureaucratic government ('public power') is either seen as necessarily limiting aristocratic power ('private power') or, conversely, aristocratic power is seen as operating according to different modes and values from royal power. This book, taking the example of Scotland as a case study, shows how the growth of royal power was not inimical to that of aristocrats, nor were they different sources of power, one representing 'public' authority, the other 'private'. It argues that the fundamental comparative dynamic to be used when analysing the various forms of medieval state is not that between public power and private power but between centrally based institutions and locally based ones.

and Ross, p. 15. This is not to say that personal relationships between aristocrats and the king have not been stressed but that this work does not look at such relationships within the context of the administration and institutions which supported them.

[95] This is even true of Barrow, *Anglo-Norman Era*, with the exception at pp. 142–3.

[96] Jennifer M. Brown [Jenny Wormald], 'Taming the Magnates?', repr. in *Essays on the Nobility*, ed. Stringer, pp. 270–80; Jennifer M. Brown [Jenny Wormald], 'The exercise of power', in *Scottish Society in the Fifteenth Century*, ed. Jennifer M. Brown (London, 1977), pp. 33–65; Michael H. Brown, 'Scotland Tamed? Kings and Magnates in Late Medieval Scotland: A Review of Recent Work', *Innes Review*, vol. 45, no. 2 (1994), pp. 120–46; Steve Boardman and Julian Goodare ed., *Kings, Lords and Men in Scotland and Britain, 1300–1625: Essays in Honour of Jenny Wormald* (Edinburgh, 2014); for a study of aristocratic power in late medieval Britain more broadly, see R. R. Davies, *Lords and Lordship in the British Isles in the Late Middle Ages*, ed. Brendan Smith (Oxford, 2009).

[97] By contrast, elements of continuity are stressed in Alexander Grant, 'The Construction of the Early Scottish State', in *The Medieval State: Essays Presented to James Campbell*, ed. J. R. Maddicott and D. M. Palliser (London, 2000), pp. 47–71.

[98] These points are developed in the conclusion to this book, particularly pp. 449–54.

This book is divided into two parts, separated thematically: the first deals with non-institutional forms of rulership, the second with the development of formal administrative institutions of government. As such, it is roughly divided into two chronological periods, although there is some crossover between them. The first part covers 1124–1230, and explores the dynamic between institutional and non-institutional forms of power. Part 1 is divided into three chapters, each of which each deals with a separate aspect of royal power. Chapter 1 examines arguments for the existence of a Scottish 'state' in the eleventh century and focuses on how the relationship between kings and their aristocrats changed over the twelfth century; Chapter 2 examines royal military resources and how they were raised; Chapter 3 examines developments in the ways in which law and order were maintained, and how the nature and authority of written law changed during the twelfth and early thirteenth centuries. It will be argued in the first part of this book that until the late twelfth century, kings did not rule, for the most part, through uniform administrative institutions across their kingdom but through the co-option, north and south of the Forth, of aristocratic power and resources. The major change over the twelfth century seems not to have been in their method of royal rulership but rather the territorialization of the basis of elite power. Only from the 1180s onwards was there an expectation that kings would rule through administrative units covering most of their kingdom.

The second part of the book covers the period 1170–1290, when uniform networks of royal officials emerged. It is devoted to outlining the development and changing shape of the institutions of royal government, and how these institutions built on the dynamics of power outlined in the first part of the book. Part II is divided into four chapters. Chapter 4 re-examines the evidence for the development of the royal officials in charge of local administration, justice and finance. It shows how institutional government developed south of the Forth but took far longer to be introduced north of it. It also stresses the roads not taken: there was no inevitable form to Scottish royal government. Chapter 5 examines the development of the common law in Scotland, and asks how this supposedly universal legal system which is thought to have developed in the thirteenth century, could work in a kingdom so accepting of non-royal jurisdictional power. Chapter 6 examines the development of a supposedly 'central' method of financial accounting, concluding that it was not so central after all; Chapter 7 deals with the nature of royal recordkeeping and the social and political profile of royal officials. Mid-thirteenth-century government looked very different from the way royal power was exercised a century earlier. There were, however, certain structural continuities: kings used and incorporated aristocratic power into the bureaucracy of their state. The developing intensity of royal government did not come at the expense of the aristocracy; the way in which kings ruled changed dramatically without affecting underlying power dynamics.

The point of the bipartite division is, essentially, to allow twelfth-century royal power to be examined from the vantage point of the thirteenth century and vice versa. This allows us to see both change and continuity over the period. The outward form of royal power changed; royal institutions of government developed, albeit at a slower pace than was once thought, and there still was an important reorientation in the methods of kingly rule in Scotland. But, despite these changes, institutional power did not fundamentally alter the relationships between, in particular, kings and lay aristocrats within the kingdom. How royal institutional power grew but yet did not diminish aristocratic power is the key question this book hopes to answer.

PART I

RULERS AND RULED, 1124–1230

1

The Early Scottish State?

How kings of Scots exercised power over their kingdom before the twelfth century is extremely contested. The issue is important in itself but the scale of disagreement is, conversely, the result of the scarcity of surviving written evidence from before the reigns of Alexander I (1107–24) and David I (1124–53).[1] There is thus much to debate and yet, simultaneously, not much to debate with. Moreover, the chronological imbalance of written evidence means that questions about the nature and geographical extent of royal power before the twelfth century have often looked back from the vantage point of the written twelfth and thirteenth centuries to the comparatively unwritten eleventh and tenth.[2] This is a methodology frequently used when historians are faced with a better-documented later period and a sparser earlier one.[3] But the approach is problematic when faced with such a significant imbalance in the evidence, as is the case for the kingdom of the Scots between the late eleventh century and the mid-thirteenth. For the methodology to work for

---

[1] The reigns of Alexander and David marked the period when kings of Scots adopted written brieves and charters to send written commands to their subordinates and give gifts to (religious) beneficiaries. For the position that pre-twelfth-century Scotland was 'charterless', see Dauvit Broun, *The Charters of Gaelic Scotland and Ireland in the Early and Central Middle Ages* (Cambridge, 1995), pp. 29–44, and Dauvit Broun, 'The Writing of Charters in Scotland and Ireland in the Twelfth Century', in *Charters and the Use of the Written Word in Medieval Society*, ed. Karl Heidecker (Turnhout, 2000), pp. 113–31, at pp. 114–20. In both these pieces, Broun was arguing against Wendy Davies's notion of a 'Celtic Charter' in Scotland, for which see Wendy Davies, 'The Latin Charter-Tradition in Western Britain, Brittany and Ireland in the Early Mediaeval Period', in *Ireland in Early Mediaeval Europe: Studies in Memory of Kathleen Hughes*, ed. Dorothy Whitelock, Rosamond McKitterick, and David N. Dumville (Cambridge, 1982), pp. 258–80. For kings (perhaps particularly Alexander I) as driving forces in the adoption of brieves (short-term written commands) in the first half of the twelfth century, see Dauvit Broun, 'The Adoption of Brieves in Scotland', in *Charters and Charter Scholarship in Britain and Ireland*, ed. Marie Therese Flanagan and Judith A. Green (Basingstoke, 2005), pp. 164–83. For the appearance of property records in gospel books more generally, see Arkady Hodge, 'When Is a Charter Not a Charter? Documents in Non-Conventional Contexts in Early Medieval Europe', in *Problems and Possibilities of Early Medieval Charters*, ed. Jonathan Jarrett and Allan Scott McKinley (Turnhout, 2013), pp. 127–49. For the argument that kings of Scots did not routinely issue charters to lay beneficiaries until late in the reign of Mael Coluim IV, if not William the Lion, see Matthew Hammond, 'The Adoption and Routinization of Scottish Royal Charter Production for Lay Beneficiaries, 1124–1195', in *ANS*, vol. 36 (2014), pp. 91–115.

[2] For the use of later evidence, see, for example, Alexander Grant, 'Thanes and Thanages from the Eleventh to the Fourteenth Centuries', in *Medieval Scotland*, ed. Grant and Stringer, pp. 39–81; for a view that eschews using much later evidence (but still necessarily extrapolates back to some extent), see Dauvit Broun, 'The Origins of the *mormaer*', in *The Earl in Medieval Britain*, ed. David Crouch and Hugh F. Doherty, forthcoming.

[3] The method was exemplified in F. W. Maitland, *Domesday Book and Beyond: Three Essays in the Early History of England* (Cambridge, 1897): 'I have followed that retrogressive method "from the known to the unknown", of which Mr Seebohm is the the apostle' (p. v).

eleventh-century Scotland, we essentially have to decide on what counts as 'early' and what counts as 'later' phenomena. If we assume that later written evidence does preserve predetermined 'early' elements accurately, those 'early' concepts and phenomena must by default be seen as static and unchanging, thus denying them the possibility of change and dynamism across the twelfth and thirteenth centuries. In the case of Scottish history, pre-decided 'native' or 'Celtic' concepts can come to be seen as unchanging 'survivals' or 'fossils' in an Anglo-Norman world.[4] As a result, there has been a move away from this retrogressive approach recently. Some historians have actively eschewed using much later twelfth- and thirteenth-century evidence to understand any aspect of the pre-twelfth-century world and, as a result, have begun to present narratives which have changed our understanding of the tenth- and eleventh-century kingdom of *Alba*.[5]

The starting point of this chapter is an exploration of the existing work on the form and structure of the early Scottish state in the tenth and eleventh centuries. It then takes the position that twelfth- and thirteenth-century written material is, first and foremost, evidence for its contemporary context. In particular, the chapter analyses two of the main 'officials' perceived as key to the form of this state: the earl (Gaelic: *mormaer*; Latin: *comes*) and the thane (probably Gaelic: *toísech*; Latin: *thanus*). It argues that the twelfth- and thirteenth-century written evidence does not provide a stable view of these figures. During the second half of the twelfth century, the title of earl (or *mormaer*) was territorialized and the title of thane (or *toísech*) expanded to mean a tenurial lord as well as the head of a local kindred and/ or an estate manager. This process of territorialization and the silent changes to the meanings of the titles and statuses of *mormaír* (or earls) and *toísig* (or thanes) challenge a particularly alluring understanding of the early Scottish state and, concurrently, provide an alternative perspective on how royal power was exercised by the early- to mid-twelfth century.

AN EARLY STATE?

Debates on the institutional form of Scottish royal power have become increasingly animated since the 1990s.[6] At their heart are competing views about the

---

[4] G. W. S. Barrow, 'The Lost Gàidhealtachd', in Barrow, *Scotland and Its Neighbours in the Middle Ages* (London, 1992), pp. 105–26; see further the remarks in G. W. S. Barrow, *The Anglo-Norman Era in Scottish History* (Oxford, 1980), pp. 156–62. Among many continuities identified, Barrow states that the earldoms 'survived intact' throughout the 'Anglo-Norman Era' and, despite some 'in the hands of families of continental origin', 'the constitutional position of the earls was preserved' (pp. 157–8, 159).

[5] Alex Woolf, 'The Moray Question and the Kingship of Alba in the Tenth and Eleventh Centuries', *SHR*, vol. 79, no. 208 (2000), pp. 145–64; Alex Woolf, *From Pictland to Alba, 789–1070* (Edinburgh, 2007), pp. 342–50; Broun, 'Origins of the *mormaer*'; and now Dauvit Broun, 'Statehood and Lordship in "Scotland" before the Mid-Twelfth Century', *Innes Review*, vol. 66, no. 1 (2015), pp. 1–71.

[6] Although from necessity this work has drawn on older scholarship, most notably: W. F. Skene, *Celtic Scotland: A History of Ancient Alban*, 3 vols (Edinburgh, 1886–90), iii, pp. 209–83; E. W. Robertson, *Historical Essays in Connexion with the Land, the Church, etc.* (Edinburgh, 1872), pp. 125–9; G. W. S. Barrow, 'Pre-Feudal Scotland: Shires and Thanes', in G. W. S. Barrow, *The Kingdom of the*

function and purpose of different ranks in Scottish society prior to the eleventh century and their relation to royal power. These ranks are the earl (Gaelic: *mormaer*; Latin: *comes*), who was attached to a regional division of the kingdom (known as a province) and the thane (probably Gaelic: *toísech*; Latin: *thanus*), who was sometimes attached to an estate. The first view sees the earl and thane as primarily administrative officials, acting at a provincial and local level on behalf of the king; the second sees the thane (or *toísech*) as the head of a local kin-group, and the earl (or *mormaer*) as drawn from the ranks of these thanes.[7] This second view sees the *mormaer* as exercising fewer and less formal administrative responsibilities on behalf of the king than the first. It may seem strange to the non-specialist that a state apparatus would rest on only two lay titles, and not include other magnates, such as bishops, seen as key to the functioning of royal power elsewhere in Western Europe, most notably Ottonian and Salian Germany, even if the unity of the 'imperial church system' has been challenged more recently in German historiography.[8] But the emphasis on earl/*mormaer* and thane/*toísech* is the result of the surviving evidence. Owing to texts like the *Chronicle of the Kings of Alba, Leges inter Brettos et Scotos*, and the Gaelic property records in the Book of Deer, we have some material (although still not a lot) on lay ranks but far less on the powers of bishops and other religious magnates. As a result, debate centres on particular lay titles, rather than any others.

The More Maximalist Views

The most recent incarnation of the first view is an article by Alexander Grant, entitled 'The Construction of the Early Scottish State', published in 2000.[9] For Grant, the fundamental unit of statehood in Scotland prior to the twelfth century

---

Scots: Government, Church and Society from the Eleventh to the Fourteenth Century, 2nd edn (Edinburgh, 2003), pp. 7–56; Kenneth Jackson, *The Gaelic Notes in the Book of Deer* (Cambridge, 1972), pp. 102–24.

  7 Most of this chapter was written before Dauvit Broun wrote his forthcoming article entitled 'The origins of the *mormaer*', forthcoming. As the volume's publication is some way off, I have only incorporated some of Broun's work here. Broun's chapter does present a more in-depth view of provincial structures back into the eighth century. His aim in this article is not the point here, which is more more focused on the twelfth and thirteenth centuries. Broun, 'Statehood and Lordship', also appeared too late to be incorporated into the arguments of this chapter but in this piece too Broun concentrates on Scotia ('Scotland') before the death of David I in 1153.

  8 Timothy Reuter, 'The "Imperial Church System" of the Ottonian and Salian Rulers: a Reconsideration', reprinted in and cited from Timothy Reuter, *Medieval Polities and Modern Mentalities*, ed. Janet L. Nelson (Cambridge, 2006), pp. 325–54.

  9 Alexander Grant has produced three important and influential studies on Scotland: Grant, 'Thanes and Thanages'; Alexander Grant, 'The Construction of the Early Scottish State', in *The Medieval State: Essays Presented to James Campbell*, ed. J. R. Maddicott and D. M. Palliser (London, 2000), pp. 47–71; and Alexander Grant, 'Franchises North of the Border: Baronies and Regalities in Medieval Scotland', in *Liberties and Identities in the Medieval British Isles*, ed. Michael Prestwich (Woodbridge, 2008), pp. 155–99. On a different theme, although using his earlier work, see now Alexander Grant, 'At the Northern Edge: *Alba* and Its Normans', in *Norman Expansion: Connections, Continuities and Contrasts* , ed. Keith J. Stringer and Andrew Jotischky (Farnham, 2013), pp. 49–85.

was the multiple estate, typologized by Glanville Jones, and made manifest in English historiography in the 'shires' of Northumbria, the 'sokes' of Yorkshire, the 'lathes' of Kent, and the *villae regales* of Bede.[10] The multiple estate is conceptualized as a group of small, sometimes disparate, settlements, all dependent on an estate centre, to which dues, food, and other services were rendered.[11] In Scottish historiography, the 'multiple estate' form has been identified not only in those estates called 'shires' (*scirae, shirae*), as it has been in England, but also 'thanages' (*thanagia*).[12] For Grant, these 'thanages' supported individuals known as thanes or *toísig*, most of whom ran them as officials of the king. The thanages, run by *toísig* (or thanes), were then 'grouped into provinces under mormaers...[which] equate to the earldoms and earls of the Anglo-Norman Era'.[13] Grant's article envisaged that each province within the kingdom of the Scots was, or could have been, controlled by a *mormaer* or earl and was made up of a large number of thanages, controlled by thanes or *toísig*, who ran them as royal officials.

Grant acknowledged that *toísig* (or thanes) could hold estates in their own right but he concentrated on those who appeared to be running them for the king. His emphasis was thus on the 'official' *toísech/*thane and *mormaer*: for him, they were

---

[10] Among many, see G. R. J. Jones, 'Multiple Estates and Early Settlement', in *English Medieval Settlement*, ed. P. H. Sawyer (London, 1979), pp. 9–40; F. M. Stenton, *Types of Manorial Structure in the Northern Danelaw* (Oxford, 1910), pp. 2–55; also for the need to do more comparative studies of 'multiple estates' (a peculiarly English term), see Chris Wickham, 'Problems of Comparing Rural Societies in Early Medieval Western Europe', *TRHS*, 6th ser., 2 (1992), pp. 221–46, at pp. 222–3. Grant's ultimate starting point, however, was the work of Geoffrey Barrow on shires and thanes in Barrow, 'Shires and Thanes'. Barrow himself drew expressly on Maitland. For the most recent critique of Glanville Jones's multiple estate see Brian K. Roberts with P. S. Barnwell, 'The Multiple Estate of Glanville Jones: Epitome, Critique, and Context', in *Britons, Saxons and Scandinavians: The Historical Geography of Glanville R. J. Jones*, ed. Paul S. Barnwell and Brian Roberts, The Medieval Countryside 7 (Turnhout, 2011), pp. 25–128, and the collected essays by Glanville Jones in the same volume. For a brief critique on the blurring of the dynamic between multiple estates, 'a unit of ownership and production', and the shire 'a political unit', see Rosamond Faith, *The English Peasantry and the Growth of Lordship* (Leicester, 1997), p. 11. For a complete re-examination of the ancient nature 'shires' in Scotland, see Broun, 'Statehood and Lordship', pp. 33–55, although this article appeared too late to be fully integrated into this chapter.

[11] In this, the multiple estate is both similar and different in conceptualization to the classic bipartite estate of the Carolingian period, divided into demesne (directly exploited) and tenant farmers (indirectly exploited), for which see Adriaan Verhulst, 'Economic Organisation', in *The New Cambridge Medieval History*, vol. 2: *c.700–900*, ed. Rosamond McKitterick (Cambridge, 1995), pp. 491–509, at pp. 488–99; see also Peter Sarris, 'The Origins of the Manorial Economy: New Insights from Late Antiquity', *EHR*, vol. 119, no. 481 (2004), pp. 279–311. The distinction between 'inland' and 'warland' in Anglo-Saxon estates is noteworthy; Faith, *English Peasantry*, pp. 15–152.

[12] 'Thanage' is a term peculiar to Scottish historiography and sometimes used as a catch-all term for Scottish multiple estates, regardless of whether the word actually appears in the surviving material. For discussion of thanages, see Grant, 'Thanes and Thanages', p. 40, and *passim*; Grant, 'Franchises', pp. 177–8. For earlier work on the subject, see Robertson, *Historical Essays*, pp. 125–9; cf. Grant, 'Thanes and Thanages', p. 40, n. 5. For the comparison between Scottish thanages and English baronies, see Rachel R. Reid, 'Barony and Thanage', *EHR*, vol. 35, no. 138 (1920), pp. 161–99. But thanage is a late term and should not be applied indiscriminately across the early and central Middle Ages, such as in Stephen Driscoll, *Alba: the Gaelic Kingdom of Scotland AD 800–1124*, Historic Scotland (Edinburgh, 2002), pp. 53, 55; and for the late appearance of the word *thanagium*, see below, pp. 66–9.

[13] Grant, 'Construction', p. 55.

royal officials; even if thanes were drawn from 'classes of local lairds', 'thane' was still the title of a royal official.[14] In this view, *mormaer* and *toísech*/thane collected revenue in the form of tribute (*cáin*) and hospitality duty (*coinnmed*) on behalf of the king and, because *cáin* and *coinnmed* were levied systematically throughout the kingdom, they could be understood as a form of taxation. In addition, *mormaer* and *toísech* also supervised justice and defence: each thanage had its own court, which operated under royal jurisdiction. The local courts came together from time to time at a provincial moot headed by the *mormaer* and the province's legal expert (Gaelic: *brithem*; Latin: *iudex*).[15] Each thanage also provided men to serve in the army of the province, and the leader of the provincial army was the *mormaer* who exercised this responsibility for the king. In all of these functions—justice, revenue collection, and military service—the *mormaer* was responsible for the whole province while the *toísech*/thane served the immediate locality.[16] This administrative structure made up the pre-twelfth-century Scottish state.

However, Grant admitted this picture of an administrative hierarchy of multiple thanes/*toísig* under a single earl/*mormaer* in each province was 'oversimplified'. He placed particular importance on the charter evidence from the twelfth and thirteenth centuries which showed that *mormaír* only had direct control over a *proportion* of the lands within their province.[17] This meant that his reconstruction of the relationship between the king's 'local agents' and the king's 'provincial agents' had to be refined because *mormaír*, despite their provincial title, were clearly *not* ultimately in charge of all the land (and thus revenue) within the province. His solution was that, by the end of the eleventh century, a 'dual territorial structure' had been introduced in the provinces.[18] This 'dual territorial structure' meant that *mormaír* held up to half the land of the province which they ran relatively autonomously through their own thanes, while the king (and church) held much of the other half, in the form of royal thanages run by thanes.[19] Because *mormaír* held only around half of all the provincial lands, and sometimes provinces did not have *mormaír*, the king emerged from Grant's reconstruction as the most powerful landholder in the kingdom, which contributed greatly to his power and status and explained why, for Grant, a single kingship had emerged in the kingdom of *Alba*.[20]

[14] Grant, 'Construction', pp. 53–4; Grant, 'Thanes and Thanages', pp. 41–2.

[15] For the 'cuthill' court, see G. W. S. Barrow, 'Popular Courts', in Barrow, *Scotland and Its Neighbours*, pp. 217–45; Grant, 'Construction', p. 55.

[16] See Alexander Grant, 'Aspects of National Consciousness in Medieval Scotland', in *Nations, Nationalism and Patriotism in the European Past*, ed. Claus Bjørn, Alexander Grant, and Keith J. Stringer (Copenhagen, 1994), pp. 68–95, at pp. 88–92.

[17] Grant, 'Construction', pp. 56–60.

[18] Grant, 'Construction', p. 60.

[19] See further, Grant, 'Thanes and Thanages', pp. 40–9, which deals with the earlier period, although his article goes up to the fourteenth century. For his later treatment of church lands see Alexander Grant, 'Lordship and Society in Twelfth-century Clydesdale', in *Power and Identity in the Middle Ages: Essays in Memory of Rees Davies*, ed. Huw Pryce and John Watts (Oxford, 2007), pp. 98–124.

[20] Grant, 'Construction', p. 60. This, for Grant, also explained the large amount of the king's *cró* (life-value) of 1000 cows, as contrasted with the *mormaer*'s 150-cow *cró* listed in *LBS* (Grant, 'Construction', pp. 61–2). The vast landed power of the king of Scots was stressed again in Grant, 'At the Northern Edge', pp. 72, 81–2.

Grant was then left with the question of when this 'dual territorial structure' had come about. He constructed a moment of transition, from a period dominated by 'regional power', in which the *mormaír* had direct control over most of the provinces, to 'one in which the land of the provinces was only partly held by the provincial rulers'.[21] Presumably this meant that, before this transition, the *mormaír's* power in the province was somehow autonomous from the king's; regardless, the king's assumption of part of the landed extent of each province increased royal power. The process of state formation was thus a process of land accumulation by the king who wrested land away from provincial *mormaír* into his own hands. The roles of the *mormaer* and the *toísech*/thane were thus readjusted:

> King's thanes or toiseachs would have run [thanages], and would also have helped to levy the cain or taxation owed from other territories—including the lands of the mormaers.... the mormaers, too, would be regarded as royal agents, whose function would have been to control the provinces on behalf of the crown; the provincial armies which they led were the king's, while the justice they and the provincial brithems [legal experts] supervised was the kingdom's. Thus, although the early Scottish state had a two-part territorial structure, both parts would, directly or indirectly, have been subject to the king's authority, in what can be considered an effectively organised state.[22]

Although there have been challenges to his view, as we shall see, Grant's work remains the most complete picture of the form of royal power in the eleventh century ever to have been published.[23] But it is based on two key assumptions. First, if the kingdom of the Scots could be called a state, that state had to have an administrative and institutional base: in order for it to exist, it had to be run by royal officials. This was why, particularly in his earlier publications, Grant only acknowledged, but did not develop, the written evidence that suggested that *toísig*/thanes did not just serve as royal officials but were a noble rank in their own right. The second assumption was that the basis of royal power was the uniform and systematic exaction of resources from land throughout the kingdom and that, most importantly, the earlier exaction of resources could be tracked by following later patterns of lordship. Thus, the administrative infrastructure of the kingdom of *Alba* allowed royal officials to exact revenue and men both from defined units of land over which they exercised direct control (the 'thanages') and from lands over which they did not (presumably lands held by other lords). The assumption that the form of administration was linked to the extraction of, essentially, tax and army service was the reason why Grant found the evidence suggesting that *mormaír* had direct control over *part* of their province so problematic. If, on the one hand, all *toísig*/thanes were subordinate to *mormaír*, who were themselves subordinate to the king, then the *mormaer* should have had control (even if not direct control) over the extraction of resources for the entire province, which demonstrably was not the

---

[21] Grant, 'Construction', p. 65; repeated in Grant, 'Franchises', pp. 177–8.
[22] Grant, 'Construction', pp. 62–3. It should be said that Grant emphasized that, within pre-twelfth century 'earldoms', 'local government was much more the earls' private responsibility'; Grant, 'Franchises', pp. 183–4.
[23] Although now, see the very recent work in Broun, 'Statehood and Lordship'.

case. So, on the other hand, if *mormaír* clearly did not have control over all land within their province and held their own land within the provinces autonomously, what was it that made them royal agents (which they had to be for the Scottish state to exist)? In line with his bipartite territorial state structure, Grant came up with a clear answer to the question of what *mormaír* had to do for the king: *mormaír* were responsible for levying taxation from their own lands in the province (and probably supervised the collection elsewhere) and were ultimately responsible for the military levy from the province and for provincial justice.

Because Grant necessarily relied on post-eleventh-century written evidence, most notably the evidence from charters, basic continuity in state structure had to be assumed throughout the twelfth and thirteenth centuries. If he had not so relied, or if *mormaír* and *toísig/*thanes had changed during this period, then the empirical foundations of the early state form he had constructed would have been weaker. Grant thus opted for continuity and the argument was as follows: most thanages survived, either in their original form or as the bases of sheriffdoms. He particularly emphasized that kings kept their control over most of their thanages: only in the fourteenth century, at a time of great political tension, did kings give them away to their subordinates. Thanes themselves survived: the title did not become 'obsolete' and, although their status was challenged because of the incoming knights and barons of the Anglo-Norman Era, they could be seen as their equivalents in rank (if not in the service they owed). The nature of the *mormaer*'s power within his lands in his province did not change much, although the ethnic profile of *mormaír/*earls did; some earldoms were taken over by Anglo-Norman incomers, who married into the title, while others remained in the hands of natives.[24] The responsibilities of *mormaír/*earls over the entire province may have lessened somewhat but, within their own lands, there was basic continuity between the eleventh-century *mormaer* and the thirteenth-century earl.[25] This therefore was Grant's view: an early Scottish state, run by the administrative officials of earl and thane, who managed the king's thanages, all of which survived in their essentials throughout the central Middle Ages.[26]

The More Minimalist Views

There have been recent challenges to Grant's position. At the same time as this view of early Scottish statehood was being put forward, Dauvit Broun was working on one of the key pieces of evidence Grant had been using, the texts known as the property-records in the book of Deer which revealed much about local and regional society in the province of Buchan in the north-east.[27] Whereas Grant had argued

[24] In a later publication, however, Grant stressed the large amount of land given to incoming French, Norman, and Breton lords during twelfth and early thirteenth centuries; Grant, 'At the Northern Edge', pp. 82–4.

[25] The aspect of earl-as-lord appears much more strongly in Grant's later article, which was on aristocratic franchises, rather than statehood; Grant, 'Franchises', pp. 184–9.

[26] For the long view, see Grant, 'Franchises'.

[27] Dauvit Broun, 'The Property Records in the Book of Deer as a Source for Early Scottish Society', in *Studies on the Book of Deer*, ed. Katherine Forsyth (Dublin, 2008), pp. 313–60, in which it is argued

that these records showed both 'the operation of local lordship' *and* the actions of *mormaer* and *toísech*/thanes as royal officials, Broun argued instead that the Deer records supported a different interpretation in which '*mormaer* and *toísech* controlled general dues and services in their own right; as leading lords, not as officials' in a kin-based society.[28] The *mormaer* in Buchan seems not to have been a great official in his own right but 'the predominant *toísech* [head of kin-dred] in the region', who was responsible for raising military service along with other *toísig*.[29]

Broun left the door open as to how far these conclusions could be taken outside the province of Buchan.[30] He was not the only historian, however, coming to a more minimal view of the eleventh-century *mormaer* and, indeed, state structures in general. At the end of his 2007 book, *From Pictland to Alba*, Alex Woolf examined a legal tract, known as 'The Laws between the Brets and the Scots' (*Leges inter Brettos et Scotos* or *LBS*). *LBS* is a difficult text which has been subject to a great deal of academic debate.[31] Opinions have varied from seeing it as law put together in the early eleventh century to regulate the relations between the Britons of Strathclyde and the Scots of Scotia to seeing it as an 'enactment' by David I upheld throughout all the areas under his control, including Strathclyde.[32] Many of the problems surrounding *LBS* (and views about when and why it was written down) are caused, however, by too much stress being placed on its title (which may possibly be apocryphal) and not enough attention paid to the various ways it appears in its two separate textual traditions, the earlier as the final chapter of *Leges Scocie* (*LS*, c.21, where it appears in French), and the later as the last few chapters of the early-fourteenth-century legal treatise, *Regiam Majestatem* (*RM*). All the textual evidence assembled thus far suggests that what we know as *LBS* may be but a remnant of a larger (written) legal tradition but which (in its earliest *LS*-incarnation) survives in a written form that cannot date earlier than the second quarter of the twelfth century.[33]

Woolf noticed that *LBS* presented the life-value (how much was owed in compensation for killing a man of a particular status rank) of a *mormaer* as only 50 per cent greater than a thane. This was a far smaller ratio than that present in similar texts from early-eleventh-century England, where an ealdorman was worth six times more than a thegn. Woolf concluded, therefore, that 'these thanes...were

---

that all interpretations of these records had, since their discovery in 1860, been fundamentally affected by a view of Scottish society that saw it governed by an administrative hierarchy of *mormaer* and *toísech* (or earl and thane) as royal officials under the king. Broun demonstrated that this view was formed in the second half of the nineteenth century before anyone had even heard of the records themselves, which were thus interpreted to fit within a pre-existing scheme. For Broun's summary of historiography, see Broun, 'Property Records', pp. 315–26.

   [28] Broun, 'Property Records', pp. 353–4.   [29] Broun, 'Property Records', p. 355.
   [30] See further, Broun, 'Origins of the *mormaer*', forthcoming.
   [31] I am exploring these issues in a forthcoming paper: 'Was the *Leges inter Brettos et Scotos* Really an Early Eleventh-Century Lawcode Written for the Britons of Strathclyde and Scots of Alba?' But for the bare bones of this argument, see Chapter 3, pp. 123–32.
   [32] For the first view, see Kenneth Jackson, 'The Britons in Southern Scotland', *Antiquity*, vol. 29, no. 114 (1955), pp. 77–88; and for the second, see Skene, *Celtic Scotland*, iii, p. 217; for other views, see the historiography cited in Chapter 3, p. 123, and notes 49–50.
   [33] See Chapter 3, pp. 123–32.

not a well developed ministerial class but, for the most part, simply wealthy landowners...in each province one among these thanes bore the title of *mormaer* and responsibility for leading the military levy and enforcing justice'.[34] For Woolf, the *mormaer* had responsibilities for justice and the army but was not of that high a rank, being drawn from among one of (many) leading kin-groups in his particular province, which were headed by *toísig*.

Neither Broun nor Woolf presented their researches as wholly overturning Grant's work. Instead, they offered ways into it and they asked important questions of it. For Broun, if the Deer records—one of Grant's pieces of evidence—did not show an administrative hierarchy in Buchan, then it should be questioned how far this structure existed elsewhere in the kingdom.[35] For Woolf, if another of the texts used by Grant—*LBS*—did not reveal the meaning of a thane/*toísech* as 'a royal agent', wider arguments about the form of the early Scottish state must also be questioned.[36] But at present neither puts forward an alternative option, although Dauvit Broun is setting out his views more fully in two publications, one very recent, the other forthcoming.[37] What both Woolf and Broun did, however, was to use evidence that did not much pre-date the mid-twelfth century. The property records in the Book of Deer were entered in Deer's gospel book between the 1130s and the 1150s and most are records of eleventh-century transactions. Woolf used *LBS* as evidence for social ranks in the tenth and early eleventh centuries.[38] *LBS*, as we have it in its earliest manuscript form, cannot, in fact, be earlier than the second quarter of the twelfth century but Woolf and Broun's basic methodology still stands: in order to understand the earlier society, one should prefer texts that pertain, or arguably pertain, to that period. Thus, whereas both Broun and Woolf used texts dating from no later than the mid-twelfth century to ask questions of state structure in late tenth- and eleventh-century *Alba*, Grant used texts from the whole of the twelfth and thirteenth centuries (and beyond) to think about the same issues. This later evidence will now be re-examined to identify potential changes in the supposedly key officials of the early Scottish state. At the end of this chapter, what these changes contribute to these debates will be examined. What follows immediately is thus not primarily focussed on the eleventh century; instead, it will examine the earl/*mormaer* and thane/*toísech* in the twelfth and thirteenth centuries, the power they exercised over land and people, and whether these roles were changing or largely continuous during this period.

EARLS AND EARLDOMS

The debates on the form of eleventh-century royal power are, in part, based on differing views of the *mormaer*: how strong his control was over the province, how

---

[34] Woolf, *Pictland to Alba*, pp. 342–50, at p. 350.   [35] Broun, 'Property records', p. 355.
[36] Woolf, *Pictland to Alba*, p. 349. Woolf here cited A. A. M. Duncan, *Scotland: the Making of the Kingdom* (Edinburgh, 1975), p. 111.
[37] Broun, 'Origins of the *mormaer*', forthcoming; Broun, 'Statehood and Lordship'.
[38] For *LBS*, see below, pp. 123–32.

far his title resulted from royal appointment, and whether he collected tribute and held provincial courts in his own right or on behalf of the king.[39] What follows takes these subjects in turn to argue for a rather different view of the *mormaer*, as the position appears in mid-twelfth-century evidence. But debating the 'early Scottish state' is, although very important, only a secondary aim of this chapter. As it takes evidence from the central Middle Ages and applies it to its contemporary context, this chapter also emphasizes how the position of *mormaer* changed over the period. The focus of recent scholarship has not, per se, been to chart differences between the *mormaer* as he appears in the mid-twelfth century and the earl as he appears in the early thirteenth, other than to stress that the period saw the emergence of patrimonial inheritance, which naturally affected *who* would be earls and on what basis they held the title.[40] In this later period, it is generally agreed that the title of earl was inherited (ideally through the male line), that the earl inherited a territorial 'earldom', which was not coterminous with the province from which his title derived, that earls received profits from the land of their earldom in similar ways to other lords, and that they dispensed justice in the court of their earldom (if they dispensed justice elsewhere it was normally because they served as a justiciar in the king's government).[41] What current scholarship has not done is address when and how this transformation occurred. In addition to putting forward a different view of the *mormaer c.*1130s–*c.*1160s (when we have most of our earliest evidence), the primary aim of this section is to understand the chronology of change in this position.

Terminological Problems

The highest socio-legal rank under the king in the central Middle Ages was described by the generic Latin word *comes* (pl. *comites*), meaning, originally, a 'companion'.[42] The title of these *comites* was attached to a province, a wide regional

---

[39] It is, however, generally accepted that he raised the army on the king's behalf; see Chapter 2, pp. 102–3.

[40] The exceptions are Grant, 'Franchises', pp. 176–89; John Bannerman, 'MacDuff of Fife', in *Medieval Scotland: Crown, Lordship and Community—Essays Presented to G. W. S. Barrow*, ed. Alexander Grant and Keith J. Stringer (Edinburgh, 1993), pp. 20–38; Richard D. Oram, 'Continuity, Adaptation and Integration: the Earls and Earldom of Mar, c.1150–c.1300', in *The Exercise of Power in Medieval Scotland, c.1200–1500*, ed. Steve Boardman and Alasdair D. Ross (Dublin, 2003), pp. 46–66, at pp. 52–6. Over the fourteenth and fifteenth centuries, the title of earl became honorific and had fewer direct associations with the province whence his title derived; see Alexander Grant, 'Earls and Earldoms in Late Medieval Scotland c.1310–1460', in *Essays Presented to Michael Roberts*, ed. J. Bossy and P. Jupp (Belfast, 1976), pp. 24–40; and now Michael Brown, 'Scottish Earldoms in the Late Middle Ages: Survival and Transformation', in *Earl in Medieval Britain*, ed. Crouch and Doherty, forthcoming.

[41] I derive this from, among many, Cynthia J. Neville, *Native Lordship in Medieval Scotland: The Earldoms of Strathearn and Lennox, c.1140–1365* (Dublin, 2005); Alan Young, 'The Earls and Earldom of Buchan in the Thirteenth Century', in *Medieval Scotland*, ed. Grant and Stringer, pp. 174–202; Oram, 'Earls and earldom of Mar'; Elsa Hamilton, *Mighty Subjects: the Dunbar Earls in Scotland, c.1072–1289* (Edinburgh, 2010).

[42] What follows is a heavily shortened version of my forthcoming article: Alice Taylor, 'The *Comes* in Medieval Scotland', in *The Earl in Medieval Britain*, ed. Crouch and Doherty, forthcoming. *Comes* was the word used to describe Anglo-Norman earls following the Norman Conquest. Previously, the Latin word preferred had been *dux*, but this caused problems, given that the new king of England

division of the kingdom of *Alba*. Thus, in the first half of the twelfth century, there is evidence, for example, of *comites* of Fife, Atholl, Mar, and Buchan, all within Scotia. By the later Middle Ages, when Scots had become the language of record, the title of *comes* was recorded as 'earl', derived partly from the Old English *eorl*.[43] Historians used to be generally comfortable calling all *comites* attested in Scotland during the central Middle Ages 'earls'. More recently, however, this has come to be seen as problematic. Within Scotia, where, until the late eleventh century, all *comites* under the authority of the king of Scots are attested, the Latin word *comes* translated a Gaelic word, *mormaer* (pl. *mormaír*).[44] *Mormaer* has the original meaning of either 'great steward' (*mór+maer*) or 'sea steward' (*mor+maer*).[45] As a

was also a Norman *dux*; see Chris Lewis, 'The Early Earls of Norman England', *ANS*, vol. 13 (1990), pp. 207–23. It is interesting that the hierarchy of *dux-comes*, present in Normandy and Anglo-Norman England, is reversed in the record of the Kirkness dispute, discussed later in this chapter, in which Soen (perhaps a local *toísech*) is described as a *dux* but the *mormaer* as a *comes*; Lawrie, *ESC*, no. 80.

[43] Later Scots language transcripts of charters always use *earl* for *comes*; see, for example, the recently discovered charter of William the Lion, printed in Arkady Hodge, 'A New Charter of William the Lion Relating to Strathearn', *SHR*, vol. 86, no. 222 (2007), pp. 314–18. Andrew Wyntoun also generally called earls 'earls', although sometimes preferred *maysterman*; Andrew Wyntoun's *Orygynale Cronykil of Scotland*, 3 vols, ed. D. Laing (Edinburgh, 1872–79), ii, book vii, ch. iii, lines 389–390; for *maysterman*, see book vii, ch. vii, lines 1387, 1389 (pp. 166, 197). Wyntoun also described Earl David of Huntingdon, William's brother, as an *erle*, although in fact was denoting his jurisdiction over the Garioch, over which he was never given the title *comes*; see *Wyntoun*, ed. Laing, ii, book vii, ch. viii, line 1680 (p. 207). The idea that the Garioch was a *comitatus* is, to my knowledge, first attested in *Gesta Annalia* I and then adopted by Walter Bower; *Gesta Annalia* I, in Skene, *Fordun*, i, p. 281; *Scotichronicon by Walter Bower*, 9 vols, gen. ed. D. E. R. Watt (Aberdeen and Edinburgh, 1989–98), v, pp. 78–9.

[44] The *mormaer* of Moray, who appears in Irish annals in the first half of the eleventh century, has been seen not as a 'regular' *mormaer* but as a solution to the particular political context of having a different *clann* hold the kingship of *Alba*; for which see Broun, 'Origins of the *mormaer*', forthcoming. The equivalence of *comes* and *mormaer* is confirmed by comparison of Gaelic and Latin sources. One Ruaídrí, *mormaer* of Mar, witnesses a gift made to Deer by Gartnait, *mormaer* of Buchan, in 1130×1131 and recorded in the Gaelic vernacular, and also attested in a Latin charter of David I, drawn up 1127×31, as *Rotheri com(es)*. See Text III in Katherine Forsyth, Dauvit Broun, and Thomas Clancy ed., 'The Property Records: Text and Translation', in *Book of Deer*, ed. Forsyth, pp. 131–43, at pp. 138–9; *CDI*, no. 33. More recently, Alasdair Ross and Richard Oram have argued for a separation between *mormaír* and *comites*, on the basis that no single text ever equates the two. While this is true, that there is no contemporary evidence for *mormaer* is not the case and the example cited above shows that Latin documents could describe a man as a *comes* whom Gaelic records had described as a *mormaer*; Alasdair Ross, *The Kings of Alba, c.1000–c.1130* (Edinburgh, 2011), p. 50; Richard Oram, *Domination and Lordship: Scotland 1070 to 1230* (Edinburgh, 2011), pp. 216–17, 219–21. Further references to *mormaír* appear in Texts II, III, and VI in the Book of Deer, in Forsyth, Broun, and Clancy ed., 'Property Records', in *Book of Deer*, ed. Forsyth, pp. 131–43. The *Chronicle of the Kings of Alba*, revised in the late tenth century, records that Dubucán, son of Indrechtach, *mormaer* of Angus, was killed in the reign of Constantín, son of Áed; see Benjamin Hudson, 'The "Scottish Chronicle"', *SHR*, vol. 77, no. 204 (1998), pp. 129–61, at p. 150. The most recent commentaries on *CKA* are D. N. Dumville, 'The Chronicle of the Kings of Alba', in *Kings, Clerics and Chronicles in Scotland, 500–1297: Essays in Honour of Margorie Ogilvie Anderson on the Occasion of her Ninetieth Birthday*, ed. Simon Taylor (Dublin, 2000), pp. 73–86; and Woolf, *Pictland to Alba*, pp. 88–93; for references to a *mormaer* of Moray, see *AT, s.a.*1020.8; of Mar, *AU, s.a.* 1014.2.

[45] The lengthy discussions over the etymology of *mormaer* are summarized in Woolf, *Pictland to Alba*, pp. 342–3; and Broun, 'Origins of the *Mormaer*', forthcoming; see also Jackson, *Book of Deer*, pp. 103–9; for the wide application of *comites* and other Latin positional words for elite groups or those with administrative responsibilities (e.g. *prefectus, prepositus, minister*), see Julia Crick, *Elders and Betters: Local Hierarchies and Royal Agents in England and the West, 800–1000*, G. O. Sayles Memorial Lecture on Mediaeval History 5, given 1 May 2009, text available at <www.academia.edu>; Julia

result, the twelfth-century 'earl' has been replaced by the twelfth-century *mormaer* in more recent work.

Mormaer was thus never regularly transposed into Latin as, for example, *mormarus*; it was instead regularly translated by the word *comes*.[46] *Comes*, which has a broad semantic range, would have been a useful generic word in the multilingual environment of twelfth-century Scotland.[47] For us, however, it causes problems in nomenclature. It now seems extremely odd to refer to *comites* in the early twelfth century as 'earls' when that was not the written word used to describe them in Gaelic vernacular records. But it equally seems bizarre to refer to *comites* in the thirteenth century as *mormaír* when we know that word was replaced by 'earl' in the increasingly dominant Scots vernacular. In addition, it would be awkward to refer to *comites* by their Latin descriptor.[48] In order to avoid the clunky solution of referring to these figures as earl/*mormaer* throughout this book, I will refer to all *comites* as *mormaír* up to *c.*1180s–*c.*1190s, and 'earls' thereafter. In the second part of this book, all *comites* will be referred to as 'earls'. In part, this decision has been taken because of the argument made in this chapter: that there was a significant reconfiguration in the basis of *mormaer*-power over the later twelfth century. This involved their power becoming territorialized, located not on the entire province (from which they took their title) but on their smaller landed holdings *within* the province, which came to be known in Latin as the *comitatus* and which is now translated as 'earldom'. Changing the name of the *comes* at this chronological point is not ideal, as it may give the impression that a silent process of territorialization was, in fact, accompanied by a simultaneous change in title, which it was not. It is, however, a solution that makes the best of a complex terminological problem that confronts any historian working on the central Middle Ages.

As a final note, this chapter takes *mormaer* to mean an individual called a *comes* whose title was attached to a broad regional division (a province) of the kingdom and whose authority was somehow subordinate to the king of Scots. It will thus exclude those *comites* who ruled areas that may have been kingdoms in their own right (such as Moray) or who were subordinate to other kings (such as the *comites* of Orkney and Caithness).[49] It will also in general exclude *comites*, such as those of

---

Crick, 'Nobility', in *A Companion to the Early Middle Ages: Britain and Ireland, c.500–c.1100*, ed. Pauline Stafford (Oxford, 2009), pp. 414–31, at pp. 417–21.

[46] *Maer*, after all, was transposed as *marus*; *LS*, c. 20.

[47] In his *vita* of Queen Margaret, written between 1100 and 1107, Turgot mentioned how Mael Coluim III translated the English of his wife to his Gaelic-speaking aristocracy because 'he knew the tongue of the English and his own equally' (Turgot, *Vita Sancte Margarete*, in *Symeonis Dunelmensis Opera et Collectanea*, ed. I. H. Hinde, Surtees Society 51 (Durham, 1868), p. 243). The witness lists to a handful of Scottish royal charters (probably drafted by a single scribe of Melrose Abbey) render some parts of some names in French; *RRS*, ii, nos. 264, 265 (and comments by Barrow at pp. 296–7). *Comes* was translated by the French *cunte* (or some other variant) in, for example, *LBS*; *LS*, c. 21.

[48] Although this was the strategy I adopted in Taylor, '*Comes* in Medieval Scotland', it does not, however, make sense in the context of this book, which covers a much longer timeframe.

[49] For Orkney and Caithness, see Barbara E. Crawford, *The Northern Earldoms: Orkney and Caithness from AD 870 to 1470* (Edinburgh, 2013). Moray represents a particularly difficult case. Was the ruler of Moray a *comes* (so described by Latin twelfth-century writers, such as Orderic Vitalis) or was he a *rí* ('king'), so called by the Irish Annalist (Orderic Vitalis, *The Ecclesiastical History of Orderic Vitalis*, 6 vols, ed. M. Chibnall, Oxford Medieval Texts (Oxford, 1968–80), iv, p. 276; *AU*, *s.a.*1130.4)?

the Lennox, Carrick, Menteith, and Ross, who are not attested until the later part of the twelfth century because this chapter argues that a profound transformation in the nature of the *comes* in Scotland took place during the twelfth century (albeit a change not reflected in nomenclature).[50] The areas under consideration are thus in Scotia north of the Forth but south and east of Moray: Angus, Atholl, the Mearns, Fife, Strathearn, Mar, and Buchan. Dunbar is not included in this list, not only because it is clearly a late-eleventh-/early-twelfth-century creation but also because, until the late thirteenth century, its *comites* predominantly took their title from a toun rather than a large regional division.[51] The basis of their authority was conceptualized differently from the other *comites* and *provinciae*; they are therefore unrepresentative and, accordingly, do not form part of the present discussion.[52]

Rank and Hierarchy

First, it has long been acknowledged that *comites* had control over provinces (*provinciae*) to which their title was attached. *Comites*, however, first appear in twelfth-century royal charters without their provincial designations. We need not, however, think that the provincial aspect of comital authority was new in the twelfth century because the property records (written 1130s–1150s), both in Gaelic and in Latin, in the Book of Deer *do*, on occasion, give the province of particular *mormaír*.[53] Thus, although the scribes of the earliest Scottish royal

With such fluidity in title, however, one should remember the warning of James Campbell: 'it would have been possible that in the eighth century [in Bede's Northumbria] for the same man to have been described by different writers and in different contexts as *rex, subregulus, princeps, dux, praefectus* and *comes*', James Campbell, 'Bede's *Reges* and *Principes*', in *Essays in Anglo-Saxon History* (London, 1986), pp. 85–98, at p. 91. This advice works well for Moray. The chronicler of Holyrood, for example, described both Óengus of Moray and Donnchad of Fife as *comites*, thus deeming them equivalent in status but Fergus of Galloway as a *princeps*, perhaps suggesting that he viewed Fergus to be of higher status than either Óengus or Donnchad. Fergus was a patron of Holyrood Abbey so this also may have affected the chronicler's choice of status descriptor. I am grateful to Matthew Hammond for this last suggestion. See, *A Scottish Chronicle Known as the Chronicle of Holyrood*, ed. M. O. Anderson, Scottish History Society, 3rd ser. vol. 30 (Edinburgh, 1938), *s.a.* 1130, 1154, 1161 (pp. 118, 126, 139).

[50] For the earliest reference to the earldom of the Lennox, datable to *c.* 1178, see *RRS*, ii, no. 205; for Menteith, see *RRS*, i, no. 243. I have also learnt much from Matthew Hammond's unpublished paper on the Lennox, 'The Origins of the Earldom of Lennox'; see also Michael Brown, 'Earldom and Kindred: the Lennox and Its Earls, 1200–1458', in *Exercise of Power*, ed. Boardman and Ross, pp. 201–24, at pp. 202–4. For Menteith as a later creation out of a greater Strathearn, see Broun, 'Origins of the *mormaer*', forthcoming.

[51] 'March', of course, represents a frontier rather than a region internal to one kingdom; Alastair J. Macdonald, 'Kings of the Wild Frontier? The Earls of Dunbar or March, *c.*1070–1435', in *Exercise of Power*, ed. Boardman and Ross, pp. 139–58; for a survey of the title evidence, see Hamilton, *Dunbar Earls*, pp. 34–6, particularly p. 35 and note 12. Hamilton argues that the earldom of Dunbar did not become 'a settled and recognised concept' until the end of the twelfth century and the beginning of the thirteenth, which parallels the argument put forward later in this chapter; Hamilton, *Mighty Subjects*, pp. 35, 115.

[52] See also Broun, 'Origins of the *mormaer*', forthcoming.

[53] Mael Ísu is styled *comes* but not *comes de Strath'* in *CDI*, nos. 33, 44, 56, 86–87; Caustantín appears as *comes* in *CDI*, no. 33, as *comes* of Fife in the Kirkness settlement; Lawrie, *ESC*, no. 80; Donnchad I appears as *comes* alone in, among others, *CDI*, nos. 53, 54, 56, 67, 68, 69, 86–90, 99, 137, 153, 156, 194. Matad (Atholl) attests as *comes* alone in *CDI*, nos. 33, 44, 54, 120; for the Property-records, see, for example, Texts VI and VII in Forsyth, Broun, and Clancy ed., 'Property

charters predominantly recorded the *rank* of *comes* alone, the contrast may be one of linguistic style and even a wish to save time, rather than a substantive difference suggesting that *mormaír* were not that closely related to their provinces.[54] It became more common (although still comparatively infrequent) to include the *mormaer's* titular province in the witness lists to Latin charters in the reign of William the Lion.[55] Early in the reign of Alexander II, however, provinces were invariably given alongside the rank of *comes* in the witness lists to royal charters.[56]

If early royal charters emphasized the rank of the *comes/mormaer*, just how high a rank was it? The text known as *LBS*, written in French in its earliest attested manuscript witness and probably compiled in this form no earlier than the mid-twelfth century, lists the ranks of Scottish society, starting with the king and moving down all the way to the peasant.[57] This text is discussed in much more detail later in this book.[58] It will suffice to say here that each rank under the king is described in two ways: as a rank in its own right and as the 'son' of the rank above.

Records', pp. 140–3 (also *CDI*, no. 136); for the scribe see Broun, 'Writing of Charters', pp. 117–18.

[54] Eleventh-century Anglo-Saxon Latin diplomas give the earl's title as *dux* without specifying to which earldom the title belonged. For some examples in the reign of Edward the Confessor (1043–66), see S 998–1006, S 1010, S 1012.

[55] Rank alone: *RRS*, ii, nos. 8–10, 12, 13 (+ 1 with provincial title), 23, 27, 29–30, 33, 37, 42, 59, 60, 72, 79, 85, 105–106, 109, 114, 116, 127, 133–135, 138–142, 143 (inflated?), 144, 148, 149 (+2 with provincial titles), 152, 153 (+2 with provincial titles), 158–159, 167–171, 173, 175, 181, 188, 190 (+1 with provincial title), 191, 197 (+2 with provincial titles), 198, 200–201, 203–204, 205 (+2 with provincial titles), 206 (+1 with provincial title), 207, 208 (+1 with provincial title), 209–211, 213–215, 222–224, 229 (+3 with provincial titles), 236, 242 (+1 with provincial title), 249–250, 251 (+3 with provincial titles), 254, 261, 266, 271 (+1 with provincial title), 272 (+2 with provincial titles), 273 (+2 with provincial titles), 274 (+ 1 with provincial title), 275, 277, 280, 281, 283, 284 (+2 with provincial titles), 287, 293–295, 298–299, 302, 308, 310, 311, 314–315, 318, 321–322 (both +1 with provincial title), 323–324, 327–331, 333–334, 335 (+2 with provincial titles), 336–339, 340 (+1 with provincial title), 344 (+1 with provincial title), 345 (+2 with provincial titles), 346 (+1 with provincial title), 347–348, 350, 355–60, 361–2 (both +1 with provincial title), 364, 368, 371, 375, 381, 383, 391–394, 396, 398, 403 (+1 with provincial title), 404, 405 (+ 2 with provincial titles), 411–412, 418, 420 [later abridgement], 421, 423, 429 (+1 with provincial title), 430–431, 460, 468, 481, 491–492 (with at least one provincial title); *RRS*, ii, nos. 13, 28, 128–129, 136–137, 149–151, 153, 190, 197, 205, 206, 208, 229, 242, 251, 271–273, 282, 284, 321, 322, 335, 340, 344–346, 361–362, 388 (authenticity is *slightly* questionable), 403, 405, 414, 428–429, 464, 470–471, 474, 489, 499, 519, 522: whereas Donnchad II was normally called *comite Dunecano* in witness lists, his son, Mael Coluim, was normally styled *comite Malc' de Fif.*

[56] See, for example, *The Chiefs of Grant*, ed. W. Fraser, 3 vols (Edinburgh, 1883), iii, no. 3 [AII/5]; *Arbroath Liber*, i, nos. 100 [AII/6], 102 [AII/214], 103 [AII/89], 105 [AII/18], 106 [AII/19], 107 [AII/20], 108 [AII/29], 113 [AII/64], 123 [AII/21], 171 [AII/118], 264 [AII/307]; *APS*, i, 87–8 [AII/7]; BL, Additional MS 33245, fos. 43r–44r [AII/8], 46v [AII/306], 149v–150r [AII/308]; NRS, GD119/2; Grant G. Simpson, *Scottish Handwriting, 1150–1650*, 2nd edn (East Linton, 1998), no. 4 [AII/12], GD1/203/1 [AII/213]; *Melrose Liber*, i, nos. 174 [AII/14], 175 [AII/167], 176 [AII/13], 184 [AII/46], 185 [AII/47], 198 [AII/239], 207 [AII/258], 231 [AII/320], 237 [AII/324], 239 [AII/309], 255 [AII/255]; ii, 366 [AII/16]; *Balmerino Liber*, nos. 1 [AII/207], 3 [AII/23], 41 [AII/191], Appendix, no. 2; *Glasgow Reg.*, i, nos. 132 [AII/25], 134 [AII/26], 174 [AII/229], 181 [AII/286], 183 [AII/283], 185 [AII/291], 186 [AII/293]; for exceptions see *Melrose Liber*, i, nos. 184–5 [AII/46,/47]; *Moray Reg.*, no. 29 [AII/119]; *Balmerino Liber*, no. 1 [AII/207], in which Earl Patrick of Dunbar (and it is always Earl Patrick) is just given the title *comite Patricio*.

[57] *LS*, c. 21.   [58] See Chapter 3, pp. 123–32, 147–52.

These ranks are given their own 'life-values' (Gaelic: *cró*), the amount owed by a slayer and his kin to compensate the slain man's kin for their loss and, presumably, to avoid their vengeance.[59] Thus, the *mormaer* (named here as a *comte* or *cunte*) was given the same life-value (*cró*) as the son of the king. The *mormaer*'s son was assessed as equal to the 'thane' (French: *thain*; Latin: *thanus*).[60] The king was assessed at 1000 cows; the *mormaer* and king's son at 150 cows; the thane and *mormaer*'s son at 100 cows; and the thane's son at two-thirds the last amount. *Mormaír* thus were conceptualized as belonging much more to the ranks of thanes than the rank of the king, a point made by Alex Woolf.[61] The localized position of the Scottish *mormaer* is contrasted with the comparatively much higher rank of the Northumbrian ealdorman, described in a similar tract on status, *Norðleoda laga*, which survives as part of a compilation put together at York in the early eleventh century.[62] In *Norðleoda laga*, the ealdorman is worth four times as much as the *worldþegnes* ('secular thegn') whereas, in *LBS*, the *mormaer* is only worth 50 per cent more than the thane.[63] Indeed, some *mormaer* were themselves *toísig* (singular: *toísech*), a Gaelic word, meaning, in this context, 'head of kindred', a title that was almost certainly what was being translated by the French *thain* and Latin *thanus*.[64] Although we might think that a *mormaer* far outranked the thane or *toísech*, he in fact could belong to their ranks and was valued at a level far closer to the thane than he was to the king.

In this more localized context, associating the *mormaer* more with heads of kin-groups, how do we understand his authority over the province? This is already a subject of some debate but, in both maximalist and more minimalist accounts of royal power, it is generally acknowledged that early-twelfth-century *comites* had some sort of jurisdictional and military responsibilities and collected tribute from their dependents. Both will be dealt with in more detail in the next two chapters (Chapter 2 concentrates on resource extraction and military duties; Chapter 3 elucidates the jurisdictional side). Chapter 2 will argue that the *mormaír* had, until roughly the third quarter of the twelfth century, ultimate responsibility for raising the army from the entire province from which he took his title. This he did by tapping into the networks of other local heads of kin (*toísig*) and other potentates, such as bishops; this type of coercive capacity could well be called extensive authority. However, military service was the primary arena in which this extensive authority operated. He collected a tribute render (*cáin*) from settlements that acknowledged his primary authority but this tribute was collected not on behalf of the king but for

---

[59] This logic is discussed below, Chapter 3, pp. 136–8. For these sorts of payments see, among many, George Garnett, '*Franci et Angli*: the Legal Distinctions between Peoples after the Conquest', *Anglo-Norman Studies*, vol. 8 (1986), pp. 109–37, at 118–25.
[60] See below, pp. 56–9.
[61] Woolf, *Pictland to Alba*, pp. 346–9.
[62] Although the core text may be older; Patrick Wormald, *The Making of English Law: King Alfred to the Twelfth Century*, vol. 1: *Legislation and its Limits* (Oxford, 1999), pp. 391–4.
[63] First noticed in Woolf, *Pictland to Alba*, pp. 348–9. For *Norðleoda laga*, see *Die Gesetze der Angelsachsen*, ed. F. Liebermann, 3 vols (Halle, 1903–10), i, p. 460; Wormald, *Making of English Law*, pp. 391–4. The word used in this text for 'life-value' is the Old English *wergeld*.
[64] See below, pp. 58–9.

himself and must have been a source of relatively independent revenue that could be used to support his position and perhaps compensate him for his military responsibility. Chapter 3 shows that, in matters of law and justice, the *mormaer* was also a figure who offered protection to those below him to guarantee protection beyond the solidarity offered by their kin-groups. His power was a focal point in the province (although importantly not the only one) whereby accusations of theft could be heard and decided upon.[65] The point running throughout the next two chapters, however, is that, although the *mormaer* exercised extensive authority over his province by the mid-twelfth century, he did not do so to the exclusion of other local potentates, both religious and lay. Indeed, the picture that emerges from the limited evidence for *mormaer* activity before the 1160s is of a figure at the ultimate head of a provincial community who also depended on other sources of authority for its cohesion.

A few examples should bear out this last point for the purpose of the present chapter. There is only one surviving record of a provincial assembly from the first half of the twelfth century.[66] Questions must be raised about how representative it is of twelfth-century assemblies, but it is all we have so we must use it. The record contains the settlement of a dispute between the monastic brethren of St Serf's (under the protection of the bishop of St Andrews) and a knight, Robert of Bourgogne, over the settlement of Kirkness, supposedly given to the brethren by Mac Bethad mac Findlaech in the mid-eleventh century.[67] The case dates to 1128×36 and the resulting record was preserved in the archives of the priory of St Andrews.[68] It was clearly drawn up from St Serf's point of view, beginning with a description of Robert as 'the furnace and fire of all evil' who had wished to take a quarter of Kirkness from the monks as a result of 'the fervour of his rapacity and unbridled tyranny'.[69] Whether Robert was indeed this harbinger of doom may be debated but his behaviour clearly troubled the monks, who sought out King David I and supplicated to him, 'that he would make just judgement between them [the monks] and the said Robert'. The king agreed, sent out his messengers to the province (*provincia*) of Fife and Fothrif, and called out 'a multitude of men' who came

---

[65] *LS*, c. 1.

[66] Lawrie, *ESC*, no. 80; cf. a brieve of David I, dating from the early 1150s, which addresses the bishop of St Andrews and the *mormaer* and men of Fife and says that they are no longer to hear cases arising from the abbot's men in Newburn in Fife, who will only answer to the court of Dunfermline Abbey. The only stipulation was that, at the abbot's court, a *iudex* (a legal expert) of Fife ('my *iudex* of that province') had to be present. Here the *mormaer* and the bishop head up the address clause, and thus the provincial community; *CDI*, no. 190. For more on *iudices*, see Chapter 3.

[67] Simon Taylor has convincingly argued that Mac Bethad was granting the land by right of his wife, Gruoch, to whom the land most probably belonged: Simon Taylor, 'The Rock of the Irishmen: an Early Place-Name Tale from Fife and Kinross', in *West over Sea: Studies in Scandinavian Sea-Borne Expansion and Settlement before 1300*, ed. B. B. Smith, S. Taylor, and G. Williams (Leiden, 2007), pp. 497–514, at p. 503.

[68] For the records relating to the founding and early benefaction of St Serf's hermitage, see *St Andrews Liber*, pp. 114–18.

[69] Lawrie, *ESC*, no. 80; *St Andrews Liber*, pp. 117–18, at p. 117; for the Loch Leven records, and their relationship with the St Andrews cartulary, see Taylor, 'The Rock of the Irishmen', pp. 497–514; Broun, *Charters*, pp. 32–3.

together in one place (*unum locum*).[70] Present was not only Caustantín, *mormaer* of Fife, but Mac Bethad, thane (*thaynetum*) of Falkland, and 'the chiefs, leaders and commanders of the bishop's army', two of whom are named—Buadach and Sluagadach—and, finally, one Soen, a leader (*dux*), who arrived with his *familia*, which can be translated as 'retinue', 'household', or, even, 'kin'. Witnesses were heard and the judgement was made by three *iudices*, who were all given further accolades: Caustantín, *mormaer* of Fife ('a great judge in Scotia'), Dubgall, son of Mocche (described as a 'just and venerable old man'), and Mael Domnaig, son of Mac Bethad, ('a good and wise judge (*iudex*)'). Although all three *iudices* participated in weighing up the witness testimonies, it was Dubgall who actually made the judgement, because he was the oldest and was deemed to have the greatest knowledge of the law.[71]

The text reveals an absence of any set official hierarchy of rank in the province itself.[72] Caustantín, *mormaer* of Fife, is the first of the 'multitude of men' to be named and is given a complimentary description but, although he is a *comes* and a *magnus iudex Scotie*, he too defers to Dubgall's judgement. Although the *comes* arrived with his 'deputies and dependents' and the army of Fife, his presence was counterbalanced by the bishop of St Andrews who, although not present himself, was represented by 'the chiefs, leaders and commanders of the bishop's army', two of whom were important enough to be named. Nor were the *mormaer* and leaders of the bishop's army the only powerful people present; there was also Soen, a *dux*, who might have been a local *toísech*.[73]

Caustantín is presented in the text as a *mormaer* of great distinction: he was *mormaer*, a *iudex* (in all Scotia, not just Fife), and was given clear preference in the composition of the record of settlement. But his position was still one that necessarily operated in relation to others of high social capital, whether military leaders or other legal specialists. These men were also focused on the provincial community, a province in which the *mormaer* held the highest socio-legal rank but still acted alongside other high-status individuals. A Gaelic record entered in the gospel book of Deer *c.*1150 shows Colbán, *mormaer* of Buchan, together with his wife and the local *toísech*, acquitting some of Deer's lands from performance of the burdens that 'apply to the chief districts of *Alba*', with 'district' almost certainly denoting the province.[74] It might be thought that the *mormaer*'s authority alone

---

[70] Archibald Lawrie, probably on the basis of *LS*, c. 16, and *SA*, c. 14, which list the judicial *caput* of Fife as Dalginch, thought that the 'one place' might be Dalginch; there is no evidence to confirm this; Lawrie, *ESC*, p. 330. For the relationship between *SA*, c. 14, and *LS*, c. 16, see Alice Taylor, 'Leges Scocie and the Lawcodes of David I, William the Lion and Alexander II', *SHR*, vol. 88, no. 226 (2009), pp. 207–88, at pp. 234–5.

[71] That all three were deemed to be judges by the writer of this settlement is demonstrated by the explanation of Dubgall's precedence: 'quia alii judices detulerunt Dufgal propter sui senectutem et juris peritiam'; Lawrie, *ESC*, no. 80.

[72] King David summoned the meeting but does not appear to have been present. Falkland was a royal settlement until Mael Coluim IV gave it to Donnchad, *comes* of Fife, between 1160 and 1162 (*RRS*, i, no. 190).

[73] As can be seen in Lawrie's text (Lawrie, *ESC*, no. 80), there is a gap in the manuscript after *dux* and before *cum familia sua* suggesting that Soen was a *dux* of *something*, perhaps a local kin-group?

[74] Text VI in Forsyth, Broun and Clancy ed., 'Property Records', pp. 140–1.

was enough to secure this acquittal, but Colbán did not just act alongside his wife; he also needed the authority of a *toísech* of the same province.

This sort of collective provincial activity can be found in Latin acts as well as Gaelic ones, and in Fife as well as Buchan. A brieve of Mael Coluim IV, datable to 1153×62, commanded a number of high-status individuals to protect and maintain the monks of Dunfermline Abbey.[75] The brieve addressed Donnchad, *mormaer* of Fife first but also Merleswain, Áed (son of Gille Míchéil), G. 'mac Sloclac' (son of Sluagadach), Ness (son of William), and one Alun.[76] Some of these luminaries are identifiable. Merleswain was the son of Colbán, who married into one of the leading kin-groups of Buchan and became the province's *mormaer*. His son, Merleswain, was quite literally the 'son of a *mormaer*' and may have thus had a *cró* (life-value) equal to that of a thane.[77] Similarly, Áed was the son of Gille Míchéil, a past *mormaer* of Fife, so again would have occupied a similar position to Merleswain.[78] Ness (son of William) was certainly lord of Leuchars in Fife, meaning that he too was of high status.[79] Geoffrey Barrow has suggested that Alun was the Alún son of Gille Críst who witnessed charters of Earl Donnchad II of Fife (d.1204).[80] The ability to protect was a quality inherent in high status itself.[81] All these men, including the *mormaer*, therefore had the capacity to offer protection to others of lower status; by commanding them all to protect Dunfermline Abbey, Mael Coluim was tapping into the social capital of the entire province, which clearly constituted a greater force than the *mormaer* alone.

Succession

How did individuals attain the title of *mormaer*? Were they appointed to the title by the king? Did they attain the title through election within their kin-groups? Or was it the norm for sons to inherit their father's title? These are difficult questions to answer. The ranking system described in *LBS* suggests, on the one hand, that the position of *mormaer* could be inherited: a son of a *mormaer* might attain the title

---

[75] *RRS*, i, no. 181.

[76] These men are discussed in some detail in *PNF*, vol. 5, pp. 111–14.

[77] Young, 'Earls and Earldom of Buchan', pp. 179–81; G. W. S. Barrow, 'Companions of the Atheling', *ANS*, vol. 25 (2003), pp. 35–47, at pp. 36–7; Matthew H. Hammond, 'A Prosopographical Analysis of Society in East Central Scotland with Special Reference to Ethnicity' (PhD Dissertation, University of Glasgow, 2005), p. 122; for a summary of their debate over the name, see Grant, 'At the Northern Edge', p. 67.

[78] Bannerman, 'MacDuff', pp. 31–2.

[79] For Ness son of William, see Duncan, *Making of the Kingdom*, p. 138; Barrow, *Anglo-Norman Era*, pp. 22–3; and Grant, 'At the Northern Edge', pp. 65–6. For the description of Ness as 'son of the countess', see G. W .S. Barrow, 'The Earls of Fife in the Twelfth Century', *PSAS*, vol. 87 (1952–53), pp. 51–62, at pp. 53, 60. Ness was listed fifth among those Scottish aristocrats who handed over hostages to Henry II in 1174. Only Donnchad, *comes* of Fife, Gille Brigte, *comes* of Strathearn, Gille Críst, *comes* of Angus, and Richard de Morville, the constable, preceded him; see the text of the Treaty of Falaise in Howden, *Gesta*, i, p. 98; *Anglo-Scottish Relations, 1174–1328: Some Selected Documents*, ed. and trans. E. L. G. Stones (Oxford, 1965, repr. with corrections, 1970), no. 1, at pp. 6–7. For the name 'Ness' in the kingdom, see Hammond, 'Prosopographical Analysis', p. 85.

[80] *RRS*, i, p. 51.   [81] See Chapter 3, pp. 147–52.

on the death of his father and henceforth be assessed and accepted as a *mormaer*. On the other hand, the high position of the *mormaer's* son may equally be indicative of the increase in status that holding the title brought his immediate kin.[82] *LBS* is inconclusive and could be read either way.

There were clearly occasions when attested *mormair* were not sons of the previous incumbent; this, however, may be indicative of the power particular kin-groups had over the title. A good example of this would be Colbán, *mormaer* of Buchan, who, as we have seen, acquitted four *dabaig* of land controlled by Deer from the common burdens of the realm in the early 1150s. Colbán had married Eva, daughter of a past *mormaer* of Buchan, Gartnait, who was himself the son of another earlier *mormaer*, Cainnech. Gartnait and Cainnech were part of Clann Channan in Buchan but there is no evidence that Colbán was part of this kindred; indeed, his son (probably from an earlier marriage) became lord of Kennoway in Fife and it may be that Colbán himself came from a kindred located in the south-east of Fife, not from a kindred in Buchan.[83] Colbán's own authority as *mormaer* of Buchan may have needed the authority of his wife and, through her, his wife's kin. We might, as stated above, think that Colbán could have acquitted Deer's lands from performing the common obligations owed throughout the kingdom himself, by virtue of his authority as *mormaer* of Buchan.[84] But Colbán did not make this quittance alone: he did so not only with the *toísech* of another leading kindred, Donnchad (demonstrating the importance of other potentates within the province other than the *mormaer*), but also with that of his wife, Eva.[85] Why Eva was needed to enforce this act, and Donnchad's wife (if he had one) was not, may well be explained by Eva's kin-authority, the weight of which was needed despite Colbán's position as *mormaer* of Buchan.

The Deer evidence from Buchan further suggests that local kindreds controlled the title of *mormaer*: in Buchan, Clann Channan seems to have monopolized the title (until the death of Gartnait sometime in the late 1140s) to the exclusion of Clann Morgainn.[86] Although sons did sometimes succeed fathers (as Gartnait did Cainnech), there was not a strict father-to-son inheritance of the title. Instead, the title seems to have been held by the most powerful member of a single kin-group or the most powerful head of kin within the province (who may not have been of the same kindred as the previous *mormaer*). The relationships between the men who held the *mormaer*-ship of Fife between the 1120s and 1150s suggest that the title was swapped between branches of the same kin-group. Three individuals held

---

[82] Alex Woolf suggests that these relationships denote that 'noble status was to some extent hereditary', but that the further away your relationship was to the thane (such as the fourth generation), the more likely you would be assessed or judged according to the status of a *rusticus* ('peasant'); Woolf, *Pictland to Álba*, pp. 347–8.

[83] See above, note 77. Dauvit Broun suggests by contrast that Colbán was part of a third kindred in Buchan; Broun, 'Origins of the *mormaer*'.

[84] Although it is important to note that Gartnait, son of Cainnech, also gave land to Deer together with his wife on two occasions; see Texts III and IV in Forsyth, Broun, and Clancy ed., 'Property Records', pp. 138–9, 140–1.

[85] Text VI in Forsyth, Broun, and Clancy ed., 'Property Records', 140–3.

[86] For Gartnait's latest attestation, see *CDI*, no. 171.

the title of *comes* of Fife between the 1120s and 1150s—Caustantín, Gille Míchéil, and Donnchad—but these men did not succeed patrilineally. John Bannerman has argued that all would have seen themselves as part of Clann Duib (kin of Dub, who was king of *Alba*, 962–66).[87] Caustantín was *mormaer* of Fife, dying at some point between the late 1120s and *c.*1136, but his relationship to his successor, Gille Míchéil, is uncertain. Gille Míchéil was not his son nor, apparently, his brother. Gille Míchéil went on to have at least two sons of his own but neither of these was the next *mormaer*; instead, Donnchad took the title, and he seems to have been Caustantín's son (although this is not provable).[88] After Donnchad died in 1154, it was Donnchad's son, also called Donnchad, who assumed the title of *comes* of Fife in *c.*1154, probably as a minor. After he died in 1204, Donnchad II's son, Mael Coluim, took the title of *comes*.[89] The title of *mormaer*, therefore, seems to have swapped between two branches of the same kindred in the first half of the twelfth century (probably represented by Caustantín and Donnchad on the one hand, and Gille Míchéil on the other) before Gille Míchéil's descendents dropped out of the running and were content to remain the admittedly powerful lords of Abernethy, then in the same province of Fife.[90]

How far the king of Scots (here mainly David I) was involved in the decisions concerning *mormaer*ship cannot be known. A reference in a charter of Alexander II (21 March 1225) to Mael Coluim, earl of Fife, the son of Donnchad II, reveals that David was throught to have 'granted' the *comitatus* of Fife to Donnchad II before David's death in 1153.[91] But given Donnchad II only became *mormaer* of Fife in *1154*, the year after David I died, the chronology of gift-giving in Alexander II's charter is inaccurate, which has some catastrophic consequences for traditional understandings of this charter. These will be set out below.[92] The key question here is: was the *mormaer*-ship in the king's power to appoint or confirm as inheritance? In both Buchan and Fife, the *mormaer*-ship appears to have been held by a single kin-group, even if different branches of that kin-group held the title (Fife) or if the kin-group absorbed outside men in order to maintain their grip on the title (Buchan).[93] It would be strange to imagine a situation where the king had no role in decisions as to who would be elected or chosen as *mormaer* of a particular province. It is likely his involvement varied, depending on his level of power within particular provinces: in some places, his support of an individual may have been

---

[87] Bannerman, 'MacDuff', pp. 27–33.

[88] Bannerman, 'Macduff', pp. 30–2, suggests that Gille Míchéil was a cousin of Caustantín.

[89] Before this, Mael Coluim was described as *filius comitis* or *filius comitis Dunecani* in royal charters, perhaps suggesting that he was acknowledged as Donnchad's intended heir; see his early attestations in the late 1180s and early 1190s; *RRS*, ii, nos. 342, 347, 356, 367.

[90] For Orm, son of Áed, lay abbot of Abernethy, see *RRS*, ii, no. 152, and Chapter 7, p. 431, note 166.

[91] Original, NRS, RH6/29 [AII/101].   [92] See below, pp. 47–51.

[93] Although Broun has argued that the Deer records show only a 'shadowy' presence for the king in Buchan (Broun, 'Property Records', p. 355), it is of note that, by the reign of Alexander III, the king had quite a bit of land in both Aberdeenshire and Banffshire, as demonstrated by a text known as the 'Alexander III Rental', discussed later in this chapter, and in Chapter 6, pp. 362, 368n, 382. For further discussion, see Broun, 'Statehood and Lordship', pp. 65–7.

enough—or he may elsewhere have acted as an arbiter between different kin-groups. There is no firm evidence that the king held ultimate power of conferrment; decisions must have reflected regional power dynamics and familial ties as much as kingly endorsement.

It is therefore possible to read the meagre evidence for *mormaír* in the first half of the twelfth century in a different way than as being royal agents in charge of a province, discharging specific responsibilities on the king's behalf. The *mormaer* was rather one among many potentates in a province and the title may have alternated between different kin-groups according to the ebb and flow of power within the province itself; sometimes one kin-group may have been dominant (particularly if it had a larger number of adult males and managed to exact more dues and tribute from the settlements under its control). While the king may have been involved in discussions as to who would be a *mormaer*, the title does not appear to be fundamentally conferred by kings nor held by one particular family. What, then, happened to the *mormaer* after the mid-twelfth century?

Provincia and *Comitatus*

Up to the *c*.1170s, it is important to distinguish between the *provincia*, whence the *comes* took the title, and the *comitatus*, a word that came to denote the land the *comes* controlled, directly or indirectly, within it. There is a tendency in the existing literature to fuse the province with the earldom. The province was the 'earl's' and thus was synonymous with his 'earldom' or, to use the Latin, his *comitatus*.[94] Or, put another way, the earl took his title from the province; his earldom was thus the province.[95] But, by the end of the twelfth century, the *provincia* and the *comitatus* were seen as different entities. *Provincia* remained a word used generally for a regional division of the kingdom (and thus still applied to the regional subdivisions of the kingdom to which *comites* were attached); *comitatus*, on the other hand, denoted explicitly the land controlled directly by the *comes* and on which his title had, by the end of twelfth century, come to depend, the geographical extent of which was not the same as that of the province. By this point, the *comitatus* of a *comes* might only be a small proportion of the province. The separation of the *comitatus* from the *provincia* therefore marks a shift in the basis of the authority of the *comes*—a silent shift as it was unaccompanied by an explicit change in the title of the individual. There was a *comes* of Fife at the beginning of the twelfth century and a *comes* of Fife at its end: during this period, however, the title had become territorialized, limited to direct control of a bounded area within the province of the same name.

The initial use of *provincia* and *comitatus* in Scottish royal charters and law in the first three quarters of the twelfth century may at first suggest that any firm and technical meaning cannot be deduced from words with such a wide semantic

[94] See, for example, G. W. S. Barrow, 'David I: the Balance of Old and New', in Barrow, *Scotland and Its Neighbours*, pp. 60–2; Barrow, *Anglo-Norman Era*, pp. 157–8.
[95] There are, of course, exceptions: see Young, 'Earls and Earldom of Buchan', p. 183.

range. *Provincia* had a wide usage: it could denote a province, a sheriffdom, part of a province, or an undefined wide geographical area.[96] The same is true of *comitatus*. The earliest appearance of the word *comitatus* is in a charter of Mael Coluim IV, dated to 1161×1164, where it denotes part of a province.[97] Yet *comitatus*—like *provincia*—could equally denote a sheriffdom, a province, or indeed part of a province in this period.[98]

But by the beginning of the thirteenth century, *comitatus* had developed a fixed meaning in royal charters, denoting the land held by a *comes* and his rights over it.[99] Indeed, the title of *comes* came to depend on control over the *comitatus*: the *comes* did not succeed to the province, he succeeded to the *comitatus* (the earldom). Thanks to their enrolment in the patent rolls of Henry III, we have the records of the agreement made over the *comitatus* of Menteith decided in the court of King William in 1213. Here, Muiredach, son of Gille Críst, earl of Menteith, resigned the *comitatus* of Menteith into the hands of his younger brother, also called Muiredach (although helpfully distinguished by the byname *iunior*).[100] When, in 1231, Alexander II addressed a brieve to Mael Coluim, *comes* of Fife, and his bailies of Fife, he commanded that Mael Coluim pay an eighth of the total fine (a monetary agreement) he had made with the king 'for the *comitatus* of Fife' to Dunfermline Abbey, which received an eighth of all monetary fines payable to the king.[101] The charter in which Alexander II confirmed Mael Coluim in his possession of Fife described the unit he held as the *comitatus* of Fife.[102] When Alexander II confirmed the *comitatus* of Lennox to Mael Domnaig, earl of Lennox, his charter stated that Mael Domnaig held the Lennox 'as freely and quietly as any of our *comites* hold and possess their *comitatus* from us'.[103] These references are to do with rights over land: the *comitatus* was a territorial designation and was the issue at stake in disputes over who had right to the title of *comes*. The link between *comes* and *comitatus* in charter diplomatic suggests that, whereas a province was a wider

---

[96] For a province, see *LS*, c. 1; for a sheriffdom, see G. W.S. Barrow, 'An Unpublished Brieve of Malcolm IV', *SHR*, vol. 84, no. 217 (2005), pp. 85–7, at p. 87; *CDI*, no. 75; for an undefined geographical area, see *LS*, c. 3.

[97] *RRS*, i, no. 245.

[98] For a sheriffdom, see *RRS*, ii, no. 80; for a province, see *LS*, c.12; for all the lands directly controlled by a *comes*, see *RRS*, ii, no. 205; for part of a province, see *RRS*, i, no. 245 and *LS*, c.1.

[99] For other examples of *comitatus* in non-royal charters, see Fraser, *Lennox*, ii, no. 14; NRS, GD 220/A1/4/6.

[100] Fraser, *Menteith*, ii, no. 7, pp. 214–15, which refers to the *comitatus de Manenthe*; also *RRS*, II, no. 519, which only refers to the *comitatus* as Muiredach's *hereditas*.

[101] *Dunf. Reg.*, no. 79 [AII/171]. It should be noted that the address clause of the brieve itself was not a provincial address, it was addressed to primarily to Mael Coluim, commanding him to pay, and his bailies of Fife (presumably the officials of his earldom). For 'second teinds', received by bishoprics and monastic houses, see Chapter 6, pp. 379–85.

[102] Original, NRS, RH6/29 [AII/101].

[103] *Lennox Cart.*, pp. 1–2 [AII/267], albeit without the castle of Dumbarton, among other things. The chronicle of Walter Bower is, although late, helpful here. While Bower was clear that armies were raised on the unit of the *provincia*, the title of the *comes* depended on his successful petition for rights over the *comitatus*. Thus, after the murder of Patrick of Atholl in 1242, David of Hastings received the *comitatus* of Atholl, having petitioned Alexander II by right of his wife; Bower, *Scotichronicon*, v, pp. 178–9.

territorial, social, and legal collective, *comitatus* denoted the lands held by the *comes* in the province whence he took his title—in short, the earldom. This explains the issue that historians have long grappled with: that the 'earldoms' of some earls were almost completely coterminous with the province whereas others, such as Fife and Angus, only occupied a very small proportion of its land.[104] The province and the earldom were not one and the same. Indeed, it is somewhat paradoxical that the scribes of royal charters started consistently recording the province to which the *comes* was attached only from the first regnal year of Alexander II, by which point many *comites* no longer had extensive control over the entire province (particularly in relation to military service and jurisdictional power) but, instead, intensive control over the lands of their earldom.[105]

From the beginning of the thirteenth century, therefore, the title of *comes* was a territorial title: its use denoted control over the *comitatus* and the link with the entire province was in symbolic title only. The fixity in the meaning of *comitatus* by the beginning of the thirteenth century corresponds to similar developments in other elements of charter diplomatic. Before the 1180s, for example, there was no word used consistently to denote the area of a sheriff's jurisdiction; during the 1180s, *ballia* became the convention.[106] If an individual did not have control over the *comitatus* but had instead responsibilities related to kin, they were described by another title. Only Carrick—hitherto outside the bounds of this enquiry—provides any clear evidence of this: here, the title of *comes* was inherited by Adam of Kilconquhar, the husband of Marjorie, who was the daughter of Niall, *comes* of Carrick (d.1256) but the title of *cenn ceneoil* (head of kin) was granted hereditably to one Roland of Carrick and his heirs.[107] The point emerging is clear: the title of *comes* went with the *comitatus*, meaning the 'land directly controlled by the *comes*'. If individuals had any other responsibilities, as Roland of Carrick did, but did not control the *comitatus*, they did not hold the title of *comes*. By the mid-thirteenth century, then, the basis of the title of *comes* had been transformed; it meant whichever man held the *comitatus* from the king.

When might this divorce of the earl and *comitatus* from the *provincia* have come about? The most obvious answer, founded on some long-standing historical assumptions, would be that it should have begun by *c*.1136, the date generally thought to be when David infeft Donnchad I in the *comitatus* of Fife. The infeftment of Donnchad in Fife is one of the foundation stones of Geoffrey Barrow's arguments about the 'beginnings of military feudalism in Scotland'.[108] Donnchad

---

[104] For Moray, see Ross, *Kings of Alba*, pp. 73–80; for comments on Fife, see Woolf, *Pictland to Alba*, p. 344; more generally, Grant, 'Construction', pp. 57–60; see also Brown, 'Scottish Earldoms', forthcoming.

[105] For the shift in titles of *comites* in charter witness lists, see above, pp. 37–8, and notes 55–6.

[106] See Chapter 4, pp. 201–5.

[107] *RMS*, i, nos. 508–509; Bannerman, 'MacDuff', pp. 37–8, drawing on Hector L. MacQueen, 'The Kin of Kennedy, "Kenkynnol" and the Common Law', in *Medieval Scotland*, ed. Grant and Stringer, pp. 274–96; see also Hector L. MacQueen, 'The Laws of Galloway: A Preliminary Survey', in *Galloway: Land and Lordship*, ed. R. D. Oram and G. P. Stell (Edinburgh, 1991), pp. 131–43.

[108] Barrow, 'Beginnings of Military Feudalism', p. 253.

I granted his earldom to King David only to have it returned to him as a feu, rendering service to the king from the earldom, and Barrow described the whole comital family of Fife as 'internal colonists'.[109] The infeftment of Donnchad in Fife by David is one of the standard 'facts' of Scottish medieval history and one might well think this would be the moment when the *comitatus* was first divorced from the *provincia*.

However, the only evidence possible to cite for David's supposed 'infeftment' of Donnchad I in Fife is a charter of Alexander II, dated 21 March 1225, confirming Mael Coluim in the *comitatus* of Fife after his father, Donnchad II, had died in 1204, which refers to David's giving the *comitatus* to Earl Donnchad by charter.[110] Barrow was, of course, aware that no charter of David I recording the infeftment of Donnchad I in Fife had survived but thought it fortunate that Alexander II's charter had done so instead because it 'show[ed] that King David granted to this same Earl Duncan [I] the earldom of Fife itself' and that the grant was recorded by a charter in which a fixed service was specified'.[111] Alexander's charter did indeed confirm the *comitatus* of Fife to Mael Coluim of Fife, explicitly invoked continuity with the past, and referred to David I giving the earldom away. However, there are serious chronological problems with the content of this charter. The text of the main body of Alexander's charter has therefore been given below:[112]

> Present and future know that I have granted and, by this, our charter, have confirmed to Earl Mael Coluim of Fife, son of Earl Donnchad [II], the earldom (*comitatus*) of Fife, just as Earl Donnchad, his father (*pater suus*), held that *comitatus*. To be held by him and his heirs from us and our heirs, in feu and heritage...with sake and soke, with gallows and pit, with toll and team and infangtheof...with all things lawfully pertaining to that earldom (*comitatus*), as <u>Earl Donnchad [II], his father (*pater suus*),</u> held that *comitatus*, to do the service from it which is owed to us from that *comitatus*, and as <u>the charter of King David concerning that comitatus, made for Earl Donnchad [II] his father (*pater eius*),</u> and the confirmation of our father, the Lord King William, made concerning this matter for the abovesaid Earl Mael Coluim, lawfully testify and confirm.

The Donnchad mentioned in Alexander II's charter was therefore *not* Earl Donnchad I but, instead, Earl Donnchad II.[113] Yet David simply could not have

---

[109] Barrow, *Anglo-Norman Era*, pp. 84–90; Duncan, *Making of the Kingdom*, p. 167. Barrow did, however, think that the earldom granted to Earl Donnchad I was far less in territorial extent than that inherited by his grandson, Mael Coluim, in 1204; Barrow, *Anglo-Norman Era*, pp. 84–6.

[110] NRS, RH6/29 [AII/101]; the lost charter of David is catalogued in *CDI*, no. 267.

[111] Barrow, 'Beginnings of Military Feudalism', p. 253; also Barrow, *Anglo-Norman Era*, pp. 84–5. Barrow was clear that Fife was exceptional, and that, *pace* Skene, it was unlikely that David treated the other earldoms in Scotia in the same way. Oram says the charter survives as a later transcription but this is not the case. The charter he cites is actually an early charter of David I to Robert I de Brus; see Oram, *Domination and Lordship*, pp. 214–15 and note 55.

[112] NRS, RH6/29 [AII/101].

[113] Keith Stringer has suggested to me that the use of *eius*, rather than *suus*, to refer to the Donnchad who was the recipient of David's charter implies that the scribe was, in this second passage, referring to Donnchad II's father, Donnchad I, and that the original interpretation is therefore correct. This seems to me to be unlikely. If Donnchad I *was* meant by *eius*, then why not be clearer, and refer to Donnchad as Mael Coluim's grandfather, his *avus*? Equally, this would mean that the charter would

given the earldom of Fife to him, something which has never been acknowledged before. There are serious chronological problems in the gifts and confirmations of the earldom of Fife listed in Alexander II's charter.[114] David I, after all, died in May 1153 but Donnchad II became the *comes* of Fife only in 1154 (and even then as a minor; he did not assume the title until 1159) after his father's death that year, an event noted by the Chronicle of Holyrood.[115] But Alexander's charter states that David did give the earldom to Donnchad II: the service Mael Coluim owed in 1225 was the same as that granted in 'the charter of David I', made 'for Earl Donnchad his father', meaning Donnchad II, father of Earl Mael Coluim. In short, David could not have given Donnchad II the earldom of Fife because he was already dead by the time Donnchad II became the *comes* of Fife. As a result, Alexander II's charter, the only evidence for David's purported 'infeftment' of the *comes* of Fife in his earldom, contains no firm evidence of this historiographically important milestone. How then do we understand the chronology of gift-giving in Alexander's charter to Mael Coluim of Fife?

The charter contains two references to two prior royal charters, drawn up for the *comites* of Fife in which they were confirmed in their possession of the earldom. The first is David's chronologically impossible one to Donnchad II; the second is one of William's to Donnchad's son, Mael Coluim, who was also the beneficiary of Alexander II's charter. There is nothing problematic about the reference to this second charter; William could well have confirmed Mael Coluim in his earldom after his father's death in 1204 by issuing him a charter of confirmation (this now lost charter would have a date range of 1204×14). What, then, of the reference to David's putative charter? Three solutions present themselves. The first is that David did issue a charter for Donnchad I but that a later scribe, writing at least seventy-two years later in 1225, confused Donnchad I with Mael Coluim's father, Donnchad II. The second is that the scribe of Alexander II's charter used a charter of King William, which confirmed the earldom of Fife to Donnchad II. This putative charter of William might have contained a reference to David giving the earldom of Fife to Donnchad I 'his (that is, Donnchad II's) father', which the scribe of Alexander II's charter to Earl Mael Coluim dutifully but erroneously copied.

not state that Donnchad II himself had received a charter giving him the earldom, but yet still refers to the 'confirmation' (*confirmatio*) made to Mael Coluim, which would be at the very least extremely obfuscating. Another charter of William, which also contains a bungled chronology, refers to Donnchad II as 'pater eius', but explicitly meaning Mael Coluim's father (*RRS*, ii, no. 472), and refers to another gift which 'King David, my grandfather', made to the same Earl Donnchad', meaning Donnchad II. It is far more probable, therefore, that the scribe of this charter of Alexander II used *eius* and *suus* interchangeably and was indeed referring to Donnchad II in the second passage, even though it was impossible for Donnchad to have received a charter in reality.

[114] The only person to my knowledge to have acknowledged chronological difficulties in other references to David in William's charters is Hammond, 'Adoption and Routinization', pp. 100–1, referring to *RRS*, ii, no. 472, also discussed below, p. 50. G. W. S. Barrow was, of course, aware of them but said that, referring to *RRS*, ii, no. 472, that 'King David's charter,...must have been in favour of Earl Malcolm's grandfather, Earl Duncan I' (*RRS*, ii, p. 436); see also Barrow, 'Earls of Fife', p. 55, note 4.

[115] *Chron. Holyrood*, s.a. 1154 (p. 126). It is improbable that Donnchad II obtained the title of *comes* immediately; see *Chron. Holyrood*, pp. 126–7, note 10; Bannerman, 'MacDuff', p. 35.

In many ways, either of these seems like the most attractive option, by virtue of their being relatively simple. But, in this particular case, simplicity may not offer the best solution. This charter of Alexander II was not the only one to make this kind of chronological error when dealing with the earls of Fife. A charter of William the Lion, which confirmed West Calder to Earl Mael Coluim after the death of the earl's father in 1204, stated that Donnchad II had been given West Calder by David I, another chronologically impossible gift.[116] What we see, therefore, are two royal charters, one of William and one of Alexander II, which both associate land-gifts made by David I to Donnchad II, earl of Fife, but these gifts simply could not have been made. If only one of these charters had survived, it would be easy to think this was an error; that two of them do suggests that we are looking at something more than a coincidence.

The final option is thus more complicated. The appeal to David's name in William's reign was a frequent feature of royal charter diplomatic, even when there is no firm evidence that David did any of the things he was credited with accomplishing (or of doing them in the particular way in which he was credited).[117] In this scenario, any potential reference to David in William's confirmation charter to Mael Coluim of Fife could well have been a claim to a longer history of confirming the *comites* of Fife in their earldom than did in fact exist. Indeed, as stated above, this had already happened to Earl Mael Coluim in William's reign: the charter by which Mael Coluim of Fife was confirmed in West Calder stated that his father, Donnchad II, had been given the land by David I, which was, again, impossible.[118] It is thus more than possible that the reference to Donnchad II and David in Alexander II's charter was copied from the 'confirmation' William issued to Mael Coluim after his father's death in 1204. It would have been this confirmation charter which originally contained the reference to the chronologically impossible charter of David I to Donnchad II, rather than Alexander II's charter. Accordingly, we should not see this charter of Alexander II as stable evidence of David's land-gifts (and his use of charters) but instead as evidence of how David's reputation was strategically used in William's reign as a way of lending strength to William's legal innovations and his own landed patronage. In short, it is just possible that David did not ever issue a charter confirming Donnchad I in the earldom of Fife—but that it was important that he was seen to have done so later in the twelfth century. In this case, the famous chartered infeftment of Donnchad I in the earldom of Fife may never have happened.

However, even if we do assume, for the sake of argument, that David I did 'give' Earl Donnchad I the earldom of Fife by charter, it is very improbable that the terms would have been those stipulated in Alexander II's charter to Donnchad I's

---

[116] *RRS*, ii, no. 472.

[117] Hammond, 'Adoption and Routinization', pp. 101, 105–6; and, in more detail, below, Part 1 Conclusion, pp. 180–1. Another possibility along the same lines would be that it was not David who issued the first charter about the earldom of Fife, but his grandson, Mael Coluim IV. Indeed, actions which we know were initiated in Mael Coluim's reign were accredited to David in William's reign as a way of claiming legitimacy back into a more distant past; see Chapter 3, p. 55 and note 210.

[118] *RRS*, ii, no. 472.

grandson, Mael Coluim. An equivalent example should bear this out: the two charters relating to the feu of Annandale in south-west Scotland, held by Robert de Brus in the reign of David I and by his son, Robert II de Brus, in the reign of William the Lion.[119] The charter of David I to Robert de Brus is very short and says that it has granted Annandale to Robert and that Robert is to hold it 'with all those customs which Ranulf Meschin ever had in Carlisle and in his land of Cumberland'.[120] It does not call Robert's holding a feu—a *feudum*—nor does it specify any military service or knightly service expected by the king as a result of the gift of land. If we turn to William's charter, drawn up around fifty years later, there could not be a more obvious difference. Annandale *was* there called a *feudum*—Robert was expected to render 10 knights when the king needed; he also had jurisdictional privileges with the right to hold his own court and, although he was not allowed to hear the king's pleas in this court, the king nominated a man from Robert's feu to collect the profits of justice for Robert when any of his men was subject to an accusation of the type which was only meant to be heard by the king's justices. The two charters therefore show a clear development in formal juridical language: in the first, land privileges, rights, and obligations are loosely defined between donor and recipient; in the second, the relationship is tightly defined, with the type of land named and the perennial services, obligations, and privileges clearly set out. Yet, as with the two 'charters' to the two Earl Donnchads, it has been assumed that the situation as recorded in William's charter must have existed at the time of David's original grant to the first Robert de Brus, despite the different content of the two charters.[121] This is partly the result of the language of William's charter itself: it *emphasizes* continuity, stressing that this was the situation which existed when Robert's father first received Annandale. But if this was so, then such language would surely have been present in the original grant which, happily, still survives.

What this means, therefore, is that we cannot be sure that David granted Donnchad I the '*comitatus*' (in its later sense) of Fife at all.[122] Even Alexander II's charter, normally taken as the key evidence for this gift, actually bungles its chronology, by referring to a charter of David drawn up for Donnchad II—which simply could not have been issued. Even if a charter had been drawn up for Donnchad I (an event for which there is now no firm evidence), we should be very

[119] *CDI*, no. 16; *RRS*, ii, no. 80.

[120] *CDI*, no. 16; for Ranulf Meschin and the extent of Cumberland, see Fiona Edmonds, 'The Emergence and Transformation of Medieval Cumbria', *SHR*, vol. 93, no. 237 (2014), pp. 195–216, at pp. 211–12; Richard Sharpe, *Norman Rule in Cumbria, 1092–1136*, Cumberland and Westmorland Antiquarian and Archaeological Society (Kendal, 2006), pp. 47–52.

[121] Broun, *Charters of Gaelic Scotland and Ireland*, pp. 15–16; there are, of course, exceptions: see, for example, Grant, 'Franchises', pp. 186–7; Oram, *Domination and Lordship*, p. 212; Hector L. MacQueen, 'Tears of a Legal Historian: Scottish Feudalism and the Ius Commune', *Juridical Review*, new series (2003), pp. 1–28, at pp. 7–9.

[122] The first example of *comitatus* meaning explicitly the land held by the *comes* is in William's charter granting the earldom of the Lennox to his brother, David, probably in 1178, although David did not hold the *comitatus* for long; *RRS*, ii, no. 205. For David's holding of the Lennox, see Keith J. Stringer, *Earl David of Huntingdon, 1152–1219: A Study in Anglo-Scottish History* (Edinburgh, 1985), pp. 13–18.

wary of assuming that it would have been expressed in the same language as that of his grandson, Alexander.[123] Indeed, the spread of the appearance of the word *comitatus* means that we should probably be looking at the last couple of decades of the twelfth century, the period when the language of relational lordship and jurisdiction was getting increasingly defined and formalized in charters.[124]

The territorialization of the *mormaer*'s authority is attested in sources other than charters, none of which dates from earlier than the last third of the twelfth century. Royal legislation from the 1170s onwards starts to treat *mormaír* as territorial lords who had similar privileges to other lords in their own lands. In 1180, William the Lion enacted that bishops, abbots, *mormaír*, barons, or any other freeholder 'who shall hold his court' would not be allowed to do so unless the king's sheriff was also present.[125] It will be shown in Chapter 2 that, by 1221, *mormaír* had lost ultimate control over the provincial levy of the common army: instead, bishops, abbots, knights, and thanes who held their land from the king had responsibility for their own lands.[126] *Mormaír* were expressly forbidden from entering the lands of any other lord; they only raised the levy from their earldoms, which they held from the king. An exception was made for the *mormaer* of Fife but the statute specified that he could only 'enter' the lands of others as the king's *maer* (steward), not as the *mormaer* of Fife. Presumably, if the *mormaer* of Fife had entered as a *mormaer*, he would have echoed his predecessors' responsibility for the levy of the entire province too strongly. The *provincia* did not become obsolete, retaining at least a symbolic unity for the writers of chronicles and poems who noted the existence of, for example, the armies of Fife and Mar; the *mormaer*, however, no longer had responsibility for raising all the provincial levy.[127]

What lands within the province, then, constituted the *comitatus*? In a recent set of articles, Dauvit Broun has put forward the existence of *mormaer*-ship lands in each province, that is, lands belonging to the *mormaer* which the most powerful *toísech* in the province would hold as a result of his position as *mormaer*. In addition, these *mormaír* would hold the lands pertaining to their kin-group. If the existence of the *mormaer*-ship lands is accepted, it seems likely that, when *comitatus* came to denote only the *lands* held by the *comes*, they included not only these earlier *mormaer*-lands but also those which he controlled as head of kindred.[128] But this did not hold true in all cases: the *comitatus* of the later twelfth century

---

[123] For David posthumously taking credit for Mael Coluim IV's activities, see Chapter 3, p. 155, note 210.

[124] For the appearance of *de me et heredibus meis* see Alice Taylor, 'Common Burdens in the *regnum Scottorum*: the Evidence of Charter Diplomatic', in *The Reality behind Charter Diplomatic in Anglo-Norman Britain: Studies by Dauvit Broun, John Reuben Davies, Richard Sharpe and Alice Taylor*, ed. Dauvit Broun (Glasgow, 2011), pp. 166–234, at pp. 168–85; for jurisdiction, see Chapter 3, pp. 157–64; see further, John Hudson, 'Legal Aspects of Scottish Charter Diplomatic in the Twelfth Century: A Comparative Approach', *ANS*, 25 (2003), pp. 121–38. This, however, is only a summary. A full study of the development of the diplomatic of royal charters will be conducted by the AHRC-funded project: 'Models of Authority: Scottish Charters and the Emergence of Government', run during 2014–17 at the Universities of Glasgow, Cambridge, and King's College London.

[125] *LS*, c. 7.

[126] Taylor, 'Common Burdens', pp. 209–19, and Chapter 12, pp. 102–11.

[127] See the references cited in Chapter 2, pp. 102–3.

[128] Broun, 'Origins of the *mormaer*'; Broun, 'Statehood and Lordship', pp. 55–7.

could also include whatever an earl's descendants had accumulated from the king in their own right, as well as kin-lands, and perhaps in addition whatever lands could pertain to the *mormaer*-ship. This seems to have been the position in Fife: a 1294 valuation of the *comitatus* of Fife included lands in the province which had been given to the earls of Fife by kings over the course of the twelfth century and which, by the 1290s, were included in the earl's *comitatus*.[129]

The title of *comes* (*mormaer*) thus became territorialized by the first couple of decades of the thirteenth century: that is, it depended on having control of a finite area of land, defined in royal charters as the *comitatus*, which, depending on circumstances, may have been made up of the earlier lands of the *mormaer*-ship (posited by Broun), any lands controlled by virtue of his status as head of kin within the province (from which he would have exacted tribute) and any lands accumulated by gift. Although *comites* under the jurisdiction of the king of Scots continued to take their title from a *provincia*, their title in fact depended on their holding of the *comitatus*. When disputes about succession to a *comitatus* arose from the end of the twelfth century onwards, the issue at hand was always who had control over the *comitatus*, a defined area of land. This explains why the territorial extent of *comitatus* could vary so much in relation to their particular provinces. Within the *comitatus*, the *comes* exercised more direct and intensive power than he had done over his *provincia*. He alone held his court in those lands; he was not *primus inter pares* in a provincial assembly. As will be shown in the next chapter, he alone raised his levy for military service within his lands but he no longer took responsibility for the province at large.[130] A process of territorialization began during the later twelfth century, that is, the formalization of military and jurisdictional power within a framework of fixed rights over land. It is this version of the *comes* which we might view as the functional predecessor of the later medieval earl.[131]

It might be thought that the territorialization of the authority of the *comes* limited his power because it came to be confined to a heritable but fixed geographical area, particularly in provinces where the *comitatus* only occupied a relatively small part of the overall area. But where this was the case, the payoff may have been an increase in autonomy from other magnates in the province: although the *mormaer* exercised less extensive power over the province, he exercised more intensive power over his *comitatus*. What happened to the second, supposedly continuous, element of the early Scottish state—the thane and his thanage—will be examined in the next section.

---

[129] Donnchad II of Fife was given Strathmiglo, Falkland, and other lands, and the farm of Kingskettle, 'in free marriage', to be inherited by the heirs born of his marriage to Ada, niece of Mael Coluim IV and (later) William the Lion; *RRS*, i, no. 190. In 1294, when a valuation was made of the earldom of Fife, these estates made up part of the earldom; see *Documents Illustrative of the History of Scotland from the Death of Alexander the Third to the Accession of Robert Bruce MCCLXXXVI–MCCCVI*, ed. Joseph Stevenson, 2 vols (Edinburgh, 1870), i, pp. 415–18; all originals in TNA, E372/141, m. 56, E 101/331/A, E101/331/B. A new edition of the documents of the 1294 valuation is in *PNF*, vol. 5, pp. 637–56, particularly pp. 651–2.

[130] Although the earl of Fife constituted somewhat of an exception: see Chapter 2, p. 103.

[131] As outlined by Grant, 'Earls and Earldoms', supported by Brown, 'Scottish Earldoms'.

THANES AND THANAGES

As stated in the introductory section to this chapter, there are two dominant trends of thought on the nature of the thane in pre-twelfth-century society. The first was put forward most emphatically by E. W. Robertson in two papers published in the third quarter of the nineteenth century and has found at least some favour ever since. Robertson saw 'little difficulty' in recognizing the thane as a leading royal official 'responsible for the rents and revenue of a [royal] thanage placed under his charge'.[132] Robertson's view of the thane has been followed and subsequently developed by Kenneth Jackson, Barrow, and Grant.[133] The thane-as-official has certainly been given more attention than the view that the thane was the head of a kin-group or a lord in his own right. Grant, for example, acknowledged that there was evidence that thanes could be autonomous lords as well as officials but concentrated on the evidence for them as officials. The opposite view—that a thane was not a royal official but, instead, the head or leader of a kin-group, paralleled in Gaelic by the word *toísech*—was put forward as early as 1872 by William Forbes Skene and has recently been resurrected by Alex Woolf and Dauvit Broun.[134] But the emphasis of this section lies, as in the earlier section on earls, in showing how the twelfth- and thirteenth-century evidence reveals changes and expansions in the meaning of 'thanes' and their supposed estates ('thanages'), which has implications for the use of this later evidence in the earlier period.

Thane as Estate Manager

In the twelfth-century record, thanes (singular: *thanus/theinus/tainus*) are most commonly listed as attached to particular estates.[135] Thus, the earliest record of a thane was in the written settlement of the dispute over the land of Kirkness (1128×36), in which one Mac Bethad, thane of Falkland, was listed as present at the provincial assembly of Fife where possession of Kirkness was assigned to the brethren of Loch Leven.[136] A further eleven thanes of individual estates, ranging from East Lothian to Moray, are recorded in the twelfth century: there were thanes at Fochabers in Moray; Arbuthnott, Ecclesgrieg, and Conveth in Kincardineshire; Inverkeilor in Angus; Strathardle in Perthshire; Dairsie, Kingskettle, and Kellie in Fife; Callendar

---

[132] E. W. Robertson, *Scotland under Her Early Kings*, 2 vols (Edinburgh, 1862), ii, pp. 444–7. For a full summary of the historiography on the subject, see Broun, 'Property Records', pp. 315–29.

[133] G. W. S. Barrow, *Feudal Britain: the Completion of the Medieval Kingdoms, 1066–1314* (London, 1956), p. 133; Barrow, 'Shires and Thanes', pp. 33–43, 55–6; Jackson, *Book of Deer*, pp. 110–14, 122–3; Grant, 'Thanes and Thanages', pp. 40–9, 55–9; Grant, 'Construction', pp. 52–6, 63–4; Grant, 'Franchises', pp. 177, 182–3.

[134] Skene, *Fordun*, ii, pp. 446–57; Skene, *Celtic Scotland*, iii, pp. 216–19, 238–42; Woolf, *Pictland to Alba*, pp. 346–9; Broun, 'Property Records', pp. 315–29, 354–6. Again, it has not been possible to take full account of the important study in Broun, 'Statehood and Lordship', pp. 33–55.

[135] As a result, thanes have been seen as a rather more glorified form of the Anglo-Saxon reeve, which are clearly described in James Campbell, 'Some Agents and Agencies of the Late Anglo-Saxon State', in James Campbell, *The Anglo-Saxon State* (London, 2000), pp. 201–25, at pp. 207–14.

[136] Lawrie, *ESC*, no. 80.

in Stirlingshire; and Haddington in East Lothian.[137] Although records of thanes continue well into the fourteenth century, Haddington remained the most southern reference to a thane in the kingdom. Thanes attached to estates are thus often seen as a phenomenon occurring particularly in Scotia but also in Moray.[138]

All these estates listed above were in the hands of the king either during the reign of David I, Mael Coluim IV, or William the Lion. All but two of them were then subsequently given to other people, which, through surviving charters of donation, is how we know about them. One exception is Strathardle in modern Perthshire, which remained in the king's hands, although proportions of its revenue were given to Scone Abbey by David and Mael Coluim, and its church later ended up in the hands of Dunfermline Abbey.[139] The other is Haddington, which appears to have been part of the queen's lands from the time of Ada de Warenne (who was not technically a queen, but the wife of Henry, son of King David).[140] Fochabers was given by David to his Benedictine foundation at Urquhart in Moray.[141] Falkland in Fife was given by Mael Coluim IV to Donnchad, earl of Fife, on the earl's marriage to Ada, the king's niece.[142] Dairsie, along with its church, was given to St Andrews, while William the Lion gave Kellie to Robert de Londres, his illegitimate son.[143] Part of Conveth was given to Agatha, wife of Humphrey, son of Theobald, by William, together with the right (*ius*) 'the thane was accustomed to have'.[144] Other gifts by William include Ecclesgrieg to William's brother, Earl David, Inverkeilor to Walter de Berkeley, and Arbuthnott to Osbert Olifard.[145]

Even this minimal twelfth-century evidence reveals that not only did these thanes collect service and revenue from their estates but they also kept at least some of this revenue themselves by what is sometimes called the 'thane's right' (*ius thani*).

---

[137] See the references in the very full appendix in Grant, 'Thanes and Thanages', pp. 72–81.

[138] This is despite the reference in a brieve-charter of David I (although issued before he became king) addressed to Bishop John of Glasgow, Brothers Cospatric, Colban, and Robert, and his faithful *thegnis et dregnis* in Lothian and Teviotdale (*CDI*, no. 10). Barrow attempted to locate thanes south of the Forth, all the way down to Berwickshire (Barrow, 'Shires and Thanes', pp. 22–32), although unsurprisingly, while he had much evidence for shires south of the Forth, he had much less for thanes. Despite the appearance of *thegns* in old Northumbria, it remains the case that all but one recorded thanes attached to an estate appear north of the Firth of Forth, in Scotia, despite the preponderance of the surviving written record originating from *south* of the Firth of Forth. For a recent article tracing the structural connections between *thegns* and later barons, see Jonathan Gledhill, 'From Shire to Barony: the Case of Eastern Lothian', in *Norman Expansion*, ed. Stringer and Jotischky, pp. 87–113.

[139] *RRS*, i, no. 243.

[140] For the development of land assigned to the queen, see Jessica A. Nelson, 'From Saint Margaret to the Maid of Norway: Queens and Queenship in Scotland, *c*.1067–1286' (PhD Dissertation, University of London, 2006), pp. 141–2, 160–2, 172–5, 286 (map); see also Jessica A. Nelson, 'Scottish Queenship in the Thirteenth Century', *Thirteenth-Century England IX* (Woodbridge, 2007), pp. 61–81.

[141] *CDI*, no. 185.   [142] *RRS*, i, no. 190.

[143] For Robert's holding of Kellie, see Alice Taylor, 'Robert de Londres, Illegitimate Son of William, king of Scots, *c*.1170–1225', *Haskins Society Journal*, vol. 19 (2008), pp. 99–119, at pp. 107–8, 112. Richard Siward later held Kellie with the title of *dominus*, see EUL, Laing Charters, Box 1, no. 19; PoMS, no. 5984, H4/26/14: <http://db.poms.ac.uk/record/source/5984/>.

[144] *RRS*, ii, nos. 344–5.

[145] *RRS*, ii, no. 352; Stringer, *Earl David*, pp. 59–60; *RRS*, ii, no. 185; *Spalding Misc.*, v, pp. 209–10.

When these estates were granted to other people, the new lord kept receiving this revenue and service in the same way as the thane had done, unless they wished to give it to a third party.[146] What we see therefore is that *some* thanes were attached to estates that were in the king's gift but from which they also received a proportion of revenue. By the beginning of the thirteenth century, thanes also appear attached to a few estates belonging to earls. The earliest charters of the earldom of Strathearn survive from the 1190s; from the start, named thanes appear attached to the estates of Dunning and Strowan, both under the control of the earl.[147]

Thane as Rank

In short, there seems to be good reason why we might think that thanes were royal estate managers and represented an administrative class of officials who had responsibility for collecting the king's income, even if a cut was reserved for them. But this would ignore a whole tranche of other evidence. Thanes were not just in charge of estates, whether royal or comital: the rank of thane was noble in its own right. The earliest evidence for this comes again from *LBS*.

As stated above, the first clause of *LBS* sets out the *cró* (life-value) of the socio-legal ranks of society under the king *de Scoce* ('of Scotia').[148] It begins (unsurprisingly) with the king, and ends with peasants (*vileyns*).[149] The ranks are as follows: king, *cunte* (*mormaer*), thane, thane's son, *ógtigern* ('little lord'), and peasants.[150] Each of these ranks are, however, preceded by a familial relation that is associated with the title of the next rung up. Thus, the *mormaer* is worth as much as the king's son, the thane as much as the *mormaer*'s son; the thane's son has his own rank, while the thane's kinsman (presumably outside his immediate line) is equivalent to the *ógtigern*.[151] Peasants were just peasants. Women were valued at a third of their husband's worth or, if they did not have a husband, their *cró* was the same as one of their brothers. The point about these ranks is they assume that the thane (as other ranks) was a noble rank, not far below that of the *mormaer*. Moreover, the title and status could be inherited and had consequences even for a thane's extended family. Sons of thanes were valued at the next rank down but, presumably, if their father died, one of them *could* obtain the rank of thane. Kinsmen of thanes were worth less than thanes' sons but still took their value from their kin-ties. We thus seem to be looking at the familial structure of thanes as being extended but still limited to a distinct structure of kin; all those lower than a thane's kinsman (it is possible that 'nephew' is meant here) were understood to be *villeyns* (peasants) and

---

[146] See also the *grescan* and service owed by the church of St Mo-Chonoc to the 'thanes of Inverkeilor' and afterwards to Walter de Berkeley: *Arbroath Liber*, no. 56; *RRS*, ii, no. 186.

[147] *Inchaffray Chrs*, nos. 9, 15–17, 19.

[148] Fergus Kelly, *A Guide to Early Irish Law* (Dublin, 1988), p. 125, note 1.

[149] Described as *vileyns* in the French *LS*, c. 21, and *rustici* in the Latin *RM*-versions.

[150] *LS*, c. 21.

[151] For an *ógtigern* in the bishopric of St Andrews, see G. W. S. Barrow, 'Witnesses and the Attestation of Formal Documents in Scotland, Twelfth–Thirteenth Centuries', *Journal of Legal History*, vol. 16, no. 1 (1995), pp. 1–20, at p. 19, note 76.

had the 'rights' of peasants (*et tu li plus en le parente et sunt vilayns et unt dreitur a vilayn*). Thanes were valued at 100 cows or 300 16*d*-ore and are thus presented as a high status rank within a society itself conceptualized as a kin-group. That this sense of thane continued throughout the twelfth century is shown by a statute enacted by Alexander II, probably in 1221, establishing the fines if individuals failed to serve in the king's common army. A thane had to pay six cows and a calf; an *ógtigern*, fifteen sheep, or six shillings; and a peasant (*rusticus*, a Latin word often used interchangeably with *villanus*), one cow and one sheep.[152] At least for thanes, *ógtigerna* and peasants, social ranks remained assessed in the same way as they appear in *LBS* well into the thirteenth century.

Thanus, as the French *thein* or *thain*, was, like *comes*, a translation of an existing word. The Latin *thanus* came into Scottish terminology from the Old English *þegnian*, meaning originally 'to serve', and was often translated by the Latin *minister* in English diplomas. By the time *thanus* appears in Scottish documentation, however, the noun *thegn* had, in England, developed a very wide meaning and denoted a noble rank whose wergeld (life-value) was at least 1200 shillings, as well as a royal servant.[153] It is possible that *thanus* entered Scottish Latin vocabulary from the use of 'thegn' in the English-speaking areas concentrated in Lothian, and, indeed, one charter of David I addressed the *thegnis et dregnis* ('thegns and dregns') of Lothian and Teviotdale.[154] However, the geographical spread of attested thanes is not predominantly in Lothian but in Scotia, meaning the area bounded by the Forth, Spey, and Druim Alban, in addition to a few in Moray. Some historians

[152] See Chapter 2, pp. 103–4; Taylor, 'Leges Scocie', pp. 240–3; see also Ross, *Kings of Alba*, pp. 53–5. For the equivalence of *rusticus* and *villanus* in the same document, see *RRS*, ii, no. 281.

[153] Ann Williams, *The World before Domesday: The English Aristocracy 900–1066* (London, 2008), chapter 2, emphasizes the types of royal service performed by thegns, but see also John Gillingham, 'Thegns and Knights in Eleventh-Century England: Who Was Then the Gentleman?', *TRHS*, 6th ser., vol. 5 (1995), pp. 129–53; the text known as *Dunsæte* also describes thegns as a noble rank, for which see Liebermann, *Gesetze*, i, pp. 374–9, at p. 376, and for the most recent commentary (and the literature cited therein), see George Molyneaux, 'The *Ordinance concerning the Dunsæte* and the Anglo-Welsh Frontier in the Late Tenth and Eleventh Centuries', *Anglo-Saxon England*, vol. 40 (2011), pp. 249–72.

[154] Late eleventh-century thegns were often identified as *milites* or *barones*, rather than *ministri*, in the immediate post-Conquest period. Address clauses in the early writs and writ-charters of William the Conqueror often translated *þegn* as *baro*; see *Regesta Regum Anglo-Normannorum: The Acta of William I (1066–1087)*, ed. David Bates (Oxford, 1998), nos. 287, 313–15, 346; to be compared with *Anglo-Saxon Writs*, ed. F. E. Harmer (Manchester, 1952), nos. 18, 115–16. See Richard Sharpe, 'The Use of Writs in the Eleventh Century', *Anglo-Saxon England*, vol. 32 (2003), pp. 247–91. *þegn* was not always translated as *baro*, sometimes the Latinization of *þegn—tainnus* or *teignus—*was used instead; *Regesta*, ed. Bates, nos. 191, 227, 341. Sometimes, however, thegns were lumped together within the community of *fideles* being addressed, and, perhaps, sometimes *minister* was used. See, for example, the bilingual writ-charter drawn up for Rochester cathedral; *Regesta*, ed. Bates, no. 226. The shire customs transcribed in the folios of Berkshire Domesday mention that if a 'thegn or knight' of the royal demesne should die, he should leave all his weapons to the king, together with two horses, one saddled, one without saddle. For different values of heriots in eleventh-century England, see Nicholas Brooks, 'Arms, Status and Warfare in Late-Saxon England', in *Ethelred the Unready: Papers from the Millenary Conference*, ed. David Hill (Oxford, 1978), pp. 81–103.

have thus sensibly assumed that *thanus*, although derived originally from an Old English word, was translating a Gaelic word.[155]

The word usually associated with *thanus* is the Gaelic *toísech* (meaning, rather opaquely, 'first' or 'leader').[156] Not all historians prefer this association and some have suggested that Scottish thanes were, in fact, *maír* ('stewards' or 'officials'), although there are various reasons for rejecting this association.[157] There is, however, no one figure called both a *toísech* in Gaelic records and a *thanus* in Latin—as there is for the equation of *comes* and *mormaer* in the figure of Ruaídrí, called both *comes* and *mormaer* of Mar—which demonstrates the equivalence of these titles.[158] The absence of an explicit connection between *thanus* and *toísech* means that some historians will always doubt whether thane really did translate *toísech*.

There are, however, similarities between the presentation of the relation between *mormaer* and *toísech* in the property records in the Book of Deer and the rank relations set out in *LBS*. These do provide strong evidence for seeing the thane as equivalent to the *toísech*.[159] *LBS* presents a clear hierarchy of rank: king, *mormaer*, thane, thane's son, thane's kinsman, and peasant.[160] A similar hierarchy between the ranks of *mormaer* and *toísech* can be seen in the Book of Deer. In one property record, entered *c*.1150, Colbán, *mormaer* of Buchan, and Eva, daughter of Gartnait (the previous *mormaer*), together with Donnchad, son of Síthech, *toísech* of Clann Morgainn, 'extinguished' the obligation for Deer to pay all the dues from four units of assessed land (the *dabach*).[161] Donnchad, as *toísech*, was the second male grantor of this quittance after Colbán, as *mormaer*. As *mormaer* was consistently translated by *comes*, it would make sense if *toísech* was translated by *thanus* (or 'thane'), rather than *toísig* clearly being a key part of the political landscape in Buchan even in the second quarter of the twelfth century only to then disappear. If *toísech* was what was meant by 'thane', then the latter word established itself quickly in written evidence.[162] The predominantly French text of *LBS* used *thain/*

[155] See, for example, Jackson, *Book of Deer*, pp. 112–14.

[156] In Ireland, for example, *toísech* was used to denote the 'first scholar': '*toísech na scolóc*'; online at the *Electronic Dictionary of the Irish language, s.v.* scolóc, toísech: <http://edil.qub.ac.uk/>.

[157] Barrow, 'Shires and Thanes', pp. 55–6 (although Barrow did recognize that thanes could be quite distinct from *maír*); Robertson, *Scotland*, ii, pp. 447–70, particularly pp. 463–4. *Maer* was latinized as *marus* and survived throughout the central Middle Ages and could be used in the same text as *thanus*, demonstrating that the two were different; see, for examples, *LS*, c. 20 and *SA*, c. 26 (the latter is discussed in Chapter 2, pp. 102–8).

[158] Text III, in Forsyth, Broun, and Clancy ed., 'Property Records', pp. 138–9; and *CDI*, no. 33. I am ignoring 'Finlayus Toschoch thanus de Glentilt', who appears in 1502, and whose name is attested simply too late to have a bearing on the *toísech*/thane in the twelfth century; *RMS*, ii, no. 2655, cited in *Moray Reg.*, p. xxviii; Grant, 'Thanes and Thanages', p. 42; C. A. Malcolm, 'The Origins of the Sheriff in Scotland: Its Origin and Early Development', *SHR*, vol. 20, no. 78 (1923), pp. 129–41, p. 134, note 9.

[159] Broun, 'Property Records', pp. 354–5.   [160] *LS*, c. 21.

[161] Text VI, in Forsyth, Broun, and Clancy ed., 'Property Records', pp. 140–3.

[162] See, for example, the reference to the thane in Fochabers (noticeably not explicitly the king's thane) in Moray, in a charter of David I, perhaps dated as late as 1152×53, but certainly after the battle of Stracathro in 1130; *CDI*, no. 185 (*que ad thain pertinet*).

thayn consistently, never *toísech*, despite leaving other Gaelic words, such as *ógtigern* in their original language.

Thanes and Kin-groups

Whereas *LBS* only presents the thane as a single status rank, the property records in Deer explicitly describe the *toísech* as 'leader' of a *clann* (or tribe or kin-group). Two clans are mentioned: Clann Channan and Clann Morgainn.[163] Broun has recently demonstrated that, despite the assertions of other historians, we should see no substantive difference between those *toísig* in Deer who are simply described as *toísech* and those called *toísech clainne*.[164] All the *toísig* attested in Buchan in the late eleventh and the first half of the twelfth century, therefore, should be seen as heads of leading kin-groups in the province. For two—Clann Channan and Clann Morgainn—we have names and these two were those which dominated the *mormaer*-ship in the period covered by the Book of Deer.

As *toísig* were heads of kin-groups, were thanes also presented as such? *LBS* does not say explicitly that thanes were anything other than a single status rank. But it is worth remembering that the text conceives socio-legal ranks on kin-lines (thus the thane is equivalent to the son of a *mormaer*). There are also three gradations related to the status of the thane: thane, thane's son, and thane's kinsman.[165] It could be that the thane had authority over all known to be his kinsmen; indeed, the life-value of these people actually depended on their kin-tie to the thane. The evidence is not wholly conclusive but it is possible to see the thane in *LBS* as heading a kin-group that extended to kinsmen of the wider *clann*. The *toísech clainne* of Buchan is not, therefore, as far removed from the thane of *LBS* as we might think. Indeed, a *mormaer* could also be a *toísech*, which one might expect if an individual both retained leadership over his kin-group and, as *mormaer*, extensive authority over all the kin-groups in his province. There is actually an example of a *mormaer* who was also a *toísech* in a record transcribed into the gospel book of Deer. Muiredach, son of Morgann, apparently, gave the 'holding of Gartnait's sons' and the scribe in the Book of Deer stated that 'he was *mormaer* and he was *toísech*'.[166]

If thanes constituted a noble rank, equivalent to some *toísig*, then why did these nobles of significant life-value and independent means also attach themselves to royal and *mormaer*-estates, even if they did receive a proportion of the resources extracted? Why would these individuals, who already had great social and economic capital in their locality, have wished to serve the king (or *mormaer*) in this way? It is possible that some sort of subordinate estate management was a type of service that someone of nobility would perform for a rank of higher status—a *mormaer* or a king—and receive the increased financial status that such service entailed. The only problem with this scenario is that it would require *all* thanes of

---

[163] Text V.3 and Text VI, in Forsyth, Broun, and Clancy ed., 'Property Records', pp. 140–1.
[164] Broun, 'Property Records', pp. 351–3, 354–5; cf. Jackson, *Book of Deer*, pp. 110–14.
[165] Broun, 'Property Records', p. 355.
[166] Text II.2 in Forsyth, Broun, and Clancy ed., 'Property Records', pp. 136–7.

individual estates already to be thanes in rank, a problem which explains why it has been thought that there were two types of thanes, one noble, one official.[167] But this solution is also problematic because it does not address the question of why the same title would then have been used to describe individuals of very high status *and* individuals who were functionaries (regardless of what their socio-legal status actually was). This is even more problematic when one considers that other words were used to describe individuals who either farmed royal estates (and delivered a set amount of revenue to the king each year) or managed them? Why were thanes of individual estates called thanes when 'farmer' (*firmarius*) or 'bailie' (*ballivus*) would do equally well?

A possible solution is, admittedly, speculative but has the advantage of not requiring thanes of estates already to be 'full' thanes nor does it envisage there being two 'separate' mutually exclusive types of thanes—one noble, one administrative—described by the same word. It is that the rank of thane (probably originally *toísech*) was a rank fundamentally associated with high status and remained so. By associating this title with a person who might otherwise be described as a functionary managing an estate on behalf of someone else (whether king or *mormaer*), the high-status nature of 'thane' became associated with service. If this was the case, then one might imagine that individuals not quite of the rank of thane might have been more inclined to manage estates for another person because it gave them the full thanely-status (essentially giving them a higher life-value) that they did not otherwise possess. Sons of thanes, thanes' kinsmen, even, perhaps, sons of *mormaer* who did not head their own kin-groups may well have seen this functional role as a way to increase their own status.[168]

Thanes, Knights, and Landed Estates

This speculation about thanes concerns a period for which we have a greater quantity of written evidence. But it becomes even harder to speculate about the pre-twelfth-century period when it is acknowledged that the word *thanus* expanded in meaning during the second half of the twelfth century (this periodization is necessarily rough because of the patchy evidence). In this later period, thanes start to be seen as equivalent in some way to knights and other lords. Sometimes, the

---

[167] Jackson, *Book of Deer*, pp. 111–13; Grant, 'Construction', pp. 53–4; Grant, 'Thanes and Thanages', pp. 40–2.

[168] None of what follows in this footnote is provable but it makes sense of the thirteenth-century evidence. If the trappings of a thane's high status had become granted along with estate management (whether by the earl or by the king), then it would follow, if high status came to be predominantly expressed in a different way, that we would, in our later evidence, see far more thanes as estate managers and far fewer thanes as primarily a status rank. This is indeed what we do see, albeit over a very long time frame of around 150 years. Thanes first become associated with other forms of lordly power, such as knighthood, in the second half of the twelfth century. By the 1260s, however, it is very rare (although still possible) to find thanes as a noble rank either in our charter evidence or in royal laws. The only potential exceptions are Simon, thane of Aberchirder (*Moray Reg.*, no. 218), and Ewan, thane of 'Rattenec' (*APS*, i, pp. 101). The 'rank' of thane appears in the thirteenth century much more commonly when the individual concerned is attached to a royal or comital estate.

equivalence is expressed very quickly and it is hard to know whether it is meaning-
ful: Earl Gille Brigte of Strathearn and his wife, Matilda d'Aubigny, for example,
recorded that they had founded Inchaffray Abbey not only with the assent of the
bishops of Dunkeld and Dunblane but also with the consent of 'our children
(*liberi*), knights and thanes'.[169] Some further examples show generic 'lords' exercising the same rights and privileges as thanes once had done, while others reveal a
conscious distinction between the position of a *thanus* and those of lower status,
on the one hand, and the relationship between a *dominus* and his men, on the
other.

In the 1170s, for example, Walter de Berkeley, then King William's chamberlain,
was infeft by William in the territory of Inverkeilor in Angus, which was, by then,
also a parish. Walter held this from the king for the service of one knight.[170]
Sometime later, probably not after 1178, Walter acquitted the parish church of
Inverkeilor, dedicated to St Mo-Chonoc, from the service he was owed (two forms
of tribute render, coupled with some rents) from the church's land. His charter
specified that the men living on the land had been accustomed to do this service 'to
the thanes of Inverkeilor and...afterwards to me'.[171] Although Walter was infeft in
the land of Inverkeilor and held the land from the king and his heirs (*de me et heredibus meis*) for the service of a single knight, he saw himself as the successor to a long
line of thanes who had held Inverkeilor. Indeed, he also collected the same dues that
the thanes had once done.[172] There was continuity in the expectations of resource
extraction between the past thanes of Inverkeilor and Walter de Berkeley.[173]

If one puts to one side the probability that Walter spoke a different language
from his thanely predecessors, it is possible that the inhabitants of Inverkeilor
would have had a hard time distinguishing Walter (who held his land for knight's
service) from the thanes who controlled the land before him. A case heard at an
ecclesiastical synod of Perth, in 1206, supports this.[174] The case turned on the
competing claims of one Donnchad, lord of Arbuthnott in the Mearns and the
bishop of St Andrews, over the Kirkton of Arbuthnott, which may have been similar in form to the church land of St Mo-Chonoc in Inverkeilor.[175] The lay parsons
and peasants (free and unfree) of the land were complaining against the actions of
Donnchad and his predecessors, who had turfed some of them off the land and
tried to turn it over to the plough. The bishop (as protector of the inhabitants)

---

[169] *Inchaffray Chrs*, no. 9.
[170] *RRS*, ii, no. 185. This charter does not survive either as an original or as a cartulary copy and is
only known from a late-eighteenth-century work on Scottish law; *RRS*, ii, p. 242.
[171] *Arbroath Liber*, no. 56. Walter later gave the church of Inverkeilor to King William's new
monastic foundation at Arbroath, hence (presumably) why his charters about remitting these services
survive in Arbroath's cartulary; *Arbroath Liber*, no. 54.
[172] *RRS*, i, no. 185. The charters are almost identical in their diplomatic (with a few more com-
mandatory phrases in the king's, which is unsurprising) and in their witness lists. The witnesses of
Walter's charter are the same as that of William's, apart from two men (Jordan Woodford and Robert
Chanterelle) who never appear again as witnesses in the entire surviving corpus of Scottish charters:
Arbroath Liber, no. 56.
[173] For more on this point, see below, p. 62.
[174] *Spalding Misc.*, v, pp. 209–13.
[175] For comparable *abthen* lands, see Barrow, 'Lost Gàidhealtachd', pp. 120–4.

eventually won the day but what is more important here is how the witnesses in the case, who were of varying status—lay and religious, educated and non-educated—conceived the authority of Donnchad and his predecessors.

Thirteen witness testimonies are recorded in the case summary and, through them, it is possible to construct the history of the lordship of Arbuthnott during the second half of the twelfth century.[176] Before 1163, Osbert Olifard had received Arbuthnott from the king 'for his service'. No witness says what this service is: other royal grants of estates coterminous with single parishes were given in return for the service of a single knight so it is probable, although not provable, that this was the stipulation for Osbert's lordship over the estate.[177] Osbert, however, wanted to go on crusade (the third crusade) and so gave the estate at farm to Isaac of Benvie, who also provided one of the longest witness statements in the 1206 case.[178] Isaac said that he held the land of Arbuthnott 'at farm from Osbert as from a lord' (*ad firmam ab Osberto tanquam a domino*).[179] Isaac held the land for six years before Osbert's son, Walter, took over. Walter gave the estate to Hugh Swinton, 'for his service' and Hugh's son, Donnchad, was the unsuccessful party in the dispute itself. Thus, Hugh and Donnchad held the estate 'for service' from the Olifards, who themselves held it from the king 'for service'.

All these men—Osbert, Walter, Hugh, and Donnchad—were called 'thanes' by some of the witnesses. Master Isaac, for example, testified that he had 'never heard that any thane had put a plough to the land before this man [Donnchad] had'.[180] A man named Felix said that he had seen thirteen 'thanes' of the land to whom the inhabitants of the Kirkton had always paid *cáin*, until, that is, the time of Isaac of Benvie, who had started to trouble them.[181] Felix here was not referring to all those *before* Isaac as thanes and all after him as non-thanes; he stated explicitly that 'no thane had ploughed the land unless by [permission] of the bishop, save this man, Donnchad', thereby describing Donnchad and all his predecessors, including Isaac, as 'thanes'. Donnchad was one of the thirteen thanes, regardless of how he was holding the land. The Arbuthnott case thus acts as a supplement to the Inverkeilor charters: in both, the 'new', 'Anglo-Norman' lords (in this case the Olifards and the de Berkeleys) take over from 'thanes' but receive exactly the same dues from the land in question. Indeed, it was because Donnchad (at the very least) was doing something different that the case had arisen: he was *not* behaving as past thanes had done. The expectations of continuity were thus so strong that the lords of Arbuthnott—whether the Olifards or their subtenants, the Swintons / Arbuthnotts—were known as the latest in a long line of twelfth-century thanes by those who either inhabited the land or were involved in some way in it.

---

[176] This has been done many times before: see, for example, Skene, *Celtic Scotland*, iii, pp. 259–61; and, most recently, in Broun, 'Statehood and Lordship', pp. 47–50.

[177] See below, pp. 74–5.

[178] For Scottish crusaders, see Alan Macquarrie, *Scotland and the Crusades, 1095–1560* (Edinburgh, 1985).

[179] *Spalding Misc.*, v, p. 210.

[180] *Spalding Misc.*, v, p. 211. One can actually get a sense of Isaac gesturing in court to Donnchad by the use of 'iste' to identify him. The phrase drips with accusation.

[181] *Spalding Misc.*, v, p. 212.

The equivalent position of lords and thanes (but also, simultaneously, a distinction between the two) in the later twelfth century is attested in another of King William's charters, issued for the bishopric of Moray, probably in 1185×89.[182] This was authenticated at Elgin and established the consequences for non-payment of teind.[183] The charter states that it was following the assize laid down by David I and the custom held 'until now' in the bishopric of St Andrews. The custom was as follows. If a peasant refused to pay teind, 'the thane under whom the peasant is, or his lord, if he has a lord' should make him pay, and fine him one cow and one sheep, which the lord or thane would keep himself. If the lord or thane failed to do this, or refused to pay teind themselves, then they had to pay a larger fine of eight cows, which would be taken by the sheriff, and this time handed over to the king. If the sheriff failed to do his job, then the king's justice (*iusticia*) was responsible for fining everybody who needed to be fined and making sure the king received the 'forfeitures' owed by thane, lord, sheriff, or justice.[184] All this was so that no one could 'diminish or take away the laws and rights of the Holy Mother church'.

This charter poses a number of interesting problems. First, there is an issue as to whether the procedure as it stands was actually that enacted by David for the bishopric of St Andrews before his death in 1153. Despite what the charter says, this is not the case. The roles of the sheriff and justice are, for one, described in ways that are anachronistic for the extent of their responsibilities under David I and the areas in which they operated.[185] Thus, although William's charter said this procedure followed David's assize, this does not mean that David's assize did actually envisage the punishment of defaulters in exactly the same framework. There is nothing to suggest that David did not enact a law on the general subject of non-payment of teind in St Andrews but the institutional specificity suggests that his assize may have, at the very least, been worded differently, and worked within different structures.[186] In addition, David was often invoked as an authority during William's reign without necessarily having performed the actions with which he was posthumously credited.[187] This has consequences for when the statement about the equivalence of thane and lord applied. If William's charter did preserve the text of David's assize, the statement would have originally applied to the early 1150s, at the latest; if it reworked it, then the statement only holds for the 1180s. Because William's charter uses diplomatic formulae that only appear in the late 1170s and

---

[182] *RRS*, ii, no. 281.
[183] The centre of the bishopric of Moray moved from Spynie to Elgin in the 1220s, for which see *Moray Reg.*, nos. 26 [AII/94], 57.
[184] For 'justice', as opposed to 'justiciar', see Chapter 4, pp. 213–15.
[185] The particularly troublesome formula is *vicecomes in cuius ballia*, which is not used to represent shrieval power until the 1180s. In addition, justices were not expected to operate north of the Forth in any defined way under David I, nor did sheriffs cover all of that area. For all this, see Chapter 4, pp. 200–5, 220–2.
[186] For the development of the structures for the enforcement of teind payments, see Chapter 3, pp. 154–7.
[187] See below, Part 1 Conclusion, pp. 180–1.

1180s, the second possibility is far more probable than the first—and is preferred here.

The key passage is the statement that if a peasant did not pay, 'the thane under whom he is or his lord if he has a lord' (*theynus sub quo ille est vel dominus eius si habuerit*) would compel him to do so, or face an even higher fine. This statement places the lord and thane in an equivalent but distinct position in relation to the peasant. The inherent distinction in the phrase has been the basis for the idea that thanes were still managers of royal estates: '[the charter shows that] the thane's role was clearly managerial; he was not the proprietor of the territory'.[188] This sugges- tion pushes the phrase too far. The distinction between the thane and lord may indicate a conceptual distinction in types of hierarchical authority over a lesser rank, not a difference between administrative and non-administrative function. *LBS* shows that peasants were, quite literally, conceived as being 'under' thanes in its presentation of Scottish society as one large kindred. Lordship, on the other hand, could be expressed in very personalized terms: some peasants were their lords' 'liege men' (*homines legii*) and performed homage to them in return for their protection.[189] The distinction between thanes and lords is an important one as it reveals live differences between the written conceptualization of socio-legal and socio-economic hierarchies: the thane as a higher rank *over* the peasant; the lord as existing in a personalized relationship of dependence *with* the peasant. There is no reason, therefore, to think that the clause denotes managerial capacity on the one hand and lordship on the other. But what is interesting is that, whatever difference existed between the status of thane and position of lord, they were meant to have similar functional responsibilities over their peasants in the province of Moray during the 1180s.

The distinction between the authority of lord and thane, present in the Moray charter, was beginning to evaporate in other documents drawn up in the king's name around the same time. By the late 1190s, William's legislation understood thanes to be lords who held their lands with formal jurisdictional privileges exer- cised in their own courts (*curiae*). In this, they were deemed equivalent to other major, secular landlords. In an assize enacted at Perth in 1197, and modelled on an English procedure announced two years earlier, William the Lion commanded that the 'bishops, abbots, earls, barons (*barones*) and thanes (*thani*)' should desist from maintaining and helping wrongdoers who were either their own men (*hom- ines proprii*) or other men who had come into their land.[190] By 1221, thanes were

---

[188] Grant, 'Thanes and Thanages', pp. 40–1; but see the different emphasis in Grant, 'Construction', p. 53, note 34. See also Robertson, *Scotland*, ii, p. 444. Geoffrey Barrow translated *villanus* and *rusticus* as 'neyf', implying that all these peasants were unfree; *RRS*, ii, p. 306. There is no evidence for this: *rusticus* in particular could denote a generic peasant, a free peasant, or an unfree peasant; see Alice Taylor, '*Homo Ligius* and Unfreedom in Medieval Scotland', in *New Perspectives on Medieval Scotland, 1093–1286* (Woodbridge, 2013), ed. Matthew Hammond, pp. 85–116, at pp. 106–8.

[189] Taylor, '*Homo Ligius*', pp. 91–101.

[190] *LS*, c. 15. That the other men would be found within these lords' own land is an inference from the text. *Homines proprii* here does not mean unfree people or people living in a state of strong dependency on their lords (if it did, the interpretation would then be that lords were expected to maintain justice for their generally unfree dependents and their free ones). For this use of *homines proprii*, see Marc Bloch, 'Les *colliberti*: Étude sur la formation de la classe servile', *Revue Historique*,

conceptualized not only as landlords but also as having equivalent responsibilities to barons and knights.[191] In this year, Alexander II held a council at Perth setting out the procedure for fining those within Scotia who had failed to answer the king's summons to serve in the common army. Those secular lords responsible for levying forces were (alongside earls) 'barons, knights and thanes who hold of (*de*) the king' who would pay their fines directly to him. Moreover, thanes were directly associated with the rank of knight (*miles*). The statute detailed the forfeiture owed from the decreasing ranks of men who should serve in the army (from thane to peasant). The king received the full fine for a defaulting thane but, from *ógtigerna* (lesser nobles) and peasants, the fine would be divided between the king and the 'thane or knight' who was responsible for those in his land.[192] Not all thanes, however, held their land 'from' the king: the 1221 statute also mentions earls' thanes, for whom the earl, not the king, had responsibility. Nothing more is said about them; indeed, the statute simply said that, while earls would receive fines from their thanes, the assembly had not decided how much the amount would be.

The majority of the thanes described in these two enactments were thus understood as tenurial lords who held their own courts in their own lands and raised army service from those lands when the king demanded it. It may well be that this way of describing thanely power was relatively new and the meanings of thane expanded in the late twelfth and early thirteenth centuries to include the thane as tenurial lord who looked rather similar to the knight and also held his land directly from the king. But even if the meaning of 'thane' had widened, no one meaning of 'thane' had completely superseded any other by the time of the 1221 statute. Thanes continued to manage royal (and comital) estates. In addition to being a tenurial lord, the thane was still conceptualized in 1221 as a noble rank (perhaps still the head of a local kin-group) in a similar way to how its status was ranked in the earlier *LBS*. So, as stated above, while *LBS* had described the lowest three ranks of Scottish society as 'thane–*ógtigern*–peasant', the 1221 record listed the fines of the defaulters in the same way: 'thane–*ógtigern*–peasant'.[193] There was thus no simple linear progression from thane-as-status-rank to thane-as-tenurial-lord nor were thanes *either* primarily estate managers *or* lords and/or heads of kin-groups. The title of thane was, even in the early thirteenth century, extremely flexible, encompassing a wide and increasing variety of statuses, functions, and lordships

vol. 157 (1928), pp. 1–48, 225–63. The general tenor of this statute is for justice to be maintained in the lands of these lords, in accordance with the 'justice of the land'.

[191] *SA*, c.26; the most recent edition is in Taylor, 'Common Burdens', pp. 224–34; and discussed (with a translation) in Chapter 2, pp. 103–11.

[192] Which might suggest that there was a financial incentive not to have all your men turn up for service.

[193] *LS*, c. 21. Sometime before 30 June 1233 in the reign of Alexander II, Mael Coluim, thane of Callendar, had his possession of Callendar confirmed by charter, although he was later stripped of the title of 'thane of Callendar' and allocated £40 worth of land within the estate, the remainder (worth 160 marks) going to Holyrood Abbey the next year. For the original quitclaim, see Fraser, *Carlaverock*, ii, no. 4, pp. 404–5. Alexander's grant to Holyrood is *Holyrood Liber*, no. 65 [AII/203]. Mael Coluim perhaps kept the *rank* of thane but not the title, 'thane of Callendar'. He is called *quondam thanus de Kalentyr* in both documents but, in the former document, he is also called 'M. Theinus', suggesting that he kept the *rank* of thane, just not the title 'thane of Callendar'.

that no doubt overlapped with one another in practice. So it is possible that the same thane could manage an estate and also have lands of his own that he held from the king. This individual *might* have seen his title as being bound up in either. But he could equally have viewed his title as stemming from his leadership of a local kin-group. Or it could have been a combination of all three: presumably, the lines between each 'type' of thane are more for our convenience than for theirs.

It is therefore possible to identify an expansion in the meaning of 'thane' by the early thirteenth century. Our twelfth-century evidence shows thanes in charge of royal and, less frequently, comital estates; it also shows that this title denoted a high status that is also attested even when thanes are *not* found running estates. It is possible that royal (or comital) service in this way had been a way for individuals to get ahead, to increase their status by obtaining the rank of thane (or Gaelic equivalent) through service even when their personal status may have been slightly below this. During the later twelfth and early thirteenth centuries, however, the meaning of thane expanded again to include thanes who held their *lands* directly from the king and who were easily associated with other types of noble rank of similar status and landed position, most notably, knights, barons (and sometimes just generic 'lords'). There is little evidence for the positional equivalence of thanes and knights until the 1170s and it was not until the 1220s that thanes are explicitly said to hold their estates directly from the king, in the same way as 'barons and knights' were thought to do. The expansion of *thanus* to include a territorial lord, therefore, seems to be a phenomenon recorded in royal charters and acts from the last quarter of the twelfth century. In this it is similar to the chronological transition from *provincia* to *comitatus* but also, unlike it, in that the expansion in the meaning of 'thane' brought together more statuses and functions than before under the same conceptual description.

Thanages

What then of the thanage? Although John of Fordun (probably drawing on a late-thirteenth-century source) saw thanages as the ancient estates of the crown, the word *thanagium* (or *theinagium*) was actually of comparatively late coinage.[194] The first reference to a 'thanage' in a royal charter is not until 1215×21, when Alexander II referred to the thanages of Dull and Fortingall in Perthshire.[195] After

---

[194] Skene, *Fordun*, i, p. 186, probably drawing on the now-lost chronicle of Richard Vairement, for which see Dauvit Broun, *Scottish Independence and the Idea of Britain from the Picts to Alexander III* (Edinburgh, 2007), pp. 252–63. This account has been noted before, for which see Grant, 'Thanes and Thanages', pp. 67–8, and Skene, *Celtic Scotland*, iii, pp. 238–45.

[195] *Scone Liber*, no. 65 [AII/28]. The testing clause of this—*teste rege ipso*—is relatively unusual and has raised questions about this document's authenticity, and whether it should be assigned to Alexander III, not Alexander II. The reason for the doubt is that the testing clause *teste me ipso* was introduced in Alexander III's reign in royal brieves from 1262. Though the evidence is again extremely slight, the earliest surviving brieves commanding the sheriff and others to hold inquests and valuations (for which see Chapter 5, pp. 318–19) included one or a very small number of named witnesses; see, for example *Newbattle Reg.*, no. 121 (1241) [AII/279]; *RRS*, iv, 1, nos. 27 (May 1260), 28 (August 1260), 32 (August 1261) but, from 1262 (the earliest example is 21 March), the scribes of similar sorts of brieves used *teste me ipso*; see, for example, *RRS*, iv, 1, nos. 36, 40, 67, 70, 76, 82, and also 85 (giving

that, the next appearance of 'thanage' is not until the 1230s. Alexander II gave the canons of Scone Abbey one net from his fisheries in his thanage of Scone in 1234, and land in his 'thanage' of Auchterarder to the monks of Lindores in 1236.[196] The word 'thanage' also appears in law at around this point in a statute produced by Alexander II and his counsellors at Stirling in October 1230.[197] The statute established the procedure for dealing with accusations of theft made by people who could not defend their accusation through trial by battle, such as monks and canons, clerks, widows, and prebendaries. Instead, such people could go to the lord of their land (*dominus feodi*), who would then summon the sheriff; the sheriff would then summon a visnet (a body of neighbours), which would find out the identity of the thief. The stolen goods would be taken from the thief and returned to the affected party and the thief's chattels would go to the person who 'ought' to have the chattels (the Latin is consciously vague on this point). The statute thus starts by dealing with accusations not made in the king's own land. It ends by saying that, if the thief was 'in demesne lands or thanages (*thanagiis*)', the sheriff of the *patria* (here translated as 'local area') should take the visnet 'to the king'. But, aside from these, thanage never appears regularly in thirteenth-century royal charters or surviving laws. It is actually used more frequently in the charters of Robert I (1306–29), who gave many of his thanages to members of his lay nobility in the first half of his reign.[198]

Despite the paucity of references in royal charters, 'thanage' was used frequently to describe royal estates in some non-royal documentation. Two revenue lists drawn up by the bishopric of Aberdeen at some point in the reign of Alexander III (one known as the 'Alexander III Rental') record eight royal thanages within the sheriffdoms of Aberdeen and Banff.[199] Both documents explicitly state that

---

the text of an inquest). For a further letter, requesting something in brieve form, written in 1283, which uses *teste me ipso*, see *RRS*, iv, 1, no. 142. However, *teste rege ipso* was used in two letters and one other brieve under Alexander II, suggesting that it was used as a testing formula under Alexander II (NRS, GD1/203/1 [AII/175]; TNA, SC1/5/29 [AII/58]; *Foedera*, I, i, 135 [AII/24]). If this is accepted then this brieve [AII/28] is the earliest reference to a thanage in Scotland. I am grateful to Dauvit Broun and Keith Stringer for discussing this with me.

[196] *Scone Liber*, no. 66 [AII/210]; *Lindores Cart.*, no. 22 [AII/241].

[197] *SA*, c. 5. This legislation is discussed in more detail in Chapter 5, pp. 277–80. If the translations given here seem to depart surprisingly from the Latin text prepared by Thomas Thomson and printed in *APS*, i, pp. 399–400, it is because I am using the text which appears within the *manuscript* compilation *Statuta Alexandri Regis*. The version in *APS* depends heavily (but not exclusively) on the version of this law in *CD*, which is itself a later updating of the statute (for which see Alice Taylor, 'The Assizes of David, King of Scots, 1124–53', *SHR*, vol. 91, no. 232 (2012), pp. 197–238, at pp. 216–21, dealing with another statute of the 1230 collection). The versions in *SA* preserve earlier forms of Alexander's legislation and so are preferred throughout this book. For more on these decisions, see Chapters 3 and 5, pp. 114–19, 271–2, and the longer exposition in the Appendix, pp. 457–60.

[198] For the suggestion that this may have been the subject of some contemporary concern, see Grant, 'Thanes and Thanages', pp. 66–70. But the contemporary context may equally have been appropriate under Alexander III, if Fordun was using a pre-1267 source (for which see note 194), if there was a shortage of alienable land in Scotia under the two Alexanders, for which see below, pp. 77–80.

[199] Aberdeen, Glendowachy, Aboyne, Boyne, Mumbrie, Netherdale, Formartine, and Aberchirder; *Aberdeen Reg.*, i, pp. 55–8. The other is a memorandum detailing how much teind the bishop could expect from these estates given their value set out in the 'Alexander III Rental'.

thanages were to be found *within* sheriffdoms. During the reign of Alexander III, the king's thanages were answerable to the sheriff for the revenue they produced for the king.[200] The transcript of a roll containing excerpts of accounts which officials (justiciars, chamberlains, sheriffs, farmers, etc.) returned between 1263 and 1266 shows that sheriffs accounted for the revenue from thanages, even when a thane was still in charge of a particular estate.[201] Andrew of the Garioch, for example, sheriff of Aberdeen in 1264, returned the account of the thane of Aberdeen (valuing £12) and the thane of Kintore (valuing £17 13s 4d).[202] The only exception was Reginald Cheyne, farmer of the thanage of Formartine, who appeared independently of any sheriff.[203] The example of Reginald shows, in addition, that there was no requirement for a thanage to be run by a thane. Other farmers of estates not called thanages also returned their accounts autonomously in 1263–66 so it is possible that Reginald did not have to answer to the sheriff of Aberdeen by virtue of his status as 'farmer' of a very large estate. But because of the abridged state of the account roll, one cannot know whether thanes, for example, ever proffered their revenue independently.[204]

'Thanages', however, were not just confined to estates within the royal demesne during the thirteenth century. From the late twelfth century at the earliest, there are references to thanages within earldoms, as part of the land controlled by the earl, directly or indirectly, within his *comitatus*. The word 'thanage' first appears, in fact, not in a royal charter but in an act of John, bishop of Dunkeld, drawn up during 1183×1203 (although a closer date of 1189×92 is often preferred).[205] John's charter stated that Henry, earl of Atholl (d. *c*.1211) had given the church of Logierait in Perthshire to Scone Abbey with all its appurtenances, with all teinds and benefices and rights.[206] These 'teinds, benefices and rights' belonging to Logierait included those from Rait (described as the 'head of the earldom') and those from the thanages of Dalmarnock and Findowie. Although the bishop of Dunkeld was confirming the rights (saving those due to his bishopric), the thanages were deemed to be in Earl Henry's earldom for it was his gift that the bishop was confirming. There were also thanages in Strathearn. As discussed earlier, these earls also had thanes who are named in their charters. In the early thirteenth century, one Anecol, thane of Dunning, was attesting the charters of Earl Gille Brigte and, by the 1280s, Dunning itself was called a thanage (although it is

---

[200] This is discussed in more detail in Chapter 6, pp. 368–71.

[201] The form of this roll is discussed in Chapters 6 and 7, pp. 351–6, 402–3.

[202] *ER*, i, p. 11; see also the thane of Forteviot defaulting in the account of John Cameron, sheriff of Perth, in 1266 (*ER*, i, pp. 17–18).

[203] For more on the multi-talented Reginald Cheyne, see Chapter 7, pp. 431–2.

[204] In 1292, there was a sack in the king's archive in Edinburgh castle that contained 23 'large and normal-sized' rolls containing the accounts of 'sheriffs, bailies, farmers, thanes, and burghs and others', but this neither confirms nor denies that thanes ever accounted independently from sheriffs during the 1260s; *APS*, i, p. 113.

[205] Grant suggested a closer dating of 1189×92, for which see Grant, 'Thanes and Thanages', p. 40, note 5.

[206] *Scone Liber*, no. 55.

not in the earlier evidence).[207] There is no further evidence of thanages in earldoms outside Atholl and Strathearn: it may be that only these places made use of the word but it is also possible that there were thanages in other earldoms within Scotia for which we just do not have written contemporary evidence. Thus, while *thanagium* was predominantly used to describe a royal estate, its use was not exclusive to the king's land: it also appeared within earldoms, at the very least, and there is no attested use of the term among bishops' estates.

The adoption of *thanagium* to describe an extensive territorial estate by the late twelfth century at the very earliest (and not until the late 1210s in royal documentation) thus coincides roughly with the adoption of *comitatus* to denote the bounded land under the control of an earl. While the *form* of these estates had probably existed for a long time, their conception as 'thanages' probably was new. While *comitatus* had developed quite a precise meaning by the end of the twelfth century (the land controlled by the *comes*), to call an estate a thanage did not necessarily mean that it was controlled by a thane. Those within Strathearn were so controlled (at least for some time) but royal thanages in the thirteenth century were run and managed by a variety of people, particularly farmers, as well as by thanes.

THE LANDED PATRONAGE STRATEGIES
OF THE KINGS OF SCOTS

The late adoption of the word *thanagium*, and the expansion of the meaning of the word 'thane', requires a rethinking of the argument that envisages both thanage and thane remaining relatively stable throughout the twelfth and thirteenth centuries. Of particular importance here is the thesis that because 'thanages' were among the early building blocks of Scottish royal government, kings of Scots were reluctant to give them away permanently to their greater and lesser subordinates. The argument for continuity was put forward by Alexander Grant in his important article of 1993.[208] In this article, Grant calculated the number of known royal 'thanages' and analysed their fate during the twelfth and thirteenth centuries. He found that very few identifiable 'thanages' were permanently alienated from the royal demesne.[209]

This was an important finding and had the potential (although Grant himself did not argue this) to modify the edifice of Barrow's Anglo-Norman Era for it

---

[207] *Inchaffray Chrs*, nos. 113–114; for Anecol, see *Inchaffray Chrs*, nos. 9, 11, 14, where Anecol is called 'thane of Dunning', 'of Dunning', and 'my [the earl's] thane' interchangeably. In 1247, Mael Ísu, earl of Strathearn, actually sent a brieve to Brice (or Mael Brigte), thane of Dunning, commanding him not to pay the 20 marks granted to Inchaffray to any of his own bailies but instead to the abbey (*Inchaffray Chrs*, no. 77). Dunning is, however, not called a 'thanage' in this brieve.

[208] Grant, 'Thanes and Thanages'.

[209] Grant, 'Thanes and Thanages', pp. 42–3, 52; Grant, 'Construction', pp. 70–1. Grant's argument was foreseen by W. F. Skene, who noted in 1872 that 'we find most of the thanages to have been in the Crown after the reign of Alexander III, and the subsequent kings seem to have converted them by degrees into a feudal holding'; Skene, *Fordun*, ii, pp. 415–19, at p. 419.

identified several important continuities that were reflective of a conscious royal policy. The kings' retention of their thanages, in light of the extensive alienations of land going on elsewhere, was an indication of their wish to retain and maintain existing structures. Where Barrow saw transformation in government (even if significant continuities remained in society writ large), Grant's work suggested a more profound governmental preservation.[210] Dramatic change only happened in the fourteenth century, under Robert I and David II. However, because the focus was on identifying 'thanages' (either those expressly called *thanagium* or those which were known to have been run by a thane), royal landed patronage writ large was not examined. But because *thanagium* appears relatively late in our sources, there were many other estates whose fate was overlooked. In addition, because 'thanages' were also identified if a particular estate had a thane attached to them, any settlements that are not known to have had such a thane were excluded, even if the settlement in question was clearly under royal control. Grant thus included 'the shire of Kellie' in Fife in his list of forty-eight thanages because one Mael Muire, thane of Kellie, is attested in a charter dated to 1150×52 but not the nearby 'shire of Ardross', also once in the king's hand, for which no thane was recorded.[211] The possibility that a number of identifiable royal estates was overlooked prompts an examination of the overall landed patronage strategies of the kings of Scots in the twelfth and early thirteenth centuries.

In what follows, I have identified more coherent and discrete settlements that were once under royal control during the twelfth and thirteenth centuries, although, because most of our evidence survives in royal charters of alienation, the king's direct control of such estates must have been temporary. In order to identify only those estates which were of similar form to that of the 'thanage' (i.e. the so-called 'multiple estate'), I have concentrated on those settlements called *manerium* ('residence'), contained *abthen* lands (essentially land belonging to the chief church of a multiple estate), and *scira* ('shire'), because these words were all used to denote large extensive settlements of a form similar to that outlined for the 'thanage'.[212] Indeed, some estates later known as 'thanages' were known in the twelfth century as either a *manerium* or a *scira* or recorded to contain *abthen* lands.[213] What follows is thus in no way a full study of royal landed patronage during the twelfth and thirteenth centuries; it is instead a bird's eye view, looking at landholding forms at the most basic level, and designed to refocus our views on what the

[210] For these continuities, see Barrow, *Anglo-Norman Era*, pp. 145–68, particularly pp. 156–62; and Barrow, 'The Lost Gàidhealtachd'.

[211] Grant, 'Thanes and Thanages', pp. 80–1; *CDI*, no. 165; *RRS*, i, no. 168.

[212] Again, it is important to stress that what follows has not been able to take account of the re-examination of shires in Broun, 'Statehood and Lordship', pp. 33–55, although Broun's re-examination pertains to the period before *c*.1160.

[213] See, for example, the *apdaine* of Kirkmichael, the head church of Strathardle, in *Dunf. Reg.*, no. 227; Scone, called a *manerium* in a charter of Mael Coluim IV, was later called a thanage (*RRS*, i, no. 243; *Scone Liber*, no. 66 [AII/210]) Longforgan was called both a *manerium* and a *scira* and had a recorded thane; see *CDI*, no. 173; *RRS*, i, no. 243; Stringer, *Earl David*, pp. 58–9. See the work that argues for a 'necessary connexion' between shire and thanage, although based on spurious Aberdeen charters: Barrow, 'Shires and Thanes', pp. 46–7; Robertson, *Historical Essays*, pp. 117–28.

kings of Scots were doing with their land-rights during the twelfth and thirteenth centuries. This approach found a further twenty estates which either were or had been part of the royal demesne. These are collected in Table 1.1.[214]

Unlike the supposed fate of the thanages, all these twenty estates were given away by the kings of Scots. The surviving evidence gives the impression that the majority of these estates were given to ecclesiastical beneficiaries but this may well be the result of the balance of surviving evidence: most comes from religious and monastic archives. One gift was extremely long-standing, that of Kilrimont to St Andrews, but most date from the late eleventh to the early thirteenth century.[215] Mael Coluim III and Queen Margaret gave the shire of Kirkcaldy to Dunfermline and the abbey was further endowed by Edgar's gift of Gellet and Alexander I's gift of Goatmilk.[216] David was responsible for Dunfermline's possession of part of Kinghorn and St Andrews's eventual possession of Rossie,[217] while William granted the shires of Arbroath, Ethie, Dunnichen, and Kingoldrum to Arbroath.[218] Alexander II granted Dollar to Dunfermline and Rait and Kinfauns to Scone.[219] Laymen were not infrequent beneficiaries and, as it is much less common for their charters to survive or, indeed, for laymen to be issued charters before the reign of William the Lion, what follows represents only the minimum number of grants.[220] The shires of Kinghorn and Crail were granted by David to Countess Ada de Warenne and after her death formed part of the queen's demesne;[221] William the Lion's brother, Earl David, held Dundee and Lindores (later given by David to his monastic foundation there);[222] while William's illegitimate son, Robert de Londres, held Aberdour as well as the already-identified 'thanage' of Kellie.[223] These grants were not (as has been suggested) confined to the king's immediate kin: Merleswain, a major potentate in Fife, was infeft in the shire of Ardross by William the Lion for the service of one knight.[224] Inverlunan was later granted by Alexander II to one Anselm of 'Camelyne' in 1247.[225]

---

[214] Obviously, estates known to be under the control of other potentates (and not in the king's gift) have not been included. For the control of, for example, Fowlis Wester and Crieff by the earls of Strathearn, see Neville, *Native Lordship*, pp. 95, 117–19.

[215] For the alienation of Kilrimont in the eighth century, see *Chronicles of the Picts, Chronicles of the Scots*, ed. W. F. Skene (Edinburgh, 1867), pp. 183–93, at pp. 186–7; a new edition of foundation-legend 'B' by Simon Taylor can be found in *PNF*, vol. 3, p. 573 (Latin), pp. 578–9 (translation).

[216] *CDI*, no. 172.

[217] *CDI*, no. 172; *RRS*, i, no. 118; *RRS*, i, no. 120; *St Andrews Liber*, pp. 53–6.

[218] *RRS*, ii, no. 197.

[219] *Dunf. Reg.*, no. 75 [AII/254]; *Scone Liber*, no. 75 [AII/278].

[220] For the adoption of charters to laymen under William, see Hammond, 'Adoption and Routinization', *passim*.

[221] *Dunf. Reg.*, no. 151; *St Andrews Liber*, p. 208.

[222] *RRS*, ii, no. 205; Stringer, *Earl David*, pp. 74–6.

[223] *Spalding Misc.*, v, p. 243; Barrow, 'Popular Courts', in *Scotland and Its Neighbours*, p. 234; Taylor, 'Robert de Londres', pp. 107–8.

[224] *RRS*, ii, no. 137; for Merleswain see Young, 'Earls and Earldom of Buchan', pp. 179–80; cf. *PNF*, vol. 5, p. 102, 112; Barrow, 'Companions', pp. 36–7; for the suggestion that gifts of thanages were limited to the king's family, see Grant, 'Thanes and Thanages', p. 52.

[225] Fraser, *Carlaverock*, ii, p. 405 [AII/318]; *RRS*, ii, no. 355; *Arbroath Liber*, i, no. 155; *RRS*, ii, no. 590.

Table 1.1. Further identifiable royal estates in the twelfth and thirteenth centuries.

	Name	Province	Date	Appellation	Evidence	Source
1	Arbroath	Angus	c.1178	*scira*	Aberbrothot cum tota schira sua per rectas diuisas in bosco et plano in terris et aquis in pratis et pascuis et cum omnibus iustis pertinentiis suis.	*RRS*, ii, no. 197
2	Dundee	Angus	1173 × 78	*syra*	gift of 'medietatem de Hadgillin in Dundesyra et de altera medietate decem solidos annuatim'.	*RRS*, ii, no. 149
3	Dunnichen	Angus	1215	*scira*	Dunechtin cum tota skyra sua per rectas diuisas et cum omnibus ad eam iuste pertinentibus.	*Arbroath Liber*, i, no. 100 [AII/6]
4	Ethie	Angus	1215	*scira*	Confirmavi eciam eis ut omnes homines in schyris de Abirboth et de Athyn manentes.	*Arbroath Liber*, i no. 100 [AII/6]
5	Inverlunan[226]	Angus	1189× 95	*abthen*	Terram ecclesie de Inuerlunan, tenendam libere et quiete scilicet terram de abthan per rectas diuisas.	*RRS*, ii, no. 590
6	Kingoldrum	Angus	1215	*scira*	Kyngoueldrum cum tota shyra sua per rectas diuisas suas.	*Arbroath Liber*, i, no. 100 [AII/6]
7	Rossie	Gowrie	1152×53	*Abbacia*	Abbacia de Rossie cum appendiciis suis et iuste pertinencibus in feodo et hereditate.	*St Andrews Liber*, 200; also *RRS*, i, no. 120
8	Rait[227]	Gowrie	1233×41	*dominium*	Granted (together with Kinfauns) cum earundem terram natiuis for an annual rent of 40 chalders of malt and 60 chalders of wheat.	*Scone Liber*, no. 75 [AII/278]
9	Kinfauns	Gowrie	1233× 41	*dominium*	As above.	*Scone Liber*, no. 75 [AII/278]

10	Aberdour	Fife	1189×99	*feudum*	central mill, cuthill court outside central vill, 'eccles' place names in dependent tributary land.	*Spalding Misc.*, v, 243.
11	Ardross	Fife	1153×62	*scira*	Pasturam in sire de Erdros sicut habent in sire de Callin	*RRS*, i, no. 168
12	Crail	Fife	1145×53	*scira*	Communem pasturam in sira de Chellin et in sira de Cherel.	*CDI*, no.165
13	Dollar	Fife [modern Clackmannanshire]	15 March 1265	*scira* *terra (1236)*	Sciram de Dolar per suas rectas diuisas in liberam forestam ac terras de Gask.	*Dunf. Reg.*, no. 434.
14	Gellet	Fife	1150×52	*scira*	schiram de Gellàd.	*CDI*, no.172
15	Goatmilk	Fife	1150×52	*scira*	schiram de Gatemilk.	*CDI*, no.172
16	Kilrimont	Fife	1163×64	*scira*	Cum capellis in tota skira de Kilrimund.	*RRS*, i, no. 239
17	Kinghorn	Fife	1236	*dominium*	In dominiis nostris de kinorn et de Carel tam in frumento farina braseo prebenda quam in denariis.	*Dunf. Reg.*, no. 75. [AII/254]
18	Kinnin-month	Fife	1160×61	*scira*	Kinninmoneth cum tota schira.	*RRS*, i, no. 174
19	Kirkcaldy	Fife	1128×36	*scira*	Toram scyram de Kircaldin quam Constantinus comes ab eis vi tenuit.	*CDI*, no.44
20	Lindores	Fife	1261	*scira*	Ad molendinum scyre de Lundors[228]	*Lindores Cart.*, no. 114

226 Although this document is an agreement between two separate parties, it is clear that Inverlunan did belong to the king, as William granted its church to Arbroath between 1189 and 1194, and Alexander II later granted the remainder to Anselm of Camelyne; *RRS*, ii, no. 355; Fraser, *Carlaverock*, ii, p. 405 [AII/318].
227 John M. Rogers, 'The Formation of the Parish Unit and Community in Perthshire' (PhD Dissertation, University of Edinburgh, 1992), p. 131.
228 Stringer, *Earl David*, pp. 59, 74; for the foundation of Lindores Abbey by Earl David, see Stringer, *Earl David*, pp. 92–101.

The existence and fate of these additional estates cause further consideration of the proposition that 'the twelfth-century kings were reluctant to alienate their thanages' (notwithstanding the problems in using the word 'thanage').[229] Grant was aware of these additional land gifts but gave a different explanation for their existence: they were forfeited comital lands, not royal 'thanages'.[230] Although many provinces did not have recorded *mormaír* during the reign of William the Lion, such as the Mearns and Gowrie, it is in general not possible to distinguish between settlements which had long been under the king's control and those which had once been under the control of a past *mormaer* or which may have been part of the lands of the *mormaer*-ship. In 1178, for example, William I granted to his new Tironensian foundation at Arbroath the shires of Arbroath, Ethie, Dunnichen, and Kingoldrum, all in Angus.[231] By this time, Gille Críst was attested as earl of Angus: had these four shires long been under the king's control or (as Grant suggested) were they settlements wrested away from the *mormaer*?[232] It is impossible to say. What is clear, however, is that the one province that enjoyed an unbroken string of *mormaír* over the twelfth century—Fife—also experienced the highest number of royal alienations of rights over settlements within it, suggesting that kings were, at least in this case, using their own resources.

How were these alienated estates held? Those granted to ecclesiastical beneficiaries were held in free alms and could be freed from the burdens of the king's services.[233] Feu-farm tenure used to be firm, often associated with the Scottish 'thanage', yet it is rare to find it among these alienations in this period.[234] The evidence in general suggests that the standard practice of the kings of Scots was to infeft certain lay individuals in their lands. Many were turned into knights' feus. Earl David held the shires of Lindores and Dundee with other lands in return for a single assessment of knight service and Robert de Londres seems to have been expected to perform similar service in return for Aberdour: he infeft Roger Freburn in land within 'my feu of Aberdour' in return for the service of one sergeand on a horse with a haubergel; this may have made up part of the service Robert owed for Aberdour.[235] Walter de Berkeley and Merleswain were granted the multiple estates of Inverkeilor and Ardross respectively in return for fulfilling the service of one knight.[236]

These last two charters are noteworthy. They record two large and extended estates, both granted by William the Lion and both held for the service of one knight. The creation of single fees based on large estates centred on a single vill was

---

[229] Grant, 'Thanes and Thanages', p. 55.

[230] Grant, 'Thanes and Thanages', pp. 53–5; first raised in G. W. S. Barrow, 'Badenoch and Strathspey 1130–1312: 1. Secular and Political', *Northern Scotland*, 1st ser., 8 (1988), pp. 1–15, at p. 2.

[231] *RRS*, ii, no. 197; *Arbroath Liber*, no. 100 [AII/6].

[232] Grant, 'Thanes and Thanages', p. 54.

[233] See Chapter 2, p. 92.

[234] For a possible example, see *RRS*, ii, no. 340; for feu-farm tenure see Skene, *Celtic Scotland*, iii, pp. 236–8.

[235] *RRS*, ii, no. 205; *Spalding Misc.*, v, p. 243.   [236] *RRS*, ii, nos. 137, 185.

Table 1.2. Royal estates granted for the service of one knight.

Estate	Province	Holder	Date	Service
Lundin	Fife	Philip de Valognes	1161 × 64	1 knight
Rossie	Angus	Henry, son of Gregory	1165 × 74	1 knight
Ardross*	Fife	Merleswain, son of Colbán	1172 × 74	1 knight
Kinnaird	Gowrie	Ralph Ruffus	1172 × 74	1 knight
Inverkeilor*	Angus	Walter de Berkeley	1173 × 80	1 knight
Madderty*[237]	Strathearn	Gile Brigte, earl of Strathearn	1187 × 89	1 knight
Fowlis Easter	Gowrie	Roger de Mortimer	1189 × 94	1 knight
Kinneff	Mearns	William de Montfort	1189 × 99	1 knight
Lenzie	Lennox	William Comyn	×1214	1 knight

* = already identified as shire/thanage.

common.[238] Mael Coluim IV is known to have created at least one feu held for the service of one knight.[239] William created at least eight, collected in Table 1.2. All these bar one were in Scotia. Eight of the nine single feus created during the twelfth century formed the basis of a later parish.[240] A feu of one knight was also the standard value when thanages were granted *in baroniam* in the reign of Robert I.[241] The twelfth-century kings (particularly William the Lion) thus anticipated their fourteenth-century successors in infefting individuals in single estates for the service of one knight.

It must be acknowledged that this bird's-eye view of royal land cession obscures much more complicated webs of landholding and competing rights over land.[242] First, some additional single feus were created which have not been included in the table because these were not single, discrete estates but conceptual assessments of the value of disparate lands brought together in a single gift. William Giffard was

[237] Madderty may be the exception here: it was resigned into the king's hands after its lord committed treason but may previously have been under the control of the earls of Strathearn, and Gille Brigte of Strathearn received it *back* after Gille Coluim the marishal had forfeited it in the late 1180s (*RRS*, ii, no. 258) for surrendering the king's castle of *Heryn* (perhaps Auldearn) to the king's enemies. Equally, it is possible that Madderty was a royal estate. Neville argues that Madderty was not part of the earldom of Strathearn; see Cynthia J. Neville, 'A Celtic Enclave in Norman Scotland: Earl Gilbert and the earldom of Strathearn', in *Freedom and Authority: Scotland, c.1050–1650: Historical and Historiographical Essays Presented to Grant G. Simpson*, ed. Terry Brotherstone and David Ditchburn (East Linton, 2000), pp. 75–92, at p. 77.

[238] Barrow, 'Beginnings of Military Feudalism', pp. 261–2.

[239] *RRS*, i, no. 255; see also *RRS*, ii, no. 472. This second charter is problematic for its reference to knight service, giving and confirming Calder and Strathleven to Mael Coluim of Fife, and so has not been included here; it reads *per seruicium militum*, with a gap before *militum*, and is a later transcription by Sir John Skene, Lord Clerk Register (1594–1604). Balfour provided the reading of *propter seruicium duorum militum*, which may have been a personal addition; see *RRS*, ii, p. 435; cf. Barrow, 'Earls of Fife', pp. 51–3, 55, 61–2, 62, note 3.

[240] P. G. B. McNeil and H. L. MacQueen, *An Atlas of Scottish History to 1707* (Edinburgh, 1996), pp. 201–7; Barrow, 'Beginnings of Military Feudalism', p. 261; for these parishes, see Ian B. Cowan, *The Parishes of Medieval Scotland* (Edinburgh, 1967), pp. 70–1, 88–9, 114, 121, 130, 142, 173.

[241] See, for example, *RRS*, v, no. 6.

[242] For discussion of this, see Grant, 'At the Northern Edge', pp. 82–3.

infeft in Tealing in Angus and Powgavie in Gowrie but held both together for the service of one knight;[243] and Richard de Montfiquet held Cargill in Gowrie and Kincardine in Menteith, also for the service of one knight.[244] Similarly, from the later twelfth century, there were more minor gifts of land which formed feus held for the service of half a knight or for sergeantry service, and many of these lands were once part of a single settlement but were separated off as a result of royal gift-giving. Agatha and Humphrey de Berkeley were granted four *dabaig* in Conveth (together with the *ius* the thane used to have) in return for performing half a knight's service.[245]

Second, not all small feus were held for the service of one knight. William I infeft William Hay in Errol in Gowrie for the service of two knights; Walter, son of Walter Scott, held Allardice in the Mearns for the service of one archer with a horse and a haubergel; and Hugh, brother of Elias, canon of Glasgow, was infeft in Benholm for the same service.[246] Kinnaber seems to have been granted to David de Graham in 1172×98 along with Borrowfield and Charleton for the service of one archer in the king's army.[247] The estate of Inverlunan in Angus was also granted by Alexander II to Anselm of Camelyn in 1247 for the service of half a knight.[248] But Anselm did not have full ownership of his feu at the time of its gift: Mary, the wife of the previous holder, Neil mac Ímair, held dower land within the estate which was a sixth of the value of the whole land and a third of the part once held by Neil.[249] These four estates form a small enough proportion of the surviving evidence to suggest that (although size and values of estates varied greatly) the value of one knight was the most common assessment of a single extensive settlement under the king's control. My approach does not thus intend to give a completely full assessment of all land given by the kings of Scots during the twelfth and early thirteenth centuries but is, I hope, representative of its broad strokes, showing that there was an extensive policy during this period of giving land to individual men, their families, and religious institutions in the kingdom's heartlands.

What does all this amount to? There was a significant practice of giving gifts of land in Scotia, particularly during William's reign. At least twenty-four of the additional twenty-nine estates identified here were alienated before 1214. Alexander II

---

[243] *RRS*, ii, no. 418.

[244] *RRS*, ii, no. 334; see also no. 200. William gave Ogilvy and Kilmundie to Gille Brigte, son of Gille Críst, earl of Angus, together with Pourie to make up a single knight's feu; *RRS*, ii, no. 140. Ogilvy and Kilmundie were part of the parish of Glamis: had they not been alienated, they might have formed part of the thanage [*sic*] of Glamis when it was recorded in 1264; *ER*, i, p. 8.

[245] *RRS*, ii, nos. 344–345, see also, no. 469.

[246] *RRS*, ii, nos. 204, 350, 404.

[247] Calendared in *HMC* 2nd report, 166, surviving in an inspection of Robert II, dated 28 July 1389. This charter is listed in *Handlist of the Acts of William the Lion 1165–1214*, ed. G. W. S. Barrow and W. W. Scott (Edinburgh, 1958), p. 27, but not the *RRS* volume itself, presumably because its diplomatic is too suspect for it to be treated, as it stands, as a genuine charter of William the Lion.

[248] Cowan, *Parishes*, pp. 89, 140; Fraser, *Carlaverock*, ii, p. 405 [AII/318].

[249] The estate had been farmed by Gilbert, the king's farmer, between Neil's tenure and its infeudation in 1247; Fraser, *Carlaverock*, ii, p. 405 [AII/318]. The formula describing this service is rather unusual: 'per medietatem seruicii unius militis'. The more common formula was *per seruicium dimidii militis* (*RRS*, ii, nos. 350, 405). Anselm had to pay £10 a year for the estate until Mary died and thereafter £12 (Fraser, *Carlaverock*, ii, p. 405 [AII/318]).

accepted the tenurial situation on his accession to the kingship in December 1214. *Gesta Annalia* I records that Alexander held a *parliamentum* at Edinburgh after Epiphany in 1215 and confirmed to 'each their rights as their feus dictated'.[250] But, despite this early confirmation, the policy of Alexander II and then Alexander III towards their estates in their kingdom's heartlands appears to have been altered considerably from that which produced the significant alienations of William's reign. As Grant demonstrated in 1993, only a few discrete settlements ever called thanages were given to individuals during the reign of these two kings: Belhelvie, Old Montrose, Strathardle, probably all in Alexander III's reign. Belhelvie did not travel far, making up part of the dowry of Alexander III's daughter, Margaret, in 1281, but Old Montrose was listed as a *baronia* ('barony') in an inquest of 1261. Strathardle (PER) was in the hands of John of Inchmartine by 1279.[251] Tannadice and Dull both seem to have been claimed or reclaimed, however, from Richard de Melville and the earl of Atholl respectively.[252]

Given that the number of estates actually called *thanagium* in the thirteenth century is comparatively small, it is interesting to note that the general pattern of alienation in the thirteenth century appears to have altered. There were far fewer estates recorded as infeudated by the crown during this period and held for a single knight's service than under William the Lion. Alexander II is recorded to have created only one single knight's feu: Netherbar in Angus (with other lands) granted to Gilleandreas MacLeóit for the service of one knight on 19 April 1232.[253] Alexander III is known to have granted the lordship of Manor in Peebleshire for the service of one knight to William of Badby, a grant later confirmed to William's heir, John.[254] But this estate lay south of the Forth in Peebleshire. Infeftments were not, in general, uncommon but it was far more usual under Alexander II and III for the service owed to be a fraction of a single knight (and so thus may have been fractions of estates).[255] There are far fewer records to confirm that land was being alienated north of the Forth and south of the Mounth during the reigns of Alexander II and Alexander III than during the reign of William the Lion.[256]

---

[250] *Gesta Annalia* I in Skene, *Fordun*, i, p. 283.

[251] *Rot. Scot.*, i, p. 19 (for Belhelvie as a royal estate prior to this, see *Aberdeen Reg.*, i, p. 55); for Old Montrose as a barony, see *APS*, i, p. 100; for Strathardle, see *Dunf. Reg.*, no. 227.

[252] For Tannadice, see *RRS*, ii, no. 333 (where it is held by Richard Melville), and *RRS*, v, no. 111 (where apparently it was farmed for the king). For Dull, see *Scone Liber*, no. 65 [AII/28], and for its farming in 1263–66 as a royal estate, see *ER*, i, pp. 3 (1263–66), 48 (1290); but for its earlier possession by Mael Coluim, earl of Atholl, see NLS, MS Adv. 15.1.18, no. 31 (*St Andrews Liber*, pp. 245–6).

[253] *Brechin Reg.*, i, no. 2 [AII/177].   [254] *RRS*, iv, 1, no. 166.

[255] Alexander II infeft Anselm of Camelyne in Inverlunan for the service of half a knight; see Fraser, *Carlaverock*, ii, p. 405 [AII/318]. He also infeft Gille Escoip mac Gille Críst in lands in Argyll, all for the service of half a knight; *Highland Papers*, vol. 2, ed. J. R. N. MacPhail, Scottish History Society, 2nd ser., vol. 12 (Edinburgh, 1916), pp. 121–3 [AII/272]. Alexander III infeft Hugh of Abernethy in the land of Lour in 1265 to be held 'as much of the service of one knight as belongs to the land'; *RRS*, iv, 1, no. 55.

[256] For the alienations by Alexander II north of the Forth see *Bamff Charters AD 1232–1703*, ed. J. H. Ramsay (Oxford, 1915), no. 1 [AII/182]; Fraser, *Carlaverock*, ii, pp. 404–5 [AII/194]; *Arbroath Liber*, i, no. 101 [AII/195]; *Holyrood Liber*, no. 65 [AII/203]; *Newbattle Reg.*, no. 165 [AII/208]; *Scone Liber*, nos. 62, 67, 75, 77 [AII/74,/223,/278,/236]; Anderson, *Oliphants*, no. 4 [AII/222]; *Lindores*

Alexander II did grant Dollar in modern Clackmannanshire and Rait and Kinfauns in Perthshire to Dunfermline and Scone Abbeys respectively, estates known to have been part of the king's demesne.[257] But these alienations are in the minority.[258] Alexander III often gave money in place of land, giving Reginald Cheyne and Alexander Comyn, earl of Buchan, an annual £20 until he could find enough land of the same value to give them instead.[259]

All this suggests that the rate of giving of land in southern Scotia slowed during the thirteenth century.[260] Of course, these conclusions are based not on any central

Cart., no. 22 [AII/241]; *Dunf. Reg.*, no. 75 [AII/254]; *ABB*, ii, p. 109 [AII/284]. The gift of Balcaskie in Kellie to Ivo the cook was originally made to Neil, cook of William the Lion by that king (The original is in the muniments of the Duke of Balcaskie but a typescript is in TNA, NRA, 7870, p. 18).

[257] *Dunf. Reg.*, no. 75 [AII/254]; *Scone Liber*, no. 75 [AII/278].

[258] The surviving evidence suggests that it was common for those lands which were given during this later period to have been resigned by a previous holder: these were not new gifts taken from the store of crown land. See, for example, the land of Callendar once held by Mael Coluim, thane of Callendar (who had charters confirming his possessions) and re-gifted to Mael Coluim and Holyrood Abbey; Fraser, *Carlaverock*, ii, 404–5 [AII/194] and *Holyrood Liber*, no. 65 [AII/203]. The various properties granted to the sacrist of Scone were once held by the king's clerk, Geoffrey, clerk of the livery (*Scone Liber*, no. 77 [AII/236]); Inverlunan had been held by Neil mac Ímair by 1195 before its grant to Anselm of Camelyne in 1247 (Fraser, *Carlaverock*, ii, p. 405 [AII/318]; *RRS*, ii, no. 590). The land in Cassingray, Fife, granted to Nicholas de Hay by Alexander III in 1282 (*RRS*, iv, 1, no. 139), was originally given by William the Lion to Robert, son of Henry the butler (*RRS*, ii, no. 286).

[259] *RRS*, iv, 1, nos. 310–11, 313; see further, *RRS*, iv, 1, no. 56 (£50 to Hugh of Abernethy). This was not a new policy by Alexander III. Alexander II and William had both done it as well, although there is only one example under William, which explicitly refers to the land which he *wishes* to give as either being south of the Firth of Forth or between the Forth and the Mounth; see *RRS*, ii, no. 514, confirmed by Alexander II in the early years of his reign in Raine, *North Durham*, App., no. 61 [AII/31]. See, further, Alexander giving a net in the king's fishery at Berwickstream to Ralph de Hauville, his falconer, until he would find £10-worth of land to give him (*Melrose Liber*, i, no. 177 [AII/336]).

[260] Nigg, in Kincardinshire, to Arbroath (*RRS*, v, no. 31; also *Arbroath Liber*, i, no. 101 [AII/195]); *Coupar Angus Chrs*, i, no. 41 [AII/196]; lands of Meikle Blair and Little Blair in Perthshire to Scone (*Scone Liber*, no. 67 [AII/223]); land and forest of Gladhouse to Newbattle Abbey (Midlothian) (*Newbattle Reg.*, no. 23 [AII/228]); waste land in Ettrick (Selkirkshire) to Melrose in 1236 (*Melrose Liber*, ii, App, no. 2 [AII/235]); the Vale of Leithen to Newbattle in 1241 (*Newbattle Reg.*, no. 120 [AII/280]); gift of land in Mossplatt in Lanarkshire to the bishop of Glasgow (*Glasgow Reg.*, i, no. 186 [AII/293]). For those gifts in the north and west of the kingdom, see, under Alexander II, Burgie in Moray to Kinloss Abbey in 1221, after its perambulation by Mael Coluim, earl of Fife, the archdeacon of Moray, two brothers of the bishop of Moray, and two local lords, Andrew, son of William Freskin, and Archibald of Duffus. It is unclear where this land came from; *Kinloss Recs.*, no. 5 [AII/66]. Alexander II also farmed the *prepositura* of Kinmylies for a yearly ferm of £10 to the bishop of Moray in 1232 (*Moray Reg.*, no. 34 [AII/180]). Lands in Elgin and Dallas (both in Moray) were given in 1235; *Moray Reg.*, no. 114 [AII/216]. Alexander II also gave Keith in Banffshire to the bishop of Moray, in exchange for Invernairn, which King William had previously taken from the bishop in order to build his 'burgh and castle' of Nairn (*Moray Reg.*, no. 25 [AII/61]), and lands in Ordiquhill, Banffshire, to Waleran de Normanville in 1242, for a quarter-knight's service (*ABB*, ii, p. 109 [AII/284]). Merkinch in Moray was given to the burgesses of Inverness in 1236 (*Moray Reg.*, no. 34 [AII/180]). Alexander also gave the lands of Auchencrieff, Burntscarthgreen, and Dargavel in Dumfriesshire to Thomas de Alneto, after William son of Derman quitclaimed them 'by rod and staff' in his court at Dumfries before 29 September 1224 (BL, Additional Charter 76700, printed in *Melrose Liber*, i, no. 205 [AII/96]). The same lands are also described as a gift of Alexander II to Melrose, so something odd was going on there (*Melrose Liber*, i, no. 207; BL, Cotton Charter xviii, 11 [AII/258]). He also gave Closeburn in Dumfriesshire to Ivo of Kirkpatrick in 1232. Alexander II seems to have acquired this land from Africa, daughter of Edgar, son of Domnall, lord of Nithsdale. See also *Melrose Liber*, i, no. 203 [AII/251]; for land in Argyll, see *Highland Papers*, ed. MacPhail, vol. 2 pp. 121–3 [AII/272].

record of land gifts kept by the kings themselves but on the archival practices of their beneficiaries. As a result, the difference between the land strategies of David, Mael Coluim, and William and those of the two Alexanders could be overstated. However, one further example may confirm the hypothesis that Alexander II and Alexander III had, quite simply, less land in the kingdom's heartlands at their disposal.

Both William and Alexander II (together with his mother, Queen Ermengarde) founded a major monastic house: Arbroath (in Angus) in 1178 and Balmerino (in Fife) in 1229.[261] Arbroath received a plethora of gifts on its foundation in 1178; all but three of the estates William gave to his new institution do not seem to have already been given away.[262] The three exceptions were the settlements of 'Achinglas', Dunnichen, and Kingoldrum (all in Angus) which were to be received 'after the death of Andrew, bishop of Caithness', given between 1178 and 1180 (the bishop died in 1184).[263] The reversion of these estates to the king suggests that they had originally been given to the now-elderly bishop at an earlier date and then expected to be returned on his death. No other expected reversions are mentioned in the lengthy confirmation charters issued by William and then Alexander II to Arbroath.[264]

In contrast, it is clear that some of the initial grants to the foundation of Balmerino by Alexander II and his mother, Queen Ermengarde, were taken from the endowment of Arbroath. Arbroath had been granted the church of Barry in Angus sometime between 1183 and 1189 but in 1231 Alexander II then gave this church at farm to his new foundation of Balmerino (on the south bank of the River Tay) on the monks' payment of 40 marks every year to Arbroath.[265] Indeed, even the lands on which the abbey was to stand were bought at considerable cost by the queen and her son. Owing to an absentee lord, Adam of Stawell, inheriting the lands of Coultra and Balmerino in Fife, Ermengarde had the option of buying these lands from Adam for a massive sum of 1000 marks in 1225–26.[266] In order to found their new abbey, therefore, Alexander and Queen Ermengarde did not dip into the existing store of royal demesne land but instead purchased at a high cost land in Fife, previously the source of much land for gift-giving, which had already been given away. The examples of Coultra, Balmerino, and Barry thus reveal a shortage of royal land in Fife and Angus

---

[261] Keith J. Stringer, 'Arbroath Abbey in Context: 1178–1320', in *The Declaration of Arbroath: History, Significance, Setting*, ed. Geoffrey Barrow (Edinburgh, 2003), pp. 116–41; Matthew H. Hammond, 'Queen Ermengarde and the Abbey of St Edward, Balmerino', *Cîteaux: Commentarii Cistercienses*, 59 (2008), pp. 11–36.

[262] See the two 'foundation' charters in *RRS*, ii, nos. 197, 513.

[263] *RRS*, ii, no. 223; for notice of Andrew's death, see *Chron. Melrose, s.a.* 1184.

[264] *RRS*, ii, no. 513; *Arbroath Liber*, i, no. 100 [AII/6]; for a survey of royal endowment of Arbroath see Stringer, 'Arbroath Abbey', pp. 123–7, with a map at p. 126.

[265] They were acquitted of this payment on 25 December 1234, with the king giving Arbroath a selection of *dabaig* and half-*dabaig* in Aberdeenshire; see *Arbroath Liber*, i, no. 102 [AII/214]. Alexander was able to increase the monks' landed endowment by granting them four- and three-quarter *dabaig* in Angus in 1234 in the same charter; for *dabaig*, see Chapter 2, pp. 94–5.

[266] *Balmerino Liber*, nos. 4–5; for comment, see Hammond, 'Queen Ermengarde', pp. 6–7.

deemed available to give even to a royal monastic foundation such as Balmerino, the first royal foundation since Arbroath in 1178, for which a large-scale endowment had been unproblematic.[267]

This suggests that land supply in the kingdom's heartlands was more of an issue by the second decade of the reign of Alexander II than it had been in the early decades of William's reign. The problem of a land-based state is that land will run out, unless an increased supply is found from elsewhere by political expansion.[268] It seems that land in the core areas of the kingdom had run out; the major grants of new land were in the north and west of the kingdom during periods of political expansion under the two Alexanders. They certainly did expand geographically, creating large lordships on the periphery of their kingdom for their greatest aristocrats. It is probable that the earldom of Ross was a creation of Mael Coluim IV's reign but there is no record of the position during William's long reign; the title was only revived after 1215 under Alexander II after a major threat in the north from Gofraid mac Domnaill meic Uilleim.[269] Sutherland was detached from the earldom of Caithness before 1222 and, in the 1230s, had become an earldom under the authority of the king of Scots, the first entirely new creation since Carrick in the late twelfth century.[270] Further large lordships were created in the north: by 1230 (probably 1229), following another period of insurgency by the descendants of Domnall mac Uilleim, Alexander II had created the lordship of Badenoch for Walter Comyn.[271] In the 1230s, the earldoms of Orkney and Caithness were inherited by the earls of Angus, and a new lordship, Strathnaver, in the north of Caithness was created for the de Moravia family.[272] Both Alexander II and Alexander III expanded into the west and this was reflected in their land patronage.[273] All this is well known and reveals that, while they continued to expand, Scottish kings retained their power by giving great swathes of land, binding lords to their service. But in the core areas of the kingdom, this was no longer possible: there was much less new land to give.

[267] Hammond, 'Queen Ermengarde', pp. 6–11.

[268] Chris Wickham, *Framing the Early Middle Ages: Europe and the Mediterranean, 400–800* (Oxford, 2005), pp. 58–9.

[269] For the argument that Ross was a creation under Mael Coluim IV, see Broun, 'Origins of the *mormaer*', forthcoming; for the notion that it was an earlier creation, see Alexander Grant, 'The Province of Ross and the Kingdom of Alba', in *Alba: Celtic Scotland in the Medieval Era*, ed. E. J. Cowan and R. A. McDonald (East Linton, 2000), pp. 88–126, at pp. 106–7, 117–26; R. Andrew McDonald, 'Old and New in the Far North: Ferchar Maccintsacairt and the Early Earls of Ross, c.1200–1274', in *Exercise of Power*, ed. Boardman and Ross, pp. 23–45, at pp. 27–36.

[270] Crawford, *Northern Earldoms*, pp. 264–6, 287.

[271] Alan Young, *Robert Bruce's Rivals: The Comyns, 1212–1314* (East Linton, 1997), pp. 27–8, 147–8.

[272] Crawford, *Northern Earldoms*, pp. 283–93; Barbara E. Crawford, 'Medieval Strathnaver', in *The Province of Strathnaver*, ed. J. R. Baldwin, Scottish Society of Northern Studies (Edinburgh, 2000), pp. 1–12, at p. 2; Barbara E. Crawford, 'William Sinclair, Earl of Orkney and His Family: A Study in the Politics of Survival', in *Essays on the Nobility of Medieval Scotland*, ed. Keith J. Stringer (Edinburgh, 1985), pp. 232–53.

[273] Alexander II seems to have given three *dabaig* of land near Oban to Harald, bishop of Argyll, in 1228, for which see *Moray Reg.*, no. 32 [AII/142].

CONCLUSION

If written evidence from the twelfth and early thirteenth centuries is applied to its contemporary context, then it is possible to identify changes in the meanings and titles of both *mormaír*/earls and *toísig*/thanes. The power of the *mormaer* over his province appears to have become territorialized at some point between the late twelfth and early thirteenth centuries. This meant that a *comes* took his title by inheriting or marrying into the family that held the *comitatus*, a defined piece of land *within* the province. The timing of this shift must have depended in part on patterns of death and the pressures of inheritance; presumably changes in how one went about defining the basic legality of the title of *comes* involved a need to do so.[274] This must have arisen when an existing *mormaer* died: who succeeded him, and what they succeeded to, produced the type of inheritance disputes that we see over Mar and Menteith in the late twelfth and early thirteenth centuries. Before the title of *comes* became territorialized, and his *comitatus* made up a significant (but not necessarily dominant) proportion of the province, the *mormaer* appears to have been *primus inter pares* in the province and to have been taken from the ranks of *toísig*. The only elements that seem to have set him apart from other local potentates and heads of kin were his particular responsibilities for the provincial military levy and, as has been argued by Broun, the existence of lands pertaining to the title of *mormaer* that he enjoyed in compensation for levying the provincial army for the king.[275] In that case, then the *mormaer* of the first half of the twelfth century would have exercised extensive rather than intensive power over the entire province through his responsibility for the provincial military levy, while still enjoying tribute revenue and hospitality from settlements that he controlled as part of his responsibility as a leading *toísech* in the province and from the lands of the *mormaer*-ship.

Similar but not identical changes can be posited for thanes and thanages: the thanage appears to have been a new Latin concept in the late twelfth and thirteenth centuries, while the meaning of 'thane' expanded to mean a tenurial lord, who could be seen as equivalent in status to a knight or baron, although 'thane' was still the title of a person who farmed an estate for the king. By the thirteenth century, it would be hard to differentiate between the function of a thane, who paid, for example, a set farm to the king each year, and the knight, who held his land in feu-farm from the king instead of by knight-service. Still other thanes held their lands as lords and, if they paid a feu-farm for these lands, it would have been even harder to distinguish them from the 'official' thanes who farmed the king's estates. This means, therefore, that we see similar changes in the meaning of 'thane' as we do in relation to the *comes* (or *mormaer*). If thanes can be linked to the *toísig* attested in the Book of Deer (a probability for which there is no real alternative), then the power that they exercised as heads of local kin-groups had equally become territorialized, centred on the land they held 'of' the king. In the thirteenth century,

---

[274] See Oram, *Domination and Lordship*, pp. 224–5.
[275] Broun, 'Origins of the *mormaer*', forthcoming.

thanes did continue to provide the king with revenue from royal estates but they did so alongside a host of other individuals who were never called thanes but, rather, farmers, bailies, or grieves. If large alienations had prompted a more limited royal landed patronage in the thirteenth century in Scotia, then the conceptualization of the thanage as a distinct part of the royal demesne was a way of deliniating these estates from others.

This chapter has also identified that kings in part maintained their power in Scotia during the twelfth century by giving away substantial gifts of land. In particular, William the Lion appears as the most significant giver of gifts. There was demonstrably no need for kings to keep hold of their 'thanages' (using Grant's terminology) during the twelfth century, as has been suggested; quite apart from the fact that *thanagium* is not an attested concept until the very end of the century, William the Lion was relatively profligate in giving away large, extensive estates, normally to be held for the service of a single knight. The land supply particularly in the heartlands of Scotia appears to have dried up in the thirteenth century, although the kingdom's expansion into the north and west meant that the policy of royal landed patronage could continue, albeit from different areas further away from the kingdom's heartlands. It makes sense that kings would give their land away, given that they were encouraging settlement from outside the kingdom, yet also needed to keep local potentates onside. How far this gift-giving contributed to the conceptualization of a new territorially defined power, and what was in it for aristocrats, will be considered in the conclusion to the first part of this book. But such a policy of land patronage did have its limits and Alexander II and Alexander III were unable to sustain the pace of William's gifts in Scotia; the necessary death of ruling through patronage in this area may have also prompted the greater intensification of royal power there (but not, importantly, on the periphery), a process which will be outlined in the second part of this book.

What does this mean for the early Scottish state? The situation outlined here for the mid-twelfth century is one where the king co-operated with regional and local potentates in a give-and-take scenario: *mormaír* had responsibility for the provincial army but controlled a small part of the province in return for this service; some *toísig* could run the king's estates but received a proportion of the estate's revenue for doing so. This meant that royal service would have been a way for local potentates to get ahead but, because it seems that the king did not have a consistent or standard role in appointing *mormaír* of provinces, the king was simultaneously tapping into existing networks to increase his presence in the locality and manage his resources more effectively. These reciprocal networks between king and provincial society could be called a state, in that they must have been enduring and relatively stable networks of power, but, if so, this state was not an administrative state nor was it based on a combination of lordship, a regular universal tribute extraction, and a class of royal agents. Instead, it was based on a systematic form of communication whereby the king used the position of *mormaer* for provincial military organization and the *toísech*/thane as an extractor of his revenue to tap into existing power networks in the provinces in a far more intensive way than he would have been able to do from his landed presence alone.

How does this differ from Alexander Grant's view of the early Scottish state? If we take away two of its elements—the bipartite province, divided into royal and comital land, and universal taxation—then what has been set forward here differs in emphasis, rather than in fundamental structure. Grant too envisaged that the positions of *mormaer* and thane would have been held by people who were regionally important. But he saw these 'offices' as created by a power struggle between provincial and royal power which the provinces lost, thus making the *mormaer* a royal agent rather than an autonomous provincial governor, and thane a royal estate manager, not primarily than a local lord. For him, the struggle between king and aristocracy had therefore created an administrative state. But royal power need not be seen in administrative and institutional terms, nor does such power have to be seen as growing at the expense of aristocratic power—and this is important. Instead, this chapter has stressed the necessary co-operation (which does not, of course, mean necessarily *peaceful* co-operation) between royal, provincial, and local power in which the king, *mormaer*, and *toísech* all had incentives to help each other out in order to increase their own standing.

This means we must set aside two key assumptions about early 'state' power, namely that it had to be administrative and institutional and that it was based on the regular extraction of a form of tax and service from all the lands within the kingdom. As will be shown in Chapter 2, kings did receive tribute and hospitality but they did not do so universally: *cáin* and *coinnmed* were not forms of universal taxation. Kings did receive 'common' burdens but these sprung from the irregular requirements of defence and military activity, a function which we already know involved *mormair* and *toísig*. Nor was royal power maintained primarily by royal administrative officials. By tapping into existing networks of power that worked below the level of the province, the king's authority could be felt in local society in a far more extensive way than through his own landholding alone. We thus should not see *mormaer* and *toísech*/thane as primarily royal officials but essentially as potentates whom the king needed in order to maintain his authority throughout the provinces of the kingdom. The *mormaer* guarded the province for the king but was only able to do so because he was the most powerful among the local kin-groups and so was worthy of this role. If he had not been, he could not have held the position. The same must have been true for the thane/*toísech*. As head of a local kin-group, a *toísech* would have had the necessary authority within the province to extract revenue from settlements under his control.

How far this picture can be taken back into the pre-twelfth century period is not the concern of this chapter and must be addressed by other historians.[276] What now follows in the next two chapters re-examines and reframes two further elements of the early Scottish state: resource extraction and the provision of justice.

---

[276] Broun, 'Origins of the *mormaer*', forthcoming; Broun, 'Statehood and Lordship', *passim*.

2

Common Burdens in the *Regnum Scottorum*

THE PROBLEM: *CÁIN* AND *COINNMED*

It is well understood that common obligations reveal much about the workings of early medieval society, how it organized its defences, resource extraction, and the coercive power of the state.[1] No full study of the nature and significance of common labour obligations (or burdens) in Scotland has yet been attempted.[2] But, despite this lacuna, it has long been assumed that there existed three burdens, levied on fiscal units of land throughout the kingdom, which aimed to support the itinerant king and provide him with money and men for the defence of the kingdom. These burdens are often thought to have been *cáin* (a tribute render, paid in kind), *coinnmed* ('conveth', a hospitality render), and *exercitus et expeditio* (army service within and outwith the kingdom).[3] This argument was put across with characteristic strength by W. F. Skene in volume three of *Celtic Scotland* but received exciting corroboration in 1969 when G. W. S. Barrow published his article on 'Northern English Society in the Twelfth and Thirteenth Centuries' (also

---

[1] This chapter is a shortened version of Alice Taylor, 'Common Burdens in the *Regnum Scottorum*: the Evidence of Charter Diplomatic', in *Reality behind Charter Diplomatic*, ed. Broun, pp. 166–234. For works on 'common burdens' in Anglo-Saxon England, see James Campbell, 'The Late Anglo-Saxon State: a Maximum View', repr. in James Campbell, *The Anglo-Saxon State* (London, 2000), pp. 1–30; Rosamond Faith, *The English Peasantry and the Growth of Lordship* (Leicester, 1997), pp. 94–9; Andrew Bell, 'The Organisation of Public Work in Society by the State in Early Medieval England *c.*800–*c.*1300' (DPhil Thesis, University of Oxford, 1996), pp. 235–40; W. H. Stevenson, '*Trinoda necessitas*', *EHR*, vol. 29, no. 116 (1914), pp. 689–703; Eric John, *Land Tenure in Early England* (Leicester, 1960), pp. 64–79; Nicholas Brooks, 'The development of military obligation in eighth- and ninth-century England', in *England before the Conquest: Studies Presented to Dorothy Whitelock*, ed. P. Clemoes and K. Hughes (Cambridge, 1971), pp. 69–84, at pp. 76–83; George Molyneaux, *The Formation of the English Kingdom in the Tenth Century* (Oxford, 2015), pp. 86–104.

[2] There have been three significant studies of the common army of Scotland: *Highland Papers*, vols 1 and 2, ed. J. R. N. MacPhail, Scottish History Society, 2nd ser. vols 5 and 12 (Edinburgh, 1914, 1916), ii, pp. 227–45; A. A. M. Duncan, *Scotland: Making of the Kingdom* (Edinburgh, 1975), pp. 376–92; G. W. S. Barrow, 'The Army of Alexander III's Scotland', in *Scotland in the Reign of Alexander III, 1249–1286*, ed. N. H. Reid (Edinburgh, 1990), pp. 132–47; and, in addition, G. W. S. Barrow, *The Anglo-Norman Era in Scottish History* (Oxford, 1980), pp. 161–2.

[3] For the role of 'cain and conveth' in the early Scottish state, see Chapter 1, pp. 29–31; see, further, W. F. Skene, *Celtic Scotland: A History of Ancient Alban*, 3 vols (Edinburgh, 1886–90), iii, pp. 227–36; G. W. S. Barrow, 'Pre-Feudal Scotland: Shires and Thanes', in G. W. S. *The Kingdom of the Scots: Government, Church and Society from the Eleventh to the Fourteenth Century*, 2nd edn (Edinburgh, 2003), pp. 7–56, at p. 36; G. W. S. Barrow, *Kingship and Unity: Scotland 1000–1306*, 2nd edn (Edinburgh, 2003), pp. 64–5.

about Scotland, despite the title).[4] Alexander Grant saw *cáin* and *coinnmed* as so systematically exacted on the king's behalf that they constituted a form of taxation.[5] But whether all these three obligations were, in fact, common burdens levied by the king remains open to debate. Since the publication of Barrow's article in 1969, there has been a tendency to assume that *cáin* and *coinnmed* were common obligations throughout the kingdom in the twelfth and early thirteenth centuries instead of examining whether this was indeed the case.[6] Although not all historians have subscribed to this view, no alternative view has developed. As long ago as 1928, William Croft Dickinson laid down a casual challenge to Skene's (and later Barrow's) position by stating that 'as in England, there seems to have been a general duty of service to castles, of repair of bridges, and of service in the army' (so somewhat different to *cáin* and *coinnmed*) but no subsequent commentator has taken this remark further.[7]

There is, then, an issue about what really constituted the common burdens of the kingdom in the twelfth and early thirteenth centuries. Particularly problematic are *cáin* and *coinnmed*. These are very often paired together in the historiography as mutually enforcing obligations paid by lower-status people, often to the king, as a relatively uniform expression of coercive power. Less often (although still quite frequently) historians associate *cáin* and *coinnmed* with army service and see all three making up the universal burdens owed to the king from all the land and people within his kingdom. There are, however, three problems with seeing *cáin* and *coinnmed* as forms of royal taxation, and with army service as somehow linked to them. First, and most importantly, it will be shown that neither *cáin* nor *coinnmed* was owed exclusively and/or universally to the king as late as the third quarter of the twelfth century. Second, *cáin* and *coinnmed* were understood as separate burdens in our twelfth- and thirteenth-century evidence. Sometimes *cáin* was mentioned in a document but *coinnmed* was not. Equally, the same person could receive both but it was also common for one party to receive the *cáin* and the other the *coinnmed*. *Cáin* and *coinnmed* thus could be, but did not have to be, mutually reinforcing: often, they must have served the opposite purpose, creating potentially conflicting claims of dominance over the same settlement and its inhabitants. Third, it is extremely rare to find *cáin, coinnmed* and army service appearing together in the charter evidence (far rarer than it is to find *cáin* and *coinnmed*

---

[4] G. W. S. Barrow, 'Northern English Society in the Twelfth and Thirteenth Centuries', in G. W. S. Barrow, *Scotland and Its Neighbours in the Middle Ages* (London, 1992), pp. 127–53; see further, W. D. H. Sellar, 'Celtic Law and Scots Law: Survival and Integration', *Scottish Studies*, vol. 29 (1989), pp. 1–27, at pp. 16–18.

[5] See Chapter 1, pp. 29–31; Richard Oram acknowledged that *cáin* could be received by lords other than the king but suggested that *coinnmed* was universally owed to the king: Richard Oram, *Domination and Lordship: Scotland 1070 to 1230* (Edinburgh, 2011), p. 226.

[6] See, for example, the references to *cáin* in Oram's *David I*, where it is assumed that the reader is aware of the meaning and distribution of *cáin*; Richard Oram, *David I: the King Who Made Scotland* (Stroud, 2004), pp. 92, 116.

[7] *The Sheriff Court Book of Fife, 1515–1522*, ed. William Croft Dickinson, Scottish History Society, 3rd series, vol. 12 (Edinburgh, 1928), p. 374; see also *PNF*, vol. 3, pp. 595–6.

together).[8] *Cáin* and *coinnmed* were levied on a different basis from army service. Whereas the basis of army service seems to have been a fiscal unit of land, *cáin* and *coinnmed* seem to have been levied on the inhabitants of settlements.[9] *Cáin* and *coinnmed* should thus be examined separately not only from army service but also from each other.[10]

The case heard at the ecclesiastical synod of Perth in 1206, discussed earlier in Chapter 1, helps to show how *cáin, coinnmed,* and army service were understood to be separate and could be owed to different parties.[11] As stated there, the case turned on the competing claims of the bishop of St Andrews and Donnchad, son of Hugh of Swinton, over the Kirkton of Arbuthnott in Kincardineshire. Donnchad, it was alleged, had expelled the men of the Kirkton in order to start ploughing the Kirkton's land. By asking a long line of witnesses, it was firmly decided that he had no right to do this and that the Kirkton rightly belonged to the bishop; it was 'in his possession and ownership' (*possessio et proprietas*).[12] The witnesses' statements provide a full understanding of what the men of the Kirkton were expected to render to Donnchad and the bishop as well as the implications of each obligation. The 'thanes' of the Kirkton (to whom Donnchad was the successor) had received *cáin* from the settlement (probably consisting of 10 cheeses per annum), half the minor judicial profits of blodwite (a fine for spilling blood), and merchet (a payment made to superiors on the marriage of daughters or widows). In addition, the thanes of Arbuthnott were accustomed to have three men from each of the eight houses collect their crops each autumn and, on occasion, they received provisions whenever the king's army was called out (no mention is made of actual army service).[13] The bishop of St Andrews, by contrast, received *coinnmed* from the Kirkton of Arbuthnott. *Coinnmed* here seems to have involved actually being hosted in the Kirkton or a payment in its place. The bishop also received the other half of the profits of blodwite and merchet.[14] The witnesses seemed to have associated the right to receive *coinnmed*—rather than *cáin*—with the right to *possessio et proprietas* over the Kirkton. Whether *coinnmed* was indeed 'worth' more in terms of establishing these rights cannot, however, be assumed: the bishop won the day and it may well have been his greater influence in the legal forum of an

---

[8] For these rare occurrences see *Lindores Cart.,* no. 42; *Arbroath Liber,* i, no. 146 (with *auxilia*); and *CDI,* no. 158 (just *coinnmed* and *exercitus*).

[9] Barrow, *Kingship and Unity,* p. 65, argues that *cáin* was levied on the *dabach* and ploughgate. The basis for this was *RRS,* ii, no. 169, which mentions *geldum,* which Barrow associated with *cáin*. But this *geldum* should instead be understood as an irregular *auxilium/auxilia,* which was one of the common burdens of the realm, for which see below, pp. 96–7.

[10] A full examination of *cáin* has recently been published; Dauvit Broun, 'Re-examining *cáin* in the Twelfth and Thirteenth Centuries', in *Princes, Prelates and Poets in Medieval Ireland: Essays in Honour of Katharine Simms,* ed. Seán Duffy (Dublin, 2013), pp. 46–62. This section of this chapter owes a significant debt to Broun's important article.

[11] *Spalding Misc.,* v, pp. 209–13; see Chapter 1, pp. 61–2.

[12] *Spalding Misc.,* v, pp. 209–10.

[13] *Spalding Misc.,* v, pp. 210–13. For the use of *thanus* in this context, see Chapter 1, pp. 61–2.

[14] *Spalding Misc.,* v, pp. 211–13.

ecclesiastical synod that decided the minds of the witnesses rather than any abstract greater worth in the obligation of *coinnmed* over that of *cáin*.[15] What the Arbuthnott case shows is that *cáin* and *coinnmed* were understood as two separable obligations that could be received by different lords, neither of whom were, in this case, the king.[16] There is no reason to think that either the bishop or the thane passed any of their *cáin* or *coinnmed* to the king; indeed, the receipt of either obligation appears to have been the basis for each of their claims over the land. The only obligation either party performed for the king in the Arbuthnott case was the collection of provisions for the army for Osbert Olifard, one of Donnchad's many predecessors as 'thane' of Arbuthnott.[17] The provisions were due to the king but clearly had no relation to Osbert's receipt of *cáin* nor the inhabitants' duty to harvest his lands elsewhere.

There were, however, similarities between the form of *cáin* and that of *coinnmed*, which may have caused confusion. In the Arbuthnott case, *cáin* was an annual render while in other examples *cáin* appears to have been a render consumable on the spot and so may have, in practice, resembled *coinnmed*. A charter of David I, issued to the bishopric of Glasgow probably in 1136, records the king's gift of a tenth of all the livestock he received from Ayrshire and Renfrewshire, except in the years 'when I come myself, stay there, and consume my *cáin*'.[18] *Cáin* could thus be used to relieve the king's (and his household's) hunger while he itinerated, seemingly in the same way as *coinnmed* could actually mean real hospitality. As a result, the practical form of the two could look very similar. But they were nonetheless separated (as they were for the witnesses in the Arbuthnott dispute) and probably became increasingly so when there were competing interests over individual settlements and groups of people.

While the Arbuthnott case presents *cáin* as an annual render of cheese, it could be paid in other forms as well, most notably grains, as well as livestock.[19] Thus, David I granted to Scone Abbey the *cáin* from his hides and cheeses from four royal settlements in Gowrie: Scone, Coupar, Longforgan, and Strathardle.[20] Earl David of Huntingdon granted the canons of St Andrews Cathedral Priory quittance from all the *cáin* and *coinnmed* he had from Ecclesgreig as if it were a render he had previously been receiving regularly from the settlement.[21] *Cáin*, however,

---

[15] A slightly different interpretation can be found in Broun, 'Re-examining *cáin*', p. 53.

[16] Dauvit Broun has suggested that the receipt of *cáin* from smaller settlements may have been a twelfth-century development or earlier, as part of a shift from 'general' to 'specific' lordship; for which see Broun, 'Re-examining *cáin*', pp. 56–62. That new lords also received *cáin* from settlements over which they were granted lordship is confirmed by the witness-testimonies in the Arbuthnott case.

[17] *Spalding Misc.*, v, p. 210.

[18] *CDI*, no. 57. Duncan thus suggested that the scribe of the charter actually meant *coinnmed* rather than *cáin*. But if he did make this mistake, he did so very consistently, for the charter refers to *cáin* throughout; Duncan, *Making of the Kingdom*, p. 154. Oram, *Domination and Lordship*, pp. 226–7, urges caution in equating *cáin* with *coinnmed* in this case.

[19] *Cáin* could be paid in livestock as well as produce. William Kapelle first identified an 'east/west' division, with western areas giving livestock and eastern areas produce (and smaller creatures); see William E. Kapelle, *The Norman Conquest of the North: the Region and Its Transformation* (London, 1979), pp. 60–1.

[20] *RRS*, i, no. 243.   [21] *St Andrews Liber*, p. 238.

does not appear everywhere: it is not found, for example, in Lothian but is in the south-west, within the bishopric of Glasgow and within greater Galloway and Argyll.[22] In these peripheral areas, *cáin* meant something other than a tribute levy owed by the inhabitants of particular settlements to lords. In Galloway and, it appears, Argyll, *cáin* denoted a very significant tribute render, paid by large regions to the king. Unlike the *cáin* examined above, this type was expected irregularly not annually. A charter of Mael Coluim IV to Dunfermline Abbey records that the abbey would receive half of the king's teind from Argyll and Kintyre 'in the same year, that is, when I myself (*ego ipse*) receive *cáin* from them', which implies that there were years when the king did *not* receive *cáin* (and the double emphasis on the king also suggests that there were others who could levy *cáin* from within the region).[23] There is actually evidence for how *cáin* was collected by the king in Galloway. Sometime in (probably) 1187×89, William the Lion set out the procedure for collecting a large, extraordinary levy of *cáin* from Galloway, when Roland, son of Uhtred, had gained control of the lordship of Galloway.[24] It is possible that these were new arrangements, imposed when a new lord, who then went on to serve as the king's justice, became lord of the province.[25] 'Whenever the lord king ought to have his *cáin* from Galloway', he would send his brieve to the province's *maír* and they would collect the *cáin* from those who owed it. Those responsible for paying Galloway's *cáin* seem to have been high-status individuals because, if they defaulted, they had to pay a massive 100-cow fine to the king, the same amount as a fine levied on lords in Scotia when they failed in duties other than the collection of *cáin*.[26] The record of this assembly, held at Lanark, has been discussed many times: the pertinent point here is that the king did expect to receive *cáin* from Galloway but this was not collected regularly nor did it preclude Roland, as its lord, from collecting *cáin* himself.[27]

---

[22] Duncan, *Making of the Kingdom*, pp. 152–7. The various types of *cáin* are identified and outlined in Broun, 'Re-examining *cáin*', pp. 51–7.

[23] *RRS*, i, no. 118; A. A. M. Duncan and A. L. Brown, 'Argyll and the Isles in the Earlier Middle Ages', *PSAS*, vol. 90 (1956–57), pp. 192–220, at p. 195. For a lord in Argyll levying *cáin, coinnmed* and army service himself (in perhaps a similar way to how service was collected from Galloway), see Appendix IV in the same article, at p. 219.

[24] For a recent account of politics in Galloway 1174–87, see Oram, *Domination and Lordship*, pp. 137–40, 146–8. The act is *LS*, c. 20, and the dating is discussed in Alice Taylor, '*Leges Scocie* and the Lawcodes of David I, William the Lion and Alexander II', *SHR*, vol. 88, no. 226 (2009), pp. 207–88, at pp. 213–14.

[25] For the titles used by lords of Galloway in the twelfth century, see Keith J. Stringer, 'Acts of Lordship: the Records of the Lords of Galloway to 1234', in *Freedom and Authority: Scotland, c.1050–1650: Historical and Historiographical Essays Presented to Grant G. Simpson*, ed. Terry Brotherstone and David Ditchburn (East Linton, 2000), pp. 203–34, at nos. 1 (*rex*, p. 212) and 26–31 (*constabularius*, pp. 221–4); the first surviving reference to a *dominus* of Galloway in Stringer's calendar and editions of the *acta* of the lords of Galloway is not until an act of Roland's son, Alan, issued in 1201×05 (ibid., no. 32, pp. 224–5). For Roland as a justice of the king of Scots, see Chapter 4, pp. 230–2.

[26] *LS*, c. 20, to be compared to *LS*, c. 1, in which lords who failed to make their men turn up when vouched to warranty were liable to a 100-cow fine. *LS*, c. 1, is discussed in more detail in Chapter 3, pp. 144–5.

[27] Broun, 'Re-examining *cáin*', p. 56 and note 62.

There were other types of *cáin* too—most notably, the *cáin* of the king's ships—in addition to the two already discussed.[28] The loose meanings of *cáin* in Scotland correspond to its use in Ireland (*cáin* is an Old Irish word), where it carried a range of meanings, from significant tribute paid by underkings to overkings to the making of law itself, as well as providing lesser levels of tribute exaction.[29] In Scotland, in the more peripheral areas of the kingdom, loosely under the king's control, *cáin* was an irregular tribute; in the core areas, the king received *cáin* from his own settlements, while other lords did from theirs.

Like *cáin, coinnmed* (Scots: 'conveth') has also been understood as a universal render owed to the king despite its receipt by lords (ecclesiastical and lay) other than the king.[30] *Coinnmed* was indeed a hospitality duty: the amount required to host the king and other high-status people when they stayed in a particular settlement. It could be commuted into a fixed render, an abstraction or representation of the expected hospitality. It was regularly paid in kind, with royal accounts from as late as 1264 recording the 'waitings' (a term that was increasingly used interchangeably with *coinnmed*) from Forfar and Glamis in Angus that were owed in kind. These comprised both animals (cows, pigs, hens, and eels) and produce (cheese, malt, wheat, and oats).[31] Like *cáin* from within Scotia, *coinnmed* was paid annually; it could also be commuted into cash.

There are some interesting similarities between the terminology used in the account roll of 1263–66 and the payment known as the 'farm of one night' in eleventh-century England, whereby the king was owed a certain number of 'nights' from particular estates that were paid in lieu of hospitality he would otherwise have received.[32] In 1264, Fettercairn was described as owning the 'waiting of one night' while Kinross owed four nights' waiting.[33] These suggest that, by the thirteenth century, there was an understanding that some settlements had heavier duties to host the king each year which resulted in their paying more. Charter attestations bear this out: Kinross is a place where we know kings throughout the period issued

[28] Broun, 'Re-examining *cáin*', p. 51.
[29] Broun, 'Re-examining *cáin*', p. 47; drawing on, among others, Robin Chapman Stacey, *The Road to Judgement: from Custom to Court in Medieval Ireland and Wales* (Philadelphia, PA, 1994), pp. 103–9; and Thomas Charles-Edwards, *Early Christian Ireland* (Cambridge, 2000), pp. 559–69.
[30] It must be emphasized that this latter aspect of *coinnmed* is normally stressed even by those who treat it fundamentally as part of the king's revenue; see *RRS*, ii, pp. 52–3; Oram, *Domination and Lordship*, p. 226.
[31] *ER*, i, pp. 6–7. The 1296 inventory of royal rolls and documents includes a reference to the roll of Abbot Archibald (which must have been made before 1198, when Archibald died), which listed 'ancient renders in cash (*in denariis*) and ancient waytingis', suggesting that 'waitings' were listed in kind in the roll; *APS*, i, p. 118. The account roll is discussed in more detail in Chapter 6, pp. 351–61.
[32] Discussed in more detail in Taylor, 'Common Burdens', pp. 190–1. For scholarship on the night's farm, see Carl Stephenson, 'The *Firma Unius Noctis* and the Customs of the Hundred', *EHR*, vol. 39, no. 154 (1924), pp. 161–74; Pauline A. Stafford, 'The "Farm of One Night" and the Organization of King Edward's Estates in Domesday', *Economic History Review*, vol. 33, no. 3 (1980), pp. 491–502; Stephen Baxter, *The Earls of Mercia: Lordship and Power in Late Anglo-Saxon England* (Oxford, 2007), pp. 130–4; Ryan Lavelle, 'The "Farm of One Night" and the Organisation of Royal Estates in Late Anglo-Saxon Wessex', *Haskins Society Journal*, vol. 14 (2005), pp. 53–82; see Ryan Lavelle, *Royal Estates in Anglo-Saxon Wessex: Land, Politics and Family Strategies*, British Archaeological Reports, British Series, no. 439 (Oxford, 2007), pp. 13–47.
[33] *ER*, i, pp. 12, 16, 20.

charters; Fettercairn, by contrast, is not, although the patchy survival of charters means that we cannot assume Fettercairn never enjoyed the king's presence.[34]

As can be surmised from the above, settlements north and south of the Forth owed a hospitality duty. In Lothian, however, the obligation was more often called 'waiting' and, by the 1170s, 'waiting' was also used as far north as Cargill in Perthshire, north of the River Tay, and here it translated *coinnmed*, and understood it to be an annual render.[35] Kings therefore could expect hospitality (or at least a substituted revenue) from both north and south of the Forth. Given that kings spent a great deal of their time south of the Forth, this is not surprising; such payments (or hospitality itself) would have supported their itineration, which heavily depended on the settlements south of the River Forth and contained a number of important settlements, such as Roxburgh, controlled directly by the king.[36]

Although attention has thus far been focussed on the *coinnmed* received by the king, he did not have a monopoly over the right to receive hospitality. The 1206 judgment over Arbuthnott even records that the bishop of St Andrews and his subordinates not only received payment *in lieu* of real hospitality but also actually enjoyed the hospitality of quite medium-status people while on their travels. One of the witnesses in that case, a man named Felix, testified that his father had hosted Arnold and Richard, successive bishops of St Andrews in his house, as well as their 'stewards, clerics and laymen'.[37] Andrew de Bas testified that he and his brother had hosted Bishop Hugh and his men, providing 'whatever was necessary' and then giving gifts on their departure in the morning.[38] One Master Isaac swore that he had been sent to Caithness, Moray, and Ross to escort their bishops down to St Andrews to attend the consecration of Bishop Roger. While on his journey, he was the guest of Elias, priest of Arbuthnott, and there learnt about the customs of the Kirkton (perhaps over dinner), about which he testified at the Perth synod.[39]

Nor was it only major bishops who thought they had the right to take *coinnmed*. Between 1153 and 1162, Mael Coluim IV issued a brieve commanding that the men of the province of Fife, including the *mormaer* and members of the leading kin-groups, protect and maintain the monks of Dunfermline Abbey, together with their lands and the abbey building itself, and forbidding them from taking *coinnmed* from the abbey's lands and tenants.[40] One explanation for this brieve is that these men were accustomed to take *coinnmed* from these lands but the specially protected status of Dunfermline meant that they were no longer allowed to.

---

[34] For Kinross as a place of issue for the royal charters under William the Lion and Alexander III, see the maps collected in the *RRS* editions; *RRS*, ii, p. 551; *RRS*, iv, 1, p. 275.

[35] *RRS*, ii, no. 154; but see Duncan, *Making of the Kingdom*, pp. 154, 449.

[36] A full study of the royal *iter* has not yet been done, but see the maps in *RRS* volumes cited earlier in this chapter, at note 34, and the commentary for Mael Coluim's reign in *RRS*, i, pp. 27–8, 80, William's reign in *RRS*, ii, pp. 28–9, 80–1, and, for Alexander III, *RRS*, iv, 1, pp. 34–6; for recent work on assemblies and the royal *iter* in Anglo-Saxon England, see Levi Roach, *Kingship and Consent in Anglo-Saxon England, 871–978: Assemblies and the State in the Early Middle Ages* (Cambridge, 2013), particularly pp. 45–76.

[37] *Spalding Misc.*, v, p. 212.   [38] *Spalding Misc.*, v, pp. 212–13.

[39] *Spalding Misc.*, v, p. 211.   [40] *RRS*, i, no. 181.

Certainly, their assumption was that they had a right to do so, even if the king then prohibited it, with the threat of a large monetary fine behind him. What all this means, therefore, is that *cáin* and *coinnmed* tell us little about any sort of obligation owed directly to the king but quite a lot about changing strategies of lordship and resource exploitation. *Cáin* and *coinnmed* were owed to the king but they were not exclusively rendered to him. In the case of *cáin*, there is a distinction to be made between the large tributes levied from loosely subordinate regions, such as Galloway and Argyll (which the king received), and *cáin* as a render owed from settlements (which ecclesiastical and lay lords could receive as well). It might therefore be doubted whether there were, in fact, any common obligations owed to the king: were there universal burdens theoretically owed by all the inhabitants of Scotland proper to the king? The answer to this is, happily, yes, although what that service entailed is somewhat different from what has been thought.

ROYAL SERVICE

The clearest evidence for a universal type of service comes first from a small and subtle change to the diplomatic of royal charters during the reign of William the Lion. This was the phrase 'salvo servicio meo' ('saving my service') found at the end of the body of the charter's text, following the holding clause and before the witness list. The earliest, clearly authentic, example of this specific formula is from 1166×70, in a charter of King William confirming the gift of Hownam in Roxburghshire made by one John, son of Orm, to Melrose Abbey.[41] William stipulated that the monks of Melrose should 'have and possess [the land] forever, so freely, quietly, fully and honourably, as...any alms are possessed in my kingdom and as John's charter well testifies and confirms, saving my service (*salvo servicio meo*)'.[42] There had been earlier statements which attempted to describe the service owed to the king but it was *salvo servicio meo* which became standard and which was the basis for any necessary deviation.[43] It was used in a further ninety-three surviving charters of William the Lion, making a total of 94, and was a continuing feature of the diplomatic of Alexander II's (although it morphed into the more mighty *salvo servicio nostro* when the royal plural was introduced as a standard part of royal charter diplomatic in 1222).[44]

---

[41]   There is an earlier example from Mael Coluim IV's reign: *RRS*, i, no. 132 (surviving as an original; NRS, GD 55/8, dated 1153×1159). This charter is, however, slightly suspect on palaeographical grounds, although this possibility has not been fully explored.

[42]   *RRS*, ii, no. 72; John's deed is printed in *Melrose Liber*, i, no. 127, and records that the monks were to pay 20 shillings yearly as rent but makes no reference to the king's service; their similar witness lists (John's having more names but all corresponding with those listed in William's confirmation charter) suggest they were drawn up on the same occasion (NRS, GD55/127).

[43]   See earlier quittances in *CDI*, nos. 156, 158; and for a precedent to the formula of *salvo servicio meo*, see *RRS*, i, no. 265.

[44]   For Alexander II, see NRS, RH6/24; *Melrose Liber*, i, nos. 184, 185 [AII/46, AII/47]; *Arbroath Liber*, i, nos. 123 [AII/21], 126 [AII/22]; *Kelso Liber*, i, no. 183 [AII/71]. The formula changed in

During the 1160s, the scribes of royal charters were actively thinking about how to express a service owed to the king that was either acquitted, remitted, or retained when the king or lord gave land to another party. A donor could give land to a religious house, for example, but could also continue to perform the king's service on their behalf. Thus, when Walter, son of Alan, gave Mauchline in Ayrshire to Melrose Abbey, William confirmed the gift but specified that Walter still owed him the service from the land. The *salvo servico meo* clause was altered accordingly: 'saving my service which Walter owes me from Walter himself and his heirs'.[45] But it was equally frequent for donors not to remit the performance of service and for a religious house to take on the burden. Seventy-one out of the ninety-four examples of *salvo servicio meo* in royal charters from William's reign are recorded in gifts of land (either made by the king or another donor) to religious houses that were held in alms.[46]

It must be stressed that the service referred to by the formula *salvo servicio meo* did not denote *cáin* or *coinnmed*. Two examples bear this out. First is an agreement drawn up in 1234 containing the settlement of a dispute which had arisen between Andrew, bishop of Moray, and Walter Comyn, earl of Menteith, over half a *dabach* of land belonging to Kincardine in Moray.[47] Walter claimed the land belonged to him, while Bishop Andrew of course thought the opposite. The half *dabach* in question owed *cáin* to the king, of which a tenth was owed to the bishop as teind.[48] The two parties agreed that Earl Walter would hold the land in feu-farm from the bishop, and would pay 34s 8d to the bishop every year as the teind of *cáin*. In addition, Walter agreed to do the 'forinsec service of the lord king belonging to the land'. In this example then, *cáin* was a separate render received by the king in addition to his 'forinsec service' ('forinsec' was a word often used to describe royal service in the thirteenth century). The same is true for *coinnmed*, which is borne out in a rather complicated dispute between David of Lumsdaine and Durham over the rents and dues of Lumsdaine, which David owed to Durham (via Coldingham Priory).[49] Part of the settlement involved the monks agreeing to pay four shillings to David to help him with the king's 'weyting', the word used predominantly south of the Forth for *coinnmed*, and agreeing to perform the king's forinsec service, thus clearly separating the king's service from *coinnmed*. In both these examples, 'service'

1222 to the royal plural—*salvo servicio nostro*—for examples, see *Arbroath Liber*, i, nos. 118 [AII/200], 120 [AII/147]; Fraser, *Southesk*, ii, no. 25 [AII/311]; *Dunf. Reg.*, no. 80 [AII/170]; *Scone Liber*, no. 63 [AII/338]; Gilbert of Stirling, a royal scribe, had used the plural of majesty in William's reign, for which see Dauvit Broun, *Scottish Independence and the Idea of Britain from the Picts to Alexander III* (Edinburgh, 2007), pp. 197–9.

45 *RRS*, ii, no. 78.

46 For laymen, see *RRS*, ii, nos. 209, 266–7, 309, 320, 330, 347, 348, 377, 411, 412, 423, 446, 451, 470, 471, 474, 484, 486, 519; for an archdeacon, see *RRS*, ii, no. 520; for ecclesiastical beneficiaries, see *RRS*, ii, nos. 72, 78, 129, 191, 195, 214, 225, 239A, 240, 241, 243, 246, 256, 257, 264, 276, 292, 296, 306, 307, 322, 331, 333, 342, 367, 373, 378, 381, 382, 385, 386, 396, 401, 413, 414, 425, 431, 434, 435, 441, 444, 445, 447, 448, 449, 456, 458, 461, 464, 466, 479, 480, 482, 483, 489, 492, 494, 495, 498, 503, 506, 508, 512, 513, 515, 516, 517, 518, 521, 522.

47 *Moray Reg.*, no. 85.

48 For second teinds, meaning a tenth of all royal revenue, see Chapter 6, pp. 379–85.

49 Raine, *North Durham*, App., no. 648.

was levied in addition to whatever was owed to other parties in *cáin* and *coinnmed*. The question now becomes, what did the king's service actually involve, if not *cáin* and *coinnmed*?

THE TRIPARTITE OBLIGATION

A royal charter, surviving as an original, provides a useful starting point. This was issued in the name of King William to Orm mac Aeda, lay abbot (*ab*) of Abernethy, between 1173 and 1178.[50] This charter survives as an original and was penned by the king's clerk, Richard of Lincoln, who was responsible for 15 of the 159 surviving original charters of William the Lion and worked in the *capella regis* between 1165 and 1182. Richard was thus well placed to know the exact nature of the king's service during the 1170s. The charter recorded the confirmation of the abbacy (or *apdaine*) of Abernethy to Orm, to be held 'from me and from my heirs in feu and heritage, freely and quietly from all services and customs, saving common aid, common army and common labour service (*excepto comuni auxilio comuni exercitu comuni operatione*)'.[51] These three burdens—*auxilium, exercitus,* and *operatio*—appear to have made up the king's service. Unlike *cáin* and *coinnmed*, aid, labour service, and army service regularly appear in some combination in the charter evidence, in Scotia, Moray, and Lothian. Between 1178 and 1187, William granted his ferryboat of Montrose with its appurtenant land to Arbroath Abbey 'to be held in free and quit and perpetual alms, freely and quietly from army and expedition and labour service and aid'.[52] Although often mentioned together, the three services were seen as separable burdens: a landholder could be granted quittance from one burden but not from another.[53] Between 1173 and 1178, William confirmed the gift of a ploughgate of arable in Kedlock, Fife, originally made by one Simon, son of Michael, to the Hospital of St Andrews and commanded that Simon and his heirs were to acquit (*adquietare*)[54] the land 'from army

---

[50] BL, Additional Charter 76697; *RRS*, ii, no. 152; for Richard of Lincoln see *RRS*, ii, pp. 85, 86–7.

[51] *RRS*, ii, no. 152. This formula has been discussed briefly in G. W. S. Barrow, 'The Beginnings of Military Feudalism', in Barrow, *Kingdom of the Scots*, pp. 250–78, at p. 272. Barrow argues that these services may have been required because 'knight-service was thought an inappropriate tenure for the abbot of Abernethy'. But what follows shows that the service required from Orm mac Aeda was not unusual; what was unusual was the high level of specification of these services, which were expressed by a more complicated form of the formula *salvo servicio meo*. For the *apdaine*, the most comprehensive account remains G. W. S. Barrow, 'The Lost Gàidhealtachd', in Barrow, *Scotland and its Neighbours*, pp. 106–26, at pp. 120–3.

[52] *RRS*, ii, nos. 228; for aids and labour-services together, see *RRS*, ii, no. 438; for 'aids and armies', see *Moray Reg.*, no. 34 [AII/180].

[53] *RRS*, ii, no. 92.

[54] The verb *acquietare/adquietare* does not mean that the service had been fully lifted; although the new landholder had been acquitted from burdens of the king's service, the donor still had to perform it, despite no longer having right in the land in question. The service from the land still had to be performed. For example, Adam de Hastings granted part of his land of Kingledoors in Peeblesshire to Arbroath Abbey between 4 December 1214 and 21 April 1222 and stated that 'ego vero et heredes mei forinsecum servicium domini regis quod ad terram illam pertinebit in omnibus adquietabimus'

services and labour services' but that the hospital would acquit the land from (i.e. perform) 'the royal geld (*geldum*—here denoting *auxilium*) which is commonly taken from lands and alms throughout the kingdom of Scotland'.[55]

Most of the time, charters record that this service was levied on 'land', whether named or unnamed. But, not infrequently, some charters show that, underneath these 'lands' or named settlements, service was levied on a fiscal unit. The names (and extent) of these units varied.[56] The *dabach* (pl. *dabaig*) appears to have been the universal measure of assessment in Scotland north of the Forth; the ploughgate for land south of the Forth.[57] The ploughgate did appear as a unit of assessment north of the Forth as well but, in this area, ploughgates were, on occasion, called *carucata Scoticana*, a 'Scottish [or Gaelic] ploughgate'.[58] It has been argued that ploughgates north of the Forth (whether explicitly called 'Scottish' or not) denoted the *dabach* and that they were different units of assessment from ploughgates south of the Forth.[59] It is impossible to prove whether all ploughgates north of the Forth could really have been described as 'Scottish ploughgates', although the general equivalence of the Scottish ploughgate with the *dabach* is accepted here. Subdivisions of ploughgates and *dabaig* were common and smaller units of land, when they were given to a third party, were also obliged to render the king's service, presumably a portion of the full amount of service.[60] The relative sizes, function, and origins of *dabaig* and ploughgates (along with other units) have been the subject of much debate in the literature and the whole topic has recently received new life.[61] Earlier scholarship, for example, assumed that *dabaig* were found predominantly

---

(*Arbroath Liber*, i, no. 122). Alexander II's confirmation charter, issued 21 April, 1215, stated that the monks were to hold the land 'freely and quietly, wholly and honourably, as the charter of Adam made for the monks on this testifies, saving my service from the aforesaid Adam and his heirs' (*Arbroath Liber*, i, no. 123; AII/21).

[55] *RRS*, ii, no. 169; the word *geldum* is rare in Scottish documentation and probably refers to *auxilium*—'aid', an equation which would make sense, given that both were assessed on land and were not extraordinary taxation; cf. *RRS*, ii, p. 53; Duncan, *Making of the Kingdom*, p. 213; Barrow, *Kingship and Unity*, p. 65. *Geldum* was often equated with *auxilium* in the charters and deeds drawn up for Arbroath Abbey: see this chapter, note 74.

[56] The most striking of these variations is the arachor, found exclusively in the Lennox. Service was also assessed upon the arachor; *Lennox Cart*, pp. 34–5: 'the forinsec service of the lord king which belongs to half of one arachor in the Lennox'.

[57] *Scone Liber*, no. 67 [AII/223]; *Coupar Angus Chrs*, i, no. 10. There has been much debate on whether the *dabach* corresponded to four or two ploughgates; for four, see Skene, *Celtic Scotland*, iii, pp. 223–4; cf. R. Dodgshon, *Land and Society in Early Scotland* (Oxford, 1981), pp. 73–89; for two, see G. W. S. Barrow, 'Rural Settlement in Central and Eastern Scotland', in *Kingdom of the Scots*, pp. 233–49, at pp. 243–4; Alexis R. Easson, 'Systems of Land Assessment in Scotland before 1400' (PhD Thesis, University of Edinburgh, 1986), pp. 53–60.

[58] *RRS*, ii, nos. 131, 469; NLS, MS Adv. 15.1.18, no. 61.

[59] Barrow, 'Rural Settlement', pp. 239–41, 247–8; Barrow, *Anglo-Norman Era*, pp. 161–2; Easson, 'Systems of Land Assessment', p. 226.

[60] *Arbroath Liber*, i, no. 67; also EUL, Laing Charters, Box 2, no. 87, calendared in *Calendar of the Laing Charters, A.D. 854–1837*, ed. J. Anderson (Edinburgh, 1899), no. 4.

[61] Kenneth Jackson, *The Gaelic Notes in the Book of Deer* (Cambridge, 1972), pp. 116–17; Barrow, 'Rural Settlement', pp. 239–42; Easson, 'Systems of Land Assessment', pp. 45–100, 197–265; Alasdair Ross, 'The *Dabhach* in Moray: A New Look at an Old Tub', in *Landscape and Environment in Dark Age Scotland*, ed. Alex Woolf (St Andrews, 2006), pp. 57–74, and Alasdair D. Ross, *The Kings of Alba, c.100–1130 (Edinburgh, 2011)*, pp. 14–33; for the arachor see Easson, 'Systems of Land Assessment', pp. 171–96, and Neville, *Native Lordship*, pp. 99–102.

in lowland areas of central and northeastern Scotland. Yet recent work by Alasdair Ross has shown that *dabaig* are found across the province of Moray in both highland and lowland areas.[62] To do justice to the complexity of this topic would require a book in its own right. What can be said here is that the levying of service on regionally particular fiscal units suggests that these burdens were imposed on pre-existing territorial units, whether arable or fiscal in origin, as the authority of the king of Scots spread.[63]

What the three burdens of army service, aid, and labour service actually entailed has to be drawn from negative evidence because many of the charters detailing these obligations only survive through their preservation in beneficiary archives and thus are more concerned with what beneficiaries did not have to do rather than what they did. The earliest example of common labour obligations comes from exactly this sort of negative evidence. A text known as foundation-legend 'B' of St Andrews, dated to 1140 × 52, recorded that King *Hungus* (Onuist) gave 'this place, that is Kilrimont to God and St Andrew his apostle…with such freedom that the inhabitants of that place should be free and quit always from army and from work on castles and bridges'.[64] The details of Onuist's grant that exempted St Andrews from labour obligations are almost certainly spurious and tell us about mid-twelfth century expectations of labour services rather than about ninth-century ones.[65] Labour services were certainly understood in the mid-twelfth century to encompass work on fortifications and bridges: charters of David I and Mael Coluim IV issued to Dunfermline Abbey both commanded that the men of Dunfermline Abbey should be quit from labour service on 'bridges, castles and all other works'.[66] In addition, both brieves stressed that labour service should not be exacted from the monks 'unless the abbot and monks should wish to perform it by

---

[62] Ross, *Kings of Alba*, pp. 25–33; Alasdair D. Ross, 'The Province of Moray, *c.*1000–1230' (PhD Dissertation, University of Aberdeen, 2003), pp. 41–52, 119–22. Dr Ross has recently published a new book on this subject, entitled *Land Assessment and Lordship in Medieval Northern Scotland*, The Medieval Countryside 14 (Turnhout, 2015), which appeared after the submission of this book.

[63] Oxgangs, for example, while clearly an arable unit, were *used* for fiscal purposes to assess service liability; see *RRS*, ii, nos. 404, 486.

[64] *Chronicles of the Picts, Chronicles of the Scots*, ed. William F. Skene (Edinburgh, 1867), pp. 186–7. A new edition of foundation-legend 'B' is in *PNF*, vol. 3, pp. 567–75 (Latin), 576–9 (translation); for the date, see Simon Taylor, 'The Coming of the Augustinians to St Andrews and version B of the St Andrews Foundation Legend', in *Kings, Clerics and Chronicles in Scotland, 500–1297: Essays in Honour of Marjorie Ogilvie Anderson on the Occasion of her Ninetieth Birthday* (Dublin, 2000), ed. Simon Taylor, pp. 115–23. For the most recent analysis of the date of the dedication to St Andrews, see James E. Fraser, 'Rochester, Hexham and Cennrígmonaid: The movements of St Andrew in Britain, 604–747', in *Saints' Cults in the Celtic World*, ed. Steve Boardman, John Reuben Davies, and Eila Williamson (Woodbridge, 2009), pp. 1–17.

[65] Although work on fortifications and bridges were obligations to ninth- and tenth-century kings, so there is nothing necessarily unusual about these demands in an earlier context. The most obvious earlier medieval examples are Offa's dyke (eighth-century) and the obligation ordinary people had to man and upkeep the fortifications listed in the Burghal Hidage (ninth/tenth-century), for which there is a vast amount of literature: see, among many, *The Defence of Wessex: The Burghal Hidage and Anglo-Saxon Fortifications*, ed. David Hill and Alexander R. Rumble (Manchester, 1996).

[66] *CDI*, no. 37; *RRS*, i, no. 213. Mael Coluim's charter was based on the diplomatic of David's charter and this suggests that either the monks brought David's charter to the royal chapel for re-issue or that the monks caused both charters to be drafted in house.

their own free will' (*spontanea voluntate*). When the monks helped the other wor-thy men of the kingdom build new royal castles in Ross (presumably in response to the invasion of Gofraid mac Domnaill meic Uilleim in 1211), a charter of William the Lion was drawn up in the aftermath to specify explicitly that this work was done at his own request (*ad peticionem meam*) and reassured the monks that the goodwill they had exhibited on this occasion would not prompt the transfor-mation into custom of an *ad hoc* performance of labour service on the king's fortifications.[67]

As with *operatio*, quittance from the burden of *auxilium* was strongly protected. On 23 April, 1201×07, William granted that all the tofts he had given to Arbroath in his 'burghs and manors (*maneria*)' should be free and quit 'from all aids and labour-services belonging to me and my heirs'.[68] This shows the king's expectation that the tofts in burghs and residences *were* liable for aid and labour service (at least) even if Arbroath had received exemption on this occasion. In 1216, Alexander had marched to Dover to join Louis, son of the king of France, during the English civil war of 1215–17.[69] The Chronicle of Melrose records that Alexander advanced to Carlisle prior to his journey to Dover 'with his whole army, saving the Scots from whom he had received supplies'.[70] Alexander needed all the resources he could get: a later charter, dated 7 March, 1217×19, informed his kingdom that he had been forced to ask the men of the monks of Arbroath to give aid alongside his burgesses and provide the king with hides that had later been sold in England 'in [the king's] great need' during his advance to Dover the previous year. But, in a phrase echoing that of William's charter to Dunfermline mentioned earlier, Alexander commanded that the *auxilium* the monks had granted *liberaliter* was against the freedom which his father, William, had granted them: yet again, the levying of aid was not to become *exemplum vel consuetudinem* ('a precedent or custom').[71]

The first clear reference to *auxilium* is in a brieve of Mael Coluim IV, datable to between 1162 and 1164, which forbade the *mormaer* of Angus and the *vicecomites* of Forfar and Scone from collecting aid from the property of the abbot of Scone.[72] Before this, however, David I's grand confirmation charter to Holyrood Abbey contains the prohibition that no one should take labour services (*operationes*) or aids (*auxilia*) or secular customs (*consuetudinibus seculares*) unlawfully from the

---

[67] *RRS*, ii, no. 500; the charter was drawn up on 18 August in 1211, 1212, or 1213. Gofraid mac Domnaill meic Uilleim had invaded *de consilio, prout dicebatur, thanorum de Ross* (*Gesta Annalia* I, in Skene, *Fordun*, i, p. 278) in 1211 and William had led a preliminary (but unsuccessful) force against him that year: *Chron. Melrose, s.a.* 1211. Gofraid was killed not long after Alexander's knighting by John on 4 March 1212; see *Rogeri de Wendouer liber qui dicitur Flores Historiarum*, ed. H. G. Hewlett, 3 vols (London, 1886–1889), ii, p. 60; *Gesta Annalia* I, in Skene, *Fordun*, i, p. 278. It is thus probable that the charter was issued either in August 1211 or August 1212 and the new castles in Ross were built specifically to deal with the threat posed by Gofraid.

[68] *RRS*, ii, no. 438.

[69] Keith J. Stringer, 'Kingship, Conflict and State-Making in the Reign of Alexander II: The War of 1215–17 and Its Context', in *The Reign of Alexander II 1214–49*, ed. Richard Oram (Leiden, 2005) pp. 99–156.

[70] *Chron. Melrose, s.a.* 1216.   [71] *Arbroath Liber*, i, no. 111 [AII/34].

[72] *RRS*, i, no. 252; *vicecomites* has been left untranslated deliberately see below, pp. 109–11. For the suggestion that this aid was raised to help subsidise the marriage of the king's sisters, see *RRS*, i, p. 54.

abbey.[73] It is probable that the 'aids', although generically referred to here along-side an even vaguer mention of 'customs', were the royal aids described as 'common' in William's charter to Orm mac Aeda. After the references in Mael Coluim IV's reign, however, aids appear relatively frequently. A brieve of King William referred to the aid 'which was fixed at Musselburgh' and there is an earlier mention of 'levied aid' in a charter of Mael Coluim IV to Coupar Angus Abbey, suggesting a process of consultation to determine the necessary amount.[74] Aid was probably rendered both in cash and in kind. That rendered in kind was, at least on occasion, sold afterwards for cash. Alexander II sold the hides given to him in 1216 as aid by the men dwelling in the tofts held by Arbroath and his own burgesses to fund his march to Dover.[75] There is no evidence that *auxilium* was ever a render taken annually: one charter, drawn up during 1223×4, described *auxilium* as a burden falling only 'when the lord king places a common aid on the whole kingdom (*totum regnum*)', suggesting its extraordinary nature.[76] Aid was levied when the king required it; it was not a regular or ordinary income.

The evidence detailing the nature of the third burden of the king's service, ser-vice in the king's common army, is the most abundant. Indeed, it is most common for royal service to be specifically equated with service in the king's common army—the host—rather than the rendering of aid or labour service.[77] Service in the common army could be commuted into a food rent, although this is compar-atively rare and most examples come from documents concerning land within the Lennox.[78] Not surprisingly, the timing of the levy depended on the king's need. Armies were raised on the royal command or summons not only for the defence of the realm but also to keep the peace within it.[79] They were sometimes geographi-cally specific: only the army of Mar, for example, was gathered in 1242 to provide a safe conduct to the king's court for Walter Bisset after Bisset had been accused of the murder of Patrick of Atholl.[80]

Ecclesiastical and monastic lands were rarely acquitted from common army ser-vice: the only house known to have been wholly exempt was the Cluniac priory on

---

[73] *CDI*, no. 147.

[74] *RRS*, ii, no. 326; *RRS*, i, no. 226. The scribes of charters of patrons issued on behalf of Arbroath Abbey (and perhaps drawn up by the abbey itself) explicitly associated *auxilium* with *geldum*, 'geld' being tax imposed upon units of assessed land (the 'hide') in late Anglo-Saxon England until 1161–2. For examples from Arbroath, see *Arbroath Liber*, i, nos. 50, 93–4; see, further, Duncan, *Making of the Kingdom*, p. 213; for danegeld, see Judith A. Green, 'The Last Century of Danegeld', *EHR*, vol. 96, no. 379 (1981), pp. 241–58.

[75] *Arbroath Liber*, i, no. 111 [AII/34]; *RRS*, ii, pp. 53–4.

[76] *Inchaffray Chrs*, no. 52.

[77] See, for example, *RRS*, ii, no. 131; *Moray Reg.*, no. 37 [AII/250]; NLS, MS Adv. 15.1.18, no. 68.

[78] The men of the Kirkton of Arbuthnott had to provide supplies *in expeditione domini regis*, although it is not explicit in the text that this was a commutation of service in the army itself; *Spalding Misc.*, v, p. 210; for an example in the Lennox, see *Lennox Cart.*, pp. 83–4.

[79] The remainder of this paragraph merely summarizes the arguments in Taylor, 'Common Burdens', pp. 200–1. See also the reference to David 'having sent out an edict throughout *Scotia*, moved all to arms' in *Gesta Stephani*, ed. K. R. Potter, rev. R. H. C. Davis (Oxford, 1976), pp. 54–5.

[80] *Scotichronicon by Walter Bower*, 9 vols, gen. ed. D. E. R. Watt (Aberdeen and Edinburgh, 1989–98), v, pp. 178–83.

the Isle of May.[81] Most houses and churches had to provide men to perform army service: Mael Coluim IV granted Kinclaith in Glasgow to its bishopric and commanded that it be held 'freely and quit...but saving my army-services' (*saluis tamen exercitibus meis*).[82] Although Arbroath Abbey was to hold 'all gifts so freely and quietly', its lands were still subject to obligations for 'the defence of my kingdom' (*defensione regni mei excepta*).[83] Before March 1238, Robert, son of Warenbald, and his wife, Richenda de Berkeley, granted their 'whole feu in the parish of Fordun in Mearns' to Arbroath but stipulated that the monks must answer for 'the forinsec service of the lord king in army and common aid'.[84] Alexander II granted his lands in Callendar to be held in feu-farm to the canons of Holyrood on 9 January 1234 'free and quit from all service, aid, custom and exaction, saving the defence of the kingdom'.[85]

By the mid-thirteenth century, men who held their land directly from the king were expected to raise troops and aids for the host from their lands, regardless of whether they held their land at feu-farm or if they were also charged with supplying knights to the king's knightly armies as a condition of tenure.[86] There were, of course, exceptions. Between 1252 and 1253, Gilbert of Cleish gave fifteen acres in Kinross to his nephew, John of Pitliver, with the stipulation that John had to perform the king's forinsec service for that land. However, John would be acquitted from the service if he served in the king's knightly army with Gilbert.[87] But it was more common for the king's service to be performed concurrently with any other military service owed from tenure of a feu than for the obligation of knights' service to render the performance of common army service unnecessary.[88] The most striking example comes from the earliest infeftment in Argyll by the kings of Scots.[89] In a charter dated 1 August 1240, Alexander II granted five pennylands in Fincharn and other territories to Gille Escoip mac Gilla Críst in return for the service of half a knight 'and to do the Scottish service as our barons and knights on the north bank of the sea of Scotland do for their lands'.[90] The burdens of knight service and common army service were thus being imposed concurrently in areas more recently under the control of the king of Scots.

[81] *RRS*, ii, no. 158, for May, see A. A. M. Duncan, 'Documents Relating to the Priory of the Isle of May, *c*.1140–1313', *PSAS*, vol. 90 (1956–57), pp. 52–80, nos. 50 (p. 73), 52 (p. 74).

[82] *RRS*, i, no. 265.

[83] *RRS*, ii, nos. 197, 513. The abbey did, however, hold the land belonging to the ferry-boat at Montrose free *ab exercitu et expeditione*; *RRS*, ii, no. 228. Donors could acquit the lands they granted to Arbroath from common army-service, providing that they performed it themselves. See *Arbroath Liber*, i, no. 50, and William's confirmation at *RRS*, ii, no. 456.

[84] *Arbroath Liber*, i, no. 261.

[85] *Holyrood Liber*, no. 65 [AII/203].

[86] *RRS*, ii, nos. 404, 474; for feu-farm, see *Coupar Angus Chrs*, i, no. 38; also NLS, MS Adv. 15.1.18, no. 61. For the development of the army levy through structures of land lordship, see below, pp. 103–8.

[87] Document printed in Barrow, 'Army of Alexander III', pp. 146–7.

[88] Barrow, *Anglo-Norman Era*, pp. 164–6.

[89] For the extension of Alexander II's power into Argyll, see Noel Murray, 'Swerving from the Path of Justice: Alexander II's Relations with Argyll and the Western Isles, 1214–49', in *The Reign of Alexander II, 1214–49*, ed. Richard Oram (Leiden, 2005), pp. 285–305.

[90] MacPhail, *Highland Papers*, ii, pp. 121–3 [AII/272].

Even if the two types of military service could be levied on the same piece of land, the relationship between the king's knightly army and the host is rather difficult to discern. Chroniclers thought that the two should be separated and modern commentators have generally followed their division.[91] Aelred of Rievaulx reported in his *Relatio de Standardo*, written by 1157, that David I himself commanded the armies of Scotia and Moray but appointed 'French and English knights' to guard his own person.[92] Jordan Fantosme separated the 'thousand armed knights' from the 'thirty thousand men without armour (*desarmez*)' raised by William the Lion in his attempt to wrest Northumberland and Cumberland from Henry II in 1173.[93] Fantosme also contrasted the Galwegians and Scots *qui sunt en Albanie* ('who are in *Alba*'), serving in the common army, with the barons who hold 'their honours directly from the king's royal person'.[94] But it is clear that men of aristocratic status were expected to serve in the common army as well. A law of Alexander II, issued in 1221 (and discussed in greater detail later in this chapter), reveals that not only were *rustici* (peasants, both free and unfree)[95] required to serve but so too were *ógtigerna* (men of middling status) and thanes, who were often held to be equivalent to knights and barons by the compilers of royal legislation and who, as we have seen, were conceptualized as the rank below a *mormaer* in *Leges inter Brettos et Scotos* (*LBS*).[96] What should be remembered, therefore, is that although there may have been separate armies, defined to outsiders perhaps by status and the military technologies each sported, the common army nonetheless contained individuals who were of very high rank indeed.

The word 'forinsec' has cropped up in the foregoing paragraphs. Maitland showed that 'forinsec' service denoted service owed to the king or overlord above what was owed to the immediate lord of the tenement.[97] 'Forinsec' was used in a similar context in Scotland to describe the common burdens of the land owed to the king and is found in charters and deeds from the early thirteenth century.[98] We thus hear of 'forinsec service', 'forinsec aid', and 'forinsec army service'. *Operaciones*, however, unlike *auxilia* or *exercitus et expeditio*, were never described as 'forinsec

---

[91] Barrow, *Anglo-Norman Era*, pp. 161–8.

[92] Aelred of Rievaulx, *Relatio de Standardo*, in *Chronicles of the Reigns of Stephen, Henry II and Richard I*, ed. R. Howlett, Rolls Series, 4 vols (London, 1884–9), iii, pp. 179–99, at p. 191.

[93] *Jordan Fantosme's Chronicle*, ed. R. C. Johnston (Oxford, 1981), lines 327–8.

[94] *Fantosme*, ed. Johnston, line 690.

[95] The word *rusticus* could be used to denote individuals of unfree status, see Alice Taylor, '*Homo Ligius* and Unfreedom in Medieval Scotland', in *New Perspectives on Medieval Scotland, 1093–1286*, ed. Matthew H. Hammond (Woodbridge, 2013), pp. 85–116, at pp. 106–8, but could also be used to mean peasant in general, free or unfree. There is no conclusive evidence that service in the common army was exclusive to free men.

[96] See Chapter 1, pp. 59–66.

[97] Sir Frederick Pollock and F. W. Maitland, *The History of English Law before the Time of Edward I*, 2nd edn, 2 vols, (Cambridge, 1923), i, pp. 238–40.

[98] 'Forinsec' service could also be called 'Scottish service' (*servicium Scotticanum*) north of the Forth; see Duncan, *Making of the Kingdom*, pp. 381–2; Barrow, 'Beginnings of Military Feudalism', p. 273; for examples of 'forinsec service', see *Arbroath Liber*, i, nos. 102 [AII/214], 122; *Dunf. Reg.*, nos. 75 [AII/254], 147; NRS, RH6/31; *Inchcolm Chrs*, no. 11; *Melrose Liber*, i, no. 137; EUL, Laing Charters, Box 2, no. 87; *Coupar Angus Chrs*, i, no. 10; NRS, RH6/16; *Inchaffray Chrs*, nos. 33, 39, 52, 72; BL, Additional MS 33245, fos. 147r–v, 152r; *Scone Liber*, no. 75 [AII/278]; Fraser, *Grant*, iii, nos. 4, 6; Fraser, *Douglas*, iii, nos. 2, 4–6.

labour-services'. The clearest example of their absence is in a note entered into the *Registrum Vetus* of the bishopric of Glasgow in the mid-thirteenth century.[99] This note states the churchmen were being forced to submit to 'secular justice' in some of their lands 'for the reason of certain army-services and common aids—or forinsec services—which the grantors of those feus had retained to themselves and their heirs'. It is clear that *operaciones* were still being levied in 1212, for the monks of Dunfermline were forced to send their men to help with the building of castles in the north to counteract the forces of Gofraid mac Domnaill meic Uilleim. But it is possible that the lack of references to *operaciones*—and 'forinsec labour-services'—may signify a general decline in their importance from the early thirteenth century onwards.

Conversely, *auxilium* is not mentioned in the earliest documentary evidence to detail the nature of the king's service. Version 'B' of the St Andrews foundation legend, mentioned earlier, recorded the gift of Kilrimont by King *Hungus* (Onuist) to St Andrews with freedom from army and labour services but made no mention of *auxilia*.[100] The grant of Kirkness by Mac Bethad, king of *Alba* (1040–57), surviving in a Latin translation in the Loch Leven property-records, was freed from the burdens of 'bridge-work and army-service' but, again, *auxilium* is not mentioned.[101] It is clear that, by the 1170s and the time of William the Lion's confirmation of the *apdaine* of Abernethy to Orm mac Aeda, the three burdens of *operaciones, auxilia*, and *exercitus et expeditio* were happily co-existing. Nevertheless, it remains possible that the levy of *auxilia* was introduced in the mid-twelfth century and that *operaciones* may have subsequently declined in importance. If so, this points to a number of interesting avenues to be followed: the growing importance of a cash economy (or produce to be converted into cash), the possible employment by the king of Scots of a more specialized labour force than one produced by social and political obligation, and the growing importance of financial aid for military operations.

What was the geographical spread of these burdens? The earliest references to army service date between 1145 and 1153; these refer to lands in Perthshire and Berwickshire.[102] Given the significance of Durham for the production of the earliest Scottish charters, the early attestation of common burdens in Berwickshire is understandable.[103] It does look as though the king's service spread as far as his brieve and charter did. There is, for example, only evidence of the king's service in the Lennox from the early thirteenth century, which also happens to be when charters started surviving for the Lennox in some detail. In 1224, Alexander confirmed a gift of Mael Domnaig, earl of Lennox (d. *c.* 1250), to Paisley Abbey with

---

[99] *Glasgow Reg.*, ii, no. 535.   [100] *PNF*, vol. 3, p. 573.
[101] *St Andrews Liber*, p. 114; *PNF*, vol. 3, p. 596.   [102] *CDI*, nos. 156, 158.
[103] For the significance of Durham, see A. A. M. Duncan, 'Yes, the Earliest Scottish Charters', *SHR*, vol. 78, no. 205 (1999), pp. 1–38; for a different perspective, see Dauvit Broun, 'The Adoption of Brieves in Scotland', in *Charters and Charter Scholarship in Britain and Ireland*, ed. Marie Therese Flanagan and Judith A. Green (Basingstoke, 2005), pp. 164–83.

the caveat *salvo servicio nostro* ('saving our service').[104] And in 1238, when Alexander II finally bestowed the *comitatus* upon Mael Domnaig in a formal charter, he commanded the earl to 'perform the forinsec service which belongs to [ ] full vills (*plenarias villas*) in army-services and aids'.[105] Thus, there is an issue about whether the patterns of documentation reflect the king's new imposition of these burdens in the Lennox or whether such burdens had long been imposed, but we do not have the documentation to confirm either hypothesis.

Galloway in the twelfth and early thirteenth centuries may have been subject to slightly different obligations, as perhaps elsewhere in the kingdom where the king's authority was looser. Galloway may have been liable to a different form of *cáin*, as well as army service, but does not seem to have been liable for *auxilium* and *operatio* in addition. As a basis, it is clear that land within Galloway, even that granted to beneficiaries within England, was still assessed for performance of the king's service. Between 12 May 1161 and *c.*1170, Uhtred, lord of Galloway gave the vill of Kirkgunzeon (east of the River Urr) to Holm Cultram Abbey for an annual rent of £6 and acquitted the land from 'the service of the king of Scotland'.[106] There are frequent references in narrative sources to contingents of Galwegian forces serving in the army of the king of Scots, strongly suggesting that this *servicium regis Scottorum* included serving in the king's common army.[107] As was shown above, Galloway was still accustomed to pay a tribute of *cáin* to the kings of Scots as late as 1187×1200.[108] It would be strange if Galloway had been liable both for *cáin* and the threefold burden of army service, aid, and labour service. A revealing deed of Uhtred, lord of Galloway, suggests that land may have been liable only for *cáin* and army service.[109] This deed was drawn up between 1161 and 1173 and recorded Uhtred's donation of the land of Loch Kindar in Kirkcudbrightshire to Richard fitz Truite in return for the service of one knight.[110] It also recorded that, whenever Uhtred rendered *cáin* from Cro and Desnes Ioan, Richard would pay Uhtred eight pounds of silver in return for quittance from 'all service and *consuetudines*' owed to both the king of Scots and also Uhtred. But whenever Uhtred was released from his responsibility to render *cáin*, Richard would hold the land for the service of one knight. It thus appears that, at least in the third quarter of the twelfth century, Galloway did not render the three burdens of army service, labour services, and *auxilia* but the older burdens of tribute and hosting, organized independently by the lord of the province.

---

[104] *Paisley Reg.*, p. 214 [AII/95].

[105] *Lennox Cart.*, pp. 1–2 [AII/267]; the reference to the unit of assessment as the vill, rather than the *dabach* or *arrachor*, is nonetheless noteworthy.

[106] Stringer, 'Acts of Lordship', p. 214, no. 7.

[107] See Howden, *Gesta*, i, p. 64, 67; ii, p. 8; Aelred of Rievaulx, *Relatio de Standardo*, in *Chronicles*, ed. Howlett, iii, pp. 187, 189–90.

[108] *LS*, c. 20.

[109] I am grateful to Dauvit Broun for sharing his thoughts on this with me.

[110] Stringer, 'Acts of Lordship', p. 215, no. 9; full text in F. W. Ragg, 'Five Strathclyde and Galloway Charters', *Cumberland and Westmorland Antiquarian and Archaeological Society Transactions*, new series, vol. 17 (1917), pp. 198–234, at pp. 218–19.

MECHANISMS FOR RAISING COMMON BURDENS

Who was responsible for raising the common army and the appurtenant burdens of *auxilia* and *operaciones* elsewhere in the kingdom? The attention this subject has thus far received has concentrated on the important role earls (or *mormaír*) played in raising the king's common army.[111] Geoffrey Barrow, mainly on the basis of chronicle evidence, has argued that 'the common army of Scotland was based on the earldoms and led by the earls'. His arguments have been generally accepted.[112] However, what Barrow actually meant by 'earldom' is now obscured given the arguments of Chapter 1. If Barrow's 'earldom' is taken to mean the more limited territory of the *comitatus*, it logically follows that there were tracts of land within each province whose inhabitants were *not* liable for army service because they were not under the direct lordship of the earl/*mormaer*. Given the vast number of references already cited demonstrating that the lands of bishoprics and abbeys were assessed, even if eventually excused, for such service, this scenario is unlikely. If the *provincia* was the basis of Barrow's statement, then the picture changes. Here, Barrow would have envisaged the provincial army being raised and led by *mormaír* (or earls, which is what they will be called in the following discussion), regardless of who had lordship over the land in question.[113]

At first glance, there is much to support this second possibility. The epic poem written by Jordan Fantosme on the 1173–4 Great Rebellion records that amongst William's army (*ost*) were Earl Colbán of Buchan and Gille Críst, earl of Angus.[114] Fantosme mentions that William summoned 'his knights, the earls (*cuntes*) of his land, all his best fighters' in 1174.[115] The Chronicle of Melrose records that the earls of Scotland sent their armies to plunder Moray while on the king's campaign against Domnall mac Uilleim in 1187.[116] In a striking deed, Donnchad, earl of Fife 'granted and confirmed' to the monks of May quittance 'from army and expedition as King Mael Coluim confirmed to them by his charter'. An explanation of this unusual deed would be that Donnchad was acting in his role of leader of the king's army of the province of Fife.[117] However, a royal enactment from 1221 attributable to Alexander II suggests a rather different procedure at work. I have re-edited this text recently in the longer exposition of the arguments offered here and there is no need to repeat the tortuous discussion of the implications of

---

[111] *RRS*, ii, p. 57.

[112] Alexander Grant, 'The Construction of the Early Scottish State', in *The Medieval State: Essays Presented to James Campbell*, ed. J. R. Maddicott and D. M. Palliser (London, 2000), pp. 47–71, at pp. 55–6; Alexander Grant, 'Aspects of National Consciousness in Medieval Scotland', in *Nations, Nationalism and Patriotism in the European Past*, ed. C. Bjørn, A. Grant, and K. J. Stringer (Copenhagen, 1994), pp. 68–95, at pp. 88–92.

[113] In what follows, I call *comites* 'earls' for the reasons put forward in Chapter 1, pp. 34–7.

[114] *Fantosme*, ed. Johnston, lines 471–6, at line 473.

[115] *Fantosme*, ed. Johnston, lines 1185–6. Johnston wrongly translates *cuntes* as 'barons'; Fantosme usually used *cunte* to describe an earl. See his mention of 'le cunte Colbein' [of Buchan] (line 472), 'le cunte d'Anegus' (line 473), and 'les cuntes d'Escocë' (line 1342).

[116] *Chron. Melrose, s.a.* 1187.

[117] BL, MS Egerton 3031, fo. 62v; Duncan, 'Documents', no. 52 (p. 74).

different manuscript witnesses of this statute. The translation of this law from its 2011 edition is therefore given as follows.[118]

The record made in the presence of the lord king at Perth by all the *iudices* of Scotia on the next Thursday of the first full week of Lent after the king was among his army at Inverness against Domnall mac Niall concerning those who had stayed away from the king's army. [It was decided] that the king shall have the forfeiture of the earls if their thanes had stayed away from the army but it was not discussed how much [the fine] should be. From all others who stayed away from the army, that is those from the lands of the bishops, abbots, barons, knights, thanes who hold of the king, the king alone shall have the forfeiture. From a thane, six cows and a calf; from an *ógtigern*, 15 sheep or six shillings but from him the king shall only have half, and the thane or knight the other half. From a peasant, one cow and sheep and this shall be shared in the same way between the king and the thane or knight. But if any stayed away by permission of the thane or knight, the king alone will have the forfeiture. No earl or earl's sergeands ought to come into the land of anyone holding of the king to exact this forfeiture unless he is the earl of Fife but he shall come to exact his rights not as the earl of Fife but as the king's third *maer* of Fife (*et ille non sicut comes de Fiffe sed sicut tercius marus Regis de Fiffe ad rectitudines suas exigendas*). From *gabhail* for which the king and earl share responsibility, the king and the earl shall have half of the forfeiture of the army and the thane the other half. But where the thane himself is in forfeiture, the forfeiture should be shared between the king and the earl.[119]

The law thus establishes the forfeitures owed from those who stayed away when the king called out his army throughout the kingdom. It deals with the responsibilities of the earls first: 'the king ought to have the earl's forfeiture if their thanes should have stayed away from the army', although it was not decided how much it should be. The law continued, 'concerning all others who stayed away from the army, *that is the lands of the bishops, abbots, barons, knights and thanes who hold of* (de) *the king*, the king alone should have the forfeiture'.[120] The distinction between the contingents of earls and those of the bishops, abbots, barons, knights, and thanes is clear. The highest status groups in society, many of which held immediately of the king, stood alongside the earls as responsible for raising his common army. Indeed, the earl was forbidden from coming into the lands of 'anyone holding of the king' to extract forfeitures, unless the earl in question was the earl of Fife and even he would answer to the king 'not as an earl but as the king's third *maer* of Fife'.[121] While there can be no doubt that earls raised armies (they no doubt provided the most substantial forces), this statute demonstrates they were responsible only for the levy from the lands of their *comitatus*, not of the whole province; other lords were responsible for the levies from the lands they themselves held immediately of the king. By the time of the promulgation of this law, the common army of

[118] Taylor, 'Common Burdens', pp. 224–34; I have, on occasion, departed from the translation given in the article. For a discussion on how this text also preserves earlier arrangements, see Dauvit Broun, 'Statehood and Lordship in "Scotland" before the Mid-Twelfth Century', *Innes Review*, vol. 66, no. 1 (2015), pp. 1–71, at pp. 62–5.
[119] For *gabhail*, see Taylor, 'Common Burdens', p. 234.   [120] My emphasis.
[121] For the earl of Fife and Culross Abbey, see note 134 of this chapter.

Scotland was organized on the basis of both earldoms and lay and ecclesiastical lordships, not by province: those who dwelt under an earl would serve in his contingent and those who dwelt in the land of a lord would serve in his, regardless of the particular province in which the lordship lay.

This law thus describes a different procedure for levying the common army from that envisaged by Barrow. Moreover, a lawsuit surviving in the cartularies of Arbroath Abbey demonstrates that the procedure as described in 1221 was in operation by 1251.[122] The case turned on the claims of one Nicholas of Inverpeffer, who accused Walter, abbot of Arbroath, of working to disinherit him from his land. It was heard in the abbot's court on 17 February 1251 (according to Lady Day dating; the text itself gives the year as 1250).[123] During the proceedings of the lawsuit, thirteen men (including one *iudex*) testified that they had seen Nicholas make suit at the court of the abbot of Arbroath. Further, they attested that Nicholas was also accustomed to perform army service (*exercitus*) and aid (*auxilium*) alongside the abbot's men, excepting the last occasion when the king (then the late Alexander II) raised an army—for his expedition to Argyll in 1249—and then 'the same Nicholas sent his men in the army with the men of the lord king from the sheriffdom (*ballia*) of Forfar'. Nicholas acted in this way because he feared the abbot was machinating against him; he thus wished to have the king act as his *defensor* in the matter and so served in the royal contingent instead of the abbot's. Whatever the particulars of this case, it demonstrates that the king's common army was being levied in 1251 according to the holdings of the great lords of the realm: by virtue of holding of (*de*) the abbot of Arbroath, and owing him suit of court, Nicholas of Inverpeffer was expected to serve in his contingent within the king's common army, although, because of his dispute with the abbot, he withdrew from him and served the king directly, thus avoiding the hefty forfeiture he—or the abbot—would otherwise have incurred.

The 1221 provisions may have been geographically limited. The text states that the legislation was enacted 'by all *iudices Scocie*', and it is probable that Scotia here excludes Galloway for it is usual in these laws to have the *iudices* of Galloway present at legislative assemblies dealing with issues concerning the province—and they were not in 1221.[124] Although there is not enough evidence to prove the rule, the common army may have been raised on the basis of lordship in Scotia alone, perhaps including Moray. The province of Carrick, after all, served in the army as a whole unit (not as separate units of lordships which would include that of the *comes*) and remained under the leadership (*duccio*) of the *comes*.[125] But the key

---

[122] *Arbroath Liber*, i, no. 250.

[123] The expedition is recorded to have occurred in 1248, which is correct according to Lady Day calendar dating. I have amended it to 1249 here. For the use of *ballia* to denote a sheriffdom, see Chapter 4, pp. 201–5.

[124] *LS*, cc. 18–19. For more on *iudices* and law-making, see Chapter 3, pp. 120–32.

[125] *RMS*, i, no. 508; see further, Hector L. MacQueen, 'The Laws of Galloway: A Preliminary Survey', in *Galloway: Land and Lordship*, ed. R. D. Oram and G. P. Stell (Edinburgh, 1991), pp. 131–43, at pp. 131–3, and Hector L. MacQueen, 'The Kin of Kennedy, "Kenkynnol" and the Common Law', in *Medieval Scotland: Crown, Lordship and Community—Essays Presented to G. W. S. Barrow*, ed.

issue is whether the legislation described an existing situation or set out new guidelines for levying the king's common army. There is only clear evidence dating in or
after Alexander II's reign to demonstrate that the common army (and its appurtenant burdens) were levied and organized according to the holdings of major landholders. The case heard at the Abbot of Arbroath's court in 1251 shows this kind
of organization to be in place. More evidence can be found. When Gilbert of
Cleish gave fifteen acres to John of Pitliver in 1252/53 to be held 'of him and his
heirs in feu and heritage', as we saw above, he commanded that 'when the common
army of the lord king should come together, John should go *with me* in his own
person and with his own horse in that army, at my expense'.[126] John, as subtenant,
served in the common army under Gilbert of Cleish, his tenurial lord and superior,
and, if he decided not to, he had to perform the service himself, presumably at his
own expense. Earls continued to raise forces from the lands of their *comitatus*:
Alexander II confirmed the *comitatus* of Fife to Donnchad's son, Mael Coluim, in
a charter dated 21 March 1225 and commanded that he 'perform the service owed
to us *de comitatu illo*'.[127] But earls may have raised this service—now confined to
their earldom—by older mechanisms which had previously operated at the level of
the entire province. This possibility will be put forward below. Even by the time
of the legislation, 'it was not decided' what penalty the earls should pay if their
thanes defaulted from the king's service.

It might therefore be thought that all this thirteenth-century evidence suggests
that the '1221' law implemented new arrangements for levying the army rather
than confirming existing ones and that, prior to its enactment, the earl/*mormaer*
was generally in charge of the levy from the province. Indeed, narrative sources
describing events before 1221 predominantly record earls leading the king's com-
mon army, although provincial lords and the king's constable are often mentioned.
Howden records Gille Críst, earl of Angus, as leading the king's army along with
Donnchad, earl of Fife, and the king's constable, Richard de Moreville, when
William was captured by Henry II's forces at Alnwick in July 1174.[128] In 1187,
Roland, lord of the province of Galloway, led the king's forces from Inverness against
Domnall mac Uilleim.[129] Most instructively, the fifteenth-century chronicler Walter
Bower reported that when William raised an army to send against Domnall mac
Uilleim's son, Gofraid, in 1211, he placed not only the earls of Atholl, Buchan, and
Mael Coluim, the son of the earl of Mar, in charge, but also Thomas of Lundie, his
doorward, who happened to be claiming the *comitatus* (meaning the 'earldom', the
landed possessions of the *comes*) of Mar along with the late earl's son.[130]

Alexander Grant and Keith J. Stringer (Edinburgh, 1993), pp. 274–96, at pp. 278–81; however, as
Carrick was a new creation of the late twelfth century, it would make sense that the whole area would
serve under its lord, who would have full responsibility for answering the levy.
[126] Printed in Barrow, 'Army of Alexander III', pp. 146–7; my emphasis.
[127] Original, NRS, RH6/29 [AII/101], discussed above, Chapter 1, pp. 47–52; see also *Lennox
Cart.*, pp. 19–20, in which cheeses are rendered to the earl for 'the common army of the lord king'.
[128] Howden, *Gesta*, i, pp. 66, 79; and *Fantosme*, ed. Johnston, lines 472–3.
[129] Howden, *Gesta*, ii, pp. 7–8.
[130] Bower, *Scotichronicon*, ed. Watt, iv, pp. 464–7; for Thomas of Lundie, see Matthew H.
Hammond, '*Hostiarii Regis Scotie*: the Durward family in the thirteenth century', in *The Exercise of*

However, charter evidence is clear that lords other than earls did have responsibility for raising their own contingents prior to the 1220s: a distinction should be made between those who were generally (but not exclusively) responsible for leading the army and those who raised it. A complex deed of Archibald, abbot of Dunfermline, drawn up between 1178 and 1198 is helpful here. The deed confirmed the land of Pinkie in Midlothian to William, son of Ingelram, and further augmented William's holdings by the gift of ten yokes of land between Pinkie and Tranent.[131] The deed continued: 'we also grant to him and his heirs the freedom of staying behind from the armies of the lord king unless the army be so common that the men of Inveresk and of the house of Monkton cannot stay behind'. It is unlikely that Abbot Archibald would have been able to grant exemption from common army service had he not been responsible for levying the men of his land when the king's need arose; indeed, the '1221' legislation provides for the possibility that men who had stayed away from the army had been given permission to do so.[132]

In an agreement confirmed *c*.2 February 1194, the bishop-elect of St Andrews and the bishop of Durham decided that all the parish churches belonging to Durham within the diocese of the bishop of St Andrews (which included part of Lothian) should be free of all exactions, including *cáin* and *coinnmed*.[133] But 'when a common aid is imposed throughout the whole bishopric of St Andrews, the Prior and convent of the church of Durham shall answer to the bishop-elect and his successors for these parish churches, as abbots and priors who hold freely within the bishopric of St Andrews do for theirs'. The parish churches within the bishopric of St Andrews thus answered through the bishop when the king imposed common aid on the whole kingdom. As parish churches were institutionally connected to the bishopric, and were not under the proprietorship of their owner, all those holding parish churches within the diocese of St Andrews had to answer the king's request for aid through the bishop. Because Durham was a bishopric outside the kingdom, a special arrangement was made for the churches in Scotland under its jurisdiction: in this case, they would answer through St Andrews, whose bishop was responsible for the aid from the other churches within his diocese and under his control. All this suggests that the army and the appurtenant burden of aid had

---

Power in Medieval Scotland, c.1200–1500 , ed. Steve Boardman and Alasdair D. Ross (Dublin, 2003), pp. 118–38, at pp. 124–5; for the dispute over Mar, see Richard D. Oram, 'Continuity, Adaptation and Integration: the Earls and Earldom of Mar, c.1150–c.1300', in *Exercise of Power*, ed. Boardman and Ross, pp. 46–66, at pp. 54–5.

[131] *Dunf. Reg.*, no. 301.

[132] Barrow stated that this deed is especially important because of 'the active part which Archibald abbot of Dunfermline took in royal government between 1178 and 1187'; *RRS*, ii, p. 57. Archibald did take an active part in royal government; in this deed, however, he was clearly acting in his capacity of abbot of Dunfermline, and we should be wary of thinking that he was acting in any direct way on behalf of the king. His deed begins with an address from 'Archibald, by God's grace abbot of the church of the Holy Trinity of Dunfermline *with all the convent of the same place*' (my emphasis) to 'all men whether cleric or lay belonging to the above church' and states that he has made the grant to William, son of Ingelram, 'with the common assent of our congregation'; *Dunf. Reg.*, no. 301.

[133] *RRS*, ii, no. 368.

been levied by tenants-in-chief and great lords, both ecclesiastical and lay, on their own holdings prior to the 1221 legislation.[134]

It is probable that a greater proportion of lay and ecclesiastical lords had begun to take responsibility for performing the king's service in Scotland in the middle decades of the twelfth century. Between 1162 and 1164, Mael Coluim IV informed Gille Críst, *mormaer* of Angus, 'M', *vicecomes* of Forfar, and 'E' (presumably Eógan), *vicecomes* of Scone, that he had granted to the abbot of Scone the right to collect *auxilia* from his own property (*pecuniae*) using his own *ministri* (officials) and commanded the *mormaer* and *vicecomites* that they were 'not [to] come into those lands to collect the aforesaid aid'.[135] The brieve assumes the *mormaer* and the king's *vicecomites* to have been accustomed to collect *auxilia* from the abbot's possessions; the command clause demonstrates emphatically that such a situation was no longer permitted and the abbot had assumed full responsibility for the collection of aid.[136] The abbot of Scone continued to have responsibility for the collection of aid from his abbey's lands well into William's reign. Another brieve in favour of Scone, issued between 1189 and 1195, commanded that no one was to retain the men of the abbot of Scone who had fled from the abbey's land because of the recent *auxilium* which had been fixed at Musselburgh; the abbot of Scone 'or his sergeands' should be able to have their men 'wherever they may find them'.[137] It is thus particularly interesting that the late 1160s was also the time when the formula *salvo servicio meo* became a standard feature in the diplomatic of royal charters giving land to lay individuals and religious institutions and confirming land given by others. Whether the introduction of *salvo servicio meo* was in some way tied to a procedural innovation, whereby lords started taking more responsibility for the levy from their own lands, cannot be proven. All it shows is that, during the third quarter of the twelfth century, the scribes of royal charters

---

[134] A brieve of Alexander II confirms that even relatively minor priories expected to have the responsibility of levying some of these burdens themselves, which complicates the expectations on St Andrews, as laid out in *RRS*, ii, no. 368. This brieve, issued on 12 November 1231, informed everyone that the monks of Culross were not to be troubled for aid, for making up forinsec service, and for their lands because the earl of Fife was responsible for the burdens, and that the person collecting aid should go to the earl with the amount. It might be thought that this brieve was a forgery, on account of the strange testing clause *teste rege ipso*—witnessed by the king himself—but see the defence of this clause in Chapter 1, note 195. The address clause ('to whom these letters should come') is, however, odd for a brieve of Alexander II, although the formula would become standard by the early fourteenth century. Even if this brieve were a concoction by the monks, it shows that they were worried about demands for aid that they were meant to answer themselves. Instead, they said it was the responsibility of the earl of Fife. This obligation should not be seen as the 'old' duty of the *mormaer* for the province of Fife but because Culross Abbey was founded by Mael Coluim, earl of Fife, and so the abbey was calling on him as their founder and patron: see NRS, GD/1/203/1 [AII/175]; partly in W. Douglas, 'Culross Abbey and Its Charters, with Notes on a Fifteenth-Century Transumpt', *PSAS*, vol. 60 (1925–26), pp. 67–94, at p. 73.
[135] *RRS*, i, no. 252; Eógan, *vicecomes* of Scone, is recorded only as 'E' in the address clause of this brieve but one Eógan, *vicecomes* of Scone, attests Mael Coluim's confirmation charter to Scone (datable 24 May 1163 x 23 May 1164), *RRS*, i, no. 243, and so was probably the 'E' of this address clause. *Vicecomes* has been left deliberately untranslated, for which, see below, pp. 109–10.
[136] An earlier example may be found, although this is less clear than the brieve of Mael Coluim IV; *CDI*, no. 158 and p. 129 for arguments for the charter's authenticity.
[137] *RRS*, ii, no. 326.

were increasingly concerned to record in writing who was (and who was not) responsible for levying common army service from their land.

The reference to the activities of the *vicecomes* in the Mael Coluim IV brieve to Scone Abbey raises another important issue: the role of royal officials in raising common burdens. It has long been assumed that sheriffs began to play as great a role in raising the common army as the earls after the introduction of the office of sheriff during David I's reign. In a recent synthesis on the role of the sheriff, Michael Brown argued that, although the sheriff's 'key role' was in judicial not military matters, contingents of the common army were nonetheless raised 'according to sheriffdom and served under local royal officials'.[138] In an article on the origins and development of the sheriff in Scotland published in 1923, C. A. Malcolm cited Clause 29 of the 1318 legislation of Robert I, and stated that the sheriff was ultimately responsible for the mustering of the common army throughout the thirteenth century.[139] Comparative evidence from Anglo-Saxon England supports Malcolm's reading, and it may well be that he was influenced by that evidence when making his deductions. It is of note that some sheriffs in late Anglo-Saxon England were, along with earls, responsible for raising and leading the *fyrd* when it was called out. The oft-cited customs of Shrewsbury, recorded in the Shropshire folios of Domesday Book, state that the sheriff was responsible for summoning the burgesses when the *fyrd* marched into Wales while those of Hereford record its sheriff as responsible for leading the free tenants of the borough again into Wales when required (although it is of note that both these were in charge of 'frontier' shires).[140] Local boroughs and later shire communities are frequently mentioned in the Anglo-Saxon Chronicle as forming distinct contingents of the king's army and fighting on his behalf.[141] But, as the role of the *mormaer* was curtailed, possibly from as early as Mael Coluim IV's reign, and as the sheriff did not have a coherent administrative unit until the 1180s, as will be argued in Chapter 4, the extent of their military responsibilities must be called into question.

It is hard to see the sheriff exercising similar levels of responsibility in Scotland to those of Anglo-Saxon England, particularly those on the Welsh borders. The legislation of Robert I is late and pertains to the war-stricken Scotland of the early fourteenth century.[142] More importantly, however, it does not say exactly what C. A. Malcolm thought it did. Sheriffs were responsible for implementing the clause (which is all about how the soldiers were to be provisioned and armed) but did so together with the 'lords of places' within their sheriffdoms, who were to ensure the same thing.[143] Indeed, it is hard to see Robert's legislation as being

---

[138] Michael Brown, *The Wars of Scotland 1214–1371* (Edinburgh, 2004), p. 96.

[139] C. A. Malcolm, 'The Origins of the Sheriff in Scotland: Its Origins and Early Development', *SHR*, vol. 20, no. 78 (1923), pp. 131–2.

[140] For the military role of the sheriff, see W. A. Morris, *The Medieval English Sheriff to 1300* (Manchester, 1927), pp. 27–8, 58–60.

[141] *ASC* A, *s.a.* 917, 1001; *ASC* C *s.a.* 1001, 1003.

[142] G. W. S. Barrow, *Robert Bruce and the Community of the Realm of Scotland*, 4th edn (Edinburgh, 2005), p. 386.

[143] *RPS*, 1318/29.

anything other than a more specific enforcement of a situation that had long been in existence: the sharing of the responsibility of the common army between the sheriffs and lords of various status. In 1251, over sixty years earlier, the sheriff was responsible for leading the 'men of the lord king of the sheriffdom of Forfar' in the case between the abbot of Arbroath and Nicholas of Inverpeffer but the men led by the sheriff were all tenants of the king's demesne.[144] Most instructively, the sheriff is nowhere to be found in the '1221' legislation: forfeitures were owed to the king and the earl if 'the thanes [of the earl] should have stayed away' and were shared between the king and the 'thane or knight' if their peasants had failed to serve. It is possible that the sheriff had a supervisory responsibility over the collection of these fines, much as he did over the collection of teind, which was primarily the responsibility of the 'thane or lord' in the bishoprics of Moray and St Andrews by the late 1180s but the responsibility of the sheriff if either of them defaulted.[145] Even if sheriffs did have this supervisory responsibility over the army levy, they evidently did not have primary responsibility for it.

The absence of sheriffs from the basic mechanisms for raising the common burdens is, however, potentially contradicted by the brieve of Mael Coluim IV to Scone, discussed above. This seems to show that sheriffs (*vicecomites*) did, at one stage, raise *auxilium* for lands outwith the king's demesne. But the *vicecomites* of Forfar and Scone referred to in the address clause should probably not be understood as 'sheriffs' in the same sense as the sheriffs who had been introduced south of the Forth and as far north as Perth in the reign of David I: the word should probably be translated in this brieve as 'thanes'.[146]

It is clear from the text of the '1221' legislation that thanes who held their land directly from the king were, along with knights, responsible for raising the king's common army in the localities. It has also long been acknowledged that the earliest sheriffdoms were centred on royal estates run by men previously, or also, known as thanes.[147] Evidence that the *vicecomites* in the brieve of Mael Coluim IV should be translated as 'thanes' is found in the Loch Leven property records, entered in the thirteenth-century cartulary of St Andrews Cathedral Priory. While these records were written in the cartulary in Latin, some of the transactions they record were considerably earlier and may well have been written originally in Gaelic. They are thus extremely problematic texts: a later scribe must have had to find equivalent Latin terms for Gaelic noblemen, heads of kindreds, and officials. The gift of King Mac Bethad of Kirkness, acquitted from the exactions of 'king and king's son, *vicecomes* and anyone else' is one of these problematic references.[148] The *vicecomes* here cannot be denoting a 'sheriff' for sheriffs were not introduced until the reign of David I and in that period they were mostly located in Scotland south of the

---

[144] *Arbroath Liber*, i, no. 250.   [145] *RRS*, ii, no. 281.

[146] For the relationship between thanes and *toísig*, see Chapter 1, pp. 59–60. A different interpretation of this address clause is favoured in Broun, 'Statehood and Lordship', pp. 62–3.

[147] Alexander Grant, 'Thanes and Thanages from the Eleventh to the Fourteenth Centuries' in *Medieval Scotland*, ed. Grant and Stringer, pp. 39–81, at p. 51.

[148] *St Andrews Liber*, p. 114; Taylor with Márkus, *PNF*, vol. 3, p. 596.

Forth.[149] So what was meant by *vicecomes* in this eleventh-century property record?[150]

A solution to this particular problem may be found by examining the so-called *Leges inter Brettos et Scotos*.[151] The first clause of *LS*, c. 21 lists the life-values of the social ranks of Scottish society with their equivalents in the kin-group. Thus, as stated in Chapter 1, a *cunte* was on the same stratum as the 'son of a king' (*Cro a un conte de Scoce u del fiz le Rei*). A thane was the equivalent of a 'son of the *mormaer*' (*Cro a un fiz a cunt ou a un thayn*). The *filius regis*, found extracting customs and burdens from the men of the vill of Kirkness in MacBethad's property record, may thus have been one and the same as the *cunte* or *mormaer*, while the *vicecomes* (literally 'sub-*mormaer*') was not a sheriff at all but a thane.[152] It is therefore just possible that the *vicecomites* of Forfar and Scone in the brieve of Mael Coluim IV were acting not in their new official capacity as sheriffs but were performing their role of extracting the common burdens of the realm alongside the *mormaer*. Indeed, that *mormaír* and *toísig* were once responsible for raising the common burdens of the realm is given added support from the evidence of the property record of the first half of the twelfth century entered in the Book of Deer, discussed in Chapter 1.[153] This recorded that Colbán, *mormaer* of Buchan, his wife, Eva, and Donnchad, son of Síthech, *toísech* of Clann Morgainn, 'extinguished all the offerings...from all burdens of that which would apply to the chief districts of *Alba* in general and on its chief churches so far as concerns four davochs'.[154] The most logical explanation of their ability to quit the lands from the common burdens of the realm is that Colbán, as *mormaer* and *toísech*, was ultimately responsible for the levy at a provincial and a local level, and Donnchad, as *toísech*, for his kin-group and local area.[155]

What we see, therefore, at some point between the mid-twelfth century and the 1221 legislation is a shift from a rather loose organization, in which *mormaer* and *toísech* were responsible for levying the army from the *mormaer*'s province to one where that levying was done on a territorial basis; the earl only raised the levy from his earldom—his *comitatus*. The exception was the *mormaer*/earl of Fife but even he exercised power over the province of Fife not as part of the general duties of earls but as a royal *maer* ('steward'). Apart from Fife, the earl was only responsible for his *comitatus*—his earldom—and the thanes who were under him; thanes who held their land directly from the king, by contrast, were solely responsible for those lands. The new landholders of the twelfth century—the new knights, the new

---

[149] Although see Taylor and Márkus, *PNF*, vol. 3, p. 596, in which this passage is translated as 'king and king's son, sheriff (*vicecomes*) and anyone else'.

[150] See also E. W. Robertson, *Scotland under Her Early Kings*, 2 vols (Edinburgh, 1862), ii, pp. 470–1.

[151] For *LBS*, see Chapter 3, pp. 123–32.   [152] *St. Andrews Liber*, p. 114.

[153] See Chapter 1, pp. 58–9.

[154] Text VI in Katherine Forsyth, Dauvit Broun, and Thomas Clancy ed., 'The Property Records: Text and Translation', in *Book of Deer*, ed. Forsyth, pp. 131–43, at pp. 140–1.

[155] For Colbán as both *mormaer* and *toísech*, see Dauvit Broun, 'The Property Records in the Book of Deer as a Source for Early Scottish Society', in *Book of Deer*, ed. Forsyth, pp. 313–60, at pp. 348–9.

abbots, and priors—were incorporated into this changing structure even if this acted against the previous existing provincial framework for the levy. This territorialization of army service gave high-status lords (both ecclesiastical and lay) sole responsibility for the obligation, which also seems to have expanded to include an extraordinary financial aid, as well as the existing burden of labour service on the king's bridges and castles. This leaves less space than might be expected to the new type of royal official to be examined in more detail in Chapter 4: the sheriff. If the sheriff was involved in the mustering of men outwith the royal demesne, he must have done so only when these territorial magnates—be they earl, bishop, knight, or thane—were unable or unwilling to fulfil their responsibilities. The thirteenth-century Scottish sheriff seems to have been responsible only for the levy from land controlled directly by the king. By the time of the 1221 enactment, it was lords who held the primary responsibility for levying the common burdens of the realm from their own lands; the sheriff seems to have been confined to the royal demesne.

CONCLUSION

This chapter has argued that the kings of Scots were well endowed with resources. Land within their kingdom was assessed fiscally, on units that may have borne different names and were named in different languages, but were still all deemed equivalent (at least from the perspective of the king). Exemption from these burdens was widely sought after and religious houses and bishoprics were sometimes but by no means always exempt from at least one obligation, if not all three. The authority of the king must have been cemented not only by his power to raise these resources but also from his authority to grant exemption from them or to transfer the obligation onto a third party. Yet aid, labour service, and army service were all extraordinary resources, demanded on occasion, not as the norm. They were for the military defence of the king's power. Kings did not retain their power by extracting aid as a regular tax: aid was an extraordinary revenue. Despite what is sometimes claimed, *cáin* and *coinnmed* did not serve the same function as the tripartite obligation of army service, aid, and labour service. Even when *cáin* was levied as a substantial tribute revenue, as it was in Galloway, there is no evidence to suggest that the king collected it on a regular basis. Within Scotia and Moray, however, *cáin* was levied as part of localized strategies of lordship and could be granted—by lords as much as the king—to third parties. Religious houses (which we know most about because they preserve most of the surviving documentation) were frequent beneficiaries of gifts of *cáin*. Both *cáin* and *coinnmed*, therefore, should, in this area, be examined as strategies of lordly exploitation, not as universal burdens received by the king from all land and people within his kingdom.

The three common obligations—of aid, labour service, and army service—were never levied exclusively or even predominantly through a network of officials. Before, roughly, the late 1160s, they were levied on a provincial basis, with *mormaír* and *toísig* particularly responsible for their performance. The type of people levying these burdens did change over the twelfth and early thirteenth centuries yet the change was not towards royal officials. Indeed, evidence presented in Chapter 4 will show that sheriff and his sheriffdom were not ubiquitous or stable enough positions and institutions to be capable of organizing and levying these obligations throughout the kingdom at this point. Instead, lords of various statuses were responsible for the land they themselves controlled: the responsibility came as a result of formalization of patterns of land tenure, which will be discussed in more detail in Chapter 3 and the conclusion to the first part of this book.

Although the earliest, unambiguous evidence for the shift from province to lordship as the basis for the levy comes from the 1220s, the crucial period for this transition seems to have begun in the third quarter of the twelfth century, and this fits well with the evidence gathered in Chapter 1. It is during the 1160s that the formula *salvo servicio meo* was introduced into the diplomatic of royal charters: service was becoming clearly attached to land lordship in the minds of scribes of royal charters and remained there throughout the thirteenth century. This situation held: no administrative infrastructure was implemented in Scotland to run underneath the heads of the lords who were responsible for levying the common army. In contrast to what has previously been thought, the sheriff was only obliged to collect common burdens from the king's lands. The sheriff is notable only by his absence in the '1221' enactment of Alexander II; the enactment was geared towards controlling and maintaining the levy from lands the king did not directly control. All this points to the conclusion that the common burdens of Scotland were not obligations performed within a kingdom-wide administrative structure but were levied instead through the structures of landholding and lordship.

Why the common burdens of the realm were levied according to lordship in the kingdom's heartlands is best answered by recalling the way in which kings maintained their power during the twelfth century. Twelfth-century kings gave their land away to cement their position. They gave their land to religious houses and bishoprics, institutions that preserved the memory of their gifts long after the particular royal gift-giver had passed away and also kept their lands 'in perpetuity' (*in perpetuum*). They gave their land to men whom they had brought with them, who joined their court later and settled and they gave and confirmed land to men and their descendents who were already in the kingdom. By the end of the twelfth century, there was little difference between 'native' and 'non-native' lords in terms of their treatment in this respect.[156] This new tenurial pattern must have prompted the beginnings of a change in the way common labour obligations were levied: there were more lords who were recorded as exercising rights over defined and discrete parcels of land both within and outwith the kingdom's heartlands, rather

---

[156] Hammond, '*Hostiarii Regis Scotie*', pp. 118–19. This point still holds despite exciting new research by Keith Stringer, showing how Norman families retained links with their holdings in Normandy for far longer than is often assumed: Keith J. Stringer, 'Aspects of the Norman Diaspora in Northern England and Southern Scotland', in *Norman Expansion: Connections, Continuities and Contrasts*, ed. Keith J. Stringer and Andrew Jotischky (Farnham, 2013), pp. 9–47.

than lords who extended their protection over people.[157] Accordingly, obligations came to be levied through territorialized lordship rather than through a looser, more personal authority over the province. This shift and its implications for the maintenance of law and order will be considered in the next chapter.

The arrangements for levying the common burdens of the realm point to a society where royal authority, although geographically extensive, did not permeate far past the *potentes* of the realm even by the beginning of the thirteenth century: only great lords had the responsibility of levying common service. In an article first written in 2007 but published in 2011, I concluded by stating that 'the lack of a stable, binding and centralising mechanism for the levying of royal obligations raises questions about how far the organisation of common burdens within the kingdom had the potential to contribute to the ultimate development of the authority of the kings of Scots'.[158] I would now revise the emphasis of this conclusion as it could be interpreted as judging this system as ineffective or as seeing the interests of kings and aristocrats as structurally opposed. Instead of seeing the lack of an administrative base as representing the failure of the king of Scots to break the hold of aristocrats on the levying of royal obligations, the use of the new tenurial pattern of lordship as the structural basis for raising extensive burdens should rather be seen as an equally effective way of levying this type of *landed* obligation as the use of an administrative structure of royal officials. It was through ecclesiastical and lay lords that the kings of Scots were able to marshal their extensive resources. Royal authority was not fragmented by the delegation of responsibility; in fact, it was maintained and made more pervasive as a result of its mediation through the *potentes* of the realm. This was in part created by the gift-giving of the twelfth century and the territorialization of aristocratic power but it was also a product of a society which had not been ruled intensively by uniform administrative units stocked by royal officials answerable to the king. How law and order were maintained in the twelfth century in the absence of such an administrative state is in part the subject of the next chapter.

---

[157] See Chapter 3, pp. 148–52, and Part 1 Conclusion, pp. 176–9, 183–7.
[158] Taylor, 'Common Burdens', p. 222.

3

Written Law and the Maintenance of
Order, 1124–1230

Perhaps surprisingly, written law has not often formed a major part of previous analyses of law and order in the kingdom of the Scots in the twelfth and early thirteenth centuries. This is because the previously recognized legal compilations attributed to kings of this period—*Assise Regis David* (*ARD*), *Assise Regis Willelmi* (*ARW*), *Statuta Regis Alexandri* (*SRA*)—have all either been shown to be later medieval fabrications or the products of the minds of the sixteenth- and nine-teenth-century lawyers who edited these texts.[1] However, just because law survives in later compilations or was reshaped by later lawyers does not mean it is worthless; it just requires more work to identify its original form. This chapter is a departure from previous scholarship because it puts the content of written law, correctly reconstructed from the manuscripts, at the forefront of its analysis of how law and order were maintained in the twelfth and thirteenth centuries.[2] The written law

---

[1] Hector L. MacQueen, 'Scots Law under Alexander III', in *Scotland in the Reign of Alexander III 1249–1286*, ed. N. H. Reid (Edinburgh, 1990), pp. 74–102; Alice Taylor, '*Leges Scocie* and the law-codes of David I, William the Lion and Alexander II', *SHR*, vol. 88, no. 226 (2009), pp. 207–88; Alice Taylor, 'The Assizes of David, king of Scots, 1124–53', *SHR*, vol. 91, no. 232 (2012), pp. 197–238; T. M. Cooper [First Baron of Culross], 'Early Scottish Statutes Revisited', in, *Selected Papers, 1922–1954* (Edinburgh, 1957), pp. 237–43, at pp. 238–9; *Regiam Majestatem and Quoniam Attachiamenta based on the text of Sir John Skene*, ed. and trans. T. M. Cooper, Stair Society 11 (Edinburgh, 1947), pp. 23–7; Bruce Webster, *Scotland from the Eleventh Century to 1603* (London, 1975), pp. 165–70; for the fourteenth-century compilation proclaiming itself to be the laws of Mael Coluim mac Cinaeda (d. 1034), see A. A. M. Duncan, 'The "Laws of Malcolm MacKenneth"', in *Medieval Scotland: Crown, Lordship and Community—Essays Presented to G. W. S. Barrow*, ed. Alexander Grant and Keith J. Stringer (Edinburgh, 1993), pp. 239–73.

[2] MacQueen's 1993 chapter on twelfth-century and early-thirteenth-century courts rarely refers to the legal material: see Hector L. MacQueen, *Common Law and Feudal Society in Medieval Scotland* (Edinburgh, 1993), pp. 33–50, 66–9. Hector L. MacQueen, 'Canon Law, Custom and Legislation in the reign of Alexander II', in *The Reign of Alexander II, 1214–49*, ed. Richard Oram (Leiden, 2005), pp. 221–51, does use the statute material but the analysis is predominantly based on the editions given in *APS*. See also Hector L. MacQueen, 'Girth: Society and the Law of Sanctuary in Scotland', in *Critical Studies in Ancient Law, Comparative Law and Legal History*, ed. John W. Cairns and O. F. Robinson (Oxford, 2001), pp. 333–52. MacQueen is also the historian who brought the existence of *Leges Scocie* to the attention of modern scholars; see MacQueen, 'Scots Law', pp. 87–93, and below, Appendix, p. 459. The historian who used the legal material the most before MacQueen is, perhaps, A. A. M. Duncan in his *Scotland: the Making of the Kingdom* (Edinburgh, 1975). Some historians, however, barely use the legal material at all. Cynthia J. Neville, *Land, Law and People in Medieval Scotland* (Edinburgh, 2010), p. 62, only uses the legal material once and here follows the editions in *APS*. Geoffrey Barrow mainly used charter material and, although he worried about the law and decided that

used as the fundamental evidence base is not from the most commonly used edition of Scottish law (volume 1 of the *Acts of the Parliaments of Scotland—APS*) but from the correct manuscript form of three major legal compilations, put together in the thirteenth and fourteenth centuries. These texts, although compiled later than any of the law they supposedly convey, contain some authentic statutes and assizes of David I, William the Lion, and Alexander II. The manuscript titles of these compilations are *Leges Scocie* (*LS*), *Statuta Regis Alexandri* (*SA*), and *Capitula Assisarum et Statutorum Domini David Regis Scotie* (*CD*).[3]

This chapter begins in 1124, which is the earliest possible date for our earliest surviving written record of a dispute settlement.[4] It concludes in 1230 when Alexander II issued four statutes at Stirling in October of that year.[5] Ending the chapter at this date is not because 1230 was a point at which lawmaking changed radically *ex nihilo*. But the 1230 legislation is the clearest and most complete representation of a change in the way lawmakers were thinking about law, order, crime, and jurisdiction, a change which had been identifiable in another type of evidence—charters—for the previous fifty years. As a result, this book has two 'law' chapters (this one and Chapter 5), which divide at the year 1230.

This chapter has two major arguments. First, twelfth-century kings started seeing themselves, rather than legal specialists, as the predominant source of law; as a result, the primary role of legal specialists in the making of written law declined and had finally ceased shortly before 1230. Second, the late twelfth and early thirteenth centuries saw another change, this time in how lawmakers (now exclusively kings with consultation) envisaged the enforcement and administration of royal law. The change during this half century or so was from a way of thinking about law and order that was based on generalized prescriptions about legal practice to one where similar sorts of prescriptions were framed within an explicit administrative and jurisdictional framework, thereby confirming the permanence of these frameworks for ordinary people's experience of government. Statements about the correct judicial forum and who wielded what jurisdictional rights were, by 1230, a fundamental and additional dimension to the abstract statements about legal practice and the righting of wrongs that had previously been the main feature of written law. As a result, law and legal procedure from 1230 look quite different from that enacted in the 1180s, with the king and his administrative judicial officials playing a much larger role in dispute settlement under Alexander II than had been the case under William. But written law looked even more different in 1230 from the vantage point of the early twelfth century, a period when I argue that legal specialists (*iudices*) still had fundamental control over the writing and the content of the law.

some of it was inauthentic, did not go beyond the texts in *APS*. See, as examples, *RRS*, ii, pp. 39–51, and G. W. S. Barrow, 'The Justiciar', in G. W. S. Barrow, *The Kingdom of the Scots: Government, Church and Society from the Eleventh to the Fourteenth Century*, 2nd edn (Edinburgh, 2003), pp. 88–92.

[3] For *ARD*, see *APS*, i, pp. 315–25; for *ARW*, see *APS*, i, pp. 369–84; for *SRA*, see *APS*, i, pp. 395–404. The only edition of *LS* is in Taylor, '*Leges Scocie*'. As stated above, if the texts do not diverge much from the *APS* text, then the *APS* reference will also be cited; otherwise the text from the manuscript compilation will be cited alone.

[4] Lawrie, *ESC*, no. 80.

[5] Their content is discussed fully below, pp. 162–4, and in Chapter 5, pp. 273–93.

Before these arguments can be made, it should be noted that using written law, a normative source, as evidence of legal practice has been increasingly problematized since the 1970s.[6] This is particularly true of most of the law examined here which, although belonging to the twelfth and early thirteenth centuries, has more in common with the written law of early medieval societies than with its common law counterparts, particularly in later twelfth- and thirteenth-century England. I therefore use early medieval here not in a chronological sense but, instead, to denote societies which produced written law but whose mechanisms for the enforcement of that law are not clear. Questions about enforcement are raised because the law-making authority is relatively weak and few other types of evidence survive to confirm that legal practice followed the prescriptive content of law in any consistent way.[7] I am not the only historian to describe societies which are not chronologically early medieval as, nonetheless, 'early medieval'; Thomas Charles-Edwards has done the same for Welsh law, a corpus of material that contains some surprising—and thus interesting—parallels with the Scottish material.[8] But 'early medieval law' has become so problematic that a group of early medieval historians based in the UK has, over the past thirty years, produced two volumes that have consciously eschewed using normative law, preferring instead the 'case' material that charter evidence can provide.[9]

I use written law here not as evidence of legal practice but as evidence of the expectations of the lawmakers, whether king-in-assembly or legal expert (*iudex*), and, accordingly, as one 'public expression of moral order'.[10] But this is more than saying that law is simply evidence of 'governing mentalities': written law is also evidence of changes in lawmaking assumptions that can themselves be evidence of not only changes in practice but also changes in the way that law could be administered

---

[6] Patrick Wormald, '*Lex Scripta* and *Verbum Regis*: Legislation and Germanic Kingship from Euric to Cnut', in *Early Medieval Kingship*, ed. P. H. Sawyer and Ian N. Wood (Leeds, 1977), pp. 105–38, reprinted and corrected in Patrick Wormald, *Legal Culture in the Early Medieval West: Law as Text, Image and Experience* (London, 1999), pp. 1–43. All citations are to the original 1977 article. Susan Reynolds, 'Medieval Law', in *The Medieval World*, ed. Peter Linehan and Janet L. Nelson (London, 2001), pp. 485–502, at pp. 486–9; Paul Dresch, 'Legalism, Anthropology and History: a View from Part of Anthropology', in *Legalism: History and Anthropology*, ed. Paul Dresch and Hannah Skoda (Oxford, 2012), pp. 1–37, at pp. 7–9.

[7] These questions are raised in Alice Rio, 'Introduction', in *Law, Custom, and Justice in Late Antiquity and the Early Middle Ages: Proceedings of the 2008 Byzantine Colloquium*, ed. Alice Rio, Centre for Hellenic Studies, King's College London (London, 2011), pp. 1–22; for a positive take on the issues raised by Wormald, see Peter Heather, 'Law and Society in the Burgundian Kingdom', in *Law, Custom and Justice*, ed. Rio, pp. 115–53, with his summary of the debate at pp. 116–17; for a view that stresses dialogue between 'central' legislative assembly and regional communities, see Levi Roach, 'Law and Legal Norms in later Anglo-Saxon England', *Historical Research*, vol. 86, no. 233 (2013), pp. 465–86; Levi Roach, *Kingship and Consent in Anglo-Saxon England, 871–978: Assemblies and the State in the Early Middle Ages* (Cambridge, 2013), pp. 109–12.

[8] T. M. Charles-Edwards, *The Welsh Laws* (Cardiff, 1989).

[9] The turn away from 'normative' law was heralded by two volumes produced by the extremely important, and anthropologically inspired, Bucknell Group; Wendy Davies and Paul Fouracre ed., *The Settlement of Disputes in Early Medieval Europe* (Cambridge, 1986); Wendy Davies and Paul Fouracre ed., *Property and Power in the Early Middle Ages* (Cambridge, 1995).

[10] The quotation is from Fernanda Pirie, *The Anthropology of Law* (Oxford, 2013), pp. 9–13, at p. 10.

and upheld.[11] Although this chapter is positing major changes to the roles the king played in the making of law over the twelfth century, the style of extant written law does not seem to have changed radically between 1180 and 1230. Thus, if the envisaged administration of law in written law itself changed during this time period, that provides strong evidence for wider changes in the ways in which kings ruled and how they expected their statutes to be administered.[12]

WRITTEN LAW AND LEGAL SPECIALISM

There are no longer any contemporary compilations of law surviving from the period 1124–1230; all are products of how later compilers organized and attributed earlier material. By 1292, the royal archives stored in Edinburgh castle did contain two rolls containing 'the laws and assizes of the kingdom of Scotland', together with laws of the burghs and 'certain statutes (*statutis*) circulated by the kings of Scots'.[13] However, none of these survives and consequently modern historians have generally neglected what twelfth-and early-thirteenth-century law there is.[14]

The first part of this section is devoted to setting out the form and content of the legal compilations used in this chapter because the current edition—that in volume 1 of *APS*—does not reflect the content of the extant manuscripts: the structure and content of the lawcodes attributed to David I, William the Lion, and Alexander II in *APS* have no manuscript authority. Yet, although no 'original' texts survive, as mentioned in the beginning of this chapter, there are three legal compilations that contain some authentic texts of royal laws of the twelfth and thirteenth centuries: *LS*, *SA*, and *CD*.[15] None of the compilations, however, is contemporary with the

---

[11] Patrick Wormald, *The Making of English Law: King Alfred to the Twelfth Century*, vol. 1: *Legislation and Its Limits* (Oxford, 1999), pp. 477–83, at p. 481: 'what [Anglo-Saxon lawcodes] were, perhaps above all, was an index of governing mentalities'.

[12] This strategy is also used in George Molyneaux, *The Formation of the English Kingdom in the Tenth Century* (Oxford, 2015), particularly chapter 4.

[13] *APS*, i, pp. 114–15, also in Chapter 7, pp. 400–17. The 1292 inventory also refers to one 'roll of statutes of Kings Mael Coluim and [gap in the manuscript]'. Innes supplied 'and King David', although there is nothing to suggest this to be the case (*APS*, i, pp. 116–17; see also Duncan, 'Laws of Malcolm MacKenneth', p. 239, note 3). 'Laws' of both Mael Coluim II and Mael Coluim III survive but the first is a compilation of the 1360s–1370s and the latter is (probably) a compilation of the mid-thirteenth century. An edition of the Laws of Malcolm MacKenneth (Mael Coluim II) can be found in *APS*, i, pp. 709–12; the laws of Mael Coluim III survive only in an unpublished version of Turgot's Life of St Margaret (Madrid, Biblioteca Real MS II 2097, fo. 11v). They survive in a mid-thirteenth-century historical compilation, probably put together at Dunfermline in Fife; for this argument, see Alice Taylor, 'Historical Writing in Twelfth- and Thirteenth-Century Scotland: the Dunfermline Compilation', *Historical Research*, vol. 83, no. 220 (2010); cf. Catherine Keene, *Saint Margaret, Queen of the Scots: A Life in Perspective* (New York, 2013); pp. 90–3, which does not acknowledge the nature of the Dunfermline compilation; for the manuscript, see *The Miracles of St Æbbe of Coldingham and St Margaret of Scotland*, ed. and trans. Robert Bartlett, Oxford Medieval Texts (Oxford, 2003), pp. xxxi–xxxiv; *Scotichronicon by Walter Bower*, 9 vols, gen. ed. D. E. R. Watt (Aberdeen and Edinburgh, 1989–1998), iii, pp. xvii–xviii.

[14] The exception is MacQueen, 'Scots Law', pp. 87–93, and see the literature cited in Note 2 of this chapter.

[15] There is another compilation attributed to King William called (rather imaginatively) *Leges Willelmi Regis* (*LW*). This has relatively the same manuscript history as *SA* and will appear in my

period of lawmaking they purportedly describe. *LS*, a twenty-one-chapter compila-tion, contains chapters dated to the period 1177–1210 but the only manuscript of the text is datable to 1267×72.[16] *SA*—the so-called statutes of Alexander II—is a compilation of twenty-nine chapters, containing nine datable laws and legal pro-nouncements of Alexander II and some enactments that should actually be attrib-uted to his father, William.[17] It is very difficult to establish a firm date for *SA*: it is probable that it was composed during the second half of the fourteenth century, although a late-thirteenth-century *terminus post quem* is possible.[18] *CD* is an early-fourteenth-century compilation, influenced by the recent legislation of Robert I, enacted at Scone in early December 1318.[19] Its chapters include some laws and enactments belonging to William and Alexander but which have been updated to suit the legal environment and language of the early fourteenth century.[20] Other chapters simply belong to the late thirteenth and early fourteenth centuries. Indeed, only one of them can be attributed to David himself while a further three can be

---

forthcoming edition. It is not used much here because most of its material is either attested in *LS* or is clearly of later date. The only possible exceptions are *LW*, cc. 10 and 11, to be discussed in Alice Taylor, *The Auld Lawes of Scotland: Compilations of Royal Laws from the Thirteenth and Fourteenth Centuries*, Stair Society (Edinburgh, forthcoming).

[16] Taylor, '*Leges Scocie*', *passim*.

[17] *SA*, cc. 12–19, 24, 27–29, are all found (with minor adjustments) in *LS* as cc. 1–19. *LS*, cc. 9–10, have been pushed into a single chapter in *SA* (c. 24). On only one occasion, *SA* preserves an earlier version of a text than *LS* (*LS*, c. 16; cf. *SA*, c. 14); on all others, there are hardly any differences between *LS* texts and *SA* ones, and those which are there are exceedingly minor (see the south of the Forth comparison between *LS*, c. 1, and *SA*, c. 12). *SA*, c. 21, is probably an enactment of William, and may have been issued at the same time as c. 20 (see note 135 of this chapter). *SA*, cc. 1–8 and 26, are all (all but one) datable to the year of enactment; *SA*, cc. 10–11, 22, 23, 25, are undated but cannot predate Alexander's reign. One long version of *SA* only contains twenty-six chapters, missing chapters 26 and 28–9; Edinburgh, NLS, MS Adv. 25.5.10, fo. 24r (only the list of rubrics remains for this version as the scribe stopped transcribing after *SA*, c. 5).

[18] The earliest manuscript of *SA* (the Bute manuscript; NLS, MS Acc. 21246) belongs to the late fourteenth century at the earliest. It is possible that Edinburgh, EUL, MS 206, is from the late four-teenth century; see *APS*, i, p. 186. It may be that the original compiler of *SA* was affected by his lexical and linguistic world, for he used the Scots word *colpdach* (meaning 'calf'), where Latin texts would give *iuvenca* (*SA*, c.11; NLS, MS Acc. 21246, fo. 144v). This use of Scots was relatively unusual in *SA*, which does also use the Latin *iuvenca*, for which see *SA*, c. 26. Scots words (including *colpdach*) were used in later fourteenth-century compilations, such as the so-called 'Laws of Malcolm MacKenneth' (*LMMK*): see Duncan, 'Laws of Malcolm MacKenneth', pp. 255–6, although Duncan comes to a different conclusion to me; and <http://www.dsl.ac.uk> (search: colpindach), although one has to ignore the first two entries in the *The Dictionary of the Scots Language* (*DSL*): the first is from *Leges Malcolmi Mackenneth*, which is dated in *DSL* to 1040 but actually is of a fourteenth-century date; the second, which is actually *SA*, c. 11, wrongly dated to 1230; otherwise, the next occurrence of the word is not until 1450. There is also similar content in *LW*, c. 5 (actually a version of *LS*, c. 15), and *LMMK*, c.10 (*APS*, i, p. 711). *LW*, c.5, is the text of an oath that magnates had to swear in 1197 not to receive and maintain wrongdoers in their own lands, on pain of losing their own courts (for which, see below, pp. 169–72). Chapter 10 of *LMMK* says much the same thing, at least as a general rule: 'no baron or earl or any other shall receive any wrongdoer within their dominion (*dominatio*) under the pain of losing their court in perpetuity'. What this shows is that the content of one chapter which found its way into the *LW* was also a concern of the compiler of the *LMMK*, working in the late 1360s/early 1370s, perhaps suggesting that *LW* and *SA* were compiled around the same time as *LMMK*, perhaps even by someone in the same circle.

[19] Taylor, 'Assizes of David', pp. 214–28. In this article, I identified three recensions of this text. All references to *CD* in this book refer to the first recension, compiled in 1318×29, if not 1318×24.

[20] Taylor, 'Assizes of David', pp. 214–23.

dated no more precisely than to the twelfth century.[21] As a result, those four chapters will be the subject of study here while the remainder of *CD* is better understood as useful for depictions of law in the reign of Robert I.

Both *LS* and *SA* thus contain chapters of authoritative date and attribution. The chapters in *LS* are datable to 1177, 1180, four to 1184, 1197, and 1210, and two belonging to (probably) the period 1185×1200.[22] In *SA*, the enactments of Alexander are datable to 1214, 1221, 1244, 1248, and four to 1230.[23] If one adds the four twelfth-century chapters from *CD*, of which only one seems to belong to David's reign, we can see a small but relatively steady production of written law from the mid-twelfth century onwards, with particular bursts in the 1180s and 1230s, when single assemblies produced multiple pronouncements.[24]

The locations of these legislative assemblies reveal a concentration at Stirling and Perth, with nearby Scone also featuring.[25] Stirling and Perth were major royal centres and burghs with Perth being the place of issue of forty-three of William's and Alexander's surviving charters combined, and Stirling being the location of ninety-nine of them.[26] Indeed, most of the law made in royal assemblies was promulgated within the limited area of the inland River Forth (with Stirling at the gateway between south and north of the river) and the inland River Tay, with Perth situated on the Tay. Dumfries and Lanark were the sites of lawmaking assemblies in the southwest but their proximity to Galloway probably determined the choice of location for both laws explicitly related only to Galloway.[27] Aberdeen was the furthest north of any of the assemblies.[28] Thus, while law could be made elsewhere, the

---

[21] *CD*, c. 28 (*ARW*, c. 26; *APS*, i, p. 379); Taylor, 'Assizes of David', pp. 223–5.

[22] Taylor, '*Leges Scocie*', pp. 210–43.

[23] The dating of *SA*, c. 1, to 1214 will be discussed in detail in Taylor, *Auld Lawes*, forthcoming, rather than here because it is not really germane in what follows. However, it may be that the law that Bower describes Alexander III enacting referred in fact to *SA*, c. 1, a law of Alexander II (Bower, *Scotichronicon*, v, pp. 422–3). There is also major confusion in the literature over which year *SA*, c. 2, was enacted. All manuscripts agree 1244 but some historians, thinking that laws use Lady Day dating for the calendar year, have dated it to *our* 1245 (see, for example, Barrow, 'Justiciar', p. 90). But, in his forthcoming edition of the *acta* of Alexander II, Keith Stringer has shown that the law should, in fact, be dated to 1244 because the year is corroborated in a charter, issued at Roxburgh, dated seven days before the statute (*Glasgow Reg.*, i, no. 186 [AII/293]), which contains a remarkably similar witness list to those who were listed in the two Latin manuscripts which do give a list of prominent attendees at the legislative assembly (**F**: BL, Additional MS 18111, fo. 149v; **G**: EUL, MS 206, fo. 89r; witnesses printed in *APS*, i, p. 403). There is no indication that Scottish laws, when they use *anno domini*, were dated according to Lady Day dating. The Roxburgh location is unsurprising, given that the statute was supposed to apply in the jurisdiction of the justiciar of Lothian, and within Lothian alone. I am extremely grateful to Keith Stringer for his help with the dating of this act. For *SA*, c. 2, see, Chapters 4 and 5, pp. 240–4, 293–4; and for the adoption of *anno domini* in statutes, see below, pp. 134–5.

[24] Two of the four *CD* chapters that must be of the twelfth century begin *si quis* (*CD*, cc. 31, 33; both printed as *ARD*, cc. 14–15, in *APS*, i, p. 320); their significance is discussed below, pp. 127–9.

[25] For Stirling, see *LS*, c. 7 [1180], *SA*, c. 3 [1248], *SA*, cc. 4–7 [1230]; for Perth, *LS*, c. 5 [*rg*. William], cc. 11–14 [1184], *LS*, c. 15 [1197], *SA*, c. 26 [1221]; for Scone, see *SA*, c. 1, and *CD*, c. 42, as well as *LW*, c. 11.

[26] These figures are drawn from the *People of Medieval Scotland* database, and were produced by searching for 'Sources', with the place-name filters and the names of each king. <http://www.poms. ac.uk/db>. Some of these charters may well have been drawn up on the same occasion.

[27] *LS*, cc. 18, 20.

[28] *LS*, c. 6. Although about Galloway, *LS*, c. 19, was made in Edinburgh, this may have been because the individual concerned was probably in custody in Edinburgh castle, for which see Taylor,

overwhelming trend was for assemblies to be held within a small area between Perth and Scone on the Tay and Stirling on the Forth. It is possible that the choice of Stirling, the symbolic (and physical) gateway between Lothian and Scotia, had a very particular purpose: to make law which would be upheld both north and south of the Forth, not in Scotia or Lothian alone.[29] We know that, by the mid-thirteenth century, Alexander II was still enacting law for individual regions of his kingdom; it is possible, then, that when a lawmaking assembly was held at Stirling, its purpose was to promulgate law to be upheld in Scotia, Moray, and Lothian.

Who made the law? The datable material in *LS* (1177–1210) shows that law was made in royal assemblies and associated with the king, as in Anglo-Saxon England.[30] The assizes were the king's assizes, even if he made it with 'the earls and barons and judges of Scotia' (*LS*, c. 5) or 'with the assent of the earls and barons' (*LS*, c. 7) or 'in the presence of all bishops, abbots, earls, barons and other worthy men of his land' (*LS*, c. 11).[31] Some manuscripts of *SA* give the names of those present at Alexander's legislative assemblies and, from them, it is clear that the generic descriptors in other legal records are not at all misleading.[32]

What, then, of legal specialism in Scotland? In twelfth- and thirteenth-century Wales, legal specialists or lawyers (Middle Welsh: *ynad*, pl. *ynaid*) not only interpreted the law but also made it, wrote it down, and compiled it.[33] In Anglo-Saxon

'*Leges Scocie*', pp. 216–18; see further, Montrose (*CD*, c. 28). Stirling also appears as the location of *CD*, c. 29, which may be broadly of late twelfth- or early thirteenth-century date.

[29] For Stirling as the symbolic gateway between north and south, see Dauvit Broun, 'Britain and the Beginnings of Scotland', Sir John Rhŷs Memorial Lecture, *Journal of the British Academy*, vol. 3 (2015), pp. 107–37, at pp. 125–6; and one of Matthew Paris's maps of Britain in BL, Cotton MS Claudius D, vi, fo. 12v, online at <http://www.bl.uk/onlinegallery/onlineex/mapsviews/mapgb/large17694.html>.

[30] *LS*, cc. 5–7, 11–15.

[31] Cf. *LS*, cc. 1–3 (*statutum est* or *dominus rex statuit*); *LS*, cc. 18–20 (*iudicatum est* or *fuit*).

[32] EUL, MS 206, fos. 88v–89r (*SA*, cc. 2 [1244]–3 [1248]); BL, Additional MS 18111, fos. 149v, 150r. Both are two fifteenth-century manuscripts which contain a text entitled *Statuta Regis Alexandri* these actually contain four chapters in one manuscript and five in the other, as opposed to the twenty-nine chapters *SA* ordinarily contained. In addition to the names found for *SA*, cc. 2–3 (enacted in 1244 and 1248 respectively), Thomson included the names of individuals who were present at the 1230 Stirling assembly in *SRA*, c. 4 (*APS*, i, p. 399). Although I have consulted the manuscripts apparently used by Thomson, I have found no Latin text of the 1230 legislation containing the names of those present. They are, however, listed in two fifteenth-century Scots manuscripts, containing Scots translations of the 1230 legislation but one is actually in the version of the 1230 legislation as attested in *CD* not in *SA* (NLS, Adv. MS 25.4.14, fo. 94v–95r, at 94v), although the other (NLS, Adv. MS 25.4.15, fo. 106r) *is* in the Alexander-compilation (for the differences between *SA* and *CD*, see Taylor, 'Assizes of David', pp. 216–21). The only conclusion is that either Thomson had viewed manuscripts which have since disappeared or he translated the names from the Scots manuscript into Latin and inserted them into his own text. The possibility that more manuscripts of early Scots law will appear in the future cannot, of course, be ruled out. However, it is of note that the Scots manuscript states that 'þe bishop of St Andrews' was present, without stating the bishop's name. In Thomson's Latin text, the bishop appears as '[W] episcopo S. Andree' (*SRA*, c.4; *APS*, i, p. 399), demonstrating that, whatever text Thomson used, the bishop's initials or name was not provided. It is thus possible that Thomson *did* use the Scots manuscripts as the basis for his Latin edition.

[33] Charles-Edwards, *Welsh Laws*, pp. 6–10, 70–1; T. M. Charles-Edwards, *Wales and the Britons, 350–1064* (Oxford, 2013), pp. 267–73. Although some are thought to be based on royal pronouncements, they are fundamentally not royal law; see Huw Pryce, *Native Law and the Church in Medieval Wales* (Oxford, 1993), p. 4: 'the Welsh lawbooks incorporate little by way of legislation; rather, they seem to consist in the main of lawyer-made law'; see further, Huw Pryce, 'Lawbooks and Literacy in Medieval Wales', *Speculum*, vol. 75, no. 1 (2000), pp. 29–67, at pp. 34–47.

England, the situation was different: bishops could be responsible for making and writing law as well as being among the 'wise men' (the *witan*) who advised the king in his lawmaking.[34] Although these bishops and abbots also served as judges, there was no sense in which they constituted a separate and self-defined group of legal specialists as in Wales.

Scotland might be thought to resemble Anglo-Saxon England more than it did twelfth- and thirteenth-century Wales in its view of legal specialism. The people who made the laws appear to have been politicians and statesmen, not lawyers. However, there were also individuals who were known in Latin as *iudices* (singular: *iudex*; Gaelic: *brithem*), a word that translates as 'judge'.[35] These judges were described as being 'learned in the law' and are found settling and presiding over cases, particularly about the boundaries of land, in the twelfth century.[36] On occasion, the legal evidence records that they also collectively 'made' the law and 'made judgements' sometimes to the exclusion of the bishops and abbots, and sometimes to the exclusion of all elite assembly-goers.[37] Thus, one chapter about waterways was made by 'the earls and barons and *iudices* of Scotia'; another was about the breach of the king's peace in Galloway and this procedure was decided on 'by the *iudices* of Galloway'. A trial of one Gillescop Mac Aedacáin, who in 1210 seems to have been engaged in some treachery against King William alongside one Thomas de Colville, was judged by the *iudices* of Scotia and Galloway.[38]

Iudices worked at a wide regional level, that of Scotia or, indeed, Galloway, but they also worked at more local levels. The Kirkness dispute, datable to 1128×36, was decided on by three *iudices* of Fife, one of whom, Caustantín, also *mormaer* of Fife, was described as a 'great judge in Scotia'.[39] One of David's charters to Dunfermline Abbey commanded that a *iudex* of Fife be present at the abbot's court.[40] There is also record of one *iudex* of Gowrie in the late twelfth century and, around the same time, one Mael Brigte appears as the king's *iudex* and attested four of William's charters, all (probably coincidentally) in the late 1180s and 1190s, just after a period of relatively intense lawmaking.[41] The spread of *iudices*, therefore,

---

[34] Ine Prol; Alf, Prol. 49.10 ('eallum minum witum þas geowde'); AGu Prol; II Ew 1; IV As Prol (*sapientes*); V As 1; II Em Prol; I Atr Prol (*Die Gesetze der Angelsachsen*, ed. F. Liebermann, 3 vols (Halle, 1903–16), i, pp. 46, 88, 126, 140, 171, 186, 216); for comment on legislative assemblies, see Roach, *Kingship and Consent*, pp. 104–21.

[35] G. W. S. Barrow, 'The judex', in Barrow, *Kingdom of the Scots*, pp. 57–67; Dauvit Broun, 'The King's *brithem* (Gaelic for "Judge") and the Recording of Dispute-Resolutions', *The Paradox of Medieval Scotland: 1093–1286*, Feature of the Month, no. 11 (April 2010), online at: <http://paradox.poms.ac.uk/feature/april10.html> (#fn13).

[36] The earliest mention of a *iudex* 'in Scotia' and *iudices* of Fife is in the Kirkness dispute, see Lawrie, *ESC*, no. 80.

[37] *Iudices* are present in LS, cc. 5, 18, 19, 20; *SA*, c. 26.

[38] LS, c. 19; for discussion about the date, see Taylor, '*Leges Scocie*', pp. 216–18. Before this, the date of 1228 was preferred: see Duncan, *Making of the Kingdom*, p. 529, note 19, on the weak basis of the 1228 attribution.

[39] Lawrie, *ESC*, no. 80.   [40] *CDI*, no. 190.

[41] *RRS*, ii, nos. 343, 454, 466, 497 (as *Bricius iudex*); *Scone Liber*, no. 21; for a *iudex* of Fife, see *St Andrews Liber*, pp. 242, 247; For a *iudex* of Buchan, see *Aberdeen Reg.*, i, pp. 14–15; for a *iudex* of Strathearn, see *Arbroath Liber*, i, no. 35, and *Inchaffray Chrs*, nos. 39, 41. For a discussion of Mael Brigte, see Broun, 'King's *brithem*', *passim*.

was across areas under differing levels of Scottish royal control: in Galloway, where the king had limited influence, but also in Scotia, where his authority ran deeper. There is no evidence of *iudices* in Lothian, where the king's authority was also strong. We should therefore question at this point how far *iudices* should be seen exclusively or even predominantly as the king's legal specialists, even in Scotia. The appearance of Mael Brigte as explicitly the *king's* judge (*iudex regis*) was a royal link that no other judge previously had.[42] The stress on Mael Brigte's position as the king's *iudex* thus suggests that, prior to this, other *iudices* were *not* exclusively the king's. Having a legal specialism which was not explicitly tied either to royal authority or to the royal person was not unusual, a point to be developed in more detail in the following paragraphs. Twelfth- and thirteenth-century Welsh judges in Deheubarth in Gwynedd were not under the direct control of the king and, although thirteenth-century kings and princes of Gwynedd gained closer links to their *ynaid* ('judges'), these judges were still autonomous when expounding the law in legal disputes.[43]

There is, however, one major problem for historians of medieval Scotland who think about *iudices*: we do not know what made a *iudex* an expert in the law. In short, what constituted their specialism? What knowledge made a *iudex* a *iudex*? We know that *iudices* were involved in pronouncing on land disputes; the Kirkness case from 1124×36 tells us as much.[44] But we do not know the nature of the knowledge that made Dubgall, for example (one of the *iudices* in Fife), so learned in the law that the other *iudices* deferred to him when making the judgment. This is a problem that historians of Welsh law, for example, never have to confront. One of the recensions of Welsh law includes within it a text known as *Llyfr Prawf Ynaid* ('The Judges' Test Book'), which contained all a trainee *ynad* (a 'judge' or legal expert) needed to know.[45] Even those versions of Welsh law which did not contain *Llyfr Prawf Ynaid* still made it clear which texts within the whole corpus of Welsh law a person needed to know before he could really call himself an *ynad* (judge). One of the Latin versions states that

> No-one ought to judge unless he knows those three which are called *tair colofn cyfraith* [the three columns of law] and the price of men and animals which are necessary in the sight of men.[46]

No one could be a judge, then, without knowledge of the lists of abetments for theft, homicide, and arson (the three columns of law), and how much men and animals were worth. But as yet we do not have any material deemed to be similar for the *iudex* in Scotia. What follows will put flesh on the *iudex* in Scotia and explain why we do not have more surviving written material about the content of legal specialism within

---

[42] Broun, 'King's *brithem*', states that 'Mael Brigte is the first known *brithem* to have been designated "king's *brithem*"'. For subsequent *iudices regis*, see the list in Barrow, 'The *judex*', pp. 61–5.

[43] Pryce, 'Lawbooks and Literacy', pp. 47–9.

[44] Lawrie, *ESC*, no. 80.

[45] Charles-Edwards, *Welsh Laws*, pp. 30–1; Pryce, 'Lawbooks and Literacy', pp. 47–65.

[46] Latin Redaction A, in *The Latin Texts of the Welsh Laws*, ed. Hywel David Emanuel (Cardiff, 1967), p. 121.

this area.[47] The argument is based on a text already mentioned in the first two chapters of this book: *Leges inter Brettos et Scotos* (*LBS*). This is a text that has generated much debate. As such, it is necessary to introduce it in some detail.

Leges Inter Brettos et Scotos: Ethnic Assimilation or Lawyers' Tractate?

The text known as *Leges inter Brettos et Scotos* (*LBS*) has long caused problems: there is no consensus about when, where, and why it was written nor are we even sure that the text *we* know as *LBS* actually circulated under this name in the twelfth and thirteenth centuries.[48] Some historians think that it was a text compiled in the eleventh century to bring together two linguistically separate peoples—the Britons of Strathclyde and the Scots of *Alba*—following the partial absorption of Strathclyde into the king of Scots' authority.[49] Earlier historians thought that it was a compilation made under the authority of David I to unify Lothian and Scotia, rather than Scotia and Strathclyde, or placed it in a rough period of 'Danish influence' in southern Scotland, based on its use of 16d-ore as a unit of calculation.[50] All of these differing views are the result of the emphasis placed on the presence of seemingly Gaelic and Britonnic technical terms in the text itself and the units of English or Danish calculation within it. These issues are, although significant, less important to understanding the text than the way it appears in its manuscripts. This is what I will concentrate on here, although the whole question about the nature of *LBS* will be developed at greater length elsewhere.[51]

As a starting point, it is rarely acknowledged that there are two versions of '*LBS*', which belong to separate textual traditions.[52] Moreover, there is textual development

[47] These arguments will be set out in more detail in a forthcoming article; Alice Taylor, 'Was *Leges inter Brettos et Scotos* really an eleventh-century lawcode held among the Britons of Strathclyde and the Scots of *Alba*?', forthcoming.

[48] See, most recently, Alex Woolf, *From Pictland to Alba, 789–1070* (Edinburgh, 2007), p. 346.

[49] Kenneth Jackson, 'The Britons in Southern Scotland', *Antiquity*, vol. 29, no. 114 (1955), pp. 77–88, at p. 88. A. A. M. Duncan is normally cited as a historian who agreed with this line but I can see nothing explicit in *The Making of the Kingdom*. He did note that the presence of 16d-ore in the first clause indicated an 'eleventh-century origin'; Duncan, *Making of the Kingdom*, p. 107, note 10. For the view that the text would have had particular relevance in Galloway, see G. W. S. Barrow, *Robert Bruce and the Community of the Realm of Scotland*, 4th edn (Edinburgh, 2005), pp. 176–7, discussed in Hector L. MacQueen, 'The Laws of Galloway: A Preliminary Survey', in *Galloway: Land and Lordship*, ed. R. D. Oram and G. P. Stell (Edinburgh, 1991), pp. 131–43, at pp. 135–6, with a verdict of 'Not Proven' (p. 136) for a Galwegian origin. The fate of Strathclyde has been re-examined in Dauvit Broun, 'The Welsh Identity of the Kingdom of Strathclyde *c.* 900–*c.* 1200', *Innes Review*, vol. 55, no. 2 (2004), pp. 111–80.

[50] W. F. Skene, *Celtic Scotland: A History of Ancient Alban*, 3 vols. (Edinburgh, 1886–90), iii, p. 217, argued that it belonged to early in David's reign as king of Scots, where he sought to unify the 'Britons of Strathclyde', whom he had ruled as prince of the Cumbrians, and the Scots north of the Forth and Clyde. For its placing in a period when there was a 'Danish connection', see Frederic Seebohm, *Tribal Custom in Anglo-Saxon Law* (London, 1902), pp. 307–18, at p. 315; for the view that it was adopted south of the Forth under Mael Coluim III's sons (and so pertained to Lothian as well), see E. W. Robertson, *Scotland under Her Early Kings*, 2 vols (Edinburgh, 1862), ii, pp. 305–6. For the deficiencies in the *LS*-text, see F. W. L. Thomas, 'Proposed Correction of the text of *Leges inter Brettos et Scottos*', *PSAS*, vol. 19 (1884–85), pp. 73–4.

[51] In particular, the linguistic element will be brought out in more detail in the forthcoming article: Taylor, '*Leges inter Brettos et Scotos*', forthcoming.

[52] This is despite all three texts appearing in *APS*, i, pp. 663–5; Seebohm, *Tribal Custom*, pp. 307–14.

within the second version. The first, and earlier, version is written in French and contains five clauses. It survives in only one manuscript: as the last chapter of *LS*, the only chapter in that compilation to be written predominantly in French.[53] The five clauses of *LBS* in *LS*, c. 21, are as follows. The first details the *cró* (life-value) of each of the ranks of Scottish society, and was discussed in Chapter 1.[54] Life-values are calculated in cows and 16d-ore. This clause is the only one in *LS*, c. 21, to contain any monetary values in addition to those in kine. The second clause lists the compensation owed to a peace-holder if someone within his peace was killed. The ranks of the peace-holder are the same as those given in clause 1 (king, *mormaer*, thane, *ógtigern*, peasant), except that peasants, unsurprisingly, are not peace-holding ranks and so do not appear in this second clause. In addition, we learn of a payment known as *gelthach*, which is equivalent to another word (*kelchin*), appearing for the first time in clause 2. Both *gelthach* and *kelchin* appear to have denoted a payment compensating for insult, equivalent to *sarhaed* and *enech* found in Welsh and Irish law respectively.[55] The third clause contains information about how much a person had to pay another if they spilt their blood either below or above the neck, again according to rank. The last two are concerned with death in battle: how was a lord to be compensated for the loss of his man in battle or if his man was homicidally killed on campaign within and outwith the kingdom? Whereas the first three clauses concentrate on rank and compensation to kin, the last two emphasize lordship, and what compensation is owed to lords, although the same payments (*cró, galanas, kelchin*) apply to both lordship and kinship.

The second version of *LBS* survives in the early-fourteenth-century legal treatise, *Regiam Majestatem* (*RM*).[56] There is still much more work to do on this text, but it is generally agreed that it was compiled in the early fourteenth century under Robert I as part of a legal propaganda effort that was going on under his kingship.[57] The two main sources of the work were the English legal tractate known as

---

[53] *LS*, c. 21. The commentary in Taylor, '*Leges Scocie*', pp. 237–43, is superseded by the following discussion.

[54] See Chapter 1, pp. 38–9, 56–7.

[55] This link has been suggested before: see Seebohm, *Tribal Custom*, p. 314, and also the rebuttal of Sir John Skene's view in Jenny Wormald, 'Bloodfeud, Kindred and Government in Early Modern Scotland', *Past & Present*, no. 87 (1980), pp. 54–97, at pp. 61–2. I have previously suggested that it might denote a protection payment (Alice Taylor, '*Homo Ligius* and Unfreedom in Medieval Scotland', in *New Perspectives on Medieval Scotland, 1093–1286*, ed. Matthew Hammond (Woodbridge, 2013), 85–116, at pp. 97–8, note 61) but am now far less sure about this, owing to the analysis of protection payments in *LBS*, discussed below, pp. 147–52, and in Alice Taylor, 'Crime without Punishment: Medieval Scottish Law in Comparative Perspective', *ANS*, 35 (2013), pp. 287–304, at pp. 296–9.

[56] Interestingly, although it has long gone under the name *Regiam Majestatem* (its opening two words), the treatise as a whole is attributed to David, and, in most manuscripts, often ends with the words *expliciunt constitutiones regis David*—here end the constitutions of King David, that is, David I, who ruled from 1124 to 1153 (see, for example, BL, Additional MS 18111, fo. 76v, known as the manuscript that preserves the earliest form of *RM* ever since 1961, for which, see in A. A. M. Duncan, '*Regiam Majestatem*: a Reconsideration' *Juridical Review*, new series, vol. 6 (1961), pp. 199–217, at pp. 199–202).

[57] Alan Harding, '*Regiam Majestatem* among Medieval Lawbooks', *Juridical Review*, new series, vol. 29 (1984), pp. 97–111, at pp. 110–11; Duncan, '*Regiam Majestatem*', pp. 210–17; Taylor, 'Assizes of David', pp. 236–8.

Glanvill (1187×89) and the Romano-canonical *Summa* of Goffredus de Trano (d.1245), composed in the early 1240s.[58] Other parts of *Regiam* were taken from existing Scottish law.[59]

RM itself is divided into four books but the text did not remain stable across its manuscript witnesses; the oldest manuscript is of the late fourteenth century at the earliest.[60] Instead, *RM* grew, both in the number of chapters and in the sophistication of the legal language within it, particularly in those chapters that are late-twelfth- and early-thirteenth-century enactments by Scottish kings.[61] Thus, although much more work remains to be done, it can still be understood at this stage that *RM* was a live text, which grew and was updated in what appear to be relatively stable recensions.

In the earliest manuscripts of *RM*, *LBS* appears as the last four chapters of book 4, that is, the last four chapters of the entire treatise. These chapters are: first, the clause on *cró*; second, breach of peace; third, *kelchin*;[62] fourth, blood spilt above and below the neck. All of these four clauses appear in the French *LS*-text, although *RM* has divided clause 2 in *LS* into two (clauses 2 *and 3* in *RM*). It might therefore be thought that we should not be concerned with the much later *RM*-tradition and concentrate instead on the earlier French text. However, such an approach would be unjustified. These *RM*-texts often contain better versions of the clauses than those preserved in *LS*. If we look carefully at clause 2 of *LS*, c. 21, and chapters 2 and 3 of *RM*, we can see that the scribe of *LS* has erred and made some slips of the eye when transcribing his text.[63] As a result of these superior readings, we cannot ignore the *RM*-texts.

Moreover, as *RM* developed, more chapters were added to the *LBS*-section at the end of the tractate. The next group of *RM*-manuscripts, of which the earliest dates from the 1430s, have one chapter not present either in *LS* or in the earliest

---

[58] For the use of Goffredus Tranensis, see Peter Stein, 'The source of the Romano-canonical part of *Regiam Majestatem*', *SHR*, vol. 48, no. 146 (1969), pp. 107–23. For the long association of David I with *Regiam* (and thus the assumption that *Glanvill* must have borrowed from *Regiam*, not the other way around), see Hector L. MacQueen, '*Glanvill* Resarcinate: Sir John Skene and *Regiam Majestatem*', in *The Renaissance in Scotland: Studies in Literature, Religion, History and Culture offered to John Durkan*, ed. A.A. MacDonald, Michael Lynch and Ian B. Cowan (Leiden, 1994), pp. 385–403.

[59] Duncan, '*Regiam Majestatem*', pp. 206–10.

[60] Edinburgh, NLS, MS Acc. 21246.

[61] I argued in an article published in 2012 that *CD* updated earlier twelfth- and thirteenth-century material to better suit fourteenth-century technical legal language. The earliest manuscripts of *RM* do not contain these updated early statutes but the later ones *do*; see, for examples, Taylor, 'Assizes of David', pp. 236–7, and notes 251, 252.

[62] The word *gelthach* does not appear in any Latin text of *RM*; instead, *kelchin* is always used; see the edition in *APS*, i, pp. 663–5.

[63] If we take BL, Additional MS 18111 (elsewhere called **F**) as our base text, we can see that it contains *better* readings than *LS*, c.21, despite being a far younger manuscript. Thus, *LS*, c. 21, states that, 'if a man is killed in the peace of the son of a thane, he pays him 26 cows'. Now, a particularly sharp-eyed person, who had looked at the relative values of the legal ranks in *LBS* would pull up at this, because 26 cows is far lower than it should be, given that the peace of a thane was valued at 60 cows, and the life-value of a thane's son was only a third lower than his father. **F**, by contrast, gives this reading: 'item, if a man is killed in the peace of a son of a thane, he should pay him 40 cows; if a man is killed in the peace of a thane's kinsman, 26 ⅔ cows pertain to him' (**F**, fo. 75v; also confirmed in the Cromertie manuscript (**H**): NLS, MS Adv. 25.5.10, fo. 73v).

manuscripts of *RM*, which is concerned with the merchets of women.[64] It appears before the chapter on *cró* and contains the same ranking system as that in the *LBS*-material in both *LS* and *RM*. So, we learn that the merchets of *mulieres*, (previously) married women, regardless of status, would consist of a calf or three shillings. But the merchet of a free woman's daughter would be one cow or six shillings.[65] If the woman were a daughter of a thane or an *ógtigern*, the merchet was set at two cows; if a daughter of a *mormaer* or a queen, twelve cows.[66] The relative values of merchets between the ranks are slightly problematic but what is important here is that not only are the ultimate ranks the same (*ógtigern*, thane, *mormaer*, queen (instead of king)) but the way they are written is also the same: *ógtigern* has been moved across into Latin without an attempt at translation; *thanus* has been transliterated; while *mormaer* and queen have been fully translated as *comes* and *regina*.

Finally, the last group of manuscripts of *RM* contain one further chapter in their '*LBS*' sections, still placed towards the end of the tractate.[67] The earliest manuscript to contain this second additional chapter is dated to 1488 but the group of manuscripts as a whole (which are all related) seem to date from an archetype that cannot predate 18 February 1370.[68] All these manuscripts also contain the chapter on merchets, again preceding the chapter on *cró*, but have an additional one, entitled in some manuscripts 'on compensating injuries and blows', which is an injury tariff list.[69] These tariffs cover loss of feet, teeth, wounds less than an inch, blows under the ear, wounds in the face, wounds under the clothes, all of which are standard subjects of compensation lists in general, including those we see in Old English laws from Æthelberht and Alfred onwards.[70] It is interesting to note that the amount to be paid for loss of life is 180 cows, the same amount for the breach of the king's peace set out elsewhere in *LBS*.[71] It is clear the injury tariff uses a 16d-ore as a unit of calculation as had the first clause of the *LBS*-material in both *LS* and *RM*, denoting a relationship between the clause on *cró* and this additional chapter.[72] The textual history of *LBS* is displayed in Table 3.1.

---

[64] See, for example, NLS, MS Adv. 25.5.10 (H), fo. 73v. This chapter is present in both Cooper's (drawing on Sir John Skene's) edition as well as Thomas Thomson's (see *Regiam Majestatem*, ed. Cooper, pp. 273–4, and ed. Thomson, *APS*, i, p. 640). It does not, however, appear in either BL, Additional MS 18111 (F), or NLS, Acc. 21246.

[65] The valuation in cows is different to the valuation in *LS*, c. 21, clause 1, where a cow was worth four shillings. This may mean that the text as it stands may have been updated to suit later conditions.

[66] The reference to *regina*, rather than *rex*, is strange, and may be a corruption of the text. All other women are described as 'daughter of' a male social rank.

[67] NLS, MS Adv. 25.5.6 (K), fo. 81r–v; BL, Harley MS 4700 (P), fo. 81r–v.

[68] Taylor, 'Assizes of David', pp. 213–14.

[69] This chapter did also develop across all its manuscript witnesses, so it was not stable. That it did, however, belong to the '*LBS*' chapter 'on the spilling of blood' (or, at the very least, circulated along with it or was linked with it in the later Middle Ages) is indicated by the earlier manuscripts of *RM* of this later recension, which end the chapter stating 'the rest [of this chapter] may be sought in the nearest rubric above, on the spilling of blood'; NLS Adv. MS 25.5.6 (K), fos. 81r–v; BL, Harley MS 4700 (P), fos. 81r–v (they are actually on the same folio numbers).

[70] Ab 33–72; Af 44–77; both printed in Liebermann, *Gesetze*, i, pp. 5–7, 78–89.

[71] K, fo. 81r.

[72] Falling as the result of a blow from a staff is valued at 16d; breaking bones was valued at 2 ore (32d).

Table 3.1. '*LBS*' chapters in *Leges Scocie* and *Regiam Majestatem*

LS, c. 21	RM—redaction 1	RM—redaction 2	RM—redaction 3
		merchets	merchets
Cró [life-value]	*Cró* [life-value]	*Cró* [life-value]	*Cró* [life-value]
Breach of peace and kelchin/gelthach	Breach of peace	Breach of peace	Breach of peace
	Kelchin	*Kelchin*	*Kelchin*
Blood spilt above and below the neck	Blood spilt above and below the neck	Blood spilt above and below the neck	Blood spilt above and below the neck
Loss of man in battle			
Loss of man while on campaign			
			Injury tariffs

What this suggests, therefore, is that *all* these chapters, spread across *LS* and the *RM*-tradition, belonged to a similar corpus of texts. However, this corpus of texts was not stable but was live and disparate: some of its chapters were preserved only in *LS*; others were preserved only in later recensions of *RM*. *RM* sometimes preserves better versions of the material it shares with *LS*, despite *LS* surviving in an earlier manuscript. The complicated and diverse textual history of *LBS* therefore demonstrates that its chapters were once widely circulated, even if this circulation can only be glimpsed from much later texts whose scribes either were not always interested in, or had available, all seven chapters which have been identified thus far as once having belonged to the same original corpus of material.

But why does it matter if this *LBS*-material did indeed belong to a larger corpus of material, which had a wider circulation than once thought?[73] In order to answer this question, it is important to establish that these chapters were not the only written material from Scotland in the central Middle Ages to show interest in compensation payments and the socio-legal ranks which would and should receive them. Indeed, there is a small but steady amount of evidence which reveals continued interest in the topics covered by *LBS*-chapters.[74] First, *CD* preserves two enactments which, although they cannot be securely attributed to David I himself, must belong to the twelfth century.[75] Both show interest in the subject of clauses 1 and 2 in the *LS* and *RM*-versions.

---

[73] It should be clear here that I disagree with Geoffrey Barrow's suspicion that 'we may have been slightly mesmerized by the tidy arithmetic of the wergild tables, which in any case come to us from tracts, often antiquarian in flavour, composed by ecclesiastics keener to display their legal lore than their knowledge of the real world'; G. W. S. Barrow, 'Pre-feudal Scotland: Shires and Thanes', in Barrow, *Kingdom of the Scots*, pp. 7–56, at p. 17. Conversely, it is clear that, even as the process of lawmaking changed, there was real engagement with the ranks and systems described in *LBS*; see below, pp. 128–32.

[74] There is also some material from the early fourteenth century which shows well that the concepts described in *LBS* were not forgotten, even after the changes which this chapter outlines had taken place. See the reference to *enach* in *RM* (BL Additional MS 18111 (F), fo. 22r; *RM*, bk II, c. 9, in *APS*, i, p. 608; *Regiam Majestatem*, ed. Cooper, p. 114); and compensation in *Scottish Formularies*, ed. A. A. M. Duncan, Stair Society 58 (Edinburgh, 2011), A76, p. 33.

[75] *CD*, cc. 31, 33; Taylor, 'Assizes of David', p. 223, note 157. *CD*, c. 31 (*APS*, i, p. 320), is discussed in MacQueen, 'Girth', pp. 334–6.

One chapter in *CD* is concerned with violence in the king's hall: if anyone draws a knife in the king's court and spills blood, he shall lose his hand.[76] If the victim was killed, the king should receive 180 cows and a calf and the perpetrator should make peace with the kin of the dead man and with the king 'following the assize of the kingdom of Scotia'. The other *CD*-chapter is on breach of peace—either sanctuary or anywhere where the king's peace or the peace of a lord has been given.[77] Compensation payments are allocated, with the king generally getting a higher payment for breach of his peace (again, 180 cows and a calf) than the victim, who was compensated according to the 'assize of the land'. It could be that, because we do not hear about any payments going to anyone apart from the king, despite references to lords' peaces, this is just a fragment of a much longer text. It could equally be that once the ratios of kingly fine and victim/kin compensation had been set out, it was expected that lower grades of peace could be worked out accordingly. Both are possible but what is significant in this context is that the amount for the king's peace is the same (with the exception of the added calf) in both *CD*-chapters as that given for homicidally breaking the king's peace in the text known as *LBS*. Moreover, both refer to compensation for loss of life which went to the dead man's kin from the slayer and, presumably, the slayer's kin, which can only refer to the type of *cró* payments we again find in *LBS*.

Finally, there is a sense that the area over which the ranking was thought to apply was limited to Scotia: not the medieval kingdom of the Scots, meaning all the area under the king's authority, but *Scotia*, the area between the Forth and River Spey (or, just possibly, greater Scotia, which encompassed Moray as well). We know this because of the statute of Alexander II, enacted in 1221 and discussed in Chapter 2, which listed the fines for failure to turn up and serve in the king's army.[78] It lists the amount of the fines owed from thanes, *ógtigerna*, and peasants: for peasants, one cow and one sheep, which appears on numerous occasions elsewhere; for *ógtigerna*, six shillings or fifteen sheep; and for thanes, six cows and a calf.[79] These are three of the ranks that we find in *LBS*. The *mormaer* and king are missing because they were often responsible for collecting the fines.[80] More important, however, is that this law was enacted *not* by the king with the consent of bishops, abbots, earls, barons, and knights, as was usual in dated enactments, but, at Perth, by 'all the *iudices* of Scotia *in the presence of the lord king*', denoting that the statute was determined by the legal experts of Scotia, and strongly suggesting that this was a ranking system and a way of fining that only applied, even in 1221, in Scotia, not the whole of the Scottish kingdom. Indeed, we do find that other areas of the kingdom had different ways of levying army-service.[81]

---

[76] *CD*, c. 33; printed (with no real differences) in *APS*, i, p. 320.

[77] *CD*, c. 31; printed (with no real differences) in *APS*, i, p. 320.

[78] See Chapter 2, pp. 102–4; and the full edition in Alice Taylor, 'Common Burdens in the *Regnum Scottorum*: the Evidence of Charter Diplomatic', in *The Reality Behind Charter Diplomatic: Studies by Dauvit Broun, John Reuben Davies, Richard Sharpe and Alice Taylor*, ed. Dauvit Broun (Glasgow, 2011), pp. 166–234, at pp. 224–34.

[79] For fines of one cow and one sheep for small offences (e.g. *birthinsake*), see *LS*, c. 8; for its levy on peasants, see *Dunf. Reg.*, no. 322, *RRS*, ii, no. 281.

[80] See Chapter 2, pp. 103–4.   [81] See Chapter 2, pp. 104–5.

Thus, far from being a relic from the eleventh century (or even earlier), other legal evidence suggests that the socio-legal ranks and concepts found in *LBS* were actively engaged with in the twelfth and early thirteenth centuries. Moreover, the geographical base for these ranks and concepts appears to have been Scotia, the very area where *mormair* (earls) and *toísig* (thanes) were attested and where we know there were also *iudices*. This begs the question: did these various chapters on compensation, injury tariffs, breach of peace, life-values, compensation for army-service, women and marriage payments, which are spread across a much later and very complicated French and Latin written tradition, constitute part of the legal specialism of the twelfth-century *iudex* in Scotia in the same way that parts of *Cyfraith Hywel* did for the thirteenth-century Welsh *ynad*?[82]

First, it has to be acknowledged that there is no direct evidence for formulating this hypothesis. If there were, then the question would have already been asked and the potential link between *LBS* and *iudices* would already have been identified. But there is, now, enough circumstantial evidence to warrant asking the question, namely the continued interest in the subjects of *LBS* in the twelfth and thirteenth centuries, the geographical focus on Scotia, and the diverse manuscript evidence. Taken together, they suggest that no single authority had control over the ultimate form of the texts, a situation in essence similar to that of Welsh law. No single manuscript of Welsh law—written in Welsh or Latin—is completely identical to another, even within the same redaction, because such manuscripts were written by lawyers for lawyers who each made partial adjustments to their texts.[83]

In order to support the possibility of a link between the *LBS*-material and legal specialism, one further point must be demonstrated. The two chapters from *CD* dealing with violence in the king's hall and breach of peace present the lists of compensation owed to kin as *assizes*—either of the kingdom or of the land.[84] They therefore conceptualize these lists of compensations as royal assizes. The word *assisa* appears to have been introduced in the late 1170s into Scottish Latin law to mean a particularly *royal* form of lawmaking, borrowed from the use of the word 'assize' under Henry II (where law was enacted at royal assemblies, some of which, such as Northampton in 1176 and the Assize of Arms in 1181, were attended by William the Lion, king of Scots).[85] All the datable pieces of law in *LS* are, indeed, called either an 'assize' or, where appropriate, 'assizes' and were made by the king in assemblies.[86] To call the list of life-values (*cró*) an assize, as the *CD*-chapters did, was thus to associate them explicitly with a particularly *royal* form of lawmaking.[87]

---

[82] Not that all *ynaid* took their authority from the same source; see Pryce, 'Lawbooks and Literacy', pp. 43–7.
[83] Pryce, 'Lawbooks and literacy', pp. 41–54.
[84] *CD*, cc. 31, 33. In a (?) late thirteenth-century brieve formula, surviving in a fourteenth-century brieve collection (1323×29), compensation payments demanded on the death of a kin-member from the slayer and his kin were called a *consuetudo*; see *Scottish Formularies*, ed. Duncan, A76, p. 33. This brieve collection, known as the 'Ayr collection', is examined in Chapter 5, pp. 301–7.
[85] See below, p. 171.
[86] *LS*, cc. 5–7, 11–14; also *RRS*, ii, nos. 281, 406.
[87] By the time of *RM*, the *LBS* chapters are presented as royal *enactments*. The first clause begins with the phrase *Statuit dominus rex* (*RM*, bk IV, c. 55, ed. Thomson, in *APS*, i, p. 640).

Given the manifest effort to present rules that look similar to those in the *LBS*-material as 'assizes' or royal laws, what do we know about the relationship between kings and *iudices* during the twelfth century? There is evidence that during the reigns of David I and William the Lion (which covers almost the entire twelfth century), kings were trying to link *iudices* more with their own authority than they had previously; that is, kings were trying to create a more formal link between legal expertise itself and their own royal authority.

Only one chapter of *CD* can be confidently attributed to David I.[88] This was enacted by the king at Montrose, and stated that the king had laid down that every *iudex* of each province of Scotia had to come to him when he entered their particular province. If they did not, they would be fined a large sum of eight cows, which, it should be noted, was larger than that owed by thanes if they failed to answer the summons to serve in the king's army. By fining them a large amount, David was acknowledging the high status of *iudices*. Moreover, the enactment was framed as something new: *iudices* were now expected to attend on the king when he came into their province, which suggests that this had not previously been an expectation and, even if it had been an expectation, there were now punitive consequences for not meeting it.[89]

There were also changes to *iudices* under the long reign of his grandson, William, which were mentioned earlier. During the 1180s, a *iudex* appears as a witness to William's charters with a previously unattested title: *iudex regis*—the king's *iudex*.[90] There is no previous record of any figure with this title. This *iudex regis* appears to have been given administrative responsibility for land perambulations under two royal justices, then operating in Scotia, in the late twelfth century.[91] That is, the king's *iudex* was not only a legal expert whose relationship with the king was stressed above his provincial or regional attachment but he was also acting under the new judicial official of the second half of the twelfth century—the royal justice.[92]

The twelfth century, then, when viewed as a whole, shows changes in the relationship between legal experts and the king, by which the king was trying to bring their expertise more firmly under the banner of his own authority. This may explain why and how chapters which look like *LBS* were called 'assizes' and, indeed, what

---

[88] *CD*, c. 28 (printed *ARW*, c. 26, in *APS*, i, p. 379, among the assizes of William). For arguments for its placing in David's reign, see Taylor, 'Assizes of David', pp. 223–5; for another interpretation see Barrow, 'The *judex*', pp. 59.

[89] See also *CDI*, no. 190, commanding the presence of his *iudex* (*iudex meus*) of Fife at the court of the Abbot of Dunfermline, when the abbot's men of Newburn pled there.

[90] For Mael Brigte, see Broun, 'King's *brithem*', *passim*. For the only Latin document in Mael Brigte's name, see the edition in Barrow, 'The *judex*', pp. 66–7.

[91] These royal justices were Gille Brigte, earl of Strathearn, and Matthew, bishop of Aberdeen (see Gille Brigte's letter edited in Barrow, 'The *judex*', p. 66), who, in Barrow's edition, were denoted as *justiciarii*. It is, however, possible that, because this survives in a cartulary whose scribe enjoyed expanding abbreviated words, that what was written in the original was *iust'*, which could easily be expanded as a *singular* royal justice, referring to Gille Brigte, earl of Strathearn alone. This would make sense as justices were, in general, laymen rather than church men.

[92] For the justification for calling justices, 'justices', rather than 'justiciars', see Chapter 4, pp. 213–16.

made them find a place among texts which were collectively called *LS*—laws of Scotland, for sure, but predominantly a collection of individual *royal laws*, made at royal assemblies. We do not need to see this process as one of conflict between king and *iudices*—kings and legal experts always needed each other's authority—but the *iudex's* positions as the transmitter of written law and its predominant practitioner were slowly being subsumed under the king's authority.[93]

This also can be linked to changes in the way law was made, which may itself explain the diverse and diffuse manuscript history of the chapters that have been known to us as *LBS*. If the chapters I have identified did indeed make up part of the content of what it meant to be a legal specialist, then it seems as if kings were trying to become the main source of lawmaking, which had previously lain pre-dominantly in the figure of the *iudex*, not the king.

If all this is deemed plausible, then a new scenario can emerge. The known chapters of *LBS*—along with, presumably, some more—would have circulated primarily among legal specialists. Written (or indeed oral) law would have been, as in Wales, for the lawyer to know and to make, not, fundamentally, the king. But kings of the twelfth century, particularly William the Lion, seem to have had a different view of how law should be made: it should be made by kings in royal assemblies, in a similar way to that of Henry II in England but also, and perhaps more importantly, to that of Anglo-Saxon kings since the early tenth century, at the latest.[94] This new way of making law eventually caused the eclipse of the *iudex* as the main source of law, although this took a long time to happen, and there were periods when *iudices* are recorded as making law at royal assemblies. But these assembly appearances were focused: during the reign of William the Lion and early in the reign of Alexander II, *iudices* made law in assemblies to the exclusion of the king or any other magnate but only about particular topics: the track of water, army service, older forms of tribute (*cáin*), and when judging individuals.[95] On other subjects, such as the courts of lords, and shrieval and justice courts, they were not even recorded as those who made the law; their legal expertise was deemed unnecessary to invoke when this type of statutory innovation was being made.[96] In these circumstances, *iudices* were

---

[93] The testimony of *The Chronicle of the Kings of Alba* states that 'in his [Domnall mac Aílpín] time, the unwritten and written laws (*iura et legis*—sic, for *leges*) of the kingdom [or kingship] of Áed mac Echdach were given (*fecerunt*) to the Gaels by [or with] their king at Forteviot' in no way contradicts this statement (I should say here that I am not attached to the translation of *iura et leges* as 'unwritten and written laws' but it is a conceivable translation.); see Benjamin Hudson, 'The "Scottish Chronicle"', *SHR*, vol. 77, no. 204 (1998), pp. 129–161, at p. 148. Kings and *iudices* were not structurally opposed; certainly the authority of Hywel Dda was invoked even in the Welsh case. The point is, who really had responsibility for transmitting and making law? I argue here that there was a transition from law-yer-made law (where reform, even if present, was not explicit) to king-in-assembly-made law, where active and explicit change was the point of lawmaking. For the identification of customary *æ* in the Anglo-Saxon kingdoms, and the role of *deman* in preserving it in seventh-century Kent and Wessex, see Tom Lambert, *Law and Order in Anglo-Saxon England* (forthcoming), chapter 2.

[94] Even the so-called 'unofficial lawcodes', such as III and VI Æthelstan, and perhaps IV Æthelstan, were made through assemblies of *witan* or *sapientes*, which had a broader meaning than 'legal expert'; see Molyneaux, *Formation*, p. 55. For these codes (and for the position that IV Æthelstan was a 'response'), see Roach, 'Law and Legal Norms', *passim*.

[95] *LS*, cc. 5, 19–20 (about Galloway); see also *SA*, c. 26, discussed in Chapter 2, pp. 102–4.

[96] *LS*, cc. 7, 14–15.

not listed as present at the assembly, even when the assembly was held within Scotia. The last occasion when we know that multiple *iudices* were the main lawmakers was in 1221, on fines for default of army-service, an area of expertise also attested in the *LBS*-text surviving as *LS*, c. 21.[97] The remainder of Alexander II's later legislation was made exclusively *by* the king *with the consent* of his bishops, earls, abbots, and barons, many of whom come to be named in the texts of Alexander's law.[98] So, in short, we may well be looking at a situation whereby parts of the text traditionally known as *LBS* were reissued by the king and reconstituted under his own authority. This was also the time when kings were trying to tie legal experts more firmly to their own authority and yet simultaneously, but not at all contradictorily, were slowly minimizing the role of legal experts in autonomously making or reforming the law, which came to be done by the king in assembly and, by 1230, not even by the *iudices* in the presence of the king.

The Promulgation of Written Law in the Late Twelfth and Thirteenth Centuries

The previous section argued that there was a quiet but still substantial change in the authorities practically responsible for making law in Scotia during the reigns of David I and William the Lion. That *iudices* stopped being the main lawmakers, and sources of law may explain why the manuscript evidence for their specialism is so sparse and has to be reconstructed so painfully; from the late twelfth century onwards, this stopped being the main legitimate way in which law was made and by 1230 it had ceased to be the way law was made. How, then, was law circulated in the period when royal lawmaking in assemblies seems to have become dominant?

By the reign of Robert I, not only were the mechanisms for the circulation of written law laid down in legislation itself but legal knowledge was expected to be obtained by everyone by hearing the content of these written texts: statutes were circulated widely. Knowledge of their written contents depended on a level of Latin literacy but they could easily be disseminated orally to others.[99] Robert I's legislation, enacted at Scone in December 1318, stated that written copies of laws would be read out repeatedly, not only in sheriffdom courts but also in other places 'where there are frequent gatherings of the people, so that all would know and observe the law, whether they were in the court of a bishop, earl, baron or any other court holder'. Copies of the statutes (*statuta*) were to be distributed in those

---

[97] *SA*, c. 26; *LS*, c. 21, clause 5.

[98] *SA*, cc. 2–7. It is important to note that one 'W. *brithem*' (perhaps Walter, the king's *iudex*) was listed as confirming the 1244 legislation in the two manuscripts which provide a list of individual names, rather than generic groups. This is interesting but it is important to stress that this was an attestation by a single *iudex*, not a group of *iudices*, as in earlier legislation; BL Additional MS 18111 (F), fo. 149v. It is thus possible that *iudices* could have still been present but were listed under the heading of, for example, *probi homines*. Indeed, the generic list of assenters to the 1244 (in all other manuscripts of *SA*) simply listed those present as 'bishops, abbots, earls, barons and worthy men of Scotland [denoting Scotland north and south of the Forth]'; *SA*, c. 2.

[99] *RPS*, 1318/1, online at http://www.rps.ac.uk/mss/1318/1.

courts so that no one could cry ignorance as an excuse if they were found not knowing their contents.[100] Arbroath Abbey certainly had and kept its own copy: the second earliest copy of Robert's 1318 legislation survives in Arbroath's cartulary, *Registrum Vetus*.[101] By 1318, therefore, the distribution of written law, from the lawmaking centre to the periphery of a local court (whether royal or aristocratic, ecclesiastical or monastic) was the way in which people were expected to know the content of law.

How long had this been happening? Written law started providing dating clauses in the late 1170s (the earliest is datable to 1177), according to the liturgical calendar. Modern calculation of the date is only possible because each act is also situated in a particular historical context. One was 'made on the next Monday before the next feast of St Margaret the virgin after the first coronation of Philip, king of the Franks'. One rather wishes the drafters of these texts had just written 1180 instead of leaving us with the task of untangling the reference.[102] Rather surprisingly, however, these idiosyncratic dates reveal that at least some if not all of these texts were drawn up long after the lawmaking assembly had been held. Thus, the series of statutes all enacted at a Perth assembly held on 30 October 1184 (*LS*, c. 11–14) begin by saying 'these are the assizes of the king made at Perth on the next Tuesday before the feast of All Saints … in the year when the Duke of the Saxons *first* came into England'.[103] Now, Henry the Lion, duke of Saxony came into England in 1184 and 1189.[104] Whoever was writing the statutes down could not have done so until after Henry's *second* visit, so thus earlier than 1189, when Duke Henry came to England a second time, thus making his 1184 visit his 'first', as the dating clause of the first assize asserts. Even our datable written material of the late twelfth century, therefore, need not and sometimes was not produced at the time of its making, suggesting that it is unlikely that, even by the end of the twelfth century, written law made at royal assemblies was circulated as systematically as it would be under Robert I, over a century later.

This being said, the king's assizes do seem to have increased in authority at the end of the twelfth century. In the last two decades of the twelfth century, William's charters also start referencing the king's own assizes and those of his predecessor, David I, in a way that had never been done before.[105] These mention William's assizes relating to burghs and to Galloway, his and David's burgh assizes (including prescriptions on buying and selling, taverns, and freedom from tolls), and his and David's assizes on teind collection.[106] There is no reason to think that William was necessarily drawing on pre-existing texts of David's laws; indeed, the one clear

---

[100] *RPS*, 1318/1.

[101] NLS, Adv. MS 34.4.2, fos. 119v–125r, also collated in *RRS*, v, no. 139.

[102] Taylor, 'Leges Scocie', p. 211; for dating by memorable event in England, see Michael T. Clanchy, *From Memory to Written Record: England, 1066–1307*, 2nd edn (Oxford, 1993), pp. 301–3.

[103] For the association of *LS*, cc. 11–14, with the same Perth assembly, see Taylor, 'Leges Scocie', pp. 211–12.

[104] Howden, *Gesta*, i, p. 316; ii, pp. 56, 62.

[105] See the example on teind fines, discussed below, pp. 154–7, and note 210.

[106] *RRS*, ii, nos. 281, 406, 475.

survival of 'David's' laws in one of William's charters is contemporary not with David's reign but with the date of the charter itself, that is, 1185×89.[107] These references to David's law may not, therefore, be indicative of an authentic tradition of Davidian lawmaking but, instead, indicative of a wish to increase the status and authority of royal law itself by associating it with a dead but illustrious predecessor.[108] But this cluster of references to royal assizes in the late twelfth century must point to the increased authority of the very concept of royal 'assizes' (written or unwritten), which allowed them to be reference points for the future.[109]

There was a subtle change to the dating of written law under Alexander II. Whereas William's laws had made a song and dance about their dates, Alexander's laws begin with *anno domini*.[110] Sometimes they even gave the day and month but it was more common for Alexander's written law to retain the tendency of William's law which was (for us) a rather complicated array of saints' days.[111] The first clear-cut example of the new legal dating system is Alexander's important 1230 legislation, discussed in more detail in Chapter 5, which states: 'in the year of grace 1230, on the next Sunday before the feast of St Luke the Evangelist, in the presence of the great men of his kingdom, King Alexander enacted...'.[112] The reference to years and saints' days, rather than historically contextual events, may have been because a written text of the law *was* drawn up at the assembly itself. This cannot be proven but the change to *anno domini* dating is nonetheless interesting, and may, at the very least, suggest that it was more important for the date of particular laws to be more easily identifiable at a later point, which would be indicative of a greater weight placed on the *text* of law as an accurate reflection of the content of a legislative assembly.

---

[107] *RRS*, ii, no. 281; for discussion, see Chapter 1, pp. 63–4.

[108] The naming of David in William's charters is often taken as unproblematic but just because David was cited as the lawmaker does not mean we should take these claims at face value. For a parallel example, see the supposed laws of Mael Coluim III that have nothing to do with Mael Coluim but instead must date either from the reign of Alexander II (after 1230) or the early years of the minority of Alexander III's government (the exemplar of the manuscript text is 1249×86); Madrid, Biblioteca Real MS II 2097, fo. 11v. For the use of David I as the lawmaking ancestor of Robert I, see Taylor, 'Assizes of David', pp. 225–35; and for David's reputation in William's reign, see also Matthew Hammond, 'The Adoption and Routinization of Scottish Royal Charter Production for Lay Beneficiaries, 1124–1195', in *ANS*, vol. 36 (2014), pp. 91–115, at pp. 105–6; see also Chapter 1, pp. 47–52, and below, pp. 154–7, 177–84.

[109] See, for example, the reference to an assize concerning waterways in a brieve of Alexander II in *Paisley Reg.*, p. 218 [AII/257], which might be a reference to *LS*, c. 5.

[110] For introduction to dating conventions and chronological ordering, see Diana E. Greenway, 'Dates in History: chronology and memory', *Historical Research*, vol. 72, no. 178 (1999), pp. 127–39; R. D. Ware, 'Medieval Chronology: theory and practice', in *Medieval Studies: An Introduction*, ed. J. M. Powell (New York, 1992), pp. 252–77. For problems with the 1230 legislation as printed in *APS*, see Chapter 5, pp. 271–2, 285–9.

[111] It is interesting that the day and month were not used in Alexander's laws because this had been the preferred method of dating charters from 1195, with the calendar year used briefly (and according to Lady Day dating) between October 1221 and April 1222, with the regnal year present during and after April 1222. Charters and laws under Alexander II were dated in different ways. For dating of charters see *RRS*, ii, pp. 81–3; Dauvit Broun, 'The Absence of Regnal Years from the Dating Clause of Charters of Kings of Scots, 1195–1222', *ANS* 25 (2003), pp. 47–63; Dauvit Broun, *Scottish Independence and the Idea of Britain from the Picts to Alexander III* (Edinburgh, 2007), pp. 191–201.

[112] *SA*, c. 4 (13 October 1230).

In sum, there was a profound shift in the identity of lawmakers over the twelfth century: from *iudices* to the king-in-assembly, which did not always require the presence and authority of *iudices*. Royal 'assizes' themselves became much more prominent in charter evidence from the late twelfth century onwards than they had been earlier in the century. But this does not mean that there was no written legal tradition before the late twelfth century. The text we know as *LBS* is only the remains of what may have been a larger written legal tradition that had less chance of being preserved by later medieval compilers because it had already been superseded by the king's law, itself a form of lawmaking that had different aims from those of the later medieval lawyers and statesmen who put together compilations of royal laws. Given that we can be sure that not all royal assizes once made were included in these compilations, the distinct legal culture of *LBS* would have had far less of a chance of inclusion; there must have been no overwhelming need to preserve it in whatever original form it had once circulated.

CRIME, PUNISHMENT, FEUD, AND FINES

While the first part of this chapter was devoted to the form of and authority behind law, this section is concerned with its content. Our twelfth-century texts—whether royal assizes or *LBS*-material—do not necessarily give us any sense of how written law was received and enforced but their content does provide evidence for what kind of social structures and relationships were envisaged to be necessary for legal prescriptions to work on the ground. Moreover, how far written law inserted the figure of the king into local legal practice (either through the collection of judicial fines or through administrative control of practice) reveals the extent to which kings of Scots of the twelfth and early thirteenth centuries aimed to control legal practice in their kingdom and the mechanisms by which they did so.[113]

Fundamental here are the concepts of crime and feud. Crime is an action defined by law as an abstract offence against the morality of a wider community.[114] The morality of a community can be delegated to the authority of a state, which makes the law (formal criminalization) and punishes criminals (substantive criminalization) through its own type of penal system.[115] A monopoly over punishment and

---

[113] The emphasis of this section is expressed more fully in Alice Taylor, '*Lex Scripta* and the Problem of Enforcement: Anglo-Saxon, Welsh and Scottish Law Compared', in *Legalism*, vol. 2: *Community and Justice*, ed. Fernanda Pirie and Judith Scheele (Oxford, 2014), pp. 47–75, where I stress that lawmakers directly tapped into the value structures and legal attachments between individuals as the method of assumed enforcement. See also Taylor, 'Crime without Punishment', pp. 287–304; for a similar approach solely focused on Anglo-Saxon England, see Lambert, *Law and Order*.

[114] For criminal law and a definition of punishment see, among many, Nicola Lacey, *State Punishment: Political Principles and Community Values* (London, 1988), pp. 4–12, 100–20.

[115] For the need for a more coherent theory of criminalisation, see Nicola Lacey, 'Historicising Criminalisation: Conceptual and Empirical Issues', *Modern Law Review*, vol. 72, no. 6 (2009), pp. 936–60. I am here favouring Lacey's Criminalization 'A'– as a pattern or outcome—but her set of distinctions also includes criminalization as a social practice. The key point here is that 'the extent of criminalisation (and hence of overcriminalisation) is *largely a function of the breadth or reach of criminal law* [my emphasis]', in Lacey, 'Historicising Criminalisation', p. 944, quoting D. Husak, *Overcriminalisation: the Limits of the Criminal Law* (Oxford, 2008), p. 8.

its consequences—even a delegated monopoly—is thus a key part of the relationship between the abstract concepts of crime and the state: if crime is an offence against the community-as-represented-by-the-state, then the state (or the state's delegates) must punish crime as it sees fit. In a medieval context, therefore, crime is defined as 'an offence subject *primarily* to royal punishment', a definition favoured recently by John Hudson and Tom Lambert, with the king as representative of the community, whose moral order his authority (rather than his physical person) protects.[116] The legal order of crime and punishment is thus vertical and top-down: law is present to enforce the obedience of the state's subjects, who are punished within defined legal limits if they are disobedient to its prescriptions.

Feud, by contrast, has often been seen as having no legal place in a society where the state has fundamental control over the definition and identification of crime and criminals, as well as the administration of punishment.[117] By feud, I mean a particular way in which a society deals with threats to the lives or status of its constituent members. In a society that supports feud, the killing or insulting of the honour of another produces the expectation and/or threat that the killing or insult will be avenged by a person's associates, often his kin, but any other socio-legal tie will do equally well.[118] There does not have to be actual retributive violence following the initial killing or insult; such violence only has to be seen as a legitimate consequence in the absence of compensation paid as part of a peace settlement. Even in this context, violent vengeance has to be appropriately focussed on the parties or associated parties who hold themselves responsible for the initial act. Appropriate violent vengeance and compensation are thus both expected consequences of an initial offence, and the whole set of norms is called feud here. In contrast to crime and punishment, feud is therefore thought of as part of a predominantly horizontal legal order because it involves reciprocity among equals or, at least, comparable persons. Two parties exchange vengeance and/or compensation for the initial act of insult, injury, or killing. Any rules or laws made to set the guidelines for feud (such as sets of compensation tariffs for particular actions, according to the status of the individuals involved) set the

---

[116] T. B. Lambert, 'Theft, Homicide and Crime in Late Anglo-Saxon Law', *Past & Present*, no. 214 (2012), pp. 3–43, at pp. 7–8, and John Hudson, *The Formation of the English Common Law: Law and Society in England from the Norman Conquest to Magna Carta* (London, 1996), p. 56.

[117] Now, when feud-like behaviour exists in Western liberal democracies, it is a phenomenon of marginalized groups: see, for example, Simon Antrobus (chair), *Dying to Belong: An In-depth review of Street Gangs in Britain*, The Centre for Social Justice (London, 2009), online at <http://www.centreforsocialjustice.org.uk/publications/dying-to-belong>. Jonas Grutzpalk, 'Blood Feud and Modernity', *Journal of Classical Sociology*, vol. 2, no. 2 (2002), pp. 115–34.

[118] For this understanding of feud, I am indebted to Paul R. Hyams, *Rancor and Reconciliation in Medieval England* (Ithaca, 2003), pp. 8–9; William Ian Miller, *Bloodtaking and Peacemaking: Feud, Law and Society in Saga Iceland* (Chicago, IL, 1990), pp. 179–81; Lambert, 'Theft, Homicide and Crime', p. 6, note 8. I am aware that some scholars argue for the abandonment of the term 'feud', seeing it as loaded with anachronistic associations. While Halsall's concept of customary vengeance is a particularly helpful thinking tool, I would argue that a dictionary definition of long-standing cyclical feuds is too narrow even to understand the range of feuding practices and so will continue to use the term in the context outlined above. See Guy Halsall, 'Violence and Society in the Early Medieval West: An Introductory Survey', in *Violence and Society in the Early Medieval West*, ed. Guy Halsall (Woodbridge, 1998), pp. 1–45, at pp. 19–28.

standards of behaviour of the two parties, rather than *necessarily* aiming to enforce these tariffs completely or punish them if either party fails to uphold the content of law. When historians, inspired by anthropologists such as Evans-Pritchard and Gluckman, started seeing feud not as a sign of social chaos but instead as a potentially ordering phenomenon (the vaunted 'peace in the feud'), societies that supported feud were by default stateless ones: the change in thinking brought by the peace-in-the-feud was the acknowledgement that stateless societies could be ordered rather than anarchic.[119]

Accordingly, the relationship between crime and feud is often viewed as a barometer of a central authority's monopoly over violence or, in other words, the extent of the state's legal power.[120] If socio-legal norms dictate that particular offences are offences and insults to people, rather than, first and foremost, transgressions against an abstract moral community, then there is necessarily no or little legitimacy for a central authority to punish those offences itself; indeed, it would be a transgression of that particular constitution of legal behaviour to do so. This is obviously ideal-type sort of stuff; moreover, the past historical narrative of the general replacement of feud and compensation by state-defined crime and punishment has been increasingly problematized in historical scholarship since the post-war era.[121] No medieval society ever completely rejected feud and vengeance as part of either its culture or its criminal justice system.[122] Indeed, thirteenth-century Welsh law prescribed the king's 'enforcing third' of all compensation payments for bloodshed, injury, and

[119] E. E. Evans-Pritchard, *The Nuer: A Description of the Modes of Livelihood and Political Institutions of a Nilotic People* (Oxford, 1940), pp. 155–9; Max Gluckman, 'The Peace in the Feud', *Past & Present*, no. 8 (1955), pp. 1–14; J. M. Wallace-Hadrill, 'The Bloodfeud of the Franks', repr. in J. M. Wallace-Hadrill, *The Long-Haired Kings and Other Studies in Frankish History* (London, 1962), pp. 121–47; for stateless societies, see R. R. Davies, 'The Survival of the Bloodfeud in Medieval Wales', *History*, vol. 54, no. 182 (1969), pp. 338–57. A very useful summary of medieval and early modern scholarship on feud can be found in Jeppe Büchert Netterstrøm, 'The Study of Feud in Medieval and Early Modern History', in *Feud in Medieval and Early Modern Europe*, ed. Bjørn Poulsen and Jeppe Büchert Netterstrøm (Aarhus, 2007), pp. 9–67.

[120] Patrick Wormald, 'Giving God and the King their Due: Conflict and Its Regulation in the Early English State', in Wormald, *Legal Culture*, pp. 333–57, at p. 342; Patrick Wormald, 'Frederic William Maitland and the Earliest English Law', *Law and History Review*, vol. 16, no. 1 (1998), pp. 1–25, at 17–22. Even those articles which do not see an opposition between king and kin have still seen authorities having the capacity to encroach on the capacity of kin to deal with these themselves; Lambert, 'Theft, Homicide and Crime'. However, in Lambert's forthcoming book, he effectively overturns the appropriateness of this analytical framework for early medieval England: Lambert, *Law and Order*. It is a shame that I have not been able to take account of this important work in this chapter, as the manuscript appeared too late to be incorporated. I have, however, made general references to individual chapters of Lambert's book where appropriate.

[121] Wormald, 'Bloodfeud'; Paul R. Hyams, 'Does It Matter When the English Began to Distinguish between Crime and Tort?', in *Violence in Medieval Society*, ed. Richard W. Kaeuper (Woodbridge, 2000), pp. 107–28; and, most importantly, Lambert, *Law and Order*.

[122] Dan Smail, 'Common Violence: Vengeance and Inquisition in Fourteenth-Century Marseilles', *Past & Present*, no. 151 (1996), pp. 28–59; Robert Bartlett, 'Mortal Enemies: The Legal Aspect of Hostility in the Middle Ages', T. Jones Pierce Lecture, University of Wales (Aberystwyth, 1998); repr. in *Feud, Violence and Practice: Essays in Medieval Studies in Honor of Stephen D. White*, ed. Belle S. Tuten and Tracey L. Billado (Farnham, 2010), pp. 197–212; William Ian Miller, 'In Defense of Revenge', in *Medieval Crime and Social Control*, ed. Barbara A. Hanawalt and David Wallace, Medieval Cultures 16 (Minneapolis, MN, 1999), pp. 70–89; Trevor Dean, 'Marriage and Mutilation: Vendetta in Late Medieval Italy', *Past & Present*, no. 157 (1997), pp. 3–36.

insult which were received by the injured kin-group, thus blurring the horizontal nature of compensation itself.[123] However, setting up crime on the one hand and feud on the other as an ideal contrast is useful because it reveals how inappropriate the distinction is in any analysis of twelfth- and early-thirteenth-century Scotland.

The distinction is, however, present in much of the existing scholarship on the 'origins' of crime. This is despite the fact that the earliest challenge to the idea that feud was a phenomenon limited to stateless societies came from a historian of early modern Scotland, Jenny Wormald.[124] The origins and early history of the category of crime in Scotland have been identified in the increasing strength of royal justice from the reign of David I and the widening of the remit of royal legislation during the reigns of William the Lion and Alexander II.[125] From the reign of David, the jurisdiction of some major monastic institutions, founded either by David or his more immediate predecessors, was explicitly subordinated to royal justice: if an abbot failed to do justice in his own court, the king would do it in his stead.[126] During the reign of William, references survive to some offences explicitly heard by the king alone: murder, arson, rape, and robbery (theft with violence).[127] In this kind of interpretation, aristocratic justice remained important but worked along-side the king's, according to the same legal norms.[128] Royal charters from William's reign also stressed that certain offences, including transgressions relating to the royal forest, unlawful poinding (seizure of goods for debt), and detention of anoth-er's neyfs, would put the perpetrator at the king's mercy, where he would suffer *plenaria forisfactura* ('full forfeiture').[129] These forfeitable offences were thus crimes in form even if not yet in name. Statutes enacted by Alexander II at Stirling in 1230 provide the clearest legal evidence of the king conceptualizing offences as against his own authority even though they did not affect his physical person.[130] The statutes themselves underscored the very existence of crime as a socio-legal category in Scotland: the word 'crime' (Latin: *crimen*) appears in them for the first time.[131] In 1244, Alexander issued a statute with force only in Lothian that

---

[123] Ior. 108/1, 3a, in *Tair Colofn Cyfraith: The Three Columns of Law in Medieval Wales: Homicide, Theft and Fire* (henceforth, *Tair*), ed. T. M. Charles-Edwards and Paul Russell (Bangor, 2007), pp. 270–1; for comment see T. M. Charles-Edwards, 'The Three Columns of Law: A Comparative Perspective', in *Tair*, pp. 26–59, at pp. 31–4.

[124] Wormald, 'Bloodfeud'.

[125] Barrow, 'Justiciar', pp. 89–91. For the importance of the statutes of Alexander II, Duncan, *Making of the Kingdom*, pp. 539–41, at p. 541; for a further examination, see Chapter 5, pp. 271–97.

[126] MacQueen, *Common Law*, pp. 42–7.

[127] *RRS*, ii, no. 80; *LS*, c. 7; for jurisdiction over more minor offences, see *RRS*, ii, pp. 48–51, no. 39 (p. 148), and below, note 244.

[128] Most recently, Alexander Grant, 'Franchises North of the Border: Baronies and Regalities in Medieval Scotland', in *Liberties and Identities in the Medieval British Isles*, ed. Michael Prestwich (Woodbridge, 2008), pp. 155–99, at pp. 184–92, distinguishing between 'kin' and 'royal' justice.

[129] *RRS*, ii, pp. 54, 71–4.

[130] Duncan, *Making of the Kingdom*, pp. 539–41; MacQueen, 'Canon Law, Custom and Legislation', pp. 239–49.

[131] For the general semantic range and history of *crimen*, see J. F. Niermeyer, *Mediae Latinitatis Lexicon Minus*, ed. C. Van de Kieft (Leiden, 1997). The word 'crimen' is also used in the spurious laws of Mael Coluim III which, although have nothing to do with that king, are good indications of legal mindsets of, perhaps, the mid-thirteenth century; see Madrid, Biblioteca Real, MS II 2097, fo. 11v.

described murder and robbery as felonies (*feloniae*) and also legislated on the offences of theft and homicide, thus confirming their existence as crimes, even if not felonies.[132]

This evidence gives little indication of why an emerging crime-and-punishment narrative might be problematic: some charters did indeed define crimes that were exclusively the king's to hear, delegated other offences to other lords and judicial fora, and expected some financial stake in the consequences. The emerging distinction between the jurisdiction of lords (religious and lay) and the king is important but is a narrative that is predominantly based on charter evidence. Written law, however, tells a neglected but different story, which will be set out here.

This section goes on to examine the written legal material to see what offences, if any, could be conceptualized as 'crimes' and what the significance of this may have been. It will then show how those who drafted the law must have envisaged its enforcement without invoking any major administrative or jurisdictional means of so doing. It will then argue that, although there were some offences which could be classed as 'crimes', most notably theft, kings did not aim to have a monopoly (even a delegated one) over their punishment. Instead, the prescriptions of written law are only understandable if it is accepted that law was not intended to enforce obedience through a top-down governmental structure but instead did so through other socio-legal ties, such as kinship and lordship, ties which were fundamentally bound up in that supposedly 'other' legal order, feud. 'Feud' and 'crime' were thus not separate legal orders; they were, instead, inseparable parts of the same whole. Sometimes the king received fines from malefactors, but this was not always the case: there was no uniform expectation that the king would regularly receive fines from or be involved in the punishment of thieves, even though they had committed what Dafydd Jenkins once called 'the great *crime*' of medieval kingdoms, theft.[133]

---

[132] *SA*, c. 2. The version in *APS* does describe theft and homicide as felonies but this reading is not present in the earliest manuscripts of *SA*. It is only present in a few later manuscripts. The scribe of one manuscript (NLS, Adv. MS 25.5.10) added in an extra *felonia* and thus may have actually obscured the meaning of the original statute in his attempt to clarify what was meant; see Taylor, *Auld Lawes*, forthcoming. For *SA*, c. 2, see Chapter 5, pp. 293–4. The word *felonia* is being used here to mean 'serious crime', as it appears in *Glanvill* in 1187×89 (for example, *Glanvill*, XIV, c. 1, p. 171), rather than breach of faith, as in the early-twelfth-century *Leges Henrici*. For this, see Sir Frederick Pollock and F. W. Maitland, *The History of English Law before the time of Edward I*, 2nd edn, 2 vols (Cambridge, 1923), i, pp. 303–4; T. B. Lambert, 'Protection, Feud and Royal Power: Violence and its Regulation in English Law, *c*.850–*c*.1250' (PhD Dissertation, University of Durham, 2009), pp. 200–1, 214–20. A charter of William's, dated 1187×89, refers to the *felonia* of Gille Coluim against the king, meaning here 'breach of faith' (*RRS*, ii, no. 258). The expansion of *felonia* to denote particular offences belonging to the king must therefore have been occurring between the late 1180s and this law of 1244. It is interesting that the 1230 legislation does not use the word *felonia* but, instead, *crimen*, to denote offences.

[133] Dafydd Jenkins, 'Crime and Tort in the Three Columns of Law', trans. T. M. Charles-Edwards, in *Tair*, pp. 1–25, at p. 3; and, most recently and emphatically, Lambert, 'Theft, Homicide and Crime', *passim*.

Crime in *Leges Scocie*

Of our twelfth-and early-thirteenth-century material, thirteen (fourteen at a push) of the twenty-one chapters of *LS* are devoted to theft and the problem of correctly identifying perpetrators. Another assize on theft, conceivably enacted sometime after 1175 (but possibly quite a long time after), is found in *SA*, at chapter 21.[134] Theft was and is a secret action: it is performed in a clandestine way and, if a person stole a cow and took it to market to sell, he was presenting the stolen goods as his own.[135] Indeed, Isidore of Seville had defined 'crimes' such as theft as offences, which were done secretly: theft's (*furtum*) etymology meant 'gloomy' (*furvus*) from the word 'dark' (*fuscus*), 'because it [theft] takes place in the dark'.[136] Because theft was secret, identifying thieves was a very tricky business, which was why it received so much attention.

LS specified repeatedly that the punishment for a proven thief was death;[137] a thief could also be killed on the spot if he had been caught in the act and pursued.[138] A thief was not to be avenged; there was to be no feud raised on his behalf because, by the act of thieving, he had proven himself to be a person without honour and, accordingly, could not be avenged: only people with honour warranted vengeance to assuage the insult done to them.[139] Petty theft was also a

---

[134] *SA*, c. 21. The reasons for placing this chapter in William's reign are rather complicated, and fundamentally cannot be proven completely, but we still need to try. I would place this assize late in the twelfth century. It was enacted 'after the deliverance of the lord king', which is normally taken as the release of William the Lion from captivity in Falaise in 1174–75. Second, this time period refers to the treatment of people accused of theft *after* this point; in this, it resembles the time limits placed on the Assize of Clarendon, enacted in 1166 (*Select Charters and Other Illustrations of English Constitutional History from the Earliest Times to the Reign of Edward I*, ed. W. Stubbs, 9th edn, revised by H. W. C. Davis (Oxford, 1921), p. 171) ('after the lord king was king'). If this link is deemed convincing (and it must be admitted it is tenuous), then it may be that the assize was not enacted immediately after William's return in 1175 but could be a number of years later, perhaps even on the lifting of the Treaty of Falaise in 1189. Although the level of detail it reveals might seem anachronistic for William's reign, it may possibly belong to it, given the probability that it is attached to the chapter above, which was enacted in Lothian alone (*SA*, c. 20: 'assisa facta per dominum regem in Laudonia'), which would make the rather strange dating clause, placed at the end of this statute, more understandable (it would lead directly to *SA*, c. 21). The reference to the *placitum justic* (the 'justice plea') in this end dating clause should be taken to mean a justice court not as evidence of a justice ayre. *LS*, c. 14, enacted in 1184, describes the introduction of high-status, irregular justice courts (so somewhat different from an itinerant ayre) as '*placita iusticiar* [*sic*]'. For discussion of these justice courts, see Chapter 4, pp. 238–40. As sheriffs in Lothian held courts from at least the reign of Mael Coluim IV (but sheriffs north of the Forth did not), the mention of the sheriff in *SA*, c.20, does not contradict the argument of this chapter. Whatever, *SA*, c. 21, could not post-date the mid-thirteenth century, as it refers to the ordeals of water and iron, see Chapter 5, pp. 280–4.

[135] Charles-Edwards, 'Three Columns of Law', pp. 39–40; T. M. Charles-Edwards, 'The Welsh Law of Theft: Iorwerth versus the Rest', in *Tair*, pp. 108–30, at pp. 108–10; Lambert, 'Theft, Homicide and Crime', pp. 8–11.

[136] *The Etymologies of Isidore of Seville*, ed. and trans. Stephen A. Barney, W. J. Lewis, J. A. Beach, and Oliver Berghof (Cambridge, 2006), pp. 122–3, at p. 123.

[137] *LS*, c. 9; see further, *SA*, c. 21 (*APS*, i, p. 371); *RRS*, ii, pp. 48–51; also *LS*, cc. 3–4, 17.

[138] *LS*, cc. 4, 9.

[139] *LS*, c. 9; for comparative material, see Ior. 115/9, in *Tair*, pp. 288–9; Lambert, 'Theft, Homicide and Crime', pp. 16–18; on honour in earlier Anglo-Saxon codes, see Stefan Jurasinski, 'Germanism, Slapping and the Cultural Context of Æthelbertht's Code: A Reconsideration of Chapters 56–58', *Haskins Society Journal*, vol. 18 (2006), pp. 51–71. Tom Lambert identifies three broad areas subject

known sub-category of graver kinds of theft: a thief was only to be fined and flogged if he stole 'a calf or ram or however much he is able to carry on his back' (*LS*, c. 8); *CD* states that a thief was not to be hanged if he had stolen less than 16d.[140] If a person was accused of theft or found with the stolen goods in his possession, he could also be subject to a mode of judicial proof to determine his guilt or innocence—the ordeals of iron, battle, or water.[141] *SA*, c. 21, also stated that the accused could only go to the ordeal if his accuser had not been able to find enough witnesses from the chief men of the vill (*homines seniores*). If the grieve of the vill summoned the witnesses himself, the accused would go to the ordeal; if the accuser managed to produce them, the thief would be hanged immediately. This shows that, by 1175 at the earliest, there was some concern that accused people should not be hanged without the sufficient weight of witness testimony. If the accuser could not produce enough backing for himself, the accused would be given up to God's judgment by the ordeal.[142]

Despite this emphasis on the punishment of thieves, chapters in *LS* and *SA* also allow for the possibility that accused thieves could buy their lives by a payment of what was explicitly called a 'thief's *wergeld* [life-value]', which was fixed at thirty-four and a half cows regardless of whether the thief was free or unfree.[143] But the option of buying one's life did not offer a simple get-out clause for the accused. *LS*, c. 3, reveals that paying a fine for theft significantly affected a person's reputation and one royal purge of thieves after 1175 (*SA*, c. 21) included anyone who was known to have 'given a redemption [payment] for theft' as well as all those who had recently been accused of theft. Later Scots translations of *SA*, c. 21, render *redemptio furti* as *thyftbote* (theft-payment).[144] This same chapter reveals that the option of buying your life could only be taken before the ordeal of whatever kind had taken place. Paying a fine to buy your life thus admitted guilt but saved your life – in a similar way to how pleading guilty now can result in a lesser sentence. It even mattered if people thought you were a thief: if a person was defamed of theft in three different provinces or accused of theft by three men of different lords, then he was to be treated as a proven thief and hanged accordingly (*LS*, cc. 3, 17).

to punishment: religious offences, procedural offences, and theft, all of which, he argues convincingly, were understood and treated as offences against the (moral) community (whether temporal or spiritual), not as offences or insults against an individual: Lambert, *Law and Order*, particularly chapters 2 and 4.

[140] *CD*, c. 1. In his edition for *APS*, Thomson printed this statement as the final sentence of the chapter on petty theft (*birthinsake*), placing it among his 'Assizes of William': *APS*, i, p. 375. However, the first attestation of this statement is as the final sentence to the first chapter of *CD*, which is, in fact, a reissue of a chapter containing stipulations on the holding of aristocratic courts (first surviving as *LS*, c. 7) and a procedure for petty theft (*LS*, c. 8 plus additional sentence). It does not, however, appear in *LS*.

[141] *LS*, cc. 9, 15; *CD*, cc. 3, 14, and 42 (*APS*, i, pp. 317, 318–19, 400–1; this last is in the Statutes of Alexander in *APS* but actually first attested in the 'David' legal tradition as *CD*, c. 42). In this period, the mode of proof ranged between the ordeals of iron, battle, or water (*LS*, cc. 9, 15) and compurgation (*CD*, c. 3), following the prohibition of clerical participation in the ordeals of iron and water in 1215; see Chapter 5, pp. 277–80.

[142] For the ordeal as last resort, see Robert Bartlett, *Trial by Fire and Water: the Medieval Judicial Ordeal* (Oxford, 1986), pp. 24–33.

[143] *LS*, c. 10.   [144] *APS*, i, p. 371.

A 'theft-payment' saved your life in the short term but the admittance of guilt stood: once a thief, always a thief.

Because theft was fundamentally a clandestine act, much attention is paid in *LS* to problems in identifying thieves. Everyone when they bought something had to have a surety who would ensure appearance and compliance if they were ever accused of having stolen the item they had bought.[145] Five chapters of *LS* were concerned with warrantors who were invoked when someone accused of theft said that another had lent or sold the item to him.[146] If that person could be found, he would 'warrant' the accused's testimony and answer the accusation in his stead (being a warrantor thus involved a degree of personal risk).[147] Not everyone could act as a warrantor: priests generally could not or, if they did, only in circumstances involving very particular types of gift-giving.[148] One chapter of *LS*, enacted after October 1184, describes a very lengthy procedure to be followed if someone vouched as his warrantor another who lived or was in another province;[149] another shows great interest in the case of a person accused of stealing a horse, who then claimed that the particular horse was lent to him by someone else.[150]

Crime and Enforcement

Written law reveals that the king was not envisaged to have a monopoly over the profits of justice. On one occasion, lords of lands received fines: for petty theft (*birthinsake*), they received a fine of one cow and one sheep from the malefactor,

---

[145] Or, even, prevent the possibility that one or both parties were partaking in the trafficking of stolen goods; *LS*, c. 2. See also the prescription that all trading should be done in a burgh in *RRS*, ii, nos. 467, 475. For comparative material from Anglo-Saxon England, see the discussion in Molyneaux, *Formation*, pp. 136–41.

[146] *LS*, cc. 1, 11–13, 16.

[147] Richard W. Ireland, 'Law in Action, Law in Books: the Practicality of Medieval Theft Law', *Continuity and Change*, vol. 17, no. 3 (2002), pp. 309–31, at p. 320–2.

[148] *LS*, c. 13, for example, records that, a priest could act as a warrantor only if they could prove that the accused had received the item from the priest or if the animal in question had been born and nurtured in the priest's house (and was able to prove this) or if the item was given to him as an oblation; or through receipt of teind. The restrictions on priests as warrantors is also found in Welsh law, in the *Llyfr y Damweiniau* translated in *The Law of Hywel Dda: Law Texts from Medieval Wales*, ed. and trans. Dafydd Jenkins (Llandysul, 1986), pp. 163–4.

[149] *LS*, c. 1. Lord Cooper questioned the authenticity of this chapter on the basis that it was unlikely that its procedure would ever work in practice because it potentially involved calling warrantors from as far away as Argyll and Caithness; *Regiam Majestatem*, ed. Cooper, p. 26; although for other defences, see William Croft Dickinson, 'The toschederach', *Juridical Review*, vol. 53 (1941), pp. 85–111, at pp. 99–105; MacQueen, 'Scots Law', pp. 88–90. I favour MacQueen's interpretation. The chapter itself is focussed on Scotia, and regional divisions within Scotia. The references to Argyll and Caithness are general rules about very particular circumstances, and have an extra level of coercion (through the warrantor's lord) to ensure their success in theory. The accused would, anyway, have an extra month to produce the warrantor if they lived in an area outwith Scotia. We should also remember that the chapter just aimed to set the rules of practice; whether it would have been easy for accused people to find their warrantors who lived in different areas is an entirely different question but not one which impinges on the authenticity of the chapter itself; see also Taylor, '*Leges Scocie*', pp. 224–5.

[150] *LS*, c. 12.

the standard fine levied on wrongdoers of peasant status.[151] Only three chapters state that the king should be the recipient of some fines for theft-related wrongs: any lord who failed to appear as a warrantor when his man had defaulted on his responsibility had to pay the king the vast sum of hundred cows and any surety who failed to make his pledgee appear to answer an accusation of theft would have to pay eight cows.[152] A further context for the king receiving a fine was when a kin-group attempted to avenge one of their members who had been adjudged a thief.[153] All these three prescriptions appear to have been laid down in William's reign. But the remainder of the theft and theft-related chapters do not mention the king at all. Instead, most are prescriptions that assume their applicability in all contexts without mentioning the figure of the king, except as the authority that set the rule in the first place. Thus, *LS*, c. 13, enacted in 1184, gave all the scenarios when a priest *could* act as a warrantor but did not mention any punitive measures if any priest failed to act in accordance with the law. *LS*, c. 12, enacted on the same occasion, set out the procedures about what should be done when borrowed horses were claimed to be stolen items but, again, nothing is stated about what would happen and who would profit from the wrongdoing if the rules were broken.

Nor is there much mention of any institutional means for administrating these prescriptions about theft. *LS*, c. 3, for example, stated that anyone 'defamed of theft' in one or two provinces, who was discovered without a lord to act as his surety, would be treated as a proven thief (i.e. killed). But what constituted defamation, who determined whether a man lacked a surety and who was to supervise the process of judgment is not stated. It is assumed that everyone would have known what to do; the content of the chapter does not appear to be concerned with the means of its own enforcement.[154] The same is true for *LS*, cc. 12–13, on priests as warrantors and borrowing horses respectively: the content of both chapters set the limits and exceptions to the rule but did not say how it was to be enforced or administered. Even a detailed procedure, like *SA*, c. 21 (enacted in or after 1175, and probably only in Lothian), which assumes that accusations of theft would be made publicly in a vill and that if the accuser did not have sufficient

---

[151] A Dunfermline charter from the 1280s stated that the abbot should have all fines of one cow and one sheep, meaning, essentially, all fines from peasants (*Dunf. Reg.*, no. 317).

[152] *LS*, c. 2: in addition, the wrongdoer would be outlawed. This may have been a *de facto* outcome anyway; it was quite easy to declare a person an outlaw formally if he/she had not appeared; for outlawry see Paul Dresch, 'Outlawry, Exile and Banishment: Reflections on Community and Justice', in *Legalism*, ed. Pirie and Scheele, pp. 97–124; Elisabeth van Houts, 'The Vocabulary of Exile and Outlawry in the North Sea Area around the First Millennium', in *Exile in the Middle Ages*, ed. Laura Napran and Elisabeth van Houts (Turnhout, 2004), pp. 13–28; Elisabeth van Houts, 'L'Exil dans l'espace anglo-normand', in *La Normandie et l'Angleterre au Moyen Âge*, ed. Pierre Bouet and Veronique Gazeau (Leiden, 2003), pp. 75–85.

[153] The 'right' is likened to the king's broken peace (*LS*, c. 9), for which, see below, pp. 149–50, 164–72. From the legal material, it would appear that breach of the king's peace was atoned for by a payment of 180 cows (£36) but, in one charter of Mael Coluim IV, the amount given was £10 and it is hard to know what to make of this discrepancy (see *LS*, c. 21; *CD*, cc. 31, 33; cf. *RM*, bk IV, c. 56, ed. Thomson, in *APS*, i, p. 640; cf. *RRS*, i, no. 230).

[154] Although, of course, the chapter was concerned with enforcement, just not through an administrative apparatus, see below, pp. 144–7, and Taylor, '*Lex Scripta*'.

backing for his accusation, the grieve (*prepositus*) would do so in their stead only brought the grieve into the process if the initial accusation lacked witnesses; nor did it envisage any further level of enforcement above the level of the vill.[155] Although theft and theft-related procedures were punished severely in the royal law in *LS*, many of the chapters are not interested at all in how such prescriptions would be enforced or who would do the punishing.

This is not to say that no chapter ever mentions *any* structures of enforcement, only that those chapters which actually contain procedural content (such as what happens when a borrowed horse was claimed as stolen) are not set within any jurisdictional or administrative structure.[156] *LS*, c. 1, is a good example for the present purposes because it is the only one that *seems* to combine detailed procedure within a rather complicated administrative structure; closer examination, however, reveals administration to be limited to extremely exceptional cases. In its current form, this chapter must have been drafted after 1184. It is a lengthy text based on a short and simple prescription; that 'stolen' goods had to be brought to the place in each earldom or province (the Latin is not entirely clear) established by David I. Once brought, the accused had fifteen days to produce his warrantor if, that is, both the accused and the warrantor lived within Scotia (which the text helpfully defines as between the Rivers Spey and Forth and the mountain range of Druim Alban).[157] The length of the chapter results not from this simple prescription but from the problem about what to do if the warrantor dwelt outside Scotia, whether in Moray, Argyll, Ross, or Caithness, or south of the Forth.[158] Accusations dealing with people south of the Forth were dealt with every six weeks at Stirling Bridge. Elsewhere, the onus was on the accused to find and produce his far-flung warrantor but, if he failed, there were fallback options. If the warrantor dwelt in Moray, Ross, Caithness, or the part of Argyll 'which pertains to Moray', then the accused had to appeal to the sheriff of Inverness, who would then go with the king's sergeands and extract

---

[155] There has been no study on grieves in Scotland. For the significance of reeves in Anglo-Saxon England, see James Campbell, 'Hundreds and Leets: A Survey with Suggestions', in *Medieval East Anglia*, ed. Christopher Harper-Bill (Woodbridge, 2005), pp. 153–67; Molyneaux, *Formation*, pp. 108–9, 180–2.

[156] *LS*, cc. 7, 14–15; for comment, see below, pp. 157–8.

[157] There is an issue about what was meant by the chapter's distinction between a *provincia* and a *comitatus*. As the statute was promulgated in 1184, it might be thought that *comitatus* meant 'earldom' and province, the regional division of the kingdom (see Chapter 1, pp. 45–53). But this is problematic because, if *SA*, c. 14 (expanded in *LS*, c.16), lists the places within the *comitatus*, as I have argued elsewhere, then not all of these were in earldoms. Rait, Dalginch (probably, because it was part of the parish of Markinch, which was in the hands of a cadet branch of the comital dynasty), and Kintillo all were, but Aberdeen was a royal burgh, Scone a royal estate, Forfar a royal burgh, and Dunnottar a royal estate. So if *comitatus* was referring to these places, it could not have denoted 'earldom', meaning the territory within the province under the direct control of an earl, which further suggests that an earlier law (of David's) lies behind this particular chapter.

[158] *LS*, c. 1, only dealt with accused people who dwelt in Scotia. Different arrangements were made for Moray, Caithness, Argyll, and Ross. Those who dwelt *ultra Forth* ('beyond the Forth'), that is, south of the Forth, had to come to Stirling Bridge every six weeks. No indication is given about how the procedure would be heard. One might imagine the sheriff of Stirling having some role here but the chapter does not say so explicitly. *LS*, c.1, was incorporated into *SA* (as c. 12); in this version, *ultra Forth* explicitly denotes 'in Lothian or in Galloway'.

the reluctant warrantor. If that failed, then the lord of the warrantor had to find him; if the lord refused to do so then he was fined the huge sum of hundred cows by the king. If the wrongdoer dwelt in Argyll 'which pertained to Scotia', he went to the abbot of Glendochart; if from Kintyre or Cowal, the earl of Menteith was responsible for producing the warrantor (or the warrantor's lord) as above.[159] None of these responsibilities of the earl, abbot, and sheriff, however, tell us anything about how the actual accusation would be heard on the ground. The stolen chattel would be brought to the particular place in the province, and the warrantor would also appear. The earl, abbot, or sheriff would be brought in *only* if the accused had failed to produce his/her warrantor and *only* if that warrantor lived outside Scotia, the area the procedure covered.[160] The chapter is silent on what happened next: if *mormaer*, as heads of provinces, were involved in the provincial procedure, they could only have done so *de facto* for the chapter does not mention them.[161] In short, the prescriptive and procedural content of the chapters on theft makes very little mention of any administrative structures of enforcement. Judicial fora are mentioned in statutes from the 1180s onwards but they are not integrated into the content of prescriptive law itself, as would be the case in the law of Alexander II, as will be shown later.[162]

If the content of individual statutes rarely outlines any institutional structures for their enforcement, how, if at all, *might* it be enforced?[163] The explanation offered here is that, instead of being overwhelmingly concerned with *who* or *what* was in charge of implementing and overseeing the procedures in the chapters (that is, administration and jurisdiction), these twelfth- (and sometimes early-thirteenth-) century chapters actually do provide a method of enforcement. This method of enforcement was not worked out within an administrative or jurisdictional frame-work but by socio-legal attachments whose existence was assumed by those who drafted written law. The expectation in written law was that all wrongdoers and, further, *all* people, wrongdoers or not, should be attached to other individuals or groups and it was a problem if they were not. Some of these attachments were primarily *legal* categories; others were bonds that would now be called 'social' but

[159] For Menteith as a new earldom, carved out of 'greater Strathearn' in the 1160s, see Dauvit Broun, 'The Origins of the *mormaer*', in *Earl in Medieval Britain*, ed. David Crouch and Hugh F. Doherty, forthcoming.

[160] *SA*, c. 14, which I have argued elsewhere is the earlier version of *LS*, c. 16, lists the provinces as Gowrie, Stormont, Atholl, Fife, Strathearn, Angus, the Mearns, and Mar and Buchan. *LS*, c. 16, adds 'Ross and Moray' as well; see Taylor, '*Leges Scocie*', pp. 234–5; and Broun, 'Origins of the *mormaer*', forthcoming.

[161] For *mormaír* and provinces, see Chapter 1, pp. 40–2.

[162] See Chapter 5, pp. 271–97.

[163] These points are developed in more detail in Taylor, '*Lex Scripta*', pp. 67–71. The issue of how early medieval law could be enforced has attracted a lot of attention. In addition to the literature cited in Notes 6, 7, 9, see Simon Keynes, 'Royal Government and the Written Word in Late Anglo-Saxon England', in *The Uses of Literacy in Early Medieval Europe*, ed. Rosamond McKitterick (Cambridge, 1992), pp. 226–57; David Pratt, 'Written law and the Communication of Authority in Tenth-Century England', in *England and the Continent in the Tenth Century*, ed. David Rollason, Conrad Leyser, and Hannah Williams (Turnhout, 2010), pp. 331–50; Catherine Cubitt, '"As the Lawbook Teaches": Reeves, Lawbooks and Urban Life in the Anonymous Old English Legend of the Seven Sleepers', *EHR*, vol. 124, no. 510 (2009), pp. 1021–49; Roach, 'Law and Legal Norms'.

which then carried legal force. Indeed, such social bonds were required for a person to claim legal personality; that is, the capacity to be both protected and punished by the law.

The main legal categories of attachment were suretyship and warranty. All people who bought or borrowed an item were expected to make the relevant seller or lender their warrantor: someone who would, if the item were claimed as stolen, warrant that the person had indeed bought or borrowed it legally and had not stolen it himself.[164] Most important was the surety: people had to have sureties who would be responsible for their appearance at judicial proceedings; if they did not and were already of bad reputation, the non-attached person was treated as guilty.[165] Under (probably) Alexander II, if an individual accused of a plea of the crown—murder, robbery, rape, or arson—fell in trial by battle, his pledges (sureties) had to satisfy the king by a payment of 180 cows and a calf, the amount (minus the calf) of killing someone in the king's peace set out in the *LBS*-material.[166] No one could buy anything without a surety; if the purchased goods were claimed as stolen, the surety was responsible for bringing their possessor to the hearing.[167] Having a surety, therefore, ensured that individuals were law-worthy, that they were deemed of good enough reputation and status to have someone insure their behaviour: the material possessions of a surety, after all, were put at risk if at any point his pledgee was considered to have transgressed the law.

LS, c. 3, prescribed that men defamed of theft who had no lord to provide a surety for them would be killed as 'proven thieves'. The assumption here is that men were expected to have lords, and lords were expected to act as sureties for their men (in this case, the position of surety would have been to ensure the accused man's appearance at the judicial proceedings). The responsibilities of 'lords' for their men extended to when a subordinate was vouched to warranty: *LS*, c. 1, states that, if a person accused of theft could not find and thus produce their warrantor, the lord of the warrantor had to try and find him and, if he refused, he had to pay the king a fine. Here, the expectation was that all warrantors, regardless of where they lived, would have lords. All individuals were also part of kin-groups which were responsible for maintaining and avenging the honour of their members. Thus, *LS*, c. 9, states that no kin (*parentes*) was allowed to pursue vengeance for one of the kin-group who had been killed while caught in the act of thieving or as punishment for judicially proven theft.[168] The assumption behind this rule was that it was legal for kin-groups to avenge their slain kinsman so long as the slain man had not already proven himself to be unworthy of honour and protection by committing theft.[169] Kin also clubbed together to help one of their members who had been accused of

---

[164] The accusation would then pass to the warrantor, for which see *LS*, c. 1.

[165] *LS*, cc. 2–3; Wendy Davies, 'Suretyship in the *Cartulaire de Redon*', in *Lawyers and Laymen: Studies in the History of Law Presented to Professor Dafydd Jenkins on his 75th birthday*, ed. T. M. Charles-Edwards, Morfydd E. Owen, and D. B. Walters (Cardiff, 1986), pp. 72–91; Chapman Stacey, *The Road to Judgement: from Custom to Court in Medieval Ireland and Wales* (Philadelphia, PA, 1994).

[166] *SA*, c. 11.   [167] *LS*, c. 2.

[168] The method of judgment explicitly referred to here was the ordeal of iron or water; for the ordeal, see Chapter 5, pp. 280–4.

[169] See further *LBS*, in *LS*, c. 21, clauses 1–2.

theft and wished to buy their lives.[170] While there is no concrete evidence that kin-members would act as sureties for one another, much as lords would do, comparative evidence from tenth-century Anglo-Saxon England and thirteenth-century Wales, however, where kin-groups *were* expected to act as sureties suggests that this would not have been unusual had it also occurred in twelfth-century Scotland.[171]

Homicide and Compensation: Separate Legal Orders?

Even these few examples, discussed in the previous section, show that written law assumed that individuals were expected to belong to kin-groups and be attached to lords.[172] People who did not have these ties were problems and so exceptions had to be made: as Paul Dresch has written, 'the unattached person... is a moral threat'.[173] It was also assumed that both types of attachment would protect individual people from violent injury or death by the hand of another. This is where feud comes in again. At the beginning of this section, I outlined how feud is often seen as belonging to a different legal world from that of 'crime'. Scottish law, although it saw theft as an action to be punished (with no necessary compensation to the victim for the act beyond restitution of the stolen goods), did not see killing and violence in the same way.[174] Homicide was not defined as a crime in Scottish law until 1244 and even then it was not a 'felony', a crime belonging to the king, but just an act that, if committed, could result in a 'conviction'.[175] Before this date (or, more likely, before this general period of lawmaking in the 1230s and 1240s), it seems that homicide—an act where the killer was known and acknowledged his responsibility—was *not* a 'crime' per se, but rather something that should be avenged if the victim's associates were not compensated appropriately.[176] Nonetheless, just as people accused of the

---

[170] In the so-called 'laws of Mael Coluim III', the second *petitio* accepted by the king was that he would no longer take a *precium* from thieves who had obtained the money from their kin (or 'nearest', the Latin is *proximi*) in order to be reconciled with the king; Madrid, Biblioteca Real, MS II 2097, fo. 11v.

[171] Taylor, '*Lex Scripta*', pp. 70–1. The evidence for sureties in Wales is vast and this one paragraph hugely simplifies the difficulties of evaluating the tractate on suretyship in *Cyfraith Hywel*; the Iorwerth, Cyfnerth, and Latin E redactions are edited in Charles-Edwards, Owen, and Walters ed., *Lawyers and Laymen*.

[172] In *LS*, c. 1, the lord is essentially acting as a surety for his man who has been vouched to warranty.

[173] Dresch, 'Outlawry', p. 105. For regulations on going out at night in Scotland, see *LS*, c. 6.

[174] Particular spaces were protected, for example, the king's hall and those spaces to which the king's peace was explicitly granted, or *girth* (*grithstol*), that is, sanctuary; for which see *CD*, cc. 31, 33, and, further MacQueen, 'Girth'. The distinction between theft and homicide is developed forcefully in Lambert, 'Theft, Homicide and Crime', an article to which I owe a great debt. The following paragraphs are basically a shorter summary of the arguments and evidence in Taylor, 'Crime without Punishment', pp. 294–9.

[175] *SA*, c. 2, a 1244 statute for Lothian, assumes that homicide normally belonged to 'earls and barons'. As stated earlier, although the *APS* text does describe theft and homicide as felonies, this reading is not present in the earliest manuscripts; see Note 131, and, for further discussion, Chapters 4 and 5, pp. 240–4, 293–4.

[176] Homicide is an openly declared act which, in a feud scenario, stakes a claim to its own legitimacy. For homicide as open killing, as opposed to murder—secret killing—see *Glanvill*, XIV, 3, at p. 174. Murder—killing in secret—was a type of killing that was wrong and so was treated differently

crime of theft were brought to face accusations through ties of suretyship and, beyond these, kinship and lordship, the same forms of horizontal and vertical socio-legal attachments were also brought into play to avenge actions, such as killing, which could initiate feud or, at the very least, demand compensation. 'Crime' and 'feud' did not belong to separate legal orders in Scotland: both relied on the same socio-legal attachments for their functioning.

A list of these compensation payments, which would assuage active and violent vengeance, survives in the final chapter of *LS* (c. 21), otherwise known as one of the manuscript witnesses of *LBS*.[177] I argued earlier that *LS*, c. 21, was a translation of a remnant of a larger corpus of texts that would once have constituted the legal expertise of the *iudex*. Some of this material was reissued as royal assizes over the course of the twelfth century. The balance of evidence suggests that this French text was compiled in its *LS*-form no earlier than the second quarter of the twelfth century, possibly as late as the last third of the century.[178]

Although *LS*, c. 21, contains five clauses, only the first two concern us here. The first clause lists the life-values of different social ranks, beginning with the king (1000 cows) and ending with *vileyns* (16 cows), and was analysed in Chapter 1.[179] The word used for 'life-value' is the Gaelic *cró*, literally meaning 'violent death' or 'compensation for violent death'.[180] Every woman, regardless of her rank, had a *cró* of exactly one-third less than her husband. If a woman did not have a husband, her *cró* was exactly the same as one of her brothers (the possibility that a family might not have any male children was clearly unthinkable). These sorts of payments can only exist in a society that deems the killing of an individual as primarily an offence against his kin. Resources have to transfer between the two parties as a result, not simply to compensate for loss but also to achieve reconciliation.

The second clause reveals the existence of another payment that could be extracted for committing homicide. It was a payment owed for killing somebody

from open killings both by the perpetrator and by the legal order. Neither vengeance nor compensation can, after all, be extracted if the perpetrator does not acknowledge the killing. Murder thus occupies the same position in relation to killing as theft does in relation to taking things. Indeed, murder was sometimes conceptualized as a particular type of theft because it carried an equivalent level of moral abhorrence: Irish law, for example, refers to murder as 'person-theft'; see Fergus Kelly, *A Guide to Early Irish Law* (Dublin, 1988), p. 128. The metaphorical link between murder and theft was not because of their fundamental similarity (to steal something was not the same as to kill somebody) but because murder was, like theft, secret and unjustifiable and so was likened to theft, the one action everybody knew was wrong. Welsh law defined killing as first and foremost an insult (*sarhaed*). As a result, the kin would expect a payment for the insult done to their kinsman before *galanas* was paid (Ior. 109/1, in *Tair*, pp. 272–3).

[177] With the exception of the first three chapters (probably four chapters, given that *LS*, c. 4, circulated with *LS*, cc. 1–3), from chapter 5 onwards, they go up in date: 5 (undatable); 6 (1177); 7 (1180); 8 (undated); 9 (undated); 10 (undated); 11 (1184); 12 (1184); 13 (1184); 14 (1184); 15 (1197); 16 (rel. to 1–3); 17 (undated); 18 (1186×1200); 19 (1187×1200); 20 (1210). It is possible that, as chapters 18–20 are all about Galloway, they were added to the end, perhaps later than the first 17 chapters, and so may be earlier than chapter 15 (1197).

[178] Taylor, '*Leges inter Brettos et Scotos?*', forthcoming.   [179] See Chapter 1, pp. 38–9, 56–7.

[180] Kelly, *Guide*, p. 125, note 1; *galanas* is a word that appears twice in the Irish legal corpus (see Taylor, '*Leges Scocie*', p. 238, note 118), despite being an Old Welsh word, again, like *cró*, having the double meaning of 'death' and 'compensation for death'.

Table 3.2. 'Peaces' in *Leges Scocie*, c. 21

King	180 [400] cows
mormaer/son of king	90 cows
thane/son of *mormaer*	60 cows
son of thane	40 cows
kinsman of thane	26 cows

protected by the peace of a particular rank.[181] These peaces are given below in Table 3.2. The penalty for breaking the king's peace was substantially higher than that for breaking the peace of any other rank. Although the *LS*-text provides the figure of 400 cows for the breach of the king's peace, this is attested in no other manuscript of this text, and is probably a scribal error; nonetheless, 180 cows still represents twice as much as the penalties enforced at the rank of the *mormaer*, the next rung down.[182] Table 3.3 reveals that the relative values of peace and *cró* were all fairly stable across the ranks. With the exception of the king, all peaces were worth roughly 60 per cent of the holder's life value. It is not surprising that the king was an exception. Because his life was so much more valuable than any other, its material worth was set at an unrealistically high level. The breach of his peace, however, was set at a high but still practical level.[183] From the perspective of those who would have been protected by these peaces, the king's offered the best protection but, for those of lower socio-economic status, the low fine of twenty-six cows offered by the kinsman of a thane would still have constituted significant protection.

These peaces do not overlap with each other: only the holder of the peace received the payment. Some prior analyses have assumed that the peaces are all decreasing ranks of the royal peace but the text explicitly contradicts this reading.[184] If you killed in 'the peace of the son of a king or in the peace of a *mormaer*',

[181] T. B. Lambert, 'Introduction: Some Approaches to Peace and Protection in the Middle Ages', in *Peace and Protection in the Middle Ages*, ed. T. B. Lambert and David Rollason (Toronto, 2009), pp. 1–18, at pp. 2–4; and, now, Lambert, *Law and Order*, chapter 2.

[182] The manuscript of *LS* gives 400 cows (xx^{xx}) (NRS, PA5/1, fo. 61v (*LS*, c. 21); changed in the printed version, *APS*, i, p. 664); the *RM*-version gives 180 (*APS*, i, p. 640; confirmed in earliest MS version of *RM*, BL, Additional MS 18111, fo. 76v); Other legal *capitula* refer to the fine for breach of royal peace as 180 cows (*CD*, cc. 31, 33; printed, *APS*, i, p. 320); *CD*, c. 31, reads 29 cows for breach of the king's peace. It is easy to explain this reading: the scribe of the archetype text may well have seen ^{xx}ix (180) in his reading, and mistakenly rendered it *xxix* (29), which was then followed in every other manuscript witness of the text (for the earliest MS witness of this chapter, see NRS, PA5/2, fo. 39r [the Ayr MS]).

[183] For other high fines, see Seebohm, *Tribal Custom*, pp. 311–12. As stated earlier, *RM*-texts often preserve better readings than *LS*, although do not contain all the chapters of *LS*, c. 21; see above, pp. 124–6.

[184] Patrick Wormald, 'Anglo-Saxon Law and Scots Law', *SHR*, vol. 88 no. 226 (2009), 192–206, at pp. 196–7, where Wormald describes *mormaír* and thanes as royal officials; thus, if their peace was broken, the breach was fundamentally that of the king's peace. Neither Seebohm nor Harding thought that these peaces were the *king's* peace. Seebohm, *Tribal Custom*, p. 311; Alan Harding, 'The Medieval Brieves of Protection and the Development of the Common Law', *Juridical Review*, new series, vol. 11 (1966), pp. 115–49, at p. 115.

Table 3.3. Relative peace and *cró* values

Rank	Protection level (cows)	*Cró* (cows)
Mormaer	90–180	150
thane	60–180	100
thane's son	40–180	66 ⅔
thane's kinsman	26–180	43 + 13 ⅔d

you paid your fine to them (*ilur a feit*): the holder of the particular peace received the cattle.[185] Two potential payments could thus result from homicide: compensation of the life-value of the slain man (to the affected kin) and a payment for breach of peace (to the protector, presumably of higher rank than the *protégé*).[186] The fine levied for breaking the peace of a particular rank by homicide was not a penalty for the act of homicide itself but rather for killing someone who was in the peace of a peace-wielding rank, thereby calling the efficacy of that peace into question. If the protector failed to extract this payment, then his reputation would be further called into question. The payment for breach of peace was thus not a penal fine for the act of homicide, as might be thought, but was instead a compensation payment for dishonouring the peace-holder, whether that protector was the king or anyone else. Two compensation payments could thus be extracted for homicide: one horizontal payment to the kin and another vertical one to the protector. If one speculates that it would have been unlikely (or at least profoundly strange) for a person to place himself under the protection of a status rank lower than himself, then the balance between these two payments (one vertical to the protector, the other horizontal to the kin) look relatively equal, as shown in Table 3.3.

Under an even more conservative assessment, whereby it would have been more common for individuals to seek the protection of a rank higher than themselves, the relative weight of the vertical compensation owed to the protector increases even further, as shown in Table 3.4.

The first two clauses of *LS*, c. 21, thus reveal at least two consequences of killing. Two parties had to be reconciled by payment of a slain individual's *cró* in order to avoid vendetta. However, there was also a third party, the protector of the individual slain. Compensation was due to both the affected kin and the protector. The amount of the latter payment was, at the very least, two-thirds of the *cró* of the slain individual. The relative values of protection and *cró* reveal that the capacity to offer protection was a stable part of status; we might thus expect that offering effective protection was part of what allowed a high-status individual to maintain

---

[185] The Latin *RM*-texts state *sibi pertinent* (*APS*, i, p. 664).

[186] *LS*, c. 21, also references four further payments: *gelthach* or *kelchin*, *enach*, *turhochret*, and *forgard*, which are not discussed here. *Enach* seems to have meant an 'honour' payment for insult. *Gelthach* was also a consequence of homicide (*LS*, c. 21, clause 2). If *gelthach* was equivalent to *kelchin*, we only know who received it in the case of the death of a free woman (her husband) or an unfree person (the lord). The *turhochret* (etymology unknown) was a payment of lesser value than the *gelthach*, which the husband of an unfree woman received instead of the *kelchin*. *Forgard* was a compensation payment a lord received on the death or wounding of his man in battle.

Table 3.4. Conservative values of balance between peace and *cró*

Rank	Protection level (cows)	Cró (cows)
Mormaer	180	150
thane	90–180	100
thane's son	60–180	66 ⅔
thane's kinsman	40–180	43 + 13 ⅔d

his social position.[187] All noble ranks, aside from the king, offered protection worth almost exactly 60 per cent of their own life: the capacity to protect was thus an intrinsic aspect of noble status. The offence against a *protégé* violated the essence of the status of the protector. In this way, protection did not necessarily diminish the possibility of further violence (presumably the protector would have to get violent if he did not receive compensation) but brought in a third party that stood in a vertical relationship to the slain person.[188]

Combining the legal material on theft and homicide, therefore, we might see at first different legal logics in the same legal system: some offences (theft) were punished; others (killing) were compensated for or avenged. But a closer look reveals that this distinction does not hold. If theft was a crime, it was not one subject to on-the-ground punishment by the rule-making authority, the king. Twelfth- and early-thirteenth-century law defined the crime without being much concerned with jurisdiction and control over its punishment. Equally, if homicide was atoned for by the reconciliation (through compensation) of two parties, there was also a third party, of higher status than the victim, to whom the killer had to answer, who could be the king but did not have to be; the third party could be a *mormaer*, a thane, or a thane's kinsman. Most importantly, the content of the chapters on theft do not assume a royal administrative structure of enforcement but, instead, the existence of other socio-legal ties, such as kinship and lordship, on which the consequences of insult, injury, and killing also depended. There were thus no 'separate' legal orders; there were only the attachments and values of socio-legal ties that avenged the honour and status of victims, their kin, and protectors and also brought accused thieves to answer.

The prescriptive statements in *LS* were thus written not with administrative structures in mind but with socio-legal attachments that were abstracted and generalized so as to be applicable in all circumstances.[189] Royal ambition for the

---

[187] Alexander Grant has suggested to me that these peaces may have covered retainers of *mormaír*, thanes, and so on (Grant, personal communication). I find this suggestion very interesting but there is not enough surviving evidence on which to base a discussion of retainers. But, even if there were, we are still very far from Wormald's view that these peace payments show that 'in Scotland, as in England, [the] seminal notion of vesting social security in the protection afforded by the king's peace may...have a very much earlier origin than has so far been conceived' (Wormald, 'Anglo-Saxon Law and Scots Law', p. 197).

[188] See, for comparison, the king's enforcing third in Welsh law is an interesting contrast here, particularly in the Cyfnerth version (Cyfn 9/19; cf. Ior. 108/1, 1a, 2 in *Tair*, pp. 248–9, 270–1).

[189] One might think that, because *LS*, c. 7, and *LS*, c. 14, do mention courts, this statement does not hold water. But the point I am making here is that these are about the *legitimacy* of holding courts

potential reach of law was not matched by a concurrent concern for its administration: there was a large gap between the making of law at assemblies and its practice in the locality. Yet uniformity in practice was not the issue or the point. Put simply, royal law in the reign of William the Lion did not depend primarily on formal structures of government. Its purpose was not administrative but ideological: to record and reinforce the legal rules and norms sanctioned by the central authority in the kingdom. This therefore necessitated the dependence of laws on the social and legal ties of lordship and kinship, which also dealt with the fallout from violence and injury. Of course, some of these ties could come into conflict with one another: as it was wrong to steal, so too was it wrong to avenge a thief, thus conferring honour upon him.[190] If there was conflict—as there clearly was in this context—the king could provide the solution. But there is absolutely no need to think about competing legal systems: the legitimacy of royal law depended not on monopolizing practice (kings simply did not have the power to do this) but on monopolizing the capacity to create rules when need arose.

CHARTERS, FINES, AND JURISDICTIONS

As stated above, it is an interesting feature of William's legislation that the king only received fines in theft-related assizes in a very few cases.[191] In contrast to royal and royally inspired laws of tenth-century England, where the king, through 120-shilling and 240-shilling fines for an increasing range of disobediences, was inserted into structures of local enforcement, the same did not happen in Scotland.[192] There were, however, a few more fines in law that showed the king expected to receive fines for offences other than theft, even if these fines have little of the conceptual unity of Anglo-Saxon fines for *oferhyrnesse* ('over-hearing' or 'disobedience'), a fine of 120s, attested in royal laws from the early tenth century.[193] *LS* records a fine of 100 cows levied on great lords within Galloway who

---

(*LS*, c. 7) and when particular courts should be held and who should attend them (*LS*, c. 14). What they do not do is set any prescriptive legal procedure in the framework of these courts. So the point is that, in *LS*, there is a distinction between prescriptive procedure (the majority) and the few statutes that do mention jurisdiction and administration but, crucially, do not give the same level of prescriptive detail that it clearly was possible to provide on an abstract level. For the melding of these two forms of statute under Alexander II, see below, pp. 162–4.

[190] Welsh law offers another interesting comparator. If someone was accused of abetting homicide, but did not injure anyone by so doing, the kin did not receive any compensation, either for the insult (*sarhaed*) or for the life-value (*galanas*) of the slain man (Ior. 106/15–21, in *Tair*, pp. 264–5). This was because (with a few adjustments) 'there is neither assault nor attack nor blood nor wound nor loss of life. And where those are not present, there is neither injury nor life-value and therefore the kindred is entitled to nothing'. Tom Lambert also explains how developing royal punishments grew out of honour cultures, and responded to their logics, rather than contradicted them: Lambert, *Law and Order*, chapter 2.

[191] For consistency in the amounts of Anglo-Saxon fines, see John Hudson, *The Oxford History of the Laws of England*, vol. 2: 871–1216 (Oxford, 2012), pp. 188–94.

[192] For the increasing presence of the king's financial involvement in the consequences of killing over the tenth century, even if kings did not 'tackle' feud directly, see Lambert, 'Theft, Homicide and Crime', pp. 27–32.

[193] Taylor, '*Lex Scripta*', pp. 54–60.

refused to pay the king's *cáin* whenever it was owed.[194] A chapter in *CD*, which is, most probably, a record of an enactment by David, prescribed another fine of eight cows on any *iudex* who left his presence without permission when the king was in his particular province.[195]

If we move away from the law, charter evidence reveals that there were even more fines owed to the king. The word invariably used for fines was *forisfactura* or *forisfactum* ('forfeiture'), although *defensio* ('defence') and *rectum* ('right') were used as well.[196] Late in the reign of David I, a charter formula appears which continued to be used well into the reign of John Balliol and beyond: *super meam forisfacturam* ('on pain of my forfeiture') or *super meam plenariam forisfacturam* ('full forfeiture').[197] The earliest offences worthy of the king's 'forfeiture' were withholding another lord's neyfs, breach of the king's peace, unlawful poinding (seizure of goods for debts), infringement of Scone Abbey's judicial rights, forcing payment of toll from those who had been given exemption by the king, and infringements of forest and warren rights, particularly from William's reign onwards.[198] The amount of the king's forfeiture could vary: some charters give the amount of 12 cows (for non-payment of teind); others 100 shillings; others £10 (for breach of peace and infringement of forest and warren rights).[199] The king was not the only high-status person to receive 'forfeitures': the large extant corpus of charters of the earls of Strathearn reveal that, in the thirteenth century, earls were meant to receive forfeitures for breach of their own peace and infringement of sanctuary rights.[200]

The charter evidence therefore shows that the king expected to receive more fines than written law records. One—breach of the king's peace—is attested in law as well as charters, although royal charters show that breach of peace did not only mean killing someone but also injuring or being generally violent to individuals or institutions within his peace. The other fines—unattested in law—are mostly dependent on gifts of land: an institution or individual could be given land with forest and warren privileges which were protected by the punitive might of the king's forfeiture.[201] Written law of the same period as these charters does not,

---

[194] *LS*, c. 20.

[195] *CD*, c. 28, discussed in Taylor, 'Assizes of David', pp. 223–5. For more on the king's peace, see below, pp. 164–72. See also *LS*, c. 7, in which the king receives a forfeiture if anyone held their court without *attempting* to summon the king's sheriff (it does not matter whether the sheriff or king's sergeand actually attended); for discussion of *LS*, c. 7, see Chapter 4, pp. 206–8.

[196] *CDI*, nos. 38 (*plenariam forisfacturam*), 188 (*defensio*), 210 (*forisfactum*); *RRS*, i, nos. 113 (*plenarium/plenum forisfactum*), 119, 125–126, and more. A full list of mentions of forfeitures in royal charters can be found by doing a simple search in the PoMS database, using the word 'forfeiture'.

[197] *CDI*, no. 38.   [198] *RRS*, i, p. 55; *RRS*, ii, p. 54.

[199] See, among many, *RRS*, i, nos. 230, 258; *RRS*, ii, no. 46.

[200] *Inchaffray Chrs*, no. 9. Under Alexander II, many of the forfeitures for which £10 was specified were for privileges of forest; see *Dunf. Reg.*, nos. 77 [AII/327]; *Glasgow Reg.*, i, no. 180 [AII/288]; Anderson, *Diplomata*, no. 30 [AII/261]; *Newbattle Reg.*, no. 22 [AII/269], 145 [AII/310], 157 [AII/275]; BL, Additional Charter 66570 [AII/331]; *Aberdeen Reg.*, i, pp. 15–16 [AII/289]; for hunting in Scotland, the main study remains John M. Gilbert, *Hunting and Hunting Reserves in Medieval Scotland* (Edinburgh, 1979), pp. 19–28.

[201] It might be thought that a scenario where the king expected to receive a fine if someone transgressed the forest privileges of a lord was a significant infringement of aristocratic rights. Certainly, jurisdictional 'immunities' are often conceptualized as lands where the king's writ or officer could not

however, deal with land: the first surviving law to do so was Alexander II's 1230 statute on novel dissaine.[202] The absence of these fines from law must be, in part, the result of the absence of legislation on property and property rights in general. Scottish law was not unique in this: Anglo-Saxon royal lawcodes of the tenth and early eleventh centuries, for example, tell us very little about 'bookland and folkland'.[203] If the argument of the previous two chapters is accepted—that elite power was increasingly conceived as territorial from the last third of the twelfth century—then one would expect to find references to forfeitures for property-related infringements, and that is indeed what charters do show. They are more an evidence of the king's support of aristocratic privilege than, at this stage, a regular insertion of the king's jurisdiction into landed disputes far down into society.

Like written law, royal charters rarely give a sense of how these fines owed to the king were to be collected. There are, however, exceptions: two brieves of Mael Coluim IV and two of William, all of which were on the collection of teind.[204] Mael Coluim's brieves were issued to St Andrews Cathedral Priory and the bishopric of Glasgow; William's to the bishoprics of Glasgow and (lengthily) Moray. William's brieve to Glasgow, however, is extremely similar to Mael Coluim's one to the same beneficiary and was probably based directly on Mael Coluim's earlier deed; it is thus not analysed in what follows.[205]

Mael Coluim's brieve to St Andrews (issued 1161×64) is addressed to 'his sheriffs and servants (*ministri*) of his whole land in whose power (*potestates*) the canons serving God and St Andrew hold churches'.[206] It states that if anyone withheld their teind or other ecclesiastical render, 'you' (meaning the sheriffs and royal servants) will collect the fine (*forisfactum*), as 'I enacted in the area (*patria*)'. Mael Coluim's brieve to Glasgow (datable no more closely than 1153×65) is somewhat longer, addressing the 'justices, barons, sheriffs, servants, French, and English, Scots, Welsh and Galwegian, and all parishioners of the church of St Kentigern of Glasgow and the bishop of the same'.[207] It too stated that everyone was to pay

---

go. This is clearly not the case here; there are no equivalents to *nec intromissionem* clauses. For the debates on Merovingian immunities, and how they were constitutive of royal power (and are so an interesting comparative example), see Barbara H. Rosenwein, *Negotiating Space: Power, Restraint and Privileges of Immunity in Early Medieval Europe* (Ithaca, 1999), particularly pp. 74–95; Paul Fouracre, 'Eternal Light and Earthly Needs: Practical Aspects of the Development of Frankish Immunities', in *Property and Power*, ed. Davies and Fouracre, pp. 53–81. See also the stimulating discussion of the question in medieval Britain and Ireland in Keith Stringer, 'States, Liberties and Communities in Medieval Britain and Ireland (*c*.1100–1400)', in *Liberties and Identities*, ed. Prestwich, pp. 5–36.

[202] See Chapter 5, pp. 285–93.

[203] For folkland, see the summary of the debates in Stephen Baxter and John Blair, 'Land Tenure and Royal Patronage in the Early English Kingdom: A Model and a Case Study', *ANS*, 28 (2006), pp. 19–46, at pp. 21–3.

[204] *RRS*, i, nos. 233, 258; *RRS*, ii, nos. 179, 281.   [205] *RRS*, i, no. 258; *RRS*, ii, no. 179.

[206] *RRS*, i, no. 233; for the use of the word *potestas* to describe the sheriff's authority under Mael Coluim IV, see Chapter 4, pp. 200–1.

[207] *RRS*, i, no. 258; for the inclusion of 'Welsh' in the address clause, see Broun, 'Welsh Identity', pp. 122–4, 142–3, 168; and Broun, *Scottish Independence*, pp. 126–8. See also Richard Sharpe, 'People and Languages in Eleventh- and Twelfth-Century Britain and Ireland: Reading the Charter Evidence', in *Reality behind Charter Diplomatic*, ed. Broun, pp. 1–119, at pp. 88–91, who stresses the linguistic element; cf. Kenji Nishioka, 'Scots and Galwegians in the "peoples address" of Scottish Royal Charters', *SHR*, vol. 87, no. 224 (2008), pp. 206–32.

teind but there was a more complicated procedure for the collection of fines for non-payment. The sheriff would take twelve cows as a fine from the wrongdoer but if the sheriff had been party to the detention or, indeed, had not given his own teind, the king's justice (*iusticia mea*) would take the fine from the sheriff.[208] William's charter to the bishopric of Moray (1185×89) contains an even more detailed procedure, which has already been discussed in Chapter 1.[209] There, it was argued that, although the charter appears to be repeating an original assize of David I, applied in the bishopric of St Andrews, the scribe of William's charter at the very least massively revised and updated the assize to fit the contemporary governmental context of the late 1180s.[210] William's charter also states that forfeitures were to be taken from those who defaulted on their teind payments: if peasants defaulted, they had to pay one cow and one sheep, which would be taken by the peasant's lord or thane. If the lord or thane refused to do this, or withheld their own teind, the sheriff would compel them to pay it and would then fine them eight cows, which went to the king. The charter emphasized that the king received the larger fine of eight cows from the 'thane or lord', which strongly suggests that he did not receive the fines of those of lower status, which were meant to be kept by the thane or lord.[211] If the sheriff failed in his responsibility, the justice would compel the wrongdoer to pay and also fine the sheriff eight cows.[212]

These three brieves/charters provide three anticipated structures for enforcing the payment of teind. Mael Coluim's brieve to St Andrews says that the sheriff would collect the fines from defaulters. His second brieve to Glasgow, perhaps around the same time, says that if sheriffs somehow failed to collect this fine, the king's justice would collect it instead. William's charter to Moray, issued around twenty years later, described a more nuanced structure than either. Thanes and lords were initially responsible for defaulting peasants; only if they failed would the sheriff come in and, again, if he failed, responsibility fell to the king's justice.

It might be thought that these three brieves/charters are extremely problematic for the validity of the argument put forward thus far in this chapter because they do show not only that fines were owed to the king for non-payment of teind but also that two types of royal official (the sheriff and justice) acted as enforcing agents in a hierarchical administrative structure should payment not be forthcoming. As this chapter has argued that written law did not show that much interest in the administration of and jurisdiction over its prescriptions, this appears to leave an

---

[208] The reference to the *iusticia* (the 'justice') is important and is developed in Chapter 4, pp. 220–2.

[209] See Chapter 1, pp. 63–4.

[210] Indeed, if anything, the king who *is* known to have enacted something on teind fines in St Andrews is Mael Coluim IV, who enacted *in patria* regulations (*RRS*, i, no. 233). William was not copying his procedure from Mael Coluim's, however, as it is much more complicated. It is nonetheless interesting that William's charter did not invoke the authority of his brother but, instead, his grandfather, David. For discussion of this example (although stressing the similarity, rather than difference, between William's and Mael Coluim's acts), see Hammond, 'Adoption and Routinization', p. 105.

[211] Fines collected from peasants or *ógtigerna* by thanes or knights if they neglected common army service were shared between the king and the thane; see *SA*, c. 26 (Taylor, 'Common Burdens', p. 230).

[212] For 'justice', rather than 'justiciar', see Chapter 4, pp. 211, 213–16.

unresolved contradiction between the evidence of royal charters on teind and that of written law.

But charters/brieves and law are different types of document.[213] Charters are for particular institutions or individuals and so reveal particular assumptions about existing local, or even regional, administrative structures; they should not, however, be taken as *prima facie* evidence for kingdom-wide structures. Laws, by contrast, provided statements at the most general level that could be upheld *regardless* of the local situation. Thus, the teind charters of Mael Coluim to Glasgow and St Andrews Priory tell us only that there were sheriffs and a justice who could operate within the bishopric of Glasgow and that there were sheriffs operating within the lands controlled by St Andrews Priory. They do not provide the information that sheriffs and justices were common throughout the kingdom; indeed the absence of the justice from Mael Coluim's brieve to St Andrews suggests that justices were not operating consistently or frequently enough in the churches of St Andrews Priory to be mentioned in Mael Coluim's brieve, as they were in the same king's brieve to Glasgow.[214] Most of the land of St Andrews Cathedral Priory lay north of the Forth and it will be shown in Chapter 4 that royal justices do not seem to have been given jurisdiction there under Mael Coluim in a way that they had been south of the Forth, where much of Glasgow's lands lay.[215] When Mael Coluim's brieve stated that he had enacted these procedures for St Andrews in the 'patria', it may well have been referring to the local area itself, rather than the kingdom; the *country*, like our modern 'countryside', rather than 'country', meaning our modern nation-state. *Patria*, after all, denoted the local area (the 'countryside') in thirteenth-century law and legal procedure.[216]

The absence of royal justices, therefore, in Mael Coluim's brieve to St Andrews may indicate their absence in reality from the political landscape north of the Forth during his reign. In contrast to charters, law would only set its prescriptions within uniform administrative and jurisdictional structures when such fora were common enough throughout the kingdom for the prescriptive content of law to be applied within them uniformly; law, in short, took longer to reflect institutional change. It is therefore important to note that William's charter to the bishopric of Moray, datable to the late 1180s, was drawn up at a time when the expectation was that although sheriffs and justices could hold their own courts, this nonetheless did

---

[213] For the rest of this section, I will refer to these brieves as charters because what follows is a point that stands for them both; the technical classification of a brieve as a command (whether addressed generally or to named individuals) and a charter as a formulaic gift, grant, or confirmation of privileges and moveable and immovable property holds. For the different languages of giving and granting in royal charters, see John Reuben Davies, 'The donor and the duty of warrandice: giving and granting in Scottish charters', in *Reality behind Charter Diplomatic*, ed. Broun, pp. 120–65.

[214] Indeed, if Mael Coluim's brieve to Glasgow was drafted by Ingelram, bishop of Glasgow (and then reissued under his successor, Jocelin), as suggested by Broun ('Welsh Identity', p. 168), then he would have known well the capacity of royal officials to intervene in his diocese.

[215] Most of the lands of St Andrews were north of the Forth, for which see the 'possession factoids' of the priory collected in the PoMS database (<http://db.poms.ac.uk/record/person/131/>). Under Mael Coluim IV, a justice only seems to have been in operation south of the Forth, see Chapter 4, pp. 217–24.

[216] See Chapter 5, pp. 305, 334–5.

not give them immediate responsibility for collecting fines from peasants who refused to pay teind. In William's charter to Moray, the responsibility first fell to thanes or lords, who appear to have kept the fines owed from their own peasants; only if they did not collect these fines did the sheriff, and then finally the justice, step in and exact fines from the high-status wrongdoer.[217] Thus, even during the 1180s, a period when we can be relatively confident that there were sheriffs and justices operating north and south of the Forth, the primary responsibility for the collection of teind fines (and the benefit of so doing) in Moray and St Andrews fell on lords, not on royal officials.[218]

The Delineation of Jurisdictions

Most of the chapters in *LS* thus provide general statements about practice without placing them within an administrative, institutional, or jurisdictional framework for their enforcement. Yet, as noted above, there are three chapters in *LS* that *do* show an interest in judicial fora and in the type of offences that could be heard within them. These chapters are rather different in tone from the majority of other *LS* chapters, which set out relatively detailed procedures to be followed when particular problems arose, but which never state in whose court the proce-dures were to take place. The 'jurisdictional' chapters in *LS* are not about pro-cedure but do set out the existence and legitimacy of magnate and royal courts. No chapter ever fully assigns particular offences to particular fora but the interest in jurisdiction is clear.[219] The three chapters are dated 1180, 1184, and 1197 respectively. *LS*, c. 15 (1197), refers to the courts of secular and ecclesiastical lords in which justice would be done.[220] *LS*, c. 7 (1180), states that neither 'bishops, abbots, earls nor barons, nor any one holding freely shall hold their court unless the king's sheriff or his sergeand are present or have been summoned there to be present to see that the court is conducted lawfully'.[221] These secular and ecclesias-tical court-holders could, apparently, hear any case, apart from four 'which belong to his [the king's] crown': rape, robbery, arson, and murder. This is the earliest statement in written law that secular and ecclesiastical lords had courts but were not allowed to hear the so-called pleas of the crown.[222] *LS*, c. 14, enacted in 1184,

[217] *RRS*, ii, no. 281.

[218] Although the brieve does just pertain to Moray, it nonetheless refers to this procedure as occurring in St Andrews diocese (*RRS*, ii, no. 281). Although it did not happen in St Andrews in David's reign in the way the charter proclaims, it is a reasonable assumption that similar regulations to those expressed in the Moray brieve were in place there by the late 1180s, when the Moray brieve was drawn up.

[219] Meaning 'power of declaring and administering law or justice; legal authority or power' and 'The extent or range of judicial or administrative power'; *Oxford English Dictionary* consulted online at <http://www.oed.com/view/Entry/102156?redirectedFrom=jurisdiction#eid>.

[220] Barrow wrote that the absence of the justiciar from this oath is surprising; Barrow, 'Justiciar', p. 89.

[221] It might be thought that this constituted quite a heavy level of shrieval supervision; however, this was at a time when there does not appear to have been a uniform expectation that all sheriffs would hold their courts. This statute and its context are discussed in more detail in Chapter 4, pp. 206–8.

[222] For pleas of the crown, see MacQueen, *Common Law*, pp. 42–3, although his view of *LS*, c. 7 (at p. 42), is compromised by the *APS* edition, which adds an additional sentence to the 1180 act, which is actually *SA*, c. 22, which states that 'no baron may hold a court of battle, water or iron unless

gave the first explicit statement in any sort of source that it was a standard requirement for sheriffs and justices to hold their own courts and gave a list of the types
of individuals who were expected to attend them. These three assizes together not
only confirm the existence of a hierarchy of offences but also reveal that there
were judicial fora to hear them, even if the majority of the remaining chapters of
LS do not mention them.

What constituted the pleas of the crown was not, however, consistent, even
within written law. *LS*, c.7 (1180), stated that the four pleas of the crown were
rape, robbery, arson, and murder, which were not to be heard by anyone other than
the king (or, presumably, his delegate). But the charter of William the Lion, issued
to Robert de Brus between 1165 and 1172, recorded six, not four, pleas of the
crown, including treasure trove and premeditated assault, in the list.[223] Whether
the king did in fact have exclusive control over his pleas is a question raised by
LS, c. 15, the text of an oath sworn at Perth in 1197, which reveals that bishops,
abbots, earls, barons, and thanes did deal with cases of murder and robbery (rape
and arson are not mentioned). This is strange on two levels: first, murder and robbery were meant to be pleas of the crown, so we should not find them mentioned
in this oath; second, if pleas of the crown were heard by magnates, why were arson
and rape not mentioned?[224] Later charter evidence shows that the king 'granted'
the right to hear the pleas of the crown to particular beneficiaries. Alexander II, for
example, confirmed the land of Nigg to his father's foundation, Arbroath Abbey,
in 1233, 'with the pleas and suits belonging to our crown'.[225]

This flexibility aside, it is clear that two legal chapters, one dated 1180 and the
other 1197, were concerned with what offences should be heard in which forum.
That they contradicted each other may well indicate that what constituted pleas of
the crown was still being worked out. Despite the uncertainty, the linking of
offences to particular fora in *LS*, cc. 7 and 15, shows an interest in jurisdiction that
is otherwise absent from *LS*, that is, from the law of the reign of William the Lion.
If we move away from laws, the diplomatic of royal charters also emphasize jurisdiction much more frequently from the 1170s onwards than do laws. William's
charter to Robert de Brus, confirming Annandale to him, also granted Robert the
privilege of sending one man (albeit one whom the king had chosen) to prosecute

the sheriff or his sergeand is present'. *SA*, c. 22, is very difficult to date, although the reference to
the ordeal may mean that it either pre-dates or cannot long post-date 1230 (for which, see Chapter 5,
pp. 280–4). If so, then it may be a *refinement* to *LS*, c. 7, made in the fifty years or so after the original
statute. But it is not in *LS*, c. 7, itself. For commentaries on this statute, see Alexander Grant, 'Murder
Will Out: Kingship, Kinship and Killing in Medieval Scotland', in *Kings, Lords and Men in Scotland
and Britain, 1300–1625: Essays in honour of Jenny Wormald* , ed. Steve Boardman and Julian Goodare
(Edinburgh, 2014), pp. 193–226, at pp. 212–13, and Chapters 4, pp. 206–8.

[223] For discussion of this charter, see Chapter 1, pp. 50–1.

[224] The later updating of this oath in the *LW* tradition (*LW*, c. 5) is interesting: it adds some variant
of *neque murdratores* after *raptores* and altering *interfectores in murthedric* to *interfectores hominium*,
thus adhering to the Glanvillian distinction between simple homicide and secret homicide (murder);
see Taylor, '*Leges Scocie*', p. 272, notes 761, 762. For more on this assize, see below, pp. 169–72.

[225] *Arbroath Liber*, i, no. 101 [AII/195]; for Arbroath's holdings see Keith J. Stringer, 'Arbroath
Abbey in Context: 1178–1320', in *The Declaration of Arbroath: History, Significance, Setting*, ed.
Geoffrey Barrow (Edinburgh, 2003), pp. 116–41, at pp. 123–9.

any crown cases occurring in Annandale before the king's justice.[226] It was also during the 1170s that William's charters start including a jurisdictional formula not only imported from England but also used by Scottish kings throughout the twelfth century in their charters to English beneficiaries, concerning lands and jurisdictional rights in England: sake, soke, toll, team, and infangentheof.

The meaning of these words have been hotly debated and discussed and this is not the place to go into them, except to note that infangentheof denoted the right to hang thieves and take their chattels.[227] The formula was not Scottish in origin (all are Old English words) but, from the 1170s onwards, it is used in Scotland both north and south of the Forth. Between 1172 and 1174, for example, Merleswain was given Ardross in Fife to be held 'with sake and soke and toll and team and infangentheof' for the service of one knight while, between 1165 and 1174, Ralph of Graham was given Cousland, Pentland, and Gogar in Lothian with the same jurisdictional privileges.[228] Predominantly north of the Forth, another alliterative formula was tacked onto the end, *furca et fossa* ('gallows and pit'), confirming the right to a gallows and also an ordeal pit.[229] During the reign of William the Lion, only two royal charters to lay beneficiaries south of the Forth included the 'gallows and pit' formula.[230] The second of these charters was actually confirming the grant of the first: between 1177 and 1185, Philip of Seton was given Seton and Winton in East Lothian and Winchburgh in West Lothian with 'gallows and pit', which was confirmed for his son, Alexander, in 1196.[231] Apart from this, gallows and pit only appear north of the Forth in the surviving evidence.[232] Although there are some examples from the 1170s, *furca et fossa* became more common in charters issued from the late 1180s onwards.[233]

---

[226] *RRS*, ii, no. 80.

[227] F. W. Maitland, *Domesday Book and Beyond: Three Essays in the Early History of England* (Cambridge, 1897), pp. 80–107, 258–90. The formula is one of the pieces of evidence for the whole debate about private jurisdiction before the Conquest of 1066; for a firm rebuttal, see Patrick Wormald, 'Lordship and Justice in the Early English Kingdom: Oswaldslow Revisited', in *Property and Power*, ed. Davies and Fouracre, pp. 114–36; Naomi D. Hurnard, 'The Anglo-Norman Franchises', *EHR*, vol. 64, nos. 252–253 (1949), pp. 289–327, 433–60; Julius Goebel, Jr, *Felony and Misdemeanor: A Study in the History of Criminal Law* (Philadelphia, PA, 1976), pp. 339–61; also discussed in Rosenwein, *Negotiating Space*, pp. 192–5. For a complete reassessment, see Lambert, *Law and Order*, chapter 7.

[228] *RRS*, ii, nos. 125, 137.

[229] *RRS*, ii, nos. 136, 152 (although relatively exceptional in detail), 185, 200, 302, 334, 335, 338, 340, 350, 375, 383, 390, 405, 418, 428, 524.

[230] Cf. *RRS*, ii, pp. 49–51; Grant, 'Franchises', pp. 189–90; and, for a brief study on baronial courts, Neville, *Land, Law and People*, pp. 13–40.

[231] *RRS*, ii, nos. 200, 390. It is very rare to be given details about ordeal pits. The exception is William's charter to Orm mac Aeda, in which we learn that Orm was only to have 'gallows and pit' in two places (as opposed to the many he had previously?), Abernethy and Inverarity. The men from Fife and Gowrie should go to the pit at Abernethy; those from his other lands should go to Inverarity (*RRS*, ii, no. 152).

[232] The simple formula—sake, soke, toll, team, and infangtheof—was used concerning lands north and South of the Forth. For the charters that did not include *furca et fossa*, see *RRS*, ii, nos. 116, 125, 135, 137, 147, 171, 204–205, 258, 459.

[233] So, for example, William's gift of Errol in Perthshire to William Hay (1178×1182) did not include the formula, but the confirmation to his son, David, did; *RRS*, ii, nos. 204, 383.

This formula confirmed not only jurisdictional rights and privileges on its holder but also, with the addition of gallows and pit, gave them a means of proof and punishment: the ordeal and the gallows. It does seem that this written emphasis on jurisdiction and judgment was new in the early years of William's reign. The corpus of David's and Mael Coluim's charters to Scottish beneficiaries contains one occurrence of the formula for each king but there is a major problem with its sole appearance under David.[234] It appears in a charter drawn up for Durham by a Durham scribe who was accustomed to using the formula in the charter diplomatic of the institution.[235] The one occurrence in Mael Coluim's corpus is in his charter granting Renfrew in Ayrshire to Walter fitz Alan for five knights, probably on 24 June 1161.[236] The almost complete absence of this formula under Mael Coluim IV and David is even more striking given that jurisdictional formulae were used in their charters to beneficiaries in England. Charters of David and Earl Henry for Tynemouth Priory, for example, or of Earl Henry and Mael Coluim IV for Uhtred of London, concerning land in Northumberland and Middlesex respectively, do contain the formula.[237] But the few charters addressed to religious institutions in Scotland that give land in feu (*in feudum*) do not use the formula.[238] Even more strikingly, the few charters to laymen under David I do not mention jurisdictional formulae despite giving land south of the Forth *in feudo et hereditate* for some sort of knight service.[239] The implication is that, although the formula may have been introduced in Scottish royal charters for beneficiaries within the bounds of the kingdom in the reign of Mael Coluim IV, it was only used

---

[234] Although most royal charters in this period were issued to religious institutions, the absence of the formula *saca et soca* (and variants) cannot be explained by the patterns of survival. We do, after all, have a few charters to laymen, and they do not use the formula: *CDI*, nos. 16, 177, 194, 210. Hammond has raised the possibility that *CDI*, no. 194, may have been a later confection, possibly drawn up at the same time as one of Countess Ada de Warenne's charters on the same subject (EUL, Laing Charters, Box 2, no. 67), but also notes that this is only one of three potential options; Hammond, 'Adoption and Routinization', pp. 98–9. For *CDI*, no. 177, being drafted on the request of the beneficiary, Walter of Ryedale, see Stephen Marritt, 'The Ridale Papal Letters and Royal Charter: A Twelfth-Century Anglo-Scottish Baronial Family, the Papacy, the Law and Charter Diplomatic', *EHR*, vol. 176, no. 523 (2011), pp. 1332–54, particularly pp. 1339–43.

[235] *CDI*, no. 31, 32 [duplicates].

[236] *RRS*, i, no. 184. It has long been accepted that *RRS*, i, no. 184 (which survives only in the notebook of Sir John Skene), was issued at the same Roxburgh assembly as *RRS*, i, no. 183 (*RRS*, i, p. 225, note 1). *RRS*, i, no. 183, survives as an original in the Durham Cathedral Archives (Durham, Dean and Chapter, Misc. Chrs., no. 7162). Matthew Hammond has argued that this charter was made at the request of Walter fitz Alan for the benefit of Durham: Hammond, 'Adoption and Routinisation', pp. 108–9. If so, then it may well be likely that he requested *RRS*, i, no. 184, on the same occasion; was that charter drawn up by a Durham scribe? If so, then it would mean that both our early examples under David and Mael Coluim were drawn up in the context of Durham charter production.

[237] *CDI*. nos. 84, 107 (no infangentheof), 144; *RRS*, i, no. 206 (no infangentheof). Even if these were compiled by beneficiaries, the concentration of the formula outside the kingdom is still noteworthy.

[238] See *CDI*, no. 53 (*dedi ⁊ concessi… in feuda(m)*); 161 (*tenere in feudo ⁊ in elemosinam*); 177 (*ad tenend' de me et heredibus meis in feudo et hereditate*), 184 (*tenendum de me in feudo*).

[239] These are problematic charters. Hammond suggests they were exceptional and were often obtained when the beneficiary was in dispute with another party: Hammond, 'Adoption and Routinization', pp. 106–9; see *CDI*, nos. 177, 194. See, under Mael Coluim, *RRS*, i, nos. 255–256.

consistently north and south of the Forth under William, and in charters from the 1170s onwards.[240]

This is not to say that royal charters of David and Mael Coluim had never mentioned the judicial capacity of many of their beneficiaries; they just did not do so in such a way as to make jurisdiction a formal and indissoluble part of the land-gift itself. David I's long charter to Dunfermline Abbey stated that the abbey was free from all royal exactions, save for defence of the realm and 'royal justice', but only if the abbot failed to do justice in his court.[241] Similar formulae are used in the charters of Mael Coluim to Dunfermline and of William to Holyrood and Arbroath.[242] Both David's and Mael Coluim's charters confirmed the privileges of Holyrood and Scone Abbeys to conduct the ordeals of iron, water, and battle, Scone with 'the liberty that no-one ought to answer outside the court'.[243] But only one surviving charter of Mael Coluim IV actually makes jurisdiction an intrinsic part of any gift of land, as became standard from the 1170s.[244]

The charter and legal evidence thus show different ways of thinking about the administration of law. While three chapters of *LS* show a concern with judicial fora, they are not integrated into the more detailed and generalized procedures characteristic of the other *LS*-chapters. Charter evidence, by contrast, was increasingly concerned with jurisdiction: from the 1160s/1170s onwards, gifts of land, often but not exclusively to secular beneficiaries, added jurisdictional formulae and started to mention particular offences which only the king could hear. Thus, if one removed the three chapters in *LS* which do refer to judicial fora and jurisdiction (although not procedure), the evidence of charters and law would run in completely opposite directions: one concerned with enforcement through administration and jurisdiction, the other assuming enforcement through the existence of

---

[240] The distinction between *RRS*, i, nos. 255–256, and Mael Coluim's charters to beneficiaries in Northumberland, Huntingdonshire, and Tottenham is remarkable. Take this as an example: 'to be held by him and his heirs in feu and heritage, freely and quite, from all which pertains to me, with sake and soke and toll and team as well as Uhtred ever held that fief' (*RRS*, i, no. 206).

[241] *CDI*, no. 33.

[242] *RRS*, i, no. 118; *RRS*, ii, nos. 39, 197, 513; also repeated in Alexander II's charter to Arbroath (*Arbroath Liber*, i, no. 100 [AII/6]). In William's charter to Holyrood, it is stated: 'and the abbot shall do full right in accusations on his man, and if he fails in this, then the sheriff and the justice shall do right on him, concerning the accusation made lawfully by the claimant on the abbot's man' (*RRS*, ii, no. 39). The reference to the sheriff and justice is not surprising here, given their south-of-Forth base in the mid-1160s, for which see Chapter 4, pp. 218–24.

[243] *RRS*, i, no. 247.

[244] It is of note that there were large numbers of smaller courts, which have often not received enough attention in the existing scholarship (nor will they do here). In general, these courts heard small pleas. *LS*, c. 7, ends by stating that 'concerning all other pleas, every free man who has a court may have all that falls there, saving the justice of the lord king'. These may well have involved *blodwite* (a fine for minor bloodshed), *birthinsake* (petty theft, also attested in *LS*, c. 8). The earliest appearance of these fines is in the Kelso cartulary, concerning land in Clydesdale, in an act dated 1147×60, but the remaining cluster in the late twelfth to early thirteenth centuries (*Kelso Liber*, i, nos. 102–4, 108–9, 112–14; ii, no. 474). The context of *Kelso Liber*, i, nos. 102–104 and 112–14, is discussed in Andrew Smith, 'The Kelso Abbey Cartulary: Context, Production and Forgery' (PhD Dissertation, University of Glasgow, 2011), pp. 63–7. See also mentions to *blodwite* in *Spalding Misc.*, v, p. 211, and *RRS*, ii, no. 39, for what looks like a Latin rendering of *blodwite* and *birthinsake*.

pre-existing socio-legal ties that could apply anywhere, regardless of in whose land or jurisdiction the offence took place. How can this be explained?

If one thinks in ideal types, there are two ways in which offences may generally be treated. The first is to make the type of offence determine the forum. This is the situation envisaged by *Glanvill* (1187×89) in England when its author described that theft, deemed a minor offence, was the preserve of sheriffs whereas felonies, deemed more serious, belonged to the king's court.[245] The second way is where persons, rather than primarily offences, determine the forum for any settlement. Thus, a powerful person could hear whatever he wanted, and do whatever justice he wanted, regardless of what the offence was.[246] In this second way, therefore, personal status determines the treatment of offences. The charter evidence from the 1170s seems to correspond with the first way and the legal evidence predominantly with the second. There were, of course, crossovers: charter evidence shows that major institutions, such as Arbroath Abbey, could hear pleas of the crown and the legal evidence is not entirely devoid of references to a hierarchy of offences and judicial fora, even if correct legal practice was not situated within this structure. Nonetheless, the distinction still holds.

What is, perhaps, difficult to grasp (or, perhaps, accept) is that these two ways of thinking—abstracted, non-jurisdictional, prescriptive law on the one hand, and jurisdictional power over land and men on the other—co-existed in Scotland during the last third of the twelfth century, a period when much of the surviving law was made and charter diplomatic shows an increased focus on jurisdictional boundaries. Yet co-exist in separate spheres they did, although they did not do so forever. Alexander II's legislation adopted the same jurisdictional framework that had been used in charters from the 1160s/1170s onwards but had not appeared in William's earlier law, as will now be shown.

All four of Alexander's statutes enacted in October 1230 are positioned in some way within all or a combination of the jurisdictions of sheriffs, justiciars, and lay and ecclesiastical lords, and the type of pleas that each authority could hear.[247] One chapter is concerned with accusations of theft and robbery. If anyone accused another of either offence and was acquitted, then the original appellant would be either in the mercy of the lord king, if it was a case of robbery, or in the mercy of the 'earl or baron' if it was a case of theft.[248] No piece of legislation under William incorporates procedure and jurisdiction in this way. Alexander's statute of novel dissasine, the procedure whereby somebody could accuse another of unlawfully dispossessing them of land and/or chattels, states explicitly that the case would be initiated by a brieve from either the king or the justiciar, and the justiciar or sheriff

---

[245] *Glanvill*, IX, 8 (p. 177).

[246] Moreover, the status of the person also determined where he would be tried if he was accused: thus high-status people would be tried by the highest authority, regardless of the type of offence in question.

[247] *SA*, cc. 4–7; for discussion of these acts, see Chapter 5, pp. 273–93.

[248] *SA*, c. 6. The exception under William may be *SA*, cc. 20–21, which are conceivably statutes enacted in Lothian (where one might expect a greater level of precision anyway); for discussion, see Note 134.

would then conduct the inquest to see whether the claimant was telling the truth.[249]

Moving beyond the 1230 legislation, another chapter attributable to Alexander II states that, if a stranger stayed more than one night in a lodging without having anyone act as his surety, and was discovered, he would be put before the sheriff or justiciar to do with him as they would (one imagines that, had this chapter appeared in *LS*, it might have simply said the stranger would be treated 'as a proven wrong-doer'—'sicut malefactore probato'—or, perhaps, a 'proven thief').[250] A law enacted in 1244 set up indictments in Lothian whereby each vill would produce a panel to accuse known wrongdoers within their locality.[251] Those indicted would then be put before the justiciar, who would supervise a visnet (a 'neighbourhood jury') to determine their guilt. If any of them were convicted of murder or robbery 'or any other like felony which pertains to the crown of the king', their chattels would be confiscated by the king and justice would be done but, if any of them were con-victed by the justiciar of theft or homicide, they would then be handed over to 'barons or their bailies' who would do justice on them 'in their free baronies', unless the king, through his mercy, intervened.[252] These indictments were done explicitly in accordance with structures of royal and aristocratic justice: kings had control over murder and robbery; lords had control over the punishment of theft and homicide and received the profits of justice. No chapter on theft in *LS* comes close to this level of integration of procedural content and administrative and juris-dictional structure.

By the end of the period discussed in this chapter, therefore, the content of written law had shifted: from setting out general rules of practice, regardless of whatever level of administrative and jurisdictional power existed, to rules being made within an explicit structure of landed jurisdictions, magnate courts, and royal administration. Did this constitute a major change on the ground? One should not assume so necessarily. If lords, for example, through their capacity to offer protection and take people into their 'peace', had long had a financial stake in the consequences of homicide, as can be seen in *LS*, c. 21 (*LBS*), then it would be possible to grant them or 'allow' them jurisdiction over homicide without too much trouble. In this context, there is structural—although not formal—continu-ity in the protection offered by lords and the jurisdictional rights given to and claimed by lords in their own courts in their own land. The same can be said for theft, a much more obvious target of royal legislative ambition. It may seem para-doxical that, by the 1230s and 1240s, theft was one offence that Alexander II and his legislative assemblies felt very comfortable 'delegating' to other lords as a juris-dictional privilege, despite theft being the main subject of his father's legislation, and the offence most subject to rule-making and punishment, understood as an abstract wrong or a crime. Seen in this light, it becomes even clearer that, in

---

[249] *SA*, c. 7; the text as in *SA* is printed and discussed in Taylor, 'Assizes of David', pp. 217–18.
[250] *SA*, c. 23.   [251] *SA*, c. 2.
[252] It is more common for legal material to refer to *baroniae* than charter material in the thirteenth century (in addition to *SA*, c. 2, see *SA*, c. 5). See also the inquests that refer to testimonies from the 'baronies', in *APS*, i, pp. 98–9; this was also noted in Grant, 'Franchises', pp. 190–1.

comparison with Alexander's, William's legislation never aimed to establish an exclusive jurisdiction over theft, just a monopoly on the formal rules for dealing with it. If his law did not aim to establish exclusive penal jurisdiction on the ground, then the later space given to lords' jurisdiction over theft would not have had much practical impact: lords and local communities would have remained responsible for dealing with theft on a large scale.

The change was, instead, one of jurisdictional linguistics and institutional apparatus. It may not seem a big jump from a scenario where law left a lot of *de facto* space for local powers—whoever they were—to one where the same would have applied in practice, but those jurisdictional powers were defined according to offence and fixed to the land and title of elite franchises and royal administrative institutions.[253] The change from a generalized and abstracted rule-making to rules negotiated between different levels of jurisdiction and administration which were in the king's power to give and confirm did, however, represent a different way of thinking about royal power over property and privileges than that evidenced by the law of William the Lion. While this shift in written law was taking place, it is clear that the power of sheriffs and justice/justiciars, the subjects of Chapter 4, had become fixed enough to be incorporated into the administration of law. The written law of Alexander II was thus able to depend on both the jurisdiction of royal officials and that of lay and ecclesiastical elites in a way that William's was not. It is in this context that the final section of this chapter will examine the king's peace.

THE KING'S PEACE

In the historiography of medieval England, the king's peace has been subject to a small but influential amount of research, influential because of the key part it plays in discussions on the origins of crime. The overall thrust of this scholarship was as follows: although it was an expectation placed on all medieval kings to maintain the peace, the king's peace could develop a stronger conceptual and ideological force if all law-worthy men in the kingdom swore an oath promising to maintain it.[254] When peace therefore became a concept actively maintained across the whole kingdom, particularly by oaths, then all types of disorder could be punished by the king as breaches of his peace. If this had happened, then homicide, for example, was no longer an offence causing dishonour to the victim and his associates but, because it constituted a breach of royal peace, it was also punished by the king or his representative. If this punishment was greater than the compensation owed to the victim, the killing could be defined as a crime. Since Sir Frederick Pollock's lecture outlining this argument, peace and its breach have become the litmus test for the existence of the category of crime in medieval England and, accordingly, a

---

[253] Compare Grant, 'Franchises', pp. 184–92.

[254] For a much more in-depth analysis of the scholarship, see Lambert, 'Protection, Feud and Royal Power', pp. 164–71; and Lambert, 'Introduction'.

state judicial system of any level of sophistication.[255] Debates have centred on when the king's peace gained conceptual force: from Alfred or from Henry II to the time of *Bracton*, whose author states that only by the king's grace could outlaws be 'inlawed' by being readmitted to the 'peace'.[256]

Scotland does not seem a particular promising example of Pollock's conceptual royal peace: *LBS*, after all, shows that different ranks exercised their own separate peace, suggesting that the king's peace did not undercut the protection offered by others. Nonetheless, Alan Harding has argued that, although there is no concrete evidence in Scotland for a strong conceptual and ideological royal peace, as in thirteenth-century England, brieves of protection issued by Scottish kings in the twelfth century show that a notion of royal peace was a *de facto* part of all written documents issued by the king.[257] The king's peace thus had a conceptual force which, if breached, was subject to punishment by the king's sheriffs. Harding's arguments and their implications must be re-examined here, because they run directly counter to those presented above, which have, in essence, argued that the authority of the king was not inserted consistently into all legal practice in this way during the twelfth century.

Brieves of Peace and Protection

Brieves of protection are defined here as formulaic written grants of the king's peace that contain a command that no one may do harm to those under royal protection (hence their broad classification as 'brieves'). They begin to survive in some form from the beginning of the twelfth century and continued to be issued under the names of successive kings throughout the central Middle Ages.[258] They all have a clear focus, although the diplomatic formulae of expression was not identical.[259] Some are grants of protection that follow a land grant from the king; some are confirmations of the king's protection to large monastic houses; others wish the beneficiary's land and men to be protected.[260] Still others grant the king's peace and protection to those travelling to markets, often in newly privileged burghs.[261]

---

[255] Sir Frederick Pollock, 'The King's Peace', in his *Oxford Lectures and Other Discourses* (London, 1890), pp. 65–90.

[256] Wormald, 'Maitland', pp. 17–18; Wormald, 'Giving God and the King'; cf. Goebel, *Felony and Misdemeanor*, pp. 7–25, 44–61, 117–22, 423–40; for further works on the king's peace, see Jack K. Weber, 'The King's Peace: A Comparative Study', *The Journal of Legal History*, vol. 10, no. 2 (1989), pp. 135–60.

[257] Harding, 'Medieval Brieves', pp. 115–21, mentioned in MacQueen, *Common Law*, pp. 107–8. T. B. Lambert has also taken issue with Harding's argument in another context, for which see Lambert, 'Protection, Feud and Royal Power', pp. 184–8, who comes to similar conclusions to those presented here by another approach.

[258] Harding, 'Medieval Brieves', pp. 115–21; *RRS*, ii, pp. 71–4; *RRS*, i, pp. 64–5.

[259] For the importance of this, see forthcoming work by Joanna Tucker on twelfth- and thirteenth-century legal/administrative brieves, which will shed more light on the subject.

[260] *RRS*, i, no. 125; *RRS*, ii, nos. 24, 32, 76, 239; *Inchaffray Chrs*, no. 53 [AII/103]; for Galloway and protection, see *RRS*, i, no. 230.

[261] *RRS*, ii, no. 442; for the inclusion of protection clauses in longer charters to burghs, see nos. 467, 475.

Harding's main argument was that the origins of the actions of trespass and lawburrows (both under the jurisdiction of the fourteenth-century sheriff) were to be found in the extension of the royal protection in Scotland from the early twelfth century onwards.[262] This argument is not the focus here but Harding made some crucial points about earlier royal protection on which his narrative of the later Middle Ages rested, which must be examined. Harding defined protection (at least for the twelfth to fourteenth centuries) as a 'written grant of the king's peace', which came into Scotland as 'an intrinsic part of the Anglo-Norman charter'; the adoption of charters by the kings of Scots being, for him, a process culminating in the reign of David I.[263] Harding then turned to the formula for the brieve of protection found in the early-fourteenth-century register of brieves in a manuscript known as the Ayr manuscript, which will be discussed in detail in Chapter 5.[264] Harding then compared this 'developed and mature' brieve with the earlier examples from the twelfth century and found that, with one exception, 'all the grants of protection appear to have emerged in Scotland...by the reign of Mael Coluim IV', having identified ten elements of this protection, including the capacity to recover fugitive neyfs.[265] For Harding, because the king's peace was inherent in *every* charter and brieve the king issued, it acted *de facto* as the conceptual underpinning of society and thus vastly increased the king's presence in the maintenance of law and order.[266]

In order to unpick this argument, we must start with the 'developed and mature' brieve of protection that underpinned Harding's understanding of protection. The 'brieve of protection of three clauses' is the first item in the Ayr register and is translated below:[267]

The king to all the worthy men of his whole land, greeting. Know that we have lawfully received such-and-such, their lands, their men, and all their earthly possessions and all their goods, moveable and immoveable, under our firm peace and protection. Whereof we firmly prohibit that anyone presume to bring any shame, evil, molestation, injury or oppression (*dampnum, malum, molestia, iniuria uel gravamen*) unlawfully on them, on pain of our full forfeiture.

On poinds. We also grant to them that no one shall take their poinds or those of their men for any debt, pledge or forfeiture, unless for their own debt, pledge or forfeiture, excepting our burghs, firmly emphasising that no one shall go against this, our grant, on pain of the same, our full forfeiture.

Compulsion. Moreover, we also command and firmly order the justiciars, sheriffs, grieves and their bailies to whom these present letters shall come that all those men

---

262 Harding, 'Medieval Brieves', pp. 124–5.
263 Harding, 'Medieval Brieves', p. 124; for the adoption of charters in Scotland, see Dauvit Broun, 'The Writing of Charters in Scotland and Ireland in the Twelfth Century', in *Charters and the Use of the Written Word in Medieval Society*, ed. Karl Heidecker (Turnhout, 2000), pp. 113–31; Dauvit Broun, The Adoption of Brieves in Scotland', in *Charters and Charter Scholarship in Britain and Ireland*, ed. Marie Therese Flanagan and Judith A. Green (Basingstoke, 2005), pp. 164–83; and now Hammond, 'Adoption and Routinization'.
264 See Chapter 5, pp. 301–7.   265 Harding, 'Medieval Brieves', pp. 121–2, 124.
266 See also Lambert, 'Protection, Feud and Royal Power', pp. 185–8.
267 *Scottish Formularies*, ed. Duncan, A1, p. 11.

who owe debts in their balliwicks or burghs to such-and-such or his sure attorney, bearer of the present letters, shall render them to him or his sure attorney, bearing the present letter, lawfully and without delay; following what such-and-such, or his said attorney has proven in their presence that the said debt is owed to him lawfully, and compel them in as much as is right so that, because of their default, we will not hear more on this suit.

Despite Harding's assurances, the first clause of the brieve of protection did not reach its register form until the 1260s.[268] Only then did the language of brieves of protection specify that the protection applied to 'moveable and immoveable goods' as well as lands, men, and generally defined possessions. The inclusion of a formulaic prohibition of injury did not become standard until the 1180s, although this formula was normally some variant or combination of *iniuria*, *violencia*, or *contumelia* (and even then the words do not regularly appear in the same form).[269] The formula *iniuria, molestia vel gravamen* did not appear until the 1200s; the first appearance of *malum* was not until the 1220s, and even then was used very inconsistently.[270] A standard, basic and formulaic protection grant seems not to have been available until the 1180s and certainly did not take the form of the Ayr register brieve until the 1260s.

If protection did not reach its attested early-fourteenth-century formula-standard until the 1260s, what, then, did it cover before this? Harding argued that the ten elements of protection included commands for the recovery of neyfs and the prohibition of poinding, despite the recovery of neyfs not ending up in the brieve formula of protection.[271] However, actions over poinding (taking a person's chattels to pay off a proven debt) and recovery of neyfs were, in fact, separate from protection though they could be added to it if the beneficiary wanted them and wanted, presumably, to pay for them. A brieve of William the Lion, dated 1189×95, should serve as a good example.[272]

William, by the grace of God, king of Scots, to all the worthy men of his land, cleric or lay, greeting. Know that I have lawfully received the church of St Cuthbert of Holy Island, the monks there serving God, and their men, and all their earthly possessions, into my firm peace and protection (*in mea firma pace et protectione juste recepisse*). I also grant to them that, wherever they be in my land, they shall be free and quit from all toll on their demesne chattels. And I command that wherever they can find fugitives of their land outside my demesne, they should have them lawfully. Whereof I prohibit firmly that anyone presume to bring any injury or violence on the monks or their men (*iniuriam uel uiolentiam aliquam inferre*), or demand toll from them for their demesne chattels or keep the fugitives of their land from them unlawfully, on pain of my full forfeiture, as the charter of King David, my grandfather, and the charter of King Mael Coluim, my brother, testify. Witness: Hugh, my chancellor,

---

[268] *RRS*, iv, 1, nos. 50, 158.　　[269] *RRS*, ii, nos. 239, 313, 316.

[270] *RRS*, ii, no. 475; *Scone Liber*, no. 70 [AII/41]; *Kelso Liber*, i, no. 184 [AII/75]; *Scone Liber*, no. 73 [AII/73]; *Inchaffray Chrs*, no. 53 [AII/103]; *RRS*, iv, 1, nos. 8, 158.

[271] Harding, 'Medieval Brieves', pp. 117–21, 122; *Scottish Formularies*, ed. Duncan, A1 (p. 11), and the developments in the Bute formulary, in *Scottish Formularies*, ed. Duncan, B28–B31 (p. 133).

[272] *RRS*, ii, no. 313.

Archibald, abbot of Dunfermline, William Lindsay, Robert of London, my son, Gervase Avenel, David Lindsay. At Roxburgh.

This generally addressed brieve contains three separate grants and three separate warnings from the king. It is a grant of the king's peace and protection; it exempts the monks from paying toll; and it further allows them to pursue fugitive neyfs outside the king's demesne. The three prohibitions correspond to their particular grant: the king prohibits anyone from bringing injury or violence on the monks (thus breaking his protection); he prohibits anyone taking toll from them (for they are exempt); he finally prohibits anyone from detaining the monks' neyfs on their land unlawfully (because the monks have the privilege of pursuing them). The separate nature of each grant stands out clearly in this single brieve. What is most important here is that the grant of peace and protection is accompanied by the prohibition of injury and violence, and the specification of a general forfeiture. That is all.

The brieve of protection was thus a very simple instrument to which much else could be added. It could be issued alone or it could be issued in addition to other grants. Simple grants of protection can be found throughout the thirteenth century. This is an example from 1222, issued by Alexander II, for Lesmahagow Priory:[273]

> Alexander, by the grace of God, king of Scots, to all the worthy men of his whole land, greeting. Know that we (*sciatis nos*) have lawfully received the prior of Lesmahagow and his men, lands and all his possessions under our firm peace and protection. Whereof we firmly prohibit that anyone presume unlawfully to bring any injury, molestation or oppression on them, on pain of our full forfeiture. Witness: William del Bois, chancellor, Earl Patrick. At Traquair, on the ninth day of December, in the ninth year of our kingship. [9 December 1222]

As in the William the Lion example mentioned earlier, much could be added to the simple protection. The next example is again from Alexander II's reign and shows how a command for the lawful recovery of neyfs could easily be added to the simple formula of protection:[274]

> Alexander, by the grace of God, king of Scots, to all the worthy men of his whole land, greeting. Know that we have lawfully received the house and abbot and canons of Inchaffray and their men, lands, and all their earthly possessions under our firm peace and protection. Whereof we firmly prohibit that anyone presume to bring injury or molestation or oppression on them on pain of our full forfeiture. We also grant to the aforesaid abbot and canons that wherever they may find their neyfs and fugitives who ought to be theirs by right (*de ratione*) outside our demesne, they shall have them lawfully. And we prohibit firmly that anyone should presume to keep them from them unlawfully, on pain of our full forfeiture. Witness: Thomas of Stirling, archdeacon of Glasgow, Henry de Balliol, chamberlain. At Stirling, on the eighth day of June, in the eleventh year of our kingship [8 June 1225].

---

[273] *Kelso Liber*, i, no. 184 [AII/75].   [274] *Inchaffray Chrs*, no. 53 [AII/103].

Royal peace and protection were not, therefore, as Harding would have it, inherent in all gifts and grants from the king but constituted a very particular grant, stating that a particular place, person, or institution and their possessions had been taken under the king's peace, prohibiting generally defined injuries, and threatening a financial penalty of an unspecified amount if anyone broke the peace. Who and what was received into the royal protection must have been a mixture of royal policy and beneficiary petition.[275] But the point is that it served as a general prohibition of injury sought by individuals or institutions (seemingly of high status) in conjunction with other privileges in order to secure their possessions and thus cement their wealth and status.[276] Nothing thus far has been said that directly impinges on the ability of aristocrats to act in a protective capacity alongside the king; indeed, thirteenth-century earls and other lords also offered their own protection in written form by the late twelfth century.[277]

Oaths

The only issue left to think about is, did Scottish kings demand an oath from all their free men to maintain their peace? One of the reasons why Henry II is credited with the creation of a wider conceptual peace in England is because of the oaths of loyalty sworn to him promising to uphold the law. Oaths to maintain the peace were a key part of Pollock's argument about its conceptual force and have been used in a different way by Patrick Wormald for Anglo-Saxon England to argue that oaths transformed all transgressions into breaches of faith against the king from the tenth century, if not from the time of Alfred.[278] The evidence presented thus far suggests that oaths were not used in this way but it is important to be sure, not least because, in 1197, William the Lion, inspired by Angevin peacekeeping legislation, summoned a mass oath-taking assembly to meet at Perth. What exactly did this ritual entail and what was its significance?

In the annal for 1197, Roger of Howden recorded in his *Chronica* that

> In the same year [1197], William king of Scots, imitating a good precedent, made the men of his kingdom (*homines regni*) swear that they would serve the peace with all their might (*pro posse suo*) and that they would not be thieves, robbers, outlaws or their

[275] The surviving brieves reveal that it was also common for the king's peace and protection to be granted to those travelling to and from markets and fairs in burghs, for example. Not all burghs which received this privilege were royal burghs—the bishop's burgh at Glasgow represents a particularly obvious exception—and thus we may envisage a situation where the king's peace automatically extended to those trading and coming to his own burghs (although it still had to be subject to a specific grant) but the extension of his protection to the burghs under the control of other lords, whether lay or ecclesiastical, had to be petitioned for and, presumably, bought: *RRS*, ii, nos. 442, 467, 475.

[276] The comments of MacQueen are important. MacQueen argues that actions of wrang and unlaw did not break the king's peace and protection but the peace and protection exercised by whatever local authority mattered on the ground, whether it be that of a lord or that of a burgh; Hector L. MacQueen, 'Some Notes on Wrang and Unlaw', in *Miscellany V*, ed. Hector L. MacQueen, Stair Society 52 (Edinburgh, 2006), pp. 13–26, at pp. 24–5.

[277] *Paisley Reg.*, p. 213; *Kelso Liber*, i, no. 254.

[278] The clearest statements of these views are Wormald, 'Maitland', pp. 17–18; Wormald, 'God and the King', and Wormald, 'Anglo-Saxon Law and Scots Law', pp. 194, 197.

harbourers, nor would they help those men in anything, and that, when they might know of any kind of wrongdoer, they would, with all their might, capture and destroy him.[279]

Howden's words echo many of the emphases of the Angevin peacekeeping assizes he transcribed into his *Chronica*. The Assizes of Clarendon (1166) and Northampton (1176) target *latrones, murdratores, roboratores,* and *eorum receptatores*.[280] However, the clearest parallel comes not from these two famous assizes but from the lesser-known *Edictum Regium*, drawn up in 1195 by Hubert Walter, archbishop of Canterbury and justiciar of England, distributed throughout the English counties and again copied by Howden into his *Chronica*.[281]

Edictum Regium is a description of an oath sworn in the county court to uphold the king's peace. It is in the tradition of the Assizes of Clarendon and Northampton, stating the form of the oath to be sworn and then moving on to logistics: Clarendon concentrated on the sheriff's responsibilities, Northampton on those of the justices, and *Edictum* on the knights of the shire appointed to oversee the oath-taking and the pursuit of criminals. In *Edictum*, all free men above the age of fifteen were to swear an oath in front of the knights of the shire, promising that they would not be thieves, robbers, outlaws, or their harbourers and that, if they knew of anyone committing these offences, they would capture them and hand them over to the knights, who would then deliver them to the sheriff.[282] Howden described the efficacy of this oath: apparently, many wrongdoers were captured as a result, although some were pre-warned and fled the county with a heavy conscience.[283]

If one follows Howden's description, the 1197 oath in Scotland was very similar in scope to *Edictum Regium* of 1195 in England. According to Howden, all men of the kingdom of Scots were to swear to uphold the king's peace *pro posse suo* and not to become thieves, robbers, outlaws, or their harbourers. But to think the same thing was being prescribed in 1197 in Scotland as in 1195 in England would be erroneous. The text of the 1197 oath actually survives as *LS*, c. 15. This shows that, although the 1197 was inspired by *Edictum*, it was far shallower in scope.[284] The chapter states that 'this is the assize of the lord king made at Perth on St Augustine's Day [27 May]' and describes how the bishops, abbots, earls, barons, and thanes swore that they would not be thieves, 'killers in secret (*interfectores in murthedric*)', or robbers, nor would they maintain or harbour such men but bring them to

---

[279] Howden, *Chronica*, iv, p. 33.
[280] *Select Charters*, ed. Stubbs, pp. 170, 179; Northampton also targets *falsoneria vel iniqua combustione*.
[281] Howden, *Chronica*, iii, pp. 299–300; *Select Charters*, ed. Stubbs, pp. 257–8.
[282] The age limit is higher than that specified in II Cnut 21, where all men of above twelve years were required to swear the oath that they would not partake in theft or harbour those who did. But there clearly was some debate about this, because Æthelstan had much earlier changed his mind on this as a result of consultation, see Roach, *Kingship and Consent*, pp. 108–9.
[283] Howden, *Chronica*, iii, p. 300.
[284] For the link between *LS*, c. 15, and Howden's oath, see Duncan, *Making of the Kingdom*, pp. 201–2; MacQueen, 'Scots Law', p. 87; Hector L. MacQueen, 'Expectations of the Law in the Twelfth and Thirteenth Century', *Tijdschrift voor Rechtsgeschiedenis*, vol. 70, nos. 3&4 (2002), pp. 279–90, at p. 282; Taylor, '*Leges Scocie*', pp. 212–13.

justice instead.[285] Moreover, they would maintain justice over their own men and not receive any monetary compensation in return for acquittal. In the pursuit of wrongdoers, each had the obligation to testify against another and to give true testimony. In order that they would uphold their oath, each offered their court as a pledge: if they 'broke the assize', they would lose their court.

The concern of both *Edictum* and *LS*, c. 15, is the identification and pursuit of wrongdoers and both use similar phrasing (*pro posse suo*).[286] It is also worth remembering that King William, his brother David, and most of his episcopacy and high aristocracy had direct experience not only of the Angevin court but also court assemblies at which the Angevin assizes were promulgated. William himself, Richard, bishop of St Andrews, Joscelin, bishop of Glasgow, Richard, bishop of Dunkeld, along with other bishops, abbots, and priors of the kingdom of the Scots were all present at the council of Northampton in 1176, where the Assize of Northampton was recorded and promulgated, for example.[287] But because William and his counsellors were so well informed about the legal developments going on at the courts of Henry II and his sons, the manner in which the Scottish 1197 oath departs from *Edictum* is even more significant. The Scottish oath was expected to be upheld within a very different administrative and jurisdictional structure than that assumed in *Edictum*.

Edictum starts with a general oath, sworn by the *homines regni Angliae*, to maintain the lord king's peace. This stipulation is not found in *LS*, c. 15: it is only Howden who says that the men of the kingdom swore the oath.[288] Given that the language and structure of *LS*, c. 15, is similar in its essentials to *Edictum*, if the 1197 oath had included a general oath-taking by all free men of the kingdom, one would properly anticipate that such a mass event would have been included and recorded in *LS*, c. 15. Its absence from the text must indicate its absence in reality. After all, *LS*, c. 15, does tell us who the oath-swearers were and they are different from those of *Edictum*. *Edictum* swears that 'all men of the kingdom of England' above fifteen years of age were to swear the oath and pursue offenders. By contrast, the oath-swearers in 1197 were the most powerful in the kingdom: the bishops, abbots, earls, barons, and thanes—all those who held a court. Howden thus contradicts *LS*, c. 15, by stating that the 1197 oath was sworn by 'all the men of the kingdom' but the text of the oath, in this case, belies the chronicler. All free adult

---

[285] The *CD*-version of this law adds 'nor any other wrongdoers in Moray or elsewhere', which is a nice indication of how Moray was viewed in the early fourteenth century; see Taylor, '*Leges Scocie*', p. 272, note 762; and Duncan, *Making of the Kingdom*, p. 201, note 31.

[286] *Select Charters*, ed. Stubbs, p. 257; *LS*, c. 15.

[287] Howden, *Chronica*, ii, p. 91; Howden, *Gesta*, i, p. 111.

[288] It should be said that Howden did not say *omnes homines regni*, just *homines regni* (Howden, *Chronica*, iv, p. 33). However, given he described *Edictum* in a similar way (*qui per sacramentum fidelium hominum de visnetis ceperunt*), when all free men above fifteen were supposed to swear the oath, it is still worth demonstrating the misleading potential of this sentence. Moreover, Howden did make some mistakes when reporting on the oath: he said it was, like *Edictum*, directed at thieves, robbers, outlaws, and their harbourers but *LS*, c. 15, shows that its targets were thieves, robbers, *murderers*, and their harbourers—there is no mention of outlaws. Murderers are listed in the Assizes of Clarendon and Northampton but not, surprisingly, in *Edictum* (Howden, *Chronica*, iii, p. 299). I have learnt much from Kenneth Duggan's work on *Edictum*.

men swore to uphold the contents of *Edictum* in England; their counterparts in Scotland did not do the same.

The structure of peacekeeping was different in *LS*, c. 15, from that in *Edictum*. *Edictum* states that knights of the shire were appointed to oversee the oath-taking, and were the first port of call if any free man managed to apprehend an offender. The knights in turn would deliver them to the sheriff and their case would be heard in front of the king's justices. This chain of command was in place from the Assize of Clarendon at the earliest, which stipulated that all suits arising from the assize would be heard by the king's justices after potential offenders had been delivered to the sheriff.[289] But *LS*, c. 15, has no role at all for justices and sheriffs; instead, it was the *potentes* of the kingdom who were required to maintain justice in their lands and testify in each other's courts, should the need arise.[290] The contents of the 1197 oath were to be implemented not in the sheriffdom—the Scottish equivalent of the county court—but in the courts of the kingdom's great men: *they* were the ones who would not deny justice to anyone. Aristocratic courts were the focus of the 1197 oath so much so that the court itself was the pledge for the upholding of the oath.

The similarity in language and focus between *Edictum* and *LS*, c. 15, should thus not be mistaken for a similarity in aim and application. The 1197 oath was directed at the main peacekeepers in the kingdom: the great lords, who caught offenders and had them judged in their own courts. It was not required for *all* free men to swear an oath. How local communities identified, pursued, and punished thieves, robbers, and murderers was, by the end of the twelfth century, still a matter to be decided on the ground; it was not a subject of royal legislative concern, although it would become so under Alexander II. The concern of the 1197 oath was that those responsible for apprehending wrongdoers would be the 'helpers' (*auxiliantes*) of the lord king and, as such, only the *potentes* of the kingdom were bound to the king by oath.

The brieve evidence thus shows that the king's peace was conceived as *limited*, covering particular people and places. By the 1180s, Scottish kings were issuing standardized brieves of peace and protection that finally reached their Ayr-register form not in the reign of Mael Coluim IV but in the 1260s. The notion that royal peace and protection were limited and sat alongside the protection offered by aristocrats was confirmed by the 1197 oath which, unlike its Angevin inspiration, was sworn only by the great lay and ecclesiastical landholders who upheld peace and justice in their own courts.

CONCLUSION

Two major shifts in the making of law and the maintenance of order have been identified in this period: the first one concerned the authority behind the law, the

---

[289] *Select Charters*, ed. Stubbs, pp. 257–8.   [290] *LS*, c. 15.

second the structures for the enforcement of laws. The first shift was one where kings gradually took the primary responsibility for actually *making* and *writing* the law away from *iudices*, hitherto the specialists who were responsible for preserving written legal rules. This is not to say that kings were not involved in law-making before the later twelfth century—kings and *iudices* must have previously drawn on each other's authority—but it is to say that the way in which law was predominantly made in the later twelfth century (by the king, in an assembly) was relatively new. This explains why *iudices* do not seem to play as important a role in the thirteenth century as they had done in the twelfth; their legal expertise had been superseded and the role that they had played in making law was minimized to the benefit of that of the king in his assembly. *Iudices* did not disappear but their activities seem to have become confined within more localized settings.[291]

The second change concerns the explicit methods of enforcement incorporated into written law: we move from the law of the later twelfth century in which legal prescriptions are not situated within an institutional and jurisdictional structure to the law of the mid-thirteenth century, where such prescriptions *are* situated within such a structure. The written law of William the Lion was mostly concerned with theft. Theft was a wrong that should be punished, although it appears that thieves could buy their lives if they essentially admitted their guilt and had the resources, presumably from friends, families, and lords, to be able pay the amount. The same socio-legal attachments of lordship and kinship which were responsible for bringing thieves to justice were also those responsible for exacting and paying compensation to parties if the need arose. We thus need not see any necessary distinction in legal order between the punishment of thieves (crime) and the pursuit of vengeance and compensation by the affected parties themselves (feud).[292] The capacity of the same value structures to support the punishment of thieves and the pursuit of feud simultaneously was made even more possible because of the relative lack of interest in jurisdiction in the law of William the Lion. Almost all the prescriptions on theft were, although procedural, made without reference to which bodies or people would enforce them in local communities. Nor was the king's authority consistently inserted through law into judicial practice on the ground by the receipt of judicial fines. The relative lack of interest in administration and jurisdiction gave a lot of space for multifarious legal solutions to be employed on the ground by those who exercised power locally.

Charter evidence, at first glance, shows a different picture from written law. In contrast to law, charters from the 1170s onwards emphasize jurisdiction over land. In these, the king's authority granted particular jurisdictional rights to individuals that were to be held in the land given or confirmed by the king, particularly jurisdiction over punishment; some lords were granted the right to an ordeal pit and gallows, the tools by which they could administer justice to thieves in particular. Royal charters also show that the king received a 'forfeiture' when privileges over land—such as retention of neyfs and forest rights—were infringed. Moreover,

---

[291] See the list and location of thirteenth-century *iudices* collected in Barrow, 'The *judex*', pp. 61–5.
[292] See also Grant, 'Murder Will Out', p. 226.

there is also evidence that royal officials collected at least some of these fines if lords had originally failed to do so.

The contradiction between written law and royal charters is present, but it need not result in one type of evidence being preferred as more correct than the other. Different types of source material can run at different tempos because of the nature of the documents in question. Charters are far more likely to reveal change than laws because they were issued on a case-by-case basis. Law, by contrast, aimed to provide universal prescriptions that could be applied in nearly all contexts and so is more likely to reveal continuity rather than change, particularly if change was piecemeal. Thus, if pleas of the crown were not fully defined in the late twelfth century (as the conflicting evidence of *LS* and charters shows), then lawmakers simply would not have integrated them into their abstract prescriptions on theft and killing. If power was only just beginning to be conceptualized territorially, as argued in Chapters 1 and 2, then it would have been unwise for lawmakers to base the content of law predominantly in the context of the formal jurisdiction, even if jurisdictions were a consistent part of charter diplomatic from the 1170s onwards. Equally, if the offices of sheriff and justice/justiciar did not cover the greater part of the kingdom, and their courts were only nascent, as will be argued in Chapter 4, then it would have been improbable that lawmakers would have incorporated their authority into the content of the law, even if such officials were well established in some areas of the kingdom; the crucial point is that they had not been established in *all* areas for long enough. Written law under William the Lion therefore contain detailed procedure but little emphasis on the institutional apparatus for enforcement. This technique allowed for the absence of administrative uniformity not to matter: everyone would have known when a priest could act as a warrantor or what to do when somebody lent a horse to another that was later claimed as stolen, regardless of whether there was a sheriff in the area or not.

The later law of Alexander II is different from that of his father. This difference was not, predominantly, a substantive change in content: Alexander's legislation remained concerned with theft, for example, even if he also covered more problems than his father and introduced different procedures, as will be shown in Chapter 5. Where the general subject of their legislation coincides, however, Alexander's was framed not only through the jurisdictional powers of lords but also through the administrative and judicial offices of sheriff and justiciar, a feature absent from William's laws. Comparison of William's and Alexander's laws therefore allows the evidence of charters to be used in a more nuanced way. The underlying argument of this chapter is thus again that there was a significant development in the conceptualization of elite jurisdiction and the development of administrative apparatus between, roughly, the 1160s and 1230, which appears in charters from the late 1160s/1170s onwards but in law only by 1230. The lag in law can be explained if it is assumed that lawmakers only started incorporating institutional apparatus when it was common enough and stable enough to be a recognizable structure throughout the kingdom. Combining the evidence of charters and law highlights the half-century or so before 1230 as a period when major administrative and jurisdictional changes were made in the institutional apparatus for the maintenance of law and order.

This institutional apparatus was both jurisdictional and administrative and included both the new definitions of aristocratic power and the structures of royal officialdom. This chapter therefore assumes that the offices of sheriff and justice/ justiciar developed more slowly and in a more piecemeal way than previous analyses have suggested. A full examination of this slower narrative of royal officialdom will be put forward in Chapter 4. The point stressed here is that when written law incorporated royal officials into its content by 1230, it did so alongside the jurisdictional powers exercised by lords. The evidence of the king's peace shows that the king wielded a high level of protection but a type of protection which did not undercut the protective powers of other lords. Aristocratic justice had, by Alexander II's reign, become key to the workings of royal justice in general: only court holders, after all, had to swear the oath in 1197 to the king to uphold justice and not do wrong. Jurisdiction over land had become an intrinsic part of written conceptualizations not only of elite power but also of royal justice and administration. Aristocratic power was thus not independent of royal power but was assumed and built into the content of royal law. How aristocratic power was incorporated into and worked through the intensive and bureaucratic ways of ruling that developed under the two Alexanders during the thirteenth century is the theme underlying the second part of this book.

Conclusion
The Anglo-Norman Era Revisited

Cumulatively, the foregoing chapters have shown that there were major changes to the definition of aristocratic power and the mechanisms through which common obligations were discharged over the twelfth century. *Mormaer*-power became territorialized: we move from a situation where *mormaír* exercised extensive power over their titular province to one where they exercised intensive power over a territorial *comitatus*. Thanely power also became territorial: thanes began to be seen as equivalent to knights, and exercised similar forms of power over their lands as knights did over their feus. There was also a reorganization in the way in which the common burdens of the kingdom were levied: *mormaír* (with the help of accompanying *toísig*) once had levied them for the king; by the 1220s, all landholders who held their land directly from the king were responsible for the levy in their own lands. While *mormaír* retained responsibility for leading these armies, they did not do so exclusively and their symbolic authority should not be confused with the underlying territorial mechanisms for the levy. We can first identify this reorganization in the early 1160s, under Mael Coluim IV: by the 1220s, it was firmly rooted enough to act as the basic structure through which fines for default of service could be levied. In addition, jurisdictional power came to be conceived as territorial over the last third of the twelfth century. Land was granted with appurtenant jurisdictional privileges and, by 1197, it was assumed that lay and religious aristocrats would take responsibility for wrongdoing committed by their own men in their own lands and would do so in their own courts. By the time of Alexander II's important laws of 1230, statutes reveal that aristocratic jurisdiction was so much a part of the political landscape that new royal legislation was supposed to be enforced through royal and magnate courts in a uniform way.

All this reveals a significant reorientation in the conceptualization of elite power over a period roughly beginning in the 1160s and ending by 1230. Power had become territorialized and defined through landholding; jurisdiction was not only a key part of the authority of the landholder but was also attached to the land itself.[1] This change is never explicitly mentioned in the charter or chronicle evi-

---

[1] For a summary of 'territoriality', insofar as it relates to states, see Rhys Jones, *Peoples/States/Territories* (Oxford, 2007), pp. 21–8; see also the notion of 'state-as-place' in Michael Mann, 'The Autonomous Power of the State: Its Origins, Mechanisms and Results', *European Journal of Sociology*, vol. 25, no. 2 (1984), pp. 185–213, at pp. 198–201. The issue, therefore, when applied to aristocratic power, is when aristocratic power was defined spatially. For territorialization elsewhere in Western

dence and thus requires some explanation. How and why could this territorialization of elite power have come about and why did it happen so silently?

These questions are best approached through a case study, which has already
been met in Chapter 1: the charters of David and William, each recording the
respective king's gift of Annandale to Robert I and then Robert II de Brus.[2]
David and William's charters are very different not only in the conceptualization
of the land-gift itself but also in the respective rights each party exercised over it.
The actual charter of David I to Robert is very short: it confirms and grants
David's gift of Annandale and some other lands to Robert and says, quite clearly,
that Robert should hold the land 'with all those customs which Ranulf Meschin
ever had in Carlisle and in his land of Cumberland'.[3] Although Robert's possession is defined as 'Annandale', the terms on which he holds it are personal; he
holds it as Ranulf Meschin held his, and presumably everybody would have
known what this would have entailed.[4] There is an obvious difference between
this charter and William's, which was drawn up almost fifty years later. Robert II
de Brus is to have Annandale as a feu (*feudum*) and is to hold it hereditably (these
are terms absent from David's charter) and 'of' the king.[5] Moreover, Robert II is
to have judicial pleas—all apart from those reserved to the king—and, even in
these cases, Robert is to have one man within his land nominated to bring those
accused of royal pleas into royal courts. William's charter also stipulated that
Robert is to hold all his land in return for the service of ten knights. Although
William's charter explicitly frames this gift as exactly the same as what had been
given in David's, the terms on which Robert II held Annandale had been
redefined and given abstract form.

As was noted in Chapter 1, this has not always been the common interpretation
of these two charters. It used to be generally assumed that the situation as recorded
in William's charter must have existed at the time of David's original grant to the
first Robert: David's charter was thus taken as one of the earliest pieces of evidence
for the 'feudalization' of Scotland.[6] This interpretation is partly the result of too

Europe, see Matthew Innes, *State and Society in the Early Medieval West: The Middle Rhine Valley
400–1000* (Cambridge, 2000), pp. 245–50. Benjamin Arnold, *Princes and Territories in Medieval
Germany* (Cambridge, 1991), pp. 112–32, argues for a change in the meaning of *comes* around 1100
'releasing it from its previous association with public justice exercised under the crown, to apply
instead to the cluster of hereditary rights which the dynasty in question exercised, although a comital
title was by no means a precondition for this kind of authority' (i.e., not all lords were counts, p. 112).
See also the wider debates discussed from a variety of perspectives in Martin Vanier ed., *Territoires,
territorialité, territorialisation: Controverses et perspectives* (Rennes, 2009).

[2] *CDI*, no. 16; *RRS*, ii, no. 80; see Chapter 1, pp. 51–2.
[3] *CDI*, no. 16.
[4] For Ranulf Meschin, see Richard Sharpe, *Norman Rule in Cumbria, 1092–1136*, Cumberland
and Westmorland Antiquarian and Archaeological Society (Kendal, 2006), pp. 43–52.
[5] *RRS*, ii, no. 80.
[6] Although it is often qualified with 'probably': e.g., G. W. S. Barrow, 'The Beginnings of Military
Feudalism', in G. W. S. Barrow, *The Kingdom of the Scots: Government, Church and Society from the
Eleventh to the Fourteenth Century*, 2nd edn (Edinburgh, 2003), pp. 250–78, at p. 251. More recently,
the difference between David's and William's charters to Robert de Brus has been noticed and ana-
lyzed, albeit with different conclusions: see Alexander Grant, 'Franchises North of the Border: Baronies
and Regalities in Medieval Scotland', in *Liberties and Identities in the Medieval British Isles*, ed. Michael
Prestwich (Woodbridge, 2008), pp. 155–99, at pp. 186–7; and Hector L. MacQueen, 'Tears of a

literal an interpretation of the language of William's charter itself, which emphasizes continuity by stressing that it recorded the original agreement between Robert I de Brus and David I. But what is clear is that William's charter contained a more detailed and formal statement of the relation between William and Robert than did the earlier charter. The formalization of the relation had solidified and was constitutive of the changing powers attached to both parties. Robert was not only given more in William's charter than his father but William also had more to give than David. The formal and permanent character of William's charter contrasts with the vague and temporary nature of David's.

William's charter to Robert de Brus is exceptional in its detail. But it is not exceptional in the broader context of an identifiable trend towards charters with tighter and more formal diplomatic over the twelfth century. Only one of the surviving charters of David I to a layman contains the jurisdictional formula of 'sake and soke' and this was drawn up by a Durham scribe who was used to including them in charter texts.[7] Apart from this one example, formal jurisdiction was not a part of any other gift of land under David I. But, under William, jurisdictional formulae were used very frequently and, indeed, were lengthened by the addition of 'gallows and pit'.[8] There was thus a major change in what rights were conceded by kings when giving away land. By making it the norm that land would be given to elites with appurtenant jurisdictional privileges, William continued his grandfather's strategy of giving land away but he had also simultaneously and fundamentally departed from it.

What was actually given when land was given away was thus greater in territorial and jurisdictional definition towards the end of the twelfth century than it had been under David I. As a result of the work of Dauvit Broun, we now know that kings of Scots did not issue formulaic Latin charters granting land either to religious institutions or to laymen until the reign of David I.[9] This picture has recently been developed: Hammond has argued that kings of Scots did not routinely issue charters granting land to their lay aristocrats until the late 1160s.[10] Thus, although we have earlier charters to laymen, these were often drawn up either at the request of the beneficiary or a party in a relevant dispute, who may well have had very particular reasons for wanting such a document. The effect of this work is to stress how slow and piecemeal was the adoption of charters over the twelfth century, even at the highest social level. Despite the significance of this work, however, the

Legal Historian: Scottish Feudalism and the *Ius Commune*', *Juridical Review*, new series (2003), pp. 1–28, at pp. 7–9.

[7] See Chapter 3, pp. 158–61.   [8] See Chapter 3, pp. 159–60.

[9] Dauvit Broun, *The Charters of Gaelic Scotland and Ireland in the Early and Central Middle Ages* (Cambridge, 1995), pp. 8–13; developed in Dauvit Broun, 'The Writing of Charters in Scotland and Ireland in the Twelfth Century', in *Charters and the Use of the Written Word in Medieval Society*, ed. Karl Heidecker (Turnhout, 2000), pp. 113–31, and Dauvit Broun, 'The Adoption of Brieves in Scotland', in *Charters and Charter Scholarship in Britain and Ireland*, ed. Marie Therese Flanagan and Judith A. Green (Basingstoke, 2005), pp. 164–83. In another context, see Cynthia J. Neville, *Land, Law and People in Medieval Scotland* (Edinburgh, 2010), pp. 74–83.

[10] Matthew Hammond, 'The Adoption and Routinization of Scottish Royal Charter Production for Lay Beneficiaries, 1124–1195', *ANS*, vol. 36 (Woodbridge, 2014), pp. 91–115.

content of these earlier twelfth-century charters has rarely been compared with later twelfth-century ones. The comparison presented here, however, reveals clear changes to the written conceptualization of the power of the king and aristocrat between the 1120s and the 1170s, identifying that the relationship had become located in landholding. Power, essentially, had become conceived as territorially based.

But this change is rarely identified in the existing literature. This can be explained in part by assumptions in the historiography. Since Geoffrey Barrow published his 1977 Ford lectures as *The Anglo-Norman Era in Scottish History*, it has been all too easy to conceive the twelfth century as a continuous but static whole, during which David I encouraged settlement from outside the kingdom, a policy then continued (but not changed) under his grandsons, Mael Coluim and William.[11] Barrow was clear that he never saw Scotland as fully 'feudalised'; the kingdom, for him, always remained a melting pot.[12] But one ingredient in Barrow's pot was feudalism, meaning not only a form of government but also a coherent system of land tenure. In Barrow's understanding, David and his grandsons were introducing feudalism to Scotland by giving land to outsiders as feus, in return for knight service.[13] Barrow's understanding of feudalism was not unique to him: even within Scottish historiography alone, it had a long pedigree stretching well back into the nineteenth century, and is identifiable in the work of William Forbes Skene and Eben William Robertson, among others.[14] But feudalism now is no longer seen as a portable socio-political or socio-legal system, which kings and nobles carried with them wherever they wanted; indeed, it is no longer seen as a unified socio-political or socio-legal system at all.[15] The notion that kings of Scots and their immigrant aristocracy could have introduced feudalism at all has thus been called into

---

[11] This assumption is most obviously exemplified in the first chapter of *The Anglo-Norman* Era, entitled 'A Land for Younger Sons', which concentrates primarily on men who came to Scotland in Mael Coluim's and William's reigns: G. W. S. Barrow, *The Anglo-Norman Era in Scottish History* (Oxford, 1980), pp. 1–29, particularly pp. 19–29. See also the treatment of scribal practice between David and William in G. W. S. Barrow, 'The Scots Charter', in G. W. S. Barrow, *Scotland and Its Neighbours in the Middle Ages* (London, 1992), pp. 91–104, at pp. 101–4. See also his remarks in 'Beginnings of Military Feudalism', p. 254, and note 22, and, in addition, Neville, *Land, Law and People*, p. 77.

[12] Hector MacQueen, 'Geoffrey Wallis Steuart Barrow, 1924–2013: A Memoir', *Innes Review*, vol. 65, no. 1 (2014), pp. 1–12, at pp. 7–10.

[13] Barrow, 'Beginnings of Military Feudalism', pp. 250–3. In addition, see Barrow's salutary criticism of 'general histories' and 'general historians' which gave the 'impression...that all these "Normans" poured into Scotland at the same time, there to establish, almost overnight, their feudalism, their administrative system and their motte-and-bailey castles'; G. W. S. Barrow, 'Scotland's 'Norman' Families', in Barrow, *Kingdom of the Scots*, pp. 279–95, at p. 280. But the critique here was of those who thought all incomers were 'Normans', and the *quickness* of the transformation.

[14] W. F. Skene, *Celtic Scotland: A History of Ancient Alban*, 3 vols (Edinburgh, 1886–90), vol. i, pp. 454, 457–60; E. W. Robertson, *Scotland under Her Early Kings*, 2 vols (Edinburgh, 1862), vol. i, p. 319.

[15] Elizabeth A. R. Brown, 'The Tyranny of a Construct: Feudalism and Historians of Medieval Europe', *American Historical Review*, vol. 79, no. 4 (1974), pp. 1063–88; Susan Reynolds, *Fiefs and Vassals: the Medieval Evidence Reinterpreted* (Oxford, 1994); and the two volumes of essays responding to the issues raised by both in *Il feudalesimo nell'alto medioevo*, 2 vols. *Settimane di Studio del Centro Italiano di studi sull'alto medioevo*, vol. 47 (Spoleto, 2000); Sverre Bagge, Michael H. Gelting, and Thomas Lindkvist ed., *Feudalism: New Landscapes of Debate* (Turnhout, 2011).

question.[16] The difficult concept of feudalism is not the point here; it is, however, important to stress that, because Barrow saw feudalism as a comprehensive system, 'steadily expanding' (his words) across the kingdom, differences in the diplomatic of charters between the earlier and the later twelfth century did not matter so much to him, although he was of course aware of them, because he knew the material so well.[17] As a result, in *The Anglo-Norman Era*, evidence from the late twelfth and thirteenth centuries is taken as evidence for earlier settlements, and later evidence is squashed together with earlier evidence. Not only did this remove more precise chronological change from his analysis, it also prevented any acknowledgement that the real and documentable changes in charter diplomatic could be indicative of wider changes in the conceptualization of the abstract bases of power.[18]

The professional difficulty historians have had in identifying the twelfth-century process of territorialization is also a product of the sources themselves, which emphasize continuity in landholding practice between David and William, rather than change. A particular feature of William's charters is their emphasis on continuity between William's rule and that of his grandfather, David. William's charters to Robert de Brus, Orm mac Aeda, and William son of Freskin all emphasize continuity: when the charter is framed as a gift or re-gift, all three state that the tenurial situation as recorded in William's charter was merely continuing what had occurred under David.[19] In some cases, it is clear that the past is being claimed, rather than accurately described. Both William's and Alexander II's charters to Earl Mael Coluim of Fife, for example, inaccurately state that David had already made gifts to Mael Coluim's father, Earl Donnchad II, which was impossible given that Donnchad II was not yet an earl on David's death.[20] These projected continuities even stretched to law: under William, David's name and authority was invoked at the expense of the legislative activity of William's predecessor and older brother, Mael Coluim.[21] The tendency among historians to see continuity must be the result of their taking these statements of continuity between David's and William's reigns at face value, rather than understanding them as strategic claims, as *presentations* of institutional continuity (and by this I mean the notion of aristocratic jurisdictional power as a social institution).[22] In the face of such change to the conceptualization

---

[16] See also MacQueen, 'Tears of a Legal Historian'; Richard D. Oram, 'Gold into Lead? The State of Early Medieval Scottish History', *Freedom and Authority: Scotland, c.1050–1650: Historical and Historiographical Essays Presented to Grant G. Simpson*, ed. Terry Brotherstone and David Ditchburn (East Linton, 2000), pp. 32–43; Neville, *Land, Law and People*, pp. 1–7.

[17] Barrow, 'Beginnings of Military Feudalism', pp. 252–4, at p. 253.

[18] A problem noted by Dauvit Broun, 'The Property Records in the Book of Deer as a Source for Early Scottish Society', in *Book of Deer*, ed. Forsyth, pp. 313–60, at p. 313.

[19] *RRS*, ii, nos. 80, 116, 152; see, in another context, *RRS*, ii, no. 153 (about guilds in Aberdeen), and no. 281 (the oft-discussed teind charter). What is nice is that each of these three examples shows continuity through different means. The charter to William, son of Freskin, is framed as a 'gift' in that it uses the word *dedisse* (*RRS*, ii, no. 116), the charter of Robert de Brus is framed as a 're-gift', by its use of *rededisse*, which perhaps was more accurate (*RRS*, ii, no. 80), while the charter to Orm was framed as a confirmation by its use of *concessisse et confirmare* but not *dedisse* or *rededisse* (*RRS*, ii, no. 152).

[20] See Chapter 1, pp. 47–52.   [21] See Chapter 3, pp. 155–7, note 210.

[22] Hannah Skoda, 'A Historian's Perspective on the Present Volume', in *Legalism: History and Anthropology*, ed. Paul Dresch and Hannah Skoda (Oxford, 2012), pp. 39–54, at pp. 43–5.

of elite power, the presentation of territorialized power as something longstanding, protected by the power of custom, would have been an understandable need for both kings and aristocrats.

These charters were not often wrong in emphasizing continuity but it was continuity in a practical, not institutional sense. What David and William both did was give land away in order to gain support, even if those gifts were framed in different ways. All our charters conceptualize the transfer of property as gifts: the king has given, granted, and confirmed the land in question to another person or institution (*dedisse, concessisse, confirmasse*).[23] Even when lay aristocrats themselves gave land to others, the king was often called upon to 'grant and confirm' (*concessisse et confirmasse*) the gift.[24] In this way, both king and aristocratic donor accepted the king's position as the ultimate gift-giver; the king's authority was used to confirm and thus sanction gifts even when they were not his own. Thus, in order to understand the real process of territorialization (as well as the symbolic claims in charters to continuity), we have to understand the functions of gift-giving.

The giving of gifts to maintain and increase the symbolic capital of a ruler is now a well-understood phenomenon of medieval kingship: paradoxically, by giving away, rulers could demonstrate their economic power (they had things to give) but also place the recipient in a subordinate position (they had received and thus accepted a demonstration of superior power and authority).[25] Since Mauss wrote his *Essai sur le don* (1925), it has also become well known (albeit also contested) that gifts carried the expectation of reciprocity.[26] The recipient had to reciprocate the gift not only to maintain the relationship which the original gift had constituted and confirmed but also to avoid the symbolic debt and position of subordination that his receipt of the gift had, albeit temporarily, bestowed upon him. In societies where status was inherently unstable, giving the wrong gift, taking too long to reciprocate, or reciprocating too generously could be interpreted as openly aggressive acts whose consequences could be severe: death, exile, mutilation, as William Ian Miller has shown in his analysis of Icelandic sagas.[27] Gifts of land

---

[23] The interplay between these verbs is discussed in a different context by John Reuben Davies, 'The Donor and the Duty of Warrandice: Giving and Granting in Scottish Charters', *The Reality Behind Charter Diplomatic: Studies by Dauvit Broun, John Reuben Davies, Richard Sharpe and Alice Taylor*, ed. Dauvit Broun (Glasgow, 2011), pp. 120–65.

[24] Davies, 'Donor and the duty of warrandice', pp. 121–31.

[25] The literature on medieval gift-giving is vast, but see Mayke de Jong and Esther Cohen ed., *Medieval Transformations: Texts, Power and Gifts in Context* (Leiden, 2001); Gadi Algazi, Valentin Groebner and Bernhard Jusson ed., *Negotiating the Gift: Pre-Modern Figurations of Exchange* (Göttingen, 2003); Wendy Davies and Paul Fouracre ed., *The Languages of Gift in the Early Middle Ages* (Cambridge, 2010); Arnoud-Jan Bijsterveld, *Do Ut Des: Gift Giving, Memoria, and Conflict Management in the Medieval Low Countries* (Hilversum, 2007). See also Lars Kjær and A. J. Watson ed., *Feasts and Gifts of Food in Medieval Europe: Ritualised Constructions of Hierarchy, Identity and Community*, Special Issue of *The Journal of Medieval History*, vol. 37, no. 1 (2011).

[26] Marcel Mauss, *The Gift: the Form and Reason for Exchange in Archaic Societies*, with a foreword by Mary Douglas (Abingdon, 2002); see further Pierre Bourdieu, *Practical Reason: On the Theory of Action* (Stanford, CA, 1998), pp. 92–123; Pierre Bourdieu, *The Logic of Practice* (Cambridge, 1990), particularly pp. 112–21; Marshall Sahlins, *Stone Age Economics* (London, 1974), pp. 149–83.

[27] William Ian Miller, 'Gift, Sale, Payment, Raid: Case Studies in the Negotiation and Classification of Exchange in Medieval Iceland', *Speculum*, vol. 61, no. 1 (1986), pp. 18–50; William Ian Miller, *Humiliation and Other Essays on Honor, Social Discomfort, and Violence* (Ithaca, 1993), pp. 15–52.

could operate on a similar although not identical scheme and Stephen D. White has shown well how, in early eleventh-century Poitou, those who had the capacity to give and bestow land could expect service from their subordinates in return; the person who controlled landed gifts could control his followers.[28] In this way, the symbolic debt created by receipt of the gift of land was institutionalized into an explicit expectation of service and subordination and, in this, the Poitevin example is very different from the scenes depicted in sagas. (Gifts to religious institutions are both similar and somewhat different because the gift is made first to God and the saints and then to the institution which serves God; the reciprocation is explicitly in the form of prayers but functions to increase the power of the donor through the creation of a close relationship with powerful and geographically sprawling institutions.[29])

The promise and receipt of gifts of land were clearly used by kings of Scots to attract men to the kingdom. If they had not been, it would be very unlikely that such men would have settled.[30] Indeed, the settlement of migrants is at the heart of the construct of Barrow's 'Anglo-Norman Era', when men of northern continental extraction were given land by kings, fundamentally changing the composition of the aristocracy within the kingdom.[31] David's encouragement of the Brus family, the Morvilles, and Walter fitz Alan, among many, has long attracted attention. It is clear that David buttressed his power in southern Scotland by giving vast swathes of land to his friends and this was the support that contemporaries claimed he particularly counted on when faced with the challenge to his rule by Mael Coluim, natural son of Alexander I.[32] Royal power in the twelfth century thus in part depended not only on land but also on the capacity of kings to give land away. Chapter 1 showed how consistent a strategy this was, even in the much-changed world of the two Alexanders, who gave land away in the new peripheries of the kingdom because they had less land to give in Scotia and Lothian.[33] Aelred of Rievaulx, who had once been the beneficiary of David's generosity, clearly knew

---

[28] Stephen D. White, 'The politics of exchange: gifts, fiefs and feudalism', in *Medieval Transformations*, ed. de Jong and Cohen, pp. 169–88. The main source of White's enquiry was the *Conventum Hugonis*. What is interesting about this Poitevin example is that Count William's status is never fully challenged as a result of his failure to hand over the gifts he has promised; evidently, his comital title gave him enough security to fail in the gift-giving game without a consequent loss in formal status. The *Conventum Hugonis* is edited in Jane Martindale, '*Conventum inter Willelmum Comitem Aquitanorum et Hugonem Chiliarchum*', *EHR*, vol. 84, no. 332 (1969), pp. 528–48.

[29] This is best demonstrated in Barbara H. Rosenwein, *To be the Neighbour of Saint Peter: the Social Meaning of Cluny's Property, 909–1049* (Ithaca, 1989).

[30] I use settled in a looser way here than 'permanent residence in the kingdom of the Scots', recalling Keith Stringer's remarks in Keith J. Stringer, 'Aspects of the Norman Diaspora in Northern England and Southern Scotland', *Norman Expansion: Connections, Continuities and Contrasts*, ed. Keith J. Stringer, and Andrew Jotischky (Farnham, 2013), pp. 9–48, at pp. 11–12.

[31] This goes back long before Barrow's concept of the *Anglo-Norman Era*, for which see R. L. G. Ritchie, *The Normans in Scotland* (Edinburgh, 1954), and also W. E. Kapelle, *The Norman Conquest of the North: the Region and Its Transformation* (London, 1979), which was published two years after Barrow gave his Ford Lectures in 1977.

[32] This example has been picked because Aelred mentions it obliquely in his *Relatio*; for which see Aelred of Rievaulx, *Relatio de Standardo*, in *Chronicles of the Reigns of Stephen, Henry II and Richard I*, ed. R. Howlett, Rolls Series, 4 vols (London, 1884–9), vol. iii, p. 193.

[33] See Chapter 1, pp. 69–80.

how important gifts were to David's power.[34] In a speech placed in the mouth of Robert de Brus in the *Relatio de Standardo* (1157), Aelred speaks through Robert by saying how well he knew David's 'generosity in giving many kinds of gift' and 'in granting estates and possessions'.[35] Aelred here, possibly drawing on his own experience, depicts Robert's understanding of his own success (and his prior support of David) in the long and deep friendship the two men had shared since childhood, which David cemented by the giving of land, among other gifts.

If the capacity to give gifts of lands to followers had become a key part of royal power under David I, then William continued this apace.[36] But in William's charters, aristocratic power came to be defined as *over* land. This is an important distinction. David's charters (small in number though they are) gave gifts of land to aristocrats; William's defined aristocratic power as essentially territorial. Although the importance of land-gifts to the mechanisms of royal power might have been a direct cause and consequence of migration to the kingdom, charters granting large estates with jurisdictional privileges were not necessarily so nor, under William, were they something that only incoming migrants and their descendants received. Men who are sometimes called 'native' lords received such gifts and redefinitions as well. The most obvious examples are Merleswain in Ardross, William, son of Freskin, in Moray, and Orm mac Aeda in Abernethy during William's reign: Merleswain appears to have received Ardross from the king 'as freely and quietly as other knights hold their feus from me'; Orm received Abernethy 'as on the year and day when King David my grandfather was alive and dead'; while William, son of Freskin, received land in West Lothian and Moray 'which his father Freskin held in the time of King David, my grandfather'.[37] In the first charter, Merleswain's gift is deemed equivalent to those made to knights in William's kingdom; in the other two, continuity between David and William is used to justify a reframing of power on explicitly relational and territorial terms.[38] The use of the language of continuity

---

[34] For the a recent assessment of Aelred's *Lamentatio* for David I, and the attitudes it conveys, see Dauvit Broun, 'Attitudes of *Gall* to *Gaedhel* in Scotland before John of Fordun', in *Mìorun Mòr nan Gall: 'The Great Ill-Will of the Lowlander?': Lowland Perceptions of the Highlands, Medieval and Modern*, ed. Dauvit Broun and Martin D. MacGregor (Glasgow, 2009), pp. 49–82, at pp. 69–71; see, more generally, Joanna Huntingdon, 'David of Scotland: *vir tam necessarius mundo*', *Saints' Cults in the Celtic World*, ed. Steve Boardman, John Reuben Davies, and Eila Williamson (Woodbridge, 2009), pp. 130–45.

[35] Aelred of Rievaulx, *Relatio de Standardo*, in *Chronicles*, ed. Howlett, vol. iii, p. 195. This was, of course, the moment when Aelred presented Robert de Brus formally renouncing his *fides* to David: in order to convince the king of his point of view, however, Robert stressed the large amount he had received from the king, thus why Robert still would support his king, so long as David took the correct action (i.e. did not go into battle). In the end, David was convinced otherwise, thus demonstrating bad lordship, and justifying Robert's renunciation of his *fides*.

[36] See Chapter 1, pp. 74–7.

[37] *RRS*, ii, nos. 116, 137, 152; see also Hammond, 'Adoption and Routinization', pp. 104–5. We have to be sceptical of all declarations of continuity with David under William.

[38] For a much more detailed study on the *sicut* clause, and what it could mean, see Dauvit Broun, 'English law and the Unification of Scotland', Breaking of Britain Feature of the Month, May 2012, online at <http://www.breakingofbritain.ac.uk/blogs/feature-of-the-month/may-2012/>; see further, Dauvit Broun, 'Britain and the Beginnings of Scotland', Sir John Rhŷs Memorial Lecture, *Journal of the British Academy*, vol. 3 (2015), pp. 107–37, at pp. 111–14. The phrase was also discussed in Barrow, *Anglo-Norman Era*, pp. 153–5.

and equivalence also explains why the major redefinition in the power and authority of the *mormaer*, put forward in Chapter 1, happened—and happened so silently. What the change from extensive power over the province to intensive power over the *comitatus* offered *mormaír* was not only relatively autonomous jurisdictional power, defined in the language of formal gift-giving, it was also power exercised over land which was protected by the king in the same way as land which had been given to incomers, or the land of existing magnates, like Orm mac Aeda, Merleswain, or Freskin, who had their lands reconfirmed along new lines.

Both David and William thus used the potential of land-gifts in similar ways; it was the conceptualization of these gifts that differed. David I did give land to his followers, particularly south of the Firth of Forth. But he appears to have done so on comparatively vague and individual terms: land-gifts do not seem to have regularly been recorded in charters nor, when they were, did the scribes of those charters deploy the same formulae in order to describe the powers given by the king to the lord over the land in question. This only seems to have happened at least a generation after the initial phases of settlement under David, perhaps when inheritance issues arose for existing settlers, when even more men came to settle, or when existing magnates wished to have their own lands confirmed along similar lines. In short, the territorialization of aristocratic power did not happen as an immediate and direct result of the initial phase of settlement under David nor from a wholesale import of Anglo-Norman 'feudalism'.[39] Rather, it occurred decades later when kings were regularly giving land away north of the Forth and were formalizing the relationship they would have with their aristocracy as a whole, not just with those who had newly come into the kingdom to settle. Not only were the 1160s and 1170s the period when charters of landed gifts start regularly including formulaic grants of jurisdiction, it was also when there are hints that the common burdens of the kingdom were starting to become organized by lordship, as would demonstrably be the case by the early 1220s.

Migration and settlement thus did not cause the redefinition of elite power directly, in the short term, but rather indirectly and in the long term. But this still does not answer the question, *how* could this have happened? It is argued here that it could only have been possible to introduce new terms and formulae that would conceptualize power and jurisdiction territorially if such terms were filling a gap in the existing lexicon.[40] It is of note that the only three Gaelic terms to make an impression in the entire corpus of surviving Latin charters were *dabach*, *cáin*, and *coinnmed* (Latinized as *davaca*, or transposed as *dauah*; *canum* or *cana*, transposed

---

[39] This is not to say that modern historians have not problematized Barrow's understanding of feudalism, which is actively eschewed in, for example, Richard Oram, *Domination and Lordship: Scotland 1070 to 1230* (Edinburgh, 2011), particularly in chapters 6 and 9.

[40] This paragraph has been inspired by the important work by Bruce O'Brien. See, in particular, Bruce O'Brien, 'Translating Technical Terms in Law-Codes from Alfred to the Angevins', in *Conceptualizing Multilingualism in England, 800–1250*, ed. Elizabeth M. Tyler (Turnhout, 2011), pp. 57–76; Bruce O'Brien, *Reversing Babel: Translation among the English during an Age of Conquests, c.800–c.1200* (Plymouth, 2011). See also John Hudson, 'Imposing Feudalism on Anglo-Saxon England: Norman and Angevin Presentations of Pre-Conquest Lordship and Landholding', in *Feudalism*, ed. Bagge, Gelting and Lindkvist, pp. 115–34.

as *chan* or *can*; and *convethe* or *convetum*).[41] All related to resource extraction. It makes sense that these words would be used by scribes in Latin charters because they were existing resources expected by lords (lay and religious) from their lands, which continued to be extracted well into the fifteenth century.[42] Their inclusion thus shows that there was a Gaelic vocabulary of domination, extraction, and assessment that was possible to represent in Latinate form. The question therefore becomes, why import the Old English charter formula of 'sake and soke, toll and team and infangentheof' to describe the jurisdictional powers exercised by lay lords, if there was, as *LBS* shows, an existing vernacular legal vocabulary to work with? The Gaelic legal terminology present in *LBS* does not appear in the Latin charter record of the twelfth and thirteenth centuries. *Cró, gelthach/kelchin, enach, forgard, turhochret* are all absent; indeed, *cró, kelchin,* and *enach* only appear once legal tractates were composed in the later thirteenth and early fourteenth centuries.[43]

This must be because all these words described phenomena which, at the broadest level, regulated the relations between people. Although the precise meaning and contexts in which *kelchin, enach, forgard,* and *turhochret* were used may never be known, all paid for some form of insult, injury, or loss. The world to which these technical and legal Gaelic words belonged was a socially personal world which was not, in theory, territorially based. Such words therefore had no or little application in a grant of landed jurisdiction. Granting the 'right' to *kelchin* to a lord would not have made sense if *kelchin* was, as suggested above, a payment for insult; *kelchin* would have gone to whoever had been insulted, who would only have been the lord of the land if he was the one who had suffered damage to his honour. The inability of these words to translate into landed jurisdiction meant that a new way of describing jurisdictional power over land had to be found and the formula chosen was one already used in Anglo-Norman and Angevin England.[44] The sake and soke formula was based on Old English words but, by the late 1160s, it was so commonly used in Anglo-Norman and Angevin charters that it had been fully incorporated into the lexical register of Latin charter diplomatic. That in some way this was not quite deemed sufficient in the kingdom of the Scots, particularly in Scotia, is evidenced by the addition of 'gallows and pit', denoting an explicit capacity to punish criminals that presumably high-status people had long exercised by virtue of their status, rather than as part of the gift or confirmation of land itself.[45]

The reframing of the legal environment did not mean that compensation payments for death, injury, and insult declined; rather, these new territorialized jurisdictions

---

[41] For *dabaig*, see *RRS*, ii, nos. 346, 423, 466, 497; *Scone Liber*, no. 67 [AII/223]; Fraser, *Douglas*, iii, no. 6; *Coupar Angus Chrs*, i, no. 38; for *cáin*, see, among many, *CDI*, no. 38; *RRS*, i, no. 242; *RRS*, ii, nos. 367, 374, 421, 590; *LS*, c. 20; for *coinnmed* see, among many, *RRS*, ii, no. 590.

[42] Dauvit Broun, 'Re-examining *cáin* in the Twelfth and Thirteenth Centuries', in *Princes, Prelates and Poets in Medieval Ireland: Essays in Honour of Katharine Simms*, ed. Seán Duffy (Dublin, 2013), pp. 46–62, at pp. 52–3.

[43] *RM*, II, c. 9; IV, c. 30, ed. Thomson in *APS*, i, pp. 608, 637. The earliest reference to these terms is technically in *LS*, whose earliest surviving MS witness is 1267×72, so technically these terms do not predate this. But this would be too harsh a reading: *LS*, c. 21.

[44] For the literature on sake and soke, see Chapter 3, p. 159, at note 227. See further Helen Cam, 'The Evolution of the Mediaeval English Franchise', *Speculum*, vol. 32 (1957), pp. 427–42.

[45] See Chapter 3, pp. 159–60.

must have lain across the top. We know that *cró* survived into the early fourteenth century; it appears in *Regiam Majestatem* both in the *RM*-texts of *LBS* and elsewhere within the tractate.[46] *Enach* also appears in *RM*, and is used in a context unattested elsewhere. It may also be that the *consuetudo* associated with David I, mentioned in an early-fourteenth-century brieve formula, referred to *cró* payments, for the brieve itself commanded the kin and friends of a certain man to help pay the fine he owed for killing another man, 'according to what was the custom in the time of King David'.[47] As at least some of the technical Gaelic terms survived into the fourteenth century, it is important to distinguish between practical continuity on the ground and significant changes to the conceptualization of jurisdictional and territorial relations at an elite level.

The effect of these chapters is thus to put forward a different view of the so-called Anglo-Norman Era. It does not deny the political importance of settlement but it does remove the need for a pre-formed political and documentary culture to act as the only catalyst of change in a helpless native environment. Nor does it require the native environment to be instinctively hostile or resistant to changes, although it does not deny the possibility of some sort of political trauma.[48] Instead, it allows the settlement of incomers to matter without assigning that process a primary, causal force. Settlement did matter not least because, in order for it to last, kings had to give away large portions of land. By doing so, David I and his grandsons engaged in a common practice of medieval kingship—gift-giving to secure support—which in fact remained a stable and consistent practice of medieval Scottish kings across the central Middle Ages, although the areas from which kings made their landed gifts shifted. But by making land-gifts one of the key support bases of royal power, aristocratic power itself came to be defined territorially from the 1160s/70s onwards in a way that it had not been previously. Indeed, it was precisely because the basis of aristocratic power had not been conceptually territorial that charter formulae from Anglo-Norman and Angevin England were used and adopted to express this new way of thinking. In both the short and the longer term, therefore, territorialization necessarily affected other magnates, most notably (but not exclusively) *mormaír*, and created the need in William's charters to claim institutional continuity with the past, particularly by invoking the name and

---

[46] It is interesting to note that one of the manuscripts that also contains the injury tariff, a chapter which may belong to the *LBS*-group, states that the chapter on 'the spilling of blood', which is also present in *LS*, c. 21, adds a sentence which says, 'all and each one of the above [compensation payments for blood spilling], which run in lords' courts, are terminated according to aid and favour (*auxilium et favorem*)': BL, Harley MS 4700, fo. 81r (*RM*, bk IV, c. 68, in that manuscript). While this would not have been included in earlier texts, it is an interesting indication of how these compensation payments were later expected to operate within the structure of defined lordly jurisdiction.

[47] *Scottish Formularies*, ed. Duncan, A76, p. 33.

[48] For native reaction, see Cynthia J. Neville, 'Charter Writing and the Exercise of Lordship in Thirteenth-Century Scotland', in *Expectations of the Law in the Middle Ages*, ed. Anthony Musson (Woodbridge, 2001), pp. 67–89; Cynthia J. Neville, 'A Celtic Enclave in Norman Scotland: Earl Gilbert and the Earldom of Strathearn', in *Freedom and Authority*, ed. Brotherstone and Ditchburn, pp. 75–92; Cynthia J. Neville, *Native Lordship in Medieval Scotland: The Earldoms of Strathearn and Lennox, c.1140–1365* (Dublin, 2005); Oram, 'Gold into Lead?', pp. 39–40; and, also extending to seal usage: Neville, *Land, Law and People*, pp. 96–9.

reputation of David I. But modern historians should not interpret claims to continuity as representations of past realities; the continuity that should in fact be identified and analysed is the fundamental practice of royal gift-giving.

The first part of this book has also by default concentrated on what appear to be informal modes of ruling, that is, ruling through elites. More will be said on this subject in the overall conclusion to this book. That kings ruled with and through elites remained a constant throughout the twelfth century, despite the major changes to the conceptualization of aristocratic power that started to occur in the 1160s and 1170s. But the last third of the twelfth century was also when governmental institutions started appearing not only south but also north of the Forth; it thus saw the beginnings and development of uniform institutions of government. The second part of this book will set out the growth and shape of these administrative and judicial institutions, how they changed over the course of the thirteenth century, and what part territorial aristocratic power played within them.

PART II

THE EMERGENCE OF A BUREAUCRATIC STATE, *c.*1170–1290?

4

The Institutions of Royal Government, *c.*1170–1290

The argument of Chapter 3 rested on an unproven premise: that the institutions of royal government took a longer time to develop than previous analyses have suggested. The assumption of longer development partly explained why the law of William the Lion did not set its administrative procedures in an institutional or jurisdictional framework whereas that of his son, Alexander II, did. The time has now come to prove this premise. This chapter will examine three royal officials in turn: the sheriff, the justiciar, and the chamberlain, of which only one—the justiciar—has previously been the subject of a full study.[1] These officials have been chosen because of their responsibilities. The sheriff covered local government and administration, the justiciar, developments in royal justice, while the chamberlain was responsible for managing the king's income and expenditure. There is more than empirical accuracy at stake in the attempt to understand when and where these officials were introduced and when they accumulated particular responsibilities. If their development took longer than previously thought, then the methods for exercising royal power in the thirteenth century must have been significantly different from those in the twelfth. The first part of this book examined changes in the conception of royal and aristocratic power over the twelfth century; this chapter provides a new narrative of institutional development to set alongside those changes. It argues that the institutional structure of government, in which chamberlains and regionally based justiciars interacted with local administrative divisions (the 'sheriffdom'), could not have been fully in the minds of those who wrote royal charters and drafted royal laws until the first two decades of the thirteenth century at the earliest.[2]

---

[1] G. W. S. Barrow, 'The Justiciar', in G. W. S. Barrow, *The Kingdom of the Scots: Government, Church and Society from the Eleventh to the Fourteenth Century*, 2nd edn (Edinburgh, 2003), pp. 68–111. The absence of a study on sheriffs was noted in and formed the basis of Alexander Grant, 'Lordship and Society in Twelfth-century Clydesdale', in *Power and Identity in the Middle Ages: Essays in Memory of Rees Davies*, ed. Huw Pryce and John Watts (Oxford, 2007), pp. 98–124; see also G. W. S. Barrow and Norman H. Reid ed., *The Sheriffs of Scotland: An Interim List to c.1306* (St Andrews, 2002).

[2] In this chapter, I take institution to mean a 'concrete organisational form', rather than as a social institution, in which practices are so common across all spectrums of society (such as marriage) that they could be called 'institutions'; see Hannah Skoda, 'A Historian's Perspective on the Present Volume', in *Legalism: History and Anthropology*, ed. Paul Dresch and Hannah Skoda (Oxford, 2012), pp. 39–54, at p. 44.

This chapter does not cover all aspects of royal government and administration. It does not examine, for example, the office of chancellor and the composition of the king's *capella*, his writing office (sometimes called a 'chancery' in modern historiography). Debates about whether kings had their own 'chancery' have often played a key part in wider conversations about the extent and strength of royal power in other European kingdoms: the most obvious case is that of Anglo-Saxon England.[3] However, although the chapel is an important subject in its own right, the concern of this chapter is what the *content* of royal charters reveals about the institutions of government not the scribes who wrote them.[4] In this context, whether most royal charters were written by scribes primarily attached to the king's chapel is of secondary importance to the issue of when and how scribes of royal charters (wherever they were based) not only started referring to governmental institutions but also did so in the same legal language ('diplomatic'). Nor will this chapter cover all the subjects pertinent to each official: thirteenth-century developments in the judicial responsibilities of the justiciar and sheriff will be developed in Chapter 5 and the chamberlain's role in the development of probative accounting will be examined in Chapter 6. The focus here is on early development and it is with the official of local government—the sheriff—that we will start.

SHERIFFS

Axiomatic in previous analyses of sheriffs and sheriffdoms is that their spread denotes the increasing reach of royal government in the periphery of the kingdom. Dickinson wrote with characteristic ease that 'the reach of the sheriffdoms represents the reach of the royal power. Each push into the unknown is marked by a...royal sheriff to hold and to organise that new district that has been gained'.[5] Even G.W.S. Barrow, who was more circumspect about the powers sheriffs wielded during the twelfth century, particularly north of the Forth, stated (together with Norman Reid) that, by the end of this century, the sheriff was 'undoubtedly a

---

[3] For examples of the differing views on the Anglo-Saxon chancery, see Pierre Chaplais, 'The Anglo-Saxon Chancery: From the Diplomat to the Writ', *Journal of the Society of Archivists*, vol. 3, no. 4 (1966), pp. 160–76; his contributions were reprinted in Felicity Ranger ed., *Prisca Munimenta: Studies in Archival and Administrative History Presented to Dr A. E. J. Hollaender* (London, 1973), pp. 28–107. For a different view, see Simon Keynes, *The Diplomas of King Æthelred 'the Unready', 970–1016. A Study in Their Use as Historical Evidence* (Cambridge, 1980), pp. 14–83; Simon Keynes, 'Regenbald the Chancellor (sic)', *ANS*, vol. 10 (1988), pp. 185–222. A useful summary of this debate can be found in Levi Roach, *Kingship and Consent in Anglo-Saxon England, 871–978: Assemblies and the State in the Early Middle Ages* (Cambridge, 2013), pp. 78–89.

[4] For a preliminary study of the Scottish writing office, see G. W. S. Barrow, 'The *Capella Regis* of the Kings of Scotland, 1107–1222', in *Miscellany V*, ed. Hector L. MacQueen, Stair Society 52 (Edinburgh, 2006), pp. 1–11, although written originally in the 1970s. A full palaeographical and diplomatic study of Scottish royal charters to 1250 will be undertaken by the Arts and Humanities Research Council-funded project, 'Models of Authority: Scottish Charters and the Emergence of Government, 1100–1250', running at Glasgow, Cambridge, and KCL in 2014–17.

[5] *The Sheriff Court Book of Fife, 1515–1522*, ed. William Croft Dickinson, Scottish History Society, 3rd ser., vol. 12 (Edinburgh, 1928), pp. 347–88, at p. 368; William Croft Dickinson, *Scotland from Earliest Times to 1603* (Edinburgh, 1961), pp. 101–3.

powerful figure in the locality ... [a phenomenon] consistent with the kings' policy of extending centralised authority throughout the realm'.[6] One assumption at work here is that the sheriffdom (often referred to as a *vicecomitatus*), a territorial area with fixed geographical and jurisdictional limits, was introduced at the same time as the office of sheriff (*vicecomes*).[7] The most recent work to engage with the medieval Scottish sheriff conflated the introduction of the office of sheriff with the development of a defined area of local administration: '*sheriffs* ... [were] on a par with the provincial earls and lords. Scotland's *sheriffdoms* were a twelfth-century innovation, appearing at the same time as the new provincial lordships', a period which could mean any time from David I's gift of Annandale to Robert de Brus between 1124 and 1128 to William the Lion's gift of the Garioch to his brother, Earl David, by 1182.[8]

Earlier work also held that a sheriff headed a court of his sheriffdom from the moment of the introduction of the office.[9] But this did not command fundamental acceptance. In 1971, Barrow argued that, although shrieval courts may have existed in an 'embryonic' form in the reign of William the Lion, royal justice was invariably administered by either the king's court (*curia regis*) or a session held by a royal justice. This situation persisted 'down to 1214', whereupon sheriffs presumably began to hold their own courts, although Barrow was not explicit on this point.[10] Barrow's thoughts were based on a magisterial command of the charter evidence but, unfortunately, he never developed his statements into a full study and his points were not influential enough to become orthodox. Thus, in 1993, Hector MacQueen stated that 'sheriff and burgh courts had emerged in the reign of William I, if not before'.[11] MacQueen did not develop his statement either and as a result the geography and chronology of the growth of shrieval courts remain opaque.[12]

---

[6] Barrow and Reid, *Sheriffs of Scotland*, p. xv; R. Andrew McDonald, 'Old and New in the far North: Ferchar Maccintsacairt and the Early Earls of Ross, *c*.1200–1274', in *The Exercise of Power in Medieval Scotland, c.1200–1500*, ed. Steve Boardman and Alasdair D. Ross (Dublin, 2003), pp. 23–45, at p. 27; *RRS*, ii, pp. 41–2.

[7] Dickinson, *Scotland from Earliest Times*, pp. 101–2; cf. R. L. G. Ritchie, *The Normans in Scotland* (Edinburgh, 1954), pp. 316–22, at 319–20, who did state that a defined territorial administrative district was not always introduced along with the office of sheriff.

[8] Alexander Grant, 'Franchises North of the Border: Baronies and Regalities in Medieval Scotland', in *Liberties and Identities in the Medieval British Isles*, ed. Michael Prestwich (Woodbridge, 2008), pp. 155–99, at p. 187; my emphasis. For David's holding of the Garioch, see Keith J. Stringer, *Earl David of Huntingdon, 1152–1219: A Study in Anglo-Scottish History* (Edinburgh, 1985), pp. 30–5, 60–8.

[9] Dickinson, *Scotland from Earliest Times*, p. 101. It is of note that even Ritchie did not separate the presence of a sheriff from the presence of his court: '[the sheriff] discharges his military duties, chiefly local defence and recruitment, holds his Court, collects the revenue and keeps the records of the lands and owners in his district which in the process of time grows into a sheriffdom': Ritchie, *Normans in Scotland*, p. 319.

[10] *RRS*, ii, pp. 42–3, at p. 42.

[11] Hector L. MacQueen, *Common Law and Feudal Society in Medieval Scotland* (Edinburgh, 1993), p. 49; cf. *Atlas of Scottish History to 1707*, ed. Peter G. B. McNeill and Hector L. MacQueen (Edinburgh, 1996), pp. 192–3.

[12] A situation summed up by Barrow's summary of his previous work on the sheriff and sheriffdom in a 2002 publication, put together with Norman Reid. This stated that, under William the Lion, the sheriff's administrative roles 'were being supplemented by an increasing judicial rôle. The sheriff's

This section will avoid seeing sheriffdoms wherever sheriffs are mentioned. It will look instead for institutional form: when do sheriffdoms, as administrative divisions with their own courts, start being mentioned as standard units throughout the kingdom of the Scots? Less attention will be paid to the spread of the office of sheriff (i.e. tracking references to sheriffs in the written record): not only has this been done before, but doing so also blurs the line between the individuals who held the office of sheriff and the existence of defined administrative units of government. We do, after all, already know the narrative of the spread of the office of the sheriff across Scotland.[13] The first example of a sheriff, Cospatric, dates from between 1120 and 1126: this Cospatric has been convincingly associated with Roxburgh.[14] Sheriffs were established in Lothian and as far north as Perth under David I but took longer to be recorded elsewhere. By the end of Mael Coluim IV's reign, there were sheriffs at Berwick, Lanark, Edinburgh, Linlithgow, Stirling, Dunfermline, Crail, Clackmannan, Perth, Scone, and Forfar.[15] By 1214, there are recorded instances of sheriffs of Selkirk, Traquair, Haddington, Ayr, Inverness, Nairn, and others associated with the provinces of Moray, the Mearns, Fife, Carrick, and Galloway.[16] All this can be consulted in map form in the *Atlas of Scottish History*.[17] By looking at the increasing spread of references to the sheriff in the kingdom of the Scots across the twelfth and early thirteenth centuries, one can understand why W.C. Dickinson and many others after him thought its development represented 'the reach of royal power'.[18]

But to leave the issue there would be problematic. A growing list, however accurate, just tells us about the spread of an office: it does not tell us about how that office changed and developed as it spread. The unconscious assumption, present in earlier Scottish historiography, that the sheriff, sheriffdom, and shrieval court were all introduced simultaneously must be acknowledged and then immediately abandoned. They are analysed here as separate, though not independent, phenomena and there is ample comparative material to support this approach. Shire communities in Anglo-Saxon England existed before their meetings became routine under King Edgar; groups of shires were headed by ealdormen long before ealdormen (or, later, earls) presided over regular and defined meetings of the shire; kings employed reeves to collect their fiscal dues and profits of justice from fortified places and royal estates before a particular type of reeve (the shire-reeve, *scirgerefa*, sheriff) was

court may not have been as developed as the supposed *Assise Regis Willelmi* would have us believe... [but] the use of the sheriff in the actual dispensation of justice was largely a later development'. Barrow and Reid, *Sheriffs of Scotland*, p. xvi. This statement gives the impression that sheriffs had courts at some unspecified time in William's reign, had increasing judicial responsibilities but did not dispense justice in their own courts, instead only aiding the king and justice. There may not be anything wrong with this interpretation, but it is confusing.

[13] *RRS*, ii, pp. 39–41; *Sheriff Court Book*, ed. Dickinson, pp. 349–68; and the maps in *Atlas*, pp. 192–4 (all prepared and commented on by Hector L. MacQueen).

[14] *Sheriff Court Book*, ed. Dickinson, p. 347 and note 2.

[15] *Atlas*, p. 192. Although it was argued earlier that the *vicecomites* of Forfar and Scone were thanes rather than sheriffs, see Chapter 2, pp. 109–10.

[16] *Atlas*, p. 193; see further Barrow and Reid, *Sheriffs of Scotland*, pp. 1–45.

[17] *Atlas*, pp. 192–4.   [18] Dickinson, *Scotland from Earliest Times*, p. 101.

given the responsibility for a single shire.[19] Likewise, while eleventh- and early twelfth-century Normandy had *vicomtes*, responsible for keeping the duke's peace, and collecting dues from the ducal estates within his county (*vicomté*), the court of the *vicomte* seems not to have had a judicial function until 1144.[20] Once the sheriff, sheriffdom, and shrieval functions are separated, the development of royal local administrative units of government in medieval Scotland becomes clearer.

The Sheriffdom

Over the past ten years, there has been something of a revolution, led by Richard Sharpe, in the interpretation of the address clauses of royal and ducal charters in England and Normandy.[21] In 2003, Sharpe put forward a new and clear definition of a type of document known as the 'writ-charter'.[22] The content of this type of document was that of a charter—a notification of a transfer of land and/or privilege—but it was *deliverable*, as writs were, to officials in charge of particular assemblies, not only addressing that forum and the people who attended it but also explicitly naming the individuals and officials who presided over it. In England, this forum was, until *c.*1170 at the latest, the shire court; in Normandy, it was the court of the *vicomté*. The king (or duke) would send his writ-charters to the officials of the shire court (or *vicomté* court), who would read the document to the assembly. The writ-charter was then taken away by the beneficiary to be archived after the meeting. Writ-charters could also be obtained by (but not addressed to) the beneficiary directly if they held land in different shires. In these cases, the writ-charter would be addressed to multiple shires and it has been suggested that the beneficiary was responsible for taking its writ-charter to the various shire courts to be read out after they received it from the king.[23] The common factor behind all these processes is that the precise address clause shows that the writ-charter was designed to be *read*

---

[19] For the introduction of regular shire meetings under Edgar, see George Molyneaux, *The Formation of the English Kingdom in the Tenth Century* (Oxford, 2015), pp. 165–72; for the points that shires formed the units of an earl's jurisdiction but that shires could be transferred between earls, see Stephen Baxter, *The Earls of Mercia: Lordship and Power in Late Anglo-Saxon England* (Oxford, 2007), pp. 62–71; for the many functions of reeves before the earliest appearances of the *scirsman* and *scirgerefa*, see W. A. Morris, *The Medieval English Sheriff to 1300* (Manchester, 1927), pp. 1–16.

[20] Mark Hagger, 'The Norman *Vicomte*, *c.*1035–1135: What Did He Do?', *ANS*, vol. 29 (2007), pp. 65–83, at pp. 79–82; Mark Hagger, 'The Earliest Norman Writs Revisited', *Historical Research*, vol. 82, no. 216 (2009), pp. 181–205, at pp. 191–4; Mark Hagger, 'Secular Law and Custom in Ducal Normandy, *c.*1000–1144', *Speculum*, vol. 85, no. 4 (2010), pp. 827–67, at pp. 859–60. See also F. Lot and R. Fawtier, *Histoire des institutions françaises au moyen âge*, II: *Institutions royales* (Paris, 1958), pp. 144–58.

[21] Richard Sharpe, 'The Use of Writs in the Eleventh Century', *Anglo-Saxon England*, vol. 32 (2003), pp. 247–91; Richard Sharpe, 'Address and Delivery in Anglo-Norman Royal Charters', in *Charters and Charter Scholarship in Britain and Ireland*, ed. Marie Therese Flanagan and Judith A. Green (Basingstoke, 2005), pp. 32–52; Richard Sharpe, 'People and Languages in Eleventh- and Twelfth-Century Britain and Ireland: Reading the Charter Evidence', in *The Reality Behind Charter Diplomatic: Studies by Dauvit Broun, John Reuben Davies, Richard Sharpe and Alice Taylor*, ed. Dauvit Broun (Glasgow, 2011), pp. 1–119; for Normandy, see Hagger, 'The Earliest Norman Writs Revisited'.

[22] Sharpe, 'Use of Writs', pp. 248–54; cf. *Regesta Regum Anglo-Normannorum, 1066–1154: Regesta Willelmi Conquestoris et Willelmi Rufi, 1066–1100*, ed. H. W. C. Davis (Oxford, 1913), p. xxxv.

[23] Sharpe, 'Use of Writs', p. 253.

out in the assembly of the formal unit of local government, thus demonstrating the very existence of that forum in the first place. The address clauses of writ-charters, therefore, have the potential to be one type of evidence for the existence and workings of very real local assemblies and administrative units themselves.

It must be noted that address clauses in England altered depending on the type of document and the forum in which it was read. A writ—as opposed to a writ-charter—in England commanded an individual or group of individuals, defined by office and function, to do something.[24] The same was true with Scottish brieves (Scots parlance for writs, from the Latin *breve*, meaning 'short document'). Writs and brieves differ from writ-charters or brieve-charters because their form was not primarily notificatory: they were written commands, giving instructions to individuals. Writs and brieves did not therefore have to be read out in particular venues; they pertained to the actions required of particular individuals, not necessarily the business of communal units of administration. A brieve could contain a notificatory summary of a particular gift but its fundamental purpose was still to command an individual to do something; the description of the gift just gave the command its context. Brieves could also follow the issue of a charter recording a particular gift. When the king gave land or privileges to a beneficiary and recorded them in a charter or brieve-charter, a parallel brieve could then be drawn up which was addressed to the official who had the responsibility for conveying the gift.[25]

The scribes of royal *acta* in Scotland during the twelfth century adopted much of the diplomatic practice of English royal *acta*, even the form of the written document itself.[26] Brieves were not adopted until late in the reign of Alexander I but, when they were, their diplomatic was influenced by that of England.[27] By the reign of David I, the written record of gift-giving had come to be recorded in documents that often adopted and mirrored the diplomatic of English royal charters. An examination of the address clauses of the *acta* of the kings of Scots is, therefore, an exciting chance to see if their *acta* were also addressed to assemblies of local government.[28] Were there any administrative units or other communities seen as

---

[24] For brieves addressed to groups of individuals defined by office and function, see *RRS*, ii, nos. 68 (officials of the church of Wedale) and 93 (fishermen who fish around the Isle of May).

[25] See, for example, the gift made by King William of three marks from his burgh ferm of Haddington to Dunfermline Abbey to contribute to the cost of lighting the abbey church. A brieve was then drawn up, addressed to the 'sheriff and provosts of Haddington', commanding them to hand the money over every year (*RRS*, ii, nos. 304–305). Another example might be *RRS*, i, no. 201, which grants Durham freedom from toll, and contains a general address clause—'justices, sheriffs, provosts, officials and all other worthy men'—but which also survives in a cartulary copy, which addressed 'the sheriff of Berwick, justices...': *RRS*, i, p. 237, no. 1.

[26] This had not always been the case: it has been argued that, until the reign of David I, royal gift-giving was recorded in different ways from those of the contemporary English chancery: Dauvit Broun, *The Charters of Gaelic Scotland and Ireland in the Early and Central Middle Ages* (Cambridge, 1995), pp. 33–45; Dauvit Broun, 'The Writing of Charters in Scotland and Ireland in the Twelfth Century', in *Charters and the Use of the Written Word in Medieval Society*, ed. Karl Heidecker (Turnhout, 2000), pp. 113–31, at pp. 117–20; Dauvit Broun 'The Adoption of Brieves in Scotland', in *Charters and Charter Scholarship*, ed. Flanagan and Green, pp. 164–83, at p. 175–9.

[27] Broun, 'Adoption of Brieves', *passim*, but particularly pp. 177–9.

[28] See the preliminary comments in Sharpe, 'People and languages', pp. 77–8; Broun, 'Adoption of Brieves', p. 165.

coherent enough to be addressed explicitly in the address clauses of Scottish brieve-charters? As the Scottish sheriffdom was based on the English shire and shire court, the chronology of address clauses in Scotland has much to reveal about the development and emergence of the sheriffdom, seen as the primary local unit of royal administration.[29]

During the reigns of David I and Mael Coluim IV, there survive brieve-charters which address a particular sheriff and the potential community of a sheriffdom. A brieve-charter of David I, issued 1140×47, addressed the sheriffs and provosts of the shire of Stirling (*Strivelinis Scyra*) and informed them that he had granted a teind of land in Airthrey.[30] This brieve-charter thus addressed the sheriff and provosts of the burgh of Stirling who exercised authority over the extensive shire (that is, extended estate) of Stirling. Some brieves also addressed a defined communal unit of the sheriffdom. David addressed brieves to the 'sheriff of Berwick, provosts and all his worthy men of the sheriffdom (*vicecomitatus*) of Berwick' and 'all men of the whole sheriffdom (*vicecomitatus*) of Perth'.[31] On occasion, the sheriffdom is referred to within the text of the charter itself but the word choice was not standard: we hear of the *provincia* and *comitatus* of Roxburgh and the *vicecomitatus* of Perth and Berwick. All sheriffdoms that were addressed in surviving brieves were, with the exception of Perth, located south of the Forth: Berwick, Edinburgh, Stirling, Linlithgow, and Roxburgh. We might think, therefore, that south of the Forth, sheriffdoms had emerged by the end of the reign of David I, and even reached across the Forth as far north as Perth.

But these 'sheriffdoms' located predominantly south of the Forth were not all called the same thing. Berwick and Perth were called *vicecomitatus*. Roxburgh was called a *comitatus* and a *provincia* on two different occasions. Edinburgh, Stirling, and Linlithgow were called 'shires', a word which may not have denoted an administrative 'sheriffdom' but, instead, a large extended estate of the type outlined in Chapter 1.[32] This is in clear contrast to the diplomatic of Scottish royal *acta* addressed to beneficiaries in England: the scribes of these 'Scottish' writ-charters adopted the conventions of English royal charter diplomatic and so addressed the

---

[29] For more on Scottish brieve-charters, see Matthew Hammond, 'The Adoption and Routinization of Scottish Royal Charter Production for Lay Beneficiaries, 1124–1195', in *ANS*, vol. 36 (2014), pp. 91–115, at pp. 93–5. Brieves in Scotland could also be addressed generally, not to particular individuals: commanding generic officials, such as 'justices and sheriffs and officials', to maintain or protect particular gifts made to another individual or institution (see, for example, King William's written command to 'the justices, sheriffs, officials, and all the worthy men of his whole land', commanding that they implead and maintain lawfully the cases of the monks of Newbattle Abbey; *RRS*, ii, no. 70). This type of document may have been obtained and kept by beneficiaries, to be produced in front of the relevant royal official if possession of the gift was ever challenged. Documents that take the form of charters—a record of a gift of land or privilege—but are addressed generally to officials, such as 'justices, sheriffs and servants', may also have served a similar function. These writs, addressed to *generic* officials, are not deliverable, like writ- or brieve-charters; the absence of an addressable venue from the address clause shows they were not intended to have been read out at any particular forum. Again, we might think that they were kept by the beneficiary and then archived and produced when possession was disputed. The address to unnamed types of royal officials may have been useful to the beneficiary because, if the gift was challenged in the future, the charter could be shown to *any* royal official, regardless of whether they were in office at the time of the original gift.

[30] *CDI*, no. 99.   [31] *CDI*, nos. 51, 188.   [32] See Chapter 1, pp. 27–8, 69–70.

comitatus, the 'county', of Cumberland and Northumberland.[33] The English 'county' court was always called a *comitatus* in English writ-charters: the scribes of David's and Mael Coluim's charters thus followed this convention in all the writ-charters they drew up for English beneficiaries. That David I and Mael Coluim IV addressed 'sheriffdoms' in Scotland using a variety of words (and only in a small area) not only suggests that there were only a few sheriffs that controlled a geographically defined unit of administration but also that even these sheriffdoms were not defined in uniform and standard ways as they were in England (otherwise why not use the word *comitatus* in Scottish royal charters, as scribes did for the counties of Northumberland and Cumberland?). Stirling, Edinburgh and Berwick were called shires because they were conceptualized as large extended estates which were commonly called shires north and south of the River Tweed. This also explains why Roxburgh (which we do not know to have been the head of a large estate) was *not* called a 'shire'; instead, the sheriffdom of Roxburgh was identified by the words *comitatus* and *provincia*. These words were used predominantly north of the Forth in the later twelfth century to distinguish between the titular province of the *comes* and his earldom, the land he controlled within it (it is thus of some importance that no sheriffdom north of the Forth in the later twelfth and thirteenth centuries was ever called a *comitatus*).[34] But the point pertinent here is that sheriffdoms south of the Forth were not deemed identical administrative units under David I: they were referred to by different words, suggesting a sensitivity on the part of the scribes of brieves and brieve-charters for the estate structures that lay underneath our early 'sheriffdoms'.

In addition, many of these early brieves and brieve-charters which appear to address a sheriffdom were, in fact, addressing a burgh community.[35] Their content addressed matters that pertained to the burgh: gifts made from the king's burgh ferm (the set amount of money he received each year from the burgh community), the establishment of markets, trading regulations, and land conveyances within the burgh itself. The standard address clause of these brieves and brieve-charters was to the 'sheriff and provosts (*vicecomes et prepositi*)' of a particular burgh, demonstrating

---

[33] For Cumberland, see *CDI*, no. 58, in which *vic'* is incorrectly expanded as *vicecomitibus*; for Northumberland, see the *acta* of Henry, David's son, when he was earl of Northumberland: *CDI*, nos. 79, which mistakenly gives *uicecomitibus* for *uicecomiti*, 80, 82 (*de comitatu Norhmbie et de honore Huntedunie*), 103, 104 (with *vic'* incorrectly expanded to *vicecomitibus*), 203 (same applies with *vic'*). I am grateful to Hugh Doherty for help with the address clauses of the acts of Henry, earl of Northumberland.

[34] For Stirling and Berwick, see G. W. S. Barrow, 'Pre-Feudal Scotland: Shires and Thanes', in *Kingdom of the Scots*, pp. 7–56, at pp. 23–4, 31–2. For the potential shire of Edinburgh, see G. W. S. Barrow, 'Midlothian—or the Shire of Edinburgh?', *The Old Edinburgh Club*, vol. 35 (1985), pp. 141–8; for the small amount of evidence for pre-burghal Perth, see Niall Robertson and David Perry, 'Perth before the Burgh', in *Perth: The Archaeology and Development of a Scottish Burgh*, ed. David P. Bowler, Tayside and Fife Archaeological Committee (Perth, 2004), pp. 10–11.

[35] For the chronology of the development of burghs, see George S. Pryde, *The Burghs of Scotland: A Critical List* (Oxford, 1965). A full study of burghs in medieval Scotland is yet to be accomplished, although see the points in Richard Oram, *Domination and Lordship: Scotland 1070 to 1230* (Edinburgh, 2011), pp. 265–94; E. Patricia Dennison, 'Burghs and Burgesses: a Time of Consolidation?', in *The Reign of Alexander II, 1214–49*, ed. Richard Oram (Leiden, 2005), pp. 253–83.

that the sheriff had provosts under him in charge of governing and monitoring the burgh itself. David addressed the 'sheriff and provosts of Stirling' when he granted a teind of his rents (*census meus*) from Stirling to Dunfermline Abbey.[36] Burgesses also appear in these address clauses, which makes the burghal—rather than shrieval—destination even more obvious. Mael Coluim IV addressed 'his sheriff and burgesses of Linlithgow, and all his other worthy men of Linlithgowshire' when he granted a toft in Linlithgow to Scone Abbey.[37] William addressed 'his sheriff and provosts of Haddington' when he commanded them to apportion three marks from the burgh ferm to Abbot Archibald of Dunfermline to light the abbey church.[38] It is easy to assume that these brieves and brieve-charters were addressing a sheriffdom for the very reason that their address clauses are similar to later mandates addressing sheriffs of particular touns who also exercised jurisdiction over a known sheriffdom. To do so, however, would be to ignore the content of these documents, concerned with burghal issues, and we should separate the development of burgh communities from that of sheriffdoms.

With the exception of Perth, all of the addressable sheriffdoms in Scottish brieves and brieve-charters were located south of the Forth in the reign of David I. If we move into the reign of Mael Coluim IV and north of the Forth, and exclude Perth, it is hard to see *sheriffdoms* being addressed north of the Forth; we only know that sheriffs were.[39] But what is interesting is that magnates north of the Forth were also addressed in brieves and brieve-charters in a similar (but not identical) way to how sheriffs were addressed south of the Forth during his reign. We have already seen in Chapter 1 how a brieve of Mael Coluim IV addressed the potentates of the province of Fife in a way that not only made sense of internal power dynamics but also commanded them to 'maintain and guard' the monks and lands of Dunfermline Abbey.[40] A brieve-charter of Mael Coluim IV, datable to 1153×62, was addressed to the abbot of Dunfermline and one Cospatric, son of Waltheof, and all the ferrymen of sea ports, informing them that the bishop of St Andrews and his men might cross the Firth of Forth without payment, on pain of the king's full forfeiture. The primary crossing of the Forth was between Queensferry

---

[36] *CDI*, no. 49.

[37] *RRS*, i, no. 253. Two acts have survived from the reign of Mael Coluim IV, the first dated 1153×62, referring to the burgesses of Linlithgow; the second, dated 1162×64, referring to the burgesses of Perth: *RRS*, i, nos. 171, 253; see further, *RRS*, ii, nos. 97, 98.

[38] *RRS*, ii, no. 305.

[39] *RRS*, i, no. 214 (sheriffs of Dunfermline and Clackmannan). No brieves survive directly addressed to a sheriff of Perth from Mael Coluim's reign but as the *vicecomitatus* of Perth is addressed under David, we can assume that the sheriff of Perth existed under Mael Coluim (*CDI*, no. 188). See also Mael Coluim's act addressed to the 'earls, barons, justices, sheriffs, provosts and the burgesses of Perth' (*RRS*, i, no. 121). Indeed, it is sometimes hard to be sure that sheriffs *were* being addressed when *vicecomites* were named north of the Forth: it has already been argued in Chapter 2 that the *vicecomites* of Forfar and Scone addressed in one of Mael Coluim's brieves may have been thanes, not sheriffs; see Chapter 2, pp. 109–10.

[40] *RRS*, i, no. 181. This act also contained a prohibition that these men were not allowed to take *coinnmed* from the abbey's lands. It is thus more personal than brieves of protection, which might have generally addressed 'sheriffs' (or even personally named them), and which would not normally have assumed the addressee would be one of the targets of the brieve (*RRS*, i, no. 220, for the sheriff of Berwick). For brieves of protection, see Chapter 3, pp. 165–9.

on the south bank and Inverkeithing (via North Queensferry) on the north. The abbot of Dunfermline controlled Queensferry; by the 1170s, one Waltheof, son of Cospatric, controlled Inverkeithing and Dalmeny (just to the east of Queensferry). Given the patronymic, it is probable that Waltheof, the later lord of Dalmeny and Inverkeithing, was the son of the Cospatric, who was addressed in Mael Coluim IV's earlier brieve-charter. If so, Cospatric had probably controlled Inverkeithing in Mael Coluim's reign before his son, imaginatively named Waltheof, did so later in William's reign. In that case, Cospatric's power over these lands would explain his position in the address clause alongside the abbot of Dunfermline: both Cospatric and Dunfermline were notified of the king's grant to St Andrews because they held the lordship of the two places affected by it: Inverkeithing (Cospatric) and Queensferry (Dunfermline). We therefore see the intermingling of royal command and the patterns of local power in Mael Coluim IV's brieve: the efficacy of royal patronage to St Andrews depended, in this case, not on officials but on local lords with whom the king communicated in the same way in which he communicated with his growing group of sheriffs, located predominantly south of the Forth.

Excluding Perth, whose sheriff controlled a *vicecomitatus* in the reign of David I, the first evidence that sheriffs north of the Forth were generally expected to have some form of coercive power over a large area occurs during the reign of Mael Coluim IV. A new formula was introduced in royal *acta* that described shrieval power generically, suggesting that the powers of sheriffs were coming to be seen as more extensive, replicable, and equivalent: this formula was 'the sheriff in whose power' (*vicecomes in cuius potestate*). During the 1160s, *potestas* was used precisely to denote a generally defined area of responsibility that was projected *outside* the toun to which the sheriff was attached. Mael Coluim IV commanded his 'sheriffs and the servants (*ministri*) of his whole land in whose powers (*potestates*) the canons serving God and St Andrews hold churches' to ensure that teinds be paid lawfully to the priory.[41] The formula of 'sheriff in whose power (*vicecomes in cuius potestate*)' continued to be a standard feature of the diplomatic of King William's charters until the 1180s.[42]

Potestas was, however, a vague word, lacking a defined territorial element and, it would appear, clear jurisdictional responsibility. This was in contrast to what was meant by *vicecomitatus* or *provincia*; the sheriffs of Perth, Berwick, Roxburgh, and Stirling did not have *potestas*, they controlled a *vicecomitatus*, a *scira*, or a *provincia*, the community of which could be addressed. A sheriff's *potestas*, it appears, could not be addressed: there are no surviving brieve-charters that address a local community defined under the *potestas* of a sheriff. Shrieval *potestas* was based on an individual: William commanded the 'sheriffs and servants of his whole land in whose powers (*potestates*) the canons serving God and St Andrew the apostle hold their churches'.[43] The power was located in the individual sheriff and projected outwards onto an ambiguous area of landed inhabitants. These shrieval *potestates*

---

[41] *RRS*, i, no. 233; see also *RRS*, i, no. 167; G. W. S. Barrow, 'An Unpublished Brieve of Malcolm IV', *SHR*, vol. 84, no. 217 (2005), pp. 85–7, at p. 87; *RRS*, i, no. 242.
[42] *RRS*, i, no. 192; *RRS*, ii, nos. 71, 132, 259.   [43] *RRS*, ii, no. 71.

were particularly located north of the Forth. The *potestas* exercised by a sheriff north of the Forth, for example, was contrasted directly with the *provincia* controlled by a sheriff south of the Forth in a brieve of Mael Coluim IV for Guisborough Priory.[44] The terminological distinction between *potestas* and *provincia* within the same document demonstrates that shrieval power north of the Forth was conceived as less defined on the land than that south of the Forth: the *potestas* of a sheriff suggests that sheriffs had particular responsibilities but not a clearly defined area over which to exercise them.

Nor, it would appear, did *potestas* include autonomous jurisdiction. The brieve of Mael Coluim IV (dated 1162×65) for Guisborough Priory is important here because it demonstrates that sheriffs south of the Forth held autonomous courts, while those north of the Forth did not.[45] The brieve recorded the grant of the king's peace to the servants of Guisborough Priory in Yorkshire who came into the land of the king of Scots to retrieve the priory's stolen goods or possessions. If the priory's servants discovered its possessions in Lothian or Teviotdale, the sheriff of the 'province' (*provincia*) in which the goods were found was to do 'justice' to the priory, whose case would be heard in the sheriff's presence, demonstrating that sheriffs south of the Forth had their own courts. But if the same were to happen within *Scotia*, denoting Scotland north of the Forth, 'the sheriff in whose power (*potestas*) the goods were discovered' should bring those goods before the justices south of the Forth, who would then hear the priory's complaint.[46] The Guisborough brieve therefore shows that, at this point in the 1160s, sheriffs north of the Forth were conceived as having fewer responsibilities than sheriffs south of the Forth. The sheriff south of the Forth could settle the priory's case himself; the sheriff north of the Forth, with his vaguely defined *potestas*, could not.[47]

Defined geographical limits to shrieval power, together with the capacity to hold a court, did emerge as standard phenomena north of the Forth but only during the 1180s. This development has been unnoticed in the existing historiography yet it is signalled by yet another change in the diplomatic of royal *acta*. Here, the *potestas* of a sheriff north of the Forth was replaced by his *ballia*—his balliwick or sheriff-dom. This is best demonstrated by two brieves, drawn up for the bishopric of Moray and concerned with the same subject: the punishment of teind avoidance within the bishopric. The first was drawn up in 1172: William addressed the sheriffs

---

[44] Barrow, 'Unpublished Brieve', p. 87.

[45] Barrow, 'Unpublished Brieve', p. 87. The PoMS database acknowledges that a wider date range of 1153×65 is possible (<http://db.poms.ac.uk/record/source/257/>). The appearance of the formula *vicecomes in cuius potestate* in the 1160s, however, makes a date towards the *terminus ante quem* of 1165 more probable.

[46] This also twins with what we know about the spread of justices in Mael Coluim IV's reign: his teind brieve to Glasgow referred to the enforcing power of the justice; in his similar brieve to St Andrews Cathedral Priory, the justice is not mentioned. See Chapter 3, pp. 154–7, and below, pp. 217–24.

[47] This is supported by a brieve of David I, addressed to the *mormaer* of Fife, the bishop of St Andrews, and the men of Fife, stating that the men of Newburn (recently given by David to Dunfermline Abbey) would no longer have to answer any accusation *except* in the abbot's court. If the sheriff had jurisdiction in Fife between 1150 and 1153 (the date of the brieve), one might expect this to be mentioned here or for the sheriff to be an addressee as well (*CDI*, no. 190).

and servants of Moray, notified them that teind and other ecclesiastical renders should be paid promptly within the diocese and commanded that, if anyone should fail to pay teind, the sheriff 'in whose power (*in cuius potestate*)' the offence occurred should distrain and fine the wrongdoer.[48] The second document was drawn up between 1185 and 1189, addressed the 'worthy and faithful men of Moray', and set out the same stipulation: teind should be paid within the bishopric and the royal official in charge of enforcing payment from peasants was the sheriff if lords had failed to do so.[49] If a peasant's thane or lord refused to distrain a defaulting individual, the sheriff 'in whose sheriffdom (*balliva*) this was done' was to compel the individual to pay the teind and take a fine from him or her.

The sheriffdom denoted by the words *balliva, baillia*, or *ballia* had a clear territorial element, projecting outwards from a royal toun or burgh. When William confirmed burghal privileges to Inverness in a charter dated 18 August and drawn up between 1205 and 1207, he laid down that 'no one within the sheriffdom (*baillia*) of Inverness shall make dyed or shorn cloth outside the burgh', showing that not only did the *baillia* of Inverness project outside the burgh but also the inhabitants of the *baillia* were expected to know that they belonged to the sheriffdom of Inverness.[50] We see that *ballia* (and its derivatives) denoted formal administrative divisions of land most demonstrably in a charter of Alexander II, again to the bishopric of Moray, in which the king listed the lands from which the bishop was accustomed to receive second teinds, a tenth of the king's revenue from his lands and profits of justice. These lands were listed according to their sheriffdom (*balliae*): the *ballia* of Inverness, the *ballia* of Nairn, the *ballia* of Forres, and the *ballia* of Elgin.[51] The lands listed in each of these sheriffdoms are shown in Map 4.1.[52]

In the early thirteenth century, the royal chapel started drawing up long charters of William the Lion to his royal burghs, both those which had newly been founded, such as Ayr, and those which had long been in existence, such as Perth. William's charter to Perth was the template of his later charter to Inverness and Alexander II's charters to Aberdeen and Stirling, while William's charter to Ayr was the model for Alexander II's later charters to Dingwall in the far north and Dumbarton in the west.[53] Only the 'Perth' group gives us a sense of the relationship between sheriffdom and burgh; no foreign merchant could buy or sell *outside* the burgh in the sheriffdom of Perth, Inverness, Aberdeen, or Stirling but could inside the burgh. If anyone was found within the sheriffdom of Perth, Inverness, Aberdeen, or Stirling trying to do so, he should be detained until the king decided what to do with him. No one should have a tavern in any vill of the sheriffdom, unless the person who wanted one was a knight and was the 'lord of the vill' in which the proposed tavern

---

[48] *RRS*, ii, no. 132.   [49] *RRS*, ii, no. 281; discussed in Chapter 1, pp. 63–4.

[50] *RRS*, ii, no. 475.   [51] *Moray Reg.*, no. 40 [AII/264].

[52] I have been greatly helped by the 'Places' search function on PoMS (<http://db.poms.ac.uk/search/>). Any errors are my own responsibility.

[53] For Inverness, see *RRS*, ii, no. 475; for Perth, see *RRS*, ii, no. 467; for Aberdeen, see *APS*, i, pp. 87–8 [AII/7] and *Aberdeen Burgh Chrs*, no. 3; for Ayr, see *RRS*, ii, no. 462; for Dumbarton, see Joseph Irving, *The History of Dumbartonshire*, 2nd edn (Dumbarton, 1860), pp. 45–6 [AII/70]; for Dingwall, *RMS*, ii, no. 2387 (abridgement) [AII/130]; for Stirling, *Stirling Charters*, no. 7 [AII/127].

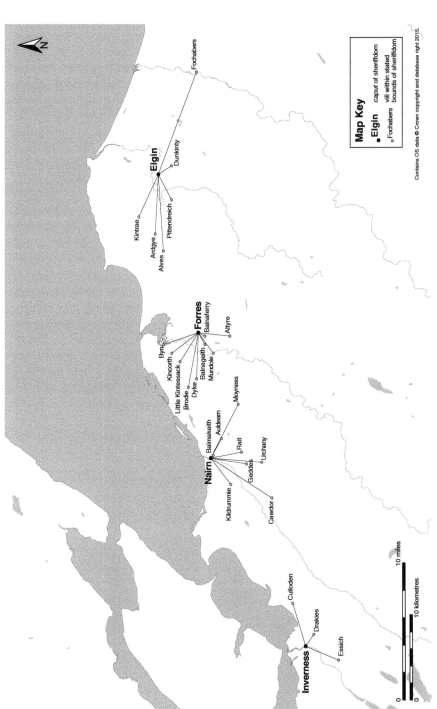

Map 4.1. Identifiable vills within the sheriffdoms of Inverness, Nairn, Forres, and Elgin according to *Moray Reg.*, no. 40 [AII/264]

was to be. No one dwelling outside the burgh of Perth, Inverness, Stirling, or Aberdeen but within their respective sheriffdoms should buy shorn or dyed cloth; that was the preserve of the burgesses. In short, the charters to the burghs of Inverness, Perth, Aberdeen, and Stirling show a real conceptual distinction between the privileges of the burgh and the surrounding sheriffdom; the sheriffdom, made up of vills but not privileged burghs, had far fewer privileges than the burgh itself. In these three charters, the word used to describe the sheriffdom was *ballia* for Inverness and *vicecomitatus* for Perth, Stirling, and Aberdeen, demonstrating that the scribes of the Stirling and Aberdeen charters were using the Perth charter as their model.[54]

Despite the textual preference for *vicecomitatus* in these charters, it is clear that *ballia* had become the standard choice for denoting the sheriffdom. The scribe of Alexander II's charter for Aberdeen used the charter for Perth as his model, adding and subtracting sentences from Perth's, so the two are, although very similar, not completely identical.[55] In particular, the scribe of the Aberdeen charter expanded the penultimate clause of the Perth charter. The penultimate clause in the Perth charter was 'I grant all these liberties and customs to [the burgesses] and confirm them by my charter.'[56] In the Aberdeen charter, by contrast, this formula has been extended. 'I grant all these liberties and customs to [the burgesses], and confirm them by my charter, excepting the liberties and free customs which, before this grant, were given to other burghs and burgesses within the sheriffdom (*ballia*) of Aberdeen.'[57] This second phrase was added as a conscious exception to the charter phrasing in the scribe's exemplar. That the scribe described the sheriffdom as a *ballia*, despite the presence of *vicecomitatus* elsewhere in his exemplar, indicates strongly that *ballia* had become the standard way of describing a sheriffdom by the first year of Alexander II's reign.[58]

The use of *balliua* (or *ballia* or *baillia*; the spelling was not standard) in place of *potestas* became a standard feature of charter diplomatic north of the Forth after its introduction in the late 1180s.[59] It was not wholly adopted: those which had previously been called a *comitatus* (Roxburgh) or *vicecomitatus* (Berwick, Perth) might well continue to be referred to as such in charter diplomatic.[60] One brieve of Alexander II did use *potestas* but it is an almost verbatim copy of an earlier—and

---

[54] *Vicecomitatus* was probably used in the case of Perth because Perth always been a *vicecomitatus*. The charter to Perth ended up heading a later medieval lawcode entitled *Constitutiones Regis Willelmi*, which contains an unstudied set of burgh regulations. The *Constitutiones* are given attention in Oram, *Domination and Lordship*, pp. 273–4; and Hector L. MacQueen and William J. Windram, 'Law and Courts in the Burghs', in *The Scottish Medieval Town*, ed. Michael Lynch, Michael Spearman and Geoffrey Stell (Edinburgh, 1988), pp. 208–27, at p. 211.

[55] These additional clauses are not found in the Stirling charter; *Stirling Charters*, no. 7 [AII/127].

[56] *RRS*, ii, no. 467.

[57] *APS*, i, pp. 87–8, at p. 88 [AII/7]; cf MacQueen and Windram, 'Law and Courts', pp. 211–12.

[58] The charter is datable to 27 February 1215.

[59] See further, *RRS*, ii, nos. 354, 475; *Arbroath Liber*, i, no. 106 [AII/19]; *Dunf. Reg.*, no. 78 [AII/134]; *Coupar Angus Chrs*, i, no. 45 [AII/273]; *Glasgow Reg.*, no. 181 [AII/286]; *Moray Reg.*, no. 40 [AII/264].

[60] *RRS*, ii, no. 467; *St Andrews Liber*, pp. 236–7 [AII/136]—there is no simple explanation for the appearance of *vicecomitatus* in this last document.

surviving—brieve of William the Lion.[61] From the 1180s, the overwhelming trend was for sheriffs to control sheriffdoms (*balliae*), known geographical areas over which sheriffs exercised their jurisdictions.[62] Haddington's excerpts from the 1263–66 account roll reveals that, by these years, the sheriff of Forfar was accounting for the *ballia de Forfar*, while the justiciar of Scotia recorded that his ayre had passed through the *balliae* of Inverness, Nairn, Forres, Elgin, Banff, Aberdeen, Kincardine, Forfar, Perth, and Fife—all, as was shown earlier, the seat of sheriffdoms, some of very long standing.[63] Nor was the word used just of sheriffdoms north of the Forth. The ayre of Stephen Fleming, justiciar of Lothian in 1264, went through the *balliae* of Ayr, Lanark, Peebles, and Roxburgh.[64] The acknowledgement that sheriffs controlled defined geographical administrative units, however, seems only to have become a standard and recognized feature of all attested shrieval jurisdictions from the 1180s when the phrase first appears in royal charters.

Shrieval Courts and Jurisdiction

If *ballia* gave the sheriffdom administrative definition, it is of note that the earliest written statement to acknowledge explicitly that sheriffs had a duty to hold their own courts, regardless of the location of the sheriffdom, is in legislation of William the Lion, issued at Perth as part of a series of four enactments on 30 October 1184, just before *ballia* first appears in the diplomatic of royal charters.[65] The assize has previously been thought to be spurious but I have argued elsewhere that this belief is mistaken, and is based on the text prepared by Thomas Thomson for volume 1 of *APS*, which itself is a spurious concoction not attested in any early legal manuscript.[66] There is no problem with the text as it appears in *LS* (as c. 14). But Thomson did not use the *LS*-text; instead, he primarily based his edition on the later revision of the statute attested in *CD*.[67] Part of the text of *LS*, c. 14, as it pertains to sheriffs is therefore given below:[68]

> The lord king [William] also enacted that each sheriff shall hold his pleas (*placita sua*) every forty days (*ad capud xl dierum*), and that the barons and knights and those holding freely, and the stewards of bishops and abbots and earls, must be present at the pleas of the sheriffs (*placitis vicecomitum*). If, however, any of them should fail to attend the sheriffs' pleas (*placita vicecomitum*), he shall incur the king's forfeiture.

[61] *Scone Liber*, no. 60 [AII/333], copying *RRS*, ii, no. 259.

[62] For the *ballia* of Nairn in 1236, see *Thanes of Cawdor*, p. 2 [AII/245]; for the *ballia* of Stirling, see *Cambuskenneth Reg.*, no. 224 [AII/184]; for the *ballia* of Lanark, see *Glasgow Reg.*, i, no. 186 [AII/293].

[63] *ER*, i, pp. 8, 18.   [64] *ER*, i, pp. 9–10.

[65] *LS*, cc. 11–14; for the arguments as to associate *LS*, c. 14, with the other three enactments of William made at Perth, see Taylor, 'Leges Scocie', pp. 211–12.

[66] For the belief that the statute is spurious, see *RRS*, ii, p. 42; for the identification of the original form of *LS*, c. 14, see Taylor, 'Leges Scocie', pp. 220–2.

[67] Taylor, 'Leges Scocie', pp. 220–2, shows how Thomson dealt with the conflicting material from *CD* and *LS*.

[68] Translation adapted from Taylor, 'Leges Scocie', p. 284.

The date of this enactment thus coincides with the earliest appearance of the word *ballia* to denote the area over which sheriffs exercised authority (1185×89, although 1187×89 is also possible).[69] It is, of course, highly probable that many sheriffs had held courts before this, and what was introduced in 1184 was for them a confirmation of an existing scenario, while also introducing uniform regulations for the running of shrieval courts.[70] This may even have been the case north of the Forth, an area which, as the Guisborough brieve showed, appears not to have supported shrieval jurisdiction even late in the reign of Mael Coluim IV.[71] But the point about the 1184 enactment is that it confirms that sheriffs north and south of the Forth were expected to hold courts: it was a requirement of the office. That it pre-dated the earliest reference to *ballia* in the diplomatic of royal charters by only a few years suggests that the first half of the 1180s was when the expectation developed that *all* sheriffs, regardless of where they held their office, should hold courts. We should not thus date the introduction of standard shrieval courts in the kingdom of the Scots until the mid-1180s at the latest, and not much before this.

What did the existence of standard shrieval courts mean for those lords who held their land with major jurisdictional privileges, which had started to be defined in royal charters around twenty years before?[72] It seems that lands which were held by these lords were, with the exception of offences belonging to the crown, exempt from appearing in front of the sheriff (although they may have had to attend his court); certainly, later evidence from the mid-thirteenth century shows sheriffs attempting to fine religious institutions for their tenants' failure to attend shrieval *placita*.[73] This, however, did not necessarily mean that 'state' and 'lordly' jurisdiction existed autonomously. Not only did the 1184 act envisage that barons and knights, as well as stewards of bishops, abbots, and earls, would have to attend shrieval courts but an earlier enactment of 1180—before shrieval courts ever appear in royal legislation—also aimed to integrate the sheriff into the courts of others. This enactment stated that:

> Concerning the assize made at Stirling on the next Monday before the next feast of St Margaret the virgin after the first coronation of Philip, king of the Franks, with the assent of the earls and barons, neither bishops nor abbots nor earls nor barons nor any

[69] *RRS*, ii, no. 281.

[70] For an example of the king's *placita* before 1184, see the brieve of William, issued 1165×71, which addressed the 'justices, sheriffs and servants' of the king and commanded them that 'wherever the monks or brethren of Newbattle should come to my pleas [held] among you, you should maintain and plead their pleas as my own' (*RRS*, ii, no. 70), strongly suggesting that in Lothian (where Newbattle held most of its land; the location of the abbey is in Midlothian) there were sheriffs and justices holding the king's pleas.

[71] John of Hastings, sheriff of Mearns, one of the witnesses in the Arbuthnott dispute, heard at the ecclesiastical synod at Perth in 1206, testified that, in the time of Bishop Richard of St Andrews (d.1178), the bailies of the bishop of St Andrews would come to him 'as for the men of the bishop and to the court of the bishop' if any of the men of the Kirkton of Arbuthnott were vexed in anything pertaining to the sheriffdom (*vicecomitatus*) or forest (*forestarium*), suggesting that there were sheriff courts in the Mearns in the 1170s; *Spalding Misc.*, v, p. 210.

[72] See above, Chapter 3, pp. 157–64, Part 1 Conclusion, pp. 177–84.

[73] The most obvious evidence for the relationship between a significant aristocratic jurisdiction and royal justice in the third quarter of the twelfth century is William's charter to Robert de Brus: *RRS*, ii, no. 80; see also, for relationship with a monastic one, *Dunf. Reg.*, no. 85.

other holding freely shall hold their court unless the king's sheriff (*vicecomes regis*) or his sergeand (*serviens eiusdem*)[74] is present or has been summoned to be present to see that the court was conducted properly. And four pleas pertaining to his crown are reserved for the king's business in all their courts: that is, rape, robbery, arson and murder. And if the sheriff does not come when summoned to baronial courts nor sends another of the king's sergeands (*aliquem de servientibus regis*), the baron may hold his court lawfully without the king's forfeiture and by lawful witness. Concerning all other pleas, every free man who has a court shall receive whatever has fallen there, saving the justice of the lord king.

[74] There are, in fact, three texts of this statute: one in *LS*, c. 7; a second and almost identical copy in *SA*, c. 18; and a third revised and updated copy in *CD*, c. 1. Thomson's text is a conglomeration of their material but, in general, when the copies in *CD* and *LS* presented different readings, Thomson invariably preferred the reading of *CD* over that of the earlier *LS*. There is one further problem with the text in *APS*. The final sentence of Thomson's text is as follows: 'Moreover, no baron may hold a court of battle, water or iron unless the sheriff or his sergeand is present to see that law and justice are upheld': *ARW*, c. 12, in *APS*, i, p. 375. Accordingly, this sentence is often treated as part of the statute itself. But it is, in fact, a separate chapter in *SA* (c. 22). Thomson, seeing that the general subject of *SA*, c. 22, was broadly similar to the 1180 enactment, presumably added it to his edition.

Only one difference between the *LS*- and *CD*- texts is relevant here. When *LS*, c. 7 states that no lord, ecclesiastical or lay, may hold his court 'unless the king's sheriff or his sergeand (*serviens eiusdem*) were present', *CD* (and accordingly Thomson) states that no one may hold his court 'unless the king's sheriff or sheriff's sergeands (*servientes vicecomitis*) were present' (*LS*, c. 7; *CD*, c. 1; *ARW*, c. 12, in *APS*, i, pp. 374–5). The statute in *LS* makes it clear that the *eiusdem* refers to the king not to the sheriff: 'if the sheriff does not come...nor does he send another of the king's sergeands (*servientes regis*)', the lord's court could continue regardless. Moreover, the reading of *serviens eiusdem* (rather than *servientes vicecomitis*) is also attested in γ group of *CD*-manuscripts, which I have argued elsewhere often contains particularly accurate readings; the same reading is also attested in the earliest surviving manuscript of *SA* (Alice Taylor, 'The Assizes of David, king of Scots, 1124–53', *SHR*, vol. 91, no. 232 (2012), pp. 197–238, at pp. 213–14). The meaning of the statute and the authority of the reading in *LS* are clear: if the sheriff could not attend a lord's court, he summoned one of the king's sergeands, not one of his own.

Preferring the original meaning of 'king's sergeands' for the previously accepted 'sheriff's sergeands', however, prompts a reinterpretation of the structure of local shrieval administration in the late twelfth century. The accepted reading of 'sheriff's sergeands' assumes that the sheriff had sergeands, known to him and subordinate to his office, whom he could command to take his place supervising a lord's court (see, for example, Dickinson, *Scotland from Earliest Times*, p. 102). The original reading of *serviens eiusdem*, denoting the *king's* sergeands, suggests that the sheriff did *not* have such well-defined subordinate officials to whom he could delegate this responsibility. In 1180, it was the king who had sergeands who could supervise lords' courts, not the sheriff. These royal sergeands could assume the duties of a sheriff; however, the language of the statute shows that they were tied to the king, not to any structure of local administration headed by the sheriff. It was, admittedly, the sheriff's responsibility to 'send' or command (*miserit*) these royal sergeands to attend a lord's court if the sheriff was unable to himself; from this, we might interpret that the *status* of the office of sergeand was subordinate to the sheriff, even if he did not report directly to him within a structure of local administration. If we were to accept this interpretation, it still remains that, if the sheriff was unable to attend a lord's court, he summoned *not* one of his subordinate officials but an official who was associated directly with the person of the king and whose status and expertise were, at the very least, assumed to be high enough to perform the task in his place. We see this in a notificatory mandate of King William, datable to between 1165 and 1171 and addressed to his justices and sheriff of Berwick. Here, the king informed the justices and sheriff that 'none of my sergeands of the sheriffdom (*vicecomitatus*) of Berwick' shall collect the customs, pleas and lawsuits pertaining to them in Coldingham and its shire, dues and fines which 'my sergeands of my other sheriffdoms (*vicecomitatuum meorum*) have in my other alms in my land' (*RRS*, ii, no. 67). While there clearly were sergeands associated with sheriffdoms (at least south of the Forth), the king perceived them as his own, not under the sheriffs.

It is impossible to know how far this statute was enforced, and whether sheriffs did regularly attend lord's courts as a result. Part of the reason for this difficulty is the rather lax nature of the statute: it anticipates that sheriffs would often not be able to attend, nor would it always be possible to send a substitute in the figure of the king's sergeand.[75] But it is also impossible to know its effect because men who were sheriffs in the late twelfth and early thirteenth centuries did not always attest agreements made in the courts of others with their titles: were they therefore present as sheriffs or as prominent lords—or a combination of both?[76] Proving the statute's relevance, however, is not as important in this context as the statute's intent: that sheriffs were to be present at the courts of major lay and religious landlords. For those who held more minor jurisdictional powers, probably encompassing the offences of *blodwite* (fines for bloodshed) and *birthinsake* (petty theft), sheriffs did not have to be present; the integration was with the courts of bigger lords.[77] The place of enactment—Stirling—seen as the gateway between north and south of the Forth—must indicate that the statute was intended to be enforced in both regions of the kingdom. If so, then it suggests a level of acceptance of lordly jurisdiction both north and south of the Forth unknown in contemporary England, as argued recently by Dauvit Broun: where Henry II's legal reforms either intended to or had the consequence of taking business out of lords' courts, this statute of William's actually protected them.[78] By legislating that a sheriff should attend a lordly court (but if he could not, the court could still go ahead), the king was, in fact, ensuring that fewer complaints of default of justice could come to him from suitors of lordly courts: the sheriff was summoned to ensure that the court was conducted properly; if he could not attend, then it would be assumed that the court had nevertheless been conducted properly and fewer appeals to the king would occur as a result. In short, this statute not only confirmed the sheriff's supervisory role over lordly jurisdiction but, at the same time, also confirmed, maintained, and protected the legitimacy of the lord's court in all cases other than those reserved for the king.

When and from what did this expected supervisory function of sheriffs over the jurisdictions of other people and institutions develop? Five or six years into William

---

[75] For a cognate example, albeit held at an ecclesiastical synod, rather than merely the 'bishop's court', see a deed of Peter of Ashby (1196×1200), quitclaiming to Dryburgh Abbey some of his land in Berwickshire or Roxburghshire (*Dryburgh Liber*, no. 223). Peter later read out his agreement in the *comitatus* of Lanark (here meaning the sheriffdom). See also the agreement between John, son of Theobald, and Arbroath Abbey, dated 1214×15, where Hugh Cameron, sheriff of Forfar was present (with his title), although the forum is not clear: London, BL, Additional MS 33245, fo. 152r. William del Bois, the king's chancellor, was also present. See also William, sheriff of Crail, present at the deeds of Morgann, earl of Mar, and his wife Agnes. Crail was a long way away from the land in question but was relatively closer to St Andrews, the beneficiary (*St Andrews Liber*, pp. 248–9).

[76] *RRS*, ii, pp. 39–40.

[77] For the fact that these 'big lords' and sheriffs were one and the same by the mid-thirteenth century (and probably by this point as well but that research is difficult to do, given that sheriffs were rarely given their title in the late twelfth century), see Chapter 7, pp. 419–34. For *blodwite* and *birthinsake*, see Chapter 3, p. 161, note 244.

[78] Dauvit Broun, 'Britain and the Beginnings of Scotland', Sir John Rhŷs Memorial Lecture, delivered at the British Academy on 5 December 2013 (text online at <https://www.academia.edu/5362455/Britain_and_the_beginning_of_Scotland._Sir_John_Rhys_Memorial_Lecture_British_Academy_5_December_2013>).

the Lion's reign, sheriffs acted in conjunction with royal justices to give justice where lordly courts had failed. Between 1165 and 1171, Holyrood Abbey was the beneficiary of a general confirmation charter in the name of William, king of Scots. The right to hold a court was among the privileges granted to the abbey and the only proviso was that, if the abbot defaulted in his judicial responsibility, then 'the sheriff and the justice would do right to [the claimant] following what the claimant had accused the abbot's man of lawfully'.[79] The superior aspect of the king's capacity to dispense justice to that exercised by lords is found earlier, in charters of Mael Coluim IV and David I, but in these there are no mentions of the sheriff or the king's justice (meaning the official, rather than the abstract concept). A general mandate of Mael Coluim IV, drawn up for Scone Abbey in 1165, forbade the king's 'worthy men' from taking poinds from anyone on the abbey's land, even for any default of payment by the abbot himself, 'unless the abbot or his man, having first been accused in the abbot's court, should default from right (*rectum*)'.[80] Similar statements are found in David's charters: the abbot of Dunfermline could have all his rights, lands, and privileges as the king possessed his own 'except if the abbot falls through any negligence of justice'.[81] What is different in William's charter to Holyrood, in contrast to either Mael Coluim's charter to Scone or David's charter to Dunfermline, is that William's provides a clear administrative mechanism for this type of supervision: if the abbot of Holyrood failed to do justice, the sheriff and justice would do right. This stipulation is absent in David I's own confirmation charter to Holyrood, suggesting that the additional formula represents a development in the structures of the administration of justice within the kingdom.[82] But, notwithstanding this development, William's confirmation charter is still the only evidence that sheriffs acted in a supervisory function alongside royal justices; it does not show that sheriffs presided over their own courts. However, it does reveal that there was a growing precision in referring to the general supervisory function of royal justice: in the charters of David and Mael Coluim, this is expressed generically; under William, the officials responsible for such supervision are identified, albeit only to a beneficiary situated south of the Forth.[83]

It has already been shown in Chapter 3 that sheriffs were expected to enforce teind payment north and south of the Forth (but not in Moray) from late in the reign of Mael Coluim IV.[84] The earliest reference to sheriffs collecting forfeitures for teind default in Moray comes from 1172.[85] In addition, the decade before the 1180s saw the inception of the idea that sheriffs would provide justice if particular religious institutions did not. This provides a context for the 1180 enactment, whereby sheriffs were encouraged to attend lordly courts or, if not, send one of the king's servants in their stead. Thus, even if the 1180 enactment did not envisage

---

[79] *RRS*, ii, no. 39; see further, MacQueen, *Common Law*, pp. 33–4, 42.
[80] *RRS*, i, no. 262.   [81] *CDI*, no. 33.   [82] *CDI*, no. 147.
[83] Which is different from the sheriff as enforcing agent, as in teind charters to Glasgow and St Andrews under Mael Coluim IV.
[84] However, the justice was not given this responsibility north of the Forth under Mael Coluim but was south of the Forth; see Chapter 3, pp. 154–7, and below, pp. 217–24.
[85] *RRS*, ii, no. 132; for further comment, see below, p. 221.

that sheriffs would *always* be present at the courts of other lords, such an enactment in theory extended the supervisory powers they were already exercising in another context.

If all this is accepted, then a chronology for shrieval executive and jurisdictional functions can be outlined. Under David I's and much of Mael Coluim IV's reign, there is little explicit evidence for what sheriffs had to do other than presumably collect and allocate the king's revenue from his estates and, under Mael Coluim, enforce teind payments. During the 1160s, however, sheriffs south of the Forth clearly held their own courts, in which cases of theft could be decided. This corresponds with their early definition as administrative units: the sheriffs of Stirling and Berwick, for example, controlled *scira* or *vicecomitatus*. Sheriffs north of the Forth did not yet have this responsibility nor did they control such units. Yet, late in Mael Coluim's reign and early in William's, the jurisdictional responsibilities of sheriffs north and south of the Forth were increasing in other ways: they collected fines from teind defaulters, provided justice if it was lacking in other jurisdictions and, from 1180, supervised the activities of other court-holders. This suggests that, before it became standard that sheriffs would hold their own courts, by 1184, regardless of location, sheriffs were interacting with other court-holders whose jurisdiction over their own lands was being increasingly defined and formalized in royal charters at the very same time, as was argued in Chapter 3. By the time shrieval courts became standard (a development made formal in law in 1184), sheriffs were expected to be involved in the courts of others. We thus should not interpret the rise of shrieval courts as being at the expense of or in opposition to the courts of other major landholders; indeed, the 1180 statute not only confirmed but also maintained and protected the legitimacy of lordly justice. We should also be aware that only from the 1180s can we talk about the kingdom—and still only stretching from Dumfries in the west to Inverness in the north—having a uniform smattering of local administrative districts in the form of sheriffdoms which also provided justice in a relatively systematic way and interacted with other jurisdictions in their immediate locality.

JUSTICIARS

The point of this section is to understand in more detail when and in what form the figure of the royal justice (later, justiciar) was introduced and when justiciars were given powers over a defined region (Scotia, Lothian, or Galloway) and started going on 'ayres' (itinerations) around the region under their jurisdiction, hearing pleas in all the sheriffdoms therein. Exactly what their responsibilities were or what pleas the king assigned them to hear will be addressed in Chapters 5 and 6.[86] As with the sheriff, then, the aim is to understand the chronological development and changes to institutional form over the twelfth and thirteenth centuries.

---

[86] See below, Chapter 5, pp. 285–94, 305–6, 308–15; Chapter 6, pp. 374–9.

In understanding the twelfth- and thirteenth-century justice/justiciar, we cannot rely on any source kept by royal government (few of which survive) but, instead, on charters, brieves, and agreements, some of which survive as originals and others as later copies in monastic, religious, and—in one case—aristocratic cartularies, the earliest of which dates from the early thirteenth century.[87] Charters, brieves, and agreements, however, pose methodological problems, particularly when they survive as later copies, made either by scribes of monastic and ecclesiastical cartularies or by later antiquaries.[88] This is particularly the case when thinking about the justiciar. The standard abbreviation for the justiciar (*iusticiarius*) was *iustic'* or *iust'* but these were also the abbreviations for the 'justice' (*iusticia*), which, as we shall see, was the word used for individuals who would be known as *iusticiarius* ('justiciar') by the early thirteenth century.[89] Later scribes, who lived in worlds where the justice was no longer called 'justice' but 'justiciar', could easily have expanded *iust'* or *iustic'* as 'justiciar' (*iusticiarius*), not as 'justice' (*iusticia*).[90] What follows therefore prefers the evidence from documents which survive as originals over the evidence from later copies because there is a real danger in relying on the accuracy of later scribes who were copying documents and expanding earlier abbreviations in a period far removed from that of their sources. But that does not mean there are no problems in dealing with original single-sheet documents. If a new version of a title appears only in the documents drawn up by a single scribe (such as 'justice of the Scots'), can we know whether such a change was actually reflective of concurrent institutional developments and not mere scribal predilection?[91]

---

[87] The earliest record of the ayre does not survive until 1493 and has recently been analysed in Jackson W. Armstrong, 'The Justice Ayre in the Border Sheriffdoms, 1493–1498', *SHR*, vol. 92, no. 223 (2013), pp. 1–37. Research into the development of Scotland's 'earliest cartulary' (the bishopric of Glasgow's *Registrum Vetus*) is being undertaken by Joanna Tucker as part of her PhD thesis, entitled 'Documentary Culture in Thirteenth-Century Scotland: the Physical Context of Cartularies'.

[88] For questions of how cartularists organized their material, often according to a common pattern, see David Walker, 'The organization of material in medieval cartularies', in *The Study of Medieval Records: Essays in Honour of Kathleen Major*, ed. D. A. Bullough and R. L. Storey (Oxford, 1971), pp. 132–50; for a different take see Patrick Geary, 'Medieval Archivists as Authors: Social Memory and Archival Memory', in *Archives, Documentation and Institutions of Social Memory: Essays from the Sawyer Seminar*, ed. Francis X. Blouin and William G. Rosenberg (Ann Arbor, MI, 2006), pp. 106–13.

[89] For *iusticia* in charter texts, see *RRS*, i, no. 258; *RRS*, ii, nos. 39, 281.

[90] We cannot take all references to 'justiciars' in the twelfth century as unproblematic if the reference in question survives in a cartulary copy or later inspection, not an original charter, brieve, or record of an agreement: the 'early' reference to a 'justiciar' may simply be the result of a later scribe instinctively expanding *iust'* as *iusticiarius*. See, for example, *RRS*, ii, nos. 148 (later summary), 162, 174, 182, 184, 222 (summary), 237, 251 (spurious, but possibly based on an authentic act; *RRS*, ii, p. 287), 275 (later summary), 334, 348, 388, 400 (inflated, *RRS*, ii, p. 387), 406, 420 (later summary).

[91] The title of *iust'* *Scott* or *iustic'* *Scott* was used by at least three scribes (but predominantly in the charters of one Gilbert of Stirling) to describe William Comyn. It is discussed below, p. 214, note 103. It appears to have been adopted early in 1210; the earliest attestation of the title is in a charter written by Gilbert of Stirling, dated 7 January, possibly 1210; *RRS*, ii, no. 489. The date of 1210 is suggested by the attestation of Thomas de Colville, who spent some months imprisoned in Edinburgh castle after machinating against William the Lion; *Chron. Melrose, s.a.* 1210, for commentary see Taylor, '*Leges Scocie*', pp. 216–18; and Matthew H. Hammond, 'The Use of the Name Scot in the Central Middle Ages. Part 1: Scot as a By-name', *Journal of Scottish Name Studies*, vol. 1 (2007), pp. 37–60, at pp. 52–4. The dating is not, however, completely secure. Thomas did ransom himself on 11 November 1210 (*Chron. Melrose, s.a.* 1210). It is unlikely that Thomas would have later attested charters of William so soon afterwards (perhaps 1211) but it is not impossible, because Thomas did attest one

The Regional Divisions

The treatise known as 'The Scottish King's Household', and written perhaps between 1292 and 1296, informs us that there should be three justiciars, one for north of the Forth (Scotia), one for south of the Forth (Lothian), and one for Galloway.[92] And, indeed, figures given the title 'justiciar of Scotia' and 'justiciar of Lothian' do appear in royal charters from *c*.1220 onwards and a formal justiciar of Galloway appears intermittently from 1258.[93] A preoccupation of modern historians, therefore, has been the origins of this regional division, and how far back its history can be pushed.

In what remains the most full and important discussion of the justiciar in the central Middle Ages, G.W.S. Barrow argued that the threefold regional division of the justiciarship was a development of the last two decades of the twelfth century.[94] A twofold one, between Scotia and Lothian, could be identified in Mael Coluim IV's reign and the beginning of William the Lion's (the late 1150s and 1160s).[95] Barrow was aware that his evidence for this early division was problematic but, based on the patterns of attestations of known 'justices' and single references to one justice of Fife and one of Scotia, he nonetheless determined that a regional division existed from earlier in the twelfth century, possibly from the reign of David I, but only attested under David's grandsons, Mael Coluim and William.[96] Barrow's

early charter of Alexander II on at Luffness on 20 March 1215; NRS, GD119/2, printed in Grant G. Simpson, *Scottish Handwriting, 1150–1650*, 2nd edn (East Linton, 1998), no. 4 [AII/12].

[92] Mary Bateson ed., 'The Scottish King's Household and Other Fragments From a Fourteenth-Century Manuscript in the Library of Corpus Christi College, Cambridge', in *Miscellany of the Scottish History Society*, Scottish History Society, 2nd ser., 44 (Edinburgh, 1904), pp. 3–43, at pp. 36–7. For a new appreciation of the treatise (and the probability that it did not accurately describe the organization of the king's household), see David Carpenter, '"The Scottish King's Household" and English Ideas of Constitutional Reform', *Feature of the Month, October 2011*, The Breaking of Britain (2011), online at <http://www.breakingofbritain.ac.uk/blogs/feature-of-the-month/october-2011-the-scottish-kings-household/>.

[93] The earliest unproblematic reference to a justice/justiciar of Scotia is 16 February 1217×21: NRS, GD 236, Gilbliston titles, no. 1 (awaiting listing [AII/30]); PoMS, no. 1827, H1/7/30 (online at <http://db.poms.ac.uk/record/source/1827>), to a justice/justiciar of Scotia, 30 November 1222 (Original, DUL, Dean and Chapter Muniments, Misc. Chr no. 624 [AII/74], Raine, *North Durham*, App., no. 64). The earliest reference to a justiciar of Lothian in a non-original charter is 11 April, 1219×21, probably 1221; *Paisley Reg.*, p. 253 [AII/57]. The earliest reference to a justiciar of Galloway is to John Comyn in 1258: see PoMS, no. 4288, H4/42/2, online at<http://db.poms.ac.uk/record/source/4288/>.

[94] Barrow, 'Justiciar', pp. 81–8; *RRS*, i, pp. 49–51; *RRS*, ii, pp. 43–7.

[95] Barrow, 'Justiciar', pp. 81–2, 84–5; see also A. A. M. Duncan, *The Kingship of the Scots, 842–1292: Succession and Independence* (Edinburgh, 2002), p. 73.

[96] Barrow, 'Justiciar', p. 84: 'we have seen that King Malcolm IV addressed one surviving brieve (concerning Perth) to a justiciar of Scotia…The guess may be hazarded—since King David's brieves and charters are addressed to "justiciars" [*sic*] in the plural—that there was a justiciar for Scotia even before 1153.' When writing this piece, which was originally published in 1971 in the *Juridical Review* Barrow did not have the evidence of the brieve of Guisborough Priory, which refers to justices of Lothian and Teviotdale (for which, see below, pp. 217–20). This was discovered by Nicholas Vincent, who then gave it to Barrow to publish in the *SHR* in 2005; see Barrow, 'Unpublished Brieve', p. 85. It might be thought that Barrow would have welcomed these references but he actually came to this conclusion: 'Although there is explicit reference for justiciars of Fife and Scotia in Malcolm's reign the brieve published here might almost suggest either that no justiciar was available benorth the Forth or that in

analysis thus started with a late thirteenth-century situation, and attempted to trace that scenario as far back as it could go. But, although Barrow's work is full of insights, this approach is problematic because it assumes that kings of Scots and their advisors would have had in mind a particular way of organizing the justiciar-ship in the mid-twelfth century which, in fact, is only attested a full century later, when a named justiciar of Galloway finally appears in the written record. But if we move away from this assumption and take the twelfth- and early thirteenth-century evidence on its own terms, a different chronology for a regional justiciarship can emerge.

The arguments put forward so far in this chapter also cause us to question immediately how far Barrow's view of an early regional justiciarship makes sense. If sheriffs were not uniformly expected to hold courts until the 1180s and, if sheriffs north of the Forth did not have autonomous jurisdictional power in the reign of Mael Coluim IV, is it likely that an official justiciarship, operating in Scotia and Lothian, could have been granted formal jurisdictional powers much earlier? (Barrow was clear that a justiciar of Galloway did not appear until the last two decades of the twelfth century.[97]) Moreover, given that our earliest evidence for the activities of justices show them operating in tandem with sheriffs only south of the Forth, and *not* north (for instance, when enforcing teind payment), then should we assume that justices really were a kingdom-wide phenomenon?[98] Chapter 3 also showed that the absence of the figures of justice and sheriff from the procedural content of William the Lion's law suggested that such officials were not so ingrained in the administrative landscape as to allow writing them into the law, as would happen later under Alexander II.[99] This again is suggestive of later development. Thus, even without looking at any more evidence for the justice/justiciar, we should be wary of Barrow's chronology for the regional justiciarship.

The evidence from royal *acta* shows that the figure we know as the justiciar was actually called the 'justice' in twelfth-century documents. Although the title was abbreviated in witness lists to *iust'* or *iustic'*, it was often written out in full in the body of the document itself and there it is rendered *iusticia*—'justice'.[100] Thus, Mael Coluim's brieve to the officials of the bishopric of Glasgow, discussed in Chapter 3, stated that if a sheriff refused to give his own teind, or failed to collect the fine from a defaulter, 'my justice shall take my forfeiture from the self-same sheriff' (*Iusticia mea de ipso vicecomite forisfactum meum capiat*).[101] Most importantly, however, this title was used without any regional designation: royal justices were just called 'justice'. In the twelfth century, fourteen men were given the title of *iusticia* in royal charters and not one of them was given a regional title.[102] The

---

some way he was judged to be insufficient for the required duties' (Barrow, 'Unpublished Brieve', p. 86). An explanation of this apparent contradiction in our evidence is attempted in this chapter.

[97] *RRS*, ii, p. 45.   [98] See the discussion in Chapter 3, pp. 154–7, and below, pp. 217–24.
[99] See Chapter 3, pp. 162–4.
[100] *RRS*, ii, nos. 80, 281; *LS*, c. 14; cf. Barrow, 'Justiciar', p. 68.   [101] *RRS*, i, no. 258.
[102] David Olifard, Robert Avenel, Donnchad, earl of Fife, Walter Olifard, Richard Comyn, Geoffrey de Melville, Robert de Quinci, Roland, son of Uhtred, Gille Brigte, earl of Strathearn, Patrick, earl of Dunbar, William Lindsay, Gervase Avenel, David Lindsay, William Comyn; see also *RRS*, ii, p. 43, and the list in Barrow, 'Justiciar', p. 110.

only two references to a named 'justiciar', holding power over a regional division, are two attestations to royal charters by a 'iusticiarius Scotie'—both referring to Donnchad, earl of Fife (d.1204). But these are later copies: one is a much later summary and the other is a copy in which all abbreviations have been expanded, the exemplar of which (now lost) may even have been contaminated on the basis of unusual and possibly anachronistic diplomatic.[103] Although there are not that many references to justices in non-royal charters, those which date to the late twelfth and early thirteenth centuries also do not use a regional title: the justice is described as *iusticia domini regis* or *iusticiarius regis*, an understandable expansion of *iustic' reg'*, given that all of these references survive in later copies.[104] Both

[103] For the summary, see *RRS*, ii, no. 275 (Balfour's seventeenth-century abridgement of Coupar Angus cartulary). In this, Alan fitz Walter's attestation is given as *Alanus Senescallus* ('Alan the Steward'), which is anachronistic for the late twelfth century, when both Walter fitz Alan and his son Alan attested as *dapifer*. For the other charter, see *RRS*, ii, no. 388, on no duels in the burgh. The charter has been printed in *APS*, volume 1, and whatever source Innes was using has now been lost (*APS*, i, 89; *RRS*, ii, pp. 379–80). The names of the witnesses do not appear with any abbreviations, which suggests either that Innes (who printed the charter in *APS*, i) was expanding an original in which the diplomatic formulae and the names of witnesses had been abbreviated, or that Innes himself used a copy which had already been expanded. But it is clear in *APS* that the original abbreviations have not been preserved. Donnchad's name is not included; he appears in the witness list as *comite de Fife justiciario Scotie*, which is an unusual form of attestation for him. He more regularly appears as *Comite Dunecano iusticia*. The charter itself is slightly problematic. It says that burgesses in Inverness should not clear themselves by trial by battle but only by compurgation. This is strange, as the *Leges Quatuor Burgorum*, cc. 7–18, among others absolutely accept trial by battle in many circumstances. See the reference in the earliest incomplete manuscript of the text in the Berne MS (1267×72); NRS, PA5/1, fo. 62r, online at <http://stairsociety.org/resources/view_manuscript/the_berne_manuscript/208>. But it could well be that Inverness secured an exception. The charter is slightly odd in other ways too: chancellors by this point normally attested above earls (with the exception of the king's brother, Earl David, and then, after 1198, William's son, Alexander: cf. *RRS*, ii, nos. 368, 383, 385, 391–392, 394), and Hugh appears here after the earls of Strathearn and Fife. Moreover, it alternates between the plural of majesty and the singular (*burgensis nos* vs *burgensis meus*). While one scribe, Gilbert of Stirling, did use the plural of majesty (*RRS*, ii, no. 493), this alternation is strange, and in general the plural of majesty was not introduced until late July 1222, after the introduction in April of dating via regnal year. Dauvit Broun has suggested that this charter was presented to the royal chapel as a draft, and was there engrossed by a royal scribe, who preserved the plural of majesty (Dauvit Broun, 'The Absence of Regnal Years from the Dating Clauses of Charters of Kings of Scots, 1195–1222', *ANS*, 25 (2003), pp. 47–63, at pp. 54–7). Otherwise, the earliest charter to use the plural of majesty was a brieve of protection, dated 21 July 1222 (Durham, DUL, Dean and Chapter, Misc. Chr, no. 626, Raine, *North Durham*, App., no. 63 [AII/72]). For a discussion of the plural of majesty in general (including some of these charters), see Dauvit Broun, *Scottish Independence and the Idea of Britain from the Picts to Alexander III* (Edinburgh, 2007), pp. 197–9, at p. 197.

[104] See, for example, William Comyn *iusticiar' domini regis* in *Arbroath Liber*, i, no. 74 (*bis*), dated *c*.1205×14; *iusticia eius* in *Newbattle Reg.*, no. 3; *iusticiarii domini regis* in G. W. S. Barrow, 'The Judex', *Kingdom of the Scots*, pp. 57–67, at p. 67 (BL, Additional MS 33245, fos. 162v–163r); *tunc iusticiar Reg'* in *Melrose Liber*, no. 244 (Original, NRS, GD 55/244); the reference to *iusticiarius* in an original charter would not be unusual in the early 1220s, which is when this deed was issued. David Lindsay was called *iusticiarius domini regis Scotorum* in *Lindores Cart.*, no. 129. The only possible exception I have found is the reference to Alexander, sheriff of Stirling, and Walter Lindsay, sheriff of Berwick, called 'then justiciars of Lothian', in a cartulary copy of a quitclaim originally given by Simon Post (a burgess of Berwick?); *Newbattle Reg.*, no. 186. The PoMS database dates this to between 1208 and 1215 (PoMS, no. 5630, H3/632/5; online at <http://db.poms.ac.uk/record/source/5630/#>). However, the reason for this date is Walter's and Alexander's time as justiciars, for which there is no firmer dating evidence in the deed itself: this is the only occasion when these two men attest with the title of justiciar in the whole corpus of surviving evidence. It is therefore unclear on what grounds this dating rests. Alexander's last attestation to a royal charter of Alexander II is dated to 1218×21 (*Melrose*

non-royal and royal charters therefore give the uniform impression that royal justices were not only called 'justice' but also were not given formal regional titles in the twelfth century. Regional division seems, on the basis of title alone, not to have been something that the scribes of Scottish charters wanted to stress.

The *absence* of formal regional jurisdictions in the title of the king's justices from royal and non-royal charters is important because they were added in the years around 1220, and thereafter always appeared, suggesting either that an *ad hoc* regional division had been given written institutional form or that there had been a real change in the way the jurisdiction of the justice was conceived. The earliest appearance of a *clear-cut* regional title in an original royal charter is not until 16 February 1217×21, when William Comyn, then earl of Buchan, was given the title 'justice [justiciar] of Scotia' in a charter concerning land in Fife and written by the king's clerk, Gilbert of Stirling.[105] This was shortly followed by the appearance of

---

Liber, i, no. 185 [AII/47]), while Walter Lindsay died in *c*.1222 (PoMS, Person ID no. 2115, online at <http://db.poms.ac.uk/record/person/2115/>). It is possible that this reference to these two justiciars was before Walter Olifard took the role of justiciar of Lothian in 1221 but after a regional division was first attested in the later years of the justiciarship of William Comyn (so the late 1210s).

[105] NRS, GD 236, Gilbliston titles, no. 1 (awaiting listing); H1/7/30 [AII/30], a reference I owe to Keith Stringer. See also the original charter dated 27 November 1219/20, where William Comyn attests as Justic' Scoc' (NRS, GD 220/2/1/3 [AII/49]). But this is still not an uncomplicated sentence. William Comyn received a different title in charters written by the royal scribe, Gilbert of Stirling, prior to this: 'justice of the Scots' (*iust' Scott*, rather than *iust' Scoc*). This title was first attested on 7 January 1210 (*RRS*, ii, no. 489; NLS, Charters, no. 36) and appears to have been introduced on that date or not long before that, perhaps as early as 18 April 1209 (see *RRS*, ii, no. 485, also written by Gilbert of Stirling; NRS, GD 45/13/250). After that, the title 'justiciar/justice of the Scots' was used two more times in royal charters. One survives as an original, written by Gilbert of Stirling; the other is a cartulary copy (*RRS*, ii, nos. 492, 523). Under Alexander II, Gilbert of Stirling wrote a further three charters before 1221/22 (when dating clauses were introduced) which contain some sort of title relating to the justice of the Scots/Scotia. The first, dated 12 February, probably 1215, called William *iust' Scott* (justice/justiciar of the Scots; Fraser, *Grant*, iii, no. 3 [AII/5]); the second (1217×21) calls him *Just' Scoc'* (justice/justiciar of Scotia; NRS, GD 236, Gilbliston titles, no. 1 (awaiting listing) [AII/30]); the third (1219/20) calls him *iustic' Scoc* (Fraser, *Lennox*, ii, no. 3 [AII/49]). Gilbert wrote one more charter in 1226, with the title *just' Scoc'* (*Ane Account of the Familie of Innes compiled by Duncan Forbes of Culloden, 1698, with Appendix of Charters and Notes* (Aberdeen, 1864), pp. 52–3 [AII/112]). The title of 'justice of the Scots' therefore causes some interesting problems. It might be thought that 'justice of the Scots' was Gilbert's own rendering of 'justiciar of Scotia', because all the references to this title 1210–*c*.1221 belong in charters written by him, even though he did not use the title consistently. However, two later charters, written by two different scribes (one writing a charter dated to 1228; the other to 1231) *also* use the title *just' Scott*, showing that the title was not simply a whimsical invention by Gilbert of Stirling (*Holyrood Liber*, no. 71; NRS, GD45/13/257 [AII/141]; BL, Campbell Charter xxx, 6 [AII/166]). It might be thought, therefore, that 'justice of the Scots' did not represent a regional division but, instead, a wider development. William Comyn was, during the 1210s, the only attested justice/justiciar in the kingdom. Did the title then mean 'justice of the Scots', meaning justice/justiciar of the whole kingdom (as *rex Scottorum*)? This is a very attractive scenario. However, it is complicated by the two later references to William as 'justice of the Scots' in the two original surviving charters (AII/141; AII/166, as shown earlier in this note) which post-date 1222, the point when Walter Olifard appears as 'justiciar of Lothian', finally confirming that a formal regional division had taken place (for which see below, pp. 215–16). If 'justice of the Scots' did mean 'justice of the whole kingdom', then the appearance of the division of the justiciarship between Scotia and Lothian *should* have meant that the wider title of 'justice of the Scots' had become redundant, which it did not. It is possible that these two later mentions of a 'justice of the Scots' were hangovers from an earlier situation but it is not provable either way. I am extremely grateful to Keith Stringer for helping me with Gilbert of Stirling and these early charters of Alexander II as well as providing me with more examples.

Walter Olifard, *iusticiario Laudonie* in a cartulary copy of a royal charter dated 11 April, 1220×22 (probably 1221).[106] Walter did not, however, start attesting regularly with the title until April 1222 and his earliest surviving attestation as 'justiciar of Lothian' to an original charter was on 30 November 1222.[107] The regional division of Lothian was used consistently thereafter, while, during the 1220s, the title of William Comyn alternated between 'justiciar of the Scots' (*iustic' Scott*) and 'justiciar of Scotia' (*iustic' Scoc*) but it is unclear whether this distinction meant anything.[108] By 1231, William Comyn's title was consistently territorial (*iustic' Scoc*—justiciar of Scotia) and we have no further evidence of any other 'justice of the Scots', whatever that title may have meant in practice. A twofold regional division is also attested in non-royal charters at around the same time in the late 1210s/early 1220s.[109] The first appearance of *iusticiar'*, rather than *iustic'*, in an original charter was on 21 July 1222, demonstrating that, by this point, 'justiciar' had obtained some purchase above 'justice'.[110] It is tempting to assume from the above that the title 'justiciar' predominated as a result of the regional division and that 'justice' was used before that when justice-power was non-regional. But we cannot assume this, neat though it is as a solution, because it was possible to expand *iustic'* either as 'iusticia' (justice) or as 'iusticiarius' (justiciar). It is, however, clear that 'justiciar' was being used by the early 1220s, at which point a regional division between Scotia and Lothian is explicitly attested. As stated above, there is no record of a justiciar of Galloway until 1258.[111]

How long had kings of Scots used justices and where did they operate? *Iusticiae* appear quite suddenly in the address clauses of Scottish royal charters in *c.*1140.[112]

[106] *Paisley Reg.*, p. 253 [AII/57].

[107] Raine, *North Durham*, App., no. 64 [AII/74]. An earlier attestation to a cartulary copy was on 20 April 1222 as *iustic' Laodon* (*Kelso Liber*, i, no. 7 [AII/68]).

[108] *Foedera*, I, i, 165 (*iustic' Scoc*) [AII/60]; *Moray Reg.*, no. 25 (*iusticiar' Scoc*) [AII/61]; *Arbroath Liber*, i, no. 113 (*iustic' Scoc*) [AII/64]; DUL, D&C, Misc Chr, no. 626, printed in Raine, *North Durham*, App., no. 63 (*Iusticiar Scott*) [AII/72]; *Arbroath Liber*, i, no. 103 (*iustic' Scoc*) [AII/89]; *Dunf. Reg.*, no. 78 (*iust' Scoc*) [AII/134]; *Dunf. Reg.*, no. 74 (*iustic' Scoc*) [AII/135]; *St Andrews Liber*, pp. 236–7 (*iusti' Scotorum*) [AII/136]; NRS, GD 45/13/257, printed in *Holyrood Liber*, no. 71 (*Iust' Scott*) [AII/141]; *Moray Reg.*, no. 32 (*iust' Scoc*) [AII/142].

[109] See, for example, the attestation of 'Lord Walter fitz Alan, the steward, justiciar of Scotia' to a charter of John de Vaux, drawn up 30 April 1230×11 September 1233 (*Arbroath Liber*, i, no. 117). The dating follows that of PoMS (H3/586/13, online at <http://db.poms.ac.uk/record/source/5530>); other examples are *Arbroath Liber*, i, nos. 227, 250.

[110] DUL, Dean and Chapter Muniments, Misc. Chrs 626, printed in Raine, *North Durham*, App., no. 63 [AII/72].

[111] PoMS, no. 4288; H4/42/2, online at <http://db.poms.ac.uk/record/source/4288>. John may have ceased in this role before 17 April 1261 (whereupon Stephen Fleming may have taken up the position), for he is described in the witness list to a joint charter of John Russell and Isabella, countess of Menteith, as *domino I cumin' tunc iusticiario galwidie* (Fraser, *Menteith*, ii, no. 6, with facsimile of original charter on the facing page).

[112] The earliest is *CDI*, no. 85, where St Andrews of Kilrimont (St Andrews Cathedral) is given the church of St Mary in Haddington (south of the Forth) between 1136 and 1140, closely followed by *CDI*, nos. 86–87. There is an earlier brieve-charter dating to 1124×36 where justices are addressed but the hand is late-twelfth- or early-thirteenth-century and was written by a Durham scribe and so it cannot be taken as an uncontroversial example of the formula (*CDI*, no. 41; and Barrow's commentary: *CDI*, p. 74). The earliest firmly datable occurrence of *iusticiae* in the address clause to beneficiaries within the kingdom of the Scots is *CDI*, no. 86, issued on 14 June, probably in 1140 (which survives as an original: BL, Cotton Charter, xviii, 12).

Previously, they had been absent in charters pertaining to Scotland. In charters of David which pre-date 1140, the only occasions when a 'justice' is addressed are in writ-charters that address either English honors or English shire courts (particularly Cumberland and Northumberland).[113] After 1140, however, *iusticiae* are addressed in some—but, importantly, not all—charters intended for someone or some institution in Scotland in which sheriffs, provosts (*prepositi*), and 'officials/servants' (*ministri*) are also addressed (sometimes along with any lay and ecclesiastical magnates).[114] While *c.*1140 therefore need not be taken as *the* date for the introduction of justices, it is probable that they had become sufficiently entrenched to be worth addressing alongside sheriffs and other officials.

But where did these justices actually operate? We should not, at this point, see their presence in address clauses as evidence of a kingdom-wide presence because sheriffs were also addressed generally in David's charters and it has already been shown that sheriffs were not introduced throughout the kingdom *ex nihilo* during his reign.[115] Indeed, the address clauses of David's charters which were drawn up for beneficiaries north of the Forth after *c.*1140 and were concerned with land or privileges north of the Forth sometimes do *not* include justices in their address clauses, suggesting that justices were not a consistent enough feature of the administrative landscape north of the Forth in David's reign to be a standard part of an address.[116] The information on justices under David I thus begs the question of when a regional division was introduced. Given that the 'justiciar' title was, in fact, *iusticia*—justice—in most of Mael Coluim IV's charters as well as all of David's and William's, was there really a regional division in their responsibilities in the mid-twelfth century, as has long been supposed? Going by this evidence alone, then, there was no formally attested regional division in the twelfth-century justice-ship.

However, during Mael Coluim IV's short reign, there are four distinct references to justices with an area-based title. The brieve of Mael Coluim IV to Guisborough Priory, discussed earlier, says that sheriffs north of the Forth could seek out the king's 'justice' (*iusticia*) of 'Lothian or of Teviotdale', which suggests that there were two justices, one for the region of Lothian and the other for Teviotdale.[117] Another brieve-charter of Mael Coluim, issued between 1161 and 1164, addressed

---

[113] All references in the following four footnotes include acts of Earl Henry. For Cumberland, see *CDI*, nos. 58, 76; Northumberland: *CDI*, nos. 79–80, 82–84, 101, 103, 143–144, 163, 169–170, 203; honour of Lancaster: *CDI*, nos. 111–112; honour of Huntingdon: *CDI*, no. 82; Carlisle: *CDI*, no. 145.

[114] *CDI*, nos. 87–89, 97–98, 116, 118–119, 122, 124–125, 127–128, 134, 151, 153, 161–162, 165, 167, 176–177, 179–181, 184–185, 192–193, 200, 204–205.

[115] Cf. Barrow, 'Justiciar', p. 84, and above, pp. 197–202.

[116] *CDI*, nos. 126 (confirmation to St Andrews Cathedral Priory), 133 (Pittenweem and St Monance to May), 135 (common wood of Clackmannan to May), 171 (Newburn in Fife to Dunfermline), 173 (Longforgan, Perthshire to St Andrews), 186 (to May, freedom from *cáin* and toll), 190 (brieve to Fife about the men of Newburn, held by Dunfermline Abbey), 195 (brieve-charter to Urquhart Priory about money from Elgin), 208 (foundation of canons at Loch Leven by St Andrews), 209 (treatment of *celi dé* at Kilrimont by St Andrews). There are, however, seven occasions when justices were addressed in charters north of the Forth: see *CDI*, nos. 88–89, 127, 153, 165, 176, 185.

[117] Barrow, 'Unpublished Brieve', p. 87.

'his justice of Fife, and his sheriff of Dunfermline and his sheriff of Clackmannan', showing there was some form of justice in Fife.[118] Finally, a further brieve-charter of Mael Coluim IV addressed 'his justice of Scotia, and his sheriff of Perth', informing them that he had given some of his revenue from Perth to the abbey of Tiron.[119] This is quite a haul, given that there are far fewer surviving charters from Mael Coluim's reign than William's. Indeed, it is normally on the basis of these three documents that the dating of the emergence of some sort of regional justiciarship to Mael Coluim's reign rests.[120] This is understandable but still leaves problems: if the references to regional justices in these brieves and brieve-charters *did* denote a regional justiciarship that survived in this form into the thirteenth century, it is quite astonishing that we have no reference to such a system in William's far more numerous charters, particularly given that justices appear in royal charters almost continuously throughout his reign. How, therefore, can the references to the supposedly regional justices under Mael Coluim IV be understood?

Mael Coluim IV, Iudices, and Royal Justices

First, it must be stressed that whatever justice-system was in place under Mael Coluim, it was very different to the regional justiciarship that had developed by the first decade of Alexander II's reign, in which a single individual held the justiciarship of either Lothian or Scotia (Galloway will be dealt with later).[121] The evidence from Mael Coluim's reign reveals instead the existence of justices of Lothian and Teviotdale, and justices of Scotia and Fife. The mid-twelfth-century justice-ship of Lothian therefore encompassed an area far smaller than that covered by the thirteenth-century justiciarship of Lothian: Teviotdale in part later corresponded to the sheriffdom of Roxburgh, which, by the thirteenth century, was very much part of the later justiciarship of Lothian.[122] In addition, Fife was included in the jurisdiction of the thirteenth-century justiciarship of Scotia; it did not have its own provincial justice.[123] Whatever is made of these justices from the early 1160s, then, the division present in these few Mael Coluim charters should not be seen as the

---

[118] *RRS*, i, no. 214.   [119] *RRS*, i, no. 223.

[120] Barrow, 'Justiciar', pp. 81–8; *RRS*, ii, pp. 43–5.

[121] Under Alexander II, the named justices on record were William Comyn, earl of Buchan (justice, 1205–10, of Scots/Scotia, 1210–31), Walter Olifard (Lothian, 1221/2×1242), Walter fitz Alan (Scotia, 1232–40×41), Robert Mowat (Scotia, 1241–42), Philip Melville (Scotia, 1242), David Lindsay (Lothian, 1243–49), Alan Durward (Scotia, 1244–51). See also the single references to Alexander, sheriff of Stirling, and Walter Lindsay (*Newbattle Reg.*, no. 186, discussed in Note 104). All careers have been calculated from their attestations to surviving royal charters. See also Barrow, 'Justiciar', pp. 110–11.

[122] For Teviotdale and Roxburghshire in the fourteenth century, see Michael Brown, 'War, Allegiance and Community in the Anglo-Scottish Marches: Teviotdale in the Fourteenth Century', *Northern History*, vol. 41, no. 2 (2004), pp. 219–38, at pp. 220–1. For Bagimond's roll for the archdeaconry of Teviotdale, see Ian B. Cowan, 'Two early Scottish taxation rolls', *Innes Review*, vol. 22, no. 1 (1971), pp. 6–11; for Bagimond, see D. E. R. Watt, 'Bagimond di Vezza and His "Roll"', *SHR*, vol. 80, no. 209 (2001), pp. 1–23. For the inclusion of Roxburgh in the ayre of the justiciar of Lothian in 1264 and 1265 see *ER*, i, pp. 9–10, 27.

[123] For the *ballia de Fyfe* in the justiciar ayre of Scotia in, probably, 1266, see *ER*, i, p. 18.

direct antecessor of the regional justiciarship as it appears in thirteenth-century material.

So what was meant by the justices of Lothian, Teviotdale, Scotia, and Fife? Lothian and Teviotdale will be taken first. Chapter 3 showed that, under Mael Coluim IV, justices were seen as enforcing agents for the collection of teind within the diocese of Glasgow, which encompassed Teviotdale.[124] Moreover, Teviotdale and Lothian were two distinguishable regions in the twelfth century: they were, after all, referred to as such in a charter of David I, before he became king. Earl David's charter, probably written by a Durham or Coldingham scribe, addressed 'John, bishop of Glasgow,... and all his faithful thegns and drengs of Lothian and Teviotdale'.[125] The centre of Teviotdale, the area around the confluence of the Rivers Tweed and Teviot, was Roxburgh; in the later Middle Ages, the sheriffdom of Roxburgh could be called the sheriffdom of Teviotdale, although there is no evidence that this was the case in the twelfth and thirteenth centuries (although the region of Teviotdale is referred to in a number of extant acts, mostly as a deanery or archdeaconry of the bishopric of Glasgow).[126] Richard of Hexham, in his *de gestis regis Stephani*, recorded that David's army in 1138 was 'wicked' and was composed 'of Normans, Germans (*Germanis*), English, of Northumbrians and Cumbrians, [men] of Teviotdale and Lothian (*de Teswetadale et Lodonea*), and of Picts, who are commonly called Galwegians, and Scots'.[127] Teviotdale could be seen as one region among many in what is now northern England and southern Scotland, suggesting an ambiguous liminality to its political location.[128] In his *Relatio* of the 1138 Battle of the Standard, written in 1157, Aelred of Rievaulx described how Henry, son of David I, lined up for battle behind the king and was joined by the men of Cumbria and the men of Teviotdale (*adjunctis sibi Cumbrensibus et Tevidalensibus*).[129]

The single brieve of Mael Coluim IV which refers to the justices of Lothian and Teviotdale was issued for Guisborough Priory in Yorkshire and was important earlier in this chapter because of the distinction it makes between shrieval *potestates*

---

[124] *RRS*, i, no. 258, discussed in Chapter 3, pp. 154–7. For Teviotdale and the bishoprics of Glasgow and Durham, see G. W. S. Barrow, 'King David I and Glasgow', in *Kingdom of the Scots*, pp. 203–13, at pp. 205–6.

[125] *CDI*, no. 10. For further references to Teviotdale, see *CDI*, nos. 42, 174, 201. The deanery or archdeaconry is attested, particularly in episcopal documents, throughout the twelfth and thirteenth centuries. D. E. R. Watt, *The Bibliographic Dictionary of Scottish Graduates to AD 1410* (Edinburgh, 1977), p. 8.

[126] *Glasgow Reg.*, i, nos. 48, 208; *Kelso Liber*, i, no. 268, 275; ii, no. 356. For all the references to Teviotdale in the corpus of surviving charters, search on <http://db.poms.ac.uk> and input 'Teviotdale' in the browse data box. For the sheriffdom of Roxburgh in the diocese of Glasgow rendering second teinds to that bishop, see *ER*, i, pp. 9–10, 27; and Chapter 6, pp. 379–85.

[127] Richard of Hexham, *De Gestis Regis Stephani*, in *Chronicles of the Reigns of Stephen, Henry II and Richard I*, ed. R. Howlett, Rolls Series, 4 vols (London, 1884–9), vol. 3, p. 152.

[128] Barrow, 'David I and Glasgow', p. 206; and, for further examinations of the Anglo-Scottish Border, see G. W. S. Barrow, 'The Anglo-Scottish Border', in *Kingdom of the Scots*, pp. 112–29; cf. Keith J. Stringer, 'The Early Lords of Lauderdale, Dryburgh Abbey and St Andrews Priory at Northampton', in *Essays on the Nobility of Medieval Scotland*, ed. Keith J. Stringer (Edinburgh, 1985), pp. 44–71.

[129] Aelred of Rievaulx, *Relatio de Standardo*, in *Chronicles*, ed. Howlett, vol. 3, p. 190.

north of the Forth and the more defined *provinciae* south of the Forth.[130] Here, it has additional relevance. The brieve gave the priory permission to send its servants to search for any stolen goods in Scotland, both north and south of the Forth.[131] If the stolen goods were found in Scotia, then the sheriffs of that area would bring the property before the justices of Lothian or Teviotdale; if they were found within 'Lothian or Teviotdale', then the particular sheriff south of the Forth could make full right to them. This brieve needs to be examined not just for its content but also from the perspective of the priory. As Lothian and Teviotdale were deemed separable regions, it makes sense that Mael Coluim's brieve would stress that not only his justices but also his sheriffs covered the two regions for stolen goods found in both those areas and those found north of the Forth (where there were no justices—or indeed sheriffs—who could do a similar job to those south of the Forth). While there clearly were justices south of the Forth under Mael Coluim IV, it is hard to determine whether there really were formal and fixed positions of 'justice of Lothian' and 'justice of Teviotdale'. It is possible that there may have been 'justices', who operated in either region but whose regional specificity was stressed in this Guisborough case because the beneficiary was located in northern England, and whose members would have been well aware that Teviotdale was a defined region in the political geography of northern England and southern Scotland, separate from a smaller notion of Lothian. Yet there is also evidence in a single brieve-charter issued early in William's reign (1165×71) that there may have been broad but perhaps ill-defined area-based responsibilities for these south-of-Forth justices: William's charter addressed '*his* justice, his sheriff, and his provosts of Roxburgh', suggesting that there was a justice linked particularly to Roxburgh, the head town of the region of Teviotdale.[132] Was this 'justice of Roxburgh' the same sort of figure as the 'justice of Teviotdale' mentioned in Mael Coluim IV's brieve to Guisborough Priory? It may well be that there were more regionalized justices operating south of the Forth in the 1160s. However, it still must be emphasized that the reference to a justice of Lothian and Teviotdale was of a very different order to the justiciar of Lothian, which was developing early in Alexander II's reign.

There is an even bigger problem with accepting at face value the references to the justices of Scotia and Fife in Mael Coluim IV's reign. These two brieve-charters are dated to 1162×20 September 1164 (Scotia), and 1161×20 September 1164 (Fife).[133] During this same period, another brieve of Mael Coluim IV was drawn up on the collection of teind, this time for St Andrews Priory.[134] This stated that, if anyone failed to pay their teind to St Andrews Cathedral Priory in Fife, the sheriff 'in whose power (*potestas*)' the defaulter lived would compel them to pay and fine them in the process.[135] The king's authority and knowledge of this process was invoked in this brieve: it ended with the first person 'as I enacted in that area'. This brieve contrasted with another brieve of Mael Coluim, issued at some point in his reign to the bishopric of Glasgow, which set out much the same

---

[130] See above, pp. 200–2.   [131] Barrow, 'Unpublished brieve', p. 87.
[132] *RRS*, ii, no. 64.   [133] *RRS*, i, nos. 214, 223.
[134] *RRS*, i, no. 233; see Chapter 3, pp. 154–7.
[135] For the *potestas* of a sheriff, see above, pp. 200–1.

procedure but additionally stated that if the sheriff failed to collect the teind and fine, the king's justice (*iusticia mea*) would do so instead. This demonstrates that justices operated within the bishopric of Glasgow but not in the area in which St Andrews Priory held most of its land, that is, in Fife.[136] What we have, therefore, is a real contradiction in our evidence. On the one hand, we have references to justices of Scotia and Fife in brieve-charters whose authenticity is not in doubt; on the other, Mael Coluim's brieves to Guisborough and St Andrews clearly anticipate that there were *no* justices in Fife (or indeed in Scotia) who could act in a way that justices south of the Forth could do. Given that three of these documents were drawn up within the same period (1161×64), this contradiction is very real, and must be understood.

The evidence from William's reign further highlights this problem. In the first few years of his reign, one of William's major confirmation charters to a monastic beneficiary, Holyrood Abbey, mentions the enforcing capacities of justices: if the abbot failed to do right in his own court on an accusation made against one of his men, 'then the sheriff and the justice will do right on him [the accused]'.[137] But Holyrood was a beneficiary situated just outside Edinburgh, on the southern side of the Firth of Forth. A comparable brieve, issued in 1172, but this time for the bishopric of Moray, states that anyone withholding teind within Moray would be compelled to pay by the sheriff 'in whose power' the defaulter lived, as also happened in the bishopric of St Andrews.[138] At this point, in the early 1170s, there is no mention of justices in Moray, as there is in Mael Coluim's earlier brieve to Glasgow and William's charter to Holyrood, both south of the Firth of Forth. While Moray is further north than Fife, it still remains that William in the early 1170s did not expect justices to be operative in his kingdom north of the Forth.[139]

In addition, William's charters and contemporaneous non-royal acts do not refer to a regional division and only refer to 'justices' as *iusticiae*. As will be shown later in this chapter, the evidence that we have for justice-courts in William's reign survives only from the 1180s and reveals that, by this late point, justice-courts were not regionally based (as we might imagine if there had then been a regional justiceship) but were instead high-status and irregular affairs which all the lay and ecclesiastical magnates were supposed to attend.[140] As a result, the evidence presents a conundrum: single references to regional justices under Mael Coluim IV cannot be allowed to discount the weight of other evidence but, equally, the references to regional justices cannot be dismissed out of hand. It is possible to understand the

---

[136] *RRS*, i, no. 258.

[137] *RRS*, ii, no. 39, discussed above, pp. 208–9. It should be noted that neither William's confirmation charter to Dunfermline Abbey nor his charter to St Andrews (*RRS*, ii, nos. 28, 30) mentions the justice but this may not be significant in itself as both charters were based on previous major confirmation charters of Mael Coluim IV and David I, neither of which mentioned the justice.

[138] *RRS*, ii, no. 132.

[139] This is made even more striking by the inclusion of justices in a similar brieve for the bishopric of Moray issued around fifteen years later in the late 1180s, by which point 'justices' were expected to hold their own courts, which all high-status people were supposed to attend; *RRS*, ii, no. 281, and below, pp. 238–40.

[140] *LS*, c. 14, and below, pp. 238–9.

reference to justices of Lothian and Teviotdale because other evidence demonstrates that justices *were* operating south of the Forth but it is far harder to understand the references to justices of Fife and Scotia, when we have contemporaneous evidence that the king himself did not believe justices could act in Fife and Scotia in a way that they could south of the Forth.

The reference to the justice of Fife is perhaps the best place to start. As stated above, even when a regional division developed, a justice of Fife was not part of that system. But we do have firm evidence from David's reign that provinces were expected to have *iudices* (the type of Gaelic legal specialist discussed in Chapter 3) and, moreover, we have two documents which refer either to *iudices* or to a singular *iudex* operating in Fife.[141] It is therefore possible that Mael Coluim was not addressing a royal 'justice' of Fife but, instead, a *iudex* of Fife.[142] It is possible, after all, that the scribes of Mael Coluim's charters were open to experimentation when attempting to render Gaelic words into vague Latin ones. They may have done this with *vicecomes*: Chapter 2 argued that the two *vicecomites* of Forfar and Scone were not 'sheriffs' but 'thanes' and that scribes quite understandably used the word *vicecomes* to describe a thane, the rank under the *comes*, as was also done in the Loch Leven property records.[143] If the *iusticia* of Fife was, in fact, a *iudex*, this would explain why contemporary evidence, to which Mael Coluim had personally attached himself, demonstrates that there were no 'justices' of Fife or Scotia with permanent enforcing power. If the *iusticia* of Fife was a *iudex* of Fife then this would still explain the absence of justices north of the Forth in two other brieves of Mael Coluim IV. This may also explain the reference to the justice of Scotia. In the Kirkness settlement discussed in Chapter 1, Caustantín, *mormaer* of Fife, was also called a *magnus iudex* in Scotia; could the reference to a *iusticia* of Scotia be to a similar figure?[144]

It is then probable that the scribes of these two *acta* of Mael Coluim IV may simply have referred to the *iudex* as a *iusticia*, a word they were more used to including by this point. When 'justices' were introduced north of the Forth under William, it would have become no longer feasible to refer to *iudices* as 'justices'; indeed, it may have then become more important to distinguish between their different legal authorities. But we should not get ahead of ourselves. Under Mael Coluim IV, there appears to have been no expectation that there should be justices north of the Forth. As a result, it is worth considering this scenario in the light of the arguments made in Chapter 3 on the changing relationship between king and *iudex* over the twelfth century.[145] If the *iusticia* of Fife was, in fact, a *iudex*, then this may well be evidence of Mael Coluim continuing David's policy of attempting to tie provincial *iudices* more closely to royal authority. By calling a *iudex* a *iusticia* in a royal brieve-charter, the brieve-charter *could* have been encapsulating all figures

---

[141] Lawrie, *ESC*, no. 80, and *CDI*, no. 190.

[142] See Chapter 3, pp. 129–32; and Barrow, 'The *judex*', Dauvit Broun, 'The King's *brithem* (Gaelic for "Judge") and the Recording of Dispute-Resolutions', PoMS Feature of the Month, no. 11 (April 2010), online at <http://www.poms.ac.uk/feature/april10.html>.

[143] See Chapter 2, pp. 108–10.   [144] Lawrie, *ESC*, no. 80.

[145] See Chapter 3, pp. 129–32.

with legal authority under the same name, thus deeming *iudices* to be equivalent—but not, importantly, the same—to the newer justices. When named justices first appear in the first two decades of William's reign, we shall see that, with one important exception, all were landholders south of the Forth (even if they had also more recently gained lands north of it) and all had relatively recently settled in the kingdom; this must have made them look very different to Gaelic-speaking *iudices* elsewhere in the kingdom.

If this is deemed plausible, a different scenario emerges. The regional justiciarship, as it appears under Alexander II, was not the same as that suggested by the brieves and brieve-charters of Mael Coluim IV. If it had been, we would no longer have to accept that a stable regional division was introduced in the mid-twelfth century only then to disappear completely from the record for the next sixty or so years. Doing so would anyway be deeply problematic because it is quite clear that the 'regional' justices of Fife, Scotia, Lothian, and Teviotdale were not one and the same as the later justiciars of Lothian and Scotia: they 'supervised' different areas. Indeed, the 'justices' north of the Forth may not have been 'justices' at all but, instead, *iudices*, cast in a different mould. It is also important to note that *iudices* do not appear in the corpus of Mael Coluim's charters, as they had done in David's. This absence may be the result of lack of survival: there *may* once have been charters of Mael Coluim which referred to *iudices* which no longer survive. But the absence of *iudices* may equally be explained by their equation with *iusticiae*, which is the only explanation for the appearance of justices of Fife and Scotia alongside contemporary information which denies that justices had enforcing power in the same areas.

Seeing *iudices* behind the references to justices in Scotia and Fife during Mael Coluim IV's reign fits in well with what happened to the status and authority of *iudices* over the twelfth and early thirteenth centuries, as set out in Chapter 3. There, it was argued that the authority of *iudices* to transmit legal knowledge may have been gradually subsumed under the figure of the king-in-assembly, who not only reissued parts of a *iudex*'s written legal specialism as his own 'assizes' but also attempted to tie *iudices* more firmly to his own authority, both by requiring them to be present when he came into his province and also, later, through the emergence of the 'king's *iudex*'.[146] The equation of *iudices* with 'justices' could have been a similar move by Mael Coluim IV: by assimilating the two, he put two forms of legal authority under the same umbrella while simultaneously respecting in practice their distinct legal authority and specialism. After all, *iudices* and justices clearly did have different types of authority and responsibility by the reign of Mael Coluim IV. Whereas justices (wherever they were) did have the power to enforce teind payment and collect fines if the sheriff defaulted, *iudices* were not given that responsibility. If *iudices* had been responsible for enforcing teind payment, we would find references to either *iudices* or 'justices' operating north of the Forth under Mael Coluim IV as his justices did south of the Forth, which we do not.

---

[146] See Chapter 3, p. 130. It is possible, as Dauvit Broun has suggested to me, that the *iudex regis* was not a *new* position per se but a reconfiguration of the position of *iudex Scotie* (or *brithem nAlban*). However, I leave this particular conundrum for another.

This therefore seems like a more complicated but fundamentally more plausible narrative than seeking the origins for the thirteenth-century regional justiciarship in the reign of Mael Coluim IV. Not only would the latter assume a much more entrenched royal administration than the evidence allows, it would also mean searching for a system attested in the thirteenth century in the very different twelfth. Emphasizing that what Mael Coluim may have been doing was different to what came later does not lessen its importance, or classify him as somehow 'failing' to create a regional justiciarship. What it means is that the early history of these offices was more fluid and more indicative of the king's slowly developing institutional control over his kingdom than we have previously imagined.

William the Lion, Earl Donnchad, and the Regional Divisions

If Mael Coluim was experimenting with the relationship between justices and existing *iudices*, this idea took a slightly different shape under William. Named justices start to appear in the witness lists to royal charters early in William's reign. The earliest two were David Olifard and Robert Avenel. Both held land south of the Forth: Robert's was the major lordship of Eskdale and David Olifard, David I's godson, was the lord of Bothwell, and held land in Roxburghshire, Berwickshire, and Lanarkshire.[147] Robert Avenel only appeared twice with the title of 'justice' (once at Kinghorn in Fife, when the king bestowed churches in Aberdeenshire to St Andrews, and once at Stirling, which involved the king's chapel in Stirling castle being given to Dunfermline).[148] David appears ten times and witnessed north of the Forth at Perth, Dunfermline, Kinghorn, and St Andrews, as well as Stirling, Berwick, and Roxburgh south of the Forth.[149] Our two earliest named justices in William's reign were thus southern lords, who both attested charters as justices north and south of the Forth and concerned themselves with business on either side. As there are no secure references to justices operating north of the Forth before William's reign, this seems to have been a departure from the situation under Mael Coluim, when royal justices appeared only south of the Forth; now, although only a permanent part of the legal landscape south of the Forth, they went north of the Firth of Forth occasionally.[150]

---

[147] Robert was the lord of Eskdale but no charter granting him this land under David survives. For comment on this, see Hammond, 'Adoption and Routinization', pp. 100, 104–5. For David Olifard, see *Glasgow Reg.* i, nos. 203, 231; for a full appreciation, see Keith Stringer, 'A Gloucestershire Archive in the Earliest Charters of Sawtry Abbey', *Journal of the Society of Archivists*, vol. 6, no. 6 (1980), pp. 325–34, at pp. 327–30, 333.

[148] *RRS*, ii, nos. 129–130. In no. 130, Robert is described as perambulating land near Stirling with Richard de Morville, the constable. Robert's title here is *justic*.

[149] *RRS*, ii, nos. 14–15, 32, 35, 37, 45–46, 67, 107–108.

[150] It is worth considering the possibility that the situation in the early years of William's reign could equally be a continuation and intensification of an already *ad hoc* situation existing before 1165, whereby justices based south of the Forth, where they were a more permanent part of the legal landscape, would deal with business north of the Forth when required (either by the king or by a disputant). It is of note that, in the early 1170s, justices were not a permanent part of the legal landscape in Moray for they do not appear in the teind charters of the bishopric (whereas sheriffs do): *RRS*, ii, no. 132. Thus, if justices did go far north of the Forth in Mael Coluim's reign, this must have been on an *ad hoc* basis.

The long justice-career of Donnchad, earl of Fife (d.1204), who first appeared as a justice between 1172 and 1173 and continued to hold the office perhaps as late as 1203, appears to have changed all this.[151] What is interesting about Earl Donnchad's pattern of attestations as *iusticia* is their regional focus, in contrast to either of his predecessors.[152] His attestations are regional in terms of both the place of issue of the particular charter and that charter's content.[153] Earl Donnchad appears as a witness to forty-three of William's surviving charters with the title of *iusticia*.[154] All but two of these charters concerned land, privileges, and beneficiaries lying north of the Forth, from Fife in the south to Moray in the north.[155] More importantly, however, he only appeared with his title of *iusticia* in four charters issued south of the Forth: two at Stirling, one at Rutherglen, and one at Haddington. When it is also appreciated that Stirling was considered as the gateway between north and south of the Forth, this becomes even more striking: by attesting at Stirling, Donnchad was attesting at the frontier of *Scotia*. In addition, the content of the charter issued at Haddington related to churches north of the Forth, in modern Perthshire. In short, Donnchad attested only one surviving charter south of the Forth which also concerned land south of the Forth in which he was given the title of justice by a charter scribe. Given that Donnchad served as a justice for around thirty years, that this happened in only one surviving charter suggests that it was far more common for Donnchad to attest royal charters *as a justice* in locations north of the Firth of Forth than in those south of that natural divide.

Most importantly, Donnchad's pattern of attestation with the title of 'iusticia' is completely at odds with his attestations where he did not bear the title 'iusticia', that is, where he appears as plain *Comes Dunecanus* (Earl Donnchad), not *Comes Dunecanus iusticia*, which continued throughout his career as a justice.[156] For example, Earl Donnchad attested ten charters of King William at Edinburgh but in none of them was he ever given the title of 'iusticia'.[157] Such numbers are extremely striking.[158]

---

[151] Earl Donnchad attests as a justice in *RRS*, ii, nos. 134–6, 148, 153, 200, 208, 213, 222, 224, 229, 242, 250–1, 261, 272–3, 275, 277, 280, 283, 322, 334, 336, 338–40, 344–8, 358, 388, 393–4, 396, 398, 403–4, 418, 420–1, 423, 429.

[152] Barrow also noted this, although we come to different conclusions (*RRS*, ii, p. 43).

[153] This was the case even in his earliest attestations, for which see *RRS*, ii, nos. 134 (land in the Mearns; issued at Kinghorn); 135 (land in Perthshire; issued at Perth); 136 (land in Perthshire; issued at Perth); 148 (land in Angus, issued at Perth); 153 (burgesses in Aberdeen and in Moray; issued at Perth).

[154] This includes the charters which are later summaries and two which are potentially suspect (*RRS*, ii, nos. 251, 388).

[155] In one charter concerning land in Lothian (and issued at Stirling), Donnchad attested as *iusticia* alongside Walter Olifard, also called *iusticia*; *RRS*, ii, no. 200.

[156] The last surviving attestation of Earl Donnchad is to *RRS*, ii, no. 429, which G. W. S. Barrow dated to 28 August 1200×03, with a caveat of 'probably 1201'; *RRS*, ii, p. 405.

[157] *RRS*, ii, nos. 37, 42, 293–5, 298–9, 308, 364, 368.

[158] Further evidence from charters issued at Roxburgh supports this. Earl Donnchad attested five charters at Roxburgh in a date range of 1159×95 (*RRS*, i, nos. 131, 184; ii, nos. 175, 314–15). In none was he given the title 'justice'. Indeed, in one of his attestations, Richard Comyn also attests the charter as *iusticia* (*RRS*, ii, no. 175).

This evidence suggests that scribes of royal charters did not use the title of 'iusticia' in a haphazard way; it was considered and used only when deemed appropriate.[159] It was *not* appropriate for Earl Donnchad to be given the title *iusticia* when attesting south of the Forth and about issues pertaining to south of the Forth, except in what appear to be special circumstances. This leaves us with yet another complicated scenario to try to explain. If we were to look at the evidence of the title alone, it would appear that a regional division was not introduced to Scottish royal government until *c*.1220. But by looking at attestation patterns and scribal deployment of the title to refer to particular individuals, we can see that Earl Donnchad was acting in a way that suggested he had charge of Scotia in practice if not in name. How can this be explained?[160]

A potential solution can be found first by looking at who exactly was given the title of *iusticia* in the first half of the reign of William the Lion, the period when we actually have *named* men on record performing this role. Putting Earl Donnchad to one side for the moment, it becomes immediately apparent that all men who served as the king's justice were not only relatively 'new men'—that is, men who were not native to Scotland and who had settled there either in David's reign or in Mael Coluim's—but also whose lands were predominantly south of the Forth (or at least that was where they gained the first holdings): David Olifard, Robert Avenel, Walter Olifard, Richard Comyn, Robert de Quincy, and Geoffrey de Melville, all of whom appear as justices in the 1170s.[161] David Olifard, the earliest of these justices, was clearly concerned with business both north and south of the Forth: he was, for example, the only justice to witness William's confirmation of

---

[159] Barrow, of course, was aware that *when* scribes included the title of justice it was 'of the greatest interest and significance' (*RRS*, ii, p. 43) but thought instead that 'charter clerks might fail to give the title of justice to a man even when he was actually holding the office'. This is a fair assumption but charter scribes were not as inconsistent as Barrow may have thought and, instead, may well have used the title when people were actually performing the role.

[160] Donnchad's attestations are very different from those of Walter Olifard, who held the title of 'justice' for a maximum period of 1173×85 (*RRS*, ii, nos. 162, 195, 197, 199–200, 233, 237, 248). Walter Olifard succeeded to his father David's holdings and Osbert Olifard's lordship of Arbuthnott, which William gave Osbert in the late 1160s or early 1170s (*Spalding Misc.*, v, p. 211; cf. Paul C. Ferguson, *Medieval Papal Representatives in Scotland: Legates, Nuncios and Judges-Delegates, 1125–1286*, Stair Society 45 (Edinburgh, 1997), Appendix IV, note 1). Walter was the father of the Walter Olifard who served as justiciar of Lothian between *c*.1222 and 1242, and Walter I had married Christina, daughter of Ferteth, *mormaer* of Strathearn (see Arkady Hodge, 'A New Charter of William the Lion relating to Strathearn', *SHR*, vol. 86, no. 222 (2007), pp. 314–18). Walter I Olifard attested as 'justice' in eight of King William's surviving acts (see also *RRS*, II, p. 43). Three survive as originals and were written by two, if not three, different scribes (*RRS*, ii, nos. 195, 199, 200, with identification of scribes taken from Barrow, *RRS*, ii, pp. 87–8, noting the possibility that Bc and Cc may be the same scribe). Walter attested, in contrast to David Olifard, predominantly south of the Forth and only once north of the Forth, at Forfar (*RRS*, ii, no. 233). But, like his father (and unlike Earl Donnchad), the business of these charters concerned land and privileges north and south of the Forth, including lands for the king's monastic foundation at Arbroath, which was mainly in Angus, and tofts in Inverness, Auldearn, Elgin, and Forres in Moray. Thus, although Walter appears to have been more restricted in his movements, the business for which his title of justice was recorded continued to range across the kingdom up into Moray.

[161] G. W. S. Barrow, *The Anglo-Norman Era in Scottish History* (Oxford, 1980), pp. 28, 44–5, 96–7, 159; for Quinci and Avenel, see G. W. S. Barrow, 'Scotland's "Norman" Families', *Kingdom of the Scots*, pp. 279–95, at pp. 281–2, 286–7.

the settlement of a dispute between two big hitters, Dunfermline Abbey and St Andrews Cathedral Priory, over the land of Balchristie in Fife.[162] What we see in the 1160s and 1170s, then, is a group of new men (although some were newer than others), whose earliest accumulated landholdings were in the south, an area where we know justices operated under Mael Coluim IV and which was also the area covered by the earliest administrative sheriffdoms. Early in William's reign, these justices went north of the Forth when required.[163] This very much mirrors the chronology of the development of sheriffs and sheriffdoms outlined earlier, which began predominantly south of the Forth under David I and stretched north-wards under Mael Coluim IV and William the Lion. In a related way, justice activity relied on men south of the Forth, where most of the new administrative local institutions had developed. These men dealt with business north of the Forth on an ad hoc basis: north of the Forth was an area where kings of Scots had less intense formal administrative reach (although still a lot of power) and which, as argued in Chapter 3, had its own form of legal specialism.[164]

The appointment of Earl Donnchad as 'justice' in the early 1170s, therefore, may have been a different move by William the Lion that continued the putative policy of his brother while also resulting in a departure from it. By the early 1170s, Earl Donnchad had become the premier *mormaer* (or earl) in Scotia.[165] His prob-able grandfather, Caustantín, had been described as a 'great *iudex*' in Scotia in David I's reign, meaning that he was knowledgeable in the law and was a judge in legal disputes.[166] By appointing Earl Donnchad as a justice, William may have been creating continuity in judicial function in an area where royal power was not yet formally channelled through local administrative sheriffdoms (which seems to have become the norm only in the mid-1180s). In this, William may have been continuing a strategy begun by his brother Mael Coluim but taking it in a different

---

[162] *RRS*, ii, no. 35 (which was itself settled in the king's presence).

[163] David Olifard is recorded with the king at Perth, Dunfermline, St Andrews, and Kinghorn (*RRS*, ii, nos. 8, 10–11, 19, 23–4, 27–8, 30, 33–4, 36). This merely highlights the need for a study of assemblies under William the Lion to develop a more nuanced understanding of when and why cer-tain individuals were given titles in *some* charters but not in others. It is interesting that, on the basis of the location of his surviving charters, William spent much of his time in the early years of his reign north of the Forth.

[164] The sheriffdom of Perth constitutes the exception north of the Forth: it is attested in David's reign as an administrative unit (a *vicecomitatus*), for which, see above, pp. 197–9. One should not also think that this means that the social worlds of the aristocracy north and south of the Forth were sep-arate. In William's reign, men either descended from 'new' men or 'new' men themselves started get-ting land north of the Forth (see Chapter 1, pp. 74–6). This was also true for marriage patterns as well, for which see the marriage of Walter Olifard (son of David Olifard) to Christina, the daughter of Ferteth of Strathearn before 1171. Marriages north of the Forth are discussed in Matthew H. Hammond, 'A Prosopographical Analysis of Society in East Central Scotland with Special Reference to Ethnicity' (PhD Dissertation, University of Glasgow, 2005), pp. 136–54, and in Matthew H. Hammond, 'Women and the Adoption of Charters in Scotland North of the Forth, *c*.1150–1286', *Innes Review*, vol. 62, no. 1 (2011), pp. 5–46, at 12–26, 27–33.

[165] For Donnchad, see John Bannerman, 'MacDuff of Fife', in *Medieval Scotland: Crown, Lordship and Community—Essays Presented to G. W. S. Barrow*, ed. Alexander Grant and K. J. Stringer (Edinburgh, 1993), pp. 20–38; and [R.] Andrew McDonald, 'Macduff Family, Earls of Fife (*per c*.1095–1371)', *ODNB*, online at <http://www.oxforddnb.com/view/article/50328>.

[166] Lawrie, *ESC*, no. 80.

direction: by *not* calling Earl Donnchad explicitly justice of Scotia or, indeed, Fife; Donnchad as a royal justice had a different authority from his grandfather, Caustantín's, as a *iudex*. But the symbolic continuity between Donnchad and Caustantín may also have provided Donnchad with the necessary status (and probably linguistic skills) to perform the role of king's judicial delegate in Scotia because he was the most important *mormaer* (or earl) in the kingdom, in contrast to people like David Olifard, Robert Avenel, or Walter Olifard.[167] As a result, Donnchad's actions as a justice appear to have been regionally focussed to a far greater extent than David Olifard's, whose career as a royal justice appears to have ceased by 1171, the year before Donnchad is first attested in the role.

There is thus a way of explaining how and why the formal titles of justiciar of Scotia/Lothian are generally absent from the record until the reign of Alexander II. Before this, justices were the king's delegates who, as will be argued later, may not even have held formal courts until, or shortly before, 1184.[168] But the appointment of Earl Donnchad created an *ad hoc* regional division: Donnchad, because of his status and perhaps his family tradition, was well placed to be the king's justice and by default took responsibility for *most* of the business occurring north of the Forth. The same must have held when he was joined for a short period of time by Gille Brigte, earl of Strathearn, who appears as a justice in one royal charter dating to 1187×95.[169] As a result of Earl Donnchad's long life, other royal justices of the last two decades of the twelfth century became more (but not exclusively) regionally focused in Lothian; they did not need to go into Scotia as justices of the king because Earl Donnchad, sometimes supported by others, was already there. We can see this hypothesis reflected in the attestation patterns of other justices.

William Lindsay, for example, justice from 1189×1195, attests only south of the Forth with his title, and about issues pertaining to that region, as did David of Lindsay and Gervase Avenel in the early 1200s, although little survives about their activity.[170] On Earl Donnchad's death in 1204, however, there was a short hiatus,

---

[167] William the Lion had a dalliance with the daughter of Robert Avenel. Their daughter was called Isabella and was married in 1183 to Robert II de Brus and then in 1191 to Robert de Ros; *Chron. Melrose*, *s.a.* 1183, 1191.

[168] See below, pp. 238–40.

[169] *RRS*, ii, no. 337 (*not* no. 433; cf. *RRS*, ii, p. 43). Gille Brigte served for longer than his single attestation suggests. In a document surviving in the unpublished cartulary of Arbroath, Gille Brigte, along (perhaps) with Matthew, bishop of Aberdeen, is described as *iusticiarii domini regis* (probably expanding *iust* or *iustic* in the original) in Mael Brigte's 1221 letter (although describing a situation 'under King William'); BL, Additional MS 33245, fo.162v–163r (printed in Barrow, 'The *Judex*', pp. 66–7; discussed in Broun, 'King's *brithem*'). For the suggestion that Gille Brigte alone was a royal justice in this document, see Chapter 3, Note 91.

[170] William Lindsay attests as *iusticia*: *RRS*, ii, nos. 316 (Roxburgh, concerning the bishopric of Glasgow), 317 (Roxburgh, concerning land in Roxburghshire for Kelso), 400 (Haddington, for Soutra; but problematic), 406 (Selkirk, about Melrose men and monks in Galloway). Roland, son of Uhtred, attests as *iusticia*: *RRS*, ii, nos. 309 (Lanark, concerning land in Ayrshire), 400 (Haddington, for Soutra; but problematic), 406 (Selkirk, about Melrose men and monks in Galloway). David of Lindsay and Gervase Avenel both attest: *RRS*, ii, nos. 481 (Traquair, neyfs of Kelso Abbey), 483 (Selkirk, agreement between Earl Patrick of Dunbar and Melrose Abbey over Leader Water). Patrick, earl of Dunbar, attests: *RRS*, ii, nos. 381 (Selkirk, about land in Langton for Kelso Abbey), 431 (Edinburgh, about land in Perthshire to Cambuskenneth Abbey), 460 (Wedale, agreement between

when two perhaps three justices appear irregularly, until William Comyn appears with the title of 'justice'. From 1210, William Comyn was the *only* justice on record until the appointment of Walter Olifard as 'justiciar of Lothian' (a title he always attested with) by 1222.[171] Until Walter's appointment, however, William Comyn attested both north and south of the Forth as justice or 'justice of the Scots'.[172] These charters were concerned with business that stretched from plough-gates in Dumfriesshire in the southwest to lands in Invernesshire in the north (this kingdom-wide role may explain why William—and no other—was given the title 'justice [or justiciar] of the Scots' for a short period of time).[173] But, on the appointment of Walter Olifard by 1222, William Comyn's appearances as justiciar again became more—but not completely—restricted to Scotia.[174] In short, a *de facto* regional division was developing in the twelfth century but may not have been formalised until later, and is only fully attested early in the reign of Alexander II. Even then, the justiciar-ship did not include Galloway as will be shown later.[175] Given attestation patterns and the references to justices of Lothian and Scotia under Mael Coluim IV, one would be forgiven for thinking that a regional justi-ciarship had developed by the mid-twelfth century but to do so would nonetheless be anachronistic and ultimately misrepresent the nature of twelfth-century royal officials. The twelfth century should be analysed not solely for the origins of a thirteenth-century system but as a dynamic period, full of experimentation regard-ing how the legal authority of *iudices* could work alongside that of the south-ern-based royal justices. This eventually resulted in the eventual predominance of the royal justice but this was far from inevitable.[176]

Durham and St Andrews). Only Earl Patrick, therefore, attests a charter which has anything to do with lands north of the Forth and this was in a charter authenticated at Edinburgh, whose beneficiary was Cambuskenneth Abbey in Stirling.

[171] David Lindsay last attests as a justice in, probably, June 1210: *RRS*, ii, no. 493.

[172] *RRS*, ii, nos. 465, 472, 475, 489 (*iustic Scott*), 490, 492 (*iustic Scott*), (?)493 (did the *iustic'* refer to *both* William Comyn and David Lindsay, as Barrow thought, or just to David Lindsay?), 497, 502 (*iustic' Scoc*, perhaps for *Scott*; it is a cartulary copy), 522. Under Alexander II, see Fraser, *Grant*, iii, no. 3 (*iust' Scott*) [AII/5]; *Balmerino Liber*, no. 3 (*iustic Scott* [*sic*], despite what the printed edition gives) [AII/23]; *Glasgow Registrum*, i, nos. 132, 134 (*iustic Scot*) [AII/25, AII/26].

[173] See Note 105.

[174] This region-based pattern to attestations is not completely maintained in the reign of Alexander III during the long justiciarship in Scotia of Alexander Comyn, earl of Buchan. Alexander Comyn attested both north and south of the Forth, although predominantly (but not exclusively) about mat-ters pertaining to Scotia (*RRS*, iv, 1, nos. 18–20, 30–31, 41, 44, 54–56, 59, 62, 73, 84, 88, 91, 129, 154, 156, 162–164, 167). Hugh de Berkeley, justiciar of Lothian, however, was more based within his region: only one of his thirteen surviving attestations was at a place in Scotia, and this also pertained to land in Perth (*RRS*, iv, 1, nos. 26, 47–8, 51–3, 55, 60, 64, 68, 73–4, 88). The power of Alexander Comyn may well have prompted his kingdom-wide attestations but by then it was far more normal for the title of justiciar to be included in all attestations made by a particular individual. For Alexander Comyn, see Alan Young, *Robert Bruce's Rivals: The Comyns, 1212–1314* (East Linton, 1997), pp. 66–86, particularly pp. 77–9.

[175] For Alan (who did not serve as a royal justice), see Keith J. Stringer, 'Periphery and Core in Thirteenth-Century Scotland: Alan Son of Roland, Lord of Galloway and Constable of Scotland', in *Medieval Scotland*, ed. Grant and Stringer, pp. 82–113.

[176] It is of note that chronicle evidence does not mention justiciars until the thirteenth century. The first reference to a justiciar of a region in *Gesta Annalia* is to Alan Durward, *iusticiarius Scocie*,

Where does all this leave the putative justiciar of Galloway, whom Barrow argued had been introduced in the last two decades of the twelfth century? The man normally taken to be the first 'justiciar of Galloway' was Roland, son of Uhtred and lord of Galloway (d.1200).[177] The evidence normally cited in support is Roland's attestation as *iusticia* to three surviving *acta* of William the Lion and his presence at a legislative assembly held at Lanark in May, sometime between 1185 and 1200.[178] It is worth giving some background about Roland. Roland was the eldest son of Uhtred, who had ruled part of the province of Galloway with his (half-)brother, Gille Brigte, before that same brother caused Uhtred to be blinded and castrated in 1174, leading to his death.[179] In 1185, Roland, on the death of his uncle, Gille Brigte, had entered the latter's part of the province with the hope of obtaining it himself.[180] This he eventually managed to do but only with the threat of invasion from Henry II of England (to whom he had to submit in 1186).[181] Only after that was he fully confirmed as *lord* of Galloway; his cousin, Donnchad, the son of his (half-)uncle Gille Brigte, had to make do with Carrick, previously part of Galloway earlier in the century but now forming its own region.[182]

Before he obtained confirmation as lord of Galloway in August 1186, Roland had appeared as a witness to only two of King William's surviving *acta*.[183] One of these was to the charter confirming (and probably re-granting on different written terms) Annandale to Robert de Brus, which was issued at the head town in Annandale, Lochmaben, and whose witness list reads as a roll call of all the major magnates of the south and south-west, and included Roland's father, Uhtred, as well as his uncle, Gille Brigte.[184] After August 1186, however, Roland attested ten charters of King William before his death in 1200 and, in three, he was given the title *iustic*—'justice', not, it should be stressed, justiciar of Galloway.[185] After August 1186, therefore, Roland was much more integrated in King William's orbit than he had been previously.

when he intervened before the inauguration of Alexander III; *Gesta Annalia* I in Skene, *Fordun*, i, pp. 293, 297. The Chronicle of Melrose only refers to a *iusticiarius*, again Alan Durward, in 1251 (*Chron. Melrose, s.a.* 1251).

[177] Oram, *Domination and Lordship*, pp. 146–8, 155; for a calendar and partial edition of Roland's acts, see Keith J. Stringer, 'Acts of Lordship: the Records of the Lords of Galloway to 1234', in *Freedom and Authority: Scotland, c.1050–1650: Historical and Historiographical Essays Presented to Grant G. Simpson*, ed. Terry Brotherstone and David Ditchburn (East Linton, 2000), pp. 203–34, at pp. 217–23.

[178] *RRS*, ii, nos. 309, 400 (inflated?), 406.   [179] Howden, *Gesta*, i, pp. 79–80, 99, 126.

[180] Howden, *Gesta*, i, pp. 339–40.   [181] Howden, *Gesta*, i, pp. 348–9.

[182] For Donnchad, see A. M. Duncan, *Scotland: the Making of the Kingdom* (Edinburgh, 1975), pp. 183–4, 186–7, 233–4; Richard Oram, *The Lordship of Galloway c.900–1300* (Edinburgh, 2000), pp. 100–5; Seán Duffy, 'The Lords of Galloway, Earls of Carrick and the Bissets of the Glens: Scottish Settlement in Thirteenth-Century Ulster', in *Regions and Rulers in Ireland, 1100–1650*, ed. David Edwards (Dublin, 2004), pp. 37–50, at pp. 37–8, 43–4.

[183] *RRS*, ii, nos. 80, 236.   [184] *RRS*, ii, no. 80.

[185] *RRS*, ii, nos. 255, 260, 299, 308–310, 367–368, 400, 406. *RRS*, ii, no. 406, calls him *justiciario* but this is alongside William of Lindsay, also *iusticia*, who is given as *iustic*, which is probably what was in the original, because this survives in the cartulary of Melrose, now held in the British Library (Harley MS 3960).

Two out of Roland's three surviving attestations as 'justice' were to royal charters which had nothing to do with Galloway. The charters were issued at Lanark and Haddington and concerned land in Ayrshire and the Hospital of Soutra in Midlothian respectively.[186] Only one attestation as 'justice' concerned Galloway. Roland witnessed a general brieve addressed to the men of Galloway, which must have been procured by the monks of Melrose and was issued on 11 December at Selkirk between 1195 and 1198.[187] In it, the king commanded that lords in Galloway should help the monks of Melrose when they came into Galloway tracking thieves, according to the king's assize of Galloway, an assize which no longer survives. The brieve was also attested by another of the king's justices, William of Lindsay. It is understandable why Roland would attest this charter (issued at Selkirk): he was not only the king's justice but also lord of Galloway and so would obviously have needed to consent to whatever statutory changes the king was imposing within his lordship.[188] Although the evidence is slight, Roland appears as 'justice' in business unconnected with Galloway as well as that concerned with it; this makes him look similar to the other justices of the late twelfth century who had no formal regional jurisdiction.

The final piece of evidence normally cited when outlining Roland's supposed role as 'justiciar of Galloway' is the record of an enactment made at Lanark which survives as the penultimate chapter of *Leges Scocie*. This enactment records the business of a royal assembly held at Lanark where, in the presence of Roland, son of Uhtred, the *iudices* of Galloway judged how the king would receive his *cáin* from the whole province.[189] Roland is not, however, given the title of 'justice' in the statute itself and, again, his presence at the king's court can be explained by his position as lord of the province, rather than justice of the king for Galloway. In short, while Roland served as a justice of the king, and was necessarily affected by any royal involved in his province (because he was its lord), there is nothing to suggest that a formal justiciarship of Galloway was in operation in the late twelfth century, as Barrow thought.[190] Our earliest evidence for a justiciar of Galloway is not until 1258, after the province had been broken up after the king and some of his nobles had quelled a serious uprising in 1235 over the king's partition of the province among the three legitimate daughters of Roland's son, Alan.[191] A. A. M. Duncan has indeed suggested that the development of the position of justiciar of

---

[186] *RRS*, ii, nos. 309, 400. Barrow deemed the charter to Soutra to be inflated, which is extremely likely; there is, however, nothing wrong with the witness list. Regardless, this attestation must be taken as problematic (*RRS*, ii, p. 387).

[187] *RRS*, ii, no. 409.

[188] Galloway, after all, was known to have its own 'special laws', which were acknowledged in 1244 (*SA*, c. 2); for the nature of these laws, see Hector L. MacQueen, 'The Laws of Galloway: A Preliminary Survey', in *Galloway: Land and Lordship*, ed. R. D. Oram and G. P. Stell (Edinburgh, 1991), pp. 131–43.

[189] *LS*, c. 20.

[190] Even though he acknowledged that there was a major gap between 1200, when Roland died (*Chron. Melrose, s.a.* 1200), and 1258, when John Comyn is attested as the 'next' justiciar of Galloway: *RRS*, ii, p. 45; Barrow, 'Justiciar', pp. 86–7.

[191] For this, see Oram, *Lordship of Galloway*, pp. 141–50; Stringer, 'Periphery and Core', p. 96; MacQueen, 'Laws of Galloway', pp. 137–8; Duncan, *Making of the Kingdom*, pp. 530–1.

Galloway was one of the many consequences of this Galwegian uprising, alongside the introduction of sheriffs of Dumfries and Wigtown, east and west of Urr Water respectively.[192] There is no evidence to confirm this because a justiciar of Galloway does not appear until 1258; it remains, however, a plausible suggestion.

What all this adds up to is a new picture of the twelfth- and early thirteenth-century justice/justiciar. Justices first appear from *c.*1140 onwards and it is thus to roughly then that we should date their introduction. Under Mael Coluim IV, justices appear to have operated with enforcing power only south of the Forth in wider Lothian as well as within the bishopric of Glasgow. They do not appear as permanent features north of the Forth; there was no formal regional division under Mael Coluim IV. Our earliest named justices under William were primarily southern-based lords (even if they later were given land north of the Forth) who appear to have served on an ad hoc basis, and heard cases north of the Forth on occasion. What we see until the 1170s is a south-focused, ad hoc system, in which the king's justices were used when necessary.

How the new form of legal authority of the justice would interact with the existing specialism of *iudices* must have been of interest to kings of Scots, as well as to others. That the king now possessed a different judicial officer—the justice—could only have raised questions about how this person would interact with the existing *iudices*, who we know were a key part of the legal landscape in Scotia.[193] One key difference between them (apart from enforcing teind payment or not) was that the justice was explicitly the king's judicial agent and representative; the authority of the *iudex*, by contrast, did not necessarily represent the king. Many solutions to negotiate the relationship between these two forms of legal authority must have presented themselves and it has been argued here that Mael Coluim IV equated these *iudices* in Fife and Scotia with the new royal justices of the southern part of his kingdom. That Mael Coluim's (or his scribes') strategy, if it can even be called so, was not permanent should not concern us. That, with the exception of the king's *iudex*, *iudices* ended up in the thirteenth century as predominantly more local figures, only attending local or regional courts, should not be seen as part of an inevitable decline. Instead, twelfth-century kings seem to have responded more actively to the *iudex*'s legal specialism by bringing them more firmly under their royal authority. That the premier royal judicial officials in Scotia, greater Lothian, and, eventually, Galloway came to be justices (later justiciars), not *iudices*, was in part the perhaps unforeseen and longer-term consequence of who held the title of justice and where they discharged this responsibility.

The justice-ship of Earl Donnchad must have been extremely important in establishing the royal justice as a permanent part of the legal landscape north of the Forth and, indeed, in laying the ground for the regional division itself. Donnchad must have been so useful in the role of justice not only because he was probably the most important earl or *mormaer* in the kingdom, but also because he descended

---

[192] Duncan, *Making of the Kingdom*, pp. 530–2.

[193] Barrow wrote that 'the ancient order of *judices*…between whom and the incoming Anglo-Norman justiciars one can trace no true organic link': Barrow, 'Justiciar', p. 84.

from a *mormaer* who had once been described as a *magnus iudex* in Scotia and who was part of a different legal order to the royal justices. While he held the justice-ship, at least one other earl, Gille Brigte of Strathearn, served alongside him. It may thus be a rather fitting consequence of Donnchad's ability to bridge symbolically a gap between *iudex* and justice (rather than practically bridging it) that he may have helped to cause the eventual disappearance of the *iudex* from the top levels of law-making (the last attested time a defined group of *iudices* made law was in 1221, the year before Walter Olifard first firmly appears as justiciar of Lothian, thereby con-firming that a regional division had emerged).[194] It was during Donnchad's tenure of the office, which lasted for most of his adult life, that the ad hoc regional divi-sion in the justice-ship developed; it was formalized by *c.*1220, just over fifteen years after his death in 1204. This formal regional division is not attested in our sources until the early 1220s and even then only concerned Scotia and Lothian; Galloway was not included at this point. It is also at this point that we can be con-fident that our justices were regularly being called justiciars. But we should not see the regional division as being planned from the very moment Donnchad first took on the role of justice. The twelfth century appears to have been a time of great innovation and experimentation, all of which is obscured if the regional division in the justiciarship is seen as nascent and emergent throughout the period. It is in the context of this much more exciting, fluid, and dynamic twelfth century that the evidence for the emergence of the justiciar's ayre will now be considered.

The Ayre

The treatise perhaps written in 1292×96, and known as 'The Scottish King's Household', not only tells us that there were three 'justices' in operation in the kingdom of the Scots—one each in Scotia, Lothian, and Galloway—but also that these justices held 'sessions' twice a year.[195] This reference to sessions heard bian-nually by regional justices has long been thought to be a reference to the 'ayre' they held: a journey around their region during which they heard pleas belonging to their jurisdiction. The justiciar's ayre has accordingly been thought to be one of the benchmarks of the administrative developments in royal justice that occurred dur-ing the central Middle Ages. But David Carpenter has recently shown that justi-ciars do not seem to have conducted an ayre twice a year; indeed, there was probably more than one year, if not more, between the periods of their formal itineration.[196]

---

[194] See Chapter 3, pp. 131–2.
[195] 'The Scottish King's Household', ed. Bateson, pp. 36–7. There is also a chapter first attested in *CD* in the early fourteenth century, which states that the lord king established that there should be 'two chief pleas of the justiciar' held each year at Edinburgh and Peebles (*CD*, c. 24, printed in *APS*, i, p. 379 as *ARW*, c. 25). There is no other confirmatory evidence for this chapter.
[196] David Carpenter, 'Scottish Royal Government in the Thirteenth Century from an English Perspective', in *New Perspectives on Medieval Scotland, 1093–1286*, ed. Matthew Hammond (Woodbridge, 2013), pp. 117–59, at pp. 133–7. Some of Carpenter's evidence is a little overstated: Hugh de Berkeley, for example, did not take office in *c.*1262 but, instead, by Christmas 1263, so his ayre of

Putting aside the question of what a more minimal view of the ayre means for our understanding of royal justice, one key question has never been fully addressed: when did it start and in what context?[197] Even G. W. S. Barrow, in his full study on the Scottish justiciar, did not comment explicitly on the ayres, nor when he thought they were introduced in the kingdom of the Scots.[198] His comments on the development of the regional justiciarship may suggest that he thought (although, importantly, he never said so explicitly) that they began to develop either late in the reign of Mael Coluim IV or early in the reign of William the Lion—either way in the 1160s. If one dispenses with the dubious tactic of trying to decipher what Barrow thought but never wrote publically about, the gap in our understanding of the early history of the ayre grows even larger.

The Justiciar's Ayre: The Evidence of the 1263–66 Account Roll

We start, for once, near the end of the chronological reach of this chapter, and head backwards through time. The best evidence for the form of the justiciar's ayre in the second half of the thirteenth century comes from a transcript of two royal account rolls from 1263–66 and 1288–90, which survive only in excerpts made by Thomas Hamilton, earl of Haddington, in the early seventeenth century.[199] The problems and possibilities this source presents will be discussed in more detail in Chapters 6 and 7.[200] For now, we only need note that accounts of four justiciars are mentioned in the 1263–66 roll (two from Lothian, one from Scotia, and one from Galloway—via a shrieval account), while the account of a single justiciar of Galloway was copied by Haddington from an original roll covering the years 1288–90.[201]

The accounts from 1263–66 show that, by this point, justiciars of Scotia and Lothian (though not Galloway, as we shall see) were collecting their profits of justice (*lucra*) by journeying through sheriffdoms. For example, Stephen Fleming, justiciar of Lothian, held a short ayre in 1263 which went through the sheriffdoms of Ayr, Lanark, Peebles/Traquair, and Roxburgh, before his ayre suddenly ceased, perhaps when Stephen died or, at the very least, gave up office.[202] In 1265, Hugh de Berkeley, his successor as justiciar of Lothian, accounted for a much more comprehensive job: he had again covered the sheriffdoms visited by Stephen the previous year but also visited Berwick, Edinburgh, Dumfries, Dumbarton, and Stirling.[203] The justiciar of Scotia also conducted his ayre by visiting the head towns of sheriffdoms. Probably in 1266, Alexander Comyn, earl of Buchan, and

---

1265 covered at the minimum one year, not the three suggested by Carpenter ('Scottish Royal Government', p. 134, although drawing on Barrow, 'Justiciar', pp. 110–11). Nevertheless, Carpenter's general and important point stands: there is no evidence that justiciars attested twice a year; the absolute maximum the accounts show them to have journeyed was once a year and it is clear that more than one year had elapsed since the last ayre of Alexander Comyn, earl of Buchan.

[197] What was heard by royal justiciars is developed in Chapter 5, pp. 285–94, 305–6, 308–15.
[198] Barrow, 'Justiciar'.   [199] NRS, E38/1; printed in *ER*, i, pp. 1–51.
[200] See Chapter 6, pp. 351–4, and Chapter 7, pp. 403–5.   [201] *ER*, i, pp. 9–10, 16–17.
[202] Hugh de Berkeley is attested as justiciar of Lothian on 25 December 1263, so Stephen must have ceased holding the office by then (*RRS*, iv, 1, no. 47).
[203] *ER*, i, p. 27. The amounts raised in these ayres are discussed in Chapter 6, pp. 374–9.

long-serving justiciar of Scotia, returned his account at Scone, having journeyed through Inverness, Nairn, Forres, Elgin, Banff, Aberdeen, Kincardine, Forfar, Perth, and Fife.[204] The profits of this ayre, returned via the sheriffdom, reveal that the sheriff of Inverness actually accounted for the profits received not only from Moray but also from the more northerly Ross and Caithness.[205] This is surprising because the 1263–66 account roll shows that there were sheriffs in Cromarty and Dingwall, who might account for Ross at the very least.[206] But these sheriffs did not return the justiciar's profits; instead, all *lucra* were funnelled through the sheriff of Inverness, suggesting that the justiciar of Scotia did not include the more northerly sheriffdoms on his ayre; instead, suitors from Ross and Caithness came to the justiciar's court at Inverness, whose sheriff was responsible for collecting all their profits of justice.[207]

The justiciar of Galloway returned his profits in 1263–66 differently from those of Scotia and Lothian, so will be left to one side for the moment. The profits returned by the justiciars of Scotia and Lothian from the sheriffdoms under their jurisdiction were, however, not physically returned by them. Instead, sheriffs had to collect the fines and confiscated chattels decided upon by the justiciar during their ayre. We know this because the justiciars' accounts expressly tell us so. The account of Alexander Comyn, justiciar of Scotia, for example, gave the total amount of money collected during his ayre (over £405) and then stated that the 'sheriffs will answer for [these sums] in their own accounts'.[208] And, indeed, sheriffs did account for the *lucra justiciarii* they owed each year.[209] Sometimes justiciars had left out one or two values of confiscated chattels and, on occasion, these missing sums were diligently reported to the royal auditors by the relevant sheriff.[210] At other times, disputes arose as to which sheriff was responsible for which profits raised by the justiciar: for example, David of Lochore, sheriff of Fife, petitioned the king's auditors for an additional £10 with which, he said, he had been unlawfully burdened in his last account because the case had not been settled in his sheriffdom, nor did the wrongdoer have any goods within Fife from which he (the sheriff) could be compelled to pay.[211] This sort of administrative error must have happened quite frequently, even if (as was not the case in the above example) the case had been heard in the right sheriffdom but the wrongdoer only had goods in another sheriffdom from which he would pay his fine. The method of accounting presented by the

---

[204] *ER*, i, p. 18.   [205] *ER*, i, pp. 13, 19.   [206] *ER*, i, pp. 19, 26.

[207] Dingwall had attained the status of a royal burgh by 1227 (for which see above, pp. 202–3, and the references cited in Note 53) For the sheriff of Dingwall, see *ER*, i, p. 26. However, this may have been a relatively recent addition because an undated account in the same roll was returned by the attorneys of Alexander Comyn, *bailie* of Dingwall (*ER*, i, p. 19). But the attorneys did not do a very good job, because, in one account as bailie of Dingwall, they admitted that they did not know whether anything more was owed 'because they were unsure of the farms of the bailie of Dingwall, as the roll of the chapel testifies, and thus the account remains unfinished' (*ER*, i, p. 19). Dingwall and Cromarty were, however, included alongside Inverness in the so-called 'Valuation of the Sheriffdoms', suggesting that they were all conceptualized together. The 'Valuation of the Sheriffdoms' was printed in 'Scottish King's Household', ed. Bateson, p. 25.

[208] *ER*, i, p. 18; see also *ER*, i, p. 10.

[209] For development of this point, see Chapter 6, pp. 374–9.

[210] *ER*, i, pp. 17, 31.   [211] *ER*, i, p. 32 and pp. 4–5.

1263–66 account roll therefore shows that there was a relatively coherent system whereby the justiciar would journey through each sheriffdom, hear cases, draw up a list of resulting fines and confiscated chattels, and give a copy of this to the local sheriff, who was then responsible for collecting the money and goods and handing them over to the king's auditors when called to account.[212] Justiciars returned statements of their own accounts individually, so that the amounts proffered and collected by sheriffs could be compared to what was owed in total.[213] Evidently the system was not perfect but it was, nevertheless, a system.

The way in which the justiciar of Galloway interacted with his region was very different. Only one justiciar of Galloway is recorded in the 1263–66 account roll transcript: Stephen Fleming, who was also concurrently justiciar of Lothian.[214] Stephen, however, either died or gave up his two justiciar offices sometime towards the end of 1263 or the middle of 1264, and his replacement as justiciar of Galloway was Aymer Maxwell, sheriff of Dumfries, who attested a royal charter, dated 9 December 1264, as 'justiciar of Galloway', alongside Hugh de Berkeley, Stephen Fleming's replacement as justiciar of Lothian, who is attested in the position by December 1263.[215] In his 1264 account, however, Aymer was responsible as sheriff of Dumfries for the profits from Stephen Fleming's last ayre in Galloway, which amounted to £13 17s 1d.[216] Stephen Fleming, as justiciar of Galloway, had only heard pleas from those parts of Galloway that fell within the bishopric of Glasgow. There is no return—and no mention of a return—from any area west of the River Urr. The power of the justiciar in Galloway had, however, extended by the time of the 1288–90 accounts. In these, William Sinclair was both sheriff of Dumfries and justiciar of Galloway and proffered *lucra* from both west and east of the Urr, although the bishop only received an eighth of the total income from east of the Urr, the most westerly border of his bishopric.[217]

During the period between the account rolls of 1263–66 and 1288–90, there was an extension of the range of the justiciar's ayre in Galloway to include west of the River Urr. But the way in which the ayre was organized in Galloway was different from that in Scotia and Lothian. In the latter two regions, the justiciar went from sheriffdom to sheriffdom, holding court, and noting down his profits, which were then collected by the relevant sheriffs throughout the region. By contrast, all

---

[212] This sort of documentation would have been different to that entered on the 'roll of the justiciar concerning (*de*) Kincardine', which is mentioned at the end of a record of dispute settlement copied into Arbroath's *Registrum Vetus*. The record had been found in the justiciar's roll at Kincardine (*Arbroath Liber*, i, no. 230). This roll, however, appears to have been accounts of disputes and their settlements, not a list of fines and chattels to be collected by the sheriff *as a result of a judgment or settlement*. For more on the justiciar's roll, see Chapter 7, pp. 412–13.

[213] Profits (*lucra*) of justiciars are mentioned in an inventory made of the records kept in Edinburgh Castle in 1292: *APS*, i, p. 114.

[214] *ER*, i, p. 17.

[215] *RRS*, iv, 1, nos. 47, 51. Although his first attestation was in 1258 (*RRS*, iv, 1, no. 26), Hugh de Berkeley later seems to have lost the office, only to regain it later.

[216] This is the total of the pleas in Galloway, not including the bishop of Glasgow's eighth, but including the value of the goods of two men, beheaded in the time of Stephen Fleming, justiciar, saving the bishop's eighth (£4 7s 6d); *ER*, i, p. 17.

[217] *ER*, i, pp. 36–7.

the profits from the justiciar of Galloway were delivered to the sheriff of Dumfries in both 1263–66 and 1288–90.[218] There is no indication that the sheriff of Wigtown, attested in both 1263–66 and 1288–90, had a responsibility in 1288–90 for collecting the profits accrued by a justiciar of Galloway while west of Urr Water, as might have been expected, given that Wigtown lies west of that water boundary.[219] The situation in Galloway seems instead to have resembled that in the far north of the kingdom, where the sheriff of Inverness took ultimate responsibility for collecting the profits from Caithness and Ross, despite Dingwall attaining the status of a royal burgh in 1227 and, later, a sheriffdom. What we are therefore seeing is that justiciar ayres depended on the existence of sheriffdoms for the collection of their profits. Where there were no sheriffdoms or, at least, sheriffdoms not deemed potent enough, justiciars had to rely on the next available one: Dumfries served for Galloway; Inverness for Ross and Caithness.

Sheriffs were also expected to bear the cost of an itinerant justiciar, although the amounts each sheriff spent varied quite significantly, probably depending on how many cases the justiciar heard, how diligent he was in hearing them, and how generous each individual sheriff was (we shall see in Chapter 6 that justiciar profits from sheriffdoms were variable). Thus, Robert Mowat, sheriff of Forfar in 1264, said that he had spent £6 18d on hosting the justiciar, while David of Lochore, sheriff of Perth, only spent 14s in the same year.[220] The sheriff returned more profits from the justiciar's ayre in Forfar than the sheriff in Perth (just over £28 as compared to just under £9 in Perth): the justiciar may have been entertained better in Forfar but it is also more likely that his pleas took less time during that particular court session.[221]

This, then, was the ayre as it appears from the 1263–66 account roll. The justiciars of Scotia and Lothian intermittently went on ayres around their region of the kingdom. Sometimes they went on ayres in successive years, as was the case when Hugh de Berkeley, justiciar of Lothian, went on a much more substantial ayre than his predecessor, Stephen Fleming, had been able to do the year before.[222] But in other cases there was a gap of more than a year, perhaps even two, between ayres. When an ayre did occur, it was organized by sheriffdom, and the justiciar held a

[218] *ER*, i, pp. 35–6.

[219] Alexander Comyn was sheriff of Wigtown in 1265; *ER*, i, pp. 30–1. His son and successor, John Comyn, also served as sheriff of Wigtown (*ER*, i, pp. 39, 48).

[220] *ER*, i, pp. 4, 8. Aymer Maxwell, sheriff of Dumfries, spent 41s 9d on Stephen Fleming, justiciar of Lothian and, probably, Galloway, who had completed an ayre of Galloway, perhaps in 1264 (*ER*, i, p. 17). However, Aymer's account also included food for prisoners, an explicit addition which suggests that this expenditure was not normally calculated alongside the expenses on the *officium justiciarii*. Hugh de Berkeley, sheriff of Berwick, accounted for prisoners' food separately and the amount came to over 16s (*ER*, i, p. 27).

[221] These figures are calculated after an eighth was shaved off in Forfar for the abbot of Dunfermline (*ER*, i, p. 4), and a tenth from Perth's profits which went to the prior of Restenneth (*ER*, i, p. 9). These figures are anyway much lower than the totals returned in the justiciar of Scotia's accounts, probably returned in 1266, in which Alexander Comyn raised £90 6s 8d from Forfar and £23 18s 4d from Perth. For the step-by-step process of collecting these debts in the sheriffdom, as well as for 'second teinds', see Chapter 6, pp. 374–8, 379–85. For the entertainment in the late-fifteenth-century ayre books, see Armstrong, 'Justice ayre', p. 4, note 16.

[222] *ER*, i, pp. 9–10, 27; also Carpenter, 'Scottish Royal Government', pp. 133–7.

court at the head town in each district to hear pleas. His clerks then drew up lists of fines which the sheriffs were supposed to collect and return to the king in stages.[223] Sheriffs were responsible for paying for the justiciar while he was on ayre in their sheriffdom and also for all the fines he had imposed; some sheriffs felt themselves to be unjustly burdened by the responsibility. In Galloway east of the Urr, and in the far north, where sheriffdoms were not firmly established enough even by the 1260s, the justiciar went on ayre but returned a copy of his profits to a sheriff who stood at the gateway to each region: Inverness for the north, Dumfries for the south-west. We will be dealing in more detail with what type of pleas the justiciar could hear in Chapter 5; certainly, the account roll showed that he, in places, dealt with thieves and the more generic *malefactores* ('wrongdoers'), had them beheaded or hanged, and confiscated their chattels to enrich the king's coffers.[224]

But this was the ayre as it had developed by the 1260s. The key question here is, when was the justiciar's ayre introduced and from what did it develop? The focus of what follows will be on Scotia and Lothian as it is clear from this section that there were significant developments in the range of the ayre in Galloway even between 1263 and 1266 and the earliest attested justiciar of Galloway does not anyway appear until 1258.

Justice Courts and the Justiciar's Ayre

Although the ayre is unlikely to have been introduced before the justiciarship became formally regionally based, it is still worth considering how justices would have held their courts. It will be remembered that we can only be confident of the existence of a uniform expectation that sheriffs would hold courts from the mid-1180s onwards.[225] This is also the period when the earliest evidence survives for justices holding their 'pleas' (*placita*). By 1184, it is also clear that the justice was supposed to hold a court but it is not at all clear that this court resembled anything like a journey through all the major sheriffdoms to hear the criminal cases of (at least) murder and robbery, some cases of theft and homicide and, in addition, cases initiated by brieves of perambulation, recognition, novel dissasine, and mortancestry, as Chapter 5 will show it would from the 1220s–1230s onwards.[226] The evidence for the formal makeup of the justice's court in the late twelfth century comes in the same statute of William the Lion, enacted at Perth on 30 October 1184, which also contained the confirmation or the establishment of regular sheriff courts to be held throughout his kingdom.[227] The section on the justice courts is as follows:

---

[223] See Chapter 6, pp. 375–8; Chapter 7, pp. 412–13.   [224] *ER*, i, pp. 4, 17, 31, 32.

[225] See above, pp. 205–6.

[226] Many aristocrats had jurisdiction over theft (rather than robbery), for which, see Chapter 3, pp. 157–64, and Chapter 5, pp. 285–94, 305–6, 308–15, 334–6.

[227] *LS*, c. 14.

At the summons of the justice (*iusticie*),... the bishops and abbots, earls, barons and knights, and the bishops' and abbots' stewards, ought to be present at the pleas of the justice (*iusticiarii*)[228] on the king's command.

Whereas shrieval courts were to be held every forty days, there is no similar temporal regulation for that of the justice. The statute merely states that, on the 'summons of the justice', bishops, abbots, earls, barons, and knights, and the stewards of bishops and abbots, ought to be present at his pleas. Unlike at the shrieval court, which bishops, abbots, and earls did not have to attend in person, attendance at the justice's court *was* required. But it was required only on the summons of the justice and on the command of the king.

In this 1184 statute, therefore, there was no direct link between sheriffdom and justice court; for sure, the two were dealt with in the same statute and at the same lawmaking assembly but there is no firm evidence in the statute showing an expectation that the justice would spend time at the head of each sheriffdom, hearing the relevant pleas there. Indeed, the types of men required to be present suggests that an itinerant and regular justice court, travelling through the sheriffdoms, was not even envisaged by this statute. Making all the bishops, abbots, and earls of the kingdom attend the 'justice's pleas' suggests that such pleas were one-off occasions, held when all the great men were summoned together on the command of the king. This could not have been the case when the justiciar's presence in the localities became more of a frequent and expected occurrence: it simply would have been an unrealistic expectation to demand that all the greatest lay and ecclesiastical magnates of the kingdom be present at the ayre. Indeed, two later but clear cases heard by the justiciar while on ayre at Kincardine and Aberdeen in 1281 and 1299 respectively show that only a few high-status people were present at the justiciar's courts: they were there, but there were just not that many of them and, in 1299, local knights made up the bulk of the witnesses.[229] But in the late twelfth century, when justice courts were probably more irregular, such a demand for high-status attendees would have made sense. The courts themselves would have been greater occasions in the late twelfth century than they came to be in the

---

[228] I have translated *iusticia* as 'justice' throughout the assize and assumed that the scribe of *LS*, writing in 1267×72, simply made a mistake and rendered *iustic*' as *iusticiarii* when the word occurred for the second time, possibly because he was more used to having justiciars than justices.

[229] The 1281 case was heard at Kincardine 'in the full court of the justiciar' and in the presence of Hugh, bishop of Aberdeen, Alexander Comyn, earl of Buchan and justiciar of Scotia, and Reginald Cheyne the elder, (once) the king's chamberlain, and 'many others' (*Arbroath Liber*, i, no. 230); for Reginald, see Chapter 7, pp. 431–2. The case heard in 1299, in the presence of John Comyn, earl of Buchan and justiciar of Scotia, was held at Aberdeen, and John Comyn was described as 'holding the pleas of his office next to the castle of Aberdeen in the place called Castleside'. The indicted man was eventually repledged to Arbroath Abbey's regality court at Tarves but those present at the justiciar's court were Henry Cheyne, bishop of Aberdeen, John, earl of Atholl, then sheriff of Aberdeen, William of Meldrum, Walter de Berkelay, Duncan of *Ferendr*, Henry his brother, John Fleming, Thomas of Monymusk, Patrick of St Michael, Waleran de Normanville, Andrew of *Raath* [all knights], Cristian the *iudex*, and many others. So, essentially, in 1299, there was one bishop, the earl who was the local sheriff, and a whole host of local knights, together with a *iudex* (*Arbroath Liber*, i, no. 231).

late thirteenth but only because they were not so regular or held so frequently in each sheriffdom.[230]

If not in the late twelfth century, then when might the justiciar's ayre have been introduced? The reign of Alexander II, particularly during the late 1220s, 1230s, and 1240s, was a time when additional formal responsibilities were being given by the king to his justiciar. Chapter 5 will show that standard judicial brieves became available from the king's chapel, brieves which addressed the justiciar and commanded him to initiate some form of legal process.[231] Although it is possible that some of these commands (such as that of perambulation) were introduced in a less standardized form in the late twelfth century, the 1230s was the decade when we have most of our early references to processes of recognition and novel dissasine.[232] In addition to these new methods for dealing with disputes over land, Alexander II introduced a new procedure for punishing criminals—in particular, those who had committed theft, homicide, murder, or robbery—that was to be put into practice by his justiciar of Lothian, then David Lindsay, who served as the king's justiciar of Lothian from 1243 to 1249.[233] This statute was issued on 15 February 1244.

The statute states that the justiciar of Lothian would conduct a series of inquests into wrongdoing within all the sheriffdoms of his jurisdiction (*vicecomitatuum in balliam vestram*).[234] Although applying only to the area south of the Forth, Galloway was still explicitly excluded on the basis that it had 'its own special laws', further adding weight to the probability that a justiciar of Galloway had not yet been introduced.[235] A panel of men in each vill of every sheriffdom in Lothian would make sworn accusations against those in their own village whom they believed to be murderers, robbers, thieves, or homicides. Those accused would be arrested and brought before the justiciar. The justiciar would then summon a visnet (a body of sworn men who would say what they perceived to be the truth of the case).[236] If the accused were found guilty of murder or robbery (here described

---

[230] Of course, when a high-status person (for example, when Donnchad, *nepos* of the earl of Fife, appeared before the justiciar of Fife, recorded in the 1263–66 accounts) was attached, high-status people might have attended the justiciar's court. If that did happen, it might have been because of the statute enacted in 1244, which suggests the rumblings of the notion that men ought only to be tried by their peers (*SA*, c. 2, states that indicted knights are only to be tried by a 'sworn visnet of knights or hereditary free tenants'). In addition, the so-called 'laws of Mael Coluim III', which probably date to the mid-thirteenth century, state that the king, in cases which concern himself, is not to appear before the judge himself nor appoint a judge of higher status than the accused (Madrid, Biblioteca Real MS II 2097, fo. 11v). Equally, however, it could be that higher-status people would have attended any trial of one of their peers simply to witness the potential scandal.

[231] See Chapter 5, pp. 285–94, 305–6, 308–15.

[232] For perambulation, see Cynthia J. Neville, *Land, Law and People in Medieval Scotland* (Edinburgh, 2010), pp. 41–64; and Broun, 'King's *brithem*'.

[233] David attests: A. A. M. Duncan and A. L. Brown, 'Argyll and the Isles in the Earlier Middle Ages', *Proceedings of the Society of Antiquaries of Scotland*, vol. 90 (1956–57), no. 1 (p. 218) [AII/292], no. 2 (p. 218) [AII/332]; *Scone Liber*, no. 81 [AII/313]; *Melrose Liber*, i, no. 266 [AII/315].

[234] The plural *vestram* is consistent with a singular justiciar of Lothian, not justiciars of Lothian and Scotia because, from mid-1222, the king himself had adopted the plural of majesty in his charters.

[235] *SA*, c. 2; see further, MacQueen, 'Laws of Galloway'.

[236] For visnets, see Cynthia J. Neville, 'Neighbours, the Neighbourhood, and the Visnet in Scotland, 1125–1300', in *New Perspectives*, ed. Hammond, pp. 161–73; and, more generally, Mike Macnair, 'Vicinage and the Antecedents of the Jury', *Law and History Review*, vol. 17, no. 3 (1999), pp. 537–90.

as 'felonies'), all their chattels went to the king and they presumably would be hanged or beheaded. If they were found guilty of theft or homicide (not described as 'felonies'), their chattels went to their lords—if, that is, their chattels were in the land of a lord other than the king. If those indicted of theft or homicide did belong to the jurisdiction of lords other than the king, they would be handed over to their lords or their lords' bailies; justice would then be done by lords in their own courts. If an indicted man was a knight, he was only to be tried by those deemed his peers. The statute had focussed only on those who had been suspected of wrongdoing since 1 December 1242, not any suspected prior to this date.

The statute itself may not have been designed to last for long: it could potentially have been a short-term measure designed to restore law and order, perhaps after the violence that had erupted in Lothian after the murder of Patrick of Atholl at Haddington earlier in 1242.[237] It is probable that any institutional change would not have been acceptable to lords with jurisdiction over theft and homicide in the longer term. We know that many lay and ecclesiastical lords had complete jurisdiction over theft and homicide and so would not have been happy if the consequence of this statute was a permanent requirement for the men of their vills to indict some of their men in front of the justiciar instead of themselves.[238] This point will be developed in more detail in Chapter 5. It is enough to say here that even evidence from the late fifteenth century shows lords of regalities repledging their men from out of the justiciar's ayre into their own courts.[239] It may have been that, for whatever reason, a series of intense indictments, to include those suspected from 1 December 1242 to the time of the enactment, was there as part of a single but intense crackdown on suspected wrongdoers in Lothian alone. What is interesting for this purpose is not whether this particular statute had long-term institutional force in the thirteenth century but its envisaged enforcement.

In the 1244 statute, indictments were supposed to be made by 'the good and sworn' men from each vill, together with its steward. Vills were then grouped according to sheriffdom, and, ultimately, all the sheriffdoms made up the justiciar of Lothian's jurisdiction. Any man or woman indicted was to be arrested and brought before the justiciar 'at a set day and place'. The justiciar would hear the indictments and convict those who should be convicted of their supposed offences. It is not made explicit that the justiciar would hear the indictments sheriffdom by sheriffdom but it is clear that the sheriffdom was the organizing administrative institution for the indictments made in the vill.

What all this suggests, therefore, is that a system of accusation, arrest, and trial, organized via the sheriffdom, was in place by 1244 which allowed the justiciar to

---

[237] For this, see Duncan, *Making of the Kingdom*, pp. 544–6; and Chapter 5, pp. 293–4.

[238] Even they did eventually receive the convicted's chattels and retained the right to 'do justice' (i.e. kill) the convicted man after the justiciar's judgment. This statute is discussed in Chapter 5, pp. 293–4, and Barrow, 'Justiciar', pp. 90–1.

[239] Jackson, 'Justice Ayre', pp. 17–19. Armstrong stresses that justiciars by default seem to have taken the regalities as belonging to the ayre. Only if the holder of the regality actively intervened would a person be repledged into another court. Jackson, however, situates this in the context of Grant's picture of a late-fifteenth-century decline in regalian powers, for which see Grant, 'Franchises', p. 199.

interact with the vills within the sheriffdoms of his jurisdiction without having to visit any of them directly. Instead, they came to him. That this process was already in operation allowed it to form the procedural basis of the 1244 statute in which *all* those indicted, regardless of in whose land they had their chattels, would be tried and convicted in front of the justiciar, even if they were then handed back to their lords for punishment. What we seem to be seeing in 1244 is the underlying presence of a basic structure for the communication of accusations, certainly for murder and robbery, from the very local level all the way up to the justiciar, via the administrative unit of the sheriffdom. This basic structure must have also under-lain the ayres we see in operation in the 1263–66 account roll.

Something similar had been applied in Scotia by the time of the 1263–66 accounts. The only bit of information we have for this is under one of Andrew of Garioch's accounts as sheriff of Aberdeen.[240] This records a remittance of £32 to the sheriff, which had been the fine on four men who failed to find pledges for their indictment at a particular time and place 'in the presence of the justiciar'. The king pardoned their fine on account of their poverty. The 1244 statute does not give any information on finable offences, such as failing to find a pledge to secure appearance, but the emphasis in the account roll on the presence of justiciar and its use of the word 'indictment', which would become far more common in the fourteenth century (and then the word 'dittay' in the fifteenth), suggests that, by 1263–66, indictments were made in Scotia via the sheriffdom and those indicted therefore had to provide sureties to guarantee their appearance before the justiciar. There are many more examples in the account rolls which detail the value of the chattels of deceased criminals, punished by death, after the justiciar had supervised the judgment upon them.[241]

It would thus be overstating the evidence to say that the 1244 statute is evidence for the introduction of the justiciar's ayre in the mid-thirteenth century. What the statute shows us is an underlying formal and replicable procedure, organized by sheriffdom, in which accused individuals were brought before the justiciar and then either punished (and their chattels confiscated) or handed back to the rele-vant lord to be tried again. Although 1244 cannot therefore be used to date the introduction of the ayre itself, it can be used to locate a point by which the struc-tures of the ayre were already in existence. When seen in the context of the addi-tional responsibilities and remedies given to the justiciars of Scotia and Lothian (responsibilities that post-date the institutional regional division of the justiciar-ship itself), the 1230s and 1240s emerge as key decades when justiciars accrued an increasing number of formal civil remedies and were expected to follow a formal procedure in criminal matters.[242] It would not be at all surprising if a more formal justiciar ayre was introduced early in these decades of great change; indeed, it may well be that a regional ayre was introduced around the same time as a regional division. That the ayre and the division went together cannot be proven; however, it makes sense to see a major and substantial change in the conceptualization of the jurisdiction of the justiciar to be accompanied by a substantial change in practice—namely, the introduction of the regional ayre.[243] Although such ayres were never held as regularly as twice a year, a relatively frequent journey through the sheriffdoms was a way in which their new responsibilities were discharged in a systematic but not overly burdensome way.

Thus, although there is evidence for justice-pleas from 1184 onwards, the regional ayre was not introduced until sometime later, probably during the 1230s or early 1240s but just possibly at the same time as, or shortly after, the royal justice of the late twelfth century had developed into the regional justiciar of the late 1210s/1220s. Justice/justiciar courts also changed in composition, from being ad hoc assemblies at which the greatest men of the kingdom were expected to be present, to being more locally based courts, held at sheriffdoms as part of a wider regional ayre, which some *potentes* attended but, perhaps more importantly, so too did the knights of the local area. This new chronology for the justiciar therefore posits that the period from the late 1210s to 1240s saw the emergence of the regional justiciars of Scotia and Lothian, who were expected to travel around their jurisdictions hearing pleas in each of the sheriffdoms under their control. This makes sense in the light of the additional responsibilities that justiciars were allocated from 1230 onwards, in response to new legislation of Alexander II, who used the office of justice/justiciar much more regularly than his father, William, had ever done. Indeed, it is hard to imagine that the changes to civil procedures that occurred from 1230 onwards could have taken place without the justiciar already having structural contact with the sheriffdoms in his jurisdiction. The remedies introduced in the 1230s will be examined in Chapter 5.

There were thus profound changes to the justice/justiciar during the reigns of Mael Coluim IV, William the Lion, and Alexander II. The office changed from involving an ad hoc royal delegate, located south of the Forth, to one who appeared north and south of the Forth, and held very high status but intermittent courts. By the end of the reign of Alexander II, a regional justiciar had emerged. This regional justiciar had more formal responsibilities and held an ayre through the sheriffdoms under his jurisdiction. The key period of change appears to have been the late 1210s/1220s–early 1240s, when justices were recorded as justiciars of Lothian or Scotia, and when an administrative base for the justiciar's ayre developed. We thus cannot push the origins of the formal regional justiciarship (and perhaps the ayre itself) much before 1220. Although it might be thought that the justice-ship of Earl Donnchad may have created an *ad hoc* regional division, Donnchad's regional specificity may reflect a real division in legal structure between north and south of the Forth, a division which was only gradually eroded during the second half of the twelfth century (justices, for example, are only attested as permanent parts of the legal landscape in Moray in the late 1180s). But even when justices were frequent features north of the Forth, they were still very different from the regional justiciars that had certainly developed between the late 1210s and 1240s. Attempting to identify a regional justiciarship in the second half of the twelfth century, therefore, misunderstands the nature of royal officialdom in this early period, as well as the

---

[243] I have benefited much from discussions with Dauvit Broun on this point.

chronology of institutional development. Justices in the second half of the twelfth century operated in both Lothian and Scotia but on a less formal basis than the regional justiciars who followed them. The jurisdiction of justices may well have been exceptional, rather than routine, whereas the jurisdiction of regional justiciars was certainly routine. Now, however, it is time to turn to the last official examined in this chapter: the chamberlain.

CHAMBERLAINS

Unsurprisingly, the treatise known as the 'Scottish King's Household' also has something to say about the chamberlain (*camerarius*; *chamberlain*). It states that the chamberlain should be chosen by the king's 'council and all the baronage' (*consail et...touz le barnage*), and should be someone who knows how to 'guide and govern the burghs, the demesne lands of the king, and his poor husbandmen in demesne, and will deal with wardships, reliefs, marriages and all other business of the kingdom to the profit of the crown'.[244] Some of this is anachronistic, even for the 1290s: there is no indication that the chamberlain, for example, had to be chosen by the king's council and the whole baronage; indeed, the magnates' role in appointing the major officials of government was a radical move, which had been among the Provisions of Oxford, imposed temporarily in England in 1258.[245] But the text may not be so far off in its description of the chamberlain's responsibilities, at least for the adult reign of Alexander III.[246] By the death of Alexander III, we have clear evidence that the chamberlain had responsibilities for both the burghs and the king's revenue, as this section will show.

The chamberlain is currently the most understudied of the three officials examined here.[247] This is because there is almost no twelfth-century evidence for his activity or for the form of the chamber (*camera*: the conceptual financial body into which revenue was paid). Thus, G. W. S. Barrow found it understandably hard to write much about the chamberlain in either of his two marvellously full introductions to the acts of Mael Coluim IV and William the Lion; the charters just did not give enough information with which he could work.[248] All they provided were the names of individual chamberlains and three references to the king's *camera*, which did reveal that the *camerarius* first appeared early in David I's reign, while the

---

[244] 'Scottish King's Household', ed. Bateson, pp. 32 (French), 38 (translation).

[245] Mary Bateson, 'The Scottish King's Household I', *Juridical Review* (1901), pp. 405–22, at p. 410, noted that 'the idea of the council's appointment of the Chamberlain would seem to be an original one. No such proposal was made in England till the time of Richard II's minority'. But for the rather radical nature of this demand, and when it was made (during the reform movement under Henry III), see Carpenter, 'Scottish King's Household', online at <http://www.breakingofbritain.ac.uk/blogs/feature-of-the-month/october-2011-the-scottish-kings-household/>.

[246] Although it may not have been so radical in the context of the recent 'guardianship' of Scotland that persisted until the death of Margaret in 1290.

[247] There are brief remarks in Duncan, *Making of the Kingdom*, pp. 159, 208–9, 599–600, 606–7.

[248] *RRS*, i, pp. 30–1; *RRS*, ii, pp. 33–4.

camera is securely attested in a royal charter to Holyrood Abbey datable to 1141×47.[249] Even the better-documented thirteenth century does not provide much more information. There is no reference to the chamber in any of Alexander II's acts and only a few in the surviving charters of Alexander III.[250] From royal and non-royal charters, we can still know the names of the chamberlains and have, in addition, one seventeenth-century transcript of a single chamberlain's account from 1264.[251] Evidence for the chamberlain really takes off only in the early fourteenth century. The earliest surviving chamberlain's roll is dated to 1328 and there survives a series of 'articles' which the chamberlain was supposed to enquire into while on his ayre of the burghs, which was compiled between 1314 and, probably, 1329.[252]

The scarcity of the evidence probably explains why the chamberlain of the central Middle Ages has never really been the object of study in its own right. However, it is hoped that even this scarce evidence can be squeezed to greater effect. This section begins with the basics: who were the chamberlains of this period? Can we identify any changes in the type of person who held the office? How did his responsibilities change over the period? And how similar was its development to that of the other 'central' officer discussed earlier, the justice/justiciar? As with the previous two sections, the aim will be to avoid the assumption of continuity in the form of office over two centuries, as was done in the introduction to the first volume of the *Exchequer Rolls*, in which we are told that 'the *camera*...presided over by the *camerarius*...was one of the institutions for which Scotland was indebted to David I....The Chamberlain of Scotland was at once the collector and disburser of the Crown revenues and continued to be so until the time of James I', which, if taken literally, suggests real and significant continuity between the twelfth and fifteenth centuries.[253]

Who Were the Chamberlains?

A list of all those who are known to have held the office of chamberlain and when they did so is provided in Table 4.1. It is mostly based on witness lists to royal charters but, where non-royal charters provide evidence of a longer tenure of office, this evidence has been preferred. It is particularly difficult to establish firm dates of tenure for the period before 1222, because charters before this date only rarely included the year in which they were issued.

This is, of course, not a complete list: it is based on patterns of attestation to royal charters and does not allow us to reconstruct a smooth pattern of succession from chamberlain to chamberlain, even if such smooth successions did actually occur. We cannot assume that one chamberlain was immediately replaced with

---

[249] *CDI*, no. 147; see also *CDI*, no. 194; for doubts about the authenticity of this charter, see Hammond, 'Adoption and Routinization', pp. 98–9.

[250] *RRS*, iv, 1, nos. 88, 147.

[251] *ER*, i, pp. 10–11; for the 1263–66 roll, in which this account survives, see Chapter 6, pp. 351–66.

[252] *ER*, i, pp. 111–22; NRS, PA5/2, fos. 15v–18v.   [253] *ER*, i, pp. xxxiii–xxxiv.

Table 4.1. Known chamberlains of David I, Mael Coluim IV, William the Lion, Alexander II, and Alexander III

Chamberlain	Time in office
Edmund	1124×29
Philip	1128×36
Herbert	1136×60[254]
Edmund	? 1157/58[255]
Nicholas	1160×64[256]
Philip de Valognes	1165×71
Walter de Berkeley	1171–*c*.1193×
Philip de Valognes (2nd term)	×1195–1215
William de Valognes	1216×19
Henry de Balliol	1221–29[257]
John Maxwell	19 March 1231–3 July 1233×early October 1235[258]
Master David de Bernham	8 October 1235×1 October 1239[259]
Henry de Balliol	11 January 1241–16 February 1246[260]
Master Richard of Inverkeithing	8 April 1249[261]
Robert Menzies	25 April 1251–?April 1252[262]
William, earl of Mar	21 April 1252–12 February 1267 [break in 1260]
Aymer Maxwell	18 August 1260–12 December 1260[263]
Reginald Cheyne	16 April 1268–?
Thomas Randolph	2 December 1273–?
John de Lindsay	2 October 1278–4 July 1280

[254] A Hugh *camerarius* attests a charter along with Herbert *camerarius* in a charter of Earl Henry datable to 1139×41. The charter had seventeen witnesses: Herbert attested in sixth place while Hugh attested in seventeenth place (*CDI*, no. 74). The surviving evidence suggests that, within Scotland, kings only had one chamberlain. Could this Hugh *camerarius* be a mistake for Hugh *de camera*, who attests other charters of David and Mael Coluim but never without a chamberlain attesting above him (*CDI*, no. 207; *RRS*, i, nos. 228, 241). Equally, as Henry's charter was issued down in Huntingdon, it may be that Hugh was a 'chamberlain' belonging to the earldom or, indeed, Henry's own chamberlain.

[255] An Edmund the chamberlain attests a charter at Carlisle in 1157/58 (*RRS*, i, no. 139) but it is not at all clear that he was the same Edmund nor that he was a permanent chamberlain of the king of Scots.

[256] *RRS*, i, nos. 176, 178, 194–195, 198–201, 204–207, 212, 214, 221, 226, 229, 233, 239, 241–243, 245, 248, 249, 252, 256. Nicholas of Roxburgh (d.1171) had become chancellor of King Mael Coluim in the year before the king's death (*RRS*, i, nos. 260–265).

[257] Henry's last recorded appearance as chamberlain was on 25 May 1229 (*Scone Liber*, no. 72 [AII/152]).

[258] David de Bernham appears as chamberlain on 8 October 1235 (*Newbattle Reg.*, no. 23 [AII/228]), indicating that John's term had come to an end. John had, nonetheless, witnessed a charter on 21 April 1235 without the title of chamberlain (*Moray Reg.*, no. 36 [AII/218]), suggesting that he may have ceased in the office long before October; his last surviving attestation with the office was on 3 July 1233 (*Dunfermline Liber*, i, no. 101 [AII/195]).

[259] David de Bernham only appears three times as chamberlain in royal charters. Given that Henry de Balliol does not appear until 1241, it is possible David continued until this point but his latest appearance as king's chamberlain is on 1 October 1239; see Theiner, *Monumenta*, no. 100.

[260] For the appointments to the chamberlainship late in Alexander II's reign, see D. E. R.Watt, 'The Minority of Alexander III of Scotland', *TRHS*, 5th ser., vol. 21 (1971), pp. 1–23, at pp. 4–5.

[261] For Richard of Inverkeithing, see PoMS, Person ID no. 2032, online at <http://db.poms.ac.uk/record/person/2032/>.

[262] Robert Menzies's last appearance to a surviving royal act was on 20 October 1251; the first appearance of his successor, William, earl of Mar, was 21 April 1252 (*RRS*, iv, 1, nos. 13–14). It is possible that Robert was one of the *quidem alii* who, along with Alan Durward, was accused of treachery (*proditio*) against Alexander III on Christmas 1251 (*Chron. Melrose, s.a.* 1251).

[263] Aymer Maxwell attests a single brieve of Alexander III on 18 August 1260 (*RRS*, iv, 1, no. 28); William, earl of Mar, then reappears on 12 December 1260 (*RRS*, iv, 1, no. 31).

another; there may well have been time between appointments. What is of note, however, is that after the career of Nicholas the chamberlain (who left the office to become Mael Coluim's and then William's chancellor), chamberlains start having surnames. This may seem like a flippant observation but it is not: it probably indicates that the chamberlains before *c*.1165 (Edmund, Philip, Herbert, and Nicholas) were clerics, who did not, in the twelfth century, often attest with any epithet other than *clericus* ('clerk') or, in this case, *camerarius*. Indeed, it is absolutely clear that Nicholas (on occasion known as Nicholas of Roxburgh) was a clerk: he first appears as *clericus* in charters of David I during the second part of that king's reign, before appearing as chamberlain under Mael Coluim IV.[264] Moreover, Nicholas accompanied William, bishop of Moray, to meet Pope Alexander III in 1159 at Anagni.[265] Following Nicholas's appointment as King Mael Coluim's chancellor in 1164, however, there appears to have been a shift from using clerics as chamberlains to using laymen: all but two of the subsequent longer-term chamberlains in the later twelfth and thirteenth centuries were laymen, starting with the appointment of Philip de Valognes in *c*.1165, and ending with John de Lindsay in the late 1270s. The only exceptions to this general pattern were Master David de Bernham (later bishop of St Andrews) and Master Richard of Inverkeithing (later bishop of Dunkeld): both highly educated men and quick to receive promotion to major bishoprics in Scotland after their tenure as royal chamberlain. Neither held the office of chamberlain for more than a few years.

The appointment of Philip de Valognes to the chamberlainship in *c*.1165, then, appears to have been the start of a long-term trend to have high-ranking laymen serve as the king's chamberlain, the very same type of men who also held the office of justiciar in the thirteenth century: a combination of earls and lords of high status who appear at the king's court. Indeed, attending the king's court and witnessing his charters appears to have been a prerequisite for obtaining the office of chamberlain; nobody appeared out of nowhere. Thus, Henry de Balliol and John Maxwell appear in the witness lists to Alexander II's charters a few years before they obtained the office of chamberlain.[266] John Maxwell, moreover, had been sheriff of Roxburgh before he became chamberlain sometime before 19 March 1231, when he first attested a royal charter with the title.[267] This suggests that the position of

---

[264] As *clericus*, see *CDI*, nos. 153, 166–7, 173, 176, 178, 180, 194, 208–9, 213–15; *RRS*, i, nos. 114 (where his fraternal relationship with Adam, chaplain of Roxburgh Castle, is stressed), 117, 119, 120–1, 124, 127–8, 131, 133–5, 137. As *camerarius*: *RRS*, i, nos. 176, 178, 194–5, 198–201, 204–7, 212, 214, 221, 226, 229, 233, 239, 241–3, 245, 248, 249, 252, 256.

[265] *Chron. Melrose, s.a.* 1159.

[266] For Henry Balliol, see Fraser, *Carlaverock*, ii, 404 [AII/53]; *CDS*, i, no. 808; *Inchaffray Chrs*, no. 40 [AII/56] (first attestation as chamberlain is in *Paisley Reg.*, p. 253 [AII/57]); for John Maxwell, see *Melrose Liber*, i, nos. 184–5 [AII/46, AII/47]; *Paisley Reg.*, pp. 47–8 [AII/160], 172–3 [AII/145], 213–15 [AII/138, AII/139], 253 [AII/57]; *Arbroath Liber*, i, no. 113 [AII/64], 134 [AII/165]; *Moray Reg.*, no. 32 [AII/142]; *Kelso Liber*, i, nos. 7, 15 [AII/68]; Raine, *North Durham*, App., nos. 63–5 [AII/72, AII/74, AII/87]; *Glasgow Reg.*, i, nos. 118 [AII/80], 119 [AII/81], 135 [AII/128], 137 [AII/102]; *Ayr Burgh Charters*, no. 3 [AII/82]; *Melrose Liber*, i, no. 245 [AII/123]; *St Andrews Liber*, pp. 232–6 [AII/143] (first attestation as chamberlain is *Melrose Liber*, i, no. 175; BL, Cotton Charter xviii, 4 [AII/167]).

[267] For John's attestations as sheriff of Roxburgh, see *Glasgow Reg.*, no. 129 [AII/106], 133 [AII/108], 138 [AII/107]; *Melrose Liber*, i, no. 278 [AII/114]; *Arbroath Liber*, i, no. 171 [AII/118].

chamberlain had become more akin to that of the justiciar than that of the chancellor, which remained the preserve of clerics and bishops. Although requiring handling of written records and substantial sums of money, the chamberlainship and the justiciarship were given to one of the king's lords and close followers, men who were also integrated into the government of the realm by accompanying the king on his itineration and often serving as other officials elsewhere. For example, Thomas Randolph, chamberlain in the 1270s, was also sheriff of three places: Roxburgh, Berwick, and Dumfries.[268] Reginald Cheyne, chamberlain in the late 1260s, was sheriff of Kincardine (or the Mearns) in the mid-1260s as well as farmer of the king's thanage of Formartine.[269] Like Alexander Comyn, earl of Buchan, and long-standing justiciar of Scotia from (during his second term) 1260 to 1285, William, earl of Mar, occupied the corresponding position of chamberlain for a lesser but comparable amount of time, certainly between 1252 and 1267.[270]

The expectation that the office of chamberlain would be held by a layman may only have developed *after* one or more laymen had served in the role. Philip was succeeded by Walter de Berkeley who during his life held land in Roxburghshire and Angus and then Galloway.[271] Although the dating cannot be precise, Walter seems to have ceased in the office shortly before 1195, whereupon Philip served for a second term.[272] Philip died in 1215, and was succeeded by his son, William de Valognes, who died four years later in 1219.[273] William's successor was Henry de Balliol, who held lands in Roxburghshire but had married one of William de Valognes's two daughters before 1233 while he was chamberlain (his last appearance was on 16 February 1246 and he died later that year).[274] Whether Henry's choice of bride was affected by the fact that he was holding the office of chamberlain, which had been in the Valognes family for the past twenty years, is not clear

---

[268] For his attestations as chamberlain under Alexander III, see *RRS*, iv, 1, nos. 87, 99, 164; as sheriff of Roxburgh, see *RRS*, iv, 1, no. 70; as Berwick, see *RRS*, iv, 1, no. 131; Dumfries, *Melrose Liber*, i, no. 206.

[269] As chamberlain, see *RRS*, iv, 1, no. 69; as sheriff of Kincardine, see *RRS*, iv, 1, no. 164; BL, Additional MS 33245, fo. 160r; *ER*, i, pp. 12–13 ('Roberti'; [*sic*] for 'Reginaldi'), 20–1; for farmer of the thanage of Formartine, see *ER*, i, p. 21.

[270] For William, earl of Mar, as chamberlain, see *ER*, i, pp. 10–11, and *RRS*, iv, 1, nos. 14–19 (break for Aymer Maxwell; *RRS*, iv, 1, nos. 28, 31), 43–44, 47–48, 54–55, 57–58, 60, 62.

[271] For Walter's lands, see Duncan, *Making of the Kingdom*, p. 176.

[272] Walter attests as chamberlain in the late 1180s and early 1190s: *RRS*, ii, nos. 284 (probably April 1189), 292 (1189×93), 293, (1189×c.1193), 295 (1189×90), 342 (1190×t.1193), 343 (1189×c.1193), 348 (1189×c.1193), 165 (1193×95, perhaps 1193); Philip de Valognes attests as chamberlain: *RRS*, ii, nos. 300 (1193×95), 347 (1189×95), 373 (1189×95), 374 (c.1193×95), 375 (1195?), 376 (17 April 1195×99, probably 1195, when day and month dating clauses were introduced), 377 (5 May 1195×99, probably 1195). Philip attests thereafter. What this shows is that Walter de Berkeley ceased as chamberlain between 1193 and 1195; from 17 April 1195, Philip de Valognes remained the only chamberlain on record until his death in 1215.

[273] Philip's last attestation is on 3–6 April 1215 (*Melrose Liber*, i, nos. 174 [AII/14], 255 [AII/15]; ii, 366 [AII/16]; NRS, RH6/24 [AII/17]). William de Valognes's first attestation as chamberlain is on 24 May, probably 1216 or 1218 (*Arbroath Liber*, i, no. 108 [AII/29]); Raine, *North Durham*, App., no. 61 [AII/31]; *Spalding Misc.*, ii, nos. 5 (pp. 305–6) [AII/32], 6 (p. 306) [AII/33]; *Arbroath Liber*, i, no. 111 [AII/34]; *Scone Liber*, i, no. 68 [AII/38].

[274] For Henry, PoMS, no. 1420, online at <http://db.poms.ac.uk/record/person/1420/>; see G. P. Stell, 'Henry de Balliol', *ODNB*, online at: <http://www.oxforddnb.com/view/article/1207>.

but it seems that, by the second chamberlainship of Philip de Valognes, it had become a general expectation that the chamberlain would be a layman, even if two high-ranking clerics held the office for short periods of time in the 1230s and 1250s respectively. The use of earls and lords as the major officials of the kingdom is a theme developed in more detail in Chapter 7; it is enough to say here that the lay chamberlain could only have become an expectation after laymen had success-fully performed the role for a while.[275] If so, then the last quarter of the twelfth century, during the chamberlainships of Walter de Berkeley and Philip de Valognes, is when we should locate this change.

There is, however, one problem with this scenario. It has become a common-place in scholarship to identify Herbert the chamberlain, not Philip de Valognes, as the first lay chamberlain. Herbert held the office for over thirty years. It was G. W. S. Barrow who, in 1960, first put forward the evidence that Herbert was not a cleric but a layman.[276] He did so on the basis that he held land (Kinneil in West Lothian) and had children: two sons (Stephen and William) and an unnamed daughter.[277] This might seem like compelling evidence for Herbert's lay behaviour. But clerics did hold land by gift of the king nor was it unusual (even if not strictly allowed) for them to have children who would consent to any gifts they might make from their land.[278] Moreover, there is other evidence that strongly suggests that, despite his capacity to father children, Herbert was a cleric. This evidence comes from charter witness lists of the reign of Mael Coluim IV. This may seem like a problematic form of evidence, because the scribes of the surviving acts of both David and Mael Coluim IV did not regularly divide witnesses into two groups, cleric and lay, as would become more frequent by the end of the twelfth century.[279] But some scribes really did take care to do so, especially in long and formal charters to religious or ecclesiastical institutions, which often contain long and quite stylized witness lists.[280]

---

[275] See below, Chapter 7, pp. 417–34.   [276] *RRS*, i, p. 30.

[277] *RRS*, ii, no. 48, records the gift Herbert had made of Borrowstoun in West Lothian to Hugh Giffard along with his daughter in marriage. Herbert, with the consent of his sons, Stephen and William, gave the church of Kinneil to Holyrood Abbey (*RRS*, i, no. 196). William is called 'William, son of Herbert the chamberlain' in *RRS*, i, no. 213 (1161×64).

[278] James A. Brundage, *Law, Sex and Christian Society in Medieval Europe* (Chicago, IL, 1987), particularly chapters 5–7.

[279] For example, David gave a net in the River Tay to St Andrews Cathedral Priory in *c.*1140, essentially giving them fishing privileges there (*CDI*, no. 88). The charter was witnessed (in order) by Hugh de Morville, Earl Donnchad (I), Herbert the chamberlain, Robert *de sigillo*, Ranulf de Sules, Robert de Bourgogne, Alwin mac Arkil, and Robert of Perth. Herbert and Robert thus appear in the middle of a group of otherwise identifiable laymen. It is certain that Robert *de sigillo* was a clerk, and had responsibility for the king's seal but what was Herbert? Was he a layman attesting generally among laymen? Or was he a cleric, attesting before the other cleric in the witness list, Robert *de sigillo*? For another ambiguous example, see *CDI*, no. 129, probably issued in 1144, which was witnessed first by Robert, bishop of St Andrews, then Earl Donnchad, then William the chaplain, then Herbert the chamberlain, then Alfwin mac Arkil, and finally Malothen the marischal.

[280] Not all did; see for example, *RRS*, i, no. 174 (1160 confirmation charter to St Andrews), wit-nessed by Gregory, bishop of Dunkeld, Andrew, bishop of Caithness, Geoffrey abbot of Dunfermline, Matthew the archdeacon, Earl Cospatric, Hugh de Morville and his son Richard, Gilbert de Umfraville, Walter fitz Alan, Herbert the chamberlain, Merleswain, Ness son of William, David Olifard, Robert de Brus, Ralph son of Dunegal, Philip de Colville, Richard Comyn, Thomas of

The strongest evidence that Herbert was simultaneously a cleric and a father is from one of these charters: Mael Coluim IV's formal confirmation to Kelso Abbey, which is famous because of the decorated first initial 'M', which depicts David I and Mael Coluim IV each enthroned underneath the two diagonal descendors of the letter, issued in 1159.[281] The scribe of this charter divided the witness list into four: bishops, the royal family, then other clerics, and finally laymen not of the royal family. Herbert the chamberlain appears among the clerics, between Thorald, archdeacon of Lothian, and Nicholas the clerk. Other people listed in this section were four abbots, the king's chancellor, the prior of St Andrews, two archdeacons, three clerks, two masters, and two chaplains.[282] The first witness among the laymen was Godred, king of the Isles, who was followed by four earls, then Uhtred, son of Fergus, the son of the then lord of Galloway, then a number of other lords who did not hold formal title. In short, if Herbert had been a layman, one would expect to find him among the laymen and not among the clerics, who are clearly divided from one another. At this point (1159), Herbert was nearing the end of his long tenure as chamberlain. Herbert should thus be seen as one of a successive series of clerical chamberlains in the reigns of David I and Mael Coluim IV and not the first of a later series of lay chamberlains, which only began in the reign of William the Lion, under the chamberlain-ship of Philip de Valognes, and probably only became a general policy after successive laymen had performed the office: Philip himself, Walter de Berkeley, Philip's son, William, and William's son-in-law, Henry de Balliol.[283]

If the type of person holding the office of chamberlain changed, can we identify similar changes in the office itself?[284] The earliest clerical chamberlains—Edmund, Philip, Herbert, and Nicholas—always attest royal charters with the title *camerarius*. Herbert and Nicholas did so extremely frequently. Herbert attested forty-one surviving charters of David I, Earl Henry, and Mael Coluim IV during his *floruit* of 1136×60 while Nicholas, as chamberlain, attested twenty-seven of Mael Coluim IV's between *c*.1160 and *c*.1164.[285] This suggests that, although these clerics may

---

Lundin, Roger de *Theruieth*, Walter the clerk, Richard of the Hospitallers, Robert, brother of the Temple.

[281] *RRS*, i, no. 131; the original is on display in the National Library of Scotland; see also *RRS*, i, no. 195. *RRS*, i, no. 131, is dated to 'the year from the Incarnation of Our Lord 1159'. Barrow assumed that this calendar year began on Lady Day (25 March), noting also that Mael Coluim crossed into Normandy on 16 June 1159 and did not return until 1160 (*RRS*, i, p. 192, note 2; *RRS*, i, pp. 114–15).

[282] The order of the witnesses is: Walter the chancellor, Robert, prior of St Andrews, Matthew, archdeacon of St Andrews, Thorald, archdeacon of Lothian, Herbert the chamberlain, Nicholas the clerk, Richard the chaplain, Master Andrew, Master Arthur, Walter, clerk of the chancellor, John, nephew of Bishop Robert (of St Andrews, perhaps his son?), Serlo the clerk, Soloman, chaplain of Bishop Herbert (of Glasgow), and Elias, clerk of Bishop Herbert.

[283] For Philip's career, see Barrow, *Anglo-Norman Era*, pp. 23–4.

[284] There has been work on the personnel of the chamber, some of whom are given the epithet *de camera*. For comment on these figures, see *CDI*, p. 34; *RRS*, ii, pp. 33–4.

[285] For Herbert, see *CDI*, nos. 53, 56, 63, 65, 67, 70, 74, 76, 80, 88–9, 91, 93–5, 100, 105, 107, 112, 113, 128–9, 135, 138, 147, 151, 153, 155, 158–9, 166, 171, 172, 206–7, 215; *RRS*, i, nos. 114, 117, 131, 134, 174. For Nicholas see *RRS*, i, nos. 176, 178, 194–5, 198–201, 204–7, 212, 214, 221, 226, 229, 233, 239, 241–3, 245, 248, 249, 252, 256.

have had surnames (whether patronymic or toponymic), scribes of royal charters stressed their primary identification of chamberlain.[286]

Our earliest lay chamberlains, however, did not always attest with the title *camerarius*. In this, they differed from their clerical predecessors. Instead, the phenomenon looks more similar to the way in which scribes gave the title of justice to the person who held the office in the second half of the twelfth century and the beginning of the thirteenth. Our earliest attested justices—David and Walter Olifard, and Earl Donnchad—appear more frequently *without* their title than they do with it. A similar but not identical trend occurs with the lay chamberlains between *c*.1165 and *c*.1188. During this period, Philip de Valognes and Walter de Berkeley frequently witnessed royal charters without their title during this period when we know they both held the office. Philip de Valognes, for example, attested nine surviving charters with the title of *camerarius* between 1165 and 1171, when he first held the office, but also attested a further ten charters without any official designation in the same period.[287] Walter de Berkeley attested nineteen surviving charters without his title and fifty-three with it throughout the period of his chamberlainship (1171–*c*.1193).[288] This may seem like a strong preference for attesting *with* his title but when one considers that Walter appears with his title in *all* charters that post-date *c*.1188, the figures look less stark when analysing the previous attestations. Before *c*.1188, Walter attested nineteen surviving charters without his title but thirty-three with it.

That Walter attested *all* the surviving royal charters issued after *c*.1188 with the title of *camerarius* suggests that the practice of giving lay chamberlains their official title when they attested royal charters had become increasingly important. The second tenure of Philip de Valognes bears out this hypothesis. Between *c*.1193 and his death in 1215, Philip attested a massive seventy-six surviving charters with the title of chamberlain but only four without it.[289] Moreover, one of the four was, in fact, the payment plan that seems to have been part of the Treaty of Norham made with King John of England in 1209.[290] Members of the aristocracy did not have

---

[286] Nicholas *camerarius* was Nicholas of Roxburgh but he never appeared in witness lists with this toponymic. The closest reference to this was his attestation to *RRS*, i, no. 114, in which his brother was listed as 'Adam, chaplain of Roxburgh Castle' and Nicholas as 'Nicholas the clerk, his brother'.

[287] As *camerarius*: *RRS*, ii, nos. 36, 45, 47–48, 59, 69, 75, 106 (although here just *Philippo camer'*), 111; without the title of *camerarius*: *RRS*, ii, no. 30, 33, 34, 39, 60, 62, 81–3, 102.

[288] With *camerarius*: *RRS*, ii, nos. 131, 134, 135–6, 148, 153, 154–5 [155 is a later summary], 158, 162, 175, 178, 181 (as Waltero Cam), 184, 190, 195, 197, 200–2, 203, 206–8, 215–16, 218–19, 222–4, 226, 228, 237–8, 240, 244–5, 248–50, 255, 266, 277, 284, 287 (Barrow deems this spurious but 'possibly based on an authentic original'; *RRS*, ii, p. 310), 292, 293, 295, 300, 342, 345, 348, 365; without *camerarius*: *RRS*, ii, nos. 130, 133, 137, 139–140, 142, 143 (inflated but authentic witness list), 146, 152, 159, 166, 194, 199, 204, 210–11, 214, 233, 234.

[289] With *camerarius*: *RRS*, ii, nos. 347, 373–8, 382–3, 385–6, 389–92, 395, 397, 408–12, 415–20, 422, 424 (inflated; *RRS*, ii, p. 402), 427–8, 434–6, 438, 443–7, 453–4, 458–64, 467, 468 (but *cancellario* for *camerario*), 469, 474, 484–5, 489, 492–5, 500–2, 506–7, 510–14, 520, 522; NRS, GD119/2 [AII/12]; *Melrose Liber*, i, nos. 174 [AII/14], 255 [AII/15]; ii, 366 [AII/16]; RH6/24 [AII/17]; without *camerarius*: *RRS*, ii, nos. 421, 429, 488, 491.

[290] *RRS*, ii, no. 488, discussed in A. A. M. Duncan, 'John king of England and the Kings of Scots', in *King John: New Interpretations*, ed. S. D. Church (Woodbridge, 1999), pp. 247–71, at pp. 256–61. The 1209 treaty was recently discovered by David Carpenter; for the text and translation see David Carpenter, *Magna Carta: A New Commentary* (London, 2015), pp. 473–5.

their internal governmental title recorded in such diplomatic documents where status seems to have mattered more than office. The general trend is thus clear: the earliest lay chamberlains were not always called by their title, in contrast to their clerical predecessors. By the end of the twelfth century, if a lay lord was a chamberlain, he was titled as such in a royal charter. This trend continued under Alexander II and Alexander III: when chamberlains were in office, they attested royal charters with their title.

It might, of course, be thought that the reason some charters included the chamberlain's title and others did not was because some charters were drafted by royal scribes and others by beneficiary scribes. If so, the change in the pattern of attestation would not have denoted any real institutional change. Even if a (controversial) division between royal scribe and beneficiary scribe (or non-royal scribe) was maintained, the evidence still would not justify this objection. Scribes who we know were key members of the king's *capella*, such as Richard of Lincoln, did enter Walter de Berkeley, for example, into a witness list without his title of chamberlain during the very period when we know he held the office.[291] Until the late 1180s, therefore, scribes did not routinely include the official title of lay chamberlains when writing out witness lists. After this period, the overwhelming trend was the opposite: the title of chamberlain was included routinely and the exceptions in this later period often prove the rule.

What are we to make of this? That the earliest lay chamberlains were not routinely entitled as such suggests that their primary identity and reason for being included in the witness lists was not their official title: it was themselves, as individuals, members of powerful families, as lords, and, above all, as people of sufficient standing and relationship with the king as to attest his charters frequently. Thus, personal status remained, on the whole, enough; official title was not always needed and may only have been deployed when required. By the end of the twelfth century, however, this had changed: the office of chamberlain had become important enough and of great enough status to be included alongside its holder's name. By this point, when a lay chamberlain witnessed a charter, he witnessed not only as himself but also as chamberlain. The only explanation for this change must be that the office itself had developed more institutional permanence and governmental importance between the 1160s and the late 1180s, by which point the title started to be used almost without exception in every surviving attestation made by a known chamberlain.

This explanation makes sense in the context of related developments. It will be argued in Chapter 6 that an early system of probative accounting and auditing developed during the 1190s: that is, officials in charge of collecting the king's revenue started being summoned to return and account for their duties at particular sessions of the king's court, where their monies were paid into the king's

---

[291] Richard of Lincoln's wonderful charter, important for Chapter 2 (discussed at pp. 93–4, 97), BL, Additional Charter 76697, gives Walter as 'Waltero de Berkel' in a period when we *know* he was the king's chamberlain (*RRS*, ii, no. 152); see further Richard's charters: *RRS*, ii, no. 133, 137. Walter is not given the title of chamberlain in either of these two charters.

chamber.[292] These sessions started being recorded on parchment rolls: the earliest accounting roll we know of probably dates from 1199 and the earliest shrieval accounts from 1204 (neither, however, survives). We can thus reasonably assume that financial auditing had begun in some form by the end of the twelfth century. The development of such a system would have required more formal and numerous responsibilities for the chamberlain to take on. As we shall see in the next section of this chapter, the chamberlain was the official with overall responsibility for the total amounts returned within the kingdom. He also supervised the audit session. By the 1260s, the chamberlain also had responsibility for doling out the king's gifts, for his entertainment, for his purchases (particularly his wine consumption), and for paying his officials. While we cannot tell if the system of accounting that developed in the late twelfth century required the chamberlain to perform all the tasks he would by the 1260s, we can be sure that the introduction of an auditing procedure would have had as its cause and consequence an increased status for the position of chamberlain. This, above all, must explain why it became necessary for the title of chamberlain to be recorded when its holder attested a royal charter: the chamberlain, the person responsible for the king's income and expenditure and who interacted with all the royal officials, had to attest the king's charter *as chamberlain* and not just as the man who also happened to perform that role.

In many ways, the developments in the position of chamberlain also mirrored (at a slightly earlier date) that of the justice/justiciar. Up to the regional division of the justiceship by, at the latest, the late 1210s/early 1220s, justices attested with and without their title. But during the early thirteenth century, William Comyn started attesting *with* his title of justice (or justice of the Scots) more frequently than he did without it.[293] After the regional division, it was so frequent for justiciars' titles to be included that one might think that the scribes of royal charters had received a policy directive: 'include the title of office!'. Even when a justiciar was an earl, as were William and Alexander Comyn, he was predominantly recorded with his title of justiciar of Scotia or Lothian. Indeed, some even adopted their justiciar-title in their own charters, which had nothing to do with their formal responsibilities as justiciar.[294] Being justiciar by this point added to a lord's status; it had an institutional permanence that increased the holder's status as well

---

[292] See Chapter 6, pp. 351–66.

[293] With the title: *RRS*, ii, nos. 465, 472, 475, 485, 489–90, 492, (?)493 (did the *iust* belong to William Comyn as well as David Lindsay?), 497, 502, 522, 523; Fraser, *Grant*, iii, no. 3 [AII/5]; *Balmerino Liber*, no. 3 [AII/23]; *Glasgow Reg.*, i, nos. 132 [AII/25], 134 [AII/26]; *Scone Liber*, nos. 68–70 [AII/38, AII/158, AII/41]; *Arbroath Liber*, i, nos. 103 [AII/89], 108 [AII/29], 113 [AII/64]; NRS, GD 236, Gibliston titles no. 1 (awaiting listing) [AII/30]; *May Recs*, no. 19 [AII/35]; Fraser, *Lennox*, ii, no. 3 [AII/49]; *Foedera*, I, i, 165 [AII/60]; *Paisley Reg.*, pp. 172–3 [AII/145], *Moray Reg.*, nos. 25 [AII/61], 32 [AII/142]; Raine, *North Durham*, App., no. 63 [AII/72]; *RMS*, i, App. 1, no. 55 [AII/93]; *RMS*, iii, no. 2132(4) [AII/129]; *Dunf. Reg.*, nos. 74 [AII/135], 78 [AII/134]; *Holyrood Liber*, no. 71 [AII/141]; *St Andrews Liber*, pp. 236–7 [AII/136]. Without the title: *RRS*, ii, nos. 466–467, 469, 474, 479, 491, (?)493 (did the *iust* belong to William Comyn as well as David Lindsay?), 496; *Coupar Angus Rental*, i, no. 22 [AII/11]; *Arbroath Liber*, i, pp. 105–7 [AII/18–20]; *Inchaffray Chrs*, App. no. 4b [AII/39]; *Kelso Liber*, ii, no. 399 [AII/42]; *Melrose Liber*, i, nos. 184–5 [AII/46–7]; *Moray Reg.*, no. 52 [AII/65].

[294] 'Willelmus Cumin comes de Buhhan Justic' Scoc' salutem' (*St Andrews Liber*, p. 252).

as socio-economic position in a way that being the king's justice had not in the preceding century. By the beginning of the thirteenth century, being a chamberlain must have performed a similar function.

The Chamberlain's Account of 1264 in Context

The development of audit sessions in the late 1190s must have affected the amount of work that went with holding the position of chamberlain. What, then, did the chamberlain have to do? It is impossible to answer this question for most of the thirteenth century because almost no evidence survives about how and when chamberlains exercised their responsibilities and how money was paid into the chamber. Indeed, the earliest relatively full piece of evidence for the chamberlain's duties comes from 1264, at which point auditing had been occurring for over half a century. In addition, there is material surviving in Haddington's second transcript of a roll containing the accounts from 1288 to 1290.

The 1264 source is in Haddington's transcripts and excerpts from an original account roll covering the years 1263–66. They contain one account of the then chamberlain, William, earl of Mar.[295] Haddington seems to have copied out Earl William's account in full; accordingly, one can get a sense of what the chamberlain was responsible for and on what he spent the king's money.[296] Earl William returned his account in 1264 at Scone on a Thursday and, although Haddington did not give the day and month of the original account, this information was present in the source he was using. The account covered three accounting terms, from Whitsun 1263 to Martinmas 1263; from Martinmas 1263 to Whitsun 1264; and then from Whitsun 1264 to Martinmas 1264. This demonstrates that Earl William's account was heard sometime after 11 November 1264.[297] We shall see in Chapter 6 that there was no expectation that officials responsible for collecting the king's revenue had to have their accounts audited every year, even by the 1260s, so this lengthy period between the chamberlain's accounts does not seem to be particularly unusual.[298]

Earl William's account was divided into two sections: receipts and expenses. His receipts seem to have been the total formal revenue received by the king during this accounting period: they covered 'general receipts' from the *balliae* (denoting here sheriffs and bailies of individual estates) on each side of the Forth; burgh ferms (that is, the set amount each royal burgh owed the king each year); and common receipts from the profits of justice, including fines made between individuals and

[295] *ER*, i, pp. 10–11.

[296] There are no 'etcs', as would become more normal as Haddington continued in his work (which he clearly did not find *that* interesting); see below, Chapter 6, pp. 352–3.

[297] *ER*, i, p. 10: 'in stipendiis seruiencium de tribus terminis finitis ad festum Martini anno etc [domini MCC] LXIIII'. This means, however, that we do not know whether the calendar year was dated according to Lady Day (25 March), Christmas (25 December), or 1 January. When scribes of charters of Alexander II temporarily adopted calendar years in their dating clauses (between October 1221 and April 1222), it was clear that they dated the year according to Lady Day; however, the dating of *SA*, c. 2, demonstrates that the calendar year began then either on 1 January or on 25 December.

[298] See Chapter 6, pp. 357–8.

the king, as well as his income from reliefs and wardships.[299] The total came to £5313 17s 1d, although William was in arrears by just over £30.[300]

The receipts are, perhaps, less interesting than the expenses, in which Earl William had to list in much more detail what he had spent the king's money on.[301] He had spent it on horses, stipends for the king's servants, dispensing the king's gifts of money, paying for monetary knight's feus, the expenses of the king's nuncios, presumably sent abroad, and a whole host of expenses concerning royal hospitality and entertainment.[302] William had spent only £16 2s 9d on royal 'games' but a huge amount, totalling over £800, on the king's wine supply.[303] Indeed, procuring this wine involved paying foreign merchants directly; we know this because a record of a wonderful case survives in English chancery documents, which contains a complaint made by a foreign merchant, John Mazun, to Edward I of England in 1284, who then followed it up with Alexander III.[304] John Mazun had claimed that he had not been paid for the wines he had sold to one Weland, clerk of the king's chamber, who had been appointed to do the job of the chamberlain and pay a number of merchants at Haddington. John appeared and named the debt he was owed but apparently refused to produce the letter patent containing the agreement he had made with members of the king's council containing the amount of wine they had purchased. Weland had apparently not paid John because John refused to hand over this letter; John then complained to Edward, who complained to Alexander. Alexander supported his clerk: if John Mazun would return to Scotland and 'account reasonably' (*rationabiliter computatur*), he would be paid. This is an interesting case, and is a chance survival from what may have been a relatively common problem (even if it did not always involve Edward I) but it breathes a bit of life into the account roll information, which simply gives the amount the chamberlain spent each year on wine. If the chamberlain was expected to go and pay the merchants personally, it is understandable why, on occasion, someone was appointed to go in his place. In this case, it was Weland, a clerk of the chamber, who must have been ruing this particular job, given that it resulted in his name being caught up in a serious complaint from king to king.[305]

An even greater proportion of the revenue was spent on hospitality than on wine; the amount, presumably, which the king consumed when travelling around

---

[299] For the growth in burgh ferms between 1264 and 1327, see Chapter 6, note 120.

[300] The total is provided in *ER*, i, p. 10.

[301] The receipts are discussed in Chapter 6, pp. 385–7.

[302] All of this would have required a huge amount of written instruction and documentation. So, for example, money from king's gifts/monetary feus would have been confirmed by a charter in which the official who was responsible for paying the amount to the beneficiary would be named. But none of these survive in Scotland; the only evidence is from a case heard in Lanercost and so preserved among English governmental documentation in the National Archives of England. John of Swinburn was given 10 marks per year for the rest of his life, and was to be paid this by the bailie of Tynedale every year (which do actually appear in the account of bailie of Tynedale); *Cal Inq. Misc.*, i, no. 2032.

[303] The figure for wine is calculated for both 1263 and 1264: *ER*, i, pp. 10–11.

[304] *RRS*, iv, 1, no. 147. Weland was described as a 'Master' in the 1292 inventory, and had been given custody of Alexander III's will and two small rolls about the King's Wardrobe in 1282; *APS*, i, p. 115.

[305] Nor did it end there; see the continuation of the dispute after Alexander III's death in Stevenson, *Documents*, i, no. 46.

his kingdom and putting up important guests. Earl William had spent over £2224 on the king's hospitality.[306] But, rather interestingly, he did not have to pay the whole amount; the king owed just under £589 himself, which he owed to the 'country' (*patria*), perhaps indicating that the king, although king, could not suck his own kingdom dry. That the king owed money to his own government perhaps explains why he and his wife were in debt to many of the royal burghs.[307] The chamberlain was also responsible for keeping track of the queen's expenses, the amount of which had been returned to him by the queen's clerk, called Alexander.[308] A large amount of money came under 'other purchases', which presumably involved clothing and victuals spent for, or on behalf of, the king.

Other incidental information shows that the chamberlain was the official who would grant respite from fines made by individuals with the king. Chapter 6 will suggest that the majority of people who made such fines were of high socio-economic status but, when these fines were made, the chamberlain could grant some respite from their payment. Thus, in 1264, Robert Mowat, sheriff of Forfar, claimed that he should be allocated an extra £14 which he had been expected to collect because this money was part of a fine the burgesses of Forfar had made with the king but the burgesses had been granted respite of £14 'by the letter of the earl of Mar', that is, by William, earl of Mar, the king's chamberlain.[309] It will thus not be surprising to learn that the chamberlain was also the official responsible for ultimately deciding any *decidenciae* (cuts or deductions) from the amounts owed by sheriffs and bailies. In the 1288–90 roll, we learn that, in 1288, John Comyn, then bailie of Jedburgh, had asked for some allocations and deductions: the auditors decided that the chamberlain should 'find out the truth' about John's claim to deductions before granting them.[310] In addition, the chamberlain was responsible for setting the king's lands at farm. That is, he visited the lands, enquired into their value, and then fixed a sum to be paid each year to the king by whoever was given the land 'at farm'. In 1263–66, William, earl of Mar, then chamberlain, had gone north into Moray and had spent quite a long time setting lands within the sheriffdoms of Inverness and Nairn at farm.[311] Alexander de Balliol, chamberlain in 1288–90, did the same, this time within the sheriffdom of Selkirk.[312]

The 1263–66 and 1288–90 rolls also give a bit more incidental information. In 1289, the chamberlain, Alexander de Balliol, had sold some of the produce renders

[306] *ER*, i, p. 11.

[307] There debts are mentioned in the 1292 inventory of all the records kept in Edinburgh castles made on the orders of Edward I. 'Item, between two plates are 19 letters patent, that is, letters of the provost and burgesses of Dingwall, letters of the burgesses of Dumbarton; letters of the burgesses of Inverness, letters of the burgesses of Forfar, letters of the burgesses of Dumfries, letters of the burgesses of Rutherglen, letters of the burgesses of Elgin, letters of the burgesses of Wigtown, letters of the burgesses of Forres, letters of the burgesses of Aberdeen, letters of the burgesses of Cromarty, letters of the burgesses of Fyvie, letters of the burgesses of Ayr, letters of the burgesses of Stirling, letters of the burgesses of Nairn, letters of the burgesses of Linlithgow, letters of the burgesses of Dundee, letters of the commune of Kintore, by which all the above letters quitclaimed the king and queen of Scotland and all their ancestors of all the debts which they owed them, until a certain time as contained in the letters.' The debts were thus temporarily cancelled; *APS*, i, pp. 115–16.

[308] *ER*, i, p. 11.   [309] *ER*, i, p. 9.   [310] *ER*, i, p. 44.

[311] *ER*, i, pp. 19, 20.   [312] *ER*, i, p. 35.

returned to him by William Sinclair, sheriff of Linlithgow and Edinburgh, in order to obtain more cash.[313] The chamberlain was also responsible in these later accounts for ordering individual sheriffs to pay the fees of various officials. Thus, in 1290, John of Kinross paid the fee of William of Dumfries, clerk of the king's rolls, in his own account but had done so on the command (probably on the written command) of the chamberlain.[314] The 1288–90 roll also shows that some sheriffs were responsible for paying the fees of other royal officials, most notably the justiciar, and it is probably reasonable to assume that they were commanded to do so, the most obvious source for his command being the chamberlain.[315] Thus, perhaps by the 1260s, and certainly by 1288–90, the chamberlain was responsible for paying other royal officials and did so by ordering local sheriffs to make the payment, a burden that must have been determined according to the size and wealth of an individual sheriffdom, but balanced by some sort of a need for equality in determining who would do so in each accounting session.

When and how the chamberlain returned his account of all the revenue is somewhat harder to see. The information presented by the 1263–66 account roll shows that he did so at the same time as other officials, most notably sheriffs, returned theirs. But Haddington's excerpts from the 1288–90 roll may suggest that, by this point, the chamberlain returned his account independently of any other official and thus commanded his own audit. There is no chamberlain's account in 1288–90 as there is in the 1263–66 roll, although it is clear that the chamberlain was still involved in much of the business of the sheriffs of the later period, as he had been in 1263–66. The account of William Sinclair, sheriff of Edinburgh, returned in 1288, referred to an earlier account (*compotus*) of the chamberlain Alexander de Balliol audited at Haddington earlier in the year.[316] There is no evidence in the 1288–90 roll that any other official returned their account on this occasion and it may be that, by the late 1280s, chamberlains' accounts, which contained all the king's revenue, had taken on a separate institutional existence from those of individual sheriffs, justiciars, and other officials.[317] This would make sense, given that the 1288–90 accounts are much more regionally focused and coherently organized than those of 1263–66, as will be argued in Chapter 6.[318]

Moreover, by the early fourteenth century, chamberlains' accounts were recorded on separate rolls from those of sheriffs, bailies, farmers, and thanes. This is in contrast to the roll of 1263–66: it will be shown later in this book that this account roll had originally contained the accounts of various officials, each with very different responsibilities, including justiciars, sheriffs, bailies, and farmers, as well as chamberlains.[319] The earliest reference to a separate roll of the chamberlain

---

[313] *ER*, i, p. 48.

[314] *ER*, i, p. 51. For more examples, see the letters of the Guardians commanding Alexander Balliol, then chamberlain, to pay various people, either for monetary feus or for official 'fees' (the word for both was the same—*feodum*, and only sometimes *officium*); Stevenson, *Documents*, i, nos. 30, 32, 34–8, 44, 58, 60, 82.

[315] See Chapter 6, pp. 385–6.   [316] *ER*, i, p. 37.

[317] William Sinclair, justiciar of Galloway, returned a separate account in 1288: *ER*, i, pp. 36–7.

[318] See Chapter 6, pp. 365–6.   [319] See Chapter 6, pp. 355–6.

survives in a later copy of a register made by Sir John Skene in 1595, which listed five chamberlain rolls of the early fourteenth century up to the death of Robert I in 1329, of which the earliest dated to 1301 which, unfortunately, does not survive.[320] This, of course, was all that was 'extant in the register' and thus available for Skene to consult. But 1301 remains the *terminus ante quem* for the introduction of separate rolls of chamberlains' accounts. In light of this, it is not inconceivable that the reference in 1288 to the account of Alexander de Balliol did refer to a separate accounting session where one of these chamberlain's rolls would have been produced. Skene's references to these early fourteenth-century chamberlains' accounts suggest that they were heard on a more frequent basis than that of William, earl of Mar, in 1264, which, it will be remembered, covered a period of at least seventeen months. Skene recorded the presence of chamberlain's accounts from 1327, 1328, and two from 1329 under Robert I (who died in June 1329).[321] In his list of the surviving rolls under David II, Skene sometimes listed two or even three rolls dated to the same calendar year.

The earliest account of the chamberlain to survive in its original form dates from 1328, when one Robert of Peebles was chamberlain.[322] His account is dated 26 June, and was audited at Scone. It is interesting to compare this longer roll with the much shorter account made by William, earl of Mar, also at Scone in 1264. First, they differ substantially in length: the 1264 account does not even make up two printed pages in its edition, while that of 1328 takes up almost twelve pages in the same volume. What caused the length is not so much the existence of additional revenue streams in 1328 compared to 1264 but the level of detail given in 1328 for revenue and expenses already attested in only general terms at the earlier date. In short, while the account of William, earl of Mar, provided his receipts under general headings, that of Robert of Peebles was broken down, burgh by burgh and sheriffdom by sheriffdom.[323] The same is true of the expenses. Where Earl William's account listed a general heading (for example, 'king's gifts') and provided the overall total, Robert of Peebles's listed each gift made, how much it was, and then totted these up to the overall total.[324] But the overall impression is that the chamberlain in 1328 was responsible for the same sort of things as in 1264: Robert of Peebles also accounted for king's gifts, the expenses of nuncios, the king's clothing, wine and entertainment, as well as monetary feus. There were a few introductions, most notably what produce renders had been sold and accounted for in cash, and the presence of lists of debtors, but the general tenor of the accounts is the same. The difference lay, quite literally, in the detail, suggesting that much more extensive expectations about accountability and recordkeeping had developed by 1328 than had existed even in 1264.

---

[320] NLS, MS Adv. 31.3.15, fo. 1r. Here Skene is said to have listed surviving chamberlain rolls from 1301, 1327, 1328, 1329, 1329, and chamberlain's rolls from throughout the long reign of David II (1329–71). The earliest chamberlain's roll to survive (from 1328) is printed in *ER*, i, pp. 111–22.

[321] NLS, MS Adv. 31.3.15, fo. 1r.   [322] *ER*, i, pp. 111–22.

[323] *ER*, i, pp. 111–13.   [324] *ER*, i, pp. 114–15.

The Chamberlain and the Burghs in the Thirteenth Century

The 'Scottish King's Household' informs us that the chamberlain was responsible for the good governance of royal burghs. But it is very hard to identify the point when the chamberlain started going on a yearly ayre around the kingdom, enquiring into the behaviour of the burgh community and hearing cases that came to his court. The earliest account of a chamberlain's ayre is not until 1399 or 1400, when the chamberlain held his pleas at Aberdeen.[325] But it is clear that chamberlain ayres had been going on long before this. The earliest reference to chamberlain's *lucra* ('profits'), as opposed to those of the sheriff or justiciar, is again in the 1263–66 account roll, when Earl William of Mar, then chamberlain, granted himself exemption from his arrears for a paltry sum of 2 marks, acquired from 'his pleas' held at Aberdeen.[326] In addition, a memorandum attached to the so-called 'rental' of Alexander III, which listed the second teinds owed to the bishopric of Aberdeen from the sheriffdoms of Aberdeen and Banff in Alexander's reign, referred to the *iter camerarii*, demonstrating that a chamberlain's ayre was occurring in the second half of the thirteenth century.[327] What pleas were heard in this ayre, however, is hard to garner from the thirteenth-century evidence.

The Ayr manuscript, datable to 1318×29, contains a list of 'articles' which the chamberlain had to enquire into while on his ayre.[328] This included general questions—whether burgh bailies were doing justice to rich and poor equally, for example—and also more precise ones, concerning the behaviour and faithful service of brewers, stallholders, millers and dyers, butchers, the status of burgesses, the behaviour of foreign merchants, and whether anyone had abjured the burgh. This list, however, as it stands cannot date earlier than 1314 because the penultimate article tells the chamberlain to enquire into those 'holding lands in their hands which they have from the king's gift before Bannock but against the recall made at Cambuskenneth', referring to Robert I's pronouncement at Cambuskenneth on 6 November 1314 that all those who had not yet come into his peace should be

---

[325] William Croft Dickinson, 'A Chamberlain's Ayre in Aberdeen, 1399×1400', *SHR*, vol. 33, no. 115 (1954), pp. 27–36. The reference to the *iter camerarii* in *Assise Regis Willelmi*, c. 39, in *APS*, i, p. 383, actually survives in one later manuscript, known as the Arbuthnott manuscript, and formed the last section of the Arbuthnott manuscript's version of *Leges Willelmi Regis* (NLS, MS Acc. 16497, fos. 209v–210r). When Innes came to compile his comments on Thomson's *Assise*, he was unable to find a manuscript witness of the text (*APS*, i, p. 283). The Arbuthnott text is not, however, the version used by Thomson, as there are several small differences between the text in *APS* and that printed by Thomson. While it bears some resemblance to the language of William's charters to burghs, it should not be taken as an authentic law of William the Lion. The text reads: 'He enacted that the merchants of his kingdom should have their merchant guild, and they should rejoice in peace with the privilege of buying and selling within the bounds of the liberties of the burghs. And that every man should be content with his privilege and no one should occupy the liberty of another unless he wishes to risk being condemned in the chamberlain's ayre (*iter camerarii*) and punished as a forestaller (*forisstallator*).'

[326] *ER*, i, p. 11.

[327] *Aberdeen Reg.*, i, pp. 56, 57. There also appears to be a reference to the chamberlain presiding over justiciar's pleas, held at Dumbarton, in RH5/19 (*CDS*, iv, App., no. 2).

[328] NRS, PA5/2, fos. 15v–18v, beginning 'de articulis inquirendis in burgo in itinere camerarii secundum usum Scocie'; for more on the Ayr MS, see Chapter 5, pp. 301–7.

disinherited and treated as the king's enemy.[329] Because this appears towards the end of the list of articles, it is hard to know whether it was a later addition to an earlier corpus or if the whole list should be dated to after November 1314, and thus would represent a more formal way of conducting the chamberlain's ayre.

Nor is the *Leges Quatuor Burgorum* of much help either. Although the core of the *Leges* is often thought to date back to David I's reign, the development of this text has not yet been fully studied and we should be wary of assuming a Davidian origin to even some of its earliest material.[330] The first full reference to the 'laws and customs of the burgh' survives in a summary of a 1223 charter of Alexander II to the burgh of Dumbarton, whereas William's charters to Perth and Inverness merely prohibit any burgess from doing anything against 'the reasonable laws and customs'.[331] The earliest manuscript of the *Leges Quatuor Burgorum* (*LQB*) dates from 1267×72 (the same manuscript as *Leges Scocie*; the Berne manuscript) but unfortunately it is there incomplete, as the end of the treatise survives in a part of the manuscript that had become detached from the surviving section at some point in the manuscript's unrecorded history.[332] There is only one chapter in *LQB* as edited in *APS* which refers to the chamberlain and if this were ever in the Berne manuscript-text, it was in the part which no longer survives.[333] Unfortunately, we cannot tell, because the Berne manuscript-text does not contain a list of rubrics from which we could analyse the overall structure and layout of the earliest text of *LQB*. The chapter does, however, appear in the next earliest manuscript of the text, the Ayr manuscript, which also contains the articles to be asked by the chamberlain when on ayre, and is also the earliest manuscript of the legal compilation attributed to David I (*CD*).[334] The relevant chapter is the last chapter in the Ayr-text, which might suggest that it is a later addition, but it is still important to examine, so on we go.

The chapter states that the grieve or provost of each burgh must elect no fewer than four liners (people who would set the boundaries of tofts within the burgh) so that 'no complaint shall come to the chamberlain of the lord king for default of lining'. The liners were to swear that they would 'line' each toft length- and width-ways, front and back, 'following the right and old bounds of the burgh'. The chapter is thus interesting not because of the procedure it is introducing but because of its underlying assumption: that the chamberlain would hear complaints when boundaries were not lawfully delineated. The new procedure, by choosing particular men,

---

[329] NRS, PA5/2, fo. 18v: 'item de tenentibus terras in manibus suis quas habuerunt ex dono domini regis ante Bannok contra reuocationem factam apud Cabuskened', online at: <http://www.stairsociety.org/resources/view_manuscript/the_ayr_manuscript/229>. The 1314 legislation has most recently been edited in *RPS* 1314/1, online at <www.rps.ac.uk/mss/1314/1>.

[330] For important preliminary remarks, see MacQueen and Windram, 'Law and Courts', pp. 209–10.

[331] *RRS*, ii, nos. 467, 475.

[332] NRS, PA5/1, fo. 62r, where it is entitled: 'Leges et consuetudines quatuor burgorum scilicet Edinburg, Rokisburg, Berewick, Striueline, constitute per dominum David regem Scocie'.

[333] *Leges Quatuor Burgorum*, c. 105, in *APS*, i, pp. 353–4.

[334] *Leges Burgorum*, c.105; *APS*, i, pp. 353–4; reading confirmed in the Ayr manuscript, NRS, PA5/2, fo. 67v (c.105).

was meant to increase the quality of the boundaries drawn, so that the chamberlain would hear no more (or, at the very least, fewer) complaints. This suggests strongly that, before the date of the Ayr manuscript at the latest (1318×29), the chamberlain was the official to appeal to if boundary disputes had occurred and were irresolvable within the burgh. We cannot know how long the office had held this responsibility but it must pre-date the Ayr manuscript by some significant length of time because the Ayr chapter seems to be reforming an existing procedure, suggesting that some time must have passed in order for such a reform to have been necessary. If, of course, the Berne manuscript-text had preserved this chapter, then it would be further firm evidence of the chamberlain's jurisdictional responsibilities over burghs during the 1260s, the very point at which we have our earliest extant evidence for chamberlain's pleas within burghs themselves. However, the Berne manuscript is not forthcoming so neither is this conclusion.

It is of note that the charters of William the Lion, which fully confirm the privileges of the burghs of Perth and Inverness, do not mention the chamberlain at all.[335] They do mention the regulations for buying and selling, the behaviour of foreign merchants, the privileges of burgesses, the location of taverns, and where and when dyed cloth could be sold. They also mention the relationship between the burgh and the sheriffdom. But they do not mention a supervisory role for the chamberlain. No other charter to a burgh issued later during the thirteenth century mentions it either, so we should not, perhaps, read too much into this absence. It is, however, important that whoever was responsible for drawing up the king's charters to Perth and Inverness did not think it necessary to mention the chamberlain. In addition, although the chamberlain, Philip de Valognes, witnessed William's charter to Perth, he did not witness that to Inverness. The relationship between chamberlain and burgh may not have been quite so close in the late twelfth and early thirteenth centuries as it would become later and, although we do not have the evidence to posit even a vague date range for the introduction of the chamberlain's ayre, it may have developed sometime after the latter stages of the reign of William the Lion (when probative accounting was generally introduced) but well before the 1264 account of William, earl of Mar (when we have the first direct and datable reference to the chamberlain's ayre).[336]

There were thus significant changes to the office of chamberlain during the twelfth and thirteenth centuries. It is just not enough to say that David I 'introduced' the office of the chamberlain to Scotland and then leave it at that. First, the general personality of the chamberlain changed, from cleric to layman. Although under Alexander II, clerical masters held the office, they did so relatively infrequently and for relatively short periods of time.[337] Nor were the lay chamberlains mere laymen: some were earls and some had previously served as sheriffs but all

---

[335] *RRS*, ii, nos. 467, 475; for further discussion, see Dennison, 'Burghs and Burgesses', pp. 256–7, 270–4.

[336] See Chapter 6, pp. 351–66.

[337] Moreover, these masters themselves went on to be holders of major bishoprics within the kingdom. David of Bernham went on to be bishop of St Andrews, while Richard of Inverkeithing became bishop of Dunkeld; for David, see A. A. M. Duncan, 'David of Bernham', *ODNB*, online at

were frequent attendees of the king's court and had substantial landed holdings of their own. The office of the chamberlain clearly increased in status: from the late 1180s onwards, it was extremely infrequent for the chamberlain to attest a royal charter without his official title, even when (as would be the case of William, earl of Mar) he was also an earl. This pattern continues to be identifiable in the witness lists to the charters of Alexander II and III. A chronology which locates greater institutional form to the chamberlain in the late twelfth century makes sense in the context of the new chronology of shrieval power outlined earlier in the chapter. The chamberlain's role could not have been so systematic if it did not have a network of local administrative units with which to interact, a phenomenon we can only see present in Scotia (including Moray) as well as Lothian from the 1180s onwards. Moreover, it will be shown in Chapter 6 that financial auditing of all royal officials began (albeit in a piecemeal way) in the very late twelfth century, a development that must have vastly increased both the status and responsibilities of the chamberlain and the institutional links the office had with each individual sheriffdom and burgh.[338]

By the time of the 1263–66 account, the chamberlain had responsibility for *all* the king's income, and *all* his expenditure. He was also expected to account for it and did so through a relatively uniform network of royal officials. What he accounted for in 1263–66 does not seem to have been that different from the earliest extant account of 1328 but the detailed and itemized lists of 1328 stand in stark contrast to the generally expressed headings of 1264, suggesting that the chamberlain was expected to be held accountable for every individual item of expenditure in 1328, which could not have been possible by consulting the more general account of 1264. By the 1320s, chamberlains seem to be accounting for more, and more frequently.

As a result of these developments, it is therefore hard to see how far early fourteenth-century evidence on the form and structure of the chamberlain's ayre around the royal burghs of the kingdom can be used confidently as evidence for the ayre in the 1260s, by which point we know some form of judicial itineration had been introduced. When and why a chamberlain's ayre developed is extremely hard to document, although it is clear that some sort of an ayre was in place by 1264. It may be doubted, however, whether a formal *iter* was in place in the twelfth century: a period when there was no formal justiciar's ayre and, until the 1180s, not even a kingdom-wide network of sheriffdoms through which to work. Thus, while the end of William the Lion's reign may have been the period when the status of the chamberlain increased (and thus might explain why prominent laymen were increasingly given the job), the reign of Alexander II may well have been when the chamberlain obtained more formal jurisdictional responsibilities, which corresponds to when the justiciar's ayre probably developed, also during the reign of Alexander II.

<http://www.oxforddnb.com/view/article/50015>; for Richard, see Watt, *Graduates*, pp. 280–2, and PoMS, Person ID no. 2032, online at <http://db.poms.ac.uk/record/person/2032>.

[338] See Chapter 6, pp. 361–6.

CONCLUSION

Taken together, this chapter has shown that each of the three offices of sheriff, justiciar, and chamberlain underwent fundamental changes between *c*.1170 and *c*.1290. The key period of change for all three, however, was the late twelfth and first half of the thirteenth centuries under William and Alexander II. From the 1180s, sheriffs north and south of the Forth were expected to exercise jurisdiction over a defined territorial administrative unit (the sheriffdom; their *ballia*) and could hold their own courts. Royal justices—first attested by name in the late 1160s—began as high-status but ad hoc royal judicial delegates and, by the early 1220s at the latest, had developed into regional justiciars. One was in charge of Scotia; the other, Lothian. By the 1240s, we can infer that these regional justiciars were each holding judicial ayres, travelling through the sheriffdoms within their region; indeed, by this point, a justiciar's territorial *ballia* ('jurisdiction') was made up of multiple shrieval *balliae*. Chamberlains started as household clerks but, by the end of the twelfth century, were predominantly laymen of similar rank to those who held the office of justice/justiciar during the same period. It is much harder to identify when and how chamberlains began travelling around the kingdom's burghs and hearing their own pleas but it is unlikely that it much pre-dated the emergence of probative accounting more generally, a process which also involved the chamberlain returning the profits from burghs in a relatively systematic way.

In short, between the late twelfth and the mid-thirteenth centuries, a uniform structure of local government had emerged in the sheriffdom, through which the two central royal officials of justiciar and chamberlain also exercised their responsibilities. The sheriffdom was the key unit of royal government: without sheriffs, the profits justiciars raised would not have been collected and the ayre would have taken a significantly different shape; without sheriffs, chamberlains could not have paid any of the king's officials nor accounted for any of the farms from royal burghs. This was a structure that first developed south of the Forth. This was, with one exception, the region where the earliest attested sheriffdoms were located and where, it would appear, royal justices were first given enforcing powers over such basic practices as teind payment. Indeed, it is clear that sheriffs south of the Forth had more responsibilities in the early 1160s than sheriffs north of the Forth; they could hold their own courts while sheriffs north of the Forth could not. It is also clear that Mael Coluim IV thought that he had royal justices working south of the Forth but not identical figures north of it.

These therefore were major changes but, equally, it is important to stress their limitations. It must be acknowledged that a uniform structure of government through the sheriff only operated from Dumfries in the south-west, Inverness in the north, and Berwick and Roxburgh in the south-east. It was primarily a government of greater Lothian, Scotia, and the lowland part of Moray. Despite the (re) introduction of earldoms in Ross and Sutherland, and the partition of Galloway, all in the reign of Alexander II, government in the far northern and far western periphery was fed through one sheriffdom which acted as the gateway to this core area: Dumfries for Galloway and Inverness for Ross, Sutherland, and Caithness.

Nor did this structure of government develop in a vacuum. Before it was confirmed that sheriffs could hold their own courts, many had been doing so for decades and, before the justiciar formally became regional, Earl Donnchad had been acting *de facto* as such. Moreover, before there were justices and sheriffs with courts north of the Forth, there were justices and sheriffs with courts south of the Forth. But there still is a difference between *de facto* responsibility and official responsibility: we cannot say that all sheriffs from Berwick to Inverness were expected to hold courts until the 1180s, nor can we say that justiciars had responsibility over a region and were expected to conduct an ayre of all the sheriffdoms within that region until the 1220s. If we accept this chronology, it becomes far less odd that the jurisdiction of justiciars and sheriffs were not included in the prescriptive content of William the Lion's law, as was argued in Chapter 3, but were in the legislation of Alexander II.

Royal power was thus exercised through very different methods in the mid-twelfth century from those of the mid-thirteenth. Mid-twelfth-century royal officials, whether they were sheriffs or royal justices, did not cover anything like the same geographical area they would do a century later nor did they have the same formal responsibilities. There is a big difference between royal power as delegated through Earl Donnchad, who may have taken responsibility for the cases north of the Forth (and may have supervised land perambulations), and royal power as expressed through formal written legal process, whereby appellants and accused would have their cases heard sheriffdom by sheriffdom, by the justiciar of the region, in the type of ayre that Alexander Comyn, earl of Buchan, would conduct as justiciar of Scotia under Alexander III.[339] Given some of our evidence, it is understandable why it might be thought that the origins of the regional justiciarship are to be found in the mid-twelfth century and were the direct result of David's innovations in royal government but, if institutional continuity is assumed from extremely sparse and contradictory evidence, we miss the ultimately changing and live development of institutional expressions of royal power, characterized as much by the roads not taken (the maintenance of the status of the *iudex*) as by those which were (the emergence of the regional justiciarship).

That these forms of royal officials developed in the way they did must be because both longstanding local and newer lords who held their land in Scotia in particular saw benefits in performing this type of service. These benefits must have been financial as well as status-driven; certainly, by the time of the accounts of the 1260s, we know that royal officials were well rewarded for their services. Both Earl Donnchad and Earl Gille Brigte served as the king's justice (Earl Donnchad for a much more substantial time than Earl Gille Brigte); Philip de Valognes and Walter de Berkeley, both of whom held land in Angus, served as the first two lay chamberlains. All these figures served in this role before the offices themselves had increased in status and responsibility. Powerful lords were co-opted and co-opted themselves into royal service before any of the offices under consideration here had developed

---

[339] For these judicial and administrative brieves, see Chapter 5, pp. 307–34.

the kinds of formal responsibilities that we see in the thirteenth century. The same conclusion can be made for the development of shrieval courts: before it was expected that sheriffs would hold courts themselves, they were expected to be present at the courts of lords in order to confirm the legitimacy of lordly jurisdiction. The administrative changes and innovations in the late twelfth and early to mid-thirteenth centuries could not even have been contemplated without the cooperation of lords, which is evident from the start. In this again, there are basic continuities in the fundamental exercise of royal power from the mid-twelfth century to the mid-thirteenth. As Chapter 1 argued, early twelfth-century kings used and depended on communication with major magnates to increase their power in the localities. The same dynamic is identifiable a century later, although the method and functions differed: kings used major lords as their officials and in so doing were able to make royal authority felt in local society in a far more intense way than they could have done through itineration alone. The following three chapters will examine in more detail further developments in royal government (law, finance, and bureaucracy) and how the incorporation of lordly power remained an underlying dynamic in all three areas throughout the thirteenth century.

5

The Development of a Common Law, 1230–90

The chronological limits of this chapter have been chosen because they bookend the period when the Scottish common law is thought to have developed. In 1230, Alexander II enacted four pieces of legislation which, according to one interpretation, heralded the point when 'royal justice...began to assert much more strongly not just ultimate but also exclusive jurisdiction within the realm in relation to secular land' and the acceptance by society at large of 'the function of the ruler to punish and make restitution'.[1] In 1264, a charter of Alexander III stated that the king wished his people to observe both 'custom and common law (*consuetudo et ius commune*)'.[2] Common law is normally taken to mean a law upheld in royal courts, which was distinct from local custom and the canon law applied in ecclesiastical courts in front of papal judge- delegates.[3] This is also the meaning of 'common law' in England, even though Scottish common law differed significantly from its English counterpart despite also taking much inspiration from it.[4]

Previous studies of the development of common law in Scotland have concentrated on its protection of free property: pursuers could obtain a type of royal brieve known as a 'pleadable' brieve to initiate a case against another in defence of their possession or to secure their inheritance. It is also thought that these 'pleadable' brieves became so important that, over the thirteenth century, a rule developed that no one could be ejected from their inheritance without first obtaining one. This rule was confirmed by legislation of Robert I in December 1318 and is known

---

[1] *SA*, cc. 4–7 (different texts in *APS*, i, pp. 399–400); first quotation from Hector L. MacQueen, 'Canon Law, Custom and Legislation in the Reign of Alexander II', in *The Reign of Alexander II, 1214–49*, ed. Richard Oram (Leiden, 2005), pp. 221–51, at p. 249; the second from A. A. M. Duncan, *Scotland: the Making of the Kingdom* (Edinburgh, 1975), p. 541.

[2] *RRS*, iv, 1, no. 49.

[3] For work on papal judge-delegates, ecclesiastical courts, and canon law in Scotland, see T. M. Cooper, *Select Scottish Cases of the Thirteenth Century* (Edinburgh, 1944), pp. xxxv–xxxix, xlix–lii; Paul C. Ferguson, *Medieval Papal Representatives in Scotland: Legates, Nuncios and Judges-Delegates, 1125–1286*, Stair Society 45 (Edinburgh, 1997); MacQueen, 'Canon Law, Custom and Legislation', pp. 229–32, 235–9; for church statutes, see Donald E. R. Watt, 'The Provincial Council of the Scottish Church, 1215–1472', in *Medieval Scotland: Crown, Lordship and Community—Essays Presented to G. W. S. Barrow*, ed. Alexander Grant and Keith J. Stringer (Edinburgh, 1993), pp. 140–55.

[4] Hector L. MacQueen, *Common Law and Feudal Society in Medieval Scotland* (Edinburgh, 1993), pp. 1–3; for the similarities and differences between England and Scotland, see W. D. H. Sellar, 'The Common Law of Scotland and the Common Law of England', in *The British Isles: Comparisons, Contrasts and Connections*, ed. R. R. Davies (Edinburgh, 1988); Cooper, *Select Cases*, pp. xli–xlv.

in historical scholarship as the 'brieve rule'.[5] In 1296, Alexander MacDonald of Islay informed the English king, Edward I, that 'many people say that, according to the laws of England and Scotland, no one ought to lose his heritage unless he has been impleaded by brieve and named in the brieve by his own name'.[6] The thirteenth century, therefore, is not only seen as when the king established himself as the authoritative source of punishment of crime and the guarantor of all free property; it was also when standard written remedies (the 'pleadable brieves') became available from the king's chapel, creating a recognizable system of royal justice.[7] As a result, not only did the king gain a real monopoly over the definition and punishment of crime (formal and substantive criminalization), he also introduced written legal instruments to initiate cases over civil matters which were heard in the king's court.[8]

Much has been written about this important period of legal change. However, the scholarship is very diverse, contains different emphases, and comes to different conclusions. It is a very live area of debate: the picture of a thirteenth-century development of a Scottish common law has recently been challenged by David Carpenter in an article published in 2013. This chapter puts forward an understanding of thirteenth-century legal developments that is different even from Carpenter's. As a result, the scholarship of the last one hundred years on the thirteenth-century common law needs be set out so that the conclusions of this chapter can be interpreted within a clear historiographical field.

VIEWS ON THE THIRTEENTH-CENTURY COMMON LAW

The scholarship of the preceding century can roughly be divided into three groups. First is the position that developed mainly in the first half of the twentieth century which is particularly associated with the Scottish judge and politician, Thomas Mackay Cooper (1892–1955), first baron of Culross, who had been appointed Lord Advocate in Scotland.[9] Cooper stressed the importance of ecclesiastical

---

[5] MacQueen, *Common Law*, pp. 106–10.

[6] *CDS*, v, no. 152, commented on in MacQueen, *Common Law*, p. 105. It should, however, be pointed out that this letter was written in rather exceptional circumstances, and may have been an attempt to subtly resist Edward I's ambition; see the discussion in J. G. Dunbar and A. A. M. Duncan, 'Tarbert Castle: A Contribution to the History of Argyll', *SHR*, vol. 50, no. 149 (1971), pp. 1–17, at pp. 3–5, and the letter printed at pp. 16–17. For a recent challenge to the existence of the brieve rule in thirteenth-century Scotland, see David Carpenter, 'Scottish Royal Government in the Thirteenth Century from an English Perspective', in *New Perspectives on Medieval Scotland, 1093–1286*, ed. Matthew Hammond (Woodbridge, 2013), pp. 117–59, at pp. 143–53, and below, pp. 345–6.

[7] For earlier adoption of brieves (although in non-judicial contexts), see Dauvit Broun, 'The Adoption of Brieves in Scotland', in *Charters and Charter Scholarship in Britain and Ireland*, ed. Marie Therese Flanagan and Judith A. Green (Basingstoke, 2005), pp. 164–83.

[8] For the terms formal and substantive criminalization, see the literature cited in Chapter 3, p. 135, Note 115.

[9] Cooper very much viewed legal historians as *lawyers*. He wrote: 'the legal historian must be both a historian and a lawyer, but he should be lawyer first': T. M. Cooper [First Baron Cooper of Culross], 'The Dark Age of Scottish Legal History, 1350–1650', in *Selected Papers, 1922–1954* (Edinburgh,

courts, papal judge delegates, and Romano-canonical law for understanding thirteenth-century legal practice in the kingdom of the Scots, not only for church and monastic lands but also for civil cases that did not just pertain to church rights. Cooper's fundamental position (although he started to revise this towards the end of his life) was that 'the efficient and ubiquitous Papal Courts heavily encroached upon the administration of civil justice' in Scotland.[10] This was in contrast to England: 'in Scotland [justices] were acting under Papal authority and administering Canon Law while in England they were acting under Royal authority and administering common law'.[11] By these 'papal courts', Cooper meant the system of papal judge delegates which had developed in Western Christendom in the late twelfth century. Within this system, ecclesiastical and monastic institutions had the capacity to appeal to the Pope when controversies arose.[12] The Pope would then appoint 'judge-delegates', often (but not always) men relatively local to the area concerned, who would then hear the case under papal authority, and would apply canon and Romano-canonical law.

Cooper acknowledged that the majority of the surviving judgments or records of dispute settlement survived in ecclesiastical or monastic archives but, by looking at the few lay collections which did survive, he nonetheless stressed the comparative lack of litigation in lay tribunals and so concluded that 'until the later years of the 13th century important civil controversies, when not settled by agreement or arbitration, were usually left to the decision of skilled and ubiquitous ecclesiastical lawyers, who in Scotland found ample scope for their activities owing to the absence of a fully organised judicial system, and a legal profession to work it'.[13]

1957), pp. 219–36, at p. 236. His views on historians are also worth remembering. In his introduction to *Regiam Majestatem*, Cooper wrote: 'it is possible to detect three different types of reader [of *Regiam Majestatem*]. First in importance and in time comes the working practitioner in search of authorities…Next comes the academic jurist, more or less competently equipped to treat his historical sources with critical impartiality…And behind the lawyers comes the patient company of harmless drudges who toil over historical and antiquarian research': *Regiam Majestatem and Quoniam Attachiamenta Based on the Text of Sir John Skene*, ed. and trans. T. M. Cooper, Stair Society 11 (Edinburgh, 1947), p. 5. What he would have made of this chapter I dread to think. For an early summary of Cooper's import, see T. B. Smith, 'The Contribution of Lord Cooper of Culross to Scottish Law', in Cooper, *Selected Papers*, pp. xxix–xlix.

[10] Cooper, *Select Cases*, p. xxii.   [11] Cooper, *Select Cases*, p. xlv.

[12] For papal judge-delegates, see James A. Brundage, *The Medieval Origins of the Legal Profession: Canonists, Civilians, and Courts* (Chicago, IL, 2008), pp. 135–63; R. H. Helmholz, *Oxford History of the Laws of England*, vol. 1: *The History of Canon Law and Ecclesiastical Jurisdiction from 597 to the 1640s* (Oxford, 2004), pp. 89–91, 93–100; Jane E. Sayers, *Papal Judges Delegate in the Province of Canterbury, 1198–1254: A Study in Ecclesiastical Jurisdiction and Administration* (Oxford, 1971); Peter Herder, 'Zur päpstlichen Delegationsgerichtsbarkeit im Mittelalter und in der frühen Neuzeit', *Zeitschrift der Savigny Stiftung für Rechtsgeschichte. Kanonistische Abteilung* 88, ed. H-J. Becker, A. Thier, and H. de Wall (2002), pp. 20–43. The major study of papal judge-delegates in Scotland is now Ferguson, *Medieval Papal Representatives*.

[13] Cooper, *Select Cases*, p. xxvi; Peter Stein, 'Roman Law in Scotland', reprinted in Peter Stein, *The Character and Influence of the Roman Civil Law* (London, 2003), pp. 269–317. As Barrow long ago noted, Cooper's views had begun to adjust when he started to study (and, indeed, publish), the formularies surviving in the Ayr and Bute manuscript: G. W. S. Barrow, 'The Justiciar', in G. W. S. Barrow, *The Kingdom of the Scots: Government, Church and Society from the Eleventh to the Fourteenth Century*, 2nd edn (Edinburgh, 2003), pp. 68–111, at pp. 70–2. At the end of the introduction to *Select Cases*, Cooper noted that, as *Select Cases* was going into print, he had gained access to the Ayr and Bute

Thus, for Cooper, delegated papal justice took the space left unoccupied by royal justice.

What Cooper did not sufficiently allow for, however, was just how much our evidence for thirteenth-century dispute settlement is framed by the patterns of survival of the evidence.[14] We know that, by the end of the thirteenth century, kings of Scots kept central records of judicial proceedings in Edinburgh castle—but almost all (with some exceptions) of this evidence has been lost.[15] This has resulted in some significant imbalances in our evidence. There are roughly 324 surviving records of dispute settlement in Scotland dating from the late twelfth and thirteenth centuries.[16] Of these, 152 concern *only* ecclesiastical participants, 157 are between a cleric and a layman, while only 15 are between lay people. The majority of these survive in ecclesiastical archives and are the product of the archival enthusiasm of monks and bishops who had their own priorities. Given that the church preserves most of (but not all) the documentation for dispute settlement, we would expect a preponderance of appeals to judge-delegates, and cases not only involving ecclesiastical participants but also heard for the most part in ecclesiastical courts. Cooper knew this but never fully developed its significance.[17]

The second position on the Scottish common law developed in part in response to Cooper's work. Whereas Lord Cooper assumed a negligible system of royal justice, Hector MacQueen set out to resurrect it. MacQueen showed in a series of publications, leading up to his *magnum opus*, *Common Law and Feudal Society in Medieval Scotland* (1993), that a Scottish common law system, run through royal courts, did in fact develop in the thirteenth century and that it not only remained firm throughout the politically tortuous fourteenth and fifteenth centuries but also continued to develop.[18] MacQueen was able to construct this picture of

formularies, which showed, among other things, that 'the assortment of remedies available to the Scottish litigant before the justiciar or sheriff in or about 1300 was far richer and more varied than other sources of information would lead us to expect'; Cooper, *Select Cases*, p. lxv. In the introduction to his edition of the brieve registers, Cooper characterized the twelfth to the fourteenth century as the period of 'initial . . . construction, which began with David I and ended with Bruce, the structure being then far from complete, and the plans being lost or destroyed'; *The Register of Brieves as Contained in The Ayr MS, the Bute MS and Quoniam Attachiamenta*, ed. T. M. Cooper, Stair Society 10 (Edinburgh, 1946), pp. 1, 3. No mention was made of papal judge-delegates or canon law.

[14] For more commentary on Cooper, see, among many, W. D. H. Sellar, 'Scots Law: Mixed from the Very Beginning? A Tale of Two Receptions', *Edinburgh Law Review*, vol. 4, no. 1 (2000), pp. 3–18, at pp. 5–7; Hector L. MacQueen, 'Legal Nationalism: Lord Cooper, Legal History and Comparative Law', *Edinburgh Law Review*, vol. 9, no. 3 (2005), pp. 395–406, at pp. 396–401.

[15] J. Maitland Thomson, *The Public Records of Scotland* (Glasgow, 1922), pp. 6–8, 15–16, 55–7, 77–9, 138, 141–4.

[16] These figures have been calculated from the PoMS database, by selecting the 'source' search function, and then by browsing all 'agreements' and 'settlements' (<http://db.poms.ac.uk>). Not all documents that come up, however, are disputes. Some, for example, were agreements for a lay person to have a chapel. As a result, some discretion was used in calculating the figures so they should be used to create an impression of the landscape of evidence, not as hard data.

[17] Cooper, *Select Cases*, p. xxvi.

[18] MacQueen, *Common Law*. In his introduction, MacQueen did not single out Cooper's thesis as one of the things he wished to challenge; instead, he wanted to contribute to the debates raised by S. F. C. Milsom, *The Legal Framework of English Feudalism* (Cambridge, 1976). Nonetheless, he later cited *Common Law* as one of the works that showed his 'significant (although not total) disagreement' with Cooper; MacQueen, 'Legal Nationalism', pp. 395–6, and note 4; Hector L. MacQueen, 'Scots

thirteenth-century development through, in part, examination of legal formularies that survive from the early fourteenth century onwards and chance references to 'royal brieves' in the very records of thirteenth-century dispute settlement that Cooper himself had analysed.[19] But MacQueen did have a very particular focus: he concentrated on three particular judicial processes, begun by brieve, that developed during the thirteenth century and were explicitly based on similar procedures in England, although they did not replicate them.[20] These remedies were categorized as *pleadable brieves*: the brieve of novel dissasine; the brieve of mortancestry; and the brieve of right. All were remedies available for the recovery of land and brought cases into royal courts. Thus, for MacQueen, these brieves were key to the 'development of regularised royal justice in the thirteenth century, and hence of a Scottish common law'.[21] In so doing, MacQueen effectively challenged Cooper's position: there *did* develop a regularized system of royal law in the thirteenth century, albeit one not so extensive as that in England, and these three types of pleadable brieves were the main evidence for it.

MacQueen's work solved many of the problems other historians had also raised with Cooper's position, most notably those identified by G. W. S. Barrow.[22] After Barrow and MacQueen's work had established the existence of a relatively strong thirteenth-century structure of royal justice, it became easier to understand the preponderance of evidence for the use of canon law and appeals to papal judge delegates as, in part, a product of the balance of surviving evidence.[23] In addition to these appeals, there *were* common law courts for laymen and lay land, even if the evidence is harder to see. But very recently, David Carpenter challenged this.[24] Carpenter noticed that not only was the brieve of right only available to tenants-in-chief (unlike in England), there were also large punitive fines (of £10) attached to another of the remedies—the brieve of novel dissasine—the counterpart of which in England was, in fact, the most popular remedy of English common law courts.[25] If a pursuer (English: plaintiff; now, claimant) brought a complaint of novel dissasine against another in Scotland and was found to be in the wrong, the pursuer was not fined a mark or half a mark—as he would have been in England—but an enormous £10, which was half the amount of an annual monetary knight's feu in Scotland. Carpenter concluded that only the very rich would have even

---

Law under Alexander III', in *Scotland in the Reign of Alexander III, 1249–1286*, ed. N. H. Reid (Edinburgh, 1990), pp. 74–102.

[19] The wish to overturn the later Middle Ages as a 'dark age' of legal history also played a part. See Cooper, 'Dark Age'. For commentary on MacQueen's impact, along with that of Barrow and Duncan, see Sellar, 'Common Law', pp. 83–7.

[20] MacQueen, *Common Law*, pp. 105–214.

[21] MacQueen, *Common Law*, p. 247; although MacQueen emphasized the role of the church (MacQueen, *Common Law*, pp. 250–1), he devoted more space to it in MacQueen, 'Canon Law, Custom and Legislation'.

[22] Barrow, 'Justiciar', pp. 70–2.

[23] Paul Ferguson argues that judge-delegates were far more important in dispensing papal justice than legates and nuncios but does not comment directly on how this affects our view of royal justice, which is not the subject of his book; Ferguson, *Medieval Papal Representatives*, pp. 204–5.

[24] Carpenter, 'Scottish Royal Government', pp. 138–54.

[25] Carpenter, 'Scottish Royal Government', pp. 148–50.

thought about using the procedure. In his words, 'In Scotland, the amercement for a false claim was a major deterrent to bringing a common law action. In England, for anyone other than the poor, it was no deterrent at all...resort to the common law in Scotland was on a much smaller scale than is usually supposed.'[26] The Scottish common law was not so common after all; it protected the rich, and particularly the tenants-in-chief of the king.

Finally, running throughout all these positions was the significant presence of aristocratic justice. MacQueen acknowledged the importance of aristocratic justice, but how this fitted in with his more maximalist view of the Scottish common law was not really fully developed; it was left as an aside to the more important issue of establishing the form of royal civil justice and how pleadable brieves worked within that structure.[27] But Alexander II's legislation on crime did, as we shall see, rely on aristocratic courts.[28] In addition, it has already been shown in Chapters 3 and 4 how governmental institutions started to develop across the kingdom at the same time as aristocratic jurisdictional power was increasingly being defined in royal charters.[29] Developments in aristocratic justice thus moved in tempo with those in royal government and royal justice. As a result, although aristocratic justice is the least well studied aspect of our current understanding of thirteenth-century justice, it is one of the most important.

In this context, this chapter offers a further re-examination of legal development in the thirteenth century. Like MacQueen and Carpenter, it focuses on the structures of and remedies offered by the royal judicial system but, unlike either, it attempts to detail how these remedies interacted with other jurisdictions. It questions whether the category of a 'pleadable brieve' was as well established in thirteenth-century Scotland as it would become in the fourteenth and fifteenth centuries and offers an alternative explanation that allows for the simultaneous importance of and development in royal, aristocratic, and papal justice within the thirteenth-century kingdom.

THE LEGISLATION OF ALEXANDER II

All the surviving pieces of legislation of Alexander II are in *Statuta Regis Alexandri* (*SA*), which contains eight securely dated statutes: one in 1214, one in 1221, four in October 1230, one in 1244, and one in 1248.[30] There is

---

[26] Carpenter, 'Scottish Royal Government', pp. 149, 154.

[27] MacQueen, *Common Law*, pp. 20, 32–66, 112–13, 115–20, 144, 172–5, 181–3, 248–9, 252–3. Alexander Grant did deal with the relationship between aristocratic justice and royal justice but mainly concentrated on criminal jurisdiction and did not discuss the effect of civil pleas on such jurisdictions; see Alexander Grant, 'Franchises North of the Border: Baronies and Regalities in Medieval Scotland', in *Liberties and Identities in the Medieval British Isles*, ed. Michael Prestwich (Woodbridge, 2008), pp. 155–99, at pp. 184–92.

[28] See Chapter 3, pp. 162–4, and below, pp. 295–7.

[29] See Chapter 3, pp. 157–64, and Chapter 4, pp. 264–5.

[30] *SA*, cc. 1–7, 26. Thomson printed them all in some form in his *Statuta Regis Alexandri*. *SA*, cc. 1–7, are all dated, and some manuscripts provide the names of those present of *SA*, cc. 2–7, all of

another undated statute which, by the people it names, can be dated confidently to the 1230s/1240s and a further three which are undated but which, by their content and place in the compilation, probably belong to Alexander's reign.[31] *SA* does not contain all the legislation that Alexander ever enacted in his assemblies (although it does contain all we have): MacQueen has argued that the procedure of mortancestry (claims to heritable succession from an ancestor) was introduced by Alexander between 1230 and 1237 but the text of this legislation does not survive.[32] Nevertheless, the following section makes do with what we have and thus is, by default, an analysis of the content and aims of Alexander's surviving legislation, rather than of his putative legislation, the texts of which no longer survive.

The original content of some of Alexander II's legislation has been obscured in the edition prepared by Thomas Thomson for *APS* and used by all modern historians. Thomson did not reproduce the material from *SA* exactly but often combined the readings of *SA* and *CD* (the 'Assizes of David') instead.[33] Unfortunately, *SA* and *CD* are different in style and substance: *CD* contains versions of Alexander's legislative material, updated to meet early-fourteenth-century conditions. Thomson thus created versions of the statutes that corresponded not only to conditions of the first half of the thirteenth century but also to those of the reign of Robert I (1306–29). Thus, many of Thomson's texts have no manuscript authority; they are, instead, ahistorical creations. This, of course, is not a problem for those chapters in *SA* which were *not* updated in *CD* but it is for those which were, and the use of the *APS*-texts has resulted in modern historians unknowingly reading some of Alexander's legislation through a fourteenth-century lens.[34]

which are consistent with what we know of Alexander's court at the date of their enactment (see, for example, BL, Additional MS 18111, fos. 149r–150v).

[31] *SA*, cc. 8–11 (*SRA*, cc. 10–13, in *APS*, i, pp. 401–2). As stated previously, a full study of *Statuta Regis Alexandri* will be forthcoming in my edition of *The Auld Lawes*. The first eleven chapters seem to belong in a discrete group. It is not possible to date *SA*, cc. 9–11, which are written more in the *si quis* style also found in *LS*; their content, however, suggests that they are of thirteenth-century date and may be authentic statements of Alexander II. At *SA*, c. 12, legal chapters attributable to other kings start to appear in the compilation (beginning with the law known as *Claremathen*, which first survives as *LS*, c. 1, and which belongs to William the Lion's reign: see Alice Taylor, 'Leges Scocie' and the Lawcodes of David I, William the Lion and Alexander II', *SHR*, vol. 88, no. 226 (2009), pp. 207–88, at pp. 223–7).

[32] MacQueen, *Common Law*, pp. 169–70. A case heard in 1235, whereby Gilbert, son of Samuel, impleaded Mael Domnaig, earl of Lennox, may be one of warrandice, in which case brieves which could be used in warrandice cases *may* have been introduced by this point. The reference to the brieve is in *Paisley Reg.*, pp. 170–1, and is discussed in Cooper, *Select Cases*, pp. 34–5; MacQueen, *Common Law*, p. 139 (who argues it is a case of dissasine); and Cynthia J. Neville, *Native Lordship in Medieval Scotland: The Earldoms of Strathearn and Lennox, c.1140–1365* (Dublin, 2005), pp. 146–8 (who suggests warrandice).

[33] Alice Taylor, 'The Assizes of David, King of Scots, 1124–53', *SHR*, vol. 91, no. 232 (2012), pp. 197–238, at pp. 216–21.

[34] Those chapters which are less of a problem (but still something of one) are *SA*, cc. 1–3, 8–11; those for which it is a problem are *SA*, cc. 4–7, 26 (to a lesser extent). These chapters are printed by Thomson among his *Statuta Regis Alexandri* (*SRA*), cc. 2, 4–7, in *APS*, i, pp. 398–400.

The 1230 Legislation

On 13 October 1230, Alexander II, together with his lay and ecclesiastical magnates, enacted four pieces of legislation at Stirling which are usually understood to have curtailed the jurisdictional power of lords over their men, cemented the role of the jury in deciding civil and criminal cases, heralded the decline of the ordeal as a normative method of proof, and established the king as the ultimate guarantor of free landed property through the introduction of novel dissasine, based on the English procedure—novel disseisin—introduced by Henry II in the 1160s.[35] All these points will be challenged or modified in what follows.[36]

The text of the 1230 legislation in *SA* is divided into four chapters, numbered 4–7. *SA*, c.4, tells us that Alexander II enacted all four pieces of legislation in the presence of the magnates of his kingdom 'by the counsel and will of the same magnates'. In two Scots manuscripts of these statutes, the names of those present are given: William, bishop of St Andrews; Mael Coluim, earl of Fife; William Comyn, earl of Buchan and justiciar of Scotia; Thomas, prior of Coldingham; Walter Olifard, justiciar of Lothian; Walter, son of Alan, the king's steward; and John Maxwell (later the king's chamberlain), along with others who are unnamed.[37]

The first of these four enactments dealt with repledging (when and under what circumstances a lord could remove an accused man from another's jurisdiction and place him in his own); the second with accusations of theft when trial by battle was not an option; the third is supposed to have instituted the jury as the regular method of proof in accusations of theft and the more serious crime of robbery; and the last introduced procedures for accusations of novel dissasine, modelled on the English procedure of novel disseisin, whereby an individual had recourse to royal justice if they claimed that their lord or anyone else had wrongly dispossessed them of their land. What follows takes each in turn.

---

[35] For the literature on the 1230 legislation see MacQueen, 'Canon Law, Custom and Legislation', pp. 239–49; Duncan, *Making of the Kingdom*, pp. 539–41; Ian D. Willock, *The Origins and Development of the Jury in Scotland*, Stair Society 23 (Edinburgh, 1966), pp. 17–18, 23–9, 36–7; George Neilson, *Trial by Combat* (Glasgow, 1890), pp. 113–16.

[36] It is still common to assign the law entitled 'Lex quomodo duellum procedet secundum condiciones personarum', printed as *SRA*, c. 8 (*APS*, i, pp. 400–1), to 1230; see for example, Willock, *Jury*, pp. 24, 28; although cf. Duncan, *Making of the Kingdom*, p. 541, note 38. George Neilson seems to be the work commonly cited for the dating to 1230. But in *Trial by Combat*, Neilson was, in fact, circumspect, writing that the statute was 'placed by the editors of the Scots Acts [i.e. *APS*], on grounds not unsatisfactory although by no means conclusive, next after a statute of the undoubted date of 1230': see Neilson, *Trial by Combat*, p. 114. Cosmo Innes, in his 'table of parliaments', did indeed place the chapter chronologically between the 1230 legislation and a judgment of 1231 between Patrick of Dunbar and Coldingham Priory: *APS*, i, p. 285. But there does not seem to be any concrete evidence for this. The chapter does not appear in the manuscript-text of *SA*. It does, however, appear as *CD*, c. 42, where it follows the updated versions of the 1230 legislation present in that compilation. The placing of the chapter on duels next to the updated 1230 legislation in *CD* is not evidence for any temporal association between them.

[37] For the manuscript tradition here, see Chapter 3, pp. 117–20, and Notes 23, 32. John Maxwell's first attestation as chamberlain was on 19 March 1231, so about six months after these enactments, for which see Chapter 4, pp. 246–7. For attestations of royal charters in the reign of Alexander II, see Keith J. Stringer, 'The Scottish "Political Community" in the Reign of Alexander II (1214–49)', in *New Perspectives*, ed. Hammond, pp. 53–84.

Replegiation and Aristocratic Jurisdiction (SA, c. 4)

The first statute is entitled 'on repledging men'.[38] It enacted that henceforth no 'bishop, abbot or clerk, earl, baron or any other' should repledge—that is remove to his own court—anyone (*aliquis*) who was accused of any wrongdoing or crime.[39] The only exception was if the accused person was the lord's 'liege man, neyf, or *manens*'. If a complaint was made against the lord's actions, the issue would be put to the 'lawful men of the country (*patria*)', who would decide whether the repledged individual *was* the lord's 'liege man, neyf or *manens*'. If the person was found *not* to be the lord's man, the lord would be at the king's mercy, and probably fined. We do not know the territorial power of the act's lordly targets but can safely assume that all those who were repledging had a level of jurisdictional authority, whether great or small.[40] The reference to 'wrongdoing' and 'crime', however, shows that the statute was explicitly concerned with criminal pleas, such as theft, homicide, and murder, not with civil ones.

The issue of aristocratic jurisdiction underlies this statute, which could be viewed as an attempt to control and discipline lords with jurisdictional power who had been flexing their muscles too vigorously: lords could, henceforth, only repledge their men in particular circumstances; if they repledged men who were not their own, they would be fined or worse. It must be admitted that there were incentives for lords to repledge whenever they could. The material benefit accrued from the resulting profits of justice—whether fines or confiscated chattels—must have been one intended outcome of repledging, even if it was not the only one.[41] Even the act of repledging could in itself be profitable. The statute was explicitly targeted at those lords who would repledge men who were technically not their own by taking a payment of 'pepper, wax, cumin or something similar' (denoting a render a lord would customarily receive) from the accused, thus making the accused one of their own men and thus a suitor of the particular aristocratic court. However, it is important to acknowledge the implicit advantages to the other side: individuals were clearly in the habit of giving such a payment to their imposter lords; accordingly, they must also have seen some benefit in being transferred to the court of another lord who was not their own. Indeed, given that some people probably had more than one tenurial lord, it is possible that repledging would have happened very frequently, as lords may have repledged the accused into their own court, not necessarily knowing that another lord technically had the right to do so instead.

As it stands, however, the act was not a blanket ban on repledging per se. Repledging was only forbidden if the 'lawful men of the land' found that the

---

[38] *SA*, c. 4.

[39] For repledging (replegiation) in general, see *The Sheriff Court Book of Fife, 1515–1522*, ed. William Croft Dickinson, Scottish History Society, 3rd ser., vol. 12 (Edinburgh, 1928), pp. 344–6; John Stuart, 'Notice of the Early System of Replegiation as Exercised in Scotland', *PSAS*, vol. 11 (1874–76), pp. 163–7.

[40] For the different levels of jurisdiction in thirteenth-century Scotland, see Chapter 3, p. 161, at Note 244.

[41] Duncan, *Making of the Kingdom*, p. 539.

wrongdoer in question was not 'the liege man or neyf or dwells (*manens*) in the land of the repledger' (thereby indicating that a recognition had taken place to determine the status of the repledgee in question). *Homo legius, nativus,* and *manens* were all legal categories of persons and were, in this statute, all deemed equivalent in a jurisdictional sense through their dependence on their lord.[42] Neyfs and liege men were categorized in law and legal documents as unfree. 'Liege' could be used to describe the tie which bound individuals to the king, above whatever tie of fealty they owed to any other lords, but in Scottish charters and agreements it is used to describe a state of unfreedom. In this statute, therefore, *legius* denoted an unfree person, bound in a personal condition of servility to a lord, a use of the word attested elsewhere in Europe.[43] There is evidence that *manentes* were a broad legal category whose unfreedom may have been, in theory, lighter than *homines legii* or *nativi*.[44] Particular *manentes* could also be described not only as 'dwellers' but also as *homines legii* ('liege men'), blurring the boundaries between the two status groups.[45] Alexander's statutes thus focussed on a court-holder's power over his unfree dependents.

The 1230 statute thus did not target replegiation in and of itself but instead set the parameters for the action. Regardless of their offence (whether theft or anything else) and jurisdiction, lords had the right to repledge their unfree or generally dependent *manentes* to their own courts. It might be thought that this enactment curtailed the powers of lay and ecclesiastical lords, limiting their capacity to repledge to unfree dependants. But the statute can actually be seen to act in the interests of elite jurisdictions, whether ecclesiastical, aristocratic, or royal. It is clear that autonomous and independent jurisdiction was at stake in this statute. Thus, if a free man of one lord stole something from a free man of another lord, this statute laid down that the first lord did not have the right to repledge his man into his own court: the case should be dealt with in the jurisdiction in which the offence was thought to have occurred. This prevented lords from taking cases away from other

---

[42] Alice Taylor, '*Homo Ligius* and Unfreedom in Medieval Scotland', in *New Perspectives*, ed. Hammond, pp. 85–116, at pp. 91–108.

[43] Taylor, '*Homo Ligius*', pp. 89–61. In addition to the references cited in that article, *ligius* was also paired with *nativus* in the *Leges Marchiarum*: see *APS*, i, p. 414.

[44] The point that some of these words (particularly *manentes*) were empty legal categories, and not necessarily descriptive of a particular type of servile work was useful for negotiation on both sides: see Alice Rio, '"Half-free" Categories in the Early Middle Ages: Fine Status Distinctions before Professional Lawyers', in *Legalism*, vol. 3: *Rules and Categories*, ed. Paul Dresch and Judith Scheele (Oxford, 2015), pp. 129–52. For *manentes* elsewhere see, among many, Chris Wickham, 'Manentes e diritti signorili durante il XII secolo: Il caso della Lucchesia', in *Società istituzioni, spiritualità: Studi in onore di Cinzio Violante*, Centro Italiano di Studi sull'Alto Medioevo (Spoleto, 1994), pt 2, pp. 1067–80.

[45] Taylor, '*Homo Ligius*', pp. 101–10. The focus on these three categories has been obscured in Thomson's edition because he includes the *familia*, which can be translated either as 'household' or 'kin-group'. But this was an addition in the *CD*-text, which seems to have been responding to Robert I's extension in the remit of this statute in 1318 to include free members of the *familia*, near kinsmen, retainers, or tenants: *RPS*, 1318/12; online at <www.rps.ac.uk/mss/1318/12>; see further, Taylor, 'Assizes of David', pp. 226–8; T. M. Cooper, 'The First Reform (Miscellaneous Provisions) Act', in Cooper, *Selected Papers*, pp. 88–92; MacQueen, *Common Law*, pp. 146–53; and now, most recently, Michael Penman, *Robert the Bruce: King of the Scots* (New Haven, CT, 2014), pp. 190–202, 315–17.

lords or, even, the king but it did not prevent any case that *should* have been heard in a particular lord's court being heard in that forum.

Repledging thus was a problem because it had the potential to infringe another's jurisdiction: by taking a customary render from the accused, lords were attempting to claim individuals as their own (presumably to gain whatever profits of justice would accrue) when the case should be heard in another's court.[46] Only if the accused thief was the lord's unfree man (or woman) did the lord have the right to repledge him or her. Far from targeting aristocratic jurisdiction, the act aimed instead at resolving conflict between competing jurisdictions, regardless of who wielded them: king, bishop, abbot, earl, or lord. What was at stake was hearing the case in the appropriate forum. If an individual was not legally dependent on a lord, then the case should be heard in whatever forum the accusation pertained (whether the king's court or the court of another lord).[47] The inquest to determine the status of the individual was thus used not to protect the parameters of royal jurisdiction but to protect multiple jurisdictions (which included that of the king's) from impinging on each other.[48] The statute protected jurisdictional integrity rather than attacked it.

There are very few surviving examples of replegiation from Scotland in the thirteenth century. One comes right at its close. When John Comyn, earl of Buchan and justiciar of Scotia, held his justiciar's court near Aberdeen in 1299, John of Pollok, steward of the abbot of Arbroath, appeared and repledged five men indicted with stealing cows and sheep to the abbot's court of regality.[49] The men were described as *manentes* in the land of the abbot, exactly the category of men envisaged in the much earlier statute of 1230. Although the abbot's court is referred to as a 'court of regality', indicating that he had explicit right to hear pleas of the crown (*regalitas* is a term that does not take on this particular meaning until the late thirteenth century), it is of interest here that the men repledged were charged with the crime of theft, a plea which kings had for long relied on lords hearing, as was argued in Chapter 3.[50] We hear of more cases of replegiation in the fourteenth and fifteenth centuries but by then the status of those repledged was generally higher, probably as the result of the extension enacted by Robert I in 1318 to include members of a lord's household, his close kin, retainers, and tenants.[51] It is more than possible that this extension of repledging in the early fourteenth century accounts for the references to high-status replegiations that we find thereafter but, in 1230, replegiation was to protect elite rights over their jurisdictions and over

---

[46] In this context, it is of interest that *LS*, c. 8, which prescribes the procedure for cases of petty theft (*birthinsake*), stated that 'a court is not to be held [for *birthinsake*]; rather, he in whose land the thief is take shall take one cow and one sheep from him, and [the thief] ought to be whipped'.

[47] This means that the statute should not be interpreted as creating the distinction between lordly courts, whose suitors were in part unfree, and royal courts, where suitors were free, that developed in England as an unintended consequence of Henry II's legal reforms; see Paul R. Hyams, *Kings, Lords, and Peasants in Medieval England: The Common Law of Villeinage in the Twelfth and Thirteenth Centuries* (Oxford, 1980), pp. 221–65.

[48] See also the points in MacQueen, 'Canon Law, Custom and Legislation', p. 242.

[49] *Arbroath Liber*, i, no. 231.   [50] For regalities, see Grant, 'Franchises', pp. 167–76.

[51] *RPS*, 1318/12.

their unfree dependents. If an unfree person was accused in the court of another, they returned automatically to the court of their lord to be dealt with but, if they were free, they remained under the power of judgment of whoever's jurisdiction they had been unlucky enough to fall under.

Theft and the Problem of Trial by Battle (SA, c. 5)

The second 1230 statute laid down the procedure to follow if those who could not defend their own accusations through trial by combat needed nonetheless to raise complaints of theft.[52] Individuals did have the option of trial by battle as a method of proof but certain types of people, particularly the clergy—although widows are also expressly mentioned—did not and so another solution had to be found for them.[53] The solution found in *SA*, c.5, was the recognition (*recognitio*), a group of 'worthy and sworn men' who would discover and swear a truthful answer to a particular question.[54] The particular procedure introduced by this statute involved the person who was unable to wage trial by battle going to their lord with their complaint of theft. The lord 'of the feu' would then summon the sheriff and conduct a recognition by the men 'of the visnet' of 'three baronies'.[55] If a wrongdoer was identified, he or she would then have to surrender the stolen goods to the complainer and the lord would confiscate his or her remaining chattels.[56] If the complainer was in the king's demesne land or his thanages, a slightly different procedure was to be followed. There, the complainer would take his or her problem directly to the sheriff, who summoned the recognition, and then took its verdict 'to the king'.[57]

There are two points to be drawn from this: one concerns the structures in which justice was done; the second concerns the method of proof. Despite its

---

[52] *SA*, c. 5.

[53] Robert Bartlett, *Trial by Fire and Water: the Medieval Judicial Ordeal* (Oxford, 1986), p. 126, argues that other legal solutions developing in the thirteenth century, rather than clerical opposition, may have prompted a less obvious decline in trial by battle; for a new discussion of how this statute affected procedures for dealing with robbery, see Andrew R. C. Simpson, 'Procedures for Dealing with Robbery in Scotland before 1400', in *Continuity, Change and Pragmatism in the Law: Essays in Memory of Angelo Forte*, ed. Andrew R. C. Simpson, Scott C. Styles, and Adelyn L. M. Wilson (Aberdeen, 2015). For a broader study on the duel in Scotland, see A. D. M. Forte, '"A Strange Archaic Provision of Mercy": The Procedural Rules for *Duellum* under the Law of *Clann Duib*', *Edinburgh Law Review*, vol. 14, no. 3 (2010), pp. 418–50.

[54] This thus differs from MacQueen's view that the context for this act was not the difficulties posed in finding legal solutions for particular types of people but 'a specific solution in a particular context—the loss and recovery of moveable property'; MacQueen, 'Canon Law, Custom and Legislation', p. 240. Given the emphasis on theft in legislation of William the Lion, discussed Chapter 3, pp. 140–2, the 'particular context' was a subset of a much larger one. For more on *recognitiones*, see below, pp. 306–7.

[55] For three baronies, see below, pp. 334–5; and further, Grant, 'Franchises', pp. 157–67, 188–91.

[56] The lord is an inference: the text says that the chattels should be 'his whose they ought to be' but since the contrast is with those wrongdoers found in the king's land—his demesne or his thanages— and the statute had previously mentioned 'the lord of the feu', it is a reasonable inference; *SA*, c. 5.

[57] The distinction between demesne lands and thanages is discussed in Chapter 1, pp. 66–7. The *CD* version contains an additional sentence about what happened if the wrongdoer fled the scene having been convicted. It also makes it clear that the wrongdoer would submit to just judgment (presumably would be killed); *CD*, c. 40.

status as a royal pronouncement, the statute envisaged a bipartite procedure, one to be upheld in the lands of lay lords, the second in the land the king directly controlled (his demesne land and his thanages). If the statute envisaged royal courts as the primary forum for this procedure, its content contradicts this putative aim. Instead, it anticipated that lords of feus would be the primary movers in administering this particular complaint of theft; they were expected to summon the visnet and, even though the local sheriff was required to be present, lords oversaw the proceedings and received the profits of justice.[58] Only if the accusation took place in the king's own land (i.e. the land he directly controlled through farming or direct management), did his official—the sheriff—summon the visnet, and send its results directly back to the king (either the judgment itself or an answer that would result in judgment). In this way, the content of the statute was mediated through the sheriff in the king's lands and the lord in his feu: it was anticipated that king and lord would act together, not independently.

The second statute also confronted the problem of the correct type of legal proof. Widows and clerics were not allowed to fight in cases of theft: how, then, was anyone to know the truth of their accusation in the absence of the alternative method of the ordeal? The solution found in written law was the visnet. This suggests, conversely, that trial by battle was, for everybody who was not a woman or a cleric, the main way of defending their accusation.[59] *SA*, c.5, thus did not present the visnet as a more rational and fair solution to contemporaries than trial by battle; it was used as a solution to the problem that women and clerics could not engage in it.[60] The fifteenth-century chronicler, Walter Bower, reported that when Walter Bisset realized in 1242 that he would be called to account for his part in the killing of the young Patrick of Atholl, he asked to be tried by battle rather than place himself on the verdict of the visnet, not wanting to be vulnerable to the 'malice of peasants' (*malicia rusticorum*).[61] Being quite literally able to fight your own battles must have seemed like an attractive option, particularly to confident members of the aristocratic class.

It appears that the procedure laid down in this second statute could not always be adhered to fully. In March 1231, a mere five months after the statute was enacted, the monks of Melrose sought the king's protection, the details of which were drawn up in a brieve which they then kept.[62] The brieve described that if the

---

[58] The supervisory functions of sheriffs in the late twelfth century are discussed in Chapter 4, pp. 206–10; see also *LS*, c. 7, §1, c. 22.

[59] Cf. Neilson, *Trial by Combat*, p. 116, who sees the institution of trial by battle as 'steadily on the wane' after the reign of Alexander II. Trial by battle was also the proof used for accusations of theft and homicide in *Leges Marchiarum*: *APS*, i, p. 414. *Glanvill* states that denied accusations of felonies, heard before the justices, should be settled *per duellum* ('by battle'); *Glanvill*, XIV, 1 (p. 172). See also M. J. Russell, 'Trial by Battle and the Writ of Right', *Journal of Legal History*, vol. 1, no. 2 (1980), pp. 111–34; M. J. Russell, 'Trial by Battle and the Appeals of Felony', *Journal of Legal History*, vol. 1, no. 2 (1980), pp. 135–64.

[60] For discussion on this, see Rebecca V. Colman, 'Reason and Unreason in Early Medieval Law', *Journal of Interdisciplinary History*, vol. 4, no. 4 (1974), pp. 571–91.

[61] *Scotichronicon by Walter Bower*, 9 vols, gen. ed. D. E. R. Watt (Aberdeen and Edinburgh, 1989–1998), v, pp. 182–3.

[62] NRS, GD55/175; printed in *Melrose Liber*, i, no. 175 [AII/167].

monks complained to a sheriff about any case of theft, that sheriff was to answer their cases as he would the king's own. If there were a need, the sheriff would also find a champion to fight in any resulting duel on the monks' behalf, unless the case was resolved either by the visnet or by monetary agreement. If the sheriff was able to resolve the case in Melrose's favour, the monks would be compensated for their loss from the chattels of the convicted and the king would receive any resulting fines and confiscations that were left over. This thus differs from the scenario outlined in the 1230 statute. Instead of holding the visnet (with the sheriff present), the monks, when they wished to, appealed to the king, who then commanded his sheriff to hear cases of theft on the monks' behalf, a responsibility which included finding a champion for the duel if required. However, it still left the option open that the issue could be resolved either by the visnet or by agreement. If the case went to trial by battle, the monks of Melrose handed over responsibility to the sheriff, thereby denying themselves the increased income from the resulting profits of justice but yet avoided the problem of being too closely connected to trial by battle in which they were not allowed to participate.

The promulgation of the 1230 statute seems to have served as a general guide to correct practice when confronted with the fact that certain people were not, technically, allowed to wage trial by battle. The issue itself might have been raised because, following the Fourth Lateran Council, William Malveisin, bishop of St Andrews (who was present at the 1230 legislative assembly at Stirling), complained heavily about the 'nefarious custom' by which the clergy partook in trial by battle and obtained a bull from Innocent III in 1216 condemning the practice.[63] What is interesting here is that the statute itself only envisaged that lords 'of feus' would supervise inquests outside the king's demesne land; it does not mention those who held their lands 'in alms', the main method of tenure of ecclesiastical institutions, whether of the institutional church or monastic or regular houses.[64] Perhaps because of this statutory lacuna, the king was, in the case of Melrose, able to interpret

---

[63] *Concilia Scotiae: Ecclesiae Scotianae Statuta tam provincialia quam synodalia quae supersunt MCCXXV–MDLIX*, ed. J. Robertson, Bannatyne Club, 2 vols (Edinburgh, 1866), i, pp. ccxcvii–ccxcviii; discussed in MacQueen, 'Canon Law, Custom and Legislation', pp. 240–1. The ambiguous relationship between royal and ecclesiastical justice will be developed below, pp. 334–43.

[64] There is a vast literature on the development of alms tenure in the twelfth century. See, among many, Sir Frederick Pollock and F. W. Maitland, *The History of English Law before the Time of Edward I* (henceforth *HEL*), 2nd edn, 2 vols (Cambridge, 1923), i, pp. 240–51; Elizabeth G. Kimball, 'Tenure in frank almoign and secular services', *EHR*, vol. 43, no. 171 (1928), pp. 341–53; Audrey W. Douglas, 'Frankalmoin and Jurisdictional Immunity: Maitland Revisited', *Speculum*, vol. 53 (1978), pp. 26–48; Audrey W. Douglas, 'Tenure *in elemosina*: Origins and Establishment in Twelfth-Century England', *The American Journal of Legal History*, vol. 24, no. 95 (1980), pp. 95–132; David Postles, 'Tenure in frankalmoign and Knight Service in Twelfth-Century England: Interpretations of the Charters', *Journal of the Society of Archivists*, vol. 13 (1992), pp. 18–28; Benjamin Thompson, 'Free Alms Tenure in the Twelfth Century', *ANS*, vol. 16 (1994), pp. 221–43. Alms tenure has not received the same amount of attention in Scotland but see the comments in Duncan, *Making of the Kingdom*, pp. 144, 288–9, 388–9; John Hudson, 'Legal Aspects of Scottish Charter Diplomatic in the Twelfth Century: A Comparative Approach', *ANS*, vol. 25 (2003), pp. 121–38, at pp. 127–8; Alice Taylor, 'Common Burdens in the *regnum Scottorum*: the Evidence of Charter Diplomatic', in *The Reality Behind Charter Diplomatic: Studies by Dauvit Broun, John Reuben Davies, Richard Sharpe and Alice Taylor*, ed. Dauvit Broun (Glasgow, 2011) , pp. 166–234, at pp. 168–75.

his own provision, made five months earlier, by allowing the abbey, on occasion, to rescind any judicial responsibility they might have had in cases of theft, appeal to the sheriff, and pursue their accusations through him in a variety of ways that included the capacity to engage (through an appointed champion) in trial by battle. Melrose was not the only monastic house which took this line; there is a similar brieve, issued by Alexander II, to Balmerino Abbey, also providing the same solution.[65] It may be more than a coincidence that both Melrose and Balmerino were Cistercian houses or it may be that monastic houses of other orders also took the same line.[66] If there had been a connection between Bishop Malveisin's complaints and the 1230 statute, it is interesting that the monks of Melrose and Balmerino did allow themselves to engage in trial by battle if the sheriff could find a champion to fight on their behalf. In terms of clerical *response* to the problem of trial by battle, therefore, there was no unified front among the ecclesiastical and religious men of the kingdom of the Scots: some, like Bishop Malveisin, condemned their participation unilaterally; others, like the houses of Melrose and Balmerino, had less of a problem, providing that they were not procuring a champion themselves. William Malveisin was present at Stirling when the 1230 legislation was enacted and so probably affected the content and direction of the legislation.[67]

Theft, Robbery, and Further Issues of Proof (SA, c. 6)

The third statute issued in 1230 concerned accusations of theft and robbery (or plunder).[68] Robbery was conceptualized as a more serious offence than theft and was listed among the pleas of the crown in legislation issued in 1180 and charters drawn up from the late 1160s at the earliest, even if, as shown in Chapter 3, some lords heard pleas of *roboria* in their own courts, either through express grant of the king or, as in the 1197 oath, through the king's general acknowledgement that they could.[69] By this 1230 enactment, people accused of theft or robbery could choose to place themselves on the verdict of the visnet (*super proportacionem visneti*). If they were purged by the visnet, the defendant would be quit of the appeal (the accusation) but the complainer would be in the mercy of *either* the lord king, if the appeal had been one of robbery, *or* the 'earl or baron' if the accusation had been of theft. If the defendant failed to be acquitted, then 'just judgment' would be done upon him.

At first glance, this statute appears to be all encompassing and clear in intent. It confirms the existence of a conceptual hierarchy of offences, the levels of which belonged to particular jurisdictions.[70] Theft was seen to belong to the 'earl or

---

[65] D. E. Easson, 'Miscellaneous Monastic Charters: Charters of Balmerino Abbey', *Miscellany VIII*, Scottish History Society (Edinburgh, 1951), pp. 1–16, at pp. 8–9, no. 2 [AII/176].

[66] Before 1216, many monastic houses had their right to hold trial by battle confirmed, most notably Scone Abbey and Arbroath Abbey: *RRS*, i, no. 243; *RRS*, ii, no. 513; *Arbroath Liber*, i, no. 220. For the 'island' where duels were held, see *Scone Liber*, no. 56.

[67] MacQueen, 'Canon Law, Custom and Legislation', pp. 240–1.   [68] *SA*, c. 6.

[69] See Chapter 3, p. 158.   [70] See Chapter 3, pp. 161–4.

baron' whereas robbery pertained to the king. Moreover, the method of determining guilt was the inquest, which would decide who was to suffer judgment for guilt or pay a fine for making a wrongful appeal. Yet even this reading shows the reliance on and incorporation of lay aristocratic jurisdiction into the very content of royal legal pronouncements. Theft was deemed to be the preserve of great lords whereas, in England, *Glanvill* was explicit that appeals of theft were heard in county courts under the sheriff and did not turn up in a court as great as the king's, even if many lords had, in practice, control over hundreds and had the jurisdiction of infangentheof—the right to hang convicted thieves in their own land.[71]

Moreover, a closer reading of *SA*, c.6, reveals that, like *SA*, c.5, it did not replace one method of proof with another. The defendant was, after all, able to *choose* his method of proof and the statute described only one of the choices available—the recognition. Trial by battle did not disappear: it remained a key mode of proof in pleas of theft and robbery into the early fourteenth century. Two chapters of *CD*, which appear to be contemporaneous with the early-fourteenth-century date of the compilation, record that theft and robbery were two *malefacta* which could be settled by battle (*duellum*).[72] The statute, therefore, covered only those cases when the defendant *chose* to place himself on the visnet. Moreover, it was concerned only with the jurisdictional rights of lay lords not ecclesiastical ones, who also heard cases of theft and, in some cases, robbery.[73] Regardless of the right of those lords who could hear 'pleas of the crown' in the thirteenth century, the statute was still, in its own terms, limited to the rights of particular groups of lay landholders and only introduced the procedure for one method of proof. But, when read alongside *SA*, c.5, it shows a fundamental interest in 1230 about regulating the modes of proof available to people when charged of theft and/or robbery.

This statute therefore raises two issues concerning proof that have attracted some historiographical attention: whether the statute outlawed the ordeal in response to the canons of Lateran IV and whether the ordeal had ever been a frequently used method of proof in Scotland in the first place.[74] The second is more easily dealt with than the first. Both the two main modern commentators on the ordeal in twelfth- and early-thirteenth-century Scotland have agreed that the ordeal had never much been in use. For Neilson, 'the ordeals of water and iron appear but seldom in the records of Scots law'; for Willock, 'the ordeal was never the most common mode of trial in Scotland and was on the wane even before

---

[71] *Glanvill*, XIV, c.8 (p. 177). For infangentheof, see Pollock and Maitland, *HEL*, i, pp. 576–82; John Hudson, *The Oxford History of the Laws of England* (henceforth *OHLE*), vol. 2: *871–1216* (Oxford, 2012), vol. ii, pp. 291–2.

[72] *CD*, cc. 14, 42; see also *CD*, c. 3; *SA*, c. 11.

[73] For ecclesiastical jurisdiction, see below, pp. 337–43.

[74] For the ordeal in general, see Bartlett, *Trial by Fire and Water*, particularly chapters 4, 5, and 7; Peter Brown, 'Society and the Supernatural: A Medieval Change', *Dædalus*, vol. 104, no. 2 (1975), pp. 133–51; Sarah Larratt Keefer, '"Ðonne se cirlisca man ordales weddigeð": the Anglo-Saxon Lay Ordeal', in *Early Medieval Studies in Memory of Patrick Wormald*, ed. Stephen Baxter, Catherine Karkov, Janet L. Nelson, and David Pelteret (Farnham, 2009), pp. 353–67; John W. Baldwin, 'The Crisis of the Ordeal: Literature, Law and Religion around 1200', *Journal of Medieval and Renaissance Studies*, vol. 24 (1994), pp. 327–53; for interesting comparative evidence, see William Ian Miller, 'Ordeal in Iceland', *Scandinavian Studies*, vol. 60, no. 2 (1988), pp. 189–218.

1216'.[75] However, it is hard to see why either came to this conclusion, given that it completely contradicts most of the available evidence. Royal charters granting and confirming land with jurisdictional rights increasingly, from early in the reign of William the Lion, add the alliterative formula 'gallows and pit' (*furca et fossa*) to the phrase borrowed from English royal charters—*saca et soca, tolla et teama et infangentheof*.[76] The conscious addition to the borrowed formula means that the inclusion of an ordeal pit and a gallows was no slavish imitation of English diplomatic practice; it bore some relation to reality. Indeed, sometimes the location of particular ordeal pits (for the ordeal of water) was spelled out in charters. Sometime between 1173 and 1178, William confirmed Abernethy to Orm mac Aeda with the stipulation that Orm only be allowed to have an ordeal pit in two places, Abernethy and Inverarity, the assumption being that Orm *also* had ordeal pits elsewhere that were no longer to be used.[77]

The prevalence of the ordeal in Scotland was not confined to the ordeal of water; iron and, as we have seen, battle were both used as well. The 1197 oath to maintain the peace, sworn by all ecclesiastical and secular lords, contained the stipulation that 'they will take no compensation through which justice can default after judgement of water, iron or battle has happened'.[78] Both William and Alexander's great confirmation charters of the lands and privileges of Arbroath Abbey, drawn up on 25 February 1213 and 17 February 1215 respectively, included the grant of '[the convent's] free court with . . . iron and duel and pit and gallows'.[79] Again, given that the normal charter formula for jurisdictional privileges was the alliterative phrase 'sake and soke, toll and team and infangentheof, and gallows and pit', why the phrase 'iron and duel' was explicitly used in William's and Alexander II's charters if there was no real context for it would be hard to understand.[80] Although there are not many miracle collections surviving from medieval Scotland, it is of note that the miracles of St Margaret, probably partly compiled before 1250, mention a carpenter, William, who on raping a woman subsequently underwent the ordeal of iron.[81] After his burnt hand was sealed, William spent the night at the tomb of Margaret in Dunfermline Abbey. The queen duly appeared, blew on his hand, and made him better, whereupon William was freed from captivity. But, because he knew himself to be guilty, William nonetheless went on a pilgrimage to the Holy Land. Pilgrimage, prayer, and piety trumped the ordeal in this case but, regardless

---

[75] Neilson, *Trial by Combat*, p. 79; Willock, *Jury*, p. 26. Lord Cooper thought that Neilson's original position was bizarre, for which see *Regiam Majestatem*, ed. Cooper, p. 37.

[76] See Chapter 3, pp. 159–61.	[77] *RRS*, ii, no. 152; see also *RRS*, i, nos. 243, 247.

[78] *LS*, c. 15.	[79] *RRS*, ii, no. 513; *Arbroath Liber*, i, no. 100 [AII/6].

[80] The phrase is also present in William's first great confirmation charter to Arbroath Abbey of *c*.1178 (*RRS*, ii, no. 197), and Lucius III's papal confirmation to Arbroath of 1182, stipulating that their court had 'ordeal of iron, trial by battle, pit and gallows' (*Arbroath Liber*, i, no. 220); see also William's charter to Scone, confirming their right to have a court with battle, iron, and water: *RRS*, ii, no. 27.

[81] *The Miracles of St Æbbe of Coldingham and St Margaret of Scotland*, ed. and trans. Robert Bartlett, Oxford Medieval Texts (Oxford, 2003), pp. 118–19; for the problems in dating the collection as a whole, see pp. xxxiv–vii; the exemplar of the manuscript must date from 1263×86, although some sections may have been earlier and it is hard to know when most of the miracles were compiled. This miracle is discussed in MacQueen, 'Canon Law, Custom and Legislation', p. 240, note 88.

of the efficacy of the method of proof, it is of note that this miracle assumes that the ordeal of iron was the way in which people could clear themselves in accusations of rape. In a charter of Fergus, son of Gille Brigte, earl of Strathearn, which was drawn up 1223×39, we learn that the men living on an oxgang in Perthshire could make suit at Fergus's court, but that (significantly) Fergus's men would carry out any dismemberment, beheading, or the judgment of iron or water if it were required.[82] Far from being an uncommon mode of proof, the ordeal—in whatever form—was commonly invoked in charters, certainly before 1230.

This, therefore, raises the question of whether this particular statute had an effect on the ordeal. The issue has thus far turned on the interpretation to the rubric of this statute. In 1966, Willock noticed that the earliest manuscript text had the rubric 'on the abolition (*deletio*) of the law of pit and iron and the introduction of the visnet'. Willock concluded that the statute itself did not quite live up to its title.[83] For Willock, while the statute did 'introduce' the visnet in cases of theft and robbery, it could not simultaneously have abolished the ordeal because this mode of proof was not much used in Scotland. The rubric, he concluded, was probably a later addition by a later scribe who knew that the ordeals of pit and iron 'had vanished at approximately this time [and] gave the impression that the ban was explicit'.[84] However, the rubric, 'delecio legis fosse et ferre et institutio visneti', is only present in *CD*-texts of this statute; the rubric in *SA* is entirely different and says nothing at all about ordeals and visnets.[85] The rubric to *SA*, c.6, merely says it is on 'complaints of theft and robbery' and this rubric is present in all manuscript witnesses of *SA*, which contains the version of the statute closer to the original text.[86]

Debates on the future of the ordeal after October 1230 should not, therefore, be based on the rubricated headings of this particular piece of legislation. That the statute abolished the ordeal is suggested not by its manuscript rubric but by its final sentence. *SA* proclaims that 'henceforth, judgement by pit or iron shall not happen on him [i.e. the accused] as was the custom in ancient times', and even *CD* states that 'henceforth, judgement by pit or iron shall not happen on him'.[87] We should not interpret 'in ancient times' as actually referring to a time long gone by but, probably, an attempt by the drafters of the legislation to separate the past from the hopefully iron- and water-free future. Certainly, the combined testimony of *CD* and *SA* suggests that it was an intention of the drafters of the original statute to ban the use of the ordeal for theft and robbery.

What, then, happened to the ordeals of iron and water after 1230? It is clear that battle long survived the decline of these two, as was the case in England, where trial by battle was only formally abolished in 1819.[88] *CD*, compiled in the reign of

---

[82] *Coupar Angus Chrs*, i, no. 35.　　[83] Willock, *Jury*, pp. 26–8.

[84] Willock, *Jury*, p. 28.

[85] *CD*, c. 39; confirmed in its earliest manuscript witness, NRS, PA5/2, fo. 40v.

[86] *SA*, c. 6; confirmed in its earliest manuscript witness, NLS, MS Acc. 21246, fo. 144r.

[87] *SA*, c. 6; *CD*, c. 39.

[88] Russell, 'Trial by Battle and the Writ of Right', pp. 111, 129 (note 11).

Robert I, gives three options of proof in cases of theft and robbery: the visnet, compurgation, or trial by battle.[89] The absence of iron and water from these chapters is noteworthy: it suggests that the ordeals of iron and pit were no longer a sanctioned option by the fourteenth century.[90] Non-royal charters post-dating 1230 reveal that accusations of theft could be proven by trial by battle, rather than iron or water, or even settled by amicable composition (agreement) and arbitration.[91]

But was this really the case? The miracle collection of Queen Margaret gives the example of William the carpenter, who underwent the ordeal of iron to prove his innocence, showing that iron was a normal mode of proof in cases of rape, and it is possible that this miracle was either reported or written down after the 1230 act itself.[92] It is possible that the statute only aimed to abolish the ordeal in 1230 in cases of theft and robbery; it may have survived longer for other cases, such as rape. Royal charters that again long post-date 1230 continue to include the formula 'gallows and pit' even in charters recording new gifts of land.[93] A legal chapter in *SA*, which re-writes an assize of William enacted in 1180, states that the sheriff or the *sheriff's* sergeand had to be present at baronial courts to supervise the ordeals of battle, water, or iron.[94] It is impossible to prove that this chapter was recorded before or after 1230. The balance of evidence therefore suggests that, although the ordeals of iron and water had dropped out of written legislation by the time of *CD*, they were, most probably, still used in practice, particularly in the decades after the 1230 legislation and despite the ambitions of the statute.[95]

---

[89] *SA*, c. 11; *CD*, cc. 3, 14, 42. For the reference to the ordeal in *CD*, see *CD*, c. 17, but expanding *LS*, c.9. Only one chapter of *CD* original to the compilation mentions the presence of an ordeal pit: *CD*, c. 21. Neville cites a charter of Alexander II issued in 1215 to the Knights Templar 'specifying that in the adjudication of serious offences they should have the right to opt for trial by visnet instead of the dangers of the ordeal pit': Cynthia J. Neville, 'Neighbours, the Neighbourhood, and the visnet in Scotland, 1125–1300', in *New Perspectives*, ed. Hammond, pp. 161–73, at p. 168. But the charter, as far as I read it, does not state this. It says that the men of the brethren should not be put to the ordeal pit 'if their lords or neighbours (*vicini*) wish to pledge them [i.e. stand as their surety]': NRS, GD 119/2; Grant G. Simpson, *Scottish Handwriting, 1150–1650*, 2nd edn (East Linton, 1998), no. 4 [AII/12]. Thus, these men would only be subject to the ordeal if they had no one to act as a surety for them, which was still a privilege, as men defamed of theft in one or more provinces but were unable to find a surety would, in *LS*, be treated as 'proven thieves' (*LS*, c. 3).

[90] See also the evidence assembled in *Regiam Majestatem*, ed. Cooper, pp. 36–8. This evidence should be read in the knowledge that Cooper believed that *RM* was a thirteenth-century treatise, probably compiled during the reign of Alexander II (*Regiam Majestatem*, ed. Cooper, pp. 43–4).

[91] *Melrose Liber*, i, no. 175 [AII/167]; 'Charters of Balmerino', ed. Easson, pp. 8–9, no. 2 [AII/176].

[92] For the date, see *Miracles*, ed. Bartlett, pp. xxxiv–xxxvii.

[93] *RRS*, iv, 1, nos. 41, 55, 126; Fraser, *Carlaverock*, ii, p. 405 [AII/318]; Fraser, *Carlaverock*, ii, pp. 404–5 [AII/194].

[94] *SA*, c. 21. This updates the law of 1180 (*LS*, c.7, and discussed in Chapter 4, pp. 206–8, and Note 74). Thomson, because he knew that *SA*, c. 21, was similar to the 1180 statute, put it as the last sentence to his edition of the 1180 statute, which he had placed among the Assizes of William (*ARW*, c. 12; *APS*, i, pp. 374–5).

[95] Cf. Hector L. MacQueen, 'Expectations of the Law in the Twelfth and Thirteenth Century', *Tijdschrift voor Rechtsgeschiedenis*, vol. 70, nos. 3&4 (2002), pp. 279–90, at pp. 287, 290.

Novel Dissasine (SA, c. 7)

The final statute enacted in October 1230 has attracted the most attention. Unlike the other three, it is a legal remedy for the recovery of possession of land, a subject absent from the legal material discussed thus far. The remedy was based on the English writ of novel disseisin—novel dissasine in Scots—through which an ejected tenant of a free landholding could complain to the king of his dispossession and seek its restoration. Although there is considerable debate surrounding its introduction in England, the procedure has been thought to date to around the same time as the Assize of Clarendon in 1166 (although the original enactment does not survive); reference in the English pipe rolls suggests the procedure became available almost immediately.[96] *Glanvill*, written 1187×89, contains a formulaic writ of novel disseisin.[97] This was addressed to the sheriff and informed him that the king had received a complaint from 'N' that 'R' had unlawfully and without judgment disseised him of his free tenement (*tenementum*) in a particular vill. The sheriff was immediately to take the disseised chattels into his hand (so that whoever was the sitting tenant would no longer have enjoyment of them while the case proceeded) and summon twelve 'free and lawful men' to appear before the king's justices to conduct a recognition, whereupon a verdict would be given. The defendant, R, was also to be summoned before the king's judges. No essoins (legitimate no-shows) were allowed in these cases; this meant that the defendant could not drag the case out by repeated non-appearance in court. If either party failed to show up, the case continued regardless and they were liable for amercement if the judgment went against them. If both parties showed up and the defendant were found guilty, he had to pay a fine, also called an amercement. If the plaintiff lost his case, he was subject to the same penalty. If the plaintiff was vindicated, a writ was sent to the sheriff commanding him to reseise him of his land.

Maitland long ago recognized that *tenementum* was an abstract word that did not have to (although it could) refer to life-long possession of a physical piece of earth.[98] *Glanvill* was clear on this as well: a disseisin of a *tenementum* included situations where someone 'raised up or knocked down' a bank, raised the level of a millpond, refused another his rights to common pasture, or, indeed, at another extreme, forcibly ejected someone from their entire landholding on which their status and livelihood depended.[99] But the range of novel disseisin in England is not the only reason for its importance in English historiography. By providing a remedy for the recovery of land available to all free men, regardless of any other tie of lordship, the king's court effectively undercut the jurisdictional rights of great landlords to have ultimate control over their tenants, subordinates, and land. There

---

[96] Pollock and Maitland, *HEL*, i, pp. 145–7; ii, pp. 47–56; Doris M. Stenton, *English Justice between the Norman Conquest and the Great Charter 1066–1215* (London, 1965), pp. 33–43, 48–9; R. C. van Caenegem, *The Birth of the English Common Law* (Cambridge, 1973), pp. 42–7; Donald W. Sutherland, *The Assize of Novel Disseisin* (Oxford, 1973), pp. 5–42; for the most recent discussion see, Hudson, *OHLE*, ii, pp. 609–19.
[97] *Glanvill*, XIII, cc. 32–39, pp. 167–70.
[98] Pollock and Maitland, *HEL*, ii, pp. 148–9.   [99] *Glanvill*, XIII, cc. 35–37, pp. 168–9.

has been much debate about whether Henry II did intend to lessen the jurisdictional power of lords or whether this consequence was unintentional.[100] These debates are less important to the argument of this chapter because, by the time of its introduction in Scotland in 1230, it was clear that, in England, the act had brought a bulk of cases, all using the new procedure, into the developing structures of the royal courts. For Maitland, the introduction of novel disseisin in England laid down the rule that 'seisin of a free tenement, no matter of what lord it be holden, is protected by the king'.[101]

Its Scottish counterpart, introduced in 1230, has also received plaudits. Its introduction was, for similar reasons to that in England, 'a crucial step towards the conversion of royal justice into a common law of the kingdom' when royal justice had become 'a matter of course or of right for the complainer'.[102] The statute establishing novel dissaine identified lords as those who would have unjustly dissaised their men, thereby suggesting that novel dissaine did increase the business of the king's courts at the expense of the tenurial power of lords. MacQueen has argued that novel dissaine also protected the church from dispossession of their land in lay courts.[103]

The version of the statute introducing novel dissaine in Scotland used in modern scholarship is that in volume 1 of *APS*. Unfortunately, this brings together two separate manuscript traditions of the text, one belonging to *SA*, the other to *CD*. As a result of this joining, the significance of the text and the structure of landholding rights described within it needs to be reconsidered.

A translation of the *APS* text is as follows:

> The lord king Alexander also enacted at the said day and place that if anyone complains to the lord king or his justiciar that his lord or any other person has dissaised him unjustly and without a judgement of any tenement of which he was previously vest and saised (*de aliquo tenemento de quo ipse prius fuerit vestitus et saisitus*) and shall find pledges for the prosecution of his claim, the justiciar or the sheriff shall, by the brieve of the king or the justiciar, cause a recognition to be done by the good men of the country [to decide] if the complainer makes a just suit (*iustam queremoniam fecerit*). And if it shall be recognosced and proved, the justiciar or the sheriff shall cause him to be resaised of the land (*de terra*) of which he was dissaised and the dissaisor shall be in the king's mercy (*misericordia*). If however, it shall be recognosced that the complainer has made an unjust suit (*iniustam queremoniam*), the complainer shall be in the king's mercy (*misericordia*) of ten pounds.[104]

[100] Milsom, *Legal Framework*, pp. 185–6; Paul Brand, 'Henry II and the Creation of the English Common Law', in *Henry II: New Interpretations*, ed. Christopher Harper-Bill and Nicholas Vincent (Woodbridge, 2007), pp. 215–41, at pp. 235–8; Paul Brand, '"Multis vigillis excogitatem et inventam": Henry II and the Creation of the English Common Law', *Haskins Society Journal*, vol. 2 (1990), pp. 197–222; J. G. H. Hudson, *Land Law and Lordship in Anglo-Norman England* (Oxford, 1994), pp. 276–9; Hudson, *OHLE*, ii, pp. 603–4, 609–20.

[101] Pollock and Maitland, *HEL*, i, p. 146.

[102] MacQueen, 'Canon Law, Custom and Legislation', p. 244.

[103] MacQueen, *Common Law*, pp. 143–4.

[104] *APS*, i, p. 400 (*SRA*, c. 7); translation based on MacQueen, 'Canon Law, Custom and Legislation', p. 243; and MacQueen, *Common Law*, p. 137.

The verbal dependence of this text of the statute on the description of novel disseisin in *Glanvill* is clear and, indeed, has been noted frequently.[105] *Glanvill*, like the *APS*-text, states that pleas of novel disseisin could be initiated when 'anyone disseised another of his free tenement unlawfully and without a judgement'.[106] However, the text in *SA* is different:

> The lord king Alexander enacted on the said day and place [13 October 1230] that if anyone complains to the lord king or his justiciar that his lord or any other person dissaised him unlawfully and without judgement and has found a pledge for the prosecution of his claim, the justiciar or the sheriff shall, by the brieve (*preceptum*) of the lord king or justiciar (*per preceptum regis vel iusticiarii*), cause a recognition to be done by the law-worthy men of the country [to decide] whether the complainer has told the truth (*verum dixerit*). And if it is so recognosced, the sheriff shall make sasine to him of that which he was dissaised (*faciet ei saisinam de qua fuit dissaisitus*). And he who dissaised him shall be at the mercy of the lord king for £10. If it is understood that the complainer said an untruth (*falsum dixerit*), he shall give the forfeiture over the matter.[107]

The *SA* text is thus more vague in its terminology and in the object of dissasine than that printed in *APS*. It does not use the word *tenementum* but instead refers to it merely as *de qua* ('of that'). Nor does it specify, as *APS* does, that the complainer has to be 'vested and saised' (that is, ceremonially invested with the land itself, often by rod and staff) in whatever has been lost.[108] Moreover, the legal language is less formal: the complainer 'tells the truth' in *SA* rather than making a *iusta queremonia*, as in *APS*. The text of the statute introducing novel dissasine was less dependent on the legal language of late twelfth-century England (as exemplified in *Glanvill*) than is usually thought.

It is easy to see why the *APS*-text diverts stylistically and substantively from *SA* when the *CD*-text is consulted. This is given below:

> Item, it was enacted and unanimously granted that if anyone complains to the lord king or his justiciar that his lord or any other person dissaised him unlawfully and without judgement of anything in which he was first vested and saised (*de aliquo quo ipse prius fuerit vestitus et saisitus*), and he should have found a pledge for the prosecution of his claim, the justiciar or the sheriff shall, through the brieve of the lord king, cause a recognition to be done by the law-worthy men of the country [to decide] whether the complainer has made a lawful suit (*iustam queremoniam*). And if it is so recognosced and proved, the sheriff or the justiciar shall make resasine to him of the thing of which he had been dissaised and the knight or other person (*miles vel alius*) who did the said dissasine shall be at the mercy of the lord king. And those chattels or land shall be restored immediately to the dissaised at the same court with damages or arrears (*dampnis seu arreragiis*). If, however, it is acknowledged that the complainer made an unlawful suit (*iniustam queremoniam*), the complainer shall be at the mercy (*misericordiam*) of the lord king, that is, for £10.[109]

[105] MacQueen, *Common Law*, pp. 136–7.   [106] *Glanvill*, XIII, c. 33 (p. 167).
[107] *SA*, c. 7, also printed in Taylor, 'Assizes of David', pp. 217–18.
[108] This stipulation is not found in *Glanvill* nor even in the later and much more comprehensive Bracton. The verb *saisire* was in use in twelfth-century Scotland, however; it just did not make much of an imprint in the diplomatic of contemporary royal charters.
[109] *CD*, c. 41.

Thomson thus used the *CD*-text as his general guide to the legal language of the statute of novel dissasine, with one exception. When preparing the *APS*-text, he did not include the sentence present in *CD* 'and those chattels or land shall be restored immediately to the dissaised at the same court with damages or arrears'. It is hard to see why Thomson ignored it because the sentence suggests that, as in England, the seizure of chattels preceded or was part of the act of dissasine itself. The *APS*-text, therefore, combines the text in *SA* and *CD*, in general preferring the language of *CD* to that in *SA*. Most importantly, the *APS*-text has no manuscript support whatsoever and, by combining texts of almost a century apart, it obscures developments in the technical language of law. Thus, in order to understand novel dissasine and its subsequent development, the *SA*-text must be our starting point.

The statute in *SA* states that if anyone wished to pursue a case of dissasine, they appealed to the king or justiciar, who then (depending on who was the point of complaint) commanded the justiciar or sheriff by written precept to call a recognition (a body of *probi homines* drawn from the locality) to determine the truth of the matter. If the complaint was upheld, the defendant had to pay a fine to the king of £10; if the complaint was dismissed, the complainer himself had to pay the substantial fine.[110]

Although the *SA*-text and the *CD*-text give us roughly the same procedure, the technicality of the language of law is more developed in *CD* than in *SA*. If we compare both these texts to the brieve formula for novel dissasine found in the same manuscript as the earliest textual witness of *CD*—the Ayr manuscript—it is clear that in places the formulaic texts mirrors that of *CD*, not *SA*.[111]

> The king to the justiciar etc. A, by his grave complaint, has shown us that B unlawfully and without judgement dissaised him of the land of C with its appurtenances in the tenement of E within the sheriffdom of B, of which he was vested and saised (*vestitus et saisitus*) for days and years as of feu or of dower or of farm for a term which has not yet past. Wherefore we command and order that, having taken safe and secure pledges from A for the prosecution of his claim, you cause a recognition to be done lawfully and following the assize of the land, by the worthy and sworn men of the locality [to decide] if it is as the said A has shown to us. If, through the said recognition, done lawfully and according to the assize of the land, you should decide it to be so, you shall cause the said A to have sasine of the said land of C with its appurtenances and, without delay, take for our need the amercement (*misericordia*) belonging to us from the above for the unlawful dissasine done by him. But if, by the same recognition, done lawfully and following the assize of the land, it appears otherwise to you, you should take for our use the amercement belonging to us from the above A for his unlawful suit (*de iniusta querimonia*).

The similarity between *CD* and the Ayr formula throws the initial flexibility of the introduction of novel dissasine into view. This is not just a matter of the presence or absence of technical language, although there is an inherent difference in

---

[110] For other £10 fines, see Chapter 3, pp. 153–4, and Carpenter, 'Scottish Royal Government', pp. 148–9.
[111] *Scottish Formularies*, ed. Duncan, A21, pp. 18–19.

formality (and, perhaps, procedure) between the injunction to 'tell the truth' and to 'make a lawful suit'. The vagueness of *SA* shows how far the procedure had been honed down and elaborated between 1230 and the reign of Robert I. This still holds even though the most recent commentator on novel dissasine in Scotland has described even the fourteenth-century brieve formula as 'vaguer and [more] open to discretion than it was in England'.[112] But if the brieve formula was 'vaguer' than its English counterpart, the original 1230 legislation was even more so. While lords were singled out as the main group of potential dissaisors in *SA*, what they were meant to dissaise is unclear.[113] By the time of *CD* and the brieve formula, novel dissasine covered anything in which the claimant had been vested and saised. The brieve formula is more precise than *CD*: the vested and saised object had become a *tenementum*, which could be a feu, a piece of dower land, or even land held at farm whose lease had not expired.

This focus on lay landholdings and the proper form of possession is absent in the original 1230 statute: it must have developed at some point between the enactment and the early fourteenth century. The first surviving appearance of the formula 'vestitus et saisitus' in a royal act is in a brieve of Alexander III of 1260, where he commanded the then justiciar, Alexander Comyn, earl of Buchan, to find out whether Hector, son of Hector, was 'vested and saised' of five pennylands in South Ayrshire.[114] 'Vested and saised' does not appear in the surviving charters of Alexander II.[115] All other appearances of the formula in royal charters appear in the 1260s or later.[116] In order for the formula to appear in the updated version of the law in *CD*, it may be surmised that it had achieved purchase in royal conceptions of lay landholding more generally. The appearance of *vestitus et saisitus* in

---

[112] Carpenter, 'Scottish Royal Government', p. 147.

[113] Carpenter, 'Scottish Royal Government', p. 147. The object of dissaine, the *tenementum*, is rarely present in any of the manuscripts containing this statute, even those of *CD*. Only MS H (normally called the Cromartie manuscript), written *c*.1470, around 250 years after the promulgation of this assize, describes the object of dissaine as *tenementum*, probably influenced by the brieve formula in the Ayr manuscript which was using this word by the early fourteenth century; NLS, MS Adv. 25.5.10, fos 21v (*CD*-version) 129r–v (*SA* version). The scribe of H was extremely well versed not only in the content of *Glanvill* but also more widely in Roman and canon law. The appearance of *tenementum* in this manuscript alone must have been an addition by the scribe of MS H, presumably because he knew the content of *Glanvill* and because he knew that *tenementum* had by then become the catchall term in cases of dissaine in Scotland.

[114] See *RRS*, iv, 1, no. 27, for the brieve and NRS, RH5/30, for the returned inquest. The brieve is retourable, for which see below, pp. 298–300.

[115] I am grateful to Keith Stringer for confirming that the formula does not appear in any of Alexander II's charters. For other examples of *vestitus et saisitus* in royal charters or documents generated by royal charters (such as inquest returns), see *APS*, i, p. 100; *Dunf. Reg.* nos. 228, 322; NRS, RH5/54 (after 1259); NRS, RH5/33; NRS, RH5/30; *Documents Illustrative of the History of Scotland from the Death of Alexander the Third to the Accession of Robert Bruce MCCLXXXVI–MCCCVI*, ed. J. Stevenson, 2 vols (Edinburgh, 1870), i, no. 68.

[116] There is one earlier appearance that I have found in an act of Alexander Stewart, dated 1252, for which see *Paisley Reg.*, pp. 90–1. The appearance of 'vested and saised' in royal charters coincides with the appearance of our earliest retourable brieves and inquests, for which see below, pp. 318–19, 323–334. This in itself may not be a coincidence but the absence of the phrase from the *SA*-text of the 1230 statute suggests that we are looking at a period 1230×52 for the most conservative estimate for when it appeared, 1230 denoting the absence of the formula from the statute, and 1252 the appearance of the formula in a non-royal act.

1260 is thus unlikely to be the moment when novel dissasine became immediately more focused and more like its fourteenth-century successor but is indicative of the slow development of the focus on novel dissasine on particular types of lay landholding and possession.

The difference between the language of the statute of novel dissasine in *SA*, *CD*, and the brieve formula in the early-fourteenth-century Ayr manuscript is important. By not stating explicitly that a person had to be 'vested and saised' in the land he or she claimed to have been unlawfully dissaised of, the *SA* statute effectively meant that pursuers were not required to prove that they had been formally invested with their land in order to make a plea. That 'vested and saised' was present in the later statute in *CD* and in the Ayr brieve formula suggests that certain qualifications of what it meant to be 'vested and saised' in a piece of land were required if a pursuer's attempt to initiate a claim were to be accepted. Equally, that *CD* stated a pursuer had to make a 'lawful suit', whereas *SA* only expected him or her to 'tell the truth', suggests that the court proceeding itself had become conceived as a *querimonia*, which, in Roman law, meant a complaint made to an imperial official or, more generally, a formal complaint made in a court for which a response was required, rather than a mere verbal statement made against another person, as suggested by 'tell the truth'.[117] All this is indicative of an increasing formalization and specialization of the language of law between 1230 and the early fourteenth century, which was not there when the statute was first introduced.

The elaboration and formalization of the technical language of novel dissasine is explicable by increasing use of this procedure. But who, in fact, did use it? Until very recently, it has been assumed that Scottish common law brieves including novel dissasine were available to all freeholders, rich and poor(ish), as their counterpart writs were in England.[118] There, the wide availability of writs of novel disseisin was both in theory and in practice: the cost of obtaining the relevant writs and the fines for making a wrongful plea were not prohibitively high; thus, even people of relatively low socio-economic status could consider appealing to royal justice.[119] As a result, low-status people could initiate pleas of novel disseisin about very small pieces of land: one writ in the Berkshire file for 1248 reveals that Isabel of Sandford and her son, Thomas, had claimed that one Hugh, son of Henry, had unlawfully disseised them of 400 (2ft by 200ft) square

---

[117] Adolf Berger, *Encyclopedic Dictionary of Roman Law* (Philadelphia, PA, 1953), p. 666.

[118] This view, however, is also relatively new and is mainly based on the work of MacQueen, beginning in the early 1980s, who did so much to illuminate the capacities of thirteenth- and fourteenth-century common law; see Hector L. MacQueen, 'The Brieve of Right in Scots Law', *The Journal of Legal History*, vol. 3, no. 1 (1982), pp. 52–70; Hector L. MacQueen, 'Dissasine and Mortancestor in Scots Law', *The Journal of Legal History*, vol. 4, no. 3 (1983), pp. 21–49; Hector L. MacQueen, 'The Brieve of Right Revisited', in *The Political Context of Law*, ed. R. Eales and D. Sullivan (London, 1987), pp. 17–25; and, of course, MacQueen, *Common Law*, particularly chapters 4–7, some of which supersedes his earlier work, in particular pp. 146–53. Although I argue for a more minimal view of novel dissasine than MacQueen does, the importance of his work cannot be overestimated and this chapter would not have been possible without it.

[119] Carpenter, 'Scottish Royal Government', pp. 148–9.

feet of land, around the size of many prohibitively expensive one-bedroom flats in London today.[120]

But was this the case in Scotland? In an extremely important article, David Carpenter has drawn attention to the large amercement of £10 levied in Scotland either on the unlawful dissaisor or on the person initiating the claim if he or she was wrong.[121] Thus, unlike in England, where the fines for initiating an unjust plea were much smaller—the largest were around £1—in Scotland, claimants stood to lose a large sum of money if they failed in their case. Under Alexander II and III, half a knight's feu could be worth £10. At some point during his reign, Alexander III created single money feus worth £20 for Reginald Cheyne and Alexander Comyn, earl of Buchan, who were both of extremely high rank.[122] Had either ever made an unlawful claim of novel dissasine, they would have stood to lose half their annual income from these money feus. Even these men might have thought twice about initiating a plea, despite having other monetary and landed resources on which to draw. Someone who *only* was of knightly status or who only had the otherwise quite substantial holdings of a single knight's feu (men such as, in the late twelfth century, Walter de Berkeley, the king's chamberlain) would have lost a great proportion of their income from their lands if they were found to have made a wrongful claim.[123] Carpenter has written: 'in Scotland, the amercement for a false claim was a major deterrent to bringing a common law action. In England, for any one other than the very poor, it was no deterrent at all'.[124]

Carpenter has drawn attention to the only clear case of novel dissasine to have survived from the thirteenth century. It mentions these fines and the effect they could have. The case does not survive in its entirety: we only know about it because Hugh de Berkeley, then justiciar of Lothian, wrote to his 'man', William de Badby, constable to Berwick, commanding him to raise £10 from the land of John Scot of

---

[120] *Roll and Writ File of the Berkshire Eyre of 1248*, ed. Michael T. Clanchy, Selden Society 90 (London, 1973), p. 408 (a24), case as no. 66, at pp. 35–6. It was decided here that Hugh did not disseise them unjustly (despite his not showing up, therefore leaving his pledges in mercy) and so Isabel and Thomas were amerced for making unlawful claim. Another case (a93, at p. 439), was concerned with an even smaller piece of land, measuring 80 square feet (4ft by 20ft).

[121] I follow the arguments and evidence provided in Carpenter, 'Scottish Royal Government', pp. 138–54. This is not needless repetition (there are no other cases). But it is necessary because, although I follow Carpenter's arguments about novel dissasine, I depart from him in part about the other common law brieves, as set out below, pp. 308–9.

[122] Bain, *CDS*, ii, nos. 1617, 1737. For a £20 feu given to Hugh de Berkeley, see *ER*, i, p. 2. In David I's reign, half a knight's feu was worth 10 marks: *CDI*, no. 194. Hammond has suggested, however, that this charter may have been compiled early in William's reign: Hammond, 'Adoption and Routinization', pp. 98–9.

[123] Anselm of Camelyne was given an estate worth £20; on its gift in 1247, he was to pay £10 a year in addition to half the service of a knight; Fraser, *Carlaverock*, ii, p. 405 [AII/318]. Other local lords were better off. Mael Coluim, thane of Callendar, was compensated for his loss of the thanage of Callendar by land worth £40, for which see *Holyrood Liber*, no. 65 [AII/203] (and Fraser, *Carlaverock*, ii, pp. 404–5 [AII/194]). For both these gifts, see Chapter 1, pp. 76, 78, note 258.

[124] Carpenter, 'Scottish Royal Government', p. 149. Carpenter seems to suggest that this fine was levied for all wrongful actions begun by pleadable brieve but such fines were not levied in cases of mortancestry, for which see below, pp. 308–9. The amount of £10, which the pursuer and defendant had to put in pledge before the plea began in court, is confirmed in *Quoniam Attachiamenta*, ed. T. David Fergus, Stair Society 44 (Edinburgh, 1996), c. 38, pp. 220–1.

Reston (modern Scottish borders) to pay for works on the king's chapel in Berwick castle.[125] The letter records that John had pledged Great Reston to the king when beginning two claims of novel dissasine against a defendant whose name is not given. The two cases of novel dissasine had thus been heard at some point before 6 March 1262, the date of the justiciar's letter to the constable of Berwick.[126] John had, prior to this, obtained 'two pairs of letters of the lord king of dissasine' and had placed his land of Great Reston in pledge to the king if he should fail in his claim.[127] Unfortunately for John, he did, both times, and thus had to pay two fines (*forisfacturae*) of £10 each, totalling the vast amount of £20. John must have already paid off one of the fines of £10: the justiciar's letter is clear that the constable should raise only £10 from the land and 'if there is anything left beyond £20 [the whole amount John owed], you must hand it over to the said John'. In the event, John could not recover any of his land and the king seized it, later granting it to Coldingham Priory. Following John's death, Coldingham then sold the vill of Great Reston back to John's brother, Patrick Scot, as 'his true inheritance', stating that John had lost the land 'judicially for the forfeitures against the lord king of Scotland'.[128] The dower land of John's stepmother, Alice, was reserved: presumably the priory could reclaim this land on Alice's death.

Coldingham Priory did well out of John's initiation of two claims of novel dissasine: they received some money from the sale to Patrick and may well have kept Alice's dower land after her death. The king also did well: he repaired his chapel at Berwick castle from John's forfeiture. Patrick Scot of Reston also did reasonably well, although at a price: he reclaimed his inheritance from his brother, via the king, the justiciar, and Coldingham Priory. John, however, did extremely badly: he lost his inheritance and died about a decade later. We cannot know whether John's loss would have been typical in cases of dissasine: comparison from the 1256 Shropshire eyre in England shows that, out of sixty-two cases, twenty-one resulted in judgment in favour of the defendant, twenty for the plaintiff, and twenty-one were dropped before they came to court, and so resulted in the plaintiff's amercement for initiating a plea that was not followed through.[129] Thus, in two-thirds of cases in this Shropshire eyre, the person who brought the case of disseisin was amerced, in a kingdom where the financial consequences of an unsuccessful plea were much lighter than in Scotland. There was no guarantee that pleas of novel disseisin would be successful and, coupling this with the large fines in Scotland, the risks of initiating a claim of novel dissasine there may have been too great for most people. In addition, the large amercement of £10 means that pursuers would

---

[125] *Cold Corr.*, no. 1.

[126] *Cold Corr.*, no. 1. The document is dated 6 March 1261; I have followed PoMS in assuming Lady Day dating. However, this is just for consistency; there is no external evidence confirming consistent use of Lady Day *anno domini*: H3/83/19, available online at <http://db.poms.ac.uk/record/source/4383/>; for commentary, see Carpenter, 'Scottish Royal Government', pp. 149–50.

[127] It is unclear what the reference to the 'pairs of letters' actually denotes. Could it have meant one brieve addressed to the justiciar, and the other from the justiciar summoning the defendant, as suggested by MacQueen? MacQueen, *Common Law*, p. 139, note 14 (at p. 162).

[128] Raine, *North Durham*, App., no. 579.

[129] *The Roll of the Shropshire Eyre of 1256*, ed. Alan Harding, Selden Society (London, 1981).

have rarely agreed to drop their plea and make an agreement once they had obtained the king's brieve and initiated the case. If they did, they risked being heavily amerced. This means not only that lower-status people would have been loath to obtain a brieve of novel dissasine but also that even higher-status people may have been reluctant to use it as a conscious strategy to push for an agreement. Novel dissasine may instead have stood as the nuclear option, something only to be used when all other options had failed; the financial fallout may not have been worth it, particularly when there were other brieve options available from the king's chapel, as we will see later in this chapter.[130]

The Remainder of Alexander II's Legislation

Not all of Alexander's legislation is discussed in this section; the result would be a rather tedious list. Instead, two themes of 1230—crime and security of possession—will be discussed to see how they were dealt with in two other important pieces of legislation.

In February 1244, Alexander II instituted an inquisition in Lothian under the supervision of his justiciar. It is clear that the inquisition was, at this point, to happen only in lands south of the River Forth and excluded Galloway, because that province 'has its own special laws'.[131] The inquisition seems to have been inspired by the juries of presentment in England, set up by the Assize of Clarendon in 1166.[132] In England, twelve 'lawful men' from each vill and hundred would identify and accuse wrongdoers, who then had to undergo the ordeal. If they failed the ordeal, they would lose a foot; even if they passed, they could be exiled if they were already of bad reputation and the local community really wanted to get rid of them.[133] The 1244 inquisition (*inquisicio*) marshalled 'good and sworn men' of each vill within each sheriffdom, together with the vill's steward.[134] These panels of oath-swearers formed visnets, who would then identify and accuse 'wrongdoers and their harbourers' who would then be tried. If those attached (i.e. accused) were convicted, the king would have the chattels of those accused of murder and robbery while the lord in whose lands the wrongdoer 'had any chattels' would have the chattels of those convicted of theft and homicide. Moreover, in these cases, the justiciar would hand over the accused 'to barons', who would do justice on them

---

[130] See below, pp. 318–19, 323–334.

[131] *SA*, c. 2; on the laws of Galloway, see MacQueen, 'Laws of Galloway'. For the implications of this act on robbery, see Simpson, 'Procedures', forthcoming.

[132] *Select Charters and Other Illustrations of English Constitutional History from the Earliest Times to the Reign of Edward I*, ed. W. Stubbs, 9th edn, revised by H. W. C. Davis (Oxford, 1921), pp. 170–3.

[133] The emphasis on community reputation led to a lot of false accusations, which were targeted in the 1170 Inquest of Sheriffs, as Kenneth Duggan has pointed out to me. By the time of the Assize of Northampton, issued in 1176, the punishment was loss of a foot and an arm. For these references see Stubbs, *Select Charters*, pp. 170–2, 176–7, 179.

[134] *SA*, c. 2. The word 'inquest' (*inquisicio*) was probably used here because the results did not lead to immediate judgment or conviction, and thus immediate punishment. If they had, then the word *recognitio* would probably have been used. For the difference between recognitions and inquests, see below, pp. 306–7.

in their own courts and take their chattels as a result. The statute also allowed for higher-status individuals to be attached by these visnets but only if they were tried by their peers: other knights or freeholders who held their lands hereditarily.[135]

At this point, this statute was applied only in Lothian. As Chapter 4 has shown, there is firm evidence that a basic process of indictments was introduced in Scotia by the 1260s and it is even possible that the ayre was introduced around the same time as the regional division in *c.*1220.[136] Together with the chattels confiscated from those convicted of murder, robbery, and similar felonies (probably arson and rape), these indictments could constitute a significant amount of income for the king from a more intense supervision of crime and its punishment than was ever indicated by the law of William the Lion. Although the statute itself does not list fines for neglect of duty in Lothian, it would be unsurprising if similar fines were also levied there.

There must be some caveats here, however. It was argued in the previous chapter that this 1244 statute may have been a short-term measure, designed to crack down on disorder following the murder of Patrick of Atholl in the local area. But even if the statute was only ever intended for the short term, many of the indictments would have profited secular lords, not the king; lords in whose lands the attached people had their chattels may not have minded the removal of accusation procedures from their own courts, as long as it was only in the short term. After all, the statute is explicit that the lords retained the profits of justice and the right to judgment in cases of homicide and theft. A comparison with the Devon eyre of 1238 in England shows that most of the criminal cases heard by royal justices were those of theft and homicide, the two crimes that the 1244 statute said would ordinarily be heard by lords.[137] If similar trends occurred in Lothian, then most of the income and justice-giving remained in the hands of lords, not the king and his justiciar. In fact, by convicting thieves and homicides by indictment, the justiciar gave lords in Lothian a hand. But it is probable that lords would not have been content with delegating the initial indictment and judgment to justiciars in the long term. Thus, while the level of co-ordination is certainly impressive and indicative of the growing responsibilities of justiciars, these responsibilities did not grow at the expense of aristocratic jurisdiction, which may well have significantly benefitted financially from the indictments in the short term.

Alexander is also known to have legislated on dower lands, the 'terce', that is, the third received by a widow of the heritable part of her late husband's estate. *SA*, c.8, is a record of a case brought into the king's presence and which resulted in the king

---

[135] Was this stipulation influenced by *Magna Carta*, clause 21? (online, with commentary, at <http://magnacarta.cmp.uea.ac.uk/read/magna_carta_1215/Clause_21>); see also *SA*, c. 3 (*APS*, i, p. 404), a 1248 enactment, in which Alexander and his magnates enacted at Stirling that 'henceforth, an oath concerning the loss of a man's life or limb shall not be made…unless by worthy and sworn men who are freeholders by charter'.

[136] *ER*, i, p. 34; see further Carpenter, 'Scottish Royal Government', pp. 131–2; Barrow, 'Justiciar', p. 90; see also, Chapter 4, pp. 240–3.

[137] In the first hundred cases in the Devon eyre, there were seven cases of murder, sixteen of homicide, and seven of theft; *Crown Pleas of the Devon Eyre of* 1238, ed. H. Summerson, Devon and Cornwall Record Society, new series, vol. 28 (Torquay, 1985).

making a new enactment 'as law' (*pro lege*).[138] The case is roughly datable to the 1230s/early 1240s, based on the *floruit* of Henry of Stirling, son of Earl David of Huntingdon, one of the protagonists in the case.[139] It states that Helen de Burnville, wife of John de Burnville, had been seeking her 'terce' [dower] in the land of *Kerinton* against Henry of Stirling who, at present, had custody of the land. Henry's position was that John's mother had been saised in this dower land since the death of her husband, whereas John had never been, and so it was not the custom for a widowed woman, as Helen was, to seek a terce 'of this kind'. Perhaps surprisingly, Alexander pronounced that widowed women did have the right to petition for this kind of terce, as well as other kinds (presumably ones which their husbands had been in sasine of before they died, when the case would be more clear-cut). Wishing there to be no more confusion on the matter, Alexander then enacted this 'as law', with 'many magnates' present.

The issue here is not that Alexander II was protecting all widows' pursuit of their terce—that was already well known—but that he was establishing a widow's right to seek the terce in lands which had belonged to her husband's father, now her mother-in-law's dower lands, but which her husband had not necessarily been saised in before their death. Presumably this case had arisen because John's mother had now died (as suggested by the pluperfect *tenuerat*), was no longer holding the third, and Henry of Stirling had been granted custody and intended to keep it. Helen, whose husband had recently died, was not happy with this and petitioned the king who, rather surprisingly, upheld her right to do so over that of his half-cousin, Henry of Stirling.

Conclusion

Like his father, Alexander legislated on theft and other crimes. But he did so in a very different framework, as was argued in Chapter 3. His legislation on crime was hierarchical: some crimes belonged to him, others to lords. He actively allowed for this in some of his 1230 legislation and his 1244 statute. The main feature of Alexander's 1230 legislation was the extent of its incorporation of lay aristocratic jurisdiction: if the king did not deal with it, his earls and barons would. If the offence took place in a lord's land, that lord would supervise the procedure; if the offence was in the king's demesne land, the sheriff took responsibility.[140] The statute on repledging limited the capacities of lords to repledge their free men but it in no way was a blanket ban on the practice. Instead, it aimed at regulating the potentially conflicting networks of jurisdiction—lay, ecclesiastical, and royal—without explicitly targeting any of them.

This may seem to be at odds at first with Alexander's concurrent introduction of novel dissasine. This procedure in England caused, in aim or in consequence, the

---

[138] *SA*, c. 8; printed in *SRA*, c. 8, in *APS*, i, pp. 401–2.

[139] It is possible that John was the father of John, who died in 1276, and whose wife, Agnes, claimed land in 1296 which *may* have been her dower land, worth 48 marks from Edward I. The location of this land is not known; Stevenson, *Documents*, ii, no 385a.

[140] *SA*, c. 5.

weakening of the jurisdiction of secular lords. But, despite the introductory statute naming lords explicitly as potential perpetrators, novel dissasine in Scotland could not have done the same because of the high amercements risked for making an unlawful claim: people, even those of relatively high status, such as John Scot of Reston, would have hesitated before bringing a complaint of novel dissasine against their lords. The introduction of novel dissasine, far from contradicting the other three statutes enacted in 1230, went some way to protect lords from their tenants. By limiting the practical use of the statute, thirteenth-century novel dissasine could only have been a remedy appealed to by the very few.[141]

But this does beg the question: if the assize of novel dissasine was so limited in Scotland, why introduce it at all? Security of heritable tenure, with the subsidiary security of lawful possession, was clearly an issue Alexander confronted.[142] If the procedure for mortancestry is also ascribed to his reign, it, combined with his legislation on dower lands and novel dissasine, reveals an interest in ensuring rightful succession and security in tenure and possession that must have lain at the heart of the discussion among the great magnates of the kingdom in October 1230.[143] As we shall see, Alexander II and Alexander III had remedies other than dissasine by which rights in land could be restored and secured. These additional remedies were not heavily amerceable, unlike novel dissasine. If novel dissasine in Scotland was practically limited to those who were either or almost of the status of the potential dissaisors, then its introduction would have gone some way to protect lordly power in their own jurisdictions while still providing a remedy against unlawful dispossessions at the highest level. Alexander's legislation was thus something of a compromise, something that did not contradict the tenor of his other statutes.[144]

The 1230 legislation as a whole, therefore, does not quite deserve its reputation as a transformative moment in the history of Scots law. Whereas it could be thought that the four pieces of legislation enacted at Stirling in 1230 *did* curtail the jurisdictional power of lords, cement the role of the jury in civil and criminal cases, outlaw the ordeal as a method of proof, and establish the king as the ultimate guarantor of all free landed property, the statutes themselves support more limited readings. It is argued here that the statutes actually protected elite jurisdictions, used the visnet only when trial by battle could not be invoked, and protected elite property rights rather than secure possession at large. Only the ordeals of iron and water may have gradually declined but even these were invoked in thirteenth-century charters on

---

[141] I deliberately echo Carpenter, 'Scottish Royal Government', 148–51. How far the potential social exclusivity of novel dissasine applied to other judicial brieves issued from the king's writing office will be developed below, pp. 308–9.

[142] Security of tenure, rather than outright possession, was the issue novel dissasine primarily confronted. The two could go together: the lawful holder of the land *could* be the same as the possessor and the possessor need not be the same person as the unlawful dissaisor. For this distinction, see MacQueen, 'Dissasine and Mortancestor', pp. 30–1; and for the effect of the 1318 legislation on third-party possession (i.e. when the possessor was not the named defendant), see MacQueen, *Common Law*, pp. 146–53.

[143] For the introduction of mortancestry in Alexander II's reign, see MacQueen, *Common Law*, pp. 167–75, and below, pp. 308–9.

[144] For its compromise nature, see Carpenter, 'Scottish Royal Government', pp. 150–2.

occasion. Thus, while the procedures introduced clearly were innovative (in that they were enacting something new), they were responding to already evident power dynamics—in particular, the importance of elite jurisdictions to the overall maintenance of law and order.

Finally, it is worth noting the *secular* tone of Alexander's legislation. Unlike his father's legislation, Alexander's legislation rarely mentions non-secular jurisdictions explicitly. While William's legislation had included the courts of 'bishops and abbots' alongside those of secular lords—earls, barons, knights, and thanes—Alexander's legislation mentions their jurisdiction only once, despite setting the prescriptive content of his legislation in an overwhelmingly administrative and jurisdictional framework. Only his 1230 statute on replegiation included any 'bishop, abbot or clerk', which makes sense, given that the statute was designed to protect elite jurisdictional integrity. All others are silent on the matter. Even a statute issued in 1214, which is more influenced by biblical language than any other piece of Alexander II's legislation, focuses only on earls, tenants-in-chief, their tenants, and peasants.[145] The statute on alternatives to trial by battle, although it involves clerks and prebendaries as potential victims, is only applicable in feus controlled by 'lords', the king's demesne land, and royal thanages; there is no mention of land held in 'alms'.[146] The statute on theft, robbery, and modes of proofs states that if the crime was one of murder or robbery, the king provided justice but if of homicide or theft, justice was done by the 'earl or baron'.[147] In 1244, those convicted of theft or homicide by the justiciar's inquisition in Lothian were to be handed over 'to barons', who would do justice in their courts.[148] Moreover, 'lords' were explicitly targeted in the statute introducing novel dissasine, as were 'knights' in the updated version in *CD*.[149] The exclusion of ecclesiastical lords from the content of Alexander's legislation did allow for some flexibility in response: the abbeys of Melrose and Balmerino adapted the content of one of the 1230 statutes to fit their own circumstances. But the secular nature of Alexander II's legislation, in comparison with William's, suggests that ecclesiastical and royal (with aristocratic) justice had become distinct. How and why this happened will be developed at the end of this chapter.

BRIEVE COLLECTIONS AND THE ALEXANDRIAN LEAP FORWARD

Although the surviving law of Alexander II reveals fewer substantial changes than previously thought, the statute of novel dissasine is evidence of a relatively new practice of royal government: the availability of formulaic brieves from the king's writing office which initiated legal processes. The 1230 legislation on novel dissasine

---

[145] *SA*, c. 1. Bower's reference to Alexander III's statutory reforms concerning field-systems may well be a misplaced one, really referring to this piece of legislation, enacted in 1214 by Alexander II (Bower, *Scotichronicon*, v, pp. 422–3).

[146] *SA*, c. 5.   [147] *SA*, c. 6.   [148] *SA*, c. 2.   [149] *SA*, c. 7; *CD*, c. 41.

states that pursuers (English: 'plaintiffs') could obtain a *preceptum* (a 'brieve') from the king or relevant justiciar which would initiate a case heard in royal courts to decide whether the pursuer had been unlawfully dissaised of his land. Novel dissasine was not the only procedure to be initiated by brieve: numerous other remedies also developed. These brieves were referred to in Latin in a number of ways: as *precepta* ('commands'), *breves* ('brieves'), and *litterae* ('letters'). These words did not denote technical differences between various 'types' of legal brieves; instead, they were all used generically, to refer to brieves purchasable from the king's chapel to initiate some form of legal process in a court.[150] The number of legal brieves increased substantially during the thirteenth century and allowed royal justice to be available in a far more regular and standard way than before.[151]

Pleadable Brieves, Retourable Brieves, and Non-Pleadable Brieves

Legal historians often divide these brieves into two types: pleadable and retourable.[152] The most powerful explanation of the distinctive quality of pleadable brieves is that put forward in 1986 by Hector MacQueen.[153] MacQueen demonstrated the intimate link between the pleadable brieve and the formal process of pleading in court. A pleadable brieve set out in general terms the contested issue between two named parties on which the court was to provide a judgment. That issue was then debated and refined by pleading in court: the pursuer set out his case and the defendant put forward exceptions to the pursuer's case. These exceptions could result in the case being dismissed before the jury judged the case. But if this did not happen and the case went to the jury, the general issue set out in the pleadable brieve had already been refined and defined by the formal process of court pleading to establish the particular issue on which the jury had to decide. MacQueen has written: 'if pleading was a debate between two parties about the facts of a case in which they defined the dispute which the jury had to determine, then such a procedure could only take place upon a brieve if it set out in general terms some dispute between two parties and invited the court to decide it'.[154] Pleadable brieves were the main evidence of the workings of the thirteenth-century

---

[150] The word *preceptum* is used in *SA*, c. 7; Fraser, *Douglas*, iii, no. 285; *RRS*, iv, 1, no. 85; *Dunf. Reg.*, no. 196; *littera* or *litterae* could be used to refer to brieves of recognition, mortancestry, brieves of dissasine, or brieves of inquest (see *RRS*, iv, 1, no. 18; *Glasgow Reg.*, i, no. 172; *Cold. Corr.*, no. 1; *Paisley Reg.*, pp. 180, 191, 192, 198; Fraser, *Keir*, pp. 197–8; *Dunf. Reg.*, no. 86). The Ayr formulary refers to *breves* and *littere*: NRS, PA5/2, fo. 18v; *Scottish Formularies*, ed. Duncan, p. 11; for *breve*, see Raine, *North Durham*, App., nos. 191, 296.

[151] Thus supposedly doing the same as judicial writs did in England, as outlined in Stenton, *English Justice*, pp. 22–53; van Caenegem, *Birth of English Common Law*, pp. 29–61.

[152] Sheriff Hector McKechnie, however, dealt with both together; Hector McKechnie, *Judicial Process Upon Brieves 1219–1532* (Glasgow, 1956), pp. 6–7. For Ian Willock, the contrast was between 'retourable brieves' and 'non-retourable brieves', although he also described them as 'pleadable and non-pleadable' brieves: Willock, *Jury*, pp. 106, 109–21, 122–32. Willock's views are discussed in Hector L. MacQueen, 'Pleadable Brieves, Pleading and the Development of Scots Law', *Law and History Review*, vol. 4, no. 2 (1986), pp. 403–22, at pp. 406–7.

[153] MacQueen, 'Pleading', pp. 407–11, 413–19; MacQueen, *Common Law*, pp. 122–4.

[154] MacQueen, 'Pleading', p. 415.

common law and affected the development of the structures of later medieval justice.[155]

For MacQueen, retourable brieves did not initiate the same process as pleadable brieves.[156] Technically, retourable refers to a brieve which commanded the addressee to return (or 'retour') a written report to the king on whatever he had been instructed to do in the original brieve. MacQueen acknowledged that retourable brieves could cover similar issues as pleadable ones—most obviously succession—but, for him, the key distinction between a pleadable brieve and a retourable brieve was in the different court process the two types of brieve initiated and, accordingly, the form of the brieve itself. Retourable brieves did not name two opposing parties (a pursuer versus a defendant) and did not result in pleading to determine 'the actual issue put to the assize'; retourable brieves did not initiate formal disputation between two parties in courts.[157] Instead, their function was administrative: an individual wishing to know a certain question about his or her rights in a particular piece of land would obtain a retourable brieve from the king's writing office which commanded the sheriff to initiate an inquest based on his or her particular question. The sheriff (or other official) would then report the facts in a written report which was sent back to the king. In this way, retourable brieves did not involve two conflicting parties debating their cases in a formal court setting. Because legal historians have seen retourable brieves having an administrative function rather than involving formal disputation (or pleading) in the court forum itself, they have been far less well studied than pleadable brieves.[158]

Retourable brieves are thus seen as non-pleadable; they did not initiate pleading. But, in addition, there were legal brieves which were *non-retourable* (in that their results were not returned in a written document) but were also *non-pleadable* (in that they did not initiate formal pleading in courts). Non-pleadable, non-retourable brieves included the brieves of perambulation and recognition, discussed later in this chapter.[159] Brieves of perambulation and recognition initiated a process to decide the lawful boundaries of particular pieces of land. But they did not initiate pleading; instead, the brieve contained a question (what are the marches of this land?), which a panel of sworn men set out to answer; this answer would be upheld as 'truth'. This is rather confusing for non-legal historians: pleadable brieves were not retourable; retourable brieves were not pleadable but, equally, there were some brieves, which initiated a legal process, which were neither pleadable nor retourable. This is an important distinction to keep in mind for this chapter as it will be shown here that the reliance on this categorization explains why a significant body

---

[155] MacQueen, *Common Law*, pp. 129, 247, 256–7.

[156] MacQueen, 'Pleading', pp. 415–16; cf. Willock, *Jury*, pp. 106, 122–32.

[157] MacQueen, 'Pleading', pp. 415–16; MacQueen, *Common Law*, pp. 123, 168–9.

[158] McKechnie, *Judicial Process*, p. 11, distinguishes between the brieves of mortancestry and succession in this way: 'All our writers until Erksine … confused this brieve [of mortancestor] with that of succession [retourable], but the two were quite distinct. Succession was only appropriate to decide who was the rightful heir of a deceased whose *title to the subjects was not challenged*: it was addressed to the sheriff and was retourable. Mortancestor was sought against a stranger *"qui terras iniuste detinet"*, came before the justiciar, and was not retourable'; my emphasis. See below, pp. 323–34.

[159] MacQueen, 'Pleading', pp. 416–17; MacQueen, *Common Law*, p. 123.

of evidence for understanding thirteenth-century legal development has been almost completely overlooked. Legal historians, interested in the substantive law as practised in courts, have often concentrated on the importance of pleadable brieves at the expense of retourable and non-pleadable brieves.[160]

None of these terms ('pleadable', 'retourable', 'non-pleadable'), however, are attested in the surviving evidence before the death of Alexander III in 1286: they are either very late thirteenth- or fourteenth-century terms or the categorizations of early modern and modern lawyers.[161] The category of 'pleadable brieve' is not attested until the 1290s, appearing in a treatise written in French known as 'the Scottish King's Household', in which pleadable brieves were distinguished from brieves *de cursu* (*les briefs de cours et pledables*), although, as Chapter 4 showed, there are problems with the testimony of this particular text.[162] The earliest unproblematic reference to a formal category of pleadable brieves does not appear until Robert I's legislation of 1318.[163] The earliest list of pleadable brieves appears in the legal treatise *Regiam Majestatem* (*RM*), which is probably of early-fourteenth-century date, compiled in the reign of Robert I.[164] *RM* states that right, novel dissasine, mortancestry, cases over neyfs, purprestures, and distress were all actions 'pleaded (*placitantur*) by brieve in the presence of the justiciar, sheriff or provosts of burghs'. By the second decade of the fourteenth century, therefore, pleadable process upon brieves was well known enough to be included in *RM*.

However, the very same period contains evidence that contemporaries were unsure about what was meant by pleading and how it related to the written documents issued from the king's writing office. A major collection of brieve formulae probably compiled in the late 1320s states that it is a collection of 'letters to be pleaded in courts' and 'brieves sent by the king from chancery'.[165] Thus, one might imagine that the 'letters to be pleaded in courts' were what historians now define as pleadable brieves. But the compiler of the collection did not maintain this distinction: the 'letters' in the collection could be simple instructions to royal officials, which were not pleadable at all, while some of the 'brieves' sent from the king's

---

[160] There are some exceptions: see Willock, *Jury*, pp. 123–32, who concentrates mainly on the brieves of perambulation and lining.

[161] As acknowledged in MacQueen, 'Pleading', pp. 406–7.

[162] 'The Scottish King's Household and Other Fragments From a Fourteenth-Century Manuscript in the Library of Corpus Christi College, Cambridge', ed. Mary Bateson, in *Miscellany II*, Scottish History Society, 1st ser., vol. 45 (1904), p. 31; MacQueen, 'Pleading', p. 407. David Carpenter, '"The Scottish King's Household" and English Ideas of Constitutional Reform', *Feature of the Month, October 2011*, The Breaking of Britain (2011), online at <http://www.breakingofbritain.ac.uk/blogs/feature-of-the-month/october-2011-the-scottish-kings-household/>; for more on the treatise, see Chapter 4, pp. 212, 233, 244.

[163] *RPS*, 1318/27.

[164] *RM*, bk I, c. 4, in *APS*, i, p. 598 (entitled *de his que per brevia placitantur coram justiciario, vicecomite vel burgorum prepositis*). The later fourteenth-century treatise, *Quoniam Attachiamenta*, also contains a longer set of pleadable brieves; see *Quoniam Attachiamenta*, ed. Fergus, c. 33, pp. 208–9. Both lists are discussed in MacQueen, 'Pleading', p. 407.

[165] *Scottish Formularies*, ed. Duncan, p. 11 (NRS, PA5/2, fo. 18v): *capitula capelle regis Scocie tam de litteris in curiis placitandis quam de brevibus per regem de cancellaria mittendis*. Henceforth, all references will be given to the *number* in Duncan's edition, followed by the page reference in brackets.

chancery correspond to those which historians would call 'pleadable brieves'.[166] So, while there was a category of pleadable brieve developing in the late thirteenth and early fourteenth centuries, we have to question how firmly it was established and what it included.[167]

The only possible evidence for thinking that the *category* of pleadable brieve, meaning a brieve that initiated pleading between two disputing parties in a court setting, was developing immediately after 1230 is the appearance of the verb *implacitare* or *impetare* ('implead' or 'bring into court' and, more generally, 'accuse') in certain records of dispute settlement.[168] However, the appearance of this word is not enough to assume that the type of formal court procedure shown by MacQueen existed later in the fourteenth century. Indeed, there is evidence that *implacitare* simply meant a person appearing in court to face some sort of accusation; it did not mean the procedure used in that court. For example, between 1261 and 1268, Alexander Baird granted to his son, Nicholas, that, among other things, if any of Nicholas's men or women were 'impleaded' in his (Alexander's) court, Nicholas would receive the forfeitures resulting from the cases.[169] There is no indication that *implacitare* meant being brought into court to answer a plea initiated by a pleadable brieve, the defence of which involved formal pleading. If we continue to use the category of pleadable brieve, we must recognize that it serves our understanding more than it served contemporaries. When examining the earliest collection of brieve formulae, then, it should be remembered that brieves were not divided or categorized in any consistent way during the thirteenth century.

Brieve Formulae in the Ayr Manuscript

The starting point here is this earliest collection of brieve formulae compiled in the early fourteenth century and known as the Ayr formulary.[170] As a later collection, it does not provide an accurate representation of the brieves available in 1230 but, because it claims to contain the range of brieve forms available from the king's 'chancery' (*cancellaria*: the earliest mention of this term) in the early fourteenth century,

---

[166] A18 (p. 17): *breve de recto*; A20 (p. 18): *breve de morte antecessoris*; A1 (NRS, PA5/2, fo. 18v): *litera de attornato*.

[167] MacQueen, 'Pleading', pp. 408, 414–15. MacQueen, however, acknowledged the conflicting evidence in the Ayr formulary; MacQueen, *Common Law*, p. 123.

[168] See, for example, *Paisley Reg.* i, p. 170; Fraser, *Douglas*, iii, no. 285; Raine, *North Durham*, App., no. 296; Fraser, *Keir*, pp. 197–8.

[169] 'Eight Thirteenth Century Texts', ed. W. W. Scott, in *Miscellany XIII*, Scottish History Society, 5th ser., vol. 14 (Edinburgh, 2004), pp. 1–41, text at pp. 33–5, with the reference to impleading and forfeitures at p. 34.

[170] NRS, PA5/2, fos. 18v–30r. The collection is known as the 'Ayr' formulary in modern scholarship because it survives in a manuscript that at one point passed through the hands of somebody very interested in the burgh of Ayr. The Ayr manuscript appears to have been compiled in the late 1320s, certainly 1318×29, although it contains some later sections which must post-date 1343 which were written in a later hand. It is also the manuscript containing the earliest surviving witness of *CD* (for which see Taylor, 'Assizes of David', pp. 201–2, 210–11). Lord Cooper edited the formulary in 1946 but his edition has now been superseded by that of A. A. M. Duncan, published in 2011: see *Register of Brieves*, ed. Cooper, pp. 33–52; *Scottish Formularies*, ed. Duncan, pp. 11–36. For a description of the Ayr MS, see *Scottish Formularies*, ed. Duncan, pp. 3–9.

it is still a useful starting point for understanding the range of brieves that had developed by this point.[171] The Ayr formulary lists the rubrics for eighty-one separate brieve forms, which are either less detailed or anonymized versions of authentic brieves or simple formulae which could be expanded or filled in as need be. Some brieves are not particularly well anonymized: one is a letter granting the merchants of 'W', count of Holland, free entry and exit at the king's ports. 'W' can be identified as William II, count of Holland and Hainault, and the original brieve was issued in 1323 as a dated copy of it survives in the count's archives.[172] Other brieves, however, are completely anonymized. An example of this is the formula commanding a sheriff to summon a general inquest (*generalis inquisicio*), which provides questions for him to ask. Not all brieves of general inquest contained all of these questions; the formula acts as a list of potential questions that could be asked in particular cases, depending on what issue had to be sorted out.[173]

> King to the sheriff. We command and order that you make a diligent and faithful inquest by the worthy and sworn men of the country (*patria*) [to discover] if a certain A de B, father, brother, uncle, sister *or* mother of B, bearer of the present letters, died vested and saised as of feu of the land of N with its appurtenances within your jurisdiction (*ballia*); *and* if his/her son [or brother, sister or nephew] B is the lawful and next heir of A in the land, is of lawful age; *and* how much the said land is worth each year; *and* from whom it is held; *and* by what service it is held, *and* in whose hands it now is: how; by whom; why and for how long; and if in any way he has done wrong towards us or our kingdom on account of which he ought not to recover his/her inheritance by law (*ius*); *and* if we have given the land to any other person and, whatever you should discover by the said inquest, conducted diligently and faithfully, you should send (*mittatis*) under the seal of the sheriff and the seals of others who were present when the inquest was done, back to our chapel with this brieve.

Before formulating any conclusions on the basis of the Ayr formulary, it should be acknowledged that the collection presents some quite significant problems. First, the brieve to William, count of Holland, shows that the Ayr collection contains datable early-fourteenth-century material that cannot necessarily be carried backwards into the thirteenth.[174] Indeed, the stipulation given in the brieve inquest above, concerning the wrong done towards the king and kingdom, is attested in the political behaviour and legal prescriptions of Robert I, not Alexander III, and so may well not have appeared in the thirteenth-century brieves.[175]

[171] The normal term is king's chapel (*capella regis*), for which see G. W. S. Barrow, 'The *Capella Regis* of the Kings of Scotland, 1107–1222', in *Miscellany V*, ed. Hector L. MacQueen, Stair Society 52 (Edinburgh, 2006), pp. 1–11. For the Scottish chancery in the later Middle Ages, see Athol L. Murray, 'The Scottish Chancery in the Fourteenth and Fifteenth Centuries', in *Écrit et Pouvoir dans les chancelleries médiévales: espace français, espace anglais*, ed. K. Fianu and D. J. Guth (Louvain-La-Neuve, 1997), pp. 133–51.

[172] A71 (p. 31); *RRS*, v, no. 243.

[173] A22 (p. 19); to be compared with *RRS*, iv, 1, nos. 27, 32, 36, 40 (and *APS*, i, p. 101), 70, 76. See also the points in David M. Walker, *A Legal History of Scotland*, vol. 1: *the Beginnings to A.D. 1286* (Edinburgh, 1988), pp. 122–3, 262–3.

[174] A71 (p. 31).

[175] *RPS*, 1318/23; see also the chapter on treason or sedition in *CD*, c. 32.

Second, the Ayr collection is incomplete: although it contains a list of eighty-one chapters, around three bifolia are missing, so thirty-six full texts do not survive.[176] Help is at hand from two later collections in fourteenth- and fifteenth-century manuscripts known as Bute and 'E', which are both longer collections and contain all but two of the missing brieve-texts from the Ayr collection.[177] However, we cannot necessarily assume that the content of Bute and E was always identical to what was once in Ayr. While many of the texts in Ayr are reproduced almost verbatim in Bute and E, others are not.[178] The brieve of protection in Bute, for instance, includes an additional clause not found in Ayr.[179] The brieve of mortancestry in Bute specifically states that the procedure of mortancestry could not be used for land held in alms, or for the services of freeholders. Neither exception is found in Ayr.[180]

However, many of the formulae in Ayr and, where applicable, E and Bute, are unproblematic for the period 1260–90 because either their entire content or elements of their diplomatic are attested in brieves of Alexander III.[181] Many of the questions asked in the formula of the general inquest, for example, are attested in the brieves of inquest and the inquest returns themselves, which survive from 1259/1260 onwards.[182] Only brieve formulae whose diplomatic corresponds with that of extant charters and brieves of Alexander III or for which there is other supporting evidence have been used. The focus of what follows is on the responsibility of particular officials and procedures they oversaw.[183] What type of official was supposed to do what? Are there identifiable types of procedure for which a particular office had responsibility? If so, what types of claims were answered by which official and what procedure was normally used?

By far the most frequently addressed official in the collection is the sheriff: sixteen brieves are addressed to him and his bailies. One is a brieve of compulsion which commanded the sheriff to compel a person to pay a debt to which the

---

[176] The last half of A24 (p. 20) does not survive, nor the first half of A59 (p. 23).

[177] Most of the Bute manuscript dates to c.1400 (before 1424) and contains 107 chapters (*Scottish Formularies*, ed. Duncan, pp. 115–21). E is datable to 1424×82 and its formulary contains 115 chapters (*Scottish Formularies*, ed. Duncan, pp. 39–45).

[178] An example of near-identical brieves is that commanding the recovery of fugitive neyfs; see A5 (pp. 12–13), compared with B12 (p. 126). The only change in Bute is that the king's name is given (as *Robertus*), and the brieve ends by saying 'presentibus post annum minime valituris'. The brieve does not appear in E.

[179] B28–31 (p. 133); cf. A1 (p. 11).

[180] B106: 'exceptis terris elemosinatis et libere tenencium serviciis' (p. 168); cf. A20 (p. 18).

[181] Some subjects in the Ayr formulary are also mentioned in extant thirteenth-century evidence, even though a particular brieve does not survive; see, for example, the appointment of a justiciar's attorney in A10 (p. 14) and *APS*, i, p. 99, issued in 1259.

[182] A22 (p. 19), to be compared with *RRS*, iv, 1, nos. 27, 32, 36, 40, 70, 75–76, 85; RH5/30, RH5/33, RH5/36, RH5/54, RH5/231; *APS*, i, pp. 97–8, 98, 98–9, 99, 99–100, 100, 101, 102; *Paisley Reg.*, pp. 191–2.

[183] Thus, some brieves in the Ayr formulary have not been included, such as those addressed to *probi homines*; A1 (p. 11), A2 (p. 12), A3 (p. 12), A4 (p. 12), A6 (p. 13), A7 (p. 13), A8 (pp. 13–14), A9 (p. 14), A61 (p. 24), A62 (pp. 24–5), A65 (p. 26), A66 (pp. 26–7), A71 (p. 31), A72 (pp. 31–2), A73 (p. 32), A75 (pp. 32–3), A78 (p. 34), A79 (p. 35). If one includes the texts from E, which may have been present in Ayr, this list is extended: E58/A33 (pp. 79–80), E44/A39 (pp. 71–2), E49/A40 (pp. 74–5), E33/A50 (p. 65).

claimant, who had obtained the brieve, had already proved his right in the sheriff's presence.[184] Sheriffs also had executive power. Royal brieves command the sheriff to give sasine to those who have proved their lawful sasine by inquest; to those who had been granted the wardship of a minor and his land; to a widow in her lawful dower; to a ward who has recently come of age.[185] The famous brieve of right was, unlike in England, addressed to the sheriff and commanded him to do 'right' to tenants-in-chief whose rights in their land had been infringed in some way; this was a remedy that protected, rather than challenged, elite power.[186]

However, the brieves in the Ayr formulary reveal that the most common processes initiated by sheriffs were inquests, in particular dealing with questions about inheritance and lawful sasine of land. The sheriff was commanded to hold an inquest, and their results would be written down, and returned to the king; brieves of inquest were thus technically retourable. A whole host of questions was contained within the formula for a 'general' inquest which the sheriff would initiate.[187] Did the relative of the 'bearer' of the king's letters (*lator presencium*) die vested and saised in his land as of feu? Is the 'bearer' the legitimate and nearest heir of the dead person? Is the bearer of the brieve of legitimate age? From whom is the land held and by what service? In whose hands is the land now, how long has it been so, and why does the current possessor hold it? Is there any reason why the procurer of the king's brieve should not receive his or her inheritance?[188] The questions in the brieve of 'general inquest' (*generalis inquisicio*), whose text was given earlier, were to determine the procurer's lawful inheritance. As a result, reports of the findings of these inquests have been thought to be responses to pleas of mortancestry or dissasine, which is not the case.[189]

---

[184] A11 (pp. 14–15). There is a summary of a charter made by James Balfour to the sheriffs of Forfar and Perth saying that they must compel all who owe debts to the abbey of Coupar Angus to pay them without delay. It was witnessed by Walter Comyn, earl of Menteith, and Alan Durward, justiciar of Scotia, on 14 March 1244; *Coupar Angus Rental*, i, no. 17, pp. 326–7 [AII/295]. The transcript of the account roll of 1263–66 states that David Lochore, sheriff of Fife, who rendered his account in 1264, 'ought not to be compelled to the payment' of the fine of 12 marks, which Donnchad, nephew of the earl of Fife, incurred in the 'presence of the justiciar', perhaps a reference to a brieve of compulsion that the sheriff would otherwise have received (*ER*, i, pp. 4–5). Lawrence Grant, sheriff of Inverness, was another who would be a future recipient of a brieve of compulsion. Haddington's transcript states that '*Memorandum* that the same sheriff [Lawrence] ought not to be compelled [to pay] the £45 for the 180 cows for the fine of the earl of Ross, which the lord king has given respite to the earl, until the lord king commands [Lawrence] specially to make compulsion' (*ER*, i, p. 20). Another brieve, this time addressed to 'all the sheriffs and bailies' of the land, tells them to compel all who owe debts to Arbroath to pay them. This was issued on 3 March 1246 (BL, Additional MS 33245, fo. 46v [AII/306]). The only difference from the Ayr formulary brieve of compulsion is that the 1246 brieve does not contain the formula *ita quod pro vestro defectu* nor does it mention that debts have already been proven in the sheriff's presence. This suggests that there was some development between the 1240s and the time of the Ayr formulary, which will be confirmed later in this chapter, see below, pp. 332–4.

[185] B54/A47 (p. 144), B55/A47 (pp. 144–5), B75/A32 (p. 155), B102/A27 (p. 166). It is not completely provable all these were addressed to the sheriff since they were on one of the missing folios of the Ayr manuscript. It is, however, probable.

[186] A18 (p. 17); and below, pp. 315–18.   [187] A22 (p. 19).

[188] This question probably relates to the reign of Robert I; it is not attested in any extant inquest or inquest return from the reign of Alexander III; see above, pp. 302–3.

[189] As pointed out in MacQueen, *Common Law*, pp. 168–9; cf. Walker, *Legal History*, i, p. 265.

The Ayr formulary also contains other commands to the sheriff to hold inquests about different issues: to establish rights in tofts, whether tofts or land had been unlawfully detained from the 'bearer' of the king's letters or whether land had been unlawfully deforced.[190] Sheriffs were also to summon inquests to discover rights to dower. Had the bearer been 'vested and saised' in her dower before her marriage at the church door? Had her dower land been unlawfully kept from her? How was she ejected from the land?[191] The preponderance of brieves addressed to the sheriff can thus be divided in two: to hold inquests into a question posed by the person who procured the king's brieve and to deliver sasine to individuals, by the king's command, sometimes in response to an inquest's findings.[192] It is clear that sheriffs held inquests into issues not just about land: one brieve formula reports the findings of a shrieval inquest into whether 'A' had killed 'H' in self-defence.[193]

In contrast to the plethora of brieves addressed to the sheriff, the Ayr formulary contains only four brieves addressed primarily to the justiciar: novel dissasine, mortancestry, recognition, and perambulation.[194] In no case was it specified, as it was in the brieves addressed to the sheriff, that the justiciar should return the results of his findings to the king: none of these brieves was thus technically retourable. Instead, the justiciar was to either make or supervise the judgment of the case. In pleas of mortancestry, the justiciar would summon a recognition (*recognitio* or *recognoscere faciatis*) to be made by 'worthy sworn and elder men of the country (*patria*)'.[195] If they found that the demandant was the lawful heir of a person who had died vested and saised of his land, the justiciar was to give sasine to the demandant following three conditions: if there was nothing lawful that would prevent the demandant from recovering his inheritance; if the cited defendant said nothing reasonable (*rationabiliter*) that prevented the recognition from concluding; and if the defendant had lawfully detained the land from the demandant. In a case of novel dissasine, the justiciar was to summon a recognition to test the validity of the pursuer's complaint of unlawful dissasine.[196] If the demandant's claims were upheld, the justiciar would uphold the verdict, deliver sasine and take an amercement from the dissaisor. If the demandant's claims were dismissed, the amercement would fall on him or her. In a case of perambulation, the justiciar was to supervise the perambulation of the bounds between two landholders and cause them to be observed.[197] In a case of recognition, the justiciar was to summon a recognition to discover what rights a

---

[190] A23 (p. 20), A24 (p. 20), E21/A48 (p. 59).

[191] B60–63 (pp. 146–7). B62 (p. 147) contains a reference to *regia dignitas*, which is a rare (but not wholly unused) phrase in the thirteenth century.

[192] Brieves addressed to provosts (or grieves) of burghs were very similar to those to the sheriff: they, like sheriffs, received brieves of compulsion, commanding them to compel other individuals to hold to the agreements they made about boundaries within burghs: A17 (pp. 16–17). Provosts also received brieves of right: A19 (p. 17). This is generally the same as the brieve of right addressed to the sheriff: it commands the provost to do 'full right' to the pursuer in his land held of the king of which another had deforced him. The king also addressed provosts and bailies in particular burghs and commanded them that they delineate boundaries within the burgh and, like the brieves of perambulation and recognition addressed to the justiciars, cause them to be observed firmly: A68 (p. 28).

[193] A75 (pp. 32–3).

[194] A20 (p. 18), A21 (pp. 18–19), B85/A25 (p. 159), B88/A26 (p. 160).

[195] A20 (p. 18).   [196] A21 (pp. 18–19).   [197] B85/A25 (p. 159).

tenant-in-chief held in their land.[198] The justiciar was to command that the land be held according to the results of the recognition.

The brieve collection in Ayr thus contains far more brieves addressed to the sheriff than to the justiciar.[199] From these brieves, one can see that the responsibilities of these officials were different when they dealt with problems over land. Sheriffs summoned inquests and returned their results and the original brieve back to the king. These inquests were often about inheritance and possession but could also discover whether the 'bearer' of the king's brieve had been unlawfully deforced or dispossessed from his or her land.[200] Once the inquest had been returned to the king, he either issued a command back to the sheriff to deliver sasine as a result of the inquest's findings or, as will be argued later, the individuals concerned could take these brieves into another court to secure their lawful rights and possession. Justiciars, by contrast, were able to conclude and judge disputes over land about direct inheritance, dissasine, or boundaries. Both justiciars and sheriffs could thus enquire into similar claims but the results were different: justiciars could terminate the cases heard in their presence whereas brieves delivered to the sheriff provided answers, not, technically, judgments.[201]

Both sheriffs and justiciars used the same method to determine the truth of an individual's claim: they used a body of *probi et fideles homines* to find out the answer to the question. This body was sometimes called a 'visnet' (*visnetum*), although this word was more frequently used to describe a group of jurors summoned to hear cases of theft, robbery, murder, and homicide, than of land.[202] But these panels of jurors were used in different ways. Jurors delivered an answer to the sheriff without determining what should be done as a result. In contrast, the answers given to the justiciar acted as a verdict, which the justiciar would uphold by giving sasine or commanding observance.[203] The distinction between these two procedures is reflected by the different words used to describe them. In general, sheriffs summoned inquests (*inquisiciones*); justiciars made 'recognitions' (*recognitiones*). Some thirteenth-century cases reveal a few exceptions to this rule. Sheriffs were expected to hold recognitions for criminal cases, while justiciars on occasion held inquests

---

[198] B88/A26 (p. 160). That there existed a brieve of recognition which was separate from those of mortancestry and dissaine has never been properly acknowledged. For more on the brieve of recognition, see below, pp. 309–12.

[199] Brieves addressed to provosts of burghs and *probi homines* were mentioned in Notes 192 and 183, respectively. In addition, for the brieves addressed to the steward (perhaps replaceable with any other aristocrat), see A16 (p. 16), E31/A46 (p. 64); to barons, E24/A38 (p. 60), to bishops or archdeacons, A64 (pp. 26–7); to bishops, A67 (p. 27); to kin and friends, A76 (p. 33); to the king's forester, A81 (p. 36); and to an unnamed officer, perhaps the sheriff, E57/A32 (p. 79).

[200] See, for example, *RRS*, iv, 1, nos. 27, 70. For deforcement in burghs, see MacQueen, *Common Law*, pp. 155–6.

[201] For this difference between a brieve of succession and mortancestry, see MacQueen, *Common Law*, pp. 168–9. But it is argued below (pp. 323–32) that the brieve of succession did more to than 'merely establish a title to inherit' (MacQueen, *Common Law*, p. 169). MacQueen also calls the brieve of succession a brieve of inquest.

[202] *Melrose Liber*, i, no. 325; *SA*, cc. 2, 5–6. The status of those on the visnet was a concern of *SA*, cc. 2–3.

[203] In the 1230 statute of novel dissasine, the sheriff is listed as the official who would deliver sasine: *SA*, c. 7.

in exceptional circumstances.[204] It also appears that sheriffs could conduct cases of novel dissasine and mortancestry in the early years after their introduction; this practice, however, did not last long.[205] But the general rule still holds for disputes over land: justiciars held recognitions, gave judgments, and delivered sasine; sheriffs held inquests but did not give judgments or deliver sasine as a direct result of the inquest.[206]

The emerging picture is that the brieves provided a number of remedies that claimants could obtain from the royal courts. However, these remedies were, by the early fourteenth century, clearly divisible by process and jurisdiction. Justiciars were to hear cases that could be concluded, either by a judgment and delivery of sasine (mortancestry, novel dissasine) or by pronouncing that the results of the recognition were to be held without challenge for all time (perambulation, recognition). Sheriffs could summon and supervise inquests into particular questions about possession and inheritance of land but could not often conclude these cases. The Ayr formulary reveals that sheriffs, unlike justiciars, could not regularly make judgment on questions concerning lawful sasine of land and inheritance.[207] But as the Ayr formulary is a late source, when these particular brieves were introduced, how they developed, and how they were used in the thirteenth century must now be considered.

Legal Brieves in the Thirteenth Century

What follows considers the thirteenth-century development and, in places, the use of the procedures of dissasine, mortancestry, recognition, perambulation, right, and the shrieval inquests. Most attention has been focussed on the brieves of novel dissasine, right, and mortancestry. But the brieves addressed to the justiciar in the Ayr formulary were not these three; they were dissasine, mortancestry, perambulation, and recognition. As stated earlier, it is clear that mortancestry and dissasine did introduce a new form of judicial process in Scotland by naming both the pursuer (in a case of novel dissasine) or demandant (in a case of mortancestry) and the defendant in the brieve, whose opposing positions would be debated during the

---

[204] For sheriffs holding inquests into non-criminal matters, see *Newbattle Reg.*, no. 170, in which John, sheriff of Stirling, had held a recognition into the lands belonging to Nicholas de Soules's saltpan in the Carse of Callendar. For a further example, see the document printed in MacQueen, 'Dissasine and Mortancestor', pp. 48–9. For justiciars holding inquests, see *APS*, i, pp. 98–9; for an inquest held in the presence of a justiciar (although it is not clear whether he conducted it), see *Dunf. Reg.*, no. 85.

[205] *SA*, c. 7; see also the comments in MacQueen, *Common Law*, pp. 139, 171.

[206] This does not mean that there was not slippage between the two in contemporary language. *Dunf. Reg.*, no. 85, is the report of a rather difficult case raised by David of Lochore, sheriff of Perth, and Dunfermline Abbey, concluded at the king's court in 1256. The process involved was an *inquisicio*—an inquest—heard in the presence of Alexander Comyn, justiciar of Scotia. The deed survives in the Dunfermline cartulary. However, the whole document was copied into the cartulary in a different hand from the main text. It concludes with the words 'hec supradicta continentur in capella domini regis scilicet in rotulo recognitionis' (NLS, MS Adv. 34.1.3A, fo. 52vb). That is, although the process was described as an inquest, the monks of Dunfermline found the text in the 'roll of recognition', kept in the king's chapel, showing there was some terminological slippage between the two processes.

[207] The exception was in cases of right, for which see below, pp. 315–18.

court proceedings themselves. As the brieve of right was addressed to the sheriff, it is with dissasine and mortancestry that we will start.

Dissasine and Mortancestry

Only the brieve of novel dissasine has a surviving statute which confirms the date of its introduction in Scotland. Dissasine has already been discussed here so what follows merely summarizes those conclusions. Comparison of the content of the original 1230 statute of dissasine with its later revision in *CD* and the brieve formula in the Ayr collection reveals that the technical language of law did significantly develop over the eighty-year period between the introduction of the procedure for unjust dissasine and the appearance of the brieve formula.[208] The statute of novel dissasine contained very large fines of £10 either for making unlawful dissasine or for making an unjust claim.[209] If the contemporary English evidence is anything to go by, pursuers would be amerced if they abandoned the plea: if the same held in Scotland, even if it did not happen very often, then the risk of being fined such a large amount would have been even higher.[210] Novel dissasine therefore worked to the advantage of lords, who would consequently had nothing like as much to fear from the introduction of novel dissasine in Scotland as their counterparts in England.

The first documented case of mortancestry is from 1253, when Emma of Smeaton brought Dunfermline Abbey into the king's presence 'by royal letters of mortancestry'.[211] MacQueen has argued that mortancestry may have been introduced between 1230 and 1237 but, although this is possible, the argument is based on reforms to the procedure made in England, which Scottish statute-makers did not adopt until 1318.[212] However, it is likely that mortancestry was introduced around the same time as dissasine (as it was in England), and sometime before its earliest attested appearance in 1253.[213] But if mortancestry was introduced in the 1230s, the brieve formula as it appears in the Ayr collection cannot have been that used during the first few decades of its life. The Ayr brieve of mortancestry commanded the justiciar to summon a recognition which would establish whether the father of the demandant had died vested and saised as 'of feu', whether the demandant was this man's nearest and legitimate heir, and whether there was anything that should prevent the demandant from recovering his sasine of the land he claimed.[214] If all this had been established, then the defendant had said nothing lawful that would *prevent* the recognition from taking place (*nichil dixit racionabile propter quod dicta recognicio non debeat de iure procedere*). This rather complicated brieve therefore suggests that the procedure for mortancestry was as follows: the demandant made his claim; the defendant, having

---

[208] See above, pp. 286–90.　　[209] See above, pp. 290–3.
[210] Sutherland, *Assize of Novel Disseisin*, pp. 65–7.
[211] *RRS*, iv, 1, no. 18; also *Dunf. Reg.*, no. 83.
[212] MacQueen, *Common Law*, pp. 169–70.
[213] MacQueen, *Common Law*, p. 169.　　[214] A20 (p. 18).

been cited, either admitted it or countered it; if his counters were deemed 'lawful', the recognition would not take place.

The diplomatic of this brieve formula is far too technical to have been introduced in the 1230s. No brieve of Alexander II comes close to its level of procedural precision. Indeed, it is of note that the only record we have of a clear-cut and explicit case of mortancestry in the entire course of the thirteenth century—that between Emma of Smeaton and Dunfermline Abbey—does not mention this particular form of process, although this may be because of the evidence produced by the abbey in its defence.[215] The documentation concerning this case survives in the cartulary of Dunfermline Abbey. The agreement drawn up as a result is a record authenticated by the lay and ecclesiastical magnates who were present, who formed part of Alexander III's minority government: Clement, bishop of Dunblane, Richard, abbot of Cambuskenneth, Walter Comyn, earl of Menteith, Alexander Comyn, earl of Buchan and justiciar of Scotia, William, earl of Mar, the king's chamberlain, Alexander Stewart, Robert de Ros, Nicholas de Soules, David de Graham, Master Gamelin, some chaplains and clerks of the king, and two knights. It states that on 17 December 1253, Emma's plea of mortancestry was heard at Stirling in the king's presence. Dunfermline Abbey produced a charter of David I, giving them the land, and 'confirmations of noble kings of Scots now dead', which the young Alexander III read out to all present. As a result of hearing these charters, Emma renounced her claim, the land was adjudged to Dunfermline, and Emma received some compensation. If there was a process of pleading in court, this case had clearly never got to the point of placing the question to the assize: the abbey produced charters and so Emma's demand was overturned.

Did a person bringing a plea of mortancestry also run the risk of high amercement? Emma of Smeaton's plea appears to have been thrown out before it was put to the jury. If this had been a case of dissaisine, Emma would probably been amerced for £10. But it appears that the same fines were not levied on cases of mortancestry. The statute introducing mortancestry does not survive; however, the brieve formula in the Ayr collection does not mention any amercements, either on the guilty defendant or on a dismissed demandant, whereas the brieve of novel dissaisine in Ayr does.[216] The brieve states only that if the demandant was vindicated in a plea of mortancestry, the justiciar was instructed only to give sasine of the land 'of the type in which "A", late father of the [demandant], had in the land on the day he was alive and dead'.[217] If the fines involved in pleas of dissaisine effectively put off people of lesser means from purusing their claims against their superiors, there seems to have been no similar financial barrier when obtaining brieves of mortancestry.

Recognition and Perambulation

Less attention has been paid to the other two brieves addressed to the justiciar—perambulation and recognition—because of the absence in the brieve of formal

---

[215] *Dunf. Reg.*, no. 83.   [216] A20 (p. 18); A21 (p. 19).   [217] A20 (p. 18).

opposition between two parties (they were not 'pleadable').[218] Neither the brieve of perambulation nor that of recognition actually names a defendant: if read on a superficial level, neither suggests a context of disputation.[219] But this does not mean that these brieves were not used to settle contentious issues. Brieves of perambulation and recognition were used to settle disputes, even if they did not initiate formal disputation between two parties in a court, as we can see most clearly in the Ayr formula for the brieve of mortancestry by the early fourteenth century. Moreover, both appear to have been introduced relatively early in Alexander II's reign.

The brieve of recognition, although it appears in the Ayr formulary, has rarely been identified as a procedure distinct from mortancestry and dissasine. This is probably because mortancestry and dissasine also involved recognitions; indeed, the verb *recognoscere* appears in both their brieve formulae.[220] This is an important distinction. Recognition was a legal process, used in a wide variety of civil and criminal procedures, *and* an autonomous procedure, initiated by brieve. Mortancestry, dissasine, and cases of theft and robbery *used* the recognition: a panel of sworn men who returned a verdict which the court-holder would then enforce and give a judgment.[221] But recognition *was* also a separate brieve, used by people in particular circumstances: the Ayr collection provides a simple rubric for a 'breve de recognitione' and this category is confirmed in *Regiam Majestatem*, which was compiled roughly contemporaneously with the Ayr formulary itself.[222] Unfortunately, this brieve was copied in the folios in the Ayr collection which have now mysteriously disappeared. However, a form of the brieve of recognition has survived in the Bute collection and is given below.[223]

Robert etc. to the justiciar north of the Forth, greeting. We command *ut supra* that you make recognition lawfully and following the assize of the land of the lands of F by all their right marches, which are A's, which he claims to hold from us in chief, between the lands of such-and-such on one side, and the lands of such-and-such on

---

[218] MacQueen, 'Pleading', pp. 416–17.

[219] MacQueen, *Common Law*, pp. 122–4, 168–9.

[220] A20–21 (pp. 18–19); cf. *SA*, c. 7.

[221] See above, pp. 278–9, 287–90, 308–9.

[222] A26 (p. 20); *RM*, bk I, c.10 (*APS*, i, p. 601), in which brieves of mortancestry, recognition and novel dissasine are all listed. MacQueen has argued that mortancestry *was* a brieve of recognition (MacQueen, *Common Law*, p. 184, note 11). While this is true (in that it used a recognition), it must not be confused with the separate remedy. MacQueen cites *RM*, bk I, c.4 (*APS*, i, p. 598), where mortancestry and dissasine are described as 'breve de recognitionibus de morte antecessoris et de nova dissasine'; however, it is clear from Book 1, chapter 10, that there *was* a separate formula, understood and defined by the compiler of *RM*. In Book 3, chapter 24, novel dissasine is called 'the recognition which is called of novel dissasine' (*RM*, bk III, c. 24; *APS*, i, p. 628). In both examples, therefore, that novel dissasine and/or mortancestry *use* a recognition is stressed but this does not mean that either *was* the brieve of recognition, which had a separate form certainly by the date of the Ayr formulary, and probably long before, if the early references to the brieve of recognition are taken as such. For the date of *RM*, see A. A. M. Duncan, '*Regiam Majestatem*: A Reconsideration', *Juridical Review*, new series, vol. 6 (1961), pp. 119–217; Alan Harding, '*Regiam Majestatem* among Medieval Lawbooks', *Juridical Review*, new series, vol. 29 (1984), pp. 97–111; Taylor, 'Assizes of David', pp. 236–7.

[223] B88 (p. 160).

the other and, just as the marches were recognosced lawfully and following the assize of the land, so you should cause them [to be held] firmly.

There is nothing worrying about the language of this brieve. 'Holding in chief' is attested in charters of Alexander II and the brieve of right addressed to the sheriff was also available only to those who claimed to hold their land directly from the king.[224] Moreover, the expectation that the recognition would be done following the 'assize of the land' is also present in references to perambulation from the very late 1190s onwards.[225] What the reference to the 'assize' of the land suggests, therefore, is that brieves of recognition, like brieves of dissasine, were introduced in Scotland as part of a statutory innovation.

There are two early and clear references to brieves of recognition in the surviving corpus of records of dispute settlement. One is in a dispute between Mariota of Chirnside and her son Patrick on one side and Coldingham Priory on the other, heard in front of the justiciar, Walter Olifard, before 1242.[226] The other is a dispute raised by Ada and Mary of Paxton, and Ada's son William, again against Coldingham Priory, between 1233×5.[227] Both cases have, however, been identified as pleas of dissasine.[228] But the records of both cases clearly state that one party obtained a 'brieve of recognition'. Mariota's case was over a ploughgate of land in Renton in Berwickshire and was heard in the presence of the justiciar, who was the official addressed in the brieve-formula of recognition in the Bute collection. Mariota eventually quitclaimed the land to the Priory, admitting that she had 'no right' in the ploughgate. Despite being over hundred acres of land, it might be thought that a ploughgate was too small a holding to hold 'in chief' from the king and so Mariota would not have been able to obtain a brieve of recognition. However, kings from William the Lion onwards would grant single ploughgates of land, thus making the beneficiary (for these lay holdings) technically tenants 'in chief'.[229] There is no other evidence to confirm that Mariota thought this land was held 'in chief' from the king but, equally, there is no evidence that she did not.

The second case was heard between 1233 and 1235. Ada, Mary, and William of Paxton obtained their brieve of recognition about a wood in Restonside which they claimed against Coldingham Priory.[230] The Paxtons lost the case but they did receive a consolation prize. Both parties drew up an agreement stating that, although the Priory held the wood in perpetuity, the Paxtons had the right to estovers 'under the view of the forester of the said prior and convent'. Again, there

---

[224] *Dunf. Reg.*, no. 77 [13 Jan 1249; AII/327]; for the brieve of right, see A18 (p. 17), and the discussion in Carpenter, 'Scottish Royal Government', pp. 142–3.

[225] The earliest reference is to a perambulation conducted 'following the assize of the land' in 1198: see *Arbroath Liber*, i, no. 89. The next reference is to a perambulation conducted on 23 September 1219: *Arbroath Liber*, i, no. 228. This document is found in a separate section of Arbroath's *Registrum Vetus*, whose documents were all copied from rolls kept in the king's chapel (NLS, MS Adv. 34.4.2, fo. 6v). For this, see Chapter 7, pp. 411–12.

[226] Raine, *North Durham*, App., no. 378.

[227] Edited in MacQueen, 'Dissasine and Mortancestor', p. 48.

[228] MacQueen, *Common Law*, pp. 138, 141; Barrow, 'Justiciar', pp. 92–3.

[229] See, for example, *RRS*, ii, no. 422.

[230] MacQueen, 'Dissasine and Mortancestor', p. 48.

is no evidence to prove one way or the other that they claimed they held the wood 'in chief' from the king but they certainly were claiming not to hold it from Coldingham Priory, which is explicitly named as the other party. The only reason for thinking that this brieve of recognition was not, in fact, a brieve of recognition was that it was held not in front of the justiciar but in front of the sheriff of Berwick, William of Lindsay. Indeed, the king's 'brieve of recognition' had been sent directly to Sheriff William, not the justiciar. But if this is a reason for thinking that the case was not initiated by a brieve of recognition, then it is equally one for questioning its status as a claim of dissasine or mortancestry. If this were a case of recognition, then it would be the earliest extant reference to recognition as a distinct procedure in its own right and would thus add to the number of new procedures that were being introduced in the 1230s.[231] The word *recognitio* had first appeared in the 1220s: the 1230 legislation refers to 'recognitions' to determine free or unfree status and 'recognitions of perambulations' survive from 1228.[232]

Perambulation itself has an even longer history than recognition. Perambulations did not need a written command from the king to occur and were a normal procedure to use when disputes over land occur.[233] Indeed, the earliest reference to a perambulation in medieval Scotland is in the Kirkness dispute, discussed many times in the first part of this book. The Kirkness dispute occurred between 1124 and 1136, a time when no one would have thought of perambulation as something that could be done only when one or both parties had obtained a brieve of perambulation from the king's chapel.[234] There is a difference, then, between perambulation as a regular part of dispute settlement (which has an extremely long history) and the point at which people or institutions could obtain a standard brieve of perambulation from the king's chapel, which would initiate the procedure in the justiciar's court (which has a shorter history). Procurement of a brieve of perambulation may well have changed the dynamic of perambulation because, if only one party obtained the brieve (which they would have to pay for), the procedure would have become more adversarial, a point which will be developed later in this chapter.

The earliest reference to perambulation being done 'according to the assize of the kingdom' is in 1198×99.[235] The results of this perambulation were inspected (by oral consultation of those who had been there) and it was confirmed in 1221 that the 1198×99 perambulation had been done 'according to the assize and

---

[231] It could be that, as MacQueen has suggested elsewhere, sheriffs did hear pleas initiated by brieves more frequently in 1230s and early 1240s than they did later on in the century (MacQueen, *Common Law*, pp. 139, 171). But it is also possible that the justiciar was unavailable, and so Ada, Mary, and William had recourse to the sheriff.

[232] *SA*, c. 4; *Arbroath Liber*, i, no. 229. Recognitions could also be done in the king's presence: see *RRS*, ii, no. 496.

[233] For a preliminary study of perambulations, see Cynthia J. Neville, *Land, Law and People in Medieval Scotland* (Edinburgh, 2010), pp. 41–71.

[234] Lawrie, *ESC*, no. 80, discussed in Chapters 1 and 3, pp. 40–2, 121–2.

[235] *Arbroath Liber*, i, no. 89. I have learnt much from discussion with Dauvit Broun, who has generously shared some of his work with me. Any errors remain my own responsibility.

custom of the kingdom'.[236] A further reference to perambulation being conducted according to the 'assize of the land' is in September 1219 and a further reference in January 1227 (Lady Day dating; 1228 in our time) refers to the 'lawful assize of King David'.[237] Given that so much was attributed to David, even by the third quarter of the twelfth century, this statement should not be accepted at face value but it is evidence that, by the end of the twelfth century, there existed a royal assize which laid down a correct perambulation procedure, which was relatively frequently referred to in the first two decades of the thirteenth century.[238]

That the justice/justiciar had something to do with the assize of perambulation (as he would do in the Bute formula) is suggested by the sole surviving piece of Latin writing under the name of a *iudex*, Mael Brigte, who appears as the king's *iudex* in royal charters of the 1190s.[239] The document is datable to 11 November 1221 and in it Mael Brigte proclaimed that certain lands had been perambulated in King William's reign in order to settle a dispute (*controversia*) between Humphrey de Berkeley and Walter, son of Sibbald. The perambulation was supervised by Matthew, bishop of Aberdeen, and Gille Brigte, earl of Strathearn and justice of the lord king (Mael Brigte was also present) 'ex precepto domini regis Willelmi'. The perambulation happened in 1198 and, if *preceptum* is taken to mean a *written* command, then it seems that perambulation by brieve had developed by the late 1190s.[240] This is not, of course, to say that the form of this brieve was identical to that which appears in the Bute formulary (like recognition, it was also written on one of the missing folios in the Ayr manuscript).[241] However, there may have been more basic similarities between the early and later brieves of perambulation than there were between the early and later brieves of dissasine and mortancestry. The Bute brieve of perambulation addressed the justiciar, commanded him to perambulate the land, and stipulated that it must be done according to 'the assize of the land'. All these elements—the *preceptum*, the justice (the precursor of the justiciar), and the assize—were present in the very late twelfth century at the earliest, and certainly by the 1220s.

Even though brieves of perambulation were not, technically, pleadable, they were still used to settle disputes over land. A clear example of this was in 1254, when the king sent his 'commanding letters' (*literas suas preceptorias*) to Alexander Comyn, earl of Buchan and justiciar of Scotia, to perambulate some of Arbroath Abbey's lands in Angus following the 'justice and assize of the land' to settle a

---

[236] The document is printed in G. W. S. Barrow, 'The *Judex*', in Barrow, *Kingdom of the Scots*, pp. 57–67, at pp. 66–7.

[237] *Arbroath Liber*, i, nos. 228–229; see also *Newbattle Reg.*, no. 119.

[238] For David's reputation, see above, Chapter 1, and Part 1 Conclusion, pp. 48–50, 177–82.

[239] Barrow, '*Judex*', pp. 66–7, discussed in more detail in Dauvit Broun, 'The King's *brithem* (Gaelic for "Judge") and the Recording of Dispute-Resolutions', PoMS Feature of the Month, no. 11 (April 2010), online at <www.poms.ac.uk/feature/april10.html>.

[240] Gille Brigte, earl of Strathearn, also wrote to Mael Brigte, the king's *iudex*, and 'Bozli', the *iudex* of the Mearns, and another individual, about another perambulation of the land of Geoffrey de Melville, done 'ex precepto domini regis' (at which Mael Brigte had been present), printed in Barrow, '*Judex*', p. 66.

[241] B85/A25 (p. 159).

dispute between the abbey and Peter Maule, lord of Panmure, and his wife Cristina.[242] Other examples can also be found, which reveal something about how the results of these perambulations were archived. In 1251, for example, Robert, then abbot of Dunfermline, inspected a roll of the king which contained the record of a dispute between the abbey of Arbroath and some of its neighbours, including Marjorie, countess of Buchan (then a widow), and Philip of Feodarg, which had been settled in 1236.[243] Both cases were over the 'boundaries and marches of certain lands' and were held in the presence of Walter fitz Alan, justiciar of Scotia at Forfar.[244] All the claims resulted in mutual quitclaims: the abbey quitclaimed Braikley in Aberdeenshire to the countess who in return quitclaimed the unidentified 'Ordbothbachfyn' to the abbot. When the boundaries were in doubt, they were given in the document. The abbey maintained its claims to the marches of 'Strathlochath', which were given in the document, having been subject to a 'recognition' by the oaths of worthy men. The resulting document was then entered into the king's rolls, where it was found almost fifteen years later by Robert, abbot of Dunfermline, who was also the king's chancellor and so would have had direct access to the rolls.[245]

Another case was also found in the king's rolls. During the compilation of a later section of Arbroath's *Registrum Vetus*, one of the scribes had gone to consult the royal records. He found a 'recognition' of 1227, made about the conduct of a perambulation that had previously been made in 1219 for his abbey and Warin of Cupar over the bounds of 'Achinglas', Arbroath, and Kinblethmont.[246] He also found this earlier record of the perambulation of 1219 in the 'rolls of the lord king'.[247] The 1227 recognition was initiated by written command (*preceptum*) of the lord king and found that the earlier 1219 perambulation had indeed been done lawfully and following the assize of perambulation attributed to David I. What is interesting is that if the scribe of this section of the *Registrum Vetus* had not included the later 1227 recognition, we would not know that the 1219 perambulation had been held for two disputing parties: the abbot of Arbroath and Warin of Cupar.[248] The 1219 record of perambulation states only that the lands had been perambulated, gives the names of the walkers, states that the land had been perambulated lawfully and then gives the names of the witnesses. But we know that these bounds must have been disputed because the 1227 record informs us that the perambulation was done for two parties, who must have had conflicting stakes in the bounds.

---

[242] *Arbroath Liber*, i, no. 366, 'seen in an ancient roll'; see also NRS, GD254/1, an agreement made in 1252 (1253, if Lady Day dating is used) after a perambulation done 'by precept of the lord king Alexander [III]'.

[243] *Arbroath Liber*, i, no. 227, where it is given the rubric 'perambulacio inter abbatem de Aberbrothoc et comitissam de Buchan super terris de Taruays'.

[244] The location at Forfar perhaps suggests that this case was heard during the justiciar's ayre. If so, then this would have been in the first two decades or so of the ayre, for which see Chapter 4, pp. 240–4.

[245] For one of his early attestations as chancellor, see *Arbroath Liber*, i, no. 250.

[246] *Arbroath Liber*, i, no. 229 (1228 if not dated according to Lady Day dating).

[247] *Arbroath Liber*, i, no. 228.

[248] This point was also made by Dauvit Broun: see Broun, 'King's *brithem*'.

These cases allow us to make sense of how perambulation—and, indeed, recognition—could be used in the context of disputation, without initiating a process of formal disputation in courts. Two (or more) parties could be engaged in a long-running dispute about the boundaries of their lands (which often meant the very land itself). One of them (or perhaps both) could obtain a brieve of perambulation from the king, ordering the perambulation to take place. The perambulation was then held: the walkers perambulated the land, swore that they were the lawful boundaries; their oaths were then supplemented by the presence of witnesses, whose names were also recorded on the document. The results of the perambulation, announced by the justiciar, would thus be the 'true' bounds of the land and the dispute between the two parties would be resolved without having recourse to any sort of formal pleading between the two contending parties in the court.[249] In a case of recognition, one party who was claiming to hold his or her land from the king (but whose sasine was challenged by another party) could obtain a brieve of recognition, which commanded the justiciar to 'make recognition' of his or her lands, 'by their right marches'. Whatever was found by the recognition, the justiciar would cause to be 'held firmly...following the assize of the land'. An important difference between recognition and perambulation, however, was that the former process was available only to people who were claiming to hold their lands in chief from the king. In this, the brieve of recognition had something in common with the brieve of right, which brought the case into the sheriff's court.

Right

As MacQueen has noted, the earliest reference to the brieve of right occurs as late as 1290.[250] Tracing its introduction is thus extremely difficult. However, the issue pertinent here is the form and purpose of the brieve of right and who could access it. The brieve of right appears in the Ayr formulary. There, it is addressed to the sheriff and commands him to do right to the 'bearer of the letters' over land which he or she claims 'to hold from us hereditarily', which another person had 'unlawfully deforced' from the pursuer.[251] As both MacQueen and Carpenter have demonstrated, this differs from the English writ of right in two ways.[252] First, the English writ of right was addressed to the court-holder, not the sheriff. Second, the

---

[249] B85/A25 (p. 159).

[250] MacQueen, *Common Law*, pp. 188–200, at p. 188. There is a lengthy formula for a 'brieve of right in the burgh', surviving in London, Lambeth Palace Library (LPL), MS 167, fos. 127v–129r, which runs in the name of King Alexander: 'Alexander dei gracia Rex Scotorum'. It is unlikely, however, that this formula, which contains some pretty detailed instructions for the process of litigation, is an authentic product of either Alexander II's or Alexander III's royal chapel (indeed, it is clear later on in the formula that it is not, for it also mentions a King 'R'). The brieve formula is, however, worthy of further study. Like the brieve of right for burghs in the Ayr formulary, it too contains the assumption that the land contested over was claimed to be held 'hereditarily' and held 'from the lord king'; LPL, MS 167, fo. 128r.

[251] A18 (p. 17). There is also a near-identical brieve of right addressed to provosts of burghs, commanding them to do right to pursuers who claimed to hold land hereditarily from the king and who had been unlawfully deforced of their land (A19; p. 17).

[252] MacQueen, *Common Law*, 189–93; Carpenter, 'Scottish Royal Government', pp. 142–3.

English writ of right was available to any free person, whereas the Scottish brieve of right was only available to people who were claiming to hold their land directly from the king. Like the brieve of recognition, therefore, this remedy was available only to those people who were of the highest tenurial (not necessarily socio-economic) status. Whereas the English writ of right cut across aristocratic jurisdiction over their men and tenants, the Scottish brieve of right protected court-holders and made the brieve available only to those who claimed to hold land directly from the king.[253]

MacQueen, however, has argued that there existed another form of the brieve of right in Scotland which was addressed to the court-holder, commanding him to do right to the person who had obtained the brieve from the king. If this brieve had existed, then it would have been quite an intrusion into aristocratic jurisdictions which, thus far, appear to have been protected.[254] It should be first acknowledged that we have no concrete evidence for the existence of this brieve: it does not survive in any extant thirteenth-century brieve drawn up before the death of Alexander III in 1286. MacQueen knew this and based his view on four cases surviving from the thirteenth century, which were initiated by one of the parties obtaining the king's (unspecified) brieves and which were all heard in non-royal courts.[255] In two out of the four cases, the sheriff is listed as a witness, which MacQueen explained by suggesting that he was there 'to do right had the prior refused to do so'.[256] However, there is nothing concrete which demonstrates that any of these cases were initiated by a brieve of right addressed to a court-holder. In one of the cases, discussed at length later in this chapter, the brieve in question is demonstrably not a brieve of right but a brieve of inquest.[257] A brieve of inquest may also have been used in another of the cases MacQueen cited where the sheriff was present.[258] Indeed, if the brieve in question had been a brieve of inquest, it would also explain why the sheriff was present—he was, after all, responsible for inquests initiated by the king's retourable brieve. The final two cases are very brief accounts of two separate cases each heard in the court of the prior of Coldingham.[259] There is nothing in either to show that the brieve was a brieve of right, addressed to a court-holder. There is thus no firm evidence that such a brieve was in use in Scotland; the evidence as it stands suggests that, even by the late thirteenth century, brieves of right could be obtained only by those who were or who claimed to be tenants-in-chief of the king.

MacQueen's suggestion that there *was* a brieve of right addressed to a court-holder may well have been based on a rather ambiguous testimony in *RM*, compiled (probably) later in the reign of Robert I.[260] In a section discussing pleadable brieves in general, *RM* states that, when both parties had appeared in court, the pursuer would begin his plea by saying: 'I, such-and-such, say against this man

---

[253] Carpenter, 'Scottish Royal Government', p. 142.
[254] Carpenter, 'Scottish Royal Government', p. 142.
[255] MacQueen, *Common Law*, pp. 193–4.
[256] MacQueen, *Common Law*, p. 193.   [257] See below, pp. 326–30.
[258] See below, pp. 330–1.   [259] Raine, *North Durham*, App., nos. 191, 296.
[260] *RM*, bk I, c. 9, in *APS*, i, p. 601; my emphasis; MacQueen, *Common Law*, p. 190.

N. that since my father *or* my grandfather *or* my brother *or* my sister *or* anyone else of my kin (*parentela*) was in sasine of that land...which I claim to hold hereditarily from the lord king *or* from any other lord, rendering each year such-and-such amount to him *or* to others.' In Cooper's edition of *Regiam Majestatem*, this chapter is entitled 'the form of petition made in court in a brieve of right'.[261] If Cooper's edition is correct, then this statement would show that, by the early fourteenth century at least, the brieve of right was available not only to tenants-in-chief, but also to those who held their land from other lords, even though this putative brieve is not attested in the Ayr formulary.

However, the earliest text of *RM*, in a manuscript now held in the British Library, does *not* provide this chapter rubric. Instead, this manuscript merely states that the chapter is concerned with 'the form of petition made in court'.[262] The chapter occurs in a section in the first book of *RM* concerned with brieves of mortancestry, recognition, and dissasine, as well as with right.[263] Indeed, that this particular chapter is concerned with other legal brieves, as well as with the brieve of right, is suggested by its end sentence, which says that 'petitions for all other lands which are petitioned for by the brieve of right of the lord king should happen in the same way and according to the same form'. If the whole chapter had been concerned with the brieve of right alone, it is odd that it and it alone would have been singled out at the end. Seeing, therefore, the initiating statement to pleas in court as something that was used in *all* the legal brieves discussed in this section of *RM* means that we can understand better the options for the pursuer's statement that the chapter presents. The chapter lists the kin-relations from whom a pursuer might make a claim (extending to 'any of my kin') and how the land was held (from the king or from anyone else, for rents payable either to the king or to anyone else). These options were clearly not all repeated in real-life petitions; instead, choices were made according to case and according to the claim that was being made. If the pursuer was claiming to hold from the king, as he or she would do in the only surviving version of the brieve of right, he or she said this; if the pursuer was claiming to hold from another lord, as he or she might do, for example, in a brieve of mortancestry or novel dissasine, then he or she said this. If the pursuer was claiming that his or her father was in sasine of the land, he or she said so; equally, if the pursuer was claiming from his or her sister, then he or she used the option present in *RM*.

This all means that the statement in *RM* that a pursuer should begin their petition by saying he or she claimed to hold their land 'hereditarily from the lord king *or* from any other lord' is certainly not unambiguous evidence for the capacity of the brieve of right to be obtained by tenants who were not claiming to be tenants-in-chief of the king. While we cannot know when the brieve of right developed, it is of interest that both the brieve of right and the brieve of recognition (which is

---

[261] *Regiam Majestatem*, ed. Cooper, pp. 75–6 (In Cooper's edition, this is chapter 10 of Book 1); in *APS*, the chapter heading is simply 'the form of petition made in court'; *RM*, bk I, c.9, in *APS*, i, p. 601.

[262] BL, Additional MS 18111, fos. 10v–11r.

[263] *RM*, bk I, cc. 4–10, in *APS*, i, pp. 598–602.

attested from the 1230s) were available only to those who held—or who claimed to hold—their land directly from the king. As both brieves did bring cases into royal courts (the sheriff and the justiciar respectively), it is important to emphasize that this too would have protected the integrity of lay aristocratic courts: only those tenants who risked claiming that they were tenants-in-chief (when they weren't) could even potentially have their cases heard in royal courts.

Inquests

Finally, we move on to the inquests addressed to the sheriff. The first return of a shrieval inquest does not survive until 1259 but the questions answered in this and subsequent returns were those later reproduced in the formula in the Ayr collection.[264] An earlier brieve of Alexander II, issued on 28 August 1241, suggests that the king was expecting written responses to his brieves but that these had not yet taken on the standard formula of those of the late 1250s and 1260s.[265] In this brieve, Alexander II commanded John de Vaux, sheriff of Edinburgh, Gilbert Fraser, sheriff of Traquair, Nigel de Heriz, forester, and W. Penicuik to go to Leithen to make an extent of the land and, having done so, 'you must make us more certain of the aforesaid extent and value of the above pasture by your letters, sealed with your seals'. By contrast, all the inquests from the late 1250s and 1260s onwards contain some variant of the phrase, 'having made the inquest, you must return it to us and to our chapel, together with this brieve, as quickly as you can, under your seal and the seals of those present during the inquest'.[266] Thus, while both brieves required some sort of return to be sent back, only the brieves from 1260 onwards required the return of the original brieve itself. Thus, while we can see germs of a retourable brieve in Alexander's brieve of 1241, the inclusion of a standard command to return the results of the inquest back to the king's writing office, together with the original brieve, is not attested until the late 1250s.

The differences between the brieves of Alexander II and Alexander III suggest that brieves of inquest were developing in the early 1240s but were not, technically, retourable until shortly before 1260.[267] Moreover, the number of people addressed in Alexander II's brieve suggests that it was not yet a generally acknowledged rule that individual sheriffs would regularly hold inquests on the king's command. This is, admittedly, speculative, for the two brieves are not exact matches in content. However, a specific brieve of extent (which is probably what Alexander II's brieve would later be classed as) survives in the Bute collection, which *is* addressed to the sheriff and *does* contain the injunction that the original brieve is to be returned to the king's chapel along with the results of the extent.[268] This therefore confirms that although sheriffs were, on occasion, asked to conduct inquests and make extents of land by the king's written command, it was sometime after August 1241

---

[264] See above, notes 181–2.
[265] *Newbattle Reg.*, no. 121 [AII/279]; year established by comparison with *Newbattle Reg.*, no. 120 [AII/280].
[266] *RRS*, iv, 1, nos. 27, 32, 36, 40, 67, 70, 76.   [267] *RRS*, iv, 1, no. 27.
[268] B97 (p. 164); a form of a 'breve de extento terre' was once in the Ayr collection: A34 (p. 21).

and before 1260 that these commands became expressly retourable and an expected part of the sheriff's responsibilities.

Like recognitions, inquests were not new procedures in Scotland in the mid-thirteenth century. John, sheriff of Stirling, is known to have conducted an inquest into the land attached to a saltpan in the Carse of Callendar in 1233×41, 'ex precepto domini regis' ('on the lord king's command'), which may have been a similar ad hoc brieve as that into the extent of Leithen issued in 1241.[269] Even earlier examples of the inquest procedure can be found.[270] David I, when prince of the Cumbrian region, had ordered an inquest into the holdings of the bishopric of Glasgow.[271] But the particular *form* of shrieval inquest is not attested until 1259. There are a further twenty-six examples, either of single brieves of inquests, or of the resulting inquest, or of cases where both the brieve and the resulting inquest survive and those which are dated to the very late 1250s–1270s.[272] It would appear that the period 1230–1250s was not only when retourable brieves of inquest developed; it was also the point when they came to be expressed in more technical legal diplomatic, something which is only attested in the surviving inquests by 1259. How these brieves were used, however, is an extremely important subject, which will be tackled in more detail later in this chapter.

The Different Forms of Process

The brieves addressed to the justiciar, therefore, included two brieves (mortancestry and perambulation) that seem to have been available to everybody and did not have any particularly punitive fines behind them. By contrast, there were two brieves that effectively excluded anyone not of the highest tenurial or socio-economic status from using them: dissasine and recognition. Tenurial exclusivity was also a feature of the brieve of right, addressed to the sheriff. In short, three out of the five processes that brought cases into royal courts were limited either to people who were claiming to be tenants-in-chief or who were of high socio-economic status, and thus may well have held some level of jurisdiction over their own lands. Far from dramatically impinging on the capacity of lords to do justice in their own courts, then, many of these remedies actually may have served to protect elite jurisdictions. In addition, brieves of mortancestry and dissasine do seem to involve a different sort of court procedure than the brieves of recognition and perambulation. Defendants were named in the brieves of mortancestry and dissasine, creating the framework for the more formal pleading for which there is firm evidence from the early fourteenth century. This sort of court process does seem to have been new in Scotland in the 1230s. Perambulation and recognition, by contrast, used older practices of perambulation and oath swearing to discover the truth—there were no formal pursuers/demandants and defendants in these cases. But brieves of perambulation and recognition were still used to settle disputes and their underlying

---

[269] *Newbattle Reg.*, no. 170.
[270] For the influence of canon law, see below, pp. 323–4.
[271] *CDI*, no. 15.   [272] These are discussed below, pp. 323–34.

procedure had been in use for a long time; the difference was that these had come to be initiated by a standard written command.

Is it possible to think about which of these brieves addressed to the justiciar were the most popular? The most obvious source would be records of the justiciar's court, which we know were kept thanks to the assiduous monks and abbots who consulted them. Unfortunately for us, however, none of these rolls survive. We are instead forced to rely on a series of inquests made in 1282, 1291, 1292, and 1296, which detail the content of the king's archives, housed at the end of the thirteenth century in Edinburgh Castle.[273] Listed in 1291 was a 'great roll of recognitions' and 'another roll of recognitions containing much business touching both the kingdom and the earl of Mar and Thomas Durward'.[274] In 1292, we find ninety-three 'small rolls, sheets, and memoranda' which include 'diverse inquests and perambulations and land extents'; one roll of twelve membranes of 'recognitions and ancient charters' of the time of Kings William and Alexander; and small rolls and sheets containing different recognitions and processes.[275] It is hard to know the type of cases that lie behind these rolls of 'recognition': recognition was both a procedure used in pleas of mortancestry and dissasine as well as criminal cases and, in addition, a separate remedy available to tenants-in-chief. Rolls of 'recognition' could, therefore, conceivably have contained pleas of mortancestry, dissasine, right, as well as recognition and perambulation. Moreover, a note in the Dunfermline cartulary reveals that inquest results could be entered on rolls called 'rolls of recognition', so it is simply impossible to know how popular the individual remedies were in relation to each other from the scant evidence we have about the king's archives.[276]

But it is possible to suggest that brieves of perambulation and recognition, which fundamentally did not introduce a different sort of judicial process into the king's courts, may have been more frequently used than the brieves of novel dissasine and mortancestry. In *c*.1274, the dean and archdeacon of Dunblane wrote to Laurence, dean of the Lennox, and commanded him to go personally to the 'pleas of the lord king at Dumbarton' to announce to all present that no one should presume to bring the abbey of Paisley into a law court without the abbey's permission.[277] The request to Laurence had not come out of the blue: the abbey of Paisley had been involved in a long and protracted dispute over the church of Kilpatrick which had involved them appearing in lay fora more times than they probably had liked. This case will be discussed in more detail later. The important point here is how the letter continued. The dean and archdeacon reassured Laurence that his message was backed up by three points: first, Alexander III had himself confirmed it in his own letters; second, 'letters of the lord king of *perambulation and recognition* have been suspended against ecclesiastical persons... with other articles similarly'; third, a recent and similar case had come up whereby the case was to be heard in an ecclesiastical forum. That is, the brieves of perambulation and recognition had recently been suspended by the king when they were

---

[273] These inquests are discussed in greater detail in Chapter 7, pp. 399–417.
[274] *APS*, i, p. 112.   [275] *APS*, i, pp. 114–15.
[276] See, for example, *Dunf. Reg.*, no. 85.   [277] *Paisley Reg.*, p. 176.

brought against ecclesiastical 'persons'. Such a suspension only makes sense if brieves of perambulation and recognition had been used so frequently as to push lay claims over supposedly ecclesiastical land that a ban had to be imposed. It is thus not inconceivable that other brieves—including those of mortancestry, dissasine, and right—were included in this ban but the emphasis on perambulation and recognition strongly suggests that these were the main targets of the ban and, as such, is evidence of their popularity in comparison with other remedies.[278] It is interesting that inquests were not explicitly mentioned in this letter, as this chapter will go on to argue for their importance. This may be because brieves of perambulation and recognition were, along with right, dissasine, and mortancestry, brieves which did directly take cases into royal courts, whereas inquests did not necessarily do the same, as we shall see. Procuring any of these other brieves *ensured* that the case would be heard in a royal court, not an ecclesiastical one. That recognition and perambulation were singled out in this context suggests their more frequent use, as opposed to the technically pleadable brieves of mortancestry, dissasine, and right.

Conclusion

Like the 'Angevin leap forward', characterized by Lady Stenton for England under Henry II, the 'Alexandrian leap forward' involved the introduction of a number of new remedies that brought business into royal courts.[279] In contrast to England, where the cases were brought before the king's justices by the sheriff, in Scotland they were addressed to sheriff and justiciar alike. There were far fewer remedies in Scotland than were introduced in England but they still represented a significant increase. But the number of remedies was not the major feature of the Alexandrian leap forward: some were new in the kingdom of the Scots, such as novel dissasine, mortancestry, and right, but many more were simply adaptations of existing procedures, particularly perambulations, recognitions, and inquests. What was new was the amount of documentation expected to be generated by these remedies: justiciars had long heard cases in the king's court or in the courts of sheriffs; now such cases could be initiated by the written word, conveyed in increasingly standardized form. This is particularly true for the inquests held by the sheriff. Kings had, since the reign of Alexander I, commanded people to do certain things through their brieve.[280] But they did not command the sheriff to make an inquest and return its result back to the king, together with the original brieve, to demonstrate the inquest had covered all the questions the king had asked in the brieve. This is what we see from 1259 onwards, at the latest, when the earliest brieves of inquests and their returns survive.

---

[278] MacQueen, however, comments that the brieves of novel dissasine, mortancestry, and right were used against ecclesiastical defendants: MacQueen, *Common Law*, pp. 142–4. Even if one does not accept some of MacQueen's cited evidence as cases of dissasine and mortancestry, it remains that the only two unambiguous cases of each procedure were against monastic institutions (Dunfermline Abbey and Coldingham Priory respectively): *RRS*, iv, 1, no. 18; *Cold Corr.*, no. 1.

[279] Stenton, *English Justice*, pp. 22–53.   [280] Broun, 'Adoption of brieves', 178–9.

The written nature of this change could not have escaped contemporaries. When bishops and other churchmen were worried about their jurisdiction, as Robert Wishart, bishop of Glasgow, was in the early 1270s (both before and after his consecration) during a dispute involving lay men and women and Paisley Abbey, the documentation took care to include explicitly in all three lay quit-claims their renunciation of 'pleas and letters sought and to be sought from the lord king of Scotland and from any other person in another place or court, ecclesiastical or secular'.[281] Bishop Robert's statement both attested to the frequency of the use of royal brieves and acknowledged that people might obtain similar brieves from kings to the detriment of the abbey's interests in the future. In *c.*1274, the dean and archdeacon of Dunblane wrote to Laurence, dean of Lennox, informing him that, under pain of excommunication, use of 'the *letters* of the lord king of perambulation and recognition' against the abbey of Paisley had been suspended by the counsel of the lord king and other bishops.[282] The ambiguous and complicated relationship between royal justice and ecclesiastical jurisdiction will be examined in the last section of this chapter; suffice it to say here that the *written* nature of royal justice was one focus of the statements of the bishop, dean, and archdeacon.[283]

The Alexandrian leap forward of the late 1220s–1250s was not simply a leap forward in the number of remedies offered by the king's chapel; it was an expansion of the conceptual areas in which the king's brieve ran in a standard form. But, although this really was a transformative development and did result in comparatively more procedures being heard in royal courts than previously, we should not overestimate the structural impact these brieves had on the underlying relationship between aristocratic and royal jurisdiction. It is important to stress that whereas in England, Lady Stenton's Angevin leap forward was also one for royal courts, whereby an increasing number of remedies available to all free individuals eventually prompted evermore complicated judicial institutions, similar developments did not happen in Scotland, where royal justice remained predominantly (but not exclusively) the preserve of a regional justiciar (sometimes supported by attorneys) during the thirteenth century.[284] The number of brieves that brought pleas into royal courts was, after all, relatively small. But the uncomplicated nature of the Scottish royal judicial system may also be explained by the nature of these brieves. Three were available only to those who claimed to hold their land directly from the king or who had significant financial resources behind them. In addition, it has been possible to suggest that the brieves of perambulation and recognition may have been more popular than dissasine, mortancestry, and right because they relied on a form of non-pleadable dispute settlement that had long been in use. It thus seems unlikely that, taken together, these brieves impinged dramatically on the capacity of lords to offer justice in land disputes in their own courts, as common law writs in England eventually would. However, Scottish kings should not be seen

---

[281] *Paisley Reg.*, pp. 182, 194–5, 200. For this case and Bishop Robert's role, see below, pp. 329–30.
[282] *Paisley Reg.*, p. 176.   [283] See below, pp. 337–43.
[284] See also MacQueen, 'Scots Law', p. 80.

as 'failing' to create a more institutionally complex judicial system that gradually eroded aristocratic jurisdiction; their power, as we have seen and will see again,
depended on aristocrats. The Alexandrian leap forward not only acknowledged
aristocratic jurisdiction, but also involved the development and use of royal brieves
of inquest that could be used within those jurisdictions without necessarily impinging on the authority of the court-holder.

INQUESTS AND DISPUTE SETTLEMENT

There are twenty-six brieves of inquest and inquest returns kept at the National
Records of Scotland in Edinburgh, under the classmark RH5. Like brieves of
perambulation and recognition, these inquests are not normally used in studies on
the Scottish common law because of their case-specific nature and the assumption
that they were not used in the context of disputation in formal court proceedings.
They were technically for uncontested issues for which proof was still required.[285]
Thus, unlike the so-called 'pleadable brieves', the jury was asked a focused question
to which they provided an answer; there was not, as there was in pleading, the
option for the pursuer and defendant to narrow down the issue that the jury was
to decide upon during the court proceedings themselves. But the focus on the
types of judicial process alone, and thus the concentration on pleadable brieves to
the exclusion of any other, means that we do not yet understand the function of
retourable brieves, how they were used as strategies in dispute resolution outwith
the courts to which they were sent, and just how important a role they played in
the interaction between the king's courts and the courts of other lords.

Inquests in criminal procedure had been used more extensively in Scotland
under Alexander II: they formed the basis of his 1244 statute and were, as Simpson
has argued, perhaps influenced by Pope Innocent III's introduction of procedure
per inquisicionem, whereby individuals could be accused not on the direct testimony of other people about a particular wrongdoing but on their reputation, their
mala fama.[286] Eight royal brieves survive initiating inquests in Alexander III's reign.
Only one is addressed to a justiciar; the remainder are addressed to sheriffs.[287]
Eighteen texts of the results of inquests survive.[288] Within these twenty-six, there
are four 'pairs': that is, cases for which the brieve and the resulting inquest record

---

[285] McKechnie, *Judicial Process*, pp. 6–7, 10–11. This does not mean that exceptions were not
raised during the inquest during the later Middle Ages; see Willock, *Jury*, pp. 109–11, and MacQueen,
'Pleading', p. 417.

[286] This point is made in Simpson, 'Procedures', forthcoming; and, for context, James A. Brundage,
Medieval Canon Law (London, 1995), pp. 144–50. However, the focus on reputation is also found in
earlier material, within and outwith Scotland, so it is possible we should not attach too much innovation
to inquest through public *fama*; see Alice Taylor, '*Lex Scripta* and the Problem of Enforcement: Anglo-
Saxon, Welsh and Scottish Law Compared', in *Legalism*, vol. 2: *Community and Justice*, ed. Fernanda Pirie
and Judith Scheele (Oxford, 2014), pp. 47–75, at pp. 66, 70–1.

[287] *RRS*, iv, 1, nos. 27 (justiciar), 32, 36, 40, 67, 70, 75–76.

[288] NRS, RH5/19, RH5/30, RH5/33, RH5/36, RH5/39, RH5/54, RH5/231; *APS*, i, pp. 98,
98–9, 99, 99–100, 100, 101 (*bis*), 102 (*bis*); *Paisley Reg.*, pp. 191–2; *RRS*, iv, 1, no. 85.

survive.[289] Of the inquest returns, four show that they were held by justiciars (or a justiciar's attorney), nine by the sheriff, and a further five which do not say which official was in charge. Why three of these inquests were heard by the justiciar is explicable: two inquests were made into land then in the crown's wardship (and thus came under the purview of the justiciar) and the third came up because the legitimacy of a shrieval inquest had been called into question and so the justiciar recalled the inquest before confirming the sheriff's findings.[290]

These brieves and inquest returns cover a range of issues. Three established the 'bearers' of the brieve as legitimate heirs. Two more were to establish the 'right' the bearer had in land in vills and burghs. Robert the Crossbowman sought the king's brieve to establish his right in the king's garden at Elgin while Agatha Spink used the king's brieve to establish her right to a house in the vill of Traquair.[291] Others were to discover whether a person had died vested and saised of his land. Another was to establish whether the bearer of the king's letters held from him in chief, what service was owed and to compel the bearer to produce the charters by which he could confirm his tenure. It is clear that some of these brieves had been obtained as part of long-running disputes with other parties. One inquest was called to discover why the 'bearer' (Hector, son of Hector of Carrick) had been ejected from his land; another to discover if the burgesses of Peebles had been deforced of their peatary by Robert Crok, a prominent local knight; and a third to discover who had plundered lands in Horndean and seized the chattels of the inhabitants.[292] The claimants were actually named in another case to settle a *contentio* (disagreement) between Walter of Moray and Soutra Hospital about renders of corn.[293] Moreover, it will be shown later that at least one of those inquests which do not name another party was in fact sought as a strategy to secure a better outcome in longstanding disputes that involved some very powerful people and institutions.[294]

There was one major benefit in obtaining the king's brieve of inquest: after its issue, the inquest was held quickly and returned quickly. In the case of Robert the Crossbowman, who wanted his 'right' secured in the king's garden at Elgin, the brieve was issued to Alexander de Montfort, sheriff of Elgin, on 13 August 1261; the resulting inquest was recorded a mere fourteen days later, on 27 August.[295] Within two weeks, therefore, Alexander de Montfort had received the brieve, summoned a group of twelve men—including two thanes, the grieve of Elgin, and five burgesses—to testify on Robert's claims at the 'full pleas of the sheriff', that is, the sheriff's court. Others happened at a slightly slower pace. A case of the burgesses of Peebles, who obtained the king's brieve of inquest on 7 October 1262 to confirm whether Robert Crok had indeed deforced them of their peatary of Waddenshope,

---

[289] *RRS*, iv, 1, no. 27, and RH5/30; *RRS*, iv, 1, no. 32, and *APS*, i, pp. 99–100; *RRS*, iv, 1, no. 36, and *APS*, i, p. 100; *RRS*, iv, 1, no. 40, and *APS*, i, p. 101.

[290] *RRS*, iv, 1, no. 27; *APS*, i, pp. 98–9; *APS*, i, p. 99; *APS*, i, p. 101. The inquest procedure continued under the guardians, see Stevenson, *Documents*, i, no. 68.

[291] *RRS*, iv, 1, no. 32; RH5/36.

[292] *RRS*, iv, 1, no. 27; *RRS*, iv, 1, no. 40; *APS*, i, p. 101; *RRS*, iv, 1, no. 70.

[293] *RRS*, iv, 1, no. 85.   [294] See below, pp. 326–34.

[295] *RRS*, iv, 1, no. 32; *APS*, i, pp. 99–100.

took just under a month to complete.[296] A brieve commanding Walter Stewart, earl of Menteith and sheriff of Dumbarton, to hold an inquest into whether three women were the nearest legitimate heirs of one Dubgall, brother of the earl of Lennox, was issued on 24 April 1271 and concluded by 15 May the same year.[297] The only inquest that is known to have taken longer than a month was that initiated by the justiciar, Alexander Comyn, into the ejection of Hector, son of Hector of Carrick, from his land in Auchensoul. The king's brieve was dated 21 May 1260 but the results of the inquest were not recorded until 22 September.[298] This, however, may have been an exception. Carrick was at this stage in the king's hands because the female heiress of the earldom, Marjory, was a minor, and would not be of age until her marriage in 1269.[299] Probably as a result, it was the justiciar, not a local sheriff, who was charged with holding the inquest and this could explain why this inquest took longer than seems normal.

All three of our surviving pairs of brieve and inquest addressed to the sheriff (the fourth is addressed to the justiciar) were completed within six weeks. This suggests that these inquests were held at the sheriff's court, which was supposed to be held every forty days, if the statute enacted by William in 1184 ever had any force in practice.[300] Indeed, some of the returns state that the inquest was done in the sheriff's court. That into the rights of Robert the Crossbowman was done 'at the full pleas of the sheriff' of Elgin.[301] An inquest completed in January 1271 was conducted in 'the full court of the sheriffdom (*comitatu comitatus*) of Roxburgh'.[302] Although Walter Stewart, sheriff of Dumbarton, does not explicitly say that the inquest was heard in his court, his rather verbose return gives Dumbarton as the location of the inquest, so it is probable that the inquest was conducted there.[303]

Even this meagre evidence reveals that inquests were conducted quickly and were probably heard at sheriff's courts. Inquests offered a quick turnaround about major issues that would have affected most free people with land at some stage: inheritance, rights in land, enjoyment of their fruits and the possibility of being dispossessed of all these things. The sheriff's court, however, was not independent: inquests were not judgments, although they did deal with issues that were contested (even if not contested as part of a judicial process, as pleadable brieves were). Even those which state that the inquest was to deal with a dispute or disagreement do not name a pursuer and a defendant: they just name parties, both of whom perhaps wanted an answer to a question.

After the inquest was completed, its results were returned to the king and the brieve collection in the Ayr manuscript reveals that there were written instruments commanding the sheriff to give sasine of the rights under discussion as a result of the

---

[296] *RRS*, iv, 1, no. 40 (7 October 1262; brieve); *APS*, i, p. 101 (6 November 1262; inquest).

[297] *Paisley Reg.*, pp. 191–2. [298] *RRS*. iv, 1, no. 27; NRS, RH5/30.

[299] Isabel A. Milne, 'An Extent of Carrick in 1260', *SHR*, vol. 34, no. 117 (1955), pp. 46–9, at 46–7.

[300] *LS*, c.14; see Chapter 4, pp. 205–6. [301] *APS*, i, p. 99: 'ad plena placita vicecomitis'.

[302] *RRS*, iv, 1, no. 85. It is of note that Roxburgh could still be called a *comitatus*, as it was in the third quarter of the twelfth century, for which see Chapter 4, p. 197.

[303] *Paisley Reg.*, pp. 191–2.

findings of an inquest. Some disputes, like that between Soutra Hospital and Walter of Moray or that between Robert Crok and the burgesses of Peebles, may have ended in this way. King and sheriff were thus rather more directly and intimately linked than they were in England, where returnable writs were, unlike in Scotland, returned by the sheriff to the king's justices, who would judge the case according to the testimony of the jurors and the sheriff's written record of his preliminary findings.[304] In this way, therefore, the returnable writ in England was part of the common law litigation process. In Scotland, retourable brieves were not part of a wider process of litigation nor was the English infrastructure present and sheriffs had direct access to the king and his writing office through this relatively simple system.

The surviving inquests show that people who obtained the king's retourable brieve were often engaged in very longstanding disputes. The Kilpatrick case had first been heard in the court of the earl of Lennox in October 1270, before the three women obtained the king's brieve and had their status as heirs confirmed as a result in April 1271, although the case itself was not terminated until July 1273.[305] Another inquest for Hector, son of Hector of Carrick, was part of a dispute that had arisen in his father's generation, namely when Hector senior fell out with his son's father-in-law, Samuel, about land purchased with the money Samuel had given Hector senior as part of his daughter's dowry.[306] This dispute had clearly been running for some years and Hector the elder was now dead. Obtaining the king's retourable brieve was thus not necessarily the first port of call for disputants; it was one option they could use, often strategically, to procure the best possible outcome for themselves.[307] Hector the younger may well have preferred to use a brieve of inquest over novel dissasine, not wishing to risk the large amercement if he was found to make a false plea. Thus, although the inquest itself was conducted extremely quickly, the disputes to which they belonged could have been raging for a very long time.

However, brieves of inquest did not only settle disputes by referring the matter back to the king (even if such settlement did not last). Their findings could also be taken into other courts and, moreover, people who were involved in cases in other courts could obtain the king's brieve as a way of buttressing or restarting their case. It is worth spending time on one particularly detailed case to show this rather surprising function of the brieves of inquest.

The Kilpatrick Case, 1270–73

The Kilpatrick case, which is unusually well documented, survives in the sixteenth-century cartulary of Paisley Abbey.[308] The dispute had begun before October 1270

---

[304] *Roll and Writ File*, ed. Clanchy, pp. lx–lxxxix.

[305] *Paisley Reg.*, pp. 180–203 (first p. 203).

[306] *RRS*, iv, 1, no. 27 (NRS, RH5/42); RH5/30.

[307] I owe this point to Dauvit Broun.

[308] There has not yet been a full study of the Paisley cartulary (NLS, MS Adv. 34.4.14); for a preliminary description, see *Paisley Reg.*, pp. vii–x. This particular dispute stemmed from an earlier one, heard in stages between 1232 and 1235. For comment on this stage of the case, see Cooper, *Select Cases*, nos. 22–25 (pp. 32–6); Ferguson, *Medieval Papal Representatives*, pp. 134–5, 169, 243–4 (nos. 85–86); Neville, *Native Lordship*, pp. 145–8.

and turned on the competing rights over five settlements pertaining to the church of Kilpatrick, which itself belonged to Paisley Abbey.[309] Six people—three women and their husbands—thought otherwise: Mary and her husband, John of the Wardrobe, Helen and her husband, Bernard of Airth, and Forbflaith and her husband, Norrin of Monorgan.[310] The claims of the men were based on the three women who were sisters and the legitimate heirs of their great-uncle Dubgall, son of Earl Ailwin of Lennox, who had once been rector of the church of Kilpatrick and whose alienations had prompted an earlier phase of this dispute, heard in part in front of papal judge delegates in the early 1230s.[311]

On 24 April 1271, Mary, Helen, and Forbflaith obtained this brieve from the chapel of Alexander III:[312]

> Alexander, by God's grace, etc. to Walter, earl of Menteith, his beloved and faithful sheriff, and his bailies of Dumbarton, greeting. We command and order that you make diligent enquiry by the worthy and sworn men of the *patria* [to discover] if Mary, wife of John of the Wardrobe, Helen, wife of Bernard of Airth, and Forbflaith, wife of Norrin of Monorgan, daughters of a certain Finlay of Campsie, are the legitimate and nearest heirs of Dubgall, brother of Mael Domnaig, earl of Lennox. And you are to send the completed inquisition, returned under your seal, and the seals of those who were present at the inquisition, to our chapel, together with this brieve.

Walter did so and had the following recorded on 15 May 1271.[313]

> To all Christ's faithful who will see or hear the present writing, Walter Stewart, earl of Menteith, eternal greeting in the lord. All should know that I received the mandate of my lord Alexander, by grace of God, king of Scots, in these words [*text of the brieve follows*]. On the authority of this mandate, by the oaths of Lords Hugh Fleming, Alexander of Dunoon, Robert Coloquhoun, knights, Gilbert son of Absalom, Donnchad son of Amlaib, Mael Coluim of Drummond, Mael Muire called 'young', Gille Micheíl mac Edolf, Adam called 'young', Donnchad son of Gille Críst, Thomas son of Somerlaith, Nevin *MacKessan*, Mael Domnaig mac Davy, Hector *MacSween*, Ewen the goldsmith, I made a diligent inquest on the abovesaid, by their oaths taken bodily on the Holy Gospels, [and] I learnt truly and became aware that the aforesaid women were the true and legitimate heiresses of the aforenamed Dubgall, by a line of consanguinity descending from the part of Mael Coluim, brother of the aforesaid Dubgall, and grandfather of the women, and that the said Dubgall had never been married to a wife (*uxorem desponsatam minime habuisse*). And that the said inquest, done by me, should not perish into darkened oblivion, through the grace of great testimony, both I and the aforesaid knights, together with Donnchad, son of Amlaib, and Mael Coluim of

---

[309] *Paisley Reg.*, pp. 180–203.

[310] There has been no full study of this case but see the preliminary comments in Cooper, *Select Cases*, no. 26 (p. 36); Neville, *Native Lordship*, p. 168; Matthew H. Hammond, 'The Use of the Name Scot in the Central Middle Ages. Part 2: Scot as a Surname, North of the Firth of Forth', *Journal of Scottish Name Studies*, vol. 6 (2012), pp. 11–50, at p. 19.

[311] Cooper, *Select Cases*, pp. 32–5.

[312] *Paisley Reg.*, pp. 191–2 (NLS, MS Adv. 34.4.14, fo. 128r–v).

[313] *Paisley Reg.*, pp. 191–2. It is quite unusual for the text of the brieve to be included in the inquest return; normally they were returned as two separate documents.

Drummond, have given greater force to the present writing by appending our seals. Done at Dumbarton on the nearest Saturday before the feast of St Dunstan the archbishop, in the year of grace 1271. With these witnesses: John of *Herchyn*, knight; Lord Adam, chaplain of the castle of Dumbarton, Gille Patraig mac Molbride, William of *Cragbayth*, Clement of Dumbarton, Walter de *Orreis*, Ingelram of Montacute, and many others.

If this document, containing both the brieve and the inquest, had been the only document to survive from this dispute, it might be thought that this was a simple brieve of succession which, in Sheriff McKechnie's words, 'was only appropriate to decide who was the rightful heir of a deceased whose title to the subjects was not challenged'; in short, it only had an administrative function.[314] But this would be completely off the mark. This brieve was obtained as a strategy in the long-running dispute between Paisley Abbey and these three women and their husbands, the documentation of which survives in Paisley's cartulary. The sixteenth-century scribe of the cartulary did not, however, present the relevant material in chronological order: he rearranged it to make the dispute look as clear-cut as possible and the abbey's position insurmountable. As a result, the case must be unravelled before it can be analysed.

Before 12 October 1270, the three couples had claimed the lands of Cochno, Faifley, Edinbarnet, 'Backen', and 'Druncreve', all then within the earldom of Lennox but which Paisley Abbey claimed belonged to the church of Kilpatrick, which in turn belonged to it.[315] The case raged 'for some time' (*aliquamdiu*) in the court of Mael Coluim, earl of Lennox. On 12 October, they finally came to an agreement: the couples agreed to quitclaim their rights in the lands forever so long as the abbot and convent paid them 140 marks in compensation. Any further pursuit of their claim would result in a fine of £100, of which half would go to the builder of the church of Glasgow, and half to the builder of Paisley Abbey. Presumably both institutions were considering refurbishment.

Then there is silence until the three women obtained the king's brieve, leading to the inquest held by Walter Stewart at Dumbarton in April–May 1271.[316] It is not stated what prompted the women and their husbands to act in this way but the most reasonable explanation at this stage is that the abbey had not paid the necessary compensation and thus the couples thought about pushing their claims to the land again but first shored them up by obtaining a brieve that *proved* they were the heirs of Dubgall, brother of Earl Mael Domnaig, and so had the most legitimate claim to the land.

Following this, the three couples eventually 'brought the abbot and convent of Paisley into a suit by royal letters' (*per litteras regias*) sometime before 11 July 1273.[317] The court in question was, again, that of the earl of Lennox.[318] Given

314 McKechnie, *Judicial Process*, p. 11. Walker, by contrast, thought it was a brieve of mortancestry: Walker, *Legal History*, i, p. 276.
315 *Paisley Reg.*, pp. 189–90.   316 *Paisley Reg.*, pp. 191–2.
317 The full date is given in *Paisley Reg.*, p. 197.
318 'Noverit universitas vestra quod nos per litteras regias trahere fecimus in litem Abbatem et conventum de Passelet coram Malcolmo comite de Levenax et ballivis suis in curia sua super terris de

that Walter Stewart's return of the inquest (and inclusion of the king's brieve) eventually ended up in Paisley Abbey's archives, and were subsequently copied into the abbey's original cartulary, these royal letters are, in all likelihood, the brieve and inquest given above and not a putative brieve of right addressed to the earl, as MacQueen has argued.[319] This probability is demonstrated by the fact that all three *conventiones* made between the abbey and each couple stated that the land was claimed by 'the name and right (*nomen et ius*) of Dubgall, once rector of the church of Kilpatrick'.[320] This claim was the first the abbey dismissed by producing charters of Dubgall and also Dubgall's father, Ailwin, which renounced his claim to all of Kilpatrick's land.[321] The authenticity of these charters was immediately accepted by all those present at the court in 1273. But the important point is that a brieve of inquest (and its results) were deemed sufficient to bring the abbey back into the court of the earl of Lennox for the case to be restarted in the same forum in which the dispute had previously been settled in 1270, almost three years earlier. In short, the three couples had been able to restart the case in the earl's court by initiating an inquest, convened by the king's sheriff, two years previously, which demonstrated they were indeed the legitimate heirs of Dubgall, brother of the late earl of Lennox, Mael Domnaig.

Unfortunately for them, the court of the earl was as little impressed with their claims as it had been in 1270. The couples again quitclaimed their rights but in addition had to pay £40 to the abbey in compensation for their expenses.[322] They had to swear 'bodily oaths' to the bishop of Glasgow that they would not go back on this agreement.[323] They did, however, receive the 140 marks they had originally been promised back in 1270, thus demonstrating that they had not previously been paid.[324] Three documents were made in each of the couples' names renouncing their claims: a *conventio* between each pair and the abbey; a *resignatio* committing them to proclaim that they would quitclaim their rights publicly at the next court of the earl and then in front of the king; and, finally, a *quieta clamacio*, which actually was a receipt confirming that each couple had received a third of the 140 marks they had originally been promised for giving up their claims to the lands. It is hard to ignore the influence of Robert Wishart, bishop of Glasgow, behind these documents. Not only was he present at the court but also the three *conventiones* were authenticated by either the seal of the cathedral chapter of Glasgow, or the seal of the bishop himself, or the seals of one of his officials.[325] In addition, each of the three couples committed themselves to his jurisdiction, allowing him to excommunicate them and place their lands under interdict if they ever raised their claim

Cocmanach, Edynbernan, Finbalauch, Backan et de Druncreue': *Paisley Reg.*, pp. 180 [agreement of John and Mary], 192 [agreement of Bernard and Helen], 198 [agreement of Norrin and Forbflaith].

[319] MacQueen, *Common Law*, p. 194.   [320] *Paisley Reg.*, pp. 180, 192, 198.
[321] *Paisley Reg.*, pp. 180, 192, 198.
[322] *Paisley Reg.*, pp. 181, 184, 193, 196, 199, 202.   [323] *Paisley Reg.*, p. 181.
[324] This was confirmed in separate agreements, called 'quieta clamacio' in the cartulary: *Paisley Reg.*, pp. 190–1, 197, 203.
[325] *Paisley Reg.*, pp. 191, 195, 201. Only one of the *conventiones* survive as an original (that of John of Wardrobe and Mary) and this has slits for three seals: Belfast, Public Record Office of Northern Ireland, D623/B/7/1/5; photocopy in Edinburgh, NRS, RH1/2/900.

again. The bishop also established an even higher penalty (200 marks) than the £100 threatened in 1270 that would be extracted if they ever broke their oath or failed to pay the £40 to the abbey that they owed for their legal expenses.[326]

The case is also an excellent evidence for the view taken by the bishop about lay claimants using royal brieves to bring religious institutions into lay courts and will be discussed in this context in the next section.[327] However, the pertinent point here is that Mary, Helen, Forbflaith, and their husbands used a retourable brieve *not* to get a subsequent judgment from the king (as might be expected) but to open up an existing dispute in another court that had never been resolved fully. Having the authority of the king and the local sheriff (who also happened to be the earl of Menteith) proclaiming the three sisters to be the lawful heirs of Dubgall allowed the couples to bring the abbot into the court of the earl a second time. It did not work out that well for any of them—they did not regain the lands—but they did, eventually, receive the 140 marks that had been promised to them back in October 1270 but which they clearly had never received. It may not have been quite the victory they wanted (they had to pay the additional £40 to the abbey) but, looking through the rhetoric of the documents, it was still a result for three couples of a cadet branch of the comital family to take on the might not only of Paisley Abbey but also of Robert Wishart, bishop of Glasgow, and come out with something at the end.

What this dispute over Kilpatrick shows is that people used retourable brieves of inquest in order to restart cases in other jurisdictions. The Kilpatrick case of the 1270s is the only absolutely unambiguous evidence that this happened. But it is likely that other cases, which are far less rich in their detail and the amount of documentation they produced, also used brieves of inquest and their returns in similar ways. For example, sometime between 1247 and 1260 (but probably towards the latter end of this time range), one Bertram, son of Henry of Ulston, impleaded (*implacitavi*) his kinsman, Waltheof, 'by letters of the lord king', over two oxgangs of land in Nether Ayton.[328] The case was heard in the court of the prior of Coldingham, and the sheriff of Berwick, David of Graham, was present among the witnesses.

What seems to have caused this dispute was that Waltheof had given Bertram money 'as an advance' (*pre manibus*)[329] for which Bertram had pledged the two oxgangs in Nether Ayton as security for repayment. Bertram clearly did not pay the money back and it appears that Waltheof took over the land from him in lieu of Bertram's repayment. In his charter, Bertram stated that he was giving Waltheof and his heirs the land 'for a certain sum of money, granted to me as an advance'. Both Bertram and Waltheof appear to have been tenants of the priory of Coldingham;

---

[326] *Paisley Reg.*, pp. 182, 194, 200. It might be thought that this £40 would be far more of a deterrent to the couples than a potential £10 amercement from a plea of novel dissaisine. But this amount was not an automatic penalty; it had not been levied in 1270, after all. Indeed, the couples would have paid it from their own compensation, lessening their overall profits, but not impinging on their own annual revenue.

[327] See below, pp. 337–8, 343.   [328] Fraser, *Keir*, pp. 197–8.

[329] For this translation of *pre manibus* as 'advance' or 'cash down', see E. D. Francis, '*Particularum quarundam varietas: prae* and *pro*', in *Studies in Latin Literature and Language*, ed. T. Cole and D. O'Ross (Cambridge, 1973), pp. 1–60, at pp. 5–6.

the case was heard in the 'full court of the lord prior of Coldingham'. This is one of the cases that MacQueen suggested might have been initiated by a brieve of right addressed to a court-holder.[330] It is possible that the 'letters' which Bertram had obtained were, as demonstrable in the Kilpatrick case, a retourable brieve of inquest and its return, which testified that Bertram had long had sasine of the land. If Bertram had obtained a brieve of inquest, this would also explain why the sheriff was present at the prior's court when the case was heard because he would have been the official that conducted the inquest. The evidence is not conclusive but, in the context of the Kilpatrick case, that Bertram obtained a retourable brieve of inquest to bring his (probably quite flimsy) case into the court of his lord, the prior of Coldingham, is at least a plausible option and perhaps more plausible than identifying the 'letters of the lord king' as a category of brieve for whose use we have no surviving evidence.

The capacity of retourable brieves of inquest and their results to restart cases in other jurisdictions has never been seen before to be a function of retourable brieves of inquest but it is very important for understanding the structures of thirteenth-century justice. This function of retourable brieves has been overlooked not only because of the scarcity of comfirmatory evidence but also because of the emphasis placed on formal court process by the scholarship of the last century, which has often been written by legal historians who are or were also trained in modern Scots law. Indeed, for Hector MacQueen and Sheriff McKechnie, the difference between a pleadable brieve and a retourable brieve lay not only in the outcome of the process but also in the formal procedure that occurred in the court itself.[331] Pleadable brieves produced judgments, which were upheld in courts; retourable brieves did not. Pleadable brieves initiated formal pleading within the court session itself, a back-and-forth between pursuer and defendant to refine the issue which would be presented to the jury. It is this emphasis on court process that has led some to say that the processes started by retourable brieves were 'uncontested' or 'unopposed' and lacked a defendant.[332]

But if we concentrate on court process alone, we risk minimizing the use of retourable brieves in settling disputes and ignoring their function as ways into the courts of other jurisdictions. The point here is that, although the procedure initiated by retourable brieve was, theoretically, uncontested, the context in which such brieves were obtained by disputants was not. The Kilpatrick case shows incontrovertibly that retourable brieves of inquests could be used in the context of disputation; their function was not, certainly by the 1270s, merely administrative; they were not only sought when 'title...was not challenged'.[333] Indeed, as the thirteenth-century kingdom of the Scots was a land of multiple and overlapping jurisdictions, both ecclesiastical and lay, it makes sense that the kings of

---

[330] MacQueen, *Common Law*, pp. 193–4; see above, pp. 298–300.

[331] McKechnie, *Judicial Process*, pp. 6–7, 11; MacQueen, *Common Law*, pp. 123–4, 168–9; MacQueen, 'Pleading', pp. 416–17; MacQueen, 'Dissasine and Mortancestor', pp. 34–5.

[332] McKechnie, *Judicial Process*, pp. 6, 11; MacQueen, *Common Law*, p. 168.

[333] McKechnie, *Judicial Process*, p. 11, writing about the brieve of succession (his way of referring to the brieve of inquest; see MacQueen, *Common Law*, p. 168).

Scots and their advisors would have introduced a flexible remedy the results of which could either be sent straight back to the king for a judgment *or* into another court which would provide the necessary judgment.

Unlike previous assessments, it has been shown here that inquests were used in disputes. As a result, the division of brieves between contested 'pleadable' and non-contested 'non-pleadable/retourable' only holds up for the technical procedure in court, *not* the context in which the participants were operating. People could bring other parties into court by the king's retourable brieve; they could also obtain a pleadable brieve that started and concluded a case in front of a royal official, and involved some level of formal disputation before the case went to a jury's verdict. Indeed, retourable brieves of inquest could result in speedy decisions or their results could be used to restart cases in other jurisdictions. In sum, therefore, while the division between 'retourable' and 'non-retourable' results in a relatively accurate view of practice (some results were returned to the king before a decision was made), the division between 'pleadable' and 'non-pleadable' or 'pleadable' and 'retourable' does not convey how retourable brieves were used in a broader context of disputation; instead it confines them anachronistically to administrative functions alone. The division between 'pleadable' and non-pleadable brieves only makes sense if, by 'pleadable', we refer to the technical meaning that pleading would take on only later in the early fourteenth century. If we continue to focus on pleadable brieves as the main procedural forms of the Scottish common law in the thirteenth century, we will miss most of the legal remedies that were available from the king's chapel and, thus, a more complete view of thirteenth-century royal justice.

The Development of Retourable Brieves

It is clear from the previous section that brieves of inquest were not used simply to provide administrative answers to unopposed questions; they were used as methods of dispute settlement. Indeed, it is very important that the inquest initiated by the three sisters in 1271 seems so straightforward and unopposed: the inquest merely found that they were indeed Dubgall's rightful heirs and it makes no mention of the longstanding case between them and the abbey.[334] If this brieve of inquest and its return were not analysed in the context of the other documentation preserved by Paisley Abbey about the Kilpatrick case, it might be thought that the three sisters simply wished to establish their unopposed right to Dubgall's lands. This puts other, supposedly straightforward, retourable brieves in another context. For example, in March 1262, five daughters of Simon, doorkeeper of Montrose, obtained a brieve of inquest from the king's chapel which commanded the sheriff of Forfar to enquire into whether the daughters were indeed the 'legitimate and nearest heirs of Simon' for his land and office and if Simon had died 'vested and saised' in them.[335] Presumably, the four daughters had obtained this brieve because

---

[334] *Paisley Reg.*, pp. 191–2.
[335] *RRS*, iv, 1, no. 36 (NRS, RH5/23). I am grateful to my special subject group in 2014–15 for discussing this case in such detail with me.

there was some question over their inheritance; as four female heiresses, their possession of their father's lands may well have been challenged by another, more distant, family member, or another unrelated person altogether. Indeed, the inquest return itself survives and shows that Simon's daughters did not all have the same mother; there may well have been inter-sibling rivalry for the inheritance or that they all needed to have their inheritance confirmed together, as a single unit, in the face of outside challenge.[336]

Although brieves of inquest may have developed into an administrative process later in their history, it makes less sense to see them as serving a purely administrative function in the period when they were introduced. Indeed, it makes far more sense to see them as introduced *first* as remedies for disputes and, only later, when their use was more common, for people to have obtained them as a matter of routine to prevent challenges to their possessions and inheritance from arising. Moreover, seeing retourable brieves of inquest as functioning primarily as methods for dispute settlement makes sense in the light of what can be known about when and why they were introduced.

It was argued earlier that, although the inquest was not a new phenomenon in Scotland in the first half of the thirteenth century, retourable brieves of inquest addressed to the sheriff developed over the 1240s and 1250s.[337] This means that they developed *after* the introduction of dissasine, recognition, perambulation, and, probably, mortancestry. If this argument is accepted, it could explain why brieves of inquest addressed to the sheriff covered so much of the same ground as those which concluded cases in the court of a royal justiciar and why brieves of inquest were used in the context of disputes as much as those which started and concluded cases in royal courts. These brieves addressed to the justiciar initiated an extremely limited number of procedures, some of which were unavailable to those not claiming to hold their land directly from the king or who did not have sufficient means to risk a plea of novel dissasine. Following but extending Carpenter's interpretation, then, many of these brieves worked for the aristocracy, and protected their jurisdictional rights, rather than working against them.

This is consistent with the extant criminal legislation of Alexander II which actively incorporated the jurisdiction of lords over homicide and theft into its content. But because some brieves were available to everyone (such as mortancestry and perambulation), it is possible that retourable brieves of inquest developed in response to some sort of demand. Indeed, the Ayr formulary itself contains only five judicial brieves which explicitly state that judgments will be made in royal courts and only three of these brieves were technically pleadable. Although the

---

[336] The inquest return survives (NRS, RH5/24; printed in *APS*, i, p. 100). It was made by representatives from sixteen baronies and 'the greater part of the worthy burgesses of Montrose'. They said that a certain man called 'Crane' held the land hereditably by gift of King William, and died in the land 'vested and saised as of feu'. His son Swain held the land after him; he too died vested and saised. Swain's son, Simon held the land, and died vested and saised. The inquest then reported that Simon 'had five daughters from two wives (*ex duabus mulieribus desponsatis*)...and...that the said women were the legitimate and nearest heirs of the said Simon, now dead'.

[337] See above, pp. 318–19.

evidence is slight, it may be that, among these five brieves, those which were the most popular were those of perambulation and recognition, which drew on a much more informal process of dispute settlement than those brieves which were technically pleadable, and involved one party taking on the role of the pursuer or demandant and bringing a defendant into court to answer a charge.[338]

By contrast, there are eleven separate inquests in the Ayr collection and one of these is the 'general inquest', which essentially contained a further seven potentially separate questions about which the sheriff could enquire. In the middle decades of the thirteenth century, therefore, a new and extremely flexible remedy was introduced in Scotland and was available from the king's writing chapel. Unlike the brieves addressed to the justiciar, retourable brieves of inquest did not necessarily take judicial business into the court of a royal official and away from any other court-holder. The king could and did pronounce on the results of brieves of inquest but the results of inquests also provided backing for disputants who were bringing cases, often long-standing ones, into the courts of others. This must have allowed royal justice to work alongside and participate informally in the courts of others, instead of ultimately taking business away from them. To develop this hypothesis, how other jurisdictions, both ecclesiastical and lay, interacted with these new procedures of royal justice and judicial process in the thirteenth century must be examined.

ARISTOCRATIC AND ECCLESIASTICAL JURISDICTIONS

As stated in the first section of this chapter, the king included aristocratic jurisdiction in the content of his own law: he expected that earls and barons would have power over cases of homicide and theft.[339] Even Alexander II's legislation of 1244, which established indictments under the justiciar in Lothian, handed over those convicted of theft or homicide to the lay lord to do judgment upon them. It is clear that lay lords could negotiate jurisdictional rights between themselves without further recourse to the king. Between 1223 and 1239, Fergus, son of Gille Brigte, earl of Strathearn, confirmed the gift of his brother, Robert, of an oxgang in Perthshire to Coupar Angus Abbey.[340] As a result of this confirmation, Fergus and the abbey agreed that the men dwelling on the land would make suit at Fergus's court, although the monastery would receive the forfeitures. Fergus was to do justice 'following the laws of the land'; there was thus no distinction between Fergus's justice and that of the king. Fergus's men would carry out any executions arising from proven guilt at the ordeal.[341]

The existence of a number of remedies involving inquests and recognitions did not happen independently of aristocratic jurisdiction. Rather, 'baronies' were integral

---

[338] For 'demandant' instead of 'pursuer' in cases of mortancestry, see MacQueen, *Common Law*, pp. 170–1.

[339] See above, pp. 295–7.   [340] *Coupar Angus Chrs*, i, no. 35; also *RRS*, ii, p. 51.

[341] See also *Coupar Angus Chrs*, i, no. 10.

parts of particular kinds of remedies, regardless of whether the case was heard in a royal court, a religious court, or a lay aristocratic court.[342] The 1230 statute establishing a mode of proof for those unable to participate in trial by battle states that, in these cases, guilt or innocence would be determined by 'the verdict of three baronies of the area (*patria*)'.[343] One of the surviving inquests gives a sense of how this might have worked. In 1271, an inquest was held in the sheriff court at Roxburgh to solve a dispute between Soutra Hospital and Walter of Moray. The men of the *patria* who 'knew the truth' were taken from three baronies (each led by one person): five from the barony of Eckford, five from Upper Crailing, and five from the barony of '*Heton*', making fifteen in total.[344] The two baronies whose names still survive in the modern landscape of the Scottish borders are both between four and five miles to the south of Roxburgh as the crow flies. In short, suitors and men of local baronies were called on to determine the case. This also held for cases heard in non-royal courts. In a detailed and fascinating charter of Alexander Stewart for Melrose Abbey, dated 25 March 1266, the nature of the jurisdictional relationship between the monks and some lands in Mauchline, 'Carentabel', and Barmuir was set out. One of the stipulations was 'and if my bailies or those of my heirs are not present [at the abbot's court] with my men to conduct the visnet or to receive the bodies of the condemned,...the baillies of the abbot and convent [of Melrose] may conduct the visnet *by the baronies whom they choose*, and may punish condemned men themselves—or through the bailies of the lord king—following what was adjudged in the court of the said abbot and convent'.[345] That is, Alexander Stewart expected that the monks would conduct visnets using men from his family, his bailies from Dundonald, and his own lordship but if these men were not present, the abbot and convent could conduct the visnet themselves, using the neighbouring baronies. The structures of lordship were thus integrated into the visnet, regardless of particular jurisdiction.

It has been shown above that brieves of inquest and their results could be used not to take cases away from secular non-royal courts but, instead, to initiate cases within them. This clearly happened in the case of Paisley Abbey and the three couples which was heard in the court of the earl of Lennox.[346] The king's brieve was thus not a move against aristocratic courts; conversely, it could be used to bring more business into them. But was it ever possible for the king's brieve to initiate an inquest within land held by a lord with major jurisdictional privileges?[347] The Kilpatrick case again suggests that it was: the land Mary, Helen, and Forbflaith claimed was in the earldom of Lennox, and their question about their status as heirs of Dubgall had knock-on effects within the earldom. But, again, because the results of an inquest were not technically a judgment, the earl's authority was not challenged *de facto*: the three women merely brought Paisley abbey into

---

[342] Grant, 'Franchises'.
[343] *SA*, c. 5.   [344] *RRS*, iv, 1, no. 85.   [345] *Melrose Liber*, i, no. 325.
[346] See above, pp. 326–34.
[347] When it was not in ward: *RRS*, iv, 1, no. 27; Milne, 'An Extent of Carrick', pp. 46–7.

his court with the authority of the king's brieve and return. Although the earl may not have wished to offend Paisley Abbey, a very powerful Cluniac house under the protection of the bishopric of Glasgow, his jurisdictional rights in his court were maintained.

But what if inquests were initiated which were based on claims against a jurisdictional holder? Dissasine may not have been risked, on account of the potential fines involved. But it does seem like the king's brieve could initiate an inquest within an earl's court concerning the behaviour of the earl himself. A brieve formula is listed in the Ayr collection but it survives fully only in Bute.[348] This states that an inquest was made *with the consent of the earl* into the claim that the 'bearer' of the brieve was vested and saised in his land but was unlawfully expelled (*expulsus*) by the earl and his bailies. The king was therefore sending 'our letters' to the sheriff commanding him to give the 'bearer' sasine.

It is hard to know when this brieve formula developed and it is impossible to know whether the Bute formula is the same as what was once in Ayr. Nonetheless, the brieve is interesting. A person could obtain a brieve of inquest about lands held within an earl's court but only with the consent of the earl. This could even involve lands which had supposedly been taken by the earl, as the Bute formula states. But the inquest was to be held in the earl's court, and the results sent back to the king, who would then command the sheriff to give sasine if the facts of the inquest were sustained in favour of the dispossessed party. There is no direct evidence that this brieve formula was ever used in the reign of Alexander III. It is not, however, inconceivable, nor does it run counter to the evidence presented thus far. If individuals could bring the king's brieve of inquest into the court of the earl, why might the court of the earl not equally have held the king's inquests, so long as the earl himself had agreed to it? The earl's control over which inquests were conducted, of course, would be a limiting factor in determining whether an inquest would be held within an earldom or not; again, the protection of jurisdictional integrity would be maintained.

In short, the evidence suggests that there were few major conflicts or shifts of business from aristocratic courts to the king's court that acted to minimize the role of lay jurisdiction in upholding the law of the land. The development of an accessible system of retourable inquests must have played a large part in this, whereby the brieves and results of inquests initiated by brieve could be taken into the courts of others, allowing for a flexible approach to their reception. Indeed, local baronial power was actively integrated into inquest procedures, whether criminal or civil, with suitors from local baronies making up the body of jurors who would conduct the inquest. Alexander II's legislation does not reveal any problems with its incorporation of aristocratic criminal justice into the workings of particular statutes. This more integrative approach to aristocratic power may explain why, if there were a widely available remedy for complaint against lords, it may have been an inquest conducted in the lord's court, with his full permission.

---

[348] B76/?A49 (pp. 155–6).

The relationship between this more intensive royal judicial system and ecclesiastical jurisdiction is much more complicated.[349] First, although bishoprics and religious houses had their own courts, some religious houses were taken under the protection of their founder, who undertook to hear criminal pleas on their behalf, sometimes in specific circumstances. The abbeys of Melrose and Balmerino, both royal foundations, sought the protection of Alexander II in the early 1230s so that royal sheriffs would hear cases of theft stemming from the monks' land and would find a champion for the accused if need be.[350] Other royal foundations, however, such as Dunfermline and Arbroath, seem not to have sought royal protection in this way and preserved their jurisdictional integrity. Other founders took on even more responsibilities. Inchaffray Abbey, the foundation of Earl Gille Brigte of Strathearn, had all the pleas of the men of the abbey heard in the earl's court; the abbot had the right to their chattels, and the bodies of convicted criminals remained on comital ground 'to preserve the justice of our court'.[351] Particularly in relation to crime, courts of the king and his major aristocrats were often intertwined with those of religious houses.

Moreover, religious houses were not just caught up in webs of lay jurisdiction; they were, along with bishops, part of a wider network of papal justice and authority. Church courts could appeal to the papacy and have cases concerning their land and alms heard in front of papal judges-delegate who invoked Romano-canonical law.[352] Much has been written about the importance of Romano-canonical law in Scotland during the thirteenth century.[353] Here is not the place to go into these debates but simply to note that the old view, which saw thirteenth-century justice as conducted primarily by papal judges-delegate because royal justice was so puny, has now been overturned, particularly as a result of the work of MacQueen.[354] Particularly in the first half of the thirteenth century, many cases involving bishoprics and religious houses were heard in front of papal judges-delegate; they did not, however, operate independently of the judicial power of the king.

An example of this is the original case that arose over the church of Kilpatrick. Paisley Abbey was, for the first time, claiming its right to the lands of Kilpatrick mainly against Dubgall, son of Earl Ailwin of Lennox in 1232–34.[355] In particular, the abbey was seeking to prove their right against Gilbert, son of Samuel of Renfrew, who held Monachkennaran, which the abbey claimed belonged to Kilpatrick.[356] The abbey had secured three judges-delegate to prove their 'intention', that 'the whole land of Monachkennaran had been alienated unlawfully into [the hands of]

---

[349] See further, Marinell Ash, 'The Church in the Reign of Alexander III', in *Scotland in the Reign of Alexander III*, ed. Reid, pp. 31–52; MacQueen, 'Scots Law', pp. 79–81.

[350] See above, pp. 278–81.   [351] *Inchaffray Chrs*, no. 25.

[352] Ferguson, *Medieval Papal Representatives*, chapters 3–5, particularly pp. 161–76.

[353] See above, pp. 267–9. In addition, see Stein, 'Roman Law in Scotland'; Peter Stein, 'The Source of the Romano-Canonical Part of *Regiam Majestatem*', *SHR*, vol. 48, no. 146 (1969), pp. 107–23; see also A. M. Godfrey, *Civil Justice in Renaissance Scotland: The Origins of a Central Court* (Leiden, 2009), pp. 371–6.

[354] See above, pp. 267–71.   [355] Cooper, *Select Cases*, nos. 22–25 (pp. 32–6).

[356] *Paisley Reg.*, pp. 166–8, 169–70, 170–1.

Gilbert son of Samuel, because it by right belonged to our church of Kilpatrick'.[357] The case was heard over two days, first in the parish church of Irvine and then in the parish church of Ayr. The abbey produced witnesses, who testified, and the judges delegate found that Monachkennaran was indeed the abbey's. Gilbert was condemned, and owed £30 to be divided between those who had testified on behalf of the abbey and to the judges-delegate 'for their assistance and guidance'. Gilbert, however, failed to turn up when cited, and never paid the £30. The judges-delegate then wrote to the king, asking him to 'extend the secular arm' against Gilbert to force him to comply with the judgment and satisfy the judges.[358] Kings could therefore be invoked to confirm and uphold the judgment of papal judge-delegates, who acknowledged their 'royal majesty' (*regia majestas*) in so doing.[359]

This also worked the other way. Some of our cases have unsuccessful claimants in royal courts taking themselves under a bishop's jurisdiction, putting their behaviour under ecclesiastical censure, and incurring large punitive fines if the judgment was infringed in the future. The case of Adam Spot, who impleaded Ranulf Bunkle for two ploughgates of land in 1247, illustrates this well.[360] The case took place in the sheriff's court at Roxburgh, although it was heard in front of David of Lindsay, justiciar of Lothian. Adam had obtained a brieve (*preceptum*) from the king to initiate the case and, although the precise brieve is not explicitly stated, it was possibly one of novel dissasine, though this cannot be proven.[361] Adam ended up quitclaiming his rights to the land, and then placed himself under the jurisdiction of the bishops of St Andrews, Glasgow, and Dunkeld 'who were there at that time'. Adam swore that, if he or his heirs ever further vexed or troubled Ranulf or his heirs about the ploughgates, they would be placed under excommunication until they ceased and would have to pay a huge penalty of £200 to Ranulf for the vexation. It was not uncommon for unsuccessful parties to place themselves under the jurisdiction of bishops, who threatened them with excommunication and vast fines if they infringed the judgment of a secular court. The three couples in the Kilpatrick case, heard in the court of the earl of Lennox, placed themselves under the jurisdiction of the bishop of Glasgow in 1273, with the threat of 200 marks payable to the bishop (not Paisley Abbey) if any of the couples went against their oath.[362] Large future fines could also be threatened without invoking episcopal jurisdiction, as happened in two cases involving the unsuccessful claimants, Bertram of Ulston and Gilbert of Ruthven, but other examples reveal that it was the bishop's authority which would implement and ensure payment of the fines.[363]

---

[357] For *intentio* in canon law, see Ferguson, *Medieval Papal Representatives*, pp. 168–9.

[358] *Paisley Reg.*, pp. 169–70; for complaints about the king revoking excommunications, see Ash, 'Church in the Reign of Alexander III', pp. 33–4, 37.

[359] *Paisley Reg.*, p. 170.   [360] Fraser, *Douglas*, iii, no. 285.

[361] MacQueen, *Common Law*, p. 140.

[362] *Paisley Reg.*, pp. 182, 194, 200; see also episcopal jurisdiction as security for gifts: *Inchaffray Chrs*, no. 76; *Dunf. Reg.*, no. 190; *Arbroath Liber*, i, no. 234.

[363] Fraser, *Keir*, pp. 197–8; see further, *Panmure Reg.*, ii, pp. 82–3; NRS, RH1/2/80 (taken directly from PoMS, no. 7872; H4/26/26, online at <http://db.poms.ac.uk/record/source/7872/>); cf. *Kelso Liber*, i, no. 271; ii, no. 339; Ferguson, *Medieval Papal Representatives*, Appendix 1, no. 127 (Cooper, *Select Cases*, nos. 49, 70); *Inchcolm Chrs*, no. 30.

However, the king's brieves were used to bring cases against bishoprics and major religious institutions and this, understandably, may not have gone down well. These disputants could often be people of relatively minor status or, at least, minor in comparison to a major bishopric. Thus, widows or women may never have married were able to use the king's brieves against, for example, the bishop of Glasgow or the prior of Coldingham, which was under the jurisdiction of the bishopric of Durham.[364] In 1253, Emma of Smeaton, a widow, used the king's brieve of mortancestry to implead Dunfermline Abbey in the king's court at Stirling.[365] Although she lost the case, she was able to secure 20 marks a year from the abbey for her maintenance. When one factors in that brieves of inquest could be used to bring cases into the religious courts of others, as may have happened to Coldingham Priory, which was impleaded by Matthew of Howburn and brought into its own court, then the king's letters could and did affect not only the nature of the cases brought by secular individuals against religious institutions but also, potentially, the judicial forum into which cases were brought.[366] Another case describes the king as the 'defender' of individuals who were having their possession of land challenged in ecclesiastical courts in front of papal judges-delegate. In 1251, Nicholas of Inverpeffer cited the king as his *defensor* when he thought the abbot of Arbroath was trying to disinherit him from his land.[367] Whether Nicholas had obtained the king's brieve or was going to the king in person is not clear: regardless of what Nicholas actually did, the abstract figure of the king offered protection against disinheritance in ecclesiastical courts. As a result, the king's brieves provided an array of remedies to trouble the hold of major episcopal and religious institutions over their own landed estates.

This, naturally, caused some opposition. By *c*.1274, we know that use of the king's brieves of recognition and perambulation against 'church men' (*contra ecclesiasticas personas*) had been suspended 'by the counsel of the lord king and the consent of the prelates'.[368] Agreements drawn up between an unsuccessful lay pursuer and a successful religious defendant often contained the stipulation that the pursuer and his heirs would not henceforth obtain any 'royal letters' which could reopen his or her case.[369] But the real sticking point seems not to have been the brieves per se but the very fact that lay men and women brought ecclesiastical institutions into secular fora for land which churches claimed was held by them 'in alms'.[370] This issue long predated the introduction of brieves: thus, although procurement of royal brieves could exacerbate the conflict, they were not the cause of it.

---

[364] *Glasgow Reg.*, i, no. 172; Raine, *North Durham*, App., no. 378.

[365] *RRS*, iv, 1, no. 18.

[366] Raine, *North Durham*, App., no. 296.

[367] *Arbroath Liber*, i, no. 250; year dated because the text is dated according to Lady Day calendar dating.

[368] *Paisley Reg.*, p. 176.   [369] See above, p. 322.

[370] For the debates about which type of alms lands were meant to pertain to ecclesiastical jurisdiction and which to royal jurisdiction in England, see the important but controversial contribution in Douglas, 'Frankalmoin and Jurisdictional Immunity'.

The question of which judicial forum was correct in cases involving one secular and one religious party had arisen in Scotland by the early thirteenth century.[371] Between 1207 and 1208, Patrick, earl of Dunbar, was engaged in a vicious struggle with Melrose Abbey over the pastureland known as Sorrowlessfield.[372] Patrick had been summoned before papal judges-delegate to answer claims that he had violently occupied the land, which the abbey claimed was its own.[373] Patrick repeatedly failed to turn up after his citation, and gave reasons for so doing, one of which was taken from Romano-canonical law: 'the actor ought to follow the jurisdiction of the *reus*'.[374] That is, as Patrick claimed Sorrowlessfield was a secular tenement (*laicum tenementum*), he should not have to answer the accusations of Melrose in front of papal judges-delegate: it was a case about secular land and should be heard in a secular court. Patrick eventually got his way, at least in part: the case was heard in King William's court at Selkirk on 6 July 1208 but Patrick ended up quitclaiming his rights in the land and granting it to Melrose Abbey.[375] Perhaps he had been too clever.

These sorts of debates could also go against secular justice as well as in its favour but, equally, we should not assume that an ecclesiastical court would necessarily look all that different from a lay one, notwithstanding the type of law and legal procedure used within each court.[376] In 1225, a case over Lhanbryde in Moray between Andrew, bishop of Moray, and a lay couple, Robert Hod and his wife, Matilda, was heard in front of three papal judges-delegate: the abbot of Deer and the dean and archdeacon of Aberdeen.[377] The case had, apparently, been going on for a long time because Alexander II kept delaying matters, insisting that Lhanbryde was a 'barony' and thus litigation over it should occur in a royal court, not an ecclesiastical one. Although Alexander lost his fight, a compromise was made between him and the judges-delegate because they allowed him to participate in the judgment.[378] The bishop retained the church of Lhanbryde but quitclaimed the land to Robert and Matilda, who compensated him with a *dabach* of land from elsewhere. The witnesses to the case, however, look like those present at a major

---

[371] For a slightly earlier example, see the case about Saer de Quinci and Leuchars: *St Andrews Liber*, pp. 350–2; Ferguson, *Medieval Papal Representatives*, App. 1, no. 24 (pp. 216–17).

[372] *Melrose Liber*, i, nos. 101–104 (NRS, GD55/101, 55/102, 55/103, 55/104); see Ferguson, *Medieval Papal Representatives*, pp. 138–40, and App. 1, no. 25 (pp. 217–18); T. M. Cooper, 'Melrose Abbey *versus* the Earl of Dunbar', in Cooper, *Selected Papers*, pp. 81–7; MacQueen, 'Canon Law, Custom and Legislation', pp. 231–2.

[373] *Melrose Liber*, i, no. 101.

[374] *Melrose Liber*, i, no. 101 (p. 88); R. H. Helmholz, 'Civil Jurisdiction and the Clergy', in R. H. Helmholz, *The Ius Commune in England: Four Studies* (Oxford, 2001), pp. 196, 201–3, 238–9. The maxim first appears in Justinian's *Codex*.

[375] *Melrose Liber*, i, no. 102.

[376] For the use of Romano-canonical procedure, see Ferguson, *Medieval Papal Representatives*, pp. 161–77, and, in general, Brundage, *Medieval Canon Law*, pp. 127–40.

[377] *Moray Reg.*, Cartae Originales, no. 6; Ferguson, *Medieval Papal Representatives*, pp. 133, 140, 181–2, and App., no. 73 (pp. 239–40); MacQueen, 'Canon Law, Custom and Legislation', pp. 236–7. The charter says it was drawn up in 1225; however, if the year was dated according to Lady Day dating, then *our* dating would be 25 March 1225×24 March 1226. This is the dating used in PoMS, no. H4/32/48, online at <http://db.poms.ac.uk/record/source/3965/>.

[378] *Moray Reg.*, Cartae Originales, no. 6.

royal assembly. The agreement was witnessed by Walter and Gilbert, bishops of Glasgow and Caithness respectively, but also Alan of Galloway, Mael Coluim, earl of Fife, William Comyn, earl of Buchan (then justiciar of Scotia), Robert, earl of Strathearn, Walter fitz Alan, the king's steward, Henry de Balliol, the king's chamberlain, Walter Comyn, the king's clerk, alongside Ingelram de Balliol, John of Maxwell, and Walter Giffard, all of whom attested the king's charters.[379] So, although the case was technically heard in front of papal judges-delegate, it looked far more like a major royal assembly, with bishops and earls attesting first, as they would do the king's charters.

Disputes about the relationship between secular and ecclesiastical justice flared throughout the thirteenth century. On 2 April 1230, before the issue of Alexander II's legislation of that year, Pope Gregory IX confirmed to the bishop of Glasgow that their men and possessions were not to be brought into secular courts, 'unless they have been granted in a manner pertaining to feus and not in pure alms (*tanquam feodalia non tanquam in puram elemosinam sint collata*)'.[380] Only a day later, he wrote directly to Alexander II asking him to enforce this grant; Alexander 'was not to allow the bishop or his men to be brought in front of secular judgment for issues concerning their possessions and other things belonging of their church', and included the same exception.[381] It is often thought that these disputes flared up in the 1220s and then again in the 1250s but were finally settled in that period to the benefit of secular power and ceased to be a problem once Alexander III attained majority.[382] There was a further papal challenge during the minority of Alexander III when Innocent IV sent similar letters to the bishop of Glasgow and the abbot of Scone in 1253.[383] Prior to this, Innocent IV had sent a letter to his delegates in England, the bishops of Worcester, Lichfield, and Lincoln, asking them in powerful language to look into complaints he had received about the young king (and, behind him, his minority government) revoking excommunications, bringing churchmen into secular courts, and extracting services other than those of the common burdens of the realm.[384] Moreover, the bishops of Scotland also petitioned the young king's authority, complaining about laymen who had despoiled the church men of their lands, 'as we heard happened recently to the prior of St Andrews'.[385] But to see these sorts of debates as being, essentially, over by the time of Alexander II's death, only flaring up again during the political instability of a minority, would be incorrect. The developing brieve system added another layer to these debates. The letter of Laurence, dean of Lennox, written in *c.*1274, reveals that the church had achieved a limited victory through the ban on brieves of recognition and perambulation being initiated against church lands, a

---

[379] For the major witnesses to Alexander II's charters, see Stringer, 'Scottish "Political Community"', pp. 81–4.

[380] *Glasgow Reg.*, i, no. 158.   [381] *Glasgow Reg.*, i, no. 161; see also *Scone Liber*, no. 120.

[382] Duncan, *Making of the Kingdom*, pp. 288–90, although he describes his position as 'tentative' (p. 290). Slightly different views are offered in Ash, 'Church in the Reign of Alexander III', pp. 36–8; MacQueen, 'Scots Law', pp. 79–81; Ferguson, *Medieval Papal Representatives*, pp. 187–90; MacQueen, 'Canon Law, Custom and Legislation', pp. 236–8.

[383] *Glasgow Reg.*, i, no. 197; *Scone Liber*, no. 112.

[384] *Moray Reg.*, no. 260.   [385] NLS, MS Adv. 15.1.18, no. 16.

ban which had been made 'by the king's counsel'.[386] Moreover, this worked both ways. There developed at some point before the early fourteenth century a remedy, attested in the Ayr formulary, whereby the king could command, in a standard and formulaic way, a bishop, archdeacon, or dean to desist from bringing individuals into their courts over lay holdings which 'by law pertains to our royal court'.[387] If the addressee persisted, the king threatened that he would seize the offender's chattels. While there may well have been peaks in complaints made to the papacy about the correct jurisdictional forum, it is hard to imagine that these sorts of complaints were not a relatively consistent feature of litigation when a lay person was set against a religious institution (and vice versa).

Why so many disputes about the status of land occurred is not hard to imagine: ambition, conflicting rights over long and complicated series of inheritances and purchases, and new and more aggressive claims to lordship from one of the parties that were unacceptable to the other. All these are rather generic reasons. It is, however, possible that the organization of common burdens in thirteenth-century Scotland made it easier to bring land held in alms into secular courts. It will be remembered from Chapter 2 that some church land was liable to army-service and aid: sometimes ecclesiastical lords organized their own resources but, on occasion, donors could remit these services and perform them themselves, when they granted land in alms.[388] Lords who had, as a result of the pious donations of their ancestors, the responsibility of raising army-service and aid from lands of which they did not enjoy possession may well have wished to pursue a claim to that land. A bull of Innocent IV, issued in 1251 and mentioned earlier, denounced those who brought clerks into secular judgment through which they were despoiled of their land and immediately followed this by stating that no lay person may take anything from secular land 'except for army service and common aid for the defence of the kingdom'.[389] A note was entered into the margins of the *Registrum Vetus* of Glasgow in a mid-thirteenth-century hand which said that 'powerful men and their bailies' who had granted 'feus' (*feoda*) to the church were compelling bishops and other ecclesiastical men to 'subject themselves to secular forums and secular justice' for the reason that these laymen 'retained army service, aid, and other kinds of forinsec service' to themselves.[390] What is interesting here are the many potential landed targets for, essentially, the same complaint. Churchmen, monks, and canons were not to be brought into secular fora for alms land nor 'by royal edicts' nor for their land held as 'feus', which owed aid and army-service which was to be performed by the original donor and his heirs.

Given the sheer range of situations where a complaint could be made that cases concerning the church had been brought into lay fora, it is interesting that there never developed in Scotland a remedy for determining the status of the landholding, the results of which would determine the appropriate judicial forum.[391] Such

---

[386] *Paisley Reg.*, p. 176.   [387] A64 (pp. 25–6).   [388] See Chapter 2, p. 92.
[389] *Moray Reg.*, no. 260.   [390] *Glasgow Reg.*, ii, no. 535.
[391] *Utrum* is found in *Regiam* (*RM*, bk III, c. 30, in *APS*, i, pp. 630–1) but in a passage directly lifted from *Glanvill*, bk XIII, cc. 23–24 (pp. 163–4). For the introduction of *utrum*, see *Select Charters*, ed. Stubbs, pp. 165–6. There is no evidence for its use in Scotland.

a remedy had developed in England: the assize *utrum*, introduced in the Constitutions of Clarendon in 1164, and in Normandy shortly afterwards, where it was known as the writ *de feodo et elemosina*.[392] This introduced a recognition (*recognitio*) to be summoned in front of royal justices to determine whether (*utrum*) the land was lay fee or alms land. If alms land, the subsequent case would be heard in an ecclesiastical court; if fee, then it would be heard in the king's court. But nothing similar seems to have developed in Scotland, which is surprising, given that it was an issue throughout the thirteenth century and resulted in a number of ad hoc statements that certain of the king's brieves did not run if raised against church men and church lands. But how to prove that the land belonged to the church and was held in alms? Kings of Scots do not seem to have developed a preliminary remedy, whereby correct jurisdiction was determined *before* the case was heard. In Scotland, the issue was integrated into the hearing itself: at the end, land could be judged to be alms, thus vindicating the claims of one party, but there was no remedy for determining the correct jurisdiction beforehand.

The case between Paisley Abbey and the three couples over Kilpatrick heard between 1270 and 1273 is again relevant. The agreement made in 1270 was heard in the court of the earl of Lennox and had been going on 'for a long time'.[393] When the case was reopened in 1273, after the three couples had initiated an inquest into their status as heirs of Dubgall, heard by the sheriff of Dumbarton in 1271, this too was heard in the earl's court.[394] In March 1265, however, the abbey of Paisley had obtained a bull of Clement IV in which he prohibited the abbey from being brought into secular judicial fora for their lands, possessions, or material goods given in alms.[395] The abbey, of course, believed that they held the lands in Kilpatrick in alms, as Dubgall had quitclaimed his right to them back in 1233: in his charter, Dubgall confirmed that Paisley should hold these lands 'freely and quietly, fully and honourably, as . . . they hold and possess other alms given and granted to them by the faithful'.[396] But the combined weight of Clement's bull and the perceived status of the lands as Paisley's 'alms' was not enough to stop the three couples (all lay men and women) from bringing the case into a secular court, presumably because they believed that the lands were not alms at all but their rightful, lay, inheritance. There was no remedy, as there was in England, for the issue about the status of disputed lands to be solved before the case was brought into court: as a result, this type of question was not, as it was in England, resolved in front of the king's officer but was resolved as cases progressed, which *could* be in royal courts, but did not have to be. Why this was so will be addressed in the conclusion to this chapter.

---

[392] For its Norman adoption (but not in the rest of France), see John W. Baldwin, *The Government of Philip Augustus: Foundations of French Royal Power in the Middle Ages* (Berkeley, CA, and Los Angeles, 1986), pp. 319–23. See also the passages in the mid-thirteenth-century *Summa de Legibus*, in *Coutumiers de Normandie: Textes Critiques. Tome II: La Summa de Legibus Normannie in curia laicali*, ed. E. J. Tardif (Rouen and Paris, 1896), XCI.3 (p. 217), CXV (pp. 295–9).

[393] *Paisley Reg.*, p. 189. [394] *Paisley Reg.*, p. 180.

[395] *Paisley Reg.*, pp. 418–19. [396] *Paisley Reg.*, p. 163.

CONCLUSION

This chapter has not dealt with brieves briefly. It has shown that, during the second quarter of the thirteenth century, standard written remedies developed that were used by free individuals to settle disputes over the lands and rights they claimed. Previous work has focussed on the pleadable brieves of mortancestry, right, and dissasine as the key procedures of the Scottish common law. These brieves have been seen as evidence of a system of 'regularised royal justice in the thirteenth century, and hence of a Scottish common law'.[397] I would not disagree that there developed in Scotland a 'regularised [system] of royal justice' and a 'Scottish common law'; I would, however, question the significance of pleadable brieves. The key brieves for the Scottish common law were not necessarily the technically 'pleadable' ones. Instead, the non-pleadable brieves of perambulation and recognition addressed to the justiciar and, in particular, the retourable brieves of inquest addressed to the sheriff should occupy a more substantial place in our understanding of the range of legal remedies available from the king's chapel, how far royal justice inserted itself into the courts of others, and how far it actually aimed to work with and alongside them.

Brieves addressed to the justiciar were comparatively few in number, which may explain why a more complicated system of courts did not develop in thirteenth-century Scotland, as it did in contemporary England. The justiciar remained responsible for the pleas within his large ayres which were confined to Lothian, Scotia, and, from 1258 at the latest, Galloway. Justiciars simply did not have responsibility over enough remedies nor were those remedies necessarily available to enough people either for greater institutional complexity to develop or for it to become necessary that the office of justiciar should be performed by more than one or two men and their deputies. Greater institutional sophistication was also probably unnecessary. The king did not have a monopoly over the practical provision of justice but, equally, he also did not need to create one: aristocratic jurisdiction remained absolutely key to the power of royal legislative ambition. The criminal legislation of Alexander II shows that, even when justiciars were given power to summon visnets to indict criminals, as the justiciar of Lothian was in 1244, they handed those they convicted back to the lords who had jurisdictional power over them. Only when the plea was 'of the crown' did the king have ultimate power over malefactors and even then the right to hear these pleas was sometimes given away. When Alexander II introduced remedies that could potentially have diminished elite secular jurisdiction, such as mortancestry, right, dissasine, perambulation, and recognition, many of the remedies were limited in theory and in practice. The introduction of right, mortancestry, novel dissasine, and recognition suggests that Alexander was concerned with securing lawful possession but these remedies actually protected elites and did not undermine their jurisdictional power. Royal power formally depended on aristocratic power to such an extent that it would have been revolutionary to direct business overwhelmingly into royal courts in this way. Moreover,

---

[397] MacQueen, *Common Law*, p. 247.

it will be shown in Chapter 7 of this book that most royal officials were not in any way a separate class of new men but entrenched aristocrats whose status was enhanced by royal service but did not depend on it. As a result, it made sense that the new remedies did not fundamentally challenge aristocratic jurisdiction and that their jurisdiction was formally incorporated into the content of Alexander II's legislation.

The introduction of retourable brieves of inquest occurred after and probably in response to the introduction of standard brieves addressed to the justiciar, including the technically pleadable ones. Although there is no direct evidence to prove this, it is plausible that the existence of a small range of remedies, which were unrestricted (perambulation, mortancestry), coupled with three that *were* restricted (dissasine, recognition, right) created a demand for more readily available procedures stemming from the king's writing office. The solution to this putative demand could well have been the retourable brieves of inquest that developed between 1241 and 1259. These set questions similar in essence to the five procedures just listed but were wider in range and availability. Yet these brieves side-stepped the issue of judgment: brieves of inquest did not produce judgments per se. Instead, they either referred the matter back to the king or provided a springboard for disputes to be initiated or raised again in the courts of others. In this way, retourable brieves either brought particular disputes into the direct purview of the king or were able to work within jurisdictions without necessarily threatening the authority of a court-holder. When seen alongside perambulation and recognition, the concentration on pleadable brieves in existing scholarship has thus overlooked some of the significant ways in which people interacted with the king's writing office.

But all this is affected by whether there was a rule that 'no freeholder could be made to answer to his lands except by an action begun by the king's brieve', as there was in England, where no person had to answer for his freeholding without a royal writ.[398] As stated at the beginning of this chapter, this rule was first laid down in Scotland in Robert I's 1318 legislation, which 'ordained and agreed' that 'no one shall be ejected from his freeholding (*liberum tenementum*) of which he claims to be vested and saised as of feu without the king's pleadable brieve or other like brieve'.[399] MacQueen, mainly interpreting pleadable as those of mortancestry, dissasine, and right, has argued that this rule had already developed throughout the kingdom by the end of the thirteenth century, and was particularly applied within burghs.[400] If so, then the argument put forward in this chapter becomes problematic for the existence of such a rule would have had the potential to cut across the jurisdiction of others, particularly lay aristocrats, bringing their business into royal courts.[401] This is the opposite of what has been argued here: that pleadable brieves were few, the use of one was limited to high socio-economic status, and all were

---

[398] MacQueen, *Common Law*, pp. 105–6.   [399] *RPS*, 1318/27.
[400] MacQueen, *Common Law*, pp. 105–11.
[401] The clear ambition of this rule, contrasted with Robert's use of aristocratic franchises, is acknowledged by MacQueen, *Common Law*, p. 106.

perhaps not so much used as other types of brieve, most obviously the brieves of perambulation and recognition, as well as the brieves of inquest that allowed claimants either to appeal directly to the king or to take the king's brieve into the court of another.

But the evidence for the development of the 'brieve rule' in the thirteenth century is, in fact, rather scarce and ambiguous. First, it must be acknowledged that even Robert I's statute did not focus only on pleadable brieves; it also mentioned any 'other like brieve'. But even if we expand Robert's statute to include *all* the legal brieves available from the king's writing office, it is still unclear that there was a 'brieve rule' operating in Scotland much before 1318.[402] The key evidence for the 'brieve rule'—in the *Leges Quatuor Burgorum*—in fact states that people within burghs *could* answer claims on their lands brought by pursuers without a royal brieve if they wanted to: a brieve was not required.[403] The first clear evidence of the rule is not until 1318, when it was 'ordained and agreed' by Robert I's Scone Parliament.

This makes Robert's enactment in 1318 look rather more innovative than first thought: he stated, for the first time, that a person could only be ejected from a free tenement by the king's pleadable brieve or any like brieve. Robert's legislation also, as MacQueen has shown, extended the range of brieves of mortancestry and dissasine and is also the first clear evidence showing that kings wished to control the form of pleading in their own courts.[404] This must have led to a vast increase in the amount of expected business in royal courts, particularly that of the justiciar; it must also have led to the intimate link between pleading and brieve that MacQueen has illuminated for the fourteenth century.[405] It is perhaps ironic that Robert I, who famously dispossessed much of his nobility of their land, may have been responsible for the extension of a variety of remedies designed to secure tenure of land on a much wider scale.[406] But there is nothing to suggest that a nascent 'brieve rule' *compelled* claimants to seek the king's brieve in the thirteenth century nor that either pleadable or retourable brieves were required to eject individuals lawfully from their free landholdings.[407] It is thus possible that pleadable brieves— and compulsion to use brieves in general—only took centre stage in the Scottish common law in the fourteenth century as a result of an attempted redirection of royal authority and justice that was occurring under Robert I.[408]

The absence of a 'brieve rule' does not, however, mean that there was no common law in thirteenth-century Scotland. Certainly, the term *communis lex* was

---

[402] Carpenter, 'Scottish Royal Government', pp. 143–4.

[403] *Leges Quatuor Burgorum*, c. 43, in *APS*, i, p. 341. This chapter is present in the Berne MS text of *Leges Quatuor Burgorum*, which is incomplete but is still the earliest surviving manuscript of the text: NRS, PA5/1, fo. 63v.

[404] MacQueen, *Common Law*, pp. 146–53 (particularly pp. 147–51), 169–70, 177–8; also G. W. S. Barrow, *Robert Bruce and the Community of the Realm of Scotland*, 4th edn (Edinburgh, 2005), p. 387.

[405] MacQueen, 'Pleading'.

[406] MacQueen, *Common Law*, pp. 177–8.

[407] It is altogether possible that increased recourse to the brieve created *ad hoc* compulsion by the early fourteenth century.

[408] Most recently, Penman, *Robert the Bruce*, pp. 190–202, 209–27, 315–24.

used. Lay aristocratic courts were supposed to operate 'following the law of the land'.[409] The common law of the land did not mean that all people interacted with the same judicial institutions in the same way but that, regardless of jurisdiction, the common law or the law of the kingdom was supposed to be upheld. Procuring a royal brieve of inquest was one way the law of the land could be upheld, even if the judgment was heard in another court and even if that judgment was not *directly caused* by the procurement of a brieve. The common law of Scotland was not upheld by a uniform jurisdiction but rather by multiple jurisdictions which were incorporated into the prescriptive content of royal statutes.

This holds only for lay aristocratic jurisdiction. When it comes to ecclesiastical jurisdiction, a different picture emerges. Aristocratic jurisdiction does not seem to have been threatened by developments in royal justice over the thirteenth century. Ecclesiastical jurisdiction was—or was at certain points and in certain contexts—, and its separate nature was deployed as a strategy of dispute resolution against lay participants. The introduction of pleadable and retourable brieves tapped into an already existing debate about jurisdiction over church lands, which was itself a dispute occurring across Western Europe since the mid-twelfth century at the latest. In Scotland, the brieves of the two Alexanders added another layer to these debates: bishoprics and religious institutions were not just to be taken into 'secular courts' for the lands they claimed to hold in alms; they were now also not to be impleaded 'by royal letters'. But one should not overestimate a picture of conflict between lay and ecclesiastical jurisdiction during this period: both king and bishop continued to reinforce the decisions of each other's courts and it would be incorrect to think that the introduction of legal brieves *caused* conflict over church lands. In many ways, it was the very combination of the separate nature of ecclesiastical jurisdiction *and* its close relationship with royal justice that may explain why *utrum* (or a similar procedure) was never introduced in Scotland. Introducing a procedure whereby the correct forum would be decided in front of royal officials would, perhaps, have given more weight to royal jurisdictional fora than was possible in Scotland, where theoretical jurisdictional separateness masked what was often significant jurisdictional integration.

Why was the second quarter of the thirteenth century the period when these remedies were introduced? We must look not only at developments in royal justice but also at developments in the institutional power of the Scottish church, in particular, its own lawmaking. It has already been shown in Chapter 4 that shrieval and justiciar jurisdiction had strengthened during the last two decades of the twelfth century and covered enough of Scotia, Moray, and greater Lothian (including Clydesdale) to be considered a common feature throughout the kingdom. But if royal justice provided the structure, the church may have prompted the timing. Following the attendance of William Malveisin, bishop of St Andrews, and Henry, abbot of Kelso, at the Fourth Lateran Council in 1215, the bishops, abbots, and priors were developing their own institutional coherence, acknowledged by the

---

[409] See above, p. 339.

establishment of a Provincial Council in Scotland in 1225.[410] It has been acknowledged that the church was a 'crucial formant' in the rise of a Scottish common law but by this it is meant that the church did justice in its own court, that it was the conduit for Romano-canonical law into Scotland, and that it provided the moral compass for the justice of secular kings.[411] But it may also have been more prosaic than that. Simply by having their own provincial council, issuing their own legislation and regularly meeting to discuss the laws and regulations of the dioceses of the kingdom of the Scots, the church in Scotland provided a model and left a gap for secular power to develop concurrently. This may have particularly acted as a spur to Alexander II as he was present at the formation of the provincial council in 1225. This, above all, must explain the relative absence of episcopal and monastic/religious jurisdiction from the law of Alexander II, as well as, perhaps, the very existence of the law itself.

The period 1230–90, therefore, saw major changes in the workings of royal justice, most notably in its use of the written word to create a set of standard procedures whereby free men and women could obtain the king's brieve to initiate cases or use such processes in their disputes with other parties. But these changes did not undercut the jurisdiction of lay aristocrats and may well have developed in response to a legislating church. Alexander's statutes and brieves both negotiated between and incorporated multiple and overlapping jurisdictions. Alexander's statutes were all made in the presence of the bishops, abbots, priors, and great lords of his kingdom. All of them probably felt well served and protected by them: churchmen (because their jurisdiction was, in general, explicitly not included) and aristocrats (because their jurisdiction was included). If the Scottish common law has been thought not particularly common either in geographical range (because it did not include the great lordships of the kingdom) or in use (because its remedies were few and limited), then this is because too much attention has been given to pleadable brieves and not enough to the retourable ones, which could be used by anyone and taken into the courts of others who were also expected to uphold the 'laws of the land'.

---

[410] D. E. R. Watt, *Medieval Church Councils in Scotland* (Edinburgh, 2000), pp. 43–78, 87–102, particularly pp. 43–9.

[411] MacQueen, 'Expectations of the Law', p. 279; MacQueen, 'Canon Law, Custom and Legislation'.

6

Accounting and Revenue, *c.*1180–1290

How kings received their revenue and from what sources they did so are key to understanding the extent of institutional power in the kingdom during the late twelfth and thirteenth centuries. Standardized ways of collecting revenue often develop in the process of greater institutional centralization. This happened in England, when the exchequer was introduced in the reign of Henry I to become a geographically fixed institution at Westminster, held almost continuously throughout the year. The revival of standard accounting at the exchequer is held to be part of the reestablishment of royal authority by Henry II after the troubles of Stephen's reign.[1] The power of the English exchequer was significant: royal officials from the most northerly and westerly reaches of the kingdom were all summoned to account at the governmental centre. The Exchequer at Westminster also ultimately controlled newly conquered areas in Wales and Ireland, albeit through a more delegated structure. When north Wales was conquered by Edward I in 1283–84, the sheriffs introduced in that area accounted at the Westminster Exchequer indirectly through the chamberlain of Caernarfon.[2] In a similar way, when sheriffs were introduced in English Ireland, they accounted at the Exchequer in Dublin under a treasurer, who then presented himself at the English Exchequer at Westminster.[3]

[1] William Stubbs, *The Constitutional History of England in its Origin and Development*, 3 vols. (Oxford, 1874–78), i, pp. 407–18; H. G. Richardson and G. O. Sayles, *The Governance of Medieval England from the Conquest to Magna Carta* (Edinburgh, 1963), pp. 163–5, 171–2, 243–50, 279–80; Judith A. Green, 'Praeclarum et Magnificum Antiquitatis Monumentum: the Earliest Surviving Pipe Roll', *Bulletin of the Institute of Historical Research*, vol. 55 (1982), pp. 1–17; also see now Mark Hagger, 'A Pipe Roll for 25 Henry I', *EHR*, vol. 122, no. 495 (2007), pp. 133–40. Judith A. Green, *The Government of England under Henry I* (Cambridge, 1986), pp. 40–50, 51–93; for exchequer in the mid-twelfth century, see Kenji Yoshitake, 'The Exchequer in the Reign of Stephen', *EHR*, vol. 103, no. 409 (1988), pp. 950–9; Emilie Amt, *The Accession of Henry II in England: Royal Government Restored, 1149–59* (Woodbridge, 1993), pp. 119–28; cf. Graeme J. White, *Restoration and Reform, 1153–1165: Recovery from Civil War in England* (Cambridge, 2000), pp. 130–60.

[2] R. R. Davies, *The Age of Conquest: Wales 1063–1415* (Oxford, 1991), pp. 364–6; E. A. Lewis, 'Account Roll of the Chamberlain of the Principality of North Wales 1304–5', *Bulletin of the Board of Celtic Studies*, vol. 1 (1921–23), pp. 256–75.

[3] Philomena Connolly, *Medieval Record Sources*, Maynooth Research Guides for Irish Local History, 4 (Dublin, 2002), pp. 18–23; *Irish Exchequer Payments, 1270–1446*, ed. Philomena Connolly, Irish Manuscripts Commission, (Dublin, 1998).

Historiographical tradition has established that the kingdom of the Scots, although not under the power of the English king, nonetheless had a similar structure of central account and audit which also went under the name 'exchequer'.[4] This idea has very recently come under challenge by David Carpenter, building on the 1970s' work of A. A. M. Duncan.[5] In his 2013 study, Carpenter concluded that 'there was no Scottish exchequer; no office, that is, staffed by its own officials, separate from the itinerant court and fixed in one place'.[6] This is quite a statement, given that the majority of evidence for thirteenth-century accounting practice can be found in a volume entitled *The Exchequer Rolls of Scotland*, which, if one follows Carpenter, refers to an institution which seems not to have existed in this period.[7] One purpose of this chapter is to show how different the audit process was in Scotland from in its southern neighbour and to question how important geographical centrality was to the emergence of standardized accounting procedure.

The link between financial means and statehood has long been acknowledged by historians and sociologists. Charles Tilly identified a causal link between the management of public finance and an increasingly centralized government, albeit for a later period.[8] Better management spawned more intensive institutions of extraction. The impetus for financial change was identified as the demands of war, the need to maintain military forces necessitating better resource extraction which itself produced more intensive—and bureaucratic—government, although the extent of such changes depended on existing factors.[9] How far war affected the relationship between public finance and central power will be considered at the end of this book. The fundamental question of this chapter, however, is what the changing structure of royal resource extraction reveals about the extent of central administrative power in the kingdom of the Scots during the thirteenth century.

---

[4] A good indication of the strength of this purchase is in works written by historians not of medieval Scotland; see, for example, Robin Frame, *The Political Development of the British Isles 1100–1400* (Oxford, 1995), p. 93. Frame's comments, however (short though they are), are remarkably clear and to the point, so I am using his work merely as a way of highlighting the appearance of the term 'exchequer'.

[5] A. A. M. Duncan, *Scotland: the Making of the Kingdom* (Edinburgh, 1975), pp. 596–600, 606–7; David Carpenter, 'Scottish Royal Government in the Thirteenth Century from an English Perspective', in *New Perspectives on Medieval Scotland, 1093–1286*, ed. Matthew Hammond (Woodbridge, 2013) , pp. 117–59, at pp. 118–26; Carpenter's earlier points are also still very instructive: David Carpenter, *The Struggle for Mastery, The Penguin History of Britain 1066–1284* (London, 2004), pp. 520–1.

[6] Carpenter, 'Scottish Royal Government', p. 121.   [7] *ER*, i.

[8] Charles Tilly, *Coercion, Capital and European States, AD 900–1992* (Oxford, 1990); Charles Tilly, 'Entanglements of European Cities and States', in *Cities and the Rise of States in Europe, AD 1000–1800*, ed. Charles Tilly and Wim P. Blockmans (Boulder, CO, 1994), pp. 1–27; Charles Tilly, 'Reflections on the History of European State-Making', in *The Formation of National States in Western Europe*, ed. Charles Tilly (Princeton, NJ, 1975), pp. 3–83.

[9] Tilly, *Coercion*, pp. 67–95; Anthony Molho, 'The State and Public Finance: A Hypothesis Based on the History of Late Medieval Florence', in *The Origins of the State in Italy 1300–1600*, ed. Julius Kirshner, supplement of *The Journal of Modern History* (Chicago, IL, 1995), pp. 97–135.

THE GROWTH OF AUDITING AND ACCOUNTING

Notwithstanding the pioneering work of A. A. M. Duncan and David Carpenter, the main reason for the absence of an in-depth study of accounting procedure is the loss of all original rolls from the period. Whether this loss was through Edward I's overlordship, fires in the 1540s, the sinking of a ship in 1660 containing records carried off by Oliver Cromwell from Stirling Castle, or the fire of the Exchequer buildings on 10 November 1811, the loss is significant and longstanding.[10] Even by the late sixteenth century, very few thirteenth-century account rolls were housed in the Register in Edinburgh. In 1595, for example, Sir John Skene completed an inventory of the Exchequer records.[11] Skene, however, listed only four yearly accounts from the thirteenth century—those returned in 1264, 1265, 1266, and 1289. The scarcity of thirteenth-century account rolls is attested even earlier in the late fourteenth century. In 1382, Robert II commanded that his rolls 'of accounts' and registers should be searched for evidence of the bishop of Aberdeen's right to collect a tenth of all royal revenue ('second teinds') but the only thirteenth-century accounts cited in the return were dated 1264 and 1266.[12] The next roll consulted contained two accounts returned in 1328 and then another of 1343.[13] The king's archives thus did not contain a full and continuous series of thirteenth-century account rolls even by the late fourteenth century.

In what is only small compensation for this absence of material, we do have transcripts made in the early seventeenth century by Thomas Hamilton, first earl of Haddington (1563–1637).[14] Haddington abridged the content of the extant rolls for the years 1263–66 and 1288–90, some of which were mentioned by Skene in his 1595 register of existing records. Skene, however, believed that accounts were only returned in 1264, 1265, 1266, and 1289, probably because he did not consult the extant rolls in great detail.[15] In fact, Haddington's transcript contains accounts from 1263, 1288, and 1290 as well as those from 1264–66 and 1289.[16] Haddington's transcripts were then edited by John Stuart in the nineteenth century before they were posthumously published by George Burnett in 1878 in volume 1 of *The Exchequer Rolls of Scotland*.[17] The transcripts are not as frequently

---

[10] J. Maitland Thomson, *The Public Records of Scotland* (Glasgow, 1922); Athol L. Murray, 'The Pre-Union Records of the Scottish Exchequer', *Journal of the Society of Archivists*, vol. 2, no. 3 (1961), pp. 89–101; David Stevenson, 'The English and the Public Records of Scotland, 1650–1660', in *Miscellany I*, Stair Society 26 (Edinburgh, 1971), pp. 156–70.

[11] Skene's list is described as 'ane tabill and repertour of the Cheker rollis extant in the Reg(ist)er collectit and put in ordour conforme to the number and ordour of kingis in quhais tyme they wer maid and of the yeiris of ilkane of the kingis forsaidis be M. Johne Skene clerk of the regis(ter) the tyme of his intermissionn with the said register 1595': see NLS, MS Adv. 31.3.15, fo. 1r; see, further, Athol L. Murray 'Sir John Skene and the Exchequer, 1594–1612', in *Miscellany I*, Stair Society 26 (Edinburgh, 1971), pp. 125–55.

[12] *Aberdeen Reg.*, i, pp. 156–74, particularly pp. 157–61, with the quotation cited at pp. 156–7, and the extracts from the 1264 and 1266 accounts at p. 158. For 'second teinds', see below, pp. 379–85.

[13] *Aberdeen Reg.*, i, p. 159.   [14] NRS, E 38/1.   [15] NLS, MS Adv. 31.3.15, fo. 1r.

[16] See below, pp. 353–61, including a reference to an earlier account held in Scone in 1262; cf. Maitland Thomson, *Public Records*, p. 10; Murray, 'Pre-Union Records', p. 94.

[17] *ER*, i, pp. 1–51.

studied as one might expect given that they are not only readily available but also the only coherent source for thirteenth-century accounting procedure. Since their first publication by Burnett, historians have held Haddington's transcripts in varying degrees of trust. Burnett stated that, although of 'great value', they were also 'in many places injudiciously abridged, and by no means free from copyists' errors'.[18] In 1975, A. A. M. Duncan stated that although the transcripts were 'invaluable', they were also 'badly transcribed'.[19] In general, historians have gutted his transcripts for the financial data they contain about the extent and sources of the king's income.[20] They have rarely, however, been used in any systematic examination of accounting procedure and the extent of the institutional framework surrounding it, which is the purpose of this section.[21]

As a result, the authority of our fundamental source, Haddington's transcripts, must be established.[22] Haddington's reputation is not good: he is berated for making scribal errors, for adopting a note-like approach to the material, and for abridging many of the accounts he only partially transcribed. But consultation of Haddington's original manuscript shows that he did take care throughout his work, scoring out his mistakes (when he made them) and copying the correct readings over the top.[23] The mistakes he made most frequently were in the names of officials when his source simply provided an initial and a surname. That being said, the mistakes Haddington made with nomenclature are rectifiable and the names he recorded correctly far outnumber those he did not.[24] Moreover, while he did abridge his material and made mistakes when expanding initials, confidence in the *content* of his transcriptions is confirmed by comparing Haddington's work with the extracts from the accounts of the sheriffdoms of Banff and Aberdeen in the royal charter of Robert II drawn up for the bishopric of Aberdeen in 1382.[25] These do indeed confirm that Haddington did not include *all* the information in his source (but we knew that anyway); the accuracy of those he did transcribe, however, is good.[26]

---

[18] *ER*, i, p. xxxvi (although acknowledging they covered 1262 to 1266).

[19] Duncan, *Making of the Kingdom*, p. 596.

[20] See, for example, Alexander Grant, 'Thanes and Thanages from the Eleventh to the Fourteenth Centuries', in *Medieval Scotland: Crown, Lordship and Community—Essays Presented to G. W. S. Barrow*, ed. Alexander Grant and Keith J. Stringer (Edinburgh, 1993), pp. 39–81, at pp. 60–3; Michael Brown, *The Wars of Scotland 1214–1371* (Edinburgh, 2004), pp. 57–61; Duncan, *Making of the Kingdom*, pp. 598–600.

[21] See the comments in Duncan, *Making of the Kingdom*, pp. 596–600, and the more detailed study in Carpenter, 'Scottish Royal Government', pp. 118–20.

[22] *ER*, i, pp. 1–34 (1263–66), 35–51 (1288–90).

[23] See, for example, NRS, E 38/1, fo. 6r, in which Haddington began to transcribe the renders in kind from the waiting of four nights from Kinross (beginning *redditus vaccarum*) before stating that these renders were part of the waiting owed. He crossed out his mistake and began again with the words 'de waitinga', as in *ER*, i, p. 16.

[24] See Chapter 7, p. 420, notes 92–3, 96.

[25] *Aberdeen Reg.*, i, pp. 157–61; for a summary of the lengthy dispute, see *ER*, i, pp. clxxv–clxxix. The extracts from the accounts in the 1382 charter can also be found in *ER*, i, pp. clxxix–clxxxii.

[26] Thus, both the 1382 charter and Haddington record the profits of the justiciar of Scotia in the sheriffdom of Aberdeen in 1264 as '100 and 14 shillings': *ER*, i, pp. 11–12; *Aberdeen Reg.*, i, p. 158. The only difference is in the account of Ranulf of Strachan, sheriff of Banff in 1264, where Haddington states that 100 cows were remitted to Walter of Moray, whereas the Aberdeen charter says that 160

Haddington also preserved the original order of the accounts he copied. This will be surprising to anyone who has consulted this material because Haddington presented it in what looks like an extremely haphazard way. The order of individual accounts within the transcript is non-chronological and entries jump from year to year. Accounts returned in 1264 are followed by those made in 1263; the roll then continues to record accounts returned in 1264, then 1266, then back to 1263, and so on.[27] This has led to the assumption that Haddington must have cherry-picked information from a number of sources, presumably one roll for each financial year (like the yearly pipe rolls of England).[28] Yet it would appear that Haddington was drawing on only two sources (one roll for the 1263–66 material, a second from 1288–90) and, in both cases, followed their order closely. About two-thirds of the way through the 1263–66 material, for example, Haddington stated that the remainder of the accounts (from various financial years) were on the *dorse* of the singular roll ('upon the bak of the forsaid roll') that he was copying.[29] That his source was a single roll containing financial accounts in non-chronological order is again confirmed by Robert II's 1382 charter to the bishopric of Aberdeen. This charter states that the 1266 account of Andrew of the Garioch, sheriff of Aberdeen, was to be found 'on the dorse of the same roll', as it was in Haddington's transcript, making it clear that a single roll had been consulted for both accounts.[30] Haddington's 'chaotic' and 'injudicious' arrangement thus seems to have been present in his original source and, although he often abridged content, he did not alter the *order* of his source and, indeed, took some care in the presentation of the material he did bother to transcribe. The seemingly chaotic and non-chronological order of the 1263–66 roll affects our views on the relationship of the centrally kept written record to the process of accounting itself, which will be set out in Chapter 7.

We can thus use Haddington's transcripts with some confidence, although their limitations still have to be acknowledged. It is still not possible, because of their excerpted state, to use them to calculate complete levels of income passing through this particular audit process at all levels of government, as one can in England. But we can use them to think about auditing structure and process, as will be done here, and we can use them to discuss the sources of the king's revenue, as will be

---

cows were remitted to Hugh of Moray (and were being paid to Mael Coluim of Moray). But these appear to be two separate transactions, not a mistake by Haddington (*ER*, i, p. 15; *Aberdeen Reg.*, i, p. 158).

[27] The significance of this rather haphazard process of recording in the 1260s is developed in Chapter 7, pp. 403–5.

[28] Although two, if not three, copies were supposed to be made, see *Dialogus de Scaccario (The Dialogue of the Exchequer) and Constitutio Domus Regis (The Disposition of the King's Household)*, ed. Emilie Amt and S. D. Church, Oxford Medieval Texts (Oxford, 2007) (henceforth, *Dialogus*), pp. 26–7.

[29] NRS, E38/1, fo. 8v; *ER*, i, pp. 23–4.

[30] *Aberdeen Reg.*, i, p. 158: 'in dorso vero eiusdem rotuli in compoto Andree de Garuiach'. It should also be noted that Skene in 1595 confirmed that the accounts of '1264–6' were 'ane roll of the sherff compt' and those of 1289 in 'ane breff roll and compt' (NLS, MS Adv. 31.3.15, fo. 1r). It is possible that the later accounts were entered on separate rolls but it is certain that those of 1264–66 were kept on a single roll.

done in the next section, even if we cannot calculate the precise amount each source provided.

Both sets of accounts from the 1260s and 1288–90 reveal that accounts were heard primarily by bishops and abbots, alongside the household officers of chamberlain and chancellor.[31] In 1264, the account of the then chamberlain, William, earl of Mar, was heard by Gamelin, bishop of St Andrews, Richard, bishop of Dunkeld, the abbot of Dunfermline, Thomas, abbot of Lindores, the abbot of Holyrood, Robert, abbot of Scone, William, abbot of Coupar Angus, Robert Menzies, once the king's chamberlain, and John Cameron, lord of Denmuir and also sheriff of Perth, who also returned his account sometime in 1264.[32] In 1290, a series of accounts were heard at Scone in front of the abbots of Coupar Angus, Arbroath, and Scone, Nicholas de Hay and Robert Cameron, 'knights', Master Thomas of Chartres, the chancellor of Scotland, and Master William Cramond, clerk, who was taking the place of the chamberlain, Alexander de Balliol.[33]

It is worth considering the people holding the audit in 1264 in more detail. Many of the churchmen were or had been household officers of the king's court: Richard, bishop of Dunkeld (d.1272), for example, was a chamberlain of Alexander II before his election to the see of Dunkeld in 1250. Robert Menzies had also been a chamberlain under Alexander II and Nicholas de Hay would occupy the same role later under Alexander III.[34] The final auditor in 1264 was John Cameron, lord of Denmuir, who rendered account that year as sheriff of Perth.[35] John does not appear as a witness to Alexander III's charters but did attest at least two of Alexander II's; his appearance as sheriff of Perth in 1264 and 1266 is at least indicative of his incorporation into the structures of royal governance.[36] While it was expected that the audit session would be presided over by two royal officials of the king's household—his chamberlain and chancellor—the remaining auditors were secular and ecclesiastical landlords, many of whom would attend the king as he travelled.[37]

Moreover, it is of note that both the 1264 and the 1290 accounts were heard at Scone. The nearest sheriff to Scone was the sheriff of Perth and, in both 1264 and 1290, the sheriff of Perth acted as an auditor: John Cameron in 1264 and Nicholas Hay in 1290, although neither was given his shrieval title among the lists of auditors.[38] Although the evidence is extremely sparse, it appears that the nearest sheriff to the location of the audit would sit alongside the chancellor, chamberlain, and others to hear the accounts. This makes sense, given that it will be shown later that local sheriffs paid for the account out of the shrieval income when the audit was heard in their sheriffdom.[39] The links between 'local' and 'central' government were even stronger than this. In 1264, the future sheriff of Perth, Nicholas Hay,

---

[31] *ER*, i, pp. 11, 22, 45.   [32] *ER*, i, p. 11.   [33] *ER*, i, p. 49.

[34] For more on the personality of office holders, see Chapter 7, pp. 417–34.

[35] *ER*, i, pp. 26–7.

[36] *Scone Liber*, no. 66 (NRS, RH6/33 [AII/210]); *Coupar Angus Chrs*, i, no. 46 [AII/276].

[37] For comparative terminology in twelfth-century England and France, see Bruce Lyon and Adriaan Verhulst, *Medieval Finance: A Comparison of Financial Institutions in Northwestern Europe* (Bruges, 1967), pp. 70–1, 90–1; also Brian Kemp, 'Exchequer and Bench in the Later Twelfth Century—Separate or Identical Tribunals?', *EHR*, vol. 88, no. 348 (1973), pp. 559–73.

[38] *ER*, i, pp. 11, 49.   [39] See below, this chapter, pp. 385–6.

was also an auditor.[40] It is of note that Nicholas's father, Gilbert Hay, had died in the office of sheriff of Perth between 27 March 1262 (when he returned his final account) and 29 September 1263 (by which point he was dead, and his account was returned by two attorneys).[41] Nicholas Hay may have been very young at this point—certainly, he lived until 1305×6—but, as the new lord of Erroll in Perthshire, his presence was nonetheless required at the audit. In 1290, Robert Cameron, John Cameron's son, was also an auditor, despite not being the sitting sheriff.[42] What this shows, therefore, is the links between the structures of local lordship, office holding, and the audit procedure.

Although accounts were heard by a mixture of ecclesiastical and lay men, it was the chancellor and the chamberlain (so, often one cleric and one layman) who really mattered. They had to be present for the audit to take place at all or, if they were not, they had to send a representative.[43] If neither they nor their attorney was present, certain transactions could not take place. For example, Hugh de Berkeley, sheriff of Berwick, returned his account at some point between 1263 and 1266, requesting the 20 marks he was accustomed to receive each year 'from the king's grace'. But Hugh, despite also being justiciar of Lothian, had to go away empty-handed since the *curia* would not grant the amount 'because of the absence of the chancellor and the chamberlain'.[44] There was thus a very formal aspect to accounting procedure: money could not be released unless the two officials who exercised this responsibility were present. The place where officials deposited their monies was called the *camera* ('the chamber'), under the supervision of the chamberlain, and the clerks who recorded the subsequent audit proceedings, at least in some form, were called the 'clerks of the king's chapel'.[45] The whole proceedings were described simply as the business of the court (*curia*): there was no Exchequer (*scaccarium*), merely the king's court and his financial *camera*.[46]

Officials of various kinds—from bailies to sheriffs to justiciars to the chamberlain himself—returned their accounts at the audit. The chamberlain did not have his accounts recorded on his own roll in 1263–66, as he would do by 1301, and more continuously from 1327.[47] The chamberlain was responsible for the sum total of the revenue, including 'ferms from *balliae* on both sides of the Scottish sea

---

[40] *ER*, i, p. 11.　　[41] *ER*, i, pp. 1–2.　　[42] *ER*, i, p. 49.

[43] For the *camera*, see *ER*, i, pp. 4, 41; for the *capella regis*, see *ER*, i, p. 51, and, more generally, G. W. S. Barrow, 'The *Capella Regis* of the Kings of Scotland, 1107–1222', in *Miscellany V*, ed. Hector L. MacQueen, Stair Society 52 (Edinburgh, 2006), pp. 1–11.

[44] *ER*, i, p. 22.

[45] There was no *cancellaria* ('chancery') nor *scaccarium* ('exchequer').

[46] *ER*, i, p. 45; the only mention of a *scaccarium* in a document issuing from the king's chapel is in Alexander II's great privilege to the Templars, issued in 1236, which is modeled on (although does not completely replicate) King John's charter to the Templars: *Aberdeen Reg.*, ii, pp. 269–71 [AII/234]; for John's (which does not contain the reference to the 'exchequer'), see *Rotuli Chartarum in Turri Londinensi Asservati Anno ab 1199–1216*, ed. Thomas Duffus Hardy, vol. 1, part 1 (London, 1837), pp. 1–2. But the charter contains so many formulae and expressions not otherwise found in Scottish royal charters that I think it fair to discount this reference here.

[47] For the possibility that the chamberlain accounted separately in 1288–90, see Chapter 4, pp. 257–8.

[the Firth of Forth]', 'ferms of burghs on both sides of the Scottish sea', 'common receipts until the day of this account, with fines and reliefs'.[48] Only the income from burgh ferms does not appear in Haddington's transcripts of the 1263–66 shrieval accounts but it does appear in sheriffs' accounts from the time of 1288, when William Sinclair, sheriff of Dumfries, proffered £20 8d from the burgh ferm of Dumfries.[49] It is unlikely that burgh ferms were not accounted for in 1263, particularly as the chamberlain's account explicitly refers to them: it may just be that Haddington did not include them under 'receipts' or that they were then accounted for separately from the justiciars, sheriffs, and bailies.

Although Haddington did sometimes abridge account records to the point of absurdity, it is still possible to identify a standard form to shrieval accounts from those fuller transcripts which appear, perhaps understandably, more frequently at the beginning of his manuscript than at its end, when he seems to have got a bit tired of transcribing. From these, it is clear that each account originally began with 'receipts', the revenue each sheriff received, often in kind, from his sheriffdom. These were interlinked with 'expenses' where appropriate. Thus, the sheriff of Forfar accounted under his receipts for thirty-two chalders and two bolls of malt as part of the king's waitings from Forfar and Glamis, which was immediately followed by his 'expenses', whereby he had already used seventeen chalders and one and a half bolls of malt in 'the king's service'.[50] After the expenses came the *adquietacio*—the discharge—in which the sheriff accounted for all the remaining monies he had received as part of his office. The totals were then added up, and if the sheriff still owed an amount, this was recorded at the end. There were links between all three sections. If a sheriff had sold some produce render in kind (which should have been entered solely in the receipts section), the cash amount he had received for so doing was entered in the 'discharge' (*adquietacio*) section.[51] Finally, *memoranda* were placed at the end of the account. These *memoranda* recorded, for example, if the sheriff had requested any additional money to be allocated to him for a particular purpose, if he had requested to be acquitted from payment of some item, or if he still owed anything outside his ordinary budget, such as if he had used additional produce when hosting the king.[52] Thus, although Haddington's transcripts are irritating in what they do not include, they still provide enough information to demonstrate that revenue was accounted for in a fairly standard way, even by 1263–66.

The audit did demand accountability. Even the king was accountable for his expenditure. In the account of the chamberlain, William of Mar, returned in 1264, Alexander III was found to owe the 'country' (*patria*) £589 9s 8½d, which he was expected to pay.[53] But so too were his officials. The accounts of all sorts of officials are scattered with references to their arrears from the last account and references to how much they owed.[54] The only exception was the justiciar, who was not found

---

[48] *ER*, i, p. 10.   [49] *ER*, i, p. 35.   [50] *ER*, i, p. 7.
[51] *ER*, i, pp. 8–9.   [52] *ER*, i, pp. 9, 10, 11, 14.
[53] For royal debt, see Chapter 4, pp. 255–6, and below pp. 356–7.
[54] *ER*, i, pp. 1, 10.

to owe anybody anything, because the profits of his justice were returned via the sheriff, as was shown in Chapter 4.[55] As a result, sheriffs were liable if they failed to deposit the justiciar's profits, not the justiciar himself. This system can only have worked if the justiciar left behind a list of amercements for the sheriff to collect once he had heard his pleas in the particular sheriffdom.[56]

Sheriffs must have been summoned by royal brieve to have their accounts audited by the king's court. A brieve formula survives in the Ayr formulary dealing with this very issue.[57] In this, the sheriff of Edinburgh (although the addressee could have been any sheriff), together with his main subordinate bailies of Linlithgow and Haddington, was summoned to appear 'promptly and prepared' at a certain place, in the presence of 'such-and-such auditors of account who will be gathered there' to render their accounts.[58] Moreover, the sheriff was to summon all other officials 'who receive our monies' within his sheriffdom to return their accounts. It is probable that some sort of similar brieve was in action in the reign of Alexander III. The formula itself says that sheriffs were to return account for all 'ferms and outgoings of your sheriffdom (*bailia*) both from [the king's] demesne lands and from wardships, reliefs, dower lands, fines and escheats', all of which sheriffs did account for in 1263–66. But the brieve formula describes the auditors as 'auditores', a word attested in the 1288–90 accounts, not those of 1263–66.[59] If this brieve in the Ayr formulary bears any resemblance to that putatively used to summon Alexander III's sheriffs, it may well have used less technical language.

The procedure attested in 1263–66 was thus relatively standard and formal, although it would become more so, as we shall see. But it was not a carbon copy of that of England. The first contrast to note with England is that sheriffs—and other officials—did not have to turn up to account each financial year. Indeed, as the Exchequer in England was open from Michaelmas through to the following summer, it was really a year-long event, with only the summer months free, so it was impossible for a sheriff in England to escape.[60] That sheriffs did not do the same in Scotland is, perhaps, surprising, given that the revenue expected from particular estates and sheriffdoms was fixed and depended on annual rent and render extraction either in kind or in cash. Although the account rolls are littered with phrases saying that particular officials returned their accounts 'from that year' (*de illo anno*) or 'from one year' (*de uno anno*), there are also occasions when sheriffs were audited for an indeterminate period (described by the formula *de illo termino*), which could either be a period within the year (say, Martinmas to

---

[55] See Chapter 4, pp. 234–5.
[56] For further comment on amercement lists, see Chapter 7, pp. 412–13.
[57] A69 (pp. 28–9); for the Ayr formulary, see Chapter 5, pp. 301–7.
[58] For the relationship between Edinburgh, Haddington, and Linlithgow, see the data collected in G. W. S. Barrow and Norman H. Reid, *The Sheriffs of Scotland: An Interim List to c.1306* (St Andrews, 2002), pp. 14–16.
[59] See below, p. 365.
[60] Hubert Hall, 'The System of the Exchequer', in *Introduction to the Study of the Pipe Rolls*, Pipe Roll Society 3 (London, 1884), pp. 35–69, at 35–6, 52–7. I have also found useful Richard Cassidy, '*Recorda Splendidissima*: the Use of Pipe Rolls in the Thirteenth Century', *Historical Research*, vol. 85, no. 227 (2012), pp. 1–12.

Whitsun) or a period encompassing several *termini* (say from Martinmas 1263 to Whitsun 1265).[61] In some cases, it is explicit that a sheriff was accounting for more than a single financial year but it is not explicit that this was a problem in any way; indeed, the lengthy financial period is merely recorded, not acknowledged as an exception. Gilbert de Hay, sheriff of Perth, returned his account at the very earliest after 29 September 1263 despite his last account being over eighteenth months earlier, on 27 March 1262.[62] We see a similar level of flexibility in the collection of income by royal officials: render dates were generally Martinmas and Whitsun and, less frequently, Michaelmas.[63] The financial year could be calculated at either of these dates. Some officials returned their accounts for a financial year finishing at Whitsun, others at Martinmas, and only a few at Michaelmas.[64] Thus, the financial year and the period between audits all appear to have been relatively flexible, although it is of note that it seems to have been rare for an official to go for more than two years between accounts. David Carpenter has recently demonstrated that justiciars, who returned the profits of justice at the same accounting sessions, did not conduct their ayres twice a year, as was previously thought, but instead did so irregularly.[65] The timing of the ayres governed the timing of their accounts so they did not account every year but rather when they had finished their ayre. Similar conclusions can be made for other officials, including sheriffs.

A second contrast with England, where the Exchequer met at Westminster, is that Scottish accounts were not heard at a single, central location. The material from 1263–66 shows accounts heard in many different places, in Scone, Arbroath, Linlithgow, Newbattle, and Edinburgh, while those of 1288–90 show them at Scone, Linlithgow, and Edinburgh.[66] It is clear that some centres were used more often, such as Scone, but no one place held a monopoly. Nor were all places used for audit, even royal centres: Arbroath, for example, was the burgh of Arbroath Abbey itself (even though the abbey was a royal foundation) and there was no 'sheriff of Arbroath', only of nearby Forfar.[67] But although the king's court did move to hear accounts, it still did so in a comparatively limited area, mainly confining itself to southern Scotia and Lothian.[68] There is no evidence to suggest that accounts were heard in the very west and north of the kingdom: thus, a sheriff of

[61] For *de illo anno*, see *ER*, i, pp. 6, 12, 13; for *de uno anno*, see *ER*, i, pp. 3, 4; for *de illo termino*, see *ER*, i, pp. 1, 5

[62] *ER*, i, pp. 1–3.

[63] For render days in charters, Whitsun was the most commonly specified, with 4/3 occurrences; then Martinmas (443); then Michaelmas (72); then Easter (61). These figures are from the database of *The People of Medieval Scotland* (PoMS), found through 'browse' function and 'factoid filter', online at <http://db.poms.ac.uk/browse/facet/renderdates/?resulttype=factoid&totitems>.

[64] *ER*, i, pp. 2, 4, 5–6. For the emergence of Whitsun and Martinmas as fixed render days, see W. W. Scott, 'The Use of Money in Scotland, 1124–1230', *SHR*, vol. 58, no. 166 (1979), pp. 105–31, at 127–8.

[65] Carpenter, 'Scottish Royal Government', pp. 133–6.

[66] This has been noticed before: Duncan, *Making of the Kingdom*, pp. 606–7; Carpenter, 'Scottish Royal Government', pp. 121–2.

[67] *RRS*, ii, nos. 197, 513.

[68] *ER*, i, pp. 1, 10–11, 18, 49–51 (Scone); 9 (Arbroath); 30, 37–45 (Linlithgow); 24–5 (Newbattle); 22, 34, 45–8 (Edinburgh); 40 (Haddington).

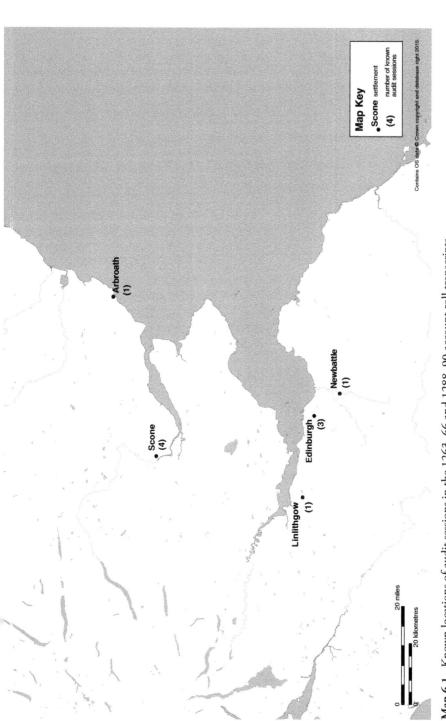

Map 6.1. Known locations of audit sessions in the 1263–66 and 1288–90 account roll transcripts

Inverness, Wigtown, and Ayr would still have had to travel quite far to return his account. The general picture is thus of a mobile accountancy but mobile within quite a limited geographical area of the kingdom's heartland. The accounts returned between 1288 and 1290 reveal a similar type of mobile accountancy. Map 6.1 reveals all the places where we know accounts were heard in 1263–66 and 1288–90.

Furthermore, and again unlike in England, not all sheriffs were expected to account at the same session.[69] The evidence for the 1289 audit session reveals that it was attended by the sheriffs of Berwick, Roxburgh, Selkirk, Traquair, Lanark, Ayr, Stirling, Linlithgow, and Edinburgh, as well as the mason and carpenter who were then doing work on Stirling castle.[70] All the accounts seem to have been heard in early February at Edinburgh.[71] It is notable that this southern venue was attended by sheriffs whose bases were exclusively south of the Firth of Forth; the exception might be seen to be Stirling, but Stirling was the focal point between north and south. By contrast, another session held at Scone in 1290 heard the accounts of the sheriffs of Kincardine, Banff, Aberdeen, Forfar, Fife, Kinross, Perth, and Dumbarton.[72] Again we see a geographic focus to the attendees at Scone: all—bar one—were sheriffs from north of the Forth. The exception was Dumbarton, a sheriffdom on the mouth of the River Clyde, west of Glasgow and south of Loch Lomond, within the jurisdiction of the justiciar of Lothian but geographically closer to Scone than most other 'south-of-Forth' sheriffdoms (and, indeed, some 'north-of-Forth' ones as well!).[73]

By the time of the 1288–90 records at the latest, the host sheriff was responsible for bearing the costs of this peripatetic accounting. The 1288 session, held in March at Linlithgow, is a good example. The last official to account was William Sinclair, the local sheriff, who proffered sixty chalders of malt, of which a tenth went to the local nunnery of Manuel, and fifteen 'were freed to the service of the present auditors, that is the chancellor, and other clerks of the court'.[74] Thirteen and a half bolls of provender were also exempt from the sheriff's expenses because they were assessed as part of 'the expenses of the clerks and others who received provender for their horses in the present account', a nice indication of how the auditors travelled around.[75] Eels were clearly the preferred energy boost after a long day's auditing, for William also accounted for '280 eels...by expenses incurred during the present account'.[76] If the costs of the audit were borne by the local sheriff, it makes sense that the king's court moved around the kingdom in order to hear them: no one sheriff could be expected to bear that much every year.[77] It is important to stress the relative intimacy of this situation. By having local sheriffs bear the costs of the 'central' audit, the boundaries between local and central government became blurred. The scant evidence also suggests that the local

---

[69] Sheriffs did not always turn up in England but they were all expected to.
[70] *ER*, i, pp. 45–8.   [71] *ER*, i, p. 46 (7 February).   [72] *ER*, i, pp. 49–51.
[73] For Dumbarton within the justiciarship of Lothian in 1265, see *ER*, i, p. 27.
[74] *ER*, i, p. 45.   [75] *ER*, i, p. 45.   [76] *ER*, i, p. 45.
[77] Because William Sinclair also served as sheriff of Edinburgh, he had to do so all over again when the audit was held in Edinburgh in 1289: *ER*, i, p. 48.

sheriff would have sat as an auditor when the court came into his locality.[78] All this suggests that it would be misleading to describe Scottish accounting as a way in which the local was called to account by the centre: the centre travelled around and, in a very real institutional way, depended on the local for its own revenue collection. Just as 'central' government was inherently localized and mobile so too was 'local' government an intrinsic part of central revenue collection.

The Development of Probative Accounting

For how long had the kings of Scots audited their accounts? The terms *camerarius* ('chamberlain') and *camera* ('chamber') are attested in the charters of David's reign. But we should not confuse the presence of these officials with the *auditing* of accounts, and also the occasion when money was paid in and out of the king's chamber.[79] It is generally assumed that auditing as a regular administrative process begun either in the 1180s or *by* the 1200s.[80] As no original accounts survive, both these views are based on some items listed in the by-no-means-comprehensive inventory of some of the contents of Edinburgh castle, drawn up in 1296.[81]

The 1296 inventory lists a number of rolls that contain records of royal financial administration. Of these, attention has focused on the 'roll of Abbot Archibald'. This was said to contain 'ancient renders in pennies and ancient waitings' (hospitality income from certain estates).[82] Archibald was abbot of Dunfermline from *c.*1182 to 1198; it is on the basis of this roll that the 1180s has been cited as the earliest date for the commencement of auditing and the recording of the accountancy session on a roll.[83] However, Abbot Archibald's roll may not have been a record of an account at all but a list of expected revenues from certain estates that may—or may not—have been royal.[84] The roll is not called a *compotum* (an 'account'), the word generally used to describe an accounting process. The absence of *compotum* may not be an important absence in itself but is more significant given that other rolls listed in the same inventory *are* called 'accounts'.[85] This suggests

---

[78] Nicholas Hay, sheriff of Perth, served as an auditor at the Scone 1290 audit (*ER*, i, p. 49). He is, alongside Robert Cameron, described as a *miles*. It is of note that the office of sheriff of Perth swapped between the Hay and the Cameron family throughout the second half of the thirteenth century: Barrow and Reid, *The Sheriffs of Scotland*, pp. 35–6.

[79] See Chapter 4, pp. 244–62.

[80] Duncan, *Making of the Kingdom*, pp. 213–14; cf. *RRS*, i, p. 30; cf. Athol L. Murray and Charles J. Burnett, 'The Seals of the Scottish Court of Exchequer', *PSAS*, vol. 123 (1993), pp. 439–52, at p. 440.

[81] *APS*, i, pp. 117–18.

[82] *APS*, i, p. 118; for waitings (*coinnmed*), see Chapter 2, pp. 89–91.

[83] Duncan, *Making of the Kingdom*, p. 213; Scott, 'Use of Money', pp. 119–20.

[84] The difference between 'prescriptive' and 'probative' accounting is discussed in Thomas N. Bisson, *The Crisis of the Twelfth Century: Power, Lordship and the Origins of European Government* (Princeton, NJ, 2009), pp. 316–48; see also T. N. Bisson, 'Les Comptes des domaines au temps de Philippe-Auguste: essai comparatif', in *La France de Philippe Auguste: Le temps des mutations. Actes du colloque international organisé par le C. N. R. S.*, ed. R.-H. Bautier (Paris, 1982), pp. 521–39, at pp. 526–9.

[85] *APS*, i, pp. 117–18; see, for example: 'unus rotulus continens iiii^xx pecies de compotis diversorum vicecomitum et aliorum ministrorum regni Scocie ab anno domini m°. cc°. xviii usque ad annum eiusdem m. cc. lxxv qui rotulus sic incipit compotum Johannis de Makeswell etc.'

that, had Abbot Archibald's roll survived, we would probably have categorized it as a similar type of document as the 'Alexander III Rental', a list of the value of the estates in the sheriffdoms of Aberdeen and Banff, rather than an early example of the audit process.[86]

There are, however, six other items listed in the 1296 inventory explicitly called *compotum*.[87] These included one roll of three pieces listing 'ancient renders in grain and other things', which started 'the account (*compotum*) of William Comyn, earl of Buchan'.[88] William was the earl of Buchan from 1212 to 1233 so his account must have been returned during this period. The inventory also lists a roll of two membranes containing the account of William Freskin, sheriff of Nairn, returned in 1204; and one of William Prat, a later sheriff of Nairn, returned in 1227.[89] There were also two rolls, each of eighty-nine membranes, containing accounts of various sheriffs and other royal officials dating to 1218–75 and 1218–42 respectively.[90] Finally, there is a rather strange reference to a roll starting in 'the third decennovial year' (probably 1199) and ending in 1215.[91] The choice of decennovial year is unusual and may have been an early experiment in dating before *anno domini* became standard. All this suggests that the recording of audits—and evidence for the process of auditing itself—began in the last few years of the twelfth century and the beginning of the thirteenth.

If auditing had been a part of royal financial administration since the early thirteenth century, it did not develop into a form of continuous government: kings travelled to have their accounts heard in short bursts every so often.[92] That auditing remained occasional partly explains why the process never became a separate institution of financial administration, as the Exchequer had done in England. Scottish accounts were paid into the king's chamber; there was no institution of the Exchequer.[93] Indeed, the earliest reference to an 'exchequer' (French: *leschequer*, *escheqier*) in Scotland is in the text known as 'The Scottish King's Household', apparently drafted in 1292×96 (although the dating is not secure), which, although containing some important information, is not a secure source

---

[86] *Aberdeen Reg.*, i, pp. 55–6. The rental is perfunctory, listing royal estates in the two sheriffdoms and stating what revenue was expected from them. When it was thought a particular estate could render more, this was merely stated, without indicating how and when more could be extracted.

[87] *APS*, i, pp. 117–18.   [88] *APS*, i, p. 118.

[89] *APS*, i, p. 118. William Prat (if it was the same person) was later sheriff of Aberdeen; PoMS, Person ID, no. 4709, online at<http://db.poms.ac.uk/record/person/4709>.

[90] *APS*, i, pp. 117–18.

[91] While 1215 is given in calendar year, the first date is rendered as *annus cicli xix iii*, the third year in a nineteen-year cycle (the *cyclus decennovalis*) dating back to Late Antiquity. There was a year one of this cycle was in 1197; the third year of the cycle would thus be 1199, although this assumes that the accounting roll spanned less than a single decennovial cycle (if it spanned two, then the year would be 1180). I take this from the *Medieval Latin Dictionary*, which gives an example from 1238, described as the fourth year of the cycle; cf. *RRS*, ii, pp. 57, 67 (at note 180), which calculates the date of 1205 from an 1843 work by N. H. Nicolas entitled *Chronology of History*. I am grateful to Richard Sharpe for discussing this with me and providing me with the evidence of 1238.

[92] I deliberately echo Timothy Reuter, 'Assembly Politics in Western Europe from the Eighth Century to the Twelfth', reprinted in and cited from Timothy Reuter, *Medieval Polities and Modern Mentalities*, ed. Janet L. Nelson (Cambridge, 2006), pp. 193–216, at pp. 194–5.

[93] A point already made by Carpenter, 'Scottish Royal Government', p. 121.

for the court, household, and administration in the thirteenth century.[94] Its testimony on the Scottish 'Exchequer', for example, which states that it met once a year in one fixed location, does not match up to the practice recorded in Haddington's transcripts of either the roll of 1263–66 or that of 1288–90.[95] It makes much more sense to see this rather more intimate form of revenue collection, in which centre and locality were blurred, as not having separate institutional form but as part of the administration of an institutionally peripatetic kingship in thirteenth-century Scotland.

This is a very different scenario to developments in England. It has long been acknowledged that 'exchequer procedure' was different in Scotland than in England, although *how* it differed is not often demonstrated.[96] This may in part be down to existing debates within English historiography. The independence of the Exchequer from the royal court has, after all, been a matter of some debate among historians of twelfth-century England. Richardson and Sayles argued that it was structurally independent from the king's court, being in general fixed in one place, '[it was] not a court of the ambulatory household'.[97] From Bishop Stubbs on, however, others have also stressed that *because* the major officials of the Exchequer were primarily and simultaneously officials of the king's household and court, the exchequer itself was a product of the court and did not have manifestly independent institutional form. For Warren Hollister, 'the twelfth-century Exchequer was not a department but an occasion'.[98] Yet, exactly *when* one thinks the Exchequer transformed from an occasion into a department is incidental to the present purpose: the point is that it *did* take on independent institutional form by the end of the twelfth century.[99] By the late 1170s, Richard fitz Nigel was able to describe the twice yearly audits of the Exchequer at Westminster as depending on a hierarchy of royal officials, then headed by the justiciar and the treasurer.[100] By the 1270s, the Exchequer contained its own chancery staff who were institutionally separate

---

[94] 'The Scottish King's Household and Other Fragments from a Fourteenth-Century Manuscript in the Library of Corpus Christi College, Cambridge', ed. Mary Bateson *Miscellany II*, Scottish History Society, 1st ser., vol. 45 (1904), pp. 1–43, at p. 32; for the supposed date, see G. W. S. Barrow, 'The Justiciar', in Barrow, *The Kingdom of the Scots: Government, Church and Society from the Eleventh to the Fourteenth Century*, 2nd edn (Edinburgh, 2003), pp. 68–111, at p. 75 and note 32; for a reassessment see David Carpenter, '"The Scottish King's Household"' and English Ideas of Constitutional Reform', *Feature of the Month, October 2011*, The Breaking of Britain (2011), online at <http://www.breakingofbritain.ac.uk/blogs/feature-of-the-month/october-2011-the-scottish-kings-household/>; see also Chapter 4, pp. 212, 233, 244.

[95] 'Scottish King's Household', ed. Bateson, p. 32. Its testimony that sheriffs were summoned by brieve, however, is plausible, and a formula of summons was included in the Ayr formulary; see Note 57.

[96] The exception is Carpenter, 'Scottish Royal Government', pp. 118–26.

[97] Richardson and Sayles, *Governance of England*, p. 250.

[98] C. W. Hollister, 'The Origins of the English Treasury', *EHR*, vol. 93, no. 367 (1978), pp. 262–75, at p. 273.

[99] See, for example, the final comments of Nicholas Karn, 'Nigel, Bishop of Ely, and the Restoration of the Exchequer after the "Anarchy" of King Stephen's Reign', *Historical Research*, vol. 80, no. 209 (2007), pp. 299–314, at pp. 313–14.

[100] *Dialogus*, pp. 22–49; for a depiction of the Exchequer table, see *Dialogus*, p. xxi; and for comment see Reginald L. Poole, *The Exchequer in the Twelfth Century: The Ford Lectures Delivered in the University of Oxford in Michaelmas Term 1911* (Oxford, 1912), pp. 100–2.

from the king's regular chancery.[101] The fixing of the Exchequer in one place, its divorce from the royal itinerary, and its staffing by officials with clearly defined roles pertaining to that governmental department alone are simply not developments identifiable in thirteenth-century Scotland. In Scotland, the king had no option but to use his chamber; it was not, as it was for King John, an alternative to an existing and permanent institution.[102] Accounting remained peripatetic, tied to the movements of the king's court. There was no need for the office of treasurer to develop in Scotland, as it did in England during the reign of Henry I, because the chamberlain presided over the chamber and thus over revenue collection. Even if the difference between England and Scotland is acknowledged, if the word 'exchequer' continues to be used to describe accounting procedure in Scotland, it distorts the way the king's court held audits and collected his revenue, aligning it unconsciously in practice and form to the Exchequer of England. Instead, Scotland exhibits a more intimate arrangement, with money coming into the king's household chamber on an irregular basis and the identity of the auditors being based on their personal relation to the king, their role in local government, and, often, the senior church hierarchy.[103]

But we should not go too far down this road and imagine that intimate and localized arrangements meant that procedure was not formal and institutionalized. Even in Haddington's transcript of the 1263–66 roll, there is clear evidence of centralization and institutionalization in the record of the audit itself. Although Haddington abridged the accounts themselves, it is clear they all followed a standard format. If there were any changes to an official's expected proffer, then the corresponding memorandum was transcribed into the record itself at the appropriate place within each section. Not all revenue in kind was or had already been commuted into cash, as might be expected. Laurence Grant, sheriff of Inverness, probably returned his account in 1266, recording the payment of 5 marks to the bishop of Caithness, 'for his teind for the 200 cows from the fine of the men of Caithness, all sent to Leith, for the king's service'.[104] The proffer of revenue in kind, transported across the kingdom, means that we should be wary of assuming that unilateral coin use was a prerequisite for the emergence of standard accounting practices.[105]

---

[101] For the development of the chancellorship of the Exchequer, first attested in the 1220s but not properly independent of chancery until the 1270s, see Nicholas C. Vincent, 'The Origins of the Chancellorship of the Exchequer', *EHR*, vol. 108, no. 426 (1993), pp. 105–21.

[102] For John's use of the chamber as a way to bypass the Exchequer after the papal interdict of 1207, see J. E. A. Jolliffe, 'The Chamber and Castle Treasuries under King John', in *Studies in Medieval History Presented to F. M. Powicke*, ed. R. W. Hunt, R. W. Southern and W. A. Pantin (Oxford, 1948), pp. 121–37, at pp. 127–8; Nick Barratt, 'The Revenue of King John', *EHR*, vol. 111, no. 443 (1996), pp. 835–55, at pp. 838–42; Nick Barratt, 'Finance on a Shoestring: The Exchequer in the Thirteenth Century', in *English Government in the Thirteenth Century*, ed. Adrian Jobson (Woodbridge, 2004), pp. 71–86, at pp. 72–3.

[103] For more on the identity of government personnel, see Chapter 7, pp. 417–34.

[104] *ER*, i, p. 19.

[105] Cf. *RRS*, ii, p. 59, in which Barrow argued that 'we must not exaggerate the advances made in royal revenue collection or bookkeeping' *because* Alexander II took an aid in hides in 1216.

Moreover, between 1263–66 and 1288–90, the language used to describe the audit procedure had become more formal.[106] Those who presided over the chamberlain's account in 1264 were described thus: Gamelin and his peers merely 'heard that account' (*istud computum audiverunt*).[107] But by 1288–90, their successors were consistently called 'auditors' (*auditores*), denoting their primary identity during the audit.[108] Indeed, only in the 1288–90 transcript is there evidence of the formula that would become such a standard part of fourteenth-century accounting procedure: that individuals had to show written authorization for new or extraordinary expenses and allowances 'on the account' (*super compotum/computum*).[109] Letters patent and mandates of the guardians of the kingdom had to be produced 'on the account' (*super computum*) for any extraordinary allowance decided in advance. If these letters were not produced, then the expected money and provisions would not be allocated. In 1288, Andrew Murray and James Stewart, together returning the account of the sheriffdom of Ayr, sought provisions and expenses for stocking Ayr castle. These were not granted because the two men did not bring 'letters of the guardians of the exact sum to be allocated' and, as a result, the auditors did not dare (*audebant*) grant them the money.[110]

A greater reliance on the authority of the written word is also more apparent in 1288–90 than in 1263–66. The 1263–66 transcripts do reveal that respite from payment and extraordinary allowances was communicated to the official coming to account in writing. The memoranda dotted throughout the rolls are clear evidence of this type of written command and allowance. Other royal letters are also referred to generically in the 1263–66 transcript. John Cameron's account as sheriff of Perth in 1266 records that 'the thane of Forteviot ought to answer for 20 marks for which he was given respite by the letter (*literam*) of the lord king until the feast of St Peter'.[111] But by 1288–90, the formality and authority of these letters was given greater emphasis. In 1288, William Sinclair returned his account as sheriff of Dumfries and, during the audit, it was decided that he should henceforth no longer be burdened with £37 10s 4d for the ward of certain lands 'because the guardians of the kingdom, by their letter, sealed with the common seal', had commanded sasine to be given to William de Ferrers, and he was to answer to the chamberlain for the sum.[112] Again in 1288, William Sinclair accounted for an expense incurred as sheriff of Edinburgh for three chalders of grain given to the friars preacher of Edinburgh, 'by letter patent of the guardians of the kingdom, signed with the common seal, and shown on the account'.[113] If the common seal of the guardians was not used, then the guardians would sign with their individual seals, and the record of the account would specify exactly who had affixed his seal to the letter patent. Thus, Nicholas Hay, sheriff of Perth, returned his account in

---

[106] See also Chapter 7, pp. 403–5. [107] *ER*, i, p. 11.

[108] *ER*, i, pp. 38, 39, 44, 45, 48, 49.

[109] *ER*, i, pp. 36, 42, 44, 46, 48, 49. See further the 'lost' mandates and letters patent of Robert I collected in *RRS*, v, nos. 507–556A.

[110] *ER*, i, p. 38; see also *ER*, i, p. 37, when the auditors refused to grant William Sinclair £8 13s 9½d in 1288 because they did not 'dare allow it without the command (*preceptum*) of the guardians'.

[111] *ER*, i, p. 18. [112] *ER*, i, p. 36. [113] *ER*, i, p. 41; also *ER*, i, pp. 42, 46.

1289 and had been granted extraordinary expenses 'by letter patent of the guardians of the kingdom of Scotland, sealed with the seals of the earl of Fife, the earl of Buchan, and John Comyn in his name and the name of their associates (*sociorum*) and shown on the account'.[114]

The greater formalization evident in 1288–90 may simply be the result of developing bureaucratic practices. But the absence of the king, following the death of Alexander III on 19 March 1286, must also have prompted greater standardization and formalization in procedure. The 1288–90 accounts were returned after the unifying focus of authority—the king—had died with no adult successor. The structure of audit itself remained intact after the death of the king despite those who returned the accounts being even more the peers of the auditors than when Alexander III was alive. Donnchad, earl of Fife, and John Comyn of Badenoch had both been made guardians of the kingdom in 1286 but yet accounted as sheriffs and bailies at the audit sessions of 1288 and 1289, despite that procedure being controlled by their own letters patent.[115] When Donnchad, earl of Fife, returned his account as farmer of the royal manor of Dull in 1289, he returned the renders for 'two years by the extent made after the king's death, on the command of the guardians'; that is, he was responding to his own command in another capacity.[116] The institutional structure of an audit procedure thus outlasted and was in fact strengthened by the loss of the individual—the king—on whom a patrimonial structure is supposed to have depended.[117] By 1288–90, audit procedure had, despite its attachment to a peripatetic court, taken on independent institutional existence even though the structure that emerged was not territorially fixed, and held at a single central location.

SOURCES OF INCOME AND EXPENDITURE

There is only one surviving chamberlain's account in the 1263–66 and 1288–90 accounts: that of William, earl of Mar, returned in 1264.[118] This was discussed in Chapter 4 and there is no need to repeat the information given there.[119] However, it is useful as a starting point here because it provides a general overview of the king's income and expenditure, and allows for an assessment of the relationship between local revenue collection and the overall accounting done by the chamberlain. Although the account was returned following the rather expensive wars

---

[114] *ER*, i, p. 49; also *ER*, i, p. 46.

[115] *ER*, i, pp. 38, 48 (Donnchad, earl of Fife); 39 (John Comyn). For a less positive assessment of the politics of this period, see Michael Brown, 'Aristocratic Politics and the Crisis of Scottish Kingship, 1286–1296', *SHR*, vol. 90, no. 229 (2011), pp. 1–26.

[116] *ER*, i, p. 48.

[117] This is despite (and perhaps because of) the sometimes violent factionalism of the late 1290s, see Brown, 'Aristocratic Politics'.

[118] *ER*, i, pp. 10–11.   [119] See Chapter 4, pp. 254–8.

with the kings of Norway (culminating in the Battle of Largs in 1263), it is of note that, with the exception of the western sheriffdoms, there are not that many references to expenses directly incurred by military activity. The chamberlain's account is divided into two sections: receipts and expenses. This section will deal with each in turn.

Income

The chamberlain's receipts were divided into general descriptive categories: he received £2896 18s 3d from 'ferms of *balliae*' from officials exercising jurisdiction on both sides of the River Forth; £675 18s 2½d from burgh ferms (the set amount owed from each royal burgh to the king); and, finally, £1808 5s ½d from 'common receipts...with fines and reliefs', denoting the non-standard revenue from profits of justice, together with the amount paid on inheritance (the 'relief') and fines imposed on individuals by the king. The chamberlain was in arrears by £32 11s 7d, so the overall amount of the receipts was £5313 17s 1d. It is important to note that burgh ferms constituted the least significant source of royal monetary revenue out of the three categories, which is important because burghs have long been thought to be the predominant source of money in the economy.[120] The fixed revenue from burghs was around a third of that received by the king from 'common receipts', which was itself just under two-thirds of the amount received from the king's demesne land.

These figures were taken from the sum total of the income paid 'into the chamber' by sheriffs, bailies, and other officials for the entire period of the chamberlain's account, which ran from Whitsun 1263 to Martinmas 1264.[121] They thus did not constitute a source of royal revenue that was separate from that received by royal officers individually. However, it did not include all the revenue the king received, as the amounts did not include proffers in kind, as will be shown later, so this represents the minimum income from the accounting period.[122] We might think that, as most of the king's income came from ferms—that is, set amounts rendered annually—royal income was relatively stable. What follows will test this hypothesis in more detail.

---

[120] For a more nuanced development of this line, see Scott, 'Use of Money'; for the use of money in rural as much as urban areas, see N. M. McQ. Holmes, 'The Evidence of Finds for the Circulation and Use of Coins in Medieval Scotland', *PSAS*, vol. 134 (2004), pp. 241–80, at pp. 246–7. In 1327, the accounts returned by burgh ferms was almost double, amounting to £1133 3s 4d, which suggests a vast urban expansion over the sixty/seventy odd years between the 1260s and late 1320s (for this figure, see the totals in *ER*, i, p. lxxxviii). This would be in line with the monetary expansion of the late thirteenth century posited by Mayhew, for which see N. J. Mayhew, 'Alexander III—a Silver Age?', in *Scotland in the Reign of Alexander III, 1249–1286*, ed. N. H. Reid (Edinburgh, 1990), pp. 53–73, at pp. 61–4; for a general economic expansion in the thirteenth century, see Wendy B. Stevenson, 'The Monastic Presence in Scottish Burghs in the Twelfth and Thirteenth centuries', *SHR*, vol. 60, no. 170 (1981), pp. 97–118, at pp. 100–4.
[121] See Chapter 4, p. 253.   [122] See below, pp. 369–71.

Ferms, Renders, and Wardships

The first item often listed in the discharge section of the sheriff's account was the income from 'small ferms' within each sheriffdom. 'Small ferms' were annual renders paid by the estate or piece of land to the king and were too small or insignificant to be listed singly; instead, they were given as a lump sum. It seems likely that 'small ferms' were discharged in each shrieval account although Haddington gives us precise figures for only four for the period 1263–66, which range from £24 6s 8d from Aberdeen to £86 from Haddington to over £136 from Forfar and over £123 from Perth.[123] Comparison with the 1288–90 material reveals that the amount collected from small ferms did vary considerably between sheriffdoms: Dumbarton was expected to provide £26 13s 4d (1 mark) each year while in 1288 the sheriffdom of Lanark rendered over £399.[124] The amount from Lanark may have been for more than a year; however, even if the number is halved, the amount from Lanark would still have been around eight times more than that from Dumbarton.[125] The varying levels of 'small ferms' must also reflect the amount of land the king had at farm within each particular sheriffdom and the size of the sheriffdom.

If a single estate within a sheriffdom paid a large annual ferm, it was listed individually in the account. Thus, Andrew of the Garioch, sheriff of Aberdeen, proffered £12 from the thane of Aberdeen and £17 13s 4d from the thane of Kintore in 1264.[126] Nor were these sorts of individual payments restricted to royal thanages. The bailie of Inverquiech accounted independently from any sheriff for his annual ferm of 83 marks (£55 6s 8d).[127] Some estates were worth even more. Thus, after a revaluation made between 1286 and 1289, Dull was worth a massive £251 16s 8d *per annum*.[128] There is only one occasion when Haddington included in his transcript both the amount of 'small ferms' and individual ferms in his account: that of Robert Mowat, sheriff of Forfar, returned in 1264, but covering an accounting year that finished at Martinmas, 1263.[129] The amount of small ferms the sheriff collected came to £136 7s 4d while those from the named estates came to £165 13s 2d, making a total of just over £300.[130]

---

[123] *ER*, i, pp. 3, 8, 12, 24; the figure for Aberdeen is a calculation based on the bishop's second teind of 48s 8d from small ferms from Aberdeen (*ER*, i, p. 12); for second teinds, see below, pp. 379–85.

[124] *ER*, i, pp. 38 (when Dumbarton accounted for two years), 39.

[125] *ER*, i, p. 39, where the amount of £399 is described 'ut patet in precedenti computo', and it is clear that the sheriff was making up for 'arrears from the last account'.

[126] *ER*, i, p. 11. It is interesting that these figures are quite a bit lower than in the 'red roll' surviving in the archives of the bishopric of Aberdeen, known as 'the Rental of Alexander III', where Kintore is valued at 101 marks and Aberdeen at 50 marks; *Aberdeen Reg.*, i, p. 55; for the description of the Alexander III rental as 'the red roll', see *Aberdeen Reg.*, i, p. 160. This is important as the rental is normally taken to be an accurate valuation of estates within the sheriffdom and how much they owe to the king: see Duncan, *Making of the Kingdom*, p. 598.

[127] *ER*, i, pp. 3–4, 16, 33. Alan Durward was to answer independently for part of the ferm from Dull; *ER*, i, p. 3.

[128] This figure is based on two years' return in 1289, by Donnchad, earl of Fife, who proffered £500 73s 4d (£503, 1 mark) for the 'redditus dicti manerii de dictis duobus annis per extentam factam post mortem regis, per preceptum custodum', that is, after the land had been revalued after Alexander III's death: *ER* i, p. 48.

[129] *ER*, i, pp. 8–9.   [130] *ER*, i, pp. 8–9.

It might be thought that this revenue, although relatively small, could be relied upon. But many of these ferms were not ferms from royal demesne but land only temporarily in the king's hands. The 'extra' ferms collected by the sheriff of Forfar in 1264 in fact contained £80 from the earldom of Angus, which had been in the king's hands following the death of Gilbert Umfraville, earl of Angus, by right of his wife, Matilda, in 1245.[131] Had the earldom of Angus not been in the king's hands, the total revenue from ferms within the sheriffdom of Forfar would have been £222 6d, of which only just over £85 came from ferms of named estates. Haddington did sometimes specify that the king was receiving money from land held in wardship but on other occasions he did not (such as the revenue received from the earldom of Angus), suggesting that the 'stability' of income from ferms may be more illusory than real.[132] Acquiring land through wardship would have significantly affected the amount the king received from each of his sheriffs. Thus, although Alexander III received £2896 18s 3d from ferms from estates in the chamberlain's account of 1264, this figure must have fluctuated, depending on how much the king held temporarily in each accounting period.

Quite separate from the revenue returned from ferms in cash was that owed in kind, either from named estates or from the sheriffdom as a whole. Haddington recorded that Perth, Forfar, Kincardine, Elgin, Inverness, Forres, Kinross, Stirling, Edinburgh, Linlithgow, and Traquair all returned named revenue in kind between 1263 and 1266.[133] This must represent the absolute minimum, for Haddington sometimes did not include this section in all shrieval accounts. These sheriffs returned a combination of livestock and waterlife (cows, pigs, hens, and eels) and grain produce (wheat, barley, and malt). On occasion, such as with the sheriffdoms of Kinross and Forfar, it is specified that the renders were for annual 'waitings', the customary amount in kind that particular estates within the newer sheriffdoms had long owed the king.[134] These waitings could be very substantial. Table 6.1 records the amount proffered in kind by Robert Mowat, sheriff of Forfar, in 1264. The first column gives the type of produce render, how much was rendered, what

---

[131] This would mean a very long minority for Gilbert III d'Umfraville, the future earl. The age of majority was twenty-one in Scotland, for which see Duncan, *Making of the Kingdom*, p. 400. Thus, if Gilbert III was a baby in 1247, then it would not have been until 1267–68 when he came into his inheritance, which would explain why the sheriff of Forfar was still accounting for the earldom in his account in 1264. The PoMS database shows that Gilbert III d'Umfraville did not make any named appearances in the charter record until the late 1260s/early 1270s: PoMS, Person ID, no. 2137, online at <http://db.poms.ac.uk/record/person/2137/>. The only exception is *Panmure Reg.*, ii, pp. 140–1, which is dated in the PoMS database to the later 1250s (probably); PoMS H 3/585/5. However, in this deed, Gilbert III is not named by name; it is the 'earl of Angus', described generically, who receives the annual rent of 3s *per annum*, suggesting that this deed was drawn up during Gilbert's minority. Indeed, that Gilbert was still underage in the mid-1260s is confirmed by the testimony of the account of Hugh of Abernethy, sheriff of Roxburgh, which says that certain lands owed nothing 'on account of the age of Gilbert d'Umfraville': *ER*, i, p. 28.

[132] For an example of stated wardships, see *ER*, i, p. 33.

[133] *ER*, i, pp. 1–2, 6–7, 12, 13–14, 15, 16, 17, 20–1, 23, 25–6, 32.

[134] For waitings, see Chapter 2, pp. 89–91.

Table 6.1. Revenue received in kind in account of the sheriff of Forfar, 1264

Render	Amount	Expenses	Purpose of Expense	Difference
Cows	24 (Forfar) 13½ (Glamis) Arrears (from last account): 21 cows T: 58½ cows	48 cows	king's service	Owes 10½ cows
Pigs	75 pigs	25 pigs	king's service	[50 pigs]

Cheese	404 cogalls
	 + Glamis: 81
	 + Kingalty: 7 cogalls, etc.
	 T: 263½ cogalls, 1½ stone
	   (sold 223½ cogalls, 1½
	   stone = £33 17s)
		10 cogalls	king's service	

Hens	291 hens	311 hens		[perhaps overspent by 20 hens]
Malt	[from Forfar and Glamis] 32 chalders, 2 bolls increment on Glamis: 2 chalders	17 chalders, 1½ bolls 4 chalders, 12 bolls	King's service Queen's service	[perhaps owes 4 chalders, 4½ bolls]
Ground barley	10 chalders, 5 bolls	3 chalders, 2 bolls, 1 firlot 9½ bolls 4 chalders, £10 6 bolls	king's service queen's service 4 young puppies and their mother porter of stones within the town	[nothing is given]
Provender	206 clevins, 3 bolls [91 chalders, 2 bolls]	38 chalders, 8½ bolls, 1 firlot 13 chalders, 10 bolls, 1 firlot 8½ chalders, ¾ boll 14 chalders, 6 bolls 4½ chalders 2 chalders	king's service queen's service. falconer for 29 weeks, 2 days king's horses pigs in wood for increment of land of Glamis	[nothing is given]
Eels	800 eels 200 in arrears from last account T: 1100 eels [sic]	700 eels 180 eels [?160?] T: 860 eels [sic][135]	king's service queen's service	to pay: 260 eels [sic: *recte* 240]

[135] This figure is clearly a mistake, either by Haddington or present in his source. If the owed figure is correct, then 160 eels would have been consumed in the queen's service, not the 180 as specified in the account: *ER*, i, p. 7.

had already been spent and for what purpose, and whether any debts can be identified (even if they were not explicitly recorded in Haddington's transcript).

The total amounts, therefore, were retrospective: the expenses had already been taken from the receipts before the time of accounting. Sheriffs were thus only liable for the amount remaining once the expenses had been subtracted.[136] Sometimes, this was a very small amount because the produce had already been consumed. Roughly two-thirds of each kind of income had already been consumed by serving the king and queen, leaving much less to account for in the chamber. We are thus looking at a retrospective accounting system in kind whereby much of the exchange between sheriff and audit process had already taken place as a result of hosting the king when he came through the sheriffdom.[137] The amount in kind was accounted for separately from the proffers in cash. The sheriff of Forfar also returned a total of £485 8s 11d from his receipts in cash that did not include the monetary value of the proffers in kind.[138] But, if a sheriff had already sold some chalders of produce or some livestock on the market, that amount would be answered for in the 'cash section' and was not factored in the total of kind revenue. In short, therefore, there existed two separate but interlinked systems of audit: one in cash, the other in kind, of which much of the exchange between king and sheriff had already taken place at the level of the sheriffdom.

Fines and Reliefs

What, then, of the income from 'common receipts', which included fines and reliefs? The amount accounted for by William, earl of Mar, in 1264 was £1808 5s ½d. Both fines and reliefs were accounted for by the sheriff and so we know something of the mechanisms by which fines were collected, and how much they were. Fines (*fines*) were made with the king, either for his mercy or for some other sort of payment.[139] In England, these fines were recorded in the 'fine rolls' but collected, as in Scotland, by the sheriff and proffered to the Exchequer.[140] In Scotland, some of these fines were recorded on 'small rolls' but none of these rolls now survive.[141] Fines appear in Haddington's transcripts as a source of income quite distinct from the profits accrued by the sheriff and justiciar. The fines are listed by debtor and amount, although do not show a clear payment plan.[142] Haddington recorded, for example, that a person was paying a *proportion* of the total fine he or she owed but not the total amount itself, nor how much he or she still had left to

---

[136] See below, pp. 386–7.   [137] See also Connelly, *Medieval Record Sources*, p. 19.

[138] *ER*, i, p. 9. The auditors acquitted the sheriff from 118s 4d, leaving him to pay £204 17s 1d in total (minus the money already spent).

[139] For another analysis of the fines in the account roll, see Carpenter, 'Scottish Royal Government', pp. 123–6, 156–9.

[140] David Carpenter, 'The Fine Rolls of Henry III: the Origins and Development of the Rolls', online at <http://www.finerollshenry3.org.uk/content/commentary/historical_intro.html>.

[141] *APS*, i, p. 114 (1292 inventory): 'item, in tercio sacculo, LII Rotuli, cedule et memoranda videlicet quidam Rotuli de finibus factis per gentes Scocie Regibus eiusdem Regni tam vaccis quam denariis'.

[142] Carpenter, 'Scottish Royal Government', pp. 123–4.

pay. This information does not ever seem to have been given on the original roll Haddington had copied so one must imagine that payment plans were recorded in other documents whose information was not included in the audit roll.[143]

Excluding reliefs and judicial amercements, there are fifteen fines in the accounts from 1263–66.[144] Of these, the smallest was just over 66s, which was imposed on Geoffrey Liddell for an unspecified offence, although this might have been part of a much larger fine for Geoffrey also later appeared in the account roll as paying 10 marks 'by the fine. for that year'.[145] A fine of eighty cows (which works out at £16 at 4s a cow or, more probably, £20 at 5s/cow) was imposed on Gilaverian, farmer of Cumbraes in Ayrshire, which he had not yet paid and so the sheriff of Ayr was holding his son as a pledge.[146] The earl of Sutherland was paying off a fine of at least £40 during 1263–66 while Earl Patrick of Dunbar owed at least £20 for paying a fine for 'the sons of Mac Galgys', suggesting that the earl had either taken on the fine owed by these sons or committed some sort of transgression which had resulted in a fine.[147] The earl of Ross owed 200 cows (either £40 or £50, depending on whether cows were valued at 4s or 5s) from which the king eventually gave him respite.[148] But these are very large sums indeed. Moreover, they were imposed on high-status individuals. Nicholas Corbet was the grandson of Earl Patrick I of Dunbar (d. 1232) and owed the king at least 75 (probably 100) marks for an unspecified offence.[149] Three earls had to pay large fines, as did one bishop and the burgesses of the burgh of Arbroath.[150] Fines in the account rolls were therefore large and appear to have been imposed on high-status individuals or very large groups, such as the 'men of Caithness', who had to pay a fine along with the earl.[151]

This is unlike England, where the fine rolls are full of very small sums for procurement of the king's writ up to much larger sums for a whole host of individual transgressions and debts owed by lower-status people.[152] The 1263–64 fine roll (48 Henry III), for example, contains multiple fines made with the king of a mark or half a mark for procuring the king's writ and up to 100 marks imposed on

---

[143] Carpenter, 'Scottish Royal Government', p. 124.

[144] The list in Carpenter, 'Scottish Royal Government', pp. 156–9, contains *all* private debts listed in the account roll of 1263–66, not just those explicitly described as fines.

[145] *ER*, i, pp. 21, 28 (where Geoffrey accounted for 10 marks from a fine, so either these two payments were part of the same fine or Geoffrey had made two separate fines with the king).

[146] *ER*, i, p. 5: for cow prices, see Elizabeth Gemmill and Nicholas Mayhew, *Changing Values in Medieval Scotland: A Study of Prices, Weights and Measures* (Cambridge, 1995), pp. 249–56. However, it is clear that on occasion cows were valued at 5s per unit, even in the 1263–66 account roll itself. Thus, the earl of Ross owed 180 cows, which were valued at £45. Indeed, it is probable that the original fine was 200 cows, but the bishop of Ross received a tenth of the income, as did the bishop of Caithness when the men of Caithness made a fine with the king of 200 cows (*ER*, i, p. 20). The individual price of each cow in the 180-cow fine was nonetheless 5s per cow.

[147] *ER*, i, pp. 13, 28. The latter figure has been calculated *inclusive* of the eighth owed to the bishop of Glasgow as part of his second teind revenue.

[148] *ER*, i, p. 20.

[149] *ER*, i, p. 21; For Nicholas, see PoMS, Person ID, no. 2092; online at <http://db.poms.ac.uk/record/person/2092/>.

[150] *ER*, i, pp. 4, 9, 13, 19, 20.   [151] *ER*, i, pp. 13, 19.

[152] Carpenter, 'Fine Rolls of Henry III'.

Gloucester Abbey for harbouring barons in the abbey's precinct without the king's permission.[153] By contrast, the fines which appear in the account rolls in Scotland were, as we have seen, only for very large sums, levied on individuals, who were either of very high status or whole groups of men organized by region (such as the 'men of Caithness') or corporation ('the burgesses of Forfar').[154] In short, the evidence of the account rolls shows that the king only imposed relatively large fines: fines were not levied for standard procurements, such as obtaining a writ, as they were in England, but for significant transgressions imposed on a case-by-case basis.

Reliefs were one-off payments made by an heir to the tenurial lord before he or she fully obtained possession of the inheritance: thus, reliefs owed to the king were theoretically owed only by tenants-in-chief whereas other lords extracted reliefs from their own tenants.[155] In England, such reliefs had been set in law and depended on the status of the landholding in question. The 1215 Magna Carta established that if the estate was a 'barony', the relief was £100, if a single knight's fee, then the relief was 100s.[156] Anything lower was paid according to custom. These rules were confirmed in the 1225 reissue of the document.[157] Reliefs paid in 1263–66 and 1288–90, however, reveal that there were no similar rates in Scotland. Roland of Carrick paid his relief of 18 marks between 1263 and 1266; £20 was owed for the relief of the land of *Serlinglaw*, owed to the bailie of Jedburgh in 1288, whereas the wife of Robert of Montgomery only had to pay 5 marks to the sheriff of Ayr in 1265.[158] The highest recorded in the account rolls was the 100 marks owed by Richard Lovell through the sheriff of Roxburgh in 1263–66.[159] Reliefs thus varied massively and could go even higher than the reliefs attested in the account roll: the earl of Dunbar had to pay £200 in 1293, for example, whereas the earl of Buchan only had to pay £120 to Edward I in 1294.[160] Duncan has shown convincingly that the amount of a relief was negotiated according to the annual value of the land in question, an argument supported by the few figures in the account rolls that give the amount owed both for wardship and for relief.[161] It is thus no surprise that reliefs varied massively and must have been the subject of negotiation, perhaps resulting in a new 'extent' (valuation) being made of the land.[162]

---

[153] Fine Roll, 48 Henry III, no. 90, online at <http://www.finerollshenry3.org.uk/content/calendar/roll_061.html>.

[154] *ER*, i, pp. 9, 19.

[155] Cynthia J. Neville, *Native Lordship in Medieval Scotland: The Earldoms of Strathearn and Lennox, c.1140–1365* (Dublin, 2005), pp. 108–10.

[156] 'The 1215 Magna Carta: Clause 02', *The Magna Carta Project*, trans. H. Summerson et al. <http://magnacarta.cmp.uea.ac.uk/read/magna_carta_1215/Clause_02>.

[157] J. C. Holt, *Magna Carta*, 2nd edn (Cambridge, 1992), p. 502; for commentary on the circumstances of the 1225 issue, see David A. Carpenter, *The Minority of Henry III* (Berkeley, CA, and Los Angeles, 1990), pp. 382–8.

[158] *ER*, i, pp. 28, 43.   [159] *ER*, i, p. 29.

[160] *Rot. Scot.*, i, 18b; *Documents Illustrative of the History of Scotland from the Death of Alexander the Third to the Accession of Robert Bruce MCCLXXXVI–MCCCVI*, ed. J. Stevenson, 2 vols (Edinburgh, 1870), i, p. 418.

[161] Duncan, *Making of the Kingdom*, pp. 400–5.

[162] Duncan, *Making of the Kingdom*, pp. 403–4.

The king did not receive the whole relief: a proportion (normally a tenth but sometimes an eighth) went to a local religious institution.[163] Thus, in 1265, Robert Mappar had to pay 40 shillings for his relief for his unnamed land within the sheriffdom of Traquair/Peebles but five shillings of this went to the bishop of Glasgow, who was accustomed to receive an eighth of all crown income.[164] In that year, however, the sheriff of Traquair also accounted for the 40s 4d from the wardship of Robert's land. Robert had come of age: the account states that 'henceforth [the ward] is not to be paid, because his age has been proven'.[165] From this, it appears that underage heirs in the Scottish kingdom still had to pay a relief to the king once they came of age, and their land stopped being held in wardship. This went against the demand put forward in Magna Carta in England, where it was stipulated that wards did not have to pay reliefs when they came of age; reliefs were due instead only from adult heirs.[166] Perhaps it was because reliefs were quite closely related to the annual value of the land, and were also comparatively lower in Scotland, that there did not develop a demand, as there did in England, that the king should not receive any more revenue from an estate from which he had already enjoyed the profits of wardship.

The system of fines and reliefs in Scotland, therefore, differed from that in England. Reliefs were calculated on a case-by-case basis, as were fines. But, unlike fines in England, Scottish fines seem only to have been levied on either high-status individuals or large groups. It is impossible to know just how large a proportion of the £1808 of 'common receipts' returned by the chamberlain in 1264 were fines and reliefs because we do not have a full set of shrieval accounts. It is probable, however, that these 'common receipts' also included the profits of justice from shrieval and justiciar courts. Each 'discharge' section in shrieval accounts the amount raised from shrieval courts and justiciar courts (the *lucra*: 'profits').

Profits of Justice from the Sheriff and Justiciar

Most of the evidence about judicial income comes from the references to *lucra* of the sheriff and justiciar returned by each individual sheriff. The justiciar performed his ayre and the sheriffs were responsible for returning the monies collected in the process.[167] But calculating any total figure is impossible and the data we do have is also problematic. On occasion, Haddington provided the proffer from both sources but more frequently he only noted that *lucra* from sheriffs and/or justiciars were returned but did not provide the full amount.[168] At other times, Haddington mentioned one set of profits but not the other.[169] However, they are, as always, what we have to work with.

The amount collected by the justiciar's ayre varied massively. A full ayre was returned by Alexander Comyn, earl of Buchan and justiciar of Scotia, probably in

---

[163] For more on this, see below, pp. 379–85.   [164] *ER*, i, p. 33.   [165] *ER*, i, p. 33.
[166] 'The 1215 Magna Carta: Clause 03', *The Magna Carta Project*, trans. H. Summerson et al, online at <http://magnacarta.cmp.uea.ac.uk/read/magna_carta_1215/Clause_03>.
[167] See Chapter 4, pp. 234–5.
[168] *ER*, i, pp. 15, 21, 33.   [169] *ER*, i, pp. 15, 31.

Table 6.2. Alexander Comyn's ayre as justiciar of Scotia in (?)1266

Sheriffdom	*lucra* of justiciar
Inverness	£95
Nairn	5 marks
Forres	*nothing*
Elgin	£15 20d [1s 8d]
Banff	£12 6s 8d [½ mark]
Aberdeen	£129
Kincardine	£25
Forfar	£90 6s 8d [½ mark]
Perth	£23 18s 4d
Fife	£11, 1 mark [13s 4d]
Total	**£405 13s 4d**

1266.[170] This covered the sheriffdoms of Inverness (accounting for Caithess and Ross as well), Nairn, Forres, Elgin, Banff, Aberdeen, Kincardine, Forfar, Perth, and Fife.[171] The ayre collected over £405, just under a tenth of the total annual revenue collected by the chamberlain in 1264. The total is broken down according to sheriffdom in Table 6.2. It does not include the proportions of the income given to bishoprics and religious houses from these profits (*lucra*; singular: *lucrum*).

Not all sheriffdoms were equally profitable and one, Forres, produced no income at all. It might be thought that differing levels of population created higher or lower judicial profits. But while population must have some impact, it does not explain every case: Perth, which accounted for only £23 18s 4d, in comparison with Aberdeen's £129, was a major trading centre and whose profits of justice from the sheriff's court in 1266 came to a whopping £49 11s 8d, including the tenths received by the abbot of Scone and the bishop of Dunkeld from different districts within the sheriff's jurisdiction.[172]

Moreover, the amount collected in each ayre also varied significantly. In 1264, Stephen Fleming, justiciar of Lothian, returned his account for an ayre he had conducted previously. At the time of his account, Stephen was no longer justiciar but still provided a record of his profits.[173] His ayre was extremely short and covered only four sheriffdoms: Roxburgh, Lanark, Peebles, and Ayr. In 1265, Hugh de Berkeley completed a much more extensive ayre of Lothian, which covered nine sheriffdoms, and accounted for it during the same year.[174] Table 6.3 compares the two and shows that, in 1265, Hugh collected just under four times as much from the sheriffdoms visited by Stephen in 1264. In only one case, Roxburgh, were their

---

[170] *ER*, i, p. 18. The account followed immediately one made in 1266 (*ER*, i, p. 17); Haddington saw the date of the justiciar's account but decided not to include it, suggesting that it was the same as the account above. However, this cannot, for obvious reasons, be demonstrated.

[171] For map of this ayre, see *Atlas*, p. 195.

[172] *ER*, i, p. 18; for trade in medieval Perth from the thirteenth century onwards see Adrian Cox et al., 'Backland Activities in Medieval Perth: excavations at Meal Vennel and Scott Street', *PSAS*, vol. 126 (1996), pp. 733–821.

[173] *ER*, i, pp. 9–10.   [174] *ER*, i, p. 27.

Table 6.3. Comparison between the ayres of Lothian in 1264 and 1265

Sheriffdom	*lucra* (Stephen Fleming, 1264)	*lucra* (Hugh de Berkeley, 1265)
Berwick		£144 13s 4d (1 mark)
Roxburgh[175]	£45	£40 6s 8d (half a mark)
Edinburgh		£129 8s 4d
Lanark	8 marks	£187
Peebles	33s 4d (or 20s, 1 mark)	£10, 1 mark (13s 4d)
Ayr	£20, 1 mark	£7 17s 4d
Dumfries		'nothing' (*nihil*)
Dumbarton		£33 6s 8d (half a mark)
Stirling		7 marks
Total [for the sheriffdoms covered by both]	**£72 13s 4d**	**£547 19s [£245 17s 4d]**

profits roughly comparable (£45 vs. £40 and half a mark). But in others there was significant disparity: Lanark rendered 8 marks in 1264 but £187 in 1265; all the figures are displayed in Table 6.3. The amount in square brackets represents the total amount Hugh collected from the sheriffdoms also visited by Stephen.

Sheriffs accounted for the profits made during the justiciar's ayre. The profits from both sheriff and justiciar were normally entered under 'discharge' in the sheriff's account, with the profits of the sheriff's court listed first and those of the justiciar listed second. Although Haddington often did not include the amount owed and collected, the frequency of mentions to *lucra* of the sheriff and justiciar shows that they were a consistent feature of shrieval accounts. The amounts discharged from sheriff's accounts from the profits of justice in both shrieval and justiciar courts are provided in Table 6.4, together with the total profits recorded by the justiciar from the next nearest ayre. However, in only one case may the profits recorded by the sheriff be those returned from datable justiciar's ayre. Notwithstanding this problem, it will be immediately apparent that the amounts recorded by the sheriff from the justiciar's ayre are significantly lower than those recorded from the ayre accounts themselves. All figures have been calculated to *include* the tenth or eighth that would normally go to the local bishop or religious house. These payments, known as 'second teinds', will be discussed later.[176]

It cannot be denied that the justiciar's *lucra* in the shrieval accounts are rarely those from the extant ayres. They were returned at different dates. But the general point remains: sheriffs returned far less in their accounts of the profits from the justiciar than those stipulated by the justiciar. This was still the case even when the justiciar's ayre did not produce much money. Thus, the justiciar collected £11, 1 mark from Fife in his eyre of 1266 but the account of David of Lochore, sheriff of Fife, which may well have been returned in 1266, recorded only £1 in total, and over a tenth of this (2s 6d) had already been received by the abbot of Dunfermline and so was not received by the chamberlain.[177] The only figure in the shrieval

---

[175] In Hugh de Berkeley's ayre, the account states that the figure was for 'profits acquired in the sheriffdom of Roxburgh in the bishopric of Glasgow': *ER*, i, p. 27.

[176] See below, pp. 379–85.   [177] *ER*, i, p. 31.

Table 6.4. Comparison between *lucra* from the ayre and *lucra* returned by sheriffs, 1263–66

Sheriffdom	Amount from justiciar's ayres (date)	*lucra* of justiciar (year) from sheriff account	*lucra* of sheriff (year) from sheriff account
Inverness	£95 (?1266)	£5 from Ross £1 from Caithness £7 from Moray (total: £13) (1263)	nothing (1263)
Forres	*nothing* (?1266)		10s (1264)
Aberdeen	£129 (?1266)	£6 6s 8d (1264)	£18 18s 1d (1264)
Kincardine	£25 (?1266)	£2 (1264)	£4 6s 8d (half a mark)
Forfar	£90 6s 8d (?1266)	£31 5s (1264)	£6 (1264)
Perth	£23 18s 4d (?1266)		£4 6s 8d (?1263, just from Gowrie) £51 11s 8d (from Gowrie, Strathearn, and Stormont) (1266)
Fife	£11, 1 mark (?1266)	£9 15s 10d (1264) £1 (not given: 1266?)	£41 (1264)
Edinburgh	£129 8s 4d (1265)		(Haddington): 33s 4d[178]
Ayr	£7 17s 4d (1265) £20, 1 mark (1264)		£3 6s 8d (?1264)
Dumfries	nothing (1265)		(covering Galloway and Dumfriesshire) within bishopric of G: £9 14s 4d outwith bishopric: 20s

accounts that comes relatively close to that of the justiciar is that in the sheriffdom of Forfar, whose sheriff accounted for a total of £31 5s from the justiciar's profits in 1264, of which a tenth (62s 6d) was to go to the prior of Restenneth, leaving the sheriff to pay £28 2s 6d.[179] When compared with other sets of figures, these from Forfar are more in line with the much larger £90 6s 8d collected from Forfar by the justiciar in (probably) 1266, unlike, for example, those from Aberdeen, where the sheriff proffered over £6 into the chamber in 1264 but whose 1266 ayre figure was £129. It is, as stated above, possible that a justiciar could receive vastly differing amounts of money from the same sheriffdom in different ayres. But sheriffs did not have to pay *all* the amount collected by the justiciar in the year of his ayre: instead, they had terms of payment. In 1264, the sheriff of Forfar established that he should not be liable to pay £28 2s 6d for the justiciar's profits 'before the terms (*terminos*) established by the justiciar'.[180] The word *terminus* is used in the accounts to denote a period of the year ending either at Whitsun or at Martinmas.[181] The surprisingly

---

[178] It is possible that even by the 1260s, Haddington and Linlithgow were all, although separate sheriffdoms, run by the same person who was also the sheriff of Edinburgh. In both 1263–66 and 1288–90, the sheriff of Edinburgh was also the sheriff of Linlithgow and sheriff of Haddington (*ER*, i, pp. 24–6, 41–3, 45, 48). Neither Haddington nor Linlithgow was listed as separate *balliae* in Hugh de Berkeley's ayre of 1265 in Lothian, so it is possible that their pleas were held at Edinburgh: *ER*, i, p. 27.

[179] *ER*, i, p. 9.

[180] *ER*, i, p. 9; see also Carpenter, 'Scottish Royal Government', p. 136.

[181] See above, Chapter 4, pp. 257–8; this chapter, pp. 357–8.

large amount from Forfar, therefore, may well have been because this was the *whole* amount imposed by the justiciar while on ayre, for which he would account in smaller portions in later audit sessions until the justiciar conducted another ayre. Sheriffs may well have paid off their debts (made up of the amercements imposed by justiciars on wrongdoers) in stages; this may explain the low figures in shrieval accounts, contrasted with the much higher ones in the ayre record.

In light of this, therefore, the income received from shrieval courts would account for a more significant part of royal revenue than that received from the justiciar's ayre each time the sheriff returned his account. In 1264, the sheriff of Aberdeen returned over £18 from his own court and just over £6 from the profits of the justiciar.[182] In 1264, David of Lochore, sheriff of Fife, proffered £41 from his own court and over £9 from the justiciar.[183] Notwithstanding that sheriffs were not always called to account every year, the few sheriffdoms in which shrieval profits of justice were recorded suggest that shrieval judicial income constituted a greater proportion of their income than that accrued by the justiciar during his ayre. Indeed, in Perth, the justiciar's ayre collected £23 18s 4d but a large £51 11s 8d from the profits of the sheriff's court.[184] But these conclusions must be tentative because shrieval profits of justice could also vary dramatically: the sheriff of Perth collected just over £4 from his district of Gowrie in 1263 but £20 from the same district in 1266.[185]

What all this amounts to, then, is that the largest proportion of the king's income came in 1264 from his estate ferms and those estates within sheriffdoms which owed him customary renders in kind. The precise proportion of this stable income in relation to the whole amount received by the chamberlain cannot be calculated not only because of the abridged state of the 1263–66 account roll but also because the seemingly stable 'ferms' could actually include the rent from land temporarily in the king's hands. Because the amounts the chamberlain dealt with were comparatively small, the effect of wardships and seizures on the size of the crown's income each year must have been very significant. A sense that royal encroachment on inheritance rights may have been a problem to landholders— although not so great a problem that laws over wardship were reformed—is suggested by the spurious 'Laws of Mael Coluim III', which were perhaps compiled in the mid-thirteenth century.[186] These state that the king should no longer put himself in the position of the adopted son of rich men and women who died, thus giving their heritage to the king rather than to their own heirs. But the crown stood to gain a lot financially from wardships, as the existing account rolls testify.

Neither did judicial income represent a particularly stable form of income. Profits of justice varied massively from ayre to ayre and from sheriffdom to

[182] *ER*, i, pp. 11–12.   [183] *ER*, i, p. 4.   [184] *ER*, i, p. 18.

[185] *ER*, i, pp. 3, 18; both these figures have been calculated to include the tenth that otherwise went to the abbot of Scone.

[186] Madrid, Biblioteca Real MS II 2097, fo. 11v; for commentary on this compilation, see Alice Taylor, 'Historical Writing in Twelfth- and Thirteenth-Century Scotland: the Dunfermline Compilation', *Historical Research*, vol. 83, no. 220 (2010), pp. 228–52, at pp. 229–36. I hope to engage with the political context of these laws on another occasion.

sheriffdom. Moreover, while the amounts the justiciar accounted for were significant, shrieval returns reveal that their payment was probably spread over a number of accounting terms, thus making the amount the king received from each individual ayre less significant when calculated on an annual basis. With this in mind, shrieval *lucra* may have been more significant from year to year than that from the justiciar, although this too could vary, probably owing to the tenacity of individual sheriffs.[187] It may be that sheriffs were able to collect comparatively large sums of money each year because their courts were more frequent but, even with this in mind, the accounts do not suggest that the *lucra* from justiciar and shrieval courts were so large as to constitute a proportion of income similar to that received from the king's own land.

Although individual fines could be very large, they appear to have been levied on high-status individuals, indicative of their capacity to access the king directly in striking a deal. If this holds, then Scottish fines were different from their counterparts in England, where people of comparatively low status could make small fines of as little as half a mark (6s 8d) with the king for obtaining his writ, although in the absence of the fine rolls, which we do know existed by 1292, this hypothesis cannot be proven. But the interesting point here is that because the stable elements of Scottish royal income only added up to just shy of £2500 (through shrieval and burghal ferms), its extraordinary parts (the fines, wards, reliefs, profits of justice) should have been ripe for exploitation by its kings in a way similar to that of the Angevin kings of the second half of the twelfth and early thirteenth centuries in England.[188] Reasons why this did not happen in Scotland to the same extent will be explored later.[189]

Expenditure

So much for revenue. What did the king spend his money on? The first thing to acknowledge is that the king did not receive the whole amount collected by his officials from landed rents, from profits of justice, or from the revenue of fines, wardships, and reliefs. The account rolls show that particular religious institutions received a proportion of royal revenue from all these sources. This income came to be called 'second teinds' and it has rarely been discussed in the context of the king's finances.

Second Teinds

The proportion of royal revenue received by religious institutions was normally a tenth but the bishopric of Glasgow and the abbot of Dunfermline received an

---

[187] For un-cooperative sheriffs on the justice ayre in the late fifteenth century, see Jackson W. Armstrong, 'The Justice Ayre in the Border Sheriffdoms, 1493–1498', *SHR*, vol. 92, no. 223 (2013), pp. 1–37, at pp. 15–17.

[188] Most obviously Holt, *Magna Carta*, chapters 2–5; and, recently, Janet S. Loengard, ed., *Magna Carta and the England of King John* (Woodbridge, 2010); David Carpenter, *Magna Carta: A New Commentary* (London, 2015), chapter 7.

[189] See below, p. 388.

eighth.[190] Most frequently, the beneficiary was the bishop in whose diocese the sheriffdom lay. Thus, the bishop of Brechin received a tenth of the profits of justice from the court of the sheriff of Kincardine in 1263–66 and the bishop of Aberdeen received a tenth of all profits of justice from the sheriffdoms of Aberdeen and Banff, as well as a tenth of the small ferms collected by both sheriffs.[191] But it was also possible for a local monastic house to receive this type of cut from royal income. The beneficiary of an eighth of profits from Fife was not the bishop of St Andrews, as might be expected, but the abbot of Dunfermline, who appears in the 1263–66 rolls as receiving an eighth from the king's income of all profits from the courts of the sheriff of Fife and the justiciar, as well as an eighth from the amercements levied by 'royal letters' on individuals within the sheriffdom.[192]

For other sheriffdoms, such as Perth, this income was split between the bishop and a religious house. The bishop of Dunkeld received a tenth of the justiciar's profits from Perth and shrieval *lucra* from the districts of Stormont and Strathearn, whereas the abbot of Scone received a tenth of sheriff's profits in Gowrie.[193] When income was proffered from a number of different districts, different religious figures received the teind. Thus, the sheriff of Inverness accounted for all the justiciar's profits from Caithness, Ross, and Moray, presumably including those profits from Elgin and Forres, also within Moray, which were visited separately on the justiciar's ayre.[194] But the bishop of Caithness received a tenth from Caithness; the bishop of Ross, the tenth from Ross; and the bishop of Moray, the tenth from Moray. Map 6.2 shows which religious institutions received what from each sheriffdom. The data is based on Haddington's transcripts of the 1263–66 and the 1288–90 rolls.

Haddington did not transcribe all instances where a tenth or an eighth was allocated to a third party. But, even from his meagre transcriptions, it becomes clear that a stable proportion of the king's income was shaved off in this way. This was as true for his fixed ferms as it was for profits of justice from courts, individual amercements, fines, wardships, and reliefs.[195] It thus seems likely that those who received a proportion of the king's profits of justice through his courts also received the same proportion of fines and reliefs. Indeed, a brieve of Alexander II, issued on 12 August 1227, informed his sheriff of Fife that the abbot of Dunfermline would receive an eighth of all *lucra* (profits) and *fines* (fines) from the sheriffdom (*ballia*)

[190] *ER*, i, pp. 4, 5, 9–10, 16–17, 21, 28, 31, 33.
[191] *ER*, i, pp. 11–12, 15, 21.   [192] *ER*, i, p. 4.
[193] *ER*, i, pp. 3, 18. The sheriffdom of Perth encompassed the districts of Stormont and Strathearn, Atholl, as well as Gowrie; see Map 6.2. For the context of this inclusion, see Broun, 'The Origins of the *mormaer*', in *Earl in Medieval Britain*, ed. Crouch and Doherty, forthcoming; and Dauvit Broun, 'Statehood and Lordship in "Scotland" before the mid-twelfth century', *The Innes Review*, vol. 66, no. 1 (2015), pp. 1–71, at p. 8 (and note 29), 37–40.
[194] *ER*, i, p. 13.
[195] The bishop of Caithness received a tenth of the fine of 200 cows paid by the men of Caithness to the king and the bishop of Glasgow received an eighth of two fines, one paid by Simon Lockhart and one by Earl Patrick of Dunbar in Ayr (*ER*, i, pp. 19, 28). The bishop of Glasgow also received an eighth of the 40s relief paid by Robert Mappar through the sheriffdom of Traquair (*ER*, i, p. 33).

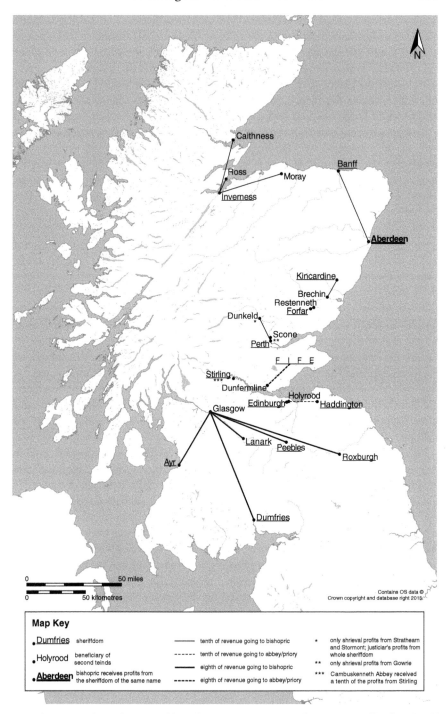

Map 6.2. Second teinds received by religious institutions in the account rolls of 1263–66 and 1288–90

of Fife which the sheriff would collect.[196] A charter of Robert I, enquiring into the privileges of Restenneth Priory in the time of Alexander III, found that the priory received a tenth of 'profits, fines and escheats from both the court of the justiciar and the sheriff within the sheriffdom of Forfar, and a teind of all wards and reliefs', even though the extent of the priory's income is not fully revealed by the 1263–66 roll, which shows the priory only receiving a tenth from one estate within the sheriffdom of Forfar and the profits of the courts of sheriff and justiciar.[197]

Religious institutions thus received proportions of the king's revenue at a scale only partially revealed by Haddington's transcripts. The 1263–66 account roll reveals that the bishop of Aberdeen received a tenth of the revenue in the sheriffdom of Aberdeen from small ferms and the profits from shrieval and justiciar courts, as well as a tenth of the revenue from Banff from the same sources.[198] But the bishop actually received far more than this. The fourteenth-century cartulary of the bishopric of Aberdeen contains the document known as the Rental of Alexander III.[199] This is a list of all revenue owed to Alexander III from his estates within the sheriffdoms of Aberdeen and Banff, together with a later memorandum from the fourteenth century listing the amount owed to the bishop from all parts of the king's income ('second teinds').[200] It is interesting because it shows that the bishop expected to receive a tenth of the revenue from all the king's estates in the sheriffdom (both those he held directly and those which he had granted as feus to others) and also a tenth of the profits from sheriff, justiciar, and chamberlain, as well as the 'wards, reliefs, escheats and other things' received by the sheriffs of Aberdeen and Banff in their sheriffdoms. Thus, although Haddington opened the door into the amount received by the bishop from the sheriffdoms of Aberdeen and Banff, the rental confirms that, under Alexander III, the bishop expected a tenth from all revenues the king received from the two sheriffdoms within his bishopric.

Bishoprics, abbeys, and priories were thus closely intertwined with royal revenue and stood to benefit from any incremental changes to it. How and why had this situation come about? In short, it had developed from royal patronage strategies.[201] Kings granted a proportion of their revenue to ecclesiastical beneficiaries, presumably for some sort of spiritual benefit but no doubt also to buttress royal control over their landholdings. These sorts of grants from royal estates were distinct from the teinds owed to parish churches which were themselves received either by bishoprics or abbeys and priories. The granting of 'second teinds' is thus a separate (although probably not fully autonomous) process from the development of parishes in Scotland, a process often tracked by the emergence of teinds payable to parish churches. The origins of parishes in Scotland has been much debated, with

---

[196] *Dunf. Reg.*, no. 78. Another brieve, this time addressed to Mael Coluim, earl of Fife, informing him that Dumfermline Abbey would have an eighth of the 'fine which you made with me', for the earldom of Fife (presumably Mael Coluim's relief, although that was probably made originally with King William after Donnchad II's death in 1204): *Dunf. Reg.*, no. 79.

[197] *RMS*, i, App. 1, no. 29; *ER*, i, p. 8.   [198] *ER*, i, pp. 11–12, 15.

[199] *Aberdeen Reg.*, i, pp. 55–8; Edinburgh, NLS, MS Adv. 16.1.10, fos. 100r–101r

[200] See above, pp. 361–2.   [201] See also Scott, 'Use of Money', p. 109.

views ranging from an *ab nihilo* introduction by David I to ones which still see David as the king who oversaw the formation of formal parish units (*parochiae*) in Scotland north of the Forth but with forms which were territorially and structurally contiguous with older forms of 'parochial' organization.[202] Here is not the place to enter these debates but, for the present purpose, all we need do is note that the earliest reference to a proportion of royal income being granted to a religious beneficiary is in David I's first confirmation charter to Dunfermline Abbey, drawn up in 1127×31.[203]

Early in David's reign, therefore, is the latest point for the development of gifts of second teinds from non-landed income. A similar grant of a tenth was made to Cambuskenneth Abbey, from the king's 'pleas and profits' from Stirling, Stirlingshire, and Callendar by David I in 1150×53.[204] In 1164, Pope Alexander III confirmed to Holyrood Abbey that the king had granted them a tenth of all royal profits between the River Avon in Stirlingshire and Cocksburnpath in Berwickshire and the sheriff of Haddington was indeed recorded giving a tenth of judicial income to the abbey in 1263–66.[205] By the late 1180s, when William was enforcing rules for teind payment in the bishopric of Moray, he granted the bishopric a teind of all his pleas throughout the diocese of Moray, a grant again confirmed by the 1263–66 account roll when the sheriff of Inverness stated that the bishop had received his tenth of all profits collected from the justiciar's ayre in Moray.[206]

These grants may well have been piecemeal, which would suggest why some sheriffdoms, such as Perth, had different institutions expecting their cut from particular sources of revenue. The units from which this revenue was taken changed according to the introduction of standard administrative units, as discussed in

---

[202] For twelfth-century innovations being fundamentally rooted in older parochial organization, see G. W. S. Barrow, 'Badenoch and Strathspey, 1130–1312, vol. 2: The Church', *Northern Scotland*, 1st ser., 9 (1989), pp. 1–16; John M. Rogers, 'The Formation of the Parish Unit and Community in Perthshire' (PhD Dissertation, University of Edinburgh, 1992); Thomas O. Clancy, 'Annat in Scotland and the Origins of the Parish', *Innes Review*, vol. 46, no. 2 (1995), pp. 91–115. Both lines are critiqued but not wholly replaced in Alasdair Ross, *The Kings of Alba, c.1000–c.1130* (Edinburgh, 2011), pp. 59–63; for a new and different view of shires and parishes, see Broun, 'Statehood and Lordship', pp. 33–55 (of which, as stated in Chapter 1, it has not been possible to take full account).

[203] *CDI*, no. 33.

[204] *CDI*, no. 214, confirmed by Pope Alexander III in 1163, in *Scotia Pontifica: Papal Letters to Scotland before the Pontificate of Innocent III*, ed. Robert Somerville (Oxford, 1992), no. 55. William exchanged the grant in 1173×77 for the church of Forteviot (*RRS*, ii, no. 161) but this seems not to have taken effect, for Innocent III again confirmed the grant in 1206 (*Cambuskenneth Reg.*, no. 26).

[205] *Holyrood Liber*, App. 1, no. 1, confirmed by Honorius III in 1217 (*Holyrood Liber*, App. 1, no. 10); *ER*, i, pp. 24, 32.

[206] *RRS*, ii, nos. 273, 281; *ER*, i, p. 13. That this was a new grant is suggested by *RRS*, ii, no. 421, issued in 1199, which extended the grant to those areas within the bishopric which had not previously been given teinds. It would appear, however, that Alexander II cancelled the second teind of the renders (*redditus*) from his estates in each sheriffdom within the bishopric of Moray in 1238. In compensation for this cancellation, he granted the bishop of Moray the land of Kildrummie, with its free court, and 24 marks from his feu-farmer of Moyness (MOR) and 16 marks from his feu-farmers of Dyke and Brodie (*Moray Reg.*, no. 40 [AII/264]). See further the grant of a teind of the king's revenues from the sheriffdom of Linlithgow to Manuel Priory (*RRS*, ii, no. 407), and a teind of the revenue from Auchterarder (called a thanage in *Lindores Cart.*, no. 23), run in the reign of Alexander II by a royal farmer, was given in 1226 to Inchaffray Abbey (*Inchaffray Chrs*, no. 54).

Chapters 3 and 4. The earlier charter references to these grants saw this revenue as being taken from particular districts or large estates, rather than administrative units like sheriffdoms. Thus, David granted to Dunfermline an eighth of his revenue from Fife and Fothrif and a tenth to Cambuskenneth from 'Stirling, Stirlingshire and Callendar'.[207] But by the 1220s, however, it was clear that bishops, abbots, and priors received their tenth or eighth from the sheriffdom. Thus, by the later 1220s, Dunfermline Abbey received its eighth *not* explicitly from the provinces of Fife and Fothrif, as it had previously, but from the *ballia* ('sheriffdom') of Fife via the sheriff of Fife.[208] In short, although second teinds may have been received continuously from the moment of their grant, the units from which this revenue was taken changed from district and estate to wider sheriffdom, a situation in full operation by the time of the 1263–66 account roll.

That bishops, abbots, and priors stood to benefit financially from the king's profits of justice may be a secondary reason why the church did not present a unified front in its reaction to the developments in thirteenth-century royal justice, discussed in the last chapter. After all, they would profit financially from a system of justice that was wider in ambition and deeper in reach at the level of both sheriff and justiciar.[209] This explanation, of course, does not preclude the fact that differences in stance taken by individuals or institutions when principled disputes arise can also be explained by strategic, moral, or emotive responses by the parties involved. Indeed, it is somewhat ironic (and perhaps revealing of the man's character) that Robert Wishart, bishop of Glasgow, who seems to have been a prime mover in his attempt to block monasteries and church land from being brought unwillingly into royal courts, actually received a greater proportion of royal revenue than most other bishoprics, abbeys, and priories, through his eighth of profits within a bishopric that spanned the sheriffdoms of Ayr, Traquair, Roxburgh, Lanark, and Dumfries.[210]

In short, the most powerful bishops, abbots, and priors gained financially from the changing levels of royal income. Unfortunately, we will never know the full amount they received in the 1260s, owing to the abridged state of Haddington's transcripts. However, it is just possible that almost every form of royal revenue had a tenth or an eighth shaved off it, received by a happy bishop, abbot, or prior. This makes sense, given that we know how integrated major church figures were in the running of the royal court and household. Bishops and future bishops served as the king's chancellors, as did some abbots; and bishops, abbots, and priors were also there at the royal assemblies where royal legislation was enacted. The limited data from 1263–66 and 1288–90 shows that abbots made up the largest category of

---

[207] *CDI*, no. 214.   [208] *CDI*, no. 33; *Dunf. Reg.*, no. 78.

[209] See Chapter 5, pp. 337–43.

[210] It was not only kings who granted away proportions of their profits of justice and their extraordinary revenues. Lay aristocrats did as well, although in their cases the principal beneficiaries of such grants were normally their own monastic foundations. Earl Gille Brigte of Strathearn granted a teind of all pleas heard in his court to his foundation at Inchaffray in the early thirteenth century (*Inchaffray Chrs*, nos. 9–10). Donnchad II, earl of Fife (d.1204), granted a teind of 'his pleas and reliefs' to North Berwick Priory (*North Berwick Chrs*, no. 3); see further, *RRS*, ii, no. 28.

auditors of royal accounts. These ecclesiastical figures, as well as being responsible for drafting law and receiving royal revenue, had a financial stake in the king's income, whether it be that received from his demesne ferms, that collected when dispensing justice or the amounts imposed on lay individuals within his kingdom in fines, wards, and reliefs. In what follows, therefore, it must be borne in mind that the first major expense for the king was the proportion of his income from his sheriffdoms received by the bishops, abbots, and priors of his kingdom.

Hosting, Entertainment, and Financial Remuneration

The chamberlain's account for 1264 reveals that most of the king's overall income was spent on his itineration and the hospitality that this would require. The total expenses for 1264 were £5467 13s 9d, of which £3783 14s 3d was spent on hosting-related expenses: horses, storage, wine, entertainment, and other expenses generally falling under the separate category of *hospicium* ('hospitality'), which constituted the greatest proportion of this type of expenditure (over £2224).[211] That an itinerant king and court would expect not only to be hosted but also to host, particularly when he was staying at royal estates, which he often did, is unsurprising.[212] But what is perhaps surprising is the sheer proportion of his income taken up by this kind of expense. Around two-thirds of the king's income was spent on consumption, entertainment, and hospitality: the figures completely dwarf the other expenses in the chamberlain's accounts. Other smaller expenses came from over £120 on 'gifts of the king', £150 on royal messengers, and a general figure of £410 on 'other purchases'. A few smaller expenses were the paying of stipends to the king's servants (*servientes*) for 'three terms', meaning Martinmas 1263, Whitsun 1264, and Martinmas 1264.[213]

The account rolls of 1263–66 give us no information about how major royal officers were compensated for their efforts. But those of 1288–90 do at least provide a snapshot. It is clear that the justiciar of Galloway was paid from the income received by the sheriff of Dumfries (the fact that the two were the same individual probably does not affect this). William Sinclair, justiciar of Galloway and sheriff of Dumfries, paid himself £66 13s 4d [100 marks] 'for his service and labour performed in the said office [of justiciar of Galloway]'.[214] The order for payment was made by the letter patent of the guardians of the kingdom and 'shown on the account'. The chancellor, Thomas of Chartres, was paid in the same way: his fee was £100, by letters patent shown 'on the account'.[215] Rather interestingly, this too was paid from two sheriffdoms: the sheriff of Edinburgh contributed £60 while the sheriff of Lanark contributed £40.[216] In 1290, the sheriffs of Perth and Kinross

---

[211] This was discussed in more detail in Chapter 4, pp. 254–8.

[212] For recent work on hosting and itineration, see Levi Roach, 'Hosting the King: Hospitality and the Royal *iter* in Tenth-Century England', in *Feasts and Gifts of Food in Medieval Europe: Ritualised Constructions of Hierarchy, Identity and Community*, Special Issue of *Journal of Medieval History*, ed. Lars Kjær and A. J. Watson, *Journal of Medieval History*, vol. 37, no. 1 (2011), pp. 34–46.

[213] All references are to *ER*, i, pp. 10–11.

[214] *ER*, i, p. 36.   [215] *ER*, i, p. 46.   [216] *ER*, i, pp. 42, 46.

paid £20 for the fee of William of Dumfries, clerk of the rolls of the chapel.[217] Now, from these few figures it is impossible to say whether all major officials were always paid from the profits of sheriffdoms and, if they were, how long this situation had lasted and which sheriffdoms bore the cost. But the meagre evidence from 1288–90 shows that, by this point, at least some royal officials were being paid set fees that were taken from the income of sheriffs. Whether the burden of payment shifted from sheriffdom to sheriffdom is unknown but the point remains: all the surviving evidence suggests that the justiciar, the major judicial officer, and the chancellor, the major officer of the king's chapel, were both paid from revenue from individual sheriffdoms, not from the sum total of crown revenue.

As stated earlier, sheriffdoms were also expected to bear some of the cost of hosting the king. William Sinclair, sheriff of Edinburgh, detailed among his expenses twenty-seven cow carcasses, six cows, eighty mutton sheep 'bought for the king's service for two colloquia held at Edinburgh in 1264'.[218] The accounts returning profits in kind are full of expenses already incurred by 'the king's service', which denoted the costs incurred from hosting and feeding the king when he came into the sheriffdoms. The host sheriffdom of the king's audit would bear the cost of the honour and sheriffs also paid when the justiciar came into their sheriffdom on ayre.[219] When the chamberlain journeyed on the king's business, most notably to evaluate lands and set them at farm, sheriffs also had to pay for his presence; presumably when he went on his ayre around the burghs, the burghs had to foot the bill.[220]

What, apart from hosting the king, and paying for the fees and hosting of his officers, did sheriffs spend their money on? Shrieval accounts were, of course, retrospective. At the time of audit, they accounted for their receipts, deducted the expenses, and the remaining amount constituted the sum of royal profits or shrieval debt. Common categories of expenditure emerge from reading shrieval accounts: repair of houses, buildings, castles, and chapels within the sheriffdom; fees of burghal and urban officers, such as doorkeepers, gardeners, and gravediggers; fees paid to the watch of royal castles; provisioning of royal castles; maintenance of hostages and prisoners; and, on occasion, monetary feus paid to individuals in lieu of land.[221] They also paid for carriage and transport of livestock and wine around the sheriffdom, often on the king's service. In addition, sheriffs also had the responsibility to pay teinds from royal estates and extraordinary expenses: thus, the sheriff of Stirling had to pay for hosting Magnus, king of Norway, when he was staying in Stirling castle.[222] The type of expenses incurred by sheriffs seem to have been relatively fixed, although they did vary from sheriffdom to sheriffdom. Sheriffdoms

---

[217] *ER*, i, p. 51.   [218] *ER*, i, p. 33.

[219] *ER*, i, p. 4; see further, above, pp. 385–6.

[220] See, for example, *ER*, i, 19: 'in the expenses of the chamberlain staying at Inverness to place the lands of the lord king at farm, 54s, 5d'; see also *ER*, i, p. 20.

[221] One such feu was that paid to Hugh de Berkeley from the sheriffdom of Perth. The word used is *feodum*; the amount £20 (*ER*, i, p. 2). This was not the *feodum* of his justiciarship, which was very firmly the justiciar of Lothian, not Scotia, and Perth was a sheriffdom in Scotia.

[222] *ER*, i, p. 24.

in Lothian and around the River Forth had to pay for more expenses than did the more northerly sheriffdoms of Aberdeen and Banff, reflecting the geography of the king's itineration, while coastal sheriffs, particularly in the west, had more to do with royal ships than inland sheriffdoms. But, in general, it would appear that there were common expectations about the categories of shrieval revenue, suggesting uniformity in categories (if not amounts) of expenditure throughout the areas of the kingdom covered by sheriffdoms.

Conclusion

What can be garnered from all this? The account roll of 1263–66 reveals that royal income was generally small: just under five and a half thousand pounds in 1264. This contrast with England, where the annual income of Henry III in 1264–65 is estimated at *c*.£11,500 (paid into the Exchequer)—and this during a civil war, when the government was on the brink of collapse and the Exchequer did not even open during its Easter session that year. Even at this financial lowpoint, English kings were bringing in twice as much as the Scottish kings in the same year (who themselves may have been affected by the demands of war). The normal disparity in their incomes would have been even greater: normally, revenue for Henry III seems to have averaged at *c*.£30,000 but the king had been able to raise a tax of £48,000 in 1248.[223] Kings of Scots do not seem to have taxed on moveables as Edward I did from 1275.[224] Instead, the only tax they levied was the *auxilium* levied for military expeditions on units of assessed land, which appears also to have been used to raise large sums on demand (and of course through consultation) for political expediency, and probably required the consent of the court.[225] Thus, an aid was 'fixed' at Musselburgh, probably to raise the 10,000 marks to pay Richard I for the Quitclaim of Canterbury in 1189; between 1209 and 1211, William had raised 11,750 marks to pay John in return for John's not building a castle at Tweedmouth.[226] In 1224, Alexander II apparently raised £10,000 in an aid for the

---

[223] J. H. Ramsay, *A History of the Revenues of the Kings of England, 1066–1399*, 2 vols (Oxford, 1925), i, pp. 345–8, at p. 348, although here miscalculating by a year, so the revenue Ramsay states to be from 1264–65 and 1265–66 actually refer to the years 1263–64 and 1264–65. I am grateful to David Carpenter and Richard Cassidy for help on this point. The figure above does not include the estimated income paid into the king or queen's wardrobes.

[224] It might be thought that Alexander III introduced a tax on wool exports between 1275 and 1282, based on the English model of 1275 (discussed in Duncan, *Making of the Kingdom*, pp. 603–4). But the only evidence for it in Alexander's reign is from the 1292 inventory, detailing 'a roll...of custom of wool and hides of Berwick' (*APS*, i, p. 114). Collection of custom seems only to have been something done at Berwick; Duncan notes that there is no evidence that '[dues] were collected generally in Scotland before 1304'; *Scottish Formularies*, ed. Duncan, pp. 23–4. The Ayr formulary contains one brieve that addresses (among other officials) 'all collectors of the new custom'; A60 (p. 23).

[225] See Chapter 2, p. 97. It might be thought that had William received permission from his magnates to contribute to the Saladin Tithe of 1188, it would have been collected by an *auxilium*; see Howden, *Gesta*, ii, pp. 44–5.

[226] G. W. S. Barrow, 'The Reign of William the Lion', in G. W. S. Barrow, *Scotland and Its Neighbours in the Middle Ages* (London, 1992), pp. 67–89, at 81–2; A. A. M. Duncan, 'John, king of England and the Kings of Scots', in *King John: New Interpretations*, ed. S. D. Church (Woodbridge, 1999), pp. 247–71, at pp. 257–62.

marriage of his sisters and, although this figure comes from a fifteenth-century chronicle, it is not improbable that Alexander raised an aid to pay for his sisters' dowries.[227] In 1264, Alexander III raised an aid on the 'hide' (presumably meaning a *dabach* or ploughgate) to help Henry III against Simon de Montfort.[228] But this revenue does not seem to have been collected frequently and was not a regularly expected part of royal income. Instead, the greatest proportion of royal income came from the ferms of royal estates and the revenue from fines, reliefs, and wardships, and the profits of justice.[229]

As this latter kind of revenue made up over a third of the king's annual income, it is hard to see why Alexander III does not seem to have exploited it more, even to the point of serious discontent. Reliefs were set at the annual value of lands but no more seems to have been done to gain extra income. While there may have been murmurs about the king's interference in inheritance strategies, these complaints did not add up to a full campaign for reform, as they did in England under King John.[230] Why this did not happen may be due to the nature of the revenue from fines, reliefs, and wardships, combined with the nature of royal rule in thirteenth-century Scotland. Reliefs and wardships were *de facto* taken from tenants-in-chief and it seems that fines were either made with relatively high-status individuals or with large groups of lower-status individuals organized according to district but over which there must have been coordinating elite figures. As Alexander's power was mediated so much through that of his aristocrats—they were his chamberlains, justiciars, and many of his sheriffs and aristocratic courts were those which had power over homicide and theft—his government simply did not have an autonomous enough institutional and administrative base to exploit the potential of extraordinary revenue fully.[231] As a result, such income, along with the profits of justice, was less substantial in the chamberlain's account of 1264 than that received from the ferms and renders from his estates taken throughout the sheriffdom.

Sheriffs and sheriffdoms played a fundamental role not only in the production of the king's revenue but also in supporting his rule and governance. Sheriffs were not only constant accounters at the audit session, they also bore much of the expense of hosting the king, the justiciar, the chamberlain, the payment of royal officials, and, even, the audit process itself. The profits of their courts may have

[227] *Scotichronicon by Walter Bower*, 9 vols, gen. ed. Watt (Aberdeen and Edinburgh, 1989–1998), v, pp. 130–1; for these aids, see Scott, 'Use of money'; Duncan, *Making of the Kingdom*, pp. 212–13, 245–6, 379–80, 388–9.

[228] *Gesta Annalia* I, in Skene, *Fordun*, i, p. 302.

[229] Kings also borrowed money. Alexander III's borrowing from his burghs has already been discussed in Chapter 4, p. 256, note 307. But William was in debt for just under £2800 to Aaron of Lincoln; *CDS*, i, no. 433. But because these are more reflective of individual policies of kings, I have not included them here as expected parts of revenue.

[230] See, particularly on reliefs and wardships, Thomas K. Keefe, 'Proffers for Heirs and Heiresses in the Pipe Rolls: Some Observations on Indebtedness in the Years before Magna Carta (1180–1212)', *Haskins Society Journal*, vol. 5 (1993), pp. 99–109.

[231] See also the similar comments in Keith J. Stringer, 'The Scottish "Political Community" in the Reign of Alexander II (1214–49)', in *New Perspectives*, ed. Hammond , pp. 53–84, at pp. 60–70, 79–80. For sheriffs midway through the reign of Alexander III, see Chapter 7, pp. 417–34.

been more substantial when calculated on a yearly basis than those of the justiciars. If the justiciar seems a more ephemeral figure from these accounts, then the sheriff becomes a much more concrete one. As sheriffs were also responsible for holding inquests which acted as gateways into other jurisdictions, as argued in Chapter 5, their role in the king's governance becomes even more important. The key institution of royal government was not any existing centrally, in one place, but the local sheriffdoms, which supported the king on his itinerary and thus had much more direct access to him than their counterparts in England. The institutional power of Scottish royal government in the thirteenth century was more in the local sheriff than it was in any central institution or office.

CONTROL OVER THE COINAGE

Given that kings received much of their income in cash, how much control did kings have over the coinage that circulated within their kingdom? The capacity of kings to issue a single coinage with a uniform design, struck at royally sanctioned mints, is normally taken as a sign of administrative strength.[232] Recoinages required an even greater level of coercive power because they involved the successful recall of circulating coins to sanctioned places to create a new type that henceforth became legitimate tender within the kingdom.[233] Given that kings of Scots only began minting coins in their own name under David I, the question of how far they were able to exert this kind of control in the twelfth and thirteenth centuries is an important one.

The first thing to acknowledge is that the 1263–66 abridged accounts reveal that royal income was mixed: it was received in both cash and kind.[234] Even more was received in kind before the audit took place, which sheriffs had previously sold at market before proffering money to the auditors when called to account. The same was true for judicial profits. The sheriff of Fife accounted for some *lucra* which had been missed out of the justiciar's account of 1264. The amount was four cows

[232] Simon Coupland, 'Charlemagne's Coinage: Ideology and Economy', in *Charlemagne: Empire and Society*, ed. Joanna Story (Manchester, 2005), pp. 211–29, at p. 227.

[233] These debates on the *renovatio monetae* particularly inform views on the Anglo-Saxon state: see James Campbell, 'Observations on English Government from the Tenth to the Twelfth Centuries', in James Campbell, *Essays in Anglo-Saxon History* (London, 1986), pp. 155–70, at pp. 155–6; and James Campbell, 'The Significance of the Anglo-Saxon State in the Administrative History of Western Europe', in Campbell, *Essays*, pp. 171–89, at pp. 186–8. But see now Rory Naismith, 'The English Monetary Economy, *c.*973–1100: the Contribution of Single Finds', *Economic History Review*, vol. 66, no. 1 (2013), pp. 198–225; George Molyneaux, *The Formation of the English Kingdom in the Tenth Century* (Oxford, 2015), pp. 116–41. It has been argued that, in England, frequent recoinages were abandoned in the twelfth century, perhaps leading to an increase in the amount of lesser quality coins circulating, for which see Mark Blackburn, 'Coinage and Currency under Henry I: a Review', *ANS*, vol. 13 (1991), pp. 49–81; and Martin Allen, 'Henry II and the English Coinage', in *Henry II: New Interpretations*, ed. Christopher Harper-Bill and Nicholas Vincent (Woodbridge, 2007), pp. 257–77. The question of how far and when kings of Scots were able to control their coinage is still a valid one because a coinage under the name of the kings of Scots was a new phenomenon in the twelfth century.

[234] See above, pp. 369–71; *ER*, i, pp. 6–10, 16, 20, 26.

which had been taken 'from the goods of hanged thieves' within the sheriffdom. These had been valued at twenty shillings, five shillings per cow.[235] But, if we only had the justiciar's accounts, we would not know that any livestock had been taken and presumably sold before it was accounted for in cash, revealing a significant level of transactions done at a local level. More pertinent here, however, is the distinction between the use of coinage in a particular society (its monetization) and the amount of *control* kings exercised over the types of coin circulating in their kingdom. What follows focuses on the latter.[236]

Coins were used in Scotland before the reign of David I but a coinage issued under the name of a king of Scots was not introduced until *c.*1136, when David I captured Carlisle, gained control over the silver mine at Alston, and began to mint coins at Carlisle which, although bearing David's name, were based on Stephen's first type.[237] Although control over Alston mine was lost in 1157, when Henry II took Cumberland back from Mael Coluim IV, Lord Stewartby has shown that kings of Scots only used Carlisle briefly as their main mint before the emergence of Roxburgh.[238] Table 6.5 records the main classification of coin types, the dates of their circulation, and what mints were used under each king. It is based on the work of Edward Burns, Lord Stewartby, D. M. Metcalf, Nicholas Mayhew, and Timothy Crafter, although most of the original typologies were created by Edward Burns and Lord Stewartby.[239]

It is immediately clear that, with one exception in the coinage introduced in 1250, only two mints were used by all five kings: Berwick and Roxburgh. Perth and Edinburgh were used by all kings apart from Alexander II, although sometimes with die reverses used at Roxburgh.[240] Minting was thus very geographically focused on the burgh quadrant of Perth, Berwick, Roxburgh, and Edinburgh until

[235] *ER*, i, p. 31.

[236] For the use of money, see Scott, 'Use of Money'; Holmes, 'Evidence of Finds', pp. 242–52; N. M. McQ. Holmes, 'A Probable Short Cross Purse Hoard from Dumfriesshire', *British Numismatic Journal*, vol. 74 (2004), pp. 180–3; D. M. Metcalf, 'The evidence of Scottish coin hoards for monetary history, 1100–1600', in *Coinage in Medieval Scotland: 1100–1600*, ed. D. M. Metcalf, British Archaeological Reprints, British Series (Oxford, 1977), pp. 1–60; Nicholas J. Mayhew, 'Money in Scotland in the Thirteenth Century', in *Coinage*, ed. Metcalf, pp. 85–102; Mayhew, 'Alexander III—A Silver Age?'.

[237] No coins minted under the name of a king of Scots have been found before those of David I. This is despite Turgot, in his *Vita Sancte Margarete*, referring to gold coins (*nummos aureos*) which Mael Coluim III used to give out on the feast of the Last Supper; Turgot, *Vita Sancte Margarete*, in *Symeonis Dunelmensis Opera et Collectanea*, ed. I. H. Hinde, Surtees Society 51 (Durham, 1868), pp. 234–54, at p. 246. Coins of Earl Henry, David's son, were minted at Corbridge and Bamburgh: see Holmes, 'Evidence of Finds', pp. 242–3.

[238] Ian Stewart, 'Scottish Mints', in *Mints, Dies and Currency: Essays Dedicated to the Memory of Albert Baldwin*, ed. R. A. G. Carson (London, 1971), pp. 165–291, at pp. 191–202. Ian Blanchard, by contrast, has argued that Carlisle was the minting centre of the 'English Empire' of David I; see Ian Blanchard, 'Lothian and beyond: the Economy of the "English Empire" of David I', in *Progress and Problems in Medieval England: Essays in Honour of Edward Miller*, ed. Richard Britnell and John Hatcher (Cambridge, 1996), pp. 23–45.

[239] Edward Burns, *The Coinage of Scotland*, 3 vols. (Edinburgh, 1887), i, pp. 1–186; also Ian [B. H. I. H.] Stewart, 'The Volume of the Early Scottish Coinage', in *Coinage*, ed. Metcalf, pp. 65–72; I. H. Stewart, *The Scottish Coinage with Supplement* (London, 1955), pp. 1–24, 132–5.

[240] The square cross (phase 1) of the Crescent coinage minted at *Dun* and Edinburgh used Roxburgh reverses, for which see Stewart, 'Scottish mints', p. 199.

Table 6.5. Types and mints of coins issued under the names of kings of Scots from David I to Alexander III

King	Coin type	Phases/Classes	Mints used
David I	*Stephen' first type* Cross fleury		Carlisle Roxburgh Berwick Edinburgh ?Perth[241]
Mael Coluim IV	Cross fleury (*c.*1140–*c.*1170)		Roxburgh ?Berwick
William the Lion	Crescent (*c.*1170–*c.*1195)	Classes a–e, plus P. Two phases (*c.*1170–80; 1180–95)[242]	Roxburgh Berwick Edinburgh Perth[243] *Dvn*[244]
	Short Cross (1195–1249)	Phases a–b	Berwick Roxburgh Perth Edinburgh
Alexander II	Short Cross (1195–1249)	Phases b–d (although only 'd' in name of Alexander II)	Roxburgh Berwick
Alexander III	Short Cross (1249?) Long voided Cross (1250–80)	Phase e Types I–VIII	Berwick Aberdeen Ayr Berwick *Dun* Edinburgh Forfar *Fres* Glasgow Inverness Kinghorn Lanark Montrose Perth Renfrew St Andrews Stirling

[241] For Aberdeen and Perth, see Stewart, 'Volume', p. 67; Stewart, 'Scottish Mints', pp. 180–81.

[242] Stewart, 'Volume', pp. 67–8, identifies two phases of the Crescent coinage, from a square cross to a cross pommée. See also Stewart, *Scottish Coinage*, pp. 10–12, 133, 192, while Crafter, 'Monetary Expansion', pp. 150–3, identified five classes, including a sixth separate one, encompassing all coins minted at Perth, which used a different die source; see also Stewart, 'Scottish mints', p. 199, see T. C. R. Crafter, 'Monetary Expansion in Britain in the Late Twelfth Century', (DPhil Dissertation, University of Oxford, 2007), pp. 150–6.

[243] There is a question as to how far the emergence of Perth as a central mint under William the Lion's Crescent coinage was because the mints at Roxburgh, Berwick, and Edinburgh were not used during the English occupation of those castles. This was first put forward in Burns, *Coinage of Scotland*, i, pp. 52–7; Stewart, *Scottish Coinage*, pp. 10–12; Stewart, 'Scottish mints', pp. 199, 200–1 (although here concluding that minting may have continued at Roxburgh). Tim Crafter, however, argues that, although some disruption occurred, the mints continued to function because mints were located in burghs (which were technically unoccupied) not castles (which were occupied): Crafter, 'Monetary Expansion', pp. 217–24.

[244] For striking of DVN on the reverse, see Stewart, 'Scottish Mints', pp. 178, 184–5; Crafter, 'Monetary Expansion', pp. 156–8. This is either thought to be Dunfermline or Dumfries; Crafter

King	Coin type	Phases/Classes	Mints used
	Long single cross (1280–1357)	Phase I (out of V)	St Andrews (named under John Balliol) [eight more][245]

the reign of Alexander III. Nor did all mints produce equal amounts of coins: the evidence from single finds and hoards suggests that Roxburgh produced most of the second stage of the Crescent coinage (this stage probably ran from *c.*1180 to 1195), at which point the Chronicle of Melrose informs us that William 'reformed his money', thus introducing the new Short Cross coinage.[246] This Short Cross coinage used a total of four mints under William the Lion: Roxburgh, Perth, Edinburgh, and Berwick.[247] But Berwick was not used until Phase e of the coinage and so was effectively discontinued as a mint from 1195 for the remainder of William's reign. Alexander II, however, continued striking the coinage (Phases c–d) but only used his own name on coins from around the mid-1230s (Phase d), and, moreover, only used Roxburgh and Berwick as mints for those coins which bore his name, with Roxburgh holding almost a complete monopoly in coin production.[248] By contrast, Berwick coins predominate in the ideosyncratic Phase e of the Short Cross coinage, which show a beardless Alexander III on the obverse.[249] Different mints also produced different phases of a single type. William's Crescent coinage, for example, reveals a shift in the type of cross shown on the obverse of the coin, presumably imitating a similar shift introduced on Henry II's coins in 1180. Perth, however, which had produced most of the first phase of Crescent coins alongside Roxburgh, is not known to have minted a single coin of the second phase of Crescent coins.[250]

favours Dunfermline. It used to be thought that Stirling was used in the Crescent coinage, for which see Stewart, *Scottish Coinage*, p. 12; but then, later, Stewart, 'Scottish Mints', p. 198, and Crafter, 'Monetary Expansion', pp. 158–9.

[245] Numismatists identify mints on the combination of points of stars and mullets on the reverse of each coin, because the mint name is not given, for which see Stewart, 'Scottish Mints', pp. 216–17. Thus it is not possible to identify the names and location of the mints with confidence; simply that there were nine *identifiable* mints in Type 1 of the Long Single Cross coinage. Lord Stewartby considered which mints were involved in Stewart, 'Scottish mints', pp. 219–21, 224. St Andrews was probably the bishop's mint, for which see Veronica Smart, *The Coins of St Andrews* (St Andrews, 1991), pp. 12–17; also J. E. L. Murray and Ian Stewart, 'St Andrew's Mint under David I', *British Numismatic Journal*, vol. 53 (1983), pp. 178–80, although Murray and Stewart use the testimony of Bower, which is suspect. Bower records that, in 1284, Alexander III granted St Andrews the right to mint its own money (Bower, *Scotichronicon*, v, pp. 416–17). This, according to Bower, had previously been granted by Alexander II (and his predecessors). It may be that Bower confused Alexander II with Alexander III, as he had done (in the opposite direction) with Alexander III's (*recte* II) statutory innovations; see Chapter 5, Note 145.

[246] *Chron. Melrose, s.a.* 1195.

[247] Mayhew, 'Money in Scotland', p. 85; Stewart, 'Volume', pp. 68–9.

[248] Stewart, 'Scottish mints', pp. 203–5.   [249] Stewart, 'Scottish mints', p. 205.

[250] Crafter has argued that Perth dies in the crescent coinage came from a different source to those used at Edinburgh, Roxburgh, and Berwick (and perhaps Dunfermline) and so should be classed differently; see Crafter, 'Monetary Expansion', pp. 150–6.

That being said, however, it is clear that it was possible to use more mints by the reign of Alexander III. Walter Bower recorded that, in 1250, the 'Scottish money was reformed so that the cross which previously had not crossed the legend of the penny now reached its outer edges'.[251] This introduced the Long Cross penny into Scotland, in which the cross on the reverse of the coin did indeed, as Bower testified, stretch to the outer edge of the coin, a move which allowed the coin to be divided into halfpennies and farthings with less difficulty and also would identify more easily which coins had been clipped.[252] But, unlike all previous types, which had been minted at a maximum of six places, type III of Alexander's Long Cross coin was minted at sixteen different places, from Inverness in the north to Ayr and Dumfries in the west.[253] Some coins were minted at different places but all by the same moneyer: thus, the moneyer Walter was responsible for the coins minted at Glasgow, Kinghorn, Montrose, *Fres*, and *Dun*, which have been identified as Dumfries and Dunbar respectively.[254] That the same moneyer was responsible for groups of these new mints suggests that the aim was to carry production of the king's coin into areas that had not been given this responsibility previously as a short-term measure to indicate the presence of the new young king in the further reaches of his kingdom rather than to establish new permanent mints in all places.[255] Alexander's court was not unaware of the political message coins could carry: the last phase of the Short Cross coinage (Phase e) shows the bust of a young unbearded man, presumably the young Alexander III, thereby identifying the youth and innocence of the king with the authority of the currency circulating under his name. Similar sorts of political messages were also to be found on Alexander III's minority seal, which was smaller in size than a normal royal seal, but also bore a biblical legend informing the viewer that they be 'as *prudens* as a serpent but as innocent as a dove'.[256]

The minority of Alexander III thus prompted a quite extraordinary response in the use of mints.[257] The contrast between Alexander's accession and that of his father in 1214 could not be clearer. Alexander II did not issue a new type of coin on his accession. More interestingly, however, he did not even bother to reissue his father's coinage under his name until the mid-1230s. Up to that point, Short Cross coins were circulating (both in Scotland and in England) that bore his father's name, not his own (Phases b–c).[258] Indeed, it was quite usual for there to be a

[251] Bower, *Scotichronicon*, v, pp. 298–9.   [252] Stewart, *Scottish Coinage*, p. 18.

[253] Type I was the Long Cross version of the beardless Alexander, and belongs to an early phase; type II also used a large number of mints (Berwick, Roxburgh, Perth, Aberdeen, Ayr, Glasgow, and Lanark) but fewer than Type III: Stewart, 'Scottish mints', pp. 205–7.

[254] Or *Fres* could indicate Forres; see Stewart, *Scottish Coinage*, p. 19.

[255] Some moneyers did work at more than one mint: Raul who minted William's crescent coinage appears to have worked at both Roxburgh and *Dun* (probably Dunfermline); see Stewart, 'Scottish Mints', p. 199; also Crafter, 'Monetary Expansion', pp. 158–9.

[256] Grant G. Simpson, 'Kingship in Miniature: A Seal of the Minority of Alexander III, 1259–57', in *Medieval Scotland*, ed. Grant and Stringer, pp. 131–9.

[257] This is not to say that all mints produced equal outputs. For an example of the distribution of mints in the Brussels Hoard, discovered in 1908, see Stewart, 'Scottish mints', p. 209. For the Brussels Hoard see, B. H. I. H. Stewart, 'The Brussels Hoard: Mr Baldwin's Arrangement of the Scottish Coins', *British Numismatic Journal*, vol. 29 (1958–59), pp. 91–7.

[258] Stewart, *Scottish Coinage*, p. 17; Stewart, 'Volume', pp. 68–9.

significant delay before a new coinage was minted under the new king's name: in England, even Henry II took four years and Richard and John never minted a coin under their own names.[259] The immediate recoinage on the accession of Alexander III was thus in context an extremely unusual action, which must have been done to stamp the new but young king's authority over the kingdom. The extensive use of mints in 1250 did not continue: after the regional mints were closed before *c.*1265, almost all the coins produced in the Long Cross type were minted at Berwick.[260] However, the use of a larger number of mints was reintroduced for Alexander III's second coinage, introduced in 1280 and known as the Long Single Cross type, for which at least nine mints were used, although it is harder to be sure where, because this type did not include the location of the mint on the reverse of the coin.

Thus, even this brief survey of minting practices shows that, until the reign of Alexander III, minting was very focussed in four urban centres (Roxburgh, Berwick, Perth, and sometimes Edinburgh), which were not all equally used even within particular coin types. Under Alexander III, this changed, probably because of the exigent situation of a minority. Excluding the 1250 recoinage, his second coinage of 1280 used far more mints than any of his predecessors had done. The reason for this must be because the amount of Scottish coins in circulation had increased vastly during his reign.[261] Nicholas Mayhew has estimated that mint output tripled in Scotland during Alexander's reign, from *c.*£50,000–£60,000 to *c.*£130,000–£150,000. Moreover, this monetary expansion had been steadily occurring since the Crescent coinage, introduced in *c.*1170, which may have had an output of £8000–£16,000 on the most recent estimate.[262]

Where did the silver come from? It used to be thought that the mine at Alston provided the bulk of silver that was later minted into Scottish coins. Recent work, however, has done much to disprove this, with Crafter arguing that most of the twelfth-century coinage was minted from silver already circulating in Scotland from as early as the eighth and ninth centuries.[263] It is generally agreed that, through the developing trade in wool and hides, the supply of Scottish silver increased through trade, which in the mid-thirteenth century seems to have been located in Flanders and in the west of Germany, particularly east of the Rhine, and

---

[259] Allen, 'Henry II', pp. 258–60. Richard did, however, issue coinages in his own name in Poitou and Aquitaine. Edward took nine years to mint his own coins after his father's death in 1272. But a delay of over twenty years is quite exceptional by the same monarch; for the early coinage of Henry II under Stephen, see Martin Allen, 'The English Coinage of 1153/4–1158', *British Numismatic Journal*, vol. 76 (2006), pp. 242–302; and, for the Angevin kings' coins of the late twelfth century (all under Henry's name), see John Brand, *The English Coinage, 1180–1247: Money, Mints and Exchanges* (London, 1994), pp. 2–5. The appreciation of Alexander III's coinage in particular is conditional until more is known about the Twynholm Hoard, uncovered in February 2014.

[260] Stewart, 'Scottish mints', pp. 209–10.

[261] For the quality of the Scottish coinage throughout this period, see D. M. Metcalf, 'The Quality of Scottish Sterling Silver, 1136–1280', in *Coinage*, ed. Metcalf, pp. 73–84.

[262] Crafter, 'Monetary Expansion', pp. 213–28, 264; for the context, see Peter Spufford, *Money and Its Use in Medieval Europe* (Cambridge, 1988), pp. 109–13.

[263] Crafter, 'Monetary Expansion', pp. 33–42.

then shifted north-west towards the Netherlands during the second half of the thirteenth century.[264] The silver of German coins was certainly the source of some of the Scottish coinage. Some Crescent sterlings minted at Roxburgh were directly struck onto German pfennigs without prior melting.[265] The large amounts of English coin circulating in Scotland also provided a ready source of silver.

The model for many of these coin types was England. The Short Cross was introduced on an English example of Henry II, which had been in circulation since 1180.[266] The Long Cross imitated the Long Cross coinage of Henry III, in circulation since 1247. The Single Long Cross was introduced in Scotland in 1280 on the example of Edward I, whose coinage had been of that type since 1279.[267] Only the Crescent coinage differed from English example: where Henry II introduced the Cross and Crosslets coinage in 1158, William's coinage of *c.*1170 deviated from it in general type.[268] There were always slight differences in design, however, between Scottish and English coins even when the former was directly imitating the latter. Whereas the English Short Cross coinage circulating in the 1190s would have pellets in the angles created by the cross on the reverse, the Scottish coins would have pointed stars, with the number of points depending on the phase and mint to which the individual coin belonged. The portrait of the king was, in Henry's Short Cross coin, a facing bust, while William's was in profile, either to the left or right, again depending on the phase and mint. William's crescent coinage settled on a French legend (often *Le Rei Willame*), which would be adopted onto his own Short Cross and continued into Alexander's reign, whereas Henry's Short Cross coinage had a Latin legend, although his Cross and Crosslets had called him *Henri* on its legend.[269] Where English coins had pellets in the angles created by the cross on the reverse, Scottish coins had stars and/or mullets. Whereas the moneyers of Edward I's Long Single Cross coins managed to keep the name of the moneyer and mint on the reverse, Alexander's 1280 coins had an extended version of the king's title running fluently from the legend on the obverse of the coin to the legend on the reverse, which, although impressive, has given numismatists serious problems when attempting to identify mints.[270]

Keeping the designs between Scottish and English coins broadly similar was probably a smart idea, given that Scottish coin was in no way the coin most

[264] David Ditchburn, *Scotland and Europe: The Medieval Kingdom and Its Contacts with Christendom*, vol. 1: *Religion, Culture and Commerce* (East Linton, 2001), pp. 176–83; Scott, 'Use of Money'; Alexander Stevenson, 'Medieval Scottish Associations with Bruges', in *Freedom and Authority: Scotland, c.1050–1650: Historical and Historiographical Essays Presented to Grant G. Simpson*, ed. Terry Brotherstone and David Ditchburn (East Linton, 2000), pp. 93–107, at pp. 93–4.

[265] Ian Stewart, 'Some German Coins Overstruck with Sterling Types', *Lagom: Festschrift für Peter Berghaus* (Munster, 1981), pp. 205–10; see further, concentrating on the later period, Ian Stewart, 'Imitation in later Medieval Coinage: the Influence of Scottish types abroad', in *Studies in Numismatic Methods Presented to Philip Grierson*, ed. C. N. L. Brooke, B. H. I. H. Stewart, J. G. Pollard, and T. G. Volk (Cambridge, 1983), pp. 303–26.

[266] Stewart, 'Scottish mints', pp. 202–3.

[267] For Edward's 1279 reform and the *Forma nove monete*, see Martin Allen, *Mints and Money in Medieval England* (Cambridge, 2012), pp. 73–8.

[268] Crafter, 'Monetary Expansion'. For recent work on Henry's coinage, see Allen, 'Henry II'.

[269] Crafter, 'Monetary Expansion', pp. 150–3.   [270] Stewart, 'Scottish mints', pp. 215–16.

frequently circulated within the kingdom. Indeed, Scotland is one of the clearest examples of the distinction between mint output and the volume of currency.[271] Mint output was much smaller than the overall estimated volume of the currency. In short, Scottish coins only made up a small proportion of the currency of Scotland: Mayhew has estimated that only 6 per cent of the circulating Scottish currency was made up of coins bearing the name of a king of Scots and that English money made up as much as 90 per cent of the circulating money within the kingdom.[272] The Dun Lagaidh hoard, discovered in 1968, comprised fourteen English pennies, eight english half-pennies (obols) but only one penny and one obol of William the Lion.[273] The records of Balmaclellan hoard in Dumfriesshire, discovered in 1924, included sixty-four English coins but only four Scottish ones.[274] In short, the evidence suggests that Scottish coins in no way dominated the total volume of coins circulating in the kingdom. That role instead went to contemporary English coins, although it is probable that they were melted down to form Scottish coins during recoinage so it is conceivable that the proportion of Scottish coins in the currency went up in the years immediately after a recoinage.

The narrative of Scottish minting practices looks rather different from that in England in the twelfth and early thirteenth centuries. There was no centralization of minting activity in twelfth-century Scotland as in twelfth-century England. The centralization of minting in England happened very quickly: forty-six mints issued Henry II's first type (the 'Awbridge' type) but only twenty-nine issued the first phase of his Cross and Crosslets in 1158. Only between six and ten mints were commanded to participate in the 1180 recoinage, introducing the Short Cross type for the first time.[275] In Scotland, the phenomenon went the other way: thus, a stable but small number of mints in operation during the late twelfth and thirteenth centuries following the introduction of the first major type in Scotland—the Crescents coinage. Throughout the period until the coinage of Alexander III, there was a particular concentration on Roxburgh and Berwick or Perth. Under Alexander III, there was a vast expansion in the number of mints used, probably because of very particular political purposes, followed again by a contraction in the

---

[271] Crafter, 'Monetary Expansion', p. 43; Metcalf, 'Scottish Coin Hoards', p. 4; see also the range of coins in Nicholas J. Mayhew, 'The Aberdeen Upperkirkgate Hoard of 1886', *British Numismatic Journal*, vol. 44 (1975), pp. 33–50, particularly pp. 43–50.

[272] This is not that unusual, although it differs from the English experience. See, for example, the coin hoard discovered at Vallon-sur-Gée, concealed 1206–07, containing only 7 per cent English coins and the vast majority were taken from nearby mints, all in the Loire valley, with one exception. It is thought that the continental Angevin lands did not have a 'single accepted currency' but instead a mixed one, albeit one with the major mints of Anjou, Britanny, and Poitou predominating. See Barrie J. Cook, '*En monnaie aiant cours*: The Monetary System of the Angevin Empire', in *Coinage and History in the North Sea World, c.AD 500–1250: Essays in Honour of Marion Archibald*, ed. Barrie J. Cook and Gareth Williams (Leiden, 2006), pp. 617–86, at pp. 621–3, 669–73.

[273] Holmes, 'Evidence of Finds', p. 244, citing E. Barlow and A. Robertson, 'The Dun Lagaidh Hoard of Short Cross Sterlings', *Glasgow Archaeological Journal*, vol. 3 (1974), pp. 78–81.

[274] J. Davidson, 'Coin Finds in Dumfriesshire and Galloway', *Transactions of the Dumfries and Galloway Natural History and Antiquaries Society*, vol. 26 (1947–48), pp. 100–13. The exception is the Baddingsgil hoard found in Peebleshire in 1834.

[275] Allen, 'Henry II', pp. 271–2, 275–7 (including the table); and Martin Allen, 'The Chronology of Short Cross Class Ia', *British Numismatic Journal*, vol. 63 (1993), pp. 54–8.

number used but still representing a substantial increase from the number in use during Alexander II's reign and reflecting the increasing amount of circulating Scottish coinage under Alexander III.

The Scottish coinage thus presents a rather interesting problem. The introduction of a coinage circulating under the names of its kings was a political statement, as much as an economic policy, and the coinages during the minority of Alexander III show the minority government's awareness of this type of power wielded by the iconography of coin faces and the importance of kingdom-wide minting. Yet, even during Alexander's reign, when mint output appears to have tripled, there was never a time when Scottish coins predominated in the currency at large; that had to wait until the second half of the fourteenth century, after David II had separated Scottish coins from English in 1357.[276] Scottish coins never occupied more than a small part of the estimated total volume of circulating currency within the kingdom and there were no more than four mints in use at any one time until the 1250 recoinage. When kings collected their revenue in cash, they must have received at least a proportion of coins not under their own name, nor did they make any effort to melt them down and reintroduce the silver into circulation as their own pennies. It is thus very important to separate the volume of Scottish coinage from the Scottish cash economy. As a result, although it is clear that kings did have control over the currency they issued, and were able to recoin it when they wished, they did not have control over the circulating currency. It may have been that the expansion of trade, particularly in wool, to the Netherlands in particular, increased the volume of the coinage in Scotland to such an extent that Scottish mints could not have recoined it all, even if they had been told to, or that, in a more integrated international market, the need for a monopolistic control over currency was lessened.[277] Regardless of why, the coinage of the Scottish kings occupied a more important ideological role than it did make up the greater proportion of coin circulating within their kingdom.

CONCLUSION

The auditing of the accounts of royal officials in Scotland seems to have begun by the early thirteenth century at the latest. But it was not a process that slavishly followed its English exemplar. There was no separate institution called the Exchequer in Scotland, royal officials did not have to account every year, and, most

---

[276] How far proportions were affected by the huge growth in the volume of the coinage under Alexander III is not clear; for comment see Metcalf, 'Scottish Coin Hoards', pp. 9–13; Mayhew, 'Alexander III', pp. 63–4.

[277] David Ditchburn, 'Trade with Northern Europe, 1297–1540', in *The Scottish Medieval Town*, ed. Michael Lynch, Michael Spearman, and Geoffrey Stell (Edinburgh, 1988), pp. 161–79, and Alexander Stevenson, 'Trade with the South, 1070–1513', in *Scottish Medieval Town*, ed. Lynch, Spearman, and Spell, pp. 180–206. The Ayr formulary (discussed in Chapter 5, pp. 301–7), also has a large number of brieves dealing with merchants and travellers with merchandise: see A55/E62 (pp. 22, 82–3), A60 (p. 23), A63 (p. 25), A71 (p. 31), A73 (p. 32), A78 (p. 34); all in *Scottish Formularies*, ed. Duncan.

importantly, the officials not only came to the king's court but the king's court also came to them. Haddington's transcript reveals that the places used for the audits between 1263 and 1266 were geographically focused in the south of the Forth and in Scotland up as far as Arbroath and Perth. It may be that more northerly places were used but, if so, record of this does not survive. The minting of coin was also very geographically located in the south: for much of the period, the most northerly mint was Perth and it was only during the reign of Alexander III, a period which saw an extraordinary expansion in the mint output of the Scottish kingdom, that more northerly mints were used.

The bulk of the king's revenue came from ferms and rents from his lands. Less regular landed income came from wardships and the reliefs owed when heirs succeeded. Judicial profits varied, with the sheriff's court seeming to provide a more substantial source of regular income than the justiciar, whose profits were returned by the sheriff in stages. The justiciar only went on ayre every few years, and the type of civil cases he heard were comparatively few, which probably explains why his profits may seem less significant than expected. Moreover, the church and monastic institutions were integrally linked with the collection of royal revenue: particular bishoprics and monastic and religious houses received a cut of the king's income, which may also explain why the heads of such institutions were the main type of people who audited the king's accounts. In terms of stakes in income, church and state were broadly on the same page.

What stands out here is the importance of the sheriffdom as the keystone of Scottish governmental structure by 1263–66. Not only did sheriffs account for almost all kinds of income eventually received by the king, their expenses were absolutely fundamental to the workings of royal power at the centre. Individual sheriffs paid not only for hosting the king but also his audit court; later, they also seem to have paid the fees of the major royal officials, such as chancellor, chamberlain, and justiciar. Indeed, the travelling audit reflects the importance of the sheriffdom as the unit of what might otherwise be called central government: 'local' sheriffs paid for the centre directly, not indirectly. So, in short, central government had no separate institutional form that existed autonomously from the sheriffdom: the justiciar relied on the structure of sheriffdoms to conduct his ayre; the king relied on the sheriffdoms to hear his audit and to pay for his itineration throughout the kingdom. Scottish royal government was inherently localized in the area covered by sheriffdoms during the thirteenth century.

How far this government was therefore bureaucratized—that is, staffed by individuals whose authority came primarily from their position within an institutional and administrative government—is the subject of the next chapter. Who were the people who acted as royal officials during the second half of the thirteenth century, by which time the structure of localized central government, based on the sheriffdom, had emerged? What records were drawn up and how far were these records produced—and kept—as part of routine governance? What types of people performed official roles and how far a written bureaucratic culture developed in the thirteenth century are the subjects addressed in the last chapter of this book.

7

A Bureaucratic Government?

Studies of medieval bureaucracies have mainly concentrated on two aspects—parchment and people—often to ask how far a particular kingdom or polity did enough recordkeeping or had sufficiently autonomous officials to develop an institutional and administrative existence separate from the rest of social life.[1] The profile of office holders is studied in this context: how far were royal officials dependent on their position for their power? And how many alternative sources of wealth and influence did they have to fall back on? This chapter takes parchment and people in turn.

ENROLMENT AND RECORDKEEPING

Enrolment is an interesting subset of the general practice of keeping records of (governmental) activity: it is a *type* of archiving the form of which—in a roll—has a shifting resemblance to the actual practice it intends to record. In the case of the enrolment of financial accounts, rolls can be the direct and primary record of auditing procedure.[2] Yet enrolment can also be at further stages removed from process. For any type of outgoing document, such as charters or records of judicial proceedings, the enrolled item is a mere copy of an 'original' document; it is a record of the contents of an existing document and thus further away from the process of drafting the original record and the actions which both records were

[1] Agnès Bérenger and Frédérique Lachaud ed., *Hiérarchie des pouvoirs, délégation de pouvoir et responsabilité des administrateurs dans l'Antiquité et au Moyen Âge* (Metz, 2012), pp. 6, 9–11; see also the essay by François Bérenger, 'Le contrôle des officiers du royaume de Sicile dans le dernier tiers du xiiie siècle (1266–1300)', in *Hiérarchie des pouvoirs*, ed. Bérenger and Lachaud, pp. 231–52, which concentrates on the varying levels of accountability and performance of officials, particularly financial ones. T. N. Bisson, 'Les comptes des domaines au temps de Philippe-Auguste: essai comparatif', in *La France de Philippe Auguste: le temps des mutations: Actes du colloque international organisé par le C. N. R. S.*, ed. R-H. Bautier (Paris, 1982), pp. 521–39; Michel Nortier, 'Les Actes de Philippe Auguste: notes critiques sur les sources diplomatiques du règne', in *La France de Philippe Auguste*, ed. Bautier, pp. 429–53; Jean Dufour, 'Peut-on parler d'une organisation de la chancellerie de Philippe Auguste?', *Archiv für Diplomatik*, vol. 41 (1995), pp. 249–61; Bruce Lyon and Adriaan Verhulst, *Medieval Finance: A Comparison of Financial Institutions in Northwestern Europe* (Bruges, 1967). For an important and recent study of officialdom, see Frédérique Lachaud, *L'Éthique du pouvoir au Moyen Âge: l'office dans la culture politique (Angleterre, vers 1150–vers 1330)* (Paris, 2010), particularly pp. 29–39. For a recent study on accountability in bureaucracies and institutions, see John Sabapathy, *Officers and Accountability in Medieval England, 1170–1300* (Oxford, 2014), particularly chapters 2–3.

[2] Michael T. Clanchy, *From Memory to Written Record: England, 1066–1307*, 2nd edn (Oxford, 1993), pp. 135–44.

supposed to convey accurately. The most important point about rolls—and central records in general—is that they are seen to be part of the process by which kings started governing continuously.[3] The creation of central archives is thought to demonstrate the use of the written word as part of routine 'governance' that, through the creation of a record of its activity, gave particular 'governments' more institutional permanence. Indeed, the keeping of written records allowed for past governmental activity to form part of government in the present: the written record became an intrinsic part of the memory of kingship and always had the potential to be called upon. So given that kings of Scots adopted methods of central government that look continuous (accountancy; judicial ayres and brieves), as Chapters 5 and 6 have argued, but which were, in fact, intertwined with local governmental units (through their dependence on the sheriff), how, if at all, was this more localized and institutionally peripatetic governmental arrangement reflected in the way in which their records were kept?

As always, there is an immediate problem in examining this subject in Scotland: a complete lack of original rolls. Not one original roll—of whatever kind—survives.[4] What we have, for the most part, are four inventories of the documents that were once kept in the king's 'treasury' at Edinburgh castle. The first inventory was drawn up on 29 September 1282, when Alexander III was still king, by the king's clerks: Thomas of Chartres, Ralph de Bosco, and William of Dumfries.[5] The remaining three inventories were compiled on the command of Edward I after he had taken the title 'superior lord of the kingdom of the Scots'.[6] These Edwardian inquests are dated 23 August 1291, 30 December 1292, and 16 December 1296. Earlier historians and antiquarians used these inventories as evidence of the complexity and sophistication 'reached' by the kingdom of Scotland before its destruction by Edward I. When William Robertson published the inventories in Edinburgh in 1798, he remarked, 'such monuments of those ancient records are still preserved...as prove incontrovertibly, that Scotland, prior to the dispute about its Crown, had reached a pitch of internal polity not inferior to that of any kingdom of Europe'.[7] Despite the level of confidence placed in them, however, the inventories have never really been fully studied, although they must be the source

---

[3] For the transition from 'brief spurt' governance and 'continuous government', see Timothy Reuter, 'Assembly Politics in Western Europe from the Eighth Century to the Twelfth', reprinted in and cited from Timothy Reuter, *Medieval Polities and Modern Mentalities*, ed. Janet L. Nelson (Cambridge, 2006), pp. 193–216, at pp. 194–5; see also Clanchy, *Memory*, pp. 44–80, particularly p. 62: 'the increasing mass of royal documents tended to enlarge and stratify the bureaucracy which produced them'; Lyon and Verhulst, *Medieval Finance*, pp. 9–10; Vincent Moss, 'Normandy and England in 1180: the Pipe Roll Evidence', in *England and Normandy in the Middle Ages*, ed. David Bates and Anne Curry (London, 1994), pp. 185–95.

[4] J. Maitland Thomson, *The Public Records of Scotland* (Glasgow, 1922), pp. 1–24; Athol L. Murray, 'The Pre-Union Records of the Scottish Exchequer', *Journal of the Society of Archivists*, vol. 2, no. 3 (1961), pp. 89–101.

[5] *APS*, i, p. 107; NRS, RH5/8/1, RH5 8/2 (1282).

[6] London, TNA E 39/3/53; E 39/3/54 (1291); Edinburgh, NRS, SP 13/1 (1292); London, TNA, E 101/331/5 (1296), all (including 1282) printed in *APS*, i, pp. 107–18.

[7] William Robertson, *An Index, Drawn Up about the Year 1629* (Edinburgh, 1798), p. ix; Maitland Thomson, *Public Records*, pp. 2, 4.

of the historical assumption that government in Scotland, during the thirteenth century, showed evidence of recordkeeping and enrolment akin to that in England, even if on a smaller scale.[8]

This section will use the evidence of the inventories to examine the development and form of the central records kept, for the most part, in Edinburgh castle by the 1280s and 1290s. It will cover three broad areas: financial records, judicial records, and the records of outgoing and incoming written documents, most notably copies of royal charters, and the charters and letters of other people. It will argue that each of these three types of record kept in Edinburgh castle were not kept as the result of systematic and routine enrolment that had occurred throughout the thirteenth century. The process of central recordkeeping of financial activity was at one stage removed from the process of government and administration; central records were not created after every accounting session. Moreover, these secondary central records seem only to have been kept from roughly midway through the reign of Alexander II. Judicial records seem only to have been kept as a matter of course from, at the earliest, the 1220s, the period when the changes to the judicial system, discussed in Chapter 5, began. Copies of royal charters do not seem to have been kept routinely until the reign of Alexander III; any charter rolls of an earlier date were *post factum*, not routine creations. In short, there appears to have been another 'leap forward' in how royal documentation was kept and archived in the mid-thirteenth century but this process was more responsive and, with the exception of judicial records, less routine than might once have been thought.

First, it must be acknowledged that the body responsible for producing royal rolls was *not* called the 'chancery' (*cancellaria*), as in thirteenth-century England, but the *capella regis*—the king's chapel.[9] From as early as the late 1240s, there was at least one clerk with particular responsibility for the 'rolls of the royal chapel'.[10] The position of 'clerk of the rolls' is recorded in an account from 1290 but, when Edward I assumed the title of 'superior lord of Scotland', the clerk had been promoted from mere *clericus* to *custos*—'guardian' or 'custodian' of the rolls.[11] Outgoing records of all kinds, including financial accounts, were compiled in the

---

[8] Richard Oram, *Domination and Lordship: Scotland 1070 to 1230* (Edinburgh, 2011), p. 363, although not stressing the similarity with England.

[9] The earliest reference to *cancellaria* is in the Ayr MS (online MS: <http://www.stairsociety.org/resources/view_manuscript/the_ayr_manuscript/229>). However, even here, the chapters containing the brieve formulae are called 'capitula capelle regis scocie'; NRS, PA5/2, fo. 18v, even though this is then followed by 'tam litteris in curiis placitandis quam de breuibus per regem de cancellaria mittendis'; see further Athol L. Murray, 'The Scottish Chancery in the Fourteenth and Fifteenth Centuries', in *Écrit et Pouvoir dans les chancelleries médiévales: Espace français, espace anglais*, ed. K. Flanu and D. J. Guth (Louvain-La-Neuve, 1997), pp. 133–51.

[10] The earliest record for a 'clerk of the chapel' is, to my knowledge, a royal charter dated to 20 April 1248 (*Melrose Liber*, i, no. 237 [AII/324]; NRS, GD55/237); the same Alexander also attests *Melrose Liber*, i, no. 322 (NRS, GD55/322); see also *ER*, i, p. 11; cf. A. A. M. Duncan, *Scotland: the Making of the Kingdom* (Edinburgh, 1975), pp. 607–8.

[11] *ER*, i, p. 51 (*clericus*); *APS*, i, p. 111 (*custos*). The 'Scottish king's household' refers to a clerk of the rolls who had control over all the documents and charters issued from the 'chancery' and all the accounts from the 'exchequer' and, although these names may be anachronistic for Scottish practice, the existence of a 'clerk of the rolls of the royal chapel' is attested in the 1288–90 account transcripts;

capella regis; there was no separation, as there was in England, between those records produced by the Exchequer and those of chancery.[12]

It is clear that Haddington's sources for the accounts of 1263–66 and 1288–90 (discussed in Chapter 6) were two rolls drawn up by a clerk (or clerks) of the king's *capella regis*.[13] But what role did these rolls play, if any, in the audit process itself? Were rolls compiled as the audit was taking place, as they were in England? There is, after all, no need to assume that Haddington's source was a direct record of the process of financial administration. As shown in Chapter 6, Haddington's transcript of the accounts from the 1260s seems to have been made from a single roll that was arranged in non-chronological order.[14] Individual accounts returned in different years are scattered throughout the transcript: 1264 follows 1265, 1264 follows 1266, and so on.[15] When it was thought that Haddington was copying from separate 'exchequer' rolls, this erratic dating could be brushed away by blaming his editorial proclivities. But Chapter 6 showed that Haddington *did* follow the order of his source: the erratic dating was present in the roll for 1263–66. How then do we explain their generally non-chronological order? The only reasonable solution is that the original rolls were *secondary* records, drawn up at a

---

'The Scottish King's Household and Other Fragments from a Fourteenth-Century Manuscript in the Library of Corpus Christi College, Cambridge', ed. Mary Bateson, *Miscellany II*, Scottish History Society, 1st ser., vol. 45 (Edinburgh, 1904), pp. 1–43, at p. 32; *ER*, i, p. 51.

[12] For those produced by the chancery see, among many, Nicholas Vincent, 'Why 1199? Bureaucracy and Enrolment under John and his Contemporaries', in *English Government in the Thirteenth Century*, ed. Adrian Jobson (Woodbridge, 2004), pp. 17–48, and David Carpenter, 'The English Royal Chancery in the Thirteenth Century', in *Écrit et Pouvoir dans les chancelleries médiévales: espace français, espace anglais*, ed. K. Flanu and D. J. Guth (Louvain-La-Neuve, 1997), pp. 25–52, repr. in *English Government*, ed. Jobson, pp. 49–69; for the distinction between Scottish and English procedures, see David Carpenter, 'Scottish Royal Government in the Thirteenth Century from an English Perspective', in *New Perspectives on Medieval Scotland, 1093–1286*, ed. Matthew Hammond (Woodbridge, 2013) , pp. 117–59, at pp. 121–2.

[13] *ER*, i, pp. 11, 19, 51.   [14] See Chapter 6, pp. 351–4.

[15] The first account to be dated is that of David of Lochore, sheriff of Fife, returned in 1264 (*ER*, i, p. 4); then Robert [E] Mowat, sheriff of Forfar, also 1264 (*ER*, i, p. 6; Stephen Fleming's ayre of Lothian was returned 'on the same day and year': *ER*, i, p. 9); then that of the chamberlain, William, earl of Mar, made at Scone on a Thursday in 1264 (*ER*, i, p. 10); the account of Andrew of the Garioch, 1264 (*ER*, i, p. 11); Lawrence Grant, sheriff of Inverness, 1263 (*ER*, i, p. 13; followed by the account of Alexander de Montfort, sheriff of Elgin 'on the same day and year': *ER*, i, p. 13); the account of William Wiseman, sheriff of Forres, 1264 (*ER*, i, pp. 14–15); John Cameron, sheriff of Perth, 1266 (*ER*, i, p. 17); Alexander Comyn, earl of Buchan, sheriff of Wigtown, 1266 (*ER*, i, p. 22; returned at Edinburgh); John Lamberton, sheriff of Stirling, 1266, then 1263 (*ER*, i, pp. 23, 24); R[oger/obert?] de Mowbray, once sheriff of Haddington, 1263 (*ER*, i, p. 24); Nicholas de Vieuxpont, bailiff of Tynedale, 1264 (*ER*, i, p. 25); R[oger/obert] de Mowbray, sheriff of Linlithgow, 1263 (*ER*, i, p. 25); Robert [W] Mowat, sheriff of Forfar, 1264 (*ER*, i, p. 26); John Cameron, sheriff of Perth, 1264 (*ER*, i, p. 26); Hugh de Berkeley, justiciar of Lothian, 1265 (*ER*, i, p. 27); William Comyn of Kilbride, sheriff of Ayr, 1265 (*ER*, i, p. 27); Alexander Sinton, sheriff of Selkirk, 1265 (*ER*, i, p. 30); John Lamberton, sheriff of Stirling, 1265 (*ER*, i, p. 30); Alexander Comyn, earl of Buchan, sheriff of Wigtown, 1265 (*ER*, i, p. 30); Simon Fraser, sheriff of Traquair, 1263 (NRS, E38/1, fo. 11r; cf. *ER*, i, p. 32); William Sinclair, sheriff of Linlithgow, 1264 (*ER*, i, p. 33); Laurence Grant, bailie of Inverquiech, 1266 (*ER*, i, p. 33); William Wiseman, sheriff of Forres, 1266 (*ER*, i, p. 34); John of Kinross, sheriff of Kinross, 1263 (*ER*, i, p. 34); R[obert] Mowat, late sheriff of Forfar, 1266 (*ER*, i, p. 34); William Comyn of Kilbride, sheriff of Ayr, made by his attorney, Fergus mac Kennedy, 1266 (*ER*, i, p. 34); David of Lochore, sheriff of Fife, 1266 (*ER*, i, p. 34). For more on these individuals, see below, pp. 417–34.

time removed from the process of accounting itself. That is, the scattergun approach to 1263–66 in particular resulted from assembling the accounts of individual officials or small groups of officials which had been returned at least two or three years previously.

It is probable that this central roll copied a range of written records made at the audit itself. Haddington's transcript reveals that 'clerks of the chapel and court of the lord king' attended the 1264 session and probably made records of its proceedings.[16] The 1296 inventory records two small rolls of two membranes each, containing the accounts of two sheriffs of Nairn, one from 1204 and the other from 1227.[17] These may well have been the type of written account that fed into the central record at a later stage. Moreover, if each of these rolls contained the account of a single sheriff, or perhaps only a few sheriffs, then this would explain why the roll created jumped around chronologically: the clerk who compiled it must have had a collection of disparate accounts in front of him which he did not sort into order before beginning his transcription. The reference to individual shrieval accounts from 1204 and 1227—when the audit process was in its early stages—suggests that the decision to consolidate individual accounts into a single central record was taken later than the decision to conduct an audit itself.[18]

The 1296 inventory lists two large rolls, each of eighty-nine membranes, which cover the periods 1218–72 and 1218–42 respectively.[19] These rolls, even though they do not survive, must have differed from English pipe rolls, in which the accounts from each financial year were recorded in separate rolls: each yearly audit had its own roll. By contrast, one of the Scottish rolls covered a period of fifty-four years and the other twenty-four years. It is inconceivable that these long rolls would have been brought to each account session: it must also be the case that they too were created from a corpus of earlier records. If so, then the process of creating these records may have begun by the year 1242, the *terminus ante quem* for the rolls mentioned in the inventory.

The probability that the account rolls produced by the mid-thirteenth century were neither arranged chronologically nor direct records of the audit process itself is strengthened by the contrast between the arrangement of Haddington's transcripts of the proceedings from 1260s and those from 1288–90. Both sets of accounts appear in non-chronological order but the accounts of the mid-1260s are decidedly *more* haphazardly arranged than those of 1288–90, which have not yet been fully discussed. Haddington seems to have been true to the order of the accounts returned between 1288 and 1290, even if, again, he got understandably bored in transcribing all of their contents.[20] At the beginning of his transcription of 1288, for example, he noted to himself that 'the first comptis [on the roll] ar

---

[16] *ER*, i, p. 11.   [17] *APS*, i, p. 118.
[18] For the development of the audit, see Chapter 6, pp. 351–66.   [19] *APS*, i, pp. 117–18.
[20] The accounts of John Comyn, earl of Buchan and sheriff of Banff, and William de Meldrum, sheriff of Aberdeen, and Walter Stewart, earl of Menteith and one-time sheriff of Dumbarton, returned at Scone in 1290, are all blank: *ER*, i, p. 49.

revin blekked ["blackened"] and can not be red'.[21] The extracts Haddington made from 1288–90 are from three separate and clearly identifiable accounting sessions: one held in Linlithgow in 1288, another in Edinburgh in 1289, and a third in Scone in 1290.[22] These proceed one from another in chronological order, with one exception: the accounts from Edinburgh in 1289 and Scone in 1290 are separated by one seemingly miscellaneous account returned in 1290, followed by two in 1289.[23] The strange placing of these accounts in Haddington's transcript suggests that he was, as in his transcripts of the 1260s, following the order in his source but his source for 1288–90 was arranged in a much more explicitly chronological way than his source for 1263–66: the bulk of it seems to have included relatively full records from three accounting sessions for 1288, 1289, and 1290. Non-chronological material appears only between 1289 and 1290. In short, the 1288–90 roll was a much more organized affair than that of 1263–66. Whereas the audit sessions of 1288–90 appear to have produced fuller records of all the accounts heard, those of 1263–66 appear to have produced separate accounts for each official (or separate accounts for small groups of officials) which were not put in order when a single roll for 1263–66 was compiled.

If this scenario is accepted, then the records of audit sessions had become more coherent by 1288–90, when a single audit session appears to have produced a single record, than they were in 1263–66, when a single audit may have produced multiple records. This conclusion ties in with one put forward in Chapter 6: that the language of audit was more technical and formal in 1288–90 than it had been in 1263–66.[24] However, even by 1288–90, the records produced by the audit would not have been quite as straightforward as all that: the presence of single accounts heard in 1290 and 1289 in the middle of the 1288–90 roll suggests that single shrieval accounts were still being produced in addition to the general record of particular sessions, which were then copied separately onto the roll. This rather complicated scenario may have arisen if the single 1290 account and the two 1289 ones were heard at different times and/or at different places than those returned at Linlithgow in March 1288, Edinburgh in 1289, and Scone in 1290.[25] The placing of the 1289 and 1290 accounts in the middle of the roll is thus a reminder that the

---

[21] *ER*, i, p. 35; for comment, see Murray, 'Pre-Union Records', p. 94.

[22] The sheriffs of Selkirk, Traquair, Dumfries, Edinburgh, Ayr, Dumbarton, Stirling, Wigtown, Lanark, Edinburgh, and Linlithgow all returned in March 1288, as did the justiciar of Galloway, the custodian of the king's castle of Kirkcudbright, the bailiff of Jedburgh, and the mason and carpenter working on the king's castle at Stirling (*ER*, i, pp. 37–45). The accounts of these sixteen royal officials of various types are all listed in Haddington's transcript *en bloc* but not all of them are dated and the location of the account recorded is not always given. They do, however, all appear to have been returned at Linlithgow in March 1288. The last entry in this block is the account of William Sinclair, sheriff of Linlithgow, which contains the expenses for the audit court session at Linlithgow (*ER*, i, p. 45). Sheriff William's account therefore must have been the last to be scrutinized by the auditors because it needed to show the expenses incurred at the audit session.

[23] Sheriff of Wigtown (29 May 1290), at *ER*, i, p. 48; and the farmer of Dull (1289) and Nicholas Hay, sheriff of Perth (1289), at *ER*, i, p. 49; followed by 'accounts heard at Scone, in the year 1290...for the year 1289' (*ER*, i, p. 49).

[24] See Chapter 6, pp. 365–6.

[25] The session at Linlithgow in 1288 was held between at least 8 and 12 March (*ER*, i, pp. 38, 40). There are no day and month dates recorded for either the 1289 session at Edinburgh or the 1290

1288–90 roll was, like that of 1263–66, a *post factum* record, compiled at a later time than the audit session itself.

Even if the mere outlines presented here are accepted, then the creation and role of central records of account were very different in Scotland from in England. Richard fitzNigel's description of two, sometimes three, copies of the pipe rolls being made at the very time of the meeting of the Upper Exchequer is evidence not only of a geographically centred accounting procedure (absent in Scotland) but also of one in which the preparation of an authoritative written record, to be kept centrally, was an intrinsic part of the process of accounting itself.[26] The contrast between English and Scottish procedure remains despite the emerging view that the pipe rolls were on occasion not the record of unassailable accuracy described in the *Dialogus*.[27] That the pipe rolls sometimes contained mistakes does not take away from the intimate connection they reveal between the creation of a central written record and the otherwise oral process of account. In Scotland, the process of compiling central records was removed from that of accounting. This is not to say that written records were not drawn up at the time of the audit—the accounts from the sheriffdom of Nairn may be our only lingering testimony of this—but that centrally kept records of the entire session were not drawn up at the time of the account. That process happened later and is witnessed by the arrangement in Haddington's transcripts. These records are less ones of the immediate activity of government; they should be seen instead as a later consolidation of that process.

A *post factum* central record must have been necessary because the king's court travelled to audit their accounts and did not hear all officials at the same sessions. Nor was every official expected to account every year. As a result, it would have been impossible for royal clerks to create the type of unified annual records of the English Pipe Rolls.[28] Instead, clerks of the audit sessions appear to have produced single records, containing either the accounts of individual officials or small groups of them (as seems to be the case in 1263–66) or for more-or-less-entire sessions (as seems to be predominantly the case in 1288–90). These were then compiled into a single roll or set of membranes some time later, often years later. Some of the accounts from 1263, for example, cannot have been entered before 1266, because they appear after those of 1266 on the original roll. The non-chronological arrangement of the central record made for 1263–66 must have made it very difficult to consult, which begs the question of why they were compiled at all. But routine and

session at Scone but the single account of the sheriff of Wigtown returned on 1290 provides the date of 29 May (*ER*, i, p. 48).

[26] *Dialogus de Scaccario (The Dialogue of the Exchequer) and Constitutio Domus Regis (The Disposition of the King's Household)*, ed. Emilie Amt and S. D. Church, Oxford Medieval Texts (Oxford, 2007) (henceforth, *Dialogus*), pp. 26–7, 52–5; for the assertion that Thomas Brown's roll was a third copy of the pipe roll, see Vincent, 'Bureaucracy and Enrolment', p. 23, note 27.

[27] Mark Hagger, 'Theory and Practice in the Making of Twelfth-Century Pipe Rolls', in *Records, Administration and Aristocratic Society in the Anglo-Norman Realm*, ed. Nicholas Vincent (Woodbridge, 2009), pp. 45–74; and now Richard Cassidy, '*Recorda Splendidissima*: the Use of Pipe Rolls in the Thirteenth Century', *Historical Research*, vol. 85, no. 227 (2012), pp. 1–12.

[28] Even if English sheriffs did not themselves turn up each year to render their account, they were still expected to.

frequent consultation was probably not the point: indeed, most records kept now are not kept for regular consultation but in order that a record be kept, to have a 'paper trail' for potential consultation, just in case need arises. The central accounting roll in Scotland under Alexander III must have been created to serve as a record of past activity: it was created to be a record, made out of other existing records, which must explain why there was no need in 1263–66 to produce a clearer internal arrangement. That 1288–90 shows a more coherent set of records probably indicates a more formal process of recording the accounts at audit sessions themselves rather than a more rationalized central record.[29]

What can then be said of other enrolment practices, in particular of outgoing charters, letters, and memoranda issued under the king's name? The enrolment of royal charters by the English chancery has long been thought to have been introduced under John, although this is not uncontroversial.[30] In Scotland, the issue is also complex. Attention has been drawn to 1195, when limited dating clauses (containing only the day and the month of issue but not the regnal year) became a standard part of royal charter diplomatic during the reign of William the Lion. Geoffrey Barrow suggested that the introduction of limited dating clauses by 17 April 1195, recording the day and month of the issue of the charter, could only be explained by 'the assumption that [from 1195] . . . the clerks of the chapel began to copy acts on rolls which were made up, or freshly headed, for each regnal year'.[31] If this had been the case, it would have meant that the kings of Scots kept charter rolls before they were introduced in England in 1199 (if 1199 is, for the sake of the present argument, the accepted date). Yet the introduction of limited dating clauses would explain only the absence of regnal years from the putative rolls, not from the sealed charters themselves. If consultation were ever a motivation for the introduction of charter rolls, it would be impossible for an enrolled copy even to be found in the rolls if the regnal year was missing from the original document. This does not prove that charter rolls were not introduced at the same time as limited dating clauses but it does make Barrow's assumption rather more unlikely.[32] If the presence of dating clauses can be linked in Scotland to the creation of charter rolls, then it makes more sense to see 1222, when royal charters began to be dated by regnal year, as a more significant date than 1195.[33] Indeed, an alternative explanation

---

[29] See Chapter 6, pp. 365–6.

[30] David Carpenter has very recently argued that chancery enrolment may have begun in the 1180s, possibly even earlier, for which see David Carpenter, '"In Testimonium Factorum Brevium": the Beginnings of the English Chancery Rolls', in *Records*, ed. Vincent, pp. 1–28, at pp. 24–7. See also Vincent's rather *terse* response in Nicholas Vincent, 'Introduction: the Record of 1204', in *Records*, ed. Vincent, pp. xiii–xx, at pp. xvi–xix. For a discussion of 'Index A' in Scotland, see Alice Taylor, 'Auditing and Enrolment in Thirteenth-Century Scotland', in *The Growth of Royal Government in the Reign of Henry III*, ed. David Crook and Louise Wilkinson (Woodbridge, 2015), pp. 85–103, at pp. 96–7.

[31] *RRS*, ii, p. 58.

[32] For a much more extensive treatment, see Dauvit Broun, 'The Absence of Regnal Years from the Dating Clause of Charters of Kings of Scots, 1195–1222', *ANS*, vol. 25 (2003), pp. 47–63, at pp. 50–7, incorporated into and developed in Dauvit Broun, *Scottish Independence and the Idea of Britain from the Picts to Alexander III* (Edinburgh, 2007), pp. 191–206.

[33] Broun, 'Absence of Regnal Years', pp. 57–8.

has been put forward for why limited dating clauses were introduced in 1195, which has nothing to do with enrolment practices.[34] It will also be shown later that there is no clear evidence for the enrolment of royal charters until the reign of Alexander III and even this was a less routine and a more retrospective activity than it was in England.

What, then, can the inventories tell us about charter enrolment? It should first be acknowledged that the four inventories are not identical in scope, purpose, or content. The 1282 inventory was made on Alexander III's command (*ex precepto Regis*) and was preceded by an oral inquest into the whereabouts of the king's documentation (Simon Fraser confessed that he had taken certain papal bulls, once at the Edinburgh treasury, to Melrose Abbey to be archived; the fact that this was recorded may suggest that this was not expected behaviour).[35] The inventory itself is divided into four sections, each concerned with the king's rights in relation to other powers: the first section deals with relations with the papacy; the second with Anglo-Scottish relations; the third with the kings of Norway; the fourth with the magnates of his kingdom. The 1282 inventory thus tells us very little about governmental administration per se but a great deal about how the king's clerks made a statement about the king's historical legal position vis-à-vis other rulers and lords.[36]

In contrast, the three Edwardian inquests (of 1291, 1292, and 1296) had simpler aims: to list what they could.[37] This was not very much in the case of 1296, more in 1291, and really quite a lot in the 1292 inventory. All list once-existing rolls, a host of bags, chests, and boxes containing single-sheet documents, as well as precious jewels and items, relics, and cloths that were also kept in the treasury, including the staff used to invest Alexander II in the county of Northumberland in 1215.[38] It is thus from the inventories of the 1290s that we learn most about the depth of the Edinburgh treasury but it is important that our own assumptions do not ascribe greater importance to the presence of rolls over single sheet, and documentary evidence more generally over precious and symbolic items. All were part of a single archive: the Edinburgh treasury.

The four inventories of the contents of the royal treasury in Edinburgh castle in fact reveal little that was similar to the rolls of letters patent and letters close found in England. This is despite the adoption of letters patent as an explicit category of document under Alexander II; indeed, each of the inventories of 1282, 1291, and 1292 all list *individual*—not enrolled—letters patents among their contents.[39] The inventories do itemize rolls of charters but these rolls are very different from the more systematic charter rolls which survive (and may have begun) in England from the first regnal year of King John (27 May 1199–17 May 1200). Some of the Scottish charter rolls are clearly the result of individual endeavour, not the more routine process of record. The 1291 inventory tells us of the existence of 'one roll

---

[34] Broun, *Scottish Independence*, pp. 193–4, 197–201, 203–6.
[35] *APS*, i, pp. 107–10, at p. 107.   [36] A point developed below, pp. 434–5.
[37] *APS*, i, pp. 111–18.   [38] *APS*, i, p. 112.
[39] *APS*, i, pp. 115–17, 118; *ER*, i, p. 20. The first reference to a letter patent is, as far as I can tell, on 25 January 1241 in *Coupar Angus Chrs*, i, no. 45 [AII/273].

of titles of all charters which by William of Dumfries ordered to be made'.[40] This appears to have been a calendar of certain charters made by William, who was described as Alexander III's clerk of the rolls in 1282 and 'custodian of the rolls of the kingdom of Scotland' in 1291; it is thus possible that he compiled this retrospective calendar as part of his office.[41] In 1292, we find a record of 'two rolls of memoranda, one great, one small' made by the chancellor, Thomas of Chartres, 'after the death of [Alexander III], king of Scots'.[42] This sort of record keeping was clearly made after, sometimes long after, the issue of the documents themselves. The rolls of charters and memoranda made by William and Thomas were not products of routine central government but lists compiled later to bring together disparate documents.[43]

Where we do have evidence of rolls containing copies of royal charters that do not, at first glance, appear to have been compiled *post factum*, these are mixed up with other types of document. In 1292, we find a record of 'one great roll of 62 membranes, written on both sides, containing diverse charters and diverse confirmation of different kings of Scotland'.[44] But this 'great roll' also contained 'charters and recognitions', 'pleas', 'inquests', 'perambulations', 'agreements', and 'concords', as well as other sorts of documents. Had this roll survived, one might imagine that these documents were grouped together with the purpose of demonstrating the ins and outs of particular gifts, disputes, and resulting settlements; on the other hand, it might have been a miscellaneous collection with no purpose other than to record disparate material in the same place. What it is not, in any case, is a roll that records the routine output of the majority of royal charters produced by the king's chapel.

Only by the reign of Alexander III do we have anything even remotely resembling the charter rolls of King John. It seems that a degree of charter enrolment had begun by midway through the minority of Alexander III: in 1253, Alexander's charter confirming the land of Smeaton to Dunfermline Abbey was copied into 'the roll of the lord king in his chapel' after a case of mortancestry had been brought by Emma, daughter of Gilbert, against the abbey.[45] The 1292 inventory records

[40] *APS*, i, p. 112.

[41] For the 1282 reference, see *APS*, i, p. 107; for the reference to William as 'custodian of the rolls', see *APS*, i, pp. 110–11.

[42] *APS*, i, p. 115.

[43] See also the roll of twelve membranes of 'recognitions and ancient charters of the time of King William and King Alexander', which included a list of 'those to whom the said kings once gave their peace and of those who stood with MacWilliam'. Both William and Alexander faced MacWilliam threats from the late 1170s to 1230; this roll too must have been a *post factum* roll, drawn up from a number of different sources of extremely varying date: *APS*, i, p. 114. For the most recent narrative of the MacWilliam claim, see Oram, *Domination and Lordship*, pp. 140–5, 170–1, 175–6, 190–4; Alasdair Ross, 'Moray, Ulster and the MacWilliams', in *The World of the Galloglass: Kings, Warlords and Warriors in Ireland and Scotland 1200–1600*, ed. Séan Duffy (Dublin, 2007); for the reconceptualization of the MacWilliam claim in the later twelfth century, see Dauvit Broun, 'Contemporary Perspectives on Alexander II's Succession: the Evidence of King-Lists', in *The Reign of Alexander II, 1214–49*, ed. Richard Oram (Leiden, 2005), pp. 79–98.

[44] *APS*, i, p. 114.

[45] *Dunf. Reg.*, no. 83; see also *Arbroath Liber*, i, no. 294; for mortancestry, see Chapter 5, pp. 308–9.

the presence of 'one roll of nine pieces, written on both sides, containing charters and confirmations of Alexander [III], last king of Scotland, of different years of his kingship'.[46] On the basis of the size of this single roll in the inventory—containing only nine 'pieces'—the scale of enrolment seems to have been small fry in comparison with John's charter rolls, organized as they were as separate rolls dated by regnal year: the first, in three parts, containing a total of sixty-eight membranes; the second, for 2 John, containing thirty-five membranes; the third, for 5 John, containing twenty-six.[47] The earlier rolls of John's reign have more membranes than the later ones because beneficiaries would have rushed to have their charters confirmed at the beginning of the reign, creating a far larger output of written documentation in the first few years than in the succeeding years.[48] We should not exaggerate the systematized production of a vast quantity of enrolled royal charters under John: the relationship between the issue of a charter and its entry on the roll is yet to be studied.[49] Even a summary survey of the structure and hands of John's charter rolls shows that charters were not copied into the roll in the order in which they were issued; enrolment appears to have been a more ad hoc process than we might imagine.[50] But there is still a vast difference in the amount of systematic enrolment in the English chancery, in which a separate roll was begun each regnal year, to the one small mention we have of charter enrolment under Alexander III. This was not organized by regnal year as the charter rolls in England were, either because of selectivity or because the Scottish king's chapel did not generate the same level of material. On the evidence of the inventories, therefore, it seems that the introduction of regnal years in 1222 in royal charter diplomatic was not caused by the enrolment of royal charters, which is not attested until the early 1250s. This should not be surprising: full dating clauses were introduced to the diplomatic of Richard I's charters in 1189 in England but clear evidence of charter enrolment does not appear until 1199.[51]

The inventories also list many single-sheet items that were not enrolled. These include charters issued by the kings of Scots, letters from burgh communities, and

---

[46] *APS*, i, p. 114. We know that other rolls were written on both sides, for example, Haddington's source for 1263–66; Edinburgh, NRS, E38/1, fo. 8v; *ER*, i, pp. 23–4, and Chapter 6, pp. 351–3.

[47] *Rotuli Chartarum in Turri Londinensi Asservati Anno ab 1199–1216*, ed. T. D. Hardy (London, 1837); 1 John is preserved in three parts: TNA, C 53/1, 53/2, 53/3; 2 John is TNA, C 53/4; 5 John is C 53/5. The charter rolls for 3 and 4 John do not survive.

[48] There are four membranes in the charter roll for 15 John; 11 for 16 John; 10 for 17 John, 1 for 18 John (John died on 19 October 1216 and his regnal year began in 1216 on 19 May).

[49] Noted in Vincent, 'Bureaucracy and Enrolment', p. 38.

[50] See, for example, the charter roll for 9 John (1207–08; TNA, C 53/8), contains a total of eight membranes with nothing written on the dorse. In 1207, John's regnal year began on 31 May. Membrane 3 contains eight charters and three clear changes of hands (although this preliminary conclusion is, of course, open to the onslaught of a full palaeographical study). Membrane 6 contains nine charters and at least six different hands of varying dates: (from the bottom of the membrane) 28 August, 19 October, 8 August, 25 October, 5 October, 27 August, 28 September, 16 June, 17 September. This demonstrates that, for example, the charters which follow 19 October, including some issued in June, could not have been entered before October.

[51] For the introduction of dating clauses in Richard I's charters, see Pierre Chaplais, *English Royal Documents: King John–King Henry VI, 1199–1461* (Oxford, 1971), p. 14; Broun, *Scottish Independence*, pp. 191–3.

aristocratic letters and charters. Most of these documents touched the king's own interests, as is most obviously evidenced by the layout and structure of the 1282 inventory. As stated above, the 1282 inventory is explicitly divided into four main sections: one concerned with papal relations, the second with Anglo-Scottish ones, the third with the king of Norway, the last recording individual charters handed over to the kings of Scots which were probably a combination of royal and non-royal charters. Documents such as the Quitclaim of Canterbury of 1189, the 1237 treaty of York, the correspondence between the king of Scots, Louis of France, and the barons of the counties of Northumberland, Cumberland, and Westmorland in the war of 1215–17 were recorded in this section.[52] But most of the letters recorded were not documents written by the king's chapel but, instead, the letters of others, whose content touched on matters pertaining to the rights of and agreements made by the king of Scots in relation to other parties, predominantly parties outside the kingdom.

We can also see this focus on single items in the other three inventories that aim for more comprehensive coverage of the treasury's content. In 1292, it was recorded that the Edinburgh treasury contained nineteen letters patent of the provosts and burgesses of nineteen Scottish burghs, kept between two boards, which temporarily had quitclaimed the king [Alexander III] and queen of the money they owed them.[53] Other single letters concerned land and offices once belonging to other individuals, now returned to the king: for example, a letter of Margaret de Ferrers, countess of Derby, resigned the office of constable into the hands of Alexander III.[54] There are also references to aristocratic deeds that seem at first to have nothing to do with the king himself but actually reveal themselves to be part of documentary chains concerned with land which eventually ended up in the king's hands. Thus, a deed of William de Vieuxpont is mentioned in the 1292 inventory in which William de Vieuxpont granted *Shollesclyve* to his kinsman, William of Horndean, and his heirs.[55] But William of Horndean then gave (*dedit*) the lands of *Shollesclyve* to Alexander III and this deed, surviving in two copies, was also listed as kept 'in a small box' in the king's treasury. This suggests that William de Vieuxpont's original gift to William of Horndean was only in the treasury because the land was now the king's and all documentation concerning *Shollesclyve* had been handed over when William of Horndean gave the king the land. The overwhelming impression given by many of the documents listed in the inventories is thus that they are to do with the king's own business. The treasury—or at least the treasury as viewed by the inventory-takers— looks as much a repository for the king's personal rights and privileges as it does a record of direct and routine archiving of all outputs of the king's chapel. Indeed, we see a clear reference to this process in a charter of Alexander III,

---

[52] *APS*, i, pp. 108–9.

[53] *APS*, i, pp. 115–16; see further, a box containing personal debts of the king and queen to various unnamed merchants: *APS*, i, p. 116.

[54] *APS*, i, p. 115. William of Horndean's only dated charter is from 1256, for which see *Melrose Liber*, i, no. 333; PoMS, H3/281/1, online at <http://db.poms.ac.uk/record/source/5361>.

[55] *APS*, i, p. 115.

probably drawn up in 1271, when Nicholas Corbet, a knight, returned and resigned the estate of Manor in Peebleshire 'by his letters patent, sealed with his seal and the seals of many of our other barons', 'which we caused to be enrolled (*inrotularia*) in our chapel (*capella*) on the Sunday in the morning of St Mark the Evangelist, in the year of grace 1271, at Kinclevin'.[56] Here, it was Nicholas's quitclaim that was enrolled, not Alexander's charter. Nicholas's letters patent were enrolled to protect the king and then William against any future challenge to the royal gift.

Moving on finally to judicial records. We know that there was a roll in the king's chapel onto which perambulations and recognitions were recorded. The earliest explicit reference to this is in a document of 1219, which stated the bounds between Kinblethmont, 'Achinglas', and Arbroath.[57] This document is found within a section of the *Registrum Vetus* of Arbroath Abbey, compiled in the early fourteenth century, possibly at the behest of Bernard, abbot of Arbroath and chancellor of Scotland.[58] The scribe of this section of the *Registrum* stated that the 1219 perambulation was 'found written in this way in the rolls of the lord king', a statement also found at the bottom of a 1228 perambulation copied into the *Registrum* just after the perambulation of 1219.[59] Documents recording the results of perambulation were, therefore, being entered into the king's roll, although this does not necessarily prove that such rolls were in existence by 1219, only that documents of this date were later entered on a roll. Dauvit Broun has recently shown that Mael Brigte, the king's *brithem* in the late twelfth century, kept records of witnesses and perambulators from 1198 at the latest; however, it is not clear that these records were ones made for and kept in the king's treasury.[60]

By the 1250s, however, the results of perambulation and inquests were being recorded on the same sort of roll. By 1251, it was clear that the rolls of recognition in the king's chapel were the source of consultation for inquisitive individuals. In 1251, Robert, abbot of Dunfermline and royal chancellor, consulted the 'roll of the king' and found a series of disputes relating to the land of Tarves and involving Arbroath Abbey, the countess of Buchan, and Philip of Feodarg.[61] Robert, as chancellor, must have received a request from the monks of Arbroath to look up the documentation surrounding the dispute over Tarves, which he did diligently, wrote down his findings, and sent them to Arbroath, whose monks must have then kept the document until it was transcribed into their *Registrum Vetus* in a section separate from the main structure of the cartulary.[62] The results of an inquest heard

---

[56] *RRS*, iv, 1, no. 166.   [57] *Arbroath Liber*, i, no. 228.

[58] Edinburgh, NLS, MS Adv. 34.4.2, fo. 6v. The 1292 inventory also includes a reference to a 'calendar of charters of Kings of Scots, which Thomas, monk of Dunfermline, has to transcribe them'; *APS*, i, p. 116. It is unclear whether Thomas had the charters themselves (and the chapel had kept an inventory of the ones which were missing), or the calendar.

[59] *Arbroath Liber*, i, nos. 228–229.

[60] Dauvit Broun, 'The King's *brithem* (Gaelic for "Judge") and the Recording of Dispute-Resolutions', PoMS Feature of the Month, no. 11 (April 2010), online at <http://www.poms.ac.uk/feature/april10.html>.

[61] *Arbroath Liber*, i, no. 227; discussed in Chapter 5, p. 314.

[62] NLS, MS Adv. 34.4.2, fo. 6r–v.

in 1256 into whether Dunfermline Abbey did indeed owe the sheriff of Perth four marks for the failure of some of the abbey's tenants to turn up at the sheriffdom court was recorded 'in the chapel of the lord king, that is, in the roll of recognition'.[63] Whether the results of perambulations, inquests, and recognition were by this point recorded as a matter of routine or on the request of participants is hard to know. In some earlier cases, it is possible that a person had requested enrolment: in 1231, David Durward had a recognition made over the land lying between his own lands of Dunduff and the contiguous lands of Dunfermline; his quitclaim ended by stating that he had caused the document to be 'noted down' in the king's chapel for greater security: did this mean that he had caused it to be recorded on the roll of recognition?[64]

Thus, some sort of recording of the results of perambulations, recognitions, and inquests had developed by 1250. By 1281, it is clear that the justiciar kept records of his activity, which may well have been the records of his ayre. A case between Arbroath Abbey on the one side and Philip of Findun and Thomas, son of the thane of Cowie, on the other was heard in the presence of Alexander Comyn, earl of Buchan, and then recorded 'in the rolls of the justiciar of Kincardine'.[65] As Kincardine was a sheriffdom, it is possible that the 'rolls of the justiciar of Kincardine' referred to the records of the justiciar's ayre when he passed through Kincardine. It might be thought that the explicit reference to Kincardine might suggest that the roll was kept in the sheriffdom. However, the reference to the roll occurs in the section of the *Registrum Vetus* in which other documents found in the king's chapel were transcribed. This suggests that the justiciar's roll of Kincardine was also kept in the king's chapel and that the proceedings of his ayres were enrolled, via sheriffdom, in the king's chapel by the 1280s.

The justiciar's ayre must have produced a number of records in order for it to function properly. The justiciar held his pleas irregularly in individual sheriffdoms: the profits of justice were later collected by the sheriff and were proffered at the audit session in increments. This must have meant that the justiciar would have left behind a list of amercements for the sheriff to which the sheriff could refer over a long period of time. The 1292 inventory records that copies of these amercement lists were also kept in the king's chapel. There, we learn that there existed in the Edinburgh treasury 'certain [rolls] concerning the profits (*de lucris*) of the justiciar and other perquisites'.[66] These rolls may have been the original amercement lists, returned by the sheriff to the king's chapel once all profits had been collected; equally, they may have been separate copies of these lists, designed to be referred to when the sheriff returned the justiciar's profits at the audit to create accountability.

[63] *Dunf. Reg.*, no. 85; Edinburgh, NLS, MS Adv. 34.1.3A, fo. 52vb.

[64] *Dunf. Reg.*, no. 196.　　[65] *Arbroath Liber*, i, no. 230.

[66] *APS*, i, p. 114. It is also of note that the 1264 account of David of Lochore, sheriff of Fife, mentioned a case heard by the justiciar of Scotia, referring to the value of the chattels of a beheaded criminal (which the sheriff should not be burdened with). If this information had been left by the justiciar in the sheriffdom, it is clear that the lists of amercements would have been more detailed than the total profits, listed by sheriffdom, returned by the justiciar to the audit: *ER*, i, p. 4.

We cannot know, but the presence of these rolls of the justiciar's *lucra* in the 1292 inventory is utterly unsurprising, given what we know about the structure of the ayre and how its profits were returned via the sheriff. These rolls must therefore have been introduced no earlier than the earliest regional ayres (set up by 1244) and obviously have a final *terminus ante quem* of 1292, when they were recorded in the inventory. It is hard, however, to imagine that the audit could have functioned without them once the ayre had been introduced; if so, then the second half of the reign of Alexander II seems the most likely time when rolls of amercements started to be kept in the king's chapel, which roughly mirrors the introduction of central account rolls, although not the charter rolls.

Many documents, however, were not enrolled. The main reason why we know about the use of inquests at all is because the original brieve and returned inquest were stored in the king's archives as single sheets.[67] It may be that, when a case was brought into another jursidiction after an inquest had been held, the king's archives no longer stored the documentation: Paisley Abbey kept the results of the inquest procured in 1271 (or a copy of it) by the heirs of Dubgall, son of Alwin, which had brought Paisley into court about some of the lands of Kilpatrick church some two years later.[68] Other inquests were enrolled, such as that obtained by Dunfermline in 1256, which may suggest that, although inquest returns could be copied in the king's chapel, there was no systematic enrolment of this sort of document if the originals were already stored on site. For example, Alexander III sent Robert Wishart, bishop of Glasgow, a verbatim copy of an inquest made in 1273 at Roxburgh, concerning a dispute between Walter Murray and Soutra Hospital.[69] Whether the king's chapel had consulted the rolls or had kept the original inquest return in their archives cannot be known; the point is that they had the return available to transcribe directly into a new charter of Alexander III, made on the special request of the bishop. It is possible that Paisley Abbey as well then requested the inquest return from the king's archives in a similar way to Robert Wishart (or even that Bishop Robert did this for them) during their wrangling with the three couples over some of Kilpatrick's lands between 1270 and 1273.

The process of enrolment and archiving of judicial records thus looks superficially similar to that of thirteenth-century England. As in England, justiciars (in England, justices) drew up lists of amercements that the sheriff would collect following a justiciar's/justice's ayre (English: eyre) in their sheriffdom (English: county).[70] As in England, copies of these lists of amercements were kept in the king's archive. As in England, there appear to have developed in Scotland records of the pleas conducted by the justiciar while on ayre, which were organized according to sheriffdom, although the only attested evidence we have for Scotland comes

---

[67] For these single-sheet documents, see above, Chapter 5, pp. 318–19, 323–34.

[68] *Paisley Reg.*, pp. 191–2.   [69] *RRS*, iv, no. 85.

[70] What follows over the next four paragraphs is, for the English side of things, fundamentally taken from *The 1235 Surrey Eyre*, ed. C. A. F. Meekings, vol.1: *Introduction and Bibliographia*, Surrey Record Society 31 (Guildford, 1979); David Crook, *Records of the General Eyre*, Public Record Office Handbooks 20 (London, 1982), pp. 1–45.

from a single reference concerning the whereabouts of a document dating from 1281. It may also be that, as in England, these justiciar plea rolls were not necessarily automatically archived in the treasury. In England, this constituted a problem and Henry III and then Edward I made efforts to ensure that the king's archives did, from the late 1250s onwards, contain at least one copy of the plea rolls from the recent eyres. In 1257, for example, Henry III commanded the barons of the Exchequer to make enquiry into the location of the rolls of the justices and return them to the treasury. Edward I went further and during his reign copies of the plea rolls, known as the 'rex' rolls, were stored in the treasury.[71] Nothing similar seems to have occurred in Scotland; this may explain why explicit references to any plea rolls of the justiciar on ayre are absent from the inventories but rolls of 'profits' returned by the justicar were noted.

However, there were also significant differences between the enrolment of judicial records in thirteenth-century England and Scotland. First, in England, the office of coroner was introduced in 1194 into counties in order to keep record of all crown pleas that occurred between eyres.[72] These records, often in roll form, were then meant to be presented to the justices while on eyre. Sheriffs also kept records of crown pleas in order to check the actions of their coroners.[73] A proportion of these shrieval and coroner's rolls were kept in the treasury. There is no evidence that such a system was used in thirteenth-century Scotland, although 'crowners' do first appear in the early fourteenth century.[74] Although Scottish justiciars went on ayre more frequently than in England, the pleas they heard were not so numerous that this type of mass record producing was required, nor did the time lag between the ayres require the production of a lot of interim material to be put before the justiciars, as it did in England. Equally, the amount of judicial work borne by sheriffs courts in Scotland, as well as by aristocratic courts, meant that again a large proportion of business would not have come in front of the justiciar. Second, there is no evidence that feet of fines (records of agreements made during the eyre in England) were ever kept in Scotland; they were in Tynedale, however, which was a liberty in England held by the Scottish king. Indeed, the 1292 inventory contains explicit reference to the 'feet of fines raised by the justice in eyre in Tynedale' but no other similar reference for the kingdom of Scots itself.[75] There is

[71] Crook, *Records*, pp. 12–13, 26–8.

[72] R. F. Hunnisett, *The Medieval Coroner* (Cambridge, 1961), pp. 1–8, 97–117.

[73] Crook, *Records*, p. 37.

[74] R. A. Houston, *The Coroners of Northern Britain, c.1300–1700* (Basingstoke, 2014), pp. 38–68, particularly pp. 42–4. A reference to a 'coroner' is printed among Thomson's *Assise Regis Willelmi*, in *APS*, volume 1 (*ARW*, *c*.30; *APS*, i, pp. 381–2). However, this chapter has nothing to do with William, and is first attested as *CD*, *c*.8. Coroners are mentioned in Edward I's 1305 Ordinance on the governance of Scotland, where we learn that their performance was to be the subject of an inquest: *Anglo-Scottish Relations, 1174–1328: Some Selected Documents*, ed. and trans. E. L. G. Stones (Oxford, 1965; repr. with corrections, 1970), pp. 246–9, no. 33. The 'Scottish King's Household', another problematic text, also informs us that justices were responsible for appointing coroners, see, 'Scottish King's Household', ed. Bateson, p. 37.

[75] *APS*, i, p. 114; for the 1279–81 eyre, see M. L. Holford and Keith J. Stringer, *Border Liberties and Loyalties: North-East England, c. 1200–c. 1400* (Edinburgh, 2010), pp. 235–6, 240, 243, note 39, 281–7.

no evidence that the justiciar's ayre in Scotland made final concords a separate part of its business, as was the case in England.

Third, it is of note that the retourable brieves sent by the king's chapel to initiate inquests were very different from the returnable writs sent by the king's chancery in England to initiate pleas before the sheriff. This affected the type of documentation produced and how it was centrally archived. The Scottish retourable brieve was sent directly to the sheriff, commanding him to hold an inquest and return its results in written form to the king, together with the original brieve. Returnable writs in England were also sent to the sheriff and were eventually returned to the king. But that is where the similarity ends. In England, a returnable writ set out the process to follow *before* a particular plea could be initiated; it was a key part of the long process of litigation. A returnable writ (often called an 'original writ') was procured by a plaintiff who wished to initiate a plea.[76] The writ then commanded the sheriff to summon sureties, secure the disputed land or chattels, arrange for a viewing of that land or chattels, and write the names of those who viewed the item under dispute on the back of the writ. Those men would then be summoned to appear before the king's justices, who would hear their testimony and would make a judgment accordingly. The writ itself would be brought to the hearing, hence why it was called 'returnable'. Those writs would then be bound together with a thong and, if all went well, the bundle (called a 'writ file') would be sent to the Exchequer after the eyre was complete in the sheriffdom, where it would be kept by the treasury.

It should be obvious that none of this occurred in Scotland. Retourable brieves initiated a much less complicated process and appear to have been kept as single sheets in the king's treasury; to the extent that their results were sometimes enrolled, the rolls appear to have contained recognitions and perambulations as well as inquests.[77] What the surviving English writ files represent, by contrast, is a significant layer of formal procedure that went on before cases even came before the justices; retourable brieves, by contrast, show process but one that occurred in a single stage (the sheriff summoned the inquest, the inquest was heard, the results returned), rather than the two stages which occurred in England. This is despite clear familiarity with the basics of the English justice system, as can be seen from the 1279–81 eyre roll in Tynedale.[78] It was possible to adopt English methods in Tynedale; that the same was not adopted in the kingdom of the Scots writ large is striking, indicative of self-conscious separation between the two legal systems.

In short, therefore, it is possible to know quite a lot about central recordkeeping in thirteenth-century Scotland. Financial rolls were not records of the actions of government itself but were later consolidations of that process. The account rolls

---

[76] *Roll and Writ File of the Berkshire Eyre of 1248*, ed. Michael T. Clanchy, Selden Society 90 (London, 1973), pp. lx–lxxxix.

[77] For more on Scottish retourable brieves, see Chapter 5, pp. 298–301, 318–19, 323–34.

[78] Holford and Stringer, *Border Liberties*, pp. 231–45, 281–7. This does not mean that Tynedale was a closed world; indeed, in Northumbrian society, it could be understood as part of the *regnum Scotie*, points stressed at pp. 244–5, 267, 287.

were central records and were made for the purpose of having central records, but they were not produced at the audit session itself, which appears to have relied on ad hoc documentation produced according to where the particular audit was held and who attended it. Although the sessions in 1288–90 produced more coherent records, the peripatetic and regionally based nature of Scottish accounting meant that this delayed production of central records was probably the only way a single central record could be created. Charter enrolment also appears to have been done in a *post factum* fashion until the reign of Alexander III: it is only during his minority reign that the inventories give us a sense that his outgoing charters were copied down on a roll to allow, presumably, another level of security against the production of forged royal charters. The enrolment of perambulations and recognitions seems to have had the longest history, going back to the 1220s, and was certainly around by the minority of Alexander III. However, in its early history it seems to have been an option, rather than a routine requirement—a way to obtain an added degree of security to the perambulation by having its written record kept by the king. By 1251 at the latest, the rolls were being consulted by major monastic institutions which wanted to recover written evidence of earlier disputes and decisions. The inventories themselves do not give a sense that judicial records were enrolled with any great precision: those rolls which did once contain agreements, settlements, perambulations, and recognitions were not divided by type; all these sorts of documents were lumped together or, at least, that was how the rolls were perceived by the inventory-takers.[79]

We must distinguish between four very different types of recordkeeping that developed in the thirteenth century. The first—that of financial rolls—appears to have developed before 1242: here, miscellaneous accounts from various accounting years were brought together to form centrally kept records that covered more than one financial year. This was a secondary process and as such gives us a sense of the importance of creating a central record even if the process of compilation happened a number of years after the original audit. Second, records of perambulation, inquest, and recognition seem to have been enrolled relatively consistently, perhaps as early as the late 1210s/early 1220s but certainly by the death of Alexander II, probably because these types of records were the ones which third parties would potentially wish to consult most frequently. The emergence of the justiciar ayre, coupled with the significant connection of the ayre with the local sheriff, would also generate its own documentation that the king's chapel would have wanted to keep. Thus, having some sort of coherent record to consult was probably deemed an important requirement, even if the form of these records was different from the plea and coroners' rolls of the English judicial system. Indeed, that these rolls probably emerged sometime between the late 1210s and 1240s makes sense, given the importance of that period for judicial development in general.[80] Third, the enrolment of outgoing letters does not seem to have occurred in any sort of systematic way until the reign of Alexander III and even then was relatively small scale. Fourth, the king's 'treasury' at Edinburgh castle also served as the king's personal repository. Charters

---

[79] *APS*, i, p. 114.
[80] See Chapter 5, pp. 321–3.

which cancelled debts, or which were quitclaims by members of his kingdom, were stored in what appears to be their original form in the treasury.

All these types of central recordkeeping in Scotland are products of royal government in roughly the middle two quarters of the thirteenth century, which is what might be expected. This is most true of the central account rolls, which were created *post factum* because the audit process itself was peripatetic and produced a lot of different records which needed to be brought together. The thirteenth century did see the development of recordkeeping by the king's chapel but it is important not to see this process as a mirror image (on a smaller scale) of developments in England, where processes of enrolment were indicative of its own government, as Scotland's were of its own.

A SNAPSHOT OF GOVERNMENT, 1263–66

The second part of this chapter examines who held shrieval office during the reign of Alexander III. This is an important topic to address, not least because most of this book has been concerned with the structures of institutional power rather than the people who exercised it. Structures and administrative positions cannot exist in a vacuum: people have to be given their roles (normally for some sort of compensation) and fulfil their responsibilities in order for official power and authority to have any meaning. This section concentrates on the sheriff not only because it is the only office for which usable data survives but also because it is a useful office against which to test the argument running through the last three chapters of this book: that there was no strong institutional separation between local and central government in thirteenth-century Scotland.

Understanding the personality of office holding is, in general, extremely difficult. We have no surviving official lists of personnel for the whole of our period. Most of our evidence for the identity of office holders comes from references in charters and other documentation (royal, non-royal, lay, and ecclesiastical) the dating of which is either not secure or where date-limits are too wide apart for us to say with confidence that a person exercised the office of, for example, sheriff of Perth between two firm dates.[81] Moreover, sheriffs sometimes attested with their official titles and sometimes they did not: this makes identifying who held office and when they did so even more difficult. The only exception in the period before Alexander III's death in 1286 is Haddington's transcript of the 1263–66 account roll. This source, as shown in Chapter 6, is not unproblematic: Haddington abridged his source, sometimes missing out the name of a particular official, and, on a few occasions, made mistakes in the names of those officials he transcribed. The mistakes in nomenclature can, happily, be corrected from other sources.[82] The account roll itself does not give us a full list of all those exercising office

---

[81] Royal and non-royal charters were the main source of the sheriffs listed in G. W. S. Barrow and Norman H. Reid ed., *The Sheriffs of Scotland: An Interim List to c.1306* (St Andrews, 2002).

[82] Haddington's mistakes are detailed below, notes 92–3, 96.

within the kingdom: it does not mention the names of any provosts of burghs nor does it mention many household officials, such as marischal, constable, and the clerks of the liverance, provender and wardrobe, although it does provide interesting information on the chancellor, chamberlain, and justiciars, some of whom were discussed in Chapter 4.[83] Despite these problems, it is still the most complete source we have of the identity of those who held the office of sheriff in the kingdom of the Scots and, as such, it is through its lens of 1263–66 that we will look at the personnel of some of Scottish local government in the reign of Alexander III.[84]

Understanding who exercised official power in the kingdom of the Scots allows us tentatively to identify patterns in the 'types' of people who more commonly occupied the office of sheriff. This is not to say that office-holding was completely predictable, that we could, if given the backgrounds and landholdings of a group of people, identify who among them was a sheriff. But it is important to ask general questions about what kind of people exercised official power because there may be identifiable patterns that can test or support the hypotheses of this book. For example, putting aside the problems in the survival of documentation for a moment, if most sheriffs in the kingdom in 1263–66 are found *not* to have witnessed royal charters, and appear in documentation *only* in their locality, then that would suggest that Scottish sheriffs were, by the reign of Alexander III, local men, connected to the area in which they exercised 'official' power. If this were the case, this in turn would cause us to question some of the conclusions of earlier parts of this book: if sheriffs were 'local' men during the reign of Alexander III, then the dependence of 'central' government on the locality, as outlined in Chapters 4–6, becomes a stranger phenomenon, which would need to be problematized, and explained. If sheriffs were so key to the workings of central government, then why was that office exercised by men who appear to have no ties at all to the king and his itineration? However, this section does not, in fact, show that sheriffs were men of only local importance, so this particular hypothetical question can be left to one side. But raising it underlines the point of this section: identifying royal officials and sketching out their background allows us to probe the conclusions made about the form of royal government as outlined in the previous three chapters.

What follows is thus not a study of the royal court under Alexander III nor will it attempt to make the so-called factionalism of the mid-thirteenth century the main explanation for the identity of royal officials, although understanding which 'lesser' men were attached to 'greater' ones is, of course, important for any

---

[83] See Chapter 4, pp. 229 (note 174), 234–7, 254–6. The treatise known as the 'Scottish King's Household', perhaps written between 1292 and 1296 (and probably as much aspirational as descriptive), tells us that the king's household consisted of fifteen types of official: chancellor, chamberlain, clerk of the rolls, steward, constable, marshal, almoner, clerks of the liverance, provender, wardrobe, and kitchen, ushers, justices (justiciars), and sheriffs: 'Scottish King's Household', ed. Bateson, pp. 31–7.

[84] *ER*, i, pp. 1–34. It should be acknowledged again here that the research which follows has been made much easier by the existence of the *The People of Medieval Scotland 1093–1314 Database*, online at <http://db.poms.ac.uk/search/>.

picture of the composition of the royal court during this period.[85] A full study of the Scottish royal court and royal assemblies over the twelfth and thirteenth centuries is still lacking, although Keith Stringer has recently conducted an examination of the court and political community under Alexander II.[86] Tackling the whole subject here would be impossible for the subject is a book in its own right, and a much needed one.[87] How the composition of the court changed, and how witnessing patterns to royal charters changed, who gained power at particular times and why they did so, are all key to understanding how the king, his household, his writing office, and his familiars interacted not only with 'local' society but also how these relationships changed as governmental structure itself developed. What is attempted below is to identify the people who held office in 1263–66, where their lands were and the potential relationship between this and their office and how far any pre-existing familial relationship determined their own with the king and his court.[88] In so doing, I hope to build on Stringer's work, which showed that many sheriffs under Alexander II were prominent members of Alexander II's court.[89] How far can this conclusion be carried over into the reign of Alexander III?

The 1263–66 roll provides the names of twenty-nine sheriffs whose names and dates are given in Table 7.1.

Three earls exercised shrieval office: William, earl of Mar, Alexander Comyn, earl of Buchan, and Walter Stewart, earl of Menteith. This was not particularly unusual: John Comyn, earl of Buchan was also sheriff of Wigtown in 1288–90 after his father, Alexander Comyn, and Donnchad, earl of Fife (d.1289) was sheriff

---

[85] For preliminary comments, see Duncan, *Making of the Kingdom*, pp. 205–6, 208–9, 211–12, 587–9; Michael Brown, *The Wars of Scotland 1214–1371* (Edinburgh, 2004), pp. 32–3, 60–2; D. E. R. Watt, 'The Minority of Alexander III of Scotland', *TRHS*, 5th ser., vol. 21 (1971), pp. 1–23; Alan Young, 'Noble Families and Political Factions in the Reign of Alexander III', in *Scotland in the Reign of Alexander III, 1249–1286*, ed. N. H. Reid (Edinburgh, 1990), pp. 1–30; Alan Young, 'The Political Role of Walter Comyn, Earl of Menteith, during the Minority of Alexander III of Scotland', in *Essays on the Nobility of Medieval Scotland*, ed. Keith J. Stringer (Edinburgh, 1985), pp. 131–49; also Alan Young, *Robert Bruce's Rivals: The Comyns, 1212–1314* (East Linton, 1997), pp. 68–75, 78–80.

[86] Keith J. Stringer, 'The Scottish "Political Community" in the Reign of Alexander II (1214–49)', in *New Perspectives*, ed. Hammond, pp. 53–84; Duncan, *Making of the Kingdom*, particularly pp. 587–9. A recent study of the later medieval justiciar has also appeared, which makes similar conclusions about this later period: see Hector L. MacQueen, 'Tame Magnates? The Justiciars of Later Medieval Scotland', in *Kings, Lords and Men in Scotland and Britain, 1300–1625: Essays in honour of Jenny Wormald*, ed. Steve Boardman and Julian Goodare (Edinburgh, 2014), pp. 93–120.

[87] We will be in a far better place to understand the Scottish royal court during the central Middle Ages when the results of the three-year Leverhulme-funded project 'The Transformation of Gaelic Scotland' are known. This project is run by Professor Dauvit Broun, Dr Matthew Hammond, Dr Cornell Jackson, and Dr John Bradley at the University of Glasgow and King's College London.

[88] For preliminary comments on the same material, see Brown, *Wars of Scotland*, pp. 60–2.

[89] Stringer, 'Scottish "Political Community"', pp. 66–7. A point about how the Comyns and their supporters dominated office holding and how this formed an 'aristocratic governing community' has been made in Young, 'Noble Families and Political Factions', pp. 9–12, 14–16, although without using the 1263–66 account roll transcript.

Table 7.1. Named sheriffs in Haddington's transcript of the 1263–66 roll

Sheriff	Sheriffdom	Date of account
Gilbert de Hay†[90]	Perth	1263
David of Lochore	Fife	1264 [][91] 1266
Walter, earl of Menteith[92]	Ayr	
Robert Mowat[93]	Forfar	1264 [1263?] 1266
Andrew of Garioch	Aberdeen	1264 [][94]
Gregory de Melville[95]	Aberdeen	
Reginald Cheyne[96]	Kincardine	
Laurence Grant	Inverness	1263 [][97]
Alexander de Montfort	Elgin	1263 [][98]
Alexander Murray	Inverness	
William Wiseman	Forres	1264, 1266
Ralph of Strachan	Banff	
John of Kinross	Kinross	[], 1263
Aymer Maxwell[99]	Dumfries	
John Cameron	Perth	1266, 1264[100]
William Mowat	Cromarty	
Alexander Murray	Nairn	
John of Fenton	Forfar	

[90] Gilbert would appear to be dead by the time of the account, which was proffered for 'the arrears of his last account, made for the sheriffdom (*ballia*) of Perth, at Scone, on the Monday before Palm Sunday, in the year etc. 62' (*ER*, i, p. 1). The account itself may have been returned in 1263. Then, Gilbert's account was returned by his son, Nicholas, and Geoffrey the clerk, who are described as Gilbert's 'attorneys' (*ER*, i, p. 1). It might be that Gilbert's account was returned after 3 April 1263, for he was still alive on that date (PoMS, no. 1049; H 1/12/1, online at <http://db.poms.ac.uk/record/source/1049>), although the biography of Gilbert there suggests that he was dead by 19 March, which is not the case.

[91] David's second account as sheriff of Fife is undated at *ER*, i, pp. 31–2.

[92] *ER*, i, p. 5; Haddington transcribes 'Willelmi', which is an error for Walter Stewart, earl of Menteith, who assumed the title of earl in 1260. Presumably Haddington's source had just put 'W', and Haddington erroneously added the rest.

[93] Haddington made a lot of mistakes when rendering Robert's name: see *ER*, i, p. 6, when Haddington, transcribed 'E de Montealto', rather than R. A second time, Haddington supplies 'W de Monte Alto', which could mean William Mowat, who was sheriff of Cromarty (*ER*, i, p. 26). However, it is more probable that it was an 'R', as Robert Mowat was sheriff of Forfar in the 1260s, for which see *RRS*, iv, 1, no. 36 (1262). William Mowat, by contrast, is never called sheriff of Forfar, despite being lord of Fern in Angus and witnessing deeds concerning land in Angus in 1269×71 (NRS, GD45/16/3036; PoMS transaction factoid, no. 66405, online at <http://db.poms.ac.uk/record/factoid/66405/>; see also *Panmure Reg.*, ii, pp. 158–9). William was the nephew of Robert Mowat and it is probable that he inherited Robert's lands in Fern from his uncle; see below, note 153. It is possible that Haddington misread R. de Monte Alto for W. de Monte Alto because he had just transcribed the account of William Mowat, sheriff of Cromarty (*ER*, i, p. 26). Haddington finally copied the initial correctly at *ER*, i, p. 34, for Robert's 1266 account.

[94] The second account is undated: *ER*, i, p. 34.

[95] *ER*, i, p. 12: Gregory is described as *quondam* sheriff of Aberdeen, so perhaps this account was returned before Andrew of Garioch's dated account in 1264.

[96] Yet another mistake by Haddington, who wrote *Roberti le Chen* for *Reginaldi*, probably expanding 'R' incorrectly, strongly suggesting that his source only contained initials: NRS, E38/1, fo. 4v (*ER*, i, p. 12, has *de* Chen, not *le* Chen, as in the manuscript). Reginald Cheyne appears again as sheriff of Kincardine, at *ER*, i, p. 20, and also served as farmer of the thanage of Formartine.

[97] *ER*, i, pp. 13, 19.   [98] *ER*, i, pp. 13–14, 33.

[99] *ER*, i, pp. 16–17, 22.   [100] *ER*, i, pp. 17–18, 26–7.

Sheriff	Sheriffdom	Date of account
Hugh of Abernethy	Roxburgh	
Thomas Randolph[101]	Roxburgh	
Hugh de Berkeley	Berwick	[] 1265[102]
Alexander Comyn, earl of Buchan	Wigtown	1266, 1265
John Lamberton	Stirling	1266, 1263, 1265[103]
R de Mowbray†[104]	Haddington	1263
	Edinburgh	
	Linlithgow	
William Comyn of Kilbride	Ayr	1265, 1266[105]
Alexander Sinton	Selkirk	1265
William, earl of Mar	Dumbarton	
Alexander Uviet	Lanark	after Nov 1264[106]
William Sinclair	Haddington	
	Linlithgow	1264
	Edinburgh	
Simon Fraser	Traquair	1263[107]

of Dumbarton in 1288 up to his murder on 10 September 1289.[108] But the remainder of the men were not of comital rank: almost all were described as *milites* ('knights').[109] This appears to have been a higher social rank in Scotland than in

[101] Haddington supplies *Thome Kauer* (*ER*, i, p. 22). *Kauer* appears to be a nickname (like Walter *Belloch*, earl of Menteith, meaning 'freckled'). There is no person in the PoMS database by the name Thomas 'Kauer', 'Kaver', 'Cauer', or 'Caver'. Thomas Randolph, later chamberlain of Scotland, appears as sheriff of Roxburgh in 1266 (*Kelso Liber*, i, no. 190), so it is probable that they are the same person.

[102] Hugh de Berkeley made two returns as sheriff of Berwick. One is undated, the other was returned in 1265 (*ER*, i, p. 27).

[103] *ER*, i, pp. 23, 24, 30.

[104] It is not possible to prove whether this 'R' was Robert or Roger: *ER*, i, pp. 24–6.

[105] *ER*, i, pp. 27, 34: William Comyn of Kilbride's 1266 account was returned at Edinburgh by his attorney, Fergus mac Cinaeda: *ER*, i, p. 34.

[106] Alexander Uviet's account referred to produce bought for the king's *colloquium* held at Edinburgh in November 1264: *ER*, i, p. 30.

[107] The printed text supplies the year 1265 but the original transcript states that the account was in fact returned in 1263 (*ER*, i, p. 32; cf. NRS E38/1, fo. 11r).

[108] James Stewart also served as sheriff of Ayr in 1288, taking over from Andrew Murray: *ER*, i, p. 37. The murder of Earl Donnchad is discussed in detail in Michael Brown, 'Aristocratic Politics and the Crisis of Scottish Kingship, 1286–1296', *SHR*, vol. 90, no. 229 (2011), pp. 1–26, at pp. 5–9.

[109] For Gilbert Hay and David of Lochore, see *Lindores Cart.*, no. 55, where they are all described as knights of William of Brechin; for Reginald Cheyne, see *Melrose Liber*, i, no. 327; for Robert Mowat, see *St Andrews Liber*, pp. 252–3; for Andrew of the Garioch, see *Lindores Cart.*, no. 116; for Gregory Melville, see *St Andrews Liber*, pp. 376–7; for Alexander Murray, see *St Andrews Liber*, pp. 109–10; for Ralph of Strachan, see *Dunf. Reg.*, no. 86; for John of Kinross, see *RRS*, iv, 1, no. 152; for John Cameron, see *Coupar Angus Chrs*, i, no. 50; for William Mowat, see *Moray Reg.*, no. 220; for John Fenton, see *Dryburgh Liber*, no. 288; for Hugh Abernethy, see *Lindores Cart.*, no. 140; for Thomas Randolph, see *Kelso Liber*, i, no. 190; for Hugh de Berkeley, see *Lindores Cart.*, no. 41; for John Lamberton, see Fraser, *Carlaverock*, ii, no. 7 (pp. 406–7); for William Comyn of Kilbride, see *Melrose Liber*, i, no. 224; for Alexander Sinton, see *Glasgow Reg.*, i, no. 216; for Alexander Uviet, see *Glasgow Reg.*, i, no. 150; for William Sinclair, see *Newbattle Reg.*, no. 50; for Simon Fraser, see *Melrose Liber*, i, no. 355. The exceptions are Laurence Grant, who is described as a *dominus* (*Moray Reg.*, no. 122); Aymer Maxwell, who was perhaps such a big cheese he never needed to be described as a *miles* (he does,

England and was often interchangeable with *baro* ('baron') in the former king-dom.[110] The holdings of knights in Scotland were, by the mid-thirteenth century, known as *baroniae* ('baronies').[111] That a Scottish *miles* was socially, rather than socio-economically, equivalent to an English baron is suggested by the fact that, in treatises and documents drawn up concerning matters that affected the kingdoms of England and Scotland, men who would have attested royal charters as *milites* are called *barones regni Scocie*, making them equivalent in rank to their English counterparts.[112]

Of these twenty-nine sheriffs listed in 1263–66, a further six exercised shrieval office elsewhere in the kingdom. We know this from their appearances as wit-nesses, jurors, court-holders, or sealers to charters and agreements of the thirteenth century. David of Lochore is attested in 1255 as a sheriff of Perth and was also sheriff of Fife in 1263–66.[113] Walter Stewart, earl of Menteith, served as sheriff of Dumbarton in 1271 as well as in Ayr, as in 1265–66.[114] Aymer Maxwell was, in addition to being sheriff of Dumfries, also sheriff of Roxburgh and sheriff of Peebles (often also called Traquair).[115] Thomas Randolph was sheriff of Berwick as well as sheriff of Roxburgh while Simon Fraser was sheriff of Perth as well as Traquair.[116] Alexander Sinton also served as sheriff of Fife, as well as holding the sheriffdom of Selkirk.[117] None of these individuals served as sheriff in faraway reaches of the kingdom: those with the furthest reach were Thomas Randolph, as sheriff of Roxburgh and Berwick, and Aymer Maxwell, sheriff of Dumfries, Peebles, and Roxburgh.

Moreover, these sheriffs also held offices other than shrieval ones. William Sinclair, sheriff of Edinburgh, Haddington, and Linlithgow, was also constable of the king's castle of Dumfries.[118] Other people held more significant offices:

---

however, appear as a *dominus*: see *Coupar Angus Chrs*, i, no. 52); William Wiseman, who barely appears on the surviving record, and Alexander de Montfort, who only appears as a sheriff; for Alexander, how-ever, see below, Note 148. All of this has been checked against the PoMS database.

[110] This also seems to relate to diplomatic correspondence in general: *RRS*, iv, 1, no. 22. Robert of Meiniers is called a *baro* in the 1266 Treaty of Perth: *RRS*, iv, 1, no. 61; *APS*, i, pp. 420–1; for changes to knighthood in thirteenth-century England, see Kathryn Faulkner, 'The Transformation of Knighthood in Early Thirteenth-Century England', *EHR*, vol. 111, no. 440 (1996), pp. 1–23.

[111] For single knight's feus being understood as 'baronies', see Alexander Grant, 'Franchises North of the Border: Baronies and Regalities in Medieval Scotland', in *Liberties and Identities in the Medieval British Isles*, ed. Michael Prestwich (Woodbridge, 2008), pp. 155–99, at pp. 190–1. *LS, c.* 15, was made in the presence of 'barons and thanes'; knights are not mentioned. Knights are equivalent to thanes in *SA, c.* 26, but here barons are not mentioned.

[112] *Anglo-Scottish Relations*, ed. Stones, pp. 60–9, at p. 62, no. 10; *RRS*, iv, 1, no. 22 (probably drawn up by the English chancery). The announcement of the betrothal of Alexander II to Joan, sister of Henry III, in 1220 also listed 'the earl of Buchan, Alan Durward, and our other barons, that is, Philip de Mowbray, Walter Olifard, Duncan of Carrick, Henry de Balliol, Thomas Durward, John of Maxwell, David Marischal, Walter Comyn, Ranulf Bunkle, and Hervey Marischal' (*Foedera*, I, i, 161).

[113] *Dunf. Reg.*, no. 85.

[114] *RRS*, iv, 1, no. 76.

[115] Raine, *North Durham*, App., no. 139 (sheriff of Roxburgh); *RRS*, iv, 1, no. 40 (sheriff of Peebles).

[116] *Melrose Liber*, i, no. 206; Raine, *North Durham*, App., no. 138; *Glasgow Reg.*, i, no. 216.

[117] *St Andrews Liber*, pp. 341–2.

[118] PoMS, no. 5033; H 3/326/6, online at <http://db.poms.ac.uk/record/source/5033/>; Factoid no. 56433.

Hugh de Berkeley, sheriff of Berwick, also served as justiciar of Lothian during the very same period of accounting in 1263–66.[119] In addition to his three (perhaps four) shrieval offices, Aymer Maxwell was justiciar of Galloway in 1264 and, indeed, returned the profits from an ayre in Galloway (although not an ayre conducted by him) while sheriff of Dumfries.[120] Robert Mowat, sheriff of Forfar in 1264, had been justiciar of Scotia in 1241–42.[121] And, of course, Alexander Comyn, earl of Buchan, served as sheriff of Wigtown but also was a long-standing justiciar of Scotia from 1258, and constable from 1275, until his death in 1289.[122] During this period, other sheriffs served as his attorneys when he was unable to fulfil the demands of his office: David of Lochore and John Cameron, sheriffs of Fife and Perth respectively in 1263–66, served in this capacity at a session of the justiciar's pleas at Perth in 1260, along with Freskin of Moray.[123] Four sheriffs also served as the king's chamberlain: Thomas Randolph (Roxburgh), William, earl of Mar (Dumbarton), Aymer Maxwell (Dumfries), and Reginald Cheyne (Kincardine).[124] In total, this means that twelve out of the total twenty-nine individuals who held shrieval office are also known to have held another royal office, ranging from constable of a royal castle to justiciar to king's chamberlain.

The careers of these twelve individuals, just over 41 per cent of the total, show how integrated the holding of shrieval office was with other governmental roles. Moreover, when one includes the evidence of the witness lists to royal charters, the relationship between the king's court and local administration by the sheriff becomes even closer. Witness lists to royal charters are not unproblematic sources: sometimes they have been curtailed or mistranscribed when later cartulary scribes copied their content.[125] Whether individuals were actually present when particular

[119] For Hugh's title as justiciar of Lothian, see *RRS*, iv, 1, nos. 26, 47–48, 51–53, 55, 60, 64, 68, 73–74, 88, covering the period 16 October 1258–20 March 1274. Hugh did not hold office for all this time, however, as there is a gap in his patterns of attestation between 16 October 1258 and 25 December 1263. Stephen Fleming held the office in the meantime (*ER*, i, pp. 9–10), and Hugh de Berkeley was back as justiciar of Lothian by Christmas 1263 (*RRS*, iv, 1, no. 47).

[120] Stephen Fleming, justiciar of Lothian, seems to have either given up the office or died sometime before Christmas 1263, when Hugh de Berkeley appears as justiciar of Lothian (see note 119). That the sheriff of Dumfries might also be justiciar of Galloway is confirmed by the 1288–90 roll, when William Sinclair was both sheriff of Dumfries as well as explicitly being justiciar of Galloway, whose ayre profits he also returned (*ER*, i, pp. 35–7); for comment, see Chapter 4, pp. 236–7.

[121] For Robert Mowat as justiciar of Scotia, see NLS, Advocates Charter A.4 [AII/282]; *Glasgow Reg.*, i, no. 179 [AII/281].

[122] Alexander first served as justiciar between 1253 and 1255: see *RRS*, iv, 1, nos. 18–20; he took up office again by 1258 and again appears with the title in royal charters in 1260, and continued to do so until 1285 (*RRS*, iv, 1, nos. 30–31, 41, 44, 54–56, 59, 62, 73, 84, 88, 91, 129, 154, 156, 162, 163–164, 167). For the Comyns in the reign of Alexander III, see Young, *Comyns*, pp. 66–89, at pp. 68–70 in particular.

[123] *St Andrews Liber*, pp. 346–7.

[124] For William, earl of Mar as chamberlain, see *RRS*, iv, 1, nos. 14–19, 43–44, 47–48, 54–55, 57–58, 60, 62; for Aymer Maxwell, see *RRS*, iv, 1, no. 28, 31; for Reginald Cheyne, see *RRS*, iv, 1, no. 69; for Thomas Randolph, see *RRS*, iv, 1, no. 87. For the other men who held the office of chamberlain under Alexander III, see Chapter 4, p. 246.

[125] See the points made about *iusticia/justiciarius* in Chapter 4, pp. 211, 213–15. For some of the scholarship on charter witness lists (and the problems inherent in using them), see David Bates, 'The Prosopographical Study of Anglo-Norman Royal Charters', in *Family Trees and the Roots of Politics: The*

charters were being authenticated or drafted is also questioned and there is evidence to show that, particularly for acts drafted for lay people, individuals could write to people asking them to attest their particular charter without ever expecting them to make the journey to authenticate it in person.[126] There is also the fact that witness lists to royal charters only reveal snapshots of the personnel actually surrounding the king. This is not just because we only have a fraction of the charters originally drawn up but also because charter witness lists, particularly to charters and brieves which did not require a large number of people to authenticate them, only record a proportion of the total number of people who actually surrounded the king at any one point. In his recent study of the 'political community' of Alexander II, Keith Stringer has drawn attention to four key members of Alexander's court who either rarely or never witnessed Alexander II's surviving charters but yet who are known from other sources to have been key members of his court.[127] Equally, as Stringer has pointed out, not all parts of the reign are represented equally by the patterns of survival. This remains true for Alexander III's acts. Of 163 surviving dated acts of Alexander III (which include personal letters), twenty-six survive from the period 1249–59, forty-six from 1260–69, fifty-six from 1270–79, and thirty-five from the period 1280–86.[128] Of these, only some actually contain witness lists. If one removes them, the numbers are as follows: twenty-five from the period 1249–59; thirty-five from 1260–69; twenty-eight from 1270–79; and fifteen from 1280–86.

Analysing the attestations of sheriffs to royal charters is even more fraught with difficulty. Sheriffs are rarely given the title *vicecomes* when they attest royal charters.[129] This did not only happen to people who held higher title and office by which they no doubt preferred to be known: Alexander Comyn, earl of Buchan,

---

Prosopography of Britain and France from the Tenth to the Twelfth Century, ed. K. S .B. Keats-Rohan (Woodbridge, 1997), pp. 89–102.

[126] Dauvit Broun, 'The Presence of Witnesses and the Writing of Charters', in *The Reality Behind Charter Diplomatic: Studies by Dauvit Broun, John Reuben Davies, Richard Sharpe and Alice Taylor*, ed. Dauvit Broun (Glasgow, 2011), pp. 235–90. On occasion, space was left for the witnesses to be filled in later, which they never were. See the original agreement in the Paisley dispute mentioned in Chapter 5, p. 329, note 325 (PRONI, D623/B/7/1/5). See also the request by Saer de Quinci to William Malveisin, bishop of St Andrews asking him to put his seal to a charter already drawn up: *Dunf. Reg.*, no. 157.

[127] Stringer, 'Scottish "Political Community"', pp. 54–5.

[128] Stringer, 'Scottish "Political Community"', p. 54.

[129] There was a burst in 1222–30 (but particularly in 1225–28) when scribes started consistently including the titles of royal sheriffs in charter witness lists. This, however, did not last, but it is interesting that it coincides with the period of intensification of justiciar-power outlined in Chapter 4, pp. 243–4. Robert of Inverkeilor, sheriff of the Mearns, attested at Kincardine on 22 December 1222 (London, BL, Additional MS 33245, fo. 147r [AII/76]); Reginald Crawford, sheriff of Ayr, attested three charters at Ayr on 8–9 May 1223 (*Glasgow Reg.*, i, nos. 118–119 [AII/80,/81]; *Ayr Burgh Charters*, no. 3 [AII/82]); John Maxwell, sheriff of Roxburgh, and William of Hartside, sheriff of Lanark, attested a charter at Cadzow on 12 November 1225 (*Glasgow Reg.*, i, no. 129 [AII/106]). John Maxwell, sheriff of Roxburgh attested at Lanark on 19 November 1225 and at Cadzow again on 22 November 1225 (*Glasgow Reg.*, i, no. 133 [AII/108], 138 [AII/107]), at Roxburgh on 7 March 1226 (*Melrose Liber*, i, no. 278 [AII/114]), at Stirling on 30 March 1226 (*Arbroath*, i, no. 171 [AII/118]). William Hartside, sheriff of Lanark, attested at Cadzow on 22 November 1225 (*Glasgow Reg.*, i, no.

always attested with his title of earl but very commonly added his title of justiciar and, from 1275, constable.[130] He never, however, attested a royal charter as a sheriff, which is understandable. But sheriffs who were not earls or justiciars also did not have their shrieval titles recorded regularly. There are a few exceptions, most of which occur in the reigns of earlier kings: Alexander, son of William, son of Thor, sheriff of Stirling under William and Alexander II, almost always attested William's and Alexander II's charters as 'Alexander, sheriff of Stirling', not his longer patronymic.[131] But because we do not have surviving lists of shrieval office-holders, which state how long each individual sheriff held office, it is almost impossible to know whether a particular sheriff was indeed a sheriff at the time of his attestation of the royal charter, thus making an analysis of the attestation patterns of the office of sheriff next to impossible.

This problem, however, can be avoided if the question is turned on its head. We cannot know when sheriffs appeared at the royal court and attested charters. What we can analyse are the attestation patterns of men who we know received the office of sheriff at some point between 1263 and 1266. Such a picture is always going to be incomplete, because the number of charters actually issued in the king's name (and thus the number of potential attestations) will always be much higher than the number of charters that survive. But this problem is insurmountable and what follows makes do with what we have. It will exclude the figures of William, earl of Mar, and Alexander Comyn, earl of Buchan, because they primarily served as chamberlain and justiciar of Scotia during the period of their accounting. These

---

133 [AII/108]), and at Cadzow again on 31 May 1226 (Anderson, *Diplomata*, plates 32–33 [AII/121]; *Lennox Cart.*, pp. 91–2 [AII/122]). Ingelram de Balliol, sheriff of Berwick, attested a charter at Stirling on 31 March 1226 (*Moray Reg.*, no. 29 [AII/119]). Maurice, earl of Menteith, and sheriff of Stirling attests a charter at Clackmannan on 27 March 1226 (*Cambuskenneth Reg.*, no. 133 [AII/117]). John Hay, sheriff of Perth, attested charters at Stirling on 30–31 March 1226 (*Arbroath Liber*, i, no. 171 [AII/118]; *Moray Reg.*, no. 29 [AII/119]). William Blund, sheriff of 'Perth and Scone', attested at Perth on 12 April 1228 (*St Andrews Liber*, pp. 236–7 [AII/136]). William Prat, sheriff of Nairn, attested as *vicarius* (perhaps an incorrect expansion of *vic'* for *vicecomes*?) of Nairn at Elgin on 30 June 1228 (*Moray Reg.*, no. 109 [AII/140]). Philip de Melville, sheriff of Aberdeen, attested at Aberdeen on 8 July 1228 (*Holyrood Liber*, no. 71 [AII/141]). Bernard Fraser, sheriff of Stirling, attested at Stirling on 22 October 1228 (*Paisley Reg.*, pp. 172–3 [AII/145]). Then there is a gap of *c.*13 years, until Robert Mowat attested as sheriff of Forfar, at Forfar on 25 February 1241 (*Coupar Angus Chrs*, i, no. 45 [AII/273]). John, sheriff of Stirling, attested at Kirkton (St Ninians, Stirlingshire) on 12 September 1242 (*Glasgow Reg.*, i, no. 180 [AII/288]). Nicholas de Soules, sheriff of Roxburgh, attested at Coldingham on 21 April 1248 (Raine, *North Durham*, App., no. 74 [AII/325]).

130 For *constabularius et justiciarius*, see *RRS*, iv, 1, nos. 91, 129, 154, 156, 162, 163.

131 For Alexander's attestations as sheriff of Stirling under William the Lion, see *RRS*, ii, nos. 308, 323–325, 373–374, 376–378, 404–405, 407, 414–415, 427, 432–433, 438, 460–461, 463–464, 467, 469, 501, 504, 507–508, 519, 524. Sheriffs did have a tendency to include their title in non-royal charters, which is understandable: those who drafted the charters would have been more likely to see the benefit of emphasizing the presence of a royal official at a particular transaction or making of an agreement than those drawn up at the king's court where everyone, by default, would have been given a royal sheen. It is also more common for sheriffs to be given their official title when they were referred to in the body of a royal charter, in contrast to their appellation in witness lists; see, for example; *RRS*, iv, 1, no. 115, referring to William Sinclair, sheriff of Edinburgh, who was still holding office in 1278.

offices have been discussed in more detail in Chapter 4.[132] The attestation patterns of 1263–66 sheriffs are given in Table 7.2.

Eighteen of the twenty-six individuals under consideration here thus attested at least one royal charter (69 per cent). Three of these sheriffs, however, only attested royal charters close to their known sheriffdom. Robert Mowat, sheriff of Forfar under both Alexander II and Alexander III, and justiciar of Scotia between 1241 and 1242, attested royal charters at Forfar, which accounts for eight out of his eleven attestations, at Inverquiech (15 miles away from Forfar), and at Arbroath (again, *c*.15 miles away).[133] John of Kinross attested at Balmerino in Fife (around 25 miles away) and John Cameron, sheriff of Perth, attested at Scone (about two miles away) and Forfar (around 30 miles away). However, such behaviour was not typical of those who did attest royal charters. Even those who attested five charters or fewer often witnessed far away from the head of their sheriffdom. William Mowat, for example, attested the king's charters in Edinburgh, Selkirk, and Scone, far away from his sheriffdom of Cromarty in Ross, as well as attesting in Elgin, which was closer.[134]

Excluding Robert Mowat, who has already been mentioned, those who attested ten charters or more were Reginald Cheyne (Kincardine, chamberlain), William Comyn of Kilbride (Ayr), Aymer Maxwell (Dumfries, Roxburgh, Peebles, justiciar of Galloway, chamberlain), Hugh of Abernethy (Roxburgh), Hugh de Berkeley (Berwick; justiciar of Lothian), John of Lamberton (Stirling), William Sinclair (Edinburgh, Haddington, Linlithgow), and Simon Fraser (Traquair, Perth). Altogether, these men held a variety of offices spreading from Kincardine to Ayr. Some of them were also chamberlains and justiciars. It thus cannot be assumed that their frequent attestation was because they held a particular type of office. Thus, Hugh de Berkeley attested sixteen charters over a thirteen-year period while Hugh of Abernethy witnessed seventeen over a nineteen-year period. The figures are roughly comparable, although on average Hugh de Berkeley witnessed more charters per year (1.23 per cent) than Hugh of Abernethy (0.89 per cent). But Hugh of Abernethy only ever appears as a sheriff of Roxburgh while Hugh de Berkeley was both justiciar of Lothian (a title he attested with on thirteen occasions) and sheriff of Berwick.[135]

The most striking observation about these attestation patterns is their geographical range. Men who were sheriffs did not, in general, stick to their locality. Reginald Cheyne, for example, attested at Kintore in Aberdeenshire but as far down as

---

[132] I have also not included R. de Mowbray because it is impossible to determine whether he was Robert or Roger; see above, note 104.

[133] *Coupar Angus Chrs*, i, no. 45 [AII/273], 46 [AII/276], 53 [AII/317] (all Forfar); *Glasgow Reg.*, i, no. 179 (Forfar) [AII/281]; NLS, Advocates Charter, A.4 (Forfar) [AII/282]; *Ayr Friars Chrs*, no. 1 (Forfar) [AII/287]; *Arbroath Liber*, i, no. 252 (Inverquiech) [AII/296]; *Arbroath Liber*, i, no. 264 (Arbroath) [AII/307]; BL, Additional MS 33245, fos. 149v–150r (Arbroath) [AII/308]; Fraser, *Southesk*, ii, no. 25 (Forfar) [AII/311]; Fraser, *Carlaverock*, ii, p. 405 (no. 5) (Forfar) [AII/318]. The two charters issued at Arbroath were both authenticated on 7 March 1246.

[134] *RRS*, iv, 1, nos. 42–43, 69, 84.

[135] For Hugh de Berkeley's attestations as justiciar, see above, p. 423, at note 119.

Table 7.2. Attestations of royal charters by 1263–66 sheriffs

Sheriff	No. of chs	Places of attestation	Periods of attestation[136]
Gilbert Hay (d.1263)	7	Kincardine, Forfar, Scone, Edinburgh, Haddington, Kinghorn	1241, 1250–51
John Cameron	2	Scone, Forfar	1234, 1241
David of Lochore	5 [3][137]	Cupar, Forfar, Roxburgh	1277–78
Walter Stewart, earl of Menteith	6	Traquair, Forfar, Scone, Roxburgh, Coupar Angus, Stirling	1260–84
Robert Mowat	11 [8][138]	Forfar, Arbroath, Inverquiech	1241–47
Reginald Cheyne	12 [10][139]	Forfar, Aboyne, Haddington, Kintore, Berwick, Stirling, Scone	1262–85
William Comyn of Kilbride	11	Melrose, Machan, Kintore, Roxburgh, Haddington, Kincardine, Dumfries, Stirling, Traquair	1264–79
John of Fenton	1	Newbattle	1271
John of Kinross	1	Balmerino	1244
Aymer Maxwell	15	Berwick, Traquair, Stirling, Scone, Balmerino, Edinburgh, Roxburgh, Newbattle, Inverness, Selkirk	1232–44, 1251–64[140]
Alexander Murray	3 [2][141]	Aboyne, Elgin	1267–68
William Mowat	4	Selkirk, Edinburgh, Elgin, Scone	1263–73
Hugh of Abernethy	17 [16]	Traquair, Rattenec, Edinburgh, Roxburgh, Linlithgow, Newbattle, Melrose, Jedburgh, Aboyne, Elgin, Haddington, Forfar, Dumfries, Stirling, Kintore	1260–79
Thomas Randolph	7	Edinburgh, Berwick, Kintore, Haddington	1266–80
Hugh de Berkeley	15 [13][142]	Linlithgow, Newbattle, Selkirk, Traquair, Perth, Edinburgh, Scone, Berwick, Haddington, Roxburgh.	1258–77[143]

(continued)

[136] Regnal years were introduced by 20 April 1222, although there were some earlier experiments in AD dating years in 1221; for which see Broun, *Scottish Independence*, pp. 199–201. The earliest surviving charter dated by regnal year is *Kelso Liber*, i, no. 7 [AII/68].

[137] The number in square brackets has been given because, although David witnessed five separate charters, three were issued on the same day and at the same place, at Cupar in Fife on 10 March 1277, and all had Dunfermline Abbey as a beneficiary (*RRS*, iv, 1, nos. 102–104).

[138] Robert attested on 29 October and 31 October 1241, both at Forfar, which were probably part of the same court visit: *Glasgow Reg.*, i, no. 179 [AII/281]; and NLS, Advocates Charters, A.4 [AII/282], on 29 October and 31 October 1241, both at Forfar, which were probably part of the same court visit. Other pairs are the two issued on 8 March 1246 at Arbroath (BL, Additional MS, 33245, fo. 46v [AII/306]; *Arbroath Liber*, i, no. 264 [AII/307]); and those issued on 3 and 7 July, at Forfar, 1247 (*Coupar Angus Chrs*, i, no. 53 [AII/317]; and Fraser, *Carlaverock*, ii, p. 405, no. 5 [AII/318]).

[139] Two charters were issued at Aboyne on 14 August 1267 (*RRS*, iv, 1, nos. 65–66); two at the same court setting at Scone, held 13–15 November 1285 (*RRS*, iv, 1, nos. 162–163).

[140] Aymer's attestations must contain a break from 1255–58 when Aymer was removed from Alexander III's minority government, for which see *Anglo-Scottish Relations*, ed. Stones no. 10, at p. 62.

[141] Alexander Murray also witnessed the two charters issued at Aboyne: see note 139.

[142] Two charters were issued on 12 December 1264 at Traquair (*RRS*, iv, 1, nos. 52–53).

[143] From September 1275, Hugh de Berkeley appears without the title 'justiciar': *RRS*, iv, 1, nos. 93, 98, 108.

Table 7.2. (Continued)

Sheriff	No. of chs	Places of attestation	Periods of attestation
John of Lamberton	16 [13]	Stirling, Edinburgh, Melrose, Linlithgow, Newbattle, Machan, Selkirk, Traquair, Scone, Cupar	1245, 1263–66 1273–77
William Sinclair	15	Kinross, Edinburgh, Newbattle, Kintore, Stirling, Kincardine, Forfar, Traquair, Roxburgh, Haddington, Dumfries, Scone.	1261–82
Simon Fraser	21 [19]	Traquair, Berwick, Haddington, Roxburgh, Haddington, Selkirk, Kincardine, Forfar, Dumfries, Stirling, Scone, Newbattle.	1264–85

Berwick.[144] Aymer Maxwell attested at northern places such as Inverness but also as far south as Roxburgh and Berwick.[145] Hugh of Abernethy ranged from Elgin in the north to Jedburgh in the south and Dumfries in the west.[146] Even if these men were not holding shrieval office at the time of their attestation, the point remains that most sheriffs, even those who did not attest particularly frequently, could follow the royal court to places far away from those in which they either did, or had, or would hold shrieval office.

The kingdom-wide prominence of many of these sheriffs is demonstrated even further by looking at the main diplomatic documents of the period: those concerning changes to the minority government of Alexander III in 1255, diplomatic documents concerning relationships between Scotland, England, Wales, and Norway and particular scandals within the kingdom itself that called upon the pope and his delegates to mediate. A proportion of the sheriffs holding office in 1263–66 appear in all of these types of documents. In 1255, following the fall of one version of the minority government, headed by John Balliol and Robert de Ros, three people who were sheriffs in 1263–66 were displaced (David of Lochore, Alexander Uviet, and Aymer Maxwell) and one, Gilbert Hay, was part of the replacement government.[147] In 1258, part of the aristocracy, led by Walter Comyn, earl of Menteith, struck up an agreement with Llywelyn, prince of Wales, promising that neither Llywelyn in Gwynedd nor the Scots would make peace with

---

[144] *RRS*, iv, 1, nos. 41, 65, 164, 66, 80, 87, 91, 124, 129, 154, 162–163.

[145] Under Alexander II: Raine, *North Durham*, App., nos. 68–70 [AII/178]; *Melrose Liber*, i, no. 248 [AII/185]; PoMS, no. 2058 H1/7/192, online at <http://db.poms.ac.uk/record/source/2058/>, [AII/188]; *Moray Reg.*, App: *Cartae Originales*, no. 10 [AII/204]; *Balmerino Liber*, no. 35 [AII/205]; *Moray Reg.*, no. 36 [AII/218]; *Melrose Liber*, ii, App., no. 2 [AII/235]; *Glasgow Reg.*, i, no. 186 [AII/293]. Under Alexander III: *RRS*, iv, 1, nos. 7, 16–17, 28, 31, 51. Aymer appears to have died by 16 April 1268 (*RRS*, iv, 1, no. 68).

[146] *RRS*, iv, 1, nos. 31, 32, 41 (in charter text), 45, 48–49, 63, 65–66, 69, 72, 74, 105, 122, 124, 167.

[147] *Anglo-Scottish Relations*, ed. Stones, no. 10; commented on in Duncan, *Making of the Kingdom*, pp. 560–76; for Robert de Ros's fate in England, see David Carpenter, 'The downfall and punishment of Robert de Ros', Breaking of Britain Feature of the Month June 2012, online at <http://www.breakingofbritain.ac.uk/blogs/feature-of-the-month/june-2012/>.

Henry III without the other's awareness: those who were responsible for this on the Scottish side included David of Lochore, Reginald Cheyne, Aymer Maxwell, William Mowat, Hugh of Abernethy, and Hugh de Berkeley.[148] When, in 1281, Alexander III issued a statement about the succession customs of the kingdom, only three knights attested the document: one was William Sinclair, sheriff of Edinburgh, Haddington, and Linlithgow in 1263–66.[149] And, when Margaret of Norway was confirmed as Alexander III's heir in 1284, following the death of Prince Alexander, his oldest son, Reginald Cheyne, William Sinclair and Simon Fraser all witnessed the accompanying document, along with Nicholas Hay, who, by then, may have obtained the sheriffdom of Perth which his father, Gilbert, had held back in 1262.[150] In short, fifteen out of the twenty-nine sheriffs were or had been intrinsically involved in the politics and government of the realm.[151]

Some of these men, such as William, earl of Mar, and Alexander Comyn, earl of Buchan, were among the top tier of the aristocracy in Scotland.[152] But others had more limited landed holdings. William Mowat, for example, inherited his father's lands in Cromarty but also held the lordship of Fern in Angus after the death of his uncle, Robert Mowat.[153] We do not know that David of Lochore held any lands other than Lochore in Fife.[154] Hugh of Abernethy represents someone who was able to accumulate a large amount of land other than his inherited holding of Abernethy, now in Kinross and Perthshire.[155] In addition to his land in Fife, Hugh was given the land of Lour in Angus by Alexander III and Oxton and Lylestone in Berwickshire by Alan Durward, who was described as his *cognatus* ('kinsman'),

[148] *Foedera*, i, I, 370; commented on in Duncan, *Making of the Kingdom*, pp. 571–2; Young, *Comyns*, pp. 57–8. See also the accusations against John Russell, and Isabella, countess of Menteith, of poisoning Isabella's husband, Walter Comyn, earl of Menteith, who died in late October/early November (Theiner, *Monumenta*, no. 237); see Young, *Comyns*, p. 59.

[149] *Edward I and the Throne of Scotland, 1290–1296: An Edition of Record Sources for the Great Cause*, ed. E. L. G. Stones and Grant G. Simpson, 2 vols (New York and London, 1978), ii, pp. 189–90; also now *RRS*, iv, 1, no. 133.

[150] *ER*, i, p. 1.

[151] Alexander Comyn, earl of Buchan, William, earl of Mar, Walter Stewart, earl of Menteith, Reginald Cheyne, Aymer Maxwell, Gilbert Hay, David of Lochore, Alexander Uviet, Hugh of Abernethy, Hugh de Berkeley, William Mowat, William Sinclair, Simon Fraser, William Comyn of Kilbride. William Comyn of Kilbride has been included because, although he does not witness these diplomatic documents, he was a frequent enough witness to Alexander III's charters to warrant inclusion.

[152] For earlier earls as sheriffs, see Maurice, earl of Menteith, who was sheriff of Stirling in 1226 (*Cambuskenneth Reg.*, no. 133 [AII/117]).

[153] Robert Mowat held Fern in Angus but by the end of the century it was held by his nephew, William (who witnesses as 'lord of Fern', in *Panmure Reg.*, ii, pp. 158–9), who was the son of Robert's brother, Michael, who had been sheriff of Inverness under Alexander II (*Moray Reg.*, no. 85). The fraternal relationship between Robert and Michael is confirmed in *Arbroath Liber*, i, no. 271. Robert must have died childless.

[154] David acts as one of the justiciar of Scotia's attorneys in 1260 (*St Andrews Liber*, pp. 346–7), and we find him present at a perambulation in 1252 (NRS, GD 254/1; H 4/26/9), and an inquest in 1256 (*Dunf. Reg.*, no. 85), described as Constantine of Lochore's heir in 1235 (1236 if the charter is dated by Lady Calendar dating; *Dunf. Reg.*, no. 179).

[155] Hugh's court at Abernethy is referred to in NRS, GD 82/6 (PoMS, no. 7702; H 3/42/7; online at <http://db.poms.ac.uk/record/source/7702>.

although the precise relationship between them is unknown.[156] He held Innernethy in the sheriffdom of Perth and part of Formartine in Aberdeenshire, as well as obtaining the terce of one Lady Eithne, whose lands were in Atholl and Argyll.[157] None of this would have made him equal in rank to an earl but he did create and maintain a landed presence from Argyll to Berwickshire to Aberdeenshire.

In short, all this would suggest that this particular group of sheriffs in 1263–66 included a significant proportion of men who did not simply hold a local office in the royal government but actually constituted the government itself. This is in some way at odds with previous assessments of sheriffs under Alexander III, which have stressed that, although a few sheriffs were 'great magnates', most sheriffs, particularly those not on the periphery of the kingdom, were local barons or lesser nobles who had strong landed ties to their sheriffdoms.[158] While this is true, it does not make up the whole picture: a great proportion of sheriffs were as committed to the governance of the entire kingdom as they were to that of the locality. Men such as David of Lochore, William Mowat, and Hugh of Abernethy may have been 'lesser nobles' in terms of their rank and inherited landholdings but, in terms of their role in regnal affairs, they were absolutely top-of-the-pile. That men with comparatively smaller landed holdings than earls could be part of minority governments, for example, reflects the integrated nature of 'centre' and 'locality' in thirteenth-century royal governance, as evidenced in the last three chapters.

Excluding the earls, some of those sheriffs who were of regnal importance often had a tradition in their family of attesting royal charters and serving the king as his sheriff. Five sheriffs had uncles or fathers who had exercised the same office under Alexander II. The father of Gilbert Hay, David Hay, was a sheriff of Forfar but his uncle, John Hay, had also been a sheriff of Perth.[159] Aymer Maxwell was sheriff of Roxburgh as well as sheriff of Dumfries; his brother, John Maxwell, had exercised shrieval office in Roxburgh before him, and his father, Herbert, before that.[160] Richard, father of Alexander Uviet, sheriff of Lanark, had also exercised the same office as his son, as had Bernard Fraser, father of Simon Fraser, sheriff of Traquair.[161]

---

[156] *RRS*, iv, 1, nos. 55–56; PoMS. no. 2057, H 1/7/193; online at <http://db.poms.ac.uk/record/source/2057> [AII/189]; Fraser, *Douglas*, iii, no. 5.

[157] Fraser, *Douglas*, iii, no. 7 (pp. 6–7); for Hugh, see PoMS, Person ID, no. 2063, online at <http://db.poms.ac.uk/record/person/2063/>.

[158] Brown, *Wars of Scotland*, pp. 60–2; Stringer, 'Scottish "Political Community"', pp. 62–7, takes his cue from work on the origins of the gentry in England, and so seems to suggest that, in Alexander II's reign, these people were of substantially lesser status than the earls. While this may be true in socio-economic terms, it may not be true in socio-political ones. The thirteenth-century English gentry was characterized by a rather different relationship with the king's court and government than in Scotland, for which see Peter Coss, *The Origins of the English Gentry* (Cambridge, 2003), particularly pp. 109–35.

[159] John Hay, sheriff of Perth, attested charters at Stirling on 30–31 March 1226 (*Arbroath Liber*, i, no. 171 [AII/118]; *Moray Reg.*, no. 29 [AII/119]). David Hay was sheriff of Forfar at the end of William the Lion's reign: *RRS*, ii, no. 503.

[160] John Maxwell attested as sheriff of Roxburgh in *Glasgow Reg.*, i, no. 129 [AII106], 133 [AII/108], 138 [AII/107]; *Melrose Liber*, i, no. 278 [AII/114], *Arbroath Liber*, i, no. 171 [AII/118]. John was also a chamberlain of Alexander II; see Chapter 4, pp. 246–7.

[161] Richard Uviet attested as sheriff of Lanark in *Newbattle Reg.*, nos. 139, 142; Bernard Fraser attested as sheriff of Stirling in *Cambuskenneth Reg.*, no. 79, and *Paisley Reg.*, pp. 172–3 [AII/145].

Thomas, son of Ranulf, the father of Thomas Randolph, sheriff of Berwick and probable sheriff of Roxburgh, had been sheriff of Dumfries in the 1230s, and was also a regular witness of the charters of Alexander II and Alexander III until December 1253.[162] William Mowat's father, Michael Mowat, had been sheriff of Inverness in 1234 and also attested the king's charters, in a greater geographical range than had his uncle, Robert Mowat.[163]

Other men appear to have been the first to receive office in their families, even though these families were of long-standing importance in their locality. David of Lochore, for example, is the first attested sheriff in his family, despite its stretching all the way back to Robert of Burgundy, who was the defeated party in the dispute over Kirkness in Fife between 1128 and 1136, mentioned several times in the first part of this book.[164] David seems to have started a tradition of shrieval office holding: his son, Constantine of Lochore, followed him as sheriff of Fife in 1288–90.[165] Hugh of Abernethy could have been the grandson or even great-grandson of Orm mac Aeda, lay abbot of Abernethy, who was himself the grandson of Gille Mícheíl, earl of Fife in the reign of David I. Despite the descent of this family from a past *mormaer*, no one before Hugh appears to have been a sheriff, although Laurence of Abernethy, a direct male relative, attested the charters of Alexander II.[166] Only one individual appears to be a 'new' man: Reginald Cheyne. Reginald's first appearance, as sheriff of the Mearns (Kincardine), was to a charter of Alexander Comyn, earl of Buchan, in 1255. Before this, he may have already had control of Inverugie, near Peterhead in Aberdeenshire.[167] Whether Reginald owed his position as sheriff to his connection with Alexander Comyn or had gained it some other way is not clear but what is clear is that, during his time as sheriff, chamberlain, and at the royal court, he obtained the patronage of Hugh of Abernethy and Alexander III, while also maintaining his connection

---

[162] For Thomas, son of Ranulf, see *Glasgow Reg.*, i, no. 187 [AII/301]; Raine, *North Durham*, App, no. 74 [AII/325]; *Melrose Liber*, i, no. 231 [AII/320]; *RRS*, iv, 1, nos. 2, 19; for his title as sheriff of Dumfries, see *Melrose Liber*, i, no. 206.

[163] For Michael Mowat as sheriff of Inverness, see *Moray Reg.*, no. 85, and for his attestations of Alexander II's charters, see *Brechin Reg.*, i, no. 2 [AII/177]; Fraser, *Lennox*, ii, no. 5, pp. 4–5 [AII/173]; Fraser, *Southesk*, ii, no. 25, pp. 477–8 [AII/311]. In 1305, a later William Mowat was described as holding the sheriffdom of Cromarty as 'de fee' ('of feu'); Stones, *Anglo-Scottish Relations*, no. 33, pp. 246–7.

[164] Lawrie, *ESC*, no. 80. For the early history of the Lochores, see G. W. S. Barrow, 'The Origins of the Family of Lochore', *SHR*, vol. 77, no. 204 (1998), pp. 252–4.

[165] *ER*, i, p. 50.

[166] How Hugh became lord of Abernethy is not entirely clear. In the 1170s, it was held by Orm mac Aeda (or Orm, son of Hugh); *RRS*, ii, no. 152. Orm was also given Glenduckie and Balmeadie in Fife, which had previously been quitclaimed by Earl Donnchad in exchange for Balbirnie (*RRS*, ii, no. 14). Orm's son and heir, Laurence, then inherited both Abernethy and these Fife properties (see *Arbroath Liber*, i, no. 35). But how Hugh then obtained Abernethy is unclear. For Laurence of Abernethy's attestations, see *Dunf. Reg.*, no. 80 [AII/170]; 'Eight Thirteenth Century Texts', ed. W. W. Scott, in *Miscellany XIII*, Scottish History Society, 5th ser., vol. 14 (Edinburgh, 2004), pp. 1–41, no. 2, at pp. 8–9 [AII/176].

[167] Reginald Cheyne the elder is called *dominus de Invirugy* in a charter of John, earl of Caithness and Orkney, in Barbara E. Crawford, *The Northern Earldoms: Orkney and Caithness from AD 870 to 1470* (Edinburgh, 2013), plate 35. I am grateful to Matthew Hammond for knowledge of this charter.

with Alexander Comyn.[168] Through marriage, he was able to lay claim to land in Ayrshire by the 1270s and marry his son, also called Reginald, to Mary Murray, heiress of Duffus in Moray.[169] Reginald Cheyne the elder, however, does appear to have been the exception: from relative obscurity in the written record, he became a sheriff and chamberlain of the king and held land from Ayrshire to Lothian to Aberdeenshire.

Not all sheriffs are known to have attended the king's court or were involved in government in any other way. Five out of the twenty-nine sheriffs in 1263–66 are not known to have attested a single royal charter nor to have occupied another role in government.[170] They were all sheriffs north of the Mounth: Gregory de Melville and Andrew of Garioch in Aberdeen, Ralph of Strachan in Banff, William Wiseman in Forres, and Laurence Grant in Inverness. With the exception of Ranulf and Gregory, the other four were local to the area and what survives of their activities suggests that they were relatively localized in their actions, only attesting charters and holding land in the vicinity of their sheriffdom.[171] Gregory de Melville represents a rather peculiar case. There is little evidence that he held land in the sheriffdom of Aberdeen: all his acts and transactions concern his holdings of Melville and Leadburn in Midlothian.[172] It is not impossible that he had land in Aberdeen: one Philip de Melville had been sheriff of Aberdeen in the 1220s and had married the daughter of Walter Sibbald, lord of Mondynes, in nearby Kincardinshire.[173] But any relationship between Gregory and Philip cannot be established from the available evidence.

It is noteworthy that all sheriffs who appear to have operated in relative isolation from the royal court and other parts of royal government were in the north of the kingdom. Certainly, it was more common for sheriffs in southern Scotia to be

---

[168] For Reginald's connections with Alexander Comyn, see Young, *Comyns*, pp. 58, 70. For his lands in Aberdeenshire, see *HMC, Mar and Kellie*, 3; PoMS, no. 7691; H 3/344/5, online at <http://db.poms.ac.uk/record/source/7691/>.

[169] Reginald Cheyne married his son, also called Reginald, to Mary, daughter of Freskin of Moray and, through her, Reginald the younger became lord of Duffus: *ABB*, iv, pp. 73–5; *RRS*, v, no. 26.

[170] Gregory de Melville, sheriff of Aberdeen; Andrew of the Garioch, sheriff of Aberdeen; Ralph of Strachan, sheriff of Banff; Laurence Grant, sheriff of Inverness; William Wiseman, sheriff of Forres. The exception is Alexander Uviet, sheriff of Lanark, who never attested a royal charter but yet was part of the minority government removed in 1255, so must have been someone of regnal importance (*RRS*, iv, 1, no. 22).

[171] For William Wiseman, see *Moray Reg.*, nos. 28, 31 (these documents are dated 1225 and 1229, so possibly his father or close relative?); *Moray Reg., Cartae Originales*, no. 7. William's brother Thomas was sheriff of Elgin (*Moray Reg.*, no. 214). For Laurence Grant, sheriff of Inverness, see *Moray Reg.*, no. 122. For Andrew of the Garioch, see *Lindores Cart.*, no. 116; *Aberdeen Reg.*, i, p. 34.

[172] For Gregory's holdings in Midlothian, see *Newbattle Reg.*, no. 195; *Dunf. Reg.*, nos. 160, 203, 206; *St Andrews Liber*, pp. 376–7. He did witness in the Mearns, however (the sheriffdom of Kincardine), along with Philip de Melville: see, *Arbroath Liber*, i, no. 128; *St Andrews Liber*, p. 277. For Ralph of Strachan, see *Arbroath Liber*, i, no. 306; *Brechin Reg.*, ii, no. 1; *St Andrews*, p. 276.

[173] Gregory was the son of one William Melville (*Dunf. Reg.*, nos. 159–60), who was connected to the Midlothian Melvilles, who were given the land of Leadburn, later held by our Gregory Melville: *RRS*, ii, no. 267–269, particularly no. 268, where Richard, son of Gregory I de Melville, is given Leadburn. Our Gregory was the grandson of Richard de Melville, confirmed in *St Andrews Liber*, pp. 376–7, at p. 376. Richard de Melville was the son of Gregory de Melville, who had a brother, Geoffrey, who had five sons, Thomas, Robert, Hugh, Richard, and Walter (*Dunf. Reg.*, no 158).

regnally important as well as locally so. The most northerly based of all the men who held shrieval office in 1263–66 and who attested ten or more of Alexander III's charters was Reginald Cheyne, sheriff of Kincardine, who had his landed roots in Aberdeenshire. The contrast between north and south should not be stretched too far, however. William Mowat, sheriff of Cromarty, and Alexander Murray, sheriff of Inverness and Nairn in the 1263–66 account, both attested royal charters and Alexander de Montfort, sheriff of Elgin, had landed interests down in East Lothian (in Athelstaneford) as well as operating as sheriff in the far north of the kingdom.[174]

Is it ever possible to see whether holding shrieval office made a noticeable difference to an individual's social and political ambit? For some prominent enough to attest royal charters anyway, such as Hugh of Abernethy or William, earl of Mar, it is hard to identify the impact that shrieval office may have had. The same applies to others who had a familial tradition both of attending the royal court and of holding shrieval office. But to others it may have made a difference, particularly to those who only had local importance beforehand. A good example of this type of man was John Lamberton, sheriff of Stirling, who attested sixteen charters of Alexander III.[175] John was involved in the sheriffdom of Stirling before his appointment and appears to have had relatively strong ties to a previous sheriff of the same area, John of Stirling.[176] John Lamberton also performed a valuation (an 'extent') of the land of Pencaitland in East Lothian in 1261 for Aymer Maxwell, then, perhaps, sheriff of Haddington, as Pencaitland was in Haddington.[177] John's only attestation to a royal charter prior to his appointment was issued in 1245, at Stirling, and for Cambuskenneth Abbey, a local beneficiary.[178] Before 1263, therefore, John's career seems to have been based firmly in Stirling and then extending outwards into northern Lothian by the 1260s. But what is interesting about his career is that he attests ten royal charters in the period 1263–66, the period when he is known to have been sheriff of Stirling. Moreover, only one of these attestations was at Stirling: the rest ranged from Scone in Perthshire to Machan in Lanarkshire to Melrose in Roxburghshire.[179] After this short burst, John of Lamberton then disappears from the witness lists until 1273, when he makes one appearance at Scone and then witnesses again in 1276 and 1277, after which he disappears again.[180] It is, of course, impossible to draw firm conclusions

---

[174] Alexander was the younger brother of John de Montfort, who held Athelstaneford (*Newbattle Reg.*, no. 196). John was the older brother, for he inherited all of Athelstaneford and gave Alexander 50 acres within the territory in 1251 (*RRS*, iv, 1, no. 12).

[175] A similar case might also be made for Hugh de Berkeley, who attested only three times after he lost his title in 1274: *RRS*, iv, 1, no. 93 (although this is a transcript by Roger Dodsworth and has an incomplete witness list), 98, 108).

[176] Fraser, *Lennox*, ii, nos. 6–8 (particularly no. 7; H3/17/40); *Newbattle Reg.*, no. 216.

[177] NRS, RH5/31; There is no direct evidence for Aymer as sheriff of Haddington; this is an inference on my part because he was supervising this extent; for John Lamberton making another extent of Pencaitland, see Fraser, *Carlaverock*, ii, no. 7 (pp. 406–7).

[178] *Cambuskenneth Reg.*, no. 171 [AII/303].

[179] *RRS*, iv, 1, nos. 43, 46–53, 58.

[180] *RRS*, iv, 1, nos. 84, 100, 102–104 (all issued on 10 March 1277 at Cupar in Fife).

about this pattern because of the loss of so many royal charters. But John's sudden burst onto the scene in 1263, a period when we *know* he started to exercise his office in Stirling, is striking and it may be that, for John, royal service gave him a prominence at the royal court that was otherwise unavailable. This represents an important point: local service had the potential to mean greater prominence at the highest internal level of political activity in the kingdom—the king's court—but it did so only for those who presumably could not achieve the same results through other means, whether through family connections and/or those of lordship.

To describe the sheriffs of the 1263–66 account roll as merely sheriffs is thus misleading. Over half were men of regnal prominence, whose connections with the royal court took them into a large triangle of royal itineration that spanned Inverness in the north to Dumfries and Berwick in the south. Many more attested the king's charters only a few times but even these took them on journeys far outside their sheriffdoms. Over 40 per cent of them held other offices in royal government: there was no 'class' of men from whom justiciars and chamberlains were drawn that was different from those who occupied shrieval office. There were, of course, some who were not important on a kingdom-wide scale: most of this type held office north of the Mounth but it would be a mistake to see this as evidence of a divide between north and south, between a self-sufficient north and a governing south. Not all sheriffs north of the Mounth are known to have confined themselves to that area and, equally, there were some sheriffs south of the Mounth who were just as self-contained or whose prominence seems to have come solely from the office. Certain families did dominate certain offices but only one sheriffdom was hereditary. In short, sheriffs were men who often did hold land in their locality but they were much more than that: most were involved in the royal court and government at the highest level of political activity.

CONCLUSION

This chapter has aimed to bring together two different aspects of bureaucracy: personnel and paperwork (or parchment). It has shown that, although enrolment developed in the latter part of Alexander II's reign, we should distinguish between different sorts of recordkeeping: keeping of incoming letters, recording the content of outgoing letters, the keeping of financial accounts and recording the business of the king's judicial officers. The royal chapel dealt with these categories in different but not mutually exclusive ways, all of which, however, differed from their English counterparts. Whereas the English pipe rolls were drawn up as part of the accounting process itself, Scottish financial accounts were far more haphazardly constructed. The reconstruction of Haddington's original source for the 1263–66 and 1288–90 accounts reveal rolls that were, most probably, consolidations of existing written records (however compiled) of past accounting sessions. They appear to have been entered on the roll with little regard for future consultation. They were recorded because they were records. We should thus not see the account rolls of the thirteenth century as records of the immediate activity of government but rather as a later consolidation of that government, recording, at least in part, its past financial rights.[181]

The same can be said for the so-called enrolment of royal charters. Inasmuch as enrolment was a routine part of royal charter production in England, Scottish kings did not adopt the practice during the thirteenth century; their enrolment was, like the enrolment of financial records, *post factum* and probably non-comprehensive. What was included must have been not every item but what was thought necessary to record at some point in the future. The wish for future consultation must explain why judicial records (those which were likely to be contested prima facie) were enrolled earlier than, for example, charters. The increased importance of the *written* record of settlement, an aspect of the Alexandrian leap forward discussed in Chapter 5, coupled with the growing use of writing to initiate legal processes, must have heightened the need to keep records centrally for future consultation. What was kept may have been, at first, determined by the wish of participants, rather than the result of recordkeeping and enrolment. By 1250, the enrolment of the results of inquests and perambulation, together with the records of the justiciar's ayre, seems to have become routine but we should distinguish, for all three types of records, between the probable form of these types of rolls and their English counterparts.

This sheds light on the relation between recordkeeping—of which enrolment was a type—and the routine of administrative government. The Scottish inventories list many single documents that were deemed part of the treasury at Edinburgh and, for Alexander's clerks in 1282, they were the most important part. These single sheets were often incoming letters of different types: records of diplomatic correspondence and charters that recorded the king's patronage and the land surrendered to him: in short, they were the records of his legal rights and privileges.[182] We should see the royal archive not only as the footprint of bureaucratic government but also as a more personal repository for safeguarding the rights and privileges of kings, in many ways more similar to the motivations for compiling great cartularies of monastic houses and bishoprics than historians of royal government might care to admit.

Studying the identity of the 1263–66 sheriffs produces complementary conclusions. Sheriffs were not just men of local importance whose fathers had sometimes held the office before them, they were predominantly men who were involved in governing the realm. Some were justiciars and chamberlains, while others formed part of minority governments. Most sheriffs were of regnal importance. Not all

---

[181] These also include rights of another sort: the link with the saintly past, through the presence of the Black Rood associated with St Margaret, queen of Scotland; the link with the northern counties, both the written record of the oaths sworn to his father, Alexander II, and also the staff with which he had been invested with Northumberland in 1215, all of which are recorded in the 1291 inventory: see *APS*, i, p. 112.

[182] This is not to say that similar conclusions cannot be made for England. The most obvious example is Bishop Stapleton's kalendar, made in 1323, which I discuss briefly in Taylor, 'Auditing and Enrolment', pp. 102–3.

were, of course, but the general trend is clear. Sometimes, serving as a local sheriff transformed an individual's sphere of activity from the local and regional to the regnal. The identity of sheriffs therefore parallels the relationship between central and local government. As central government depended on sheriffs for royal itineration, audit procedure, and judicial ayres, so too were sheriffs connected with the royal court and other areas of royal government. This differs from the fate of the sheriff in thirteenth- and fourteenth-century England, where the status of those holding office in general declined.[183] Men who attended the king's court frequently and held important office (such as chamberlain or justiciar) stopped holding shrieval office; instead, sheriffs predominantly became men who were important knights in their county and who rarely had a strong connection to the king's court.[184] By contrast, many of Scotland's sheriffs in 1263–66 were men who were absolutely involved in the governance of the realm and often held more than one office. The high status of sheriffs in the kingdom of the Scots is thus indicative not only of the importance of the sheriffdom in the operations of central government, highlighted in Chapters 4–6, but also of how integrated the locality was with the centre; they were institutionally co-dependent.

All this therefore raises questions about how far thirteenth-century Scotland could be called a 'bureaucratic' government, as has been claimed.[185] How far was there a state apparatus separate from civil society if the leading members of civil society were also the leading members of government? How far was routine recordkeeping really a part of *government* if the king's archives resembled a patrimonial repository as much as a state institution? The solution here would be to take a cue from Max Weber and describe thirteenth-century Scotland as a patrimonial state, one in which neither the political and economic status of its officials nor the written products of governmental activity fits neatly into the 'public' or the 'private' sphere.[186] But to do so would be to miss the clear categorical separation between 'official' title and 'inherited' title. Thus, when Walter, earl of Menteith, served as sheriff of Dumbarton in 1271, he was addressed by the king in his brieves as 'Walter, earl of Menteith, his beloved and sworn sheriff, and his bailies of Dumbarton': Walter was both earl and sheriff.[187] When Donnchad, earl of Fife and guardian of the kingdom after Alexander III's death, returned his account as farmer of the manor of Dull in 1289, he had to return two years' revenue accord-

---

[183] W. A. Morris, *The Medieval English Sheriff to 1300* (Manchester, 1927), pp. 77–87, 113–14, 161–4, 176–8; revised in David A. Carpenter, 'The Decline of the Curial Sheriff in England 1194– 1258', *EHR*, vol. 91, no. 358 (1976), pp. 1–32; see also the summary of the debates in Richard Gorski, *The Fourteenth-Century Sheriff: English Local Administration in the Late Middle Ages* (Woodbridge, 2003), pp. 1–10.

[184] See Carpenter, 'Decline of curial sheriff', pp. 30–2.

[185] Most recently, Oram, *Domination and Lordship*, p. 363, and the introduction by Cynthia Neville to *RRS*, iv, 1, pp. 3–36.

[186] Max Weber, *Economy and Society: An Outline of Interpretative Sociology*, ed. Guenther Roth and Claus Wittich, 2 vols (Berkeley, CA, and Los Angeles, 1987), ii, pp. 1006–110. For a recent study on patrimonialism, seeing it as one of the causes for failures of democracy, see Eric Budd, *Democratization, Development and the Patrimonial State in the Age of Globalization* (Oxford, 2004).

[187] *RRS*, iv, 1, no. 76.

ing to a new valuation done 'on the command of the guardians', thus referring to an order sanctioned by himself acting in another capacity.[188] Donnchad here was earl, guardian, and farmer. He was also a sheriff, and had to perform that office as well. In all these functions, he was responding to royal authority vested partly but not wholly in himself as guardian. Describing thirteenth-century Scotland as a patrimonial state instead of a bureaucratic one, therefore, misses the real historical change that has been the subject of the last three chapters: the formation and development of more complex administrative, judicial, and financial institutions and procedures that took their authority and legitimacy from that of the king. The dynamic between aristocratic and royal power within institutional state structures is developed in the conclusion to this book.

[188] *ER*, i, p. 48.

Conclusion
The Shape of the State in Medieval Scotland

This book has discussed some fairly standard practices and concerns of medieval kingship: gift-giving, relations with the aristocracy, military organization, law and order, resource extraction, and the administration of royal resources and interests. Its fundamental purpose has been to demonstrate how these practices of kingship shaped the state in the kingdom of the Scots in the central Middle Ages. But, because kings of Scots were not exceptional in their interests, practices, or responses, the conclusion not only synthesizes the book's main arguments but also draws out some features of the medieval Scottish state to act as the basis for future comparative work.

It would not be too dramatic to say that the way in which kings ruled was completely transformed over the twelfth and thirteenth centuries. On the accession of David I in 1124, we have no record of any sheriffs, justices, chamberlains, chancellors, common law brieves, audit sessions, or governmental archives in the kingdom. By 1290, even though the royal line descending directly from Mael Coluim III had failed and the aristocracy was in political turmoil, royal government included all these officials, institutions, and remedies. By 1290, the king's chapel communicated with sheriffdoms from Wigtown in the southwest to Cromarty in the north and Berwick in the south. In addition, there were three justiciars, whose jurisdiction covered Scotia (and, in addition, Moray, Ross, and Caithness), Lothian (including Clydesdale), and Galloway (west and east of the Urr) and these officials heard the king's pleas while on ayre in their regions. The king's revenue had come to be monitored in a peripatetic audit session to which sheriffs and other officials would be called to account for the monies and produce they had collected and spent on the king's behalf. Royal and aristocratic courts proclaimed themselves to be upholding the law of the kingdom of the Scots; disputants could obtain legal brieves from the king's chapel which either took cases into royal courts or produced verdicts that could bring cases into courts of others. None of this could have been imagined on David's accession in 1124.

How and when this happened has required quite a lengthy explanation so it is worth summarizing the key features of this process.[1] For much of the twelfth century, kings did not rule through administrative units. David I did support

---

[1] What follows will not, in general, cross-reference the chapters of this book as it is their collective rather than particular import which is discussed here.

himself by introducing sheriffs south of the Forth (and, exceptionally, Perth as well) but perhaps more important to his kingship were the large lordships he gave to his followers in the south of his kingdom. In terms of the spread of administration and the creation of large new lordships, David looked primarily south of the Forth. It is probable that he ruled north of the Forth in similar ways to his predecessors, by systematically communicating with local and regional magnates who performed particular functions on his behalf, perhaps attempting to attach existing figures (such as *iudices*) more firmly to his royal person, but doing no more than that. Kings of Scots do not seem to have ruled *Alba* (meaning north of the Forth) through administrative institutions either during or prior to David's reign and we should not view the *mormaer* and *toísech* as the key officials of an unambiguous state apparatus of *Alba*.

During the second half of the twelfth century, particularly in the first two and a half decades of William's reign, kings gave more gifts of land north of the Forth. This period saw a reconfiguration of, rather than a dramatic revolution in, power relations: aristocratic power came to be conceived as territorial, defined over land and held of the king, even if this was, in some cases, no more than a reformalization and reification of existing power structures on different terms. Whereas David I had given landed gifts in large swathes mostly to incoming aristocrats south of the Forth, William the Lion predominantly gave smaller gifts of land north of the Forth not only to the descendants of settlers and people who had newly appeared in his kingdom but also to men whose existing familial status placed them among the major players in those areas.[2] The process of territorialization did not just affect lesser magnates; *mormaer*-power, for example, became more intensively focused on the earldom, the lands *mormaír* held of the king. By the thirteenth century, the title of *comes* depended on holding the *comitatus*, the land of the *comes*. In this way, while David had secured support for his kingship by giving away land to his followers mostly south of the Forth, William the Lion continued this policy, refocused it on Scotia, and in so doing reconfigured the fundamental basis of aristocratic power. By the time of our earliest surviving financial sources, kings were profiting from defined aristocratic landholding, particularly through reliefs and wardships.

Over the twelfth century, kings did not rule solely through patronage; their power was not exercised through lordship alone. A unit of local governance and administration (the sheriffdom) was first introduced south of the Forth but, under Mael Coluim and William, developed north of it. Under Mael Coluim IV, sheriffs south of the Forth could hold their own courts; however, it only became a standard expectation that sheriffs would hold courts across the kingdom by the mid-1180s. As with shrieval courts, justices were first introduced south of the Forth. Only by the mid/late 1180s is there any evidence for the expectation that justices would hold their courts throughout the kingdom. During the early 1190s, the status of the chamberlain, the king's official responsible for all his revenue, also increased. It

---

[2] Some lordships created or re-gifted by William were large, such as the Garioch, given to the king's brother, David, but this gift very much constitutes an exception; see above, Chapter 1, pp. 69–80.

cannot be accidental that this rise in official status coincided with the introduction of probative accounting, the process involving all royal officials coming to account for the revenue they had collected on the king's behalf.

Institutional government was also supported by other changes in the relationship of royal power to other status groups during the later twelfth century. In particular, the statute evidence shows a gradual reorientation in the way law was made. It appears that, at the beginning of our period, written law was made and transmitted by legal specialists—*iudices*—who were also involved in lawmaking in some of our earliest surviving statutes from the 1170s onwards. However, the role *iudices* had once played in making law lessened over the late twelfth and thirteenth centuries; instead, kings in assemblies came to fulfil that function. In the few statutes that survive from this period, *iudices* only made law concerning particular subjects that may long have been under their authority. In contrast, the majority of the surviving law made under Alexander II in both criminal and civil spheres did not mention *iudices* as a key group in the lawmaking process. By the end of Alexander II's reign, law was made in assemblies, mostly with the consent of great laymen and great churchmen. In this way, kings supported their developing governmental institutions over the twelfth century by gradually taking primary control over the way law was made and transmitted in their kingdom.

The structures of the Scottish state were not static in the thirteenth century any more than in the twelfth. In particular, there were major changes in the organization, processes, and practices of royal justice during the reign of Alexander II, albeit not in the way that has previously been thought. Early in Alexander II's reign, the ad hoc royal justices were reconstituted as two regional justiciars, who journeyed around their regions on ayres every year or few years. Royal justice began to be obtained through the king's written and standardized brieves; pursuers and claimants could seek the king's brieve and initiate legal processes, sometimes in the king's courts and sometimes in the courts of other aristocrats, both lay and, it appears, ecclesiastical. The second two-thirds of Alexander II's reign may well have been when most of these new remedies were introduced and they ushered in a period when people of varying status could interact with the king's writing chapel in pursuit of their own interests. Perhaps in response to this, the king's chapel started keeping its own records, not necessarily as a routine part of their own government, as in England, but instead to create an institutional memory of the actions of royal government.

The adoption of Latin documents as tools of kingship and governance was key to the changing capacities of institutional government across the period. It should be stressed how piecemeal a process this was. Thus, while kings used brieves to command their officials and magnates from the reign of Alexander I, they appear only to have started issuing Latin charters to religious beneficiaries in David's reign and only routinely to lay beneficiaries in the first few decades of William's.[3] Under Alexander II, it is clear, however, that the function of Latin records had extended

---

[3] For this last, see Matthew Hammond, 'The Adoption and Routinization of Scottish Royal Charter Production for Lay Beneficiaries, 1124–1195', *ANS*, vol. 36 (2014) pp. 91–115.

into the realm of brieves initiating legal processes in courts. This did constitute a change: by this process, government through the written word meant not only command and notification but now also anticipation of, and provision for, the needs of the people. Writing had become the way in which such provision could be accomplished in standard ways. Equally, during the reign of Alexander III, we can see routine commands issued through the written word in a way that it is not possible to see earlier: all monetary outgoings, for example, came to be documented by the king's letters patent.[4] That we can see provision as well as command in thirteenth-century Scottish government owes much to the expanding purposes of the documents produced by the king's chapel.

As these institutional and routine structures of rule developed in Scotia, greater Lothian (including Clydesdale), and Moray in the thirteenth century, royal gifts of land from this area declined in frequency and extent, particularly in Scotia. This is important: gifts of land had been one of the main ways kings could gain support from their aristocracy. But, as Wickham has noted, the problem with 'political reward [being] dominated by the "politics of land"' is that land—the very source of patronage—can run out.[5] This above all may explain why Alexander II and Alexander III gave far less of their land away from Scotia than William the Lion had done. The decline of the practice of ruling through landed patronage in Scotia, however, had two major consequences. First, the new periphery of the kingdom was used in a similar way: during the thirteenth century, the west and north sea-based periphery seem to have been used as a source of landed gifts, much as Lothian and Clydesdale had been used previously by David I and Mael Coluim IV, and Scotia by William the Lion. Second, the developing structures of royal government meant that governmental institutions offered their own culture of political rewards. Power and status could be cemented, confirmed, or gained by political service, rather than through land patronage, and we find that by 1263–66 a large proportion of the local sheriffs in this area were in fact major members of the king's court and had kingdom-wide political importance.

The way in which kings ruled thus changed as significantly over the thirteenth century as it had done in the twelfth. One of the contentions outlined at the start of this book should therefore have become clear: it is inaccurate to say that David I was responsible for the form of Scottish government in the central Middle Ages. Although David did introduce sheriffs and justices to his kingdom, they operated mainly south of the Forth: there is no evidence that he and his counsellors intended these units to be an intensive way of ruling his whole kingdom all the way north into Moray; the most northern point where sheriffs are documented during his reign was Perth. Indeed, the evidence from Mael Coluim IV's reign shows that justices in particular were not expected to operate north of the major boundary of the Forth in the mid-twelfth century; that area was still the preserve of *iudices*. It is worth emphasizing this point not because I think most historians

---

[4] See Chapter 6, pp. 365–6.
[5] Chris Wickham, *Framing the Early Middle Ages: Europe and the Mediterranean, 400–800* (Oxford, 2005), pp. 58–9.

now support the long-standing contention that David I directed a stable trajectory of governmental change, essentially leaving an unwritten policy directive for his grandsons to follow, for they do not. However, because previous work on Scottish government has been so focused on particular aspects of change, the overall importance of David I's reign has retained some hold on the subject from which it should now be released.

That being said, it is still important to acknowledge that the later twelfth century—and thus the reign of William the Lion—emerges from this study as a key period for the early development of governmental institutions. It was at this point that uniform units of local government—the sheriffdoms—covered most of the kingdom and were called to financial account by the chamberlain, one of the king's household officers. It is also at this point that a judicial hierarchy developed across the kingdom: if the sheriff failed to enforce justice, then the official justice would. If only one of these developments had occurred, this period might not seem so key but, as there are identifiable changes to three officials (the sheriff, justice, and chamberlain) in the same two decades or so, the later twelfth century stands out as a period when the methods of kingship were changing dramatically. This is not to suggest that we should depose David from the position of founder of Scottish government and replace him with William;[6] one could pinpoint the 'leap forward' in the use of legal brieves in the reign of Alexander II as being equally important. However, as a number of key developments occurred during the late 1170s–late 1190s, it is worth briefly thinking about why this particular period might have witnessed such explicit consolidation and expansion of the new institutional structures of royal rule across the kingdom.

William faced two major political problems during this period: one concerned Lothian, the other Moray and Ross. The whole of the kingdom of the Scots (and Galloway) was under English overlordship following William's defeat and capture at Alnwick in 1174 as part of what is now known as the 'Great Rebellion' against Henry II; the overlordship was only finally lifted in 1189.[7] More importantly, three castles in southern Scotland—Edinburgh, Berwick and Roxburgh—were occupied by English garrisons.[8] There is some debate about how far the occupying garrisons affected the day-to-day running of the burghs (including mint output) to which they were attached.[9] What is clear, however, is that the occupation affected

---

[6] A caveat also made about the relative positions of Alfred and Edgar with regard to the formation of the English kingdom in George Molyneaux, *The Formation of the English Kingdom in the Tenth Century* (Oxford, 2015), pp. 193–4.

[7] For the Treaty of Falaise-Valognes and the Quitclaim of Canterbury, see *Anglo-Scottish Relations, 1174–1328: Some Selected Documents*, ed. and trans. E. L. G. Stones (Oxford, 1965, repr. with corrections, 1970), nos. 1–2; discussed in, among many, A. A. M. Duncan, *The Kingship of the Scots, 842–1292: Succession and Independence* (Edinburgh, 2002), pp. 99–102; Richard Oram, *Domination and Lordship: Scotland 1070 to 1230* (Edinburgh, 2011), pp. 135–40.

[8] Edinburgh was given back in 1186 on William's marriage, for which see Howden, *Gesta*, i, p. 351; D. W. Hunter Marshall, 'Two Early English Occupations of Southern Scotland', *SHR*, vol. 25, no. 97 (1927), pp. 20–3, 37.

[9] Edward Burns, *The Coinage of Scotland*, 3 vols (Edinburgh, 1887), vol. i, pp. 52–7; T. C. R. Crafter, 'Monetary Expansion in Britain in the Late Twelfth Century' (DPhil Dissertation, University of Oxford, 2007), pp. 217–24.

the king's movements. Edinburgh, a popular place for assemblies and the issue of William the Lion's charters, declined in this period; its place appears to have been taken by Perth.[10] In addition, William's hold on his kingship was significantly challenged by Domnall mac Uilleim, grandson of Donnchad II, the son of Mael Coluim III through his first marriage who had briefly been king in 1094.[11] Donnchad's grandson, Domnall, violently challenged William on three occasions between 1179 and 1187 and the focus of his challenge was the north. The first and the last, in 1179 and 1186–87, were at Ross north of the Beauly Firth.[12] There is no doubt that Domnall's claims to the kingship of the Scots were taken seriously; they not only prompted a defensive programme of major castle-building up in Moray and Ross but also an ideological one, which presented Donnchad II as bastard whose descendants would thus have no legal claim to the kingship of the Scots.[13]

These two events in combination added up to a political cataclysm which must have prompted a need to intensify and regularize governmental structures. As shrieval courts and justices had long operated south of the Forth, and had begun to operate in Scotia, the main area affected by the proclamations that sheriffs and justices should hold regular courts must have been particularly Moray. As Domnall mac Uilleim made his known incursions into Ross, Moray represented a liminal area, separated from the more intensely governed Scotia and Lothian but also geographically separated from the Black Isle and Ross by the Beauly Firth. The need to regulate governmental structures in Moray in order to unify them with those of Scotia and the now occupied Lothian must have been at least one factor in determining a number of identifiable processes: the changes in charter diplomatic to the definitions of shrieval power north of the Forth; the expectation that sheriffs everywhere would hold courts; and, even, the greater focus in royal assizes on the issue of teind default that pertained to the bishopric of Moray, which symbolically realigned it with practices in other dioceses in the south.[14]

The political needs of government were also supported by an increasing monetization of the economy. William's Crescent coinage, which ran from the 1170s to 1195, had a higher estimated output than any previous issue of the kings of Scots; his Short Cross issue which followed in 1195 was even larger.[15] Although Scottish coins never made up the majority of coins circulating in Scotland, the production

---

[10] That William was well aware of this is suggested by the major assemblies held at Edinburgh and Roxburgh after the lifting of the overlordship in 1189, reconstructed from the patterns of attestation to royal charters. For Roxburgh (1189×95) see *RRS*, ii, nos. 313–18; Edinburgh, *RRS*, ii, nos. 292–9, 300, 308, 364.

[11] See A. A. M. Duncan, *Scotland: the Making of the Kingdom* (Edinburgh, 1975), pp. 194–8; Alasdair Ross, 'Moray, Ulster and the MacWilliams', in *The World of the Galloglass: Kings, Warlords and Warriors in Ireland and Scotland 1200–1600*, ed. Séan Duffy (Dublin, 2007); Oram, *Domination and Lordship*, pp. 140–5.

[12] Howden, *Gesta*, i, pp. 277–8; ii, pp. 7–9; *Gesta Annalia* I, in Skene, *Fordun*, i, p. 268.

[13] Dauvit Broun, 'Contemporary Perspectives on Alexander II's Succession: the Evidence of King-lists', in *The Reign of Alexander II, 1214–49*, ed. Richard Oram (Leiden, 2005), pp. 79–98, at pp. 92–5.

[14] Discussed respectively in Chapter 4, pp. 201–2, 205–10, and Chapter 3, pp. 155–7.

[15] See the literature cited in Chapter 6, pp. 389–97.

of a larger volume can only be understood if coin use was increasing more broadly. If coin use was increasing, then it would have been easier for kings to standardize, make routine, and collect the income they expected from their sheriffs. Political pressure and circumstance, which forced William and his counsellors to look far into the north, coupled with increasing monetization, must have prompted the kingdom-wide definition of a particular form of local government, whose officials discharged relatively uniform responsibilities, who all began to collect the king's revenue in similar ways, and whose activities started to be documented in records produced by the king's chapel. That government continued to change and develop over the thirteenth century should not blind us to the importance of the late twelfth in any history of institutional government in the kingdom of the Scots.

The narrative of change in the methods of kingship has thus been the primary subject of this book. However, although the dynamic nature of royal government over the twelfth and thirteenth centuries has been stressed here, it is worth highlighting three important aspects of royal government in the 1260s, midway through the reign of Alexander III. Once set out, these will allow identification of important but underlying continuities in the way royal power was exercised in the kingdom of the Scots, despite the transformation in the methods of royal rulership.

First, Alexander III's government was still geographically and regionally focused. It was a government primarily of greater Lothian (including Clydesdale), Scotia, and Moray. Although we have evidence of sheriffs in Galloway, Ross, and Caithness, who in general accounted independently in the 1263–66 accounts, the profits of justice from the judicial ayre were returned through other sheriffs who were located on the very edges of the core region. In this way, the area under the maximum institutional authority of the kings of Scots in the 1260s was very similar to the areas under the symbolic authority of the kings of Scots two centuries earlier, when Mael Coluim III, king of Scots, controlled Scotia, had gained control over Lothian and Clydesdale, and had some sort of domination over Moray in the north. In addition, despite this real growth in the uniform expectations of what government could do in this area, there was also an even sharper geographical focus on the locations for governmental rituals.[16] We should distinguish between the location of large ritual assemblies (held for the purposes of making law, for example), which were more likely to occur in Scotia and greater Lothian than in Moray, and the area covered by governmental institutions. How far the geographical focus of these known legislative assemblies is borne out by the locations and personal make-up of royal assemblies more generally cannot be known, given the state of present knowledge: a full study on assemblies and the royal *iter* is a pressing need in Scottish historiography of the period.[17] That kings ruled through institutions by the mid-thirteenth century is clear; however, their power would also have been legitimized

---

[16] See Chapter 3, pp. 119–20.

[17] Only Alexander II's reign has received attention; see Keith J. Stringer, 'The Scottish "Political Community" in the Reign of Alexander II (1214–49)', in *New Perspectives on Medieval Scotland, 1093–1286*, ed. Matthew Hammond (Woodbridge, 2013), pp. 53–84. Work on twelfth-century royal assemblies by Matthew Hammond is forthcoming.

through assemblies, particularly if those attending were not just the great men of the realm but also people known to have operated only in localized settings. Assemblies, after all, were one major way that medieval kings could legitimate their power in the widest possible sense.[18] A study on Scottish assemblies would no doubt illuminate further the arguments presented in this book concerning the structures of institutional government.

Second, Scottish government was inherently localized even by the mid-1260s. The sheriffdom has emerged clearly in the second part of this book as the key unit of Scottish government. It was on the basis of sheriffdoms that justiciars went on ayres. Sheriffs not only had their accounts audited after collecting the king's income, they also paid for that audit directly and paid the fees of 'central' governmental officials out of the profits of individual sheriffdoms, rather than the total income received. In this way, sheriffdoms were the key political structures on which central government depended directly. Sheriffdoms were also the units whereby kings reached into other jurisdictions. The shrieval inquests initiated by royal brieve could be taken by disputants into the courts of others. In addition, baronies were also key to the workings of the sheriffdom and representatives from baronies would make up shrieval visnets; the sheriffdom was thus the conduit into baronies and vice versa. In short, although there existed central officials, who covered the whole (the chamberlain) or part (the justiciars) of the kingdom, these officials worked directly with and depended on the sheriffdom; central offices had little institutional existence that could operate autonomously from local units of government.

Finally, and most importantly, Scottish government had not grown at the expense of aristocratic power. What we can know about royal power before the mid-twelfth century suggests that it functioned through co-opting powerful people to discharge particular responsibilities on the king's behalf at a provincial and local level. This fundamental dynamic is identifiable across the central Middle Ages, although the methods of achieving this and the structures in which this dynamic operated undoubtedly did change. Thus, when sheriffdoms were introduced north of the Forth, aristocratic power was becoming formally territorial; William gave and confirmed significant gifts of land to his aristocracy at the same time as institutionalizing the governance of his kingdom. Aristocratic power remained key to achieving the ambitions of royal law not only in the period when that law was not yet set within an explicit jurisdictional and administrative structure but also, most importantly, when it was: whereas William had implicitly relied on other powerful people following the prescriptive content of his laws, Alexander II explicitly incorporated lay aristocratic jurisdiction into his legislation. Military service was levied according to lordship; the king only took responsibility for his own land. The common law of the kingdom did not, as it did in England, take a large number of cases out of aristocratic courts and into royal courts. Many of the 'common' law brieves were limited to those of high socio-economic and socio-political

---

[18] Levi Roach, *Kingship and Consent in Anglo-Saxon England, 871–978: Assemblies and the State in the Early Middle Ages* (Cambridge, 2013), pp. 27–44, 212–38.

status; other brieves could be used indirectly to initiate cases in aristocratic courts without challenging the legitimacy of the elite court-holder. This affected, therefore, the profile of lay office holders: many major lords, who held their land directly from the king, served as his officials both at a local and at a central level. The state which had developed midway through the reign of Alexander III had not involved a reorganization of existing power relations; instead, it was a different manifestation of them, in which aristocratic power was formally territorial and jurisdictional and was explicitly built into the structures of royal government, itself growing through and with the power of aristocrats.

Scottish royal government was thus mediated and maintained not only through administrative and bureaucratic institutions but also through its reliance on defined aristocratic power. During the late twelfth century, kings defined and formalized aristocratic power in relation to their own. When the king of Scots took, for example, oaths of loyalty from his men, requiring them to keep the peace and not to harbour wrongdoers, he did so not from all the free adult males of his kingdom—as was the practice elsewhere—but only from major lay and ecclesiastical courtholders.[19] The personal ties binding lords to the king took on permanent infrastructural form: bureaucratic institutions and the devolution of power to individuals were not inherently different in ultimate function by the reign of Alexander III. Indeed, aristocratic power was the precondition for institutional and bureaucratic government. The necessity of aristocratic power to the medieval Scottish state produced, in traditional terms, a more limited and mediated government but it was nonetheless a conceptually unified government, the shape of which was fundamentally affected by the kingdom's structural inheritance from the eleventh century. This means that, although the form of government changed dramatically, the twelfth century was not so dramatic a period of change in underlying power dynamics as earlier views on the twelfth-century 'feudalization' of Scotland once supposed.

There are two points here that can be taken further into a comparative history of royal government in the central Middle Ages. The first arises out of an older narrative which stresses the influence of English governmental structures on the outward shape of government in Scotland. This process is labelled 'Anglicization', and it essentially explains change through recourse to a 'core–periphery' dynamic. That is, the political culture of an economically, socially, and politically more complex 'core' region is adopted into the political culture of a 'peripheral' region, often seen (from the perspective of the 'core') as less complex in all these areas.[20] English

---

[19] For other general oaths, see Alan Harding, *Medieval Law and the Foundations of the State* (Oxford, 2001), pp. 69–108; Thomas N. Bisson, *The Crisis of the Twelfth Century: Power, Lordship and the Origins of European Government* (Princeton, NJ, 2009), pp. 471–84; Tom Lambert, *Law and Order in Anglo-Saxon England* (forthcoming), chapter 5.

[20] See the important studies in Nora Berend ed., *Christianization and the Rise of Christian Monarchy: Scandinavia, Central Europe and Rus', c.900–1200* (Cambridge, 2007); and, among many, Sverre Bagge, 'The Europeanization of Europe: the Case of Scandinavia', in *European Transformations: the Long Twelfth Century*, ed. Thomas F. X. Noble and John van Engen (Notre Dame, 2012), pp. 171–93.

influence in Scotland has been seen as a product of a latent imperial reality of English political, social, economic, and cultural domination that affected medieval Wales, Ireland, but particularly Scotland over the central Middle Ages. Sir Rees Davies wrote that '[Anglicization's] greatest and most immediate triumph was neither in Wales nor in Ireland, but in Scotland.'[21] While Davies acknowledged that Scottish kings did not adopt English methods indiscriminately, his overwhelming impression was of Anglicization: 'it was in Scotland, or rather a good part of the most densely populated and prosperous areas of it, that the influence of England— *in law, institutions,* tenurial custom, burghal development, coinage, trade patterns, language, and so forth—was arguably most profound'.[22]

This book does not seek to deny English influence; indeed, that Scottish kings did, broadly speaking, use English methods of government—the sheriffdom, the justices, common law brieves—is clear and has been emphasized throughout the second part of this book. But it is a clear view only when glimpsed from afar; it does little to help us understand the changing form of Scottish government as a subject in its own right. Such a view also further cements an ethnic interpretive framework, distinguishing some elements of government and society as 'native' and some as 'incoming', which does not take us very far in understanding form.[23] After all, the form and structure of Scottish government were different from that of England: the borrowings were not mere borrowings, they were adaptations, and were adapted to meet particular circumstances. Existing patterns of status and authority were not static; they responded to and were changed by the more intensive governmental strategies of Scottish kings in the central Middle Ages.

By now, this point should not come as a surprise. The kingdoms of England and Scotland were indeed very different at the beginning of the twelfth century. At the time of the Norman Conquest, the kingdom of England was predominantly divided into administrative shires up to the northern boundary of Yorkshire.[24] By the death of Henry I in 1135, Northumberland and Cumberland had also been shired, although Cumberland's boundaries had not yet been set.[25] This was not the case in the kingdom of the Scots.[26] There were people in charge of collecting revenue from royal estates (how else were kings to enjoy their revenue?) but there were no standard units of local government with which the king would interact through his brieve and brieve-charter as there were in England. In Scotland, such units

---

[21] R. R. Davies, *The First English Empire: Power and Identities in the British Isles 1093–1343* (Oxford, 2000), pp. 142–71, at p. 160; see also the critiques of Davies's position in the literature cited in Introduction, p. 19, at note 91.

[22] Davies, *First English Empire*, pp. 170–1; my emphasis.

[23] See, further, Matthew H. Hammond, 'Ethnicity and the Writing of Medieval Scottish History', *SHR*, vol. 85, no. 219 (2006), pp. 1–27.

[24] Most obviously witnessed in the range of Domesday book itself; see Molyneaux, *Formation*, pp. 2–9, 199–201, 211–13.

[25] For Northumberland and Cumberland, see Richard Sharpe, *Norman Rule in Cumbria, 1092–1136*, Cumberland and Westmorland Antiquarian and Archaeological Society (Kendal, 2006), *passim*; For the shiring of East Anglia under Cnut in the earlier eleventh century, see Lucy Marten, 'The Shiring of East Anglia: an Alternative Hypothesis', *Historical Research*, vol. 81, no. 211 (2008), pp. 1–27.

[26] See Chapter 4, pp. 195–205.

developed as the century progressed and did so at the same time as developments in the role of officials normally considered as 'central', such as the justice/justiciars and the chamberlain. By contrast, in England, central developments, such as the exchequer in the reign of Henry I or the itinerant justices in the reign of Henry II, overlay a local structure of government that had existed, in places, for over one hundred years. This gave the centre in England the potential to take on a real institutional existence separate from the local.

In late-twelfth- and thirteenth-century Scotland, central government did not take on an institutional form that was spatially and institutionally distinguishable from the local. In England, the development of a real separation between the personnel of local government and that of the centre motivated many political movements which prompted institutional change in that kingdom, most notably the emergence of Parliament as a contextually representative institution.[27] The socio-economic difference between regnal and local aristocracies created a complex and stratified nobility in England, which in itself has prompted modern historiographical debates about the nature of the 'gentry' class in thirteenth- and four-teenth-century England.[28] Such debates are far less part of the historiography of thirteenth-century Scotland:[29] this must be in part because there was less of a social and economic separation between the knights who were prominent in local government and the barons of central government. Indeed, it is significant that, in the kingdom of the Scots, many of the men who held governmental rank were simply called 'knights' (*milites*) but when they appeared in English diplomatic documents, they were described as 'barons' (*barones*).[30]

What this meant in England was that, when there were reform movements, they were directed at all levels of government and were devoted to stamping out the king's abuses of his own governmental structures. The series of reforms known as the Provisions of Oxford, directed at Henry III in 1258–59, took away the king's fundamental control of virtually all his governmental institutions to reform them both at the centre and in the localities.[31] This did not happen in Scotland. The only possible document that we might identify as a reform document in mid-thirteenth-century Scotland—the so-called 'Laws of Mael Coluim III'—did not, by contrast, target

[27] J. R. Maddicott, *The Origins of English Parliament, 924–1327* (Oxford, 2010).

[28] See, among many, Peter Coss, *The Origins of the English Gentry* (Cambridge, 2003); Peter Coss, 'The Formation of the English Gentry', *Past & Present*, no. 147 (1995), pp. 38–64; Christine Carpenter, *Locality and Polity: A Study of Warwickshire Landed Society 1401–1499* (Cambridge, 1992); David Crouch, *The Image of Aristocracy in Britain, 1000–1300* (London, 1992), pp. 23–38, and Part 1; David Crouch, *The English Aristocracy 1070–1272: A Social Transformation* (New Haven, CT, 2011), pp. 13–19, 37–61.

[29] The exception is Stringer, 'Scottish "Political Community"'.

[30] See Chapter 7, pp. 411–12, and notes 110, 112.

[31] *Documents of the Baronial Movement of Reform and Rebellion, 1258–1267*, Oxford Medieval Texts, ed. R. F. Treharne and I. J. Sanders (Oxford, 1973), no. 5, see also no. 3; for commentary, see David A. Carpenter, 'What Happened in 1258?', in David A. Carpenter, *The Reign of Henry III* (London, 1996), pp. 183–97, and H. W. Ridgeway, 'Mid Thirteenth-Century Reformers and the Localities: the Sheriffs of the Baronial Regime, 1258–1261', in *Regionalism and Revision: The Crown and Its Provinces in England, 1250–1650*, ed. P. Fleming, A. J. Gross and J. R. Lander (London, 1998), pp. 59–86.

institutions.[32] The potential abuses of royal officials and their potential abuse by the king were simply not part of the rhetoric of this Scottish document; instead, it targeted the king alone. He was not to abuse wardships, accept compensation from proven thieves, nor lift penal exile in return for money. Thus, in England, aristocratic reformers concentrated on the king's use of institutions; in Scotland, putative reformers concentrated on the king independently of his governmental institutions. That aristocratic power was so closely entwined with these institutions would have meant that any attack on the king that focused on royal institutions of government would have been an attack on one major base of aristocratic power.

All this means that a narrative which sees the form of Scottish government as a direct product of Anglicization—and thus sees it as an English government in miniature—misunderstands how royal power was exercised in Scotland and how that changed over the central Middle Ages. The process of Anglicization relies on the capacity of a core, more powerful area to dominate a peripheral, less powerful area, whether that dominating power is defined culturally, politically, or both.[33] In this, the process of Anglicization resembles the process of Europeanization, in which the political culture of the 'core areas' of Europe, expanded into the periphery of Europe in the east, north, and centre.[34] A narrative of Anglicization is one lens through which to view the history of the British Isles from the late eleventh to the early fourteenth century but it has its limits in this case because it does not aid real understanding of the changing form of royal government in the kingdom of the Scots. Scottish government was not the same as English: it raised less money, it was more localized, it was more dependent on aristocratic power. That a core-periphery explanatory framework can only take us so far in understanding changes in power structures is one fundamental conclusion of this book. This is why national histories—or, to use a less loaded or anachronistic term, the history of individual polities—still matter in any comparative history project.

This brings the book to its final point: the medieval state. As stated in the introduction, medieval historians often start with definitions of modern states for their understanding of medieval ones, even if they do problematize such an approach.[35] Important here are the notions that states are those in which a single, centralized

---

[32] Madrid, Biblioteca Real MS II 2097, fo. 11v. That these so-called 'laws of Mael Coluim III' might represent a previously unacknowledged 'reform' movement in mid-thirteenth-century Scotland is a speculation but one I hope to develop on another occasion.

[33] Davies, *First English Empire*, pp. 142–5; cf. Nora Berend, 'Introduction', in *Christianization*, pp. 1–46, at pp. 19–23, 36–9.

[34] Robert Bartlett, *The Making of Europe: Conquest, Colonization and Cultural Change, 950–1350* (London, 1994), pp. 269–91.

[35] See, for example, the varying positions adopted in Walter Pohl and Veronika Wieser ed., *Der frühmittelalterliche Staat—europäishe Perspektiven*, Forschungen zur Geschichte des Mittelalters 16 (Vienna, 2009); Susan Reynolds, 'The Historiography of the Medieval State', in *Companion to Historiography*, ed. Michael Bentley (London, 1997), pp. 118–21; critiqued in R. R. Davies, 'The Medieval State: the Tyranny of a Concept?', *Journal of Historical Sociology*, vol. 16 (2003), pp. 287–93; Thomas Ertman, *Birth of the Leviathan: Building States and Regimes in Medieval and Early Modern Europe* (Cambridge, 1997), which advocates difference. For an example of the chronology of the development of states in the modern meaning of the word, see Harding, *Medieval Law*, pp. 1–5; Paul-Ludwig Weinacht, *Staat. Studien zur Bedeutungsgeschichte des Wortes den Anfängen bis ins 19. Jahrhundert* (Berlin, 1968).

authority has a monopoly over legitimate violence and in which exist abstract, impersonal administrative institutions, staffed by (specialized) officials, who are the delegations and manifestations of the areas (justice and defence, for example) over which the state claims the authority to provide for the public.[36] Scottish royal government could, by 1290, claim to cover both areas. That these aims were manifested in different ways from modern states and were often mediated through aristocratic jurisdictions as much as by royal officials should not be surprising. For the sociologist Michael Mann, one fundamental difference between modern states and 'feudal [medieval] states' was that in modern states legitimate power is exercised primarily in the abstract 'public' realm: no power can be exercised legitimately in the private realm if it is not already defined or definable as legitimate by the state, which represents the public. In 'feudal states', by contrast, *both* 'public' and 'private' spheres controlled the exercise of legitimate power. Mann commented: 'much remained hidden from the state, excluded from the public realm, *private*. Political-power networks were not unitary but dual, part public, part privately controlled by a class of local magnates'.[37] In Mann's assessment, medieval states operated a smaller public sphere than could be possible in modern states; lordship (the private world) occupied a larger space which could set the standards for the legitimacy of its own behaviour and which would not be seen as a legitimate source of power in modern states. For Mann, then, it was not that 'feudal states' were not states, it was just that power was organized differently; legitimate power ran in two parallel channels, one public, the other private.[38] It is to Mann's notion of 'dual political power networks' that the example of the kingdom of the Scots provides an important corrective.

Mann's position is one example among an extremely large body of work on states undertaken not only by sociologists but also by medieval historians. But his points do highlight the importance of the relationship between aristocratic and royal power in these debates. Scholarship on the Carolingian Empire and post-Carolingian Europe, for example, is now rejecting a view of government which analysed it according to modern definitions of states. This older narrative saw the Carolingian empire as a nascent modern state, one whose Roman inheritance preserved a sense of the public order which was manifested in its governmental structure: royal agents were placed over large administrative divisions where public courts were held and the central areas of the empire communicated with the periphery by *missi*—delegates sent out to supervise the maintenance of public law and order in the courts.[39] When the Carolingians eventually lost control of the

[36] Timothy Reuter, 'All Quiet on the Western Front? The Emergence of Pre-Modern Forms of Statehood in the Central Middle Ages', in Timothy Reuter, *Medieval Polities and Modern Mentalities*, ed. Janet L. Nelson (Cambridge, 2006), pp. 432–58.

[37] Michael Mann, *The Sources of Social Power*, 2 vols (Cambridge, 1986, 1993), vol. i, pp. 373–449, at p. 393.

[38] Although Mann did think that *early* feudal states were far weaker than ancient or modern ones and so 'in some ways it is misleading to call any of them "states," so decentralized were political functions, and so lacking in territoriality were they': Mann, *Sources of Social Power*, i, p. 392.

[39] See, among many, Karl Ferdinand Werner, '*Missus—Marchio—Comes*: Entre l'administration centrale et l'administration locale de l'Empire carolingien', in *Histoire comparée de l'administration (IVe–XVIIIe siècles)*, ed. W. Paravicini and K. F. Werner (Munich, 1980), pp. 191–241.

kingship, as they did in the late tenth century, the public order they had created remained for about a century, at which point it finally fragmented, leaving public power privatized into the hands of lesser lords and kingship itself a much less weighty political force.[40]

This narrative has been problematized and almost wholly reconceived along new lines.[41] At the heart of its transformation is a different view on the aims and capacities of kingship and the relationship between aristocratic and royal power.[42] Many historians no longer think that aristocratic power weakened the capacities of kings or vice versa. Instead, aristocrats necessarily collaborated with and were agents of the king and/or emperor: kings needed aristocrats to work for them as much as aristocrats needed to work for the king in order to increase their own power and status.[43] Major assemblies were one of the main settings in which kings could achieve consensus, the fundamental way in which they could rule over large areas.[44] The making of law was itself a consensus-driven activity undertaken by a wide stratum of elites.[45] In this way, ritual and symbolic consensus were among the main tools available to kings in an early medieval world in which the public and private realms were not defined as the fundamental binary which legitimated

---

[40] Georges Duby, *La Société aux xie et xiie siècles dans la régione mâconnaise*, in Georges Duby, *Qu'est-ce que la société féodale?* (Paris, 2002), pp. 7–597; Jean-Pierre Poly and Éric Bournazel, *La mutation féodale X^e–XIIe siècles*, 3rd edn (Paris, 2004); cf. Régine Le Jan, 'Continuity and Change in the Tenth-Century Nobility', in *Nobles and Nobility in Medieval Europe: Concepts, Origins, Transformations*, ed. Anne J. Duggan (Woodbridge, 2000), pp. 53–68.

[41] Thomas N. Bisson, 'The 'Feudal "Revolution"', *Past & Present*, no. 142 (1994), pp. 6–42, with responses by Dominique Barthélemy and Stephen D. White in *Past & Present*, no. 152 (1996), pp. 196–223, and by Timothy Reuter and Chris Wickham in *Past & Present*, no. 155 (1997), pp. 177–208; see also Dominique Barthélemy, *La mutation de l'an mil a-t-elle eu lieu?: Servage et chevalerie dans la France des Xe et XIe siècles* (Paris, 1997), and his *The Serf, the Knight and the Historian*, trans. G. Robert Edwards (Ithaca, 2009). Stephen D. White, 'Tenth-Century Courts at Mâcon and the perils of structuralist history: re-reading Burgundian judicial institutions', in *Conflict in Medieval Europe*, ed. Warren C. Brown and Piotr Górecki (Aldershot, 2003), pp. 37–68; Charles West, *Reframing the Feudal Revolution: Political and Social Transformation between the Marne and the Moselle, c.800–c.1100* (Cambridge, 2013).

[42] See the critique in Matthew Innes, *State and Society in the Early Medieval West: the Middle Rhine Valley 400–1000* (Cambridge, 2000), pp. 241–50; also Régine Le Jan, *Famille et Pouvoir dans le monde franc (viie–xe siècle): Essai d'anthropologie sociale* (Paris, 1995), pp. 126–41; see also the different and important approach taken in Rosamond McKitterick, *The Carolingians and the Written Word* (Cambridge, 1989), pp. 23–75; and Rosamond McKitterick, 'Charlemagne's *missi* and Their Books', in *Early Medieval Studies in Memory of Patrick Wormald*, ed. Stephen Baxter, Catherine Karkov, Janet L. Nelson, David Pelteret (Farnham, 2009), pp. 253–67.

[43] Stuart Airlie, 'The Aristocracy in the Service of the State in the Carolingian Period', in *Staat im frühen Mittelalter*, ed. Stuart Airlie, Walter Pohl, and Helmut Reimitz, Forschungen zur Geschichte des Mittelalters 11 (Vienna, 2006), pp. 93–112; Stuart Airlie, 'Charlemagne and the Aristocracy: Captains and Kings', in *Charlemagne: Empire and Society*, ed. Joanna Story (Manchester, 2005), pp. 90–102; Stuart Airlie, '*Semper fideles?* Loyauté envers les Carolingiens comme constituant de l'identité aristocratique', in *La Royauté et les élites dans l'Europe carolingienne (début IXe siècle aux environs de 920)*, ed. Régine Le Jan (Lille, 1998), pp. 129–43; Gerd Althoff, *Friends, Family and Followers: Political and Social Bonds in Medieval Europe* (Cambridge, 2004).

[44] Janet L. Nelson, 'How Carolingians created consensus', in *Le monde carolingien: Bilan, perspectives, champs de recherches*, ed. Wojciech Fałkowski and Yves Sassier (Turnhout, 2009), pp. 67–81; Janet L. Nelson, *Charles the Bald* (Harlow, 1992), p. 48.

[45] Janet L. Nelson, 'Legislation and Consensus in the Reign of Charles the Bald', in *Ideal and Reality in Frankish and Anglo-Saxon Society: Studies Presented to J. M. Wallace-Hadrill*, ed. P. Wormald, D. A. Bullough, and R. Collins (Oxford, 1983), pp. 202–27.

political life and in which administrative institutions also did not have much coercive power beyond what aristocrats could offer by serving within them.[46] Seeing early medieval kingship as weak, then, because it relied on the 'private' power of lordship, is to misunderstand how power could be exercised in this particular period of history.

Scholarship on the central Middle Ages has, to some extent, seen a similar transformation.[47] Like the scholarship on the early Middle Ages, there has been an increased focus on lordship and aristocratic power. It has been repeatedly stressed that royal power was, particularly in the long twelfth century, conceptualized as a form of lordship: kings were the most important aristocrats.[48] But overall changes in the methods of royal rule are still seen along relatively traditional lines, even if the causes of this change have recently been seen as a consequence of the position of lordship as a primary source of legitimate power rather than as a move against the phenomenon of lordship itself.[49] Regardless as to why, the late twelfth and thirteenth centuries are, for many polities in Western Europe, seen as the period when kings started to rule (again) through institutions, delegating their capacity to do justice to more uniform networks of royal courts, raising their revenue through more standard units of local administration, condemning (unnecessary or unlawful) aristocratic violence, and supervising the collection of their revenue in order to make sure that their officials were morally good agents, well able to serve the 'public order' that had resurrected itself again and was manifested in governmental institutions and mediated through aristocratic consultation.[50]

What has, perhaps, transformed more obviously in the scholarship on the central and, particularly, the later Middle Ages is the understanding of the functions of aristocratic power itself, particularly when that power was manifested as violence. Instead of seeing aristocrats as fundamentally opposed to the aims of kings and their governments, whole generations of historians, mostly influenced by anthropology, have seen aristocratic (or seigneurial) feuds or violence as legitimate disputing

---

[46] See, among many, Innes, *State and Society*, pp. 4–12, 254–63.

[47] See the important comments in Janet L. Nelson, 'Liturgy or Law: Misconceived Alternatives', in *Early Medieval Studies*, ed. Baxter et al., pp. 433–47.

[48] Davies, 'Medieval State', pp. 293–6; T. N. Bisson, 'Medieval Lordship', *Speculum*, vol. 70, no. 4 (1995), pp. 749–54.

[49] T. N. Bisson, 'Celebration and Persuasion: Reflections on the Cultural Evolution of Medieval Consultation', *Legislative Studies Quarterly*, vol. 7, no. 2 (1982), pp. 181–204; and now Bisson, *Crisis*, pp. 425–572.

[50] Most recently, Bisson, *Crisis*, particularly chapters 5 and 6; see also the earlier summary in Reuter, 'All Quiet on the Western Front', pp. 453–8; for earlier positions, see Heinrich Mitteis, *The State in the Middle Ages*, trans. H. F. Orton (Amsterdam, 1975 [first published in German in 1940]), and Joseph R. Strayer, *On the Medieval Origins of the Modern State*, with forewords by Charles Tilly and William Chester Jordan (Princeton, NJ, 2005), pp. 3–56; Fredric L. Cheyette, 'The Invention of the State', in *The Walter Prescott Memorial Lectures: Essays on Medieval Civilisation*, ed. R. E. Sullivan, B. K. Lachner, and K. R. Philp (Austin, TX, and London, 1978); for important corrective positions, see Timothy Reuter, 'Mandate, Privilege, Court Judgement: Techniques of Rulership in the Age of Frederick Barbarossa', in Reuter, *Medieval Polities*, ed. Nelson, pp. 413–31; John Gillingham, 'Elective kingship and the unity of medieval Germany', *German History*, vol. 9, no. 2 (1991), pp. 124–35; see also the survey in John Watts, *The Making of Polities: Europe, 1300–1500* (Cambridge, 2009), pp. 23–34.

processes that were part of social order itself.[51] A different understanding of the function of violence is key to this reconfiguration. Whereas earlier generations of historians saw violence as primarily disruptive of the order symbolically promoted by kings, historians from the 1950s and 1960s onwards have seen such violence and intra-magnate feuds as a type of social order in and of itself: satisfaction performed the same function as justice, violence the same as formal court process.[52] Thus, people could use courts as they had once used feud and mortal enmity; the ends were the same, only the means were different.[53] The more recent change in the scholarship has seen kings not only coming into conflict with this different form of dispute settlement but also – and more importantly – tapping into it, and inserting themselves into its rhythms.[54] Thus, a recent study examining how French kings dealt with and related to the seigneurial violence that characterized Languedoc in 1250–1400, during which the region came fully under royal control, has concluded that 'the royal/seigneurial relationship was primarily one of mutual accommodation and even benefit'.[55] Aristocratic power and royal power are thus now no longer seen as opposed spheres; they remain, however, separate sources of power.[56]

The example of Scotland adds to this picture and introduces one important point. The institutional changes Scotland underwent in the twelfth and thirteenth centuries can be said to encompass elements highlighted by the scholarship on the Carolingians and post-Carolingian Europe and that on violence in the central and later Middle Ages. Like the Carolingians, Scottish kings needed aristocrats in order to rule; indeed, aristocratic power could not be excluded from royal government, it was a necessary part of it.[57] But early medieval scholarship has still explained this

[51] Most recently, Warren C. Brown, *Violence in Medieval Europe* (Harlow, 2011); the earlier important studies by Stephen D. White, 'Feuding and Peace-Making in the Touraine around the Year 1100', *Traditio*, vol. 42 (1986), pp. 195–263; and, not focusing on violence per se but extremely influential, Fredric L. Cheyette, 'Suum cuique tribuere', *French Historical Studies*, vol. 6, no. 3 (1970), pp. 287–99.

[52] Although it should be said that this has a far longer history than the 1950s–1960s, most notably in Otto Brunner, *Land and Lordship: Structures of Government in Medieval Austria*, trans. H. Kaminsky and J. Van Horn Melton (Philadelphia, PA, 1992), which was first published in 1939, translation based on the 4th edn (1959); see also the survey in Jeppe Büchert Netterstrøm, 'The Study of Feud in Medieval and Early Modern History', in *Feud in Medieval and Early Modern Europe*, ed. Bjørn Poulsen and J. B. Netterstrøm (Aarhus, 2007), pp. 20–8; and, most importantly, Howard Kaminsky, 'The Noble Feud in the Later Middle Ages', *Past & Present*, no. 177 (2002), pp. 55–83.

[53] Daniel Lord Smail, 'Hatred as a Social Institution in Late Medieval Society', *Speculum*, vol. 76, no. 1 (2001), pp. 90–126; Paul R. Hyams, *Rancor and Reconciliation in Medieval England* (Ithaca, 2003).

[54] Most importantly, Justine Firnhaber-Baker, *Violence and the State in Languedoc, 1250–1400* (Cambridge, 2014), pp. 180–4. For a recent incarnation of the realities of later aristocratic power being a product of Carolingian ideals of rulership, see West, *Reframing*; for a study of later medieval aristocratic power which does not stress overly the role of violence, see R. R. Davies, *Lords and Lordship in the British Isles in the Late Middle Ages*, ed. Brendan Smith (Oxford, 2009).

[55] Firnhaber-Baker, *Violence and the State*, p. 184; see also Justine Firnhaber-Baker, 'Seigneurial Warfare and Royal Power in Later Medieval Southern France', *Past & Present*, no. 208 (2010), pp. 37–76.

[56] Although see the important remarks for the later Middle Ages in Watts, *Making of Polities*, pp. 95–8.

[57] A similar study on aristocratic violence in Scotland during the central Middle Ages would thus be extremely useful; there has, after all, been much work done on this subject on the late medieval/early modern period.

phenomenon through the absence of any real institutional basis to royal power; kings ruled through aristocrats because that was the only available mechanism for them to do so. As Innes has written, 'kings and elites were bound together because both lacked an institutional basis for the exercise of local power, and so both dominated socially rather than administratively...on an extensive stage that they shared'.[58] But the example of Scotland shows that the structural co-dependence of kings and aristocrats cannot just be explained by the predominance of social, rather than institutional, expressions of power. By 1290, Scottish royal power *was* expressed institutionally but aristocratic territorial jurisdictions were also explicitly set up as one among many fora through which royal authority was conveyed.

Equally, the development of royal administrative institutions did not transform aristocratic power into some other form of power, which was expressed in different ways from that of the king. This is something that scholarship on the central Middle Ages has tended to accept: aristocratic power was a different 'mode' of power from that of kings, more likely to dispute through violence and to end those disputes by compromise and settlement rather than judgment. The kingdom of the Scots in the central Middle Ages shows, however, that the growth of governmental institutions did not have to result in the formation of a public sphere occupied by government and bureaucracy which defined itself against a private sphere, occupied by lordship, that was either outside the state or exercised power in a different, sometimes conflicting, sometimes cooperative, way. In Scotland, aristocratic power was not separate from the state.[59] As such, any future study on aristocratic faction and violence in Scotland should analyse it in this context. That aristocratic power was indispensable to kings does not just mean that the aristocrats were employed in the king's government and served as his officials (which they did and also did elsewhere). Nor does it just denote that the royal power was enabled by the king's pursuit of consensus, often through the means of high-status assemblies (which it was, although a full study is lacking, and also was elsewhere). It above all means that aristocratic power in Scotland was a formal part of royal governmental ambitions: the institutions of royal government developed with and alongside the jurisdictional power that kings expected aristocrats to exercise in their own lands.

This has the potential to remove institutionalization and bureaucratization as forces which necessarily change the relationship between kings and aristocrats, with the former wielding public, abstract, and impersonal power and the latter wielding private, affective, and/or personal power. In some medieval states, such as England, this was the case but in others, such as Scotland, it was not. Because 'central' government in Scotland remained dependent on local

---

[58] Innes, *State and Society*, p. 261.

[59] Matthew Innes wrote, primarily about Carolingian royal power, that 'the system as a whole required symbiosis between king and aristocracy...the metaphor of a balance of power between king and aristocracy...is misleading precisely because we are not measuring *two discrete and separate forms of power in competition with one another*, but attempting to assess ultimate control of a kind of power which encompassed both king and aristocracy': Innes, *State and Society*, p. 259; my emphasis. Innes's point could well be applied to Scotland *across* the twelfth and thirteenth centuries.

society (both through the sheriffdom and through aristocratic courts), there was no space for aristocratic power to become part of the private realm, defined as somehow outside the purview of government. The dynamic between central and local, not that between aristocratic and royal, should accordingly be the basis of any future comparative history of states in Europe during the central Middle Ages.

In sum, during the twelfth and thirteenth centuries, a political structure developed in the kingdom of the Scots which functioned and endured owing to the co-dependence of elite social ranks, administrative institutions, and the central authority—the king. While the king's governmental structure was based on aristocrats and their landed power, aristocratic landed and jurisdictional power was based on royal authority. It is so easy to miss the role that formal aristocratic power played in the Scottish state because governmental service (and delegated responsibility more broadly) was described in a different political vocabulary from that used to express aristocratic power and status. The same men who held royal offices and substantial economic resources of their own fell under different Latin categories when acting in either capacity. Officials were *vicecomites, ballivi, iusticiae, camerarii, auditores*; lords were *magnates, proceres, barones, milites, comites, nobiles*, and *potentes*. No better evidence should be needed to show that the distinction between official and unofficial power (or delegated and non-delegated power) was in some way real. Yet at the same time as the relations between the king and his magnates were becoming more formalized and defined in charter diplomatic, so too were kings issuing pronouncements about standardizing the meeting times of shrieval courts, making formal reference to local administrative boundaries, and starting to keep a record of their activity themselves.

The state that had emerged in Scotland by 1290 was a symbolically centralized power structure based on royal authority. In it, the personal bonds between aristocrats and the king and the supposedly impersonal delegated responsibility of officials had become institutionalized and more formally defined. There was thus no developmental progression from a state based on mediated royal power through aristocrats to an institutional government run by royal officials. Aristocratic power and royal governmental structures developed together in a dynamic relationship to serve the same functions under the king: justice and order, defence and resource extraction. Both changed over the period studied in this book: kings started ruling through institutions and aristocrats' power came to be essentially territorial, defined as applying *over* land held from the king. Royal power did not simply depend on aristocrats to build consensus and serve as its officials; their lands and jurisdictions were part of royal government. Above all, this explains why the newer administrative and judicial institutions could reach into local society without undercutting the regional and local power of lords. Aristocratic power was the key basis on which royal institutional government rested. The relationship between aristocratic and royal power had, quite literally, shaped the state in medieval Scotland.

APPENDIX

A Note on the Legal Sources

It has been possible to write a new narrative of governmental development because of the recovery of a neglected corpus of evidence: the early law of Scotland (sometimes called the *Auld Lawes*).[1] These texts have been edited previously, once in the early seventeenth century and once in the first half of the nineteenth century. Despite the existence of these editions, it was still thought that the manuscript tradition of these legal texts was too late and too complicated to find within it any authentic material belonging to the twelfth and thirteenth centuries.[2] What follows provides a brief narrative of why and how the current editions of the laws are so problematic but shows how, nonetheless, the law itself, once properly identified and analysed, can and should be used by historians of medieval Scotland, as it has been in this book.

The first appearance in print of any early Scottish law was within the edition of *Regiam Majestatem* (*RM*) and other items of Scottish *Auld Lawes*, edited by Sir John Skene (*c.*1540–1617) in a Latin text of 1609, followed by a Scots translation of the same material in the same year. In these volumes, Skene published two collections of assizes which he attributed to William and Alexander II respectively.[3] The '*Statuta sive Assisae*' of William had thirty-nine chapters; the *Statuta* of Alexander II comprised twenty-five chapters. Skene neglected to publish any text of the *Assise Regis Dauid*, which contemporaries were aware existed. This was a significant omission noted much later by Lord Hailes in 1769 in what was the first critical appraisal of Skene's work.[4]

Skene's texts of the laws of William and Alexander remained standard until the appearance of the first volume of the *Acts of the Parliaments of Scotland* in 1844, edited by Cosmo Innes.[5] *APS*, volume 1, contained Thomas Thomson's editions of *Assise Regis David* (*ARD*:

---

[1] T. M. Cooper [Lord Cooper of Culross], '*Regiam Majestatem* and the Auld Lawes', in *An Introductory Survey of the Sources and Literature of Scots Law by Various Authors*', Stair Society 1 (Edinburgh, 1936), pp. 70–81.

[2] *Regiam Majestatem Scotiae: Veteres Leges et Constitutiones ex archivis publicis [etc]*, ed. Sir John Skene (Edinburgh, 1609); for comment, see T. M. Cooper, 'Early Scottish Statutes Revisited', in *Selected Papers, 1922–1954* (Edinburgh, 1957), pp. 238–42; *Regiam Majestatem and Quoniam Attachiamenta Based on the Text of Sir John Skene*, ed. and trans. T. M. Cooper, Stair Society 11 (Edinburgh, 1947), p. 23; Bruce Webster, *Scotland from the Eleventh Century to 1603* (London, 1975), pp. 165–6.

[3] *Regiam Majestatem*, ed. Skene, pars II, 1–17, 22–8.

[4] Sir David Dalrymple [Lord Hailes], *An Examination of Some of the Arguments for the High Antiquity of Regiam Majestatem and an Inquiry into the Leges Malcolmi* (Edinburgh, 1769), pp. 15–16.

[5] Despite the clear and deep friendship between the two men, Thomson refused to correspond with Innes about completion of the volume (including his texts of the laws), owing to his own complex feelings about the stigma of his forced resignation from the Record Commission. See *APS*, i, pp. 58–9, and Cosmo N. Innes, *Memoir of Thomas Thomson, Advocate* (Edinburgh, 1854), pp. 222–8. Innes wrote in his memoir of Thomson, published in 1854, that '[Thomson] never again entered the Register House; and though he was generously communicative on every other point where his assistance or advice was desired, he told me, soon after I had been employed to complete the first volume of his great work [*APS*, i], that it must be a forbidden subject between us' (p. 228). There is an important distinction between the work completed by Thomson and that by Innes; they did not collaborate: see

thirty-five chapters), the *Assise Regis Willelmi* (*ARW*: forty-two chapters) and *Statuta Regis Alexandri* (*SRA*: fifteen chapters).[6] Thomson's edition of the Auld Lawes surpassed Skene's both in the amount of material published and the number of manuscripts consulted and became the standard printed version of these texts.

The contents of the compilations published by Skene and Thomson were different but neither represented accurately either the content or the structure of the legal compilations in their manuscript form. They have thus served, albeit unintentionally, to distort the nature and content of the compilations for those who wish to use them. Although Innes assured his readers that he and Thomson had always taken their text from 'the oldest manuscript in which it occurs, where it was consistent and free from suspicion', it has been shown repeatedly in this book that this standard was not always maintained.[7] There is a consensus that Thomson 'did what he could to sift the evidence' but his editorial practices were firmly located in his own time and his brief was to find the most developed text of Scottish law, which he did, by putting together older and newer versions of the same material (but without making it in any way clear that he had done so).[8] When historians use the laws in *APS*, Thomson's methodology means that they are often using texts that have no manuscript authority whatsoever and are, instead, conflations of a number of different readings from manuscripts of varying date.[9] Doubts about the accuracy of Thomson's work had already started to surface in the late nineteenth and early twentieth centuries: in his 1910 *Annals of the Reigns of Malcolm and William*, A. C. Lawrie had noticed that the manuscripts containing a legal compilation attributed to William the Lion bore no resemblance to what Thomson had assembled.[10] Lord Cooper remarked in 1946 that 'easy as it is to apply destructive criticism to past efforts to date the "statutes", we are no nearer a reliable substitute arrangement of the material, and it is very doubtful whether we ever shall be'.[11] Bruce Webster commented in 1975 that assizes printed in *APS* were underused because they 'conceal[ed] a formidable series of problems'.[12]

By the 1970s, therefore, historians were aware that there existed three legal compilations attributed to three kings of the twelfth and thirteenth centuries: David I, William the Lion, and Alexander II. However, what was not clear was whether these texts were anything other than the product of a much later nineteenth-century imagination and, as a result, historians had a choice of not using them at all, using them extremely gingerly, or using them but running the risk that they would cite material that in fact had no manuscript authority. All three approaches were used but never to such an extent that the legal material became an

---

the list in *APS*, i, pp. 56–9. For Innes's editorial methods when editing some of the major episcopal cartularies and registers, see Alasdair Ross, 'The Bannatyne Club and the Publication of Scottish Ecclesiastical Cartularies', *SHR*, vol. 85, no. 220 (2006), pp. 202–30. For the context and significance of Innes's work on *APS*, see Richard A. Marsden, *Cosmo Innes and the Defence of Scotland's Past, c.1825–1875* (Farnham, 2014), pp. 55–90.

[6] For *ARD*, see *APS*, i, pp. 315–25; for *ARW*, see *APS*, i, pp. 369–84; for *SRA*, see *APS*, i, pp. 395–404.

[7] *APS*, i, p. 38.

[8] The quotation is from J. Maitland Thomson, *The Public Records of Scotland* (Glasgow, 1922), p. 29; also *Annals of the Reigns of Malcolm and William, Kings of Scotland, AD 1153–1214*, ed. Archibald C. Lawrie (Glasgow, 1910), pp. xii–xiii, 204–5.

[9] See Alice Taylor, '*Leges Scocie* and the Lawcodes of David I, William the Lion and Alexander II', *SHR*, vol. 88, no. 226 (2009); Alice Taylor, 'The Assizes of David, King of Scots, 1124–53', *SHR*, vol. 91, no. 232 (2012).

[10] *Annals*, ed. Lawrie, p. 205.   [11] *Regiam Majestatem*, ed. Cooper, p. 23.

[12] Webster, *Scotland*, pp. 165–8, at p. 166.

important source for Scotland in this period.[13] However, in 1990, new light was thrown on the matter when Hector MacQueen published a preliminary study of an otherwise neglected legal compilation, known as *Leges Scocie* (*LS*).[14]

Leges Scocie ('the laws of Scotland') had generally been unnoticed by historians before MacQueen's work. First, it had escaped the clutches of Skene. Its manuscript had only been discovered in Bern in the late eighteenth century and was brought to the attention of Scottish historians in 1799.[15] It contained a legal compilation of twenty-one chapters containing some datable statutes which, as a result of the work of A. A. M. Duncan, Hector MacQueen, and now myself, have now all been dated to the period 1177–1210, that is, the reign of William the Lion.[16] The immediate importance of *LS* lay in the date of its manuscript (1267×72), which showed an interest in relatively recent Scots law mid-way through the reign of Alexander III (1249–86). For the first time, therefore, historians had a compilation of Scottish law to work with which survived in a manuscript which was written between fifty-seven and sixty-two years after the latest datable statute the compilation contains. Moreover, I showed in an edition of *LS* published in 2009 that its content had some devastating consequences for the authority of Thomson's editions in *APS*. Many of the statutes edited by Thomson had long puzzled historians because of their complex legal language which seemed to be anachronistic for the later twelfth and early thirteenth centuries.[17] But the versions of these chapters in *LS* contained none of this worrying language. The evidence of *LS* thus demonstrated that many of our most problematic texts of law were actually Thomson's own concoctions, drawn together from a number of later manuscript texts.

By looking at the manuscript evidence for the legal compilations attributed to David I, William the Lion, and Alexander II, it has also been possible to show that they, like *LS*, were coherent compilations but which (unlike *LS*) had all undergone several later stages of development over their manuscript history, which lasted for around two hundred years in each case. I have argued elsewhere that the compilation attributed to David I (the lengthily named *Capitula Assisarum et Statutorum Domini David Regis Scocie* or *CD*) was in fact compiled in the reign of Robert I (1306–29) in a direct effort to associate Robert's own legal innovations with the posthumous authority as a lawmaker that David had by then come to wield.[18] Moreover, comparing the content of the overlapping material between *CD* and *LS* revealed that *LS*-chapters had been *updated* in *CD*, to reflect fourteenth-century conditions more accurately.[19] Nonetheless, the compilation itself contained four chapters of twelfth-century date which have proved very important for understanding legal development in this period.[20]

---

[13] Before Hector MacQueen, the historian who made most use of the 'Auld Lawes' was A. A. M. Duncan, in his *Making of the Kingdom* (1975); see further the work cited in Chapters 3 and 5.

[14] Hector L. MacQueen, 'Scots Law under Alexander III', in *Scotland in the Reign of Alexander III, 1249–1286*, ed. N. H. Reid (Edinburgh, 1990) , pp. 74–103.

[15] NRS, PA5/1, fos. 59v–61v; for correspondence over the manuscript, acquired from Switzerland in 1799, see NLS, MS Adv. 24.5.11A; for suggestions on the original provenance of the 'Berne' manuscript, see T. M. Cooper, 'The Authorship of the Berne MS', *SHR*, vol. 27, no. 104 (1948), pp. 114–23; MacQueen, 'Scots Law', pp. 85–6. No definitive statement on the provenance of the manuscript has yet been put forward.

[16] Duncan, *Making of the Kingdom*, pp. 185–6, 200–3, 207, 529; MacQueen, 'Scots Law', pp. 87–93; Taylor, '*Leges Scocie*', pp. 207–46.

[17] Taylor, '*Leges Scocie*'.   [18] Taylor, 'Assizes of David', pp. 225–35.

[19] For an example, see Taylor, '*Leges Scocie*', pp. 214–15, and notes 70–75; Taylor, 'Assizes of David', pp. 214–23.

[20] See Chapter 3, pp. 128–31.

In addition, it has been possible to show that the compilation attributed to Alexander II (*Statuta Regis Alexandri—SA*) was originally a compilation of twenty-nine chapters which contained eight securely datable statutes and a further four which, from internal evidence, probably belong to Alexander II's reign.[21] The compilation itself cannot be dated to before the second half of the fourteenth century; it can just perhaps be placed in the 1360s. Nonetheless, there is good reason to think that, despite the late date of compilation, it preserves early material well. Material which is shared between *CD* and *SA* is updated in *CD* but preserved in an earlier version in *SA*.[22] *SA* also reproduces some later-twelfth-century material first attested in *LS* but, unlike *CD*, the compiler of *SA* made extremely few adjustments to the *LS*-text, which makes it likely that he also left alone the Alexander-material that is original to this compilation.[23] Finally, it has also been possible to show that *Leges Willelmi Regis* (*LW*) was originally a compilation of eleven chapters and seems also to have been compiled at some point during the second half of the fourteenth century. Unlike *SA*, *LW* contains early-fourteenth-century material that is first attested in *CD*, as well as some late-twelfth-century material also attested in *LS*. It contains only two chapters that are original to the compilation and as such provides less evidence with which to work.

Leges Scocie and the lawcodes of David I, William the Lion, and Alexander II are still complicated texts. But uncovering their true manuscript form at least allows for their material to be used in a history of royal government in Scotland, which has been one of the main purposes of this book.

Table A.1 The relationship between *LS*, *LW*, *SA*, *CD*, and the texts published in *APS*, vol. 1. Bold type indicates difference between manuscript text and *APS*
ARD = *APS*, i, pp. 315–25; *ARW* = *APS*, i, pp. 369–84; *SRA* = *APS*, i, pp. 395–404.

(1) *Leges Scocie (LS)*

Ch.	Content	APS	Ch	Content	APS
LS, c. 1	Procedure for warranty of stolen goods ('Claremathan')	*ARW*, c. 3	*LS*, c. 11	Accusations of theft and warranty procedure (1184)	*ARW*, c. 16
LS, c. 2	All purchases to be made with lawful pledge	*ARW*, c. 5	*LS*, c. 12	Warranty of borrowed horses (1184)	*ARW*, c. 17
LS, c. 3	Defamation of theft	*ARW*, c. 6	*LS*, c. 13	Procedure to follow when priests are vouched as warrantors (1184)	*ARW*, c. 18
LS, c. 4	Thieves caught red-handed with hue and cry	*ARW*, c. 7	*LS*, c. 14	Composition of Shrieval and Justiciar courts (1184)	**ARW, c. 19**

[21] I am preparing a full edition and discussion of *LS*, *LBS*, *CD*, *SA*, and *LW* in a volume provisionally entitled *The Auld Lawes of Scotland: Compilations of Royal Laws from the Thirteenth and Fourteenth Centuries*, to be published by the Stair Society. For preliminary comment, see Chapter 3, pp. 117–20, and Chapter 5, pp. 271–3.

[22] Taylor, 'Assizes of David', pp. 216–21.

[23] These similarities and differences can, at present, be tracked by referring to the critical apparatus of the current edition of *Leges Scocie* in Taylor, '*Leges Scocie*', pp. 246–88. However, the forthcoming edition of *SA* will supersede those notes.

Ch.	Content	APS	Ch	Content	APS
LS, c. 5	Assize of waters	*ARW*, c. 10	*LS*, c. 15	Oath sworn forbidding the maintenance of criminals by lords (1197)	*ARW*, c. 20
LS, c. 6	Curfew regulations (1177)	*ARW*, c. 11	*LS*, c. 16	Places for warrantors to come	*ARW*, c. 4
LS, c. 7	Supervision of aristocratic courts (1180)	*ARW*, c. 12	*LS*, c. 17	Accusation of theft made by three men of different lords	*APS*, i, p. 737
LS, c. 8	*Birthinsake*	*ARW*, c. 13	*LS*, c. 18	Breaking of the king's peace in Galloway and duel regulations (?1187×1200)	*ARW*, c. 22
LS, c. 9	Vengeance killing after lawful killing	*ARW*, c. 15	*LS*, c. 19	Judgment against Gillascop (1210)	*SRA*, c. 3
LS, c. 10	Thieves' wergelds	*ARW*, c. 14	*LS*, c. 20	Collection of *cáin* in Galloway (1 May 1187×1200)	*ARW*, c. 23
			LS, c. 21	'Leges inter Brettos et Scottos'	*APS*, i, pp. 663–636.

(2) *Leges Willelmi Regis (LW)*

Ch.	Content	APS
LW, c. 1	Accusations of theft and warranty procedures	*ARW*, c. 16
LW, c. 2	Warranty of borrowed horses	*ARW*, c. 17
LW, c. 3	Procedure for priests to be vouched as warrantors	*ARW*, c. 18
LW, c. 4	Composition of shrieval and justiciar courts	*ARW*, c. 19
LW, c. 5	Record of oath to keep peace and not to receive or maintain wrongdoers	*ARW*, c. 20
LW, c. 6	Alienation of royal demesne	*ARW*, c. 24
LW, c. 7	On attachments and summons	*ARW*, c. 30
LW, c. 8	On answering summons in court	*ARW*, c. 31
LW, c. 9	On accusations of robbery, rape, and hamsoke	*ARW*, c. 32
LW, c. 10	On lawful charges of hamsoke	*ARW*, c. 33
LW, c. 11	On unlawfully detained neyfs	*ARW*, c. 34
LW, c. 12	Regulations on mills and multures	*ARW*, c. 35
LW, c. 13	Protection of church and religious, etc.	*ARW*, cc. 36–42

(3) *Statuta Regis Alexandri (SA)*

Ch.	Content	App. in *APS*	Ch	Content	App. in *APS*.
SA, c. 1	On the cultivation of land. (1214)	*SRA*, c. 1	*SA*, c. 15	Defamation for theft	*ARW*, c. 6
SA, c. 2	Inquisition into wrongdoers (1244)	*SRA*, c. 14	*SA*, c. 16	Thieves caught red-handed and with hue and cry.	*ARW*, c. 7

(continued)

Ch.	Content	App. in *APS*	Ch.	Content	App. in *APS*.
SA, c. 3	Assize of life and limb (1248)	*SRA*, c. 15	*SA*, c. 17	Curfew regulations (1177)	*ARW*, c. 11
SA, c. 4	Repledging (1230)	**SRA, c. 4**	*SA*, c. 18	Supervision of aristocratic courts (1180)	*ARW*, c. 12
SA, c. 5	Procedures for those unable to fight a duel. (1230)	**SRA, c. 5**	*SA*, c. 19	*Birthinsake*	*ARW*, c. 13
SA, c. 6	Theft, Robbery and Methods of Proof (1230)	**SRA, c. 6**	*SA*, c. 20	Stolen possessions discovered without warrant.	*ARW*, c. 1
SA, c. 7	Dissasine (1230)	**SRA, c. 7**	*SA*, c. 21	Punishment of thieves.	*ARW*, c. 2
SA, c. 8	Helen de Burnville *vs.* Henry of Stirling.	*SRA*, c. 10	*SA*, c. 22	Regulations on the holding of aristocratic courts.	*ARW*, c. 12.
SA, c. 9	Wrang and unlaw.	*SRA*, c. 11	*SA*, c. 23	Hospitality Regulations.	*ARD*, c. 3
SA, c. 10	Pledging in cases of life and limb	*SRA*, c. 12	*SA*, c. 24	Wergeld of a thief and vengeance killings	*ARW*, cc. 14-15.
SA, c. 11	Pleas of the crown and trial by battle.	*SRA*, c. 13	*SA*, c. 25	Laws in the burghs.	Not in *APS*.
SA, c. 12	*Claremathan*	*ARW*, c. 3	*SA*, c. 26	Fines for absence from the common army (1221)	*SRA*, c. 2
SA, c. 13	All purchases to be made with lawful surety.	*ARW*, c. 5	*SA*, c. 27	Assize of Waters	*ARW*, c. 10
SA, c. 14	Places for warrantors to come.	*ARW*, c. 4	*SA*, c. 28	Breaking of King's peace in Galloway.	*ARW*, c. 22
			SA, c. 29	Judgement against Gillescop (1210)	*SRA*, c. 3.

(4) *Capitula Assisarum et Statutorum Domini David Regis Scocie (CD—α-text)*

Ch.	Content of *Capitula*	APS	Ch.	Content of *Capitula*	APS
CD, c. 1	Supervision of aristocratic courts (1180) *Birthinsake* Value of stolen goods to evade hanging	*ARW*, c. 12 *ARW*, c. 17 *ARW*, c. 17	*CD*, c. 23	Fines for absence from common army (1221)	*SRA*, c. 2
CD, c. 2	Unlawful hangings	*ARD*, c. 1	*CD*, c. 24	Justiciar's court to be held biannually at Edinburgh and Peebles	*ARW*, c. 25
CD, c. 3	Accusations of theft to be decided by duel or compurgation	*ARD*, c. 2	*CD*, c. 25	Assize of waters	*ARW*, c. 10

CD, c. 4	Stolen possessions discovered without warrant	*ARW*, c. 1	*CD*, c. 26	Composition of Shrieval and Justiciar courts (1184), with a later addition	*ARW*, c. 14
CD, c. 5	Curfew regulations (summary)	Not given	*CD*, c. 27	Oath sworn forbidding the maintenance of criminals by lords (1197)	**ARW, c. 20**
CD, c. 6	Hospitality Regulations	*ARD*, c. 3	*CD*, c. 28	*Iudices* of the provinces ought to be with the king's person when he comes into their province	*ARW*, c. 26
CD, c. 7	Procedure for lawful pleas of robbery, hamsoke, and rape	**ARW, c. 32**	*CD*, c. 29	Procedures for ensuring lawful poinding on both sides of the Forth	*ARW*, c. 27
CD, c. 8	On attachments and summons	*ARW*, cc. 30–31	*CD*, c. 30	On the freedom of sons of merchants and chaplains	*ARW*, c. 28
CD, c. 9	On lawful pleas of hamsoke	*ARW*, c. 33	*CD*, c. 31	On the penalties for breaking the peace of the king or lord in places where it has been granted	*ARW*, c. 27
CD, c. 10	Justiciars, sheriffs, grieves. or bailies may not be present while court is deliberating	*ARD*, c. 4	*CD*, c. 32	Law enacted against *lèse-majesté* and against treachery against the kingdom or king's army, or the treachery of a man against his lord	*ARW*, c. 29
CD, c. 11	Peers must be judged by peers	*ARD*, c. 5	*CD*, c. 33	Penalties for violence raised in the king's court	**ARD, c. 15**
CD, c. 12	Quittance from accusations of theft of chattels if the amount claimed is exaggerated	*ARD*, c. 6	*CD*, c. 34	Thieves caught red-handed and with hue and cry	**ARW, c. 7**
CD, c. 13	On an ascertainable loss claimed by an appellant	*ARD* c. 7	*CD*, c. 35	Sons not accomplices to their father's felony may recover their patrimony in certain circumstances	*ARW*, c. 9
CD, c. 14	On the accusation of theft, robbery, or any wrongdoing from which a duel might arise	*ARD*, c. 8	*CD*, c. 36	Law enacted against forgery of charters, depending on whether they be royal charters or private deeds	*ARW*, c. 8
CD, c. 15	Freedom may be given up but without the possibility of recovery	*ARD*, c. 9	*CD*, c. 37	Disputed chattels ought to be brought to the place in each *comitatus* where King David established they should be brought	**Edited first line of ARW, c. 3**

(continued)

(4) Continued

Ch.	Content of *Capitula*	APS	Ch.	Content of *Capitula*	APS
CD, c. 16	No sheriff or sheriff's sergeand shall involve himself with matters belonging to the king which occur outside his sheriffdom	ARD, c. 10	CD, c. 38	Repledging of accused criminals (1230)	SRA, c. 4
CD, c. 17	Regulations over vengeance killings	ARW, c. 15	CD, c. 39	Abolition of the ordeal of pit or iron and introduction of visnet (1230)	SRA, c. 6
CD, c. 18	Breaking of the king's peace in Galloway and duel regulations (?1187✕1200)	ARW, c. 22	CD, c. 40	Procedure to follow for those unable to fight but who make accusations of despoilation (1230)	SRA, c. 5
CD, c. 19	Judgment against Gillascop (1210)	SRA, c. 3	CD, c. 41	Unlawful dissasine (1230)	SRA, c. 7
CD, c. 20	On the accusations of felony or pleas of life and limb by the king	ARD, c. 11	CD, c. 42	Law of duelling, depending on the status of an individual	SRA, c. 8
CD, c. 21	Bailies and grieves (and those who hold private courts) may not involve them-selves with pleas belonging to the crown unless by special mandate to the bailies and grieves and permission is given to those who hold their own courts	ARD, cc. 12–13	CD, c. 43	Law concerning a man accused of killing his wife	ARD, c. 34
CD, c. 22	Those infeft by the king may only lose their land by a brieve of right	ARW, c. 24	CD, c. 44	On an indictment brought by three, two, or one baronies for robbery, theft, or any infamous wrongdoing.	ARW, c. 21

Bibliography

MANUSCRIPT SOURCES

Belfast

Public Record Office of Northern Ireland
  D623/B/7/1/5

Edinburgh

National Library of Scotland (NLS)
  Accessions (MS Acc.)
    16497
    21246
  Advocates Manuscripts (MS Adv.)
    15.1.18, nos. 16, 27
    16.1.10
    25.4.14
    25.4.15
    25.5.6
    25.5.10
    24.5.11A
    31.3.15
    34.1.3A
    34.4.2
    34.4.13
    34.4.14
  Advocates Charters
    A.4
  Charters
    36

National Records of Scotland (NRS)
  E 38/1
  GD 1/203/1
  GD 45/13/247,/250,/257.
  GD 55/101,/102,/103,/104,/127,/237,/244,/322
  GD 119/2
  GD 220/A1/4/6
  GD 236, Gilbliston titles, no. 1 [awaiting listing]
  GD 254/1
  PA5 /1,/2
  RH1 /1/1,/2/80,/2/900
  RH5 /8/1,/8/2,/19,/23,/24,/30,/33,/36,/39,/54,/231
  RH6 /16,/24,/29,/31,/33,/41
  SP 13/1

University Library (EUL)
> EUL, Laing Charters, Box 1, no. 19; Box 2, no. 67, no. 87
> MS 206

London

The British Library
> Additional MS 33245, 18111
> Additional Charter 66570, 76697
> Campbell Charter xxx, 6
> Egerton MS 3031
> Harley MS 4700

Lambeth Palace Library (LPL)
> MS 167

The National Archives (TNA)
> C 47/22/5
> C 53/1–5, 53/8
> E 39/3/53, 3/54, 3/55, 3/56, 3/58
> E 101/331/5, 331/A

Madrid
> Biblioteca Real MS II 2097

PRINTED PRIMARY SOURCES

Accounts of the Lord High Treasurer of Scotland, vol. 1: *A.D. 1473–1498*, ed. T. Dickson (Edinburgh, 1877).

The Acts of the Parliaments of Scotland, vol. 1: *1124–1423*, ed. T. Thomson and C. N. Innes (Edinburgh, 1844).

Adam of Dryburgh, *De tripartito tabernaculo*, in *Patrologia Latina Cursus Completus*, ed. J. P. Migne, 221 vols (Paris, 1844–64), vol. 198, cols 609–796.

Andrew Wyntoun's Orygynale Cronykil of Scotland, 3 vols, ed. D. Laing (Edinburgh, 1872–79).

Ane Account of the Familie of Innes compiled by Duncan Forbes of Culloden, 1698, with Appendix of Charters and Notes (Aberdeen, 1864).

Anglo-Saxon Charters: An Annotated List and Bibliography, ed. P. H. Sawyer (London, 1968), revised by Susan E. Kelly in *The Electronic Sawyer*, online at <http://esawyer.org.uk/about/index.html>.

The Anglo-Saxon Chronicle: A Collaborative Edition, vol. 3: *MS A*, ed. Janet M. Bately (Cambridge, 1986); vol. 5: *MS C*, ed. Kathleen O'B. O'Keeffe (Cambridge, 2001); vol. 7: *MS E*, ed. Susan Irvine (Cambridge, 2004).

Anglo-Saxon Writs, ed. F. E. Harmer (Manchester, 1952).

Anglo-Scottish Relations, 1174–1328: Some Selected Documents, ed. and trans. E. L. G. Stones (Oxford, 1965, repr. with corrections, 1970).

Annals of the Reigns of Malcolm and William, Kings of Scotland, AD 1153–1214, ed. Archibald C. Lawrie (Glasgow, 1910).

The Antient Kalendars and Inventories of the Treasury of His Majesty's Exchequer, ed. Sir F. Palgrave (London, 1836).

Bamff Charters, AD 1232–1703, ed. J. H. Ramsay (Oxford, 1915).

Bede, *Ecclesiastical History of the English People*, ed. and trans. B. Colgrave and R. A. B. Mynors (Oxford, 1969).

The Book of Carlaverock: Memoirs of the Maxwells, Earls of Nithsdale, Lords Maxwell and Herries, ed. William Fraser, 2 vols (Edinburgh, 1873).

The Book of the Thanes of Cawdor: A Series of Papers Selected from the Charter Room at Cawdor, 1236–1742, ed. C. N. Innes (Edinburgh, 1859).

Calendar of Documents Relating to Scotland, Preserved in Her Majesty's Public Record Office, ed. J. Bain, 5 vols (Edinburgh, 1881–88).

Calendars of Entries in the Papal Registers Relating to Great Britain and Ireland, vol. 2: *1305–42*, ed. W. H. Bliss (London, 1895).

Calendar of Inquisitions Post Mortem, vol. 1: *Henry III*, ed. J. E. E. S. Sharp (London, 1904).

Calendar of the Laing Charters, A.D. 854–1837, ed. J. Anderson (Edinburgh, 1899).

Cartularium Comitatus de Levenax ab initio seculi decimi tertii usque ad annum M.CCC. XCVIII, ed. J. Dennistoun (Edinburgh, 1833).

Charters and Other Documents Relating to the Royal Burgh of Stirling, A.D. 1124–1705, ed. R. Renwick (Glasgow, 1884).

Charters and Other Writs Illustrating the History of the Royal Burgh of Aberdeen MCLXXI–MDCCCIV, ed. P. J. Anderson (Aberdeen, 1890).

Charters, Bulls and Other Documents Relating to the Abbey of Inchaffray, ed. W. A. Lindsay, J. Dowden and J. Maitland Thomson, Scottish History Society, 2nd ser., vol. 56 (Edinburgh, 1908).

Charters of the Abbey of Coupar Angus, ed. D. E. Easson, 2 vols, Scottish History Society, 3rd ser., vols. 40–41 (Edinburgh, 1947).

Charters of the Abbey of Inchcolm, ed. D. E. Easson and A. Macdonald, Scottish History Society, 3rd ser., vol. 32 (Edinburgh, 1938).

The Charters of David I: the Written Acts of David I, King of Scots, 1124–53, and of His Son, Henry, Earl of Northumberland, 1139–52, ed. G. W. S. Barrow (Woodbridge, 1999).

Charters of the Royal Burgh of Ayr, ed. W. S. Cooper, Ayrshire and Wigtownshire Archaeological Association (Edinburgh, 1883).

Chartulary of the Abbey of Lindores 1195–1479, ed. J. Dowden, Scottish History Society, 1st ser., vol. 42 (Edinburgh, 1903).

The Chiefs of Grant, ed. W. Fraser, 3 vols (Edinburgh, 1883).

Chronica Magistri Rogeri de Houedene, ed. W. Stubbs, 4 vols (London, 1868–71).

The Chronicle of Melrose: A Stratigraphic Edition, vol. 1: *Introduction and Facsimile*, ed. D. Broun and J. Harrison, Scottish History Society (Woodbridge, 2007).

Chronicles of the Picts, Chronicles of the Scots, ed. W. F. Skene (Edinburgh, 1867).

Chronicles of the Reigns of Stephen, Henry II and Richard I, ed. R. Howlett, Rolls Series, 4 vols (London, 1884–89).

Collections for a History of the Shires of Aberdeen and Banff, ed. J. Robertson, and *Illustrations of the Topography and Antiquities of the Shires of Aberdeen and Banff*, ed. J. Roberton, 5 vols in total (Aberdeen, 1843–69).

Concilia Scotiae: Ecclesiae Scotianae Statuta tam provincialia quam synodalia quae supersunt MCCXXV–MDLIX, ed. J. Robertson, Bannatyne Club, 2 vols (Edinburgh, 1866).

The Correspondence, Inventories, Account Rolls and Law Proceedings of the Priory of Coldingham, ed. J. Raine, Surtees Society (London, 1841).

Coutumiers de Normandie: Textes Critiques. Tome II: La Summa de Legibus Normannie in curia laicali, ed. E. J. Tardif (Rouen and Paris, 1896).

Crown Pleas of the Devon Eyre of 1238, ed. H. Summerson, Devon and Cornwall Record Society, new series, vol. 28 (Torquay, 1985).

'Culross Abbey and Its Charters, with Notes on a Fifteenth-Century Transumpt', ed. W. Douglas, *Proceedings of the Society of Antiquaries of Scotland* (*PSAS*), vol. 60 (1925–26), pp. 67–94.

Dialogus de Scaccario and Constitutio Domus Regis, ed. Emilie Amt and S. D. Church, Oxford Medieval Texts (Oxford, 2007).

Die Gesetze der Angelsachsen, ed. F. Liebermann, 3 vols (Halle, 1903–16).

Diplomata Scotiae: Selectus Diplomatum et Numismatum Scotiae Thesaurus, ed. J. Anderson (Edinburgh, 1739).

Documents Illustrative of the History of Scotland from the Death of Alexander the Third to the Accession of Robert Bruce MCCLXXXVI–MCCCVI, ed. J. Stevenson, 2 vols (Edinburgh, 1870).

Documents of the Baronial Movement of Reform and Rebellion, 1258–1267, Oxford Medieval Texts, ed. R. F. Treharne and I. J. Sanders (Oxford, 1973).

The Douglas Book, ed. W. Fraser, 4 vols (Edinburgh, 1885).

Early Scottish Charters Prior to A.D. 1153, ed. A. C. Lawrie (Glasgow, 1905).

'Eight Thirteenth Century Texts', ed. W. W. Scott, in *Miscellany XIII*, Scottish History Society, 5th ser., vol. 14 (Edinburgh, 2004), pp. 1–41.

Edward I and the Throne of Scotland, 1290–1296: An Edition of Record Sources for the Great Cause, ed. E. L. G. Stones and Grant G. Simpson, 2 vols (New York and London, 1978).

The Etymologies of Isidore of Seville, ed. and trans. Stephen A. Barney, W. J. Lewis, J. A. Beach, and Oliver Berghof (Cambridge, 2006).

Facsimiles of the National Manuscripts of Scotland, ed. W. G. Craig, 3 vols (Edinburgh, 1867–71).

Foedera, Conventiones, Literae, et cuiuscunque generis acta publica intere reges Angliae et alios quosvis imperatores, reges, pontifices, principes vel communitates, ed. T. Rymer (London, 1704–45).

Geoffrey of Monmouth: The History of the Kings of Britain, ed. Michael D. Reeve and trans. Neil Wright (Woodbridge, 2009).

Gesta Regis Henrici Secundi Benedicti Abbatis: The Chronicle of the Reigns of Henry II and Richard I AD 1169–1192, ed. W. Stubbs, Rolls Series, 2 vols (London, 1867).

Gesta Stephani, ed. K. R. Potter, rev. R. H. C. Davis (Oxford, 1976).

Handlist of the Acts of William the Lion 1165–1214, ed. G. W. S. Barrow and W. W. Scott (Edinburgh, 1958).

Highland Papers: Volumes 1 and 2, ed. J. R. N. MacPhail, Scottish History Society, 2nd ser., vols. 5 and 12 (Edinburgh, 1914, 1916).

The History and Antiquities of North Durham, as Subdivided into the Shires of Norham, Island and Bedlington, ed. James Raine (London, 1852).

History of the Carnegies, Earls of Southesk, ed. W. Fraser, 2 vols (Edinburgh, 1867).

Icelandic Sagas and Other Historical Documents, ed. Gudbrand Vigfusson, 4 vols. (London, 1887–94).

Irish Exchequer Payments, 1270–1446, ed. Philomena Connolly, Irish Manuscripts Commission (Dublin, 1998).

Johannis de Fordun Chronica Gentis Scotorum, 2 vols, ed. W. F. Skene, trans. Felix Skene (Edinburgh, 1871–72).

Jordan Fantosme's Chronicle, ed. R. C. Johnston (Oxford, 1981).

The Latin Texts of the Welsh Laws, ed. Hywel David Emanuel (Cardiff, 1967).

The Law of Hywel Dda: Law Texts from Medieval Wales, ed. and trans. Dafydd Jenkins (Llandysul, 1986).

The Lennox, ed. William Fraser, 2 vols (Edinburgh, 1874).

Liber Cartarum Prioratus Sancti Andree in Scotia e Registro ipso in Archivis Baronum de Panmure hodie asservato, ed. O. Tyndall Bruce and T. Thomson (Edinburgh, 1841).

Liber Cartarum Sancte Crucis: Munimenta Ecclesie Sancte Crucis de Edwinesburg, ed. C. N. Innes (Edinburgh, 1840).

Liber ecclesie de Scon: Munimenta Vetustiora monasterii Sancte Trinitatis et Sancti Michaelis de Scon, ed. W. Smythe (Edinburgh, 1843).

Liber S. Marie de Balmorinach ed. W. B. D. D. Turnball (Edinburgh, 1840).

Liber S. Marie de Calchou: Registrum Cartarum Abbacie Tironensis de Kelso 1113–1567, ed. C. N. Innes, 2 vols (Edinburgh, 1846).

Liber S. Marie de Dryburgh: Registrum Cartarum Abbacie Premonstratensis de Dryburgh, ed. J. Spottiswoode (Edinburgh, 1847).

Liber S. Marie de Melros: Munimenta Vetustiora Monasterii Cisterciensis de Melros, ed. C. N. Innes, 2 vols (Edinburgh, 1837).

Liber S. Thome de Aberbrothoc, ed. P. Chalmers, 2 vols (Edinburgh, 1848–56).

The Miracles of St Æbbe of Coldingham and St Margaret of Scotland, ed. and trans. Robert Bartlett, Oxford Medieval Texts (Oxford, 2003).

Miscellany of the Spalding Club, vol. 2, ed. J. Stuart (Aberdeen, 1842); vol. 5, ed. J. Stuart (Aberdeen, 1852).

'Miscellaneous Monastic Charters: Charters of Balmerino Abbey', ed. D. E. Easson, *Miscellany VIII*, Scottish History Society, 3rd ser., vol. 43 (Edinburgh, 1951), pp. 1–16.

Orderic Vitalis, *The Ecclesiastical History of Orderic Vitalis*, 6 vols, ed. M. Chibnall, Oxford Medieval Texts (Oxford, 1968–80).

'Original Charters of the Abbey of Cupar, 1219–1448', ed. James Wilson, *SHR*, vol. 10, no. 39 (1913), pp. 272–86.

The Property Records in the Book of Deer, in Katherine Forsyth, Dauvit Broun, and Thomas Clancy ed., 'The Property Records: Text and Translation', in Forsyth ed., *Book of Deer*, pp. 131–43.

Quoniam Attachiamenta, ed. T. David Fergus, Stair Society 44 (Edinburgh, 1996).

Records of the Monastery of Kinloss, ed. J. Stuart (Edinburgh, 1872).

The Records of the Parliaments of Scotland to 1707, ed. K. M. Brown, G. H. MacIntosh, A. J. Mann, P. E. Ritchie, and R. J. Tanner (St Andrews, 2007–09).

Records of the Priory of the Isle of May, ed. J. Stuart, Society of the Antiquaries of Scotland (Edinburgh, 1868).

The Red Book of Menteith, ed. W. Fraser, 2 vols (Edinburgh, 1880).

Regesta Regum Anglo-Normannorum: The Acta of William I, 1066–1087, ed. David Bates (Oxford, 1998).

Regesta Regum Anglo-Normannorum, 1066–1154: Regesta Willelmi Conquestoris et Willelmi Rufi, 1066–1100, ed. H. W. C. Davis (Oxford, 1913).

Regesta Regum Scottorum, vol. 1: *The Acts of Malcolm IV, 1153–65*, ed. G. W. S. Barrow (Edinburgh, 1960).

Regesta Regum Scottorum, vol. 2: *The Acts of William I, 1165–1214*, ed. G. W. S. Barrow with collaboration from W. W. Scott (Edinburgh, 1971).

Regesta Regum Scottorum, vol. 4, part 1: *The Acts of Alexander III, King of Scots, 1249–86*, ed. Cynthia J. Neville and Grant G. Simpson (Edinburgh, 2013).

Regesta Regum Scotorum, vol. 5: *The Acts of Robert I 1306–29*, ed. A. A. M. Duncan (Edinburgh, 1988).

Regiam Majestatem and Quoniam Attachiamenta Based on the Text of Sir John Skene, ed. and trans. T. M. Cooper, Stair Society 11 (Edinburgh, 1947).

Regiam Majestatem Scotiae: Veteres Leges et Constitutiones, ed. Sir John Skene (Edinburgh, 1609).

The Register of Brieves as Contained in The Ayr MS, the Bute MS and Quoniam Attachiamenta, ed. T. M. Cooper, Stair Society 10 (Edinburgh, 1946).

Registrum de Dunfermelyn, ed. C. N. Innes (Edinburgh, 1842).

Registrum de Panmure: Records of the Families of Maule, de Valoniis, Brechin and Brechin-Barclay, United in the Line of the Barons and Earls of Panmure, compiled H. Maule, ed. J. Stuart (Edinburgh, 1874).

Registrum Episcopatus Aberdonensis: Ecclesie Cathedralis Aberdonensis Regesta que extant in unum collecta, ed. C. N. Innes, 2 vols (Edinburgh, 1845).

Registrum Episcopatus Brechinensis cui accedunt Cartae quamplurimae originales, ed. P. Chalmers, J. I. Chalmers, and C. N. Innes, 2 vols (Edinburgh, 1856).

Registrum Episcopatus Glasguensis: Munimenta Ecclesie Metropolitane Glasguensis, ed. C. N. Innes, 2 vols (Edinburgh, 1843).

Registrum Episcopatus Moraviensis e pluribus codicibus consarcinatum circa AD MCCCC, ed. C. N. Innes (Edinburgh, 1837).

Registrum Magni Sigilli Regum Scotorum: The Register of the Great Seal of Scotland, ed. J. M. Thomson, J. B. Paul, J. H. Stevenson, and W. K. Dickson, 11 vols (Edinburgh, 1882–1914).

Registrum Monasterii S. Marie de Cambuskenneth A.D. 1147–1535, ed. W. Fraser (Edinburgh, 1872).

Registrum Monasterii de Passelet: Cartas, Privilegia, Conventiones, ed. C. N. Innes (Edinburgh, 1832).

Registrum S. Marie de Neubotle: Abbacie Cisterciensis Beate Virginis de Neubotle Chartarium Vetus, 1140–1528, ed. C. N. Innes (Edinbugh, 1849).

Rental Book of the Cistercian Abbey of Cupar-Angus with the Breviary of the Register, ed. C. Rogers, 2 vols (London, 1879–80).

Rogeri de Wendouer liber qui dicitur Flores Historiarum, ed. H. G. Hewlett, 3 vols (London, 1886–89).

Roll and Writ File of the Berkshire Eyre of 1248, ed. Michael T. Clanchy, Selden Society 90 (London, 1973).

The Roll of the Shropshire Eyre of 1256, ed. Alan Harding, Selden Society (London, 1981).

Rotuli Chartarum in Turri Londinensi Asservati Anno ab 1199–1216, ed. Thomas Duffus Hardy (London, 1837).

Rotuli Scaccarii Regum Scotorum: The Exchequer Rolls of Scotland, vol. 1: *AD 1264–1359*, ed. J. Stuart and G. Burnett (Edinburgh, 1878).

Rotuli Scotiae in Turri Londonensi et in Domo Capitulari Westmonasteriensi Asservati, vol. 1, ed. D. MacPherson (London, 1814).

Scotia Pontifica: Papal Letters to Scotland before the Pontificate of Innocent III, ed. Robert Somerville (Oxford, 1992).

Scotichronicon by Walter Bower, 9 vols, gen. ed. Watt (Aberdeen and Edinburgh, 1989–98).

A Scottish Chronicle Known as the Chronicle of Holyrood, ed. M. O. Anderson, Scottish History Society, 3rd ser., vol. 30 (Edinburgh, 1938).

Scottish Formularies, ed. A. A. M. Duncan, Stair Society 58 (Edinburgh, 2011).

'The Scottish King's Household and Other Fragments from a Fourteenth-Century Manuscript in the Library of Corpus Christi College, Cambridge', ed. Mary Bateson, *Miscellany II*, Scottish History Society, 1st ser., vol. 45 (1904), pp. 1–43.

Select Charters and Other Illustrations of English Constitutional History from the Earliest Times to the Reign of Edward I, ed. W. Stubbs, 9th edn, revised by H. W. C. Davis (Oxford, 1921).

The Sheriff Court Book of Fife, 1515–1522, ed. William Croft Dickinson, Scottish History Society, 3rd ser., vol. 12 (Edinburgh, 1928).

The Stirlings of Keir and Their Family Papers, ed. W. Fraser (Edinburgh, 1858).

The Sutherland Book, ed. W. Fraser, 3 vols (Edinburgh, 1892).

Symeonis Monachi Opera Omnia, ed. T. Arnold, 2 vols (London, 1882–85).

Tair Colofn Cyfraith: The Three Columns of Law in Medieval Wales: Homicide, Theft and Fire, ed. T. M. Charles-Edwards and Paul Russell (Bangor, 2007).

The Treatise on the Laws and Customs of the Realm of England, Commonly Called Glanvill, ed. and trans G. D. G. Hall, with comments by M. T. Clanchy, Oxford Medieval Texts (Oxford, 1993).

Turgot, *Vita Sancte Margarete*, in *Symeonis Dunelmensis Opera et Collectanea*, ed. I. H. Hinde, Surtees Society 51 (Durham, 1868), pp. 234–54.

Vetera Monumenta Hibernorum et Scotorum historiam illustrantia 1216–1547, ed. A. Theiner (Rome, 1864).

PRINTED SECONDARY LITERATURE

Abels, Richard P., *Lordship and Military Obligation in Anglo-Saxon England* (London, 1988).

Airlie, Stuart, '*Semper fideles?* Loyauté envers les Carolingiens comme constituant de l'identité aristocratique', in *La Royauté et les élites dans l'Europe carolingienne (début IXe siècle aux environs de 920)*, ed. Régine Le Jan (Lille, 1998), pp. 129–43.

Airlie, Stuart, 'Charlemagne and the Aristocracy: Captains and Kings', in *Charlemagne: Empire and Society*, ed. Joanna Story (Manchester, 2005), pp. 90–102.

Airlie, Stuart, 'The Aristocracy in the Service of the State in the Carolingian Period', in *Staat im frühen Mittelalter*, ed. Stuart Airlie, Walter Pohl, and Helmut Reimitz, Forschungen zur Geschichte des Mittelalters 11 (Vienna, 2006), pp. 93–112.

Algazi, Gadi, Groebner, Valentin, and Jusson, Bernhard ed., *Negotiating the Gift: Pre-Modern Figurations of Exchange* (Göttingen, 2003).

Allen, Martin, 'The Chronology of Short Cross Class Ia', *British Numismatic Journal*, vol. 63 (1993), pp. 54–8.

Allen, Martin, 'The English Coinage of 1153/4–1158', *British Numismatic Journal*, vol. 76 (2006), pp. 242–302.

Allen, Martin, 'Henry II and the English Coinage', in *Henry II*, ed. Harper-Bill and Vincent (2007), pp. 257–77.

Allen, Martin, *Mints and Money in Medieval England* (Cambridge, 2012).

Althoff, Gerd, *Friends, Family and Followers: Political and Social Bonds in Medieval Europe* (Cambridge, 2004).

Amt, Emilie, *The Accession of Henry II in England: Royal Government Restored, 1149–59* (Woodbridge, 1993).

Anderson, M. O., 'Lothian and the Early Scottish Kings', *SHR*, vol. 39, no. 128 (1960), pp. 98–112.

Anderson, M. O., *Kings and Kingship in Early Scotland*, rev. edn (Edinburgh, 1980).

Antrobus, Simon (chair), *Dying to Belong: An In-Depth Review of Street Gangs in Britain*, The Centre for Social Justice (London, 2009), online at <http://www.centreforsocialjustice.org.uk/publications/dying-to-belong>.

Armstrong, Jackson W., 'The Justice Ayre in the Border Sheriffdoms, 1493–1498', *SHR*, vol. 92, no. 223 (2013), pp. 1–37.

Arnold, Benjamin, *Princes and Territories in Medieval Germany* (Cambridge, 1991).

Ash, Marinell, 'The Church in the Reign of Alexander III', in *Scotland in the Reign of Alexander III*, ed. Reid (1990), pp. 31–52.

Bagge, Sverre, 'The Europeanization of Europe: the case of Scandinavia', in *European Transformations: the Long Twelfth Century*, ed. Thomas F. X. Noble and John van Engen (Notre Dame, 2012), pp. 171–93.

Bagge, Sverre, Gelting, Michael H., and Lindkvist, Thomas, ed., *Feudalism: New Landscapes of Debate* (Turnhout, 2011).

Baldwin, John W., 'The Crisis of the Ordeal: Literature, Law and Religion around 1200', *Journal of Medieval and Renaissance Studies*, vol. 24 (1994), pp. 327–53.

Baldwin, John W., *The Government of Philip Augustus: Foundations of French Royal Power in the Middle Ages* (Berkeley, CA, and Los Angeles, 1996).

Bannerman, John, 'MacDuff of Fife', in *Medieval Scotland*, ed. Grant and Stringer (1993), pp. 20–38.

Barratt, Nick, 'The Revenue of King John', *EHR*, vol. 111, no. 443 (1996), pp. 835–55.

Barratt, Nick, 'Finance on a Shoestring: The Exchequer in the Thirteenth Century', in *English Government*, ed. Jobson (2004), pp. 71–86.

Barrow, G. W. S., 'The Earls of Fife in the Twelfth Century', *PSAS*, vol. 87 (1952–3), pp. 51–62.

Barrow, G. W. S., *Feudal Britain: the Completion of the Medieval Kingdoms, 1066–1314* (London, 1956).

Barrow, G. W. S., *The Anglo-Norman Era in Scottish History* (Oxford, 1980).

Barrow, G. W. S., 'Midlothian—or the Shire of Edinburgh?', *The Old Edinburgh Club*, vol. 35 (1985), pp. 141–8.

Barrow, G. W. S., 'Badenoch and Strathspey, 1130–1312, vol. 1: Secular and Political', *Northern Scotland*, 1st ser., 8 (1988), pp. 1–15.

Barrow, G. W. S., 'Badenoch and Strathspey, 1130–1312, vol. 2: The Church', *Northern Scotland*, 1st ser., 9 (1989), pp. 1–16.

Barrow, G. W. S., 'The Army of Alexander III's Scotland', in *Scotland in the Reign of Alexander III*, ed. Reid (1990), pp. 132–47.

Barrow, G. W. S., *Scotland and Its Neighbours in the Middle Ages* (London, 1992).

Barrow, G. W. S., 'Kingship in Medieval England and Scotland', in Barrow, *Scotland and Its Neighbours* (1992), pp. 23–44.

Barrow, G. W. S., 'David I: the Balance of Old and New', in Barrow, *Scotland and Its Neighbours* (1992), pp. 45–65.

Barrow, G. W. S., 'The Reign of William the Lion', in Barrow, *Scotland and Its Neighbours* (1992), pp. 67–89.

Barrow, G. W. S., 'The Scots Charter', in Barrow, *Scotland and Its Neighbours* (1992), pp. 91–104.

Barrow, G. W. S., 'The Lost Gàidhealtachd', in Barrow, *Scotland and Its Neighbours* (1992), pp. 105–26.

Barrow, G. W. S., 'Northern English Society in the Twelfth and Thirteenth Centuries', in Barrow, *Scotland and Its Neighbours* (1992), pp. 127–53.

Barrow, G. W. S., 'Popular Courts', in Barrow, *Scotland and Its Neighbours* (1992), pp. 217–45.

Barrow, G. W. S., 'Witnesses and the Attestation of Formal Documents in Scotland, Twelfth–Thirteenth Centuries', *Journal of Legal History*, vol. 16, no. 1 (1995), pp. 1–20.

Barrow, G. W. S., 'The Pattern of Non-Literary Manuscript Production and Survival in Scotland, 1200–1300', in *Pragmatic Literacy, East and West, 1200–1330*, ed. Richard Britnell (Woodbridge, 1997), pp. 131–45.

Barrow, G. W. S., 'The Origins of the Family of Lochore', *SHR*, vol. 77, no. 204 (1998), pp. 252–4.

Barrow, G. W. S., 'Companions of the Atheling', *ANS*, vol. 25 (2003), pp. 35–47.

Barrow, G. W. S., *The Kingdom of the Scots: Government, Church and Society from the Eleventh to the Fourteenth Century*, 2nd edn (Edinburgh, 2003).

Barrow, G. W. S., 'Pre-Feudal Scotland: Shires and Thanes', *Kingdom of the Scots* (2003), pp. 7–56.

Barrow, G. W. S., 'The *Judex*', *Kingdom of the Scots* (2003), pp. 57–67.

Barrow, G. W. S., 'The Justiciar', *Kingdom of the Scots* (2003), pp. 68–111.

Barrow, G. W. S., 'The Anglo-Scottish Border', *Kingdom of the Scots* (2003), pp. 112–29.

Barrow, G. W. S., 'King David I and Glasgow', *Kingdom of the Scots* (2003), pp. 203–13.

Barrow, G. W. S., 'Rural Settlement in Central and Eastern Scotland', *Kingdom of the Scots* (2003), pp. 233–49.

Barrow, G. W. S., 'The Beginnings of Military Feudalism', in Barrow, *Kingdom of the Scots* (2003), pp. 250–78.

Barrow, G. W. S., 'Scotland's "Norman" Families', in Barrow, *Kingdom of the Scots* (2003), pp. 279–95.

Barrow, G. W. S., *Kingship and Unity: Scotland 1000–1306*, 2nd edn (Edinburgh, 2003).

Barrow, G. W. S., 'Scotland, Wales and Ireland in the Twelfth Century', in *The New Cambridge Medieval History IV c.1024–1198*, ed. David Luscombe and Jonathan Riley-Smith (Cambridge, 2004), pp. 581–610.

Barrow, G. W. S., 'An Unpublished Brieve of Malcolm IV', *SHR*, vol. 84, no. 217 (2005), pp. 85–7.

Barrow, G. W. S., *Robert Bruce and the Community of the Realm of Scotland*, 4th edn (Edinburgh, 2005).

Barrow, G. W. S., 'The *Capella Regis* of the Kings of Scotland, 1107–1222', in *Miscellany V*, ed. Hector L. MacQueen, Stair Society 52 (Edinburgh, 2006), pp. 1–11.

Barrow, G. W. S. and Reid, Norman H. ed., *The Sheriffs of Scotland: An Interim List to c.1306* (St Andrews, 2002).

Barthélemy, Dominique, *La mutation de l'an mil a-t-elle eu lieu?: Servage et chevalerie dans la France des Xe et XIe siècles* (Paris, 1997).

Barthélemy, Dominique, *The Serf, the Knight and the Historian*, trans. G. Robert Edwards (Ithaca, 2009).

Bartlett, Robert, *Trial by Fire and Water: the Medieval Judicial Ordeal* (Oxford, 1986).

Bartlett, Robert, *The Making of Europe: Conquest, Colonization and Cultural Change, 950–1350* (London, 1994).

Bartlett, Robert, 'Mortal Enemies: The Legal Aspect of Hostility in the Middle Ages', T. Jones Pierce Lecture, University of Wales (Aberystwyth, 1998), repr. in *Feud, Violence and Practice: Essays in Medieval Studies in Honor of Stephen D. White*, ed. Belle.S. Tuten and Tracey L. Billado (Farnham, 2010), pp. 197–212.

Bates, David, 'The Prosopographical Study of Anglo-Norman Royal Charters', in *Family Trees and the Roots of Politics: The Prosopography of Britain and France from the Tenth to the Twelfth Century*, ed. K. S. B. Keats-Rohan (Woodbridge, 1997), pp. 89–102.

Bautier, R-H., 'Cartulaires de chancellerie et recueils d'actes des autorités laïques et ecclésiastiques', in *Les cartulaires: Actes de la table ronde organisée par l'Ecole nationale des chartes et le G.D.R. 121 du C.N.R.S.*, ed. O. Guyotjeannin, L. Morelle and M. Parisse (Paris, 1993), pp. 363–77.

Baxter, Stephen, 'The Earls of Mercia and Their Commended Men in the Mid-Eleventh Century', *ANS*, vol. 19 (1999), pp. 181–202.

Baxter, Stephen, *The Earls of Mercia: Lordship and Power in Late Anglo-Saxon England* (Oxford, 2007).

Baxter, Stephen and Blair, John, 'Land Tenure and Royal Patronage in the Early English Kingdom: A Model and a Case Study', *ANS*, vol. 28 (2006), pp. 19–46.

Baxter, Stephen, Karkov, Catherine, Nelson, Janet L., and Pelteret, David, ed., *Early Medieval Studies in Memory of Patrick Wormald* (Farnham, 2009).

Beam, Amanda, *The Balliol Dynasty, 1210–1364* (Edinburgh, 2008).

Berend, Nora, ed., *Christianization and the Rise of Christian Monarchy: Scandinavia, Central Europe and Rus', c.900–1200* (Cambridge, 2007).

Bérenger, Agnès and Lachaud, Frédérique, ed., *Hiérarchie des pouvoirs, délégation de pouvoir et responsabilité des administrateurs dans l'Antiquité et au Moyen Âge* (Metz, 2012).

Bérenger, François, 'Le contrôle des officiers du royaume de Sicile dans le dernier tiers du xiiie siècle (1266–1300)', in *Hiérarchie des pouvoirs*, ed. Bérenger and Lachaud (2012), pp. 231–52.

Berger, Adolf, *Encyclopedic Dictionary of Roman Law* (Philadelphia, PA, 1953).

Bijsterveld, Arnoud-Jan, *Do Ut Des: Gift Giving, Memoria, and Conflict Management in the Medieval Low Countries* (Hilversum, 2007).

Binchy, D. A., 'Celtic Suretyship: A Fossilized Indo-European Institution?', *Indo-European and Indo-Europeans*, ed. G. Cardona, H. M Hoenigswald, and A. Senn (Philadelphia, PA, 1970), pp. 355–67.

Bisson, T. N., 'Celebration and Persuasion: Reflections on the Cultural Evolution of Medieval Consultation', *Legislative Studies Quarterly*, vol. 7, no. 2 (1982), pp. 181–204.

Bisson, T. N., 'Les comptes des domaines au temps de Philippe-Auguste: essai comparatif', in *La France de Philippe Auguste: le temps des mutations: Actes du colloque international organisé par le C.N.R.S.*, ed. R-H. Bautier (Paris, 1982), pp. 521–39.

Bisson, T. N., 'The 'Feudal Revolution'', *Past & Present*, no. 142 (1994), pp. 6–42.

Bisson, T. N., 'Medieval Lordship', *Speculum*, vol. 70, no. 4 (1995), pp. 743–59.

Bisson, Thomas N., *The Crisis of the Twelfth Century: Power, Lordship and the Origins of European Government* (Princeton, NJ, 2009).

Blackburn, Mark, 'Coinage and Currency under Henry I: a Review', *ANS*, vol. 13 (1991), pp. 49–81.

Blanchard, Ian, 'Lothian and beyond: the Economy of the 'English Empire' of David I', in *Progress and Problems in Medieval England: Essays in Honour of Edward Miller*, ed. Richard Britnell and John Hatcher (Cambridge, 1996), pp. 21–45.

Bloch, Marc, 'Les *colliberti*: Étude sur la formation de la classe servile', *Revue Historique*, vol. 157 (1928), pp. 1–48, 225–63.

Boardman, Steve and Goodare, Julian, ed., *Kings, Lords and Men in Scotland and Britain, 1300–1625: Essays in Honour of Jenny Wormald* (Edinburgh, 2014).

Boardman, Steve and Ross, Alasdair D., ed., *The Exercise of Power in Medieval Scotland, c.1200–1500* (Dublin, 2003).

Bourdieu, Pierre, *The Logic of Practice* (Cambridge, 1990).

Bourdieu, Pierre, *Practical Reason: On the Theory of Action* (Stanford, CA, 1998).

Brand, John, *The English Coinage, 1180–1247: Money, Mints and Exchanges* (London, 1994).

Brand, Paul, '"Multis vigiliis excogitatem et inventam": Henry II and the Creation of the English Common Law', *Haskins Society Journal*, vol. 2 (1990), pp. 197–222.

Brand, Paul, 'Henry II and the Creation of the English Common Law', in *Henry II*, ed. Harper-Bill and Vincent (2007), pp. 215–41.

Brooks, Nicholas, 'The Development of Military Obligation in Eighth- and Ninth-Century England, in *England before the Conquest: Studies Presented to Dorothy Whitelock*, ed. P. Clemoes and K. Hughes (Cambridge, 1971), pp. 69–84.

Brooks, Nicholas, 'Arms, Status and Warfare in Late-Saxon England', in *Ethelred the Unready: Papers from the Millenary Conference*, ed. David Hill (Oxford, 1978), pp. 81–103.

Brotherstone, Terry and Ditchburn, David, ed., *Freedom and Authority: Scotland, c.1050–1650: Historical and Historiographical Essays Presented to Grant G. Simpson* (East Linton, 2000).

Broun, Dauvit, *The Charters of Gaelic Scotland and Ireland in the Early and Central Middle Ages* (Cambridge, 1995).

Broun, Dauvit, 'The Birth of Scottish History', *SHR*, vol. 76, no. 201 (1997), pp. 4–22.

Broun, Dauvit, 'Dunkeld and the Origin of Scottish Identity', *Innes Review*, vol. 48, no. 2 (1997), pp. 112–24.

Broun, Dauvit, 'Defining Scotland and the Scots before the Wars of Independence', in *Image and Identity: The Making and Re-Making of Scotland through the Ages*, ed. Dauvit Broun, R. J. Finlay, and Michael Lynch (Edinburgh, 1998), pp. 4–17.

Broun, Dauvit, 'Anglo-French Acculturation and the Irish Element in Scottish Identity', in *Britain and Ireland, 900–1300: Insular Responses to Medieval European Change*, ed. Brendan Smith (Cambridge, 1999), pp. 135–53.

Broun, Dauvit, *The Irish Identity of the Kingdom of the Scots in the Twelfth and Thirteenth Centuries* (Woodbridge, 1999).

Broun, Dauvit, 'A New Look at *Gesta Annalia* attributed to John of Fordun', in *Church, Chronicle and Learning in Medieval and Early Renaissance Scotland*, ed. B. E. Crawford (Edinburgh, 1999), pp. 9–30.

Broun, Dauvit, 'The Writing of Charters in Scotland and Ireland in the Twelfth Century', in *Charters and the Use of the Written Word in Medieval Society*, ed. Karl Heidecker (Turnhout, 2000), pp. 113–31.

Broun, Dauvit, 'The Changing Face of Charter Scholarship: A Review Article', *Innes Review*, vol. 52, no. 2 (2001), pp. 205–11.

Broun, Dauvit, 'The Absence of Regnal Years from the Dating Clause of Charters of Kings of Scots, 1195–1222', *ANS*, vol. 25 (2003), pp. 47–63.

Broun, Dauvit, 'The Welsh Identity of the Kingdom of Strathclyde *c*.900–*c*.1200', *Innes Review*, vol. 55, no. 2 (2004), pp. 111–80.

Broun, Dauvit, 'The Adoption of Brieves in Scotland', in *Charters and Charter Scholarship in Britain and Ireland*, ed. Marie Therese Flanagan and Judith A. Green (Basingstoke, 2005), pp. 164–83.

Broun, Dauvit, '*Alba*: Pictish Homeland or Irish Offshoot?', in *Exile and Homecoming: Papers from the 5th Australian Conference of Celtic Studies*, ed. Pamela O'Neill (Sydney, 2005), pp. 234–75.

Broun, Dauvit, 'Contemporary Perspectives on Alexander II's Succession: the Evidence of King-lists', in *Reign of Alexander II*, ed. Oram (2005), pp. 79–98.

Broun, Dauvit, 'Becoming Scottish in the Thirteenth Century: The Evidence of the Chronicle of Melrose', in *West over Sea: Studies in Scandinavian Sea-Borne Expansion and Settlement before 1300. A Festschrift in Honour of Dr Barbara E. Crawford*, ed. Beverley Ballin Smith, Simon Taylor, and Gareth Williams (Leiden, 2007), pp. 19–32.

Broun, Dauvit, *Scottish Independence and the Idea of Britain from the Picts to Alexander III* (Edinburgh, 2007).

Broun, Dauvit, 'The Property Records in the Book of Deer as a Source for Early Scottish Society', in *Book of Deer*, ed. Forsyth (2008), pp. 313–60.

Broun, Dauvit, 'Attitudes of *Gall* to *Gaedhel* in Scotland before John of Fordun', in *Mìorun Mòr nan Gall: 'The Great Ill-Will of the Lowlander?': Lowland Perceptions of the Highlands, Medieval and Modern*, ed. Dauvit Broun and Martin MacGregor (Glasgow, 2009), pp. 49–82.

Broun, Dauvit, ed., *The Reality behind Charter Diplomatic: Studies by Dauvit Broun, John Reuben Davies, Richard Sharpe and Alice Taylor* (Glasgow, 2011).

Broun, Dauvit, 'The Presence of Witnesses and the Writing of Charters', in *Reality behind Charter Diplomatic*, ed. Broun (2011), pp. 235–90.

Broun, Dauvit, 'Re-Examining *cáin* in the Twelfth and Thirteenth Centuries', in *Princes, Prelates and Poets in Medieval Ireland: Essays in Honour of Katharine Simms*, ed. Seán Duffy (Dublin, 2013), pp. 46–62.

Broun, Dauvit, 'Statehood and Lordship in 'Scotland' before the Mid-Twelfth Century', *Innes Review*, vol. 66, no. 1 (2015), pp. 1–71.

Broun, Dauvit, 'Britain and the Beginnings of Scotland', Sir John Rhŷs Memorial Lecture, *Journal of the British Academy*, vol. 3 (2015), pp. 107–37.

Brown, Elizabeth A. R., 'The Tyranny of a Construct: Feudalism and Historians of Medieval Europe', *American Historical Review*, vol. 79, no. 4 (1974), pp. 1063–88.

Brown, Michael, 'Scotland Tamed? Kings and Magnates in Late Medieval Scotland: a Review of Recent Work', *Innes Review*, vol. 45, no. 2 (1994), pp. 120–46.

Brown, Michael, 'Earldom and Kindred: the Lennox and Its Earls, 1200–1458', in *Exercise of Power*, ed. Boardman and Ross (2003), pp. 201–24.

Brown, Michael, *The Wars of Scotland 1214–1371* (Edinburgh, 2004).

Brown, Michael, 'War, Allegiance and Community in the Anglo-Scottish Marches: Teviotdale in the Fourteenth Century', *Northern History*, vol. 41, no. 2 (2004), pp. 219–38.

Brown, Michael, 'Aristocratic Politics and the Crisis of Scottish Kingship, 1286–1296', *SHR*, vol. 90, no. 229 (2011), pp. 1–26.

Brown, Peter, 'Society and the Supernatural: A Medieval Change', *Dædalus*, vol. 104, no. 2 (1975), pp. 133–51.

Brown, Warren C., *Violence in Medieval Europe* (Harlow, 2011).

Brundage, James A., *Law, Sex and Christian Society in Medieval Europe* (Chicago, 1987).

Brundage, James A., *Medieval Canon Law* (London, 1995).

Brundage, James A., *The Medieval Origins of the Legal Profession: Canonists, Civilians, and Courts* (Chicago, 2008).

Brunner, Otto, *Land and Lordship: Structures of Government in Medieval Austria*, trans. H. Kaminsky and J. Van Horn Melton (Philadelphia, PA, 1992).

Budd, Eric, *Democratization, Development and the Patrimonial State In the Age of Globalization* (Oxford, 2004).

Burns, Edward, *The Coinage of Scotland*, 3 vols (Edinburgh, 1887).

Cairns, John, 'Historical Introduction', in *A History of Private Law in Scotland: Introduction and Property*, ed. Kenneth Reid and Richard Zimmerman (Edinburgh, 2000), pp. 14–184.

Cam, Helen, 'The Evolution of the Mediaeval English Franchise', *Speculum*, vol. 32 (1957), pp. 427–42.

Campbell, James, 'Bede's *Reges* and *Principes*', in James Campbell, *Essays in Anglo-Saxon History* (London, 1986), pp. 85–98.

Campbell, James, 'Observations on English Government from the Tenth to the Twelfth Centuries', in Campbell , *Essays in Anglo-Saxon History* (1986), pp. 155–70.

Campbell, James, 'The Significance of the Anglo-Saxon State in the Administrative History of Western Europe', in Campbell , *Essays in Anglo-Saxon History* (1986), pp. 171–89.

Campbell, James, 'The United Kingdom of England', in *Uniting the Kingdom? The Making of British History*, ed. Alexander Grant and Keith J. Stringer (London, 1995), pp. 31–47.

Campbell, James, 'The Late Anglo-Saxon State: a Maximum View', in James Campbell, *The Anglo-Saxon State* (London, 2000), pp. 1–30.

Campbell, James, 'Some Agents and Agencies of the Late Anglo-Saxon State', in Campbell, *Anglo-Saxon State* (2000), pp. 201–25.

Campbell, James, 'Hundreds and Leets: A Survey with Suggestions', in *Medieval East Anglia*, ed. Christopher Harper-Bill (Woodbridge, 2005), pp. 153–67.

Campbell, Stuart D., 'The Language of Objects: Material Culture in Medieval Scotland', in *New Perspectives*, ed. Hammond (2013), pp. 183–201.

Carpenter, Christine, *Locality and Polity: A Study of Warwickshire Landed Society 1401–1499* (Cambridge, 1992).

Carpenter, David A., 'The Decline of the Curial Sheriff in England 1194–1258', *EHR*, vol. 91, no. 358 (1976), pp. 1–32.

Carpenter, David A., *The Minority of Henry III* (Berkeley, CA, and Los Angeles, 1990).

Carpenter, David A., 'What Happened in 1258?', in David A. Carpenter, *The Reign of Henry III* (London, 1996), pp. 183–97.

Carpenter, David A., 'The English Royal Chancery in the Thirteenth Century', in *Écrit et Pouvoir dans les chancelleries médiévales: espace français, espace anglais*, ed. K. Flanu and D. J. Guth (Louvain-La-Neuve, 1997), pp. 25–53, reprinted in *English Government*, ed. Jobson (2004), pp. 49–69.

Carpenter, David, *The Struggle for Mastery, The Penguin History of Britain 1066–1284* (London, 2004).

Carpenter, David, 'In "Testimonium Factorum Brevium": the Beginnings of the English Chancery Rolls', in *Records*, ed. Vincent (2009), pp. 1–28.

Carpenter, David, 'Scottish Royal Government in the Thirteenth Century from an English Perspective', in *New Perspectives*, ed. Hammond (2013), pp. 117–59.

Carpenter, David, *Magna Carta: A New Commentary* (London, 2015).

Cassidy, Richard, '*Recorda Splendidissima*: the Use of Pipe Rolls in the Thirteenth Century', *Historical Research*, vol. 85, no. 227 (2012), pp. 1–12.

Chaplais, Pierre, 'The Anglo-Saxon Chancery: From the Diplomat to the Writ', *Journal of the Society of Archivists*, vol. 3, no. 4 (1966), pp. 160–76.

Chaplais, Pierre, *English Royal Documents: King John–King Henry VI, 1199–1461* (Oxford, 1971).

Chapman Stacey, Robin, *The Road to Judgement: from Custom to Court in Medieval Ireland and Wales* (Philadelphia, PA, 1994).

Charles-Edwards, T. M., *The Welsh Laws* (Cardiff, 1989).

Charles-Edwards, T. M., *Early Christian Ireland* (Cambridge, 2000).

Charles-Edwards, T. M., 'The Three Columns of Law: A Comparative Perspective', in *Tair Colofn Cyfraith*, ed. Charles-Edwards and Russell (2007), pp. 26–59.

Charles-Edwards, T. M., 'The Welsh Law of Theft: Iorwerth versus the Rest', in *Tair Colofn Cyfraith*, ed. Charles-Edwards and Russell (2007), pp. 108–30.

Charles-Edwards, T. M., *Wales and the Britons, 350–1064* (Oxford, 2013).

Charles-Edwards, T. M., Owen, Morfydd E., and Walters D. B., ed., *Lawyers and Laymen: Studies in the History of Law Presented to Professor Dafydd Jenkins on His 75th birthday* (Cardiff, 1986).

Cheyette, Fredric L., 'Suum cuique tribuere', *French Historical Studies*, vol. 6, no. 3 (1970), pp. 287–99.

Cheyette, Fredric L., 'The Invention of the State', in *The Walter Prescott Memorial Lectures: Essays on Medieval Civilisation*, ed. R. E. Sullivan, B. K. Lachner, and K. R. Philp (Austin, TX, and London, 1978), pp. 143–78.

Clanchy, Michael T., *From Memory to Written Record: England, 1066–1307*, 2nd edn (Oxford, 1993).

Clancy, Thomas O., 'Annat in Scotland and the Origins of the Parish', *Innes Review*, vol. 46, no. 2 (1995), pp. 91–115.

Colman, Rebecca V., 'Reason and Unreason in Early Medieval Law', *Journal of Interdisciplinary History*, vol. 4, no. 4 (1974), pp. 571–91.

Connolly, Philomena, *Medieval Record Sources*, Maynooth Research Guides for Irish Local History 4 (Dublin, 2002).

Cook, Barrie J., '*En monnaie aiant cours*: The Monetary System of the Angevin Empire', in *Coinage and History in the North Sea World, c. AD 500–1250: Essays in Honour of Marion Archibald*, ed. Barrie J. Cook and Gareth Williams (Leiden, 2006), pp. 617–86.

Cooper, T. M. [First Baron Cooper of Culross], '*Regiam Majestatem* and the Auld Lawes', in *An Introductory Survey of the Sources and Literature of Scots Law by Various Authors*, Stair Society 1 (Edinburgh, 1936), pp. 70–81.

Cooper, T. M. *Select Scottish Cases of the Thirteenth Century* (Edinburgh, 1944).

Cooper, T. M. 'The Authorship of the Berne MS', *SHR*, vol. 27, no. 104 (1948), pp. 114–23.

Cooper, T. M. *Selected Papers, 1922–1954* (Edinburgh, 1957).

Cooper, T. M. 'Melrose Abbey *versus* the Earl of Dunbar', in Cooper, *Selected Papers* (1957), pp. 81–7.

Cooper, T. M. 'The First Reform (Miscellaneous Provisions) Act', in Cooper, *Selected Papers* (1957), pp. 88–92.

Cooper, T. M. 'The Dark Age of Scottish Legal History, 1350–1650', in Cooper, *Selected Papers* (1957), pp. 219–36.

Cooper, T. M. 'Early Scottish Statutes Revisited', in Cooper, *Selected Papers* (1957), pp. 237–43.

Cooper, T. M. 'From David I to Bruce, 1124–1329: the Scoto-Norman law', in *Introduction to Scottish Legal History*, Stair Society 20 (Edinburgh, 1958), pp. 3–17.

Coss, Peter, 'The Formation of the English Gentry', *Past & Present*, no. 147 (1995), pp. 38–64.

Coss, Peter, *The Origins of the English Gentry* (Cambridge, 2003).

Coupland, Simon, 'Charlemagne's Coinage: Ideology and Economy', in *Charlemagne: Empire and Society*, ed. Joanna Story (Manchester, 2005), pp. 211–29.

Cowan, Ian B., *The Parishes of Medieval Scotland* (Edinburgh, 1967).

Cowan, Ian B., 'Two Early Scottish Taxation Rolls', *Innes Review*, vol. 22, no. 1 (1971), pp. 6–11.

Cowan, E. J., 'Norwegian Sunset—Scottish Dawn: Hakon IV and Alexander III', in *Scotland in the Reign of Alexander III*, ed. Reid (1990), pp. 103–31.

Cowan, E. J. and McDonald, R. Andrew, ed., *Alba: Celtic Scotland in the Medieval Era* (East Linton, 2000).

Cox, Adrian, et al., 'Backland Activities in Medieval Perth: excavations at Meal Vennel and Scott Street', *Proceedings of the Society of Antiquaries of Scotland*, vol. 126 (1996), pp. 733–821.

Crawford, Barbara E., 'Medieval Strathnaver', in *The Province of Strathnaver*, ed. J. R. Baldwin, Scottish Society of Northern Studies (Edinburgh, 2000), pp. 1–12.

Crawford, Barbara E., *The Northern Earldoms: Orkney and Caithness from AD 870 to 1470* (Edinburgh, 2013).

Crawford, Barbara E., 'The Earldom of Caithness and the Kingdom of Scotland, 1150–1266', in *Essays on the Nobility*, ed. Stringer (1985), pp. 25–43.

Crawford, Barbara E., 'William Sinclair, Earl of Orkney and His Family: A Study in the Politics of Survival', in *Essays on the Nobility*, ed. Stringer (1985), pp. 232–53.

Crick, Julia, 'Nobility', in *A Companion to the Early Middle Ages: Britain and Ireland, c.500–c.1100*, ed. Pauline Stafford (Oxford, 2009), pp. 414–31.

Crook, David, *Records of the General Eyre*, Public Record Office Handbooks 20 (London, 1982).

Crouch, David, *The Image of Aristocracy in Britain, 1000–1300* (London, 1992).

Crouch, David, *The English Aristocracy 1070–1272: A Social Transformation* (New Haven, CT, 2011).

Cubitt, Catherine, '"As the Lawbook Teaches": Reeves, Lawbooks and Urban Life in the Anonymous Old English Legend of the Seven Sleepers', *EHR*, vol. 124, no. 510 (2009), pp. 1021–49.

Dalrymple, Sir David [Lord Hailes], *An Examination of Some of the Arguments for the High Antiquity of Regiam Majestatem and an Inquiry into the Leges Malcolmi* (Edinburgh, 1769).

Davidson, J., 'Coin Finds in Dumfriesshire and Galloway', *Transactions of the Dumfries and Galloway Natural History and Antiquaries Society*, vol. 26 (1947–48), pp. 100–13.

Davies, John Reuben, 'The Donor and the Duty of Warrandice: Giving and Granting in Scottish charters', in *Reality behind Charter Diplomatic*, ed. Broun (2011), pp. 120–65.

Davies, R. R., 'The Survival of the Bloodfeud in Medieval Wales', *History*, vol. 54. no. 182 (1969), pp. 338–57.

Davies, R. R., *Domination and Conquest: The Experience of Ireland, Scotland and Wales 1100–1300* (Cambridge, 1990).

Davies, R. R., *The Age of Conquest: Wales 1063–1415* (Oxford, 1991).

Davies, R. R., *The First English Empire: Power and Identities in the British Isles 1093–1343* (Oxford, 2000).

Davies, R. R., 'The Medieval State: the Tyranny of a Concept?', *Journal of Historical Sociology*, vol. 16 (2003), pp. 280–300.

Davies, R. R., *Lords and Lordship in the British Isles in the Late Middle Ages*, ed. Brendan Smith (Oxford, 2009).

Davies, Wendy, 'The Latin Charter-Tradition in western Britain, Brittany and Ireland in the early mediaeval period', in *Ireland in Early Mediaeval Europe: Studies in Memory of Kathleen Hughes*, ed. Dorothy Whitelock, Rosamond McKitterick, and David N. Dumville (Cambridge, 1982), pp. 258–80.

Davies, Wendy, 'Suretyship in the *Cartulaire de Redon*', in *Lawyers and Laymen*, ed. Charles-Edwards, Owen and Walters (1986), pp. 72–91.

Davies, Wendy and Fouracre, Paul, ed., *The Settlement of Disputes in Early Medieval Europe* (Cambridge, 1986).

Davies, Wendy and Fouracre, Paul, ed., *Property and Power in the Early Middle Ages* (Cambridge, 1995).

Davies, Wendy and Fouracre, Paul, ed., *The Languages of Gift in the Early Middle Ages* (Cambridge, 2010).

Dean, Trevor, 'Marriage and Mutilation: Vendetta in Late Medieval Italy', *Past & Present*, no. 157 (1997), pp. 3–36.

de Jong, Mayke, and Cohen, Esther, ed., *Medieval Transformations: Texts, Power and Gifts in Context* (Leiden, 2001).

Dennison, E. Patricia, 'Burghs and Burgesses: A Time of Consolidation?', in *Reign of Alexander II*, ed. Oram (2005), pp. 253–83.

Dickinson, William Croft, 'The Toschederach', *Juridical Review*, vol. 53 (1941), pp. 85–111, at pp. 99–105.

Dickinson, William Croft, 'A Chamberlain's Ayre in Aberdeen, 1399×1400', *SHR*, vol. 33, no. 115 (1954), pp. 27–36.

Dickinson, William Croft, *Scotland from Earliest Times to 1603* (Edinburgh, 1961).

Ditchburn, David, 'Trade with Northern Europe, 1297–1540', in *Scottish Medieval Town*, ed. Lynch, Spearman and Spell (1988), pp. 161–79.

Ditchburn, David, *Scotland and Europe: The Medieval Kingdom and Its Contacts with Christendom*, vol. 1: *Religion, Culture and Commerce* (East Linton, 2001).

Dodgshon, R., *Land and Society in Early Scotland* (Oxford, 1981).

Douglas, Audrey W., 'Frankalmoin and Jurisdictional Immunity: Maitland Revisited', *Speculum*, vol. 53 (1978), pp. 26–48.

Douglas, Audrey W., 'Tenure *in elemosina*: Origins and Establishment in Twelfth-Century England', *The American Journal of Legal History*, vol. 24, no. 95 (1980), pp. 95–132.

Dresch, Paul, 'Legalism, Anthropology and History: a View from Part of Anthropology', in *Legalism: History and Anthropology*, ed. Paul Dresch and Hannah Skoda (Oxford, 2012), pp. 1–37.

Dresch, Paul, 'Outlawry, Exile and Banishment: Reflections on Community and Justice', in *Legalism: Community and Justice*, ed. Pirie and Scheele (2014), pp. 97–124.

Driscoll, Stephen, 'Church Archaeology in Glasgow and the Kingdom of Strathclyde', *Innes Review*, vol. 49, no. 2 (1998), pp. 95–114.

Driscoll, Stephen, *Alba: the Gaelic Kingdom of Scotland AD 800–1124*, Historic Scotland (Edinburgh, 2002).

Duby, Georges, *La Société aux xie et xiie siècles dans la régione mâconnaise*, in Georges Duby, *Qu'est-ce que la société féodale?* (Paris, 2002), pp. 6–597.

Duffy, Seán, 'The Lords of Galloway, Earls of Carrick and the Bissets of the Glens: Scottish Settlement in Thirteenth-Century Ulster', in *Regions and Rulers in Ireland, 1100–1650*, ed. David Edwards (Dublin, 2004), pp. 37–50.

Dufour, Jean, 'Peut-on parler d'une Organisation de la chancellerie de Philippe Auguste?', *Archiv für Diplomatik*, vol. 41 (1995), pp. 249–61.

Dumville, D. N., 'The Chronicle of the Kings of Alba', in *Kings, Clerics and Chronicles*, ed. Taylor (2000), pp. 73–86.

Dunbar, J. G. and Duncan, A. A. M., 'Tarbert Castle: A Contribution to the History of Argyll', *SHR*, vol. 50, no. 149 (1971), pp. 1–17.

Duncan, A. A. M., 'Documents Relating to the Priory of the Isle of May, c.1140–1313', *Proceedings of the Society of Antiquaries of Scotland*, vol. 90 (1956–57), pp. 52–80.

Duncan, A. A. M., '*Regiam Majestatem*: A Reconsideration', *Juridical Review*, new series, vol. 6 (1961), pp. 199–217.

Duncan, A. A. M., *Scotland: the Making of the Kingdom* (Edinburgh, 1975).

Duncan, A. A. M., 'The Battle of Carham, 1018', *SHR*, vol. 55, no. 159 (1976), pp. 20–8.

Duncan, A. A. M., 'The "Laws of Malcolm MacKenneth"', in *Medieval Scotland*, ed. Grant and Stringer (1993), pp. 239–73.

Duncan, A. A. M., 'John king of England and the Kings of Scots', in *King John: New Interpretations*, ed. S. D. Church (Woodbridge, 1999), pp. 247–71.

Duncan, A. A. M., 'Yes, the Earliest Scottish Charters', *SHR*, vol. 78, no. 205 (1999), pp. 1–38.

Duncan, A. A. M., *The Kingship of the Scots, 842–1292: Succession and Independence* (Edinburgh, 2002).

Duncan, A. A. M. and Brown, A. L, 'Argyll and the Isles in the Earlier Middle Ages', *Proceedings of the Society of Antiquaries of Scotland*, vol. 90 (1956–57), pp. 192–220.

Dunshea, Philip M., '*Druim Alban, Dorsum Britanniae*—"the Spine of Britain"', *SHR*, vol. 92, no. 235 (2013), pp. 275–89.

Edmonds, Fiona, 'The Emergence and Transformation of Medieval Cumbria', *SHR*, vol. 93, no. 237 (2014), pp. 195–216.

Ertman, Thomas, *Birth of the Leviathan: Building States and Regimes in Medieval and Early Modern Europe* (Cambridge, 1997).

Evans-Pritchard, E. E., *The Nuer: A Description of the Modes of Livelihood and Political Institutions of a Nilotic People* (Oxford, 1940).

Faith, Rosamond, *The English Peasantry and the Growth of Lordship* (Leicester, 1997).

Faulkner, Kathryn, 'The Transformation of Knighthood in Early Thirteenth-Century England', *EHR*, vol. 111, no. 440 (1996), pp. 1–23.

Ferguson, Paul C., *Medieval Papal Representatives in Scotland: Legates, Nuncios and Judges-Delegates, 1125–1286*, Stair Society 45 (Edinburgh, 1997).

Firnhaber-Baker, Justine, 'Seigneurial Warfare and Royal Power in Later Medieval Southern France', *Past & Present*, no. 208 (2010), pp. 37–76.

Firnhaber-Baker, Justine, *Violence and the State in Languedoc, 1250–1400* (Cambridge, 2014).

Forsyth, Katherine, ed., *Studies on the Book of Deer* (Dublin, 2008).

Forte, A. D. M., '"A Strange Archaic Provision of Mercy": The Procedural Rules for *Duellum* under the Law of *Clann Duib*', *Edinburgh Law Review*, vol. 14, no. 3 (2010), pp. 418–50.

Fouracre, Paul, 'Eternal Light and Earthly Needs: Practical Aspects of the Development of Frankish Immunities', in *Property and Power*, ed. Davies and Fouracre (1995), pp. 53–81.

Frame, Robin, *The Political Development of the British Isles 1100–1400* (Oxford, 1995).

Francis, E. D., '*Particularum quarundam varietas: prae* and *pro*', in *Studies in Latin Literature and Language*, ed. T. Cole and D. O'Ross (Cambridge, 1973), pp. 1–60.

Fraser, James E., 'Rochester, Hexham and Cennrígmonaid: The Movements of St Andrew in Britain, 604–747', in *Saints' Cults in the Celtic World*, ed. Steve Boardman, John Reuben Davies, and Eila Williamson (Woodbridge, 2009), pp. 1–17.

Ganshof, F. L., *The Carolingians and Frankish Monarchy: Studies in Carolingian History*, trans. J. Sondenheimer (London, 1971).

Garnett, George, '*Franci et Angli:* The Legal Distinctions between Peoples after the Conquest', *ANS*, vol. 8 (1986), pp. 109–37.

Geary, Patrick, 'Medieval Archivists as Authors: Social Memory and Archival Memory', in *Archives, Documentation and Institutions of Social Memory: Essays from the Sawyer Seminar*, ed. Francis X. Blouin and William G. Rosenberg (Ann Arbor, MI, 2006), pp. 106–13.

Gemmill, Elizabeth and Mayhew, Nicholas, *Changing Values in Medieval Scotland: A Study of Prices, Weights and Measures* (Cambridge, 1995).

Gilbert, John M., *Hunting and Hunting Reserves in Medieval Scotland* (Edinburgh, 1979).

Gillingham, John, 'Elective Kingship and the Unity of Medieval Germany', *German History*, vol. 9, no. 2 (1991), pp. 124–35.

Gillingham, John, 'Thegns and Knights in Eleventh-Century England: Who Was Then the Gentleman?', *TRHS*, 6th ser., vol. 5 (1995), pp. 129–53.

Gillingham, John, 'Killing and Mutilating Political Enemies in the British Isles from the Late Twelfth to the Early Fourteenth Century: A Comparative Study', in *Britain and Ireland, 900–1300*, ed. Brendan Smith (Cambridge, 1999), pp. 114–34.

Gledhill, Jonathan, 'From Shire to Barony: the Case of Eastern Lothian', in *Norman Expansion*, ed. Stringer and Jotischky (2013), pp. 87–114.

Gluckman, Max, 'The Peace in the Feud', *Past & Present*, no. 8 (1955), pp. 1–14.

Godfrey, A. M., *Civil Justice in Renaissance Scotland: the Origins of a Central Court* (Leiden, 2009).

Goebel, Julius, Jr, *Felony and Misdemeanor: A Study in the History of Criminal Law* (Philadelphia, PA, 1976).

Gorski, Richard, *The Fourteenth-Century Sheriff: English Local Administration in the Late Middle Ages* (Woodbridge, 2003).

Grant, Alexander, 'Earls and Earldoms in Late Medieval Scotland c.1310–1460', in *Essays Presented to Michael Roberts*, ed. J. Bossy and P. Jupp (Belfast, 1976), pp. 24–40.

Grant, Alexander, 'Thanes and Thanages from the Eleventh to the Fourteenth Centuries', in *Medieval Scotland*, ed. Grant and Stringer (1993), pp. 39–81.

Grant, Alexander, 'Aspects of National Consciousness in Medieval Scotland', in *Nations, Nationalism and Patriotism in the European Past*, ed. C. Bjørn, A. Grant, and K. J. Stringer (Copenhagen, 1994), pp. 68–95.

Grant, Alexander, 'The Construction of the Early Scottish State', in *The Medieval State: Essays Presented to James Campbell*, ed. J. R. Maddicott and D. M. Palliser (London, 2000), pp. 47–71.

Grant, Alexander, 'The Province of Ross and the Kingdom of Alba', in *Alba*, ed. Cowan and McDonald (2000), pp. 88–126.

Grant, Alexander, 'Lordship and Society in Twelfth-century Clydesdale', in *Power and Identity in the Middle Ages: Essays in Memory of Rees Davies*, ed. Huw Pryce and John Watts (Oxford, 2007), pp. 98–124.

Grant, Alexander, 'Franchises North of the Border: Baronies and Regalities in Medieval Scotland', in *Liberties and Identities in the Medieval British Isles*, ed. Michael Prestwich (Woodbridge, 2008), pp. 155–99.

Grant, Alexander, 'At the Northern Edge: *Alba* and its Normans', in *Norman Expansion*, ed. Stringer and Jotischky (2013), pp. 49–85.

Grant, Alexander, 'Murder Will Out: Kingship, Kinship and Killing in Medieval Scotland', in *Kings, Lords and Men*, ed. Boardman and Goodare (2014), pp. 193–226.

Grant, Alexander and Stringer, Keith J., ed., *Medieval Scotland: Crown, Lordship and Community—Essays Presented to G. W. S. Barrow* (Edinburgh, 1993).

Green, Judith A., 'The Last Century of Danegeld', *EHR*, vol. 96, no. 379 (1981), pp. 241–58.

Green, Judith A., 'Praeclarum et Magnificum Antiquitatis Monumentum: the Earliest Surviving Pipe Roll', *Bulletin of the Institute of Historical Research*, vol. 55 (1982), pp. 1–17.

Green, Judith A., *The Government of England under Henry I* (Cambridge, 1986).

Green, Judith A., 'Anglo-Scottish Relations, 1066–1174', in *England and Her Neighbours, 1066–1453: Essays in Honour of Pierre Chaplais*, ed. Michael Jones and Malcolm Vale (London, 1989), pp. 53–72.

Greenway, Diana E., 'Dates in History: Chronology and Memory', *Historical Research*, vol. 72, no. 178 (1999), pp. 127–39.

Grutzpalk, Jonas, 'Blood Feud and Modernity', *Journal of Classical Sociology*, vol. 2, no. 2 (2002), pp. 115–34.

Hagger, Mark, 'The Norman *Vicomte*, c.1035–1135: What Did He Do?', *ANS*, vol. 29 (2007), pp. 65–83.

Hagger, Mark, 'A Pipe Roll for 25 Henry I', *EHR*, vol. 122, no. 495 (2007), pp. 133–40.

Hagger, Mark, 'The Earliest Norman Writs Revisited', *Historical Research*, vol. 82, no. 216 (2009), pp. 181–205.

Hagger, Mark, 'Theory and Practice in the Making of Twelfth-Century Pipe Rolls', in *Records*, ed. Vincent (2009), pp. 45–74.

Hagger, Mark, 'Secular Law and Custom in Ducal Normandy, *c.*1000–1144', *Speculum*, vol. 85, no. 4 (2010), pp. 827–67.

Hall, Hubert, 'The System of the Exchequer', in *Introduction to the Study of the Pipe Rolls*, Pipe Roll Society 3 (London, 1884), pp. 35–69.

Halsall, Guy, 'Violence and Society in the Early Medieval West: An Introductory Survey', in *Violence and Society in the Early Medieval West*, ed. Guy Halsall (Woodbridge, 1998), pp. 1–45.

Hamilton, Elsa, *Mighty Subjects: the Dunbar Earls in Scotland, c.1072–1289* (Edinburgh, 2010).

Hammond, Matthew H., '*Hostiarii Regis Scotie*: the Durward Family in the Thirteenth Century', in *Exercise of Power*, ed. Boardman and Ross (2003), pp. 118–38.

Hammond, Matthew H., 'Ethnicity and the Writing of Medieval Scottish History', *SHR*, vol. 85, no. 219 (2006), pp. 1–27.

Hammond, Matthew H., 'The Use of the Name Scot in the Central Middle Ages. Part 1: Scot as a By-Name', *Journal of Scottish Name Studies*, vol. 1 (2007), pp. 37–60.

Hammond, Matthew H., 'Queen Ermengarde and the Abbey of St Edward, Balmerino', *Cîteaux: Commentarii Cistercienses*, vol. 59 (2008), pp. 11–36.

Hammond, Matthew H., 'Women and the Adoption of Charters in Scotland North of the Forth, *c.*1150–1286', *Innes Review*, vol. 62, no. 1 (2011), pp. 5–46.

Hammond, Matthew H., 'The Use of the Name Scot in the Central Middle Ages. Part 2: Scot as a Surname, North of the Firth of Forth', *Journal of Scottish Name Studies*, vol. 6 (2012), pp. 11–50.

Hammond, Matthew, ed., *New Perspectives on Medieval Scotland, 1093–1286* (Woodbridge, 2013).

Hammond, Matthew, 'Domination and Conquest? The Scottish Experience in the Twelfth and Thirteenth centuries', in *The English Isles: Cultural Transmission and Political Conflict in Britain and Ireland, 1100–1500*, ed. Seán Duffy and Susan Foran (Dublin, 2013), pp. 80–95.

Hammond, Matthew, 'The Adoption and Routinization of Scottish Royal Charter Production for Lay Beneficiaries, 1124–1195', *ANS*, vol. 36 (Woodbridge, 2014), pp. 91–115.

Hamp, E. P., 'Scottish Gaelic *morair*', *Scottish Gaelic Studies*, vol. 14 (1986), pp. 138–41.

Harding, Alan, 'The Medieval Brieves of Protection and the Development of the Common Law', *Juridical Review*, new series, vol. 11 (1966), pp. 115–49.

Harding, Alan, '*Regiam Majestatem* among Medieval Lawbooks', *Juridical Review*, new series, vol. 29 (1984), pp. 97–111.

Harding, Alan, *Medieval Law and the Foundations of the State* (Oxford, 2001).

Harper-Bill, Christopher and Vincent, Nicholas, ed., *Henry II: New Interpretations* (Woodbridge, 2007).

Haskins, C. H., *Norman Institutions* (Cambridge, MA, 1918).

Heather, Peter, 'Law and Society in the Burgundian Kingdom', in *Law, Custom, and Justice*, ed. Rio (2011), pp. 115–53.

Helmholz, Richard H., 'Civil Jurisdiction and the Clergy', *The Ius Commune in England: Four Studies* (Oxford, 2001).

Helmholz, Richard H., *Oxford History of the Laws of England*, vol.1: *The History of Canon Law and Ecclesiastical Jurisdiction from 597 to the 1640s* (Oxford, 2004).

Herbert, Máire, '*Rí Éirenn, Rí Alban*: Kingship and Identity in the Ninth and Tenth centuries', in *Kings, Clerics and Chronicles*, ed. Taylor (2000), pp. 62–72.

Herder, Peter, 'Zur päpstlichen Delegationsgerichtsbarkeit im Mittelalter und in der frühen Neuzeit', *Zeitschrift der Savigny Stiftung für Rechtsgeschichte. Kanonistische Abteilung* 88, ed. H-J. Becker, A. Thier, and H. de Wall (2002), pp. 20–43.

Hill, David, and Rumble, Alexander R., ed., *The Defence of Wessex: The Burghal Hidage and Anglo-Saxon Fortifications* (Manchester 1996).

Hodge, Arkady, 'A New Charter of William the Lion Relating to Strathearn', *SHR*, vol. 86, no. 222 (2007), pp. 314–18.

Hodge, Arkady, 'When Is a Charter Not a Charter? Documents in Non-Conventional Contexts in Early Medieval Europe', in *Problems and Possibilities of Early Medieval Charters*, ed. Jonathan Jarrett and Allan Scott McKinley (Turnhout, 2013), pp. 127–49.

Holford, M. L., and K. J. Stringer, *Border Liberties and Loyalties: North-East England, c.1200–c.1400* (Edinburgh, 2010).

Hollister, C. W., 'The Origins of the English Treasury', *EHR*, vol. 93, no. 367 (1978), pp. 262–75.

Holmes, N. M. McQ., 'The Evidence of Finds for the Circulation and Use of Coins in Medieval Scotland', *PSAS*, vol. 134 (2004), pp. 241–80.

Holmes, N. M. McQ., 'A Probable Short Cross Purse Hoard from Dumfriesshire', *British Numismatic Journal*, vol. 74 (2004), pp. 180–3.

Holt, J. C., *Magna Carta*, 2nd edn (Cambridge, 1992).

Houston, R. A., *The Coroners of Northern Britain, c.1300–1700* (Basingstoke, 2014).

Howlett, David, *Caledonian Craftsmanship: The Scottish Latin Tradition* (Dublin, 2000).

Hudson, Benjamin, 'The "Scottish Chronicle"', *SHR*, vol. 77, no. 204 (1998), pp. 129–61.

Hudson, John, *Land Law and Lordship in Anglo-Norman England* (Oxford, 1994).

Hudson, John, *The Formation of the English Common Law: Law and Society in England from the Norman Conquest to Magna Carta* (London, 1996).

Hudson, John, 'Legal Aspects of Scottish Charter Diplomatic in the Twelfth Century: A Comparative Approach', *ANS*, vol. 25 (2003), pp. 121–38.

Hudson, John, *The Oxford History of the Laws of England*, vol.2: *871–1216* (Oxford, 2012).

Hudson, John, 'Imposing Feudalism on Anglo-Saxon England: Norman and Angevin Presentations of Pre-Conquest Lordship and Landholding', in *Feudalism*, ed. Bagge, Gelting, and Lindkvist (2011), pp. 115–34.

Hunnisett, R. F., *The Medieval Coroner* (Cambridge, 1961).

Hunter Marshall, D. W., 'Two Early English Occupations of Southern Scotland', *SHR*, vol. 25, no. 97 (1927), pp. 20–40.

Huntingdon, Joanna, 'David of Scotland: *vir tam necessarius mundo*', in *Saints' Cults*, ed. Boardman, Davies, and Williamson (2009), pp. 130–45.

Huntingdon, Joanna, 'St Margaret of Scotland: Conspicuous Consumption, Genealogical Inheritance and Post-Conquest Authority', *Journal of Scottish Historical Studies*, vol. 33, no. 2 (2013), pp. 149–64.

Hurnard, Naomi D., 'The Anglo-Norman Franchises', *EHR*, vol. 64, nos. 252–253 (1949), pp. 289–327, 433–60.

Husak, D., *Overcriminalisation: the Limits of the Criminal Law* (Oxford, 2008).

Hyams, Paul R., *Kings, Lords, and Peasants in Medieval England: The Common Law of Villeinage in the Twelfth and Thirteenth Centuries* (Oxford, 1980).

Hyams, Paul R., 'Does It Matter When the English Began to Distinguish between Crime and Tort?', in *Violence in Medieval Society*, ed. Richard W. Kaeuper (Woodbridge 2000), pp. 107–28.

Hyams, Paul R., *Rancor and Reconciliation in Medieval England* (Ithaca, 2003).

Il feudalesimo nell'alto medioevo, 2 vols *Settimane di Studio del Centro Italiano di studi sull'alto medioevo*, vol. 47 (Spoleto, 2000).

Innes, Cosmo N., *Memoir of Thomas Thomson, Advocate* (Edinburgh, 1854).

Innes, Matthew, *State and Society in the Early Medieval West: the Middle Rhine Valley 400–1000* (Cambridge, 2000).

Ireland, Richard W., 'Law in Action, Law in Books: the Practicality of Medieval Theft Law', *Continuity and Change*, vol. 17, no. 3 (2002), pp. 309–31.

Irving, Joseph, *The History of Dumbartonshire*, 2nd edn (Dumbarton, 1860).

Jackson, Kenneth, 'The Britons in Southern Scotland', *Antiquity*, vol. 29, no. 114 (1955), pp. 77–88.

Jackson, Kenneth, *The Gaelic Notes in the Book of Deer* (Cambridge, 1972).

Jenkins, Daffydd, 'Crime and Tort in the Three Columns of Law', trans. T. M. Charles-Edwards, in *Tair Colofn Cyfraith*, ed. Charles-Edwards and Russell (2007), pp. 1–25.

Jobson, Adrian, ed., *English Government in the Thirteenth Century* (Woodbridge, 2004).

John, Eric, *Land Tenure in Early England* (Leicester, 1960).

Jolliffe, J. E. A., 'The Chamber and Castle Treasuries under King John', in *Studies in Medieval History Presented to F. M. Powicke*, ed. R. W. Hunt, R. W. Southern, and W. A. Pantin (Oxford, 1948), pp. 121–37.

Jones, G. R. J., 'Multiple Estates and Early Settlement', in *English Medieval Settlement*, ed. P. H. Sawyer (London, 1979), pp. 9–40.

Jones, Rhys, *Peoples/States/Territories* (Oxford, 2007).

Jurasinski, Stefan, 'Germanism, Slapping and the Cultural Context of Æthelbertht's Code: A Reconsideration of Chapters 56–58', *Haskins Society Journal*, vol. 18 (2006), pp. 51–71.

Kaminsky, Howard, 'The Noble Feud in the Later Middle Ages', *Past & Present*, no. 177 (2002), pp. 55–83.

Kapelle, W. E., *The Norman Conquest of the North: the Region and Its Transformation* (London, 1979).

Karn, Nicholas, 'Nigel, Bishop of Ely, and the Restoration of the Exchequer after the "Anarchy" of King Stephen's Reign', *Historical Research*, vol. 80, no. 209 (2007), pp. 299–314.

Keefe, Thomas K., 'Proffers for Heirs and Heiresses in the Pipe Rolls: Some Observations on Indebtedness in the Years before Magna Carta (1180–1212)', *Haskins Society Journal*, vol. 5 (1993), pp. 99–109.

Keefer, Sarah Larratt, '"Ðonne se cirlisca man ordales weddigeð": the Anglo-Saxon lay ordeal', in *Early Medieval Studies*, ed. Baxter et al. (2009), pp. 353–67.

Keene, Catherine, *Saint Margaret, Queen of the Scots: A Life in Perspective* (New York, 2013).

Kelly, Fergus, *A Guide to Early Irish Law* (Dublin, 1988).

Kemp, Brian, 'Exchequer and Bench in the Later Twelfth Century—Separate or Identical Tribunals?', *EHR*, vol. 88, no. 348 (1973), pp. 559–73.

Keynes, Simon, *The Diplomas of King Æthelred 'the Unready', 978–1016: A Study in Their Use as Historical Evidence* (Cambridge, 1980).

Keynes, Simon, 'Regenbald the Chancellor [sic]', *ANS*, vol. 10 (1988), pp. 185–222.

Keynes, Simon, 'Royal Government and the Written Word in Late Anglo-Saxon England', in *The Uses of Literacy in Early Medieval Europe*, ed. Rosamond McKitterick (Cambridge, 1992), pp. 226–57.

Kidd, Colin, *British Identities before Nationalism: Ethnicity and Nationhood in the Atlantic World 1600–1800* (Cambridge, 1999).

Kimball, Elizabeth G., 'Tenure in Frank Almoign and Secular Services', *EHR*, vol. 43, no. 171 (1928), pp. 341–53.

Kimball, Elizabeth G., 'The Judicial Aspects of Frank Almoign Tenure', *EHR*, vol. 47, no. 185 (1932), pp. 1–11.

Kjær, Lars and Watson, A. J., ed., *Feasts and Gifts of Food in Medieval Europe: Ritualised Constructions of Hierarchy, Identity and Community*, Special Issue of *Journal of Medieval History*, vol. 37, no. 1 (2011).

Lacey, Nicola, *State Punishment: Political Principles and Community Values* (London, 1988).

Lacey, Nicola, 'Historicising Criminalisation: Conceptual and Empirical Issues', *Modern Law Review*, vol. 72, no. 6 (2009), pp. 936–60.

Lachaud, Frédérique, *L'Éthique du pouvoir au Moyen Âge: l'office dans la culture politique (Angleterre, vers 1150–vers 1330)* (Paris, 2010).

Lambert, T. B., 'Introduction: Some Approaches to Peace and Protection in the Middle Ages', in *Peace and Protection in the Middle Ages*, ed. T. B. Lambert and David Rollason (Toronto, 2009), pp. 1–18.

Lambert, T. B., 'Theft, Homicide and Crime in Late Anglo-Saxon Law', *Past & Present*, no. 214 (2012), pp. 3–43.

Lavelle, Ryan, 'The "Farm of One Night" and the Organisation of Royal Estates in Late Anglo-Saxon Wessex', *Haskins Society Journal*, vol. 14 (2005), pp. 53–82.

Lavelle, Ryan, *Royal Estates in Anglo-Saxon Wessex: Land, Politics and Family Strategies*, British Archaeological Reports, British Series 439 (Oxford, 2007).

Layfield, Sarah, 'The pope, the Scots and Their "Self-Styled" King: John XXII's Anglo-Scottish policy, 1316–34', in *England and Scotland in the Fourteenth Century*, ed. A. King and M. A. Penman (Woodbridge, 2007), pp. 157–71.

Le Jan, Régine, *Famille et Pouvoir dans le monde franc (viie–xe siècle): Essai d'anthropologie sociale* (Paris, 1995).

Le Jan, Régine, 'Continuity and Change in the Tenth-Century Nobility', in *Nobles and Nobility in Medieval Europe: Concepts, Origins, Transformations*, ed. Anne J. Duggan (Woodbridge, 2000), pp. 53–68.

Lewis, Chris, 'The Early Earls of Norman England', *ANS*, vol. 13 (1990), pp. 207–23.

Lewis, E. A., 'Account Roll of the Chamberlain of the Principality of North Wales 1304–5', *Bulletin of the Board of Celtic Studies*, vol. 1 (1921–23), pp. 256–75.

Loengard, Janet S., ed., *Magna Carta and the England of King John* (Woodbridge, 2010).

Lot, F. and Fawtier, R., *Histoire des institutions françaises au moyen âge*, II: *Institutions royales* (Paris, 1958).

Lustig, Richard I., 'The Treaty of Perth: a Re-Examination', *SHR*, vol. 58, no. 165 (1979), pp. 35–37.

Lynch, Michael, Michael Spearman, and Geoffrey Stell, ed., *The Scottish Medieval Town* (Edinburgh, 1988).

Lyon, Bruce, and Verhulst, Adriaan, *Medieval Finance: A Comparison of Financial Institutions in Northwestern Europe* (Bruges, 1967).

Macdonald, Alastair J., 'Kings of the Wild Frontier? The Earls of Dunbar or March, c.1070–1435', in *Exercise of Power*, ed. Boardman and Ross (2003), pp. 139–58.

McDonald, R. Andrew, *Outlaws of Medieval Scotland: Challenges to the Canmore Kings, 1058–1266* (East Linton, 2003).

McDonald, R. Andrew, 'Old and New in the far North: Ferchar Maccintsacairt and the Early Earls of Ross, c.1200–1274', in *Exercise of Power*, ed. Boardman and Ross (2003), pp. 23–45.

McKechnie, Hector, *Judicial Process Upon Brieves 1219–1532* (Glasgow, 1956).

McKitterick, Rosamond, *The Carolingians and the Written Word* (Cambridge, 1989).

McKitterick, Rosamond, 'Charlemagne's *missi* and Their Books', in *Early Medieval Studies*, ed. Baxter et al. (2009), pp. 253–67.

Macnair, Mike, 'Vicinage and the Antecedents of the Jury', *Law and History Review*, vol. 17, no. 3 (1999), pp. 537–90.

McNeil P. G. B. and MacQueen H. L., *An Atlas of Scottish History to 1707* (Edinburgh, 1996).

Macquarrie, Alan, *Scotland and the Crusades, 1095–1560* (Edinburgh, 1985).

MacQueen, Hector L., 'The Brieve of Right in Scots Law', *The Journal of Legal History*, vol. 3, no. 1 (1982), pp. 52–70.

MacQueen, Hector L., 'Dissasine and Mortancestor in Scots Law', *The Journal of Legal History*, vol. 4, no. 3 (1983), pp. 21–49.

MacQueen, Hector L., 'Pleadable Brieves, Pleading and the Development of Scots Law', *Law and History* Review, vol. 4, no. 2 (1986), pp. 403–22.

MacQueen, Hector L., 'The Brieve of Right Revisited', in *The Political Context of Law*, ed. R. Eales and D. Sullivan (London, 1987), pp. 17–25.

MacQueen, Hector L., 'Scots Law under Alexander III', in *Scotland in the Reign of Alexander III*, ed. Reid (1990), pp. 74–102.

MacQueen, Hector L., 'The Laws of Galloway: A Preliminary Survey', in *Galloway: Land and Lordship*, ed. R. D. Oram and G. P. Stell (Edinburgh, 1991), pp. 131–43.

MacQueen, Hector L., *Common Law and Feudal Society in Medieval Scotland* (Edinburgh, 1993).

MacQueen, Hector L., 'The Kin of Kennedy, "Kenkynnol" and the Common Law', in *Medieval Scotland*, ed. Grant and Stringer (1993), pp. 274–96.

MacQueen, Hector L., '*Glanvill* Resarcinate: Sir John Skene and *Regiam Majestatem*', in *The Renaissance in Scotland: Studies in Literature, Religion, History and Culture offered to John Durkan*, ed. A. A. MacDonald, Michael Lynch, and Ian B. Cowan (Leiden, 1994), pp. 385–403.

MacQueen, Hector L., 'Girth: Society and the Law of Sanctuary in Scotland', in *Critical Studies in Ancient Law, Comparative Law and Legal History*, ed. John W. Cairns and O. F. Robinson (Oxford, 2001), pp. 333–52.

MacQueen, Hector L., 'Expectations of the Law in the Twelfth and Thirteenth Century', *Tijdschrift voor Rechtsgeschiedenis*, vol. 70, nos. 3&4 (2002), pp. 279–90.

MacQueen, Hector L., 'Tears of a Legal Historian: Scottish Feudalism and the *Ius Commune*', *Juridical Review*, new series (2003), pp. 1–28.

MacQueen, Hector L., 'Legal Nationalism: Lord Cooper, Legal History and Comparative Law', *Edinburgh Law Review*, vol. 9, no. 3 (2005), pp. 395–406.

MacQueen, Hector L., 'Canon Law, Custom and Legislation in the Reign of Alexander II', in *Reign of Alexander II*, ed. Oram (2005), pp. 221–51.

MacQueen, Hector L., 'Some Notes on Wrang and Unlaw', in *Miscellany V*, ed. Hector L. MacQueen, Stair Society 52 (Edinburgh, 2006), pp. 13–26.

MacQueen, Hector, 'Geoffrey Wallis Steuart Barrow, 1924–2013: A Memoir', *Innes Review*, vol. 65, no. 1 (2014), pp. 1–12.

MacQueen, Hector, 'Tame Magnates? The Justiciars of Later Medieval Scotland', in *Kings, Lords and Men*, ed. Boardman and Goodare (2014), pp. 93–120.

MacQueen, Hector L. and Windram, William J., 'Law and Courts in the Burghs', in *The Scottish Medieval Town*, ed. Lynch, Spearman, and Stell (1988), pp. 208–27.

Maddicott, J. R., *The Origins of English Parliament, 924–1327* (Oxford, 2010).

Maitland, F. W., *Domesday Book and Beyond: Three Essays in the Early History of England* (Cambridge, 1897).

Maitland Thomson, J., *The Public Records of Scotland* (Glasgow, 1922).

Malcolm, C. A., 'The Origins of the Sheriff in Scotland: Its Origins and Early Development', *SHR*, vol. 20, no. 78 (1923), pp. 129–41.

Mann, Michael, 'The Autonomous Power of the State: Its Origins, Mechanisms and Results', *European Journal of Sociology*, vol. 25 (1984), pp. 185–213.

Mann, Michael, *The Sources of Social Power*, 2 vols (Cambridge, 1986, 1993).

Marritt, Stephen, 'The Ridale Papal Letters and Royal Charter: A Twelfth-Century Anglo-Scottish Baronial Family, the Papacy, the Law and Charter Diplomatic', *EHR*, vol. 176, no. 523 (2011), pp. 1332–54.

Marsden, Richard A., *Cosmo Innes and the Defence of Scotland's Past, c.1825–1875* (Farnham, 2014).

Marten, Lucy, 'The Shiring of East Anglia: an Alternative Hypothesis', *Historical Research*, vol. 81, no. 211 (2008), pp. 1–27.

Martindale, Jane '*Conventum inter Willelmum Comitem Aquitanorum et Hugonem Chiliarchum*', *EHR*, vol. 84, no. 332 (1969), pp. 528–48.

Mauss, Marcel, *The Gift: the Form and Reason for Exchange in Archaic Societies*, with a foreword by Mary Douglas (Abingdon, 2002).

Mayhew, Nicholas J., 'The Aberdeen Upperkirkgate Hoard of 1886', *British Numismatic Journal*, vol. 44 (1975), pp. 33–50.

Mayhew, Nicholas J., 'Money in Scotland in the Thirteenth Century', in *Coinage*, ed. Metcalf (1977), pp. 85–102.

Mayhew, Nicholas J., 'Alexander III—a silver age?', in *Scotland in the Reign of Alexander III*, ed. Reid (1990), pp. 53–73.

Meehan, Bernard, 'The Siege of Durham, the Battle of Carham and the Cession of Lothian', *SHR*, vol. 55, no. 159 (1976), pp. 1–19.

Meekings, C. A. F., *The 1235 Surrey Eyre*, vol. 1: *Introduction and Bibliographia*, Surrey Record Society 31 (Guildford, 1979).

Metcalf, D. M., ed., *Coinage in Medieval Scotland: 1100–1600*, British Archaeological Reprints, British Series (Oxford, 1977).

Metcalf, D. M., ed., 'The Evidence of Scottish Coin Hoards for Monetary History, 1100–1600', in *Coinage*, ed. Metcalf (1977), pp. 1–60.

Metcalf, D. M., ed., 'The Quality of Scottish Sterling Silver, 1136–1280', in *Coinage*, ed. Metcalf (1977), pp. 73–84.

Miller, William Ian, 'Gift, Sale, Payment, Raid: Case Studies in the Negotiation and Classification of Exchange in Medieval Iceland', *Speculum*, vol. 61, no. 1 (1986), pp. 18–50.

Miller, William Ian, 'Ordeal in Iceland', *Scandinavian Studies*, vol. 60, no. 2 (1988), pp. 189–218.

Miller, William Ian, *Bloodtaking and Peacemaking. Feud, Law and Society in Saga Iceland* (Chicago, IL, 1990).

Miller, William Ian, *Humiliation: and Other Essays on Honor, Social Discomfort, and Violence* (Ithaca, 1993).

Miller, William Ian, 'In Defense of Revenge', in *Medieval Crime and Social Control*, ed. Barbara A. Hanawalt and David Wallace, Medieval Cultures 16 (Minneapolis, MN, 1999), pp. 70–89.

Milne, Isabel A., 'An Extent of Carrick in 1260', *SHR*, vol. 34, no. 117 (1955), pp. 46–9.

Milsom, S. F. C., *The Legal Framework of English Feudalism* (Cambridge, 1976).

Mitteis, Heinrich, *The State in the Middle Ages*, trans. H. F. Orton (Amsterdam, 1975 [first published in German in 1940]).

Molho, Anthony, 'The State and Public Finance: A Hypothesis Based on the History of Late Medieval Florence', in *The Origins of the State in Italy 1300–1600*, ed. Julius Kirshner, supplement of *The Journal of Modern History* (Chicago, IL, 1995), pp. 97–135.

Molyneaux, George, 'The *Ordinance Concerning the Dunsæte* and the Anglo-Welsh frontier in the Late Tenth and Eleventh Centuries', *Anglo-Saxon England*, vol. 40 (2011), pp. 249–72.

Molyneaux, George, *The Formation of the English Kingdom in the Tenth Century* (Oxford, 2015).

Morris, W. A., *The Medieval English Sheriff to 1300* (Manchester, 1927).

Moss, Vincent, 'Normandy and England in 1180: the Pipe Roll Evidence', in *England and Normandy in the Middle Ages*, ed. David Bates and Anne Curry (London, 1994), pp. 185–95.

Murray, Athol L. and Burnett, Charles J., 'The Seals of the Scottish Court of Exchequer', *Proceedings of the Society of Antiquaries of Scotland*, vol. 123 (1993), pp. 439–52.

Murray, Athol L., 'The Pre-Union Records of the Scottish Exchequer', *Journal of the Society of Archivists*, vol. 2, no. 3 (1961), pp. 89–101.

Murray, Athol L., 'The Procedure of the Scottish Exchequer in the Early Sixteenth Century', *SHR*, vol. 40, no. 130 (1961), pp. 89–117.

Murray, Athol L., 'Sir John Skene and the Exchequer, 1594–1612', in *Miscellany 1*, Stair Society 26 (Edinburgh, 1971), pp. 125–55.

Murray, Athol L., 'The Scottish Chancery in the Fourteenth and Fifteenth Centuries', in *Écrit et Pouvoir dans les chancelleries médiévales: Espace français, espace anglais*, ed. K. Flanu and D. J. Guth (Louvain-La-Neuve, 1997), pp. 133–51.

Murray, J. E. L. and Stewart, Ian, 'St Andrew's Mint under David I', *British Numismatic Journal*, vol. 53 (1983), pp. 178–80.

Murray, Noel, 'Swerving from the Path of Justice: Alexander II's Relations with Argyll and the Western Isles, 1214–49', in *Reign of Alexander II*, ed. Oram (2005), pp. 285–305.

Naismith, Rory, 'The English Monetary Economy, c.973–1100: the Contribution of Single Finds', *Economic History Review*, vol. 66, no. 1 (2013), pp. 198–225.

Neilson, George, *Trial by Combat* (Glasgow, 1890).

Nelson, Janet L., 'Legislation and Consensus in the Reign of Charles the Bald', in *Ideal and Reality in Frankish and Anglo-Saxon Society: Studies presented to J. M. Wallace-Hadrill*, ed. P. Wormald, D. A. Bullough, and R. Collins (Oxford, 1983), pp. 202–27.

Nelson, Janet L., *Charles the Bald* (Harlow, 1992).

Nelson, Janet L., 'How Carolingians Created Consensus', in *Le Monde carolingien: Bilan, Perspectives, champs de recherches*, ed. Wojciech Fałkowski and Yves Sassier (Turnhout, 2009), pp. 67–81.

Nelson, Janet L., 'Liturgy or Law: Misconceived Alternatives', in *Early Medieval Studies*, ed. Baxter et al. (2009), pp. 433–47.

Nelson, Jessica A., 'Scottish Queenship in the Thirteenth Century', *Thirteenth-Century England IX* (Woodbridge, 2007), pp. 61–81.

Netterstrøm, Jeppe Büchert, 'The Study of Feud in Medieval and Early Modern History', in *Feud in Medieval and Early Modern Europe*, ed. Bjørn Poulsen and J. B. Netterstrøm (Aarhus, 2007), pp. 9–67.

Neville, Cynthia J., 'A Celtic Enclave in Norman Scotland: Earl Gilbert and the Earldom of Strathearn', in *Freedom and Authority*, ed. Brotherstone and Ditchburn (2000), pp. 75–92.

Neville, Cynthia J., 'Charter Writing and the Exercise of Lordship in Thirteenth-Century Scotland', in *Expectations of the Law in the Middle Ages*, ed. Anthony Musson (Woodbridge, 2001), pp. 67–89.

Neville, Cynthia J., *Native Lordship in Medieval Scotland: The Earldoms of Strathearn and Lennox, c.1140–1365* (Dublin, 2005).

Neville, Cynthia J., *Land, Law and People in Medieval Scotland* (Edinburgh, 2010).

Neville, Cynthia J., 'Neighbours, the Neighbourhood, and the visnet in Scotland, 1125–1300', in *New Perspectives*, ed. Hammond (2013), pp. 161–73.

Niermeyer, J. F., *Mediae Latinitatis Lexicon Minus*, ed. C. Van de Kieft (Leiden 1997).

Nishioka, Kenji, 'Scots and Galwegians in the "Peoples Address" of Scottish Royal Charters', *SHR*, vol. 87, no. 224 (2008), pp. 206–32.

Nortier, Michel, 'Les Actes de Philippe Auguste: notes critiques sur les sources diplomatiques du règne', in *La France de Philippe Auguste*, ed. Bautier (1982), pp. 429–53.

O'Brien, Bruce, *Reversing Babel: Translation among the English during an Age of Conquests, c.800–c.1200* (Plymouth, 2011).

O'Brien, Bruce, 'Translating Technical Terms in Law-Codes from Alfred to the Angevins', in *Conceptualizing Multilingualism in England, 800–1250*, ed. Elizabeth M. Tyler (Turnhout, 2011), pp. 57–76.

Oram, Richard, *The Lordship of Galloway c.900–1300* (Edinburgh, 2000).

Oram, Richard D., 'Gold into Lead? The State of Early Medieval Scottish History', in *Freedom and Authority*, ed. Brotherstone and Ditchburn (2000), pp. 32–43.

Oram, Richard D., 'Continuity, Adaptation and Integration: the Earls and Earldom of Mar, c.1150–c.1300', in *Exercise of Power*, ed. Boardman and Ross (2003), pp. 46–66.

Oram, Richard, *David I: the King Who Made Scotland* (Stroud, 2004).

Oram, Richard, ed., *The Reign of Alexander II, 1214–49* (Leiden, 2005).

Oram, Richard, *Domination and Lordship: Scotland 1070 to 1230* (Edinburgh, 2011).

Oram, Richard, *Alexander II, King of Scots, 1214–1249* (Edinburgh, 2012).

Penman, Michael, *Robert the Bruce: King of the Scots* (New Haven, CT, 2014).

Pirie, Fernanda, *The Anthropology of Law* (Oxford, 2013).

Pirie, Fernanda and Scheele, Judith, ed., *Legalism*, vol. 2: *Community and Justice* (Oxford, 2014).

Pohl, Walter and Wieser, Veronika, ed., *Der frühmittelalterliche Staat—europäishe Perspektiven*, Forschungen zur Geschichte des Mittelalters 16 (Vienna, 2009).

Pollock, Sir Frederick and Maitland, F. W., *The History of English Law before the Time of Edward I*, 2nd edn, 2 vols (Cambridge, 1923).

Pollock, Sir Frederick, 'The King's Peace', *Oxford Lectures and Other Discourses* (London, 1890), pp. 65–90.

Poly, Jean-Pierre, and Bournazel, Éric, *La mutation féodale Xe–XIIe siècles*, 3rd edn (Paris, 2004).

Poole, Reginald L., *The Exchequer in the Twelfth Century: The Ford Lectures Delivered in the University of Oxford in Michaelmas Term 1911* (Oxford, 1912).

Postles, David, 'Tenure in frankalmoign and Knight Service in Twelfth Century England: Interpretations of the Charters', *Journal of the Society of Archivists*, vol. 13 (1992), pp. 18–28.

Pratt, David, 'Written Law and the Communication of Authority in Tenth-Century England,' in *England and the Continent in the Tenth Century*, ed. David Rollason, Conrad Leyser, and Hannah Williams (Turnhout, 2010), pp. 331–50.

Pryce, Huw, *Native Law and the Church in Medieval Wales* (Oxford, 1993).

Pryce, Huw, 'Lawbooks and Literacy in Medieval Wales', *Speculum*, vol. 75, no. 1 (2000), pp. 29–67.

Pryde, George S., *The Burghs of Scotland: A Critical List* (Oxford, 1965).

Ragg, F. W., 'Five Strathclyde and Galloway Charters', *Cumberland and Westmorland Antiquarian and Archaeological Society Transactions*, new series, vol. 17 (1917), pp. 198–234.

Ramsay, J. H., *A History of the Revenues of the kings of England, 1066–1399*, 2 vols (Oxford, 1925).

Ranger, Felicity ed., *Prisca Munimenta: Studies in Archival and Administrative History Presented to Dr A. E. J. Hollaender* (London, 1973).

Reid N. H., ed., *Scotland in the Reign of Alexander III, 1249–1286* (Edinburgh, 1990).

Reid N. H., 'Alexander III: the Historiography of a Myth', in *Scotland in the Reign of Alexander III*, ed. Reid (1990), pp. 181–213.

Reid, Rachel R., 'Barony and Thanage', *EHR*, vol. 35, no. 138 (1920), pp. 161–99.

Reuter, Timothy, *Medieval Polities and Modern Mentalities*, ed. Janet L. Nelson (Cambridge, 2006).

Reuter, Timothy, 'The "Imperial Church System" of the Ottonian and Salian Rulers: a Reconsideration', reprinted in and cited from Timothy Reuter, *Medieval Polities and Modern Mentalities*, ed. Janet L. Nelson (Cambridge, 2006), pp. 325–54.

Reuter, Timothy, 'Assembly Politics in western Europe from the eighth century to the twelfth', in Reuter, *Medieval Polities*, ed. Janet L. Nelson (Cambridge, 2006), pp. 193–216.

Reuter, Timothy, 'The "Imperial Church System" of the Ottonian and Salian Rulers: a Reconsideration', in Reuter, *Medieval Polities*, ed. Janet L. Nelson (Cambridge 2006), pp. 325–54.

Reuter, Timothy, 'All Quiet on the Western Front? The Emergence of Pre-Modern Forms of Statehood in the Central Middle Ages', in Reuter, *Medieval Polities and Modern Mentalities*, ed. Janet L. Nelson (Cambridge, 2006), pp. 432–58.

Reuter, Timothy, 'Mandate, Privilege, Court Judgement: Techniques of Rulership in the Age of Frederick Barbarossa', in Reuter, *Medieval Polities*, ed. Janet L. Nelson (Cambridge 2006), pp. 413–31.

Reynolds, Susan, *Fiefs and Vassals: the Medieval Evidence Reinterpreted* (Oxford, 1994).

Reynolds, Susan, 'The Historiography of the Medieval State', in *Companion to Historiography*, ed. Michael Bentley (London, 1997), pp. 117–38.

Reynolds, Susan, 'Medieval Law', in *The Medieval World*, ed. Peter Linehan and Janet L. Nelson (London, 2001), pp. 485–502.

Reynolds, Susan, 'Fiefs and Vassals in Scotland: A View from the Outside', *SHR*, vol. 82, no. 214 (2003), pp. 176–93.

Reynolds, Susan, 'There Were States in Medieval Europe: A Response to Rees Davies', *Journal of Historical Sociology*, vol. 16 (2003), pp. 550–5.

Richardson, H. G. and Sayles, G. O., *The Governance of Medieval England from the Conquest to Magna Carta* (Edinburgh, 1963).

Richardson, H. G. and Sayles, G. O., *The Administration of Medieval Ireland, 1172–1377* (Dublin, 1973).

Ridgeway, H. W., 'Mid Thirteenth-Century Reformers and the Localities: the Sheriffs of the Baronial Regime, 1258–1261', in *Regionalism and Revision: The Crown and Its provinces in England, 1250–1650*, ed. P. Fleming, A. J. Gross, and J. R. Lander (London, 1998), pp. 59–86.

Rio, Alice, '"Half-Free" Categories in the Early Middle Ages: Fine Status Distinctions before Professional Lawyers', in *Legalism*, vol. 3: *Rules and Categories*, ed. Paul Dresch and Judith Scheele (Oxford, 2015), pp. 129–52.

Rio, Alice, ed., *Law, Custom, and Justice in Late Antiquity and the Early Middle Ages: Proceedings of the 2008 Byzantine Colloquium*, Centre for Hellenic Studies, King's College London (London, 2011).

Ritchie, R. L. G., *The Normans in Scotland* (Edinburgh, 1954).

Roach, Levi, 'Hosting the King: Hospitality and the Royal *iter* in Tenth-Century England', *Journal of Medieval History*, vol. 37, no. 1 (2011), pp. 34–46.

Roach, Levi, *Kingship and Consent in Anglo-Saxon England, 871–978: Assemblies and the State in the Early Middle Ages* (Cambridge, 2013).

Roach, Levi, 'Law and Legal Norms in Later Anglo-Saxon England', *Historical Research*, vol. 86, no. 233 (2013), pp. 465–86.

Roberts, Brian K. with Barnwell, P. S., 'The Multiple Estate of Glanville Jones: Epitome, Critique and Context', in *Britons, Saxons and Scandinavians: The Historical Geography of Glanville R. J. Jones*, ed. Paul S. Barnwell and Brian Roberts, The Medieval Countryside 7 (Turnhout, 2011), pp. 25–128.

Robertson, E. W., *Scotland under Her Early Kings*, 2 vols (Edinburgh, 1862).

Robertson, E. W., *Historical Essays in Connexion with the Land, the Church, etc* (Edinburgh, 1872).

Robertson, Niall and Perry, David, 'Perth before the Burgh', in *Perth: the Archaeology and Development of a Scottish Burgh*, ed. David P. Bowler, Tayside and Fife Archaeological Committee (Perth, 2004).

Robertson, William, *An Index, Drawn up about the Year 1629* (Edinburgh, 1798).

Rosenwein, Barbara H., *To Be the Neighbour of Saint Peter: the Social Meaning of Cluny's Property, 909–1049* (Ithaca, 1989).

Rosenwein, Barbara H., *Negotiating Space: Power, Restraint and Privileges of Immunity in Early Medieval Europe* (Ithaca, 1999).

Ross, Alasdair, 'The Bannatyne Club and the Publication of Scottish Ecclesiastical Cartularies', *SHR*, vol. 85, no. 220 (2006), pp. 202–30.

Ross, Alasdair, 'The *Dabhach* in Moray: A New Look at an Old Tub', in *Landscape and Environment in Dark Age Scotland*, ed. Alex Woolf (St Andrews, 2006), pp. 57–74.

Ross, Alasdair, 'The Identity of the Prisoner at Roxburgh: Malcolm son of Alexander or Malcolm Macheth?', in *Fil súil nglais: A Grey Eye Looks Back. A Festschrift in Honour of Colm Ó Baoill*, ed. Sharon Arbuthnot and Kaarina Hollo (Ceann Drochaid, Brig o Turk, 2007), pp. 269–82.

Ross, Alasdair, 'Moray, Ulster and the MacWilliams', in *The World of the Galloglass: Kings, Warlords and Warriors in Ireland and Scotland 1200–1600*, ed. Seán Duffy (Dublin, 2007), pp. 24–44.

Ross, Alasdair, *The Kings of Alba, c.1000–c.1130* (Edinburgh, 2011).

Ross, Alasdair, *Land Assessment and Lordship in Medieval Northern Scotland*, The Medieval Countryside 14 (Turnhout, 2015).

Russell, M. J., 'Trial by Battle and the Writ of Right', *Journal of Legal History*, vol. 1, no. 2 (1980), pp. 111–34.

Russell, M. J., 'Trial by Battle and the Appeals of Felony', *Journal of Legal History*, vol. 1, no. 2 (1980) pp. 135–64.

Sabapathy, John, *Officers and Accountability in Medieval England, 1170–1300* (Oxford, 2014).

Sahlins, Marshall, *Stone Age Economics* (London, 1974).

Sarris, Peter, 'The Origins of the Manorial Economy: New Insights from Late Antiquity', *EHR*, vol. 119, no. 481 (2004), pp. 279–311.

Sayers, Jane E., *Papal Judges Delegate in the Province of Canterbury, 1198–1254: A Study in Ecclesiastical Jurisdiction and Administration* (Oxford, 1971).

Scott, W. W., 'The Use of Money in Scotland, 1124–1230', *SHR*, vol. 58, no. 166 (1979), pp. 105–31.

Seebohm, Frederic, *Tribal Custom in Anglo-Saxon Law* (London, 1902).

Sellar, W. D. H., 'The Common Law of Scotland and the Common Law of England', in *The British Isles: Comparisons, Contrasts and Connections*, ed. R. R. Davies (Edinburgh, 1988), pp. 82–99.

Sellar, W. D. H., 'Celtic Law and Scots Law: Survival and Integration', *Scottish Studies*, vol. 29 (1989), pp. 1–27.

Sellar, W. D. H., 'Scots Law: Mixed from the Very Beginning? A Tale of Two Receptions', *Edinburgh Law Review*, vol. 4, no. 1 (1996), pp. 3–18.

Sharpe, Richard, 'The Use of Writs in the Eleventh Century', *Anglo-Saxon England*, vol. 32 (2003), pp. 247–91.

Sharpe, Richard, 'Address and Delivery in Anglo-Norman Royal Charters', in *Charters and Charter Scholarship*, ed. Flanagan and Green (2005), pp. 32–52.

Sharpe, Richard, *Norman Rule in Cumbria, 1092–1136*, Cumberland and Westmorland Antiquarian and Archaeological Society (Kendal, 2006).

Sharpe, Richard, 'People and Languages in Eleventh- and Twelfth-Century Britain and Ireland: Reading the Charter Evidence', in *Reality Behind Charter Diplomatic*, ed. Broun (2011), pp. 1–119.

Simpson, Grant G. 'Kingship in Miniature: A Seal of the Minority of Alexander III, 1259–57', in *Medieval Scotland*, ed. Grant and Stringer (1993), pp. 131–9.

Simpson, Grant G., *Scottish Handwriting, 1150–1650*, 2nd edn (East Linton, 1998).

Skene, W. F., *Celtic Scotland: A History of Ancient Alban*, 3 vols (Edinburgh, 1886–90).

Skoda, Hannah, 'A Historian's Perspective on the Present Volume', in *Legalism: History and Anthropology*, ed. Paul Dresch and Hannah Skoda (Oxford, 2012), pp. 39–54.

Smail, Daniel Lord, 'Common violence: Vengeance and Inquisition in Fourteenth-Century Marseilles', *Past & Present*, no. 151 (1996), pp. 28–59.

Smail, Daniel Lord, 'Hatred as a Social Institution in Late Medieval Society', *Speculum*, vol. 76, no. 1 (2001), pp. 90–126.

Smart, Veronica, *The Coins of St Andrews* (St Andrews, 1991).

Smith, T. B., 'The Contribution of Lord Cooper of Culross to Scottish Law', in Cooper, *Selected Papers* (1957), pp. xxix–xlix.

Soffer, Reba N., *Discipline and Power: the University, History and the Making of an English Elite, 1870–1930* (Stanford, CA, 1994).

Spufford, Peter, *Money and Its Use in Medieval Europe* (Cambridge, 1988).

Stafford, Pauline, 'The "Farm of One Night" and the Organization of King Edward's Estates in Domesday', *Economic History Review*, vol. 33, no. 3 (1980), pp. 491–502.

Stein, Peter, 'The Source of the Romano-Canonical Part of *Regiam Majestatem*', *SHR*, vol. 48, no. 146 (1969), pp. 107–23.

Stein, Peter, 'Roman Law in Scotland', reprinted in his *The Character and Influence of the Roman Civil Law* (London, 2003), pp. 269–317.

Stenton, Doris M., *English Justice between the Norman Conquest and the Great Charter 1066–1215* (London, 1965).

Stenton, F. M., *Types of Manorial Structure in the Northern Danelaw* (Oxford, 1910).

Stephenson, Carl, 'The *Firma Unius Noctis* and the Customs of the Hundred', *EHR*, vol. 39, no. 154 (1924), pp. 161–74.

Stevenson, Alexander, 'Trade with the South, 1070–1513', in *Scottish Medieval Town*, ed. Lynch, Spearman, and Spell (1988), pp. 180–206.

Stevenson, Alexander, 'Medieval Scottish Associations with Bruges', in *Freedom and Authority*, ed. Brotherstone and Ditchburn (2000), pp. 93–107.

Stevenson, David, 'The English and the Public Records of Scotland, 1650–1660', in *Miscellany I*, Stair Society 26 (Edinburgh, 1971), pp. 156–70.

Stevenson, Wendy B., 'The Monastic Presence in Scottish Burghs in the Twelfth and Thirteenth centuries', *SHR*, vol. 60, no. 170 (1981), pp. 97–118.

Stevenson, W. H., '*Trinoda necessitas*', *EHR*, vol. 29, no. 116 (1914), pp. 689–703.

Stewart, B. H. I. H. [Ian] [I. H.] [Lord Stewartby], *The Scottish Coinage with Supplement* (London, 1955).

Stewart, B. H. I. H. [Ian] [I. H.] [Lord Stewartby], 'The Brussels Hoard: Mr Baldwin's Arrangement of the Scottish Coins', *British Numismatic Journal*, vol. 29 (1958–59), pp. 91–7.

Stewart, B. H. I. H. [Ian] [I. H.] [Lord Stewartby], 'Scottish Mints', in *Mints, Dies and Currency: Essays Dedicated to the Memory of Albert Baldwin*, ed. R. A. G. Carson (London, 1971), pp. 165–291.

Stewart, B. H. I. H. [Ian] [I. H.] [Lord Stewartby], 'The Volume of the Early Scottish Coinage', in *Coinage*, ed. Metcalf (1977), pp. 65–72.

Stewart, B. H. I. H. [Ian] [I. H.] [Lord Stewartby], 'Some German Coins Overstruck with Sterling Types', *Lagom: Festschrift für Peter Berghaus* (Munster, 1981), pp. 205–10.

Stewart, B. H. I. H. [Ian] [I. H.] [Lord Stewartby], 'Imitation in Later Medieval Coinage: the Influence of Scottish Types Abroad', in *Studies in Numismatic Methods Presented to Philip Grierson*, ed. C. N. L. Brooke, B. H. I. H. Stewart, J. G. Pollard, and T. G. Volk (Cambridge, 1983), pp. 303–26.

Strayer, Joseph R., *On the Medieval Origins of the Modern State*, with forewords by Charles Tilly and William Chester Jordan (Princeton, NJ, 2005).

Stringer, Keith J., 'A Cistercian Archive: the Earliest Charters of Sawtry Abbey', *Journal of the Society of Archivists*, vol. 6, no. 6 (1980), pp. 325–34.

Stringer, Keith J., *Earl David of Huntingdon, 1152–1219: A Study in Anglo-Scottish History* (Edinburgh, 1985).

Stringer, Keith J., ed., *Essays on the Nobility of Medieval Scotland* (Edinburgh, 1985).

Stringer, Keith J., 'The Early Lords of Lauderdale, Dryburgh Abbey and St Andrews Priory at Northampton', in *Essays on the Nobility*, ed. Stringer (1985), pp. 44–71.

Stringer, Keith J., 'Periphery and Core in Thirteenth-Century Scotland: Alan son of Roland, Lord of Galloway and Constable of Scotland', in *Medieval Scotland*, ed. Grant and Stringer (1993), pp. 82–113.

Stringer, Keith J., 'State-Building in Twelfth-Century Britain: David I, King of Scots, and Northern England', in *Government, Religion and Society in Northern England, 1000–1700*, ed. John C. Appleby and Paul Dalton (Stroud, 1997), pp. 40–62.

Stringer, Keith J., 'Nobility and Identity in Medieval Britain and Ireland: the de Vescy Family, c.1120–1314', in *Britain and Ireland, 900–1300: Insular Responses to Medieval European Change*, ed. Brendan Smith (Cambridge, 1999), pp. 199–239.

Stringer, Keith J., 'Acts of Lordship: the Records of the Lords of Galloway to 1234', in *Freedom and Authority*, ed. Brotherstone and Ditchburn (2000), pp. 203–34.

Stringer, Keith J., 'Reform Monasticism and Celtic Scotland, c.1140–c.1240', in *Alba*, ed. Cowan and McDonald (2000), pp. 127–65.

Stringer, Keith J., 'Arbroath Abbey in Context: 1178–1320', in *The Declaration of Arbroath: History, Significance, Setting*, ed. Geoffrey Barrow (Edinburgh, 2003), pp. 116–41.

Stringer, Keith J., 'Kingship, Conflict and State-Making in the Reign of Alexander II: the War of 1215–17 and Its Context', in *Reign of Alexander II*, ed. Oram (2005), pp. 99–156.

Stringer, Keith J., 'States, Liberties and Communities in Medieval Britain and Ireland (c.1100–1400)', in *Liberties and Identities in the Medieval British Isles*, ed. Michael Prestwich (Woodbridge, 2008), pp. 5–36.

Stringer, Keith J., 'Aspects of the Norman Diaspora in Northern England and Southern Scotland', in *Norman Expansion*, ed. Stringer and Jotischky (2013), pp. 9–48.

Stringer, Keith J., 'The Scottish "Political Community" in the Reign of Alexander II (1214–49)', in *New Perspectives*, ed. Hammond (2013), pp. 53–84.

Stringer, Keith J. and Jotischky, Andrew, ed., *Norman Expansion: Connections, Continuities and Contrasts* (Farnham, 2013).

Stuart, John, 'Notice of the Early System of Replegiation as Exercised in Scotland', *Proceedings of the Society of Antiquaries of Scotland*, vol. 11 (1874–76), pp. 163–7.

Stubbs, William, *The Constitutional History of England in Its Origin and Development*, 3 vols (Oxford, 1874–78).

Sutherland, Donald W., *The Assize of Novel Disseisin* (Oxford, 1973).

Tanner, Roland J., 'Cowing the Community? Coercion and Falsification in Robert Bruce's Parliaments, 1209–1318', in *The History of the Scottish Parliament: Parliament and Politics in Scotland, 1235–1560*, ed. K. Brown and R. J. Tanner (Edinburgh, 2004), pp. 50–73.

Taylor, Alice, 'Robert de Londres, Illegitimate Son of William, King of Scots, *c.*1170–1225', *Haskins Society Journal*, vol. 19 (2008), pp. 99–119.

Taylor, Alice, '*Leges Scocie* and the Lawcodes of David I, William the Lion and Alexander II', *SHR*, vol. 88, no. 226 (2009), pp. 207–88.

Taylor, Alice, 'Historical Writing in Twelfth- and Thirteenth-Century Scotland: the Dunfermline Compilation', *Historical Research*, vol. 83, no. 220 (2010), pp. 228–52.

Taylor, Alice, 'Common Burdens in the *regnum Scottorum*: the Evidence of Charter Diplomatic', in *Reality behind Charter Diplomatic*, ed. Broun (2011), pp. 166–234.

Taylor, Alice, 'The Assizes of David, King of Scots, 1124–53', *SHR*, vol. 91, no. 232 (2012), pp. 197–238.

Taylor, Alice, 'Crime without Punishment: Medieval Scottish Law in Comparative Perspective', *ANS*, vol. 35 (2013), pp. 287–304.

Taylor, Alice, '*Homo Ligius* and Unfreedom in Medieval Scotland', in *New Perspectives*, ed. Hammond (2013), pp. 85–116.

Taylor, Alice, '*Lex Scripta* and the Problem of Enforcement: Anglo-Saxon, Welsh and Scottish Law Compared', in *Legalism*, ed. Pirie and Scheele (2014), pp. 47–75.

Taylor, Alice, 'Auditing and Enrolment in Thirteenth-Century Scotland', in *The Growth of Royal Government in the Reign of Henry III*, ed. David Crook and Louise Wilkinson (Woodbridge, 2015), pp. 85–103.

Taylor, Simon, ed., *Kings, Clerics and Chronicles in Scotland, 500–1297: Essays in Honour of Marjorie Ogilvie Anderson on the Occasion of Her Ninetieth Birthday* (Dublin, 2000).

Taylor, Simon, 'The Coming of the Augustinians to St Andrews and version B of the St Andrews Foundation Legend', in *Kings, Clerics and Chronicles*, ed. Taylor (2000), pp. 115–23.

Taylor, Simon, 'The Rock of the Irishmen: an Early Place-Name Tale from Fife and Kinross', in *West over Sea: Studies in Scandinavian Sea-borne Expansion and Settlement before 1300*, ed. B. B. Smith, S. Taylor, and G. Williams (Leiden, 2007), pp. 497–514.

Taylor, Simon with Márkus, Gilbert, *The Place Names of Fife*, vol. 3: *St Andrews and the East Neuk* (Donnington, 2009).

Taylor, Simon with Márkus, Gilbert, *The Place-Names of Fife*, vol. 5: *Discussion, Glossaries, Texts* (Donnington, 2012).

Thomas, F. W. L., 'Proposed Correction of the Text of *Leges inter Brettos et Scottos*', *Proceedings of the Society of Antiquaries of Scotland*, vol. 19 (1884–85), pp. 73–4.

Thompson, Benjamin, 'Free Alms Tenure in the Twelfth Century', *ANS*, vol. 16 (1994), pp. 221–43.

Tilly, Charles, *Coercion, Capital and European States, AD 900–1992* (Oxford, 1990).

Tilly, Charles, 'Reflections on the History of European State-Making', in *The Formation of National States in Western Europe*, ed. Charles Tilly (Princeton, NJ, 1975), pp. 3–83.

Tilly, Charles, 'Entanglements of European Cities and States', in Charles Tilly and Wim P. Blockmans, ed., *Cities and the Rise of States in Europe, AD 1000–1800* (Boulder, CO, 1994), pp. 1–27.

van Caenegem, R. C., *The Birth of the English Common Law* (Cambridge, 1973).

van Houts, Elisabeth, 'L'Exil dans l'espace anglo-normand', in *La Normandie et l'Angleterre au Moyen Âge*, ed. Pierre Bouet and Veronique Gazeau (Leiden, 2003), pp. 75–85.

van Houts, Elisabeth, 'The Vocabulary of Exile and Outlawry in the North Sea Area around the First Millennium', in *Exile in the Middle Ages*, ed. Laura Napran and Elisabeth van Houts (Turnhout, 2004), pp. 13–28.

Vanier, Martin ed., *Territoires, Territorialité, Territorialisation: Controverses et Perspectives* (Rennes, 2009).

Veitch, Kenneth, '"Replanting Paradise": Alexander I and the Reform of Religious Life in Scotland', *Innes Review*, vol. 52, no. 2 (2001), pp. 136–66.

Verhulst, Adriaan, 'Economic Organisation', in *The New Cambridge Medieval History*, vol. 2: *c.700–900*, ed. Rosamond McKitterick (Cambridge, 1995), pp. 491–509.

Vincent, Nicholas C., 'The Origins of the Chancellorship of the Exchequer', *EHR*, vol. 108, no. 426 (1993), pp. 105–21

Vincent, Nicholas, 'Why 1199? Bureaucracy and Enrolment under John and His Contemporaries', in *English Government*, ed. Jobson (2004), pp. 17–48.

Vincent, Nicholas, ed., *Records, Administration and Aristocratic Society in the Anglo-Norman Realm* (Woodbridge, 2009).

Vincent, Nicholas, 'Introduction: the Record of 1204', in *Records*, ed. Vincent (2009), pp. xiii–xx.

Walker, David, 'The Organization of Material in Medieval Cartularies', in *The Study of Medieval Records: Essays in Honour of Kathleen Major*, ed. D. A. Bullough and R. L. Storey (Oxford, 1971), pp. 132–50.

Walker, David M., *A Legal History of Scotland*, vol. 1: *the Beginnings to A.D. 1286* (Edinburgh, 1988).

Wall, Valerie, 'Queen Margaret of Scotland (1070–93): Burying the Past, Enshrining the Future', in *Queens and Queenship in Medieval Europe*, ed. Anne Duggan (Woodbridge, 1997), pp. 27–38.

Wallace-Hadrill, J. M., 'The Bloodfeud of the Franks', reprinted in J. M. Wallace-Hadrill, *The Long-Haired Kings and Other Studies in Frankish History* (London, 1962), pp. 121–47.

Ware, R. D., 'Medieval Chronology: Theory and Practice', in *Medieval Studies: An Introduction*, ed. J. M. Powell (New York, 1992), pp. 252–77.

Watt, D. E. R., 'The Minority of Alexander III of Scotland', *TRHS*, 5th ser., vol. 21 (1971), pp. 1–23.

Watt, D. E. R., *The Bibliographic Dictionary of Scottish Graduates to AD 1410* (Edinburgh, 1977).

Watt, D. E. R., 'The Provincial Council of the Scottish Church 1215–1472', in *Medieval Scotland*, ed. Grant and Stringer (1993), pp. 140–55.

Watt, D. E. R., *Medieval Church Councils in Scotland* (Edinburgh, 2000).

Watt, D. E. R., 'Bagimond di Vezza and his "Roll"', *SHR*, vol. 80, no. 209 (2001), pp. 1–23.

Watts, John, *The Making of Polities: Europe, 1300–1500* (Cambridge, 2009).

Weber, Jack K., 'The King's Peace: A Comparative Study', *The Journal of Legal History*, vol. 10, no. 2 (1989), pp. 135–60.

Weber, Max, *Economy and Society: An Outline of Interpretative Sociology*, ed. Guenther Roth and Claus Wittich, 2 vols (Berkeley, CA, and Los Angeles, 1987).

Webster, Bruce, *Scotland from the Eleventh Century to 1603* (London, 1975).

Weinacht, Paul-Ludwig, *Staat. Studien zur Bedeutungsgeschichte des Wortes den Anfängen bis ins 19. Jahrhundert* (Berlin, 1968).

Werner, Karl Ferdinand, '*Missus—Marchio—Comes*: Entre l'administration centrale et l'administration locale de l'Empire carolingien', in *Histoire comparée de l'administration (IVe–XVIIIe siècles)*, ed. W. Paravicini and K. F. Werner (Munich, 1980), pp. 191–239.

West, Charles, *Reframing the Feudal Revolution: Political and Social Transformation between the Marne and the Moselle, c.800–c.1100* (Cambridge, 2013).

West, Francis, *The Justiciarship in England, 1066–1232* (Cambridge, 1966).

White, Graeme J., *Restoration and Reform, 1153–1165: Recovery from Civil War in England* (Cambridge, 2000).

White, Stephen D., 'Feuding and Peace-Making in the Touraine around the Year 1100', *Traditio*, vol. 42 (1986), pp. 195–263.

White, Stephen D., 'The Politics of Exchange: Gifts, Fiefs and Feudalism', in *Medieval Transformations*, ed. de Jong and Cohen (2001), pp. 169–88.

White, Stephen D., 'Tenth-Century Courts at Mâcon and the Perils of Structuralist History: Re-Reading Burgundian Judicial Institutions', in *Conflict in Medieval Europe*, ed. Warren C. Brown and Piotr Górecki (Aldershot, 2003), pp. 37–68.

Wickham, Chris, 'Problems of Comparing Rural Societies in Early Medieval Western Europe', *TRHS*, 6th ser., vol. 2 (1992), pp. 221–46.

Wickham, Chris, 'Manentes e diritti signorili durante il XII secolo: Il caso della Lucchesia', in *Società istituzioni, spiritualità: Studi in onore di Cinzio Violante*, Centro Italiano di Studi sull'Alto Medioevo (Spoleto, 1994), pt 2, pp. 1067–80.

Wickham, Chris, *Framing the Early Middle Ages: Europe and the Mediterranean, 400–800* (Oxford, 2005).

Wickham, Chris, 'The Early Middle Ages and National Identity', in *Die Deutung der mittelalterlichen Gesellschaft in der Moderne (19–21 Jahrhundert)*, ed. Natalie Fryde, Pierre Monnet, Otto Gerhard Oexle, and Leszek Zygner (Göttingen, 2006), pp. 107–22.

Wickham, Chris, 'Problems in Doing Comparative History', reprinted in *Challenging the Boundaries of Medieval History*, ed. Patricia Skinner (Turnhout, 2009), pp. 5–28.

Williams, Ann, *The World Before Domesday: The English Aristocracy 900–1066* (London, 2008).

Willock, Ian D., *The Origins and Development of the Jury in Scotland*, Stair Society 23 (Edinburgh, 1966).

Wilson, D., 'Notice of St Margaret's Chapel, Edinburgh Castle', *PSAS*, vol. 21 (1887–88), pp. 291–316.

Wilson, P. A., 'On the Use of the Terms "Strathclyde" and "Cumbria"', *Transactions of the Cumberland and Westmorland Antiquarian and Archaeological Society*, vol. 66 (1966), pp. 57–92.

Woolf, Alex, 'The "Moray Question" and the Kingship of Alba in the Tenth and Eleventh Centuries', *SHR*, vol. 79, no. 208 (2000), pp. 145–64.

Woolf, Alex, 'The Origins and Ancestry of Somerled: Gofraid mac Fergusa and "The Annals of the Four Masters"', *Medieval Scandinavia*, vol. 15 (2005), pp. 199–213.

Woolf, Alex, 'Dún Nectáin, Fortriu and the Geography of the Picts', *SHR*, vol. 85, no. 220 (2006), pp. 182–201.

Woolf, Alex, *From Pictland to Alba, 789–1070* (Edinburgh, 2007).

Woolf, Alex, Review of G. W. S. Barrow, *The Kingdom of the Scots: Government, Church and Society from the Eleventh to the Fourteenth Century*, *SHR*, vol. 86, no. 223 (2007), pp. 126–7.

Woolf, Alex, 'Geoffrey of Monmouth and the Picts', in *Bile ós Chrannaibh: A Festschrift for William Gillies*, ed. W. McLeod, A. Burnyeat, D. U. Stiubhart, T. O. Clancy, and R. O Maolalaigh (Ceann Drochaid, 2010), pp. 269–80.

Woolf, Alex, 'Reporting Scotland in the Anglo-Saxon Chronicle', in *Reading the Anglo-Saxon Chronicle: Language, Literature, History*, ed. Alice Jorgensen (Turnhout, 2010), pp. 221–39.

Woolf, Alex, 'The Song of the Death of Somerled and the Destruction of Glasgow in 1153', *Journal of the Sydney Society for Scottish History*, vol. 14 (2013), pp. 1–11.

Wormald, Jenny, 'Bloodfeud, Kindred and Government in Early Modern Scotland', *Past & Present*, no. 87 (1980), pp. 54–97.

Wormald, Jenny, 'Taming the Magnates?', reprinted in *Essays on the Nobility*, ed. Stringer (1985), pp. 270–80.

Wormald, Jenny, [as Jennifer M. Brown] 'The Exercise of Power', in *Scottish Society in the Fifteenth Century*, ed. Jennifer M. Brown (London, 1977), pp. 33–65.

Wormald, Patrick, '*Lex Scripta* and *Verbum Regis*: Legislation and Germanic Kingship from Euric to Cnut', in P. H. Sawyer and Ian N. Wood (ed.), *Early Medieval Kingship* (Leeds, 1977), pp. 105–38, reprinted and corrected in Patrick Wormald, *Legal Culture in the Early Medieval West: Law as Text, Image and Experience* (London, 1999), pp. 1–43.

Wormald, Patrick, 'Lordship and Justice in the Early English Kingdom: Oswaldslow Revisited', in *Property and Power*, ed. Davies and Fouracre (1995), pp. 114–36.

Wormald, Patrick, 'Frederic William Maitland and the Earliest English Law', *Law and History Review*, vol. 16, no. 1 (1998), pp. 1–25.

Wormald, Patrick, *The Making of English Law: King Alfred to the Twelfth Century*, vol. 1: *Legislation and Its Limits* (Oxford, 1999).

Wormald, Patrick, 'Giving God and the King their Due: Conflict and its Regulation in the Early English State', in Wormald, *Legal Culture* (1999), pp. 333–55.

Wormald, Patrick, 'Anglo-Saxon Law and Scots Law', *SHR*, vol. 88 no. 226 (2009), pp. 192–206.

Yoshitake, Kenji, 'The Exchequer in the Reign of Stephen', *EHR*, vol. 103, no. 409 (1988), pp. 950–9.

Young, Alan, 'The Political Role of Walter Comyn, Earl of Menteith, during the Minority of Alexander III of Scotland', in *Essays on the Nobility*, ed. Stringer (1985), pp. 131–49.

Young, Alan, 'Noble Families and Political Factions in the Reign of Alexander III', in *Scotland in the Reign of Alexander III*, ed. Reid (1990), pp. 1–30.

Young, Alan, 'The Earls and Earldom of Buchan in the Thirteenth Century', in *Medieval Scotland*, ed. Grant and Stringer (1993), pp. 174–99.

Young, Alan, *Robert Bruce's Rivals: The Comyns, 1212–1314* (East Linton, 1997).

Unpublished and Forthcoming Secondary Literature

Baxter, Stephen, 'Earls in Late Anglo-Saxon England, c.1016–1066', in *Earl in Medieval Britain*, ed. Crouch and Doherty, forthcoming.

Bell, Andrew, 'The Organisation of Public Work in Society by the State in Early Medieval England', c.800–c.1300 (DPhil Dissertation, University of Oxford, 1996).

Broun, Dauvit, 'The Origins of the *mormaer*', in *Earl in Medieval Britain*, ed. Crouch and Doherty, forthcoming.

Brown, Michael, 'Scottish Earldoms in the Late Middle Ages: Survival and Transformation', in *Earl in Medieval Britain*, ed. Crouch and Doherty, forthcoming.

Crafter, T. C. R., 'Monetary Expansion in Britain in the Late Twelfth Century', (DPhil Dissertation, University of Oxford, 2007).

Crouch, David, and Doherty, Hugh F. ed., *The Earl in Medieval Britain* (forthcoming).

Easson, A. R., 'Systems of Land Assessment in Scotland before 1400' (PhD Dissertation, University of Edinburgh, 1986).

Hammond, Matthew H., 'A Prosopographical Analysis of Society in East Central Scotland with Special Reference to Ethnicity' (PhD Dissertation, University of Glasgow, 2005).

Hammond, Matthew, 'The Origins of the Earldom of Lennox', unpublished paper.

Lambert, Tom, *Law and Order in Anglo-Saxon England* (forthcoming).

Lambert, T. B., 'Protection, Feud and Royal Power: Violence and Its Regulation in English Law, *c*.850–*c*.1250' (PhD Dissertation, University of Durham, 2009).

Nelson, Jessica A., 'From Saint Margaret to the Maid of Norway: Queens and Queenship in Scotland, *c*.1067–1286' (PhD Dissertation, University of London, 2006).

Rogers, John M., 'The Formation of the Parish Unit and Community in Perthshire' (PhD Dissertation, University of Edinburgh, 1992).

Ross, Alasdair D., 'The Province of Moray, *c*.1000–1230' (PhD Dissertation, University of Aberdeen, 2003).

Simpson, Andrew R. C., 'Procedures for Dealing with Robbery in Scotland before 1400', in *Continuity, Change and Pragmatism in the Law: Essays in Memory of Angelo Forte*, ed. Andrew R. C. Simpson, Scott C. Styles, and Adelyn L. M. Wilson (Aberdeen, forthcoming).

Smith, Andrew, 'The Kelso Abbey Cartulary: Context, Production and Forgery', (PhD Dissertation, University of Glasgow, 2011).

Taylor, Alice, *The Auld Lawes of Scotland: Compilations of Royal Laws from the Thirteenth and Fourteenth centuries*, Stair Society (Edinburgh, forthcoming).

Taylor, Alice, 'Was *Leges inter Brettos et Scotos* Really an Eleventh-Century Lawcode Held among the Britons of Strathclyde and the Scots of *Alba*?', forthcoming.

Taylor, Alice, 'The *Comes* in Medieval Scotland', in *The Earl in Medieval Britain*, ed. Crouch and Doherty, forthcoming.

ONLINE CITATIONS

Primary Sources

'The 1215 Magna Carta', *The Magna Carta Project*, trans. H. Summerson et al., online at <http://magnacarta.cmp.uea.ac.uk/read/magna_carta_1215/>.

The Annals of Ulster AD 431–1202, electronic edition compiled by Pádraig Bambury and Stephen Beechinor, CELT: The Corpus of Electronic Texts, online at <http://www.ucc.ie/celt/published/T100001A/index.html>.

The Annals of Tigernach, ed. and trans. Gearóid Mac Niocaill; electronic edition compiled by Emer Purcell and Donnchadh Ó Corráin, online at <http://www.ucc.ie/celt/published/T100002A/index.html>.

The Ayr Manuscript, online at <http://www.stairsociety.org/resources/view_manuscript/the_ayr_manuscript>.

The Berne Manuscript, online at <http://stairsociety.org/resources/view_manuscript/the_berne_manuscript>.

The Electronic Sawyer. Anglo-Saxon Charters: An Annotated List and Bibliography, ed. P. H. Sawyer (London, 1968), revised by Susan E. Kelly in *The Electronic Sawyer*, online at <http://esawyer.org.uk/about/index.html>.

Henry III Fine Rolls Project, AHRC-funded project, produced by David Carpenter, Louise Wilkinson, David Crook, Harold Short, Paul Dryburgh, and Beth Hartland, online at <http://www.frh3.org.uk/home.html>.

Matthew Paris's map of Britain in BL, Cotton MS Claudius D, vi, fo. 12v, online at <http://www.bl.uk/onlinegallery/onlineex/mapsviews/mapgb/large17694.html>.

The People of Medieval Scotland 1093–1314 Database, AHRC-funded database produced by Dauvit Broun, Matthew Hammond, Roibeard Ó Maolalaigh, Keith J. Stringer, John Bradley, David Carpenter, Amanda Beam, John Reuben Davies, Michele Pasin, Beth Hartland, et al., online at <http://db.poms.ac.uk/search/>.

The Records of the Parliaments of Scotland to 1707, Scottish Parliament Project, University of St Andrews, produced by Keith M. Brown, Gillian H. MacIntosh, Alan R. MacDonald, Alastair J. Mann, Pamela E. Ritchie, Roland J. Tanner et al., online at <http://www.rps.ac.uk/>.

Secondary Literature

Broun, Dauvit, '"Absent" and Dead Charter-Witnesses', PoMS Feature of the Month, no. 10 (March, 2010), online at <http://www.poms.ac.uk/feature/march10.html>.

Broun, Dauvit, 'The King's *brithem* (Gaelic for "Judge") and the Recording of Dispute-Resolutions', PoMS Feature of the Month, no. 11 (April 2010), online at <www.poms.ac.uk/feature/april10.html>.

Broun, Dauvit, 'English Law and the Unification of Scotland', Breaking of Britain Feature of the Month, May 2012, online at <http://www.breakingofbritain.ac.uk/blogs/feature-of-the-month/may-2012/>.

Carpenter, David, '"The Scottish King's Household" and English Ideas of Constitutional Reform', *Feature of the Month, October 2011*, The Breaking of Britain (2011), online at <http://www.breakingofbritain.ac.uk/blogs/feature-of-the-month/october-2011-the-scottish-kings-household/>.

Carpenter, David, 'The Downfall and Punishment of Robert de Ros', Breaking of Britain Feature of the Month June 2012, online at <http://www.breakingofbritain.ac.uk/blogs/feature-of-the-month/june-2012/>.

Carpenter, David, 'The Fine Rolls of Henry III: the Origins and Development of the Rolls', online at <http://www.finerollshenry3.org.uk/content/commentary/historical_intro.html>.

Crick, Julia, *Elders and Betters: Local Hierarchies and Royal Agents in England and the West, 800–1000*, G. O. Sayles Memorial Lectures on Mediaeval History 5, given on 1 May 2009, text available online at <https://www.academia.edu>.

Duncan, A. A. M., 'David of Bernham', *ODNB*, online at <http://www.oxforddnb.com/view/article/50015>.

McDonald, R. Andrew, 'Macduff Family, Earls of Fife (*per c.*1095–1371)', *ODNB*, online at <http://www.oxforddnb.com/view/article/50328>.

Stell, G. P., 'Henry de Balliol', *ODNB*, online at <http://www.oxforddnb.com/view/article/1207>.

Online Reference Tools

The Dictionary of the Scots Language, online at <http://www.dsl.ac.uk>
Electronic Dictionary of the Irish Language, online at <http://edil.qub.ac.uk>.
Oxford English Dictionary, online at <http://www.oed.com>.

Individual Citations from Online Primary Sources

The People of Medieval Scotland (PoMS) Database:

PoMS, no. 1049; H 1/12/1 (<http://db.poms.ac.uk/record/source/1049>).
PoMS, no. 1827; H 1/7/30 (<http://db.poms.ac.uk/record/source/1827>).
PoMS, no. 2057; H 1/7/193 (<http://db.poms.ac.uk/record/source/2057>).

PoMS, no. 2058; H1/7/192 (<http://db.poms.ac.uk/record/source/2058/>).
PoMS, no. 3965; H 4/32/48 (<http://db.poms.ac.uk/record/source/3965>).
PoMS, no. 4288; H4/42/2 (<http://db.poms.ac.uk/record/source/4288>).
PoMS, no. 4733; H 3/131/1 (<http://db.poms.ac.uk/record/source/4733/>).
PoMS, no. 5033; H 3/326/6 (<http://db.poms.ac.uk/record/source/5033/>).
PoMS, no. 5361; H 3/281/1 (<http://db.poms.ac.uk/record/source/5361>).
PoMS, no. 5530; H 5/586/13 (<http://db.poms.ac.uk/record/source/5530>).
PoMS, no. 5630; H3/632/5 (<http://db.poms.ac.uk/record/source/5630/>).
PoMS, no. 5984; H 4/26/14 (<http://db.poms.ac.uk/record/source/5984/>).
PoMS, no. 7702; H 3/42/7 (<http://db.poms.ac.uk/record/source/7702>)
PoMS, no. 7691; H 3/344/5 (<http://db.poms.ac.uk/record/source/7691/>).
PoMS, no. 7872; H 4/26/26 (<http://db.poms.ac.uk/record/source/7872/>).
PoMS, Person ID no. 131 (<http://db.poms.ac.uk/record/person/131/>).
PoMS, Person ID no. 1420 (<http://db.poms.ac.uk/record/person/1420/>).
PoMS, Person ID no. 2032 (<http://db.poms.ac.uk/record/person/2032/>).
PoMS, Person ID, no. 2063(<http://db.poms.ac.uk/record/person/2063/>).
PoMS, Person ID no. 2115 (<http://db.poms.ac.uk/record/person/2115/>).
PoMS, Person ID no. 2137 (<http://db.poms.ac.uk/record/person/2137/>).
PoMS, Person ID, no. 2092 (<http://db.poms.ac.uk/record/person/2092/>).
PoMS, transaction factoid, no. 66405 (<http://db.poms.ac.uk/record/factoid/66405/>).
Render feast days: <http://db.poms.ac.uk/browse/facet/renderdates/?resulttype= factoid& totitems>.

Henry III Fine Rolls Project:

Fine Roll 48 Henry III, no. 90, online at <http://www.finerollshenry3.org.uk/content/calendar/roll_061.html>.

The Magna Carta Project

'The 1215 Magna Carta: Clause 02', *The Magna Carta Project*, trans. H. Summerson et al. <http://magnacarta.cmp.uea.ac.uk/read/magna_carta_1215/Clause_02>.
'The 1215 Magna Carta: Clause 03', *The Magna Carta Project*, trans. H. Summerson et al. <http://magnacarta.cmp.uea.ac.uk/read/magna_carta_1215/Clause_03>.
'The 1215 Magna Carta: Clause 21', *The Magna Carta Project*, trans. H. Summerson et al. <http://magnacarta.cmp.uea.ac.uk/read/magna_carta_1215/Clause_21>.

Index

All place names have, where possible, been given their local county location, following the information provided in the database of *The People of Medieval Scotland, 1093–1314*. A list of all abbreviations used can be found at www.poms.ac.uk/information/county-abbreviations-list/. Where possible and appropriate, all dates of death have been checked against the PoMS database (accessed October 2015).